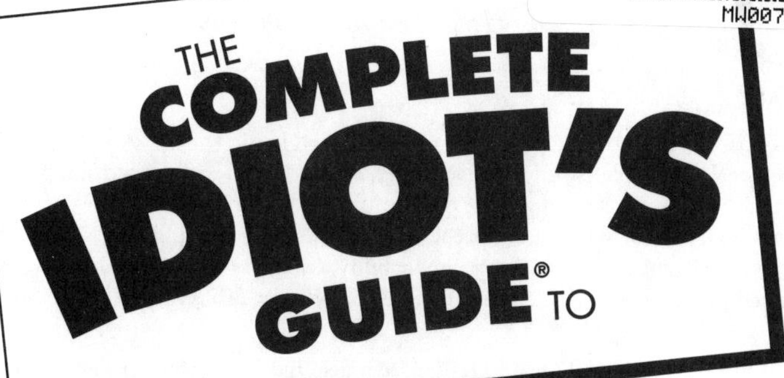

Mixing Drinks

Second Edition

by Alan Axelrod and The Players

For Anita—Here's looking at you, kid.

International Standard Book Number: 0-02-864468-9
Library of Congress Catalog Card Number: 2002117443

05 04 03 8 7 6 5 4 3 2 1

Interpretation of the printing code: The rightmost number of the first series of numbers is the year of the book's printing; the rightmost number of the second series of numbers is the number of the book's printing. For example, a printing code of 03-1 shows that the first printing occurred in 2003.

Printed in the United States of America

Publisher: *Marie Butler-Knight*
Product Manager: *Phil Kitchel*
Managing Editor: *Jennifer Chisholm*
Senior Acquisitions Editor: *Renee Wilmeth*
Production Editor: *Katherin Bidwell*
Copy Editor: *Rhonda Tinch-Mize*
Illustrator: *Chris Eliopoulos*
Cover/Book Designer: *Trina Wurst*
Indexer: *Julie Bess*
Layout/Proofreading: *Megan Douglass, Becky Harmon, Ayanna Lacey*

Contents at a Glance

Contents

Foreword

When the first edition of this book was released in 1997, the world was a relatively kinder and gentler place. Today, as the great Sean O'Casey's character Captain Boyle would say, "Th' whole worl's in a terrible state o' chassis." (Since The Players is a theatrical club, I thought I would sneak in a subtle theatrical reference.)

With the state of the world the way it is, we all need to find a way to relax, put our feet up once in a while, watch "The Sopranos" and, most importantly, have a cocktail. (This reference is not only theatrical and subtle but "Uncle Junior" himself—Dominic Chianese—is a member of The Players.) This is the book that will teach us how to do it.

Since this book, wonderfully and clearly written by Alan Axelrod, first came out, it has proven itself to be one of the best books ever on how to mix the numerous and enjoyable cocktails that exist. Unlike most "how to" books, this one is fun and readable.

Of course, I can't help but feel that this is due not only to Alan's great talent as a writer, but also to the fact that the co-author of record is The Players itself. I have had the honor and pleasure of being a member of this most wonderful and convivial of clubs since 1988 and Executive Director of said club since 1993. Not only is our Grill the best bar in the City of New York, but our history, traditions, and roster of members since its founding in 1888 is astonishing—a virtual who's who of the American Theater. From Edwin Booth and Mark Twain to the Barrymore brothers, Humphrey Bogart, James Cagney, Spencer Tracy, Jason Robards, Jose Ferrer, Walt Disney, Frank Sinatra—and today, Tony Bennett, Kevin Kline, James Earl Jones, Timothy Hutton, Walter Cronkite, Tommy Lee Jones, Tony Randall, and Jack Klugman. Like most clubs throughout the world, women were not given admittance until recent times. Since 1988, however, our list of female members includes Helen Hayes, Julie Harris, Lauren Bacall, Angela Lansbury, Carol Burnett, and Judy Collins. This, of course, is just a very partial list, but with our cast of characters how could there not be some wonderful stories.

I know that the membership of our beautiful clubhouse in Gramercy Park is proud and delighted to be a partner in this book. I'm sorry that many of our late members aren't around to see it. I can picture Jason and Jim (never Jimmy) Cagney and Spence and Bogie having a wonderful time sitting around one of the long tables in the Grill, trying each recipe and debating the merits of each one. Certainly, it would have prompted the great John Barrymore to lift a glass in its honor and proclaim it an outstanding and necessary work of literature.

Enjoy!

—John Martello
Executive Director, The Players

Introduction

The very last person who should pick up a *Complete Idiot's Guide* is a complete idiot. These books are for people smart enough and sensitive enough to *feel* like complete idiots about certain subjects. Most people find quantum physics an intimidating subject, but even more are snowed by mixology: the art and science of creating alcoholic—we prefer the term *spirituous*—drinks. What liquor to buy, what drinks to mix, how to measure them, how to mix them, how to pour them, how to serve them, to whom to serve them, and how to plan a party—these are bewilderments sufficient to reduce Albert Einstein himself to a quivering mass of Jell-O. (By the way, you will find recipes for splendid Jell-O Shots in Appendix B.)

The Complete Idiot's Guide to Mixing Drinks is not just about buying, measuring, mixing, and pouring. It's about confidence and authority. It's about acquiring the expertise required to serve—and savor—spirituous drinks with maximum pleasure.

And although confidence, authority, and pleasure are the principal aims of this book, you'll also find what every adult needs to know about drinking and serving drinks responsibly. Included, too, are generous chapters for calorie counters and those who want to enjoy adult beverages *without* alcohol.

How to Use This Book

The first part of this book gives you all the background you need to start mixing drinks and to enjoy—responsibly—the drinks you mix. Most of the rest of the book gives you the recipes for the most interesting and popular drinks, arranged by type of spirit. Special sections discuss dessert drinks, drinks for the calorie conscious, and drinks for nondrinkers. You'll also find advice on planning and managing a party and even what to do if you decide to pursue a part-time or full-time bartending career.

Part 1, "Belly Up to the Bar!" includes chapters on what you might like to drink and how you should drink it. You'll also find information on just what happens to you when you drink, how to prevent a hangover, and how to serve and enjoy liquor responsibly. For the truly curious, there is also a chapter on the chemistry and history of drinkable alcohol. Chapters 4 and 5 are a concise course on the basic equipment of bartending—including glassware, garnishes, mixers, and spirits—and on the secrets of measuring, mixing, and pouring like a pro.

Part 2, "Clear Choices," contains chapters on mixing drinks using the clear or so-called "white" spirits, gin and vodka. Included is a special chapter devoted to the martini in its many varieties.

Part 3, "Whiskey World," is about making drinks with bourbon, Tennessee Whiskey, American and Canadian blended whiskeys, rye, scotch, and Irish whiskey. Connoisseurship, including such key issues as straight versus blended bourbons and blended versus single-malt scotches, is thoroughly covered, together with the historical background of these great traditional spirits.

Part 4, "Almost Tropical," covers two of the most popular but least understood spirits: rum and tequila. In addition to the most popular tropical drinks, you'll find a discussion of the wide variety of rums available from New England to the Caribbean islands and the nations of Central and South America. As for tequila, it emerges here from the murk of its undeservedly shady reputation and into the sunlight as one of the world's most delectable—and carefully crafted—spirits, the basis of many delicious drinks.

Part 5, "Just Desserts," presents a panoply of after-dinner and dessert drinks, made with brandy and with liqueurs. You'll also learn about creating comforting hot drinks and spectacular flaming drinks, as well as *pousse-cafés*, the multilayered masterpieces served in pony glasses to *oohs* and *ahhs* of appreciation.

Part 6, "A Fresh Round," contains a pair of chapters for those who want to create tempting drinks without losing count (or control) of their caloric intake, and for those who want to create and enjoy satisfying, alcohol-free adult beverages. But the section starts off with a new look at champagne, wine, and beer, and how you can combine them with "hard" liquor to create new and exciting drinks.

Part 7, "Putting It All Together," begins with a chapter on planning a party—including what spirits to buy and how much to buy. What follows is a chapter devoted to elevating punch from a dull substitute for individual drinks to the centerpiece of the party. This section concludes with advice for those who want to make the transition from amateur host to professional bartender, whether full- or part-time.

At the back of the book, you'll find **Appendix A, "Buzzed Word Glossary,"** a compendium of words either essential or helpful to choosing, serving, and enjoying liquor, and **Appendix B, "Last Call,"** a catalog of some new or out-of-the-ordinary drinks.

No one will be offended if you don't read this book cover to cover. Look at the chapters that interest you—or consult the index for an alphabetical list of the drinks you want to make.

Extras

In addition to recipes, advice, guidance, and explanations, this book offers other types of information to help you mix drinks and enjoy the "pleasures of the spirit." These include definitions of key terms, tips from the world of professional bartending, a collection of popular toasts, and choice barroom humor. Look for these easy-to-recognize signposts in boxes:

Special Thanks to the Technical Reviewer

The Complete Idiot's Guide to Mixing Drinks was reviewed by a professional bartender who double-checked the technical accuracy of what you'll learn here, to help us ensure that this book gives you everything you need to know to become a confident bartender.

Special thanks are extended to Andrew Gouldn, self-proclaimed "King of the Random Job," from cooking to cleaning, acting to acting up, decorating sets to deconstructing them. Along the way he has found a need for a bartender in every port (pun intended), including an extended run at The Players.

Trademarks

All terms mentioned in this book that are known to be or are suspected of being trademarks or service marks have been appropriately capitalized. Alpha Books and Penguin Putnam Inc. cannot attest to the accuracy of this information. Use of a term in this book should not be regarded as affecting the validity of any trademark or service mark. The following trademarks and service marks have been mentioned in this book:

7-Up, Absolut, Angostura, Appleton, Asbach-Uralt, Bacardi and Company, Bailey's Original Irish Cream, Black Barrel, Benedictine, Bermudez, British Navy Pusser's, Cacique Ron Anejo, Cameroun Brig, Captain Morgan, Chartreuse, Cherry Marnier, Coca-Cola, Cointreau, Dr Pepper, Dubonnet, Finlandia, Glenfiddich, Glenmorangle, Godiva Liqueur, Grand Marnier, Hudson's Bay, Irish Mist, Invergordon, K.W.V., Knockando, Laphroaig, Lemon Hart & Sons, Loch Lomond, Macallan, Mandarine Napoleon Liqueur, Metaxa, Midori, Mount Gay, Myers's Rum, Old Overholt, Pernod, Peter Heering, Peychaud's , Pisco, Presidente, Rhum Barbancourt, Ron Medellin, Rose's Lime Juice, Seagram's 7-Crown, Smirnoff, Stolichnaya, Strathclyde, The Glenlivet, Tia Maria, Wyborowa, Zubrowka.

Part 1

Belly Up to the Bar!

Okay, so maybe you don't *need* a book to tell you why, what, and how you should drink, but that's how this opening section begins: with some reasons for drinking, a descriptive inventory of the range of distilled spirits, and some guidelines for enhancing your enjoyment of liquor.

Handling, serving, and consuming alcoholic beverages are all adult activities, and this section discusses what happens when you drink, how you can prevent or minimize a hangover, and, most importantly, how to serve and enjoy liquor responsibly.

You'll also find a thorough discussion of everything the home bar and bartender needs, including the correct glassware, essential garnishes, requisite mixers, and choice spirits. Then you can find out how to use all these things—how to stir, shake, measure, and generally *move* like a pro.

Chapter 1

What to Drink and Why

In This Chapter

- Three reasons to drink (if you want to)
- Respecting the rights of nondrinkers
- Liquor: your basic choices
- How to taste, judge, and savor your drink

The great jazz trumpeter Louis Armstrong had a celebrated exchange with a society matron, who asked him to define *jazz*. “Lady,” Satchmo is said to have replied, “if you gotta ask, you’ll never know.”

There are those who will tell you that something like this is also the appropriate reply to the question, “What should I drink?”

But that’s not what we’ll say to you.

Although this book is mostly about mixing drinks, before we get to the *how*, we think the *what* and the *why* are well worth talking about. Here goes.

Should I?

Going into the neighborhood bar and ordering an aqua vitae will produce unpredictable results. If the bartender is on the surly side, at the very least your request will elicit a dirty look. If, however, your neighborhood mixologist is up on his Medieval Latin, he will recognize *aqua vitae* as a term for strong distilled alcohol, such as whiskey or brandy. Depending on the neighborhood, he might even go on to discuss the etymology of this phrase. *Aqua* is, of course, water, and *vitae* is a form of *vita*—life: Water of Life.

For untold centuries, *spirits* have been associated with vitality, conviviality (another word rooted in a Latin original, *vivere*, "to live"), life, or, more accurately, the enhancement of life's pleasures.

Buzzed Words

Aqua vitae is not to be confused with **aquavit**, which is a very strong Scandinavian liquor distilled from potatoes and grain and flavored with caraway seeds. It is always served very cold, typically with the bottle frozen into a block of ice

Buzzed Words

Spirits or **spirit** is a generic term for an alcoholic beverage based on distilled **liquor**.

Bar Tips

When it comes to alcohol, the operative word—you guessed it—is *moderation*. As is true of many adult pleasures, drinking can enhance your life or it can destroy it. Irresponsible drinking can reach well beyond *your* life to destroy other lives as well. Please read the next chapter carefully.

A Toast: To Tradition!

To partake of alcoholic refreshment is to partake of tradition. Drinking is part and parcel of our culture. Alcohol, in the form of sacramental wine, plays a role in both the Jewish and Christian traditions, and other alcoholic beverages figure in the rites and rituals of numerous Native American and non-Western religions, both ancient and modern—although it is also true that some religions, including certain Protestant Christian churches, the Mormon faith, and Islam, generally forbid the consumption of alcohol.

In secular life, too, liquor plays a kind of sacramental role. Good friends traditionally cement their friendship with a drink. Business deals are "made official" with good-faith sips all around. Bride and groom are toasted with champagne or whatever else is handy. And on and on. Drinking is part of our social language.

Our Pleasure

As you will see in the next chapter, alcohol is a depressant. But, for most people, first among the mind's faculties to be depressed are those that tend to inhibit, that say "No," that draw us back from the company of others, and that check our speech and actions. The paradoxical result in most of us is that, taken in moderation, this depressant *seems* to invigorate, energize, and generally cheer. In moderation, drink heightens our enjoyment of food, music, our surroundings, and the people we're with. Even though few drinkers enjoy every kind of liquor, so many varieties of spirits can be mixed with so many other flavorful things in so many ways that just about everyone can take pleasure in the drink itself—in its taste and in its glow.

A Good Time Had by All

Conviviality—a fondness for good times among good company—can be enhanced by moderate drink. Most of us converse more freely (for better or worse) and are more emotionally generous when we bask in the glow of a drink. Alcohol has a long history as a social lubricant. Sharing spirits with friends can create social bonds and a sense of community.

But It's Always Okay Not To

Despite the long lineage of alcoholic beverage, its firm position in our culture, and the pleasure it can afford, many choose not to drink. Some people make the choice for reasons of diet, health, religion, moral belief, or simply taste. As you would want others to respect your choice to drink, you must respect absolutely the choice not to drink. Never coax, cajole, or urge alcohol on anyone. Not even jokingly. If you are hosting a party or tending bar, always have a variety of appealing nonalcoholic beverages on hand. Offer these freely and up front: "Can I get you anything? Scotch, a martini, soft drink?" (See Chapter 21.)

Bar Tips

Sophisticated hosts have always known that it is always okay not to drink. These days, it's more okay than ever because many people just feel better without alcohol in their lives. A professional bartender will not hesitate to honor a request for a nonalcoholic drink, and, certainly, no host should feel insulted if a guest chooses not to imbibe.

What Should You Drink?

What should you drink? The short answer is you'll have a much better idea after you read this book, which offers a wide range of potables. But mixed drinks are to the drinker what chemical compounds are to the chemist. Before you can appreciate them fully, you need to get acquainted with the elements from which they are made. Let's start by differentiating hard liquor from beer and wine, and then explore the "elements" themselves.

Hard Liquor vs. Beer and Wine

An alcoholic beverage is *hard* if it contains a relatively high concentration of alcohol, as measured by its *proof*. An ounce of 100-proof bourbon (or other 100-proof hard liquor), for example, contains as much alcohol as 12 ounces of beer, five ounces of wine, or three ounces of sherry. Wow! Does that make bourbon *12 times* more potent than beer?

Buzzed Words

Hard liquor is a beverage with a high alcoholic content. Gin, vodka, bourbon, sour mash whiskey, scotch, blended whiskey, rye, rum, and tequila are the most common hard liquors.

Proof is the alcoholic content of a spirit. It is determined by multiplying the percentage of alcoholic content by two; so, for example, liquor that is 40 percent alcohol is 80 proof.

The answer is yes—and no. Yes, an ounce of bourbon is 12 times more alcoholic than an ounce of beer. But who drinks beer by the ounce? A usual "serving" of bourbon is one or one and a half ounces, whereas a usual serving of beer is 12 ounces: one bottle. So a "serving" of bourbon is roughly equivalent to a "serving" of beer in terms of alcoholic content.

Your choice of hard liquor versus beer or wine should be based on taste or occasion rather than on alcoholic content. For example, a bourbon or other hard liquor can make a pleasant prelude to a dinner, but you probably won't want to wash down the meal itself with spirits. Beer or wine, in contrast, go well with food.

Straight vs. Mixed

Another choice to make is whether you want your drink mixed or straight. You can mix hard liquor with a bewildering range of other fluids: water, carbonated water, fruit juices, soft drinks, other hard liquors, and even wine and beer. If you choose not to mix the liquor with anything, you are drinking it *straight* or *neat*. If you pour it over ice, you're drinking it *on the rocks*.

Why mix liquor with anything?

Well, why not? You might take your beef "straight"—let's say a plain, medium-rare New York Strip—or you might enjoy it "mixed"—for instance, with paté de foie gras and served in a pastry shell as Beef Wellington. As sauces and other ingredients add character to basic foods, mixers add a variety of flavors, textures, and sensations to basic liquor. Moreover, some people like to drink, but they really don't care for the taste of hard liquor. For these folks, mixers make the alcohol palatable.

Finally, whereas some mixed drinks combine two or more alcoholic beverages into a particularly potent blend, nonalcoholic mixers dilute the alcoholic content of the drink—an effect some people want. This, however, can be deceptive. Sugary mixers do dilute the alcohol, but the sugar also tends to accelerate the body's absorption of the alcohol, speeding its entry into the bloodstream. The result might be more of a "buzz" than you expected.

However, there's nothing wrong with an unadorned New York Strip. If you like the taste of alcohol, the best way for you to enjoy a drink might be straight, straight-up (poured over ice to chill and then poured into a serving glass, through a strainer that holds back the ice cubes), or on the rocks. That said, it's time to turn from the "compounds" and look at the "elements": the basic varieties of hard liquor.

Bar Tips

Should you buy expensive, premium-label liquors or cheaper "bar brands"? This is a matter of taste and budget. In general, the cheaper brands will taste almost as good as the more expensive brands when mixed with fruit juices or soft drinks, whereas the premium brands are usually significantly more enjoyable if you're drinking the liquor straight, on the rocks, or mixed with water, club soda, or certain other alcoholic beverages.

Transparently Yours

Gin is a clear spirit, whose name is derived from the French *genièvre*, meaning juniper berry. There's a good reason for this: Gin is produced from corn and rye (sometimes other grains as well) distilled into a *neutral* (flavorless, odorless, and colorless) spirit, and then flavored with juniper berries. Various gin distillers add other botanicals as well to produce a surprisingly wide variety of subtle flavors.

Some people love the taste of gin; others can't stand it. Spirits that evoke this kind of love-hate relationship are typically called "drinker's drinks." If you plan to drink gin in a martini or on the rocks (it is rarely consumed straight—unchilled—though it can be drunk straight-up), you'd better like its taste. That's less important if you drink it with a strongly flavored mixer. Recently, some distinctively flavored premium gins have come on the market, including Tanqueray No. 10, which is subtly highlighted by the flavor of grapefruit, orange, lime, and chamomile in addition to the traditional juniper. Such gin is best enjoyed without a mixer.

Buzzed Words

Distillation is a process of evaporating a liquid, and then condensing the vapor to purify and concentrate the liquid, called the **distillate.** Manufacturers of spirits are called **distillers.** The distillate is a **neutral spirit**—flavorless, odorless, and colorless alcohol. **Aging** in wood and, sometimes, the addition of natural and artificial flavorings impart color, aroma, and flavor to such spirits as whiskey and dark rum.

From Russia (and Poland, Finland, and Sweden) with Love

Another clear spirit, vodka, is strongly associated with Russia, although it was probably invented in Poland and is now produced in several countries—most notably Sweden, Finland, and the United States—as well as Russia.

The word *vodka* is a "diminutive" form of the Russian *zhizennia voda*, meaning *aqua vitae*, which (thanks to our classically educated barkeep) you know means "water of life." Russians use diminutives to name people and things they really like (for example, "Nikolai" is Nicholas, but "Kolya" is "Nicky"), and *vodka* can be translated as "dear little water" or "dear little water of life."

Like gin, vodka is distilled from grain—although almost any fermented carbohydrate can be used, including potatoes—to a very high proof (at least 190). The resulting *grain neutral spirits* are cut with distilled water to a strength of 80 to 100 proof and then charcoal filtered to remove any vestige of flavor.

Whereas gin is deliberately flavored with juniper berries and other botanicals, the distillation, dilution, and filtering process used to make vodka deliberately *removes* all aroma and taste. Almost, anyway. Dedicated vodka drinkers will tell you that different brands have distinctive characters, and this is certainly true because the quality of the raw materials varies. Nevertheless, drinking vodka straight or on the rocks is not a strongly flavorful experience. This is precisely what appeals to many vodka drinkers, however, who enjoy the light, clean, refreshing "nontaste" of this spirit.

Whiskey

Whiskey comes in a wide range of varieties and variations in taste; however, all whiskey production involves the same four basic steps:

1. Malting
2. Fermenting
3. Distilling
4. Aging

The last step, the aging process—in wooden barrels—turns the clear distillate tawny brown and imparts whiskey's characteristic flavor and aroma. Aging is a chemical reaction between the alcohol and the wood; even though time marches on, the aging process stops as soon as the whiskey is bottled—removed from contact with the wood.

Buzzed Words

Whiskey versus **whisky**: American and Irish distillers spell the word with an *e*, whereas Scotch and Canadian distillers jump right from the *k* to the *y*.

Buzzed Words

Malting is the practice of allowing the grain (usually barley) to sprout before fermentation. In whiskey production, this produces a variety of characteristic flavors in the finished product. **Fermenting** is the chemical process whereby complex organic substances are split into relatively simple compounds. In the manufacture of alcohol, special yeasts are used to ferment—convert—the starches and sugars of grain (or some other organic substance) into alcohol.

We will discuss the subject of whiskey varieties in much greater detail in Part 3, but here's a quick rundown on the range of whiskies available. Let's begin with the American varieties:

- **Bourbon** derives its name not directly from the French royal dynasty interrupted by the Revolution and Napoleon Bonaparte, but from Bourbon County, Kentucky, where this liquor originates. Only whiskey made in Kentucky can be legally called bourbon, just as only the sparkling wine originating in the Champagne region of France can properly be called champagne.

  Bourbon is distilled from *mash*, a fermentable, starchy mixture, consisting of at least 51 percent corn, with the balance of the mash consisting of another grain (typically a combination of rye and barley). Bourbon is aged in oak barrels—the cheaper stuff for as little as two years, and the premium brands for up to 12. It is usually bottled at 80 to 90 proof, but never more than 160 proof. The typical flavor is dark and rich, with a distinct undertone of corn.

- **Corn whiskey** varies from bourbon in that the mash must contain at least 80 percent corn rather than 51 percent. It tends to taste sweeter and feel thicker than bourbon. Not surprisingly, the taste of corn is more recognizable.

Buzzed Words

Mash is the starchy mixture—usually including grain and corn, or some other organic substance—that is subjected to fermentation to produce alcohol.

- **Sour mash whiskey** comes from Tennessee (and thus is often termed "Tennessee Whiskey"). The mash from which it is distilled contains some portion of previously fermented (that is, "sour") yeast (fresh yeast produces *sweet mash*). The result is a liquor with a mellower, smoother taste and feel than bourbon. This is ideal "sippin'" whiskey.
- **Rye whiskey** (usually just called *rye*) is made from a mash that contains at least 51 percent rye grain. Its aggressive, sharp-toothed, somewhat musty flavor has appealed to fewer and fewer people over the years, and it has a reputation as a *serious* drinker's drink.
- **Bottled-in-bond whiskey** is "straight" whiskey bottled at 100 proof and aged a minimum of four years in a warehouse that is bonded by the United States government.
- **Scotch** is—surprise, surprise—the whisky of Scotland and perhaps the most popular kind of whisky in the world. Based on barley (and sometimes corn), scotch acquires its characteristic smoky flavor as a result of the barley malt's having been roasted over fires fueled by peat. The smoked malt is then mixed with water to form the mash, which is then fermented, distilled, and aged for at least three years in uncharred oak barrels or in casks left over from sherry aging.

  The better scotches are aged at least 12 years, and the premium brands, called *single malt*, contain only whisky distilled at one time and by a single distiller, as opposed to *blended scotch*, which consists of a blend of whiskies distilled at various times by more than one distiller. Scotch is usually bottled at 80 to 86 proof. The flavor of scotch—especially single-malt versus blends—varies so widely as to defy description. In general, though, it is at once sweeter and smokier than bourbon, and you should know that *many* dedicated scotch drinkers don't care much for bourbon and vice versa.

Buzzed Words

Single-malt scotch contains only whisky distilled at one time and by a single distiller. **Blended scotch** consists of a combination of whiskies distilled at various times by more than one distiller.

- **Irish whiskey** is becoming increasingly popular. Like scotch, it is based chiefly on barley and is produced by a similar roasting process; however, the malt is roasted in coal-fired kilns rather than over open peat fires, so it does not acquire the smoky flavor—although it tastes more like scotch than like bourbon. Aged five to ten years in used sherry casks, Irish whiskey is bottled at 86 proof. If you like scotch, you'll probably like Irish whiskey; it has a sweeter, sharper flavor.

- ***Canadian whisky*** is blended from a variety of straight whiskies *and* neutral, flavorless whiskies. You'd think that the taste of such a blend would be more complex and richer than the taste of unblended whiskies. Not true. Canadian whisky has a simpler, lighter taste than either scotch or bourbon and is usually consumed in mixed drinks rather than taken straight.

Buzzed Words

Blended whiskey can be a confusing term. A blended whiskey might be a combination of **straight** whiskies and neutral, flavorless whiskies (this is true of Canadian whisky) or it might be a combination of similar whiskey products made by different distillers at different times (as in blended scotch).

Rum

Rum is produced chiefly in Puerto Rico, Barbados, and Jamaica, and the process of production varies from place to place—with Puerto Rican rums being the lightest and driest, Barbados rums darker and heavier, and Jamaican rum quite dark, heavy, and sweet. These differences will be discussed in greater detail in Chapter 13. All rum is based on sugarcane juice and molasses, which is fermented and distilled, and sometimes aged as well. It is bottled at anywhere from 80 proof to a fist-pounding 150 proof.

Tequila

Tequila has a rather shady reputation, with suggestions that it is akin to the illicit hallucinogen mescaline.

Wrong.

To be called *tequila*, this liquor must meet strict standards set by the Mexican government, which means (among other things) that it must be made from blue agave plants (the blue variety of *Tequila weber*) grown in an officially designated area, centered on the town of Tequila. As you can't get blood from a turnip, neither can you get mescaline from agave. The Mexican government further decrees that the tequila mash must contain 51 percent blue agave juice (the balance can be as much as 49 percent sugarcane juice), must be fermented, *twice* distilled, and, finally, charcoal filtered. It can then be either bottled or aged from one to seven years in used oak barrels before bottling.

Aged tequila, which is called *anejo*, is golden rather than clear and generally has a rich flavor that makes it more agreeable straight or on the rocks than unaged tequila, which is better consumed with a mixer. Tequila imported into the United States is 80 proof, whereas that sold domestically in Mexico is 96 proof.

Bar Tips

We've all heard about "The Worm" in "real Mexican" tequila. Well, there *is* a worm, but not in tequila. It is often put in mescal, which is made from agave, but not necessarily in the Tequila region or under government control. The worm lives in the agave plant, and it is traditional to throw one into each bottle. Despite its name, mescal, like tequila, has nothing to do with the drug mescaline.

Savor, Don't Swill

Like fine wines, good liquor, whether consumed straight or mixed with other things, is usually best enjoyed when it is sipped and savored. The exceptions are certain "shooter" drinks and other drinks served in a shot glass, which are meant to be downed in a single, eye-popping, bar-slapping swallow.

Bar Tips

When taste testing liquor, it is important to ensure that no soap or detergent residue left over from washing remains in the glass. Do not use ice, which might impart an unwanted flavor to the drink; the cold temperature will also dull the taste buds.

The Nose Knows

The art of wine tasting provides another guideline for savoring good liquor. *Nose* is the term wine connoisseurs use to describe the *aroma* (in younger, simpler wines) or *bouquet* (in older, more complex wines) of the beverage. Take time to enjoy the "nose" of a good glass of liquor. Scent should be very much a part of the drinking experience.

"Professional" Tasting

If you want to get more serious about enjoying liquor, here are some suggestions. Evaluate and compare unmixed spirits this way:

- Into a very clean, thoroughly rinsed sherry glass (called a *copita*; glassware is discussed in Chapter 4), mix equal portions of the liquor under consideration with demineralized, distilled water. Use a different glass for each liquor you evaluate.
- Look at the color. Is it appealing?
- Evaluate the aroma—the "nose."
- Savor the flavor—as well as the body and the aftertaste.

The components of flavor, body, and aftertaste include

- Intensity of flavor.
- Smoothness; also called "finish."

- "Off-tastes"—suggesting chemical additives and including excessive woodiness (from the barrel), sweetness, acidity, astringency, musty flavor (unavoidable to some extent in rye), corkiness, or bitterness.
- "High notes"—pleasant characteristics, including overtones of spice, a nutty flavor, and so on. It is fun to try to identify overtones as specifically as possible.

In contrast to unmixed liquors, evaluating mixed drinks does not involve as great a need for a sophisticated palate. Pay attention to the following:

- Appearance: Does the drink *look* appealing?
- Aroma: Does it have an appealing, inviting smell?
- Flavor: Does it taste great?
- Refreshment value: Is it refreshing?
- Aftertaste: Is it pleasant or not?
- Staying power: Does the drink taste good sip after sip? Or does it quickly cloy?

Pacing

In the next chapter, we will discuss responsible drinking and responsible bartending. One key to responsible drinking—and to maximize the enjoyment of liquor—is to *pace* yourself. Alcoholic beverages, even those mixed with sweet, refreshing, and delicious juices, are not meant to be guzzled or consumed in rapid succession, one after the other. The consequences of failing to pace range from making a fool of yourself, to getting sick, to getting dangerously drunk and becoming party to a potentially lethal accident. At the very least, poorly paced drinking greatly diminishes the pleasure to be derived from the liquor. Enjoy responsibly.

The Least You Need to Know

- In moderation, drinking is a traditional pleasure that can enhance your social life, but it should never be considered a prerequisite to a good time.
- Hard liquor has a greater percentage of alcohol by volume than wine or beer, but, in terms of the amount of wine, beer, or hard liquor that constitutes a "serving," is neither more nor less potent.
- The range of hard liquor choices is great. If you have any interest in drinking at all, you will almost certainly find more than one basic liquor to please you.
- With a few exceptions, hard liquor is best sipped and savored, rather than gulped down Wild West–style.

Chapter 2

Acting Like an Adult: Responsible Drinking and Responsible Bartending

In This Chapter

- What your body does with alcohol
- How to sober up
- Dealing with a hangover
- Drinking and your health
- Your responsibilities as a drinker and a host
- Drinking and driving

If you enjoy drinking, you are not alone. Two-thirds of adult Americans consume alcoholic beverages. Most of them do so responsibly enough to avoid ravaging their lives and the lives of others. However, nearly 14 million (1 in 13 adults) abuse alcohol or suffer from alcoholism, and in 2001, 17,488 Americans were killed in crashes involving drunk drivers—41 percent of all traffic fatalities.

Drinking should be a part of good times and civilized company. But the decision to drink—and to serve drinks—is one of the heaviest responsibilities an adult can take on.

A Physiology Lesson

Take a drink, and the alcohol is immediately absorbed into your bloodstream. Unlike most other substances you ingest, alcohol does not require digestion before it is absorbed and circulated. While it circulates throughout the body, alcohol is diffused in proportion to the water content of the various tissues and organs, appearing in greatest concentration in the blood and the brain.

Bar Tips

You've heard the advice before: Don't drink on an empty stomach. The presence of food in the stomach delays the absorption of alcohol. However, mixing alcohol with carbonated beverages actually speeds absorption.

Buzzed Words

Blood-alcohol concentration (abbreviated BAC and sometimes called blood-alcohol level or BAL) is the concentration of alcohol in the blood, expressed as the weight of alcohol in a fixed volume of blood. It is used as an objective measure of intoxication.

Just as it is quick to soak up the alcohol, your body wastes little time in starting to eliminate the substance. Some alcohol—very little—is exhaled, and a slightly larger amount is secreted in sweat. Even more is excreted by the kidneys and (as anyone who has anxiously queued up for the rest room at the local club knows) soon finds its way out in urine. Nevertheless, no more than 10 percent of the alcohol is eliminated through breathing, sweating, and urination.

The rest—at least 90 percent—is processed metabolically, chiefly by the liver. In the liver, enzymes convert the alcohol to *acetate*, which enters the bloodstream and is eventually transformed into carbon dioxide and water and then disposed of.

In a man of average size, about half an ounce of alcohol—the equivalent of an ounce of hard liquor, a 12-ounce bottle of beer, or a four-ounce glass of wine—can be *metabolized* (processed and eliminated) per hour. If you drink more than one drink per hour, unprocessed alcohol will accumulate in the bloodstream and continually affect the organs, particularly the brain.

Let's go back to that average-size man and say that he drinks four ounces of 100-proof bottled-in-bond whiskey within an hour. This will put 1½ ounces of alcohol in his body, and, by the end of the hour, the concentration of alcohol in his blood will be 0.07 percent. If he continues to drink—another four ounces in the next hour—the blood-alcohol concentration will rise to 0.11 percent.

So what?

At 0.05 blood-alcohol concentration, inhibitions fade, and judgment becomes clouded. At 0.10, speech is slurred, and staggering is apparent. Behold! A drunk.

The following table shows what you can expect at various blood alcohol levels.

Immediate Effects of Alcohol Consumption

BAC (percent)	Probable Effect
.05	Loss of inhibitions; clouded judgment
.10	Impairment of coordination; staggering; slurred speech; visual impairment
.20	Senses dulled; loss of control over emotions
.30	"Blackout" (memory impairment); possible loss of consciousness
.35–.45	Coma; possible death
.60	Death

The following table shows you how much drinking it takes to get to each level.

Alcohol Consumption, Gender, Weight, and BAC

Alcohol	Drinks/hour*	Female 100 lbs.	Female 150 lbs.	Male 150 lbs.	Male 200 lbs.
½ oz.	1	.045	.03	.025	.019
1 oz.	2	.09	.06	.05	.037
2 oz.	4	.18	.12	.10	.07
3 oz.	6	.27	.18	.15	.11
4 oz.	8	.36	.24	.20	.15
5 oz.	10	.45	.30	.25	.18

** Drink = 1 oz. 100 proof spirits*
12 oz. beer
5 oz. wine
3 oz. sherry

Right to the Brain

Let's leave the blood now and enter the brain. What's happening here?

Alcohol, like barbiturates, minor tranquilizers, and general anesthetics, is a central nervous system depressant. However, in low concentrations, its effects are usually perceived as those of a stimulant because it tends first and foremost to depress inhibitions. However, as an increasing amount of alcohol is consumed, the depressant effect becomes more general and more apparent, leading to drowsiness, stupor, and coma. (Good thing for the coma. If you're passed out, you can't drink any more and, therefore, might escape ingesting a *lethal* dose of alcohol.)

Sobering Up

"Put on a pot of coffee—*black* coffee, *very black* coffee. Hot. Hot, *very*, *very black* coffee, and keep it coming! Hot, I tell you!"

Black coffee is a traditional cure, but not a very good idea. In the first place, the coffee will do nothing to sober you up. In the second place, the acids in the coffee will probably irritate your already precariously balanced stomach. A better idea is to drink water, but only to help minimize the inevitable hangover. Water won't "dilute" the alcohol or sober you up any more than coffee.

Sobering up is just a matter of time. The body metabolizes alcohol at the rate of a half ounce per hour. You can't do anything to speed that up significantly.

Anatomy of a Hangover

Of course, even if you survive a hefty drinking bout—you didn't get into a fight, get into a car wreck, or insult your boss and lose your job—you might still find yourself *wishing* you were dead.

Throbbing head, pounding heart, cotton mouth, burning eyes, nausea, dizziness, stomach cramps, thirst, and a liberal shot of remorse. This is a hangover. And now you know why they call getting drunk *intoxication. Toxic* is in the middle of that word. You've been poisoned.

Many of the hangover symptoms are not so much because of the alcohol itself, but because of dehydration induced by alcohol consumption. The process of metabolizing alcohol uses up a lot of water. Alcohol is a diuretic: It makes you pee.

The nausea and stomach cramps that often accompany a hangover are in part because of the irritating effects of the alcohol itself. It's hard on the stomach and intestinal linings. But the various flavorings and spices that find their way into liquor—and mixers—don't help the situation, and if the liquor you've been drinking is cheap, it's bound to have additives and out-and-out impurities that also upset your stomach.

First Aid for a Hangover

Your uncle knows how to cure a hangover. It's invariably some concoction involving tomato juice, Tabasco, and Worcestershire sauce—not something easily downed if your stomach's awash on the high seas.

The sad fact is that no sovereign cure for a hangover exists—except time. With the passage of some hours, you *will* feel better. If possible, take a nap.

This said, you can take some additional soothing—but not curative—steps:

1. Don't drink too much in the first place. (Okay! But we *had* to say it.)
2. When you drink, try to consume plenty of water as well.
3. If you go to bed realizing that you've overindulged, drink as much water as possible before retiring. Keep a glass of water beside your bed. If you wake up during the night, drink more of it. Minimize dehydration now, and you will almost certainly suffer less of a hangover later.
4. Avoid acidic fluids, including orange juice, tomato juice, and cola drinks.
5. In the morning, take a hot shower or (you should be so lucky) a sauna or steam bath. This will soothe and refresh you by increasing your circulation.
6. Take an aspirin. However, be aware that aspirin can be hard on your stomach. And if that's already upset, you could make things worse. Also, people who regularly take aspirin (for example, as part of a medically prescribed cardiovascular regimen) are usually advised to avoid alcohol. Popular nonaspirin pain relievers based on acetaminophen (for example, Tylenol) should be avoided after drinking because alcohol transforms acetaminophen into chemicals that could cause liver damage. This is usually a problem with chronic drinkers, but why take a chance?

Bar Tips

"To cure the bite of the dog, take a hair of the dog that bit you." For generations, misguided folk have recommended more alcohol to "cure" a hangover. Although this might dull the immediate pain, it will only make your condition worse and might turn a temporary illness into a chronic one. If you've overindulged and are suffering, avoid alcohol (at least until you are feeling 100 percent better).

To Your Health!

Drinking in moderation has never been shown to have pathological—disease causing—effects in "normal," healthy people. (There's a *very big* exception: If you are pregnant, it is important that you avoid alcoholic beverages altogether! Alcohol consumption is dangerous to the development of the fetus.) And even getting a little tipsy *on occasion* will probably produce no long-term ill effects. However, frequent drinking to the point even of moderate intoxication can result in damage to the tissues of the mouth, esophagus, and stomach and might increase your chances of developing cancer. The liver is alcohol's primary target, and it could be seriously damaged by its owner's chronic bouts of drunkenness. Heart muscle could also suffer.

> **Bar Tips**
>
> You're drunk. You can't stand the thought of how you'll feel come morning. Should you induce vomiting? Although evacuating your stomach contents *will* reduce the aftereffects of the alcohol, inducing vomiting is almost never healthy. It can damage the throat and esophagus, it can make you choke, and it can harmfully change your body's pH balance. Don't do it.

Overindulgence over a prolonged period also creates nutritional problems—not the least of which is that, with its high calorie content, alcohol promotes weight gain without supplying nutritional value. (See Chapter 20 for information on low-calorie drinks.)

Alcoholism

People who drink hard and long enough to cause major organ damage are undoubtedly classifiable as alcoholics. There has been considerable debate as to just what *alcoholism* is, but the simplest generally accepted definition is the repetitive intake of alcoholic beverages to such an extent that repeated or continued harm to the drinker occurs.

> **Buzzed Words**
>
> The medical definition and the criteria for diagnosing **alcoholism** vary, but in general, this complex chronic psychological and nutritional disorder can be defined as continued excessive or compulsive use of alcoholic drinks.

Most experts believe that alcoholism is a disease, not some "moral weakness" on the part of the sufferer, though some also view it as a drug addiction, a learned response to crisis, a symptom of an underlying psychological or physical disorder, or a combination of these. There is evidence that alcoholism is, at least in part, a hereditary disorder. Certainly, the children of families in which alcohol abuse is present are most at risk for developing alcoholism.

The following list shows the warning signs of alcoholism. If you exhibit *any* of the signs, you have reason to suspect that you suffer from alcoholism. Consult a physician.

Warning Signs of Alcoholism

1. You indulge in binges—bouts of uncontrolled or clearly excessive drinking.
2. You drink for the purpose of getting drunk.
3. You are unable to stop drinking after one or two drinks.
4. You need to consume greater and greater quantities of alcohol to achieve the same effect.
5. You suffer problems caused by drinking: inability to concentrate on your job; lateness and absenteeism; arguments with colleagues, friends, and family.
6. You avoid family and friends when drinking.
7. You become irritated when your drinking is discussed by family and friends.
8. You are unable to keep promises made to yourself about curbing your drinking.
9. You feel guilty or remorseful about your drinking.
10. You *"black out"* frequently: can't remember what you did while you were drinking.
11. You eat irregularly during periods of drinking.
12. You use drinking to escape your problems.

What happens to alcoholics? Acute, immediate effects range from hangover to delirium tremens—the DTs—the symptoms of which resemble heroin withdrawal and involve shaking, fever, unspeakable panic, and terrifying hallucinations. *Polyneuropathy*, a degenerative disease of the nervous system, is likewise common, as are a host of other irreversible diseases of the central nervous system. The most familiar long-term effects attack the liver. They include diseases such as *acute hepatitis*—inflammation of the liver—and *cirrhosis*, which is in effect scarring of the liver. If enough damage is inflicted, the diseases associated with alcoholism are fatal.

Buzzed Words

A **blackout** is not a loss of consciousness. It is an inability to remember, even after you are sober, what you did and said while intoxicated.

Alcoholics also suffer high accident rates and are more susceptible to infection. They readily lose jobs, friends, and spouses. They mess up the lives of their children, and they typically shorten their own lives by a decade or more.

Health Benefits of Drinking?

Periodically, we hear on TV newscasts or read in popular magazines of studies that reveal some positive health *benefits* of alcohol consumption. The scientific jury is still out on the claims of a number of studies that *moderate* alcohol consumers enjoy a 40 to 50 percent lower risk of having or dying of a heart attack than total nondrinkers. This statistic is similar to the results obtained from taking a low dose of aspirin daily. In addition, some studies suggest that *moderate* alcohol consumers of alcohol have a 10 percent lower death rate from all causes than do abstainers.

Some physicians dispute these claims. Others point out that the dangers and potential dangers of alcohol abuse far exceed the benefits of moderate alcohol consumption, and that it is foolish to take up drinking in hopes of improving your health. Still others suggest that the statistics might say more about the general health and attitude of people who drink moderately than about any health benefit to be derived from alcohol. That is, those who drink moderately might naturally suffer less stress than those who abstain; moderate drinking can be a characteristic of less stressed individuals, whereas abstinence might be more typical of people who are a bit more uptight.

Neither the author nor the publisher of this book make any positive health-benefit claims concerning drinking. Remember also that "general" therapeutic or dietary advice is of very limited use and could even be harmful. Issues of diet and drinking need to take into consideration your particular state of health and any conditions or disorders you might have. We advise those interested in the subject of alcohol and health to seek out the latest responsible studies *and* to consult their professional health-care provider.

Buzzed Words

If you believe that you suffer from a drinking problem, seek help. Your best first resource is your physician, but you also might want to consult such organizations as Alcoholics Anonymous. Alcoholism is such a widespread problem that you will find it as a listing category in most Yellow Pages.

Responsibilities and Obligations

As a drinker, your first responsibility and obligation is to know when to say enough. Your second responsibility and obligation is never to drive when you drink, even if you have been drinking in moderation. (We'll discuss drinking and driving later in the chapter.)

As a host who serves drinks, you also have responsibilities and obligations. (Key ethical and legal responsibilities of professional bartenders are discussed in Chapter 24.) Let's put it this way: You want to show your guests and friends a good time. You don't want to make them look foolish, you don't want to make them sick, you don't want to hurt their families, you don't want to see them injured or killed, and you don't want them to injure or kill anyone else. This being the case, you must serve alcohol responsibly:

- Offer food with the drinks you serve.
- Offer a wide range of appealing nonalcoholic beverages.
- Never "push" drinks on any guest.
- Do not serve drinks to a guest who is intoxicated.
- Do not allow an intoxicated guest to drive. Provide the services of a "designated driver," who has not had alcohol to drink, or call a taxi.

Drinking and Driving

The statistics speak loudly. Nearly 20,000 people are killed each year in the United States in alcohol-related automobile accidents. Of this number, approximately 7,000 are nondrinking victims. The cost of alcohol-related accidents, in terms of legal, medical, and property expenses, is about $16 billion per year.

Not loud enough for you? Consider this: Given the present statistics and the trend they suggest, there is a 40 percent chance that *you* will be involved in an alcohol-related car wreck at some point in your life.

Most states have established standards for defining intoxication based on blood-alcohol concentration (BAC). In many states, you are deemed intoxicated—and therefore illegally driving under the influence (DUI)—if your BAC is .10 percent or higher; in a number of other states, the level is .08 percent (see the following table).

BAC and the Law

By law, .08 percent BAC is per-se (*conclusive*) evidence of DUI in		
Alabama	Illinois	Oregon
California	Kansas	Texas
District of Columbia	Maine	Utah
Florida	New Hampshire	Vermont
Georgia	New Mexico	Virginia
Hawaii	North Carolina	Washington
Idaho		

By law, .10 percent BAC is per-se (*conclusive*) evidence of DUI in		
Alaska	Maryland	Ohio
Arizona	Michigan	Oklahoma
Arkansas	Minnesota	Pennsylvania
Colorado	Mississippi	Rhode Island
Connecticut	Missouri	South Dakota
Delaware	Montana	Tennessee
Indiana	Nebraska	West Virginia
Iowa	New Jersey	Wisconsin
Kentucky	New York	Wyoming
Louisiana	North Dakota	
By law, .08 percent BAC is evidence (but not per-se evidence) of DUI in		
Massachusetts		
By law, .10 percent BAC is evidence (but not per-se evidence) of DUI in		
South Carolina		

All legislation is subject to change.

Note that all 50 states now have BAC limits under .02 percent for drivers under age 21. In Alaska, Arizona, District of Columbia, Illinois, Minnesota, North Carolina, Oregon, Utah, and Wisconsin, even a BAC of .00 can result in a DUI charge against drivers under age 21 if officers find any evidence of alcohol consumption.

Penalties for DUI vary widely, ranging from fines, license suspensions, and license revocations to serious jail time. And the trend is toward stricter laws and increasingly severe penalties.

As bad as getting caught is, the legal consequences of DUI are far less terrible than the potential human consequences: loss of life, injury, permanent disability, shattered families, and devastated finances.

And as strict as many DUI BAC standards are, they don't even kick in before your blood-alcohol concentration begins to impair your …

- Reaction time
- Judgment
- Coordination
- Reflexes

- General motor control
- Eyesight

At a mere .05 percent BAC, you are two to three times more likely to become involved in an automobile accident than you are at .00 percent BAC. At .08 percent—still below the legal DUI definition in many states—you are five to six times more likely to get into a wreck. At the legal definition point for the majority of states—.10 percent—your risk jumps to seven to eight times the risk at .00 percent. Beyond this, if your BAC is higher than .10 percent, you are 20 to 50 times more likely to get into an accident.

If this isn't enough to make you think, consider that these figures represent the *lowest, most conservative* estimates of risk. They are the *best-case* scenario. Depending on your mood, your metabolism, the level of your fatigue, and your age, your risk can be much greater—even if everyone else on the road is sober, which is highly unlikely.

What's the bottom line? Driving drunk is incredibly stupid, criminal, immoral, selfish, self-destructive, destructive to others, suicidal, and homicidal. Do not do it. Do not let others do it.

Bar Tips

Chronic abusers of alcohol are seven times more likely to suffer a fatal accident as persons in the general population. They are 30 times more likely to suffer accidental poisoning, 16 times more likely to die from a fall, and 4.5 times more likely to die in a car accident.

See You in Court?

As if the human, humane, and moral motives for serving drinks responsibly weren't sufficient, you are, to a significant degree, legally liable for the actions of people to whom you serve alcohol.

Increasingly, lawmakers in every state have been shifting much of the responsibility for exercising good judgment from the consumers of alcohol to the servers of alcohol. So-called *dram shop laws* make it legally possible to prosecute those who serve drunks. Such laws also open the gates to civil litigation: You could get sued. Criminal and civil penalties do not apply only to saloons and professional bartenders. The hosts of private parties have also been found liable for the mayhem inflicted by their drunk guests.

How can you protect yourself?

One sure way is to refuse to serve alcohol. Short of this extreme measure, take the steps outlined a little earlier in this chapter:

- Offer food with the drinks you serve.
- Offer a wide range of appealing nonalcoholic beverages.
- Never "push" drinks on any guest.
- Do not serve drinks to a guest who is intoxicated.
- Do not allow an intoxicated guest to drive. Provide the services of a "designated driver," who has not had alcohol to drink, or call a taxi.

You do not have to assume a morally superior tone to shut off the flow of alcohol to a drunk. Although it is true that some people become hostile, even belligerent, when they drink too much, most are pretty jolly—"feeling no pain"—and the best approach is a light and good-humored one. You see that Bill has had a bit too much. Approach him with a glass of water (*plain* water; seltzer or club soda—carbonated water—might accelerate the absorption of the alcohol already sloshing around inside him). Put your arm around his shoulder, hand him the glass, and say, "Bill, you'd better have some of this, or the furniture will start to gang up on you."

Do *not* pose the classic rhetorical question—"Don't you think you've had enough?"—because the automatic answer is "No!" Tipsy folks don't need to be quizzed; they need guidance—and they'll usually accept it. Offer a glass of water along with some good-humored attention and conversation.

The Least You Need to Know

- Your body processes alcohol at a specific rate (about a half-ounce an hour), and you can do nothing to effectively accelerate this natural process.
- The only cure for intoxication—and, subsequently, for a hangover—is the passage of time.
- Drinking plenty of water after overindulging will not sober you up, but it should lessen the severity of a subsequent hangover.
- You have moral and legal responsibilities both as a drinker and as a host.
- Never drink and drive.

Chapter 3

Chemistry 101, History 101: A Short Course in Alcohol

In This Chapter

- Fermentation and distillation
- Potable and nonpotable alcohol
- The earliest alcoholic beverages
- Early development of the major alcoholic beverages

You don't need to know any of the stuff in this chapter to enjoy, mix, or serve drinks—just as you don't need to know the history of the internal combustion engine to drive your car. But if you're interested, here's some more about the nature, composition, and evolution of booze.

CH_3 CH_2 OH

Wines, beers, and spirits all contain CH_3 CH_2 OH—*ethyl alcohol*—also called *ethanol*. The alcohol is produced by *fermentation*, in which yeast enzymes decompose carbohydrates into carbon dioxide and ethanol. The carbohydrate source in wines is the sugars in fruits or berries (usually grapes); in beers, it's grains. In spirits, the carbohydrate source is also grains, but spirits differ in that they are put through an additional process in which the alcoholic beverage is *distilled* from the fermented carbohydrate material.

Buzzed Words

Liquor is an alcoholic beverage made by fermentation *and* distillation rather than fermentation alone (as is the case with wine and beer).

Buzzed Words

Ethyl alcohol is the potable alcohol obtained from fermentation. To produce hard liquor, ethyl alcohol is purified and concentrated by distillation. **Congeners** are acids, aldehydes, esters, ketones, phenols, and tannins that are by-products of fermentation, distillation, and aging. These "impurities" might add character and flavor, but they also can cause undesirable physiological effects on the drinker—notably, increasing the intensity of a hangover.

Although ethyl alcohol is the chief ingredient of all potable alcoholic beverages, very small amounts of amyl, butyl, propyl, and methyl alcohol also find their way into some beverages. You'll also find *congeners*—acids, aldehydes, esters, ketones, phenols, and tannins—along with occasional vitamins and minerals (but that doesn't make beer for breakfast a good idea). The various combinations of these substances—especially the congeners—produce the characteristic flavors, odors, and colors that differentiate one alcoholic beverage from another.

Fermentation

Fermentation has been known for at least 10,000 years, but not until the nineteenth century did the great French chemist Louis Pasteur describe the process in detail, defining it as chemical changes brought about by yeasts and other microorganisms growing *anaerobically* (that is, in the absence of air). Acting on carbohydrates, yeast fermentation produces alcohol, but by selecting various carbohydrates and other microorganisms, you can create a variety of products from fermentation, including glycerol, carbon dioxide, butyl alcohol, acetone, lactic acid, monosodium glutamate, citric acid, gluconic acid, and small amounts of antibiotics, vitamin B_{12}, and riboflavin (vitamin B).

Distillation

Okay. Fermentation is a *natural* process in which organic materials containing carbohydrates are decomposed by yeasts. However, the process of fermentation produces only a relatively low concentration of alcohol: no more than 14 percent by volume. Only by means of an *artificial* process—*distillation*—is it possible to raise the concentration of ethyl alcohol above that of the original fermented mixture.

It works this way. Alcohol boils at 173.3 degrees Fahrenheit, whereas water boils at 212 degrees. If the product of fermentation—a liquid containing ethyl alcohol—is heated to a temperature above 173.3 degrees, but below 212 degrees, and the vapor coming off the liquid is condensed, the condensed vapor (the *condensate*) will have a higher alcohol concentration than the original liquid.

The process of distillation is old enough to have been mentioned by Aristotle—who lived from 384 to 322 B.C.E.—but Pliny the Elder (23–79 C.E.), a Roman, first described a *still*, a vessel specifically made to carry out distillation.

At its most basic, a still consists of a *retort*, in which the liquid to be distilled is heated; a coil, called a *condenser*, at the top of the still, to cool and condense the vapor; and a *receiver*, a vessel that collects the distillate. Over the centuries, various elaborate industrial stills have been created, but they all consist essentially of the same three parts.

At its most basic, a still consists of the following:

- A *retort*—Where the liquid to be distilled is heated.
- A *condenser*—A coil at the top of the still that cools and condenses the vapor.
- A *receiver*—A vessel that collects the distillate.

Over the centuries, various elaborate industrial stills have been created, but they all consist essentially of the same three parts.

Bar Tips

Ethyl alcohol is valuable as a solvent, but federal law requires costly tax stamps on all potable alcohol. To get around this, toxic solvents, such as acetone or methanol, can be added to ethyl alcohol to make it toxic and, therefore, unfit for consumption. This is called *denatured alcohol.*

Poison vs. Potable

Ethyl alcohol, or ethanol, is the only type of alcohol that's safe to drink. The two other principal types—*methyl* (wood) *alcohol* and *isopropyl* (rubbing) *alcohol*—are highly toxic. Drinking wood or rubbing alcohol can result in blindness, severe gastric damage, or death.

In the Beginning, There Was Spit ...

Although distillation was known to the ancients, it didn't become popular in the West as an adjunct to producing alcoholic beverages until the Middle Ages. As far as anyone can tell—or guess—the production and consumption of fermented (but not distilled) alcoholic beverages far predates recorded history. It is believed that, many thousands of years ago, certain folks chewed and spat out grain, and then let the resulting "mash" ferment. There are plenty of yeasty enzymes in saliva, and the result was the conversion of the grain starch first into sugar and then into alcohol. Wouldn't you like to shake the hand of the first person with nerve enough to sample the brew produced by rotting grain and spit? Well, maybe not.

Babylonian Booze

The first evidence of the production of wine comes from Asia Minor about 4000 B.C.E., and the oldest known systematic code of laws, promulgated about 1770 B.C.E. by King Hammurabi of Babylonia, included statutes regulating drinking houses. Even earlier, about 2100 B.C.E., Sumerian physicians prescribed beer for what ailed (no pun intended) their patients. Egyptian doctors also prescribed wine and beer, circa 1500 B.C.E.

Early on, alcoholic beverages found their way into religious worship, doubtless inducing a state of ecstasy and trance in the celebrants. However, in ancient Mesopotamia as well as ancient Egypt, drinking as well as drunkenness spread beyond the temple and into common practice.

Land of Milk and Honey

The Jews of the Old Testament used alcoholic beverages for a host of sacramental purposes, from celebrating an eight-day-old boy's circumcision to toasting the soul of the recently deceased. Drinking also took place at weddings, and wine marked the arrival and departure of each Sabbath and festival. Like so much else in ancient Jewish life, drinking was strictly regulated. Drunkenness was frowned upon and condemned.

Bar Tips

Alcohol is the oldest and most widely used drug.

Greek Wine and Roman Orgies

The literature and art of the ancient Greeks and Romans is full of references to the copious consumption of wine by gods and people alike. The cult of Dionysus, or Bacchus, god of wine, was the most popular of Greek as well as Roman religious cults.

The Greeks and Hebrews generally enjoyed their wine cut 50/50 with water, but a minority took it straight. Whether diluted or not, wine was far more popular than straight water—not surprising in an age when the communal water source was also the communal sewer.

Buzzed Words

The **Bacchanalia** was the ancient Roman festival in honor of Bacchus (Roman version of the Greek god Dionysus). A drunken orgy with a specific religious purpose, it gave the literary English a word (spelled with a small *b*) to describe a drunken orgy.

The Middle East, Africa, and Asia

The Middle East gave rise to the first religion to actively condemn wine, Islam, although pre-Islamic Arabs developed a distillation method that was used to produce a distilled beverage from wine. In Africa, maize, millet, bananas, honey, palm and bamboo saps, and many fruits were used to ferment thick, rich beers and wines—including Kaffir beer and the highly potent palm wines that are still enjoyed today.

The people of Asia produced wines in prehistoric times, using barley and rice as raw materials. By 800 B.C.E., the Chinese produced the earliest recorded *distilled* liquor, a strong beverage from rice beer.

In the New World

While the Old World was busy imbibing, many of the peoples of the New World—the pre-Columbian Indians of North America—were without booze. When Europeans introduced them to it, the results were often tragic, and alcoholism remains a serious problem among Native Americans.

In the American Southwest, the Papago Indians fermented wine from cactus, and the Tarahumara of northern Mexico made beers from corn and from the agave—the plant that would eventually be used to produce tequila. Farther south, in Central and South America, people made *chicha* and other alcoholic beverages from maize, tubers, fruits, flowers, and saps.

Toast

May the grass grow long on the road to hell for the want of use.

Spiritual Origins

Where did the spirits we enjoy come from? The ancient Greeks and Romans knew about distilling, but distilled liquor doesn't seem to have been very popular with them. The Romans have no written references to distilled beverages before 100 C.E. In Britain, distilled spirits were produced before the Roman conquest, and Spain, France, and Western Europe also produced distilled spirits, but these didn't become popular until the early Middle Ages—about the eighth century.

Whence Whiskey?

The Middle Ages also saw the production of the first distilled spirits made from starchy grains, as opposed to sugar-based materials such as grapes and honey (the bases, respectively, of grape brandy and distilled mead, which is fermented honey and water). Distilling liquor from grains is the origin of whiskey. By the seventeenth century, various European governments were beginning to regulate the distilled spirits industry, which soon became a rich source of tax revenue.

The first whiskeys seem to have come from Ireland and Scotland. Indeed, the word *whiskey* is derived from the Celtic *usquebaugh*, similar to the Irish Gaelic (*uisce beathadh)* and the Scots Gaelic (*uisge beatha)*, all of which came from—guess what?—the Latin phrase *aqua vitae*, "water of life." The earliest account of whiskey making is found in Scottish writings dating from 1494.

Commercial whiskey production hit America by the early eighteenth century and soon became an industry associated with what was then the Western frontier: Kentucky, Pennsylvania, and Indiana. Canada joined the party in the early nineteenth century, producing characteristically blended products.

Genesis of Gin

As mentioned in Chapter 1, the name *gin* comes from the French name for the juniper berry, *genièvre*. It is the only spirit whose origin can be traced to a single inventor: one Franciscus Sylvius, a seventeenth-century professor of medicine at the University of Leiden in Holland (where, incidentally, *genièvre* is called *genever* or *jenever)*. Sylvius distilled the juniper berry with spirits in order to create a cheap medicine with the diuretic properties of much more costly juniper-berry oil.

Soon the medicine became popular as a beverage, and English soldiers marching through Holland during the wars of the later seventeenth and early eighteenth centuries took a liking to the drink and brought it back to England, where its name was contracted to *gin*. (The soldiers called it "Dutch courage.") Although all classes enjoyed the beverage, the cheap spirit was especially popular with the less privileged, and its widespread use gave rise to an epidemic of alcoholism.

Vodka's Unveiling

Vodka was first distilled some time in fourteenth-century Poland, and soon spread throughout Poland, Russia, and the Balkans. It became popular in the United States and Western Europe, however, only after World War II.

Rum's Reign

Rum originated in the West Indies and is first mentioned in records from Barbados dating from about 1650. At first, it was called "kill-devil" and "rumbullion," but, by 1667, it appeared in written records as simply "rum."

Rum was an enormously popular commodity and was soon exported to the North American mainland. In Puritan New England, a rum-distilling industry developed, becoming one of the three legs of the infamous "triangle trade": slaves were brought from Africa and traded to the West Indies for molasses; the molasses was sold in New England, where it was made into rum; and the rum was in turn traded to African-based slavers for more slaves. The rum industry received a major boost in the eighteenth century, when the British Royal Navy instituted a policy of issuing a rum ration to all sailors.

A Tale of Tequila

The native peoples of Mexico had been fermenting the juice of the *agave* for untold years before the Spanish invasion of the sixteenth century. Among the many cultural innovations the Spanish introduced to the Indians was distillation, and soon the Mexicans put distillation to work on the fermented juice of the *blue agave*. The result was a liquor named for the town of Tequila in the Mexican state of Jalisco, where the beverage is still produced under strict government control.

The Bona Fides of Brandy

The word *brandy* is of Dutch origin; *brandewijn* means "burnt wine," a reference to the application of heat in distilling the beverage from wine. Brandy was first distilled commercially in the sixteenth century. It is said that a particularly enterprising Dutch sea captain, seeking to reduce cargo costs, hit upon the idea of distilling wine in order to concentrate it. His plan was then to reconstitute the wine by the addition of water when he reached port. However, somebody sampled the concentrated beverage, liked it, spread the good news, and brandy was born. It was immediately successful.

Soon, most wine-producing countries began making brandy. Best known and most prized are the great French brandies, and outstanding among these are cognac—from the Charente and Charente–Maritime *départements* (administrative districts)—and Armagnac, from the Gers region. Spain and Portugal also produce distinctive brandies, as does Greece: *Metaxa* is sweetened and usually darkened with caramel, and *ouzo* is colorless, flavored with anise or licorice.

Liqueur Lineage

The source of the word *liqueur*, in Church Latin, *liquefacere* ("to make liquid"), betrays its origin in the world of the medieval monks and alchemists, who first produced these beverages commercially in the Dark Ages. Originally, they were used as medicines, balms, elixirs, tonics, and—above all—aphrodisiacs. The range of available liqueurs will be described in detail in Chapter 16; however, you should know that the formulas of the great proprietary liqueur brands are closely guarded secrets, dating to the Renaissance in some cases. French Bénédictine, for example, was first produced in 1510; its formula has remained a closed book since that year. Chartreuse debuted in 1607, and other famous liqueurs followed, including Cointreau, Grand Marnier, and Vieille Cure. Drambuie, derived from scotch, is made in Scotland from a French formula obtained in 1745.

No News?

Will the coming years see the evolution of truly new spirits? Probably not soon. But even though the basic spirits may remain the same, the possibilities of new mixed drinks remain virtually without limit, and, each year, enterprising mixologists develop novelties of temptation.

The Least You Need to Know

- Alcohol is produced by the action of yeasts on carbohydrates—a process called fermentation.
- Spirits are alcoholic beverages in which the alcohol content has been concentrated by distilling alcohol-bearing liquid produced by fermentation.
- Alcoholic beverages predate recorded history and are certainly as old as civilization.
- Fermented beverages have ancient lineage. Distilled spirits did not come into wide use in the West until the Middle Ages.

Chapter 4

Of Ponies, Garbage, and Garnishes: The Basic Equipment of Bartending

In This Chapter

- Stocking a basic liquor cabinet
- What you need for an advanced bar
- The basic and advanced mixers
- Glassware and other equipment

There is no "right" way to stock your bar. The liquor and the equipment you select depend on your personal needs, your taste, what you and your friends enjoy, and your budget. This chapter gives you suggestions ranging from the bare minimum to the truly well-stocked bar.

As for quantities, you might want to weigh the savings of buying large bottles against the opportunity to sample more brands and kinds of liquor if you buy smaller bottles.

A Portfolio of Potables: Price vs. Value

We're not going to say much about specific brands here, except to point out that the price of liquor varies substantially from brand to brand. You should base your buying decisions on two factors:

1. **Are you mixing it with something?** It makes no sense to spring for a premium rum if you're going to mix it with Coke. If you intend to drink liquor straight, on the rocks, with water, with seltzer or club soda, with mildly flavored mixers, or in such mixed drinks as martinis and Manhattans, your enjoyment will be enhanced by investing in the better, more expensive brands. But see #2.
2. **What's more important to you, price or value?** Old Rotgut whiskey might have the lowest price, but if it tastes like something nasty squeezed through a dirty sock, it's not a good value. At a higher, but still moderate price level, you might find a whiskey to your liking. For you, *that* could represent good value. If, however, you enjoy the flavor and feel of a fine sippin' whiskey, a premium price might be an even *better* value because (as far as you're concerned) it delivers significantly more of what you want than the moderately priced brand.

You must decide whether price or value is more important to you. Here's our suggestion: First decide what you want from a drink. If you're after an unalloyed pleasurable experience, "value" means spending enough to make drinking worth your time, and we suggest trying some of the premium or near-premium brands in an effort to decide on the ones you like best.

Bar Tips

Each chapter in Parts 2 through 5 is devoted to a major type of liquor, including advice on what qualities to look for in that type of liquor.

Drinking shouldn't be a solitary pleasure. When you are a guest in a friend's home, and you are offered a drink, be sure to take note of brands. This is one way of expanding your knowledge of available spirits without having to spring for a lot of experimental bottles yourself.

The Basics: Liquor

At its most basic, the home bar can be a kitchen-cabinet collection of the two or three kinds of mixers and spirits you and your friends enjoy. A single step more advanced is this "starter bar" selection:

- ❑ 1 (750 ml.) bottle of bourbon
- ❑ 1 (750 ml.) bottle of Canadian whisky

- ❑ 1 (750 ml.) bottle of blended scotch
- ❑ 1 (1.75 liter) bottle of gin
- ❑ 1 (1.75 liter) bottle of light rum
- ❑ 1 (1.75 liter) bottle of white tequila
- ❑ 1 (1.75 liter) bottle of vodka
- ❑ 1 (750 ml.) bottle of brandy

The Basics: Liqueurs

Even a basic bar should stock small bottles of the most popular liqueurs. Include the following:

- ❑ triple sec
- ❑ crème de menthe
- ❑ crème de cacao
- ❑ amaretto
- ❑ Kahlùa
- ❑ Drambuie
- ❑ Bénédictine
- ❑ Cointreau
- ❑ Grand Marnier

The Basics: Wine and Beer

The subjects of wine and of beer are vast, and you'll find *Complete Idiot's Guides* devoted to both. For the purposes of mixing some drinks, you will need wine and beer, so we need to give them at least a mention here. For the "starter bar," stock at least the following:

- 1 small bottle of dry vermouth
- 1 small bottle of sweet vermouth
- 2 bottles of white wine
- 2 bottles of red wine
- 1 bottle of champagne or sparkling wine
- 2 six-packs of beer
- 1 six-pack of lite beer

The Basics: Mixers

You will want to stock at least five carbonated mixers:

- 2 (1 liter) bottles of cola
- 2 (1 liter) bottles of diet cola
- 2 (1 liter) bottles of tonic water

These mix well with light alcohols, such as gin, vodka, and rum.

For the dark spirits—such as scotch and bourbon—have on hand the following:

- 3 (1 liter) bottles of club soda
- 2 (1 liter) bottles of ginger ale
- 2 (1 liter) bottles of 7-Up (or the equivalent)

You may substitute seltzer, soda water, or sparkling spring water (such as Perrier) for plain soda water. And please note carefully: This basic stock of five carbonated beverages is what you need for mixing drinks. In addition to these, be certain to have plenty of cola, ginger ale, 7-Up (or the equivalent), and other soft drinks to offer guests as an alternative to alcoholic beverages.

You'll also need five basic juices. If possible, purchase them just before use so that they'll be fresh:

- 3 quarts of orange juice
- 2 quarts of grapefruit juice
- 1 large can of pineapple juice
- 1 large bottle of cranberry juice
- 3 large bottles of tomato juice

(You'll need the tomato juice for Bloody Marys, but that's not all. See Chapter 7 for more on the ingredients that make for a great Bloody Mary.)

A number of drinks call for *sour mix* or *bar mix* (which is the same thing). You can buy this bottled or in ready-to-mix powdered form at liquor stores or grocery stores, or, if you prefer, you can prepare it yourself. There are two basic recipes.

Commercial powdered sour mix adds powdered egg white to the product to make the drink foam up. Shaking the cocktail vigorously should provide plenty of foam, even without the egg white, but if you want to ensure a foamy sour, use the second recipe:

Sour Mix Recipe #1

Juice of ½ lemon per drink

1 tsp. sugar per drink

Combine these with other drink ingredients in a shaker with ice. Shake vigorously, and then strain into serving glass.

Sour Mix Recipe #2

12 oz. lemon juice (juice of 6 lemons)

18 oz. distilled water

¼ cup refined sugar

1 egg white*

Blend all ingredients in blender. Refrigerate.

Note: The mix will keep for about 1 week under refrigeration. You must shake or blend before each use.

** Raw egg may be a source of salmonella bacteria. You may wish to avoid drinks calling for raw egg yolk or white.*

Round out the "starter bar" basic mixer arsenal with the following items:

- 1 small bottle of Rose's lime juice
- Superfine granulated sugar
- Coarse (not table) salt (for margaritas and Salty Dogs)
- Grenadine
- Sugar syrup (also known as simple syrup)

Bar Tips

Raw eggs may be a source of **salmonella**, a type of bacteria that causes food poisoning. The only way to avoid the risk of salmonella infection is to cook the egg. For this reason, you may wish to avoid all drinks made with raw egg white, raw egg yolk, or raw whole egg. You may wish to use commercially prepared sour mix, which uses powdered egg white (not associated with salmonella).

Finally, don't neglect water and ice. If the water that comes from your tap tastes great, use it. If not—and plenty of us have less than gourmet tap water—buy a couple of half-gallon bottles of good spring water or invest in a filtration system. Don't foul good liquor with bad water.

Even if the ice that comes from your freezer tastes okay—that is, has no flavor whatsoever—you will want to buy a couple of large bags for any party. Commercial ice is more reliable, as far as flavorlessness, and you'll probably need more than you can produce in your freezer—unless you really plan ahead or you are expecting only a few people.

One Step Beyond

If "basic" isn't enough for you, here's the next logical step. To the "starter bar," add the following spirits:

- 1 bottle of Dutch (Genever) gin
- 1 bottle of premium English gin
- 2 bottles of premium Scandinavian or Russian vodka
- 1 bottle of specially flavored gin, such as Tanqueray No. 10 or Bombay Sapphire
- 1 or more bottles of flavored vodka, such as Stolnichaya Peppar and Absolut Citron
- 1 bottle of rye
- 1 bottle of Irish whiskey
- 1 bottle of single-malt scotch
- 1 bottle of bourbon or Tennessee whiskey
- 1 bottle of gold rum
- 1 bottle of dark (Jamaican) rum
- 1 bottle of gold tequila (*tequila anejo*)

Bar Tips

You can buy sugar syrup ready-made or prepare it at home. In a saucepan, gradually dissolve 2 cups of sugar in a cup of water. Simmer for 10 minutes, stirring frequently. Refrigerate until needed.

A wide range of exotic liqueurs is available. Consider the following additions to the basic roster:

- framboise
- kirschwasser
- slivovitz
- crème de cassis
- sambuca
- peppermint schnapps
- peach schnapps
- Galliano
- Frangelico

You can add any number of great wines and beers to your collection. Do consider these:

- aperitif wines (Dubonnet, Lillet, and Campari are the most popular)
- 1 bottle of cream sherry
- 1 bottle of port

- 1 bottle of madeira
- 1 bottle of amontillado

Get at least two or three flavored brandies:

- 1 bottle Calvados or applejack (apple brandy)
- 1 bottle apricot brandy
- 1 bottle peach brandy

In addition to the most-requested mixers, you might also keep on hand the following:

- coffee
- cream (heavy and light)
- cream of coconut
- Falernum (a spicy, lime-flavored sweetener)
- orgeat syrup (orange-almond syrup)
- passion fruit nectar
- *bitters*

Bar Tips

Bitters is an *alcoholic* mixer (Angostura bitters is the best known) that gives a special piquance to Manhattans, old-fashioneds, and even Bloody Marys. Because all bitters contain alcohol, be careful *not* to use them to flavor nonalcoholic drinks for nondrinkers.

Although Angostura Aromatic Bitters is the most famous and popular bitters, you might want to stock Abbott's and Bokers as well. Campari is an aperitif wine that many people class with the bitters. You will also want to know about Jaegermeister, another aperitif that is often deemed a bitters. For drinks with a Cajun accent, invest in a bottle of New Orleans's classic Peychaud's Bitters.

Garnishes and Garbage

Many mixed drinks have solid as well as liquid components. If a piece of fruit or vegetable added to a drink actually changes the way it tastes, it is called a *garnish*. If it's just for visual decoration, it's called *garbage*.

The basic bar should have the following garnishes and garbage available:

Lemon twists All you use is the peel. The way to get the most peel from each lemon is to slice off the ends, and then use a spoon to force the fruit out one end. Now you have an empty lemon peel. Slice it lengthwise into strips one-quarter inch wide. When a drink calls for a "twist," take one of the strips, twist it over the drink, rub the inside of the peel around the edge of the glass, plunk it in, and then stir. It is best to have some strips prepared and ready to go.

Lime wedges Lime is rarely cut into twist strips; you use it in wedges. Think of the two bumps at either end as the poles of the lime; then cut the fruit at the equator. Quarter each hemisphere. The result is eight wedges. Use one per drink, squeezing the lime over the drink, rubbing it around the rim of the glass, and then dropping it in. Because lime wedges are such a popular garnish, you should have several limes cut and on hand.

Orange slices Oranges are typically sliced. Create as many ¼-inch–thick semicircles as possible from each orange. Cut the orange in half, starting at the stem. Put each half flat-side down, and then cut widthwise to make your semicircles. Notch a small cut in the fruit side of each slice so that you can slide it onto the rim of the glass. Do not squeeze the orange into the drink.

Buzzed Words

A **garnish** is a bit of fruit or vegetable added to a drink principally to enhance its flavor. **Garbage** is a bit of fruit or vegetable added to a drink primarily for the sake of appearance. It does not significantly enhance the flavor of the drink.

Maraschino cherries These super-sweet, surrealistically red (-dyed) little numbers are garbage; that is, they add no flavor to the drink. However, drinkers like to pull them out of the drink and eat them, so make certain that you leave the stems on. Have at least two jars of maraschino cherries on hand.

Olives Most martini drinkers like their libation with an olive or three. Use medium-size green pitted olives—with or without the pimento (it may discolor but will not materially harm the drink). Usually, the olive(s) are skewered on a toothpick or little plastic sword and placed in the drink. Some drinkers like their martini "dirty," meaning that they like some olive juice splashed in.

Pearl onions A martini harboring a pearl onion (or two or three) rather than an olive or olives is properly called a Gibson. Have a little jar of pearls handy. Stored under refrigeration in their own juice, they'll keep almost indefinitely. The pearls may be skewered on a toothpick.

Celery stalks These add the finishing touch to a Bloody Mary. The width and length of the stalk should suit the glass you use. To add some visual flair, leave the stalk's leafy end on. Yes, the celery may be eaten.

Cucumber peel A curlicue peel is used to decorate a few specialty drinks.

Inedible Additions

Don't forget cocktail toothpicks or, if you yearn for a touch of kitsch, little plastic cocktail swords. You'll also need swizzle sticks or cocktail straws. And, for tropical drinks, don't forget the paper parasols. These little touches will make you the consummate host.

Tools of the Trade

There's a load of gadgets and glassware a bartender can buy. Some of them are even useful.

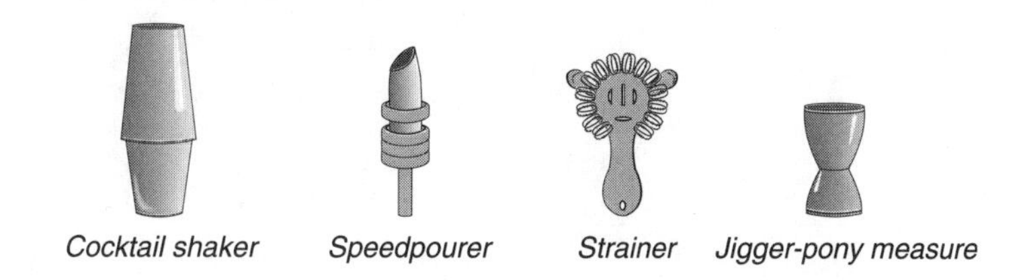

Shaker Upper

The trademark of the pro is the cocktail shaker. You'll need one to make sours, daiquiris, margaritas, and a straight-up martini à la James Bond ("Shaken, not stirred"). Buy one with a stainless steel shell—the bigger, outer part—and glass, the smaller, inner part. A 12-ounce shaker should be ample.

You'll also need a cocktail strainer that fits over the shaker so that you can pour the chilled drink without disgorging the ice cubes into the serving glass. This is called pouring a drink "straight-up."

Other Essentials

If you're going for that pro look, you'll also want a number of *speedpourers*—the plastic gadgets that fit into the mouth of a liquor bottle, allowing you to pour the liquor at an even, measured rate without spilling.

While you're at it, why not buy a genuine *bar spoon*? This has a small paddle spoon at one end of long handle that is twisted in the middle. The spoon is the bartender's Swiss army knife: drinks can be stirred with the handle, garnishes can be manipulated with the spoon (if you don't want to use your fingers), and the swirled part can be used to pour the ingredients of layered drinks—such as pousse-cafés—in which it is important to not mix the layers.

Speaking of Swiss army knife-type things, you might pick up a combination corkscrew/ bottle opener/can opener, commonly called a *captain's knife*. You're bound to need all three.

Finally, there is the *jigger-pony* combination measure. The larger cone is a jigger (1½-ounce measure), and the smaller is the pony (1 ounce).

Other useful equipment you are likely to already have in your kitchen:

- A paring knife for cutting fruit garnishes
- An electric blender
- An ice bucket with ice tongs (for the fastidious and hygienic)
- A juice squeezer

A Glass Act

True, you could get by with a collection of jelly jars, but a wide range of glassware has evolved to accommodate a wide range of drinks.

Glassware is far less critical in serving liquor than it is in serving fine wine. However, glass size and shape can enhance or detract from the experience of enjoying straight liquor as well as mixed drinks. Let's go over the basics.

Highball and Low

The *highball glass* is the one you'll use most. Highball glasses are used for scotch and soda, scotch and water, bourbon and water, gin and tonic, vodka and tonic. You get the picture. The orthodox highball glass is a tall 8 ounces; however, some hold 12 ounces.

Only slightly less popular is the *lowball glass*, which some bartenders call a *rocks glass* because it is used for many drinks served on the rocks. Ranging from 4 to 9 ounces, this short, clear glass is used for martinis on the rocks, various whiskey-rocks combinations, Manhattans on the rocks, and so on.

Both the highball and lowball glasses should be clear, not frosted. How many of both you purchase depends on your hosting plans, but a dozen of each is a good minimum number for the committed host.

Collins and Old-Fashioned

The *Collins glass* is not just for the Tom Collins, but for any of the larger mixed drinks that benefit from a cooling, refreshing image. This includes the various fizzes and a wealth of tropical drinks. The 10- to 14-ounce Collins glass is frosted (sometimes with an icy pebble effect as well) to about ¾" from the top. This top portion is left clear, partly, perhaps, to caress the drinker's lips, but mainly to remind the bartender to add soda water to the very top of the Tom Collins.

Old-fashioned glasses come in two sizes, large (7-ounce) and small (4-ounce), and are similar to the lowball glass, except for the bump at the base of the glass. Presumably, this is to remind the bartender to prepare the fixings for the old-fashioned.

Although the Collins glass is not an ideal substitute for the highball glass, the old-fashioned glass can certainly do double duty as a lowball or "rocks glass." The frugal host will, in fact, choose one or the other. As for the Collins glass, it's a good idea to have at least a half-dozen of these in addition to your highball glassware.

Bar Tips

The Collins glass would be the same as a large (12-ounce) highball glass, except that the highball glass is entirely clear, whereas the Collins glass is partially frosted.

Cocktail and Sour

The classic *cocktail glass* is so classic—an inverted cone perched on a long stem—that it is, quite literally, *the* icon of the cocktail lounge, often immortalized in neon signs. The 4-ounce glass is used for any cocktail ordered straight-up. Its stem is more than decorative: Because drinks served in cocktail glasses have no ice in them, the stem enables you to hold the glass without warming the contents with your hands. Six to 12 of these should be adequate for the moderately serious host.

You might add a few 4- or 5-ounce *sour glasses* to your collection. These are stemmed glasses with elongated bowls that make whiskey sours (and other foamy sour drinks) more inviting.

Wine and Sherry

The subject of wine glasses is complex. If you enjoy fine wines, read *The Complete Idiot's Guide to Wine*, which includes a discussion of glassware. For the basic bar, however, the sturdy, stemmed, globe-bowled glasses of a Parisian-style bistro are adequate.

You may also stock some sherry glasses. These 2½- to 3½-ounce stemmed glasses can be used for aperitifs and port as well as sherry. The best kind of sherry glass is the *copita*, which features a narrow taper that captures the wine's aroma. If you prefer, however, you might serve these drinks in the smaller pony or cordial glasses.

Champagne: American Style and in the European Mood

Like wine, the subject of champagne lies beyond the scope of this book; however, basic bar equipment should include a minimum of a dozen champagne glasses. The question is, which style?

Americans tend to favor a stemmed glass that looks like a shorter, wider, shallower version of the cocktail glass. It holds 4 to 6 ounces of bubbly. Europeans, however, prefer a very different glass, the champagne flute, which is tall and fluted—bulging gracefully at the bottom and tapering toward the rim.

Bar Tips

Using champagne flutes results in less spillage than American-style champagne glasses.

Patriotism notwithstanding, we recommend the European flute over the American champagne glass. Not only does it hold more of a good thing (capacities vary from 7 to 11 ounces), but, more importantly, its tapered profile reduces the surface area and slows the dissipation of the bubbles.

Buzzed Words

A **jigger** is the glass or the metal measuring cup used to measure drinks. It is also what you call the amount the jigger measures: 1½ ounces. Strictly speaking, a **pony** is a 1-ounce measure; however, pony glasses range in capacity from 1 to 2 ounces.

Small Stuff: The Cordial Pony and Your Best Shot

Every bar should have a supply of shot glasses, which you can use not only to serve shots, but also to measure drinks. Shot glasses come in one- to two-ounce sizes, and your wisest choice is 1½ ounces—a *jigger*—because this is the ideal size for measuring most drinks.

If you enjoy bitters, cordials, or sherry, stock either sherry glasses or some of the smaller pony glasses.

Snifter Story

The *brandy snifter* is a particularly elegant piece of glassware. It ranges anywhere from about 5 to 25 ounces; however, no snifter is meant to hold so vast an amount of brandy. Opt for about a 16-ounce snifter, in which you serve no more than 1 or 2 ounces of brandy. The idea is that the oversized balloon shape will waft, accumulate, and funnel the aroma of the wine into the drinker's nose. If you use a snifter smaller than 16 ounces, reduce the amount of brandy proportionately. Snifters larger than 16 ounces are unwieldy, tend to be fragile, and add nothing special to the drinking experience.

Unless you have a lot of brandy- or cognac-drinking friends, you shouldn't need many snifters. Fine brandy or cognac is best enjoyed in an intimate group, anyway.

Mugs and Pilsner Glasses

As with wine, the subject of beer is too vast for this book; fortunately, *The Complete Idiot's Guide to Beer* is available. But while we're on the subject of glassware, be sure to have a dozen 10-ounce beer glasses on hand.

Should you choose mugs, Pilsner glasses, or both? Mugs won't break as easily, but if you are serving really wonderful premium beer, the tall, elegant *Pilsner glass* can enhance the drinking experience. It's your call. In either case, drinking beer from a mug or glass is far more enjoyable than sucking on a bottle or slurping from a can.

Other Specialized Glassware

Now that you've had a rundown of the basic bar glassware, you should also know about the following specialized glasses.

- **Pousse-café glass** A three- to four-ounce stemmed glass with little or no flare or tapering of the bowl. It is handy for layered dessert drinks.
- **Parfait glass** A slightly larger version of the pousse-café glass, the parfait glass usually has a flared lip. It is also used for layered dessert drinks.
- **Fizz glass** This five-ounce stemmed glass is shorter but wider than a five-ounce sour glass. It is useful if you want to serve fizz drinks in something smaller than a Collins glass.
- **Martini glass** Some people prefer their martini in this modified version of a cocktail glass rather than in a cocktail glass. Typically four ounces, the martini glass tapers to a very shallow point at the stem, unlike the cocktail glass, which tapers to an acute point.
- **Eggnog mug** This large, barrel-shaped mug is a fun way to enjoy eggnog drinks.

Do you really need any of these specialized glasses? Base your decisions on your taste, on what you and your guests like to drink, and on just how "complete" a host/bartender you want (and can afford) to be.

The Least You Need to Know

- The basic bar stock recommended here should be sufficient for most casual hosts.
- Err on the side of stocking more soft-drink mixers than you think you need. Ensure that you always provide alternatives to alcohol.
- Ice is the most frequently neglected ingredient in drinks. Too many hosts have too little of it, and what they do use too often tastes of nasty things in the freezer.
- If you must reduce glassware to a *sub* minimum, make sure that you at least have highball and lowball glasses.

Chapter 5

Mixology Demystified: Secrets of Measuring, Mixing, and Pouring

In This Chapter

- The three basic kinds of drinks
- Methods of measuring
- When (and how) to stir, when (and how) to shake
- Pouring like a pro
- Preparing your glassware

If you've comparison shopped before buying this book—or if (shame on you!) you've been sufficiently disloyal and mistrustful to consult another book after purchasing this one—you may have been overwhelmed by the sheer number of drinks it is possible to mix.

Don't panic. The fact is, almost all of those hundreds, even thousands of "different" drinks are actually variations on three basic themes: the highball, the stirred cocktail ("lowball"), and the shaken cocktail. Master the basic themes, and you'll have no trouble with the variations. This chapter shows you how.

Your First Highball: A Seminar in Measurement

Most of your guests who order mixed drinks will ask for a highball. They won't *call* it that. They'll ask for a rum and Coke, a gin and tonic, a scotch and soda, a screwdriver—something like that—but they're all highballs.

So what's your primary piece of equipment? The highball glass, obviously. Grab one and proceed.

A Firm Foundation

Fill the highball glass about two-thirds with ice. Ice is the foundation of most mixed drinks. Anyone thinking about buying a house has at least some awareness of the importance of a sound and solid foundation. Yet the foundation, below ground and out of sight, probably gets the least attention from the prospective buyer, who is far more interested in what lies above. Similarly, drinkers as well as bartenders give little thought to ice—yet it is probably the most critical component of any drink poured over or chilled by it.

Ice for mixed drinks is often plagued by two problems:

- Bad taste
- Insufficient supply

Bar Tips

Almost all the drinks you'll mix will be highballs.

Bar Tips

Buy one pound of ice per each guest at a four-hour party, unless you're primarily expecting a beer-and-wine crowd.

Both problems can be solved with a single solution. Buy bags of commercial *cocktail* (small-cube) ice. First, it's flavorless, as ice should be, but most home freezer ice is not. Ice made at home typically takes on disagreeable odors or tastes. If your refrigerator has an icemaker, consider hooking it up to a water filter. That will greatly improve the flavor of the ice—and by "improve," what we really mean is eliminate. But even if you filter your ice making water, freezer burn takes its toll. Whereas most food keeps indefinitely in the freezer, exposed ice cubes do not. If they are not freshly made, they tend to go "stale," acquiring an almost musty taste.

Bagged ice is pure, tasteless, and also available in virtually *unlimited* quantities! But if you absolutely must mix a drink with refrigerator freezer ice, take the extra step of rinsing the cubes under cold tap water. This gets rid of freezer burn and many of the superficial tastes or odors that might cling to the surface of the ice.

The Jigger Method

Having laid your two-thirds–ice foundation, pour in one jigger (that is, 1½ ounces) of liquor. Either use a jigger measure or a jigger-size shot glass. (Be careful! Some so-called "shot glasses" are really pony glasses, 1 ounce instead of 1½. Make sure that you have the right measure.) Then pour in the mixer—right to the top. Not only will this give you the proper liquor-to-mixer proportion for taste, but also it *looks* generous. Most importantly, it will keep you from mixing your drinks too strong. Your object is to dispense enjoyment, not intoxication.

If the mixer is carbonated, your work is almost done (unless the drink calls for the addition of a garnish) because the bubbles, not you, do most of the mixing. If you feel the need to stir, do so gently to avoid accelerating the dissipation of the bubbles and giving the drink a flat taste.

If the mixer is noncarbonated, either give the drink a few quick stirs with your bar spoon or just put a straw in the glass and let the drinker stir to his or her heart's content.

The Two-Finger Method

Nothing is *wrong* with measuring out liquor with a jigger, and the method certainly ensures a high degree of accuracy. However, it has four drawbacks:

- It's slow. This is not a problem if your guests are few, but it can cause a backup at the bar (and monopolize too much of your time) if you are hosting a large party. For *professional* bartending, the jigger method is almost always unacceptably slow.
- It's messier; you dirty more barware, and you can drip all over the place.
- Measuring out each drink jigger by jigger might be perceived as amateurish.
- Worse, it might be perceived as cheap—as if you're rationing out the liquor guest by guest.

One alternative to jigger measurement is the "two-finger method." Just wrap your two fingers together around the bottom of the glass and pour the liquor until it reaches the top of your fingers. If you have especially slender digits, leave a little air between them when you wrap them around the glass. If you're fat-fingered, stop pouring *before* the liquor tops off at the horizon of your fingers. Don't get fanatical over accuracy. You're a bartender, not a pharmacist.

> **Toast**
>
> May you live as long as you want to, and want to as long as you live.

The two-finger method is fast and at least roughly accurate. It's also inconspicuous and looks reasonably professional.

The Three-Count Technique

If you use a speedpourer (see the previous chapter), which provides a steady, controllable, even flow of liquor, you might want to use the Three-Count Technique. Of the three measuring techniques, it's the only one that calls for practice. Here's how to do it:

1. After filling a highball glass two-thirds with ice, grab the liquor bottle firmly by the neck. The bottle *must* have a speedpourer inserted!
2. In a single, quick motion, invert the bottle—*completely upside down*—over the glass.
3. Count three. (Not out loud. And, please, try not to move your lips.)

> **Bar Tips**
>
> It pays to practice the Three-Count Technique. When you match three counts with a 1½-ounce pour, you can match a one count to one-half ounce, and you'll find that four counts will give you two ounces—should you ever need to deviate from the standard jigger.

The object is to practice to the point that a three count ("one-thousand one, one-thousand two, one-thousand three …") will dispense 1½ ounces. You'll probably want to practice with water in a shot glass until you've got the cadence matched with the pour rate.

Why bother?

This is a virtuoso method that makes you look like a thoroughgoing pro. Moreover, after you've got it down, you won't have to think about counting. Your sense of timing will kick in automatically. The result will be effortless and rapid drink preparation.

Shaken, or Stirred?

So what's the big deal when Agent 007 suavely orders his martini, specifying that it be "shaken, not stirred"? It's unorthodox, that's what. It's bold and daring—as befits a secret agent who has license to kill.

For the classic martini is stirred, not shaken. Arguably, shaking rather than stirring the martini "improves" its taste by aerating the drink. Maybe. But it also might cloud the martini with tiny air bubbles—which some drinkers find displeasing to the eye. Here's the accepted rule of thumb: If a drink consists of clear, relatively thin ingredients (such as the gin and vermouth of a martini), use the "least invasive" blending method—that is, stirring. If, however, a drink contains thicker fluids, such as fruit juice, shaking is required to blend the drink properly.

Toast

There was a college that had the reputation of being a fountain of knowledge. Everyone went there to drink.

The Stirred Cocktail

Stirred drinks can be prepared on the rocks or straight-up. Let's walk through the mixing of a vodka gimlet as an example of a stirred cocktail prepared and served on the rocks:

1. Fill a lowball glass almost to the rim with ice.
2. Pour in 2 ounces of vodka.
3. Add ¼ ounce of Rose's lime juice.
4. Stir *well.*
5. Garnish with a lime wedge; drop it in.

That's one way to do it. You can also prepare on-the-rocks, stirred cocktails in a two-step proccss. Another vodka gimlet, please:

1. Fill a shaker glass (the small, inner part of a cocktail shaker) two-thirds with ice.
2. Add 1 ounce of Rose's lime juice.
3. Pour in 5 ounces of vodka.
4. Stir vigorously. The objective is to let the ice thoroughly chill the drink.
5. Strain the gimlet into a lowball glass large enough to accommodate it—or divide the drink between two smaller lowball glasses. (You'll learn how to use a cocktail strainer just a little later in this chapter.)
6. Garnish with a lime wedge.

Bar Tips

Tips on preparing lemon twists, lime wedges, orange slices, and other garnishes and "garbage" are found back in Chapter 4.

The process of making a drink straight-up is identical to the two-step method of preparing a drink on the rocks, except that, instead of straining the chilled drink into a glass filled with ice, you just pour it into an empty, preferably chilled, glass. (Want to know how to chill a glass? See "Glassware Prep," later in this chapter.) The key step is stirring vigorously and for a generous span of time—perhaps a count of 10 or 15. The drink really has to chill.

Great Shakes

Serious bartenders have always taken considerable pride in the panache with which they wield the cocktail shaker. And, despite the risk of catastrophic spillage, the secret is to be bold, vigorous, and even aggressive. Shake *hard.*

The following is the procedure for shaking a classic shaken drink, the whiskey sour:

1. Into a shaker glass two-thirds full of ice, pour 2 ounces of Canadian whisky.
2. Add 1½ ounces of sour mix.
3. Take the stainless steel shell of the cocktail shaker and put it on top of the glass. Press down *firmly* in order to create a leakproof seal. The beauty of the steel shell is that it will contract during shaking because the icy fluid lowers its temperature.
4. Use both hands. Put one hand on top of the shaker, and the other on the bottom. Grasp firmly. Shake hard for at least six counts.
5. If you've done everything right, the laws of physics will have created a stout seal between the stainless steel top and the glass bottom of the shaker. To break the seal so that you can get at the drink, look for the frost line on the steel shell. That demarcates the point at which the top and bottom are sealed. Firmly tap this line with the heel of your hand. You should hear the sharp *snap* of the seal breaking.
6. The shell will now come off very easily. *But don't take it off yet.* First turn the shaker over so that the steel shell is on the bottom. This will prevent spillage. *Now*, go ahead and take the glass out.
7. Strain the drink from the steel shell into a lowball glass or into a whiskey-sour glass, if you have one. The advantage of the whiskey-sour glass is that, if the drinker handles it by the stem, the straight-up drink will stay colder longer.
8. Garnish. The classic finishing touches are a maraschino cherry inside the glass and an orange or lemon slice perched on the lip of the glass.

Bar Tips

See Chapter 4 for sour mix recipes.

There is a downside to shaken drinks: the cleanup. Unless you are making one right after the other of the same drink, you'll need to clean the shaker immediately. It will get gummy and nasty if you don't. Rinse it with water, and then wipe it out.

Toast

Here's to wives and sweethearts—may they never meet!

Mix, Blend, and Puree!

Given a shaker and enough elbow grease on the part of the bartender, shaking is sufficient to blend most drinks. However, if you want to prepare frozen drinks, such as a frozen margarita, a frozen daiquiri, or a frozen piña colada, you'll need an electric blender.

First, ensure that your blender is up to the task of handling ice. A heavy-duty model is best. Then,

1. Make sure that the motor is off. Pour the liquor into the blender. Next come the mixers, and then the fruit. Last: Add ice—enough to fill the blender to three-quarters full.
2. Make sure that you put the lid on properly. Hold it down with one hand and start the machine at low speed. After the initial mixing is complete, switch to high until everything is thoroughly blended.
3. Pour the drink directly into glasses. No straining is necessary because the ice has been crushed and blended with the drink.

Popping Your Cork

To open wine, begin by completely removing the foil "capsule" from the top of the bottle. If you are using the popular waiter's corkscrew, insert the point of the helical screw (called a "worm") into the cork *slightly* off center. Bore deeply into the cork, and then pull straight up, twisting slightly to loosen the cork. An easier alternative is to use either a twin-lever corkscrew or a screwpull-type corkscrew. These are available in most stores that sell food-preparation utensils.

Opening champagne is at once easier and more challenging than opening a bottle of wine. It's easier because you don't have to use a corkscrew. It's more challenging because the contents of the bottle are under great pressure.

Buzzed Words

Frozen drinks are also called **freezes**.

- Inspect the bottle before opening it. Look for deep scratches or nicks. Deep imperfections in the glass might cause the bottle to explode.
- Do not chill champagne below 45 degrees. Chilling below this temperature increases the potential for an explosion.
- During the uncorking process, point the bottle away from you and others.

To remove the cork, point the bottle away from you and others, and remove the foil "capsule" covering the top. Next, untwist the wire cage that is over the cork. While doing this, place your palm over the cork to keep it from shooting out of the bottle. Now, still pointing the bottle away from all living beings, gently twist the cork, cupping your palm over it. As the cork works free, it will press against your palm. Do not release the cork. Do not let it pop. It should clear the bottle with a barely audible hiss or very muffled pop, which people old enough to remember Maurice Chevalier like to call a "lover's sigh."

Pouring

Pouring is easy. If you aren't using a speedpourer, prevent spillage by turning the bottle slightly as you come to the end of the pour and bring the bottle upright. For the sake of an appearance that is both professional and generous looking, try to accomplish the pour in one motion rather than with tentative dribs and drabs.

Using the Speedpourer

We've already discussed the speedpourer as absolutely required for bartenders using the Three-Count Method. Even if you don't use that method, however, speedpourers make your job quicker and neater. Do take time to put the speedpourer in the bottle so that the slant of the mouth is at a right angle to the label. This will put more speed into your pour by allowing you to grab the bottle without having to check which way the stream of liquor will emerge. Moreover, your guests will be able to see the label as your pour—a nice touch, especially if you are serving premium liquor.

Using a Cocktail Strainer

You've seen that little paddle-like metal gadget with the Slinky-style spring running around it. It's a cocktail strainer, and its function is to hold back the ice as you pour a finished drink from the shaker. The strainer is intended to fit neatly over the mouth of the shaker so that you can hold it in place with one finger.

Developing a Multiple Personality

If you've admired the speed of the super-fast bartender who can prepare multiples of the same drink simultaneously, now is your chance to admire yourself. *You* can do it!

Just line up X number of glasses in a row. They should be filled with ice, and they should be standing rim to rim. Make sure that a speedpourer is in the bottle of booze. Grab the bottle by the neck. Do a smooth inversion over the first glass, count three, move the still-inverted bottle smoothly to the next glass, count three, go on and on and on.

Unfortunately, because you can't put a speedpourer into most mixer bottles, you'll have to pour this ingredient in one glass at a time. Same goes for dispensing the garnish.

Pouring the Pousse-Café

The delicately layered pousse-café presents the ultimate pouring challenge. We'll discuss the actual creation of these dessert drinks in Chapter 18, but here's a glimpse of the pouring technique.

You have to pour each ingredient in the drink slowly and carefully so that the layers don't combine. Always start with the heaviest or thickest liquid (bottom layer), proceed to the next heaviest (middle), and then on to the lightest (top). Use a twisted bar spoon to guide the liquor into the pousse-café glass. Hold one end of the handle against the bottle containing the ingredient, and place the tip of the handle against the edge of the pousse-café glass. Now let the fluid gently slide from the bottle, down the twisted bar spoon, and into the glass. Take care, but have confidence. This works. Your skill will be a subject of slack-jawed wonder and reverential praise.

Glassware Prep

The most important item of glassware preparation is cleanliness. Ensure that your bar glassware is spotless and, equally important, thoroughly rinsed so that no soap or detergent taste or aroma lingers in the glass.

Certain drinks call for additional preparation.

Chilling

If you want to chill a glass before pouring a drink into it, refrigerate the dry glass for an hour or longer, and then fill the glass with ice water. Prepare the drink. When you are ready to pour the drink, dump out the ice water.

Frosting

Frosting is a step beyond chilling. Dip the glass in water, and then put it in the freezer for half an hour. This will give it a frosty white appearance. If the glass has a stem, hold it by the stem to avoid melting any of the frost.

Salting

Salting means rimming the glass with salt—something you might want to do for a Salty Dog or a margarita. It's easy if you remember to use rock salt rather than table salt.

Pour rock salt on a plate. Take a lime wedge and rub it around the rim of the glass. Roll the glass rim around in the salt. But before you do any of this, ask your guest if he or she *wants* the rim salted. Some drinkers don't like it.

Flavoring the Rim

Aside from salting, you can flavor the rim of any glass with the fruit used to garnish the drink. Just run the orange, lime, or lemon peel on the rim. It will impart a subtle flavor and aroma to the drink.

Sugar and Spice (Plus a Little Cocoa)

A few specialty drinks can be rimmed with sugar, cinnamon, and even cocoa. In these cases, it is usually sufficient to moisten the rim with a little of the main liquor ingredient in the drink, and then roll the glass in a plate of the flavoring.

The Least You Need to Know

- Most drinks are variations on three basic types: the highball, the stirred cocktail ("lowball"), and the shaken cocktail.
- Mastering either the Two-Finger Method or the Three-Count Method of measuring makes you look like a pro and speeds the mixing process.
- Practice using your cocktail shaker before you use it. Prevent embarrassing accidents.
- Ensure that glassware is clean and free from soap or detergent residue.

Part 2

Clear Choices

Gin and vodka are the crystalline spirits—colorless, but hardly without character. They vie with one another for first place as the most popular of all mixed-drink ingredients. This section provides guidance in choosing the right gin as well as making great gin-based drinks. From there, you launch into the "vorld of vodka," a spirit even subtler in character than gin.

Perhaps no mixed drink is more discussed and debated than the martini—the "Silver Bullet." Controversial ever since it developed from the nineteenth-century Martinez, the martini simply cannot be dry enough for some, whereas others painstakingly search for the magic perfect ratio of vermouth to gin. We try to represent the claims of all sides in the great martini controversy, and we include some of the newest, trendiest martini incarnations.

Chapter 6

Brother Juniper: The Joys of Gin

In This Chapter

- How gin is made
- The difference between London dry and Dutch (genever) gin
- The range of flavorfulness of gin
- Gin recipes

A deeply aromatic spirit, gin doesn't appeal to everybody, but those who admire it cherish its bracing, refreshing qualities, redolent of juniper berries and a host of other *botanicals*—an often exotic collection of extracts from roots, barks, seeds, and leaves—that give gin its character. Unlike vodka, which is (or should be) flavorless, the character of gin varies greatly from brand to brand and invites a lot of "comparison shopping."

Distiller's Secrets

The creation of a fine gin almost has more in common with the creation of a great perfume than other alcoholic beverages. And, as with the formula used to create Chanel No. 5, the recipes behind the world's great gins are closely guarded.

British and American Varieties

The gins made in England and the United States start with fermented malt, which yields a beer that is distilled into a *malt wine*. This is purified to produce an almost neutral spirit that, like vodka, is without flavor or aroma. Next, the distillate is diluted with distilled water. At this point, it may be combined with flavoring agents, which we will discuss in a moment. The concoction is distilled again, and once again reduced with water, to yield a final product of 40 to 47 percent alcoholic content: 80 to 94 proof. Although most gins are not aged, some American producers do age their product, which gives it a pale golden coloring. Some British distillers create this effect with the addition of a small amount of caramel coloring.

Buzzed Words

Gins are often designated **dry gin** or **London dry gin**. These originated when "sweet" (called **Old Tom**) as well as "dry" gin was available. Today, the distinction is mainly superfluous because almost all English and American gin is now dry. Also note that London dry gin doesn't have to be made in London or even England. This describes a manufacturing style, not a place of origin.

There's more than one way to get the flavoring agents into the gin. If they are not added prior to the second distillation, they can be suspended from special racks *during* the second distillation so that the flavors are percolated by the distillate as it condenses. In this way, the flavor of the botanicals permeates the spirit. Makers of some less expensive American gins mix the spirits with essential oils and do not redistill. Others add the flavorings to the mash from which the malt wine is fermented. In this case also, the gin is distilled only once.

All gins share a base flavoring of juniper berries, but they diverge widely in combining such other botanicals as orris, angelica and licorice roots, lemon and orange peels, cassia, cinnamon bark, caraway, coriander, cardamom, anise, bergamot, cocoa, and fennel.

We don't like recommending one brand over another; the choice is highly subjective. If you like gin, you'll almost certainly enjoy all the premium brands as well as many of the less expensive brands—especially when combined with tonic or other mixers.

That said, it might help you choose your favorites to know that of the three most popular *premium* brands—Beefeater, Tanqueray, and Bombay—Beefeater is the least distinctively flavored and Bombay the most highly and complexly flavored, with Tanqueray somewhere in between. This is not a judgment of quality. Many people prefer the relatively "clean" taste of Beefeater to the more complex, "spicy" quality of Bombay, whereas others prefer to straddle the fence with Tanqueray. Sampling all three gives you a good idea of the range of flavoring possible in fine gin.

Dutch Varieties

Dutch gin—called Hollands, genever, geneva, jenever gin, or Shiedam gin (after the distilling center just outside of Rotterdam)—is widely consumed in the Netherlands, but is less popular in the United States. In smaller U.S. cities, you might have trouble finding a liquor store that stocks it.

Bar Tips

Unlike American and English gins, genever does *not* go well with mixers. It is meant to be enjoyed neat or, if you wish, on the rocks. All the gin recipes in this book are meant to be mixed with American or English dry gin.

In contrast to the bracing, crisp, clean taste and feel of American and English gins, genever is thick, full-bodied, and, barley-born, savors of malt. Something of an acquired taste, devotees find it delicious, and it is well worth looking for.

Genever gin is also worth a try because it is your opportunity to taste what the "original" gin must have been like. Invented by Franciscus de la Boe—better known as Dr. Franciscus Sylvius—as a diuretic medicine, it was carried back to England by British soldiers, who called it "Dutch courage."

Bar Tips

Don't look for a martini here. It gets its own chapter: Chapter 8.

Gin and ...

Although not everyone likes the taste of gin by itself, it vies with vodka as the most mixable of spirits. It can be combined with just about anything.

Gin and Bitters

Also called Pink Gin, Gin and Bitters is a singularly bracing and sophisticated combination.

Serve straight-up, strained into an old-fashioned or lowball glass.

2 oz. gin

½ tsp. Angostura bitters

Stir the gin and bitters in a glass with ice cubes until well chilled. Strain into the serving glass.

Gin and Campari

Another refreshingly astringent drink combines gin with Campari. If you enjoy Campari, you'll love this. Unlike Gin and Bitters, it is meant to be served on the rocks.

Serve in a lowball glass.

1½ oz. gin

1½ oz. Campari

Orange slice or twist of orange

Combine gin and Campari in a cocktail shaker with ice. Shake vigorously, and then strain into the serving glass filled with ice. Garnish with an orange slice or a twist of orange.

Gin and Sin

Yet another piquant drink with gin is served straight-up in a cocktail glass. It's seductively dubbed Gin and Sin.

Serve straight-up, strained into a cocktail glass.

2 oz. gin

1 TB. Cinzano

Combine gin and Cinzano in a glass with ice, stir until well chilled, and then strain into the serving glass.

Negroni

Probably the most frequently requested "bitter" gin drink is the provocatively puckering Negroni.

Serve straight-up in a chilled cocktail glass.

2 oz. gin

½ oz. sweet vermouth

¾ oz. Campari

Splash of club soda (optional)

Orange peel

Combine all ingredients, except the orange peel, in a shaker with ice. Shake vigorously, and then strain into the serving glass. Twist the orange peel and drop into the glass.

Gin and Ginger

Ginger ale is just sweet enough to leaven the bitterness of gin, but not so sweet that it entirely overpowers or clashes with the spirit. This is a favorite drink with many.

Serve on the rocks in a chilled highball glass.

1½ oz. gin

Ginger ale to fill

Lemon twist

Combine gin and ginger ale in the serving glass filled with ice. Drop in the lemon twist.

A lot of folks confuse tonic water with soda water. The two are quite different. Tonic is carbonated sugar water flavored with a bit of lemon and quinine, which gives this mixer a provocatively bitter taste. Soda water, in contrast, is nothing but unflavored carbonated water.

No great disaster will result if you mix gin with soda water. What you get is a—guess what?—Gin and Soda.

Bar Tips

An open bottle of tonic water or club soda is only good for about a day. To make sure that they're always crisp, consider buying them in six packs of small bottles, which you can finish before they get flat. For a big party, go for the larger bottles.

But the *real* thing is Gin and Tonic—next to the martini, the most popular gin-bearing drink. The key to a successful Gin and Tonic is *fresh* tonic water. Carbonated mixers quickly go flat, and none goes flatter more quickly than tonic water. To a sun-parched drinker eagerly anticipating the refreshment of a sparkling G&T, few things are more disappointing than a flat, bitter drink. Make certain that you use freshly opened tonic water. After you open a bottle, keep it refrigerated; this will retard the dissipation of the bubbles.

Gin and Soda

Serve on the rocks in a highball glass.

1½-2 oz. gin

Club soda to fill

Lemon twist

Pour the gin into the serving glass filled with ice. Add club soda, and garnish with the lemon twist.

Gin and Tonic

Serve on the rocks in a highball glass.

2-2½ oz. gin

Tonic water to fill

Lime wedge or lemon twist

Pour the gin into the serving glass filled with ice. Add tonic, and garnish with a lime wedge (traditional) or, if you prefer, a lemon twist.

Gin Daiquiri

Serve on the rocks in a lowball glass.

1½ oz. gin

½ oz. light rum

2 tsp. lime juice

1 tsp. sugar

Pour the liquid ingredients into a shaker with ice. Add the sugar. Shake, and then strain into the serving glass and garnish with the lime slice.

Gimlet Eye

Gimlet is a word that goes back to Middle English and has to do with sharpness and the quality of penetration. A gimlet is a sharp little hand tool for boring holes, and a "gimlet-eyed" individual possesses a piercing gaze. Take your cue from the history of this word: A gimlet should meet the taste buds with an eye-opening sharpness.

The best gimlets are made from freshly squeezed lime or, for a delicious variation, freshly squeezed *limon* (the offspring of a lime-lemon cross).

If you don't have fresh limes or don't want to exert the effort to squeeze them, use Rose's lime juice.

Gimlet with Fresh Lime

Serve in a chilled old-fashioned or lowball glass.

2 oz. gin

½ oz. fresh lime (or limon) juice

Lime twist or lime slice

Stir gin and juice very vigorously in a mixing (shaker) glass with cracked ice; pour into the serving glass. Garnish with a lime twist or lime slice. May also be served straight-up: Stir with ice cubes, and then strain into the serving glass.

Gimlet with Rose's Lime Juice

Serve in a chilled old-fashioned or lowball glass.

2 oz. gin

½ oz. Rose's lime juice

Lime slice

Use a shaker or blender to mix the gin and Rose's with cracked ice; pour into the serving glass. The best garnish is a lime slice, which gets more of the natural juice into the drink. May also be served straight-up: Strain the shaken or blended ingredients into the serving glass.

Tom Collins

Once popular enough to deserve its own glass, the appeal of this drink has waned over the years, but it remains a part of the standard repertoire nevertheless.

Serve on the rocks in a Collins or highball glass.

2-3 oz. gin

1½ oz. lemon juice

1½ oz. sugar syrup

Club soda to fill

Maraschino cherry

Combine all ingredients, except club soda and cherry, in the serving glass with ice. Stir well. Fill with club soda, and garnish with the cherry.

Aviation

Serve in a chilled cocktail glass.

1½ oz. gin

½ oz. lemon juice

½ tsp. maraschino liqueur

½ tsp. apricot brandy

Combine all ingredients in a shaker or blender with cracked ice. Shake or blend. Strain into the serving glass.

Juices (Mostly)

Most of us are familiar with vodka and orange juice (the screwdriver) and with vodka and grapefruit juice. No law says that you can't substitute gin for vodka in these faithful standbys.

Gin Screwdriver

Serve on the rocks in a highball glass.

1½ oz. gin

2-3 oz. orange juice

Stir well. If you like, add a dash or two of Angostura bitters.

Orange Blossom

The cocktail variation on the Gin Screwdriver is called the Orange Blossom.

Serve in a chilled cocktail glass.

1½ oz. gin

1 oz. orange juice

Orange slice

Combine all ingredients, except the orange slice, in a shaker with ice. Shake vigorously, and then strain into the serving glass. Garnish with the orange slice.

Gin and Grapefruit Juice

Serve on the rocks in a highball glass.

1½ oz. gin

2-3 oz. grapefruit juice

Combine all ingredients in a serving glass filled with ice. Stir well.

Abbey

This adds an extra dimension to the Gin Screwdriver.

Serve on the rocks in a lowball glass.

1½ oz. gin

1½ oz. orange juice

Dash or 2 of orange bitters

Maraschino cherry

Combine all ingredients, except for the cherry, in a shaker with ice. Shake vigorously, and then strain into the ice-filled serving glass. Garnish with the cherry.

Abbey Cocktail

This is a cocktail version of the Abbey.

Serve straight-up in a chilled cocktail glass.

1½ oz. gin

¾ oz. orange juice

¼ oz. sweet vermouth

Dash or 2 of Angostura bitters

Maraschino cherry

Combine all ingredients, except for the cherry, in a shaker with ice. Shake vigorously, and then strain into the serving glass. Garnish with the cherry.

Bronx Cocktail

Its name notwithstanding, the Bronx Cocktail is a product of upscale Manhattan. Johnnie Solon, legendary bartender at the old Waldorf-Astoria Hotel, invented it. It's simple and delicious.

Serve straight-up in a chilled cocktail glass.

1½ oz. gin

½ oz. orange juice

Dash of dry vermouth

Dash of sweet vermouth

Combine all ingredients, with ice, in a shaker. Shake vigorously. Strain into the serving glass. Some drinkers prefer more of the vermouths—½ ounce each—and a full ounce of orange juice. If you want a dry cocktail, skip the sweet vermouth.

Atomic Bomb

Want something stronger? Get bombed.

Serve on ice in a lowball glass.

2 oz. gin

1 oz. Benedictine

4 dashes curaçao

Combine all ingredients in a lowball glass, which is about one third filled with ice.

Lone Tree

A variation on the Bronx Cocktail is the Lone Tree, which omits the orange juice and adds orange bitters. If you like martinis, you'll want to try this.

Serve straight-up in a chilled cocktail glass.

¾ oz. gin

¾ oz. dry vermouth (optional)

¾ oz. sweet vermouth

Several dashes of orange bitters (optional)

Olive (optional)

To a shaker filled with cracked ice add all ingredients except for the olive. Shake vigorously. Strain into the serving glass and garnish with the olive.

Island Magic

Gin and the islands—almost *any* islands—seem made for each other.

Antibes

If you like the taste of gin and Benedictine, but aren't quite prepared for nuclear war with the Atomic Bomb, take a cruise to Antibes.

Serve in a chilled old-fashioned glass.

1½ oz. gin

½ oz. Benedictine

2 oz. grapefruit juice

Orange slice

In a shaker or blender combine all ingredients, except the orange slice, with cracked ice. Shake or blend, and then pour into the serving glass. Garnish with the orange slice.

Diamond Head

Let's not forget our own fiftieth state. Diamond Head is the most famous volcanic crater in the world.

Serve in a chilled cocktail glass.

1½ oz. gin

½ oz. curaçao

2 oz. pineapple juice

1 tsp. sweet vermouth

Combine all ingredients in a shaker or blender. Blend or shake, and then strain into the serving glass.

Bali Hai

Another favorite island is the one celebrated in Rodgers and Hammerstein's *South Pacific*. Bali Hai is a "special island," and the Bali Hai is a special drink. The only question is, will your local liquor store have the secret ingredient? Okolehao is a liqueur made by distilling the fermented extract of the ti tree, which is also known as an oke.

Serve in a chilled Collins glass.

1 oz. gin

1 oz. light rum

1 oz. okolehao

1 oz. lemon juice

3 oz. lime juice

1 tsp. orgeat (may substitute sugar syrup)

Brut champagne

Combine everything, except the champagne, in a shaker or blender with cracked ice. Shake or blend, and then pour into the serving glass. Top off with the champagne.

Beekman Place Cooler

Yet another island: Manhattan. And a dandy address on Beekman Place. Served in a Collins glass, this one is tall and refreshing.

Serve in a chilled Collins glass.

1½ oz. gin

1 oz. sloe gin

3 oz. grapefruit juice

½ oz. sugar syrup

Club soda

Combine everything, except the club soda, in a shaker or blender with cracked ice. Shake or blend, and then pour into the serving glass. Top off with club soda.

Barnegat Bay Cooler

Barnegat Bay might sound like a long haul from Manhattan, but it's really not that far—a pleasant drive to the Jersey shore. Here's a refreshing gin-and-juice cooler named for it.

Serve in a large chilled glass, such as a double old-fashioned glass.

2 oz. gin

3 oz. pineapple juice

½ oz. lime juice

1 tsp. maraschino liqueur

Club soda (may substitute 7-Up or ginger ale)

In a shaker or blender combine all ingredients, except the soda, with cracked ice. Shake or blend. Pour into the serving glass, and then top off with the soda.

Gin Sour

Sours aren't just made with whiskey. Gin makes a great sour, too.

Serve straight-up in a whiskey sour glass or lowball glass.

2-3 oz. gin

1 oz. lemon juice

1 tsp. sugar syrup

Orange or lemon slice

Maraschino cherry

In a shaker, with ice, combine all ingredients except the garnishes. Shake vigorously. Strain into the serving glass. Garnish with an orange slice and maraschino cherry.

Damn the Weather

Serve in a chilled old-fashioned glass.

1 oz. gin

½ oz. sweet vermouth

1 oz. orange juice

1 tsp. curaçao

In a shaker or blender combine all ingredients with cracked ice. Shake or blend, and then pour into the serving glass.

Costa del Sol

Serve in a chilled old-fashioned glass.

1½ oz. gin

1 oz. apricot brandy

1 oz. Cointreau (may substitute curaçao)

In a shaker or blender combine all ingredients with cracked ice. Shake or blend, and then pour into the serving glass.

Drake Gin Sour

Here's the gin sour invented at Chicago's Drake Hotel.

Makes two drinks. Serve in chilled cocktail glasses.

4 oz. gin

2 tsp. lemon juice

2 tsp. orgeat syrup (may substitute sugar syrup)

1 egg white*

Combine all ingredients in a blender or shaker with cracked ice. Shake or blend, and then strain into two serving glasses.

**Raw egg may be a source of salmonella bacteria. You may wish to avoid drinks calling for raw egg yolk or white.*

A Few Fizzes, a Rickey, and Sidecar

A "fizz" is cousin to the Collins. It is made with sour mix, sugar, and club soda. Everybody's heard of the Sloe Gin Fizz. Well, you won't find it in this chapter because sloe gin isn't gin, but a liqueur (check out Chapter 16). Nevertheless, the Gin Fizz—with *real* gin—is a classic, which you *should* know how to make.

Buzzed Words

A **rickey** is any drink with soda water and lime—and sometimes sugar.

Gin Fizz

Serve on the rocks in a Collins or tall highball glass.

1½ oz. gin

1 TB. powdered sugar

3 oz. sour mix

Club soda to fill

Maraschino cherry

Orange slice

To a shaker filled with ice add the gin, sugar, and sour mix. Shake vigorously. Pour into the ice-filled serving glass, and then add club soda. Garnish with a maraschino cherry and an orange slice.

And more fizzes follow…

Brittany Fizz

Serve in a chilled highball glass.

1 oz. gin

1 oz. brandy

1 oz. dry vermouth

½ oz. lemon juice

Club soda

Lemon peel

Combine all ingredients, except the soda and lemon peel, in a shaker or blender with cracked ice. Shake or blend, and then pour into the serving glass. Top off with club soda, twist the lemon peel over the drink and drop it into the glass.

Danish Gin Fizz

Serve in a chilled Collins glass.

1½ oz. gin

¾ oz. Peter Heering

¼ oz. kirsch

½ oz. lime juice

½ oz. sugar syrup

Club soda

Lime slice

Combine all ingredients, except the soda and lime slice, in a shaker or blender with cracked ice. Shake or blend, and then strain into the serving glass. Top off with soda and garnish with the lime slice.

Golden Fizz

Serve in a chilled Collins glass.

2-3 oz. gin

1 oz. lemon or lime juice

1 tsp. sugar syrup

1 egg yolk*

Club soda

Lemon or lime slice

Combine all ingredients, except the soda and fruit slice, in a shaker or blender with cracked ice. Shake or blend, and then pour into the serving glass. Top off with soda, stir gently, and garnish with the fruit slice.

**Raw egg may be a source of salmonella bacteria. You may wish to avoid drinks calling for raw egg yolk or white.*

Mandarin Fizz

Serve in a chilled highball glass.

1 oz. gin

1 oz. Mandarine Napoleon

2 oz. orange juice

½ oz. sugar syrup

Club soda

Tangerine wedge

Combine all ingredients, except the soda and tangerine wedge, in a shaker or blender with cracked ice. Shake or blend, and then pour into the serving glass. Top off with soda, and garnish with the tangerine wedge.

Peach Blow Fizz

Serve in a chilled highball glass.

3 oz. gin

1 oz. lemon juice

1 oz. heavy cream

1 tsp. sugar syrup

4 strawberries, mashed

Club soda

Combine all ingredients, except the soda, in a blender with cracked ice. Blend, and then pour into the serving glass. Top off with soda. Stir gently.

Gin Rickey

The Gin Rickey is a must for any mixologist's repertoire. Fortunately, it's quick and simple to make.

Serve on the rocks in a highball glass.

1½ oz. gin

Club soda to fill

Juice of ½ fresh lime

Fill a highball glass half full of ice cubes; pour in the gin and then the club soda to fill. Add the lime juice.

Gin Sidecar

A Gin Sidecar is a variation on the simple Rickey.

Serve in a chilled old-fashioned or lowball glass.

1½ oz. gin

¾ oz. triple sec

1 oz. lemon juice

Pour all ingredients into a shaker with cracked ice. Shake vigorously. Pour into the serving glass.

Gin Daisy

A near relation to the Gin Fizz family is the Gin Daisy—as in "fresh as a." This is a thoroughly delightful drink.

Serve in a chilled highball glass.

2-3 oz. gin

1 oz. lemon juice

¼ oz. raspberry syrup or grenadine

½ tsp. sugar syrup

Club soda to fill

Orange slice

To a shaker filled with cracked ice, add all ingredients except for the club soda and orange slice. Shake vigorously. Pour into the serving glass. Add club soda to fill, and then garnish with the orange slice.

Surprising Gin

"Bracing," "astringent," "clean," and "bitter" are words you've already heard to describe the taste of gin. But this sharp-toothed libation has some softer surprises in store. What follows is not your father's "gin and …"

The Admirals

Admiral Benbow

The Admiral Benbow is a hybrid cross between a gimlet and a martini.

Serve straight-up in an old-fashioned or low-ball glass.

2 oz. gin

1 oz. dry vermouth

½ oz. lime juice

Maraschino cherry

Stir gin, vermouth, and lime juice vigorously with ice, strain into the serving glass, and garnish with a Maraschino cherry.

Admiral Cocktail

Bet you didn't know that gin can go very nicely with cherry liqueurs such as Peter Heering or Cherry Marnier. Try the Admiral Cocktail.

Serve straight-up in a chilled cocktail glass.

2 oz. gin

¾ oz. lime juice

½ oz. Peter Heering or Cherry Marnier

Shake all ingredients vigorously with ice in a shaker or use a blender; strain into the serving glass.

Liqueur Refreshed, Brandy Rebranded—and a Dash of Dubonnet

Liqueur: heavy, sweet, and ideal for dessert drinks. That's a true assessment as far as it goes, but, if you know how to combine gin and liqueur, you'll see that this truism just doesn't go far enough. Neither liqueur nor flavored brandy need be reserved just for desserts.

A gin and liqueur combination that deserves wider recognition is the Cornell Cocktail. Because you'll need an egg white, it's easiest to make two of these at a time.

Bar Tips

Most drinks that call for egg white require half an egg white. But it's almost impossible to get *half* an egg white; therefore, all recipes in this book calling for egg white make *two* drinks. (You really shouldn't drink alone.)

Cornell Cocktail

Serve straight-up in a chilled cocktail glass.

4 oz. gin

1 oz. maraschino liqueur

1 egg white*

Vigorously shake all ingredients with ice in a shaker or blend; strain into the serving glasses. *Recipe makes two drinks.*

**Raw egg may be a source of salmonella bacteria. You may wish to avoid drinks calling for raw egg yolk or white.*

Coco Chanel

Serve straight-up in a chilled cocktail glass.

1 oz. gin

1 oz. Kahlúa or Tia Maria

1 oz. heavy cream

In a shaker or blender, mix all ingredients with cracked ice. Strain into a chilled cocktail glass.

Gin Sling

Slings are sweet drinks made with brandy, whiskey, or gin. Here's the gin version.

Serve in an old-fashioned or lowball glass.

2-3 oz. gin

1 oz. lemon juice

½ oz. orgeat or sugar syrup

Club soda to fill

Fill serving glass half full with cracked ice. Add all ingredients except club soda. Stir. Add club soda to fill. If you don't want a fizzy drink, substitute plain water for the club soda.

Buzzed Words

A **sling** is any brandy, whiskey, or gin drink that is sweetened and flavored with lemon.

Tropical Heritage

Back when the sun never set on the British Empire, Royal Navy physicians mixed gin with quinine (tonic) water, bitters, or a lot of things in the belief that it would stave off a host of terrible tropical diseases that felled sailors, soldiers, and colonial administrators alike. Gin bombed out as a medicine, but it has had tropical connections ever since. Here are some exotic temptations.

Bermuda Cocktail

Serve in a chilled old-fashioned or lowball glass.

1½ oz. gin

1 oz. apricot brandy

½ oz. lime juice (fresh or Rose's)

1 tsp. Falernum or sugar syrup

Dash of grenadine

Orange peel

½ tsp. curaçao

To a shaker filled with cracked ice, add all ingredients except the orange peel and curaçao. Shake vigorously. Pour into the serving glass. Garnish with the orange peel twist, and then carefully top with curaçao so that it floats.

Singapore Sling

By far the best-known "tropical" gin drink is the Singapore Sling. It's sweet, fun, and it's your big chance to deploy some of those little paper parasols.

Serve on the rocks in a chilled Collins or highball glass.

2 oz. gin

1 oz. cherry brandy or Peter Heering

Juice of ½ lemon

Dash of Benedictine

Club soda to fill

Lemon slice

Mint sprig

In a shaker with cracked ice, combine all ingredients except for the lemon slice and mint sprig, but include a splash of club soda. Shake vigorously. Strain into the serving glass. Add ice cubes and club soda to fill. Garnish with lemon slice and mint sprig.

Pink Lady

People love "retro" drinks, and nothing's more retro than the Pink Lady.

Serve straight-up in a chilled cocktail glass.

3 oz. gin

3 oz. applejack or Calvados

2 oz. lemon juice

2 tsp. sugar syrup

2 tsp. grenadine

1 egg white*

Combine all ingredients, with ice, in a shaker. Shake vigorously. Strain into serving glasses. Recipe makes two drinks.

**Raw egg may be a source of salmonella bacteria. You may wish to avoid drinks calling for raw egg yolk or white.*

Gin on the Fringe

At the dawn of the new millennium, these gin-based drinks were creating excitement.

Feelers

Serve on the rocks in a highball glass.

2 oz. gin

1 tsp. sugar syrup

Combine in the serving glass, stir, and drink.

Bachelor Bait

Serve on the rocks in a large glass, such as a double old-fashioned glass.

2 oz. gin

½ tsp. grenadine

2 dashes orange bitters

1 egg white*

Combine all ingredients in a shaker with cracked ice. Shake vigorously, and then strain into the serving glass.

** Raw egg may be a source of salmonella bacteria. You may wish to avoid drinks calling for raw egg yolk or white.*

Red Raider

Serve in a chilled cocktail glass.

1½ oz. gin

½ tsp. finely ground cinnamon

2 drops Tabasco

Combine in a shaker with cracked ice. Shake vigorously and strain into the serving glass.

Flesheater

Serve in a chilled cocktail glass.

2 oz. gin

½ oz. vodka

½ oz. dry vermouth

3 drops Tabasco

Combine in a shaker with cracked ice. Shake vigorously and strain into the serving glass.

Hit and Run

Serve in a chilled cocktail glass.

2 oz. gin

2 TB. port wine

2 drops anisette

Combine in a shaker with cracked ice. Shake vigorously and strain into the serving glass.

Dunce Cap

Serve in a chilled cocktail glass.

1½ oz. gin

1 oz. vodka

1 tsp. raspberry syrup

Combine in a shaker with cracked ice. Shake vigorously and strain into the serving glass.

The Least You Need to Know

- The premium gins are distilled twice—with the special flavoring added in the second distillation process.
- Use premium gins with subtle mixers and the less expensive gins with sweet or strongly flavored mixers.
- Dutch (genever) gin is well worth trying, but, in contrast to British or American gin, it does not make a good mixer.
- Every bartender should know how to make a Gin Gimlet, a Gin Rickey, a good Gin Fizz, and a Tom Collins.

Chapter 7

Na Zdorovye!: The World of Vodka

In This Chapter

- Vodka comes to America
- The art of flavoring vodka
- The Bloody Mary—history and recipes
- Favorite vodka recipes

Colorless, tasteless, and aromaless, vodka outsells every other category of spirits in the United States. This might strike you as surprising when you consider that vodka was rarely consumed here before World War II.

It would make for exciting reading if we could tell you that American soldiers brought the stuff home from war-torn Russia, but that's not the case. World War II saw the American people subjected to rigorous rationing of almost every product they had previously taken for granted. Alcoholic beverages were no exception. With peace came an end to rationing, but, after four years of war, liquor dealers had precious little product to offer.

Smirnoff Takes Off

After the war—that's when serious drinkers, as well as dealers in spirits, discovered a small distillery with a Russian name, which had been making vodka in the United States since shortly after the end of Prohibition. The label on their bottles proudly proclaimed that the Smirnoff family had been distilling vodka for the czars since the nineteenth century. (The label did not explain that the Smirnoffs and their product had fled the Bolshevik Revolution.)

The Smirnoffs plied their trade on this side of the Atlantic, purveying vodka to what was then the relatively small Russian community in the United States. Little of the product broke through the ethnic barriers and into the mainstream—until 1946.

Once discovered, the Smirnoffs promoted their spirit with one of the most memorable slogans ever to appear in liquor advertising: "*It leaves you breathless.*" The double entendre was unmistakable. Not only did the product deliver a buzz, it left no aftertaste—nor any telltale after odor. The Smirnoffs also came up with the Moscow Mule, a drink you, too, can make. (We'll show you how later in this chapter.)

Vodka today is more popular than ever, and dozens of brands have followed Smirnoff into the fray. There are now a number of American brands, and enthusiasts can choose from such premium imported labels as Russia's Stolichnaya, Poland's Wyborowa, Sweden's Absolut, France's Grey Goose, and Finland's Finlandia.

While sales of vodka have risen steadily since 1946, they exploded in the 1980s, despite a general decline in liquor consumption. Although many professionals were opting for bottled waters instead of scotch with lunch, others refused to forsake alcohol, but did retreat from the more flavorful spirits to the cleaner, lighter taste of vodka.

Bar Tips

Vodka is becoming increasingly popular as an alternative to gin in martinis, but don't look for your vodka martini here. You'll find it, with its gin-based brethren, in Chapter 8.

Of course, as enthusiasts already know, vodka can also be had in flavors. In the United States, vodkas flavored with peppercorns, lemon peel, raisins, anise, basil, berries (especially black currants), and caraway are popular.

Straight, No Chaser

By U.S. law, all nonflavored vodka consumed here must be filtered after distillation to remove all distinctive character, aroma, taste, and color. However, even the flavorless vodkas—especially the premium brands—do have a certain character, an undertone of flavor, that partisans of particular brands prize.

It's worth sampling the premium brands to discover what you like best. Serve the vodka in a lowball glass on the rocks—or, better yet, put the vodka in the freezer to get it *very* cold, and enjoy it straight.

Remember, for most mixing purposes, any decent vodka will do, especially if you are using strongly flavored mixers. Don't waste a premium-priced vodka on a cocktail: the flavor undertone is so subtle that almost any flavored mixer will overpower it.

Bloody Mary

Mary I ruled England from 1553 to 1558. A staunch Roman Catholic, she came to the throne determined to undo the Protestant Reformation her father, Henry VIII, had begun. During her reign, she ordered the execution—by public burning at the stake—of some 300 Protestants.

Thus, the name "Bloody Mary" was bequeathed to history and was snatched up to describe one of the most popular drinks ever invented. The drink is usually credited to Fernand Petiot, a bartender at Harry's New York Bar in Paris—the 1920s gathering place of F. Scott Fitzgerald, Ernest Hemingway, e.e. cummings, and other expatriate literary luminaries.

Now, some folks just throw a little vodka and a little tomato juice together and hand you what they call a Bloody Mary. But that's, at best, a vodka and tomato juice, not a Bloody Mary. The classic recipe, evolved and elaborated upon from Harry's original, follows.

Bar Tips

Most shaker drinks should be shaken vigorously, but not the Bloody Mary. Shake *too* hard, and the tomato juice could separate. Go gently.

Bloody Mary

Serve in a chilled Collins glass.

2 oz. vodka

4-6 oz. tomato juice

1 tsp. lemon juice

¼ tsp. Worcestershire sauce

Few dashes Tabasco sauce

Pinch white pepper

Pinch or two of celery salt

½ tsp. dried or fresh chopped dill

Celery stalk

Combine all ingredients (except for the celery stalk) with cracked ice in a shaker. Shake gently. Pour into the serving glass. Garnish with the celery stalk and, if you wish, add two or three ice cubes.

Variations on a Bloody Theme

The Algonquin Bloody Mary is the creation of a bartender at the Blue Bar in New York City's celebrated Algonquin Hotel—once a favored watering hole of the literati, most notably the so-called "Algonquin Wits," which included Dorothy Parker, Robert Benchley, and James Thurber, among others. The Bloody Blossom adds orange juice.

Algonquin Bloody Mary

Serve straight up in a Collins glass.

1½ oz. vodka

4 oz. tomato juice

Salt and ground pepper (to taste)

Juice of half a lime

1 tsp. Worcestershire sauce

4-6 dashes of Tabasco sauce

Lime wedge

In a shaker, combine all ingredients except the lime wedge. Shake gently. Strain into the serving glass, and garnish with the lime wedge.

Bloody Blossom

Serve in a Collins glass.

1½ oz. vodka

3 oz. orange juice

3 oz. tomato juice

Mint sprig

In a shaker, combine all ingredients, except the mint sprig, with cracked ice. Shake gently. Pour into the serving glass, and garnish with the mint.

Red Snapper

Serve in a highball glass.

1½ oz. vodka

2 oz. tomato juice

Dash lemon juice

2 pinches black pepper

2 pinches cayenne pepper

2 pinches salt

3 dashes Worcestershire sauce

Optional celery stalk garnish

First, combine the peppers, salt, Worcestershire, and lemon juice in a shaker. Next, add ice, vodka, and tomato juice. Shake vigorously, and then pour into the serving glass. Garnish with a celery stalk, if you like.

Bloody Bull

Serve in a chilled old-fashioned glass.

2 oz. vodka

3 oz. V-8 juice

3 oz. beef bouillon (may substitute consommé or broth)

½ oz. lemon juice

Dash Tabasco sauce

Dash Worcestershire sauce

Pinch white pepper, freshly ground

Combine all ingredients with cracked ice in a mixing glass. Stir, then pour into the serving glass.

Bloodhound

Serve on the rocks in a Collins glass.

1½ oz. vodka

½ oz. dry sherry

4 oz. tomato juice

Dash lemon juice

Pinch salt

Pinch white pepper

Lime slice

Combine all ingredients, except the lime slice, in the serving glass with ice. Garnish with the lime slice.

Clam Digger

Serve in a chilled highball glass.

2 oz. vodka

4 oz. V-8 juice

2 oz. clam juice

2 tsp. lemon juice

Dash Worcestershire sauce

3-4 dashes Tabasco sauce

Dash white pepper, freshly ground

Combine all ingredients with cracked ice in a mixing glass. Stir, and then pour into the serving glass.

Smoky Mary

Serve in a large glass, such as a double old-fashioned glass.

1½ oz. vodka

Tomato juice

½ oz. lemon juice

½ oz. barbecue sauce

Dash Tabasco sauce

Dash Worcestershire sauce

Lemon slice

Combine all ingredients with cracked ice in the serving glass. Stir, and then garnish with the lemon slice.

Ginza Mary

Serve in a chilled old-fashioned glass.

1½ oz. vodka

1½ oz. tomato juice or V-8

1½ oz. sake

½ oz. lemon juice

Few dashes Tabasco

Few dashes soy sauce

Pinch white pepper

Combine all ingredients in a mixing glass. Stir, and then pour into serving glass.

Cock 'n' Bull Shot

Here is one of the newest incarnations of the ageless Bloody Mary.

Serve in a chilled old-fashioned glass.

1½ oz. vodka

2 oz. chicken consommé

2 oz. beef bouillon (may substitute broth or consommé)

½ oz. lemon juice

Dash Tabasco sauce

Dash Worcestershire sauce

Dash white pepper, freshly ground

Pinch celery salt

Combine all ingredients with cracked ice in a mixing glass. Stir, then pour into the serving glass.

Don't limit yourself to the variations listed here. If you like, try substituting other spirits for vodka. People have enjoyed the O Sole Maria (made with Galliano), the Shamrock Mary (made with Irish whiskey), the Sake Mary (with sake), the Bonnie Mary (with scotch), the Bloody Maria (with tequila), and La Bonne Marie (with cognac). Also try your favorite juice variations, Clamato, Snappy Tom, or V-8 instead of ordinary tomato juice.

Russians Black and White

Two frequently requested vodka drinks are the Black Russian and the White Russian. They are simple to make.

Black Russian

Serve in a chilled old-fashioned glass.

1½ oz. vodka

¾ oz. Kahlúa

Combine the two ingredients with cracked ice in a shaker. Shake vigorously, and then pour into the serving glass. Optionally, add a few dashes of lemon juice for a "Black Magic." Garnish with a lemon twist, if desired.

White Russian

Serve in a chilled cocktail glass.

1½ oz. vodka

1 oz. white crème de cacao

¾ oz. heavy cream

Combine the ingredients with cracked ice in a shaker. Shake vigorously, and then strain into the serving glass.

White Lady

A subtle variation on the White Russian is the White Lady.

Serve in a chilled cocktail glass.

½ oz. vodka

½ oz. crème de cacao

2 oz. heavy cream

Combine the ingredients with cracked ice in a shaker. Shake vigorously, and then strain into the serving glass.

White Spider

One more variation on the theme.

Serve in a chilled cocktail glass.

2. oz vodka

1 oz. white crème de menthe

Combine the ingredients with cracked ice in a shaker. Shake vigorously, and then strain into the serving glass.

Citrus Productions

Vodka mixes beautifully with citrus juices. Don't invest in premium-label vodka for citrus drinks; instead, spend a little extra to buy freshly-squeezed juices or spend a little extra time to squeeze the juice fresh yourself. You'll taste the difference.

Moscow Mule and Other Mostly Lime Juice Drinks

The Moscow Mule is the drink that kicked vodka into the American drinking mainstream. The classic recipe that follows originated in Los Angeles, at the Cock 'n' Bull Restaurant.

Ever since the Ocean Spray company became closely associated with cranberry juice, drinks made with that juice have been given names savoring of the sea and seashore. The Cape Codder starts out with vodka and a dash of lime juice.

The gimlet is among the most popular of vodka vehicles. If at all possible, squeeze a fresh lime directly into the drink. The taste is irresistibly refreshing. If you must use concentrated lime juice, try the Vodka Gimlet with Rose's Lime Juice.

Moscow Mule

Serve in a chilled highball glass or a chilled coffee mug.

3 oz. vodka

1 tsp. lime juice

Ginger beer to fill

Lime wedge

Combine the vodka and lime juice in the serving glass one-third filled with ice cubes. Add ginger beer to fill, and garnish with the lime.

Cape Codder

Serve in a large (double) chilled old-fashioned glass.

1½ oz. vodka

Dash lime juice

4 oz. cranberry juice

1 tsp. sugar syrup

Combine all ingredients in a shaker with cracked ice. Shake vigorously, and pour into the serving glass.

Vodka Gimlet with Fresh Lime

Serve on the rocks in a lowball glass.

2 oz. vodka

1 oz. fresh lime juice

Combine all ingredients in a shaker. Shake vigorously. Pour into the serving glass. *Or,* combine both ingredients in the serving glass and stir.

Vodka Gimlet with Rose's Lime Juice

Serve in a chilled cocktail glass.

2 oz. vodka

½ oz. Rose's lime juice

Combine both ingredients with ice in a mixing glass. Stir. Strain into the serving glass.

Cayman Cup

Serve in a chilled Collins glass.

1½ oz. vodka

½ oz. triple sec

2 oz. mango nectar

2 oz. orange juice

½ oz. lemon juice

Mango and/or peach slices

In a shaker or blender combine all ingredients except fruit slices. Blend or shake with cracked ice, and then pour into serving glass. Garnish with the fruit slices.

These two are fairly new ideas for the tried-and-true vodka-lime combination. The first is pretty simple, the second requires a little more work.

The Bottom Line

Serve on the rocks in a highball glass.

1½ oz. vodka

½ oz. Rose's lime juice

Tonic water

Lime slice

Combine the vodka and lime juice over ice in the serving glass. Stir gently, fill with tonic water, and then garnish with the lime slice.

Belmont Stakes

Serve in a chilled cocktail glass.

1½ oz. vodka

½ oz. gold rum

½ oz. lime juice

½ tsp. grenadine

Orange slice

Combine all ingredients, except the orange slice, in a shaker with cracked ice. Shake well, and then strain into the serving glass. Garnish with the orange slice.

Salty Dog and Other Mostly Grapefruit Juice Drinks

Vodka and grapefruit juice are a natural combination; the puckery acidity of the grapefruit juice makes a perfect complement to the alcohol. You can keep it simple and just fill a highball glass with ice, pour in two fingers of vodka, add grapefruit juice to fill, and down the hatch. Or you can be more ambitious. The best-known vodka and grapefruit juice drink adds a bit of salt and sugar.

Salty Dog

Serve in an old-fashioned glass with a salted-sugared rim.

Salt

Granulated sugar

Lime wedge

2 oz. vodka

Grapefruit juice to fill

Prepare the glass by rubbing the lime wedge on the rim and salting the glass (see Chapter 5 for more information about salting). Fill glass one-third with ice cubes. Pour in vodka, sugar, and grapefruit juice, stir, and garnish with the lime wedge used for rimming.

Sea Breeze with Juice

Once again, the addition of cranberry evokes salt air and high seas.

Serve in a chilled highball glass.

2 oz. vodka

3 oz. grapefruit juice

3 oz. cranberry juice

Combine all ingredients in a shaker with cracked ice. Shake vigorously. Pour into the serving glass.

Russian Wolfhound

Serve in a chilled wine goblet.

Salt for rim of glass

1½ oz. vodka

2 oz. bitter lemon soda

2 oz. grapefruit juice

Salt the rim of the serving glass by moistening the rim with some bitter lemon soda and rolling the rim in the salt. Put ice cubes in the serving glass, and then add all ingredients. Stir gently.

Crimea Cooler

Serve in a chilled Collins glass.

1½ oz. vodka

3 oz. grapefruit juice

½ oz. crème de cassis

Ginger ale

Orange slice

Combine all ingredients, except the orange slice and ginger ale, in a shaker or blender with cracked ice. Shake or blend, and then pour into the serving glass. Top off with ginger ale and garnish with the orange slice.

The two that follow might not be very new, but they're also not very familiar.

Petrograd Punch

Serve in a chilled wine goblet.

1½ oz. vodka

3 oz. grapefruit juice

2 oz. concord grape wine

Combine the vodka and grapefruit juice in a shaker or blender with cracked ice. Shake or blend, and then pour into the serving glass. Carefully top with the wine as a float. Do not stir!

Serge's Sunshine

Serve in a highball glass.

1½ oz. vodka

4 oz. grapefruit juice

½ oz. triple sec

Combine all ingredients in a shaker or blender with cracked ice. Shake or blend, and then pour into the serving glass.

Screwdrivers, Wallbangers, and Other Mostly Orange Juice Drinks

To think of vodka and orange juice is to think of a screwdriver, a very basic drink named for a very basic tool. It's best if the orange juice is freshly squeezed!

Screwdriver

Serve on the rocks in a chilled highball glass or in a large (double) chilled old-fashioned glass.

1½ oz. vodka

4 oz. orange juice

Orange slice

Fill serving glass one-third with ice cubes. Pour in vodka and orange juice, stir, and garnish with the orange slice.

Harvey Wallbanger

The Harvey Wallbanger is a screwdriver with the addition of Galliano, the popular Italian liqueur that comes in a ridiculously tall bottle.

Serve on the rocks in a chilled Collins glass.

1½ oz. vodka

4 oz. orange juice

½ oz. Galliano

Fill serving glass one-third with ice cubes. Pour in vodka and orange juice, and stir. Carefully add the Galliano so that it floats. Do not stir!

Fuzzy Navel

A little thought will tell you where the name of this drink comes from, a combination of a fruit that sports a "belly button" and a fruit covered with fuzz.

Serve on the rocks in a highball glass.

¾ oz. peach schnapps

¾ oz. vodka

Orange juice to fill

Combine all ingredients in the serving glass and stir.

Fuzzy Navel Variation

If you like your vodka less fuzzy, try this variation.

Serve in a chilled Collins glass.

1 oz. vodka

½ oz. peach schnapps

6 oz. orange juice

Orange slice

Combine all ingredients, except the orange slice, in a shaker or blender with cracked ice. Shake or blend, and then pour into the serving glass and garnish with the orange slice.

Bar Tips

Before we leave the navel, be aware that some folks leave out the vodka altogether and just go with 1½ ounces of peach schnapps combined with orange juice.

Fuzzy Pierced Navel

Substitute tequila or dark rum for the vodka, and you have the Fuzzy Pierced Navel.

Serve in a chilled Collins glass.

1 oz. tequila or dark rum

1½ oz. peach schnapps

6 oz. orange juice

Combine the ingredients in a shaker or blender with cracked ice. Shake or blend, and then pour into the serving glass. If you like, add a few ice cubes.

Sex on the Beach

This certainly sounds more inviting than vodka and pineapple juice, which is what it is. You won't find a *Kama Sutra* full of versions of this drink, but there are a few. We'll begin with what most authorities agree is the original.

Original Sex on the Beach

Serve in a chilled highball glass.

1 oz. vodka

½ oz. Midori melon liqueur

½ oz. Chambord (substitute other raspberry liqueur if necessary)

1½ oz. pineapple juice

1½ oz. cranberry juice cocktail

Combine all ingredients in a shaker with ice. Shake vigorously and pour into the serving glass.

Alternative Sex on the Beach

Serve on the rocks in a highball glass.

¾ oz. peach schnapps

¾ oz. vodka

3 oz. pineapple or grapefruit juice

3 oz. cranberry juice cocktail

Combine all ingredients in the serving glass with ice and stir.

Sex on the Beach in Winter

Serve in a wine goblet or Collins glass.

¾ oz. vodka

3 oz. pineapple or grapefruit juice

3 oz. cranberry juice cocktail

1 tsp cream of coconut

Combine all ingredients in a blender with cracked ice. Blend until smooth, and then pour into the serving glass.

Kamikaze

Another popular shooter is the Kamikaze. Banzai!

Serve in a shot glass.

1 oz. vodka

1 oz. triple sec

1 oz. lime juice

Shake with ice; strain into *three* shot glasses.

Some people prefer their Sex on the Beach as a *shooter* (a drink served as a single shot). To make one, use the "original" recipe, but reduce the juices by a half-ounce each. *Strain* into three shot glasses.

Buzzed Words

A **shooter** is a drink meant to be downed in a single shot, often accompanied by table banging and gasps of pleasurable pain.

Coffee Combo

Here are a couple coffee and vodka drinks you'll enjoy.

Russian Coffee

Serve in a chilled brandy snifter.

½ oz. vodka

1½ oz. coffee liqueur

1 oz. heavy cream

Combine all ingredients in a blender with ice. Blend until smooth, and then pour into the snifter.

Russian Espresso

Serve on the rocks in a lowball glass.

1½ oz. vodka

2 tsp. espresso coffee liqueur

Few drops lemon juice

Lemon twist

Combine all ingredients, except the lemon twist, in a shaker with cracked ice. Shake vigorously, and then strain into the serving glass. Garnish with the lemon twist.

Russian Winter in the Tropics

The spirit associated with the frozen North is also an apt vehicle for tropical libations.

Melonball

Serve in a cocktail glass.

¾ oz. vodka

½ oz. melon liqueur

2 oz. orange juice

Mix ingredients in a shaker with ice. Pour into a cocktail glass. Garnish with an orange slice.

With Brandy, Liqueur, or an Aperitif

A neutral spirit, vodka mates beautifully with more flavorful alcoholic beverages and gives an added kick to brandies, liqueurs, and aperitifs.

Alexander Nevsky was a thirteenth-century Russian hero who halted an invasion of Germans and Swedes. For this, the Eastern Orthodox church made him a saint. As a bonus, somebody else, about 800 years later, named a vodka drink after him.

Alexander Nevsky

Serve in chilled snifter or wine goblet.

1 oz. vodka

1 oz. apricot liqueur

½ oz. lemon juice

4 oz. orange juice

Orange slice

Combine all ingredients, except orange slice, in a shaker with cracked ice. Shake vigorously and pour into the serving glass. Garnish with the orange slice.

Bar Tips

When you are instructed to drop a fruit wedge into a drink, release more of the flavor by first scoring—scraping—the peel with the tines of a fork.

Saint Petersburg

Doubtless, when the Saint Petersburg hit the scene, its namesake city was still called Leningrad. Now the Soviet Union has dissolved, Leningrad is Saint Petersburg again, and we can all celebrate with this simple combination of vodka and bitters. It tastes best with a premium vodka.

Serve straight up in a chilled old-fashioned glass.

2 oz. vodka

¼ tsp. orange bitters

1 orange wedge

Combine vodka and bitters in mixing glass one-third full of ice. Stir well. Strain into the serving glass. Drop the orange wedge into the drink.

The Vodka ...

A vast panoply of drinks not originally made with vodka have time-tested and taste-certified vodka versions.

The Tom Collins can be made with vodka instead of gin. Thus incarnated, it is always called a Vodka Collins, *never* a Vodka Tom Collins.

Vodka Collins

Serve on the rocks in a Collins glass.

1 oz. vodka

2 oz. sour mix

Club soda to fill

Maraschino cherry

Combine all ingredients, except for the cherry, in the serving glass filled with ice. Stir. Garnish with the maraschino cherry.

Vodka Cooler (Simple)

Serve on the rocks in a Collins glass.

1 oz. vodka

½ oz. sweet vermouth

7-Up to fill

Combine the vodka and sweet vermouth in a shaker with ice. Shake vigorously. Strain into serving glass filled with ice. Add 7-Up to fill.

The Grasshopper has seen its heyday come and go. Nevertheless, it survives as a fun retro drink. The traditional Grasshopper is strictly a liqueur drink, but here are two Grasshoppers that add vodka.

Vodka Grasshopper

Serve in a chilled cocktail glass.

½ oz. vodka

¾ oz. green crème de menthe

¾ oz. white crème de menthe

Combine the ingredients with cracked ice in a shaker. Shake vigorously, and then strain into the serving glass.

Flying Grasshopper

Serve in a chilled old-fashioned or lowball glass.

1½ oz. vodka

½ oz. green crème de menthe

½ oz. white crème de menthe

Combine all the ingredients with cracked ice in a shaker. Shake vigorously, and then pour into the serving glass.

Jungle Jim

Serve in a chilled old-fashioned or lowball glass.

1 oz. vodka

1 oz. crème de banana

1 oz. milk

Combine all the ingredients with cracked ice in a shaker. Shake vigorously, and then pour into the serving glass.

Bar Tips

If you don't want to use store-bought sour mix, see Chapter 4 for a fresh recipe.

Vodka Sour

In the last chapter, you saw that you can easily substitute gin for the traditional whisky in a sour. Nothing wrong with vodka, either.

Serve straight-up in a chilled sour glass.

1½-2 oz. vodka

¾ oz. lemon juice

1 tsp. sugar syrup

Lemon slice

Maraschino cherry

Combine all ingredients, except the lemon slice and cherry, in a shaker with cracked ice. Shake vigorously. Strain into the serving glass and garnish with the lemon slice and maraschino cherry.

The traditional stinger combines brandy with white crème de menthe. Vodka does the job, too.

The words "Gin and Tonic" roll off the tongue so naturally that you might have to stop and think—think *hard*—in order to ask for a *Vodka* Tonic. Make sure the tonic water is fresh and hasn't lost its fizz.

Vodka Stinger

Serve in a chilled cocktail glass.

1½ oz. vodka

1 oz. white crème de menthe

Combine all ingredients in a shaker with cracked ice. Shake vigorously and strain into the serving glass.

Vodka Tonic

Serve on the rocks in a highball glass.

1½ oz. vodka

Tonic water to fill

Lime wedge

Pour the vodka into a serving glass one-third full of ice. Add tonic to fill, and garnish with the lime wedge.

Vodka Visions

Vodka goes with just about anything—as today's edgiest barkeeps will tell you. Here are some vodka drinks suited to the twenty-first century.

Johnson

Serve on the rocks in an old-fashioned glass.

2 oz. vodka

½ oz. curaçao

1 oz. sloe gin

Combine in a shaker with cracked ice. Shake vigorously, and then strain into the serving glass.

Russian Roulette

Serve on the rocks in a highball glass.

¾ oz. Galliano

½ oz. orange juice

½ oz. banana brandy

1 TB. lemon juice

½ oz. vodka

Combine in a shaker with cracked ice. Shake vigorously, and then strain into the serving glass.

Submariner

Serve on the rocks in an old-fashioned glass.

2 oz. vodka

½ oz. light rum

½ oz. spiced rum

1 TB. melon liqueur

1 tsp. lemon juice

Lime twist

Combine all ingredients, except the lime twist, in a shaker with cracked ice. Shake vigorously, and then strain into the serving glass. Garnish with the lime twist.

Vampire's Kiss

Serve on the rocks in an old-fashioned glass.

2 oz. vodka

½ oz. dry gin

½ oz. dry vermouth

1 TB. tequila

2 oz. tomato juice or V-8

Pinch salt

Combine in a shaker with cracked ice. Shake vigorously, and then strain into the serving glass.

Murder Juice

Serve on the rocks in a Collins glass.

2 oz. vodka

½ oz. light rum

½ oz. tequila

Cranberry juice

Lemon slice

Combine the spirits over ice in the serving glass, and then top off with cranberry juice. Garnish with the lemon slice.

Be inventive. The range of possible vodka combinations is limited only by your imagination. Remember, vodka is a neutral spirit, which, as you've just seen, means that you can mix it with almost anything. If you need a little help, see Appendix B for more ways to quench your thirst.

The Least You Need to Know

- Vodka, which today outsells any other spirit in the United States, achieved popularity only after World War II.
- Although nominally colorless, tasteless, and without aroma, vodkas do differ subtly in character. It pays to sample, especially the premium brands.
- Most drinkers enjoy vodka libations very, very cold. Consider storing your vodka in the freezer.
- Because it adds so little flavor and aroma of its own, vodka is a universal mixer.

Chapter 8

The Silver Bullet

In This Chapter

- The martini's ancestor
- Martini controversies
- How dry is a *dry* martini?
- The basic martini
- Variations on the martini

The once-classic "three-martini lunch" has diminished in popularity since the IRS reduced the allowable deduction on business entertaining—and employers realized that *three* martinis at lunch do have a certain impact on the workday. But the martini nevertheless remains at once the most sophisticated, variable, refined, controversial, and popular of cocktails. Moreover, its popularity cuts across generational, gender, and social lines. Trendy restaurants and bars tout their "traditional" martinis even as they trumpet a panoply of innovative variations, some of them, like the extraordinarily popular Cosmopolitan, bearing little resemblance to the traditional martini, but nevertheless having become a staple of the martini bar.

The innovations notwithstanding, self-proclaimed purists have a lot to say about how a "real" martini should be made, and that includes forbidding vodka as an ingredient. "You can make a very nice drink with vodka and vermouth," they say, "but it's not a martini."

Well, this chapter aims to please the purists, but it will also cover the vodka as well as the gin martini—and a good many variations on these. After all, the people have spoken, and the will of the people must be served. We trust that we will give no lasting offense, but purists might want to shield their eyes.

The Martini's Controversial Past

As modern mixed drinks go, the martini is pretty old. It probably originated as the *Martinez*, which was invented in San Francisco during the wild Gold Rush years by a celebrated local bartender named Jerry Thomas. Purists—ye who advocate a *dry* martini—take note: Thomas's recipe was anything but dry. It consisted of four parts vermouth to one part Old Tom (*sweet* gin)—practically a mirror opposite of today's drink—and, horror of horrors, it also sported a dash of bitters and two dashes of maraschino liqueur in addition to the vermouth.

Bar Tips

The Players, steeped as it is in history, offers this historical re-creation of the ancestor of the modern martini, the Martinez. Good luck tracking down a bottle of Old Tom:

In a shaker with cracked ice, shake …

1 dash bitters
2 dashes maraschino liqueur
1 pony Old Tom
1 wine glass sweet vermouth

Strain into a chilled cocktail glass and garnish with ¼ slice of lemon.

By the 1920s, the Martinez had become the martini, but even a "standard" martini, 1920s-style, went pretty heavy on the vermouth: four parts gin to one part vermouth. And if the opinion of literary scholar Bernard DeVoto is given credence, the standard had not changed much by 1949. In that year, DeVoto published a classic essay on the martini in *Harper's*, decreeing the perfect ratio as 3.7 parts gin to 1 part vermouth.

Buzzed Words

A **dry martini** is one with relatively little vermouth versus gin. Some drinkers prefer 12 parts gin to 1 part vermouth, whereas others insist on a 20-to-1 ratio. Extremists do away with the vermouth altogether and have a gin and olive on the rocks.

Even in the 1940s—and, one suspects, earlier as well—there were champions of the truly dry martini. Gin to vermouth ratios of 12 to 1 and 20 to 1 were proposed. Sir Winston Churchill, who had strong opinions about everything, from how best to deal with Herr Hitler to the proper placement of prepositions, believed that a dry martini should be prepared by merely casting a glance toward an unopened bottle of vermouth while pouring the gin into the mixing glass.

> **Quick One**
>
> During World War II, a certain Army Air Force pilot always packed gin and vermouth, olives, a mixing spoon, and a chrome-plated cup on each mission. One day, his co-pilot asked, "What good will all that do if we crash in the jungle?" The pilot answered, "We go down in the middle of nowhere, I start making a martini, and somebody will show up and say, '*That's* no way to make a martini!'"

And, speaking of mixing, there is the controversy over whether the drink should be stirred or shaken. Agent 007, of course, has always insisted on having his martini "shaken, not stirred." Many bartenders believe that aerating alcohol by shaking it improves taste, even as others claim that shaking (or even overly vigorous stirring) "bruises the gin"—whatever that means. Vigorous shaking can indeed cloud the martini, a strictly cosmetic effect that some drinkers nevertheless find objectionable. The cloudiness, caused by the thousands of tiny air bubbles that form in the drink, does settle—but, by that time, the martini will have started to go warm, and you'll still be thirsty. (Cloudiness can also be caused by failing to strain out the cracked ice when you pour the drink from a shaker into the serving glass. Some drinkers find the presence of a little cracked ice refreshing, but, for most, it is unwelcome. Strain carefully.)

You'll also hear differing opinions on just how to chill the drink. Some drinkers prefer their martini on the rocks, whereas others insist that the real thing *must* be served straight-up—stirring (or shaking) the ingredients with ice, and then straining them into the serving glass. Some claim that the ice that melts while shaking actually "marries" the gin to the vermouth, and is therefore crucial to the preparation. Others protest the dilution that occurs by merely *stirring* the drink with ice, and insist that the only way to chill a martini is by storing the gin in the freezer so that ice becomes wholly unnecessary.

And then there's the issue of added ingredients and garnishes. Wars have been fought with less cause.

Most drinkers welcome a lemon twist or an olive, though some insist that the olive compromises the purity of the drink. A few accept the lemon peel, but insist that it remain un-twisted, lest the expressed lemon essence defile the absolute virtue of the libation. A minority insists that no garnish of any kind should contaminate their martini. On the other hand, some drinkers favor a "dirty" martini, one with olives *and* a dash of olive juice.

Imagine the discomfiture of such a thoroughly chaste drinker confronted by such accents as a few drops of scotch, curaçao, Pernod, bitters, or liqueur! Only the truly heartless can take pleasure from such a scene.

Martini Secrets

Reader, you've been patient. This is a how-to book, after all, and all we've done thus far is tell you how you might—or might not—make a martini. Here at last are the 10 Secrets of Making a Great Martini:

Quick One

"Let me slip out of these wet clothes and into a dry martini."

—Robert Benchley, Algonquin wit

Bar Tips

Glasses stored for a long time in a closed cabinet sometimes acquire a musty, dusty taste. Rinse out even clean glasses if they have been stored for any length of time.

1. For a gin martini, use a premium-label gin. Which one you use is up to you. As you might recall from Chapter 6, they range in degree of flavorfulness. If you like a martini redolent of aromatic botanicals, veer toward the Bombay end of the gin spectrum. (And if you want a really strong martini, try Bombay Sapphire, which is 100 proof, versus the conventional 80.) If you prefer a cleaner taste, lean toward Beefeater. Something in between? Taste Tanqueray. The super-premium Tanqueray No. 10 is the most flavorful of all readily available gins. Purists will be nervous about putting it into a martini, but it makes a very definite statement. There are also many smaller-label, more exotic—and more expensive!—gins on the market. Try whatever varieties your favorite club offers, and then bring home what you like best.
2. For a vodka martini, use a premium-label vodka. The variations in flavorfulness and character among these are less pronounced than among premium-label gins, but you might want to sample several to find a favorite. Flavored vodkas such as lemon, pepper, or berry flavor do not make a classic vodka martini, but you might enjoy experimenting with these nonetheless.
3. Use a dry vermouth that you would enjoy drinking by itself, on the rocks. Two brands, Noilly-Prat and Martini and Rossi, dominate the market. Both are excellent. Sample and decide.
4. Use super-clean barware and glassware for mixing as well as for serving. Make certain that there is no detergent or soap aftertaste.

5. Whether you serve your martini straight-up or on the rocks, use ice entirely free from freezer burn or freezer-borne smells and tastes. Commercial bagged ice is always best.
6. Never use olives stuffed with pimento. They will discolor the drink and give it an unwanted flavor.
7. But … never say never. Some martini lovers like pimento in their olive and don't mind the drink's pinkish hue and peppery flavor one bit. Some even insist that it is essential to the "look" of the drink, the skewered pimento olive recumbent in a martini glass serving as an icon of the traditional drink.
8. If you are the host, *listen* to the drinker. Based on your taste and experience, you might suggest this or that ratio and this or that gin, but don't force anything on anyone. Accommodate the drinker.
9. Don't let *anyone* tell you there's only one "right" way to make a martini.
10. Whatever you make, it's not worth fighting over. Give peace a chance.

Bar Tips

To chill a glass, fill it with ice, add water, and let it sit while you mix the drink. When ready to pour, dump the water and ice, shake the glass to remove the excess, and pour the drink!

The Classic Dry Martini

We believe that the "dry" martini is the closest thing there is to a "standard" martini. Here's how it's done. (If you want to taste more of the vermouth, make the martini less dry by adding more vermouth. Many drinkers favor a 5-to-1 ratio.)

Dry Martini

Serve in a chilled cocktail glass.

2 oz. gin

½ tsp. dry vermouth

Olive or lemon twist

Combine the gin and vermouth in a mixing glass at least half full of ice. Stir well, and then strain into the cocktail glass. Garnish with the olive or the lemon twist. If your olives are very small, spear three on a toothpick.

Dry Vodka Martini

A dry vodka martini should be drier than the dry gin martini. Here's a starting point most drinkers will enjoy.

Serve in a chilled cocktail glass.

3 oz. vodka

Dash of dry vermouth

Olive or lemon twist

Combine the vodka and vermouth in a mixing glass at least half full of ice. Stir well, and then *quickly* strain into the cocktail glass. Garnish with the olive or the lemon twist. If your olives are very small, spear three on a toothpick.

Perfect Martini

There's the *perfect* martini, and then there's the *Perfect* Martini. The presumptuous name comes from the exquisite yin and yang of the sweet versus the dry vermouth.

Serve in a chilled cocktail glass.

1½ oz. gin

½ tsp. dry vermouth

½ tsp. sweet vermouth

Olive

Combine all ingredients, except the olive, in a mixing glass with ice. Stir well and strain into the serving glass. Garnish with the olive. If you prefer, use a shaker to mix the drink.

Bar Tips

Both the gin and vodka martinis—but especially the vodka martini—benefit from quick stirring with a lot of ice rather than prolonged stirring with a few ice cubes. The object is to minimize meltage, which dilutes the drink. One of the few things martini drinkers agree on is that a watery drink stinks.

The Really Dry Martini

There are at least three ways to make a *really* dry martini:

1. Using the same amount of gin or vodka as for the basic dry martini, add just two or three *drops* of vermouth. No, you don't need an eye dropper. Just put your thumb over the mouth of the bottle and sprinkle.
2. Pour an ounce or so of dry vermouth into a chilled cocktail glass. Swirl the vermouth to coat the glass. Pour out the excess vermouth. Stir the gin or vodka in a mixing glass with ice. Strain into the coated cocktail glass.
3. Forget the vermouth altogether. Serve straight gin or vodka on the rocks or straight-up (having stirred the spirit with ice). Call it a *really* dry martini (but it's really just cold gin).

Gibson

The Gibson is the most common variation on the martini theme. At its most basic, it's just a martini with a few (three or more, depending on size and preference) pickled pearl onions instead of the olive or lemon twist. The conscientious Gibson maker, however, varies the underlying martini recipe slightly, yielding a somewhat larger drink that is *always* on the very dry side.

Gibson

Serve in a chilled cocktail glass.

2½ oz. gin

Dash or two of dry vermouth

Pickled pearl onions

Combine the gin and vermouth in a mixing glass at least half full of ice. Stir well, and then *quickly* strain into the cocktail glass. Garnish with the pearl onions. If you prefer, use a shaker to mix the drink.

Vodka Gibson

The Vodka Gibson is almost identical to the Gin Gibson. Just add a bit more vodka.

Serve in a chilled cocktail glass.

3 oz. vodka

Dash or two of dry vermouth

Pickled pearl onions

Combine the vodka and vermouth in a mixing glass at least half full of ice. Stir well, and then *quickly* strain into the cocktail glass. Garnish with the pearl onions. If you prefer, use a shaker to mix the drink.

Vodka Varieties

Now that we've laid out the basic gin and vodka martinis, together with the most basic variation in the form of the Gibson, let's go on to variations on the vodka martini. Indeed, in some future edition of *The Complete Idiot's Guide to Mixing Drinks*, vodka might have supplanted gin as the martini ingredient of choice. (Perish the thought!) An increasing number of drinkers prefer the cleaner, simpler taste (or non-taste) of vodka to the more assertive and complex savor of gin.

The chief thing to remember about a vodka martini—whatever form it takes—is that the vermouth or other additives and the garnishes occupy center stage. It is *their* flavor that shines through the neutral spirit that is vodka.

The Cajun Martini takes some advance preparation and the acquisition of a few jalapeño peppers.

Cajun Martini

Serve in a chilled cocktail glass.

3 oz. vodka

Dash dry vermouth

Thin slice of garlic

Several slices of pickled jalapeño peppers

Pickled pearl onions

At least one hour before serving, prepare the vodka by steeping the garlic, jalapeño, and onions in it. The steeping vodka should be stored in a closed container in the freezer. Combine the steeped vodka and vermouth in a mixing glass at least half full of ice. Stir well, and then *quickly* strain into the cocktail glass. Garnish with a jalapeño slice or with some pearl onions.

Spanish Vodka Martini

Serve in a chilled cocktail glass.

2½ oz. vodka

½ oz. dry sherry

Lemon twist

Combine the vodka and sherry in a mixing glass at least half full of ice. Stir well, and then *quickly* strain into the cocktail glass. Garnish with the lemon twist.

Ochi Chernya

"Dark Eyes"—"*Ochi Chernya*"—is a favorite old Russian song, and the name seemed appropriate to the proprietors of Manhattan's celebrated Russian Tea Room to describe a *vodka* Martini that uses a *black* olive instead of green. But that's not all.

Serve in a chilled cocktail glass.

2 oz. vodka

¼ oz. dry vermouth

¼ oz. sweet vermouth

Large black olive

Combine the vodka and vermouths in a mixing glass at least half full of ice. Stir well, and then *quickly* strain into the cocktail glass. Garnish with the black olive.

Exotic Variations

By now, we've either reeducated (fat chance) or thoroughly alienated the martini purists out there, so let's plunge ahead boldly into the depths of decadence with a catalogue of martini exotica.

Dutch, Fino, and Marsala

In Chapter 6, we observed that Dutch—or genever—gin is not generally a good mixer. The sole exception is the Dutch Martini. If you like the extremely full-bodied taste of genever, you'll enjoy this drink.

Dutch Martini

Serve in a chilled cocktail glass.

2 oz. genever gin

½ tsp. dry vermouth

Lemon peel

Combine the gin and vermouth in a mixing glass at least half full of ice. Stir well, then *quickly* strain into the cocktail glass. Garnish with the lemon peel.

Fino Martini

If dry gin can be unseated as a principal Martini constituent, so can vermouth. We've seen something like this in the Vodka Spanish Martini. Here's the Fino Martini.

Serve in a chilled cocktail glass.

2 oz. gin

¼ oz. fino sherry

Lemon twist or olive

Combine the vodka and sherry in a mixing glass at least half full of ice. Stir well, and then *quickly* strain into the cocktail glass. Garnish with the lemon twist or olive.

Marsala Martini

The town of Marsala in western Sicily is surrounded by vineyards. Since 1773, the Marsalans have been producing Marsala, a rich, full-bodied, blood-red blended wine of high alcoholic content. In the Marsala Martini, this wine supplements, but does not supplant, the traditional dry vermouth.

Serve in a chilled cocktail glass.

¾ oz. dry Marsala

¾ oz. gin

1 TB. dry vermouth

Lemon twist

Combine all ingredients, except the lemon twist, in a shaker with ice. Shake vigorously. Strain into the serving glass and garnish with the lemon twist.

Fore!

If you like the taste of bitters, try several different kinds in your Martini and see what happens. The best-known bitters augmented Martini is the Golf.

Golf Martini

Serve in a chilled cocktail glass.

1½ oz. gin

1 tsp. dry vermouth

2-3 dashes Angostura bitters

Olive

Combine the gin, vermouth, and bitters in a mixing glass at least half full of ice. Stir well, and then *quickly* strain into the serving glass. Garnish with the olive.

Pacific Rim and Bowl

As a love of sushi has spread across the United States, so has an affection for *sake*, the Japanese beverage made from fermented rice. Most of us enjoy it hot, but it is also quite delicious on the rocks, and if you substitute it for the vermouth in a traditional Martini, you have—what else?—a Saketini.

Perhaps you've never thought of the Martini in a tropical context. The addition of pineapple juice to the Martini makes it downright Hawaiian.

Saketini

Serve in a chilled cocktail glass.

2 oz. gin

¼ oz. sake

Olive or lemon twist

Combine the gin and sake in a shaker with ice. Shake well, and then strain into the serving glass. Garnish with the olive or lemon twist.

Hawaiian Martini

Serve in a chilled cocktail glass.

1½ oz. gin

1 tsp. dry vermouth

1 tsp. sweet vermouth

1 tsp. pineapple juice

Combine the ingredients in a shaker with ice. Shake well, and strain into the serving glass.

From Medici to Medoc (with a Touch of Paisley)

The Medicis ruled Florence and, subsequently, Tuscany, from 1434 to 1737, with two brief interruptions. They did things in a big way, furnishing the Church with four of its popes and marrying into most of the royal families of Europe while generally living the high life and acting as patrons to the great Florentine artists. It is only fitting that the Martini variation named for the family is the most elaborate you can make. Rome—or, in this case, *Firenza*—wasn't built in a day, so this cocktail needs some advance preparation.

Cordial Médoc is a liqueur produced in the Médoc wine district of southwestern France, on the left bank of the Gironde River estuary, northwest of Bordeaux. Don't use it instead of dry vermouth, but *with* it.

Martini Melonzona a la Medici

Serve in a chilled brandy snifter.

3 oz. gin

Few drops of white wine vinegar (see directions)

Lemon twist

Drain a jar of preserved baby eggplant. Replace the liquid with white wine vinegar, close the jar, place in the refrigerator, and steep for several days. Pour the gin into a mixing glass with ice; add a few drops of the steeped white wine vinegar. Stir well, and then strain into the serving glass. Garnish with two baby eggplants (blot dry with paper towel to remove the excess white wine vinegar) and the lemon twist.

Médoc Martini

Serve in a chilled cocktail glass.

1½ oz. gin

½ tsp. dry vermouth

½ oz. Cordial Médoc

Combine the ingredients in a mixing glass with ice. Stir well and *quickly* strain into the serving glass.

Paisley Martini

Serve in a chilled cocktail glass.

2 oz. gin

½ tsp. dry vermouth

½ tsp. Scotch

Combine the ingredients in a shaker with ice. Shake well and strain into the serving glass.

Viva la France!

We've been to France briefly with the Médoc Martini. Let's return with Marguerite, a Martini variation that uses *French* rather than Italian vermouth—and quite a lot of it. Lovers of *dry* Martinis, steer clear.

Marguerite

Serve in a chilled cocktail glass.

1½ oz. gin

1 oz. French vermouth

Dash orange bitters

Orange peel

Combine all ingredients, except the orange peel, in a mixing glass with ice. Stir well and strain into the serving glass. Garnish with the orange peel.

Peggy Cocktail

The Peggy Cocktail makes good use of those French aperitifs, Dubonnet and Pernod.

Serve in a chilled cocktail glass.

1½ oz. gin

½ oz. dry vermouth

Few dashes Dubonnet

Few dashes Pernod

Combine the ingredients in a mixing glass with ice. Stir well and strain into the serving glass.

Palm Island and Perfect

In the Palm Island, an ordinary Martini collides with white crème de cacao. The results are tropical.

Palm Island Martini

Serve in a chilled old-fashioned glass.

1½ oz. gin

½ oz. dry vermouth

¼ oz. white crème de cacao

Combine the ingredients in a shaker with cracked ice. Shake well and pour into the serving glass.

Add some Benedictine, ditch the olive, and the Perfect Martini (discussed in "The Classic Dry Martini") becomes a Rolls-Royce.

Rolls-Royce

Serve in a chilled cocktail glass.

1½ oz. gin

½ tsp. dry vermouth

½ tsp. sweet vermouth

Few dashes Benedictine

Combine all ingredients in a mixing glass with ice. Stir well and strain into the serving glass.

Romana and Rum

We've visited Sicily and Florence; now let's get to the capital, Roma. It's the Campari that nationalizes this Martini variation.

Martini Romana

Serve in a chilled cocktail glass.

1½ oz. gin

½ tsp. dry vermouth

Few dashes of Campari

Combine all ingredients in a mixing glass with ice. Stir well and strain into the serving glass.

Rum Martini

For a revolutionary Martini, leave Italy for the Caribbean.

Serve in a chilled cocktail glass.

2 oz. white rum

Several drops of dry vermouth

Olive

Lime twist

Combine the ingredients, except the olive and lime twist, in a mixing glass with ice. Stir well and strain into the serving glass. Garnish with the olive and lime twist.

Boola Boola

Give this one the old college try.

Yale Cocktail

Serve in a chilled cocktail glass.

1½ oz. gin

½ oz. dry vermouth

Few dashes orange bitters

Few dashes maraschino liqueur

Combine all ingredients in a mixing glass with ice. Stir well and strain into the serving glass.

The Tequini and the Sweeter Side

If the Saketini bows to Japan, the Tequini doffs a sombrero to the country south of the border. It's a Martini made with tequila instead of gin.

Tequini

Serve in a chilled cocktail glass.

2½ oz. tequila

½ oz. dry vermouth

Olive or lemon twist

Combine all ingredients, except the olive or lemon twist, in a mixing glass with ice. Stir well and strain into the serving glass. Garnish with the olive or lemon twist.

Atta Boy

Those searching for a sweet Martini will enjoy the Atta Boy, one of the truly classic Martini variations. It takes a liberal dose of grenadine.

Serve in a chilled cocktail glass

2 oz. gin

1 oz. dry vermouth

½ tsp. grenadine

Lemon twist

Combine all ingredients, except the lemon twist, in a shaker with ice. Shake well, and strain into the serving glass. Garnish with the lemon twist.

Gin and It

The simplest route to a sweet Martini is to use sweet vermouth, mixed in equal proportion to the gin.

Serve in a chilled cocktail glass.

1 oz. gin

1 oz. sweet vermouth

Combine all ingredients in a mixing glass with ice. Stir well and strain into the serving glass.

Sweet Martini

If Gin and It strikes you as too simple, add a little something else.

Serve in a chilled cocktail glass.

2 oz. gin

½ oz. sweet vermouth

Dash orange bitters

Orange peel

Combine all ingredients, except the orange peel, in a mixing glass with ice. Stir well and strain into the serving glass. Twist the orange peel over the drink and garnish.

Imperial

The Imperial balances tart Angostura bitters with sweet maraschino liqueur.

Serve in a chilled cocktail glass.

1½ oz. gin

1½ oz. dry vermouth

Several dashes maraschino liqueur

Several dashes Angostura bitters

Olive

Combine all ingredients, except the olive, in a shaker with ice. Shake well and strain into the serving glass. Garnish with the olive.

Chocolate Martini

What the—a *chocolate* martini? You bet!—and it's quite popular among the ladies. Simple yet sublime … chocolate and cocktails are a girl's best friend.

Serve in a martini glass.

2 oz. vodka

½ oz. crème de cacao

Combine both ingredients in a shaker filled with ice. Shake, and then pour into the serving glass.

The Silver Bullet Reloaded

The old-school martini crowd will run for cover, but here are some of the trendier offerings of twenty-first-century watering holes. Let's get perhaps the most popular down first. Should the Cosmopolitan be called a martini? Well, most urban bars serve it in a martini glass, and it is ordered by people who at least drink in the company of conventional gin-and-vermouth imbibers.

Cosmopolitan

Serve in a martini or cocktail glass.

½ oz. vodka

½ oz. triple sec

1 oz. cranberry juice

½ oz. lime juice

Lemon twist

Combine all ingredients, except the lemon twist, in a cocktail shaker with cracked ice. Shake, and then strain into the serving glass. Garnish with the lemon twist.

Submarine Cocktail

Serve in a martini or cocktail glass.

1½ oz. dry vermouth

1¼ oz. gin

¼ oz. Dubonnet

Combine all ingredients in a cocktail shaker with cracked ice. Shake, and then strain into the serving glass. If you prefer, stir this cocktail instead of shaking it.

Knockout Punch

Serve in a martini or cocktail glass.

1 oz. gin

1 oz. dry vermouth

2 tsp. Pernod

1 tsp. white crème de menthe

Combine all ingredients in a cocktail shaker with cracked ice. Shake, and then strain into the serving glass. If you prefer, stir this cocktail instead of shaking it.

Fifty-Fifty

Serve in a martini or cocktail glass.

1½ oz. gin

1½ oz. dry vermouth

Olive

Combine the gin and vermouth in a cocktail shaker with cracked ice. Shake, and then strain into the serving glass. If you prefer, stir this cocktail instead of shaking it. Garnish with the olive.

Leap Year

Serve in a martini or cocktail glass.

1½ oz. gin

½ oz. Grand Marnier

½ oz. sweet vermouth

1 tsp. lemon juice

Combine all ingredients in a cocktail shaker with cracked ice. Shake, and then strain into the serving glass.

Victor

The following is a variation on the more traditional Victor Cocktail, found in Chapter 19.

Serve in a martini or cocktail glass.

1 oz. gin

1 oz. brandy

½ oz. sweet vermouth

Combine all ingredients in a cocktail shaker with cracked ice. Shake, and then strain into the serving glass. If you prefer, stir this cocktail instead of shaking it.

Mexican Martini

Here is a more contemporary version of the Tequini, which appeared earlier in this chapter.

Serve in a martini or cocktail glass.

1½ oz. tequila

1 TB. dry vermouth

1 tsp. vanilla extract

Combine all ingredients in a cocktail shaker with cracked ice. Shake, and then strain into the serving glass.

Tango

Serve on the rocks in a lowball glass.

1½ oz. gin

¾ oz. orange juice

½ oz. dry vermouth

¼ oz. sweet vermouth

2 dashes curaçao

Combine all ingredients in a cocktail shaker with cracked ice. Shake, and then strain into the serving glass. If you prefer, stir this cocktail instead of shaking it.

Dare Cocktail

Serve on the rocks in a lowball glass.

¾ oz. dry vermouth

¾ oz. dry gin

1 TB. apricot brandy

1 tsp. lemon or lime juice

Combine all ingredients in a cocktail shaker with cracked ice. Shake, and then strain into the serving glass.

Gambler's Cocktail

Serve in a martini or cocktail glass.

1 oz. dry gin

½ oz. dry vermouth

½ oz. lemon juice

Lemon twist

Combine all ingredients, except the lemon twist, in a cocktail shaker with cracked ice. Shake, and then strain into the serving glass. If you prefer, stir this cocktail instead of shaking it. Garnish with the lemon twist.

Plaza

Serve in a martini or cocktail glass.

1 oz. gin

1 oz. dry vermouth

1 oz. sweet vermouth

1 TB. pineapple juice

Combine all ingredients in a cocktail shaker with cracked ice. Shake, and then strain into the serving glass. If you prefer, stir this cocktail instead of shaking it.

Newbury

Serve in a martini or cocktail glass.

1 oz. gin

1 oz. sweet vermouth

2 dashes curaçao

Combine all ingredients in a cocktail shaker with cracked ice. Shake, and then strain into the serving glass. If you prefer, stir this cocktail instead of shaking it.

Racquet Club

Serve in a martini or cocktail glass.

1½ oz. gin

¾ oz. dry vermouth

2 dashes orange bitters

Combine all ingredients in a cocktail shaker with cracked ice. Shake, and then strain into the serving glass. If you prefer, stir this cocktail instead of shaking it.

Bazooka

And, as the final heresy, a martini—with bourbon.

Serve in a martini or cocktail glass.

1½ oz. bourbon

1 oz. dry vermouth

1 TB. lime juice

Combine all ingredients in a cocktail shaker with cracked ice. Shake, and then strain into the serving glass. If you prefer, stir this cocktail instead of shaking it.

The Least You Need to Know

- The martini is an American institution: venerable, popular, and subject to endless controversy.
- Most martini "purists" insist that drier is better, but they won't find historical precedent for this in the martini's direct ancestor, the decidedly sweet Martinez.
- James Bond may like his martini "shaken, not stirred," but most drinkers will object to the clouding this brings to their gin.
- Vodka is catching up to gin as the primary ingredient of choice in a martini.

Part 3

Whiskey World

In the world of whiskey, time is measured in slow years of oak-barrel aging, and art is defined by the patient skill of distillers and master blenders. It is a world with a language all its own—*bottled in bond*, *straight*, *blended*, *single malt*, *Coffey still*, *pot still*, *wort*, and so on—yet with old and familiar boundaries: in Kentucky, Tennessee, Canada, Scotland, and Ireland. It is a world filled with strong and varied opinions, tastes, biases, and favorites.

This section walks you through the world of whiskey, bourbon, Tennessee whiskey, blended whiskey, Canadian whisky, scotch, and Irish whiskey, and provides historical background as well as tips on connoisseurship. And, of course, the drinks. There are a lot of them!

Chapter 9

Bourbon and Tennessee Whiskey: Produce of the Bluegrass and Volunteer States

In This Chapter

- Bourbon's ancestors
- Bourbon vs. Tennessee whiskey
- How to enjoy whiskey neat
- Bourbon and whiskey recipes

"The United States is the world's largest producer and consumer of whiskey," the *Encyclopaedia Britannica*'s article on "whiskey" concludes matter-of-factly. The numbers, however, are anything but matter of fact: Americans have more than *500 brands* of the great American whiskey, bourbon, to choose from. How many other products can you think of that are offered in 500 brands?

Nor is there any product more American than bourbon. It is rooted in colonial times and was among the very first of American industries. It was also among the first products the Feds hit on as a source of tax revenue. And *that* practically caused a war.

This chapter tells you what all the fuss has been about for all these years.

Let's Talk Whiskey

If you walk into Otto's Bar in Louisville's grand old Seelbach Hotel and ask for a "good Kentucky bourbon," you'll meet with what is best described as the bartender's courteous reproof: "*All* bourbon is Kentucky bourbon, sir (or ma'am)." You certainly can't go wrong thinking of bourbon as *Kentucky* whiskey (and, in Louisville, it's the *only* way you can think of it), but, looked at another way, you might think of sour mash and other whiskies made in Tennessee as additional varieties of bourbon. In any event, 80 percent of what is called bourbon is, in fact, made in Kentucky.

Why Kentucky?

During the early eighteenth century, before there was any such thing as the United States, Scotch, Irish, and Dutch colonists were distilling whiskey throughout Maryland, Virginia, and Pennsylvania. Farmers not only made money selling rye and barley to distillers, but also often cut out the middleman and set up a still themselves; the farmer's cart could carry no more than four bushels of grain to market, but it could transport two kegs of whiskey, which represented more than a dozen bushels of grain. With a few dismal rutted roads linking farmer and market, this was strong incentive to go into the whiskey business.

By the time the nation achieved independence from Britain, more than 5,000 stills were steaming away in Western Pennsylvania alone—a fact that excited Treasury Secretary Alexander Hamilton, who persuaded Congress to levy an excise tax on whiskey in 1791.

The farmer-distillers responded angrily with the so-called Whiskey Rebellion in 1794, and President Washington dispatched troops to enforce the law. In short order, the Whiskey Rebellion was extinguished, the authority of the federal government was affirmed, and the United States has collected liquor taxes ever since.

Not that all the farmers meekly complied. Some lit out for the territories, settling in Kentucky. Not only were the revenuers there fewer and farther between, but also the land was rich and abundant—perfect for growing corn—and the water was extraordinarily pure. Much of the state rests on a limestone mantel, a porous rock that makes for great natural filtration of ground water.

It is said that the first man to give up farming in Kentucky for a career as a distiller was Evan Williams, whose fine brand of Tennessee sippin' whiskey is still marketed. (Williams's original product, however, was apparently none too tasty, since the Louisville town council officially reprimanded him in 1783 not just for bringing whiskey to a meeting, but for bringing *crummy* whiskey.)

But a short time after this, in 1789, Elijah Craig, a Baptist minister and distiller, discovered the enormous boon of aging whiskey in a charred oak barrel. (Hitherto, distillers had aged their product in plain wooden vessels.) The charred oak imparted a smoky, smooth, mellow flavor to the liquor. Realizing he had something very good, Reverend Craig sought a name for his whiskey. The name of his home county had a regal ring to it: Bourbon.

A County in Kentucky

Not all bourbon is produced in Bourbon County, but Kentuckians continue to vigorously defend what they deem their exclusive privilege: to label as bourbon *only* that whiskey originating within the state borders. By federal—not state—law, bourbon can be made anywhere in the United States, but it must contain at least 51 percent corn—the grains that make up the balance of the mash are usually rye and barley—and it must be aged in new charred oak barrels.

Like scotch, bourbon comes in "straight" and "blended" varieties. All the whiskey in straight bourbon must have been distilled by a single distiller during a single time period, whereas blended bourbon may contain whiskeys distilled by various distillers at various times—with the proviso that the age given on the bottle label must be that of the *youngest* whiskey in the blend. Speaking of age, bourbons are aged anywhere from two to twelve years; generally, the older the better (and more costly). As with scotch, straight bourbon is usually preferable to—and more expensive than—blended brands.

Deep in Tennessee

Tennessee produces many bourbon-like whiskies, but it is best known for its fine sour mashes; the most widely marketed of which are Jack Daniel's, George Dickel, and Evan Williams (whose name was appropriated from neighboring Kentucky). The most distinctive Tennessee whiskies, like these, are readily distinguishable from Kentucky bourbon. They are very mellow, savor less of the aging barrel, and tend to bring the undertones of corn closer to the surface.

Let's Talk Proof

The term *proof*, a designation of alcoholic content, comes from the way early American distillers estimated the strength of what they distilled. "Proving" the alcoholic content of whiskey was accomplished by mixing a sample of the liquor with some gunpowder, lighting the mixture, and observing the resulting flame. Weak whiskey burned with a flickering yellow flame. Whiskey that was *too* strong went up in bright blue flame that soon burned itself out. Whiskey that was just right—that is, "100 proof"—burned with a steady blue flame. You can buy bourbon and other whiskey in proofs ranging from 80 to 100 proof and even somewhat more.

Neat, Rocks, Branch, Soda

Really good whiskey is a pleasure to enjoy neat (straight, no ice, no water), on the rocks, with club soda, or with what Southerners like to call *branch* or *branch water*, which, these days, is usually just plain tap water.

What do you need to know about enjoying whiskey unadorned? Just a little:

1. Invest in a premium-label bourbon or Tennessee whiskey. With some 500 brands, you have a lot of sampling to do.
2. Generally speaking, higher-proof whiskies are best for sipping.
3. Use scrupulously clean and thoroughly rinsed glassware.
4. Use ice that is free from freezer burn and freezer odors and tastes. Commercial bagged ice is usually the safest bet.
5. If your tap water tastes good, use it. Otherwise, consider bottled spring water. If you are *really* serious about sampling a variety of whiskies, use distilled water, which is the most neutral mixer available.
6. If you want effervescence, you can mix your whiskey with club soda, soda water, seltzer, or unflavored sparkling water, such as Perrier. If you want the most neutral carbonated mixer, use soda water.

Bar Tips

The cowpoke thrusts aside the swinging saloon doors, moseys up to the bar, orders a shot of whiskey, and downs it in a gulp. You can do this, too. But why waste *really good* whiskey? Fine whiskey, like fine wine, is meant to be savored and is best enjoyed slowly.

Bar Tips

To **muddle** is to mash and stir. Mint leaves and other solids are muddled in order to make a suspension or a paste with fluid. A special pestle-like wooden **muddler** can be used to muddle, but any spoon will do.

Juleps: The Schools of Thought

As the subject of the martini sparks debate in the snowy North, so, in the sunny South, the Mint Julep is a source of many genteelly heated and arcane discussions. Three juleps that claim to be "standard" follow.

A Mint Julep should be cold and refreshing. If it's a *really* hot day, your guests will cherish their Frozen Juleps.

Mint Julep #1

Serve in an old-fashioned glass.

½ tsp. fine-grained sugar

2½ oz. bourbon

Splash club soda

Mint sprig

Put the half teaspoon of sugar in the bottom of the mixing glass. Fill the glass one-third full with ice cubes. Add bourbon. Add the splash of club soda. Garnish with the mint sprig.

Mint Julep #2

Serve in a Collins glass.

6 mint leaves

½ oz. sugar syrup

2 oz. bourbon

Mint sprig

Place the mint leaves in the bottom of the serving glass and add the sugar syrup. Mash the leaves in the syrup. Add half the bourbon, and then fill the glass with crushed ice. Add the balance of the bourbon and stir vigorously. Garnish with the mint sprig.

Mint Julep #3

Serve in an old-fashioned or Collins glass.

1 cube sugar

3 oz. bourbon

Mint sprigs

Dissolve the sugar cube in the bottom of the serving glass with a few drops of plain water. Add a few mint sprigs. Fill the glass with ice (cubes or crushed), and then add the bourbon. Stir well. Cut up some more mint sprigs and add these to the drink. Stir, and then allow to stand several minutes before serving.

Frozen Julep

Even julep purists may not object to the frozen variation.

Serve in a large (double) old-fashioned glass.

6 small mint leaves

2 oz. bourbon

1 oz. lemon juice

1 oz. sugar syrup

Mint sprig

In a mixing glass, muddle the mint leaves together with the bourbon, lemon juice, and sugar syrup. Put the muddled ingredients in a blender with crushed ice. Blend until ice becomes mushy. Pour into the serving glass and garnish with a mint sprig.

Here are five juleps for the adventurous.

Argentine Julep

Serve over crushed ice in a highball glass.

1 oz. brandy

1 oz. light claret

1 oz. orange juice

1 oz. pineapple juice

¼ oz. Cointreau

1 tsp. sugar or 1 oz. sugar syrup (or to taste)

1 mint sprig

Combine all ingredients, except the mint, in a shaker with cracked ice. Shake vigorously, and then strain into serving glass about one-third filled with crushed ice. Garnish with the mint sprig.

Las Vegas Julep

Hardcore southerners might choke on this one from Las Vegas.

Serve over crushed ice in a highball glass.

1 oz. bourbon

1 oz. lemon juice

2 tsp. Galiano

1 tsp. sugar syrup

1 mint sprig

Combine everything, except the mint sprig, in a shaker with cracked ice. Shake vigorously, and then strain into serving glass about one-third filled with crushed ice. Garnish the mint sprig.

Virginia Julep

Closer to home, and somewhat simpler, is the Virginia Julep.

Serve over crushed ice in a double old-fashioned glass.

2 oz. bourbon

1½ tsp. sugar syrup

Several mint sprigs

Soak some of the mint sprigs in bourbon for about one hour, and then combine the minted bourbon with the sugar syrup in a shaker with cracked ice. Shake vigorously, and then strain into serving glass about one-third filled with crushed ice. Garnish with one or two *fresh* mint sprigs.

Jocose Julep

Whether made in Virginia or Nevada, the julep is, above all, a state of mind, as conveyed in the name of this one.

Serve on the rocks in a highball glass.

2½ oz. bourbon

1 oz. lime juice

2 tsp. green crème de menthe

1½ tsp. sugar syrup

6 mint leaves, chopped finely

Club soda

Several mint sprigs

Combine all ingredients, except the club soda and mint sprigs, in a shaker with cracked ice. Shake vigorously, and then strain into the serving glass. Add a few ice cubes and top off with the club soda. Garnish with a few mint sprigs.

Champagne Julep

Not a drop of bourbon in this one, but who can say no to champagne?

Serve in a champagne glass.

Several mint sprigs

1 TB. sugar syrup

1½ oz. brandy

Champagne

Crush some of the mint in the sugar syrup at the bottom of the serving glass and add brandy. Fill with crushed ice. Slowly add the champagne. Stir gently and garnish with a mint sprig or two.

The Classic Bourbon and Tennessee Cocktails

You can use bourbon or Tennessee whiskey to make any of the recipes in this chapter. Throughout, we've called for "bourbon"; add the equivalent amount of Tennessee whiskey if you prefer. For drinks that include strongly flavored mixers, there is little reason to splurge on premium-label whiskey. Ordinary "bar bourbon" will do just fine.

The idea of *bourbon* and citrus may take a little getting used to, but, aided by a bit of sweet liqueur, the result is a satisfying, full-bodied drink.

Bluegrass Cocktail

Serve in a chilled cocktail glass.

1½ oz. bourbon

1 oz. pineapple juice

1 oz. lemon juice

1 tsp. maraschino liqueur

Combine all ingredients in a shaker with ice. Shake vigorously, and then strain into the serving glass.

Brighton Punch

Serve in a chilled highball glass.

1 oz. bourbon

1 oz. cognac

¾ oz. Benedictine

Juice of ½ lemon

Juice of ½ orange

1 tsp. sugar syrup

Club soda

Orange slice

Combine all ingredients, except soda and orange slice, in a shaker or blender with cracked ice. Shake or blend, and then pour into the serving glass. Top off with soda and gently stir. Garnish with the orange slice.

Here are two without liqueur.

Sweet and Sour Bourbon

Serve in a whiskey sour glass.

1½ oz. bourbon

4 oz. orange juice

Generous pinch of sugar

Small pinch of salt

Maraschino cherry

Combine all ingredients, except the cherry, in a shaker or blender with cracked ice. Shake or blend, and then pour into the serving glass and garnish with the cherry.

Key West Cocktail

Serve in a chilled old-fashioned glass.

1½ oz. bourbon

1 oz. orange juice

1 oz. pineapple juice

1 tsp. lemon juice

Few dashes Angostura bitters

Orgeat syrup to taste

Combine all ingredients in a shaker or blender with cracked ice. Shake or blend, and then pour into the serving glass.

Buzzed Words

Traditionally, a **cobbler** is an iced drink made of wine or liqueur plus sugar and fruit juice.

Strictly speaking, a *cobbler* is an iced drink made with wine or liqueur plus sugar and fruit juice; however, no one is likely to complain if you throw in some bourbon. Beware. Like the Mint Julep, this is a potent blend. Sugar and carbonated water speed the absorption of alcohol into the bloodstream. The drink goes down so easily that you and your guests will be tempted to gulp. Sip! Please!

Bourbon Cobbler

Serve in a chilled highball glass.

1½ oz. bourbon

1 oz. Southern Comfort

1 tsp. peach-flavored brandy

2 tsp. lemon juice

1 tsp. sugar syrup

Club soda to fill

Peach slice

Combine all ingredients, except the club soda and peach slice, in a shaker with cracked ice. Shake vigorously, and then pour into the serving glass. Add several ice cubes, and then the club soda to fill. Garnish with the peach slice.

Paducah Palooka

Here is a sweeter approach to the cobbler.

Serve in a chilled old-fashioned glass.

1½ oz. bourbon

½ oz. apricot brandy

Juice of ½ lime

1 tsp. sugar syrup

Dash of grenadine

Lime slice

Maraschino cherry

Combine all ingredients, except the lime slice and cherry, in a shaker or blender with cracked ice. Shake or blend, and then strain into the serving glass. Garnish with the fruit.

Made with the traditional gin, it's called a Tom Collins. With bourbon, some call it a John Collins—a nod, doubtless, to the spirit of John Barleycorn, traditional personification of alcohol. You can have yours relatively subdued or jet-assisted, with higher-proof bourbon and a Peychaud's send-off.

Bourbon Collins (Unadorned)

Serve in a chilled Collins glass.

1½ oz. bourbon

½ oz. lime juice

1 tsp. sugar syrup

Club soda to fill

Lime peel

Combine all ingredients, except lime peel and club soda, in a shaker with cracked ice. Shake vigorously, and then pour into the serving glass. Add club soda to fill and garnish with the lime peel.

Bourbon Collins (Augmented)

Serve in a chilled highball glass.

2 oz. 100-proof bourbon

½ oz. lemon juice

1 tsp. sugar syrup

Few dashes of Peychaud's bitters

Club soda to fill

Lemon slice

Combine all ingredients, except the lemon slice and club soda, in a shaker with cracked ice. Shake vigorously, and then pour into the serving glass and garnish with the lemon slice.

The Manhattan is traditionally made with blended—especially Canadian—whiskey, which has much less body than bourbon. We'll look at plenty of Manhattans in the next chapter, but, first, why *not* a Bourbon Manhattan?

Bourbon Manhattan

Serve in a chilled cocktail glass.

2 oz. bourbon

½ oz. sweet vermouth

Dash Angostura or other bitters

Maraschino cherry

Combine all ingredients, except the cherry, in a mixing glass with ice. Stir well, and then strain into the serving glass. Garnish with the cherry.

Biscayne Manhattan

Two ounces of orange juice is sufficient to move Manhattan to Miami.

Serve in a chilled cocktail glass.

1½ oz. bourbon

½ oz. sweet vermouth

2 oz. orange juice

Few dashes yellow Chartreuse

Orange slice

Combine all ingredients, except the orange slice, in a shaker or blender with cracked ice. Shake or blend, and then strain into the serving glass. Garnish with the orange slice.

Bourbon Old-Fashioned

Bourbon is the spirit of choice for the old-fashioned, which is still a much-requested libation. The drink can also be made with rye, blended whiskey, or Canadian whisky.

Serve on the rocks in an old-fashioned glass.

1½ oz. bourbon

Splash of water

Dash sugar syrup

Liberal dash Angostura bitters

Combine all ingredients over ice in the serving glass. Stir well.

Bourbon Sidecar

The Sidecar started out life as a brandy drink, but bourbon will do it for you, too.

Serve in a chilled cocktail glass.

1½ oz. bourbon

¾ oz. curaçao or triple sec

½ oz. lemon juice

Combine all ingredients in a shaker with cracked ice. Shake vigorously, and then strain into the serving glass.

These florally named drinks look, smell, *and* taste great.

Bourbon Rose (Dark)

Serve in a chilled highball glass.

1½ oz. bourbon

1 oz. triple sec

4 oz. orange juice

Grenadine

Combine all ingredients, except grenadine, in a shaker with cracked ice. Shake vigorously, and then pour into the serving glass. *Carefully* pour a float of grenadine on top. Do not stir.

Bourbon Rose (Pale)

Serve in a chilled old-fashioned glass.

1½ oz. bourbon

½ oz. dry vermouth

½ oz. crème de cassis

¼ oz. lemon juice

Combine all ingredients in a shaker with cracked ice. Shake vigorously, then pour into the serving glass.

The Whiskey Sour remains one of the most popular sweet mixed drinks. Because it *is* sweet, most folks don't think of using bourbon for this drink; blended whiskey, lighter and thinner than bourbon, is the traditional choice. The Bourbon Sour has more body and depth than the blended whiskey version. It also makes for a more tart sour—hence the lemon instead of lime.

Bourbon Sour

Serve in a chilled Sour glass.

2 oz. bourbon

Juice of ½ lemon

½ tsp. sugar syrup

Orange slice

Maraschino cherry

Combine all ingredients, except the fruit, in a shaker with ice. Shake vigorously, and then strain into the serving glass. Garnish with the fruit.

New Traditions

Bourbon has a not entirely undeserved reputation as a man's drink—or, more precisely, an "old boy's drink." It summons up visions of conservative gentlemen reading their papers in darkly paneled club rooms thick with cigar smoke. The following are some recipes designed to update the bourbon profile.

Although most committed bourbon drinkers shy away from scotch, they usually enjoy gin well enough and have been known to down the occasional martini. Behold—the Dry Mahoney!

Dry Mahoney

Serve in a chilled cocktail glass.

2½ oz. bourbon

½ oz. dry vermouth

Lemon twist

Combine all ingredients, except the lemon twist, in a mixing glass filled with ice. Stir vigorously, and then strain into the serving glass. Garnish with the lemon twist. It is recommended that the drink be served with a few ice cubes on the side, in a second glass.

Blizzard

Think of bourbon as a warmer-upper rather than a cooler-downer? Reconsider with a Blizzard.

Serve in a chilled highball glass.

3 oz. bourbon

1 oz. cranberry juice

1 TB. lemon juice

1 TB. sugar syrup

Combine all ingredients in a shaker or blender with cracked ice. Shake or blend, ensuring that drink becomes frosty. Pour into the serving glass.

Blue Grass Glues

Kentucky is the Bluegrass State. Can you make bourbon blue, too?

Serve in a chilled old-fashioned glass.

1 oz. bourbon

1 oz. dry vermouth

Few dashes Angostura bitters

Few liberal dashes blue Curacao

Lemon peel

Combine all ingredients, except the lemon peel, in a shaker or blender with cracked ice. Shake or blend, and then pour into the serving glass. Twist the lemon peel over the drink and drop it in.

Millionaire Cocktail

The addition of Pernod—always an elegant experience—curaçao, and grenadine earn this concoction the title of Millionaire Cocktail.

Serve in chilled cocktail glasses.

3 oz. bourbon

1 oz. Pernod

Few dashes curaçao

Few dashes grenadine

1 egg white*

Combine all ingredients in a mixing glass with cracked ice. Stir well, and strain into the serving glasses. *Recipe makes two drinks.*

**Raw egg may be a source of salmonella bacteria. You may wish to avoid drinks calling for raw egg yolk or white.*

Bar Tips

Most drinks that call for egg white require half an egg white. But it's almost impossible to get *half* an egg white; therefore, all recipes in this book calling for egg white make *two* drinks.

Bank Holiday

When things start to get hairy, even millionaires declare a bank holiday.

Serve in a chilled cocktail glass.

½ oz. bourbon

½ oz. Galliano

½ oz. crème de cacao

½ oz. brandy

1½ oz. sweet cream

Combine all ingredients in a shaker or blender with cracked ice. Shake or blend, and then strain into the serving glass.

Churchill Downs Cooler

Serve in a highball or Collins glass.

1½ oz. bourbon

1 oz. crème de banana

½ oz. triple sec

3 oz. pineapple juice

½ oz. lemon juice

Club soda

Pineapple slice

Maraschino cherry

Combine all ingredients, except soda, pineapple slice, and cherry, in a shaker or blender with cracked ice. Shake or blend, and then pour into the serving glass. Top off with soda and garnish with the fruit.

Presbyterian

What is the origin of the name of the following drink? We have so far failed to discern the religious significance of combining ginger ale with club soda. Still, it's a pretty good drink.

Serve on the rocks in a highball glass.

3 oz. bourbon

Equal portions of ginger ale and

Club soda to fill

Pour bourbon into serving glass half filled with ice cubes. Add equal portions of ginger ale and club soda to fill.

Brighton Punch

Serve in a chilled highball glass.

1 oz. bourbon

1 oz. cognac

¾ oz. Benedictine

Juice of ½ lemon

Juice of ½ orange

1 tsp. sugar syrup

Club soda

Orange slice

Combine all ingredients, except soda and orange slice, in a shaker or blender with cracked ice. Shake or blend, and then pour into the serving glass. Top off with soda and garnish with the orange slice.

Buzzed Words

Absinthe is an aromatic, bitter, very strong liqueur flavored chiefly with wormwood and other botanicals. Absinthe was outlawed in many countries early in the twentieth century because of its apparent toxicity.

Sooner or later, you'll encounter the legendary Sazerac from the city of New Orleans. The classic version involves some effort, but the effort is worthwhile. Let's work our way up to the classic by beginning with the Simple Sazerac.

The original Sazerac was made with *absinthe*, a powerfully aromatic, bitter liqueur with a high alcoholic content. Its name and principal flavoring come from *Artemisia absinthium*—wormwood—but the beverage also includes licorice, hyssop, fennel, angelica root, aniseed, and star aniseed.

Absinthe was widely consumed in Paris and elsewhere, even though it seemed to have a nasty knack for inducing convulsions, hallucinations, general mental deterioration, and psychosis. It was subsequently determined that these symptoms were caused not by the liquor itself, but by *thujone*, a toxic substance present in wormwood. A number of substitutes were created, including Pernod, anisette, pastis, ouzo, and raki.

Now, except for the absinthe, here is the original Sazerac. You'll need two old-fashioned glasses. Herbsaint is an absinthe stand-in that might be hard to find outside of New Orleans; you may substitute Pernod.

Simple Sazerac

Serve in a chilled old-fashioned glass.

¼ tsp. Pernod or other absinthe substitute

½ tsp. sugar

1 TB. water

Dash Peychaud's bitters

2 oz. bourbon (may also use rye or blended whiskey)

Lemon peel

Coat the serving glass by swirling the Pernod in it. Add the sugar, water, and Peychaud's. Muddle these until the sugar is completely dissolved. Add bourbon with a few ice cubes. Stir vigorously. Garnish with the lemon peel.

Original Sazerac

Serve in a chilled old-fashioned glass.

1 sugar cube

2 dashes Peychaud's bitters

Dash Angostura bitters

2 oz. 100-proof bourbon (may substitute rye or blended whiskey)

Dash Herbsaint (may substitute Pernod)

Lemon peel

Use crushed ice to chill *two* old-fashioned glasses. Pour out the ice from one glass. In the bottom of that glass, put the sugar cube with a few drops of water. Add the bitters, and muddle the sugar and bitters until the sugar is dissolved. Add bourbon and ice cubes. Stir well. Empty the second glass of ice and add a liberal dash of Herbsaint, swirling to coat the glass. Discard the excess bitters and pour in the mixture from the first glass. Twist the lemon peel over the glass, but *do not garnish with the lemon peel*; discard.

Ward Eight

The name of this classic cocktail was meant to suggest that it is just what the doctor ordered.

Serve in a chilled cocktail glass.

2 oz. bourbon

1 oz. lemon juice

1 oz. orange juice

Sugar syrup to taste

Dash grenadine

Combine all ingredients in a shaker with ice. Shake vigorously and strain into the serving glass.

Beyond Tradition

As many drinkers see it, bourbon and Tennessee whiskey are icons of the old school. Introducing "new traditions" is pushing the envelope. But to leave tradition altogether behind is to burst the envelope. Well, so be it.

Huntress Cocktail

Serve in a chilled cocktail glass.

1 oz. bourbon

1 oz. cherry liqueur

1 oz. heavy cream

Dash of triple sec

Combine all ingredients in a shaker or blender with cracked ice. Shake or blend, and then strain into the serving glass.

Mississippi Mist

Serve in an old-fashioned glass.

1½ oz. bourbon

1½ oz. Southern Comfort

Combine the spirits in the serving glass. Add crushed ice to fill. Stir.

Little Colonel

Serve in a chilled cocktail glass.

2 oz. bourbon

1½ oz. Southern Comfort

1 oz. lime juice

Combine all ingredients in a shaker or blender with cracked ice. Shake or blend, and then strain into the serving glass.

Italian Stallion

Serve in a chilled cocktail glass.

1½ oz. bourbon

½ oz. Campari

½ oz. sweet vermouth

Dash Angostura bitters

Lemon peel

Combine all ingredients, except the lemon peel, in a pitcher or large glass with ice. Stir well. Strain into the serving glass. Twist the lemon peel over the drink, and then drop it in.

Southern Ginger

Serve in a large glass, such as a double old-fashioned glass.

1½ oz. 100-proof bourbon

1 tsp. ginger-flavored brandy

1 tsp. lemon juice

Ginger ale

Lemon peel

Combine all ingredients, except the lemon peel, in a shaker or blender with cracked ice. Shake or blend, and then pour into the serving glass. Top off with ginger ale. Twist the lemon peel over the drink, and then drop it in.

Country Girl

Serve on the rocks in an old-fashioned glass.

2 oz. bourbon

1 oz. Southern Comfort

½ oz. lemon juice

1 tsp. grenadine

Maraschino cherry

Combine all ingredients, except cherry, in a shaker with cracked ice. Shake vigorously, and then strain into the serving glass. Garnish with the cherry.

Country Boy

Serve on the rocks in an old-fashioned glass.

2 oz. bourbon

1 oz. Southern Comfort

½ oz. lemon juice

Combine all ingredients in a shaker with cracked ice. Shake vigorously, and then strain into the serving glass.

Fake Blood

An interesting-looking drink that is even more interesting to taste.

Serve on the rocks in a Collins glass.

1 oz. bourbon

½ oz. lime juice

Tomato juice

1 tsp. tequila

Combine the bourbon and lime juice over ice in the serving glass, and then top off with tomato juice. Stir, and then add the tequila.

Vagabond

Serve on the rocks in a lowball glass.

1½ oz. bourbon

2 TB. triple sec

1 tsp. brown sugar

Combine all ingredients in a shaker with cracked ice. Shake vigorously. Strain into the serving glass.

Tantalizer

Serve on the rocks in a lowball glass.

1 oz. brandy

1 oz. bourbon

½ oz. lemon juice

Combine all ingredients in a shaker with cracked ice. Shake vigorously. Strain into the serving glass.

Philly Special

If you like to chew your drink, try the Philly Special.

Serve in a chilled cocktail glass.

1 oz. bourbon

1 oz. heavy cream

1 oz. dark crème de cacao

Combine all ingredients in a shaker with cracked ice. Shake vigorously. Strain into the serving glass.

Black Beauty

For the horsey set.

Serve in a cocktail glass.

1½ oz. kirsch

1½ oz. bourbon

Dash sugar

Combine in the serving glass. Stir. No ice.

Bucking Bronco

Serve in a chilled cocktail glass.

2 oz. tequila

½ oz. bourbon

Combine in a shaker with cracked ice. Shake, and then strain into the serving glass.

These last two are for serious drinkers—with a sense of humor.

Crop Duster

Serve in a chilled cocktail glass.

1 oz. bourbon

1 oz. dark rum

½ oz. Southern Comfort

Combine in a shaker with cracked ice. Shake, and then strain into the serving glass.

Moron

Serve in a chilled cocktail glass.

2 oz. tequila

1 oz. bourbon

1 tsp. sugar syrup

Maraschino cherry

Combine all ingredients, except cherry, in a shaker with cracked ice. Shake, and then strain into the serving glass. Garnish with the cherry.

The Least You Need to Know

- Bourbon might not be the most popular spirit in America, but it is the most original. Its precursors have been distilled on American shores since the early eighteenth century.
- Strictly speaking, only whiskey made in Kentucky can properly be called bourbon, although you can consider Tennessee whiskey a bourbon variation.
- The flavor and character of bourbon and Tennessee whiskey comes mainly from the aging process. Freshly distilled, whiskey is essentially a neutral spirit.
- Bourbon and Tennessee whiskey work well as mixers as long as you remember that they are strongly flavored and full bodied. Some people will prefer the lighter, less characterful flavor of blended whiskey in their mixed drinks.

Chapter 10

'Round the Blend: Canadian and American Blended Whiskeys

In This Chapter

- How blended whiskey is made
- Why blended whiskey is a great mixer
- How to select a blended whiskey
- Blended whiskey recipes

Americans tend to enjoy a lighter beverage than Europeans; for example, in the United States, ale and stout have never been as popular as pilsner-style beer. So it is with whiskey. To be sure, many Americans love their bourbon and scotch, but blended whiskey is a North American phenomenon, a beverage that is less filling and lighter in body than bourbon, scotch, or rye. Some of the most popular U.S. and Canadian whiskeys are blended. They make great mixers, as you'll see.

The Master Blender at Work

Blended whiskeys could combine various straight whiskeys (whiskeys distilled from the mash of a single grain) only, or could involve combinations of straight, mixed-grain whiskeys, grain neutral spirits, and so-called *light whiskeys*. The latter are whiskeys distilled at high proof—more than 160—and stored in used charred oak barrels. The result is more flavorful than neutral spirits, but not as strong as straight whiskey. In a blend, light whiskey imparts character without compromising the light, dry quality desired in a blend.

> **Buzzed Words**
>
> The **master blender** is the craftsperson in charge of selecting and proportioning the component whiskeys that make up a blended whiskey.

The creation of a fine blended whiskey is as much art as science; a *master blender* directs the creation of a blended whiskey. The blender might combine as many as 50 whiskeys drawn from a "library" of hundreds of products.

Not Whiskey, but Whisky: Enjoying the Canadian Difference

So far as the quality of lightness goes, the Canadian distillers of blended *whisky* (that's how Canadians spell it) have taken the beverage to its extreme. Light, delicately flavored, and extremely smooth, Canadian whiskeys are ideal mixers.

> **Bar Tips**
>
> You can make the recipes in this chapter with American or Canadian blended whiskey; however, at the end of the chapter, you'll find a group of recipes in which the ultra-light Canadian product works best.

The flavor qualities of blended whiskeys, although often subtle, are greatly varied. You would do well to sample a range of these products. Don't forget to use your nose, not just your taste buds. The aroma of a fine blended whiskey is complex and rewarding, and, precisely because of the liquor's light body, much of the pleasure of the product comes from its "nose"—its scent.

Neat, Rocks, Soda, Ginger

You'll want to devote a good deal of pleasurable effort to discovering your favorite blends, particularly if you intend to enjoy the whiskey neat, on the rocks, or with plain soda. Soapy glasses, chlorine-laden tap water, or freezer-burned ice will spoil the taste of delicately flavored American and Canadian blends.

Buzzed Words

Straight whiskey is made from mash containing at least 51 percent of a certain grain; however, straight corn whiskey mash contains 80 percent corn. With **mixed-grain whiskeys**, no single grain predominates. **Light whiskey** is distilled in excess of 160 proof and aged in charred oak barrels. An important component in blended whiskey, it is more flavorful than neutral spirits, but not as strong as straight whiskey.

Ginger ale has always been a popular mixer with blended whiskey. Just pour a jigger of whiskey into a highball glass filled with ice and add ginger ale to fill. If you want something a little fancier and quite a bit stronger, try the Horse's Neck.

Horse's Neck

Serve in a Collins glass.

1 lemon

3 oz. blended whiskey

Ginger ale to fill

Peel the lemon in one continuous strip and place it in the serving glass. Fill glass one-third with ice cubes. Add whiskey. Squeeze a few drops of lemon juice over the whiskey, and then add ginger ale to fill.

Boilermaker

Another simple way to enjoy blended whiskey is the celebrated Boilermaker, a macho rite of passage since time immemorial.

Serve in a shot glass.

1½ oz. blended or Canadian whisky

12 oz. beer

Drink a shot (1½ oz.) whisky. Chase with a 12-ounce beer.

Depth Charge

Serve in a beer mug or large glass.

1½ oz. blended or Canadian whisky.

12 oz. beer

Pour whisky into a shot glass. Drop the shot glass into a 12 oz. mug or glass of beer. Drink.

Manhattan Varieties

The woodwind tones of a good blended or Canadian whiskey are perfectly suited to the Manhattan. Made carefully, the Manhattan is a delicate and subtle drink, despite its essential sweetness. Although many people have theirs on the rocks, it is best enjoyed well-chilled, straight-up. The basic, unadorned recipe follows.

Manhattan

Serve in a chilled cocktail glass.

2 oz. blended whiskey

½ oz. sweet vermouth

Dash Angostura bitters

Maraschino cherry

Combine all ingredients, except the cherry, with ice in a mixing glass. Stir well, and then strain into the serving glass and garnish with the cherry.

As with the dry vermouth in a martini, the amount of sweet vermouth in a Manhattan should be adjusted to suit your taste. Some drinkers specify *Canadian* whisky in their Manhattan. Make it the same way and call it a Canadian Manhattan.

Dry Manhattan

For some hard-bitten Manhattan drinkers, sweet vermouth is just too sweet. For these folks, a Dry Manhattan is called for. If necessary, the Angostura bitters may be excluded, though we prefer to keep this ingredient, even in the *Dry* Manhattan.

Serve in a chilled cocktail glass.

2 oz. blended whiskey

½ oz. dry vermouth

Dash Angostura bitters (optional)

Lemon twist

Combine all ingredients, except the lemon twist, with ice in a mixing glass. Stir well, and then strain into the serving glass and garnish with the lemon twist.

Some drinkers prefer to garnish the Dry Manhattan with a green olive.

Dubonnet Manhattan

You can substitute Dubonnet for sweet vermouth to make a Manhattan sweeter than a Dry Manhattan, but not as sweet as the standard Manhattan.

Serve in a chilled old-fashioned glass.

1½ oz. blended whiskey

1 oz. Dubonnet rouge

Maraschino cherry

Combine ingredients, except the cherry, in a blender with cracked ice. Shake vigorously, and then pour into the serving glass and garnish with the cherry.

Old-Fashioned Manhattan

The Old-Fashioned Manhattan balances the whiskey against the sweet vermouth for a much sweeter drink. If you like old-fashioneds, this one is for you.

Serve in a chilled cocktail glass.

1½ blended whiskey

1½ oz. sweet vermouth

Maraschino cherry

Combine ingredients, except the cherry, in a shaker with cracked ice. Shake vigorously, and then pour into the serving glass and garnish with the cherry.

Perfect Manhattan

Taking its cue from the Perfect Martini, the Perfect Manhattan balances dry and sweet vermouth. But don't make the proportions *quite* equal.

Serve in a chilled cocktail glass.

2 oz. blended whiskey

½ oz. sweet vermouth

¼ oz. dry vermouth

Dash Angostura bitters

Maraschino cherry

Combine all ingredients, except the cherry, in a mixing glass with ice. Stir well, and then strain into the serving glass and garnish with the cherry.

Manhasset

Those familiar with New York City and Long Island know Manhasset as one of the older towns along the island's North Shore. It's moneyed and sedate, and it has a Manhattan variation of its very own.

Serve in a chilled cocktail glass.

1½ oz. blended whiskey

¼ oz. dry vermouth

¼ oz. sweet vermouth

½ oz. lemon juice

Lemon twist

Combine all ingredients, except the lemon, in a shaker with ice. Shake vigorously, and then strain into the serving glass and garnish with the lemon twist.

Maria's Manhattan

Serve in a chilled cocktail glass.

1½ oz. blended whiskey

½ oz. dry vermouth

½ oz. strawberry liqueur

Combine all ingredients with ice in a mixing glass. Stir well, and then strain into the serving glass.

Rosy Manhattan

You can try raspberry liqueur for a Rosy Manhattan.

Serve in a chilled cocktail glass.

1½ oz. blended whiskey

½ oz. dry vermouth

½ oz. raspberry liqueur

Combine all ingredients with cracked ice in a shaker. Shake vigorously, and then strain into the serving glass.

Swiss Manhattan

Kirsch is a Swiss liqueur. *Very* cherry.

Serve in a chilled old fashioned glass.

1½ oz. blended whiskey

½ oz. dry vermouth

½ oz. kirsch

Liberal dash Angostura bitters

Combine all ingredients with cracked ice in a shaker. Shake vigorously, and then pour into the serving glass.

Danish Manhattan

From Switzerland to Denmark …

Serve in a chilled cocktail glass.

1½ oz. blended whiskey

¼ oz. kirschwasser

¼ oz. Peter Heering

Combine all ingredients with cracked ice in a shaker. Shake vigorously, and then pour into the serving glass.

Parisian Manhattan

And on to New York's sister city …

Serve in a chilled cocktail glass.

1½ oz. blended whiskey

½ oz. sweet vermouth

Few dashes Amer Picon

Maraschino cherry

Combine all ingredients, except cherry, with cracked ice in a shaker. Shake vigorously, and then pour into the serving glass. Garnish with the cherry.

The Land of Nog and a Sea of Grog

Mention eggnog, and you think, first, of eggs, and, second, of rum. But a zippy eggnog can be made with whiskey instead. Bourbon works well, and so does blended whiskey.

Buzzed Words

Grog was originally nothing more than rum diluted with water and rationed to sailors of the eighteenth-century Royal Navy. Its namesake was Admiral Edward Vernon (1684–1757), who first ordered the ration: Vernon's nickname was Old Grogram, after his habit of wearing a grogram (coarse wool) cloak.

Whiskey Eggnog

Serve in a chilled highball glass.

1 egg*
1½ oz. blended whiskey
Grated nutmeg
1 tsp. sugar
6 oz. milk

Combine all ingredients, except nutmeg, in a shaker with ice. Shake vigorously, and then strain into the serving glass. Sprinkle with nutmeg.

You can also experiment with combinations of blended whiskey and rum or brandy.

**Raw egg is a source of salmonella bacteria. You may wish to avoid drinks calling for raw egg yolk or white.*

Henry Morgan's Grog

Like eggnog, grog is traditionally thought of as a rum-based drink, but Henry Morgan's Grog, a most potent libation, is based mainly on blended whiskey. Don't substitute bourbon; you need a light whiskey. Canadian would work well here, too.

Serve in a chilled old-fashioned glass.

1½ oz. Canadian whisky
1 oz. Pernod
½ oz. Jamaica (dark) rum
1 oz. heavy cream
Ground nutmeg

Combine all ingredients, except nutmeg, in a shaker with cracked ice. Shake vigorously, and then pour into the serving glass. Sprinkle with the nutmeg.

Fizzes

Blended whiskey is the perfect choice among the "dark spirits" for fizz drinks because its light qualities complement effervescence and don't fight sweet mixers.

Japanese Fizz

What's so Japanese about this fizz drink? Only the name.

Serve in a chilled highball glass.

2 oz. blended whiskey
¾ oz. port
1 tsp. sugar syrup
Orange peel
½ oz. lemon juice
Club soda to fill
Pineapple stick

Combine all ingredients, except the club soda and fruit, in a shaker with cracked ice. Shake vigorously, and then pour into the serving glass. Add club soda to fill. Twist the orange peel over the drink and garnish with it and the pineapple stick.

Summer Fizz

The Summer Fizz is generous with the grapefruit juice and club soda, making for a light and refreshing warm weather drink. It's easy to make, too.

Serve in a chilled highball glass.

1½ oz. blended whiskey
3 oz. grapefruit juice
1 tsp. strawberry liqueur
Club soda to fill

Combine all ingredients in the serving glass one-third full of ice cubes. Add club soda to fill.

Whiskey Curaçao Fizz

Another drink that's especially welcome on a summer evening is a combination of whiskey and curaçao. Consider using Canadian whiskey for a feather-light drink.

Serve in a chilled Collins glass.

2 oz. blended whiskey

½ oz. curaçao

1 oz. lemon juice

1 tsp. sugar

Club soda to fill

Orange slice

Combine all ingredients, except the orange slice and club soda, in a shaker with cracked ice. Shake well, and then pour into the serving glass. You may add additional ice cubes, if you wish. Add club soda to fill. Garnish with the orange slice.

Whiskey Fizz

The Whiskey Fizz is the classic whiskey fizz drink. The bitters counterpoint the sugar syrup nicely.

Serve in a chilled highball glass.

1½ oz. blended whiskey

Few dashes Angostura bitters

½ tsp. sugar syrup

Club soda to fill

Combine all ingredients, except the club soda, in the serving glass one third full of ice. Stir well, and then add club soda to fill.

Imperial Fizz

Serve in a chilled champagne glass.

1 oz. bourbon

½ oz. lemon juice

½ tsp. sugar

Champagne

Combine all ingredients, except the champagne, in a shaker with cracked ice. Shake, and then strain into the serving glass. Top off with champagne.

Fiji Fizz

Serve on the rocks in a Collins glass.

1½ oz. dark rum

½ oz. bourbon

1 tsp. cherry brandy

3 dashes orange bitters

4 oz. cola

Lime slice

Combine all ingredients, except the cola and lime slice, in shaker with cracked ice. Shake, and then strain into the serving glass over ice. Top off with the cola. Garnish with a lime slice.

Grapefruit Combos

Although the combination of bourbon or scotch with grapefruit juice might raise some eyebrows, the cleaner, lighter taste of blended whiskey makes it all seem perfectly natural.

Grapefruit Cooler

Most coolers contain a relatively small amount of alcohol. The Grapefruit Cooler packs a full two ounces.

Serve in a chilled Collins glass.

2 oz. blended whiskey

4 oz. grapefruit juice

½ oz. red currant syrup

¼ oz. lemon juice

½ orange slice

½ lemon slice

Combine all ingredients, except the fruit, in a shaker with cracked ice. Pour into the serving glass, adding ice cubes, if you wish. Garnish with the orange and lemon.

Indian River Cocktail

The Indian River of south Florida runs through the heart of citrus country, which is where the half ounce of grapefruit juice in the Indian River Cocktail comes from.

Serve in a chilled old-fashioned glass.

1½ oz. blended whiskey

¼ oz. raspberry liqueur

¼ oz. sweet vermouth

½ oz. grapefruit juice

Combine all ingredients in a shaker with cracked ice. Shake vigorously and pour into the serving glass.

Old-Fashioneds and a Rickey

As some people see it, only an old-fashioned made with bourbon is a *real* old-fashioned. They like the full body of the Kentucky whiskey and the play of the sugar syrup and bitters against a spirit with loads of character and strong flavor. Others prefer to lighten up with blended or Canadian whiskey.

A rickey is a drink made with sugar and lime juice. The classic spirit is gin, and although most drinkers would find bourbon or scotch too rich for their rickey, blended whiskey or Canadian works just fine.

Blended Whiskey Old-Fashioned

Serve on the rocks in an old-fashioned glass.

1½ oz. blended whiskey

Dash water

Dash sugar syrup

Liberal dash Angostura bitters

Combine all ingredients in a serving glass half full of ice.

Canadian Old-Fashioned

For a Canadian Old-Fashioned, use Canadian whisky, of course, and make a few other adjustments.

Serve in a chilled old-fashioned glass.

1½ oz. Canadian whisky

½ tsp. curaçao

Dash lemon juice

Dash Angostura bitters

Lemon twist

Orange twist

Combine all ingredients, except twists, in a shaker with cracked ice. Shake vigorously, and then pour into the serving glass. Garnish with the twists.

New Orleans Old-Fashioned

Serve in a chilled old-fashioned glass.

½ tsp. sugar syrup

Few dashes Angostura bitters

2 tsp. water

2 oz. blended whiskey

Few dashes Peychaud's bitters

Lemon twist

Combine the sugar syrup, Angostura bitters, and water in a mixing glass and stir until the sugar is dissolved. Add the whiskey and one-third glass of ice cubes. Stir well, and then dash on the Peychaud's and garnish with the lemon twist.

Whiskey Rickey

Serve on the rocks in a Collins glass.

1½ oz. blended whiskey

Juice of ½ lime

1 tsp. sugar syrup

Club soda to fill

Lime twist

Combine all ingredients, except the lime twist and club soda, in the serving glass at least half filled with ice. Stir well. Add club soda to fill and garnish with the lime twist.

Pucker Up

The Whiskey Sour might be the most popular blended whiskey cocktail. The basic sour can be made with commercial powdered sour mix or with freshly prepared sour mix. Check out Chapter 4 for a sour-mix recipe.

Whiskey Sour

Serve in a chilled sour glass.

2 oz. blended whiskey
1 oz. sour mix
Maraschino cherry
Orange slice

Combine all ingredients, except fruit, in a shaker with cracked ice. Shake vigorously. Pour into the serving glass and garnish with fruit.

If you don't want to use commercial sour mix or make sour mix yourself, just use lemon juice and sugar syrup. You will sacrifice the creamy foam.

Alternative Whiskey Sour

Serve in a chilled sour glass.

2 oz. blended whiskey
1 oz. lemon juice
1 TB. sugar syrup
Orange slice
Maraschino cherry

Combine all ingredients, except fruit, in a shaker with cracked ice. Shake vigorously. Pour into the serving glass and garnish with fruit.

Whiskey Sour in the Rough

Serve in a chilled old-fashioned glass.

2 oz. blended whiskey
1 tsp. sugar
Orange slice
Lemon slice
Maraschino cherry

In the shaker glass, muddle—mash and stir—the sugar, orange slice, and lemon slice. Add one half glass of ice and the whiskey. Shake vigorously. Pour into the serving glass and allow a few moments to settle. Then garnish with the cherry.

Frisco Sour

The cocktails that have emerged from San Francisco tend to be fairly elaborate and very sweet. That city's version of the Whiskey Sour is no exception.

Serve in a sour glass.

1½ oz. blended whiskey
¾ oz. Benedictine
1 tsp. lemon juice
1 tsp. lime juice
Dash grenadine
Orange slice

Combine all ingredients, except orange slice, in a shaker with ice. Shake vigorously, and then strain into the serving glass. Garnish with the orange slice.

New York Sour

In contrast to the products of San Francisco, those of New York are characteristically more reserved and astringent.

Serve in a sour glass.

2 oz. blended whiskey

1 tsp. sugar syrup

½ slice lemon

½ oz. lemon juice

½ oz. dry red wine

Combine all ingredients, except the lemon slice and red wine, in a shaker with cracked ice. Shake vigorously, and then pour into the serving glass. Add the wine and garnish with the lemon slice.

On the Sweet Side

The mild flavor of blended whiskey makes it a natural for the sweeter mixers.

New Yorker

If you like the New York Sour, try the New Yorker.

Serve in a chilled cocktail glass.

1½ oz. blended whiskey

½ oz. lime juice

1 tsp. sugar syrup

Dash grenadine

Lemon twist

Orange twist

Combine all ingredients, except fruit, in a shaker with ice. Shake vigorously, and then pour into the serving glass and garnish with the twists.

Rattlesnake

The Rattlesnake is a foamy classic for people who want something a little different from the usual Whiskey Sour. Because the recipe calls for egg white, and egg white is pretty hard to divide in half, this recipe yields two drinks.

Serve in chilled old-fashioned glasses. (Yields 2 drinks.)

3 oz. blended whiskey

2 tsp. lemon juice

2 tsp. sugar syrup

1 egg white*

Several dashes Pernod

Combine all ingredients in a shaker with cracked ice. Shake vigorously, and then pour into the serving glasses.

** Raw egg is a source of salmonella bacteria. You may wish to avoid drinks calling for raw egg yolk or white.*

Whiskey Daisy

Daisy drinks feature a float of liqueur. Golden liqueur is traditional—hence the name—but you can float any light liqueur on a daisy, including curaçao, maraschino liqueur, Grand Marnier, green Chartreuse, Benedictine, Galliano, or others.

Serve in a chilled highball glass.

2 oz. blended whiskey

1 tsp. red currant syrup (may also use raspberry syrup or grenadine)

½ oz. lemon juice

Club soda to fill (optional)

1 tsp. yellow Chartreuse (or other light liqueur)

Lemon slice

Combine all ingredients, except liqueur, club soda, and lemon slice, in a shaker with cracked ice. Shake vigorously and pour into the serving glass. Carefully add the liqueur for a float. Do not stir. Garnish with the lemon slice.

Buzzed Words

A **daisy** is a whiskey- or gin-based drink that includes some sweet syrup and a float of (usually golden) liqueur.

Canadian Daisy

For lovers of Canadian whisky, there is the Canadian Daisy.

Serve in a chilled highball glass.

1½ oz. Canadian whisky

½ oz. lemon juice

1 tsp. raspberry syrup

Club soda to fill

1 tsp. brandy

Whole raspberries

Combine all ingredients, except the raspberries, brandy, and club soda, in a shaker with cracked ice. Shake vigorously and pour into the serving glass. Add club soda to fill, and then carefully float the brandy on top. Garnish with the raspberries.

Aunt Grace's Pacifier

Then there's sweet old Aunt Grace, who had a way of making her guests feel warm, cozy, and calm. It wasn't her personality that did it.

Serve in a chilled old-fashioned glass.

2 oz. blended whiskey

1 oz. raspberry syrup

Club soda to fill

Pour the whiskey and syrup into the serving glass one third filled with ice cubes. Add club soda to fill.

Black Hawk

From Chicago, the classic Black Hawk, named after the hotel that was, in turn, named for the combative early nineteenth-century leader of the Sac and Fox Indian tribes.

Serve in a chilled cocktail glass.

1 oz. blended whiskey
1 oz. sloe gin
½ oz. lemon juice
Maraschino cherry

Combine all ingredients, except the cherry, in a shaker with ice. Shake vigorously and strain into the serving glass. Garnish with the maraschino cherry.

7&7

Long a favorite among mainstream blended whiskeys, Seagram's 7-Crown soon developed a natural affinity for its soft drink counterpart, 7-Up. Can you use a different blended whiskey in a 7&7? Sure, but then it wouldn't really be a *Seven* & 7, would it?

Serve on the rocks in a highball glass.

1½ oz. Seagram's 7-Crown
4 oz. 7-Up

Pour the whiskey into the serving glass filled with ice. Add 7-Up.

With Wines and Liqueurs

If the 7&7 has a reputation as a working person's drink, blended whiskeys also contribute to a battery of more genteel creations.

Ladies' Cocktail

The Ladies' Cocktail was born of an age when it was assumed that women were "ladies" who liked their alcohol with frills and frou-frous. Today, the Ladies' Cocktail makes a marvelous "retro" drink.

Serve in a chilled cocktail glass.

1½ oz. blended whiskey
1 tsp. anisette
Few dashes Pernod
Few dashes Angostura bitters
Pineapple stick

Combine all ingredients, except the pineapple stick, in a shaker with cracked ice. Shake vigorously and strain into the serving glass. Garnish with the pineapple stick.

The Lawhill

The Lawhill is practically the definition of a cocktail: a combination of diverse ingredients on top of an alcohol base.

Serve in a chilled cocktail glass.

1½ oz. blended whiskey
½ oz. dry vermouth
¼ oz. Pernod
½ oz. orange juice
Dash Angostura bitters
Pineapple stick
¼ tsp. maraschino liqueur

Combine all ingredients, except pineapple stick, in a shaker with ice. Shake vigorously and strain into the serving glass. Garnish with pineapple stick.

Madeira Cocktail

Malmsey is the sweetest of the fortified wines named for their place of origin, the Portuguese island of Madeira in the Atlantic. Madeira is fortified with brandy during fermentation and achieves an alcoholic content of 18 to 20 percent.

Serve in a chilled old-fashioned glass.

1½ oz. blended whiskey

1½ oz. Malmsey Madeira

1 tsp. grenadine

Dash lemon juice

Orange slice

Combine all ingredients, except the orange slice, in a shaker with cracked ice. Shake vigorously and pour into the serving glass. Garnish with the orange slice.

Los Angeles Cocktail

Foamy and sweet, the sunny Los Angeles Cocktail could never have been made in dour old New York City. This recipe, which calls for one egg, yields two drinks.

Serve in chilled old-fashioned glasses. (Yields 2 drinks.)

4 oz. blended whiskey
1 oz. lemon juice
2 oz. sugar syrup
1 raw egg*
Few dashes sweet vermouth

Combine all ingredients in a shaker with cracked ice. Shake vigorously and pour into the serving glasses.

**Raw egg is a source of salmonella bacteria. You may wish to avoid drinks calling for raw egg yolk or white.*

Stonybrook

Another foamy creation, thanks to the action of egg white.

Serve in chilled cocktail glasses. (Yields 2 drinks.)

3 oz. blended whiskey
1 oz. triple sec
1 oz. crème de noyaux
1 egg white*
Lemon twists
Orange twists

Combine all ingredients, except twists, in a shaker with ice. Shake vigorously and strain into serving glasses. Garnish with twists. *Recipe makes two drinks.*

**Raw egg is a source of salmonella bacteria. You may wish to avoid drinks calling for raw egg yolk or white.*

Sunset Gun

Traditionally, day's end is marked at many military installations by firing a howitzer salute as the flag is lowered: the sunset gun. Here's another way for two people to commemorate the occasion, but you'll need about an hour's head start on the setting sun.

Serve in chilled cocktail glasses. (Yields 2 drinks.)

4 oz. blended whiskey (may substitute bourbon or rye)

6 whole cloves

1 oz. curaçao

Few dashes orange bitters

Steep the cloves in the whiskey for about an hour; keep the glass covered. Strain the steeped whiskey into a shaker with ice. Set the cloves aside. Add the curaçao and shake vigorously. Strain into the serving glasses, and then dash on the bitters. Return the cloves to the glasses.

Temptation Cocktail

Resplendent with wonderful liqueurs and a popular aperitif, the Temptation Cocktail more than deserves its name.

Serve in a chilled cocktail glass.

1½ oz. blended whiskey

½ oz. Dubonnet rouge

Few dashes curaçao

Few dashes Pernod

Orange twist

Lemon twist

Combine all ingredients, except twists, in a shaker with ice. Shake vigorously and strain into the serving glass. Garnish with the twists.

Whiskey Cobbler

The cobbler is to liquor what "comfort food" is to cuisine—sort of warm, a little fuzzy, and all around feel-good.

Serve in a goblet or large snifter.

1 tsp. sugar syrup

1 tsp. orgeat syrup or amaretto liqueur

2 oz. blended whiskey

Dash curaçao

Mint sprig

Fill goblet or snifter with crushed ice. Add the sugar and orgeat (or amaretto). Stir well. Add whiskey. Stir again so that frost forms on the outside of the serving glass. Dash on curaçao and garnish with the mint sprig.

O, Canada!

All the recipes in this chapter can be made with Canadian whisky instead of American blended whiskey, if you prefer. But here are a few drinks especially for Canadian whisky.

Dog Sled

Serve in a chilled old-fashioned glass.

2 oz. Canadian whisky

2 oz. orange juice

1 TB. lemon juice

1 tsp. grenadine

Combine all ingredients with cracked ice in a shaker. Shake vigorously, and then pour into the serving glass.

Frontenac Cocktail

Frontenac was an early colonial governor of Canada; it's possible that this orangey cocktail was named for him.

Serve in a chilled cocktail glass.

1½ oz. Canadian whisky

½ oz. Grand Marnier

Few dashes kirsch

Dash orange bitters

Combine all ingredients with cracked ice in a shaker. Shake vigorously, and then pour into the serving glass.

Saskatoon Stinger

Saskatoon is a city in south-central Saskatchewan, founded in 1883 as the proposed capital of a temperance colony. The best-laid plans ....

Serve on the rocks in an old-fashioned glass.

2 oz. Canadian whisky

1 oz. peppermint schnapps (may substitute white crème de menthe)

Lemon twist

Pour the whisky and schnapps into the serving glass half filled with ice cubes. Stir well, and garnish with the lemon twist.

Blended Remix: Some New Drinks

Here's a blended trio that's definitely "out there."

Herpetologist's Dream

Serve on the rocks in a Collins glass.

2½ oz. blended whiskey

1 TB. dry vermouth

½ oz. dark rum

Grapefruit juice

Combine the spirits over ice in the serving glass. Top off with grapefruit juice. Stir well.

Alien

Serve on the rocks in any large glass.

1½ oz. vodka

Grapefruit juice

½ oz. blended whiskey

2–3 olives

Combine the spirits over ice in the serving glass. Top off with grapefruit juice. Stir well, and then drop in the olives.

Locomotive

Serve on the rocks in an old-fashioned glass.

1½ oz. blended whiskey

1 oz. scotch

2 oz. pineapple juice

½ oz. prune juice

Maraschino cherry

Combine all ingredients, except cherry, in a shaker with cracked ice. Shake well, and then strain over ice into serving glass. Garnish with the cherry.

The Least You Need to Know

- Blended whiskey and Canadian whisky are considerably lighter in flavor and body than bourbon, scotch, or rye; therefore, many people find them more "mixable."
- Fine blended whiskey is the work of a master blender, who chooses and proportions a variety of whiskeys to create the blend.
- Clean glassware, pure water, and pristine ice cubes are essential to making a good drink with a subtly flavored blended whiskey.
- In most recipes, U.S. and Canadian blends can be used interchangeably; just be aware that Canadian whisky is generally lighter and more subtly flavored than its U.S. counterparts.

Chapter 11

Comin' Through the Rye: Enjoying the Drinker's Drink

In This Chapter

- Why rye is a "drinker's drink"
- Where rye comes from
- A good reason to avoid *cheap* rye
- Rye recipes

Rye whiskey is one of those spirits people call a "drinker's drink," which means that a lot of folks just don't like the stuff. It does come on strong, but if you like scotch, rye is worth giving a chance. This chapter has some suggestions for enjoying this black sheep among whiskies.

The Black Sheep

Rye is a cereal grain that has been cultivated at least since 6500 B.C.E. Despite its lengthy lineage, it's always been something of a second-class grain, grown mainly where the climate and soil are unsuited to other, more favored cereals, or cultivated as a winter crop in places too cold to grow winter wheat. You can make a loaf of bread with rye, but, even here, it doesn't measure up to wheat because it lacks the requisite elasticity. The so-called "rye bread" most of us eat is almost always a blend of rye and wheat; traditionally, black bread, made entirely from rye, has been associated with poverty (though the moderately increasing popularity of pumpernickel in the United States has upgraded the stature of rye grain somewhat).

Quick One

Commuter to train conductor: "This morning I accidentally left a small bottle of rye on the train. Was it turned into the Lost-and-Found?"

"No," the conductor replied, "but the guy who found it was."

So there it is: the rather sad story of this hearty, but hard-pressed cereal grain. And it gets even sadder.

While pumpernickel bread has increased in popularity in the United States over recent years, the popularity of rye whiskey has steadily declined. Most liquor stores carry but few brands, and many drinkers give it scarcely a thought.

Rye, Unadorned

The fact is, rye offers a full-bodied, up-and-at-'em alternative to scotch and Irish whiskey, the two whiskey types it most resembles in flavor. Invest in a good rye. Cheap brands give new meaning to the term *rotgut* and are characterized by a distinctly musty taste—like sipping something that's been sitting in a damp basement far too long. Drinking rye should not be a punishment. In many liquor stores, you'll find but a single premium brand, Old Overholt, the most widely marketed rye. Fortunately, it's quite good.

Bar Tips

Rye has fallen so far out of the loop that drinkers who ask for "rye and ginger," are probably expecting to be served a blended whiskey with ginger ale. Respond to the request thus—"Do you want rye or blended whiskey?"

Serious drinkers take their rye neat, period: in a shot glass, at room temperature. Like other whiskies, it can also be served on the rocks, straight-up (having been chilled on ice), with club soda, or with ginger ale. The usual rules and recommendations apply:

- Use scrupulously clean glassware
- Use pure water
- Use unsullied ice cubes

Rock and Rye: What It Is and What to Do with It

Some day, if it hasn't occurred already, you will have a conversation something like this:

You: Have you ever tried rye?

Them: I've heard of *rock* and rye. Is that what you mean?

You: No.

Rock and rye is not rye whiskey on the rocks. It is a liqueur, marketed under various brand names, made with rye whiskey, whole fruits—you'll see them in the bottle—and rock candy. Since every time you say *rye*, the phrase "rock and rye" will jump up like a leg whose knee has been tapped by a physician's rubber mallet, you'd better know what to do with rock and rye.

Basically, there are two things you can do. You can make a *cooler* or you can make a *heater*—a libation to cool yourself down or one to heat yourself up.

Certain old-timers swear by the Rock and Rye Toddy as very comforting to cold sufferers. We make absolutely no claim to any health benefits, but just pass on this fragment of folk wisdom.

Buzzed Words

A **toddy** is a hot drink consisting of liquor (often rum), water, sugar, and spices.

Rock and Rye Cooler

Serve in a highball glass.

1½ oz. vodka

1 oz. rock and rye

2 tsp. lime juice

Lemon-lime soda to fill

Lime slice

Combine all ingredients, except soda, in a shaker with ice. Shake vigorously, and then strain into the serving glass half filled with ice cubes. Add lemon-lime soda to fill and garnish with a lime slice.

Rock and Rye Toddy

Serve in a heat-proof mug.

2 oz. rock and rye

3 oz. boiling water

2 dashes Angostura bitters

Lemon slice

Cinnamon stick

Grated nutmeg

Combine rock and rye with bitters in the mug. Drop in the lemon slice, and then pour on boiling water. Garnish with the cinnamon stick and grated nutmeg.

Fizz and Flip

Buzzed Words

Flip drinks contain liquor, sugar, spice, and egg. They were most popular in the eighteenth and nineteenth centuries.

A *fizz* is just about any drink made with sugar and soda, and a *flip* is a drink with liquor, sugar, spice, and egg. Both types of drinks have pleasantly old-fashioned qualities, which makes them perfect for rye—itself an old-fashioned spirit.

Rye Fizz

Serve on the rocks in a highball glass.

1½ oz. rye

Dash Angostura bitters

Dash sugar syrup

Club soda to fill

Combine all ingredients, except the soda, in a mixing glass. Stir well and pour into the serving glass filled with ice. Add club soda to fill.

Rye Flip

Serve in a chilled brandy snifter.

1½ oz. rye

1 egg*

1 tsp. sugar syrup

Ground nutmeg

Combine all ingredients, except nutmeg, in a shaker with ice. Shake vigorously, and then strain into the serving glass. Sprinkle with nutmeg.

**Raw egg is a source of salmonella bacteria. You may wish to avoid drinks calling for raw egg yolk or white.*

Red Top

The Red Top is a flip variation.

Serve in chilled whiskey sour glasses. (Yields 2 drinks.)

3 oz. rye

1 oz. lemon or lime juice

2 tsp. sugar syrup

1 egg white*

1 oz. claret

Combine all ingredients, except the claret, in a shaker or blender with cracked ice. Shake or blend, and then strain into the serving glass. Top with the claret, but do not stir.

** Raw egg may be a source of salmonella bacteria. You may wish to avoid drinks calling for raw egg yolk or white.*

Bar Tips

The best way to chill a brandy snifter is with crushed ice. Pour it into the snifter, allow the snifter to chill, and then pour out the ice when you are ready to pour in the drink. Putting a delicate snifter in a refrigerator or freezer might crack it.

Fortifiers

The assertive quality of rye gives you the distinct feeling that you are, indeed, having a *drink*. For that reason, rye works well in the kind of drinks people used to call pick-me-ups.

Hesitation

The Hesitation, like the Kungsholm cocktail (which you'll learn about later in the chapter) combines rye with a characteristic Swedish liqueur called *punsch*. Why hesitate?

Serve in a chilled cocktail glass.

1½ oz. rye

1½ oz. Swedish *punsch*

Few liberal dashes lemon juice

Combine all ingredients in a shaker with cracked ice. Shake vigorously, and then pour into the serving glass.

Old Pepper

Add chili and Tabasco to rye, and you get an Old Pepper.

Serve in a whiskey sour glass or wine goblet.

1½ oz. blended whiskey

¾ oz. rye

1 oz. lemon juice

Dash Worcestershire sauce

Dash chili sauce

Dash Tabasco

2 dashes Angostura bitters

Combine the ingredients in a shaker with plenty of cracked ice. Shake, and then pour into serving glass. No need to strain out the ice.

Hunter's Cocktail

The Hunter's Cocktail is an old-timey classic. Not only is it meant to recruit flagging energies after a ride to hounds, but also its bright red maraschino cherry is intended not to clash with the color of one's riding coat.

Serve on the rocks in an old-fashioned glass.

1½ oz. rye

½ oz. cherry brandy

Maraschino cherry

Combine rye and brandy over ice in the serving glass. Stir, and then garnish with the cherry.

Yashmak

Another classic pick-me-up.

Serve in a chilled highball glass.

¾ oz. rye

¾ oz. dry vermouth

1 TB. Pernod

Dash Angostura bitters

3–4 drops of sugar syrup

In a shaker combine all ingredients with cracked ice. Shake vigorously, and then strain into serving glass. Add ice cubes to taste.

Lisbon Cocktail

Movie buffs may remember the 1956 film *Lisbon*, which featured Grace Kelly and Ray Milland, and brought into the world the popular melody "Lisbon Antigua," which has graced elevator music systems ever since. It also lent brief popularity to the Lisbon Cocktail, which is something very much worth reviving.

Serve in chilled old-fashioned glasses. (Yields 2 drinks.)

3 oz. rye

4 oz. port

1 oz. lemon juice

2 tsp. sugar syrup

1 egg white*

Combine all ingredients in a shaker with cracked ice. Shake vigorously, and then pour into the serving glasses.

**Raw egg may be a source of salmonella bacteria. You may wish to avoid drinks calling for raw egg yolk or white.*

Lafayette

The addition of Dubonnet rouge is French enough to honor an imported hero of the American Revolution.

Serve in a chilled old-fashioned glass.

1½ oz. rye

¼ oz. dry vermouth

¼ oz. Dubonnet rouge

Liberal dashes Angostura bitters

Combine all ingredients in a blender or shaker with cracked ice. Shake or blend, and then pour into the serving glass.

Monte Carlo

If you like the Lafayette, you'll also want to try the Monte Carlo.

Serve in a chilled cocktail glass.

1½ oz. rye

½ oz. Benedictine

Liberal dashes of Angostura bitters

Combine all ingredients in a blender or shaker with cracked ice. Shake or blend, and then strain into the serving glass.

Here are two that blend rye with just a touch of grenadine.

Opening

Serve in a chilled cocktail glass.

1½ oz. rye

¼ oz. sweet vermouth

Dash grenadine

Dash Maraschino liqueur

Combine all ingredients in a blender or shaker with cracked ice. Shake or blend, and then strain into the serving glass.

New York

Serve in a chilled old-fashioned glass.

1½ oz. rye

½ oz. lime juice

1 tsp. sugar syrup

Liberal dash or two of grenadine

Orange peel

Combine all ingredients, except orange peel, in a blender or shaker with cracked ice. Shake or blend, and then strain into the serving glass. Twist the orange peel over the drink and drop in.

Bar Tips

Drinks calling for egg white generally require half an egg white, but because it is almost impossible to separate half an egg white from a whole one, the smart thing is to make two drinks.

Citrus Varieties

The origin of rye whiskey, in a cereal grain that thrives at high altitudes and in cold, inhospitable climates, is about as far from the realm of citrus as one can get. Nevertheless, the two worlds meet joyously in a few good drinks.

Bal Harbour is a Florida coastal community so upscale that it had to spell its name the British way. Its namesake cocktail smacks of easy living among old money.

Bal Harbour Cocktail

Serve in a chilled cocktail glass.

1½ oz. rye

½ oz. dry vermouth

1 oz. grapefruit juice

Maraschino cherry

Combine all ingredients, except the cherry, in a shaker with cracked ice. Shake vigorously, and then strain into the serving glass. Garnish with the maraschino cherry.

Toast

Here's to you and here's to me
And here's to love and laughter.
I'll be true as long as you
But not a minute after.

Founded in 1868 as a New York City drinking club, the Benevolent and Protective Order of Elks is the most venerable of the "Big Three" American lodge-type orders named after wildlife. (The others are the Moose and the Eagles.) With 1.5 million members, mostly in smaller towns across the country, the Elks certainly *deserve* their own cocktail. (You don't have to know the secret handshake to partake.)

Elk's Own

Serve in a chilled old-fashioned glass.

1½ oz. rye
1 egg white*
¾ oz. port
1 tsp. powdered sugar
Juice of ½ lemon
Pineapple stick

Combine all ingredients, except the pineapple stick, in a shaker with cracked ice. Shake vigorously, and then pour into the serving glass and garnish with the pineapple stick.

Note that the Elk's Own is an *exception* to the rule governing most drinks that include egg white. You'll need one egg white—not half—per drink.

**Raw egg is a source of salmonella bacteria. You may wish to avoid drinks calling for raw egg yolk or white.*

Algonquin

The Algonquin is named after the Manhattan hotel celebrated as the gathering place of 1920s New York literati.

Serve on the rocks in an old-fashioned glass.

2 oz. rye

1 oz. dry vermouth

1 oz. pineapple juice

Combine the ingredients with cracked ice in a shaker. Shake, and then strain over ice into the serving glass.

The Devil

Vivid red and orange mark this diabolical cocktail.

Serve in a chilled cocktail glass.

1 oz. rye
Grenadine
Orange juice
1 maraschino cherry

Combine the rye and orange juice in a shaker with cracked ice. Shake, and then strain into serving glass. Drizzle grenadine and garnish with the cherry.

Blinker

Drinks made with grapefruit juice are sometimes enjoyed even before the noon hour and are collectively called "eye openers." Here's a variation on that collective name.

Serve on the rocks in a lowball glass.

1½ oz. rye
1 TB. grenadine
2 oz. grapefruit juice

Combine the ingredients with cracked ice in a shaker. Shake, and then strain into a lowball glass. Add more ice to taste.

Indian River Rye Cocktail

You've already seen an Indian River Cocktail made with blended whiskey (in Chapter 10). The version based on rye uses orange juice rather than grapefruit juice and adds dry rather than sweet vermouth.

Serve in a chilled old-fashioned glass.

1 oz. rye

1 oz. dry vermouth

2 oz. orange juice

Few dashes raspberry syrup

Combine all ingredients in a shaker with cracked ice. Shake vigorously, and then pour into the serving glass.

Rocky River Cocktail

Or travel down another river.

Serve in a chilled cocktail glass.

1 oz. rye
Sugar syrup to taste
1 oz. apricot brandy
Maraschino cherry
1 tsp. lemon juice

Combine all ingredients, except the cherry, in a shaker with cracked ice. Shake vigorously, and then strain into the serving glass. Garnish with the cherry.

With Liqueurs and Bitters

Rye really comes into its own when combined with liqueurs and bitters. These drinks are decidedly not for people who want a "lite" experience. They'll take you the whole nine yards.

Frisco Cocktail

True to form, the cocktail named for the City by the Bay is decidedly on the sweet side.

Serve in a chilled cocktail glass.

1½ oz. rye

1½ oz. Benedictine

½ oz. lemon juice

Orange twist

Combine all ingredients, except the orange twist, in a shaker with ice. Shake vigorously, and then strain into the serving glass and garnish with the twist.

High Hat

The strong note of good rye in this flavorful drink might well prompt you to raise your hat.

Serve on the rocks in an old-fashioned glass.

1 oz. Cherry Herring

4 oz. rye

3 TB. lemon juice

Combine the ingredients with cracked ice in a shaker. Shake, and then strain over ice into an old-fashioned glass.

Lord Baltimore's Cup

Lord Baltimore's Cup is probably the best known rye cocktail, and it remains popular. Made with care, it is nothing less than spectacular.

Serve in a chilled large wine glass or wine goblet.

½ tsp. sugar syrup

Few dashes Angostura bitters

1 oz. rye

Champagne to fill

1 tsp. Pernod for float

Combine the sugar and bitters in the serving glass. Add rye, along with several ice cubes, and then fill with champagne. Carefully add Pernod as a float. Do not stir.

Pink Rye

Bitters bring out the best in really good rye. The name of the Pink Rye comes from the tinge added by the Angostura.

Serve on the rocks in an old-fashioned glass.

1½ oz. rye

Liberal dashes Angostura syrup

Combine the ingredients in the serving glass filled with ice. Stir well.

Ten Ton Cocktail

Can we explain the name of this drink? In a word, no.

Serve in a chilled cocktail glass.

1½ oz. rye

1 TB. dry vermouth

1 TB. grapefruit juice

Maraschino cherry

Combine all ingredients, except the cherry, in a shaker with cracked ice. Shake, and then strain into serving glass. Garnish with the cherry.

Rye Manhattans

The versatile Manhattan can be made with bourbon, blended whiskey, scotch, and rye. The basic recipe follows.

Rye Manhattan

Serve in a chilled cocktail glass.

1½ oz. rye

¼ oz. sweet vermouth

Maraschino cherry

Combine the rye and vermouth in a mixing glass filled with ice. Stir well, and then strain into the serving glass and garnish with the cherry.

Dry Rye Manhattan

A variation on the Rye Manhattan is the Dry Rye Manhattan. Rye combines amazingly well with dry vermouth.

Serve in a chilled cocktail glass.

1½ oz. rye

¼ oz. dry vermouth

Maraschino cherry

Combine the rye and vermouth in a mixing glass filled with ice. Stir well, and then strain into the serving glass and garnish with the cherry.

Perfect Rye Manhattan

"Perfect" Manhattans, like Perfect Martinis, combine sweet and dry vermouths.

Serve in a chilled cocktail glass.

2 oz. rye

½ tsp. sweet vermouth

½ tsp. dry vermouth

Few dashes Agnostura bitters

Maraschino cherry

Combine all ingredients, except cherry, in a shaker with cracked ice. Shake vigorously, and then strain into the serving glass and garnish with the cherry.

Shaker Heights

Shaker Heights is outside of Cleveland, Ohio, but think of this drink as another variation on the rye Manhattan.

Serve in a chilled cocktail glass.

½ oz. rye

½ oz. gin

½ oz. brandy

Few dashes of orange bitters

Combine all ingredients in a shaker with cracked ice. Shake vigorously, and then strain into the serving glass.

Rye Revisited

Despite the decline in the popularity of rye, it has found its way into a few new drinks. Here are some of the most amusing.

Flashback

Serve on the rocks in an old-fashioned glass.

1 oz. whiskey

½ oz. rye

½ oz scotch

2 TB. cranberry juice

Lemon peel

Combine all ingredients, except the lemon peel, in a shaker with cracked ice. Shake vigorously, and then strain over ice into the serving glass. Twist the lemon peel over the drink and drop in.

Rye and Dry

Serve on the rocks in an old-fashioned glass.

2 oz. dry vermouth

1 oz. rye

2 dashes orange bitters

Combine all ingredients in a shaker with cracked ice. Shake vigorously, and then strain over ice into the serving glass.

Alarm Clock

Serve in a chilled cocktail glass.

1 oz. rye

1 oz. dark rum

½ oz. Drambuie

Combine all ingredients in a shaker with cracked ice. Shake vigorously, and then strain into the serving glass.

Romulac

Serve on the rocks in a highball glass.

1 oz. rye

1 oz. sweet vermouth

½ oz. maraschino liqueur

Maraschino cherry

Combine all ingredients, except the cherry, in a shaker with cracked ice. Shake vigorously, and then strain over ice into the serving glass.

Dice Thrower

Serve in a chilled cocktail glass.

1 oz. rye

1 oz. scotch

Combine the spirits in a shaker with cracked ice. Shake vigorously, and then strain into the serving glass.

Referee's Revenge

Serve on the rocks in an old-fashioned glass.

¾ oz. rye

¾ oz. vodka

3 oz. grapefruit juice

1 tsp. lemon juice

Combine all ingredients in a shaker with cracked ice. Shake vigorously, and then strain over ice into the serving glass.

The Least You Need to Know

- Rye is the most neglected of the whiskies, but it is well worth reviving as a change of pace from bourbon or scotch.
- Rye is often confused with rock and rye, which is a rye-based liqueur laden with fruit and rock candy.
- Although the cheaper brands of bourbon and scotch aren't all that bad, cheap rye is terrible. Invest in a premium brand.
- Although dedicated rye drinkers usually prefer their rye neat, the whiskey mixes very well with bitters, liqueurs, and, surprisingly, citrus.

Chapter 12

Scotch Snobs and Irish Spirits: Blends and Single Malts

In This Chapter

- How scotch is made
- Malt vs. grain scotch, and single-malt vs. blended scotch
- Scotch vs. Irish whiskey
- Scotch recipes

As with wine, scotch commands a legion of connoisseurs, who are both dedicated and disputatious. Also as with wine, creating scotch is theoretically quite simple. There is fermentation, distilling, aging, and then bottling. In the case of blended scotch, there is the added complication of blending 15 to 50 whiskies. Nevertheless, as the saying goes, this isn't rocket science. Yet it is undeniable that scotch varies greatly in taste from label to label, and just why this is the case is a subject of deep mystery.

As to Irish whiskey, its following is much smaller than the host of scotch fanciers; yet, thanks to the great popularity of a number of liqueurs based on Irish whiskey (paramountly Irish Mist and Bailey's Original Irish Cream), the whiskey itself is enjoying increasing demand in the United States. If you enjoy scotch and have yet to sample Irish whiskey, why not take the plunge?

Scotland the Brave

No one has yet been able to make truly satisfying scotch whisky (remember, that's how the Scots prefer to spell it) outside of Scotland. Is there magic there? Or is it just the right barley, water, and peat for the barley roasting? Most authorities attribute at least some of the variation among whiskeys of the great scotch-producing regions—Highlands, Lowlands, Campbeltown, and the Isle of Islay—to differences in a variety of elements including the barley, the peat, the water, and the aging.

Speaking of *malt*, there are two broad categories of scotch, defined by their use of malted versus unmalted grain.

The process of malting barley goes like this:

1. The grain is soaked for two or three days in water, and then allowed to sprout.
2. As a result of sprouting, the barley releases an enzyme called *diastase*, which renders the starch in the barley soluble and therefore readily converted into sugar.
3. After 8 to 12 days, the sprouting process is stopped by drying the malted barley in a kiln (oven) fired with peat fuel. This ultimately imparts a smoky savor to the finished whisky.
4. Once it has been dried, the malt is ground in a mill and mixed with hot water.
5. After eight hours, a soluble starch (called the *wort*) is drawn off and transferred to fermentation vats, where it is fermented by yeast for 48 hours.
6. The result is a weak alcohol called *wash*, which is now distilled into whisky.

Buzzed Words

Malt is grain (usually barley) that has been allowed to sprout. **Wort** is a soluble starch in the form of an infusion of malt. It is used in the fermentation processes of making whiskey and beer.

Buzzed Words

The **continuous still** (also called a **Coffey still**, after the inventor, Aeneas Coffey) allows for continuous high-volume production, as opposed to the **pot still**, which must be emptied and "recharged" one batch at a time.

Malt scotches are made entirely from malted barley and are laboriously distilled, like cognac, one batch at a time, in relatively small *pot stills*. *Grain scotches* combine malted barley with unmalted barley and corn and are distilled in greater volume in more modern *"continuous" stills*.

The raw whisky that comes from the still is aged in oak casks, which may be new or used (having been used either to age sherry or even American bourbon). By Scottish law, the whisky must age for at least 3 years, but 6 to 8 years is deemed optimum for grain whisky and 14 to 15 years for malt whisky.

Grain scotches are not nearly as popular as malt scotches, and there are only about eight grain distilleries currently operating in Scotland. Such grain scotches as Black Barrel, Cameroun Brig, Invergordon, Loch Lomond, and Strathclyde are produced in relatively small quantities. The casual scotch drinker may or may not be familiar with the distinction between malt and grain scotches, but all except the neophyte have heard something about *single-malt* versus blended scotches.

By far, most scotch consumed in the United States (and in Scotland, for that matter)—such brands as Johnny Walker and Dewar's—is blended from products produced by several different distilleries. As with blended whiskey (see Chapter 10), blending is the painstaking work of a highly skilled master blender, who ensures uniformity of brand and a high level of quality control. After blending, the scotch is typically aged in wooden vats for another six to nine months to "marry" the blend. Nothing is arbitrary about blending. A premium blended scotch is a delicately orchestrated combination of malt and grain whiskies from the characteristic regions of Scotland, each combined in exacting proportion.

Buzzed Words

Malt scotches are made entirely from malted barley and are distilled in relatively small pot stills. **Grain scotches** combine malted barley with unmalted barley and corn and are distilled in "continuous" stills.

Despite the effort that goes into creating blended scotch, it is much less expensive than single-malt scotch, which, despite growing American popularity, accounts for a scant two percent of scotch sales in the United States. As the name implies, single-malt scotch is made exclusively from malted barley, which means that it is aged at least 14 years. The whisky in a bottle of single-malt scotch has been distilled and aged during a single period and by a single distillery. The best-known names among the malted scotches ring out with Celtic grandeur: The Glenlivet, Knockando, Glenfiddich, Laphroaig, Glenmorangie, and Macallan. They cost as much as *very* fine wine, and you will want to enjoy them neat, on the rocks, or with unflavored mixers.

Bar Tips

For mixed drinks, use blended scotch. There is no sane reason to expend the precious nectar of single-malt scotch in combination with strongly flavored mixers.

Ireland the Source

As we first observed in Chapter 1, Ireland is where whiskey was born; it was given its modern name in the twelfth century by soldiers of England's Henry II returning from an Irish campaign. Today's Irish whiskey starts out much the way scotch does, with barley (some malted, some not) and water. The drying process, however, is carried out in smokeless kilns rather than over a peat fire. The result: Irish whiskey lacks the smoky flavor of scotch (and is therefore perceived as less sharp, mellower, and lighter than most scotches). The barley is mixed with other grains (especially rye, wheat, and corn), fermented, distilled, and aged from 4 to 15 years. Good Irish whiskey has a predominantly barley malt flavor and is very mellow.

Unmixed Pleasure: Neat, Rocks, Water, Soda

For the lover of fine scotch, few gustatory pleasures exceed that of sampling the many blended and single-malt varieties available. Any of the premium-priced blended labels make for enjoyment, especially served on the rocks or with a plain mixer. The single-malt scotches are best enjoyed neat—and absolutely *any* of these is sure to delight. Irish whiskey is likewise rewarding neat or on the rocks. Just remember the rules of enjoying fine whiskey in its unadorned state:

- Use super-clean glassware that is free from soap and detergent residue.
- Make certain any water that you add has no unwanted flavors or odors.
- Use the best ice possible. If you must take it from your freezer, run some water over it to get rid of freezer burn and any stray odors or flavors.

Wine-tasting parties have been around for a long time. Scotch is sufficiently varied and complex in flavor that it, too, can become the focus of a tasting party. Practiced connoisseurs cut the scotch 50/50 with distilled water—and they don't feel obliged to swallow all they sample. The object of a scotch-tasting party is to experience refined enjoyment, not to get hammered. Much of the "tasting" is done with the nose. The "bouquet" of the scotch speaks volumes. Another word of advice: A scotch-tasting party is often a BYOB (bring your own bottle) affair. To supply a dozen or more bottles of premium scotch will strain any pocketbook. Work out a list of scotches to try, and arrange for each guest to bring a bottle.

Quick One

Two men meet in a sleazy dockside bar.

"Lemme tell ya. It's gotten to the point where I get drunk mostly on water."

"That's crazy," the other man said. "Impossible!"

"It's a fact. Especially when you're cooped up with nothin' but men on the ship."

Classic Scotch Concoctions

Scotch is as mixable as you let it be and certainly as mixable as bourbon. Because it has loads of character and stands so perfectly on its own, its repertoire is somewhat more limited than blended whiskey's. Nevertheless, there are plenty of great scotch drinks. See Appendix B for some scotch versions of the usual classics, and below for a few unique scotch specialties.

The Rob Roy is essentially a Manhattan made with scotch instead of bourbon or blended whiskey. The drink commands a small but intensely loyal following. The namesake, Robert Macgregor (1671–1734), was a ruthless Highland outlaw who called himself Rob Roy and who achieved the kind of exaggerated fame conferred earlier on Robin Hood (and, later, on Jesse James). In 1818, Sir Walter Scott based a sensational novel—*Rob Roy*—on his exploits.

Rob Roy

Serve in a chilled cocktail glass.

2 oz. scotch

½ oz. sweet vermouth

Maraschino cherry

Combine the scotch and sweet vermouth in a mixing glass with ice. Stir well, and then strain into the serving glass and garnish with the cherry.

Dry Rob Roy

Serve in a chilled cocktail glass.

2 oz. scotch

½ oz. dry vermouth

Dash Angostura bitters

Lemon peel

Combine all ingredients, except the lemon peel, in a mixing glass with ice. Stir well, and then strain into the serving glass. Twist the lemon peel over the glass and drop in.

Royal Rob Roy

If these Rob Roys aren't grand enough for you, take the royal road.

Serve in a chilled cocktail glass.

1½ oz. scotch

1½ oz. Drambouie

¼ oz. dry vermouth

¼ oz. sweet vermouth

Maraschino cherry

Combine all ingredients, except the cherry, in a shaker with cracked ice. Shake, and then strain into the serving glass. Garnish with the cherry.

Rusty Nail

This simple combination of scotch and scotch liqueur is among the most popular of scotch-based mixed drinks.

Serve on the rocks in an old-fashioned glass.

1½ oz. scotch

1 oz. Drambuie

Combine ingredients in the serving glass half filled with ice cubes. Stir. (If you prefer, the Drambuie can be floated without stirring.)

Rust

A recent variation on the old Rusty Nail is Rust.

Serve in a chilled cocktail glass.

1½ oz. scotch

½ oz. white crème de menthe

Combine in a shaker with cracked ice. Shake, and then strain into the serving glass.

Highland Fling with Milk

Highland Fling is the name attached to two scotch drinks, which have nothing in common, aside from the fact that both are based on a jigger of scotch.

Serve in a chilled old-fashioned glass.

1½ oz. scotch

3 oz. milk

1 tsp. sugar syrup

Ground nutmeg

Combine all ingredients, except nutmeg, in a shaker with cracked ice. Shake vigorously, and then pour into the serving glass and sprinkle with the ground nutmeg.

Highland Fling with Sweet Vermouth

Serve in a chilled cocktail glass.

1½ oz. scotch

½ oz. sweet vermouth

Few dashes orange bitters

Olive

Combine all ingredients, except the olive, in a shaker with cracked ice. Shake vigorously, and then strain into the serving glass and garnish with the olive.

Scotch with Liqueurs

Scotch marries well with liqueurs, especially Drambuie, Scotland's immensely popular scotch-based liqueur.

A *bairn* is what the Scots call a child, and the word has become an expression of particular affection. Here's a wee drink worth cherishing—pronounce it *bear-r-r-r-r-r-nnn*, trilling the 'R' thoroughly.

Toast

Women have many faults, but men have only two: everything they say and everything they do!

Bairn

Serve in a chilled cocktail glass.

1½ oz. scotch

¾ oz. Cointreau

Few dashes orange bitters

Combine all ingredients in a shaker with ice. Shake vigorously, and then pour into the serving glass.

Blackwatch

Named in honor of a famous Scottish military regiment, the Blackwatch is both highly unusual and highly refreshing.

Serve on the rocks in a highball glass.

1½ oz. scotch

½ oz. curaçao

½ oz. brandy

Lemon slice

Mint sprig

Combine all ingredients, except the lemon slice and mint sprig, in the serving glass half filled with ice cubes. Stir gently, and then garnish with the lemon slice and mint sprig.

Highland Morning

Serve in a chilled old-fashioned glass.

1 oz. scotch

¾ oz. Cointreau

3 oz. grapefruit juice

Combine all ingredients in a shaker or blender with cracked ice. Shake or blend, and then pour into the serving glass.

Gretna Green

Serve in a chilled cocktail glass.

½ oz. Falernum or honey

1½ oz. scotch

½ oz. green Chartreuse

1 oz. lemon juice

Dissolve the Falernum or honey in a little water, and then combine with the other ingredients in a shaker or blender with cracked ice. Shake or blend. Strain into the serving glass.

Blue Firth

Serve in a chilled cocktail glass.

1½ oz. scotch

½ oz. blue curaçao

Dash dry vermouth

Dash orange bitters

Combine all ingredients in a shaker with cracked ice. Shake, and then strain into the serving glass.

Eric the Red

Serve in a chilled old-fashioned glass.

1½ oz. scotch

½ oz. Peter Heering

1 tsp. dry vermouth

Combine all ingredients in a shaker with cracked ice. Shake, and then strain into the serving glass.

Ardmore Cocktail

Serve in a chilled cocktail glass.

1 oz. scotch

½ oz. Cherry Marnier

½ oz. sweet vermouth

2 oz. orange juice

Combine all ingredients in a shaker with cracked ice. Shake, and then strain into the serving glass.

Dundee Dram

Dundee is a large industrial city that is also noted for its marmalade. None of that here, however, in the Dundee Dream, a bracing combination of scotch and gin.

Serve in an old-fashioned glass.

1 oz. scotch

1 oz. gin

½ oz. Drambuie

1 tsp. lemon juice

Lemon twist

Maraschino cherry

Combine all ingredients, except fruit, in a shaker with cracked ice. Shake vigorously, and then pour into the serving glass and garnish with the twist and cherry.

Culloden Cheer

Culloden Moor was hardly a cheery place when the Scots suffered a disastrous defeat at the hands of the English in 1746, but the drink named for it is most warming.

Serve in a chilled cocktail glass.

1 oz. scotch

1 oz. dry sherry

½ oz. lemon juice

½ oz. La Grande Passion

In a shaker or blender combine all ingredients. Shake or blend. Strain into the serving glass.

The Godfather

The addition of an Italian liqueur makes this an offer you can't refuse.

Serve in a chilled old-fashioned glass.

1½ oz. scotch

3/4 oz. Amaretto di Saronno

Combine with several ice cubes in the serving glass.

On the Sweet Side

Scotch is naturally the sweetest of whiskies and takes well to the more sugary mixers. The Scotch Orange Fix, for example, pairs scotch with sugar syrup and curaçao.

Scotch Orange Fix

Serve in a chilled large (double) old-fashioned glass.

2 oz. Scotch

½ oz. lemon juice

1 tsp. sugar syrup

1 tsp. curaçao

Orange peel curlicue

Combine all ingredients, except the orange peel and curaçao, in a shaker with cracked ice. Shake vigorously, and then pour into the serving glass. Prepare a long spiral length of orange peel and garnish. Add a few ice cubes, and then carefully top with the curaçao.

Inverness Cocktail

Another sweet note sounded.

Serve in a chilled cocktail glass.

2 oz. scotch

½ oz. lemon juice

1 tsp. orgeat syrup

1 tsp. curaçao (may substitute triple sec)

Combine all ingredients, except for the curaçao, in a shaker or blender with cracked ice. Strain into serving glass. Float the curaçao on top. Do not stir!

Sangaree is the Anglicized version of the word *sangria*, which, in Spanish, pertains (unappetizingly enough) to the act of bleeding and has, therefore, lent itself to naming the rich red combination of sweetened red wine and fruit we enjoy in Mexican, Spanish, and Cuban restaurants. Unlike the Hispanic *sangria* drinks, however, the Scotch Sangaree has no red wine and is merely garnished with a lemon twist. It is a spiritous drink graced by nutmeg.

Scotch Sangaree

Serve in a large (double) old-fashioned glass.

1 tsp. heather honey

1½ oz. scotch

Lemon twist

Club soda to fill

Grated nutmeg

Mix the honey and a few splashes of the club soda in the serving glass. Stir until the honey is dissolved. Add the scotch and lemon twist, along with a few ice cubes. Stir. Add club soda to fill, and sprinkle with the nutmeg.

Scotch Smash

Smashes are drinks with loads of crushed ice.

Serve in a large (double) old-fashioned glass.

6 mint leaves

Heather honey (may substitute sugar syrup)

3 oz. scotch

Orange bitters

Muddle (mash and stir) the honey (or sugar syrup) with the mint leaves in the serving glass, and then fill the glass with finely crushed ice. Add scotch and stir well. Dash on a topping of orange bitters and garnish with the mint sprig.

Vermouth Combinations

Both sweet and dry vermouths are used in a number of scotch-based mixed drinks. In addition to those we've already seen, here's a collection of some of the best.

Blood and Sand

Blood and Sand is named for the smash-hit Rudolph Valentino film about the doomed romance of a Spanish bullfighter. Serve in a chilled old-fashioned glass.

¾ oz. scotch

¾ oz. cherry brandy

¾ oz. sweet vermouth

¾ oz. orange juice

Combine all ingredients in a shaker with cracked ice. Shake vigorously, and then pour into the serving glass.

Bobby Burns

Robert Burns, the perpetual poet laureate of Scotland, is another hero who lends his name to a scotch-and-vermouth combination.

Serve in a chilled cocktail glass.

1½ oz. scotch

½ oz. dry vermouth

½ oz. sweet vermouth

Dash Benedictine

Combine all ingredients in a shaker with ice. Shake vigorously, and then strain into the serving glass.

Bonnie Prince Charlie

Charles Edward Louis Philip Casimir Stuart, son of the "Old Pretender" James Stuart, secured the support of Scots in his bid to restore the Stuarts to the British throne. In 1745, as Bonnie Prince Charlie, he began the uprising against the English that ended in bloody defeat at Culloden Moor on April 16, 1746. Defeated or not, the young man is commemorated in a drink.

Serve in a chilled martini glass.

1½ oz. scotch

½ oz. dry vermouth

Few dashes Pernod

Lemon peel

Combine all ingredients, except the lemon peel, in a shaker with cracked ice. Shake vigorously, and then strain into the serving glass. Twist the lemon peel over the drink and drop in.

Brigadoon

Blood and Sand was a popular film that had nothing to do with Scotland, whereas *Brigadoon* was a 1947 Broadway hit musical by Lerner and Loewe that had *everything* to do with the Highlands. How *are* things in Glocamora, anyway?

Serve in a chilled old-fashioned glass.

1 oz. scotch

1 oz. grapefruit juice

1 oz. dry vermouth

Combine all ingredients in a shaker with cracked ice. Shake vigorously, and then pour into the serving glass.

Loch Ness

Serve in a chilled old-fashioned glass.

1½ oz. scotch

1 oz. Pernod

¼ oz. sweet vermouth

Combine all ingredients in a shaker with cracked ice. Shake vigorously, and then pour into the serving glass.

The Irish Collection

You could easily substitute Irish whiskey for scotch in the drinks for which we've just given the recipes. However, a good many drinks are especially suited to the mellow, lighter, drier taste of Irish whiskey.

Liqueur and Aperitif Drinks

The thinner, lighter quality of Irish whiskey combines well with a variety of liqueurs and aperitifs. Best known among the Irish whiskey-aperitif combinations is the Blackthorn.

Blackthorn

Serve in a chilled old-fashioned glass.

1½ oz. Irish whiskey

1½ oz. dry vermouth

Liberal dashes Pernod

Liberal dashes Angostura bitters

Combine all ingredients in a shaker with cracked ice. Shake vigorously and pour into the serving glass.

Innisfree Fizz

County Sligo is mostly rugged pastureland, mountainous and punctuated by peat bogs. It includes the wild island of Innisfree, celebrated in a poem by no less a figure than William Butler Yeats.

Serve in a large wine glass or goblet.

2 oz. Irish whiskey

1 oz. lemon juice

1 oz. curaçao

½ tsp. sugar syrup

Club soda to fill

Combine all ingredients, except the club soda, in a shaker with ice. Shake vigorously, and then strain into the serving glass and add club soda to fill.

Cocktail Na Mara

The Gaelic name means "Cocktail of the Sea."

Serve in a chilled highball glass.

2 oz. Irish whiskey

2 oz. clam juice

4 oz. tomato juice

½ oz. lemon juice

Few dashes Worcestershire sauce

Dash Tabasco sauce

Pinch white pepper

Into a mixing glass combine all ingredients. Stir well with cracked ice, and then pour into serving glass.

Irish Rainbow

The Irish Rainbow combines liqueurs and Pernod, which provide a spectrum of tastes and color.

Serve in a chilled old-fashioned glass.

1½ oz. Irish whiskey

Liberal dashes Pernod

Liberal dashes curaçao

Liberal dashes maraschino liqueur

Liberal dashes Angostura bitters

Orange twist

Combine all ingredients, except the twist, in a shaker with cracked ice. Shake vigorously, and then pour into the serving glass. Garnish with the orange twist.

Mists

Irish Mist is a highly popular and readily available liqueur based on Irish whiskey. Combined with more of its mother ingredient, it makes for some tempting whiskey-and-liqueur libations.

Ballylickey Belt

Serve in an old-fashioned glass.

½ tsp. heather honey

1½ oz. Irish whiskey

Club soda to fill

Lemon twist

Dissolve the honey with a few splashes of the club soda in the bottom of the serving glass. Add the whiskey, a few ice cubes, and then club soda to fill. Garnish with the twist.

Irish Fix

Serve in a chilled old-fashioned glass.

2 oz. Irish whiskey

½ oz. Irish Mist

½ oz. lemon juice

½ oz. pineapple syrup (may substitute pineapple juice sweetened with a little sugar)

Orange slice

Lemon slice

Combine all ingredients, except fruit, in a shaker with cracked ice. Shake vigorously, and then pour into the serving glass. Garnish with the fruit slices.

Sweet Drinks

Here is a nosegay of sweet drinks.

Bow Street Special

Serve in a chilled cocktail glass.

1½ oz. Irish whiskey

¾ oz. triple sec

1 oz. lemon juice

Combine the ingredients in a shaker with cracked ice. Shake vigorously, and then pour into the serving glass.

Grafton Street Sour

Serve in a chilled cocktail glass.

1½ oz. Irish whiskey

½ oz. triple sec

1 oz. lime juice

¼ oz. raspberry liqueur

Combine all ingredients, except the raspberry liqueur, in a shaker with ice. Shake vigorously, and then strain into the serving glass. Carefully top with the liqueur.

Paddy Cocktail

Serve in a chilled cocktail glass.

1½ oz. Irish whiskey

¾ oz. sweet vermouth

Liberal dashes Angostura bitters

Combine the ingredients in a shaker with cracked ice. Shake vigorously, and then pour into the serving glass.

Wicklow Cooler

Serve in a chilled Collins glass.

1½ oz. Irish whiskey

1 oz. dark Jamaica rum

½ oz. lime juice

1 oz. orange juice

1 tsp. orgeat syrup

Ginger ale

Combine all ingredients, except ginger ale, in a shaker or blender with cracked ice. Shake or blend, and then pour into serving glass. Add a few ice cubes, if desired. Top off with ginger ale.

Irish Kilt

Can't decide between Irish whiskey and scotch? Don't try.

Serve in a chilled cocktail glass.

1 oz. Irish whiskey

1 oz. scotch

1 oz. lemon juice

1½ oz. sugar syrup

Few dashes orange bitters

Combine all ingredients with cracked ice in a shaker or blender. Shake or blend, and then strain into the serving glass.

Not Your Father's Scotch

Here are four cutting-edge scotch libations and a final nod to an Irish stereotype.

Double Trouble

Serve on the rocks in a highball glass.

1½ oz. scotch

1½ oz. Southern Comfort

2 drops grenadine

Combine in a shaker with cracked ice. Shake, and then strain over ice into the serving glass.

Miami Vice

Serve in a chilled cocktail glass.

1 oz. scotch

¾ oz. dry vermouth

1 TB. grapefruit juice

Combine all ingredients in a shaker with cracked ice. Shake vigorously, and then strain into the serving glass. May add a single ice cube.

Gunrunner

Serve on the rocks in a highball glass.

1 oz. scotch

1 oz. Drambuie

½ oz. amaretto

1 TB. gold rum

Combine all ingredients in a shaker with cracked ice. Shake vigorously, and then strain over ice into the serving glass.

Nerd's Delight

Serve on the rocks in an old-fashioned glass.

1 oz. scotch

1 oz. tequila

1 oz. grapefruit juice

1 TB. grenadine

Maraschino cherry

Combine all ingredients, except the cherry, in a shaker with cracked ice. Shake vigorously, and then strain over ice into the serving glass. Garnish with the cherry.

Irish Cop

Serve in a chilled cocktail glass.

1 oz. scotch

1 oz. green crème de menthe

Combine in a shaker with cracked ice. Shake, and then strain into the serving glass.

The Least You Need to Know

- Scotch comes in blended varieties and in an unblended variety known as single-malt scotch.
- Ideal for sipping neat, expensive single-malt scotch is wasted on most mixed drinks.
- Blended scotch is the work of a master blender, and not only are the constituent whiskies aged before blending, but the blended product is also aged for several months to "marry" the combined whiskies.
- Irish whiskey is similar to scotch and can be substituted for it in many recipes calling for scotch. However, it lacks the smoky flavor of scotch.

Part 4

Almost Tropical

Whereas the nature of the ideal martini is the subject of endless debate, and whiskey is a topic of which some people never tire, the two light spirits of the tropics, rum and tequila, are understood by few and fully appreciated by even fewer. Here is your introduction to the wonderfully complex, rich, and flavorful realm of rum, in which each country of origin defines its own style and taste.

As for tequila, it has long lived in the shadows, tainted by an unfounded reputation as slightly sleazy. The spirit is actually produced in a legally defined region of Mexico in accordance with stringent standards. Good tequila is carefully crafted, and sometimes even aged.

It pays to know something about rum and tequila: not only have both gained greatly in popularity in the United States, but also they are the key ingredient in a host of much-requested, delicious, provocative, and refreshing drinks.

Chapter 13

Caribbean Sugarcane: A Rum Resumé

In This Chapter

- Rum—a spirit of great variety
- The distinctive characters of rums from different countries
- Rums to drink straight and rums to mix
- Rum recipes

If you think of rum only as a clear, sweet liquor to mix with a Coke or throw into a daiquiri, you've got a vast tropical and semitropical world to explore. The fact is, even drinkers who are sophisticated in the nuances of bourbon and Tennessee whiskey and blended versus single-malt scotches often know very little about rum. Far from being a simple, sweet spirit, it is produced in a dazzling variety and subtle gradation of flavor and body—and colors, from clear to gold to brown to virtually black, reflecting flavor and body—in countries spanning the Caribbean and the Atlantic coast of Central and South America. This chapter opens the door to the varied realm of rum.

A Little Travelogue

The existence of rum was first reported in records from Barbados about 1650. By the early eighteenth century, rum was made part of the official ration of Royal Navy sailors, and British Navy Pusser's Rum was the Royal Navy's official rum purveyor for almost three centuries, until the rum ration was discontinued in 1970. In 1862, operating a small still at Santiago de Cuba, Bacardi and Company produced the first clear, light-bodied rum. Today, Bacardi rum—in its light-bodied as well as darker incarnations—is the most widely distributed rum in the world, penetrating markets in at least 175 countries.

Buzzed Words

A **daiquiri** is a rum, lime juice, and sugar drink named after the Cuban town near the original Bacardi rum distillery.

Bacardi makes a very fine product, but it is not the only rum whose acquaintance you should make. Unfortunately, even well-stocked liquor stores in major U.S. cities rarely carry more than a few brands. You'll probably find Mount Gay, which is a fine example of the smooth, mellow gold rums produced in Barbados; you might find Bermudez, from the Dominican Republic; Rhum Barbancourt, from Haiti; and perhaps one or two of the products of Martinique. Jamaican rums, including Myers's, Appleton, Captain Morgan, and British Navy Pusser's, are also stocked in the large stores—with Myers's and Captain Morgan receiving quite wide distribution. Guyana's remote Demerara River produces a 151-proof product distilled and marketed by Hudson's Bay and Lemon Hart & Sons. Large liquor stores often stock it.

If this sounds like quite a few rums are available, wait till you run down a list of countries noted for their rums: Antigua, Barbados, Bermuda, Cuba, Colombia, Costa Rica, Dominican Republic, Guyana, Haiti, Jamaica, French West Indies, Panama, Puerto Rico (home base for Bacardi since the advent of Castro in Cuba), St. Lucia, St. Vincent, British Virgin Islands, U.S. Virgin Islands, Trinidad, and Venezuela. Many of these countries produce several brands of rum, most of which, however, are consumed domestically and never exported.

Toast

May you have health, love, money, and time to spend it!

So Near and Yet So Far

As with most spirits, the basic process of making rum is simple. Most rums are made from molasses, which is the residue that remains after sugar has been crystallized from sugarcane juice.

It is significant that the sugar necessary for fermentation is present in the molasses, which means that, more than any other distilled spirit, rum retains the flavor of the raw material from which it is made. This accounts in large part for the great variation in flavor, color, and character among rums produced in different regions.

Another determinant of taste and character is the type of yeast employed to trigger the fermentation process. Each producer of rum closely guards its unique strain of yeast. Finally, distillation methods, aging duration and conditions, and blending also contribute to distinctive flavor. As with the blending of whiskey, the blending of rum is the work of a master blender, who tests, chooses, and combines the products of various distilleries and various ages to achieve a rum of distinctive character and consistent quality.

As I said, the process *looks* simple, but the variables involved are *so* varied—geography, climate, natural processes, human invention, and human judgment—that the making of a fine rum is, as much as the creation of a great whiskey, an art.

Colonial Benders

While Royal Navy grog—a combination of rum and water—might be considered the first rum highball, legend holds that it was the Welsh buccaneer Henry Morgan (1635?–1688) who invented the first rum *cocktail*. Mixing the grog with lime juice and sugar, he created the ancestor of the daiquiri. But it was in colonial America that rum first became popular as the primary ingredient of a genuine mixed drink. George Washington, Ben Franklin, Thomas Jefferson—just about everyone who was anyone—flipped for something called Flip. It could be made cold or hot, although hot Flip was by far the favorite: Rum was mixed with beer (at a time when beer was a common substitute for water of uncertain purity), beaten eggs, cream, and spices, and then *mulled* (heated and spiced) with a red-hot poker. "Flip-iron" pokers were made especially for this purpose.

Buzzed Words

To **mull** a drink is to heat and spice it. Traditionally, the heating was done by inserting a hot poker into the drink; today, mulled drinks are usually heated on a stove.

Rum Solo

In general, the characteristic rums of Jamaica and the Demerara River region of Guyana are dark, heavy, and sweet. Barbados rums are golden or dark amber and neither as heavy nor as sweet as those of Jamaica or the Demerara region. Today, the characteristic rums of Puerto Rico and the Virgin Islands follow the pattern set by

Bacardi in the mid-nineteenth century in that they are dry and light. Long-aged rums—some of the best of which are produced in Colombia (Ron Medellin) and Venezuela (Cacique Ron Anejo)—take on a rich golden-amber color from the American Oak barrels in which they are aged for as much as 10 years.

It is a pleasure to sample golden and dark rums on the rocks or, like fine cognac, neat, in a snifter. As for the light rums, most people enjoy them in mixed drinks. However, although light rum works with most mixed rum drinks, a number of recipes call for dark or gold rum, some call for rum from a specific country, and others even call for a particular brand. These specifications should not be ignored. Rum flavors vary widely, so you will get the most pleasing results if you follow the recipe recommendations.

Bacardis

Not surprisingly, the most widely known name in rum has lent itself to one of the most frequently requested rum drinks. The Bacardi can be made with Bacardi light or gold rum.

Bacardi

Serve in a chilled cocktail glass.

1½ oz. light or gold Bacardi rum

½ oz. lime juice

½ tsp. grenadine

Combine all ingredients in a shaker with cracked ice. Shake vigorously, and then pour into the serving glass.

Bacardi Special

Light rum marries well with gin. Here's the Bacardi Special.

Serve in a chilled cocktail glass.

1½ oz. light Bacardi rum

¾ oz. gin

½ oz. lime juice

½ tsp. grenadine

Combine all ingredients in a shaker with cracked ice. Shake vigorously, and then pour into the serving glass.

Cuba Libre!

In a more innocent age ("more innocent age" being that period of time in which you happened to reach adulthood), rum and Coke was a common introduction to alcoholic beverages. The virtue and vice of rum and Coke is that it goes down, well, like Coke, and inexperienced drinkers might quickly consume far more than they should.

If you wish to reduce calories in the rum and Coke, use diet cola. And if you want to add a touch of sophistication to the drink, transform it into a Cuba Libre.

Cuba Libre

Serve on the rocks in a highball glass.

1½ oz. light or gold rum

Coca-Cola or other cola soft drink to fill

Lime wedge

Combine all ingredients, except the lime, in the serving glass filled with ice. Garnish with the lime wedge.

No, you haven't misread the recipe: A Cuba Libre is a Rum and Coke—garnished with a wedge of lime.

Cherry Cola

If you really want to transform this familiar drink into something special, use dark rum and some cherry brandy plus cola for the Cherry Cola.

Serve on the rocks in a lowball glass.

2 oz. dark rum

½ oz. cherry brandy

2 oz. Coca-Cola or other cola soft drink to fill

Lemon twist

Combine the ingredients in the serving glass filled with ice. Garnish with the twist.

Playboy Cooler

Still too much like a run-of-the-mill rum and Coke? Try the Playboy Cooler or the Pensacola Cola.

Serve in a chilled highball glass.

1½ oz. gold rum

1½ oz. Kahlúa

3 oz. pineapple juice

½ oz. lime juice

Cola

Maraschino cherry

Combine all ingredients, except the cola and cherry, in a shaker or blender with cracked ice. Shake or blend, and then pour into the serving glass. Top off with cola and garnish with the cherry.

Pensacola Cola

Serve on the rocks in a Collins glass.

1½ oz. gold rum

½ oz. Cherry Marnier

Cola

Lemon peel

Combine all ingredients, except the cola and lemon peel, over ice in the serving glass. Stir. Add cola, and then gently stir again. Twist the lemon peel over the drink and drop it in.

Coladas

The piña colada might be the most popular rum cocktail, and it has spawned a number of variations. These can be made with light or gold rum. The first recipe is specially adapted to light rum; the second, to gold.

Piña Colada with Light Rum

Serve in a chilled Collins glass.

1½ oz. light rum

1 oz. cream of coconut

2 oz. canned pineapple chunks

2 oz. pineapple juice

Splash cream

Maraschino cherry

Orange slice

Pineapple stick

Combine all ingredients, except fruit, in a blender with 3 oz. crushed ice. Blend until smooth, and then pour into the serving glass and garnish with fruit.

Piña Colada with Gold Rum

Serve in a chilled Collins glass.

2 oz. gold rum

2 oz. cream of coconut

4 oz. pineapple juice

Pineapple stick

Maraschino cherry

Combine all ingredients, except fruit, in a shaker with crushed ice. Shake vigorously, and then pour into the serving glass. Garnish with fruit.

Kilauea Kup

The following are close cousins of the piña colada, though some lack the pineapple, whereas others have no coconut: Those that retain both combine them in unconventional ways. These are genuinely exotic tropical drinks.

Serve in a chilled Collins glass.

1½ oz. gold rum

½ oz. crème de banana

4 oz. pineapple juice

1 tsp. coconut rum

Orange slice

Maraschino cherry

Combine all ingredients, except the coconut rum and fruit, in a blender with cracked ice. Blend thoroughly, and then pour into the serving glass. Top with the coconut rum—do not stir—and garnish with the orange slice and cherry.

Isle of the Blessed Coconut

Serve in a large, saucer-style chilled champagne glass.

1½ oz. light rum

½ oz. lime juice

½ oz. lemon juice

½ oz. orange juice

1 tsp. cream of coconut

1 tsp. orgeat syrup

Combine everything with cracked ice in a blender. Blend until smooth, and then pour into the serving glass.

Fern Gully

Serve in a chilled cocktail glass.

1 oz. dark Jamaica rum

1 oz. light rum

½ oz. coconut cream

1 oz. orange juice

½ oz. lime juice

½ oz. amaretto

Combine all ingredients in a blender with cracked ice. Blend thoroughly, and then pour into the serving glass.

Arawak Punch

Serve in a chilled old-fashioned glass.

1½ oz. gold Jamaica rum

½ oz. pineapple juice

½ oz. lime juice

1 tsp. orgeat syrup

Combine all ingredients in a shaker or blender with cracked ice. Shake or blend, and then pour into the serving glass.

Calypso Cocktail

Serve in a chilled cocktail glass.

1½ oz. gold Trinidad rum

1 oz. pineapple juice

½ oz. lemon juice

1 tsp. Falernum

Dash Angostura bitters

Pinch grated nutmeg

Combine all ingredients, except nutmeg, in a shaker or blender with cracked ice. Shake or blend, and then pour into the serving glass. Sprinkle with the nutmeg.

Guanabara Guava

Serve in a chilled Collins glass.

2 oz. gold rum

½ oz. maraschino liqueur

1½ oz. guava nectar

Juice of ½ lemon

½ oz. pineapple juice

1 tsp. coconut syrup

Lemon-lime soda

Lemon slice

Combine all ingredients, except the soda and lemon slice, in a shaker or blender with cracked ice. Shake or blend, and then pour into the serving glass. Top off with the soda, stir gently, and garnish with the lemon slice.

Black Witch

Serve in a chilled cocktail glass.

1½ oz. gold rum

½ oz. pineapple juice

1 tsp. dark Jamaican rum

1 tsp. apricot brandy

Combine all ingredients in a shaker or blender with cracked ice. Shake or blend, and then pour into the serving glass.

Batida de Piña

Serve in a chilled large glass, such as a double old-fashioned glass.

3 oz. light rum

⅔ cup crushed pineapple

1 tsp. sugar syrup

Mint sprig

Combine all ingredients, except the mint sprig, in a shaker or blender with cracked ice. Shake or blend, and then pour into the serving glass. Garnish with the mint sprig.

Daiquiris

To love and laughter and happily ever after!

Named for the little Cuban town near Santiago de Cuba, where the first Bacardi began operation, the daiquiri has a deceptively genteel reputation. Often considered a "ladies' drink," an unsweetened daiquiri made with 151-proof rum was a favorite of no less a macho figure than Ernest Hemingway.

Daiquiri

The classic daiquiri uses light rum. Shake long and hard in order to get a thoroughly chilled drink.

Serve in a chilled cocktail glass.

2 oz. light rum

½ tsp. sugar syrup

Juice of ½ lime

Orange slice

Combine all ingredients, except the orange slice, in a shaker with ice. Shake vigorously, and then strain into the serving glass.

Banana Daiquiri

A delightful and popular variation on the classic Daiquiri is made with banana.

Serve in a chilled cocktail glass.

1½ oz. light rum

½ oz. lime juice

1 tsp. sugar syrup

½ ripe banana, sliced

Combine all ingredients in a blender with cracked ice. Blend until smooth, and then pour into the serving glass.

Daiquiri Dark

If you prefer dark rum, try the Daiquiri Dark.

Serve in a chilled Collins glass.

2 oz. Jamaica rum

½ oz. lime juice

½ tsp. sugar syrup

Combine all ingredients in a shaker with ice. Shake vigorously, and then strain into the serving glass.

Strawberry Daiquiri

Serve in a chilled cocktail glass.

1½ oz. light rum

½ oz. lime juice

1 tsp. sugar syrup

6 large strawberries (fresh or frozen)

Combine all ingredients in a blender with cracked ice. Blend until smooth, and then pour into the serving glass.

Bar Tips

Exotic rum drinks are best served in fun vessels—the kitschier the better. Comb flea markets and second-hand stores for Hurricane glasses, totem cups, and the like. Freely substitute these for the glassware recommended in this chapter.

Peach Daiquiri

Peach-flavored drinks are gaining in popularity.

Serve in a chilled cocktail or wine glass.

2 oz. light rum

½ oz. lime juice

1 tsp. sugar syrup

½ oz. peach juice

Combine all ingredients in a blender with cracked ice. Blend until smooth, and then pour into the serving glass.

Frozen Daiquiri

As some folks see it, the only way to make a daiquiri is frozen. You'll need a blender and, for each drink, at least four ounces of ice. Let's begin with the generic Frozen Daiquiri, and then venture forth.

Serve in a chilled saucer champagne glass.

2 oz. light rum

½ oz. lime juice

1 tsp. sugar

Combine all ingredients in a blender with at least 4 oz. crushed ice. Blend at low speed until the mixture is snowy. Pour into the serving glass.

Frozen Peach Daiquiri

Serve in a chilled saucer champagne glass.

1½ oz. light rum

½ oz. lime juice

1 TB. diced peaches (may use fresh, canned, or frozen)

1 tsp. lemon juice

Combine all ingredients in a blender with at least 4 oz. crushed ice. Blend at low speed until the mixture is snowy. Pour into the serving glass.

Frozen Apple Daiquiri

Serve in a chilled saucer champagne glass.

½ oz. apple juice

½ oz. lime juice

1½ oz. light rum

½ tsp. sugar

Combine all ingredients in a blender with at least 4 oz. crushed ice. Blend at low speed until the mixture is snowy. Pour into the serving glass.

Frozen Banana Daiquiri

Serve in a chilled saucer champagne glass.

1½ oz. light rum

½ oz. lime juice

1 oz. banana liqueur

¼ banana, sliced

1 tsp. sugar (may omit, if desired)

½ oz. cream

Lime slice

Combine all ingredients, except lime slice, in a blender with at least 4 oz. crushed ice. Blend at low speed until the mixture is snowy. Pour into the serving glass. Garnish with the lime slice.

Frozen Chambord Daiquiri

Serve in a chilled saucer champagne glass.

¾ oz. Chambord

¾ oz. light rum

Juice of ½ lime

1 tsp. powdered sugar

4 black raspberries

Combine all ingredients, including fruit, in a blender with at least 4 oz. crushed ice. Blend at low speed until the mixture is snowy. Pour into the serving glass.

Frozen Cherry Daiquiri

Serve in a chilled saucer champagne glass.

1½ oz. light rum

½ oz. cherry brandy

½ oz. lime juice

Several dashes of kirsch

Lime slice

Combine all ingredients, except lime slice, in a blender with at least 4 oz. crushed ice. Blend at low speed until the mixture is snowy. Pour into the serving glass. Garnish with the lime slice.

Frozen Mint Daiquiri

Serve in a chilled saucer champagne glass.

2½ oz. light rum

2 tsp. lime juice

1 tsp. sugar

6 mint leaves

Combine all ingredients in a blender with at least 4 oz. crushed ice. Blend at low speed until the mixture is snowy. Pour into the serving glass. Garnish with the lime slice.

Frozen Gin Daiquiri

Rum not enough for you? Try this potent combination.

Serve in a chilled saucer champagne glass.

1½ oz. gin

½ oz. light rum

2 tsp. lime juice

1 tsp. sugar

Lime slice

Combine all ingredients, except lime slice, in a blender with at least 4 oz. crushed ice. Blend at low speed until the mixture is snowy. Pour into the serving glass. Garnish with the lime slice.

Frozen Fruit Daiquiri

For this one, choose fresh fruit to your liking, and then have at it!

Serve in a chilled saucer champagne glass.

1½ oz. light rum

½ oz. whiskey sour mix

1 oz. fruit liqueur of your choice

1 oz. honey

½ oz. cream

Fresh fruit of your choice

Combine all ingredients, except lime slice, in a blender with at least 4 oz. crushed ice. Blend at low speed until the mixture is snowy. Pour into the serving glass. Garnish with the lime slice.

Citrus Creations

Not surprisingly, the spirit of the tropics has a natural affinity for the fruit of the tropics. Black Stripe is a rich, thick combination of dark rum, molasses (whence the rum came), and lemon juice.

Black Stripe

Serve in a chilled cocktail glass.

2 oz. dark Jamaica rum

½ oz. golden molasses

½ oz. lime juice

Combine all ingredients in a blender with cracked ice. Blend until smooth, and then pour into the serving glass.

Javier Saavedra

Serve in a chilled cocktail glass.

1 oz. dark Jamaica rum

1 oz. white tequila

2 oz. pineapple juice

1 oz. grapefruit juice

Orange slice

Combine all ingredients, except the orange slice, in a shaker or blender with cracked ice. Shake or blend, and then strain into serving glass. Garnish with the orange slice.

Navy Grog

The original Navy Grog was nothing more than rum cut with water. The following version, for civilian consumption, is rather more elaborate.

Serve in a chilled large (double) old-fashioned glass.

1 oz. light rum

1 oz. dark Jamaica rum

1 oz. 86-proof Demerara rum

½ oz. orange juice

½ oz. guava juice

½ oz. lime juice

½ oz. pineapple juice

½ oz. orgeat syrup

Lime slice

Mint sprig

Combine all ingredients, except the lime slice and mint sprig, in a shaker with cracked ice. Shake vigorously, and then pour into the serving glass and garnish with the lime slice and mint sprig.

Buzzed Words

Grog was originally nothing more than rum diluted with water and rationed to sailors of the eighteenth-century Royal Navy. Its namesake was Admiral Edward Vernon (1684– 1757), who first ordered the ration: Vernon's nickname was Old Grogram, after his habit of wearing a grogram (coarse wool) cloak.

A zombie is one of the walking dead, a soulless body reanimated by voodoo. One of the most famous rum drinks combines three kinds of rum with curaçao and Pernod, as well as a host of citrus juices to create a libation whose effect can indeed rob one of consciousness, if not soul. The Zombie takes a bit of effort to build.

Zombie

Serve in a chilled Collins glass.

2 oz. light rum	1 oz. pineapple juice
1 oz. dark Jamaican rum	½ oz. papaya juice
½ oz. 151-proof Demerara rum	¼ oz. grenadine
1 oz. curaçao	½ oz. orgeat syrup
1 tsp. Pernod	Mint sprig
1 oz. lemon juice	Pineapple stick
1 oz. orange juice	

Combine all ingredients, except the pineapple stick and mint sprig, in a blender with 3 oz. cracked ice. Blend until smooth, and then pour into the serving glass and garnish with the mint sprig and pineapple stick.

Island Hopping

The allure of rum is that it's the tropics in a bottle and can transform any social gathering into an exotic vacation. Here's a collection of drinks that summon up faraway places.

Elvis Presley devotees will want to sample the Blue Hawaiian, which you might like to think was named after the King's 1961 film. Go ahead. Think what you want.

Blue Hawaiian

Serve in a chilled Collins glass.

2 oz. light rum

1 oz. blue curaçao

1 oz. sour mix

1 oz. orange juice

1 oz. pineapple juice

Combine all ingredients in a blender with 3 oz. cracked ice. Blend until smooth, and then pour into the serving glass.

Hurricane

Long a favorite tourist drink in New Orleans, this is the straight-up cocktail version of the Hurricane.

Serve in a chilled cocktail glass.

1 oz. light rum

1 oz. gold rum

½ oz. passion fruit syrup

½ oz. lime juice

Combine all ingredients in a shaker with ice. Shake vigorously, and then strain into the serving glass.

Little Dix Mix

Serve in a chilled old-fashioned glass.

1½ oz. dark Jamaica rum

½ oz. crème de banana

½ oz. lime juice

1 tsp. curaçao

Combine all ingredients with cracked ice in a shaker or blender. Shake or blend. Pour into serving glass.

Mai Tai

The featured drink of kitschy "Oriental" restaurants all across North America, the Mai Tai is a classic that belongs in every bartender's repertoire. Break out the miniature paper umbrellas. The first recipe is the "original" Mai Tai, as prepared in the Trader Vic's restaurant chain.

Serve in a chilled old-fashioned glass.

1 oz. Jamaica rum

1 oz. Martinique rum

½ oz. curaçao

¼ oz. rock-candy syrup

¼ oz. orgeat syrup

Lime twist

Mint sprig

Pineapple stick

Combine all ingredients, except the twist, sprig, and stick, in a shaker with cracked ice. Shake vigorously, and then pour into the serving glass and garnish with the lime, mint, and pineapple.

Rum with Liqueurs and Brandy

We begin with the following salaciously named drink. Enough said.

Between the Sheets

Serve in a chilled cocktail glass.

¾ oz. light rum

¾ oz. brandy

¾ oz. Cointreau

½ oz. lemon juice

Combine all ingredients with ice in a shaker. Shake vigorously, and then strain into the serving glass.

Outrigger

Nothing savors more of the islands than an Outrigger.

Serve in a chilled cocktail glass.

1 oz. gold rum

1 oz. brandy

1 oz. triple sec

½ oz. lime juice

Combine all ingredients in a shaker with ice. Shake vigorously, and then strain into the serving glass.

Tiger's Milk

A fabled drink, Tiger's Milk is something you really should know how to make.

Serve in a chilled wine goblet.

1½ oz. Bacardi Anejo gold rum

1½ oz. cognac

4 oz. half-and-half

Sugar syrup to taste

Grated nutmeg

Combine all ingredients, except nutmeg, in a shaker with cracked ice. Shake vigorously, and then pour into the serving glass. Dust with grated nutmeg.

Toast

All that we have drank, sang, and dance, no one will ever take away from us.

Planter's Punch Variations

Planter's Punch is claimed as the property of the folks who make Myers's Rum. This is the recipe you'll find on a bottle of their dark rum.

Planter's Punch

Serve in a chilled Collins glass.

2 oz. Myers's dark rum

3 oz. orange juice

Juice of ½ lemon or lime

1 tsp. sugar

Dash grenadine

Orange slice

Maraschino cherry

Combine all ingredients, except fruit, in a shaker with cracked ice. Shake vigorously, and then pour into the serving glass. Garnish with the orange slice and maraschino cherry.

Plantation Punch

The Plantation Punch throws Southern Comfort and brown sugar into the mix.

Serve in a chilled Collins glass.

1½ oz. dark Jamaica rum

¾ oz. Southern Comfort

1 tsp. brown sugar

1 oz. lemon juice

Club soda to fill

Orange slice

Lemon slice

1 tsp. port

Combine all ingredients, except club soda, fruit, and port, in a shaker with cracked ice. Shake vigorously, and then pour into the serving glass. Add club soda to fill and garnish with the fruit. Top off with the port.

Coffee Drinks

Jamaican Coffee (a.k.a Calypso)

Jamaican coffee is also called a Calypso and makes a splendid after-dinner drink.

Serve in a coffee mug.

¾ oz. Tia Maria

¾ oz. Jamaican rum

Hot coffee

Whipped cream

Pour Tia Maria and rum into the mug and add coffee. Top with whipped cream.

Café Foster

1 oz. light or dark rum

½ oz. crème de banana

Hot coffee

Whipped cream

Pour rum and crème de banana into mug. Add coffee to fill, and then top with whipped cream.

The Rum Millennium

Rum wants to mix with just about anything in any number of ways. Redolent of the islands, it invites exploration.

In addition to the many original mixed drinks featuring rum, the tropical spirit can stand in for a variety of liquors in familiar drinks. See Appendix B for all the rum variations of classics like the martini, the Collins, and the screwdriver. Here are five exciting new drinks.

Yachtsman's Proverb

Serve in a wine goblet.

1 oz. dark rum

1 oz. gold Jamaican rum

2 oz. cream of coconut

1 oz. pineapple juice

Maraschino cherry

Combine all ingredients, except cherry, in a blender with at least 4 oz. crushed ice. Blend at low speed until the mixture is snowy. Pour into the serving glass. Garnish with the cherry.

Thunder Lover

Serve in a wine goblet.

2 oz. dark rum

1 oz. gold rum

2 oz. cream of coconut

1 TB. 151-proof rum

Combine all ingredients in a shaker with cracked ice. Shake vigorously, and then strain into the serving glass.

Septic Tank

Serve in a highball glass.

2 oz. Bailey's Irish Cream

1 oz. green crème de menthe

2 TB. dark rum

Combine all ingredients in a shaker with cracked ice. Shake vigorously, and then strain into the serving glass.

Fig-Leaf Flip

Serve on the rocks in an old-fashioned glass.

1½ oz. sweet vermouth

1 oz. light rum

1½ TB. lime juice

Few dashes Angostura bitters

Combine in a shaker with cracked ice. Shake, and then strain over ice into the serving glass.

Organ Grinder

Serve over crushed ice in a large glass, such as a double old-fashioned glass.

1 oz. dark rum

1 oz. light rum

1 oz. whiskey

1 TB. white crème de menthe

2 oz. cream of coconut

Coconut shavings

Combine all ingredients, except coconut shavings, in a blender with cracked ice. Blend thoroughly, and then into the serving glass pour over crushed ice. Sprinkle with the coconut shavings.

The Least You Need to Know

- Few people know or appreciate the wide variety of rums produced; unfortunately, only a relatively small fraction of these spirits are available in most American liquor stores.
- Rum starts out as molasses, which contains the sugar that is the basis of the spirit's fermentation. For this reason, you will taste more of the raw ingredient in rum than in any other spirit.
- The taste and character of rum varies greatly from one country of origin to the next.
- Light or gold rum is usually best for mixing; except in a few special recipes, the dark rums are best enjoyed on the rocks or in a snifter, like brandy.

Chapter 14

From the Halls of Montezuma: Tequila!

In This Chapter

- How to drink tequila, Pancho-Villa style
- The origin of tequila
- How tequila is made
- Tequila in white and gold
- Tequila recipes

Tequila—at least on the U.S. side of the border—has long been tainted by disreputable myth. The truly callow still regard it as a hallucinogen—rendered particularly vile by the inclusion of a worm in the bottle—but, even among more sophisticated drinkers, tequila often has a reputation as a crude, harsh beverage redolent of raw yeast and industrial solvent.

The mistaken idea that tequila is a hallucinogen comes from confusing it with another spirit, *mescal*, which, like tequila, is made from the *agave* plant (a spineless cactus), albeit a different species. But the only things mescal shares with *mescaline*—a true hallucinogen—are the first two syllables of its name. The origin of mescal is agave, whereas mescaline comes from peyote.

What's more, reports of raw, harsh, and otherwise disagreeable qualities are unfounded as far as genuine tequila is concerned. The quality of this spirit must meet strict standards set by the Mexican government. The standards came about partly because tourists were often sold cheap, inferior products, which gave tequila a bad rap. As to the worm, you might find it in a bottle of mescal, but, by Mexican law, never in tequila.

If you're surprised by what you've read so far, there's quite a bit more to tell you about this pungent, faintly sweet, deliciously yeasty spirit, which continues to grow in popularity north of the border.

The Mexican Itch

As mixologist John J. Poister describes in *The New American Bartender's Guide*, the "Mexican Itch" is the "original" way to imbibe tequila. You walk into any Mexican *cantina*, belly up to the bar, and say, "*Tequila estilo Pancho Villa, por favor.*" Tequila, Pancho-Villa style.

It seems that Villa (1878–1923), a folk hero who combined the roles of bandit and revolutionary guerrilla, enjoyed his tequila in shots served with a lime wedge and coarse salt. In Villa's day, this was known as the Mexican Itch. Nowadays, we call the "Mexican Itch" a tequila shooter, and here's how you do it:

1. The tequila part is easy. Just pour a shot—a jigger—of white tequila in a shot glass.
2. Take a lime wedge between the thumb and forefinger of your left hand. (Unless you're left-handed. You're doing the shot with your good hand.)
3. Put a liberal pinch of coarse kitchen salt (not fine table salt) directly behind the held wedge, in the little hollow on the back of your hand between the base of your thumb and the base of your forefinger. (It helps to lick your hand first, so the salt stays put.)
4. Pick up the shot of tequila in your right hand.
5. Lick the salt, immediately down the tequila in a gulp, and then suck the lime.

At this point, feel free to bang the bar several times as you struggle to resume normal respiration.

Tequila's Royal Heritage

The Toltec people ruled central Mexico from the tenth to the twelfth centuries. They amassed an empire, which was subsequently invaded and conquered by the Aztecs in the middle of the twelfth century.

Some Toltec person—legend says he was of royal blood—discovered what he called a miracle plant, the pineapple. Like agave, the base of the pineapple plant fills with sweet sap, which this Toltec called *agua miel*—"honey water." The Toltecs fermented the honey water to produce what Mexicans today call *pulque*, a refreshing and only mildly alcoholic beverage.

Anyway, the rest of the story goes that the Toltec discoverer of honey water sent his daughter, the beautiful Princess Xochitl, to the principal ruler of the Toltecs. The ruler liked the honey water, and he loved Xochitl, whom he made his queen. Presumably everyone lived happily ever after.

Until, of course, the Aztecs invaded.

Four hundred years after they conquered the Toltecs, the Aztecs made the mistake of welcoming a band of highly dubious Spanish visitors led by one Hernan Cortés. Aztec-Spanish relations quickly deteriorated, and eventually the great Indian empire was pillaged, ravished, and conquered.

Although they destroyed Aztec civilization, the Spanish conquistadors did do something constructive. They introduced distillation into the conquered realm and tried it out on fermented honey water. Tequila was born.

Geography South of the Border

Or *something* was born. Maybe it was mescal. By Mexican law, to be called *tequila*, the spirit must have been distilled from mash derived exclusively from the blue agave, a plant that takes a full 10 years to mature and is cultivated in a strictly defined region surrounding the town of Tequila in the state of Jalisco. In contrast, mescal production is not subject to strict government regulation or geographical restrictions.

To make tequila, the hearts of the agave are harvested and taken to steam ovens for roasting. They are then shredded, and their juice expressed; sugar is added to promote fermentation; and then, after four days, the fermented fluid is double-distilled to produce a clear spirit that, after filtration, can be bottled directly or aged in oak casks for less than a year or as long as seven.

Tequila Varieties

Sample the various tequila brands imported into this country and choose your favorite. You should be aware of the two basic varieties, whatever the brand: the white tequila and the gold. White is unaged, bottled immediately after distillation. The gold, which sometimes shades into the brown range, called *tequila añejo*, is aged in oak casks. It acquires its color just as whiskey does, from the chemical interaction with the oak.

Buzzed Words

Tequila añejo is tequila that has been aged in oak casks, acquiring a gold or brown coloring. Unaged tequila is clear and called **white** tequila.

The difference between white tequila and *tequila añejo* is immediately apparent to the drinker. The aged product is much smoother and mellower, and the longer it has aged, the smoother and mellower it will be. It also costs more. White tequila is not a sipping drink. Either mix it or take it as a shooter, with salt and a lime wedge. *Tequila añejo*, however, can be mixed or savored slowly, like good whiskey or a fine cognac.

Tequila Estilo Pancho Villa con Sangrita, Por Favor!

Before we get into the tequila recipes, let's take note of way to enhance your experience of the simple "Mexican Itch"—the shooter. Consider chasing your shooter with *sangrita*, a traditional Mexican concoction sans alcohol. Sangrita is available premixed in stores that specialize in Mexican foods, or you can mix your own:

Sangrita

Yields 3½ cups.

2 cups tomato juice

1 cup orange juice

2 oz. lime juice

2 tsp. Tabasco sauce (or to taste)

2 tsp. very finely minced onion

2 tsp. Worcestershire sauce (or to taste)

3 pinches white pepper

Pinch celery salt (to taste)

Combine all ingredients in a blender. Blend thoroughly, and then strain into a container for chilling in the refrigerator.

The idea is to take a shot, and then drink down some *sangrita.*

By the way, sangrita makes an extremely fiery Bloody Mary or Tequila Maria mix. Just add 1½ oz. vodka (for a Bloody Mary) or tequila (for a Tequila Maria) to 4 oz. Sangrita. (You'll find another recipe for a tequila-based Bloody Mary later in the chapter.)

Margaritas

The margarita, the most popular tequila cocktail, is a natural evolution from the tequila shooter. It is essentially tequila combined with lime. The combining takes place not in your mouth and gullet—the case with the shooter—but more genteelly, in a glass. A half-ounce of triple sec sweetens the deal.

The following margarita recipes are all served in glasses rimmed with coarse salt. See Chapter 5 for information on how to rim a glass.

Some prefer their margarita on the rocks, but it goes down great as a frozen drink and is often requested as such. You'll need a *large* cocktail glass or a *large* wine goblet to serve one.

Bar Tips

Traditionally, bartenders rim margarita glasses with coarse salt. (See Chapter 5 for information on how to rim a glass.) Many drinkers find a 50/50 mixture of salt and sugar more palatable. Try it.

Margarita

Serve in a chilled cocktail glass, optionally rimmed with coarse salt.

1½ oz. tequila (white or gold)

½ oz. triple sec

Juice of ½ large lime (or whole small lime)

Coarse salt

Lime slice

Combine all ingredients, except the lime slice, in a shaker with ice. Shake vigorously, and then strain into the serving glass. Garnish with the lime slice.

Frozen Margarita

Serve in a large chilled cocktail glass or large chilled wine goblet rimmed with salt.

1½ oz. white tequila

½ oz. triple sec

1 oz. lemon or lime juice

Coarse salt

Lime slice

Put approximately 2 cups cracked ice in a blender. Add all ingredients except salt and lime slice. Blend until slushy. The mixture should be firm rather than watery. Pour into the serving glass. Garnish with the lime slice.

Frozen Fruit Margarita

An exciting variation on the Frozen Margarita is the Frozen *Fruit* Margarita. *You* pick the fruit—such as raspberries with raspberry liqueur, or bananas with banana liqueur.

Serve in a large, chilled cocktail glass or wine goblet rimmed with salt.

1½ oz. white tequila

½ oz. triple sec

½ oz. sour mix

Fresh fruit to taste

1 oz. fruit liqueur to harmonize with fresh fruit chosen

Dash Rose's lime juice

Coarse salt

Lime slice

Put approximately 2 cups cracked ice in a blender. Add all ingredients except salt and lime slice. Blend until slushy. The mixture should be firm rather than watery. Pour into the serving glass. Garnish with lime slice.

Blue Margarita

You can also depart from the familiar straight-up margarita. This blue one should shake things up.

Serve in a large, chilled cocktail glass or wine goblet rimmed with salt.

2 oz. white tequila

¾ oz. blue curaçao

2 oz. sour mix

½ oz. lime juice

Coarse salt

Lime slice

Combine all ingredients, except salt and lime slice, in a shaker with ice. Shake vigorously, and then strain into the serving glass. Garnish with the lime slice.

Strawberry Margarita

Serve in a wine goblet.

1½ oz. tequila

½ oz. triple sec

½ oz. strawberry schnapps
(may substitute a strawberry liqueur)

1 oz. lime juice

6 strawberries (if desired)

In a shaker or blender with cracked ice, combine all ingredients except the strawberries. Shake or blend, and then pour into serving glass. Garnish with strawberries.

Top-Shelf Margarita

Serve in a chilled cocktail glass rimmed with salt.

1½ oz. gold tequila

½ oz. Grand Marnier

1 oz. sour mix

1 oz. lime juice

Coarse salt

Lime slice

Combine all ingredients, except the salt and lime slice, in a shaker with ice. Shake vigorously, and then strain into the serving glass. Garnish with the lime slice.

Margarita, My Honey

Serve in a chilled cocktail glass rimmed with salt.

1½ oz. gold tequila

¾ oz. Cointreau

Juice of ½ lime

Juice of ½ lemon

2 drops honey

Drop orange juice

Coarse salt

Lime slice

Combine all ingredients, except the salt and lime slice, in a shaker with ice. Shake vigorously, and then strain into the serving glass. Garnish with the lime slice.

Ultimate Margarita

Serve in a chilled cocktail glass rimmed with salt.

1½ oz. premium tequila añejo

¾ oz. Cointreau

1 oz. freshly squeezed lemon juice

½ oz. freshly squeezed lime juice

½ tsp. sugar

Coarse salt

Lime slice

Combine all ingredients, except the salt and lime slice, in a shaker with ice. Shake vigorously, and then strain into the serving glass. Garnish with the lime slice.

Other Tequila Classics

The margarita might be the only tequila cocktail many people know, but it is hardly the end of this spirit's repertoire.

What the Doctor Ordered

A popular soft drink is the key ingredient in the Mexican Pepper Pot.

Mexican Pepper Pot

1½ oz. tequila

Dr Pepper

Lime wedge

Into a highball glass half filled with ice cubes pour tequila, and then top off with Dr Pepper. Squeeze the juice of the lime wedge into the drink and drop in the lime husk.

Sneaky Pete

A lot of tequila's off-color rep derives from its confusion with mescal, which, in days gone by, was often indifferently made and palmed off on unsuspecting tourists, who discovered that the libation had all the charm of a Mickey Finn. "It just snuck up on me," many a groggy gringo must have said. Anyway, cheap mescal was christened Sneaky Pete—and that name is all it shares with this modern drink.

Sneaky Pete

Serve in a chilled cocktail glass.

2 oz. white tequila

½ oz. white crème de menthe

½ oz. pineapple juice

½ oz. lime or lemon juice

Lime slice

Combine all ingredients, except the lime slice, in a shaker with cracked ice. Shake vigorously, and then pour into the serving glass. Garnish with lime slice.

Fur Bath

If you are looking for something with an effect closer to the original Sneaky Pete, here are some especially potent formulas.

Serve on the rocks in an old-fashioned glass.

2 oz. tequila

1 oz. bourbon

Pulpy orange juice

½ tsp. grenadine

Combine the tequila and bourbon over ice in the serving glass. Fill with orange juice. Stir. Float the grenadine. Do not stir again.

Alice in Wonderland

Serve in a chilled highball glass.

1 oz. vodka

1 oz. tequila

1 oz. light rum

1 oz. gin

1 tsp. raspberry syrup

Chill all ingredients in the refrigerator for two hours. Slowly pour into the serving glass in the order listed. Do not mix or stir, but try to achieve a layered effect.

Double Trigger

Serve on the rocks in a highball glass.

1 oz. vodka

1 oz. tequila

2 oz. sweet vermouth

½ oz. orange juice

Combine the spirits in a shaker with cracked ice. Shake, and then strain over ice into the serving glass. Top off with orange juice.

Border Crosser

Serve on the rocks in a lowball glass.

1½ oz. tequila

1½ oz. blended whiskey

2 TB. orange juice

Combine all ingredients with cracked ice in a shaker. Shake, and then strain over ice in the serving glass.

Destiny Special

Serve on the rocks in a Collins glass.

1 oz. vodka

½ oz. sloe gin

½ oz. sweet vermouth

½ oz. tequila

1 tsp. lime juice

Club soda

Maraschino cherry

Combine all ingredients, except the cherry, over ice in the serving glass, topping off with the club soda. Garnish with the cherry.

Tequila Sunrises

A popular drink that's pretty to look at, the Tequila Sunrise is not so much layered as it is shaded, one level dissolving into another. Make it carefully, and you'll quickly see where the name came from.

Tequila Sunrise

Serve in a chilled Collins glass.

1½ oz. white or gold tequila

Juice of ½ lime

3 oz. orange juice

¾ oz. grenadine

Lime slice

Combine all ingredients, except grenadine and lime slice, in a shaker with cracked ice. Shake vigorously, and then pour into the serving glass. *Carefully* add the grenadine. *Do not stir!* Garnish with lime slice.

Alternate Tequila Sunrise

An alternate take.

Serve on the rocks in a highball glass.

1½ oz. tequila

2 dashes lime juice

2 drops lemon juice

Orange juice

½ oz. grenadine

Carefully pour in order over ice in the serving glass, floating the grenadine last. *Do not stir!*

Embellished Tequila Sunrise

An embellished sunrise.

Serve in a Collins glass with cracked ice.

1½ oz. tequila

Juice of ½ lime

Club soda

½ oz. crème de cassis

2 dashes Cointreau

Lime slice

In a Collins glass one-third filled with cracked ice combine the tequila, cassis, and lime juice. Add soda to fill, and then top off with the Cointreau. Do not stir. Garnish with the lime slice.

Tequila Sunset

The tequila also sets, as shown in the Tequila Sunset.

Serve in a chilled Collins glass.

1½ oz. white tequila

3 dashes lime juice

Orange juice to fill

½ oz. blackberry brandy

Combine the tequila and lime juice in the serving glass filled with ice. Add orange juice to fill. Stir. *Carefully* pour the blackberry brandy into the drink down a twisted-handle bar spoon (see Chapter 5). Allow the brandy to rise from the bottom. *Do not stir!*

Citrus Mixers

You can combine tequila with any drinkable citrus juice and have a refreshing, great-tasting beverage. An ounce and a half of tequila to four ounces of orange, grapefruit, or pineapple juice makes a fine on-the-rocks libation. A few more inventive concoctions follow.

Matador

Serve in a chilled cocktail glass.

1½ oz. white or gold tequila

3 oz. pineapple juice

1 oz. lime juice

½ tsp. sugar syrup

Combine all ingredients in a shaker with ice. Shake vigorously, and then strain into the serving glass.

If you prefer, the Matador can be sweetened with the likes of honey, grenadine, coconut syrup, triple sec, or other sweeteners instead of the simple sugar syrup.

Royal Matador

Serve in pineapple shell.

1 whole pineapple

3 oz. gold tequila

1½ oz. framboise

Juice of 1 lime

1 tsp. amaretto

This recipe makes two drinks.

Remove the top from the pineapple and set top, with leaves, aside. Scoop out the pineapple, taking care to avoid puncturing the shell. Put the pineapple chunks into a blender and extract the juice. Strain the juice, and then pour back into blender. Add the other ingredients with cracked ice. Blend thoroughly, and then serve in the pineapple shell. Add additional ice to taste. Replace the top of the pineapple shell and serve with long straws.

Changuirongo

Serve on the rocks in a Collins glass.

1½ oz. white or gold tequila

Citrus-flavored soda

Lime or lemon wedge

Combine tequila and soda over ice in the serving glass. Garnish with the fruit wedge.

Sauzaliky

Serve in a wine goblet.

1½ oz. tequila

3 oz. orange juice

Dash lime juice

½ banana, ripe

Combine all ingredients in a blender with cracked ice. Blend until smooth, and then pour into the serving glass.

Gringo Swizzle

Serve on the rocks in a large (14 oz.) Collins glass.

2 oz. tequila

½ oz. crème de cassis

1 oz. lime juice

1 oz. pineapple juice

1 oz. orange juice

Ginger ale

Combine all ingredients, except ginger ale, in a blender with cracked ice. Blend until smooth, and then pour over ice into the serving glass. Top off with ginger ale.

Can Can

Serve in a large glass, such as a double old-fashioned glass.

1½ oz. white tequila

½ oz. dry vermouth

4 oz. grapefruit juice

½ tsp. sugar syrup

Orange slice

Combine all ingredients, except the orange slice, in a shaker or blender with cracked ice. Shake or blend, and then pour into the serving glass. Garnish with the orange slice.

Chapala

Serve in an old-fashioned glass.

1½ oz. tequila

¾ oz. orange juice

¾ oz. lemon juice

½ oz. grenadine

Orange slice

Combine all ingredients, except the orange slice, in a shaker or blender with cracked ice. Shake or blend, and then pour into the serving glass. Garnish with the orange slice.

Caramba

Serve in a highball glass.

1½ oz. white tequila

3 oz. grapefruit juice

1 tsp. sugar

Club soda

Combine all ingredients, except the soda, in a shaker with cracked ice. Shake, then pour into the serving glass. Top off with the soda.

Tequila with Liqueur

Tequila blends beautifully with a number of liqueurs including Kahlúa, anisette, and brandy.

Brave Bull

Serve in a chilled old-fashioned glass.

1½ oz. white tequila

¾ oz. Kahlúa

Lemon twist

Combine all ingredients, except the twist, in a shaker with cracked ice. Shake vigorously, and then pour into the glass. Garnish with the twist.

Torridora Mexicano

Coffee-flavored brandy is another unlikely—but delectable—mate for tequila.

1½ oz. tequila

¾ oz. coffee-flavored brandy

Juice of ½ lime

In a shaker or blender with cracked ice, combine all ingredients. Shake or blend, and then strain into a chilled cocktail glass.

Crazy Nun

Mexico has a pervasive Catholic heritage, which influenced the naming of this drink: *Monja Loca*—Crazy Nun.

Serve in an old-fashioned glass filled with finely crushed ice.

1½ oz. white or gold tequila

1½ oz. anisette

Combine all ingredients in the serving glass filled with finely crushed ice. Stir well.

The Crazy Nun can be made drier by adding less anisette.

Quick One

Man at the bar is coughing and sneezing over his tequila-and-orange juice.

"Sick?" asks the fellow on the next stool.

"Doc told me that the only way to kill these kind of germs is plenty of orange juice."

"Oh, I see."

"Trouble is: How do I get *them* to drink it?"

Tequila with Rum—Yes, Rum

Mexico is quite a distance from the islands of the Caribbean, but tequila has made the acquaintance of rum, and these two light spirits marry beautifully.

Berta's Special is also called a Taxco Fizz and was invented at Bertita's Bar in Taxco, a town in south-central Mexico. The town had been a silver mining center since pre-Columbian times. It is still renowned for its silver—and for little saloons like Bertita's. The Berta's Special requires an entire egg white for one drink.

The Coco Loco—crazy coconut—is a blast to make and great fun to drink. You'll need some straws! And, please, read the directions before you tackle the coconut. (Don't try handling the saw after you've had one of these!)

Berta's Special

Serve in a chilled tall Collins glass.

2 oz. tequila

Juice of 1 lime

1 tsp. sugar syrup (may substitute honey)

Liberal dashes orange bitters

1 egg white*

Club soda to fill

Lime slice

Combine all ingredients, except the club soda and lime slice, in a shaker with cracked ice. Shake vigorously, and then pour into the serving glass. Add club soda to fill. Garnish with the lime slice.

**Raw egg is a source of salmonella bacteria. You may wish to avoid drinks calling for raw egg yolk or white.*

Coco Loco

Serve in a coconut (see directions).

1 coconut

1 oz. white tequila

1 oz. gin

1 oz. light rum

1 oz. pineapple juice

Sugar syrup to taste

½ fresh lime

Prepare the coconut by carefully sawing off the top. Do not spill out the coconut milk. Add cracked ice to the coconut, and then pour in the liquid ingredients. Squeeze in the lime juice, and then drop in the lime shell. Stir. Sip through straws.

As popular as it has become in the United States, tequila is still *relatively* new to American drinkers, and there is a great deal of room for new tequila inventions. In the meantime, bold bartenders and drinkers have found places for tequila in a host of trusted stand-bys. For example, the sour turns out to be a natural with tequila. Don't use sour mix, but lime or lemon juice instead. The Tequila Manhattan requires a premium-label *tequila añejo.* Go easy on the sweet vermouth. See Appendix B for a full list of classic tequila variations.

Bar Tips

You'll find a recipe for a tequila martini—the Tequini—in Chapter 8.

New Ideas from Old Mexico

As with rum, tequila has found favor among the more adventurous mixologists of the new millennium. Here are a few ideas.

Killer's Cocktail

Serve in a chilled cocktail glass.

1½ oz. tequila

1½ oz. Tennessee whiskey

Combine in a shaker with cracked ice. Shake, and then strain into the serving glass.

False Hope

Serve on the rocks in a highball glass.

2 oz. tequila

1 oz. sloe gin

1 tsp. grenadine

Combine in a shaker with cracked ice. Shake vigorously, and then strain over ice into the serving glass.

Arizona Special

Serve in a shot glass.

1½ oz. tequila

¼ oz. Jagermeister

Combine in the shot glass. Drink.

Cobra Venom

Serve in a chilled cocktail glass.

2 oz. tequila

1 TB. lemon juice

1 TB. gin

Combine in a shaker with cracked ice. Shake, and then strain into the serving glass.

Fists of Stone

Serve on the rocks in a highball glass.

1½ oz. tequila

Lemon slice

1½ oz. sweet vermouth

Combine the spirits in a shaker with cracked ice. Shake, and then strain over ice into the serving glass. Garnish with the lemon slice.

The Least You Need to Know

- Contrary to its reputation in some quarters, tequila is a highly refined spirit, which is made in conformity with strict standards set by the Mexican government.
- Tequila was born when the Spanish conquistadors began distilling the fermented juice of the agave.
- Folklore aside, tequila contains no hallucinogens.
- Choose gold tequila—*tequila añejo*—for sipping and for selected mixed drinks; white tequila is for shooters and most mixed drinks.

Part 5

Just Desserts

Most drinkers enjoy different spirits at different times of day and evening. After dinner is the hour for brandy or cognac and perhaps a cordial. And it is the festive time, too, for hot or flaming drinks or, perhaps, the layered miniatures known as *pousse-cafés.*

Here is a chapter on what to look for in good brandy or fine cognac, and how to use these spirits in a delicious array of mixed drinks. Next, we turn to the liqueurs, exploring their origins in medieval medicine and describing the palette of flavors available to those who would drink them.

Then there comes a time in every bartender's life when he or she wants to do something truly spectacular. The last two chapters in this section teach you how to flame drinks safely and splendidly and how to create magically layered drinks sure to command grateful awe from anyone you want to impress.

Chapter 15

Snifter's Bouquet: The Brandy/Cognac Mystique

In This Chapter

- V.S.O.P. and other coded messages
- How brandy is made
- The brandy-producing regions
- Brandy vs. cognac
- "Flavored" or "fruit" brandies
- Brandy and cognac recipes

Brandy used to be a lot more important than it is now. It was called "water of life" in French—*eau de vie*. Brandy was employed as a tonic and as a medicine. That's why the St. Bernard dogs of the hospice founded by Saint Bernard of Montjoux in the Pennine Alps carried miniature brandy kegs. In 300 years of service as rescuers and pathfinders, these animals carried *eau de vie* to some 2,500 snowbound or lost travelers.

Even more importantly, through the many centuries when Europe's water supplies were rife with disease, brandy was mixed with the water to render it potable. Brandy was, in fact, Europe's first distilled spirit and was almost universally consumed.

Today, brandy—and especially its regal incarnation as cognac—is regarded with feelings ranging from respect to awe, and, like fine champagne, it has earned a place of honor as a ceremonial libation, typically reserved for special occasions. That's fine, but brandy also makes a delicious and very useful mixer in a host of drinks that you can enjoy any time.

That's VSOP, Not RSVP

Part of the brandy/cognac mystique is locked within the letters *V.O.* or *V.S.O.P.* printed on the label. You need be puzzled no longer. V.O. just stands for *very old*, but is, in fact, applied to brandies of a rather young age (as brandy goes), at least four and a half years. V.S.O.P. stands for *very superior old pale* and indicates a truly old brandy, usually 10 years old or more.

Costly premium cognacs sport a few additional appellations, the best-known of which is "Napoleon." At one time, a "Napoleon brandy" really was one that had been put in the cask during the reign of the great French emperor, 1804–1814. Nowadays, it just indicates a very, very old brandy. There is no standard, but some Napoleons exceed 50 years!

Bar Tips

Unlike wine, brandy stops aging once it is removed from the wooden cask and bottled, so the bottling date is of no significance. There is a practical limit to how long brandy may age. After about 60 years, aging becomes deterioration.

What does aging do to brandy? The effect is twofold. To begin with, there is simply something magical about consuming a drink that was prepared years ago. You're dipping, quite literally, into history. Speaking more practically, however, aging renders the flavor of brandy or cognac more complex, more subtle, more interesting, and makes the drink smoother and mellower.

The Story of Eau de Vie

Like basic wine, basic brandy is the product of fermented grape juice. Unlike wine, the fermented liquid is distilled, thereby significantly raising its alcohol content, before aging in wooden casks.

Those are the basics. But brandy comes in many variations, in terms of region, distillation method, aging duration and method, and even the fruit used for brandies are hardly limited to the grape.

Brandies from France and Elsewhere

The most celebrated brandy-producing nation in the world is France, but brandies are also distilled in Switzerland, Germany, Hungary, Spain, Italy, Greece, Peru, Mexico, South Africa, and the United States. Three out of every four bottles of brandy sold in America come from California.

Cognac—the Regal

In France, the Cognac region produces the most universally esteemed brandy in the world, cognac. Now, the Cognac region is large, and the label of a bottle of cognac will give a further indication of the spirit's place of origin: Grande Champagne, Petite Champagne, Borderies, Fin Bois, Bois Ordinaires, and Bois Communs. Of these districts, the Grande and Petite Champagnes are considered to produce the finest cognacs.

Everything about cognac takes time and care. Not only are the grapes carefully cultivated and selected, but also distillation is carried out in alembics, which are ancient devices that turn out distillate one batch at a time (in contrast to modern continuous stills, which are suited to mass production). Less expensive brandies are distilled in continuous stills rather than in the much more labor- and time-intensive alembics.

Buzzed Words

Champagne, as applied to cognac, has nothing to do with the sparkling wine. The word is French for flat, open country, and its English equivalent is *plain*.

Cognac is aged in storehouses above ground, in casks made of particularly porous wood. Much of the distillate simply evaporates over the years. Cognac distillers accept this loss as a cost of doing business and refer to it as *la part des anges*—the angels' share.

After 10 years or more, the cognac is bottled, and, as with other distilled spirits, once the liquid is removed from contact with the wood, the aging ceases.

Armagnac—the Nutty

Armagnac, in the southwestern quadrant of France, is renowned for its namesake brandy. Armagnac is made by a process almost identical to that used to create cognac, but the raw materials and the subsequent blending process produce a brandy that has a distinctively nutty flavor, with earthy undertones and, many insist, high notes redolent of violets, plum, and peach.

Calvados—the Big Apple

Due north of Armagnac, in northwestern France, the coastal region of Normandy produces a distinctive brandy from apples. Americans have made applejack (apple brandy) since colonial times, but the Norman Calvados is a much subtler, mellower product, the result of 10 to 15 years of aging. If you see a label indicating "Calvados du Pays d'Auge," you will know that you are drinking Calvados from the region recognized as the source of the finest.

Although it is traditional to enjoy most brandies after a meal, the Norman French typically drink Calvados in the midst of a large meal. It clears the palate while simultaneously whetting the appetite for more.

The Brandies from Elsewhere

Although most drinkers deem French cognac and (to a lesser degree) Armagnac the brandies of choice, connoisseurs also admire the light California brandies (especially good in mixed drinks) and the interesting products of other nations. Italian *grappa* is a very strong, aggressive, and bracing brandy (as is another product of France, Burgundian *marc*). Spanish brandies recall sherry (the greatest sherries are produced in Spain), and the most highly prized is *amontillado*, made famous (or infamous) by Edgar Allan Poe's story of a man who buries his enemy alive in a cellar containing a "Cask of Amontillado." Like Armagnac, amontillado has a delicious, nutlike quality. Farther afield, you'll find *Metaxa*, a Greek brandy sweetened with sugar; *Asbach-Uralt* from Germany; *Pisco* from Peru; *Presidente* from Mexico; and *K.W.V.* from South Africa. All are worth sampling, although some might be difficult to find in the local wine or liquor store.

Flavored Brandies

Calvados is an example of a *flavored brandy*—that is, a brandy based on a fruit other than the grape. The French—as well as distillers in other countries—offer a wide range of flavored or "fruit" brandies, including pear brandy (which typically comes bottled with an entire Bartlett pear inside), raspberry brandy (known as *framboise*), strawberry brandy (*fraise*), plum brandy (*mirabelle*), and cherry brandy (*kirsch*). Burgundy's *marc* is made from the *pomace* (skin and pulp) of grapes, rather than the grape juice. The result is a most aggressive and flavorful brandy.

Numerous drinks that include brandy call for flavored or fruit brandies. For those that require ordinary brandy, however, you are best off choosing a reasonably priced V.O., perhaps from a California distiller. Reserve the V.S.O.P. cognacs and the Armagnacs for snifter savoring and for the select group of subtle mixed drinks that truly benefit from the premium spirit.

Versatile as a mixer, brandy makes a provocative and refreshing stand-in for "the usual" in a variety of standard drinks. See Appendix B for recipes for the Brandy Julep, Brandy Collins, Brandy Sour, and other brandy versions of the classics.

The Alexanders

The Alexander family consists of a brother and sister. The Brandy Alexander is one of the most popular brandy-based mixed drinks—and perhaps the most popular dessert drink as well.

Brandy Alexander

Serve in a chilled cocktail glass.

1½ oz. brandy

1 oz. crème de cacao

1 oz. heavy cream

Combine all ingredients in a shaker with ice. Shake vigorously, and then strain into the serving glass.

Some drinkers prefer a straight 1-1-1 ratio—one ounce of brandy to one ounce of liqueur to one ounce of cream.

Now, although the Alexander family is small—a brother and sister—there is some doubt as to the precise identity of the sister. Here are two opinions:

Alexander's Sister de Menthe

Serve in a chilled cocktail glass.

1½ oz. brandy

1 oz. white crème de menthe

1 oz. heavy cream

Combine all ingredients in a shaker with ice. Shake vigorously, and then strain into the serving glass.

Alexander's Sister Kahlúa

Serve in a chilled cocktail glass.

1½ oz. brandy

1 oz. Kahlúa

1 oz. heavy cream

Combine all ingredients in a shaker with ice. Shake vigorously, and then strain into the serving glass.

Again, for either of these, you may use a 1-1-1 ratio, if you prefer.

Other Brandy Classics

Brandy is an eminently mixable spirit. Why not venture beyond the familiar territory of the Alexanders?

A simple brandy and soda is one of the most popular brandy drinks.

Brandy and Soda

Serve on the rocks in a lowball glass.

1½ oz. brandy

4 or 5 oz. club soda

Combine the ingredients over ice in the serving glass.

Sidecar

A sidecar can be made with whiskey, but it was born as a brandy drink.

Serve in a chilled cocktail glass.

1½ oz. brandy ½ oz. lemon juice

¾ oz. curaçao

Combine all ingredients in a shaker with ice. Shake vigorously, and then strain into the serving glass.

Stinger

We've seen a Whiskey Stinger, but, by birthright, it is a brandy drink.

Serve in a chilled cocktail glass.

1½ oz. brandy

1½ oz. white crème de menthe

Combine all ingredients in a shaker with ice. Shake vigorously, and then strain into the serving glass.

Brandy Flip

Flips made with all kinds of spirits were all the rage—about 200 years ago. Today, only the Brandy Flip survives as a reasonably popular drink.

Serve in a chilled wine glass.

2 oz. brandy

1 egg*

1 tsp. sugar syrup

½ oz. cream (optional)

Ground nutmeg

Combine all ingredients, except nutmeg, in a blender with cracked ice. Blend until smooth, and then pour into the serving glass. Sprinkle with nutmeg.

**Raw egg is a source of salmonella bacteria. You may wish to avoid drinks calling for raw egg yolk or white.*

Alabama Slamma

You'll find a recipe for the Alabama Slammer, a popular amaretto and Southern Comfort libation, in Chapter 16. The brandy-based version has nearly the same name, but is a very different drink.

Serve in a chilled brandy snifter.

1 oz. cognac ½ oz. dry vermouth

½ oz. blackberry brandy ½ oz. amaretto

1 oz. coffee brandy 1 oz. lime juice

Combine all ingredients in a shaker or blender with cracked ice. Shake or blend, and then pour into the serving glass.

Brandy Gump

Created by cartoonist Sidney Smith, Andy Gump first appeared in a comic strip distributed by the Chicago Tribune Syndicate in 1917. He faded from view in 1959, but his memory lingers in the drink sort of named for him.

Serve in a chilled cocktail glass.

3 oz. brandy

½ tsp. grenadine

½ oz. lemon juice

Combine all ingredients in a shaker with cracked ice. Shake, and then strain into the serving glass.

Ambassador West

The Ambassador East is one of two of the most celebrated hotels in Chicago. The other is the Ambassador West.

Serve in a chilled cocktail glass.

1½ oz. brandy

1 tsp. dry vermouth

1 oz. gin

Green olive

Combine all ingredients, except the olive, in a mixing glass over ice cubes. Stir, and then strain into the serving glass. Garnish with the olive.

Ambrosia

Something a little smoother.

Serve in a chilled wine glass.

1½ oz. brandy

1½ oz. apple brandy

Few dashes raspberry liqueur

Champagne

Combine all ingredients, except champagne, in a shaker with cracked ice. Shake vigorously, and then pour into the serving glass. Top off with champagne.

Baltimore Bracer

And smoother still.

Serve in chilled cocktail glasses. (Yields 2 drinks.)

2 oz. brandy

2 oz. anisette

1 egg white*

Combine all ingredients with cracked ice in a shaker or blender. Shake or blend, and then pour into the serving glasses.

**Raw eggs may be a source of salmonella bacteria. You may wish to avoid drinks calling for raw egg yolk or white.*

Betsy Ross

This one savors of the eighteenth century.

Serve in a chilled cocktail glass.

1½ oz. brandy

1½ oz. port

1 egg yolk*

1 tsp. sugar syrup

Few dashes curaçao

Few dashes Angostura bitters

Ground nutmeg

Combine all ingredients, except nutmeg, in a shaker or blender with cracked ice. Shake or blend, and then strain into the serving glass. Sprinkle with the nutmeg.

**Raw eggs may be a source of salmonella bacteria. You may wish to avoid drinks calling for raw egg yolk or white.*

Ambulance Chaser

Serve in a chilled cocktail glass.

2 oz. cognac

¼ oz. port

1 egg yolk*

Few dashes Worcestershire sauce

Several pinches white pepper

Blend all ingredients with cracked ice and pour into serving glass.

**Raw eggs may be a source of salmonella bacteria. You may wish to avoid drinks calling for raw egg yolk or white.*

Apple Blossom with Juice

Applejack and calvados are among the most popular flavored or fruit brandies. And even if you don't have apple brandy, regular brandy and apple juice make a surprisingly good drink. Like regular brandy, apple brandy or applejack can be used as the principal ingredient in a host of traditional drinks.

Serve in a chilled cocktail glass.

1½ oz. brandy

1 oz. apple juice

1 tsp. lemon juice

Lemon slice

Combine all ingredients, except the lemon slice, in a shaker with ice. Shake vigorously, and then strain into the serving glass. Garnish with the lemon slice.

Apple Cart

Serve in a chilled cocktail glass.

1 oz. applejack

¾ oz. Cointreau

½ oz. lemon juice

Combine all ingredients in a shaker or blender with cracked ice. Shake or blend, and then strain into the serving glass.

Apple Buck

Serve in a chilled highball glass.

1½ oz. applejack

½ oz. lemon juice

1 tsp. ginger-flavored brandy

Ginger ale

Preserved ginger

Combine all ingredients, except ginger ale and ginger, with cracked ice in a shaker. Shake vigorously, and then pour into the serving glass. Top off with the ginger ale and garnish with the ginger.

Apple Knocker

Serve on the rocks in a chilled Collins glass.

3 oz. apple brandy

½ oz. sweet vermouth

4 oz. orange juice

½ oz. sugar syrup

1 tsp. lemon juice

Combine all ingredients with cracked ice in a shaker. Shake vigorously, and then pour over ice into the serving glass.

Apple Dubonnet

Serve in a chilled old-fashioned glass.

1½ oz. calvados

1½ oz. Dubonnet rouge

Lemon slice

Combine the spirits with cracked ice in a shaker. Shake, and then pour into the serving glass and garnish with the lemon slice.

Apple Byrrh

Serve in a chilled old-fashioned glass.

1½ oz. calvados

½ oz. dry vermouth

½ oz. Byrrh

½ tsp. lemon juice

Lemon peel

Combine all ingredients, except the lemon peel, in a shaker or blender with cracked ice. Shake or blend, and then pour into the serving glass. Twist the lemon peel over the drink and drop in.

Apricot Excursions

If you're accustomed to thinking about apricot brandy as something your maiden aunt imbibes, here are a few recipes to help you revise your thinking.

Apricot Brandy Fizz

Serve in a chilled old-fashioned glass.

2 oz. apricot brandy

Liberal dash or two grenadine

Orange slice

Lemon twist

Club soda to fill

Combine brandy and grenadine in the serving glass one third filled with ice. Garnish with orange slice and lemon twist, and then add club soda to fill.

Apricot Brandy Sour

Serve in a chilled cocktail glass.

2 oz. apricot brandy

1 oz. lemon juice

1 tsp. sugar syrup

Lemon slice

Combine all ingredients, except the lemon slice, in a shaker with ice. Shake vigorously, and then strain into the serving glass. Garnish with the lemon slice.

Bronx Cheer

Serve in a chilled Collins glass.

2 oz. apricot brandy

6 oz. raspberry soda

Orange peel

In a chilled Collins glass, combine brandy, soda, and a few ice cubes. Stir gently. Twist the orange peel over the drink and drop it into the glass.

California Dreaming

Best served in a parfait glass.

2 oz. apricot brandy

4 oz. orange soda

1 scoop orange sherbet

Blend ingredients with cracked ice until smooth. Pour into serving glass.

Apricot

Serve in a chilled cocktail glass.

2 oz. apricot brandy

1 oz. orange juice

1 oz. lemon juice

Dash or two of gin

Combine all ingredients with in shaker or blender with cracked ice. Shake or blend, then pour into the serving glass.

Apricot Pie

Serve in a chilled old-fashioned glass.

1 oz. apricot brandy

1 oz. light rum

½ oz. sweet vermouth

1 tsp. lemon juice

Few dashes grenadine

Orange peel

Combine all ingredients, except orange peel, in a shaker or blender with cracked ice. Shake or blend, and then pour into the serving glass. Twist the orange peel over the drink and drop in.

Cherry Mixtures

These cherry brandy drinks are worth your attention.

Cherry Blossom

Serve in a chilled cocktail glass.

1½ oz. brandy

¾ oz. cherry brandy (may substitute cherry liqueur)

½ oz. curaçao

½ oz. lemon juice

¼ oz. grenadine

1 tsp. sugar syrup

Combine all ingredients in a shaker with cracked ice. Shake vigorously, and then strain into the serving glass. If you wish, rim the glass with brandy and powdered sugar.

Cherry Hill

Serve in a chilled cocktail glass.

1 oz. brandy

1 oz. cherry brandy (may substitute cherry liqueur)

½ oz. dry vermouth

Orange twist

Combine all ingredients, except orange twist, in a shaker with cracked ice. Shake vigorously, and then pour into the serving glass. Garnish with orange twist.

Cherry Ginger Frappe

Here's one that combines tangy ginger brandy with cherry liqueur.

Serve over crushed ice in a martini glass.

1 oz. cherry liqueur

1 tsp. krischwasser

1 tsp. ginger brandy

1 piece preserved ginger

Maraschino cherry

Combine all ingredients, except the ginger and cherry, in a shaker with cracked ice. Shake vigorously, and then pour over crushed ice in the serving glass. Spear the ginger and the cherry with a toothpick and bridge the toothpick over the glass.

Toast

May you never lie, cheat, or drink—but if you must lie, lie in one another's arms, and if you must cheat, cheat death, and if you must drink, drink with all of us.

Peachy Potables

Peach brandy forms the perfect foundation for some *very* sweet drinks.

Peach Fizz

Serve in a chilled Collins glass.

1½ oz. brandy

1½ oz. peach brandy

½ oz. lemon juice

1 tsp. creme de banana

1 tsp. sugar syrup

Club soda to fill

Fresh or brandied peach slice

Combine all ingredients, except soda and peach slice, in a shaker with cracked ice. Shake vigorously, and then pour into the serving glass. Add club soda to fill and garnish with the peach slice.

Peachtree Sling

Serve in a chilled Collins glass.

1½ oz. brandy

1½ oz. peach brandy

½ oz. lemon juice

½ oz. sugar syrup

Club soda to fill

Brandied or fresh peach slice

1 tsp. peach liqueur

Combine all ingredients, except soda, peach slice, and peach liqueur, in a shaker with cracked ice. Shake vigorously, and then pour into the serving glass. Add club soda to fill, then garnish with the peach slice. Spoon on the peach liqueur as a float. Do not stir.

Peach Fuzz

Serve in a chilled cocktail glass.

1½ oz. peach brandy

½ oz. white crème de cacao

1 oz. heavy cream

1 tsp. apple schnapps

Combine all ingredients, except the schnapps, in a shaker with cracked ice. Shake vigorously, and then pour into the serving glass and float the schnapps on top.

B&B Variations

B&B is a classic combination of Benedictine and brandy—preferably premium-label cognac. It is a delicious after-dinner drink.

B&B

Serve in a snifter.

1 oz. cognac

1 oz. Benedictine

Combine all ingredients in snifter and swirl.

B&B Collins

Another B&B favorite is the B&B Collins. Brandy works well here, but, for a special treat, use cognac.

Serve in a chilled Collins glass.

2 oz. cognac

1–2 oz. lemon juice

1 tsp. sugar syrup

Club soda to fill

½ oz. Benedictine

Lemon slice

Combine all ingredients, except soda, Benedictine, and lemon slice, in a shaker with cracked ice. Shake vigorously, and then pour into the serving glass. Add club soda to fill. Carefully pour on the Benedictine as a float. Do not stir. Garnish with the lemon slice.

Brandy and Champagne

Brandy and champagne make a sophisticated combination. You might begin with a Champagne Cooler.

Champagne Cooler

Serve in a chilled wine goblet.

1 oz. brandy

1 oz. Cointreau

Champagne to fill

Mint sprig

Combine brandy and Cointreau in the serving glass. Add champagne to fill and stir very gently. Garnish with mint sprig.

King's Peg

The simplest thing to do with brandy and champagne is just to mix 'em. Use brut champagne and good-quality cognac for a royal treat.

Serve in a chilled wine goblet.

3 oz. cognac

Brut champagne to fill

Pour cognac into the serving glass, and then add champagne to fill. Optionally, include two or three ice cubes.

Chicago

The Chicago is a classic brandy and champagne combination.

Serve in a chilled wine goblet rimmed with sugar.

Lemon wedge

Superfine sugar

1½ oz. brandy

Dash curaçao

Dash Angostura bitters

Champagne to fill

Run the lemon wedge around the serving glass rim to moisten. Roll the moistened rim in sugar to coat. Combine brandy, curaçao, and bitters in a mixing glass with ice. Stir well, and then strain into the serving glass. Add champagne to fill.

Mayfair Cocktail and Other Brandy Drinks

The famed Mayfair Cocktail is named for one of London's traditionally most fashionable districts. It leads off our small collection of brandy-and-bitters, brandy-and-aperitif drinks.

Mayfair Cocktail

Serve in a chilled cocktail glass.

1 oz. cognac

1 oz. Dubonnet rouge

½ oz. lime juice

1 tsp. sugar syrup

Liberal dashes Angostura bitters

Orange twist

Combine all ingredients, except orange twist, in a shaker with ice. Shake vigorously, and then pour into the serving glass. Garnish with the twist.

East India

The East India summons up the days when the sun never set on the British Empire.

Serve in a chilled cocktail glass.

1½ oz. brandy

½ oz. curaçao

½ oz. pineapple juice

Dash Angostura bitters

Combine ingredients in a shaker with ice. Shake vigorously, and then strain into the serving glass.

Phoebe Snow

The Phoebe Snow is a delicate drink that needs to be violently shaken in order to get it thoroughly chilled.

Serve in a chilled cocktail glass.

1½ oz. cognac

1½ oz. Dubonnet rouge

Dash Pernod

Combine all ingredients in a shaker with ice. Shake vigorously, and then strain into the serving glass.

Phoebe's Snow Mist

Consider this Phoebe Snow variation.

Serve in chilled old-fashioned glasses. (Yields 2 drinks.)

2 oz. cognac

2 oz. Dubonnet rouge

½ oz. Pernod

1 egg white*

2 lemon peels

Combine all ingredients, except the lemon peels, with cracked ice in a shaker or blender. Shake or blend, and then pour into the serving glasses. Twist the lemon peels over the drinks and drop in.

**Raw eggs may be a source of salmonella bacteria. You may wish to avoid drinks calling for raw egg yolk or white.*

Extravagances

Staid old brandy has found a flamboyant role in a host of new drinks. Here are some to try.

Moon River

Serve on the rocks in a Collins glass.

1½ oz. brandy

½ oz. peppermint schnapps

Lemon-lime soda

Dash grenadine

Combine brandy and schnapps over ice in the serving glass. Stir. Fill with soda, and then stir again, gently. Dash on the grenadine.

The Mooch

Serve on the rocks in a highball glass.

2 oz. apricot brandy

6 oz. lemon-lime soda

Lemon peel

Combine the brandy and soda over ice in the serving glass. Twist the lemon peel over the drink and drop in.

Purple Cow

Serve on the rocks in an old-fashioned glass.

1 oz. blackberry brandy

1 oz. light cream

1 tsp. almond extract

Combine all ingredients in a shaker with cracked ice. Shake, and then strain over ice into the serving glass.

Kahlúa Toreador

Serve on the rocks in an old-fashioned glass.

2 oz. brandy

1 oz. Kahlúa

1 egg white*

Combine all ingredients in a shaker with cracked ice. Shake, and then strain over ice into the serving glass.

**Raw eggs may be a source of salmonella bacteria. You may wish to avoid drinks calling for raw egg yolk or white.*

Lava

Serve on the rocks in an old-fashioned glass.

2 oz. vodka

1 oz. cherry brandy

1 oz. heavy cream

2 drops Tabasco sauce

Combine all ingredients, except the Tabasco, in a shaker with cracked ice. Shake, and then strain over ice into the serving glass. Drop on the Tabasco sauce.

Jersey Lightning

Serve on the rocks in an old-fashioned glass.

2½ oz. apple brandy

3 dashes Angostura bitters

Liberal pinch sugar

Combine all ingredients in a shaker with cracked ice. Shake, and then strain over ice into the serving glass.

Dracula's Bride

Serve on the rocks in an old-fashioned glass.

2 oz. cherry brandy

1 oz. vodka

½ oz. sloe gin

Liberal pinch salt

Combine all ingredients, except the salt, in a shaker with cracked ice. Shake, and then strain over ice into the serving glass. Add salt.

The Least You Need to Know

- The designation *V.O.* on a bottle of brandy means that the brandy has been aged for at least 4½ years; *V.S.O.P.* is reserved for cognac aged at least 10 years.
- Brandy ages only in contact with the oak of the aging casks. Once bottled, it no longer ages.
- Although the most celebrated brandies come from France, the product of other nations is very much worth sampling as well.
- A variety of fruits besides grapes can form the basis of brandy; most widely used is the apple, from which American applejack and French Calvados are made.

Chapter 16

Cordially Yours: The Liqueurs

In This Chapter

- Origin and history of liqueurs
- How liqueurs are made
- Liqueur innovations
- A guide to liqueurs
- Liqueur recipes

Liqueurs—also called cordials—occupy a realm between the commercial manufacture of spirits and the esoteric lore of alchemy. Ounce for ounce, you won't find stronger, more compelling, or more varied flavors than those distilled into liqueur. No distilled spirit has a more varied, more venerable, or more interesting past than the liqueurs, which partake both of ancient tradition and modern top-secret technology.

It is a great delight to shop around and taste a variety of liqueurs to identify those that will become your favorites. And don't just look in this chapter for liqueur recipes. You'll find them used throughout this book, in conjunction with many other spirits. Here, however, they take center stage.

Good for What Ails You

During the Dark Ages, distillation was a way of extracting and preserving the essences of such powerful medicinals as roots, barks, seeds, leaves, herbs, spices, fruit, and flowers. Indeed, distillation is the basis of modern pharmacology as well as modern chemistry because it allows the extraction of the active portion of many natural materials, which then can be combined and compounded in new ways.

Buzzed Words

Cordial is a synonym for **liqueur**, but the word originally designated only those liqueurs thought to have tonic or medicinal use.

During the Middle Ages, alcohol, especially alcohol in which herbal and other natural substances had been distilled, was regarded as a medicine. And for good reason: many alcoholic concoctions made people feel good—at least for a while. Even better, many of these potables tasted good. So, even after their medicinal virtues fell into doubt and disrepute, liqueurs remained popular.

A good example is curaçao. In the 1600s, British navy "surgeons" (as military physicians were officially called) noticed that scurvy appeared among crew members when their supplies of fresh citrus fruit ran out. In an era before refrigeration, what better way to preserve fruit than in alcohol? Curaçao distills dried orange peel in alcohol. Unfortunately, it doesn't distill the vitamin C along with the orange flavor, so curaçao proved wholly ineffective against scurvy—but that didn't prevent its becoming a popular drink nonetheless, and it survives as a widely used liqueur.

How Liqueurs Are Made

Liqueurs combine alcohol with various natural substances in one of four ways:

1. **Infusion** The flavoring agents are steeped in water, and then combined with alcohol.
2. **Maceration** The flavoring agents are steeped in alcohol, thereby extracting the essence of the agent.
3. **Distillation** The flavoring agents are mixed with alcohol and then distilled together.
4. **Percolation** Alcoholic spirits are percolated or dripped through flavoring agents in order to extract the essence of the agents.

In addition to the flavoring agents, all liqueurs are sweetened. In the United States, this is actually regulated by law. A liqueur must contain at least 2.5 percent sugar by weight—though most are considerably sweeter than this.

State of the Art

Although liqueur production is rooted in the Dark Ages, it is still a source of new ideas. For example, innovations in distillation technology have produced a series of dairy cream-based liqueurs, which require no refrigeration and have a remarkably long shelf life. Chocolate liqueurs, including the sumptuous Godiva Liqueur, have become popular in recent years. As for *schnapps*, not long ago it was something your grandparents remembered fondly from "the Old Country." Today, thanks to innovations in processes for extracting flavors from botanicals, a rainbow of flavored schnapps has emerged, offering remarkably natural fruit flavors.

Buzzed Words

Schnapps can be used to describe any number of strong, dry liquors, but, recently, has been applied to a variety of flavored liqueurs. The word derives from the German original, spelled with one *p* and meaning "mouthful."

Generic vs. Proprietary Liqueur

The range of liqueurs can be sharply divided into two broad categories: *generic* and *proprietary*.

The generic category accounts for somewhat less than half of all liqueurs on the market and encompasses the basic and most popular flavors, including almond, anise, peppermint, and others.

Buzzed Words

Generic liqueurs are prepared according to standard formulas by a number of distillers. **Proprietary liqueurs** are "brand-name" products prepared according to closely guarded trade-secret formulas that are the property of specific distillers.

The proprietary liqueurs include Benedictine, Chartreuse, Drambuie, Grand Marnier, and Cointreau. There are many more, each made from closely guarded secret formulas—family recipes handed down over many generations. The Benedictine liqueur-making "family," for example, is the Benedictine order of monks, who still produce this popular cordial by faithfully following a recipe formulated in 1510.

Review of the Essential Liqueurs

Chapter 4 lists the bare-bones essential set of liqueurs that should form a part of your spiritous arsenal. But if you're at all serious about mixing liqueur-based drinks, you'll need more.

The most widely used generic liqueurs include the following:

- amaretto (made with almond extract)
- anisette (anise)
- crème de banana (banana)
- crème de cassis (black currants)
- crème de cacao (cocoa and vanilla)
- crème de menthe, white or green (peppermint)
- curaçao (Curaçao orange peel)
- sambuca (coffee beans)
- chocolate (available in white and dark)
- triple sec (oranges)
- crème de café (coffee beans)
- sloe gin (sloe berries)

In addition, some authorities would class the fruit-flavored brandies not with brandy, but with generic liqueurs. Fruit-flavored brandy is conventional brandy, distilled from grapes, but flavored with the essences of other fruit. In contrast, the fruit brandies discussed in the preceding chapter are actually distilled from the fermented juice of fruit other than grapes.

There is another difference between fruit liqueurs and fruit-flavored brandies. Fruit liqueurs are very sweet and relatively low in alcoholic content, at 48 to 60 proof. Fruit-flavored brandies are less sweet and higher in alcoholic content than fruit liqueurs—around 70 proof or higher. Finally, the "true" fruit brandies are not sweet and pack a proof well in the range of hard liquor, anywhere from 86 to 100 proof.

Bar Tips

Some European producers do offer "true" fruit brandies that are sweetened and bottled at a low 48 proof. These are still considered brandies rather than liqueurs.

The best-known proprietary liqueurs include the following:

- Benedictine
- Chartreuse
- CocoRibe
- Cointreau
- Drambuie
- Frangelico
- Galliano
- Grand Marnier
- Irish Mist
- Kahlúa
- La Grande Passion
- Midori
- Peter Heering
- Southern Comfort

Bar Tips

If you or a guest spills a sticky, colored liqueur on a fancy suit or dress, immediately soak the stain with club soda. Follow with plain water, and rub a bit of Ivory bar soap directly on the stain. Rinse with cold water, and then blot dry.

Liqueurs with Brandy

Liqueurs combine very naturally with brandy or cognac to make delicious dessert or after-dinner drinks. The most often requested brandy-liqueur combination, B&B, is covered in Chapter 15. Our first offering is decidedly different from that dignified, even rather staid libation.

Acapulco Joy

Serve in a chilled wine goblet.

1½ oz. Kahlúa

1 oz. peach brandy

1 scoop vanilla ice cream

½ banana, sliced

Pinch ground nutmeg

Maraschino cherry

Combine all ingredients, except the nutmeg and cherry, in a blender. Blend until smooth, and then pour into the serving glass. Sprinkle with nutmeg and garnish with the cherry.

Blue Angel

The name of the next drink is appealing in itself, especially to fans of Marlene Dietrich.

Serve in a chilled cocktail glass.

½ oz. blue curaçao

½ oz. creme de violette

½ oz. brandy

½ oz. lemon juice

½ oz. cream

Combine all ingredients in a shaker with ice. Shake vigorously, then strain into the serving glass.

Cap Martin

The Cap Martin is a delightful combination of crème de cassis, cognac, and pineapple juice.

Serve in a chilled cocktail glass.

1 oz. crème de cassis

½ oz. cognac

1 oz. pineapple juice

Orange slice

Combine all ingredients, except the orange slice, in a shaker with ice. Shake vigorously, and then strain into the serving glass. Garnish with the orange slice.

Festival

The aptly named Festival is a bright, delicious, and highly refreshing fruity, creamy drink.

Serve in a chilled cocktail glass.

¾ oz. crème de cacao

1 oz. apricot brandy

¾ tsp. cream

1 tsp. grenadine

Combine all ingredients in a shaker with cracked ice. Shake vigorously, and then pour into the serving glass.

Rolls-Royce

Serve in a chilled cocktail glass.

1 oz. Cointreau

1 oz. cognac

1 oz. orange juice

Combine all ingredients in a shaker with cracked ice. Shake vigorously, and then pour into the serving glass.

Hoopla

Serve in a chilled cocktail glass.

¾ oz. Cointreau

¾ oz. Lillet blanc

¾ oz. brandy

¾ oz. lemon juice

Combine all ingredients in a shaker or blender with cracked ice. Shake or blend, and then pour into the serving glass.

Culross

The Culross is another drink based on Lillet blanc.

Serve in a chilled cocktail glass.

1 oz. apricot-flavored brandy

1 oz. light rum

1 oz. Lillet blanc

½ oz. lemon juice

Combine all ingredients in a shaker or blender with cracked ice. Shake or blend, and then pour into the serving glass.

Café Ligonier

Cold coffee is the essence of the next two.

Serve in a chilled highball glass.

¾ oz. crème de cacao

¾ oz. cognac

1 cup cold black coffee

Cinnamon stick

Combine all ingredients, except the cinnamon stick, in a shaker or blender with cracked ice. Shake or blend, and then pour into the serving glass. Garnish with the cinnamon stick.

Blackjack

Serve in a chilled wine glass.

1 oz. kirsch

½ oz. brandy

1 cup cold black coffee

Combine all ingredients in a shaker or blender with cracked ice. Shake or blend, and then pour into the serving glass.

Amsterdamer

You might have to hunt for the Dutch liqueur that forms 50 percent of this drink.

Serve in a chilled cocktail glass.

1½ oz. Advocaat egg liqueur

1½ oz. cherry brandy

Combine all ingredients in a shaker or blender with cracked ice. Shake or blend, and then pour into the serving glass.

Liqueur with Liquor

Combinations of liqueur with hard liquor are deceptively potent. The liqueur makes the liquor go down easy and, before you know it, you're buzzed. Enjoy—but pace yourself by drinking responsibly.

Afraid of sharks? Try tangling with a Barracuda! You can serve this tropical drink in a highball glass, in a novelty tropical drink glass, or—most fun of all—in a freshly carved-out pineapple shell.

Barracuda

Serve in a carved-out pineapple shell.

½ oz. Galliano
1 oz. gold rum
1 oz. pineapple juice
¼ oz. lime juice
¼ oz. sugar syrup
Champagne to fill
Lime slice
Maraschino cherry
Pineapple shell

Combine all ingredients, except champagne, lime slice, and cherry, in a shaker with cracked ice. Shake vigorously, and then pour into the pineapple shell. Add champagne to fill. Garnish with the lime slice and the cherry.

Café Kahlúa

Kahlúa is a delicious coffee liqueur that takes on a tawny appearance and velvety texture when combined with gold rum and fresh cream in a Café Kahlúa.

Serve in a chilled old-fashioned glass.

3 oz. Kahlúa

1½ oz. gold Jamaica rum

2 oz. cream

Cinnamon stick

Combine all ingredients, except cinnamon stick, in a shaker with cracked ice. Shake vigorously, and then pour into the serving glass. Garnish with the cinnamon stick.

Grand Hotel

Grand Hotel! The name of this libation summons up the opulence of an age gone by—not to mention yet another Marlene Dietrich movie. This is a drink to be savored slowly and, preferably, in delightful company.

Serve in a chilled cocktail glass.

1½ oz. Grand Marnier
1½ oz. gin
½ oz. dry vermouth
Dash lemon juice
Lemon twist

Combine all ingredients, except the twist, in a shaker with cracked ice. Shake vigorously, and then pour into the serving glass. Garnish with the twist.

Mazatlán

They call Mazatlán the Pearl of the Pacific. Bring a little of Mazatlán to your own private Peoria with its namesake drink.

Serve in a chilled cocktail glass.

1 oz. white crème de cacao

1 oz. light rum

½ oz. coconut cream

1 oz. cream

Combine all ingredients in a shaker with ice. Shake vigorously, and then strain into the serving glass.

Melon Ball

Melon liqueur—especially Midori—has become increasingly popular. Join the Melon Ball crowd in the Melon Patch.

Serve on the rocks in a highball glass.

1 oz. vodka

½ oz. Midori melon liqueur

5 oz. orange juice

Combine the vodka and Midori in the serving glass filled with ice. Add orange juice and stir well.

Melon Patch

Serve in a chilled highball glass.

1 oz. Midori melon liqueur

½ oz. triple sec

½ oz. vodka

Club soda to fill

Orange slice

Combine all ingredients, except club soda and orange slice, in the serving glass one third full of ice. Stir well, and then add club soda to fill and garnish with the orange slice.

Arctic Joy

Serve in a chilled cocktail glass.

1 oz. peppermint schnapps

1 oz. white crème de cacao

1 oz. light cream

In a shaker or blender combine all ingredients. Shake or blend, then strain into serving glass.

Waldorf

Don't confuse the Waldorf with the Waldorf Cocktail, a bourbon drink you'll find in Appendix B.

Serve in a chilled cocktail glass.

2 oz. Swedish Punsch

1 oz. gin

1 oz. lemon juice

Combine all ingredients in a shaker or blender with cracked ice. Shake or blend, and then pour into the serving glass.

Red Dane

Serve in a chilled cocktail glass.

2 oz. vodka

1 oz. Peter Heering

Combine all ingredients over ice in a mixing glass. Stir, and then strain into the serving glass.

Turkey Trot

Serve on the rocks in a chilled old-fashioned glass.

2 oz. Wild Turkey bourbon liqueur

1½ oz. Wild Turkey

Lemon peel

Pour the spirits into the serving glass over ice. Stir. Twist the lemon peel over the drink and drop in.

Strega Satin

Serve in a chilled parfait glass.

1½ oz. Strega

1 oz. vodka

2 oz. orange juice

Generous scoop vanilla ice cream

Combine all ingredients in a blender. Blend until smooth, and then pour into the serving glass. Provide a straw.

Tuaca Cocktail

Serve in a chilled cocktail glass.

1 oz. vodka

1 oz. Tuaca

½ oz. lime juice

Combine all ingredients in a shaker or blender with cracked ice. Shake or blend, and then strain into the serving glass.

Liqueurs with Other Liqueurs

Not surprisingly, one of the best mixers to combine with liqueur is another liqueur. Here are some combinations to try.

Blue Lady

Serve in a chilled cocktail glass.

1½ oz. blue curaçao

½ oz. white crème de cacao

½ oz. light cream

Combine all ingredients in a shaker with cracked ice. Shake vigorously, and then pour into the serving glass.

Bar Tips

Serve drinks containing dairy products fresh, just as you would serve milk alone.

Kiss Me Quick

Is it "Kiss Me Quick" or "Kiss Me, Quick"? Grammarians need not apply.

Serve in a chilled brandy snifter.

2 oz. Pernod

½ oz. curaçao

Liberal dashes Angostura bitters

Club soda to fill

Combine all ingredients, except club soda, in a shaker with cracked ice. Shake vigorously, and then pour into the serving glass. Add club soda to fill.

Mocha Mint

Serve in a chilled cocktail glass.

¾ oz. Kahlúa

¾ oz. white crème de menthe

¾ oz. crème de cacao

Combine all ingredients in a shaker with ice. Shake vigorously, and then strain into the serving glass.

Pernod Cocktail

The Pernod Cocktail is another classic—as are most drinks built on Pernod.

Serve in an old-fashioned glass.

½ oz. water

Liberal dashes sugar syrup

Liberal dashes Angostura bitters

2 oz. Pernod

Into the serving glass half filled with crushed ice, add water, sugar syrup, and bitters. Stir well, and then add the Pernod. Stir again.

Sombrero

Simple and frequently requested, the Sombrero.

Serve on the rocks in an old-fashioned glass.

1½ oz. Kahlúa

1 oz. cream

Pour Kahlúa into the serving glass half filled with ice. Use a spoon to float the cream onto the Kahlúa. *Do not stir!*

Velvet Hammer

The Velvet Hammer, one of the most celebrated liqueur-plus-liqueur drinks, is also among the simplest.

Serve in a chilled cocktail glass.

1 oz. Cointreau

1 oz. white crème de cacao

1 oz. heavy cream

Combine all ingredients in a shaker with ice. Shake vigorously, and then strain into the serving glass.

Pernod Frappé

Want a bit more bite? The icy Pernod Frappé might be just the ticket.

Serve in a chilled cocktail glass.

1½ oz. Pernod

½ oz. anisette

Few dashes Angostura bitters

Combine all ingredients in a shaker with cracked ice. Shake very thoroughly, and then strain into the serving glass.

Yellow Chartreuse Nectar

Serve on the rocks in a chilled old-fashioned glass.

¾ oz. yellow Chartreuse

¾ oz. apricot schnapps

Combine the spirits over ice in the serving glass. Stir well.

Summertime

Serve in a chilled parfait glass.

1 tsp. white crème de menthe

1 tsp. green crème de menthe

Generous scoop vanilla ice cream

Combine all ingredients in a blender. Blend until smooth, but avoid over blending. Pour into the serving glass.

River Club

Here's a blend of peppermint, coffee, and cocoa flavors.

Serve in a chilled cocktail glass.

¾ oz. peppermint schnapps

¾ oz. Kahlúa

¾ oz. white crème de cacao

Combine all ingredients in a shaker with cracked ice. Shake vigorously, and then pour into the serving glass.

South Bend

South Bend, Indiana, is the home of Notre Dame and its famed "Fighting Irish."

Serve in a chilled parfait glass.

1½ oz. Irish cream

1½ oz. Frangelico

1 oz. orange juice

1 oz. cream

Combine all ingredients in a shaker or blender with cracked ice. Shake or blend, and then pour into the serving glass.

Liqueur with Fruit Juices

Based on fruit to begin with, most liqueurs are delightful when combined with fruit juices. Here are some examples.

Abbot's Delight

Serve in a chilled parfait glass.

1½ oz. Frangelico

3 oz. pineapple juice

½ banana, sliced

Liberal dashes Angostura bitters

Combine all ingredients in a blender with ice. Blend until smooth, and then pour into the serving glass.

Bar Tips

Use only ripe bananas in recipes calling for banana.

Cape Cod Cooler

The Cape Cod Cooler is as sweet as they come.

Serve in a chilled Collins glass.

2 oz. sloe gin

1 oz. gin

5 oz. cranberry juice

½ oz. lemon juice

½ oz. orgeat syrup

Lime slice

Combine all ingredients, except the lime slice, in a shaker with cracked ice. Shake vigorously, and then pour into the serving glass. Garnish with the lime slice.

Lemonade Moderne

Serve in a chilled highball glass.

1½ oz. sloe gin

1½ oz. sherry

2 oz. lemon juice

1 oz. sugar syrup

Club soda

Lemon peel

Combine all ingredients, except soda and lemon peel, in a shaker or blender with cracked ice. Shake or blend, and then pour into the serving glass. Top off with the soda. Twist the lemon peel over the drink and drop in.

Chartreuse Cooler

Serve in a chilled Collins glass.

1½ oz. yellow Chartreuse

4 oz. orange juice

½ oz. lime juice

Lemon-lime soda

Orange slice

Combine all ingredients, except soda and orange slice, in a shaker or blender with cracked ice. Shake or blend, and then pour into the serving glass. Top off with the soda, gently stir, then garnish with the orange slice.

Kowloon

Serve in a wine glass over cracked ice.

1 oz. Grand Marnier

1 oz. Kahlúa

3 oz. orange juice

Orange slice

Combine all ingredients, except the orange slice, in a mixing glass. Stir, and then pour into the serving glass, about half filled with cracked ice. Garnish with the orange slice.

Jacaranda

Serve in a chilled cocktail glass.

1 oz. Haitian rum

½ oz. peppermint schnapps

1½ oz. mango nectar

½ oz. cream

1 tsp. peach schnapps

Combine all ingredients, except the peach schnapps, in a shaker or blender with cracked ice. Shake or blend, and then pour into the serving glass. Spoon the peach schnapps on top.

Cordial Favorites

The following is a clutch of classics—some of the liqueur drinks that are most often requested.

Alabama Slammer Highball

The Alabama Slammer may be made as a highball or as a shooter.

Serve in a highball glass.

½ oz. sloe gin
½ oz. Southern Comfort
½ oz. triple sec
½ oz. Galliano
3 oz. orange juice
Maraschino cherry
Orange slice

Combine all ingredients, except fruit, in a shaker fill with ice. Shake vigorously, and then strain into the serving glass. Add more ice, if you wish. Garnish with the cherry and orange slice.

Alabama Slammer Shooter

Serve in shot glasses.

1½ oz. sloe gin
1½ oz. amaretto
1½ oz. Southern Comfort
1½ oz. orange juice

Combine all ingredients in a shaker with ice. Shake vigorously, and then strain into shot glasses. Yields four shots.

Sloe Gin Fizz

Serve in a chilled Collins glass.

1 oz. sloe gin
2 oz. sour mix
Club soda to fill
Maraschino cherry

Combine the sloe agin and sour mix in a shaker filled with ice. Shake vigorously, and then strain into the serving glass. Add club soda to fill, and then garnish with the cherry.

Grasshopper

Reach into the retro closet, and you'll find the Grasshopper. This green, creamy drink is long past its heyday, but nostalgia is evergreen—and these drinks may well be coming back into vogue.

Serve in a chilled cocktail glass.

1 oz. green crème de menthe
1 oz. white crème de cacao
1 oz. light cream

Combine all ingredients in a blender with ice. Shake vigorously, and then strain into the serving glass.

Pink Squirrel

Let's close with another retro favorite: the Pink Squirrel.

Serve in chilled cocktail glass.

1 oz. crème de noyaux
1 oz. white crème de cacao
1 oz. cream

Combine all ingredients in a shaker with ice. Shake vigorously, and then strain into the serving glass.

Ballylickey Dickie

Serve in chilled wine goblet.

1½ oz. amaretto

1 oz. Irish cream

1 scoop vanilla ice cream

1 oz. slivered almonds

Pinch ground nutmeg

Pinch powdered cinnamon

Maraschino cherry

Blend all ingredients, except the nutmeg, cinnamon, and cherry, with cracked ice until very smooth. Pour into serving glass, sprinkle with the spices, and garnish with the cherry.

Coconut Cove

1½ oz. CocoRibe

½ oz. lime juice

1 tsp. orgeat

½ ripe banana, sliced

Scoop vanilla ice cream

Blend all ingredients with cracked ice until smooth. Pour into a chilled parfait glass.

The Newer Wave

Liqueur is all about flavor, and some of the latest liqueur drinks are not shy about introducing new tastes. Be warned; the following are definitely high octane.

Military Maneuvers

Serve in wine goblets. (Yields 2 drinks.)

2 oz. vodka

2 oz. brandy

1 oz. banana liqueur

½ oz. orange juice

½ oz. apricot juice

Liberal dash prune juice

Combine all ingredients in a blender with plenty of cracked ice. Blend on high, and then pour into the serving glasses.

Dead Girl Scout

Serve on the rocks in an old-fashioned glass.

2 oz. vodka

1½ oz. green crème de menthe

½ oz. cherry brandy

Crushed cherries

Combine all ingredients, except the cherries, in a shaker or blender with cracked ice. Shake or blend, and then strain over ice into the serving glass. Garnish with the crushed cherries.

Aggravated Wound

Serve in a highball glass piled high with ice cubes or cracked ice.

1½ oz. Kahlúa

1 oz. scotch

1 TB. milk

3 drops Tabasco sauce

2 drops lemon juice

Combine all ingredients over ice in the serving glass. Stir.

Esophagus Clogger

Serve on the rocks in an old-fashioned glass.

2 oz. Bailey's Irish Cream

½ oz. green crème de menthe

½ oz. light rum

1 TB. amaretto

Combine all ingredients in a shaker or blender with cracked ice. Shake or blend, and then strain over ice into the serving glass.

The Least You Need to Know

- Liqueur started out as medicine in the Middle Ages.
- Liqueurs are compounded by infusion, maceration, distillation, or percolation.
- Try a wide variety of liqueurs. Compile your own personal list of favorites.
- Liqueurs fall into two broad categories: generic (marketed under many brand names and made according to standard recipes) and proprietary (prepared according to jealously guarded trade secrets and marketed under a single brand name).

Chapter 17

Up in Flames: Hot and Flaming Drinks

In This Chapter

- Attractions of hot drinks
- Fortified coffee drinks
- How to flame drinks dramatically and safely
- Hot drink recipes

The human body is a furnace. Heat is precious to it, and what is precious feels good. That, in essence, is the attraction of hot drinks, whether it's tea, coffee, or hot chocolate. Add alcohol to a hot drink, and that thermal glow spreads, mellows, and is sustained. In the days before central heating, no self-respecting inn would fail, in wintertime, to offer toddies or mulled drinks. The flip, an American colonial favorite consisting of spirits, ale, eggs, sugar, cream, and assorted spices, was heated on demand with a "flip iron"—a special poker kept hot on the fireplace grate and reserved for the exclusive purpose of heating and frothing drinks.

While it may no longer be customary or practical to offer hot alcoholic drinks at all times, such libations are welcome and delightful on chilly or rainy evenings or as après-ski relaxers. Sharing a warm drink seems to invite good conversation and general conviviality. A special class of hot drinks add the element of drama as well. Offer even the most jaded of adults a flaming drink, and you are sure to get plenty of childlike ooohs and ahhhs.

Fortified Coffees of All Nations

Bar Tips

When mixing spirits with coffee, always pour the spirit in first. Then add the coffee.

The most obvious hot drink vehicle is America's favorite hot beverage: coffee. The most popular fortified coffees have national themes, derived from the kind of spirit used to fuel them.

The Italian part of the Italian Coffee is amaretto. The Mexican part of Café Mexicano is Kahlúa. Your favorite coffee will do, regardless of its nationality.

Amaretto Café (Italian Coffee)

Serve in a coffee mug.

1½ oz. amaretto

Hot coffee to fill

Whipped cream

Pour the amaretto into the mug and add hot coffee to fill. Top with whipped cream.

Roman Coffee

Combine Galliano with hot coffee for a Roman libation.

Serve in a coffee mug.

1½ oz. Galliano

Coffee to fill

Whipped cream

Pour Galliano into the mug. Add coffee to fill and top with whipped cream.

Vesuvio

Serve in a coffee cup.

1 cup hot black coffee, strong

1 oz. sambuca

1 cube sugar

Fill a cup with coffee, and then float half of the sambuca on top of the coffee. Do not stir! Put a sugar cube in a spoon and pour the rest of the sambuca into the spoon. Ignite.* Carefully dip the flaming spoon into the cup so that the sambuca float ignites. After the drink flames for a few seconds, stir to extinguish. Serve.

**Please observe instructions and cautions under "Going to Blazes."*

Café Mexicano

Café Mexicano hails from south of the border.

Serve in a coffee mug.

1 oz. Kahlúa

½ oz. white or gold tequila

Hot coffee

Whipped cream (optional)

Pour the Kahlúa and tequila in the mug. Add coffee. Top with whipped cream, if you wish.

Café Bonaparte

The French love their coffee, and although the Café Bonaparte and Café Marnier don't proclaim their nationality in their names, their Gallic identity is unmistakable.

Serve in a coffee mug or hot drink glass.

1½ oz. brandy

Cappuccino to fill

Pour the brandy into the serving glass, and then fill with cappuccino.

Café Marnier

Serve in a coffee mug.

1½ oz. Grand Marnier

Espresso to fill

Whipped cream (optional)

Pour the Grand Marnier into the mug. Add espresso to three-fourths full. Stir and add whipped cream, if you wish.

Café Zurich

In the name of Switzerland, we have the Café Zurich, the most elaborate of the national coffee drinks.

Serve in a coffee mug.

1½ oz. anisette

1½ oz. cognac

½ oz. amaretto

Coffee

1 tsp. honey

Whipped cream

Pour the spirits into the coffee mug. Add hot coffee to three-fourths full. Float a teaspoon of honey on top of the drink, and then top the honey with whipped cream.

Irish Coffee

By far, Irish Coffee is probably the most popular hot spiritous drink. Here's the classic version.

Serve in a coffee mug.

1½ oz. Irish whiskey

1 tsp. sugar

Coffee

Whipped cream

Pour whiskey into the mug. Add sugar. Add coffee to fill and top with whipped cream.

Creamy Irish Coffee

If you prefer a smoother drink, use Bailey's Irish Cream liqueur, which is made with Irish whiskey. Do not add extra sugar.

Serve in a coffee mug.

1½ oz. Bailey's Irish Cream

Coffee to fill

Whipped cream

Pour the liqueur into the mug. Add coffee to fill and top with whipped cream.

Jamaican Coffee

Flavors Jamaican have become more and more popular of late, whether it's jerked chicken or Jamaican Coffee.

Serve in a coffee mug.

1 oz. Tia Maria

¾ oz. rum (white, gold, or dark)

Coffee to fill

Whipped cream

Grated nutmeg

Pour Tia Maria and rum into the mug. Add coffee to fill, top with whipped cream, and sprinkle with nutmeg.

The following follow no particular flag, but are also among the most popular of coffee drinks.

Comfort Mocha

What is more comforting than a hot cocoa? Well …

Serve in a mug.

1½ oz. Southern Comfort

1 tsp. instant cocoa

1 tsp. instant coffee

Boiling water to fill

Whipped cream

Combine all ingredients, except the whipped cream, in a mug with boiling water. Top with whipped cream.

Café Diable

Serve in 4 demitasse cups. (Yields 4 small drinks.)

2 cinnamon sticks

8 whole cloves

6 whole coffee beans

2 oz. cognac

1 oz. Cointreau

1 oz. curaçao

1 pt. hot coffee, black, strong

Combine all ingredients, except the coffee, in a chafing dish and warm over a low flame. Ignite.* Allow to blaze for several seconds, and then add the coffee. Stir well, and then ladle into the serving cups.

**Please observe instructions and cautions under "Going to Blazes."*

Café Brülot

Serve in 4 demitasse cups. (Yields 4 small drinks.)

3-4 cinnamon sticks

8 whole cloves

4 sugar cubes

Zest of ½ orange

Zest of ½ lemon

4 oz. cognac

1 pt. hot coffee, black, strong

Combine all ingredients, except the cognac and coffee, in a chafing dish. Add a little water to soften the sugar cubes. Mash (muddle) the sugar into the zest of orange and lemon. Pour in warmed cognac. Thoroughly mix with the other ingredients, and then ignite the mixture.* Allow to blaze for several seconds, and then add the coffee. Ladle into the serving cups.

**Please observe instructions and cautions under "Going to Blazes."*

Café Amaretto

Serve in a coffee cup.

1 cup hot coffee, black, strong

1 oz. amaretto

½ oz. cognac

1 TB. whipped cream

Pour the amaretto into the coffee and stir. Float—do not stir—the cognac on top. Add whipped cream.

Café Royale

Serve in 4 demitasse cups. (Yields 4 small drinks.)

4 sugar cubes

1 pt. hot coffee, black, strong

4 oz. cognac

Rinse each serving cup in boiling water, and then place 1 sugar cube in each. Fill each cup half full with hot coffee. Float 1 oz. cognac in each cup. Ignite.* Let flame for several seconds, and then stir with a spoon to extinguish the flame.

**Please observe instructions and cautions under "Going to Blazes."*

Hot Rum Drinks

In its simplest original incarnation, grog was nothing more than rum diluted with water, and in Chapter 13 we introduced a more elaborate recipe. But grog can also be served hot.

Hot Buttered Rum

Hot Buttered Rum is talked about a lot more than it is actually served.

Serve in a mug.

1 tsp. sugar

1 tsp. butter

2 oz. white, gold, or dark rum

Boiling water to three-fourths full

Put the sugar and butter in the mug, and then add the rum. Pour in boiling water to three-fourths full. Stir.

Hot Grog

Serve in a mug.

1 tsp. sugar

1½ oz. rum

Juice of ¼ lemon

Boiling water to three-fourths full

Place sugar in the mug, and then add rum and the lemon juice. Finally, add boiling water to three-fourths full. Stir.

Coffee Grog

If you still can't get enough coffee with your hot liquor, try the Coffee Grog.

Serve in 4 flameproof mugs. (Yields 4 drinks.)

1 tsp. butter

1 TB. brown sugar

Nutmeg, grated

12 whole cloves

4 cinnamon sticks

4 small slices of lemon peel

4 small slices of orange peel

1 cup dark Jamaica rum

Hot coffee, black, strong

Whipped cream

Cream butter with brown sugar and a few pinches of the nutmeg. Add this mixture to each of 4 serving cups and drop into each 3 cloves, 1 cinnamon stick, 1 slice of lemon peel, 1 slice of orange peel, and 2 oz. rum. (Warm the rum before adding. This ensures that it will flame.) Stir each well. Ignite each.* Let blaze for several seconds, and then pour in the coffee. Stir. Top with whipped cream.

**Please observe instructions and cautions under "Going to Blazes."*

Buzzed Words

A **hot toddy** is any alcohol-based sweetened hot drink. It can be shortened simply to **toddy.** There is no such thing as a cold toddy.

Toddy Collection

Originally, a *hot toddy* was a hot drink made from the fermented sap of certain Asian palm trees. Nowadays, a toddy is any alcohol-based sweetened hot drink. Here are some classic toddies. (You may vary either of these toddies by using brandy, rum, gin, or vodka instead of blended whiskey or bourbon.)

Your Basic Hot Toddy

Serve in a mug.

1 tsp. sugar

2 oz. blended whiskey

Boiling water to three-fourths full

Put the sugar in the mug, and then add the whiskey. Add boiling water to three-fourths full. Stir.

Hot Toddy with Bourbon

Serve in a mug.

1 tsp. sugar

3 whole cloves

Cinnamon stick

Lemon slice

4 oz. boiling water

1 oz. bourbon

Grated nutmeg

Put the sugar, cloves, cinnamon stick, and lemon slice into the mug. Add 1 oz. of the boiling water and stir. After letting the mixture steep for five minutes, pour in the bourbon and the rest of the boiling water. Stir. Dust with nutmeg.

Bar Tips

Wine and most liqueurs cannot endure boiling. The flavor as well as much of the alcoholic content will go up in steam.

Hot Apple Toddy

Serve in a 10 oz. mug.

2 oz. apple brandy

2 oz. hot baked apple

2 tsp. cider (choose sweet or hard)

Piping hot water

Grated nutmeg

Heat the serving glass, and then combine the brandy and baked apple in it. Fill with hot water and stir. Sprinkle with nutmeg.

Hot Brick Toddy

Serve in a 10 oz. mug.

2 oz. blended whiskey

1 tsp. sweet butter

1 tsp. powdered sugar

1 TB. hot water

Dash cinnamon

Combine all ingredients, except the whiskey, in the serving glass. Stir well. Add the whiskey and top off with enough hot water to fill.

Hot Gin Toddy

Serve in a 10 oz. mug.

2½ oz. gin

1½ oz. lemon juice

2 sugar cubes

Boiling water

Lemon slice

In the serving glass dissolve the sugar in the lemon juice. Add gin, and then top off with boiling water. Garnish with the lemon slice.

Comfort Drinks

Just about any hot drink you can make is soothing, but the following recipes will summon up visions of true nirvana.

To mull a drink is to spice and heat it. We begin with two ways of mulling claret. The first recipe is for an individual drink; the second, for a batch.

Mulled Claret

Serve in a mug.

5 oz. red Bordeaux

1 oz. port

¾ oz. brandy

Pinch ground cinnamon

Pinch grated nutmeg

A few whole cloves

Lemon twist

Combine all ingredients in a saucepan and heat, but do not boil. Pour into the mug.

Mulled Claret Batch

Yield: 13 drinks

2 oz. honey

1 (750 ml.) bottle red Bordeaux

1 pt. ruby port

1 cup brandy

6 whole cloves

Few cinnamon sticks, broken

½ tsp. grated nutmeg

Lemon twist

In the flaming pan of a chafing dish over direct heat, dissolve the honey with 1 cup water. Add the Bordeaux, port, brandy, spices, and lemon. Heat over a low flame, stirring occasionally. Do not allow to boil.

Simple Mulled Cider

A delicious Mulled Cider can be made quite simply.

Serve in mugs.

3 oz. sugar

3 pints hard cider

4 oz. rum

1 cinnamon stick per mug

Pinch allspice per mug

Combine ingredients in a pot. Heat and stir, but do not boil. Strain into the mug. The recipe yields three large or five smaller drinks.

Mulled Cider (Single Serving)

If you prefer your Mulled Cider one drink at a time, here is a very elegant recipe.

Serve in a mug.

2 oz. gold rum

Dash Angostura bitters

4 whole cloves

Cinnamon stick

Pinch ground allspice

1 tsp. honey

1 cup apple cider

Lemon twist

Heat all ingredients in a saucepan and stir well. Strain into the mug.

Mulled Vermont Cider

Serve in mugs. (Yields approximately 4 drinks.)

2 qts. sweet cider

1 TB. brown sugar

Cinnamon sticks

Ground cloves

Allspice

8 oz. apple brandy

In a large saucepan, dissolve the sugar in the cider. Bring to a boil. Wrap the spices in a fine cheesecloth bag and infuse in the boiling cider for a full 15 minutes while stirring. Separately, warm the brandy. Remove the spice bag and add the brandy to the boiled cider. Serve piping hot.

Buzzed Words

Hard cider is fermented cider and, therefore, alcoholic. **Sweet cider** is nonalcoholic apple cider.

The classic hot drink Tom and Jerry predates the cartoons by many years and takes its name from two characters—Corinthian Tom and Jerry Hawkins—in Life in London, a popular novel by Pierce Egan. Some authorities believe the Egan characters are less important to the name of the drink than the apparent fact that it was invented by a bartender named Jerry Thomas. The Tom and Jerry has long been enjoyed as a punch. (See Chapter 23 for a punch recipe.)

Here are two popular versions:

Tom and Jerry #1

Serve in a mug.

1 egg white*

2 tsp. sugar

Pinch baking soda

2 oz. rum

Hot milk

½ oz. cognac

Grated nutmeg

Combine in a bowl the egg white, sugar, baking soda, and ½ oz. of the rum. Beat until stiff. Combine this mixture with an additional 1½ oz. rum and 2 TB. hot milk. Pour into the mug, and then add hot milk to fill. Float cognac on top and dust with nutmeg.

**Raw egg may be a source of salmonella bacteria. You may wish to avoid drinks calling for raw egg yolk or white.*

Tom and Jerry #2

The alternative recipe that follows is simpler.

Serve in a mug.

1 egg*

½ oz. sugar syrup

1 oz. dark Jamaica rum

1 oz. cognac

Boiling water to fill

Grated nutmeg

Separate the egg and beat white and yolk separately, and then fold white and yolk together. Add sugar syrup, and then pour mixture into the serving mug. Add the rum and cognac, followed by boiling water to fill. Dust with nutmeg.

**Raw egg may be a source of salmonella bacteria. You may wish to avoid drinks calling for raw egg yolk or white.*

Glüwein

Relax! Relax. Relax …

Serve in a warmed mug.

5 oz. Madeira

Lemon peel orange peel

Small cinnamon stick, broken

Few whole cloves

Pinch ground nutmeg

1 tsp. honey

Heat all ingredients in a saucepan, stirring until the honey is completely dissolved. Do not allow to boil. Pour into serving glass.

Fuzzy Nut

Serve in a warmed mug.

1½ oz. DeKuyper Peachtree Schnapps

½ oz. amaretto

5 oz. hot chocolate

Whipped cream

Pinch ground cinnamon

Combine all ingredients, except the whipped cream and cinnamon, in the serving glass. Stir. Top with whipped cream and garnish with the cinnamon.

Black Stripe

Serve in a mug.

2 tsp. molasses

Boiling water

Lemon peel

Cinnamon stick

3 oz. dark Jamaica rum

Pinch ground nutmeg

Put molasses in the serving glass, and then dissolve with a little boiling water. Add the lemon peel and cinnamon stick, and then pour in more boiling water. Float the rum on top. If desired, blaze this drink by igniting the rum and allowing to burn for several seconds.* Sprinkle with nutmeg.

**Please observe instructions and cautions under "Going to Blazes."*

Highland Hot Milk Punch

Serve in a mug.

2 oz. scotch

1 oz. Drambuie

½ oz. sugar syrup

1 whole egg, beaten*

1 cup milk

Pinch powdered cinnamon

Combine all ingredients, except the cinnamon, in a saucepan. Heat over low flame while occasionally stirring. Pour into the serving glass and sprinkle with cinnamon.

**Raw egg may be a source of salmonella bacteria. You may wish to avoid drinks calling for raw egg yolk or white.*

Alhambra Royale

Serve in a cup.

1 cup hot chocolate

Orange peel

1½ oz. cognac

1 TB. whipped cream

Add the orange peel to a cup of hot chocolate. Warm cognac in a ladle, and then ignite.* While blazing, pour into the cup of hot chocolate. Stir. Top with whipped cream.

**Please observe instructions and cautions under "Going to Blazes."*

Locomotive

Serve in a mug.

6 oz. dry red wine

½ oz. curaçao

½ oz. maraschino liqueur

½ oz. honey

1 egg*

Lemon slice

Pinch ground cinnamon

In a saucepan combine the wine, curaçao, maraschino liqueur, and honey. Stir until the honey is completely dissolved, and then gradually heat the mixture. Do not allow to boil. When hot, add the egg, slightly beaten. Bring mixture to a simmer. Pour into the serving glass, garnish with the lemon slice, and sprinkle with the cinnamon.

**Raw egg may be a source of salmonella bacteria. You may wish to avoid drinks calling for raw egg yolk or white.*

Going to Blazes

Few acts of mixology are more impressive than setting a drink ablaze. The effect is not only theatrical; done correctly, it enhances the flavor of the drink and, most importantly, results in no injury to oneself or one's guests.

Don't Try This at Home!

Most liquor has a relatively low concentration of alcohol. If what you're working with is 80 proof, the liquid is only 40 percent alcohol. This means that it probably won't burn unless it is vaporized; therefore, your first step is to heat a *small* amount of alcohol before igniting it.

This said, it must be observed that *vaporized* alcohol, even at relatively low concentrations, is *very* flammable. So, before we get into the details of how to flame drinks, let's take time for a safety check:

Bar Tips

The flaming drink is definitely not child's play. *Flaming alcohol is intensely hot and can cause serious burn injuries!* In addition to safety, it is important to flame drinks properly in order to preserve as well as enhance their flavor.

- Use the smallest amount of liquor possible to flame drinks. For a single drink, an ounce is sufficient.
- Respect alcohol as a flammable liquid, which can cause severe injury or property damage.
- Do not flame drinks near draperies, curtains, paper banners, bunting, streamers, or other combustible materials.
- When flaming or heating spirits in a saucepan or chafing dish, stand back. Do not put your face directly over the pan. The vapors might flare up!
- Never heat or flame spirits in a chafing dish at the serving table. If the hot or flaming liquid should spill, you could end up burning a number of people. Instead, heating and flaming should be done on a stable cart or serving table apart from guests.
- Do not keep uncorked spirits near an open flame.
- Never add spirits into a flaming dish! There is a good chance that the vapors will ignite and the fire will blow back on you or someone else.
- Alcohol burns with a pale flame. If the lights in the room are bright, you and your guests might not see the flame. This is not only dangerous, but insufficiently spectacular. Dim the room lights before flaming.
- When flaming drinks, be especially careful of small children in the area.
- Generally, alcohol burns off quickly; however, always have a sufficiently large lid on hand to cover the chafing dish in order to put out a fire gone awry.
- Although you can expect the alcohol to burn off quickly, never leave a flaming drink—especially in a large chafing dish—unattended.

Bar Tips

A flaming drink is *never* to be consumed while it is flaming! This may sound like superfluous advice. Who'd be dumb enough to drink fire? But in some college bars and elsewhere, the idea is to down a flaming drink at once so that the alcohol vapor burns off above the glass, while the liquor is safely downed. Raising a flaming drink to your face, and then trying to drink it, is always a very bad idea.

Ignition ... Lift Off!

To flame a drink successfully and safely, begin by taking a single teaspoonful of the liquor you want to flame. Warm this over a lighted match in order to vaporize some of the alcohol. Ignite the liquor in the spoon, and then carefully pour the flaming alcohol over the prepared recipe. Do *not* put your face near the drink you are flaming. Stand back.

Buzzed Words

As a verb, **flambé** means to drench with liquor and ignite. The word may also be used as a noun, synonymous with flaming drink.

Achieving Spectacular Effects

Flaming drinks can appear disappointing if you fail to ...

- Heat a small amount of the liquor first, in order to vaporize it.
- Turn down the lights. An alcohol flame is pale. Make certain that you and your guests can see it.

A lot of the spectacle of the flambé is in the performance rather than the flame. Make the flambé a full-dress presentation. Put on a show, and look like you're enjoying what you're doing. (Be certain, too, to observe the safety rules listed previously.)

Flaming Rum

Rum is well suited to the flambé because the flaming process creates a delicious collection of concentrated natural flavors.

Burning Blue Mountain

Serve in a egg nog-style mug.

5 oz. dark Jamaican rum

2 tsp. powdered sugar

Orange rind, cut up

Lime rind, cut up

Lemon twist

Pour rum into a chafing dish and warm. Add sugar and fruit rinds. Stir to dissolve sugar, and then ignite. Ladle the drink into the serving glass and garnish with the lemon twist.

Christmas Rum Punch

Serve in a punch bowl.

6 oranges

Cloves

1 bottle dark rum

Sugar to taste

½ gallon sweet cider

Powdered cinnamon

Grated nutmeg

Prepare the oranges by sticking them with cloves, and then baking until the oranges begin to brown. Slice the oranges and place in a punch bowl. Add rum. Add sugar to taste. Carefully ignite and allow to burn for a few minutes before extinguishing with the cider. Garnish with cinnamon and nutmeg.

Flaming Brandy

Brandy is the most frequently used fuel for flamed drinks.

Big Apple

Serve in a warmed 10 oz. mug.

3 oz. apple juice

Pinch ground ginger

3 TB. baked apple

1 oz. apple brandy

Combine the apple juice and ginger in a saucepan. Heat and let simmer for a few minutes. Put the baked apple in the serving mug. Pour the apple brandy into a ladle. Warm the ladle over a match or a low gas flame. Ignite the brandy in the ladle, and then pour over the baked apple. Extinguish the fire with the warm ginger-spiced apple juice. Stir. Serve warm, with a spoon for eating the apple.

Coffee Blazer

Serve in an old-fashioned glass.

1 TB. Kahlúa

1 TB. cognac

Sugar

Lemon slice

Hot coffee to fill

Whipped cream

Warm the Kahlúa and cognac over a match or low gas flame. Moisten the rim of the serving glass with the lemon slice, and then roll the rim in sugar; drop the lemon slice in the glass. Warm the glass over a low flame to melt the sugar on the rim. Pour in the warmed Kahlúa and cognac and ignite. Extinguish with the coffee. Stir well and top with whipped cream.

Flaming Et Cetera

Some folks just like to see things burn, and inventive mixologists are no exception. Here's a variety of nontraditional flaming drinks.

Aberdeen Angus

Serve in an egg nog–style mug.

½ oz. lime juice

½ oz. heather honey

Boiling water

2 oz. scotch

1 oz. Drambuie

Into a heat-proof mug, pour the lime juice and honey. Add sufficient boiling water to dissolve the honey. Into a small ladle, combine the two spirits. Ignite. Pour the flaming mixture into the mug. Top off with boiling water. Stir, and serve hot.

Flames Over New Jersey

Serve in a punch bowl.

1 qt. Apple brandy

Several dashes Angostura bitters

8 oz. sugar

1 qt. boiling water

Begin by warming the brandy. Then combine it with the bitters and sugar in a punch bowl. Stir to dissolve the sugar. Ignite. Allow to burn for several seconds, then extinguish with the boiling water. Stir. Ladle into punch cups while hot.

Fresh Flames

Hot drinks may seem old fashioned, but they are alive and well—and, often, pretty wild.

Galway

Serve in a mug.

1½ oz. Irish whiskey

½ oz. Frangelico

1 TB. amaretto

1 TB. Kahlúa

Coffee, black, hot

Whipped cream

Combine the spirits in a mug, and then add the coffee. Stir. Top with whipped cream.

Bulgarian Sludge

Serve in a mug.

Hot chocolate

2 oz. tequila

1 TB. 151-proof rum

1 TB. cherry syrup

Whipped cream

Fill a mug half full with hot chocolate. Add the other ingredients, except for the whipped cream. Stir. Top with a generous portion of whipped cream.

Fugari

Serve in a teacup.

Hot tea

1 oz. Campari

1 tsp. lime juice

3 chocolate morsels (chocolate chips)

Mint sprig

Fill a teacup ¾ full of tea. Add the other ingredients, except for the mint sprig. Stir well. Garnish with the sprig.

Stetson

Serve in a mug.

Coffee, hot, black

1½ oz. Jack Daniels

½ oz. amaretto

1 TB. maple syrup

Fill a mug ¾ full with coffee. Add the other ingredients. Stir well.

Organ Warmer

Serve in a mug.

1½ oz. cognac

1 oz. light crème de cacao

Hot chocolate

Combine the spirits in a mug, and then fill with hot chocolate. Stir.

Hot Banana Smoker

Serve in a mug.

1½ oz. vodka

1 oz. light crème de cacao

1 oz. banana brandy

1 TB. cream of coconut

Coffee, hot, black

1 peeled banana

Whipped cream

Combine the spirits in a mug, and then fill with hot coffee. Stir. Insert banana and top with whipped cream.

The Least You Need to Know

- Hot liquor-based drinks were most popular in the days before central heating.
- Before the advent of convenient refrigeration, more drinks were served hot than on ice.
- Today, coffee and liquor combinations are the most popular hot drinks.
- Flambés—flaming drinks—make for high drama and fun, but it is important to flame and serve them safely.

Chapter 18

Architectural Masterpieces: Building the Pousse-Café

In This Chapter

- The pousse-café challenge
- Skills and equipment required to build a pousse-café
- Pouring the pousse-café
- Pousse-café problems and how to overcome them
- Pousse-café recipes

For mountaineers, it's Everest. For concert pianists, it's the Rachmaninoff Third Piano Concerto. For a Renaissance painter, it was a great cathedral ceiling. For the bartender, it's the pousse-café.

These little gems—little, because they are characteristically served in pony glasses (1-2 oz.) or pousse-café glasses (3-4 oz.)—evoke unbridled admiration for the bartender and his or her art. They are colorful layers of liquid. Liquid! In layers! It's magic!

Actually, it's specific gravity, and this chapter shows you how to take advantage of the laws of physics to create tasty and visually appealing dessert drinks.

Many-Layered Drinks

Pousse-cafés are drinks made with two, three, four, or more liqueurs and, often, cream. Because the different spirits have differing specific gravities, some will float on top of some others. Poured carefully and in the proper order—from heaviest to lightest—the liqueurs will remain unmixed, layered like a wedding cake, some strangely beautiful geological formation, or a miniature work of architecture, depending on your imagination.

Buzzed Words

A **pousse-café** is a drink made with two or more liqueurs and, sometimes, cream. The different spirits vary in specific gravity, so float in discrete layers if carefully combined. The layered effect is novel and pretty.

These drinks are miniature spectaculars, and, as such, they require practice, patience, and a bit of good luck. It is almost impossible to create pousse-cafés in a busy bar humming with jarring and jolting activity. Although making a pousse-café is not as difficult as building a model clipper ship in a bottle, you will need some measure of peace and quiet.

Do You Have What It Takes?

In addition to peace and quiet, to make a pousse-café you'll need …

- A steady hand
- A little patience
- A good sense of humor
- Guests with a little patience and as good a sense of humor as yours
- Practice
- A twisted-handle bar spoon
- A set of pony glasses or, better yet, pousse-café glasses

Let's address the last two requirements. (The necessity and nature of the other prerequisites will become self-evident as soon as you start experimenting with these drinks.) In Chapter 4, we described the bar spoon. That long handle with its spiral twist serves an important purpose in pulling off a successful pousse-café. Here's how you use the bar spoon:

1. Measure out the appropriate amount of the first liqueur. (We'll talk about amounts in just a minute or two.)

2. From the measuring glass, pour the first—that is, the heaviest—ingredient into the serving glass.
3. Measure out the next—lighter—liqueur.

Okay. That was easy. But there are two schools of thought about just how to use the bar spoon to add the next—and subsequent—layers. Here are steps 4 and 5 according to School of Thought #1:

4. Hold the spoon upside down; that is, with the bottom of the spoon facing up. Place the handle of the spoon nearest the bowl against the mouth of the measuring glass containing the liquid you want to pour. The handle should cover the entire diameter of the measuring glass. Insert the other end of the spoon handle into the serving glass, against the inside wall of the glass and just above the level of the liquid already inside the glass.
5. *Slowly* pour so that the liqueur slides down the handle, is slowed by the spiral twist, and then slips down along the inside wall of the glass. This avoids agitating the liquids, enabling the lighter liquid to float on the heavier one without blending with it. Do this for each successive layer of liqueur, always proceeding, of course, from light, to lighter, to lightest spirit.

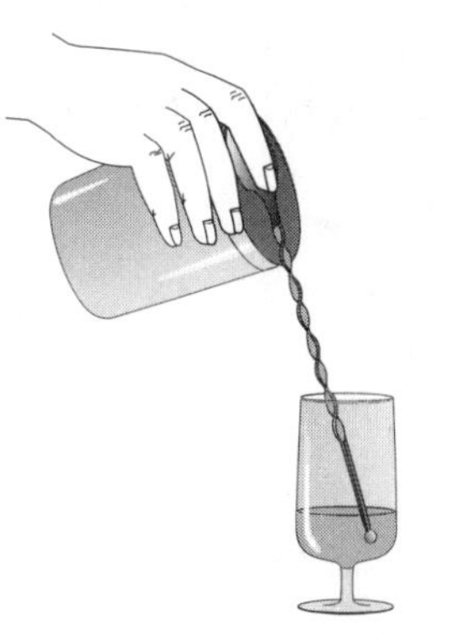

Pousse-café pouring method #1.

Here are steps 4 and 5 according to School of Thought #2:

4. Hold the bar spoon so that the bowl of the spoon will be inserted into the serving glass. The convex back of the bowl should be toward you so that the liqueur will slip around the back of the bowl. Put the other end of the spoon, the handle, against the measuring glass so that it spans the entire diameter of the glass. Insert the bowl end into the serving glass, touching the back of the bowl against the inside wall of the glass, just above the level of the liqueur already present in the glass.

5. Pour *slowly* so that the liqueur slides down the handle, is slowed by the spiral twist, and then slips down over the back of the spoon bowl, along the inside wall of the glass, and onto the first layer of liqueur. This avoids agitating the liquids, enabling the lighter liquid to float on the heavier one without blending with it. Do this for each successive layer of liqueur, always proceeding, of course, from light, to lighter, to lightest spirit.

Pousse-café pouring method #2.

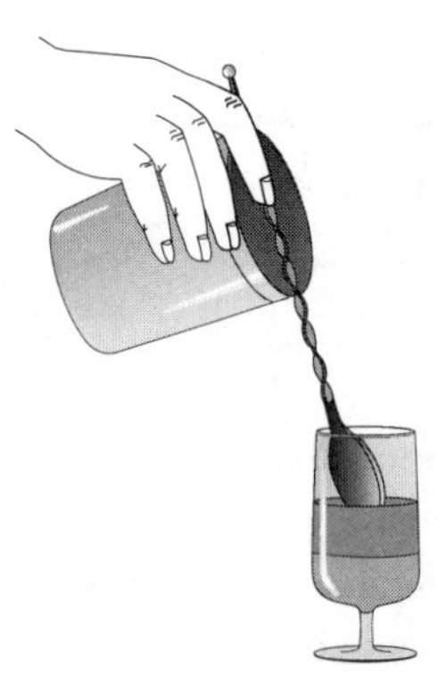

Now to the glasses. A large pony glass (2 oz.) or a small pousse-café glass (3 oz.) is best. To create and maintain the layering effect, it is crucial that the glass be quite a bit taller than it is wide. A cylindrical, tube like configuration is best.

The foundation of your creation.

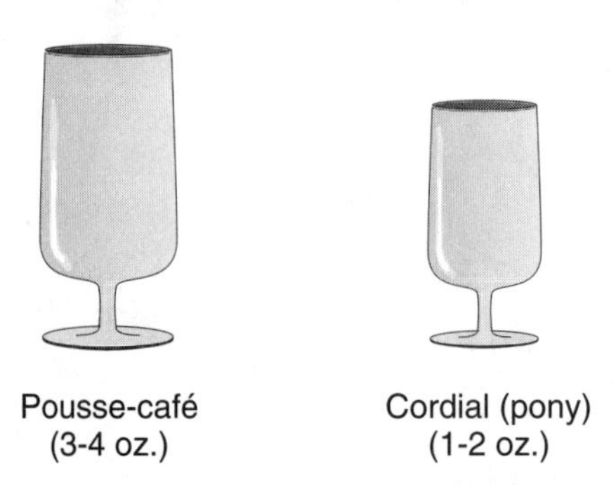

You see, although one layer of liquid is lighter than the layer that preceded it, each layer still has weight. The surface tension of each of the lower layers helps support and maintain separation of layers. To the extent that the surface of the liquid is made larger—by a wider-mouthed glass—the weaker the surface tension and the less stable the layering becomes.

Pousse-café recipes usually call for a teaspoon—that is, ¼ ounce—of liqueur for each layer. That's why a 3-ounce serving glass is ideal. A 1-ounce pony will severely limit the number of layers you can build, and if you try to compensate for this by reducing the amount of liqueur in each layer, you'll end up with layers that are either too thin to sustain or simply too thin to have much visual impact. A 4-ounce pousse-café glass is fine for many-layered drinks, but a three- or four-layer creation will get lost in such a glass—unless you increase the amount of liqueur in each layer, which is perfectly acceptable.

If you can't obtain 3-ounce glasses, adjust the amount of each liqueur to fill a larger glass adequately or, if your glass is small, restrict the number of layers you build.

Bar Tips

You can get along without a bar spoon. You'll probably get satisfactory results pouring your layers down a long, glass stirring rod. If you're skilled, you might be able to tilt the serving glass slightly, and pour each succeeding layer slowly down the side of the glass. But why don't you just go out and get a bar spoon? Accessories make the bar.

Layering Logistics

In all the recipes you'll find here, ingredients are listed in descending order, with the heaviest ingredient listed first, and the lightest last. It is imperative that the ingredients be added in order—the top-listed ingredient first, the next one next, and so on.

What can go wrong with a pousse-café?

- You can inadvertently pour the ingredients out of order. The result: total disaster (although nobody will be permanently injured).
- An over-eager guest can slap a hand on your back while you are pouring. Result: Ditto.
- A rowdy guest can slap a hand down on the bar or table on which you are preparing the drink. Result: Ditto again.
- You discover that you are in the flight path of a major airport. Result: Double ditto.
- You become overconfident and pour too fast. Result: More ditto.
- The bar spoon slips into the drink. Result: Ditto upon ditto.
- You complete your work, and then move the glass too quickly. Result: Ditto, ditto, ditto.
- Your guest seizes the drink you have so lovingly prepared, grabs a swizzle stick, and …

A Host of Angels

Pousse-cafés are by nature small, delicate, airy, and ephemeral of taste and appearance divine—at least more or less. For these reasons, a number of the classic pousse-cafés are called Angel's something-or-other.

Remember to pour the ingredients of the Angel's Delight exactly in the order listed. Grenadine is heaviest, the cream is the lightest.

Angel's Delight

Serve in a 3 oz. pousse-café glass.

½ oz. grenadine

½ oz. triple sec

½ oz. Crème Yvette

½ oz. cream

Use a bar spoon to pour each layer into the serving glass, exactly in the order listed. One layer should float upon another. *Do not stir!*

Angel's Kiss

Be certain to use cognac, not only for taste, but to ensure the proper specific gravity of the Angel's Kiss.

Serve in a 3 oz. pousse-café glass.

½ oz. white crème de cacao

½ oz. Crème Yvette

½ oz. cognac

½ oz. cream

Use a bar spoon to pour each layer into the serving glass, exactly in the order listed. One layer should float upon another. *Do not stir!*

Simple Angel's Kiss

Feel the need for training wheels? You might try the Simple Angel's Kiss as your first pousse-café.

Serve in a 3 oz. pousse-café glass.

1½ oz. Kahlúa

1 oz. heavy cream

Float the cream on top of the Kahlúa in the serving glass.

First Angel's Tit

There are two popular versions of the Angel's Tit.

Serve in a 3 oz. pousse-café glass.

¾ oz. brown crème de cacao

¾ oz. cream

Maraschino cherry

Use a bar spoon to pour each layer into the serving glass, exactly in the order listed. One layer should float upon the other. *Do not stir!* Pierce the cherry through with a toothpick and balance it across the glass as a garnish.

Second Angel's Tit

Serve in a 3 oz. pousse-café glass.

¾ oz. brown crème de cacao

¾ oz. maraschino liqueur

¾ oz. cream

Maraschino cherry

Use a bar spoon to pour each layer into the serving glass, exactly in the order listed. One layer should float upon another. *Do not stir!* Pierce the cherry through with a toothpick and balance it across the glass as a garnish.

Angel's Tip

If modesty leads you away from the two drinks just mentioned, there is also the Angel's Tip—in every way a more modest drink.

Serve in a 3 oz. pousse-café glass.

1½ oz. crème de cacao

1 oz. heavy cream

Float the cream on top of the crème de cacao in the serving glass.

Slippery Nipple

For those who have very few modesty issues, there is the following.

Serve in a 3 oz. pousse-café glass.

1½ oz. sambuca

1 oz. Bailey's Irish Cream

Drop grenadine

Use a bar spoon to pour the sambuca and then the Bailey's into the serving glass, exactly in the order listed. One layer should float upon the other. *Do not stir!* Add a drop of grenadine in the center.

Buttery Nipple

Serve in a 3 oz. pousse-café glass.

1¼ oz. Butterscotch schnapps

1¼ oz. Bailey's Irish cream

Use a bar spoon to pour the schnapps and then the Bailey's into the serving glass, exactly in the order listed. One layer should float upon the other. *Do not stir!*

Angel's Wing

The Angel's Wing is one part of the angel's anatomy no one finds objectionable in mixed company.

Serve in a 3 oz. pousse-café glass.

¾ oz. white crème de cacao

¾ oz. cognac

¾ oz. cream

Use a bar spoon to pour each layer into the serving glass, exactly in the order listed. One layer should float upon another. *Do not stir!*

Royal Palaces

The gaze of some folks is directed earthward, to corporeal rather than angelic glories. Here are some regal pousse-café creations.

King Alphonse

The King Alphonse is a First Angel's Tit without the cherry.

Serve in a 3 oz. pousse-café glass.

1¼ oz. brown crème de cacao

1¼ oz. cream

Use a bar spoon to pour each layer into the serving glass, exactly in the order listed. One layer should float upon the other. *Do not stir!*

King's Cup

The King's Cup is a simple drink, for a pousse-café, which calls for two-thirds Galliano and one-third cream.

Serve in a 3 oz. pousse-café glass.

1½ oz. Galliano

1¼ oz. cream

Use a bar spoon to pour each layer into the serving glass, exactly in the order listed. One layer should float upon the other. *Do not stir!*

Princess

The Princess is another modest libation.

Serve in a 3 oz. pousse-café glass.

1½ oz. apricot brandy

½ oz. cream

Use a bar spoon to pour each layer into the serving glass, exactly in the order listed. One layer should float upon the other. *Do not stir!*

Savoy

Regal, too, is the Savoy.

Serve in a 3 oz. pousse-café glass.

¾ oz. crème de cacao

¾ oz. Benedictine

¾ oz. cognac

Use a bar spoon to pour each layer into the serving glass, exactly in the order listed. One layer should float upon the other. *Do not stir!*

Aunt Jemima

Sometimes it's better to shun the palace and take a trip down home.

Serve in a 3 oz. pousse-café glass.

¾ oz. brandy

¾ oz. white crème de cacao

¾ oz. Benedictine

Use a bar spoon to pour each layer into the serving glass, exactly in the order listed. One layer should float upon the other. *Do not stir!*

Patriot's Pride: Red, White, and Blue Creations

Here is a trio of patriotic pousses. (Patriotic, provided that you are American—or French—with a fondness for your national colors.)

Stars and Stripes Version #1

Serve in a 3 oz. pousse-café glass.

¾ oz. grenadine

¾ oz. heavy cream

¾ oz. Crème Yvette

Use a bar spoon to pour each layer into the serving glass, exactly in the order listed. One layer should float upon the other. *Do not stir!*

Stars and Stripes Version #2

Serve in a 3 oz. pousse-café glass.

¾ oz. grenadine

¾ oz. maraschino liqueur

¾ oz. Parfait Amour

Use a bar spoon to pour each layer into the serving glass, exactly in the order listed. One layer should float upon the other. *Do not stir!*

Stars and Stripes Version #3

Serve in a 3 oz. pousse-café glass.

¾ oz. creme de cassis

¾ oz. green Chartreuse

¾ oz. maraschino liqueur

Use a bar spoon to pour each layer into the serving glass, exactly in the order listed. One layer should float upon the other. *Do not stir!*

Old Glory

Serve in a 3 oz. pousse-café glass.

¾ oz. grenadine

½ oz. heavy cream

¾ oz. Crème Yvette

Use a bar spoon to pour each layer into the serving glass, exactly in the order listed. One layer should float upon the other. *Do not stir!*

Traffic Light

Only slightly less emblematic of the U.S. of A. than the Red, White, and Blue is the all-too familiar Red, Yellow, and Green. The Traffic Light is one of the most amusing of pousse-cafés.

Serve in a 3 oz. pousse-café glass.

¾ oz. green crème de menthe

¾ oz. crème de banana

¾ oz. sloe gin

Use a bar spoon to pour each layer into the serving glass, exactly in the order listed. One layer should float upon the other. *Do not stir!*

Spectaculars

Here are three of the more spectacular pousse-cafés you can make.

The Classic

Serve in a 3 oz. pousse-café glass.

¼ oz. grenadine

¼ oz. crème de cacao

¼ oz. maraschino liqueur

¼ oz. curaçao

¼ oz. green crème de menthe

¼ oz. Parfait Amour

¼ oz. cognac

Use a bar spoon to pour each layer into the serving glass, exactly in the order listed. One layer should float upon the other. *Do not stir!*

St. Moritz Pousse-Café

Serve in a 3 oz. pousse-café glass.

¼ oz. raspberry syrup

¼ oz. anisette

¼ oz. Parfait Amour

¼ oz. yellow Chartreuse

¼ oz. green Chartreuse

¼ oz. curaçao

¼ oz. cognac

Use a bar spoon to pour each layer into the serving glass, exactly in the order listed. One layer should float upon the other. *Do not stir!*

Rancho Mirage

Serve in a 3 oz. pousse-café glass.

½ oz. blackberry brandy

½ oz. gin

½ oz. crème de banana

½ oz. cream

Use a bar spoon to pour each layer into the serving glass, exactly in the order listed. One layer should float upon the other. *Do not stir!*

Pousse L'Amour

This last drink includes a bright yellow layer. Some people like it. Some don't. Certainly, this is one pousse-café that will raise eyebrows.

Serve in a 3 oz. pousse-café glass.

¾ oz. maraschino liqueur

1 unbroken egg yolk*

¾ oz. Benedictine

¾ oz. cognac

Pour the maraschino liqueur into the serving glass. Carefully float on the unbroken egg yolk, and then use a bar spoon to pour the next two layers, one after the other. Add all ingredients exactly in the order listed. One layer should float upon the other. *Do not stir!*

**Raw egg may be a source of salmonella bacteria. You may wish to avoid drinks calling for raw egg yolk or white.*

Build Your Own Pousse-Café

As with a child and building blocks, there are few limits to the possible combinations of piling one liqueur upon another. To be exact, there are three limitations:

1. The relative weight of the liqueur
2. What tastes good—and does not taste good—to you
3. Your sense of color combination

The first limitation is rather easy to understand. The following is a list of popular pousse-café ingredients, from heaviest to lightest:

1. Anisette
2. Crème de noyaux
3. Crème de menthe
4. Crème de banana
5. Crème de cacao
6. Maraschino liqueur
7. Coffee liqueur
8. Kahlúa
9. Cherry liqueur
10. Parfait Amour
11. Blue curaçao
12. Blackberry liqueur
13. Apricot liqueur
14. Bailey's Irish Cream
15. Orange curaçao
16. Triple sec
17. Coffee brandy
18. Peach brandy
19. Cherry brandy
20. Blackberry brandy
21. Apricot brandy
22. Sambuca
23. Rock and Rye
24. Ginger brandy
25. Peppermint schnapps
26. Kummel
27. Peach liqueur
28. Sloe gin
29. Cream

Note that anisette and crème de noyaux have almost identical specific gravities; it might be difficult to layer these two together. The same is true for …

- cherry brandy and blackberry brandy
- blackberry brandy and apricot brandy
- apricot brandy and rock and rye
- peach liqueur and sloe gin
- cherry liqueur and Parfait Amour
- orange curaçao and triple sec

In general—subject to your taste, of course—you are best off layering liqueurs that are separated by at least three others in this list. For example, put maraschino liqueur on top of anisette rather than trying to put coffee liqueur on top of maraschino liqueur. This should ensure stable separation of layers.

How many liqueurs are you allowed to layer? As many as you dare. Just remember that liqueurs adjacent to one another in this list might not maintain their separation because their specific gravities are similar.

Do you really want to do this?

If you make a mistake, all of your work will be spoiled, and you'll be a laughingstock. The fact is that most pousse-cafés have three to five layers, with a few venturing to as many as seven. If you spend all of your time building pousse-cafés, you won't have much time left to *enjoy* the drink.

But experimenting can be fun—and the drinks still *taste* just good, even if the layers blend. Practice before entertaining—and drink your mistakes before they become common knowledge.

The Least You Need to Know

- Pousse-cafés require patience, a steady hand, and a relatively quiet place to build them. A busy bar setting is not conducive to creating a successful layered drink.
- Pousse-café recipes must be followed exactly, in order to ensure that the heaviest layer is poured first, the next heaviest next, the lighter layer after that, and so on.
- A twisted-handle bar spoon is an invaluable aid to pouring pousse-cafés.
- Small-diameter glassware is important in order to increase the surface tension that helps to separate each layer of liquid.

Part 6

A Fresh Round

Let's not lower an iron curtain between distilled spirits and fermented beverages. Brought together intelligently, "hard liquor" and wine, champagne, and even beer can create some lovely drinks. Many of these have been around for a very long time, but they have been rediscovered only recently. Others are quite new.

As the fermented spirits can be used to expand a mixed-drink vocabulary based on hard liquor, so thoughtful choice can be exercised to allow dieters to enjoy spirits without breaking the caloric bank. Here's a chapter full of delicious and varied recipes.

But mixing and enjoying adult beverages doesn't have to be all about liquor. A thoughtful host and bartender provides ample and tasty alternatives to alcohol, and this section closes with some of the most delightful adult drinks without spirits.

Chapter 19

More of a Good Thing: Wine, Champagne, and Beer Drinks

In This Chapter

- The emergence of wine as a mixer
- Ancient traditions of flavoring wine
- How wine, champagne, and beer can expand your mixed-drink repertoire
- Recipes with wine, champagne, and beer

Over the past two decades or so, wine has come to be regarded not just as the object of cultivated connoisseurship, to be consumed, discussed, and enjoyed for its own sake, but as an ingredient in mixed drinks. This new orientation may scandalize some wine snobs, but it has significantly expanded the repertoire of bartenders as well as drinkers.

Less numerous, but also with a substantial history, are the ways of combining beer with spirits. If it does nothing else, this chapter will give you a fresh perspective on wine (including champagne) as well as beer.

Wine as a Mixer

Not long ago, in the United States, the world of alcohol was neatly divided into the realm of *distilled* spirits and *fermented* beverages, which includes wine and beer. The twain rarely met. More recently, however, the New World has been catching up with the Old, and wine is being combined routinely with distilled spirits to create a host of mixed drinks.

But we've got a lot of catching up to do because, across the Atlantic, wine has been used as a mixed-drink ingredient since ancient times. The Greeks, Romans, and peoples of the Old Testament all routinely mixed wine with honey and spices. Many of today's *fortified wines* (wines to which a distilled spirit has been added), such as sherry, port, and Madeira, and *apéritifs* (spiritous beverages taken before meals) such as Dubonnet, developed directly out of the tradition of flavored wines.

Standard table wines as well as dessert wines, champagne and other sparkling wines, and apéritifs all figure in modern mixed drinks. Nothing is off-limits anymore.

Buzzed Words

A **fortified wine** is a fermented wine to which a distilled spirit, usually brandy, has been added. Brandy itself is often considered a fortified wine.

An **apéritif** is a spiritous beverage taken before a meal as an appetizer. Its origin, in French, is hardly appetizing, however, originally denoting a purgative.

The Classics

The recipes that follow are rediscovered classics. They've recently reemerged from the mixing glasses of American bartenders and hosts.

Kir, pronounced *keer*, is one of the best-known, wine-based mixed drinks. It is named for Canon Félix Kir, the much-honored mayor of Dijon, France. It is a simple combination of a liqueur with dry white wine.

Every bartender and host should be familiar with the *spritzer*, a light drink for people who want a dash of summer refreshment without much alcohol. The spritzer is customarily made with white wine.

Buzzed Words

A **spritzer** is a combination of wine—usually Rhine wine or other white wine—and club soda or seltzer. The word comes from the German for *spray*.

Kir

Serve in a large wine glass.

½ oz. crème de cassis

5 oz. dry white wine

The liqueur and the wine should be well chilled beforehand. Combine them in the serving glass.

Kir Royale

You can gild the Kir lily with a little champagne.

Serve in a large wine glass.

5 oz. champagne

½ oz. crème de cassis

Lemon peel

Chill the champagne and crème de cassis well, and then combine in the serving glass. Twist the lemon peel over the drink and drop in.

Spritzer

Serve on the rocks in a highball glass.

1 part white wine

1 part club soda to fill

Lemon twist

Fill the serving glass with ice. Pour wine to fill half way. Add club soda to fill. Garnish with the twist.

Rhine Wine Spritzer

Traditionalists insist on using sweetish Rhine wine for the spritzer. After all, the name of the drink is German.

Serve on the rocks in a highball glass.

4 oz. Rhine wine

Club soda (may substitute sparkling mineral water) to fill

Lemon spiral

Pour wine into the serving glass filled with ice. Add club soda or sparkling mineral water to fill. Garnish with a long lemon peel curlicue; hang over the side of the glass.

Rosé Spritzer

Don't neglect rosé. It makes an attractive and refreshing spritzer.

Serve on the rocks in a highball glass.

1 part rosé wine

1 part club soda to fill

Lemon twist

Fill the serving glass with ice. Pour wine to fill half way. Add club soda to fill. Garnish with the twist.

Apéritif Assortments

The dry sophistication of the apéritif makes it a pleasure that can be enjoyed unmixed—or mixed.

Americano

Serve in an old-fashioned glass.

2 oz. sweet vermouth	Club soda to fill
2 oz. Campari	Orange twist

Combine vermouth and Campari in a mixing glass filled with ice. Stir, and then strain into the serving glass one-third full of ice. Add club soda to fill and garnish with the twist.

Appetizer

When making an Appetizer, resist the easy out of using orange juice from a bottle or carton. Squeeze fresh oranges!

Serve in a chilled cocktail glass.

3 oz. Dubonnet rouge

Juice of 1 orange

Combine the Dubonnet and orange juice in a shaker with ice. Shake vigorously, and then strain into the serving glass.

Weep No More

Serve in a chilled cocktail glass.

1½ oz. Dubonnet rouge

1½ oz. cognac

1½ oz. lime juice

Dash maraschino liqueur

Combine all ingredients in a shaker with ice. Shake vigorously, and then strain into the serving glass.

B.V.D.

With a nod toward the maker of celebrated briefs, the initials of the next drink reflect the principal ingredients: *B*yrrh (an aromatic French apéritif redolent of orange and quinine) and *V*ermouth—*D*ry. The rum goes unrepresented in this monogram.

Serve in a chilled cocktail glass.

1 oz. Byrrh (may substitute Dubonnet)

1 oz. dry vermouth

1 oz. light rum

Orange twist

Combine all ingredients, except the twist, in a mixing glass or small pitcher with ice. Stir, and then strain into the serving glass. Garnish with the twist.

Ante

Dubonnet is quite possibly the most mixable of the apéritifs.

Serve in a chilled cocktail glass.

1 oz. Dubonnet

½ oz. triple sec

1 oz. apple brandy

Combine all ingredients in a mixing glass with ice. Stir well, and then strain into the serving glass.

Wedding Belle

Serve on the rocks in a lowball glass.

½ oz. gin

½ oz. Dubonnet

¼ oz. cherry-flavored brandy

½ oz. orange juice

Combine all ingredients in a shaker with cracked ice. Shake well, and then strain over ice into the serving glass.

Bentley

Serve in a chilled cocktail glass.

1½ oz. apple brandy

1½ oz. Dubonnet

Combine over ice in a mixing glass. Stir, and then strain into the serving glass.

Oom Paul

Serve on the rocks in a lowball glass.

1 oz. apple brandy

1 oz. Dubonnet

Several dashes Angostura bitters

Combine ingredients in a shaker with cracked ice. Shake well, and then strain over ice into the serving glass.

Mary Garden

Serve on the rocks in a lowball glass.

1½ oz. Dubonnet

¾ oz. dry vermouth

Combine ingredients in a mixing glass with ice. Stir well, and then strain over ice into the serving glass.

Dubonnet Negroni

Serve in a wine glass.

1½ oz. Dubonnet

1½ oz. gin

1½ oz. Campari

Lemon peel

Combine all ingredients, except the lemon peel, over ice in a mixing glass. Stir, and then strain into the serving glass. Twist the lemon peel over the drink and drop in.

Sanctuary

Serve on the rocks in a lowball glass.

1½ oz. Dubonnet rouge

¾ oz. Amer Picon

¾ oz. Cointreau

Combine ingredients in a shaker with cracked ice. Shake well, and then strain over ice into the serving glass.

Vancouver Cocktail

Serve in a wine goblet.

2 oz. Canadian whisky

1 oz. Dubonnet rouge

2 TB. orange juice

½ egg white*

½ tsp. maple syrup

Several generous dashes Angostura bitters

Combine ingredients in a shaker with cracked ice. Shake well, and then strain over ice into the serving glass.

**Raw egg may be a source of salmonella bacteria. You may wish to avoid drinks calling for raw egg yolk or white.*

Temptation

Serve in a chilled cocktail glass.

2 oz. blended whiskey

¼ oz. triple sec

¼ oz. Pernod

¼ oz. Dubonnet

Combine ingredients in a shaker with cracked ice. Shake well, and then strain over ice into the serving glass.

Soul Kiss

Serve on the rocks in a lowball glass.

1 oz. blended whiskey

1 oz. dry vermouth

½ oz. Dubonnet

¾ oz. orange juice

Combine ingredients in a mixing glass with ice. Stir well, and then strain over ice into the serving glass.

Dubonnet Manhattan

Dubonnet can even be pressed into service for a new slant on the old Manhattan.

Serve in a chilled cocktail glass.

1 oz. Dubonnet

1 oz. blended whiskey, bourbon, or Jack Daniels

Maraschino cherry

Combine all ingredients, except the cherry, in a shaker with cracked ice. Shake well, and then strain over ice into the serving glass. Garnish with the cherry.

Sherry Anyone? Port Perhaps?

Sherry is a fortified Spanish wine, with a nutlike flavor, that takes its name from an Anglicization of Jerez, a city in southwestern Spain, where sherry originated and from which the best sherry still comes. Port is also called *porto* and is named for the Portuguese town of Oporto, where true port is aged and bottled; however, other places also produce port wines. Like sherry, port is a fortified wine, but it is invariably sweet, whereas sherry ranges from dry to sweet.

Sherry, both in its dry and "cream" (sweet) incarnations, has enjoyed uninterrupted popularity. Port, in contrast, used to be a regular after-dinner or late evening tradition, and then receded in popularity. During the last decade or two, however, it has been widely rediscovered. Both sherry and port make excellent mixers.

A *philomel* is a nightingale, and this cocktail can be served at about the time the nightingale sings. Because you won't find any nightingales here in North America, drink this any time.

Philomel Cocktail

Serve in a chilled wine goblet.

2½ oz. amontillado

1½ oz. St. Raphael (a French proprietary liqueur)

1 oz. light rum

1½ oz. orange juice

Pinch cayenne pepper

Combine all ingredients, except cayenne pepper, in a shaker with ice. Shake vigorously, and then strain into the serving glass. Sprinkle with cayenne.

Sherry Cobbler

Amontillado takes well to sweetening, as in the Sherry Cobbler.

Serve in a chilled wine goblet.

Liberal dashes pineapple syrup

Liberal dashes curaçao

4 oz. amontillado

Lemon twist

Pineapple stick

Mint sprig

Fill the serving glass with crushed ice. Dash in pineapple syrup and curaçao, and then stir with a bar spoon until the glass is well frosted. Add amontillado and continue stirring. Garnish with the twist, pineapple stick, and mint sprig.

Here is a trio of traditional sherry and port cocktails, followed by some more unusual essays in the sherry medium.

Straight Law Cocktail

Serve in a chilled cocktail glass.

2 oz. fino sherry

1 oz. gin

Lemon twist

Combine gin and sherry in a mixing glass or small pitcher with ice. Stir, and then strain into the serving glass and garnish with the twist.

Tuxedo Cocktail

Serve in a chilled cocktail glass.

3 oz. fino sherry

½ oz. anisette

Liberal dashes maraschino liqueur

Liberal dashes Angostura bitters

Combine all ingredients in a mixing glass or small pitcher with ice. Stir, and then strain into the serving glass.

Tinton Cocktail

Serve in a chilled cocktail glass.

2 oz. port

2 oz. Calvados (may substitute applejack)

Combine in a mixing glass or small pitcher with ice. Stir, and then strain into the serving glass.

Adonis

Serve in a chilled cocktail glass.

1½ oz. dry sherry

¾ oz. sweet vermouth

Dash orange bitters

Combine all ingredients in a mixing glass with ice. Stir, and then strain into the serving glass.

Reform

Serve in a chilled cocktail glass.

1½ oz. dry sherry

¾ oz. dry vermouth

Dash orange bitters

Combine all ingredients in a mixing glass with ice. Stir, and then strain into the serving glass.

Andalusia

Serve in a chilled cocktail glass.

1½ oz. dry sherry

½ oz. brandy

½ oz. light rum

Combine all ingredients in a mixing glass with ice. Stir, and then strain into the serving glass.

Cadiz

Serve on the rocks in a lowball glass.

¾ oz. blackberry brandy

¾ oz. dry sherry

½ oz. triple sec

¼ oz. cream

Combine all ingredients in a shaker with ice. Shake, and then strain into the serving glass.

Quarter Deck

Serve on the rocks in a lowball glass.

1½ oz. light rum

1 TB. sherry

1 tsp. lime juice

Combine all ingredients in a shaker with ice. Shake, and then strain into the serving glass.

Renaissance Cocktail

Serve in a chilled cocktail glass.

1½ oz. gin

½ oz. dry sherry

1 TB. cream

Ground nutmeg

Combine all ingredients, except nutmeg, in a shaker with ice. Shake, and then strain into the serving glass. Sprinkle with nutmeg.

Betsy Ross

Serve in a brandy snifter

1½ oz. brandy

1½ oz. port

2 dashes Angostura bitters

2 drops blue curaçao

Combine all ingredients in a mixing glass with ice. Stir, and then strain into the serving glass.

Montana

Serve on the rocks in a lowball glass.

1½ oz. brandy

2 tsp. dry vermouth

2 tsp. port

Combine all ingredients in the serving glass with ice. Stir.

Vermouth Variations

Vermouth, in its sweet as well as dry forms, is a versatile mixer. It can carry a drink as the principal note, or it can serve in any number of supporting roles.

Achampañado

Serve in a chilled Collins glass.

3 oz. dry vermouth

½ tsp. sugar syrup

Juice of ¼ lime

Club soda to fill

Fill serving glass to one third with ice cubes. Add vermouth, sugar syrup, and lime juice. Stir, and then add club soda to fill.

Adonis Cocktail

Serve in a chilled cocktail glass.

3 oz. fino sherry

1 oz. sweet vermouth

Dash orange bitters

Orange twist

Combine sherry, vermouth, and bitters in a mixing glass or small pitcher with ice. Stir, and then strain into the serving glass. Garnish with the twist.

Chrysanthemum Cocktail

One of the loveliest of vermouth cocktails is the Chrysanthemum.

Serve in a chilled cocktail glass.

2 oz. dry vermouth

1½ oz. Benedictine

Liberal dashes Pernod

Orange twist

Combine vermouth and Benedictine in a small pitcher or mixing glass with ice. Stir well, and then strain into the serving glass. Garnish with the orange twist.

Satan's Whiskers

Even more interesting is the wicked Satan's Whiskers.

Serve in a chilled wine glass.

1½ oz. sweet vermouth

1½ oz. dry vermouth

1 oz. gin

½ oz. Grand Marnier

3 oz. orange juice

Dash orange bitters

Combine all ingredients in a shaker with ice. Shake vigorously, and then strain into the serving glass.

Third Rail

Third Rail? Shocking!

Serve in a chilled cocktail glass.

3 oz. dry vermouth

Liberal dashes curaçao

Liberal dashes peppermint schnapps

Lemon twist

Combine vermouth, curaçao, and schnapps in a small pitcher or mixing glass with ice. Stir well, and then strain into the serving glass. Garnish with the twist.

Vermouth Cassis

The Vermouth Cassis is quiet and reserved, whereas the Victor Cocktail packs more "spiritual" authority.

Serve on the rocks in a highball glass.

3 oz. dry vermouth

1 oz. crème de cassis

Club soda to fill

Combine vermouth and crème de cassis in the serving glass over ice. Stir, and then add club soda to fill.

Victor Cocktail

Serve in a chilled cocktail glass.

1½ oz. sweet vermouth

¾ oz. brandy

¾ oz. gin

Orange twist

Combine all ingredients, except the twist, in a shaker with ice. Shake vigorously, and then strain into the serving glass. Garnish with the twist.

Zanzibar

Serve in a chilled cocktail glass.

3 oz. dry vermouth

1 oz. gin

¾ oz. lemon juice

1 tsp. sugar syrup

Liberal dashes orange bitters

Lemon twist

Combine all ingredients, except the twist, in a shaker with ice. Shake vigorously, and then strain into the serving glass. Garnish with the twist.

Bubbly Blends

Who hasn't seen *Casablanca* several dozen times? Well, maybe you've at least seen it enough to have noticed that the Champagne Cocktail is the drink ordered most—and seems to have been the particular favorite of the heroic freedom fighter Viktor Laszlo. Champagne, one of the greatest pleasures among fermented beverages, is a surprisingly versatile mixer.

Every host who serves champagne should be familiar with the Champagne Cocktail and Mimosa.

Buzzed Words

Champagne is *the* classic sparkling wine. Named for its place of origin, the Champagne region of northeastern France, champagne is also produced in other nations; however, most connoisseurs agree that the finest champagne is still produced in the Champagne of France. Champagne ranges from dry (**brut**) to sweet and fruity.

Champagne Cocktail

Serve in a champagne flute.

1 sugar cube

Liberal dashes Angostura bitters

Champagne to fill

Lemon twist

Drop cube in the serving glass and dash on the bitters. Add champagne to fill, stirring gently until the sugar dissolves. Garnish with the twist.

Mimosa

The refreshing Mimosa is probably the most frequently requested champagne cocktail. Use dry—brut—champagne and freshly squeezed orange juice.

Serve in a chilled wine goblet.

6 oz. brut champagne

3 oz. orange juice (freshly squeezed)

Orange slice

The champagne and orange juice should be thoroughly prechilled. Combine them in the serving glass. Garnish with the orange slice.

Midori Mimosa

If you prefer a sweeter Mimosa, dash in some triple sec. And if you want something a little different, bring on the Midori melon liqueur.

Serve in a chilled wine goblet.

2 oz. Midori

2 tsp. lime juice

Champagne to fill

Lime wedge

The champagne and Midori should be thoroughly prechilled. Combine them in the serving glass. Add the lime juice, and then garnish with the lime wedge.

Bellini

Serve in a chilled champagne flute.

3 oz. chilled peach nectar

Dash lemon juice

Dash grenadine

3 oz. chilled champagne

Combine the chilled peach nectar, lemon juice, and grenadine in the serving glass. Stir, and then add the chilled champagne.

Champagne Fizz

The Champagne Fizz features an innovative use for champagne: a stand-in for soda!

Serve on the rocks in a highball glass.

2 oz. gin

1 oz. sour mix

Champagne to fill

Combine the gin and sour mix in a shaker with ice. Shake vigorously, and then strain into the serving glass. Add champagne to fill.

Toast

"Here's looking at you, kid." —Humphrey Bogart to Ingrid Bergman in *Casablanca,* 1942

Creative Coolers

Like a spritzer, a cooler is essentially a drink well diluted with sparkling water. All of these should be served on the rocks in tall glasses. If you have frosted glasses, use them.

Pineapple Wine Cooler

Serve on the rocks in a highball glass.

2½ oz. dry white wine

2½ oz. pineapple juice

1 oz. light rum

Club soda to fill

Lemon spiral

Orange spiral

Combine ingredients, except club soda and fruit, in the serving glass filled with ice. Stir. Add club soda to fill, and garnish with long lemon and orange curlicue spirals.

Red Wine Cooler

Serve on the rocks in a highball glass.

2 tsp. sugar syrup

1 oz. orange juice

Red wine to ¾ full

Club soda to fill

Combine ingredients, except club soda, in the serving glass filled with ice. Stir. Add club soda to fill.

Toast

"There's many a toast I'd like to say, If only I could think it; So fill your glass to anything, And thank the Lord, I'll drink it!"

White Wine Cooler

Serve on the rocks in a highball glass.

1 tsp. sugar syrup

White wine to ¾ full

Club soda to fill

Mint sprigs

Combine ingredients, except club soda and mint sprigs, in the serving glass filled with ice. Stir. Add club soda to fill. Garnish with mint sprigs.

Champagne Cooler

The Champagne Cooler packs a punch.

Serve on the rocks in a highball glass.

1 oz. brandy

1 oz. Cointreau

Champagne to fill

Mint sprigs

Combine ingredients, except champagne and mint sprigs, in the serving glass filled with ice. Stir. Add champagne to fill and garnish with the mint sprigs.

Beer—a Mixer?!

Maybe you're persuaded about the possibilities of wine as a mixer, but *beer*? It can be done. You can serve all of these drinks in a beer mug or a Pilsner glass, depending on your mood and inclination.

Most folks have heard of the Boilermaker, the classic drink of steel-mill hands and those who want you to think they're steel-mill hands.

Boilermaker

Serve in a beer mug (if you know what's good for you).

1½ oz. blended whiskey

12 oz. beer

Pour the beer into the mug. Add the whiskey.

You can transform the Boilermaker into a Depth Charge by dropping the whiskey—shot glass and all—into the beer.

Sneaky Pete

What some folks call a Sneaky Pete is not the Sneaky Pete made with tequila, which we showed you in Chapter 14. This one is applejack and beer.

Serve in beer mug.

1½ oz. applejack

12 oz. beer

Pour beer into a mug. Add applejack.

Black Velvet

The Black Velvet is a layered drink, but it's no pousse-café.

Serve in a tall Pilsner glass.

5–8 oz. porter or stout

Equal amount of extra brut champagne

Pour in the porter or stout, and then *carefully* pour in the champagne, slowly, down the side of the glass in order to make two separate layers. Do not stir.

Hop, Skip & Go Naked

If you consume a drink like this immoderately, hopping, skipping, and going naked is the kindest fate you may expect.

Serve on the rocks in a beer mug or Pilsner glass.

1 oz. vodka

1 oz. gin

Juice of ½ lime

Beer to fill

Combine all ingredients, except beer, in the serving glass half filled with ice. Stir, and then add beer to fill.

Anything Goes

How about trying something new?

Union League

Serve on the rocks in a lowball glass.

2 oz. gin

1 oz. port

2 dashes orange bitters

Orange peel

Combine all ingredients, except orange peel, over ice in the serving glass. Stir. Garnish with orange peel.

Poop Deck

Serve in a chilled cocktail glass.

1 oz. blackberry brandy

½ oz. port

½ oz. brandy

Combine all ingredients in a shaker with cracked ice. Shake well, and then strain into the serving glass.

Morning Becomes Electric

Serve in a chilled cocktail glass.

2 oz. dry vermouth

1 oz. brandy

2 tsp. port

Dash curaçao

Combine all ingredients in a mixing glass with ice. Stir well, and then strain into the serving glass.

Soviet Cocktail

Serve in a chilled cocktail glass.

1½ oz. vodka

½ oz. amontillado sherry

½ oz dry vermouth

Combine all ingredients in a shaker with cracked ice. Shake well, and then strain into the serving glass.

Xerxes Cocktail

Serve in a chilled cocktail glass.

2½ oz. dry sherry

Dash orange bitters

Combine in a mixing glass with ice. Stir, and then strain into the serving glass.

Lager 'n' Lime

Serve in a Pilsner glass.

½ oz. Rose's lime juice

Cold beer

Combine in the serving glass.

Modern Lemonade

Serve on the rocks in a highball glass.

1½ oz. sloe gin

1½ oz. sherry

2 oz. lemon juice

1 oz. maple syrup

Club soda

Lemon slice

Combine all ingredients, except soda and lemon slice, in a shaker with cracked ice. Shake well, and then pour over ice into the serving glass. Top with club soda, and garnish with the lemon slice.

A Yard of Flannel

Serve in warmed beer mugs. (Yields 3 drinks.)

1 qt. ale

4 oz. gold rum

3 oz. superfine sugar

4 eggs*

½ tsp. grated nutmeg

½ tsp. ground cinnamon

Carefully warm ale in a large saucepan. Use low heat, and do not boil! In a bowl, combine rum, sugar, eggs, nutmeg, and cinnamon. Beat, and then pour into a heat-resistant pitcher. Slowly add ale, stirring constantly. Continue stirring until mixture is creamy. Pour into the warmed mugs.

**Raw egg may be a source of salmonella bacteria. You may wish to avoid drinks calling for raw egg yolk or white.*

The Least You Need to Know

- The notion of combining wine with other flavorings and other spirits to create mixed drinks might be relatively new in the United States, but it is rooted in ancient practices.
- Kir, spritzers, and coolers are all lightly alcoholic alternatives to the heavier and more potent mixed drinks.
- Beer can serve as a mixer in a variety of drinks, the simplest, best-known, and most potent of which is the Boilermaker.

Chapter 20

Lo Cal: Drinks for Dieters

In This Chapter

- Alcohol and calories
- How to cut calories without giving up spirits
- Quick and easy low-calorie alternatives
- Low-cal recipes

Every few years, some book or magazine article comes along to trumpet a miracle "alcohol" diet—a way that drinking spirits can actually help you lose weight. If you believe in these diets, we've got a little Three-Card Monte game we'd like to get you into.

Either way, you can't win.

Although it is true that chronic abusers of alcohol sometimes become very thin indeed, liver disease and the loss of interest in food that accompanies it is not an attractive means of slimming down. The practical truth is that spirits will not help you lose weight. This chapter suggests ways to minimize, control, or at least be aware of your alcohol-related caloric intake.

The Truth About Alcohol and Calories

Here's the way it works. One gram of alcohol yields seven calories as it is metabolized by your body. This works out to some 200 calories per fluid ounce of absolute alcohol, but pure alcohol is something you wouldn't be drinking—so let's knock it down to a more realistic 100 calories per fluid ounce of 100-proof distilled spirits. Assuming that proof and volume are constant, all distilled spirits—whiskey, rum, gin, vodka—contain the same number of calories. Beer contains a few more calories per ounce (about four), as do liqueurs.

Bar Tips

Liquor has as many calories *per ounce* as its proof; thus, 80-proof blended whiskey contains 80 calories per ounce. Just be aware that one drink is usually the equivalent of at least 1½ ounces of liquor.

Alcohol-related calories count just as much as food-related calories, except that (unfortunately) alcohol-related calories are "empty"—without nutritional value.

Counting Calories

If you're going to count calories, you'll need figures for the typical serving of an alcoholic beverage. The following table shows you the calorie counts of many liquors and mixers.

Calorie Counts

Ingredient	Serving	Calories
Apéritif	2 oz.	80
Beer, lager	12 oz.	151
Beer, light	12 oz.	98
Bitters	Liberal dash (½ tsp.)	7
Champagne, 25-proof	3½ oz.	91 (approx.)
Club soda	10 oz.	0
Cola	12 oz.	144
Cola, diet	12 oz.	0
Cranberry juice cocktail	2 oz.	37
Ginger ale	12 oz.	113
Heavy cream	1 TB.	53

Ingredient	Serving	Calories
Lemon juice, fresh	1 TB.	4
Lime juice, fresh	1 TB.	4
Liqueurs	1 fluid oz.	66-106
Liquor (gin, rum, tequila vodka, whiskey), 80-proof	1½ oz.	97
Liquor, 86-proof	1½ oz.	105
Liquor, 90-proof	1½ oz.	110
Liquor, 94-proof	1½ oz.	116
Liquor, 100-proof	1½ oz.	124
Orange juice, fresh	2 oz.	28
Pineapple juice (unsweetened)	2 oz.	34
Sherry	2 oz.	80
Tomato juice	2 oz.	12
Tonic water	12 oz.	113
Vermouth, dry	1 oz.	33
Vermouth, sweet	1 oz.	44
Wine, dessert	2 oz.	80
Wine, dry	3½ oz.	87
Wine, sweet	2 oz.	80

If that doesn't make it clear enough, here's a short list of popular drinks and their approximate calorie count:

Cocktail	Serving Size (oz.)	Approximate Calories
Bloody Mary	5	115
Daiquiri	4.5	250
Gin and Tonic	7.5	170
Martini	2.5	155
Piña Colada	4.5	260
Screwdriver	7	175
Tequila Sunrise	5.5	190
Tom Collins	7.5	120

Mixers/Juices	Serving	Cholesterol	Total fat	Saturated fat
Whole milk	1 cup	34 mg.	8.0 g.	4.9 g.
Apple	1 cup	0	0.3	0
Cranberry	1 cup	0	0.1	0
Lemon	1 cup	0	0	0
Lime	1 cup	0	0	0
Orange	1 cup	0	0.5	0.1
Pineapple	1 cup	0	0.2	0
Tomato	1 cup	0	0.2	0
Egg white	1 (large)	0	0	0
Egg yolk	1 (large)	213	5.6	1.6

Cutting Calories

The numbers are the numbers, and no amount of wishful thinking will make them smaller. But you can take steps to reduce your caloric intake:

- Don't drink.
- Reduce the amount of alcohol in simple mixed drinks. Make your Scotch and Soda with 1 ounce of scotch instead of 1½.
- Make smaller drinks. Instead of a Gin and Tonic consisting of 1½ ounces of gin and 6½ ounces of tonic (enough to fill a highball glass on the rocks), start out with an ounce of gin and add enough tonic to fill the glass to two thirds only.
- Enjoy spritzers (see Chapter 19) and some of the other drinks recommended in this chapter. The White Wine Spritzer—essentially white wine combined 50/50 with club soda—is an excellent low-calorie alternative.
- Reduce the amount of liquor in your highballs: one ounce instead of an ounce and a half. Use the pony jigger instead of the full jigger, pour to just below two fingers instead of at the two-finger mark, or count two instead of three when you use the speed pourer. (If none of this makes sense to you, reread—or read—Chapter 5.)

Bar Tips

Low-alcohol drinks—even *very* low-alcohol drinks—are *not* no-alcohol drinks. Do not serve them to guests who want (or require) non-alcoholic beverages. See Chapter 21 for nonalcohol recipes.

As with most other of life's pursuits and pleasures, the principle of the Golden Mean is a valuable guide. Enjoy your empty alcohol calories in moderation.

Ye Olde Standbys

You should be prepared to offer your guests a variety of low-calorie alcoholic beverages. Here are a few that have stood the test of time.

- Splash some Campari in a lowball glass half filled with ice, and then add club soda to fill. Garnish with a lime wedge.
- Squeeze half a lemon into a lowball glass. Add ice and club soda to fill, and then dash in two or three dollops of Angostura bitters.
- Start with half a lowball glass of ice. Add Perrier almost to the top. Squeeze in the juice of a quarter lemon or lime, then liberally dash in crème de cassis. Garnish with a fresh lemon or lime wedge.
- Take a four-ounce can of tomato juice and combine it in a lowball glass one-half full of ice with two ounces of dry vermouth. Stir, and garnish with a lime wedge.

Bar Tips

For extra zing, consider substituting V-8 Juice for ordinary tomato juice—and, if you want to reduce your sodium intake as well as your caloric intake, look for special Low-Sodium V-8.

Lightweights: Drinks Under 80 Calories

A surprising array of drink possibilities weigh in at under 80 calories.

Apéritif Drinks

Campari Special

Serve on the rocks in a lowball glass.

1½ oz. Campari

Ginger ale to fill

Dash orange bitters

Orange slice

Combine all ingredients, except the orange slice, in the serving glass filled with ice. Stir. Garnish with the orange slice.

Pansy

Serve on the rocks in a lowball glass.

½ oz. Pernod

Dash grenadine

Liberal dash Angostura bitters

Lemon twist

Combine all ingredients, except the twist, in the serving glass filled with ice. Stir. Garnish with the twist.

Lite Liquor Drinks

Versatile gin can be used—in relatively low volume—to make a raft of wonderful drinks for the calorie-conscious.

For those watching their calorie intake, rum might seem like an extra-high-calorie drink. In reality, it has no more (and no fewer) calories than any other distilled spirit. Use 86-proof rum rather than the 151-proof blockbusters for recipes calling for rum.

Biffy

Serve in a cocktail glass filled with crushed ice.

½ oz. gin

2 TB. pineapple juice

1 TB. lemon juice

Combine all ingredients in a shaker with ice. Shake well, and then strain into the serving glass filled with crushed ice.

Bloody Pick-Me-Up

An alternative to the Bloody Mary is this gruesomely named 50-calorie libation.

Serve in a cocktail glass filled with crushed ice.

½ oz. gin

1 TB. ketchup

1 TB. lemon juice

Dash Worcestershire sauce

Combine all ingredients in a blender. Blend at high speed for at least 15 seconds. Pour into the serving glass filled with crushed ice.

Tropical Sling

Serve on the rocks in a highball glass.

½ oz. gin

1½ tsp. lime juice

1 tsp. grenadine

½ tsp. maraschino bitters

Club soda to fill

Mint sprigs

Combine all ingredients, except the club soda and mint sprigs, in a shaker with ice. Shake vigorously, and then strain into the serving glass filled with ice. Add club soda to fill and garnish with the mint sprigs.

Pink Squirrel

Serve on the rocks in a lowball glass.

½ oz. gin

1 tsp. crème de noyeaux

1 oz. lemon juice

Combine ingredients in a shaker with cracked ice. Shake well, and then pour over ice into the serving glass.

Gin Cocktail

Serve on the rocks in a lowball glass.

¾ oz. gin

Several drops orange bitters

Lime peel

Combine the gin and bitters over ice in the serving glass. Stir. Twist the lime peel over the drink, and then drop in.

Planter's Cocktail

Serve in a cocktail glass filled with crushed ice.

½ oz. light rum

1 tsp. lemon juice

1 TB. orange juice

Mint sprig

Combine all ingredients, except mint sprig, in the serving glass over crushed ice. Garnish with the mint sprig.

Dill Mary

Serve on the rocks in a lowball glass.

3 oz. tomato juice

1 TB. vodka

½ tsp. crushed dill

Pinch salt

Liberal dash Tabasco sauce

Pinch black pepper

Begin by placing the dill in a shaker. Add vodka and tomato juice. Let stand at least 15 minutes. Add salt and Tabasco, together with several ice cubes. Shake well, and then strain over ice into the serving glass. Sprinkle pepper over drink.

Wine and Vermouth Drinks

Wine is probably the ideal foundation for low-cal drinks. The calories here aren't even entirely devoid of nutritional value. Fermenting does not strip away vitamins and minerals as distilling does.

Traditionally, a *posset* is served hot and contains sweetened milk curdled with wine or ale. The English Posset doesn't go quite that far.

Buzzed Words

A **posset** is a traditional English drink made with sweetened milk that has been curdled by the addition of wine or ale. It is usually served hot.

English Posset

Serve in a chilled sherry glass.

1 oz. dry sherry

½ oz. light cream

Pinch grated nutmeg

Combine the sherry and cream in a mixing glass with ice. Stir, and then strain into the serving glass. Garnish with the nutmeg.

West Indian

Serve in a chilled sherry glass.

1 oz. dry sherry

1 tsp. guava nectar

1 tsp. limeade

2 oz. dark tea (cold)

Combine all ingredients in a shaker filled with ice. Shake vigorously, and then strain into the serving glass.

Cardinal

The lordly Cardinal weighs in at a mere 45 calories.

Serve in a chilled cocktail or martini glass.

¾ oz. dry vermouth

1 TB. orange juice

1 TB. tomato juice

Olive

Prechill the vermouth and juices. Combine in the serving glass and garnish with the olive.

Country Club Cooler

The Country Club Cooler weighs in at only 50 calories.

Serve in a chilled cocktail or martini glass.

1½ oz. dry vermouth

¼ oz. grenadine

2 oz. club soda

Lime slice

Prechill the vermouth and juices. Combine in the serving glass and garnish with the lime slice.

Cynthia

Serve on the rocks in a lowball glass.

1 oz. dry vermouth

½ oz. sweet vermouth

1 tsp. gin

Mint sprigs

Combine the vermouths and gin in the serving glass filled with ice. Stir well, and then garnish with mint sprigs.

Island Tea

Serve on the rocks in a lowball glass.

3 oz. green tea

1 oz. grenadine

1 tsp. lemon juice

Sprig mint

Combine all ingredients, except the mint, over ice in the serving glass. Stir. Garnish with the mint.

Barbie's Special

Serve in a chilled cocktail glass.

1½ TB. apricot nectar

1 oz. defrosted vanilla ice milk

Several drops of gin

Combine ingredients in a shaker with cracked ice. Shake, and then pour into the serving glass.

Clare's Cup

Serve in a hollowed-out cucumber.

2 oz. white wine, well chilled

1 large cucumber

Club soda, well chilled

Several mint leaves

1 lemon slice

Lime zest

Hollow out a large cucumber, and flatten one end. Pour in the chilled wine and top with chilled club soda. Garnish with the mint, lemon slice, and lime zest.

Carthusian Cooler

Serve in ½ hollowed honeydew melon.

½ honeydew melon

1 oz. port, chilled

Club soda, well chilled

Hollow out ½ honeydew melon, reserving the melon that has been scooped out. In a blender, combine the scooped-out melon with the port. Blend, and then pour into the melon shell. Top with well-chilled club soda.

Weighing In: 80–100 Calorie Drinks

Between 80 and 100 calories, the drinks get stronger and the options more varied.

Brandy Drinks

As a spirit for the calorie conscious, brandy hits its stride in drinks just under a hundred calories.

Shriner

The Shriner is traditional, and relatively low in key and low in calories (90 of them). George's Beauty adds 5 calories to that.

Serve in a chilled cocktail glass.

½ oz. brandy

½ oz. sloe gin

Dash Peychaud's bitters

1 tsp. grenadine

Combine all ingredients in a mixing glass with ice. Stir well, and then strain into the serving glass.

George's Beauty

Serve on the rocks in a lowball glass.

½ oz. brandy

2 tsp. lemon juice

1 tsp. grenadine

1 egg white*

Combine all ingredients in a shaker with cracked ice. Shake well, and then strain over ice into the serving glass.

**Raw egg may be a source of salmonella bacteria. You may wish to avoid drinks calling for raw egg yolk or white.*

Northern Honey Bee

The Northern Honey Bee weighs in just over the 100-calorie mark (103).

Serve in an eggnog-style mug.

1 oz. brandy

1 tsp. honey

½ oz. lemon juice

Warm the honey well in a ladle over a low gas flame. Combine in the mug with the juice and brandy. Serve warm.

Toast

"Here's to your health, and your family's good health, and may you all live long and prosper."

—Joseph Jefferson, nineteenth-century American matinee idol and member of The Players

Champagne Drinks

Feel deprived by having to count calories? These champagne drinks should banish all such negative emotions.

Alfonso Cocktail

Serve on the rocks in a lowball glass.

1 oz. champagne

2 oz. grape juice

Liberal dash Angostura bitters

Combine all ingredients in the serving glass filled with ice. Stir.

Champagne Cobbler

Serve in an American-style (saucer) champagne glass.

2 oz. champagne

1 oz. lemon sherbet

Fill glass with crushed ice. Combine champagne and sherbet in the serving glass.

Count Currey

Serve in a chilled cocktail glass.

2 oz. champagne

½ oz. gin

1 tsp. maple syrup

Mint sprig

Prechill the champagne and gin. Combine with the maple syrup in a shaker and shake vigorously. Pour into the serving glass and garnish with mint sprig.

Bar Tips

Lowering the calorie count of the drinks you make is only half the battle. Drinkers get the munchies, and alcohol tends to make us less conscious of how much we eat. Consider supplying your guests with some low-calorie snacks to go along with their low-calorie drinks.

The Hard Stuff

Applejack Daisy

The Applejack Daisy is rich and sweet but still manages to slide in at under a hundred calories (99, to be exact).

Serve in a cocktail glass filled with crushed ice.

½ oz. gin

½ oz. applejack

1 TB. lemonade

Combine all ingredients in a mixing glass with ice. Stir well, and then strain into the serving glass filled with crushed ice.

Cherry Rum

The Cherry Rum weighs in just over the 100-calorie mark (106).

Serve in a chilled cocktail glass.

½ oz. light rum

2 oz. canned sour cherries in syrup

1 TB. light cream

3 oz. crushed ice

Combine all ingredients in a blender. Blend at low speed, and then strain into the serving glass.

Honolulu Sling

Serve in cocktail glass filled with crushed ice.

1 TB. vodka

1 oz. sherry

1 oz. Hawaiian Punch (original flavor)

Combine all ingredients in a mixing glass filled with ice. Stir well, and then strain into the serving glass filled with crushed ice.

Lumberjack

Serve in a chilled cocktail glass.

½ oz. blended whiskey

1 oz. apple juice

1 tsp. brown sugar

Powdered cinnamon

Ground nutmeg

Combine all ingredients, except the spices, in a shaker with cracked ice. Shake well, and then strain into the serving glass. Sprinkle with the spices.

Bar Tips

You might think that aromaless and flavorless vodka is a "dietetic" spirit, but don't kid yourself. An ounce of 80-proof vodka contains just as many calories as an ounce of 80-proof whiskey—namely, 80.

Lorenzo

Serve on the rocks in a lowball glass.

½ oz. vodka
2 tsp. lime juice
1 TB. Tuaca
1 tsp. grenadine

Combine over ice in the serving glass. Stir.

Dieter's Cuba Libre

Serve on the rocks in a lowball glass.

½ oz. 86-proof rum
2 tsp. lime juice
½ oz. grenadine

Combine over ice in the serving glass. Stir.

Coronet Cocktail

Serve in a chilled cocktail glass.

1 oz. port
½ oz. gin
3 liberal dashes orange bitters

Combine a shaker with cracked ice. Shake well, and then strain into the serving glass.

Currier

Serve in a chilled cocktail glass.

½ oz. blended whiskey
1 tsp. lime juice
1 tsp. kummel

Combine a shaker with cracked ice. Shake well, and then strain into the serving glass.

Light Liqueur Drinks

Crème de Cacao Float

Serve in a chilled cocktail glass.

½ oz. crème de cacao
1 tsp. chocolate ice milk

Pour the liqueur into the serving glass first, and then float the ice milk on top of it. Do not stir.

Fire and Ice

Serve in a cocktail glass.

½ oz. Cherry Heering
Orange slice
1 TB. kirsch

Place a single large ice cube in the serving glass. Add liqueurs and stir until the ice cube is melted. Garnish with the orange slice.

Waverly

Serve over crushed ice in wine goblet.

½ oz. gin
1 TB. orange juice
1 tsp. crème de cassis
Orange slice

Fill serving glass ⅓ with crushed ice. Pour liquid ingredients. Garnish with the orange slice.

Fig Leaf Flip

Serve in a parfait glass.

1 oz. crème de menthe
1 oz. water
1 tsp. unflavored gelatin
3 oz. crushed ice

Boil water. Combine with gelatin, and then blend in blender for 30 seconds at high speed. Add crème de menthe. Blend again. Add ice. Blend again.

Coronation Cocktail

Serve over crushed ice in a cocktail glass.

2 TB. apricot nectar

½ oz. crème de menthe (white or green)

Fill the serving glass one-third with crushed ice. Pour on nectar and crème de menthe.

Lite Drinks: The New Outlook

Here are some new ideas for the calorie-conscious.

Cranberry Splash

Serve on the rocks in a lowball glass.

3 oz. vodka

Cranberry juice cocktail

Lime slice

Pour vodka over ice in the serving glass. Splash cranberry juice. Garnish with the lime slice.

French Summer

Serve over crushed ice in a wine goblet.

¾ oz. Chambord

3 oz. Perrier

Several drops lemon juice

Lemon slice

Fill serving glass three-quarters with crushed ice and add Chambord. Top off with Perrier, and add several drops of lemon juice. Garnish with a lemon slice.

Good and Plenty

Serve in a brandy snifter.

1 oz. anisette

1 oz. ouzo

Combine the liqueurs in the serving glass. Swirl and serve.

Tequila Popper

Serve in a shot glass as a shooter.

1 oz. tequila

½ oz. 7-Up

Combine the ingredients in the serving glass.

Lion Tamer

Serve in a shot glass as a shooter.

¾ oz. Southern Comfort

¼ oz. lime juice

Combine the ingredients in a mixing glass with ice. Stir, and then strain into the serving glass.

Java Cooler

Serve on the rocks in a highball glass.

1 oz. gin

½ oz. lime juice

Several dashes Angostura bitters

Tonic water

Combine all ingredients, except tonic water, over ice in the serving glass. Stir, and then top off with tonic water.

Green Lizard

Serve in a shot glass as a shooter.

1 oz. green Chartreuse

½ oz. 151-proof rum.

Combine the ingredients in a mixing glass with ice. Stir, and then strain into the serving glass.

The Least You Need to Know

- Although drinking will not help you lose weight, you can enjoy many relatively low-calorie alcoholic beverages.
- Counting alcoholic calories is easy: The caloric content is equal to the proof of the spirit (per ounce). An ounce of 100-proof vodka or whiskey contains 100 calories.
- Reducing the amount of alcohol in a drink or making smaller drinks are the easiest and surest ways of reducing the calorie count in a mixed drink.
- Remember that low-alcohol drinks are not *no*-alcohol drinks. Do not serve them to guests who do not want (or cannot have) alcohol-based beverages.

Chapter 21

Spiritless Yet Delicious: Drinks Without Alcohol

In This Chapter

- How to make your nondrinking guests comfortable
- How to make nonalcohol drinks exciting
- Nonalcoholic recipes

Let's face it: This book exists because of alcohol. The drinks you've found here are, well, spirited. But not everyone likes to drink liquors, not everyone *should* drink them, not everyone *can* drink them, and even people who enjoy alcohol don't *always* feel like having a drink.

Your job as a host is to offer tempting and thoroughly satisfying alternatives to alcohol-based libations. The drinks should be delicious, and they should appeal to adults. That's what we intend to supply in this chapter.

The Gracious Host

What does it mean to be a gracious host? It means, above all else, making your guests comfortable.

That last word deserves discussion. Of course, you want to see to your guests' physical comfort: pleasant places to sit, good food to eat, a temperate room. But "comfort" extends to the emotions as well—to providing a sense of well-being and ease, and at all times a feeling of welcome.

So far as drinks are concerned, this means providing alcoholic drinks for those who want them and nonalcoholic alternatives for those who don't. If you fail to provide attractive, appealing alternatives to beer, wine, and hard liquor, you fail to make all of your guests comfortable.

Bar Tips

Use the same glassware and garnishes for nonalcohol drinks as you do for drinks with spirits. Doing so enhances the drinking experience, elevating it above the ordinary.

There are many reasons why people choose not to drink. They range from momentary preference, to taste, to upbringing, to social or religious conviction, to issues of health—issues that might be based on a general inclination not to drink or an acute condition: ulcer, diabetes, alcoholism, whatever. It is not your business to investigate the motives behind your guests' choices. It *is* your business to ensure that those choices can be made comfortably.

To Refresh and Satisfy Sans Spirits

Sure, you could discharge your "hostly" obligations by seeing to it that plenty of soft drinks are available to your guests. And that *is* a good idea, as far as it goes. But does it go far enough?

If you take the time and effort to prepare exciting mixed drinks for your alcohol-consuming guests, shouldn't you do the same for those who prefer drinks *without* spirits? You want to show everyone a good time, which means ensuring that no one feels like a second-class guest.

Bar Tips

Water is so obvious an alternative to alcohol that you may overlook it. Today, many people enjoy bottled water. Provide a small variety of still and sparkling waters for your guests. This is not only great for nondrinkers, but also provides your drinking guests with a way to "slow down."

Almost any soft drink will refresh. But, in a social setting, it takes something a little out of the ordinary to *satisfy*. That's why you should devote time and effort to making appealing nonspirituous drinks.

There's another reason to prepare exciting nonalcoholic drinks. People come to a party expecting a variety of spirits, wine, and beer to be served. Soft drinks, however, hardly get a second look. Come up with something more than the usual cola and fizzy drinks, and your guests will not only be grateful for your thoughtfulness, but will talk, long after the event, about the imagination that went into every detail.

Cider Surprises

Sweet apple cider has long been served as an alternative to booze. Really good cider tastes great on its own, but the following recipes make it even more tempting and delicious.

Aileen Peterson's Cider Cup

Serve in mugs. (Yields 2 drinks.)

1 cup fresh apple cider

1 cup hot tea

1 tsp. brown sugar

Dash orange juice

Dash lemon juice

Pinch powdered cinnamon

Pinch grated nutmeg

2 cinnamon sticks

Combine all ingredients, except the cinnamon sticks, in a saucepan over low heat. Let simmer, and then pour into 2 warmed mugs. Garnish with cinnamon sticks.

Cider And

Serve on the rocks in a Collins glass.

2 oz. pineapple juice

2 oz. white grape juice

1 oz. cider

2 TB. orgeat

1 TB. lemon juice

Lime slice

Combine liquids over ice in the serving glass. Stir, and then garnish with the lime slice.

Mulled Cider

Mulled cider, with or without alcohol, is a traditional token of hospitality. It's great for cold-weather get-togethers.

Serve in cups. (Yields 16 cups.)

2 cinnamon sticks, broken

12 whole cloves

1 tsp. allspice berries

½ gallon apple cider

½ cup brown sugar

Dried apple rings

Whole cinnamon sticks

Place the broken cinnamon sticks, cloves, and allspice berries into a cheesecloth bag. Place the bag into a saucepan with the cider and brown sugar. Heat over a low flame, stirring constantly. Allow to simmer for several minutes, and then remove the spice bag. Ladle the cider into cups. Garnish with whole cinnamon sticks.

Bar Tips

Make sure that the glass ware or mugs in which you serve hot drinks are heat-resistant.

Coffee Concoctions

Coffee makes a comfortable and appropriate alternative to spirits. You can dress it up in a number of ways to make it a very special alternative offering.

Café Viennoise

Serve in a wine goblet.

1 cup strong, cold black coffee

1 oz. heavy cream

1 tsp. chocolate syrup

½ tsp. powdered cinnamon

Pinch grated nutmeg

Whipped cream

Combine all ingredients, except nutmeg and whipped cream, in a blender. Blend until smooth, and then pour into the serving glass. Sprinkle with nutmeg and top with whipped cream.

Mocha Coffee

Serve in a coffee mug.

½ cup strong black coffee

½ cup hot chocolate

1 TB. whipped cream

Pinch powdered cinnamon

Pinch grated nutmeg

Pinch grated orange peel

Combine the coffee and hot chocolate in a mug. Stir, and then top with whipped cream and add pinches of cinnamon, nutmeg, and grated orange peel.

Fruit Flavors

Fruit juice, of course, is frequently mixed with spirits because it tastes so good. Some drinkers think it's the best part of the drink! Why not showcase fruit juices in nonalcoholic drinks?

Beach Blanket Bingo

Serve on the rocks in a highball glass.

4 oz. cranberry juice

4 oz. grape juice

Lime wedge

Combine the cranberry and grape juices in the serving glass filled with ice. Garnish with the lime wedge.

Gentle Sea Breeze

If it's made with cranberry juice, it inevitably gets the sea in its name. Thank you, Ocean Spray!

Serve in a tall Collins glass or large tumbler.

½ cup cranberry juice

½ cup grapefruit juice

Combine juices in a blender until smooth and foamy. Pour into the serving glass one-third full of ice.

Fruit Juice Combo

With its battery of eight juices (plus a little something more), the Fruit Juice Combo is aptly named. Because it would require a set of laboratory glassware to measure out all the ingredients for a single small serving, this recipe makes enough to fill four highball glasses.

Serve on the rocks in highball glasses.

½ cup tomato juice

½ cup V-8 juice

½ cup apple juice

½ cup cranberry juice

½ cup grapefruit juice

½ cup lemonade

½ cup orange juice

½ cup pineapple juice

4 dashes Tabasco sauce

Pineapple slices

Orange slices

Apple slices

Combine all ingredients in a pitcher half full of ice. Prepare a skewer of the fruit slices. Use it to stir the pitcher and leave in as a garnish. Pour into serving glasses filled with ice. *Makes four drinks.*

Virgin Mary

The Virgin Mary, a nonalcohol incarnation of the Bloody Mary, may well be the most frequently requested drink sans spirits. Every bartender and host should have a zesty, tempting recipe on hand—not just a can of tomato juice poured into a glass.

Serve in a chilled highball glass.

6 oz. V-8 juice

1 tsp. chopped dill

1 tsp. lemon juice (freshly squeezed)

¼ tsp. Worcestershire sauce

Few pinches celery salt

Pinch white pepper

Liberal dash or two Tabasco sauce

Combine all ingredients in a mixing glass with ice. Stir well, and then pour into the serving glass. Add additional ice cubes, if necessary.

Down East Delight

Serve in a chilled old-fashioned glass.

½ cup fresh orange juice

2 oz. grapefruit juice

2 oz. cranberry juice

1 oz. orgeat syrup

Maraschino cherry

Combine all ingredients, except cherry, in a shaker or blender with cracked ice. Shake or blend, and then pour into the serving glass. Garnish with the cherry.

Sunset Cooler

Serve on the rocks in a chilled Collins glass.

½ cup cranberry juice

3 oz. orange juice

Dash lemon juice

Ginger ale

Lemon slice

Combine the juices in a shaker with cracked ice. Shake, and then strain over ice in the serving glass. Top off with ginger ale, and garnish with the lemon slice.

Transfusion

Serve on the rocks in a highball glass.

3 oz. grape juice

6 oz. ginger ale

Few dashes lime juice

Lime slice

Combine the juices and ginger ale over ice in the serving glass, and garnish with a lime slice.

Palm Grove Cooler

Serve in a chilled Collins glass.

2 oz. orange juice

1 oz. guava nectar

1 oz. grapefruit juice

1 oz. pineapple juice

½ oz. lime juice

½ oz. grenadine

Few dashes Angostura bitters

Club soda

Pineapple slice

Maraschino cherry

Combine all ingredients, except the soda and fruit, in a blender with cracked ice. Blend, and then pour into the serving glass. Top off with club soda, and garnish with the pineapple and cherry.

Plum Joy

Serve on the rocks in a Collins glass.

Juice of 2 plums

½ cup water

1 oz. lemon juice

½ oz. sugar syrup

2 TB. plum jelly

Lemon-lime soda

Combine all ingredients in a blender with cracked ice. Blend, and then strain over ice into the serving glass.

Hot Stuff

Hot stuff in this instance has nothing to do with thermal temperature. Drinks without alcohol often lack a certain zing—the bracing clash between spirit and palate. That's why the Indians called liquor "firewater."

Fortunately, there are plenty of fiery stand-ins for this aspect of the spirituous drink. Here are some suggestions.

Sunset

Serve in lowball glasses.

3 cups V-8 juice

½ tsp. horseradish

½ tsp. Worcestershire sauce

Combine all ingredients in a pitcher half full of ice. Stir well and pour into serving glasses. Add additional ice, if necessary. *Makes four servings.*

Poor Suffering Bastard

Serve on the rocks in an old-fashioned glass.

Dash Angostura bitters

6 oz. ginger beer

1 tsp. Rose's lime juice

Cucumber slice

Lemon slice

Mint sprig

Dash sufficient bitters into the serving glass to swirl. Empty the glass, and then add several ice cubes. Fill glass with ginger beer and add lime juice. Garnish with the cucumber, lemon slice, and mint sprig. Stir.

Jones Beach Cocktail

Serve in a chilled highball glass.

5 oz. beef consommé or bouillon

3 oz. clam juice

Juice of ½ lemon or lime

½ tsp. horseradish

Liberal dashes Worcestershire sauce

Pinch celery salt

Combine all ingredients in a shaker with cracked ice. Shake vigorously, and then pour into the serving glass. Add additional ice, if necessary.

Keyport Cocktail

Serve in a chilled old-fashioned glass.

6 oz. clam juice

1 oz. cocktail sauce

½ oz. lemon juice

Few dashes Tabasco sauce

Few dashes Worcestershire sauce

Generous pinch or two celery salt

Lemon slice

Combine all ingredients, except lemon slice, in a blender with cracked ice. Blend, and then strain into the serving glass. Garnish with the lemon slice.

Lone Prairie Oyster

Serve in a chilled wine goblet.

1 tsp. Worcestershire sauce

½ tsp. cider vinegar

1 tsp. cocktail sauce

Few dashes Tabasco sauce

Pinch celery salt

Pinch cayenne pepper

Dash Angostura bitters

1 egg yolk*

Combine all ingredients, except the egg yolk, in the serving glass. Stir well. Add the egg yolk without breaking it. The idea is to drink this down in gulp, yolk and all.

**Raw egg may be a source of salmonella bacteria. You may wish to avoid drinks calling for raw egg yolk or white.*

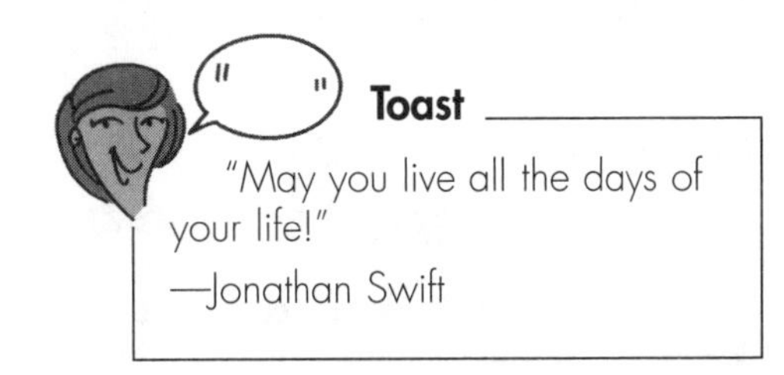

Ice Cream, Milk Drinks, and Nogs

Some drinks fire up the palate; others caress it. And this is true for drinks with as well as without spirits. Here are some soothing nonalcohol alternatives.

Don't worry, the name of the Aryan has nothing to do with the Third Reich or skinheads. *Aryan* refers to the Indo-Iranian people who probably gave the world yogurt—the primary ingredient of this drink.

Aryan

Serve in a chilled wine goblet.

½ cup plain yogurt

½ cup cold spring water

2 tsp. mint, finely chopped

Pinch salt

Combine all ingredients in a blender. Blend until smooth, and then pour into the serving glass. Add ice, if necessary.

Black Cow

You may remember the Black Cow as a childhood favorite—or maybe you called it a Brown Cow, or just a plain old root beer float. It's definitely retro, and it's definitely devoid of alcohol.

Serve in a well-chilled large root beer mug or other large tumbler.

2 scoops vanilla ice cream

Root beer to fill

Put the ice cream in the serving glass. Add root beer to fill. Stir a few times with a long-handled spoon. Serve with the spoon.

Breakfast Eggnog

Serve in a chilled wine goblet.

2 oz. frozen orange juice concentrate (unthawed)

¾ cup whole milk

1 egg*

Grated nutmeg

Combine all ingredients, except nutmeg, in a blender. Blend until smooth and foamy. Pour into the serving glass and garnish with nutmeg.

**Raw egg may be a source of salmonella bacteria. You may wish to avoid drinks calling for raw egg yolk or white.*

Mickey Mouse

Serve in a Collins glass or other large tumbler.

1 scoop vanilla ice cream

Cola to fill

Whipped cream

2 maraschino cherries

Put the ice cream in the serving glass and add cola to fill. Stir a few times with a long-handled spoon, and then top with whipped cream and add cherries. Serve with the spoon.

The Classic Malted

Anyone who doubts that chocolate is a mood-altering substance hasn't eaten enough of it. The Classic Malted dispenses much pleasure. Use no ice, but do make sure that the milk is well chilled.

Serve in a tall tumbler with a straw.

1 cup whole milk

2 scoops chocolate ice cream

¼ cup chocolate syrup

2 TB. malt powder

Combine all ingredients in a blender. Blend until smooth, and then pour into the serving glass.

Milkmaid's Cooler

For a milk drink a little less ordinary, there is the Milkmaid's Cooler.

Serve in a chilled Collins glass.

¾ cup buttermilk

¾ cup tomato juice

Dash lemon juice

Pinch white pepper

Pinch dried basil

Dash Worcestershire sauce

Chill all ingredients, and then combine in a blender until smooth. Pour into the serving glass.

Embellished Soft Drinks

We observed at the outset of this chapter that too many hosts provide nothing more than a few soft drinks as the only alternatives to their spirituous offerings. Soft drinks *are* good options, but why not dress them up?

Faux Champagne

Serve in champagne glasses.

½ cup sugar

1 cup water

1 cup grapefruit juice

Juice of ½ lemon

Dash grenadine

1 (28 oz.) bottle ginger ale

Combine all ingredients, except ginger ale, in a large pitcher with ice. Stir. Add ginger ale just before serving, and pour into champagne glasses. *Makes eight drinks.*

Pony's Neck

Serve in a highball glass or other tall glass.

1 lemon or orange zest in a long spiral

Ginger ale to fill

½ tsp. lime juice

Dash Angostura bitters

Maraschino cherry

Carefully cut away the zest (outer peel layer) of an orange or lemon in a long spiral. Place it in the serving glass, with one end draped over the rim. Fill glass to one third with ice cubes. Add chilled ginger ale to fill. Add lime juice and dash in bitters. Stir very gently so that carbonation is not dissipated. Garnish with the cherry.

Here they are, two of the all-time classic drinks for kids to enjoy while Mom and Dad imbibe something stronger. You should learn them by heart. In an age before political correctness, Roy was for the boy, and Shirley for the girl.

Roy Rogers

Serve on the rocks in a highball glass.

Dash grenadine

Cola to fill

Maraschino cherry

Combine grenadine and cola in the serving glass filled with ice. Garnish with the cherry.

Shirley Temple

Serve in a chilled wine glass.

4 oz. ginger ale

1 tsp. grenadine

Orange slice

Lemon twist

Maraschino cherry

Combine ginger ale and grenadine in the serving glass with a single ice cube. Garnish with the orange slice, lemon twist, and maraschino cherry.

The Vanilla Cola uses vanilla extract, which often contains alcohol. Check the label. If alcohol is present, do not offer this drink to people who cannot drink any alcohol.

Vanilla Cola

Serve on the rocks in a highball glass.

Splash vanilla extract (May contain alcohol! Check label.)

Cola to fill

Combine vanilla and cola in the serving glass filled with ice.

Bar Tips

Flavoring agents such as bitters and (usually) vanilla extract contain alcohol. Even a dash of these might be harmful to people who, for health reasons, must avoid alcohol. Make certain that a dash of bitters is okay with your guest before serving the drink.

Tropical Alternatives

Why should those who choose not to drink miss out on the kitschy revelry of elaborate tropical drinks? Bring on the little paper parasols!

Innocent Passion

Serve on the rocks in a highball glass.

4 oz. passion fruit juice

Splash cranberry juice

Splash orange juice

Juice of ½ lemon

Club soda to fill

Pour the passion-fruit juice over ice in the serving glass. Add all other ingredients except the club soda. Stir, and then add the club soda to fill.

Virgin Colada

Behold another "virgin" version of a popular drink.

Serve in chilled highball glass.

4 oz. coconut cream

4 oz. pineapple juice

Maraschino cherry

Pineapple chunk

Combine all ingredients, except the maraschino cherry and pineapple chunk, in a blender with cracked ice. Blend until smooth, and then pour into the serving glass.

Planter's Paunch

Serve in a chilled Collins glass.

2 oz. pineapple juice

2 oz. orange juice

1 oz. lime juice

1 oz. coconut syrup

1 oz. passion fruit juice

½ oz. grenadine

Club soda to fill

6 maraschino cherries

Pineapple slice

Orange slice

Combine all ingredients, except club soda and fruit, in a shaker with cracked ice. Shake vigorously, and then pour into the serving glass. Add club soda to fill. Garnish with the fruit.

Party Punches

The punch bowl is a particularly welcoming and inviting way to serve any party drink, especially those without alcohol. The nonalcohol punch bowl offering says to your guests that they are special, but not unusual or weird for not choosing spirits.

Bar Tips

You'll find spirit-bearing punches in Chapter 23.

Florida Punch

Serve in a large punch bowl.

2 qt. fresh orange juice

1 qt. fresh grapefruit juice

2 liter bottle ginger ale

1 cup lime juice (freshly squeezed)

1 cup orgeat syrup

½ cup grenadine

Prechill the punch bowl and all ingredients. Place a cake of ice in the punch bowl. Combine all ingredients and stir well. *Makes 46 servings.*

Red Rooster Punch

Serve in lowball glasses.

4 cups V-8 juice

10 oz. ginger ale

1 TB. lime juice

1 tsp. Worcestershire sauce

Dash Tabasco sauce

Combine all ingredients in a pitcher half full of ice. Stir well and pour into serving glasses. Add additional ice, if necessary. *Makes six servings.*

At the Boozeless Frontier

Here's a trio of new-wave nonalcoholic refreshments for those who want more than a soft drink.

Samurai Cooler

Serve on the rocks in a Collins glass.

3 oz. apple juice

1 oz. pineapple juice

1 oz. orange juice

Ginger ale

1 tsp. ginseng extract

Maraschino cherry

Combine juices over ice in the serving glass. Stir, and then top off with ginger ale. Float the ginseng extract. Do not stir. Garnish with the cherry.

Cranberry Bomber

Serve on the rocks in a Collins glass.

4 oz. cranberry juice

½ oz. orange juice

2 TB. grenadine

Cola

1 tsp. honey

Lemon slice

Combine the juices and grenadine over ice in the serving glass. Stir, and then top off with cola. Spoon in honey, and garnish with the lemon slice.

Devil's Juice

Serve on the rocks in a Collins glass.

3 oz. cranapple juice

3 oz. tomato juice

1 tsp. Tabasco sauce

1 tsp. lemon juice

2 dashes black pepper

Dash salt

Lemon slice

Sprig parsley

Combine the juices over ice in the serving glass. Stir. Dash in pepper and salt, and garnish with the lemon and parsley.

The Least You Need to Know

- Devote as much effort and imagination to preparing nonalcohol drinks as you devote to making spirituous beverages.
- Strive for variety in the nonalcohol beverage alternatives you provide.
- Present and garnish nonalcohol drinks the same way you would present alcoholic drinks.
- If you are making nonalcohol drinks for adults, make *adult* drinks—not too sweet, and with complex, rather than simple, flavors.

Part 7

Putting It All Together

If mixing one drink at a time is a challenge, what about deploying a spread for an entire party? Here's help with planning and logistics: how to figure out what to buy and how much to buy.

Many hosts have turned their backs on punch, which has acquired a reputation as a cheapskate substitute for individual drinks. But, traditionally, punch has served as the centerpiece of a party. Prepared with care, imagination, and knowledge, a great punch can fuel a party. You'll find here a chapter with the best traditional punch recipes and a few from the cutting edge.

The finale? How about an opportunity to turn pro? We end with a chapter on the bartender's vocation—everything you need to know if you want to tend bar and get paid for it. And even if a bartending career is not in your plans, this chapter gives you some tips to make your *amateur* bartending a lot more professional.

Chapter 22

It's My Party: Planning a Great Time

In This Chapter

- Setting up your bar
- What—and how much—liquor to buy
- How season influences your choice of liquor
- How to close the party

Just because a party should be fun doesn't mean that you won't have to do plenty of work. Fortunately, most of your hard work comes *before* the party—in the planning. The time you spend planning will proportionately reduce the amount of work you have to do when you should be having fun with your guests. Panic? A little planning can reduce that to nil.

This book is about mixing drinks, not about the art of entertaining, so the emphasis in this chapter is on planning your guests' experience at the bar. Alpha Books publishes *The Complete Idiot's Guide to Throwing a Great Party* and *The Complete Idiot's Guide to Entertaining*, which cover just about everything else.

The Setup

Begin with the party space. Can you rearrange it to accommodate everyone? Do you have enough seating? If necessary, rent chairs—and think about renting some folding tables for setting out food and drink and even for setting up the bar. You can purchase inexpensive disposable tablecloths, or you can rent more elegant linen at most party stores.

Now let's begin to talk about the bar. You've got some basic decisions to make first:

- Do you want a self-service bar or a tended bar? For parties with fewer than 15 people, a self-service bar usually makes the most sense. Parties with 20 or more benefit from the services of a bartender. With 100 or more guests, you'll need at least two barkeeps.
- Do you want to tend bar? A lot of hosts *really* enjoy tending bar. They feel that they are genuinely giving of themselves to their guests, and, because the guests come to the bartender, the job offers an opportunity for the host to circulate without moving. On the other hand, some hosts find that tending bar keeps them too busy to entertain their guests adequately. It is possible for the bartender host to end up missing the party!

Bar Tips

Consider compromising on the question of tending bar. While the party is just warming up, tend bar. Once you sense that it's rolling on its own, open up the bar to self-service.

- If you don't want to tend bar yourself or you are throwing a large party, consider hiring a professional bartender. Most party stores can help you find a good one, or you can consult your local Yellow Pages.

Give serious consideration to the placement of the bar:

- If it's a table—especially a folding table—make absolutely certain that it can support the weight of bottles and glassware, as well as the weight of guests leaning on it. It should also be stout enough to withstand the inevitable bumps to which people will subject it.
- If the table is a valued piece of furniture, be sure to protect it from spills by spreading a plastic tablecloth over it. The setup will be more attractive if, over the plastic table cloth, you spread a tablecloth of real linen.
- Avoid locating the bar close to a doorway. People sweeping in and out might cause spills or block access to the bar.

- If possible, shove the tended bar almost against the wall, with just enough room behind for the bartender. You want to discourage guests from sneaking around the bar to make their own drinks. This will quickly torpedo your bar setup.
- If you have a self-service bar in operation, push it *all* the way against the wall. Guests should prepare drinks from the front of the bar only; otherwise, any semblance of order in the setup of the bottles, glassware, and utensils will soon dissolve into an ugly mob scene.

For a party of fewer than 100 guests, one bar should be sufficient. If the party is larger, consider setting up an additional bar at the other side of the room.

Glassware: Real or Plastic?

We discussed glassware basics in Chapter 4, but you might have to recalculate your needs based on the size of the party. You have two decisions to make at the outset:

- Will you use real glass glassware or disposable plastic glassware?
- If you opt for real glass, should you buy or rent?

The first question depends in part on the feeling you wish to create at your party. Although plastic is acceptable at all but the very highest-brow gatherings, genuine glass adds a substantial touch of elegance to the party and enhances the pleasure of drinking. Aside from expense, of course, the chief disadvantage of glass is the possibility of breakage, which might result in injury.

If you opt for plastic, you need to purchase only two types, which will be pressed into duty for all the drinks you serve. Get lowball glasses, which hold about nine ounces, and highball glasses, with a 12-ounce capacity. Figure that you will need two glasses per person for a four-hour party, and for every three highball glasses you buy, purchase one lowball glass.

If you opt for real glassware, decide whether you want to buy or rent. Most party stores—and many general rental agencies—have glassware available for rental and will even deliver and pick up.

Bar Tips

If you are serving drinks outdoors, especially around a swimming pool, insist on plastic glassware. Broken glass is dangerous to barefoot guests!

Bar Tips

If you are throwing a dance party, increase the glassware-to-guest ratio from 2-to-1 to 3-to-1. Dancing guests typically set down their glasses, and then forget them.

To calculate your needs, use the glass-to-guest ratios just given, and consider renting some specialty glassware in addition to the lowball and highball glasses. This depends on the size of the party, its level of formality, and the kinds of drinks you intend to serve.

Bar Basics

In addition to glassware, make sure that you have all the bar utensils you'll need. (Review Chapter 4 for a list.) Unless your party is large enough to warrant two bartenders, the basics should be quite sufficient—with the addition of …

- A large trash barrel
- A larger ice bucket than the one you probably already own
- An ice tub for keeping beer cold (if you don't buy a keg)
- A pitcher for water
- Two bar towels
- An ashtray or two at the bar

Bar Tips

Cocktail napkins are essential. Professional caterers deploy them in a stack at the bar and elsewhere. For an elegant touch, put down a stack of napkins, make a fist, press your knuckles into the napkins, then twist clockwise. The result will be an attractively fanned stack. Some folks use the bottom of a shot glass, rather than their knuckles, to fan the napkins.

Some hosts fear that including an ashtray at the bar encourages smoking, but unless you prohibit smoking in your house, some of your guests *will* smoke, and you don't want them flicking (or just losing) ashes on your floor, rugs, or furniture while they wait in line at the bar.

Front Bar

In organizing a bar, professionals think in terms of a "front bar" and "back bar." They put the most frequently accessed items—and spirits—in the front bar and the less often used stuff in back. This concept may be adapted to the home party situation.

The self-service bar can be arranged in four tiers:

- Glasses and ice should be front and center, with bar towels and mixers available on either side of the glasses.
- Just behind this first tier, put garnishes and, on either side of them, pitchers of water.

◆ Along the third tier, array the liquor. A symmetrical arrangement is most effective so that, facing the bar, your guests will see (from left to right) scotch, gin, bourbon, vodka, dry vermouth, sweet vermouth, vodka, bourbon, gin, and scotch.

◆ On either side of this array, place cocktail napkins and a couple of ashtrays.

◆ In the fourth tier, farthest from the guests, store extra mixers.

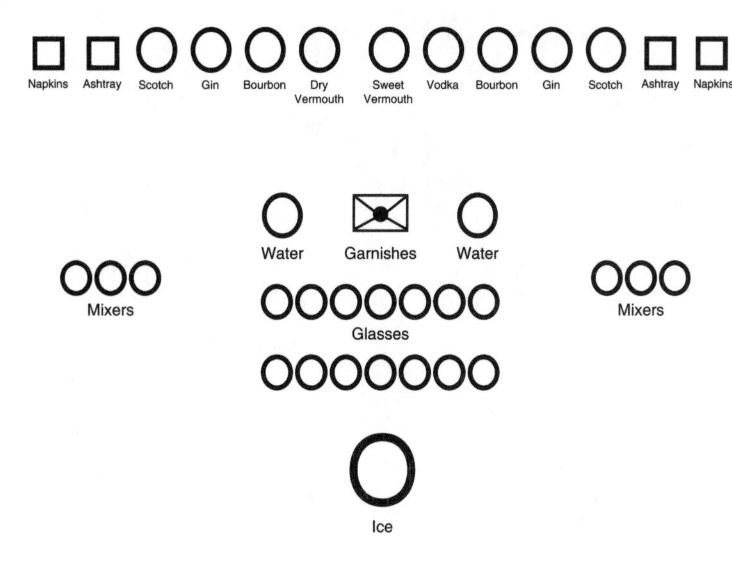

Set up your self-service bar like this.

The setup for a one-bartender bar differs from the self-service bar:

◆ The bartender should be positioned behind the bar, facing the guests.

◆ Out of sight, on either side of the bartender, place receptacles for wet trash and dry trash.

◆ Directly in front of the bartender, position the utensils, a towel to the left of these, and the lowball glasses to the left of the towel.

◆ To the right of the utensils, place a bucket of ice, and to the right of that, the highball glasses.

◆ Garnishes can be positioned directly in front of the utensils.

◆ In the next tier away from the bartender and closer to the guests, arrange the spirits most often used (from the bartender's left to right): bourbon, blended whiskey, scotch, rum, vodka, and gin.

◆ In the next tier, arrange the mixers (from the bartender's left to right): ginger ale, club soda, sweet vermouth, dry vermouth, tonic, and cola.

Unlike table settings, which are governed by rules of etiquette, there's nothing hard and fast about setting up a bar. Create a layout that's convenient for you and your guests.

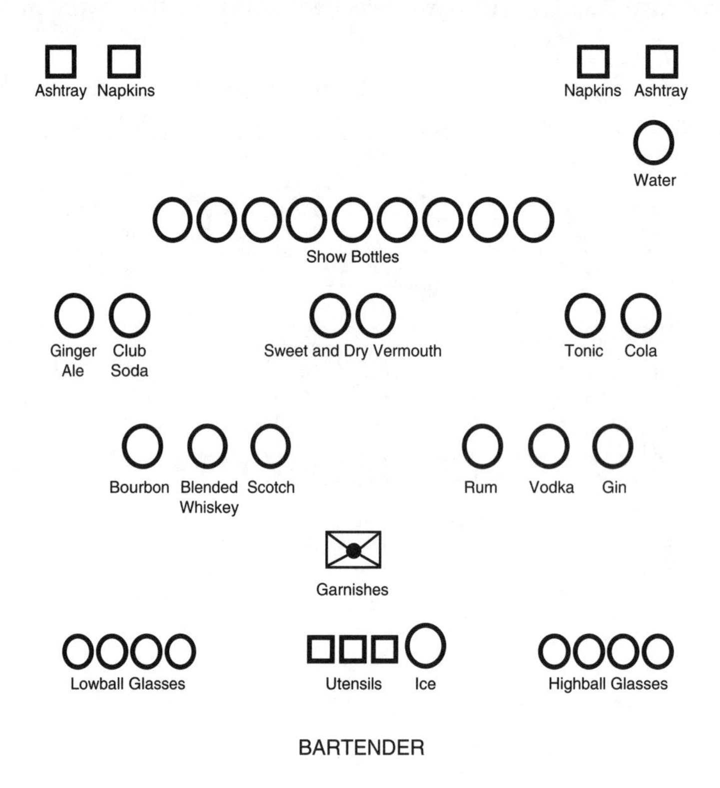

If you or someone else will be tending bar, set it up like this.

"Show" Bottles

In a saloon bar, "show" bottles—the less frequently used spirits, such as liqueurs, tequila, rye, and, often, the premium-label scotches and bourbons—are arranged up high and in the back, very much on display, but farthest from the bartender's reach. In the party bar, these show bottles are also arranged farthest from the bartender, but that means closest to the guests. It's an opportunity to display the best you have to offer.

Liquor Logistics

Unless you're springing for professional entertainment, spirits will be the most expensive ingredient in your party. You need to plan in order to ensure that you have enough on hand for your guests, but not a lot of surplus.

The Basic Cocktail Bar

There is no magic formula to put your buying decisions about type and quantity of liquor on automatic pilot. Review Chapter 4 and assess the contents of your current bar. Then consider the following rules of thumb:

- Professional caterers calculate the overall liquor requirement on the basis of 2.5 cocktails per guest.
- Stock a minimum of two kinds of light spirit—at least gin and vodka.
- Stock a minimum of two kinds of dark spirit—at least scotch and bourbon.
- Provide dry and sweet vermouths.
- Provide white and red wine. Bear in mind that a bottle of wine pours 4.5 glasses.
- Provide beer.
- Always supply a variety of nonalcoholic drinks.

Be sure to break the seals on all bottles. If you don't, your guests might hesitate to help themselves and will, consciously or not, question your hospitality.

Party Time

The season influences what people drink. In warm weather, people will veer toward the light alcohols, so stock proportionately more gin, vodka, rum, and/or tequila. Cut back on bourbon and scotch. Beer and white wine are also favored in warm weather.

In winter, the dark spirits predominate, and you should add blended whiskey and Irish whiskey to your supply of scotch and bourbon. Coffee drinks and mulled drinks are welcome, as are red wine, sherry, and brandy.

Time of day is important, too. If you're giving a brunch party, expect to be making mimosas, screwdrivers, Bloody Marys, and the like, rather than Manhattans and Zombies. Drinks before dinner range from wine and apéritifs to the lighter cocktails. Later-evening parties require an even greater variety of drinks.

What's the Occasion?

The occasion or theme will provide a key to your selection of food and drink. You don't need to lay in a supply of Irish whiskey for a Mexican Fiesta, but you'd better have more than one kind of tequila available for such an occasion. On Valentine's Day, sweet drinks will probably be in order; at Christmas time, mulled wine or eggnog might set the tone.

Who Are Your Guests?

The average age of your guests might also influence your liquor-buying decisions. Younger guests generally prefer the light spirits, as well as wine and beer. Sweet drinks are also in order for this group. Older guests tend toward the darker spirits, often preferring them unmixed. If you are expecting an older, well-established, and more conservative crowd, invest less in mixers and more in premium-label scotch and bourbon.

Bar Tips

Where local laws permit, some liquor stores make it easy for you to match volume with number of guests. Ask the store if it will sell you the liquor on consignment. That way, you can return surplus, unopened, sealed bottles for a refund.

There is no substitute for knowing what your friends like and don't like. To the degree that you are familiar with your guests' preferences, let this knowledge guide you.

Don't Ever Forget Soft Drinks

Whatever else you buy, never fail to supply ample quantities of soft drinks, including a variety of still and sparkling bottled waters. You never want to make a guest feel coaxed or coerced into drinking spirits.

How Much Do You Need?

Assume a party duration of four hours. Purchase one 1-liter bottle of each "front bar" liquor for every six guests. Unless you are inviting substantially more than a hundred guests, one bottle each of sweet and dry vermouth is sufficient. These days, expect the demand for vodka to be heaviest—especially in warmer weather.

Bar Tips

If finances are a problem, consider giving a BYOB—Bring Your Own Bottle—party. You'll still want to prime the pump with a bottle of each of the basics and all the mixers. Work out with the core group of your closest friends just who will bring what. That way, you'll be certain to strike a balance between light and dark spirits, bourbon and scotch, gin and vodka, and so on.

Still assuming the four-hour party, buy one case of beer (24 servings) for every 10 guests. Purchasing a keg becomes economical once your guest list hits 35 people or more. For 35 guests, a quarter-keg should suffice. A full keg serves 70.

Wine consumption varies widely, depending on the season and on the age of the group. Figure that a case of wine—12 bottles—contains 60 individual servings.

Order mixers on the assumption that you'll need two quarts of mixers for every liter of light alcohol you have. Buy extra.

Garnish needs can be calculated this way: You'll need one lime for every five guests, one orange for every 25, and one lemon for every 50. A full jar each of olives, cocktail onions, and maraschino cherries should be sufficient for most cocktail parties.

And don't forget the ice! For the four-hour party, you'll need one pound of ice per guest. If you're expecting a fair-sized crowd, consult your Yellow Pages to find a company that will deliver.

Bar Tips

Unless you have a huge, chest-type freezer, you'll be hard-pressed to store the ice, and in warm weather this can be a problem. Here's an idea: If you've got a washing machine, run it without clothes or detergent through two full cycles to rinse it out thoroughly. Then dump your ice into it (or leave the ice in the bags) and close the lid. This will retard melting. You can simply let any leftover ice melt away. Also: An inexpensive alternative to the metal party tubs party stores sell is a large metal washtub from your local hardware store—great for icing wine bottles and beer and soda cans and bottles.

Food, Glorious Food

It is essential that you offer food at the party, not just because it is the hospitable thing to do, but because spirits should not be consumed, even moderately, on an empty stomach. A plentiful supply of food will help prevent your having a gang of tipsy guests on your hands.

- Offer peanuts or bar nuts, chips, pretzels, and other snack foods. This is the bare minimum.
- Dress up snack foods with easy-to-prepare dips.
- Take a significant—but still easy—step beyond snack food with crudités. These are nothing more than crisp raw vegetables, such as carrot sticks, celery sticks, small whole radishes, cauliflower, edible-pod peas, cucumber sticks, blanched fresh asparagus spears, and green onions.
- A tasty dip—or, better yet, assortment of dips—will make snack food more appealing and is absolutely essential to enjoying crudités. You can purchase ready-made dips, you can make a dip from onion soup mix and sour cream, or you can prepare something more ambitious.

Quick One

Overheard at a cannibal cocktail party—

Guest: "Can this hors d'oeuvre be eaten with the fingers?"

Host: "No. Eat the fingers separately."

- Tasty hors d'oeuvres elevate the party substantially above the level of chips-and-dip. Many cookbooks have excellent sections on hors d'oeuvres, and you will find a good many cookbooks solely devoted to the hors d'oeuvre.

The Party's Over

The final ingredient of a successful party is an end. There are times when, after everyone else has left, you enjoy the company of a few intimate friends only. There are also parties that you wish would go on, full steam, into the daylight hours. But, usually, there comes an hour to call it quits.

Bar Tips

Be sure to read or review Chapter 2 about responsible behavior. Never let a tipsy or drunk guest drive home! You'll find more advice on "shutting off" drunks in Chapter 24.

Signal the end of the party by packing up the bar. Begin with the extra liquor and mixers, and then remove any speedpourers you might have in the active bottles, and put the caps back on. Your guests will soon decamp.

The Least You Need to Know

- Suit the bar setup to self-service or tended bar. In either case, try to put the bar against a wall and away from doorways.
- Offer spirits appropriate to the weather of the season and the time of day.
- Be sure to have enough spirits, mixers, ice, and nonalcoholic beverages on hand for the number of guests.
- Always offer food at any party where spirits are served. For cocktail parties and informal parties, a variety of finger foods is best.

Chapter 23

Packing a Punch: Festive Recipes by the Bowlful

In This Chapter

- Restoring the festive role of punch
- Learning from the "Rule of Five"
- Guidelines for making any punch
- Punch recipes

Alas, poor punch! Once a source of festive delight, punch has degenerated into a sickly-sweet, money-saving substitute for "real" spirits. At their worst, many contemporary punches are just plain awful; at best, they're inoffensive and dull. Let's change that with this chapter.

There was a time—during the first half of the twentieth century and through the whole of the nineteenth—when punch was a gracious expression of hospitality and festivity. The punch bowl was a place where guests could meet to partake communally of something delicious, and, while dipping into the bowl, could speak, arrange their dance cards, and flirt. They were never stuck for something to say because the punch could always be depended on as the opening focus of a pleasant conversation. Nowadays, punch, more often than not, is seen as nothing more than a demonstration of the host's lack of imagination—and generosity.

The Rule of Five

Noted mixologist John J. Poister believes the word *punch* derived from *puncheon*, a small cask in which British Royal Navy crews stored their wines and spirits; however, Poister also alludes to another popular theory, which holds that *punch* comes from a Hindustani word, *panch*, meaning "five." A *panchamrit* is a mixture of five ingredients, and, according to certain mixologists, this is the origin of the Rule of Five. The rule holds that a successful punch should balance five elements:

1. One sour component
2. Two sweet components
3. Three strong components
4. Four weak components
5. A variety of spices

Is it possible to obey the Rule of Five? Sometimes. Is it always desirable? Probably not. But the point of the rule is well taken: Create a punch in which no single component dominates to the point of becoming cloying or tiresome. If, ideally, the punch bowl is a community cocktail, the punch itself should be a community of flavors—all living happily together.

New Life to a Festive Tradition

Your mission, should you choose to accept it, is to redeem the tradition of the punch. If you serve a punch at your party, decide that it will not be a mere shortcut, a labor-saving move, or a bid to save money. Treat the punch with care, and it will become one of the lively hubs around which your party forms. Guests will actually start talking *about* the punch.

Planning Your Attack

A successful punch takes planning and preparation. You have certain questions to answer and some choices to make.

- Who will drink the punch? If your guests will be of many age groups, go easy on the alcohol. If your guests are older and more experienced drinkers, a stronger punch is in order.
- To calculate how much punch you'll need, assume that each quart of punch will yield eight four-ounce servings. In cool or cold weather, assume that each guest will consume three servings—then multiply the resulting number by two. In hot weather, multiply it by three.

- Let's talk about replenishing the punch bowl. Many a host has ruined a decent punch by repeatedly topping off the bowl as it gets lower. When the punch gets low in the bowl, remove it, take it into the kitchen, spill out the dregs, rinse the bowl, and either add a new batch that you have prepared or prepare a new batch.

Bar Tips

If you provide an alcohol-based punch, offer a non-alcoholic alternative as well. See Chapter 21 for some tasty recipes.

- Do not let the bowl run dry before you replenish it. A dry bowl signals the end of the party.
- For cold punches: Chill all ingredients in advance, and chill the bowl, too. Do not use ice cubes in punches! They will melt quickly, diluting the punch. Use blocks of ice, which melt much more slowly.

Bar Tips

For larger parties, consider using two punch bowls, each filled, so that you can rotate one to the serving table while the other is getting refilled.

- For hot punches, use a heat-resistant bowl. The punch should be *hot*, not warm, and you don't want to pour piping hot liquid into a glass or mug that will crack.
- Squeeze all fruit juices in advance, and strain them. Punch should be clear rather than murky.
- Sugar does not dissolve easily in alcohol. That is why drinks are usually sweetened with sugar syrup rather than dry sugar. When working with large quantities of spirits and sugar for a punch, dissolve sugar in the mixers first. Then add the spirits to this mixture.
- Try to hold off adding the spirits to the punch until about an hour before serving. Evaporation significantly reduces the refreshment's alcohol content.
- Carbonated mixers, champagne, and sparkling wines should be added to the punch *immediately* before serving. In a bowl, which has a large surface area, the bubbles will rapidly dissipate, and the punch will go flat quickly.
- An attractive and appropriate bowl will enhance enjoyment of the punch. If you rent a bowl for the occasion, choose carefully. For outdoor events, a rugged bowl—even a bucket or stock pot—is appropriate (and fun). Be certain to use a heat-resistant bowl for serving hot punch!

Bar Tips

Prepare ice blocks or slabs for punches by freezing water in your freezer's ice trays *without* the cube dividers. Another method: Thoroughly rinse out milk cartons, pour in water, and put them in the freezer. Tear away the carton, and you'll have a block of ice. Be certain that the water you use is free from odor or taste.

Brandy Based

Brandy makes a strong base for the more assertive punches.

Bombay Punch

Yields 50-60 servings.

12 lemons

Sugar to taste

1 (750 ml.) bottle cognac

1 (750 ml.) bottle medium-dry sherry

½ cup maraschino liqueur

½ cup curaçao

4 (750 ml.) bottles brut champagne, well chilled

2 (1 liter) bottles club soda

Place block of ice in a punch bowl, squeeze lemon juice over it, and sweeten to taste. Add everything except champagne and club soda. Stir. Add the champagne and club soda immediately before serving. You can decorate with festive fruits in season.

Brandy Punch

Yields 35-50 servings.

Juice of 12 lemons

Juice of 4 oranges

Sugar to taste

1 cup grenadine

1 cup triple sec

2 liters brandy

2 cups tea (optional)

1 quart club soda

Lemon slices

Orange slices

Combine the lemon and orange juice with the sugar, and then combine with the other ingredients over an ice block in the punch bowl. Add the club soda immediately before serving. Garnish with the fruit slices.

Applejack Punch

Makes 45 servings.

2 (750 ml.) bottles applejack

1 pt. light rum

1 pt. peach-flavored brandy

1 pt. lemon juice

1 cup brandy

½ cup maple syrup

2 liters lemon-lime soda

½ thinly sliced red apple

Chill all ingredients. Combine all ingredients, except the sliced apple, over a cake of ice in a chilled punch bowl. Stir, then garnish with the apple slices.

Cardinal Punch

Makes 45 servings.

2 (750 ml.) bottles dry red wine

1 pt. cognac

1 pt. Jamaica gold rum

3 oz. sweet vermouth

½ cup sugar syrup

1 (750 ml.) bottle brut champagne

2 liters club soda

Sliced oranges

Chill all ingredients. Combine wine, cognac, rum, vermouth, and sugar syrup over a cake of ice in a chilled punch bowl. Stir well. Immediately before serving, add champagne and club soda. Garnish with the orange slices.

Shanghai Punch

Yields 35 servings.

2 qt. hot black tea

1 (750 ml.) bottle cognac

1 pt. curaçao

1 pt. dark Jamaica rum

2 cups lemon juice

1½ oz. orgeat syrup

1 oz. orange flower water

Orange peel

Lemon peel

Cinnamon sticks

Combine all ingredients, except the orange and lemon peels and cinnamon sticks, in the flaming pan of a chafing dish. Heat to simmer over direct flame. Serve steaming hot in mugs. Garnish each serving with orange peel, lemon peel, and cinnamon sticks.

St. Cecelia Society Punch

Yields 70 servings.

6 limes, thinly sliced

4 lemons, thinly sliced

Thin slices from one small pineapple (cored and skinned)

1 cup superfine sugar

1 (750 ml.) bottle cognac

1 (750 ml.) bottle peach brandy

1 qt. iced tea

1 pt. dark Jamaica rum

1 cup curaçao

4 (750 ml.) bottles brut champagne

2 liters club soda

In a large pot with a snug lid, place the sliced fruit. Sugar the fruit, and then muddle so that the sugar is evenly pressed into the fruit slices. Add the cognac. Cover and let sit for 24 hours. After 24 hours, pour the contents of the pot into a chilled punch bowl with a large cake of ice. Add the peach brandy, tea, rum, and curaçao. Stir well. (For best results, chill these ingredients before adding.) Immediately before serving, add chilled champagne and club soda.

Champagne Punches

Champagne is a very popular festive base for punches. All too often, however, champagne punches are uninspired. This means that they are typically left out too long so that the champagne bubbles dissipate, and the punch, dull from the get-go, becomes flat as well as boring. The punches that follow are much better than the usual.

Bar Tips

If practical, prepare champagne punches immediately before serving. At the very least, the champagne must be added only moments before serving. The bubbles dissipate rapidly in a bowl.

Champagne Punch

Yields 25-35 servings.

2–3 bottles champagne, well chilled

½ cup curaçao

½ cup lemon juice

1 quart club soda, well chilled

½ lb. confectioners' sugar

Prepare punch immediately before serving, combining all ingredients in a punch bowl. No ice is needed.

Champagne Punch (# 2)

Yields 12-15 servings.

½ cup brandy

½ cup Cointreau or triple sec

2 bottles champagne, well chilled

Combine all ingredients in a small punch bowl, adding the champagne immediately before serving. No ice is needed.

Champagne Rum Punch

Yields approximately 40 servings.

2 liters rum

1 (750 ml.) bottle sweet vermouth

1 quart orange juice

1 bottle champagne, well chilled

Sliced bananas

Combine all ingredients, except bananas, in a punch bowl, adding champagne and ice block immediately before serving. Garnish with sliced bananas.

Holiday Punch

Yields approximately 30 servings.

1 (8 oz.) can crushed pineapple with juice

1 quart raspberry sherbet

1 bottle champagne, well chilled

2 quarts ginger ale, well chilled

Prepare immediately before serving. Put the pineapple and sherbet in a chilled punch bowl, and then add the champagne and ginger ale. No ice is needed.

Trader Vic's Tiki Punch

Yields 35 servings.

1 pt. Cointreau

1 pt. gin

¾ cup lime juice

4 (750 ml.) bottles champagne

Chill all ingredients and then pour everything, except the champagne, over a cake of ice into a chilled punch bowl. Stir. Immediately before serving, add the champagne.

Bar Tips

Often, if the principal ingredients of champagne punches are well chilled—and the bowl is chilled as well—no ice is needed. This will prevent dilution and retard dissipation of bubbles. Some champagne punches are better with ice, however. Follow the suggestions in the recipes.

Liqueur Punches

Liqueur-based punches are strongly flavored, sweet, and rich. They are not great thirst quenchers for sultry days, but are festive energizers that will please a crowd.

French Cream Punch

Yields 15-20 servings.

1 cup amaretto

1 cup Kahlúa

¼ cup triple sec

½ gallon softened vanilla ice cream

Combine all ingredients in a punch bowl without ice. Stir well.

Southern Comfort Punch

Yields approximately 30 servings.

1 (750 ml.) bottle Southern Comfort

2 cups grapefruit juice

1 cup lemon juice

2 quarts 7-Up or Sprite (may substitute ginger ale)

Combine all ingredients in a punch bowl with a block of ice, adding the soda immediately before serving.

Devil's Cup

Yields 27 servings.

1 cup cognac

½ cup lemon juice

2 oz. green Chartreuse

2 oz. yellow Chartreuse

2 oz. Benedictine

2 oz. sugar syrup

2 (750 ml.) bottles brut champagne

1 liter club soda

Chill all ingredients and combine all, except the champagne and soda, over a cake of ice in a punch bowl. Stir. Immediately before serving, add champagne and club soda.

Rum Punches

Rum is the punch ingredient par excellence. It is naturally sweet without being cloying, and its heavy consistency holds its own among many other ingredients. For tropically accented drinks, it adds just the right touch of warm-weather exoticism.

Fish House Punch is a true classic. It is a very potent punch and should be served in gatherings of mature and responsible drinkers. This is not for a frat party.

Fish House Punch

Yields 25-35 servings.

1 liter rum

1 (750 ml.) bottle brandy

½ cup peach brandy

2–3 quarts cola (may substitute other flavored soda, lemonade, or strong tea)

Lemon slice

Lime slice

Orange slice

Combine all ingredients, except fruit, in a punch bowl with a block of ice. If you use cola or other soda, add this immediately before serving. Garnish with fruit slices.

Old Navy Punch

Yields 45 servings.

Juice of 4 lemons

1 can sliced pineapple

1 (750 ml.) bottle dark Jamaica rum

1 pt. cognac

1 pt. Southern Comfort

Orgeat syrup to taste

4 (750 ml.) bottles brut champagne

Combine all ingredients, except champagne, in a punch bowl. Immediately before serving, add a cake of ice and pour in the champagne.

Tropical Punch

Yields approximately 100 servings.

5 bottles white wine

1 lb. brown sugar

1 quart orange juice

1 pint lemon juice

5 sliced bananas

1 pineapple, cut or chopped

3 liters light rum

1 pint dark rum

2 cups crème de banana

Assorted fruit slices (banana, pineapple, orange, lime)

Combine the wine, brown sugar, juices, and fruit in a *large* mixing bowl, or perhaps more than one (store backups in the refrigerator). Stir very thoroughly, cover, and let stand overnight. Add the rums and liqueur, and then strain into a large punch bowl containing a block or two of ice. Garnish with assorted fruit slices.

Old Colonial Hot Tea Punch

Yields 30 servings.

1 liter dark Jamaica rum

1 pt. brandy

3 pt. hot tea

1 pt. fresh lemon juice

½ cup honey

3 oz. curaçao

½ thinly sliced lemon

In a saucepan over low flame, combine all ingredients except the lemon slices. Stir until the honey is dissolved. Allow to cool, then pour over an ice cake in a punch bowl. Garnish with the lemon slices.

Celebrity Punch

Yields 43 servings.

1 (750 ml.) bottle gold rum

1 (750 ml.) bottle gin

1 liter grape juice

1 pt. orange juice

2 liters ginger ale

Jar maraschino cherries

6-8 orange slices

6-8 lemon slices

Chill spirits and juice, and then combine over a cake of ice in a punch bowl. Stir. Immediately before serving, add ginger ale and cherries. Garnish with the fruit slices.

Vodka Punches

As many hosts see it, vodka, the great clean, neutral spirit, is the ideal vehicle to propel any punch to success. It goes especially well with any fruit you wish to add.

Fruit Punch

Yields approximately 40 servings.

1 liter vodka

1 bottle white wine

2 (12 oz.) cans frozen fruit juice concentrate (pineapple, grapefruit, or orange)

2 quarts club soda

Combine all ingredients, except club soda, in a punch bowl with a block of ice. Add the club soda immediately before serving.

Velvet Hammer Punch

Yields approximately 30 servings.

1 bottle sauterne

12 ounces apricot brandy

1 liter vodka

1 bottle champagne, well chilled

1 quart ginger ale

Combine all ingredients in a punch bowl with a block of ice, adding the champagne and ginger ale immediately before serving.

Wedding Punch

Yields approximately 35 servings.

1 liter vodka

3 cups orange juice

1 cup lemon juice

2 quarts ginger ale

Cherries

Lemons

Orange slices

Combine vodka and juices in a punch bowl. Add the ginger ale and a block of ice immediately before serving. Garnish with cherries, lemons, and orange slices.

Dubonnet Vodka Punch

Yields 17 servings.

1 (750 ml.) bottle Dubonnet rouge

1 pt. vodka

½ cup curaçao

Juice of 6 limes

1 pt. club soda

Spiral-cut lime peel

Thinly cut orange slices

Chill all ingredients, and then combine everything, except club soda and fruit, over a cake of ice in the punch bowl. Stir well. Immediately before serving, add club soda and garnish with fruit.

Whiskey Punches

Whiskey punches mean business. They appeal to a more mature group.

Whiskey Punch

Yields 60-65 servings.

2 liters bourbon

½ cup curaçao

1 quart apple juice

Juice of 6 lemons

2 ounces grenadine

4 quarts ginger ale

Cherries

Combine all ingredients, except cherries, in a punch bowl, adding the ginger ale with a block of ice immediately before serving. Garnish with cherries.

Old-Fashioned Whiskey Punch

Yields 30 servings.

1 liter blended whiskey

1 pt. dark Jamaica rum

1 pt. fresh lemon juice

1 pt. chilled black tea

1 cup orgeat syrup

4 oz. curaçao

1 (750 ml.) bottle brut champagne

6 thin orange slices

6 thin lemon slices

Combine all ingredients, except the fruit and champagne, in a punch bowl. Cover and chill in the refrigerator for at least 4 hours. Immediately before serving, add cake of ice and pour in champagne. Garnish with the fruit slices.

Artillery Punch

Yields 40 servings.

1 liter bourbon

1 liter dry red wine

1 liter chilled strong black tea

1 pt. dark Jamaica rum

1 pt. orange juice

1 cup brandy

1 cup gin

1 cup lemon juice

4 oz. Benedictine

Sugar syrup

Several lemon peels

Chill all ingredients, except lemon peels, and then combine over a cake of ice in a punch bowl. Stir. Garnish with the lemon peels.

Harvard Punch

Yields 32 servings.

1 liter blended whiskey

1 pt. brandy

1 cup Grand Marnier

1 cup orange juice

½ cup lemon juice

½ cup orgeat syrup

2 liters club soda

Several orange slices

Several lemon slices

Combine all ingredients, except soda and fruit slices, in a punch bowl. Stir, cover, and refrigerate at least 4 hours. Immediately before serving, add club soda over a cake of ice. Garnish with the fruit slices.

Victoria Parade Punch

Yields 33 servings.

1 (750 ml.) bottle scotch

1 (750 ml.) bottle dark Jamaica rum

1 (750 ml.) bottle Benedictine

1 (750 ml.) bottle cherry brandy

1 pt. chilled Darjeeling tea

1 cup orange juice

4 oz. lemon juice

4 oz. pineapple syrup

Several orange slices

Several lemon slices

Chill all ingredients, and then combine over a cake of ice in a punch bowl. Stir.

Wine Punches

Wine punches appeal to a broad group of drinkers, of all ages and tastes. The degree of aggressiveness depends on the additional spirituous ingredients.

The Buddha Punch is refreshing without being overbearing. It is mild and as close to universally appealing as any punch can get.

Buddha Punch

Yields 25-30 servings.

1 bottle Rhine wine

½ cup curaçao

½ cup rum

1 cup orange juice

1 quart soda water

Angostura bitters to taste

1 bottle chilled champagne

Mint leaves

Orange slices

Combine all ingredients, except champagne, mint, and orange slices, in punch bowl. Add the champagne just before serving. Garnish with mint leaves and orange slices

Burgundy Punch

Yields 22 servings.

2 (750 ml.) bottles red Burgundy

½ cup lemon juice

1 pt. orange juice

1 oz. sugar syrup

1 cup port

1 liter club soda

1 cup cherry brandy

Several orange slices

Chill all ingredients. Combine everything, except club soda and orange slices, over a cake of ice in a punch bowl. Stir. Immediately before serving, add the club soda and garnish with the orange slices.

Hot Mulled Wine

A mulled wine punch is a classic for a party on a cold winter's eve. This one goes well at Christmastime.

Yields 15-25 servings.

2 cups water

2 cinnamon sticks, whole

8 cloves

1 lemon peel cut into a long spiral

½ cup sugar syrup

2 bottles dry red wine

Cognac (see directions)

Lemon slices (see directions)

Combine all ingredients, except wine, lemon slices, and cognac, in a large saucepan. Allow to boil for 10 minutes. Add the wine, and then resume heating, but do not bring to a boil. Serve hot in cups or glasses, garnishing each with a lemon slice and adding a splash of cognac.

Wassail Bowl

The Wassail Bowl is a traditional Christmas punch and a treat that summons up visions of the brighter aspects of the world of Charles Dickens.

Yields 25-30 servings.

1 cup brown sugar

2 tsp. grated nutmeg

2 tsp. powdered ginger

3 cinnamon sticks, broken

½ tsp. mace

6 whole cloves

6 allspice berries

3 (750 ml.) bottles Madeira, Marsala, sherry, or port

7 eggs*

1 cup cognac (may substitute gold rum)

4 baked apples

Preheat oven to 300°F. Core apples and bake for 35 minutes or until they're soft inside, but still hold their shape. Set aside. Add sugar and spices to a saucepan over direct heat and add 1 to 2 cups of water. Bring to a boil, stirring until the sugar is dissolved. Add the wine and continue heating, but do not boil. Separate the eggs, beat egg yolks and egg whites, and then fold together and pour the folded eggs into a heat-resistant punch bowl. Slowly add the heated wine mixture to the bowl. Stir to blend wine with the eggs. Add cognac. Stir. Add the baked apples. Stir. To serve, add a bit of the baked apple to each cup of punch.

**Raw egg may be a source of salmonella bacteria. You may wish to avoid drinks calling for raw egg yolk or white.*

Traditional Sangria

Sangria is popular even with people who claim not to like punch. Here is a traditional recipe and a "blonde" departure.

Yields 24 servings.

2 (750 ml.) bottles dry red wine

3 oz. curaçao

2 oz. brandy

Juice of 1 orange

Juice of 1 lemon

4 oz. sugar syrup

1 liter club soda

6 thin orange slices

6 thin lemon slices

1 thinly sliced peach

Chill all ingredients. Combine all liquid ingredients except club soda. Stir well, and then strain over a cake of ice in a punch bowl. Immediately before serving, add the soda and garnish with the fruit slices.

Blonde Sangria

Yields 25 servings.

2 (750 ml.) bottles Chablis

3 oz. curaçao

1 oz. kirschwasser

½ cup orange juice

2 oz. lemon juice

2 oz. sugar syrup

1 liter club soda

½ thinly sliced orange

Chill all ingredients. Combine everything, except club soda and sliced orange, over a cake of ice in a punch bowl. Allow to stand for ½ hour. Immediately before serving, add the club soda. Garnish with the orange slices.

Bengal Lancer's Punch

Yields 24 servings.

1 liter dry red wine

3 oz. gold Barbados rum

3 oz. curaçao

½ cup lime juice

½ cup pineapple juice

½ cup orange juice

2 oz. orgeat syrup

1 (750 ml.) bottle champagne

1 pt. club soda

Several lime slices

Chill all ingredients. Combine everything, except soda, champagne, and lime slices, over a cake of ice in a punch bowl. Stir. Immediately before serving, add champagne and soda. Garnish with the lime slices.

Ascot Cup

Yields 37 servings.

2 (750 ml.) bottles red Bordeaux

1 pt. fino sherry

½ cup cognac

½ cup curaçao

½ cup raspberry syrup

½ cup lemon juice

1 oz. framboise liqueur

2 qt. club soda

Several thin orange slices

Several thin lemon slices

Chill all ingredients. Combine everything, except club soda and fruit slices, over a cake of ice in a punch bowl. Stir. Immediately before serving, add club soda and garnish with the fruit slices.

Great Eggnogs

Like punches, eggnogs have fallen on hard times. During the holiday season, supermarket shelves are lined with thick yellow nogs in cartons, loaded with sugar and much too much nutmeg. Do yourself and your guests a favor by reminding them—or revealing to them—what an eggnog is *supposed* to taste like.

Whiskey Eggnog

Serve in a chilled highball glass.

1 egg*

1 tsp. sugar

1½ oz. blended whiskey

6 oz. milk

Grated nutmeg

Combine all ingredients, except nutmeg, in a shaker with ice. Shake vigorously, and then strain into the serving glass. Sprinkle with nutmeg.

**Raw egg may be a source of salmonella bacteria. You may wish to avoid drinks calling for raw egg yolk or white.*

Your Basic Eggnog Punch

Yields 45-65 servings.

1 lb. confectioners' sugar

12 eggs*, separated

1 pint brandy

1 pint light rum

1½ quarts milk

1 pint heavy cream

Grated or powdered nutmeg

In the punch bowl, beat confectioners' sugar in with egg yolks only, and then slowly stir in the brandy, rum, milk, and cream. Chill. Fold in stiffly beaten egg whites immediately before serving. Punch must be well chilled. Do not serve with ice. Sprinkle nutmeg on top.

**Raw egg may be a source of salmonella bacteria. You may wish to avoid drinks calling for raw egg yolk or white.*

Planter's Punch (Times 2)

Planter's Punch is so popular that it merits its own section. The Myers's rum people popularized this drink, and you can't go wrong making it with their dark Jamaican rum.

Bar Tips

You'll find Planter's Punch recipes for individual drinks in Chapter 13.

Planter's Punch

Yields approximately 30 servings.

1 liter light rum

1 pint Myers's dark Jamaican rum

1 pint fresh lime juice

1 pint sugar syrup

1 quart club soda

Orange slices

Cherries

Combine all ingredients except club soda and fruit. Add the club soda immediately before serving and garnish with orange slices and cherries.

Variation on Planter's Punch

Yields approximately 20 servings.

1 liter light rum

1 cup Myers's dark Jamaican rum

1 cup curaçao

1 pint lemon juice

1 cup orange juice

1 cup pineapple juice

Orange slices

Cherries

Combine all ingredients except fruit in a punch bowl. Garnish with orange slices and cherries.

Punch: Rethinking an Old Standby

Here's a trio of refreshingly innovative punches.

Barbados Bowl

Yields 24 servings.

8 ripe bananas

8 oz. lime juice

1 cup sugar

12 oz. light rum

12 oz. dark rum

48 oz. pineapple juice

12 oz. mango nectar

2 thinly sliced limes

Chill all ingredients except bananas. Thinly slice 6 of the bananas. Combine the banana slices, lime juice, and sugar in a blender and blend until smooth. Pour over a cake of ice in a punch bowl. Add the light and dark rum, pineapple juice, and mango nectar. Stir, and then refrigerate for 2 hours. Before serving, thinly slice the remaining bananas. Float these together with the lime slices in the punch.

Mountain Red Punch

Yields 24 servings.

3 bottles California red wine

4½ oz. amaretto

4½ oz. brandy

4½ oz. cherry-flavored brandy

16 oz. ginger ale

Toasted almonds, chopped

Combine the spirits over a cake of ice in a punch bowl. Refrigerate for 1 hour. Immediately before serving, add cold ginger ale. Garnish with chopped almonds.

Interplanetary Punch

Yields 24 servings.

24 oz. light rum

4 oz. dark rum

8 oz. peppermint schnapps

1 qt. mango nectar

12 oz. cream

1 qt. orange juice

8 mint sprigs

1 fresh mango, sliced

1 thinly sliced orange

Combine the liquids in a punch bowl. Stir well, and then add a cake of ice. Garnish with the fruit. If possible, refrigerate 1 hour before serving.

The Least You Need to Know

- Too many party punches are uninspired. Take the time and effort to create a special punch, and you will delight and surprise your guests.
- Do not view punch as a cheap, time-saving alternative to serving individual drinks. Use quality ingredients and take the time to prepare the punch from scratch.
- Cold punches should begin with chilled ingredients and should use block ice rather than cubes, which melt quickly and dilute the punch.
- Be careful with hot punches. They should be served piping hot, so make certain that the punch bowl you use is thoroughly heat resistant.
- Create a punch to suit your guests (in terms of their ages and preferences), the season (warm weather or cold), and the occasion (holiday, special celebration, whatever).

Chapter 24

Turning Pro: The Barkeep's Vocation

In This Chapter

- The challenge of professional bartending
- How much money do bartenders make?
- Breaking in as a bartender
- Dealing with customers
- The bartender's legal responsibilities

Amateur. Now there's a perfectly nice word that has gotten some very bad press. The word summons up images of bumbling, unprofessional incompetence. Actually, *amateur* comes from the Latin *amator*, which means lover. Nothing wrong with that, eh? An amateur is someone who does something not because it's a job, but because he or she *loves* it.

And so this book was written mainly with the *amateur* bartender in mind—the person who wants to mix drinks, not for cash, but for the pleasure of it, or, more to the point, for the pleasure of entertaining and refreshing good friends and convivial companions

But who says we can't do what we enjoy to make a living or supplement one? Here's a brief chapter on the *profession* of bartending.

Do You Really Want to Do This?

Ask us if the jigger is half empty or half full, and we'll give the pessimist's reply. Do you really want to spend hour after hour on your feet—pouring, measuring, and pushing a damp towel into the small hours? Do you want to endure the noise and inhale the smoke? Do you want to dwell perpetually in the company of those who "feel no pain"? And are you willing to listen to the same conversations over and over: spouse trouble, boyfriend trouble, girlfriend trouble, financial woes, and a blow-by-blow history of this lady's brand-new Bimmer and that guy's cherished Corvette?

Toast

"Let us toast the fools; but for them, the rest of us could not succeed."

—Mark Twain

Professional Bartending: What It Takes

If none of this daunts and discourages you, maybe you have what it takes to be a good—and happy—professional bartender. At the very least, you'll need:

- Manual dexterity
- Good eyesight
- Good hearing
- Good short-term memory—and, in local joints with plenty of "regulars," a good long-term memory as well
- Good feet
- Stamina
- Excellent communication skills
- A pleasant manner—an enjoyment of talking to strangers

Bartending is a lot less about pouring and shaking than it is about people. If you don't have people skills, get them. And if you can't get them, don't even think about tending bar for a living. The well-worn cliché about the bartender being the poor-man's psychiatrist is well worn for a reason: It's true. You'll listen to hours of problems, both petty and profound. With some people, you'll sympathize. You'll probably take a liking to many customers. But you can also count on running across a sizable number of jerks. To them you must also give attention and never let on what you may really feel.

This is not the only demand that will be placed on your people skills. After all, what are you serving? A substance that inhibits inhibitions. Usually, a bar is a happy and sociable place. But there will come times when you'll have to deal with drunks—some swaggering, some stubborn; others defiant, macho, obnoxious, pathetic, or downright scary. It is your responsibility to keep an eye on your customers, to recognize when someone has had enough or more than enough, and it is your responsibility to refuse to give them more. If serving customers is demanding, *not* serving them can be even more challenging.

The Rewards—and Risks—of Bartending

Let's cut to the chase. What kind of money can a bartender expect? Despite what you might have heard about bartenders who really rake in the tips, pay often starts out at around $10,000 a year (the low average is about $7,000), with $17,000 the middle range, and the top level coming in at under $29,000 a year. Of course, in the right setting, with big tippers and heavy traffic, you *can* make much, much more. As with most jobs in the food and beverage service industry, salary is typically supplemented by gratuities.

> **Bar Tips**
>
> Beware of the attraction of cash income—tips. Although tips leave no paper trail for the IRS to sniff at, the feds are quite sophisticated at calculating reasonable tip income, and they have their feelers out for waiters, bartenders, and others who might under report tip income.

The average bartender works just under a 40-hour week. However, bartending is one of those jobs that usually can be worked part time or overtime.

Although you'll probably never get rich as a full-time bartender—unless you use the job as a stepping stone to a management or ownership position—bartending can be an excellent part-time profession. Hours are often flexible, as are opportunities for mobility: Few populated places on the globe are very distant from a bar. Nor are you restricted to working in a single type of environment. A bar might be set in the corner tavern; the local disco; the hottest, hardest-to-get-into nightclub; a motel off the interstate; a hotel on the Grand Boulevard; a fine restaurant; an airport—you name it. You don't even have to work *in* a bar. Catering services set up bars in people's homes, in auditoriums and convention halls, at outdoor events, and so on.

Bartending's biggest challenge—dealing with a lot of people on an intimate level—is also, for most professionals, its greatest attraction. You'll meet a cross-section of humanity. You'll make friends. You'll make contacts you would not make in any other profession. You'll have the opportunity to watch people interact and be—*people*.

In most bars, bartending is not a particularly hazardous job. Although it is true that the potential exists for unpleasant or even violent events, most larger bars employ some form of security personnel: a bouncer. In many popular and thickly populated clubs, off-duty police officers serve as the security staff.

Bar Tips

The sixth edition (2002) of the *Jobs Rated Almanac* by Les Krantz rates the vocation of bartender as only moderately stressful: 68 jobs are less stressful, ranging from medical records technician (the least stressful) to physicist (only slightly less stressful than bartender). One hundred eighty-one jobs are more stressful, ranging from antique dealer and philosopher (just a bit more stressful than bartender) all the way to president of the United States (the most stressful).

Despite the presence of professional security personnel, a bartender can be at some personal risk. Women bartenders especially may find themselves fending off unwanted advances from customers. Such attention is often fairly benign, if annoying, but it can become intimidating and even threatening.

Dangers are also associated with any late-night job, as you travel to and from work or even walk from the bar to your car at two in the morning (or even later in some locales).

Bartending can be hazardous to your health in other ways. Possible assaults on your constitution include sleep deprivation, prolonged exposure to second-hand cigar and cigarette smoke, and hearing loss as a result of sustained bombardment by multidecibel music.

There is also a downside to being around so much liquor. A bartender who samples the wares rarely lasts long as a bartender. Not only are you drinking up profits, but also you simply cannot do your job well if you're chronically buzzed. Manual dexterity deteriorates, and short-term memory takes a vacation. But let's say that you somehow get away with it. A bartender who drinks night after night is headed for all the ills alcohol can bring. Bartending is not a profession for people with addiction-prone personalities.

Breaking In to Bartending

The good news is that bartending is a high-turnover profession. Jobs open up all the time. The bad news is that bartending is a high-turnover profession. Plenty of bartenders burn out or get fired. Most just go on to something else, never having intended to make this job their life's work.

Starting at the Bottom

So bartending is hardly a closed-shop profession. You can break in fairly easily. You just can't expect to start at the top, which is probably exactly where you'd *like* to start.

But just where is the bottom? And how bad is it?

To answer the second question first, it's not that bad. In many professions, starting out at the bottom means doing all the dirty, disgusting, back-breaking, mind-numbing work nobody else wants to do. In bartending, it just means working in settings that don't pay much.

The easiest way to break into bartending is to apply to a catering service. The folks behind the portable bars set up at parties, cocktail receptions, and the like are usually not very experienced—and not very well paid. Tips at "catered affairs" are small or nonexistent. But you can use the experience to hone your craft, even as you find out, firsthand, whether bartending is really right for you.

A step up from catering work is a job with a hotel banquet facility. This is similar to tending bar for a catering service, but the work is usually more regular and frequent. The pay? Probably not much better than casual catering gigs.

Beyond the banquet bar are the cocktail lounges and bars found in airports and train stations. Here's a step up in salary, but tips in these way stations are usually dismal, and the customers are rarely jolly. They're stressed, tired, bored, just numbing the pain and killing some time. But at least you're working at a real bar.

Bars in hotels and restaurants offer more attractive salaries and a more varied work experience, but because many of the drinks you prepare are served by waiters and waitresses, you won't deal directly with the public as much as in a standalone bar. You might regard this as a minus or a plus, though undeniably on the minus side. Without direct customer contact, you won't be pulling in the tips—although you may be "tipped out" by the servers, sharing in a portion of the tips they receive.

You can experience "real" bartending—where you're dealing face to face with your customers—at local bars and neighborhood taverns. The crowds might be small, and the tip pool commensurately shallow, but the environment can be laid back and pleasant, and the experience valuable, enabling you, at some point, to make the leap into a major hot spot.

The crowds at large, popular bars create pressure and an unremitting pace, but they also tip well. The potential for making a decent living is greatest in such venues, and, if you're the type, the level of excitement, atmosphere, and activity can be highly energizing.

Getting In

The only way to get any job is to apply. In most bartending situations, this means talking to the manager. If you talk to a bartender—instead of the manager—he or she will almost certainly tell you "they aren't hiring." Don't waste your time. Go to the manager.

Bar Tips

Don't ask to see the manager during peak business hours. Show the savvy of a pro by dropping by between three and five in the afternoon, when most bars are pretty slow.

Present yourself and your skills to the manager. If the place isn't hiring at present, leave a resumé. Or if the place isn't hiring a *bartender* at present, see if you can get a job as a barback—an apprentice bartender and gofer—and work your way up from there.

Buzzed Words

A **barback** is an assistant or apprentice bartender, who does the bartender's **scut work**, including tapping beer kegs, running ice, replacing glassware, preparing and stocking garnishes, restocking shelves, and so on.

Another way to ease yourself in is to offer to take the slow shift. Working the lunch crowd, Sunday brunches, and Monday and Tuesday evenings won't net you much in the way of tips, but it's a way to break in because the more experienced bartenders don't want to put in hours during such slack time.

Conversely, you might look for work during peak periods. Bars in places that have a highly seasonal trade—summer and winter tourist resorts, for example—are likely to need extra help during the high season. But don't wait until then to start looking. Get the drop on the competition by applying early.

Looking the Part

As a customer-contact position, bartending demands a professional appearance. Present yourself as neat, clean, well-groomed, and attractively dressed. Most bar managers will tell you what constitutes appropriate dress for the bar, and some even supply clothes. "Appropriate" varies from bar to bar and depends on clientele; however, here's what to expect:

Bar Tips

Unless the bar promotes an "alternative" atmosphere, avoid any extremes in dress.

- For men: dark pants and shoes with a white shirt. If a tie is required, either wear a bow tie or a long tie "GI style"—that is, neatly tucked into your shirt just below the second button from the collar. A long tie dangling loose will inevitably end up in somebody's drink.

- For women: dark skirt or slacks with a white blouse. Avoid dangling jewelry.
- For men and women: Long hair is probably fine, but tie it back neatly.

The best thing to do is scout out the bar before you apply for a job. Look at how the bartender and customers are dressed, and then dress accordingly when you apply.

Acting the Part

The successful bartender continuously broadcasts three messages:

- I am friendly and courteous and want to serve you.
- I am competent and efficient and will serve you well.
- I am supremely confident and will serve you with authority.

The last item is perhaps the most important. Act vague, confused, or tentative, and customers will question the quality of the drinks you mix (even if nothing is wrong with them). You will also find yourself in trouble when it comes time to refuse a drunk "one more for the road."

Project confidence in the way you move. Keep your bar well arranged so that you can grab the right bottle in a single motion, quickly and firmly by the neck. Pour without hesitation, speak clearly, and always express yourself positively.

None of this means that you have to be infallible. Obviously, the more you know about mixing drinks, the better, and you should certainly know the most frequently requested drinks by heart. But if you're stumped, boldly ask the customer: "You've got me there. What goes into a Sazerac?" Never reply that you don't know how to make such-and-such. Instead, ask the customer. If the customer doesn't know either, ask, "Well, do you mind if I look this one up?" Then consult this book!

Customer Relations

In most bars, your success—measured by customer satisfaction, which, you can easily gauge by the quantity and magnitude of your tips—depends on how you treat your "guests."

A "Feel Good" Job

Your number-one customer-relations task is to make the patron feel good. This starts with a courteous, smiling greeting, and a "What can I get for you?" Did we say a bartender needs a good short-term memory? An accurate long-term memory is useful, too. Get to know the names of your repeat or regular customers, and get to know what they usually ask for: "Hi, Jill. Will it be the usual?"

Never intrude on customers' conversation. After serving the drink, step back. However, if you are actively sought in conversation, handle it as courteously and attentively as time and the needs of other customers permit. Remember, even customers who want to use you as their psychiatrist don't really need *answers* from you. They want a sympathetic ear—someone to whom they can vent.

Generally, to the degree that you do get involved in conversation, avoid expressing opinions on politics, religion, race, sex, and just about anything controversial or potentially offensive. Avoid giving advice, never talk disparagingly about another customer, and don't gossip.

If customers cause you grief, handle them with firm tact. Address the offensive behavior, remark, or action, not the personality, intellect, or character of the offender. If a customer hits on you, turn him or her off with cool thanks: "Thank you, but my boyfriend/girlfriend/husband/wife would not approve." Or: "I appreciate the compliment, but I don't socialize with my customers."

If a customer is rude to you, it is usually best to ignore it. If he or she persists, try something simple and neutral: "I'd appreciate it if you wouldn't talk to me that way." Make this even more effective by asking the customer his or her name, and then use the name in your reply: "Mr. Johnson, I'd appreciate it if you wouldn't talk to me that way." After the veil of anonymity is lifted, it's harder for a customer to persist in being abusive. Sometimes, obnoxious behavior is directed at other customers. Again, try to address behavior rather than personality: "Sir, I'm sorry, but language like that disturbs the other guests."

The bartender is an authority figure. Calm words directed toward correcting behavior are usually sufficient. Do not pick a fight. Do not hurl threats. If you cannot quickly and calmly deal with a bad seed, summon security. If necessary, tell the customer that you will call the police. If this warning fails to produce instant results, make the call.

Customer Service

Adopt a the-customer-is-always-right attitude, even if the customer is wrong. If a patron insists that you make a drink a certain way—even if it's the wrong way—don't argue. Just do it. If you are sure that the result will be absolutely awful, reply this way: "That's interesting. I've never made one that way. Have you ever tried it with ...?" This will give the customer a chance to save face if he realizes he is wrong. If the customer still wants it *his* way, give it to him his way without another word.

If you are asked to recommend a drink or a brand of liquor, do so, but never suggest to a customer that he or she has made a bad choice.

And accept that smoking and drinking go together. Never comment on smoking, pro or con. If a customer goes for a cigarette, light it, if you can. Keep the ashtrays clean, changing them by putting the clean ashtray over the dirty one, lifting both from the bar, putting the dirty one down behind the bar, and putting the clean one in its place. This is called *capping* the ashtray; it keeps ashes from fluttering out of the dirty one as you move it.

Bar Tips

If a telephone call comes for a customer, *never* tell the caller that the customer is at the bar. Instead, tell the caller that you'll see if So-and-so is present. Then inform the customer of the call. Leave it up to the customer to take the call or not.

Handling Cash

In a busy bar, handling cash can be as tricky as making drinks. You'll need to polish your mental calculating skills to do this smoothly, efficiently, and accurately. Unless the bar has a tab system, collect cash right after you serve the drink. Always announce the amount due, and announce it again when the customer hands you the money: "That's three-twenty-five out of five." This is not only for the customer's benefit, but for the benefit of your short-term memory. Put the bill on top of the cash register until you hand the customer change. Not only will this remind you of the amount from which you need to make change, it will settle any dispute if the customer claims to have handed you a larger bill. Count the change back to the customer.

Bar Tips

Accept tips graciously, thanking the customer as he or she gets up to leave. Never comment on the amount of the tip, great or small.

Dealing with Drunks

Review Chapter 2, which contains useful advice for dealing with people—whether party guests or bar patrons—who've had too much to drink. *Shut off* or *cut off* someone who's had enough in a matter-of-fact way and with as light a touch as possible. Don't moralize. Offer a glass of water instead of a drink: "I can't serve you another martini this evening."

Buzzed Words

Professional bartenders call refusing to serve an intoxicated patron **shutting off (or cutting off) a drunk**.

You probably won't get an argument, let alone a hostile reaction, but either one is *possible*. Don't argue, don't exchange threats, and don't get into a fight. Summon the bouncer, if necessary, before the situation gets out of hand. Or call the police.

Bartending and the Law

While you're looking back at Chapter 2, review the discussion of the legal liability incurred by those who knowingly serve liquor to an intoxicated person. Bartending can be fun, but knowing when to "shut off a drunk" is serious business, with potentially life-saving benefits.

The Least You Need to Know

- Bartending is hard work and often pays modestly; however, it is a great job if you like to meet—and please—people.
- Prepare to break into bartending from the bottom up, beginning (perhaps) in a temp job with a caterer and working through the ranks to a job in a large public bar.
- Your number-one money-making responsibility is to satisfy the customer.
- Your number-one legal and moral responsibility is to ensure (kindly, gently, but firmly) that intoxicated customers get no more to drink at your bar.

Appendix A

Buzzed Word Glossary

absinthe An aromatic, bitter, very strong (containing 68 percent alcohol) liqueur flavored chiefly with wormwood (*Artemisia absinthium*) and containing other botanicals—licorice, hyssop, fennel, angelica root, aniseed, and star aniseed. Famed as the favorite drink of Henri de Toulouse-Lautrec, absinthe was outlawed in many countries early in the twentieth century because of its apparent toxicity.

aging The storage of the distilled alcohol in wooden casks, most often oak. Over months or years, the wood reacts with the alcohol, imparting to it a distinctive color, aroma, and flavor.

alcoholism The medical definition and the criteria of diagnosis of this condition vary, but, in general, this complex, chronic psychological and nutritional disorder may be defined as continued excessive or compulsive use of alcoholic drinks.

apéritif A spirituous beverage taken before a meal as an appetizer. Its origin, in French, is hardly appetizing, however, originally denoting a purgative.

aquavit Aquavit is a very strong Scandinavian liquor distilled from potatoes and grain and flavored with caraway seeds.

arrack A strong alcoholic beverage distilled from palm sap, rice, or molasses. It is popular in the Middle and Far East and is available in larger liquor stores.

Bacchanalia The ancient Roman festival in honor of Bacchus. A drunken orgy with a specific religious purpose, it gave the literary English a word (spelled with a small *b*) to describe your everyday drunken orgies.

barback An assistant or apprentice bartender, who does the bartender's scut work, including tapping beer kegs, running ice, replacing glassware, preparing and stocking garnishes, restocking shelves, and so on.

blackout Not a loss of consciousness, but an inability to remember, even after you are sober, what you did and said while intoxicated.

blended whiskey A blended whiskey might be a combination of *straight* whiskeys and neutral, flavorless whiskeys (this is true of Canadian whisky) or it might be a combination of similar whiskey products made by different distillers at different times (as in blended scotch).

blood-alcohol concentration (BAC) The concentration of alcohol in the blood, expressed as the weight of alcohol in a fixed volume of blood. Sometimes called *blood alcohol level* or BAL. It is used as an objective measure of intoxication.

bottled-in-bond Whiskey that, by federal law, must be a 100-proof, straight whiskey aged at least four years and stored in a federally bonded warehouse pending sale. Not until the whiskey is sold—withdrawn from the bonded warehouse—does the distiller have to pay the federal excise tax. Beyond these requirements, the "bottled-in-bond" designation says nothing about the quality or nature of the whiskey.

branch water Water withdrawn from the local "branch," or stream. Sadly, in most U.S. locations, this would be a risky undertaking these days, and "branch" or "branch water" is just a romantic appellation to describe what comes out of the faucet.

champagne As applied to cognac, champagne has nothing to do with the sparkling wine. The word is French for flat, open country, and its English-language equivalent is *plain.*

cobbler Traditionally, an iced drink made of wine or liqueur plus sugar and fruit juice.

Coffey still *See* continuous still.

congeners Acids, aldehydes, esters, ketones, phenols, and tannins that are by-products of fermentation, distillation, and aging. These "impurities" can contribute to the character and flavor of the spirit, but they cause undesirable effects in some people, notably increasing the intensity of hangover.

continuous still Also called a Coffey still, after the inventor, Aeneas Coffey. A type of still for whiskey distillation that allows for continuous high-volume production, as opposed to the *pot still,* which must be emptied and "recharged" one batch at a time.

cordial In modern usage, a synonym for *liqueur*; however, the word originally designated only those liqueurs thought to have tonic or medicinal efficacy.

"cutting off (a drunk)" *See* "shutting off (a drunk)."

daiquiri A rum, lime juice, and sugar drink named after the Cuban town near the original Bacardi rum distillery.

daisy A whiskey- or gin-based drink that includes some sweet syrup and a float of—usually golden—liqueur.

distilling The process of evaporating the alcohol produced by fermentation, and then condensing the evaporated fluid to concentrate and purify it. The increase in alcohol concentration is usually great.

dry martini A martini with relatively little vermouth versus gin. Some drinkers prefer 12 parts gin to 1 part vermouth, whereas others insist on a 20-to-1 ratio. Extremists do away with the vermouth altogether and have a gin and olive on the rocks.

dry gin You will often encounter the expression *dry gin* or *London dry gin* on bottle labels. These designations originated when gin was widely available in "sweet" (called *Old Tom*) as well as "dry" forms. Today, the distinction is mainly superfluous because almost all English and American gin is now dry. Also note that a gin does not have to be made in London or even in England to bear the "London dry gin" designation on its label. This describes a manufacturing style, not a place of origin.

DUI or **DWI** In some jurisdictions, drunk driving is called driving under the influence—*DUI*—in others, it's driving while intoxicated—*DWI*.

ethyl alcohol The potable alcohol obtained from the fermentation of sugars and starches. For producing hard liquor, the ethyl alcohol is purified and concentrated by distillation.

fermenting The chemical process whereby complex organic substances are split into relatively simple compounds. In the manufacture of alcohol, special yeasts are used to ferment—convert—the starches and sugars of grain (or some other organic substance) into alcohol.

fizz Any drink made with soda and a sweetener.

flambé As a verb, *flambé* means to drench with liquor and ignite. The word can also be used as a noun, synonymous with flaming drink.

flip A drink containing liquor, sugar, spice, and egg. Often served hot. Flips were most popular in the eighteenth and nineteenth centuries.

fortified wine A fermented wine to which a distilled spirit, usually brandy, has been added. Brandy itself is often considered a fortified wine.

freeze A frozen drink.

garbage A bit of fruit or vegetable added to a drink primarily for the sake of appearance. It does not significantly enhance the flavor of the drink.

garnish A bit of fruit or vegetable added to a drink principally to enhance its flavor.

generic liqueurs Liqueurs prepared according to standard formulas by a number of distillers.

grog Originally, grog was nothing more than rum diluted with water and rationed to sailors of the eighteenth-century Royal Navy. Its namesake was Admiral Edward Vernon (1684–1757), who first ordered the ration: Vernon's nickname was Old Grogram, after his habit of wearing a grogram (coarse wool) cloak.

hard liquor A beverage with a high alcoholic content. Gin, vodka, bourbon, sour mash whiskey, scotch, blended whiskey, rye, rum, and tequila are the most common "hard liquors."

hard cider Fermented—and therefore alcoholic—apple cider.

jigger The glass or the metal measuring cup used to measure drinks. It is also what you call the amount the jigger measures: 1½ ounces.

light whiskey Whiskey distilled at a high proof (in excess of 160 proof) and aged in used charred oak barrels. Light whiskey is more flavorful than neutral spirits, but not as strongly flavored as straight whiskey. It is an important component in blended whiskey.

liquor Any alcoholic beverage made by fermentation *and* distillation rather than fermentation alone (as is the case with wine and beer).

London dry gin *See* dry gin.

macerate To make soft by soaking in liquid. Applied to the production of liqueurs, maceration is a process of soaking botanicals in the distilled alcohol to extract their flavor.

malt Grain (usually barley) that has been allowed to sprout. Used as material for fermentation to produce beer or certain distilled spirits.

malting The practice of allowing the grain (usually barley) to sprout before fermentation. In whiskey production, this produces a variety of characteristic flavors in the finished product.

mash The fermentable starchy mixture from which an alcoholic beverage is produced.

master blender The craftsperson in charge of selecting and proportioning the component whiskies that make up a blended whiskey.

mixed-grain whiskey Whiskey distilled from a mash in which no single type of grain predominates. Contrast straight whiskey, which is made from mash containing at least 51 percent of a certain grain.

muddle To mash and stir. One muddles such things as mint leaves and other solids in order to make a suspension or a paste with fluid. A special pestle-like wooden *muddler* can be used, but any spoon will do.

muddler *See* muddle.

mull To heat and spice a drink. Traditionally, the heating was done by inserting a hot poker into the drink; today, *mulled* drinks are usually heated on a stove.

Old Tom A special form of gin, slightly sweetened. It is not widely enjoyed today and might be quite hard to find.

pick-me-up Many spirituous drinks advertise themselves as a *pick-me-up*. Typically acting first to suppress inhibitions, alcohol can, indeed, make you feel energized. Just be aware, however, that alcohol is ultimately a sedative or depressant.

pony Strictly speaking, a 1-ounce measure; however, pony glasses range in capacity from 1 to 2 ounces.

port (also called *porto*) Named after the Portuguese town of Oporto, birthplace of this fortified wine and the origin of "true" port today—though other regions also produce port wines. Port is sweet, whereas sherry ranges from dry to sweet.

posset A traditional English drink made with sweetened milk that has been curdled by the addition of wine or ale. It is usually served hot.

pot still *See* continuous still.

pousse-café A drink made with two or more liqueurs and, sometimes, cream. The different spirits vary in specific gravity, so float in discrete layers if carefully combined. The layered effect is novel and pretty.

proof The alcoholic content of a spirit. It is determined by multiplying the percentage of alcoholic content by two, so liquor that is 40 percent alcohol is 80 proof.

proprietary liqueurs "Brand-name" products prepared according to closely guarded trade-secret formulas that are the property of specific distillers.

rickey Any alcohol-based drink with soda water and lime—and sometimes sugar.

sangria A cold drink made with red (sometimes white) wine mixed with brandy, sugar, fruit juice, and soda. Its blood-red color and red-blooded robustness are underscored by the meaning of the word in Spanish: the act of bleeding.

schnapps A word used to describe any number of strong, dry liquors, but, recently, applied to a variety of flavored liqueurs. The word derives from the German original, spelled with one *p* and meaning "mouthful."

scut work The menial chores behind the bar, such as tapping beer kegs, running ice, stocking shelves, and so on; often performed by a *barback*.

sherry A fortified Spanish wine with a nutlike flavor. Its name is an Anglicization of Jerez, a city in southwestern Spain, where sherry was first produced and from which region the most highly respected sherry still comes.

shooter A drink meant to be downed in a single shot, often accompanied by table banging and gasps of pleasurable pain.

"shutting off (a drunk)" Professional bartenders call refusing to serve an intoxicated patron "shutting him off." Also called "cutting off."

sling Any brandy, whiskey, or gin drink that is sweetened and flavored with lemon.

sloe gin Despite the name, *sloe gin* is not a gin at all, but a sweet liqueur. Its principal flavoring is the sloe berry, the small, sour fruit of the blackthorn.

specific gravity Applied to liquids, *specific gravity* is the ratio of the mass of the liquid to the mass of an equal volume of distilled water at 39° Fahrenheit.

spirits (or *spirit*) A generic term for an alcoholic beverage based on distilled *liquor*.

spritzer A combination of wine—usually Rhine wine or other white wine—and club soda or seltzer. The word comes from the German for *spray*.

still A device for distilling liquids (including alcohol) to concentrate and purify them. In its simplest form, it consists of a vessel in which the liquid is heated to vapor, a coil (or other apparatus) to cool and condense the vapor, and a vessel to collect the condensed vapor (called the distillate). Stills are made in a great many varieties, ranging from small batch stills to huge industrial continuous stills, capable of producing large volumes of distillate.

surface tension A molecular property of liquids by which the surface of the liquid tends to contract, taking on the characteristics of a stretched elastic membrane.

sweet cider Nonalcoholic apple cider.

tequila añejo Tequila that has been aged in oak casks. It acquires a deep gold coloring and is therefore often called gold tequila; however, not all gold tequila is aged. Unaged tequila is clear and called *white* tequila.

toddy A hot drink consisting of liquor—often rum—water, sugar, and spices.

whiskey versus whisky American and Irish distillers spell the word with an *e*, whereas Scotch and Canadian distillers jump right from the *k* to the *y*.

wort A soluble starch in the form of an infusion of malt. It is used in the fermentation processes of making whiskey and beer.

Appendix B

Last Call

The recipes presented in the main body of this book are all tried and true. For the more adventurous bartender and drinker, however, we have collected some very intriguing new or out-of-the-ordinary drinks.

This is the place to come when you're stumped behind the bar, or just looking for something unusual to knock the socks off your guests. You've become familiar with most of the recipes commonly associated with each spirit. Now explore some variations on the original recipe—or stroll down entirely new avenues with intoxicating combinations such as Between the Sheets, the Woo Woo, or the impressive Ramos Gin Fizz.

Walk on the Wild Side

Some of the following are new, some not so new, but all are—shall we say—highly stimulating. They are not for the scotch-and-water or Whiskey Sour crowd.

Apocalypse Cocktail

Serve in a chilled cocktail glass.

1½ oz. vodka

1 oz. calvados

½ oz. cognac

Combine all ingredients in a shaker with cracked ice. Shake, and then strain into the serving glass.

B-52

Serve straight-up in a shot glass.

½ oz. Grand Marnier

½ oz. Bailey's Irish Cream

½ oz. Kahlùa

Combine ingredients in a mixing glass, stir, and then pour into the shot glass.

Bahama Mama

Serve in a chilled Collins glass.

1 oz. pineapple juice

1½ oz. light rum

2½ oz. orange juice

1½ oz. gold rum

1½ oz. dark rum

2 oz. sour mix

Dash grenadine

Maraschino cherry

Orange slice

Put a dash of grenadine in the bottom of the serving glass and set aside. Combine all ingredients, except the cherry and orange slice, in a shaker filled with ice. Shake vigorously, and then pour into the serving glass. Garnish with the cherry and orange slice.

Brain

Serve straight-up in a shot glass.

¾ oz. Kahlùa

¾ oz. vodka

Splash Bailey's Irish Cream

Combine the Kahlùa and vodka in the shot glass, and then splash in the Bailey's. Do not stir. The swirling of the Bailey's creates the texture that suggests a brain.

Burp 'n' Squirt

Serve in a chilled cocktail glass.

1½ oz. Jagermeister

1½ oz. dark rum

Combine all ingredients in a shaker with cracked ice. Shake, and then strain into the serving glass.

Ignorance

Serve on the rocks in a double old-fashioned glass.

1½ oz. tequila

1½ oz. vodka

1 oz. Galliano

Grapefruit juice

Pour the tequila and vodka over ice into the serving glass. Top off with grapefruit juice. Stir. Float the Galliano.

Jell-O Shots

Serve solid and eat with a spoon, or serve semigelatinous in shot glasses.

12 oz. vodka

12 oz. water

6 oz. Jell-O gelatin mix (choose flavor)

Combine 6 oz. vodka with 6 oz. water in a saucepan. Bring to a boil and stir in Jell-O gelatin mix. Remove from stove and add remaining 6 oz. of water and 6 oz. of vodka. Let set in the refrigerator overnight.

Note: Whether in fully gelled or in semiliquid/semigelatinous form, this drink tends to retard the body's absorption of the alcohol, making it more difficult to tell when you have had "enough."

Kamikaze

Serve in a chilled cocktail glass.

1 oz. triple sec

1 oz. vodka

1 oz. lime juice

Combine all ingredients in a shaker with ice. Shake vigorously, and then strain into the serving glass.

Long Island Iced Tea

Serve in a chilled Collins glass.

½ oz. gin

3 oz. sour mix

½ oz. vodka

½ oz. white tequila

½ oz. light rum

¼ oz. white crème de menthe

Cola

Lemon wedge

Mint sprigs

Combine all ingredients, except the cola, lemon wedge, and mint sprig, with cracked ice in a blender. Blend well, and then pour into the serving glass. Add cola to fill, and garnish with the lemon wedge and mint sprig.

Mace

Serve in a chilled cocktail glass.

1½ oz. tequila

1½ oz. gin

1 TB. lemon juice

Combine all ingredients in a shaker with cracked ice. Shake, and then strain into the serving glass.

Mauler

Serve on the rocks in an old-fashioned glass.

2 oz. brandy

1 oz. light rum

2 TB. chocolate syrup

Combine all ingredients in a shaker with cracked ice. Shake, and then strain over ice into the serving glass.

Melon Ball Sunrise

Serve on the rocks in a highball glass.

1 oz. vodka

½ oz. Midori melon liqueur

Orange juice to fill

Drop grenadine

Combine vodka and Midori in the serving glass filled with ice. Add orange juice to fill. Stir well. Insert bar spoon into drink and slide a drop of grenadine down it. Allow the grenadine to rise from the bottom of the drink for the sunrise effect. Do not stir.

Midori Sour

Serve in a chilled whiskey sour glass.

2 oz. Midori
1 tsp. sugar syrup
1 oz. lemon juice

Combine all ingredients in a shaker with ice. Shake vigorously, and then strain into the serving glass.

Sex on the Beach

Serve on the rocks in a highball glass.

1½ oz. vodka
1 oz. peach schnapps
Cranberry juice to ¾ full
Orange juice to fill

Combine all ingredients in the serving glass full of ice. Stir.

Toasted Almond

Serve in a chilled highball glass.

½ oz. Kahlùa
2 oz. cream
½ oz. amaretto

Combine all ingredients in a shaker filled with ice. Shake vigorously, and then strain into the serving glass. Add more ice, if you wish.

Woo Woo

Serve on the rocks in a highball glass.

¾ oz. vodka
¾ oz. peach schnapps
3 oz. cranberry juice cocktail

Combine the ingredients over ice in the serving glass. Stir well.

Worth Mixing

The following drinks are less in demand than those in the main body of the book, and some take a bit of effort to make, but they are well worth mixing, drinking, and enjoying.

More Joys of Gin

Alexander II

Serve straight-up in a chilled cocktail glass.

1 oz. gin
1 oz. heavy cream
1 oz. crème de cacao

Vigorously shake all ingredients with ice in a shaker or blend; strain into the serving glass.

Alexander III

Serve straight-up in a chilled cocktail glass.

1½ oz. gin
½ oz. white or green crème de menthe
¾ oz. heavy cream

Vigorously shake all ingredients with ice in a shaker or blend; strain into the serving glass.

Bermuda Highball

Serve on the rocks in a chilled highball glass.

1 oz. gin
1 oz. dry vermouth
1 oz. brandy
Club soda or ginger ale to fill

Stir the ingredients, except for the club soda/ginger ale, with ice in the serving glass. Pour in the club soda or ginger ale to fill.

Dubonnet Cocktail

Serve straight-up or on the rocks in a chilled old-fashioned or lowball glass.

1½ oz. gin
1½ oz. Dubonnet rouge
Lemon twist

Vigorously shake the gin and Dubonnet, with ice, in a shaker or blend; pour into the serving glass. Garnish with a lemon twist.

Gin Cobbler

Serve in an old-fashioned or lowball glass.

2 oz. gin
1 tsp. orgeat syrup
Club soda to fill
Orange slice

Stir the gin and orgeat in the serving glass with ice; cracked ice works best. Fill with club soda. Garnish with an orange slice.

Harlem

Serve in an old-fashioned glass.

1½ oz. gin
Pineapple chunks
1 TB. pineapple juice
½ tsp. maraschino bitters

Combine all ingredients in a shaker with cracked ice. Shake well, and then pour over into the serving glass.

Ramos Gin Fizz

Serve in a Collins or highball glass. (Yields 2 drinks.)

4 oz. gin
1 oz. lime juice
1 oz. lemon juice
2 tsp. sugar syrup
2 tsp. heavy cream
Several dashes orange flower water
1 egg white*
Club soda to fill

In a shaker or blender with cracked ice, combine all ingredients except for the club soda. Shake or blend vigorously. Pour into the serving glasses. Add club soda to fill. Recipe makes two drinks. (Orange flower water is an extract of orange blossom and is available at gourmet stores.)

**Raw egg may be a source of salmonella bacteria. You may wish to avoid drinks calling for raw egg yolk or white.*

Red Lion Cocktail

Serve in a chilled cocktail glass.

1 oz. gin
1 oz. Grand Marnier
½ oz. orange juice
½ oz. lemon juice

Combine all ingredients in a shaker or blender with cracked ice. Shake or blend vigorously. Strain into the serving glass.

Tender Mercies

Serve on the rocks in an old-fashioned glass.

1½ oz. gin

1 TB. apple brandy

1 TB. apricot brandy

2 drops lemon juice

2 drops lime juice.

Combine all ingredients in a shaker with cracked ice. Shake well, and then strain over ice into the serving glass.

Tiger Shark

Serve on the rocks in an old-fashioned glass.

2 oz. gin

½ oz. sloe gin

½ oz. sweet vermouth

1 TB. apple brandy

1 TB. cherry brandy

Combine all ingredients over ice in the serving glass.

The Vider Vorld of Vodka

Cosmopolitan

Serve in a cocktail glass.

¾ oz. vodka

½ oz. triple sec

1 oz. cranberry juice

½ oz. lime juice

Shake with ice; serve up in a cocktail glass. Garnish with a lemon twist.

Dubonnet Fizz

Serve on the rocks in a highball glass.

1 oz. vodka

3 oz. Dubonnet rouge

Club soda to fill

Lemon peel

Combine the vodka and Dubonnet in the serving glass one-third full of ice. Add the club soda to fill and garnish with the lemon twist.

Eggflower Soup

Serve on the rocks in a brandy snifter.

3 oz. vodka

3 tsp. apricot brandy

Combine over ice in the serving glass.

Highstepper

Serve on the rocks in a Collins glass,

2 oz. vodka

1 oz. Kahlùa

1 oz. dark rum

½ tsp. lime juice

Cola

Maraschino cherry

Combine all ingredients over ice in the serving glass, top off with the cola and garnish with the cherry.

Pit and Pendulum

Serve on the rocks in an old-fashioned glass.

2 oz. vodka

1½ oz. Kahlùa

1 oz. dark crème de cacao

Combine all ingredients in a shaker with cracked ice. Shake, and then strain over ice into the serving glass.

Russian Cocktail

Serve in a chilled cocktail glass.

1 oz. vodka

1 oz. white crème de cacao

1 oz. gin

Combine the ingredients with cracked ice in a shaker. Shake vigorously, and then strain into the serving glass.

Russian Bear

Serve in a chilled cocktail glass.

1 oz. vodka

1 oz. dark crème de cacao

1 oz. heavy cream

Combine all the ingredients with cracked ice in a shaker. Shake vigorously, and then strain into the serving glass.

Russian Rose

Serve straight-up in a chilled cocktail glass.

2 oz. vodka

½ oz. grenadine

Dash of orange bitters

Combine all ingredients in a shaker with cracked ice. Shake vigorously. Strain into the serving glass.

Sea Breeze with Cranberry Liqueur

Serve in a chilled highball glass.

1½ oz. vodka

4 oz. grapefruit juice

1 oz. cranberry liqueur

Orange slice

Combine all ingredients, except the orange slice, in a shaker with cracked ice. Shake vigorously. Pour into the serving glass, and garnish with the orange slice.

Vodka Grand Marnier

Serve in a chilled cocktail glass.

1½ oz. vodka

½ oz. Grand Marnier

½ oz. lime juice

Orange slice

Combine all ingredients, except the orange slice, in a shaker with cracked ice. Shake vigorously and pour into the serving glass. Garnish with the orange slice.

More Produce from Kentucky and Tennessee

Aftertaste

Serve on the rocks in an old-fashioned glass.

1½ oz. bourbon

1½ oz. tequila

½ oz. Galliano

Grapefruit juice

Combine all ingredients in a shaker with cracked ice. Shake well, and then strain over ice into the serving glass.

Bourbon Cooler

Serve in a chilled Collins glass.

3 oz. bourbon

½ oz. grenadine

1 tsp. sugar syrup

Few dashes peppermint schnapps

Club soda to fill

Maraschino cherry

Pineapple stick

Orange slice

Few dashes orange bitters (optional)

Combine all ingredients, except the fruit and club soda, in a shaker with cracked ice. Shake vigorously, and then pour into the serving glass. Fill with club soda. Garnish with the fruit.

Bourbon Milk Punch

Serve in a chilled old-fashioned glass.

1½ oz. bourbon

3 oz. half-and-half

1 tsp. honey

Dash vanilla extract

Grated nutmeg

Combine all ingredients, except the nutmeg, in a shaker with cracked ice. Shake vigorously, and then pour into the serving glass and sprinkle with nutmeg.

Champagne Julep

Serve in a Collins glass.

6 mint leaves

1 tsp. sugar syrup

3 oz. bourbon

Brut champagne

Mint sprig

In the bottom of the serving glass, *muddle* (stir and mash) six mint leaves in the sugar syrup. Fill glass two thirds with cracked ice. Add bourbon. Stir vigorously. Add champagne to fill. Garnish with a mint sprig.

Commodore Cocktail

Serve in a chilled cocktail glass.

1½ oz. bourbon

¾ oz. white crème de cacao

½ oz. lemon juice

Combine all ingredients in a shaker with cracked ice. Shake vigorously and strain into the serving glass.

I Don't Care

Serve in a chilled cocktail glass.

1 oz. bourbon

1 oz. white crème de menthe

½ oz. grenadine

Combine all ingredients in a shaker with cracked ice. Shake well, and then strain over ice into the serving glass.

Kentucky Windage

Serve on the rocks in a Collins glass.

2 oz. bourbon

1 tsp. lime juice

Lemonade

Pour the bourbon and lime juice over ice in the serving glass. Top off with lemonade. Stir.

Southside

Serve in a lowball glass.

6 mint leaves

2 oz. bourbon

1 tsp. sugar syrup

Plain water

Juice of ½ lemon

Mint sprig

In the serving glass, muddle the mint leaves together with the lemon juice and sugar syrup. Add bourbon and a splash of water. Add crushed ice to fill. Muddle again. Garnish with a mint sprig.

Waldorf Cocktail

Serve in a chilled cocktail glass.

1½ oz. bourbon

½ oz. sweet vermouth

¾ oz. Pernod

Dash of Angostura bitters

Combine all ingredients in a mixing glass with ice. Stir well and strain into the serving glass.

Whirlaway

Serve in a chilled old-fashioned glass.

2 oz. bourbon

1 oz. curaçao

Few dashes Angostura bitters

Club soda to fill

Combine all ingredients, except soda, in a shaker with ice. Shake vigorously and strain into the serving glass. Add club soda to fill.

Whiskey Cobbler

Serve in a goblet or large snifter.

1 tsp. sugar syrup

2 oz. blended whiskey

1 tsp. orgeat syrup or amaretto liqueur

Dash curaçao

Mint sprig

Fill the goblet or snifter with crushed ice. Add the sugar and orgeat (or amaretto). Stir well. Add whiskey. Stir again, so that frost forms on the outside of the serving glass. Dash on curaçao and garnish with the mint sprig.

'Round the Blend—Again

Action Juice

Serve on the rocks in a Collins glass.

2 oz. blended whiskey

1 oz. dark rum

1 oz. sloe gin

Orange juice

Pineapple juice

Grapefruit juice

Lime slice

Lemon slice

Pour the spirits over ice into the serving glass. Top off with the juices. Pour everything into a shaker. Shake well, and then pour back into the serving glass and garnish with the lime and lemon slices.

Frisco Sour

Serve in a sour glass.

1½ oz. blended whiskey

¾ oz. Benedictine

1 tsp. lime juice

1 tsp. lemon juice

Dash grenadine

Orange slice

Combine all ingredients, except orange slice, in a shaker with ice. Shake vigorously, and then strain into the serving glass. Garnish with the orange slice.

Horse's Neck

Serve in a Collins glass.

1 lemon

3 oz. blended whiskey

Ginger ale to fill

Peel the lemon in one continuous strip and place it in the serving glass. Fill the glass one third with ice cubes. Add whiskey. Squeeze a few drops of lemon juice over the whiskey, and then add ginger ale to fill.

Los Angeles Cocktail

Serve in chilled old-fashioned glasses.

4 oz. blended whiskey

1 oz. lemon juice

Few dashes sweet vermouth

1 egg*

2 oz. sugar syrup

Combine all ingredients in a shaker with cracked ice. Shake vigorously and pour into the serving glasses.

**Raw egg may be a source of salmonella bacteria. You may wish to avoid drinks calling for raw egg yolk or white.*

Mount McKinley

Serve on the rocks in a highball glass.

1½ oz. blended whiskey

1 TB. sweet vermouth

4 drops Pernod

3 drops cherry brandy

Combine all ingredients in a shaker with cracked ice. Shake, and then strain over ice into the serving glass.

New Orleans Old-Fashioned

Serve in a chilled old-fashioned glass.

½ tsp. sugar syrup

Few dashes Angostura bitters

2 tsp. water

2 oz. blended whiskey

Few dashes Peychaud's bitters

Lemon twist

Combine the sugar syrup, Angostura bitters, and water in a mixing glass and stir until the sugar is dissolved. Add the whiskey and one-third glass of ice cubes. Stir well, and then dash on the Peychaud's and garnish with the lemon twist.

New York Sour

Serve in a sour glass.

2 oz. blended whiskey

½ oz. lemon juice

1 tsp. sugar syrup

½ oz. dry red wine

½ slice lemon

Combine all ingredients, except the lemon slice and red wine, in a shaker with cracked ice. Shake vigorously, and then pour into the serving glass. Add the wine and garnish with the lemon slice.

Nut

Serve in a chilled cocktail glass.

1½ oz. blended whiskey

½ oz. lime juice

½ oz. grenadine

½ tsp. sugar syrup

Lemon peel

Rim the serving glass with sugar. Combine all ingredients, except lemon peel, in a shaker with cracked ice. Shake well, and then strain into the serving glass. Twist lemon peel over drink and drop in.

Orient Express

Serve on the rocks in an old-fashioned glass.

1½ oz. blended whiskey

1 oz. sweet vermouth

2 tsp. lime juice

1½ tsp. lemon juice

1½ tsp. curaçao

2 dashes orange bitters

Lemon peel

Combine all ingredients, except the lemon peel, in a shaker with cracked ice. Shake well, and then strain over ice into the serving glass. Twist lemon peel over drink and drop in.

Temptation Cocktail

Serve in a chilled cocktail glass.

1½ oz. blended whiskey

½ oz. Dubonnet rouge

Few dashes curaçao

Few dashes Pernod

Orange twist

Lemon twist

Combine all ingredients, except twists, in a shaker with ice. Shake vigorously and strain into the serving glass. Garnish with the twists.

Thunderbird

Serve on the rocks in an old-fashioned glass.

2 oz. blended whiskey

2 TB. banana brandy

1 oz. heavy cream

Combine all ingredients in a shaker with cracked ice. Shake well, and then strain over ice into the serving glass.

Whiskey Zipper

Serve on the rocks in an old-fashioned glass.

2 oz. blended whiskey

½ oz. Maraschino liqueur

1 TB. Drambuie

1 tsp. lemon juice

Combine all ingredients over ice in the serving glass. Stir.

Wire Walker

Serve on the rocks in a highball glass.

1 oz. blended whiskey or Canadian whisky

1 TB. orange curaçao

1 oz. grapefruit juice

Few dashes orange bitters

Combine all ingredients in a shaker with cracked ice. Shake well, and then strain over ice into the serving glass.

Scotland and Ireland Revisited

Affinity Cocktail

Serve in a chilled cocktail glass.

1 oz. scotch

1 oz. dry sherry

1 oz. port

Liberal dashes Angostura bitters

Lemon twist

Maraschino cherry

Combine all ingredients, except fruit, in a mixing glass with ice. Stir well, and then strain into the serving glass and garnish with the twist and cherry.

Bald Plumber

Serve on the rocks in an old-fashioned glass.

1½ oz. scotch

1 oz. Drambuie

Pineapple juice

Prune juice

Pour the spirits into a shaker with cracked ice. Shake, and then strain over ice into the serving glass. Top off with the juices. Stir.

Flying Scot

Serve in a chilled old-fashioned glass.

1½ oz. scotch

1 oz. sweet vermouth

Few dashes sugar syrup

Few dashes Angostura bitters

Combine all ingredients in a shaker with cracked ice. Pour into the serving glass.

Irish Hunter's Cocktail

Serve on the rocks in an old-fashioned glass.

1½ oz. Irish whiskey

1 TB. cherry brandy

Maraschino cherry

Pour spirits over ice in the serving glass. Stir, and then garnish with the cherry.

Kinsale Cooler

Serve in a chilled Collins glass.

1½ oz. Irish whiskey

1 oz. Irish Mist

1 oz. lemon juice

Equal portions club soda and ginger ale to fill

Lemon twist

Combine all ingredients, except the sodas and the twist, in a shaker with cracked ice. Shake vigorously, and then pour into the serving glass and add equal portions of club soda and ginger ale to fill. Garnish with the twist.

Royal Rob Roy

Serve in a chilled cocktail glass.

1½ oz. scotch

1½ oz. Drambuie

¼ oz. dry vermouth

¼ oz. sweet vermouth

Maraschino cherry

Combine all ingredients, except the cherry, in a shaker with cracked ice. Shake vigorously, and then strain into the serving glass and garnish with the cherry.

Scottish Horse's Neck

Serve on the rocks in a Collins glass.

Lemon peel curlicue

3 oz. scotch

½ oz. sweet vermouth

½ oz. dry vermouth

Arrange the long lemon peel curlicue so that it hangs off the rim of the serving glass. Fill with ice, and then pour in the scotch and vermouths. Stir well.

Scotch Julep

Serve in a chilled large (double) old-fashioned glass.

6 mint leaves

1 oz. Drambuie

Splash water

2 oz. scotch

Mint sprig

Muddle (mash and stir) the mint leaves, Drambuie, and a splash of water in the bottom of the serving glass. Fill glass with *finely* crushed ice. Add the scotch, and then muddle again to work the scotch and Drambuie through the ice. If you want a stronger drink, add as much as another ounce of scotch. Garnish with the mint sprig.

Scotch Mist

Serve in an old-fashioned glass filled with finely crushed ice.

2 oz. scotch

Lemon twist

Pour the whiskey into the serving glass filled with finely crushed ice. Garnish with the twist.

Scotch Sour

Serve in a chilled sour glass.

1½ oz. scotch

½ oz. lemon juice

1 tsp. sugar syrup

Orange slice

Maraschino cherry

Combine all ingredients, except fruit, in a shaker with ice. Shake vigorously, and then strain into the serving glass. Garnish with the orange slice and cherry.

Rum Round Two

Cocoa-Colada

Serve in a chilled Collins glass.

1½ oz. Myers's rum

1 oz. Kahlùa

1 oz. cream of coconut

2 oz. pineapple juice

Orange slice

Combine all ingredients, except the orange slice, in a blender with a scoop of crushed ice. Blend until smooth, and then pour into the serving glass and garnish with the orange slice.

Iced Coffee Devastator

Serve on the rocks in a Collins glass.

1½ oz. dark rum

1 oz. gold rum

1 oz. vodka

1 tsp. light cream

Iced coffee

Combine the spirits over ice in the serving glass. Stir, and then top off with the iced coffee. Stir again.

Frozen Daiquiri

Serve in a chilled cocktail glass or in an American-style (saucer) champagne glass.

2 oz. light rum

½ oz. lime juice

1 tsp. sugar

Combine all ingredients in a blender with at least 4 oz. of crushed ice. Blend at low speed un-til snowy, and then pour into the serving glass.

Pineapple Daiquiri

Serve in a chilled cocktail glass or wine glass.

2 oz. light rum

½ oz. Cointreau

3 oz. pineapple juice

¼ oz. lime juice

Combine all ingredients in a blender with at least 3 oz. of cracked ice. Blend with ice on frappé. Pour into the serving glass.

Peach Daiquiri

Serve in a chilled cocktail glass or in an American-style (saucer) champagne glass.

1½ oz. light rum

½ oz. lime juice

1 TB. diced peaches (fresh, canned, or frozen)

1 tsp. lemon juice

Combine all ingredients in a blender with at least 4 oz. of crushed ice. Blend at low speed until snowy, and then pour into serving glass.

Kitchen Sink

Serve on the rocks in a Collins glass.

½ oz. dark rum

½ oz. light rum

½ oz. spiced rum

½ oz. vodka

½ oz. gin

½ oz. tequila

½ oz. sweet vermouth

Pineapple juice

Orange juice

Grapefruit juice

Assorted fruit

Combine all spirits in a shaker with cracked ice. Shake well, and then strain over ice into the serving glass. Top off with the juices, and then garnish with fruit of your choice.

Mathematician

Serve on the rocks in an old-fashioned glass.

2 oz. light rum
1½ oz. dark rum
½ oz. tequila
2 oz. grapefruit juice

Combine all ingredients in a shaker with cracked ice. Shake, and then strain over ice into the serving glass.

Mexico City

Serve on the rocks in an old-fashioned glass.

2 oz. light rum
1½ oz. tequila
1 TB. orange juice

Combine all ingredients in a shaker with cracked ice. Shake, and then strain over ice into the serving glass.

Nutty Colada

Serve in a chilled Collins glass.

2 oz. amaretto
1 oz. gold rum
1½ oz. cream of coconut
2 oz. pineapple juice
Pineapple slice

Combine all ingredients, except the pineapple slice, in a blender with a scoop of crushed ice. Blend until smooth, and then pour into the serving glass and garnish with the pineapple slice.

Rum Collins

Serve in a chilled Collins glass.

2 oz. light rum
½ lime
1 oz. sugar syrup
Club soda to fill

Combine the rum and sugar syrup in the serving glass. Stir. Squeeze in lime juice, and then drop in peel as garnish. Add a few ice cubes and club soda to fill.

Rum Old-Fashioned

Serve in a chilled old-fashioned glass.

1 tsp. sugar syrup
Splash water
3 oz. gold rum
Liberal dashes Angostura bitters
Lime twist
Orange twist

Combine sugar syrup and water in the serving glass. Stir. Add bitters and rum. Stir, and then add several ice cubes. Garnish with the twists.

Rum Screwdriver

Serve in a chilled Collins glass.

2 oz. light rum
5 oz. orange juice
Orange slice

Combine rum and juice in a blender with cracked ice. Blend until smooth, and then pour into the serving glass. Garnish with orange slice.

Scorpion

Serve in a chilled wine goblet.

2 oz. light rum
1½ oz. lemon juice
1 oz. brandy
½ oz. orgeat syrup
2 oz. orange juice
Gardenia (if available)

Combine all ingredients, except the gardenia, in a blender with 3 oz. of shaved ice. Blend until smooth, and then pour into the serving glass. Garnish with the gardenia.

Rum Sour

Serve in a chilled sour glass.

2 oz. light or dark rum

Juice of ½ lime

1 tsp. sugar syrup

1 tsp. orange juice

Orange slice

Maraschino cherry

Combine all ingredients, except fruit, in a shaker with ice. Shake vigorously, and then strain into the serving glass and garnish with the orange slice and cherry.

Strawberry Colada

Serve in a chilled pilsner glass.

3 oz. gold rum

4 oz. commercial Piña Colada mix

1 oz. strawberries (fresh or frozen)

1 oz. strawberry liqueur or strawberry schnapps

Whole strawberry

Combine all ingredients, except liqueur or schnapps and whole strawberry, in a blender with cracked ice. Blend until smooth, pour into the serving glass, top with the liqueur or schnapps, and garnish with the whole strawberry.

Return to the Halls of Montezuma

Golden Margarita

Serve in a chilled lowball glass rimmed with salt.

2 oz. gold tequila

1 oz. curaçao

¾ oz. lime juice

Coarse salt

Lime slice

Combine all ingredients, except salt and lime slice, in a shaker with cracked ice. Shake vigorously, and then pour into the serving glass. Garnish with the lime slice.

Lakewater

Serve in a chilled cocktail glass.

1½ oz. tequila

½ oz. gin

½ oz. lemon juice

Combine all ingredients in a shaker with cracked ice. Shake well, and then strain into the serving glass.

Tequila Collins

Serve on the rocks in a tall Collins glass.

1½ oz. white tequila

1 oz. lemon juice

Sugar syrup to taste

Club soda to fill

Maraschino cherry

Pour tequila, lemon juice, and sugar syrup over ice in the serving glass. Stir, and then add club soda to fill. Garnish with the cherry.

Tequila Gimlet

Serve on the rocks in an old-fashioned glass.

1½ oz. white or gold tequila

1 oz. Rose's lime juice

Lime wedge

Combine the tequila and lime juice over ice in the serving glass. Stir, and then garnish with the lime wedge.

Tequila Sour

Serve in a chilled cocktail glass.

1½ oz. tequila

1 oz. lime or lemon juice

1 tsp. confectioner's sugar

Combine all ingredients in a shaker with ice. Shake vigorously, and then strain into the serving glass.

Tequila Manhattan

1½ oz. gold tequila

Dash or two sweet vermouth

Lime slice

Combine tequila and vermouth in a shaker with ice. Shake vigorously, and then strain into the serving glass. Garnish with the lime slice.

Tequila Stinger

Serve in a chilled cocktail glass.

1½ oz. gold tequila

¾ oz. white crème de menthe

Combine all ingredients in a shaker with cracked ice. Shake vigorously, and then pour into the serving glass.

Tequila Maria

Serve in a chilled large (double) old-fashioned glass.

1½ oz. white or gold tequila

4 oz. tomato juice

Juice of ¼ lime

½ tsp. fresh grated horseradish

Liberal dashes Worcestershire sauce

Liberal dashes Tabasco sauce

Pinch white pepper

Pinch celery salt

Pinch oregano

Combine all ingredients in a mixing glass half filled with cracked ice. Stir, and then pour into the serving glass.

Vengeance

Serve on the rocks in an old-fashioned glass.

1½ oz. tequila

1 oz. sloe gin

½ oz. blended whiskey

1 oz. lemon juice

Lemon peel

Combine all ingredients, except lemon peel, in a shaker with cracked ice. Shake well, and then strain over ice into the serving glass. Twist lemon peel over drink and drop in.

Another Snifter

Between the Sheets

Serve in a chilled cocktail glass.

1½ oz. cognac

1 oz. light rum

¾ oz. curaçao (may substitute triple sec)

½ oz. lemon juice

Combine all ingredients in a shaker with ice. Shake vigorously, and then strain into the serving glass.

Bombay

Serve in a chilled old-fashioned glass.

1 oz. brandy

1 oz. dry vermouth

½ oz. sweet vermouth

½ tsp. curaçao

Dash Pernod

Orange slice

Combine all ingredients, except orange slice, in a shaker with cracked ice. Shake vigorously, and then pour into the serving glass. Garnish with the orange slice.

Brandy Fizz

Serve in a chilled highball glass.

3 oz. brandy

1½ oz. lemon juice

½ oz. sugar syrup

Club soda to fill

Combine all ingredients, except soda, in a shaker with cracked ice. Shake vigorously, and then pour into the serving glass. Add club soda to fill. Additional ice cubes are optional. Omit the club soda, and you have a Brandy Fix.

Brandy Milk Punch

Serve in a chilled large (double) old-fashioned glass.

2 oz. brandy

8 oz. milk

1 tsp. sugar syrup

Pinch ground nutmeg

Combine all ingredients, except nutmeg, in a shaker with cracked ice. Shake vigorously, and then pour into the serving glass. Sprinkle with nutmeg.

Brandy Julep

Serve in a chilled large (double) old-fashioned glass.

6 mint leaves

1 tsp. honey

Splash water

Brandy to fill

Mint sprig

Powdered sugar

Combine the mint leaves, honey, and a splash of water in the serving glass. Muddle (mash and stir) until the leaves are well bruised. Fill serving glass with shaved ice. Add brandy to fill. Stir well so that glass frosts. Add additional brandy and ice as necessary to fill. *Glass should be full and thoroughly frosted.* Garnish with sprig, and then dust with powdered sugar.

Brandy Manhattan

Serve in a chilled cocktail glass.

2 oz. brandy

Dash Angostura bitters

½ oz. sweet or dry vermouth

Maraschino cherry

Combine all ingredients, except cherry, in a mixing glass one-third full of ice. Stir well, and then strain into the serving glass. Garnish with the cherry.

Brandy Old-Fashioned

Serve in a chilled old-fashioned glass.

1 sugar cube

Liberal dashes Angostura bitters

Splash water

3 oz. brandy

Lemon twist

Put sugar cube in the serving glass, dash on bitters, and add a splash of water. Muddle (mash and stir) until the sugar cube is dissolved. Half fill glass with ice cubes and add brandy. Garnish with twist.

Hot Sauce

Serve in a mug.

Coffee, strong, hot, black

1 oz. cherry brandy

1 oz. cinnamon schnapps

1 tsp. Tabasco sauce

1 tsp. powdered cinnamon

Whipped cream

Additional pinch cinnamon

Fill mug ½ with hot coffee, and then add all ingredients, topping with whipped cream and dusting with the pinch of cinnamon.

Tiger's Milk

Serve on the rocks in a double old-fashioned glass.

1 oz. brandy

1 oz. Jamaican rum

3 tsp. sugar syrup

3 oz. heavy cream

Combine all ingredients in a shake with cracked ice. Shake, and then strain over ice into the serving glass.

Index

A

B

C

G

H

I

J

K

L

M

N

Q-R

S

T

U-V

W

X-Y-Z

A Little Knowledge Goes a Long Way ...

Check Out These Best-Selling COMPLETE IDIOT'S GUIDES®

0-02-863639-2
$16.95

0-02-862743-1
$16.95

0-02-864382-8
$18.95

0-02-864339-9
$18.95

0-02-864244-9
$21.95 w/CD-ROM

0-02-864374-7
$19.95

0-02-864316-X
$24.95 w/CD-ROM

0-02-864453-0
$19.95

0-02-864232-5
$19.95

More than *400 titles* in *26 different categories*
Available at booksellers everywhere

Decision Modeling with Microsoft® Excel

SIXTH EDITION

Jeffrey H. Moore
Stanford University

Larry R. Weatherford
University of Wyoming

Prentice Hall
Upper Saddle River, New Jersey 07458

To Ashley and Aaron;

To Jenny, for her incredible support and eternal companionship; and Maria, Carolyn, Laura, Bob, Paul, Amy and Josh, for their love and enthusiasm

Library of Congress Cataloging-in-Publication Data

Decision Modeling with Microsoft Excel.—6th ed. / Jeffrey H. Moore, Larry R. Weatherford.
p. cm.
Includes bibliographical references and index.
ISBN 0-13-017789-X
1. Management—Mathematical models. 2. Management science. I. Moore, Jeffrey H. (Jeffrey Hillsman) II. Weatherford, Lawrence R.

HD30.25 .I63 2001
658.4′033—dc21

00-049153

Acquisitions Editor: Tom Tucker
Assistant Editor: Jennifer Surich
Editorial Assistant: Margarita Martinez
Media Project Manager: Cindy Harford
Senior Marketing Manager: Debbie Clare
Marketing Assistant: Jessica Pasquini
Managing Editor (Production): Cynthia Regan
Senior Production Editor: Richard DeLorenzo
Production Assistant: Dianne Falcone
Permissions Coordinator: Suzanne Grappi
Associate Director, Manufacturing: Vincent Scelta
Production Manager: Arnold Vila
Design Manager: Pat Smythe
Interior Design/Cover Design: Blair Brown
Cover Illustration/Photo: Blair Brown
Manager, Print Production: Christy Mahon
Composition: UG / GGS Information Services, Inc.
Full-Service Project Management: UG / GGS Information Services, Inc.
Printer/Binder: R.R. Donnelley & Sons

10 9 8 7 6 5 4 3
ISBN 0-13-017789-X

About the Authors

Jeffrey H. Moore

Jeffrey Moore joined the faculty at Stanford's Graduate School of Business in 1972 after more than 10 years work as a Communications Engineer, Computer Systems Analyst, and Management Analyst. Since joining Stanford, he has designed and taught courses in the Operations and Information Technology area at the Executive, MBA and PhD levels. He teaches the core course in modeling and analysis and is a popular lecturer in six of Stanford's Senior Executive programs. In his research, he concentrates on decision support systems and computer use by senior executives. He has written more than 40 papers in these and other areas, and has done extensive consulting for private industry both nationally and internationally in the application of information technology and modeling for decision support. He has worked on several courseware projects to introduce Excel for modeling and decision support to graduate level MBA's and executives. This has included work under several grants from Microsoft, IBM, and Hewlett Packard, and early work with Frontline Systems in the testing and development of Excel's Solver, particularly the linear optimization options. In the late 1970s he pioneered one of the first courses to use spreadsheet modeling in a business school, and soon thereafter, orchestrated Stanford's conversion of its modeling core course to spreadsheets, the first major business school to do so. Since that time, he has been involved in the development of modeling and statistical applications of spreadsheets, and has developed GLP, Stanford's Graphical LP Optimizer, and Regress, an Excel-based regression add-in now used at Stanford, Duke, UCLA, and elsewhere. Earlier he served on the INFORMS Business School Educational Task Force which surveyed more than 300 university instructors in the teaching of management science and has made presentations at its conferences on the important role spreadsheets should play in management education. He is also the Director of SunTELL, the Stanford Business School's Technology Educational Learning Laboratory, a facility funded by SUN Microsystems devoted to understanding the use of technology in management and in management education.

In 1996 and again in 1998, he received Stanford's Sloan Teaching Excellence Award for his core course in Decision Support Modeling. Dr. Moore holds a BSEE with specialty in digital circuit design from the University of Cincinnati, a joint MBA/CS degree from Texas A&M University, and a PhD in Business from the University of California at Berkeley. He also holds a Professional Engineer certification (E.E., Ohio).

Larry R. Weatherford

Larry is an Associate Professor in the College of Business at the University of Wyoming. He received his BA from Brigham Young University in 1982, and his MBA and PhD from the Darden Graduate School of Business at the University of Virginia in 1991. He received the Outstanding Teaching Award for the College of Business in his first year as a professor. In the ensuing years he has also earned the "Outstanding Faculty Member" award by Alpha Kappa Psi, the Outstanding Junior Research Award for the College of Business, and more recently the University wide Ellbogen Meritorious Classroom Teaching Award. He has published 17 scholarly articles in such journals as *Operations Research, Decision Sciences, Transportation Science, Naval Research Logistics, Cornell Hotel and Restaurant Administration Quarterly, International Journal of Technology Management, Journal of Combinatorial Optimization* and *Omega.*

On the practitioner side, he has made over 48 presentations on five different continents to professional organizations. He has consulted with such major corporations as

American Airlines, Northwest Airlines, Lufthansa German Airlines, Swissair, Scandinavian Airlines, Air New Zealand, South African Airways, Unisys Corporation, Walt Disney World and Hilton Hotels, as well as many other smaller corporations.

On the personal side, Larry is married to the lovely Jenny and they have 7 children (yes, they are all from the same union)! Most of his outside interests are centered in his family and church. Any other spare time is spent playing racquetball or golf or reading a fun book.

Brief Contents

CD-ROM ENRICHMENT TOPICS

Contents

APPENDICES

CD-ROM CHAPTERS

CD-ROM ENRICHMENT TOPICS

Preface

TO THE STUDENT OF MANAGEMENT:

The building of explicit models for analysis and managerial decision making has traditionally been called *management science.*

Webster's New World Dictionary defines *oxymoron* as "a figure of speech in which opposite or contradictory ideas or terms are combined." Common examples include sweet sorrow, thunderous silence, jumbo shrimp, sport sedan, bureaucratic efficiency, proprietary standard—you can probably think of many more. And management science?

The same dictionary says that *management* is "the act, art, or manner of managing, or handling, controlling, directing, etc." If management is an art, is management science then an oxymoron—a contradiction in terms?

Not to us!

Science is the process of using observation and testing to establish principles and then using these principles to answer questions. Much of business is based on the same approach. Actuaries use statistical models to set insurance rates. Organizations use discounted cash flow models to make decisions on capital expenditures. Sales executives use models based on demand elasticity to determine prices, and managers use investment models to control their personal investment portfolios.

This book is devoted to modeling concepts that may apply to a variety of different management situations. Indeed, many of the models we will study are generic models. Just as the model for discounting cash flows can be used for situations with different time periods, different interest rates, and different cash flows, so can the models and concepts studied in this textbook be used in widely different situations.

As you work your way through this text, you will find that it is so full of specific example models as to appear to be a modeling cookbook. Our goal in writing this book, however, was not to produce good recipes but to produce good cooks. Thus, you should avoid becoming so immersed in the technical details of the models and their Excel representation that you lose track of the general skills that you must develop to be both a good modeler and a good manager. We believe that you will find this book useful to the extent that you focus upon (1) the *real-world setting* that motivated the creation of the spreadsheet model in the first place, and (2) actively engage in the *model building and analysis.* Doing one without the other is a common, and mistaken, approach employed by managers because it leads to inadequate comprehension needed for good decision making and learning.

It is possible to do the assignments in this book, and not have the concepts affect you in your career. To avoid this, you must work to personally *own* these modeling concepts. To do this requires "hands-on" work with Excel modeling. The responsibility for maintaining this focus rests with you. Learning to be *both* a good modeler and a good manager is far more challenging than learning the mechanics of Excel modeling. We will help by focusing on both management and model, but you can achieve that same focus only with personal effort.

TO THE INSTRUCTOR:

As evident in our message above, Excel-based management science has a lot to offer your students. We believe a good textbook coupled with your teaching and enthusiasm can play a critical role in helping to shape the attitudes of tomorrow's managers towards the proper use of quantitative modeling in business. Certainly, spreadsheets have become the near-exclusive tool used by millions of managers in analyzing business problems. They now contain many powerful tools that can be used to analyze more sophisticated models and make better decisions. Given the pervasive use of spreadsheets in management, our task is to focus students upon developing their modeling skills—how to "paint" onto the blank canvas of the worksheet to develop helpful, practical business models—and not upon algorithms or mathematical puzzles.

This textbook is designed for introductory courses in applying the Microsoft Excel spreadsheet to management decision modeling at the upper undergraduate, executive, or MBA level. It introduces students to the key ideas of modeling and management decision making that will be important to them throughout their careers. Addressing the needs of readers interested in either general management or more specialized decision science careers, the book emphasizes

- The importance of strong conceptual foundations for all topics, as opposed to just "cookbook" spreadsheet prescriptions
- Role of spreadsheet modeling in the larger context of management decision making, as opposed to algorithmic techniques.

With this in mind, the sixth edition was revised to make it state-of-the-art in the Excel tools that it teaches and to help you make it more relevant to the management careers your students face. With this in mind, content has further shifted away from solution procedures and other mathematical details toward additional case material. For example, over a dozen new cases have been added across the chapters. We have added an expanded number of new problems at the end of most chapters (both basic skill problems and more advanced application problems). For more advanced classes we include Enrichment Topics on the book's CD-ROM for such things as treatment of degeneracy, branch-and-bound algorithms, Evolutionary Solver advanced features, and conditional probability and Bayes' theorem.

We have adopted a very "hands-on" approach to modeling many different challenges a business may face in the areas of operations, finance, human resources, marketing, and the public sector, to name a few. Students strongly prefer this approach because (1) they learn marketable skills they will use immediately in their careers, and more importantly, (2) they develop valuable modeling habits and insights of longer-term benefit. Many students have called us to say that this was one of the most valuable courses they took in college because it combines tangible applications and modeling philosophy with learning by doing.

The book has a strong focus on models—what they are, how they are created, how they are used, what kinds of insights they provide—and on the critical importance of managerial judgment in utilizing those insights. At the same time, for readers interested in the more in-depth aspects of the subject, there is an unparalleled treatment of optimization and decision analysis techniques.

In addition to revising the pioneering chapter on general modeling with Excel introduced in the previous edition, this edition has added two entirely new chapters. To complement our coverage of Monte Carlo simulation, a new chapter introduces discrete event simulation with Excel and with Extend. A new chapter on implementation that focuses on organizational and management issues surrounding institutionalization of a model has been added, which includes an extensive real-world case for class discussion of this critically important topic. We have also significantly revised two chapters—Project Management has been expanded to include both approaches to project modeling, activities on arcs and activities on nodes via use of the software package, MS Project for Windows and the Monte Carlo simulation chapter has been expanded to include examples on optimization of Excel simulation models via OptQuest.

Continuing the fine tradition of previous editions, the text offers unequaled coverage of optimization and introduces the concept of a "theme case" at the end of each chapter (Ebel Mining) in which a multi-part case's model is made increasingly more sophisticated in building block fashion as more concepts are developed in chapters.

The merging of topics begun with the previous edition has been continued in this edition in recognition of the increasing teaching pressure to streamline topic coverage. This edition combines the previously separate chapters on graphical and sensitivity analysis into a single integrated chapter that introduces SolverTable. Developed at Stanford's GSB five years ago, SolverTable is an add-in that extends Excel's Data Table to perform parametric analysis, including tabulations of Sensitivity Report values, of optimization models.

Finally, this edition increases its coverage of chapter examples, particularly by adding simpler, introductory models to facilitate learning, and maintains its Macintosh-friendly tone of documenting differences for those students modeling in Excel for Macintosh. Chapters are filled with marginal "Tips" to help students avoid pitfalls in Excel while avoiding a break in the conceptual developments in the chapters. In addition, detailed appendices on Solver and the special features of Excel for modeling not normally covered in mechanics-of-spreadsheets courses have been expanded to enable the student to improve their spreadsheet skills and gain a greater appreciation for the modeling capability of Excel.

Spreadsheet applications and examples in Microsoft Excel, including the use of popular spreadsheet add-ins (Solver, Crystal Ball, @Risk, and TreePlan), are integrated throughout as the modeling paradigm. This edition introduces Evolutionary Solver, based upon a genetic search algorithm, to illustrate applications that previously frustrated student attempts to analyze highly nonlinear models that make use of Excel's nonsmooth functions, such as =IF( ).

Considerable attention has been paid to the procedural (almost tutorial) steps to build and analyze decision-making models in Excel. The emphasis again is "hands-on" use of Excel and its add-ins. Updated to include the latest Excel version, Excel 2000, the book provides more than 500 screen "shots" of Excel models. (Most examples are applicable to earlier versions of Excel.) Importantly, the book includes more than *ten* software application packages students will use long after the course is completed:

- A graphic visualization program, GLP, for interactive optimization of linear programming models—software included with the book.
- Premium Edition Solver for Education including infeasibility and nonlinear diagnostic reports to aid students in debugging their optimization models—software included with book.
- SolverTable add-in software for parametric analysis, including Sensitivity Report values, of optimization models—software included with book.
- Evolutionary Solver (part of Premium Edition Solver for Education) for performing genetic search on models having highly nonlinear or nonsmooth relationships—software included with book.
- *Professional* version (140 day time-limit) of the Monte Carlo simulation add-in, Crystal Ball—software included with the textbook. This version includes the Monte Carlo simulation optimizer OptQuest.
- Decision analysis add-in software, TreePlan—software included with the book.
- Excel templates for queuing model calculations—software included with book.
- The discrete event simulation package Extend LT—software included with textbook.
- The Manufacturing and Business Process Reengineering simulation library extensions to the simulation package Extend LT—software included with textbook.
- Microsoft Project 2000 (120 day time-limit)—software included with the book.

The book is divided into four parts: the first deals with general modeling issues, the second with deterministic models, the third with probabilistic (stochastic) models; and the fourth with implementation issues for applying models in organizations. This provides a logical organizational framework for the material while allowing for greater emphasis on and enhanced coverage of currently "hot" areas such as genetic optimization, AHP, Monte Carlo simulation, discrete event simulation, multi-objective decision making, and the general use of spreadsheets in modeling. There is more material than can be covered in a typical first course. We believe our organization of topics allows each instructor the flexibility to tailor their course to different audiences and needs.

ACCOMPANYING MATERIALS

New copies of the book include a CD-ROM containing the following software and courseware at no extra charge:

- The graphic visualization program, GLP, for interactive optimization of linear programming models for the material in Chapters 4 and 6.
- Premium Edition Solver for Education including infeasibility and nonlinear diagnostic reports for the material in Chapters 3, 4, 5, 6, and 7.
- SolverTable add-in software for parametric analysis of optimization models for the material in Chapters 4, 5, 6, and 7.
- Evolutionary Solver (part of Premium Edition Solver for Education) for performing genetic optimization for the material in Chapter 7.
- *Professional* (140 day) version of the Monte Carlo simulation add-in, Crystal Ball for the material in Chapter 9. This includes the Monte Carlo simulation optimizer OptQuest (also for Chapter 9).
- Decision analysis add-in software, TreePlan for the material in Chapter 8.
- The discrete event simulation package Extend LT for the material in Chapter 10.
- 120 day *Evaluation* version of Microsoft Project 2000.
- Excel templates for queuing models.
- Excel spreadsheet files for all in-text examples and any relevant data for end-of-chapter problems and cases.

Supplementary items for text adopters:

- Excel Solutions (for the Instructor) to every example, problem, and case in the book. Instructors may use these as is, take out some of the detail, or modify them as desired.
- Presentation slides for each chapter in PowerPoint with the appropriate Excel spreadsheets (ISBN: 0-13-040631-7)
- Access to protected Web Page for more timely supplementary materials and additional cases.
- Instructor's Solutions Manual (ISBN: 0-13-040627-9)
- Test Item File (ISBN: 0-13-040629-5)
- Prentice Hall Custom Test for Windows (ISBN: 0-13-040620-1)

ACKNOWLEDGMENTS FOR THE SIXTH EDITION

We would like to thank the original authors of the first four editions, Gary Eppen and F.J. Gould, joined in later editions by Charles Schmidt, for their arduous efforts in creating a classic textbook that was worthy of being revised.

We would like to thank our editor, Tom Tucker, for his commitment to bringing this revision to pass and for his patient good humor as deadlines raced by. We believe if it wasn't for his guidance and direction, the book would not be nearly the product that it is.

We would like to thank our many reviewers of this edition (see the list below) for their insightful comments and ideas. This is a much better book because of them.

We thank the more than 300 instructors who participated in the extensive INFORMS Management Science Teaching Survey. Their comments and suggestions have validated many of the changes made in this edition.

We would also like to thank our secretaries, Stephanie O'Dell and Hiromi Yampol, for the long hours of dedicated service in the editing and logistics support a project such as this requires. We also thank Kevin Lewis for his help and the creation of numerous problems and examples. The Sloan Executives at Stanford deserve our thanks for pilot-testing this edition of the book. In particular, we thank Professors James Patell and Michael Harrison for class-testing some of the newest material in this book.

We are grateful to Professors Charles Bonini, Evan Porteus, Krishnan Anand, James Patell and Haim Mendelson for agreeing to make their case material available in this book, and to Professor Stephen Bradley for his cooperation in creating the implementation case. We thank Professors David Ashley and Mike Middleton for providing the queuing templates and the TreePlan software, respectively.

Also, we would like to thank Daniel Fylstra and John Watson of Frontline Systems and Software Engines for making Solver a reality. They have been a joy to work with. We are especially grateful to Dan for making Solver Premium Edition for Education available to students as a generous and gracious commitment on his part to facilitating management education.

Finally, at Microsoft, former Stanford students, Steve Ballmer and Pete Higgins, deserve thanks for their instrumental roles in creating the Excel tools that have made it the preferred choice for modeling and analysis by managers. Their cooperation with and receptivity to suggestions from academics in determining Excel's and Solver's product design and feature set is a model that we wish more software companies would follow.

We hope you find that this text and its supporting materials enhance your teaching efforts. We always like to hear from you—especially when it's to pass along your ideas for how the text can be improved—so, please feel free to send along your reactions.

Jeffrey Moore, Palo Alto, CA
Email: moore_jeffrey@gsb.stanford.edu
Phone: (650) 723-4058
FAX: (650) 725-7979

Larry R. Weatherford, Laramie, WY
Email: lrw@uwyo.edu
Phone: (307) 766-3639
FAX: (307) 766-3488

REVIEWERS FOR THE SIXTH EDITION

Sid Deshmukh, Northwestern University; James Drosen, North Michigan University; John Kottas, College of William and Mary; Rita Kumar, California State University-Northridge; Benjamin Lev, University of Michigan-Dearborn; Jerrold May, University of Pittsburgh; Danny Myers, Bowling Green University; Gary Reeves, University of South Carolina; Sam Roy, Moorhead State University; David A. Schilling, The Ohio State University; Glen Zabowski, McGill University

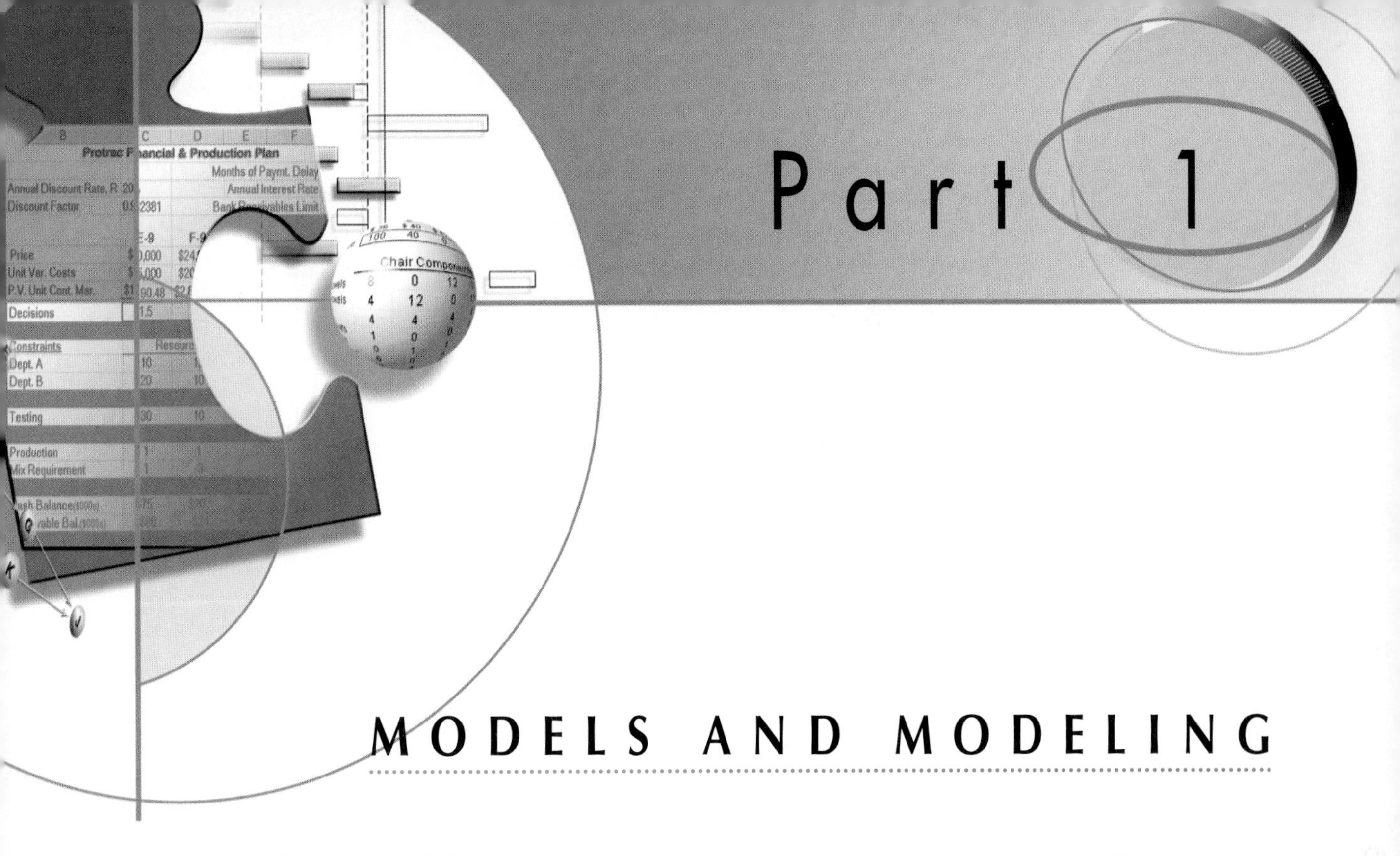

Part 1

MODELS AND MODELING

In this part we initiate the modeling approach to applying Excel for managerial decision support. Our approach consists of developing an Excel model of a management situation, analyzing the model 1with the tools of Excel, and decision making based upon that analysis. The early chapters are devoted to a class of models, called deterministic models. So it makes sense to ask, "What do we mean by *deterministic*?"

The word *deterministic* means that all aspects of the model are *known with certainty*. For example, in a production planning model we will assume that we know *exactly* how long it takes to produce a particular part, say, 20 minutes each, or equivalently, 3 parts per hour. We thus know that in 8 hours of work we can produce: 8 hours * 3 parts per hour = 24 parts.

All of us have used deterministic models. From the first time we deduced that four 25-cent pieces of candy cost a dollar, we always knew the exact value of all the factors in our analysis. Indeed, we naturally tend to assume that the world around us is deterministic. On reflection, however, we realize that it is not. In the previous example, we know that some of those part production times are going to be 19 minutes and others 23. Perhaps it will take only 7 hours and 41 minutes to produce our 24 parts.

Why, then, do we use deterministic models when we know that they do not perfectly describe reality? The answer is simple—the models are useful. Deterministic models may not be perfect, but they are often a reasonably good approximation of reality, almost always better than no model at all. The results they yield make it well worth the time and effort required to construct and analyze such models. For this reason, deterministic models are the workhorses in applying spreadsheets to analyzing management situations, and we devote both Parts 1 and 2 of the book to their study. Later, in Part 3 of the book we will relax this deterministic assumption for models that require us to consider uncertainty explicitly.

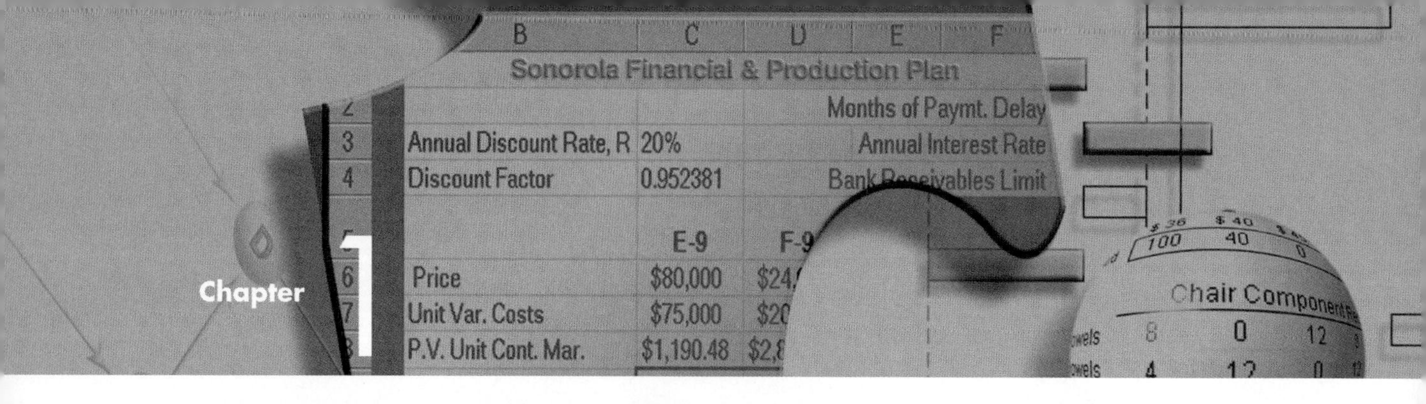

INTRODUCTION TO MODELING

CHAPTER OUTLINE

APPLICATION CAPSULE **Credit and Collections Decisions at AT&T Capital Corporation**

Owning and managing over $12 billion in assets, AT&T Capital Corporation (AT&T CC) is the largest publicly held leasing and financing company in the United States. Small-ticket commercial leasing, involving capital equipment valued at $50,000 or less, is a multi-billion dollar strategic segment of AT&T CC's business. In this highly competitive market, AT&T CC must make credit approval decisions quickly (or risk losing customers to another lessor), accurately (or risk bad debt losses), and cost effectively (or risk decisioning costs that erode profits). In addition, management of collections activities on delinquent accounts must be cost-effective to control bad-debt losses, reduce financial servicing costs, and improve cash flow.

Taking a life-cycle approach, AT&T CC developed a computer-based decision support system to manage each customer's credit risk throughout the course of the relationship. Models and systems were developed to support three phases of the relationship: (1) making initial credit decisions, (2) managing the credit line and subsequent credit decisions, and (3) collecting accounts. For each phase risk-prediction and decision-making models determine what decision to make. Benefits included quicker response times to the customer, gains in AT&T CC business volume, and increases in profitability.

For initial credit decisions, credit profile information and credit reports are used to predict a customer's future payment performance. An optimization model is used to determine the sourcing of credit information from different credit bureaus. Another optimization model determines approval decisions and assigned credit lines. The approval decision making uses the dollar exposure and credit score prediction to determine decisions of Approve, Reject, or Refer for Review. This process now automates about 68% of initial credit decisions, permitting an increase of $40 million in annual business volume while cutting costs of decision making by $550,000 annually. Another division at AT&T CC used the model to decrease its costs by over $600,000 annually, including a 40% reduction in the cost of obtaining credit reports.

Managing the customer credit line involves continuous evaluation of the customer's credit worthiness to reclassify their credit line into credit "buckets." Customers are ratcheted up to the next level or down to a lower level of credit when the credit-scoring model predicts a new threshold. The credit-line management model has resulted in an annual savings of $300,000 per year while supporting a $6 million increase in business volume.

The collections from customers in arrears is managed by a suite of statistical models that recommend one of up to five treatment scenarios for collection activity. A portfolio management model automatically selects and queues customers in arrears for a service representative's work list. This has resulted in a productivity gain of 15%, yielding a sustained reduction in delinquent receivables of $16 million and corresponding cash flow increase of $1 million per month. With the model AT&T CC's provision for doubtful accounts declined by 15% while the business volume grew by 23%.

Overall, applications of these risk analysis, statistical, optimization, and portfolio management models have reduced credit management decision costs by $3.5 million annually while supporting business volume gains of $86 million annually and reducing bad debt losses by $1.1 annually. According to AT&T CC these investments in "decision automation and optimization are now viewed as a significant source of competitive advantage and profitability improvement." (See Curnow et al.)

1.1 INTRODUCTION

Congratulations! By learning Excel you have joined the 100 million users who have made spreadsheets the *lingua franca* of management, a revolution in management that is barely two decades old. This book is not about the mechanics of Excel; it is about how you can use Excel to build models for the analysis of management situations. And spreadsheet-based management models is what we are going to study—what they are, how they are constructed, how they are used, and what they can tell us. For example, at the heart of AT&T's success in the Application Capsule above is a collection of management models for supporting credit decision making. Like AT&T, our approach will consist of developing and then analyzing a model of the situation. From this analysis, recommended decisions to improve the situation will be considered.

Historically, however, managers have long regarded modeling for decision making with mixed emotions. While acknowledging the benefits of models, general managers have often viewed the modeling process itself as a "black art" to be practiced only by mathematicians, high-paid consultants, or computer specialists. Unfortunately, this delegation of modeling to specialists removes the manager from the process, a step that often leads to misapplication or nonapplication of the results. This, in turn, leads to increased skepticism by managers as to the real value of modeling, except to provide boilerplate appendices of model results—that frequently age like fine wine—in unread reports. Money and effort is thus wasted in ceremonial modeling activities that ultimately have little or no impact upon the client manager, nor the organization that commissioned the model, because neither learns from nor is changed by the modeling process.

The spreadsheet revolution has changed this by allowing managers to construct and analyze models for themselves. The previously required analytical skills of advanced mathematics, computer programming, algorithmic thinking, and other technical training have nearly vanished as a prerequisite for managers to do their own modeling. This direct **decision-support** use of models not only leads to better management decisions, but in addition, managers themselves gain important insights that previously were lost. This learning-from-modeling approach allows a manager to address the *most* important issue of any decision-making situation: determining what fundamental questions to ask, what alternatives to investigate, and where to focus attention.

A wide range of models will be developed in this book along with the appropriate concepts to allow you to generalize these examples to the variety of situations that you will encounter as a manager. The key ingredient, however, in successfully modeling management situations with Excel is you. Remember, you are in "competition" with the 100 million others who preceded you in this revolution by mastering spreadsheet mechanics. But how many of them can use Excel to successfully model a challenging management situation and defend their analysis on sound conceptual grounds?

It is clearly possible to do the work assignments in this book, and still have the material make no impact on you or your career. To avoid this tragic result, you have to own these modeling ideas, which means you must make them a part of your intuition. We will help, of course, but ultimately you have to do it on the basis of your own "hands-on" work with Excel modeling. For our part, we have tried to keep the focus on *the relationship between management and model.* As you work your way through this text, you will find that it is full of specific models. It is easy to become so immersed in the technical details of the models and their Excel representation that you lose track of the general skills that you must develop to be either a good manager or a good modeler. We believe that you will find this book interesting (to say nothing of useful) to the extent that you (1) focus upon *real-world situations* and the role of spreadsheet models in addressing such situations, and (2) engage in the hands on building and analysis of these models. Much of the responsibility for maintaining this focus, however, rests with you. Learning something is, after all, a personal experience, and you can achieve it only with personal effort.

By modeling various alternatives for future system design, Federal Express has, in effect, made its mistakes on paper. Computer modeling works; it allows us to examine many different alternatives and it forces the examination of the entire problem.

Frederick W. Smith
Chairman and CEO of Federal Express Corporation

1.2 THE MODELING PROCESS

Figure 1.1 presents the steps of managerial decision making. When faced with a situation involving conflicting or competing alternatives, the situation is analyzed by the manager; decisions are reached to resolve the conflicts; the decisions are implemented; and the organization receives the consequences in the form of payoffs, not all of which are monetary. In this book we focus upon applying spreadsheet modeling to decision support, that is, the first two stages of analyzing the situation and reaching decisions about it. Implementation of the resulting decisions is also important, and we devote Chapter 11 to that topic.

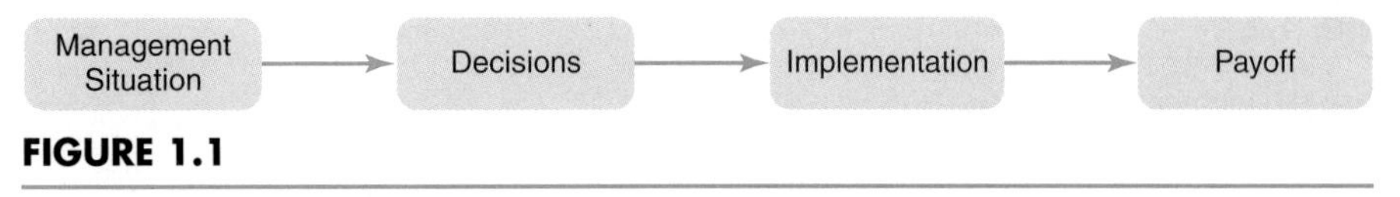

FIGURE 1.1

Managerial Approach to Decision Making

Figure 1.2 defines the **modeling process** applied to the first two stages that we will use throughout this book. Note that the diagram is divided into a top and bottom half separated by a dashed line. Below the dashed line is the real, chaotic, everyday world faced by managers who must decide how to deal with a challenging situation, such as the allocation of resources to competing tasks, the scheduling of activities, or designing a marketing strategy. The process starts in the lower left corner with the challenging management situation.

Historically, managers relied almost exclusively on their own intuition as the primary vehicle for making decisions. Although of great value, especially for experienced managers, intuition is by definition devoid of a rational analytic process. A manager practicing intuition alone for decision making learns only from the feedback of final outcomes, an expensive and unforgiving teacher.

The modeling process, as represented by the "Symbolic World" half of Figure 1.2 above the dashed line, recommends a course of action to supplement (not replace) the use of intuition in making decisions. This indirect route involves abstracting the problematic aspects of the management situation into a quantitative model that represents the essence of the situation.

After building the (quantitative) model, it is analyzed to generate some results or conclusions that emanate from the model alone, that is, without regard to the abstractions previously made. Next, interpretation of the model-based results back to the real-world situation occurs, taking into account what was left out during the earlier abstraction phase. When augmented by the manager's intuition and experience, this modeling process leads to better decisions, and insights that affect learning.

As illustrated in Figure 1.3, the modeling process itself is not a scientific-method endeavor that can be left entirely to specialists. Managerial judgment pervades all aspects of the process. Hence, intimate involvement by the manager throughout the modeling process is critical for success back in the real world.

The crucial role of managers occurs during the abstraction, model formulation, interpretation, and later, the implementation of decisions. Therefore, it is essential that you understand

1. What sorts of management situations are amenable to modeling,
2. What the prospects are for gathering or retrieving data and analyzing the model to obtain recommendations or results (within an affordable amount of time and money), and
3. What you can do to get the greatest possible value out of the model in terms of model interpretation and decision implementation.

FIGURE 1.2

The Modeling Process

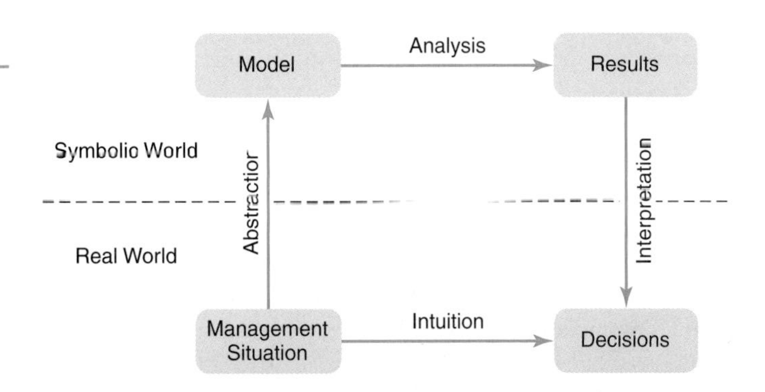

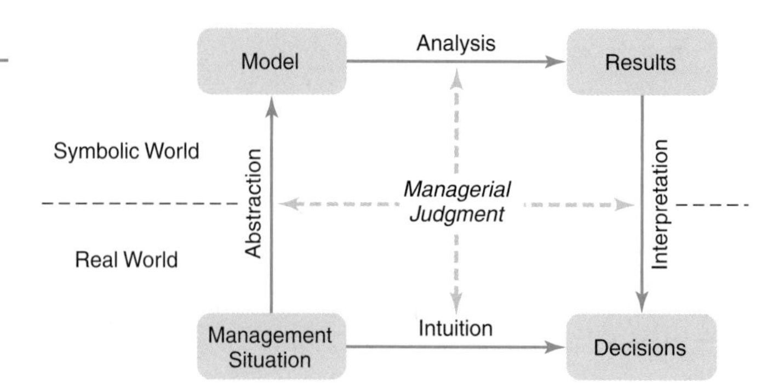

FIGURE 1.3

The Role of Judgment in the Modeling Process

MODELS IN THE FIRM

Models often play different roles at different levels of the firm. At the top levels, models more typically provide information in the form of results and insights, not necessarily recommended decisions. They are useful as strategic planning tools: to help forecast the future, explore alternatives, develop multiple contingency plans, increase flexibility, and decrease reaction time. At lower levels, models are more frequently used to provide recommended decisions. In many plants, for example, assembly-line operations are completely automated. In some cases, such as the AT&T example, decisions are produced by a model of the operation and immediately implemented with only exceptional managerial involvement. More commonly, however, automation's contribution to modeling is the ready collection of operational data. These data are then used by managers to update their spreadsheet model periodically. The revised model is then reanalyzed to produce new recommended decisions, followed by managerial reinterpretation and implementation of new decisions.

Models have different uses at different levels of the firm for a number of reasons. At progressively lower levels of an organization, alternatives and objectives are apt to become clearer. Interactions are easier to specify quantitatively, accurate data are often more available and the future environment more certain. Also, the frequency of repeated decision making is high, affording the opportunity to amortize the cost of model development and data collection over many decision-making opportunities. For example, at the bottom of the hierarchy a decision may concern the scheduling of a particular machine. We know the products that will be run on it and the costs of changing the machine from the production of one product to any other product. The goal of the model may be to find a schedule that produces the necessary amounts by the due dates and minimizes changeover and storage costs.

Contrast the clarity and explicitness of that problem with a multi-billion-dollar top-management decision between "invest and grow" and "produce to generate current earnings." Models can certainly be applied to such broad and fuzzy problems, but the models themselves are loaded with questionable assumptions and uncertainties. In such cases, the validity of the model and agreement on objectives may be as difficult to determine as the appropriate decision.

MODELS AND MANAGERS

Models are used in as many ways as there are people who build them. They can be used to sell an idea or a design, to order optimal quantities of nylon hosiery, or to better organize a giant multinational corporation. In spite of these differences, a few generalities apply to all decision-support models. All such models provide a framework for logical and consistent analysis and are used for at least seven reasons:

1. Models force you to be explicit about your objectives.
2. Models force you to identify and record the types of decisions that influence those objectives.
3. Models force you to identify and record interactions and trade-offs among those decisions.
4. Models force you to think carefully about variables to include and their definitions in terms that are quantifiable.
5. Models force you to consider what data are pertinent for quantification of those variables and determining their interactions.
6. Models force you to recognize constraints (limitations) on the values that those quantified variables may assume.
7. Models allow communication of your ideas and understanding to facilitate teamwork.

It follows from these features that a model can be used as a consistent tool for evaluating and communicating different policies. That is, each policy or set of decisions is evaluated by the same objective according to the same formulas for describing interactions and constraints. Moreover, models can be explicitly adjusted and improved with historical experience, a form of adaptive learning.

A final point: Spreadsheet models provide the opportunity for the systematic use of powerful analytical methods never before available to general managers. They can handle a large number of variables and interactions. The mind alone is capable of storing and communicating only so much information.

Models allow us to use the analytical power of spreadsheets hand in hand with the data storage and computational speed of computers.

1.3 A WORD ON PHILOSOPHY

"Philosophy" represents our effort to bridge the gap between this book's use of models and your experiences as a manager in the real world. In this book all the problems are clearly stated (at least we intend them to be so), all the data are neatly given, and the solution may be a single number in the back of the book. Of course, absolutely none of this is true "below the line" of Figure 1.2 in the real world. It thus pays to take a moment to comment further about the role of models in the real world.

REALISM

We start with a theme sounded earlier. No model captures all of reality. Each model is an abstraction. That is, it includes only some of the possible interactions, and only approximately represents the relationships among them. This provides us with a very simple and pragmatic explanation of why and when models are used.

A model is valuable if you make better decisions when you use it than when you don't.

The approach is much like that of science or engineering. The models may not exactly describe the lift on an airplane wing, but we design better planes with the models than without them. The same concept holds for managerial decision models.

INTUITION

Some managers continue to think that models and management intuition stand in opposition to each other: "Either we will be creative in addressing this situation or we will model it with a computer." Nothing could be further from the truth. The effective (and creative) use of models depends crucially on good management judgment and intuition.

Intuition plays a major role in problem recognition and model formulation. You have to "see" the potential for using a quantitative model to get the process started; that is, you must have an intuitive feeling that a model will capture the essence of the situation and yield a useful result before you are willing to invest in the modeling process.

Intuition is also crucial during interpretation and implementation. Although analysis of many of the models in this book produces "optimal" decisions, it is important to understand that such decisions are the optimal solution to the symbolic abstraction "above the line" in Figure 1.2. They may or may not be a good response to the real-world situation.

The term optimality is a model-related rather than a real-world concept. One optimizes models, but rarely, if ever, real-world situations.

Only rarely is it meaningful to talk about "optimal solutions" for the real-life situations of business (much less of government) management. That is why it is crucial that you as a manager make sure that the decisions suggested by a model make sense by satisfying your intuition. If the recommendations do not appeal to your managerial intuition, then it is necessary to decide whether the model is wrong. Indeed, a crucial aspect of your managerial role is to evaluate the model itself and to determine just how much weight should be accorded to its recommendations. The situation, or even the formulation of the model, may need to be rethought. The point is that modeling does not provide an opportunity for a manager to put intuition on hold. In fact, one of the worst mistakes a manager can make is to blindly allow a model to make his or her decisions because "Excel says so." The environment might change, and a model that was producing perfectly good results could start producing bad advice. You must always be alert to the possibility that something has changed and that the old answers just won't work anymore. Indeed, there is much evidence that the modeling process works best when the environment surrounding a business situation changes enough to render standard policies or rules of thumb inadequate.

Of course, there is no guarantee that using a "good" model will always give a good outcome; but without perfect clairvoyance it is the most rational approach that can be taken. Moreover, like the modeling process itself, management situations are really circular not strictly sequential. This means that they keep coming up and have to be revised and reworked. This fact provides one of the major motivations for studying quantitative models. Your chances for anticipating when a model will and will not yield good real-world results are dramatically improved by understanding the concepts that are used in the model.

To better understand what we have covered on the modeling process, assume you are the manager in the following manager-modeler dialog.

MANAGER: Let me make sure I understand. Essentially, you are saying that because managers have not been actively involved in the modeling process, many modeling efforts have been wasted, at least in terms of their impact upon the real world of final decision making and upon the managers themselves.

Right.

MANAGER: And that the development of powerful personal computers and spreadsheets now makes it possible for managers like me to do their own modeling in a fast and easy way without relying upon a technical specialist.

Yes, in many situations.

MANAGER: And that the indirect route—building a model, analyzing it, and interpreting it—should augment but not replace my own intuition.

Correct, particularly where some aspects of the situation can be quantified into a model that will supplement your intuitive treatment of the nonquantifiable aspects of the situation.

MANAGER: I see. So, in conclusion, adopting this modeling process will give me the answers I need to my problem.

Surprisingly . . . , no!

MANAGER: What? Are you teasing me with that answer? You and I both know that working with spreadsheets is never as fast nor as easy to use as claimed. And now you are telling me that spreadsheet modeling is *not* going to provide the answer to my management problem?

In a sense, yes, that is what I am saying.

MANAGER: Well, congratulations! You have just unsold me on using modeling by saying it is irrelevant to answering my problem.

Hold on! You have just touched upon a central misunderstanding about the modeling process for decision support. Look at the first two figures again. It is not an accident that neither the word "problem" nor the word "answer" appears in either. Our ultimate goal is to address overall improvement in decision making for managerial situations and not just give "answers."

MANAGER: Look, I don't have the time for a meaningless academic debate about semantic distinctions.

That is not my point. Of course, we will devote considerable attention in this book to providing "an" answer, if not "the" answer, to a given problem. My point is that the very articulation of your real-world situation into a problem statement has already launched you up the abstraction ladder into the modeling process. That is, problems, as such, do exist above the dashed line in the figure, *and hence, answers to those problems exist,* but only above the dashed line—*outside of the real world that you face. However, "answers" to your abstracted "problem" are rarely, if ever, solutions to your management situation by themselves. The answers must be carefully interpreted in the real-world context that you face before making a final decision. And, as a result, that final implemented decision may be quite different from the answer produced by analyzing the model.*

MANAGER: OK, I see what you are saying. In other words, I must understand what specific abstract problem the model's answers are addressing, and how those answers were arrived at, before I can properly interpret them as decision aids to help me resolve my more chaotic real-world situation.

Precisely. Think of the answers not as results in and of themselves, but coupled with the problem statements they address, as important ways to update your intuition about the managerial situation that motivated you in the first place. This "intuition updating" has benefits that transcend the immediate payoff from better decision making in the current situation because enhancing one's intuition is at the core of learning. Moreover, the benefits of learning are cumulative across situations, culminating in the wisdom we all seek. So, the commitment to modeling should be driven by your desire to understand the situation at a deeper level, not only for the immediate benefit of better decision making, but also as an important step in refining your management intuition. Refined intuition—wisdom, if you will—about management situations is the hallmark of a successful manager. Never forget the modeler's creed:

"The goal of modeling is insight, not just answers."

MANAGER: Well, it sounds to me that you just built a verbal "model" to help me get "insight" into the proper role my involvement should play in modeling in order to "refine my intuition" about the modeling process.

Touché!

MANAGER: Earlier you said that the modeling process was not scientific. I thought the whole purpose of quantitative modeling was to be more scientific.

On the contrary, I said that the modeling process was not an application of the scientific method. *The purpose of the classic scientific method is to eliminate human judgment as a polluting or biasing influence upon knowledge and understanding. As a result, verification of theories or results through repeated, controlled experimentation is at the core of knowledge acquisition in the sciences. Unfortunately, managerial situations almost never permit the luxury of replicated, controlled experiments because of cost or time constraints. So, we must substitute management judgment as an imperfect control or guide at* every step *in the modeling process. The analysis-of-the-model phase of the modeling process will be scientific in the sense that logic and computation to yield rational deductions will be employed, but otherwise judgmental influences are pervasive.*

MANAGER: In other words, modeling and analysis alone cannot protect me from the consequences of "garbage in-garbage out" in decision making.

Correct. And you, the manager, must be completely involved in the process, because only you can be the arbitrator of the GIGO content of the abstraction, the resulting model, the analysis of it, the relevance of the results, and their interpretation. After all, you are the one who ultimately will be held responsible for the final decision, right?

MANAGER: You bet I am! OK, this has been very helpful in clearing up the role I need to play and the benefits I can expect from modeling.

Actually, there is another extremely important benefit to the modeling process we haven't discussed, the usefulness of a model as a communication aid. Important decisions are rarely made in isolation, but involve the cooperation and concurrence of others, especially those charged with implementing the final decision. Properly done, the model-building process, resulting model, and the decision-making rationale it provides can be a powerful teamwork-building tool for explaining and communicating ideas and conclusions to others, and getting their feedback and cooperation.

MANAGER: OK, OK, you've got me involved! Now can we get on with spreadsheet modeling? I have decisions to make . . .

Not yet. There are some more considerations to address first: some of the different kinds of quantitative models available, the steps in building a model, and the important role played by data in spreadsheet modeling.

1.4 TYPES OF MODELS

There are three types of models. Engineers build model airplanes, and urban planners build model cities. Both of these are **physical models**. We use a second type of model so frequently that we often fail to recognize it, an **analog model**. Analog models represent a set of relationships through a different, but analogous, medium. A highway road map is an analog model of the terrain, a car's speedometer represents speed by analogous displacement of a needle on a gauge, and a pie chart represents the magnitude of several cost components by wedge-shaped areas.

The most abstract is the **symbolic model**, in which all concepts are represented by quantitatively defined variables and all relationships are represented mathematically, instead of physically or by analog. For example, physicists construct quantitative models of the universe, and economists build quantitative models of the economy. Because they use

1.5 BUILDING MODELS

Whether simple or complex, a model must be constructed by people. Unfortunately, there are no automatic "Expert Systems" for model building except in narrow, highly specialized applications. The computer revolution and accompanying software developments may someday lead to automated model-building packages for general managers. Currently, however, model building involves a great deal of art and imagination as well as a bit of technical know-how.

To model a situation, you first have to frame it. That is, you must develop an organized way of thinking about the situation. Remember, most management situations come to us in the form of symptoms, not as clear problem statements. Your sales representative in Los Angeles tells you that your chief competitor is beating you by offering e-commerce transaction processing over the Internet. In the everyday sense of the word, that is a management problem. In our language, that is a symptom. A **problem statement** involves possible decisions and a method for measuring their effectiveness, two key ingredients of a model. The art of moving from a symptom to a crisp problem statement is called **framing**. It is an essential skill of an effective manager in developing models.

In a business environment, quantitative modeling involves specifying the interactions among many variables. To accomplish this quantification, the model must be stated mathematically. We shall see many examples of model building in the chapters that follow. Do not be misled by the specific examples in the text, for in the real world there is usually no single "correct way" to build a model. Different models may give a different perspective on the same situation in much the same way that paintings by Picasso and van Gogh would make the same view look different. Although model building is an art, like art the fundamentals can be taught. As an overall guide, you can break down the process of building a model into three steps:

1. Study the environment to frame the managerial situation.
2. Formulate a selective representation.
3. Construct a symbolic (quantitative) model.

STUDYING THE ENVIRONMENT

Those new to modeling often undervalue the first of the steps, a study of the environment to frame the situation. The stated problem is often not a proper abstraction of the real situation. Often, the stated problem is really a description of a symptom. A variety of factors, including organizational conflicts, differences between personal and organizational goals, and the overall complexity of the situation, may stand between the manager and a clear understanding of the situation. Many times it is assumed that the facts are known when they really aren't. Framing requires the model builder to select or isolate from the total environment those aspects of reality relevant to the situation at hand. Prior experience is the most essential ingredient for success—both experience in building models and working experience in the environment to be studied.

FORMULATION

The second step, formulation of a selective representation, involves basic conceptual analysis, in which specific assumptions and simplifications have to be made. Because the management situations we are concerned with involve decisions and objectives, these must be explicitly identified and defined. There may be various ways to define the decision variables, and the most appropriate definition may not be apparent initially. The objectives, too, may be unclear. Even the most capable managers may not know precisely what results they want to achieve. Equally problematic, there may be too many objectives to be satisfied, and it may be necessary to choose one out of many. (It will become evident that it is usually impossible to optimize two different objectives at the same time. Thus, generally speaking,

FIGURE 1.4

The "Black Box" View of a Model

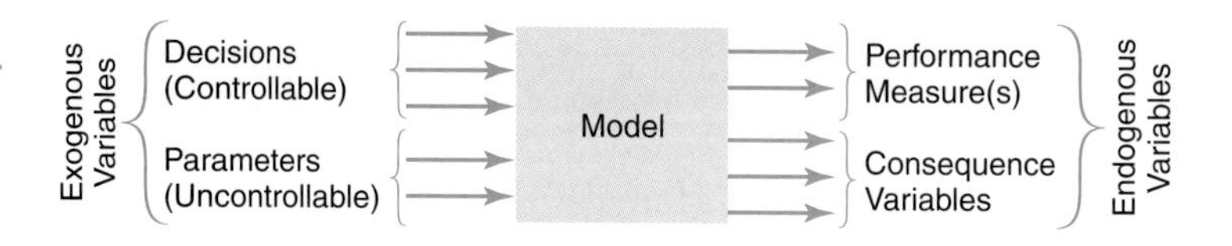

it is nonsensical to seek to obtain "the most return for the least investment" or the "greatest good for the most people.")

Figure 1.4 presents the first (and often most crucial) step in formulating a management decision model, the identification of the model's major conceptual ingredients. In this first step, we postpone creating the working details of the model. Instead, we focus on identifying (1) the model's **inputs**, the things to be worked on by the model, and (2) the model's **outputs**, the things to be produced by the model. For this reason, the model at this point is called a "black box" because we do not know (yet) what logic will be put inside the box.

Once we have identified the model's inputs and outputs, we must refine them into two subdivisions. Inputs, called **exogenous variables**, are divided into (a) **decisions**, variables that you, the manager, control, that is, the decision variables, and (b) **parameters**, variables that others, including "Mother Nature," control.[1] Examples of decision variables would be the prices to charge for your product, the location of a proposed facility, or the decision to sell a subsidiary or not. Examples of parameters are the prices charged by competitors for a similar product or service, a physical capacity constraint on a warehouse, the unit cost of raw materials, or next month's rainfall. Many uncontrolled input values may not be known in advance. Treating these inputs as parameters allows the model to be built as if they were known. Later, numeric values for these quantities can be specified after analyzing data to estimate their values, or simply given assumed values during analysis of the model.

Outputs, called **endogenous variables**, are divided into (a) **performance measures**, variables that measure the degree of goal attainment, and (b) **consequence variables**, variables that display other consequences that aid in understanding and interpreting the model's results. Performance measures are especially important because they are the criteria used to gauge how well you are meeting your ultimate objectives. For this reason performance measures are often called **objective functions**. Examples are revenue, market share, total cost, worker morale, customer satisfaction, and return on investment. Examples of consequence variables are revenue breakdown, number of items shipped, taxes paid, and other "want to know" quantities.

As simple as the black box conceptual ingredients framework is, it forces managers to consider early in the modeling process what to include and what to exclude from the model, and how to classify or frame the relevant factors. Here are some questions that illustrate how thought-provoking the simple ideas of Figure 1.4 are:

- For my private-sector company, is profit a decision or is it a performance measure?
- What exactly are the relevant sets of decision variables, as opposed to the ones of secondary or tertiary importance? For example, is the price of my product the single significant decision to consider, assuming, say, my promotion budget is fixed (by someone else?) at some given amount? Or should both product price and size of the promotion budget be considered as decisions to be made by me simultaneously?

[1] We use "parameter" here in its broadest managerial sense: "exogenous factors, such as market price or tax rate, that help define a model and determine its behavior." Some modelers prefer to substitute "uncontrolled exogenous variable" or "random variable" instead of parameter. This permits a more restrictive definition for "parameter" to characterize the underlying uncertainty in an uncontrolled exogenous variable.

- Do I, the manager, really control the price of my product, in which case price is a decision variable? Or is my product's price determined by competitive market forces, in which case price is a parameter?
- Is quantity of the product to sell a decision variable, and therefore, a controllable input to the model? Or is product quantity sold an output of the model (consequence variable), given its price as an input?
- Is worker morale a performance measure, and thus something I can influence managerially via human resource decisions? Or is it a parameter that I must accept as given? Either way, how do I measure morale? If morale is too slippery a concept to define into a variable precisely, then should I leave it out of the model and consider it later as part of the model interpretation phase? Or should I use, say, worker absenteeism as a surrogate or proxy measure for morale? In that case, what factors might affect absenteeism? And which subset of them are my decision variables?
- If market share is to be a performance measure, then what exactly is the definition of the market whose share my decisions will affect? Do I mean regional, national or international market share? Or all three? Do I mean market share this year, next year or five years hence? Should I measure market share in units sold or in revenue?
- Should I include competitor sales as input parameters in the model? But, if competitor sales are exogenous inputs, that implies I cannot affect them and must accept them as given. But, surely, I can affect my competitors' sales volumes by aggressive price discounting or expanded advertising, both of which could be my decision variables. In that case, competitor market share should be an endogenous output (consequence variable) instead of an exogenous input to my model. But, if it is an output, then should competitor market share be considered a performance measure—to be minimized?
- Should I use my own performance measures, time scale, and world view in my model or the ones preferred by my boss?
- Should the model focus on day-to-day operational decisions, longer-run strategic planning decisions, or both?
- What should I include in the way of performance measures or parameters from external stakeholder constituencies, such as government regulators, consumer groups, and shareholders?

The techniques we will develop for modeling are applicable no matter how the model inputs and outputs are defined. However, the questions illustrate the importance of management judgment in clearly defining the elements of the black box.

A suggested approach to the formulation step is to define the objective and its performance measure(s) first, that is, the critical model outputs. Then consider what model inputs (decision variables and parameters) are related to achieving that objective by influencing the performance measure(s). From that base the critical step of defining the decision variables and parameters that influence goal attainment follow more naturally. This backward reasoning ultimately produces the same black box formulation of the model. However, this working backwards approach is often easier because managers naturally think about situations in terms of objectives and performance measures.

MODEL CONSTRUCTION

Once a formulation is accomplished (and this may be a verbal or written process), a symbolic model must be constructed.

Experience has shown that generalist managers founder in model building at the point that the mathematical equations within the black box relating the variables must be developed. Like writer's block, "modeler's block" is overcome by pushing ahead often with oversimplified relationships initially that are refined later. This refinement requires some care because, along with data, these relationships become the "guts" of the whole modeling process. This topic is important enough that we will devote considerable attention to it in the remaining chapters of the book. Indeed, the central theme throughout this book is that many practical models can be built and analyzed by a single manager using modern spreadsheet techniques. Even in more complex situations requiring an interdisciplinary team, preliminary modeling can be initiated by a generalist manager.

One reason for this belief is that most relationships within a model are simple accounting equations (Profit = Revenue − TotalCost) or physical definitions (NumberMonths = 12 * NumberYears), and therefore, are well within the easy grasp of any manager. The remaining relationships in the model are sometimes more difficult to develop. However, most managerial models have only a few complicated equations. In these cases, some practice is required to develop the correct mathematics for interrelating two or more variables as part of the model's logic. A useful technique is to exploit your ability to sketch a graph giving a picture of the desired relationship(s). That is, you start, not with the final mathematical equation, but with a graph of it, and then you (or a talented colleague) deduce an acceptable equation from that graph.[2] The technique for accomplishing this also works for analyzing raw data, such as might be necessary for estimating the values of parameters. We call this technique "modeling with data," a topic important enough to warrant its own development in the next section.

1.6 MODELING WITH DATA

Managerial decisions are based to a large extent on the evaluation and interpretation of data. However, data can be interpreted only through the lens of some conceptual framework. It is difficult to say which comes first, the framework or the gathering of data. Certainly, data are required for effective modeling. Efforts toward better modeling often lead to the acquisition and storage of more or new types of data. The existence of data increases the potential for the use of models. C. West Churchman, an early advocate of management modeling, has claimed that there exist in reality no truly "raw" data in the sense that the act of collecting and tabulating the data always reflects the biases of some framework's world view, that is, a (mental) model. Nevertheless, one of the characteristics of advanced civilization, at least in terms of technology, seems to be the simultaneous acquisition and use of both data and models.

Symbolic models provide a way to evaluate and interpret data consistently and with greater attention to detail than afforded by mental models. Symbolic models can also be used to generate data, and data are usually required to build a model, for example, to estimate model parameters. In fact, it is not uncommon for the success or failure of a modeling effort to be related to issues of data availability, accuracy, and relevance. A great deal of attention should center on the subject of data in the practical building and use of management models. For example, a model requiring detailed data could be rendered useless if the data are not available or are costly and time consuming to collect.

To introduce some of the issues pertinent to the use of data in model building, consider a hypothetical firm, called HiTech. Decisions at HiTech are based to a large extent on available information, that is, on the evaluation and interpretation of data. Previously, we stated that from the modeling point of view, a recommended decision by a model is defined to be a number, such as a price or a quantity to sell. Keep this very precise definition in mind. We also want you to be very clear on what we mean by **data**. For our purposes, the word data also means numbers, in this case numbers that reflect quantitative facts about the environment of a management situation.

---

[2] As we will see in Chapter 2, Excel provides some tools to assist equation development from such graphs.

FIGURE 1.5

HiTech European Marketing Expenditures and Sales Revenue (thousands of U.S. dollars)

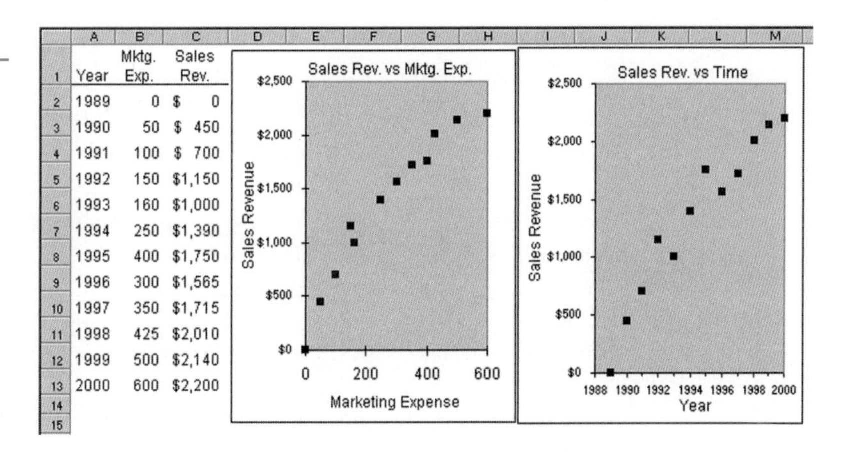

	A	B	C
1	Year	Mktg. Exp.	Sales Rev.
2	1989	0	$ 0
3	1990	50	$ 450
4	1991	100	$ 700
5	1992	150	$1,150
6	1993	160	$1,000
7	1994	250	$1,390
8	1995	400	$1,750
9	1996	300	$1,565
10	1997	350	$1,715
11	1998	425	$2,010
12	1999	500	$2,140
13	2000	600	$2,200
14			
15			

To see how numbers and models become intimately connected, consider a HiTech management decision on how much money to allocate to European marketing. Before making such a decision, management may want to have some idea of the effect of this allocation on total European sales. Therefore, an executive has queried data on European marketing expenditures and total European sales revenue for a 12-year period from the corporate enterprise-database and has imported the data into her Excel spreadsheet and created two charts, as presented in Figure 1.5.

Suppose that after studying the data in Figure 1.5, the executive assumes or hypothesizes some relationship between marketing expenditures and sales revenue. She may feel, for example, that her product total sales revenue in a given year depends directly only on the marketing expenditure in that year and not the sales revenue nor marketing expenditures in prior years. Numerous other possible relationships could be hypothesized. For example, she could assume that sales revenue follows a secular trend independent of marketing expense, or she could consider some combination of marketing expense and secular trend as influencing sales revenue. The appropriate relationships would obviously depend on many factors associated with the actual HiTech environment. And what about other relevant factors, such as general economic conditions? What real-world factors might lie behind these different degrees of effectiveness in the different years? That is, what real-world interactions do the data reflect? There could be differences in advertising techniques, or differences in market softness and demand, which, in turn, could be due to different economic conditions, weather, or government policies.

As a manager, you must consider these kinds of questions as soon as you begin to interpret data. But the point of the present discussion is this: As soon as you begin to hypothesize *any* relationship among your data, you are beginning to formulate the equation(s) of a model. That is, you are beginning to interpret the data as reflecting important underlying relationships. Therefore, Figure 1.5 takes on a special significance: It becomes a selective representation of reality. As such, a simple table of the data fits our earlier definition of a model. It is important to emphasize that the data by themselves do not represent a model. The numbers by themselves do not mean anything aside from records of fact. It is only when some relationship is ascribed to the data that a model, at least in embryonic form, exists.

1.7 DETERMINISTIC AND PROBABILISTIC MODELS

We know that this book is devoted to management decision models. There is, however, a large and diverse body of knowledge that falls under this general heading. For example, models for decision making are often classified by the business function they address or by applications discipline or industry involved. Table 1.2 gives a few of these classifications.

Table 1.2

Some Classifications of Models

CLASSIFICATION	EXAMPLES
Business Function	Finance, Marketing, Cost Accounting, Operations
Discipline	Science, Engineering, Economics
Industry	Military, Transportation, Telecommunications, Nonprofit
Time Frame	One Time Period, Multiple Time Periods
Organizational Level	Strategic, Tactical, Operational
Mathematics	Linear Equations, Nonlinear Equations
Representation	Spreadsheet, Custom Software, Paper and Pencil
Uncertainty	Deterministic, Probabilistic

Each such classification provides added insight to the uses and applicability of modeling. We will use the last example in Table 1.2 to organize our approach to modeling in this book, deterministic versus probabilistic models.

DETERMINISTIC MODELS

Deterministic models are those models in which all of the relevant data are assumed to be known with certainty. That is, deterministic models presume that when the model is analyzed all the needed information for decision making will be available. An example of a deterministic model would be the assignment of airline crews to each of an airline's daily flights over the next month, given flight schedules, staff available, legal constraints on work hours, union work rules, and so forth. As we will see in the chapters on deterministic modeling, such models can handle complex situations with many decisions and constraints. Deterministic models tend to have highest utility when there are few uncontrolled model inputs that are uncertain. As a result, deterministic models are often, but not always, used for decision making internal to an organization, such as the air crew scheduling example.

Deterministic models are covered in Parts 1 and 2 of this book. The rest of Part 1 is devoted to general spreadsheet modeling, while most of Part 2 is devoted to constrained optimization models. In Part 2 you will be introduced to **linear programming** (LP), which is the workhorse of constrained optimization models.[3] In Part 2 you will learn to formulate LP models, optimize them, and interpret the solution. A variety of other models also appear in Part 2. These include integer, nonlinear, and multi-objective programming, which are first cousins of LP.

Deterministic models are important for six reasons:

1. An amazing variety of important management problems can be formulated as deterministic models.
2. It is easy to incorporate constraints on variables in deterministic models.
3. Software exists to optimize constrained deterministic models, that is, find optimal decisions. For large LP models this can be done very quickly and reliably.
4. The techniques for analysis produce as a by-product a great deal of information that is useful for managerial interpretation of results.
5. Constrained optimization in particular is an extremely useful way to frame situations even when you are not going to build a model and optimize it.
6. Practice with deterministic models helps to develop your ability to formulate models in general.

Because basic Excel plays a central role in our development of models, the book requires knowledge of the mechanics of Excel. The Appendix B to this book provides a brief overview of those Excel features most useful for modeling.

[3] The "linear" in LP refers to the requirement that every relationship in the model be specified as a linear equation. The "programming" in LP has nothing to do with computer programming nor software development. Rather, its origin is related to "finding a schedule or *program* of activities to accomplish a task efficiently."

PROBABILISTIC MODELS

In **probabilistic**, or stochastic, models some inputs to the model are not known with certainty. Thus, probabilistic models presume that some important variables will not have their values known before decisions are made, and this ignorance must be incorporated into the model. An example of a probabilistic model would be the decision to take a startup Internet company public by an initial public offering, that is, offering shares of stock for sale, before it is known whether the market for such offerings will be favorable (bull market) yielding a high stock price or unfavorable (bear market) yielding a low stock price. As we will see in Part 3 of the book, such models incorporate uncertainty via probabilities on these "random" variables, in this case the future condition of the stock market. These models tend to have highest utility when there are only a few uncertain model inputs and few or no constraints. As a result, uncertainty models are often used for strategic decision making involving an organization's relationship to its (uncertain) environment, such as the public stock offering example.

In Part 3 of the book you will learn what kinds of criteria you can use when there is uncertainty, and how to find an optimal decision in that context. Here again we have quantitative decision models in which we are trying to optimize some function of the decision variables. Topics in this part of the book include decision analysis, queuing, two types of simulation, project management, and forecasting. Because uncertainty plays a central role in these models, this part of the book requires some knowledge of probability and statistics. The Appendix A to this book provides a brief overview of the subject. Although it certainly will not make you an expert, it does provide an introduction to (or a review of) the key concepts required for an understanding of these chapters.

1.8 ITERATIVE MODEL BUILDING

To further understand how models fit into the modeling process it will be convenient for us to classify symbolic models along the dimensions illustrated by the diamond in Figure 1.6. The right versus the left of the diamond refers to the polar extremes of building Deterministic Models versus building Probabilistic Models.

Of course, no model is either completely deterministic (no uncertainty in any variables) nor completely probabilistic (uncertainty attached to all variables' values). Returning to the previous examples, weather or sickness could disrupt flights or the availability of crew members in unexpected ways, thereby compromising the model's proposed crew assignments. Similarly, market conditions for a stock offering might be foreseeable with adequate certainty or the model could include a decision to postpone the offering at the last minute if conditions become unfavorable, thereby mitigating the effects of the uncertainty.

The top versus the bottom of the diamond refers to the polar extremes of Deductive Modeling versus Inferential Modeling. **Deductive modeling** presumes that the model can be initially developed by focusing upon the variables themselves, interrelating them in the model by making assumptions about the algebraic relationships and the values of any parameters. As a result, deductive modeling tends to be "top down" in development, placing a premium upon the modeler's prior knowledge and judgments of both mathematical relationships and data values, and of the future applicability of such prior knowledge. The resulting models tend to be "data poor" initially, involving only tens or hundreds of data items, often expressed as assumed parameters of the model.

Instead of starting with assumptions, **inferential modeling** presumes that the model can be developed by focusing upon variables themselves as reflected in existing data collections, interrelating them in the model by analyzing the data to determine the relationships and to estimate the values of any parameters. As a result, inferential modeling tends to be "bottom up" in development, placing a premium upon accurate, readily available data and judgments about the future applicability of the data. The resulting models tend to be "data

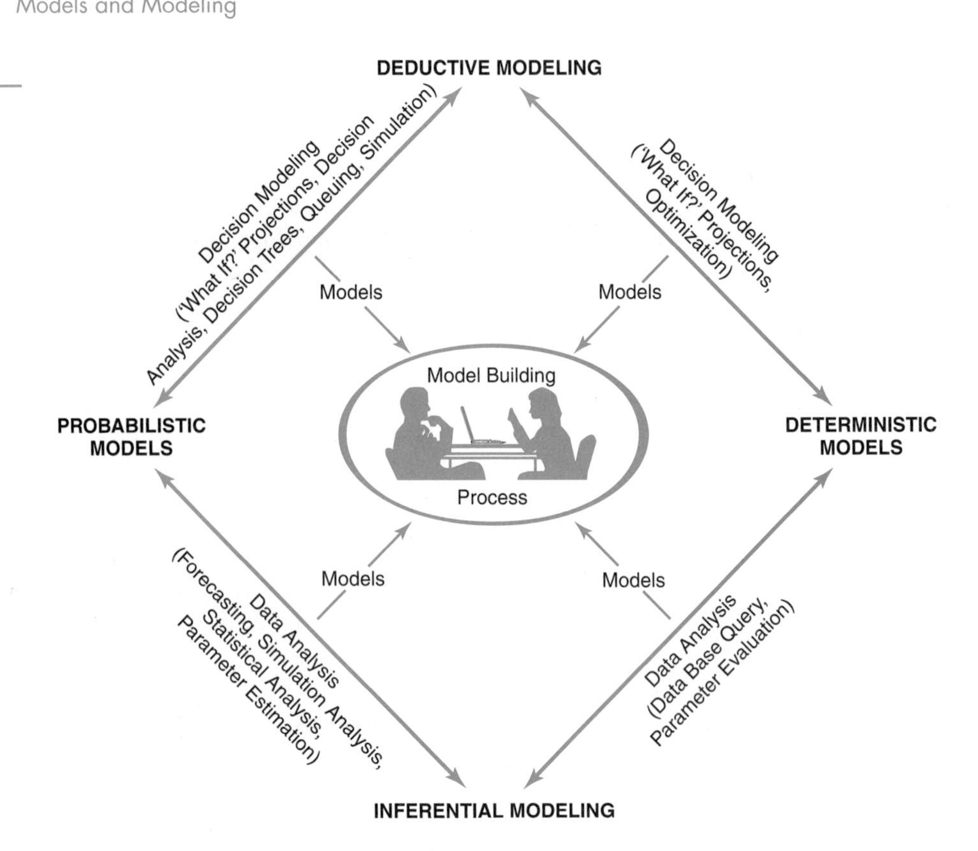

FIGURE 1.6

Types of Models

rich" initially, involving hundreds or many thousands of data items, often ultimately refined to estimate parameters of the model by a process often called data mining.

The diamond also illustrates that *all* four of the faceted dimensions of the diamond are addressed by managers in the model-building process, particularly in the early formative stages. That is, model building is rarely done by using only one dimension or by following a simple "cookbook" recipe for combining the dimensions. Instead, model elements are tried, tested, evaluated (often subjectively at first), revised, retested, and so forth in an iterative fashion by jumping or cycling from one "facet" of the diamond to another in a creative or brainstorming manner. For example, a manager at HiTech might start to build a product costing model via Decision Modeling by assuming or by (deductive) reasoning that Total Cost of Goods Sold is 60% of Total Revenue, where the 60% "cost-of-goods" percentage is known (deterministic). This sends her from the top of the diagram to the right facet of a deterministic model. Later in the modeling process, she might elect to "have a look at some historical data on revenues and costs," thereby moving down to the right-hand Data Analysis facet of the diamond in the diagram. After analyzing the historical data (inference), she might elect to revise the percentage to, say, 63%. Next, she might decide to examine the effect that revision has upon overall costs or profitability for the HiTech model as a whole. This would send her back to the right-hand Decision Modeling facet ("What if?" projections of total costs and profitability) to subjectively evaluate the model's veracity.

Still later in the model-building process, her colleagues might convince her that the cost-of-goods percentage is not fixed at 63%, but varies somewhat randomly because of variability in the commodity prices HiTech pays for raw materials. This would send the modeling process over to the left half in the diagram for her to iteratively develop cost-of-goods percentages and commodity price relationships (deduction) and analyze data to test them (inference) concerning the parameters of the probability distribution governing the values for the cost-of-goods percentage.

The trial-and-error, iterative approach to model building is highly creative. It is what makes managerial model building more of an art than a science. And, like art, you learn by looking critically at examples done by others and by practice, practice, practice.

1.9 MODELING AND REAL-WORLD DECISION MAKING

Generally speaking, the successful application of modeling to real-world decision making can be broken down into four stages that closely parallel the items in the modeling process of Figure 1.1:

1. The three model building steps of studying the environment, model formulation and model construction, for example, the process of taking real-world managerial situations, abstracting and framing them into a formulation, and then developing the mathematical terms of a symbolic model;
2. Analysis of the model to generate results;
3. Interpretation and validation of model results, making sure that the available information obtained from the analysis is understood in the context of the original real-world situation; and
4. Implementation, putting the validated knowledge gained from the interpretation of model results to work in real-world decision making.

As with model building itself, the four stages above are almost never performed sequentially. Instead, managers execute the stages iteratively, at least the first three stages. A model is built iteratively as described in the previous section. It is then analyzed to produce results, which are interpreted critically to produce recommendations that often fail to pass the simplest of validation tests: Do the interpreted results and recommendations violate common sense?

Common sense is the most obvious litmus test for validating a model. Barring easily identified logic errors in the model, if the results or recommendations violate common sense, there is no choice but to return to stage one to diagnose whether the managerial situation was inadequately defined, too much realism was lost in formulation, the model itself is deficient, or the like. More than a few iterations are commonly made among the first three stages of modeling before an acceptable model is produced, or on occasion, before a manager realizes that his or her common sense was inadequate originally. Either way, it is wrong to conclude that the iterations were wasted: Substantial learning occurs during the process itself as both models and managerial understanding are improved.

MODEL VALIDATION

Common sense alone is hardly a scientific way to validate a modeling effort. Unfortunately, other techniques for validation have their shortcomings, as well. For example, a frequent validation claim is that an organization saved $X in costs or made $Y in profit after using a model for decision making. This begs the question of whether that much performance improvement (or more!) would have happened without the model.

Because controlled experimentation is typically infeasible, one imperfect way to validate a model is to use it to "predict history." That is, historical data on decisions, parameters, and outcomes for a similar situation are taken from a known decision-making epoch and input into the model. Next, the two sets of outcomes, one from the model and the other from known historical outcomes, are compared for similarity as validation. Finally, the model is analyzed and any additional payoff from an improved decision-making recommendation becomes evidence for the worth of the model, assuming, of course, that historical validity implies future validity.

In the final analysis, it must be remembered that managerial performance is subjectively evaluated every day under ill-defined decision-making conditions. As a decision-support technology for those same managers, it is unreasonable to hold modeling to a higher, nearly unreachable scientific standard. In the final analysis, the validation of a model, like the worth of modeling, is a value judgment. Experience has shown that managers who commit to active involvement in the process have very little difficulty making these value judgments.

1.10 A FINAL PERSPECTIVE

Constrained optimization and *decisions under risk* are two important and useful frames we will cover in Parts 2 and 3 that apply to a wide variety of management situations. Unfortunately, it does not seem possible merely to describe the frames and assume that you can then use them correctly. You have to understand how the models are created and the relationships between decisions and results before you can advance to using the frames in an intuitive way. You have to learn about the models and how they are used in various situations before you can make the ideas your own. This requires taking the time to critically review the works of others and practice on your own. Thus, the book is full of examples and their spreadsheet representation, and cases and problems for you to sharpen your own spreadsheet-modeling skills.

In this text you will encounter many business models, and you will see that analysis of these models produces "optimal" decisions. That sounds great—what could be better than an "optimal" decision? But language can be deceptive if you do not have a thorough understanding of the concepts behind it. In this context, an *optimal decision* is one that gives the best answer to the abstract problem formulated in the model—for example, an answer that maximizes profits. But is it the best answer to the real-world situation that prompted you to build the model in the first place? This is what you must decide—preferably, *before* implementing the recommendations of the model. Whether or not to implement a particular recommendation is always a judgment call, but the quality of this judgment will depend heavily on how well you understand the relationship between the model and the real situation it is designed to mirror.

It is also important to assess the sensitivity of the result—that is, how much the decisions recommended by a model depend on the particular parameter values used for the model's inputs. Managers are usually most comfortable with decisions that hold for a wide range of input values, so that a good decision cannot suddenly be transformed into a bad one by a small change in one model input. **Sensitivity analysis** is thus an important topic throughout the book.

One of the basic building blocks for the models you will construct is costs. You will have the opportunity to work with the concepts of fixed, sunk, marginal, and opportunity costs. Determining the proper cost relationships in a model is crucial to arriving at good decisions. It is a skill that will stand you in good stead in your career.

While you may choose to emphasize different parts of the book, remember we emphasize the managerial approach shown in Figure 1.1 throughout the book. This managerial approach to modeling is more concerned with identifying situations, formulating models, analyzing them, interpreting the results, and implementing decisions than with the mastery of any one modeling technique. The central thrust behind our coverage of model building is an interest in applying these approaches to the real world. Without that, you, the spreadsheet user, would be a pure mathematician/programmer, and you, the manager, would be without a job.

With this introduction we think that you are just about ready to turn to Chapter 2, which begins the examination of building managerial models in Excel. However, let us close this chapter with two important caveats: unnecessary use of jargon and a healthy skepticism.

While most of the terms we have defined in describing modeling are straightforward, a given model's terminology necessarily becomes increasingly precise as model building

Table 1.3

Modeling Terminology

MODELING TERM	MANAGEMENT LINGO	FORMAL DEFINITION	EXAMPLE
Decision Variable	Lever	Controllable Exogenous Input Quantity	Investment Amount
Parameter	Gauge	Uncontrollable Exogenous Input Quantity	Interest Rate
Consequence Variable	Outcome	Endogenous Output Variable	Commissions Paid
Performance Measure	Yardstick	Endogenous Variable Used for Evaluation (Objective Function Value)	Return on Investment

evolves. This is caused by the need to carefully define the model's variables and relationships. Unfortunately, this requirement comes at a price: The use of model building jargon (e.g., "decision variable," "parameter," "exogenous," etc.) is viewed as discordant by other managers, who are often key players during implementation. Table 1.3 presents a few modeling terms, their definitions, and examples, along with suggested management phrases for colloquial use. The more colorful management lingo is often very useful in communicating black box modeling ideas to others.

Also, as a manager it is important to be skeptical. Learn to beware of experts, of solutions provided by computer models—yours and especially another's—and certainly of your own intuition. Your most valuable colleagues are those who say, "You can't be right! If you were right, then we would know that the following condition must be true, and it obviously isn't, and thus, you are wrong." Working directly with models—hands on—enhances your ability to analyze and dissect the route from assumptions to conclusions. The cases after each chapter are specifically designed to illustrate this concept. Asking the right questions is the first step in reaching a good decision. As you practice modeling, you will have the opportunity to work on developing this essential managerial skill.

1.11 SUMMARY

This chapter has provided an overview of the use of quantitative decision-making models, with special emphasis on their role as tools for the manager. The interaction between manager and model has been stressed, with attention given to the manager's role as ultimate decision maker and as a builder, user, and evaluator of models. We have explored the relationship between modeling and managerial intuition in the decision-making process.

Models are a limited representation of reality, and for this reason the results from analyzing a model are not necessarily the solution for the original management situation. In particular, we have emphasized that the notion of "optimal" is a mathematical, as opposed to real-world, concept. If a model is properly formulated and its output carefully interpreted, however, it can provide a wealth of valuable information to a decision maker.

We have introduced the concepts of decision variables, parameters, constraints, objectives, and performance measures, all of which are important components of models. We have introduced different types of models and the critical role played by data in modeling. We have discussed the iterative process by which models are created, the role played by different kinds of models in business organizations, and issues surrounding model validation. Importantly, we have emphasized the role models play in increasing managerial understanding, in the communication of ideas to others, and in facilitating teamwork.

Key Terms

Decision Support. The use of data, models, and analysis to give insights that aid decision making.

Modeling Process. The iterative application of abstraction, model building, analysis, and interpretation, coupled with intuition and judgment, to help make decisions.

Management Science. The systematic application of the modeling process to managerial situations.

Physical Model. A model, such as a model airplane, whose components are physical artifacts of an entity's actual properties.

Analog Model. A model using different media to represent actual properties, such as displacement of a clock's hands to represent time.

Symbolic Model (Quantitative Model). A model using data, variables, and mathematical relationships to represent abstracted situations, such as a model of a country's economy.

Black Box Model. An incomplete symbolic model in which only its input and output variables are defined, but without defined mathematical relationships.

Exogenous Variables. Quantitative variables whose values are determined external to a symbolic model, for example, inputs to a symbolic model.

Endogenous Variables. Quantitative variables whose values are determined by the relationships of a symbolic model, for example, outputs of a symbolic model.

Decision (Decision Variable). An exogenous variable whose value is under the control of and determined by a decision maker.

Parameter. An variable whose value is not determined by a decision maker, but is set exogenously.

Performance Measure (Objective Function). An endogenous variable that gauges the degree of goal attainment for a model.

Decision Model. A symbolic model with decision variables and at least one performance measure.

Consequence Variable. An endogenous variable providing additional information to assist managerial interpretation of model results.

Data. Numbers that reflect quantitative facts about the environment of a management situation.

Problem Statement. Identification of possible decisions and a method for measuring their effectiveness.

Framing. The art of moving from symptoms to a crisp problem statement.

Deterministic Model. A model in which all data are known with certainty.

Probabilistic Model. A model in which some data are not known with certainty, but whose uncertainty is captured by known probabilities.

Linear Program (LP). A deterministic model consisting of linear equations and a single performance measure (objective function) to be optimized subject to satisfaction of a given set of constraints.

Symbolic LP Model. The algebraic representation of an LP.

Deductive Modeling. Symbolic model building in which the values of variables, parameters, and the mathematical relationships among them are assumed from prior knowledge.

Inferential Modeling. Symbolic model building in which variables, parameters, and the mathematical relationships among them are estimated by analysis of data.

Sensitivity Analysis. Calculating the effect a (small) change of an exogenous variable has upon another variable.

Self-Review Exercises

True-False

1. **T F** The more complicated the model, the more useful it generally is.
2. **T F** Models usually ignore much of the world.
3. **T F** Decision models produce numerical values for decision variables.
4. **T F** A decision model often captures interactions and trade-offs between certain variables or quantities of interest.
5. **T F** There is usually no single correct way to build a model of a management situation.
6. **T F** One advantage of the modeling process is that it often eliminates the need to be very familiar with the environment being studied.
7. **T F** In practice, models are sometimes built by teams of individuals drawn from different disciplines.
8. **T F** By definition, optimization models always provide the best decision for the real-world situation.
9. **T F** A model is a good substitute for a manager's judgment and experience.
10. **T F** An important role of management can be the evaluation of a model (determining whether a model should be used and its results implemented).
11. **T F** Although spreadsheets make calculations easy, they have no real impact on decision making.
12. **T F** "What if" models are only useful for examining changes in the values of decision variables.
13. **T F** Data are needed only after the model is built.
14. **T F** As soon as you begin to hypothesize *any* relationship among your data, you are beginning to formulate the equation(s) of a model.

15. **T F** Data are used in building models.

16. **T F** A model provides a consistent means to interpret and evaluate data.

17. **T F** Aggregated data contain more information than do disaggregated data.

18. **T F** Models can be used to generate data.

Multiple Choice

19. A model is
- **a.** a selective representation of reality
- **b.** an abstraction
- **c.** an approximation
- **d.** an idealization
- **e.** all of the above

20. Decisions are often based on
- **a.** an evaluation of numerical data
- **b.** numbers produced by models
- **c.** the use of intuitive models that are never written down
- **d.** all of the above

21. A model
- **a.** cannot be useful unless it mirrors a real situation in great detail
- **b.** is a tool for the decision maker
- **c.** is rarely revised once it has been constructed
- **d.** all of the above

22. A model
- **a.** forces a manager to be explicit about objectives
- **b.** forces a manager to identify explicitly the types of decisions that influence objectives
- **c.** forces a manager to recognize explicitly constraints placed on the values that variables can assume
- **d.** all of the above

23. Models
- **a.** play different roles at different levels of the firm
- **b.** are rarely used in the strategic-planning process
- **c.** are a costly way of making routine daily decisions
- **d.** all of the above

24. Constrained optimization means
- **a.** that the underlying model is a very precise representation of reality
- **b.** achieving the best possible (mathematical) result considering the restrictions
- **c.** both of the above

25. Consider a prospective manager with interests and abilities that lie far from the quantitative techniques field. The point of studying a quantitative modeling course might be
- **a.** to be able to knowledgeably accept or reject the use of quantitative tools
- **b.** to acquire new ways of looking at the environment
- **c.** to become more familiar with the kind of assistance a spreadsheet might provide
- **d.** all of the above

26. With a "What if?" analysis, we are sure to find
- **a.** an optimal solution
- **b.** a good solution
- **c.** a feasible solution (if one exists)
- **d.** none of the above

27. In a probabilistic model, some element of the problem
- **a.** is a random variable with known distribution
- **b.** is a random variable about which nothing is known
- **c.** takes on various values that must be precisely calculated before the model can be solved
- **d.** will not be known until the model has been clearly formulated

28. A manager who wishes to maximize profit and minimize cost
- **a.** needs two objectives in her model
- **b.** can get the desired result by maximizing (profit minus cost)
- **c.** has an impossible goal and must choose one objective
- **d.** must make use of a probabilistic model

29. Linear programming models in general
- **a.** can be solved even if they are large
- **b.** are more useful for analyzing problems than for solving them
- **c.** are probabilistic in nature
- **d.** are rarely solved by a computer

30. Every quantitative model
- **a.** represents data of interest in numerical form
- **b.** requires the use of a computer for a full solution
- **c.** must be deterministic
- **d.** all of the above

31. The use of decision models
- **a.** is possible only when all variables are known with certainty
- **b.** reduces the role of judgment and intuition in managerial decision making
- **c.** requires managers to have a high degree of proficiency with computers
- **d.** none of the above

Answers

1. F, **2.** T, **3.** T, **4.** T, **5.** T, **6.** F, **7.** T, **8.** F, **9.** F, **10.** T, **11.** F, **12.** F, **13.** F, **14.** T, **15.** T, **16.** T, **17.** F, **18.** T, **19.** e, **20.** d, **21.** b, **22.** d, **23.** a, **24.** b, **25.** d, **26.** d, **27.** a, **28.** c, **29.** a, **30.** a, **31.** d

Discussion Questions

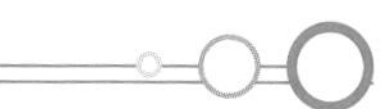

1-1. "The difficult managerial situations are those for which models do not exist." Interpret this statement. Give some examples.

1-2. What is the relationship between data and models?

1-3. At what point do the spreadsheet entries comprising a table of given data begin to take on the role of a model?

1-4. Why would a manager want to use a model to predict historical outcomes?

1-5. Suppose that you want to become a managerial decision maker but your special abilities and interests are far from the quantitative field. What is the point to your studying an introductory spreadsheet-modeling text?

1-6. What reasons can you think of to explain the fact that many models are built and never implemented? Does the absence of implementation mean that the entire model development activity was a waste of time and resources?

1-7. What is your interpretation of the phrase "a successful application of a model"?

1-8. Profit maximization is commonly taken as the performance measure for the (private-sector) firm. Is this necessarily the case? Can you think of other objectives that might be appropriate? (Do not worry about whether they are readily quantifiable.)

1-9. It is often said that there are no optimal decisions for the complex problems of business. Yet optimization models produce "optimal decisions." In what sense, then, are such decisions optimal?

1-10. Consider the following statement: "Our production policy should be to achieve maximum output at minimum cost" Comment on this statement.

1-11. What is the meaning of a mathematical equation when the data (parameter values) are not known with precision? What kinds of assumptions would tend to justify the use of models in such situations?

1-12. "Quantifying the elements of a decision problem is the easy part; the really difficult part is analyzing the model." Do you agree? Why or why not?

1-13. You are in the middle of a presentation to your company's chief executive officer in which you are justifying your request for approval of a multi-million dollar project to market a new invention. He interrupts you in mid-sentence, "Let's just cut to the chase. What levers do you want and what yardstick should I use if I approve this project?" Interpret his request in the context of modeling.

1-14. ABC Consulting specializes in building and analyzing decision models for a fee paid by their manager clients. "It's a very profitable business," says Rick James, ABC's president. "We go into the organization, get briefed by the client manager on the problem at hand. Then we assess the problem, and gather the necessary data. Next, we build a model on our ABC computers, or adapt one in our growing library of models, analyze it and return to the client and make a presentation to management with our recommendations." He continues, "Do we ever go over the equations of the model itself with the client manager or give a copy of the spreadsheet model to the client? Of course not! Are you crazy?" Why would ABC not want to give the model itself to the manager? Why might their clients not demand such delivery? What are the advantages and disadvantages of this approach to modeling? Answer this last question first from the viewpoint of Rick James and then from the viewpoint of a client manager.

1-15. Under what organizational circumstances do you believe that the modeling process would be more or less successful in supporting business decision making? To help you structure your discussion, consider the following:

   a. A collegial organization involving decision making by consensus versus an internally competitive organization in which decisions are made by adversarial arguments.

   b. A large centralized organization in which all decisions are made by a committee at the top versus a large decentralized organization in which most decision making is made by local managers.

   c. A small organization run by a single entrepreneur versus a larger organization run by functional managers in Finance, Accounting, Marketing, Manufacturing, etc.

   d. A line manager versus a staff manager.

   e. A company introducing a new product into a new market versus a company marketing a mature product into a traditional market.

   f. An organization in which all the managers are spreadsheet literate versus one in which they are not.

g. An organization with a central planning department of experts who do all business model development for the company versus one with no such department.

h. An organization with high levels of management job turnover versus one with little job turnover.

i. An organization experiencing rapid growth in revenues versus one with slowly growing revenues.

j. A highly profitable organization versus one that is experiencing losses.

k. A service organization versus a manufacturing organization.

l. An organization in a "first world" economy, such as France, versus one in a "newly emerging" economy, such as Vietnam.

m. An organization in which the managers have engineering or science college degrees versus an organization in which the managers have college degrees in liberal arts.

1-16. "As managerial situations become more complex and sophisticated, *details* become increasingly important." Why would this be true? What relevance does this statement have to modeling?

1-17. What does C. West Churchman mean when he says that raw data don't exist?

1-18. Your new boss, the VP of International Sales, has called you into her office and informs you, "I have definitely decided to open a new sales office in Singapore. But, I need to convince our boss, the Senior VP of Marketing, to go along with this decision in a meeting next Friday. I will ask you to join us, and I want you to build me a spreadsheet model with lots of equations, charts, and other stuff that will help me convince him. Make no mistake: I want that Singapore office approved!" Is this tactic an appropriate use of modeling? What would you do in response to this request by your boss and why?

1-19. It has been said that no validation study ever causes a model to be rejected, no matter how disconfirming are the data. The only thing that causes one model to be rejected is another model. Do you agree or disagree? Why or why not? Assuming the statement were true, what role does validation play in model building?

1-20. Federal Reserve Board Chairman Alan Greenspan made a speech on October 14, 1999 concerning the measurement of risk in the twenty-first century.[4] In the speech he discussed the application of models to measure risk.

> "More important, boards of directors, senior managers, and supervisory authorities need to balance emphasis on risk models that essentially have only dimly perceived sampling characteristics with emphasis on the skills, experience, and judgment of the people who have to apply those models. Being able to judge which structural model best describes the forces driving asset pricing in any particular period is itself priceless. To paraphrase my former colleague Jerry Corrigan, the advent of sophisticated risk models has not made people with grey hair, or none, wholly obsolete."

In a brief essay, relate Mr. Greenspan's comments to the process of developing models presented in this chapter.

1-21. What are the advantages and disadvantages associated with physical and symbolic models?

1-22. Given the advantages associated with symbolic models, how can you as a modeler exploit those advantages to build better models?

References

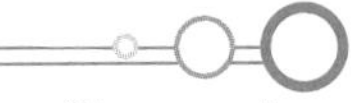

George Curnow, Gary Kochman, Steven Meester, Debashish Sarkar, and Keith Wilton, "Automating Credit and Collections at AT&T Capital Corporation," *Interfaces* 27, no. 1 (1997): 29–52.

Peter Horner, "Eyes on the Prize," *OR/MS Today* (August 1991): 34–35.

[4] Entire speeches are archived on the Federal Reserve Board Web site (http://www.federalreserve.gov/).

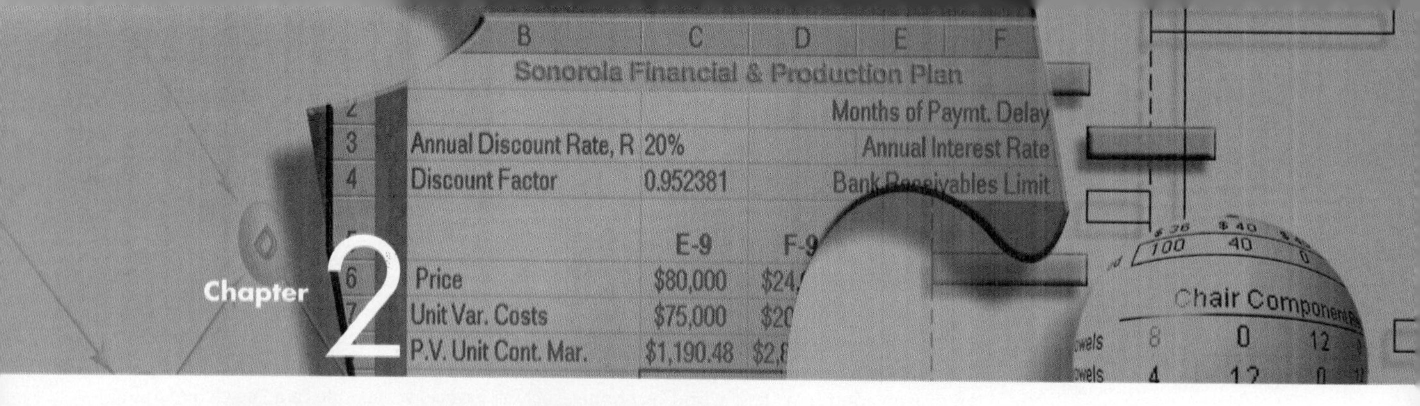

SPREADSHEET MODELING

CHAPTER OUTLINE

APPLICATION CAPSULE Modeling Coast Guard Tender Operations

One function of the United States Coast Guard is to maintain the 50,000 aids to navigation, or navaids, used by mariners to navigate United States (U.S.) waterways around the continental United States, Alaska, Hawaii, and U.S. territories, such as those in the Caribbean and the western Pacific. These navaids include lighthouses, lighted and unlighted buoys, lights, and day beacons. A navaid or aid to navigation (ATON) is either a floating buoy secured by a chain to sinkers or a fixed structure on land or pilings. Navaids mark underwater hazards and vessel traffic lanes. Large open-ocean buoys can be as large as nine feet in diameter, 38 feet tall, and can weigh over 10 tons. Each navaid is serviced once a year to keep them operational. For a permanent buoy this involves verifying the buoy's latitude and longitude, replacing missing letters or numbers, and repainting. The average time to service a buoy ranges from 25 to 260 minutes, depending on the nature of the servicing, as well as the weather and environment in which it is done.

The Coast Guard employs a variety of buoy tender classes to (1) deploy federal navaids, (2) perform routine servicing, and (3) respond to random outages. The Coast Guard needed to replace the two largest vessel classes in its buoy tender fleet (i.e., the seagoing buoy tender and the coastal buoy tender). They currently had 26 seagoing and 11 coastal tenders that serviced 7,500 navaids. The estimated replacement cost was $50 million for each seagoing tender and $20 million for a coastal tender. A model was created on a desktop computer to help support the Coast Guard's planned replacement of this 37 vessel fleet. The model analyzed the scheduling of the fleet in order to most efficiently service the navaids. The model had to consider many things, including the maintenance that would be expected, how far the tenders would have to travel to service each buoy and the associated cost.

Complicating factors included the fact that the buoy tenders perform other missions as well, like search and rescue, enforcement of laws/treaties, and oil-spill cleanup. Each type of vessel had different capabilities. For example, the seagoing tender could lift up to 20 tons of weight, could work in seas of up to 6 feet, and could stay at sea for up to 45 days; while the coastal tender primarily works closer to the coast in shallower waters that the seagoing tender could not transit. They also have less lift capacity and endurance.

Another complication to the model was trying to estimate the effects of bad weather. The total number of hours lost in a year depended on whether the buoys were fully exposed to the weather, partially exposed or completely protected.

The resulting decision-support model recommended that the optimal mix would be a fleet of 16 seagoing and 14 coastal tenders. As long as the tenders were efficiently scheduled, the new fleet would provide sufficient coverage. This represented a decrease of seven tenders in the fleet for a savings of $350 million in capital acquisition costs, as well as a reduction of 500 personnel billets (positions) and its associated savings. (See Bucciarelli et al.)

2.1 INTRODUCTION

Chapter 1 introduced some basic ideas and rationale for symbolic modeling and reviewed the art of model building as being an iterative process. This chapter will focus upon building spreadsheets for some deterministic models by means of several extended examples. In the process you will be exposed to several ideas:

- Suggested ways to translate a black box representation into a spreadsheet model,
- Recommendations for good spreadsheet model design and layout,
- Suggestions for documenting your models, and
- Useful features of Excel for modeling and analysis.

Importantly, you will also see several examples of models. Recall, modeling is an art form, learned in part by critical review of examples, and, ultimately, by practice.

A final comment before we begin. The spreadsheet models we will review are small, primarily for pedagogical convenience. Modern spreadsheets, like Excel, are capable of supporting much larger, even gargantuan, models. Indeed, there are many instances of successful use of enormous models. However, neither size of the model nor its mathematical sophistication alone necessarily imply usefulness. Simple, small models can also have great utility if they assist decision making. Moreover, successful, large, sophisticated models almost always evolve from successful management experience with a rudimentary precursor.

No manager will take seriously a model he or she does not understand or that is cumbersome to use and maintain. The biggest mistake a manager can make initially is to build a spreadsheet model with too much detail in a vain attempt to avoid losing any realism. Simplicity should be kept in mind, especially in the early stages of modeling. Remember, at least initially, a spreadsheet model must compete successfully against its popular predecessor, the "back of an envelope."

2.2 EXAMPLE 1—SIMON PIE

A startup company, Simon Pie Company generates profit from combining two purchased ingredients (fruit and frozen dough) into apple pies, processing the pies (cooking, packaging, delivery, etc.), and selling them to local grocery stores. The company's founder, Samuel Simon intends to build an Excel model to explore his options. He starts by undertaking the three steps of model building.

STEP 1: STUDY THE ENVIRONMENT AND FRAME THE SITUATION

Simon applies the model-building ideas in Chapter 1 by thinking about his business plan and the nature of dessert food manufacturing and wholesale distribution. Simon's need for immediate profits makes the performance measure choice of weekly profit easy. In thinking through the situation, Simon concludes that, all else considered, setting the wholesale pie price is his most critical decision. Simon's marketing plan precludes altering the size or the quality of its pies, and the grocery stores merely mark up their pie cost (Simon's wholesale price). Thus, quantities, and hence costs, of pies sold are determined by Simon's (wholesale) pie price. From this Simon concludes that price of the apple pies is the decision variable and that, plus the cost parameters, will determine Simon's profit.

STEP 2: FORMULATION

Recall, model formulation is defining the model's input and output variables comprising the black box picture of the model. Simon begins by defining a black box diagram shown in Figure 2.1. To do this he worked backward from his weekly profit performance measure to define his model's conceptual elements. The cost parameters consist of Simon's monthly fixed overhead cost including monthly rent, monthly interest expense on a commercial loan, and so forth; the unit cost per pie of fruit and dough; and the unit cost of pie processing, which includes pie baking, packaging, and delivery.

The next step below is model building, developing the logic inside the black box. Many managers experience "modeler's block" at this point, a curse in every way similar to writer's block. The cure to each is the same: start writing. Because model building is iterative, first attempts will be revised many times before a satisfactory model is developed; the trick is to start.

Some managers new to modeling find Influence Diagrams useful to help further structure their formulation, and coincidentally break through modeler's block. Influence Diagrams provide a good way to organize an approach to modeling and have the side benefit of beginning the model documentation useful in communicating its ideas to others. An

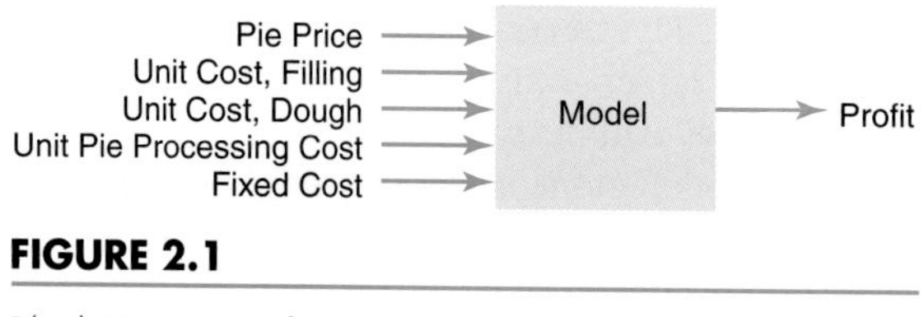

FIGURE 2.1

Black Box View of Simon Pie Model

Influence Diagram pictures the connections between the model's exogenous variables and a performance measure, but postpones defining the model's mathematical logic. An Influence Diagram is created by starting with a performance measure variable. (If there are multiple performance measures, pick one of them.) Then decompose the performance measure variable into two or more **intermediate variables** that combine mathematically in the model to define the value of that performance measure. These intermediate variables will eventually reside inside the black box logic of the model. Next, further decompose each of the intermediate variables into still more related intermediate variables. This decomposition process continues until an exogenous variable is defined, that is, until you pop out of the black box by defining an input decision variable or a parameter.

There are no hard and fast rules for how much detail to include in an Influence Diagram; its purpose is to aid the start of model building and facilitate communications about the model to others, not to completely identify every intermediate variable in the final model. Later, during model development appropriate details will emerge as more of the logic is formalized. Let us illustrate this process for Simon Pie.

Starting with the performance measure, weekly Profit, Simon defines its two components, Revenue and Total Cost. In turn, Simon decomposes each of these two intermediate variables into constituent parts, and in turn, each of them into parts, and so on, as shown in Figure 2.2. Simon's diagramming stops when all the model's input variables are defined.

Inspection of Figure 2.1 and Figure 2.2 reveals a lot about Simon's thinking. Not only does it include the factors he considers relevant for turning pies into profits, but by excluding other factors, the diagram represents his business world view as a selective representation of reality. For example, the diagram makes clear that neither competitor reactions nor the general economy are relevant to his profits, at least in the short run. Also, there are no inventories, presumably because pies are baked and sold fresh. Working capital and other cash flow variables are missing, and so must not materially affect his profits. The details of procurement, baking schedules, deliveries, spoilage, marketing, and human resources are all missing. Of course, he may be planning to add these and other factors in later iterations of the modeling process in order to simplify the initial model, a wise tactic.

FIGURE 2.2

Simon Pie Model Influence Diagram

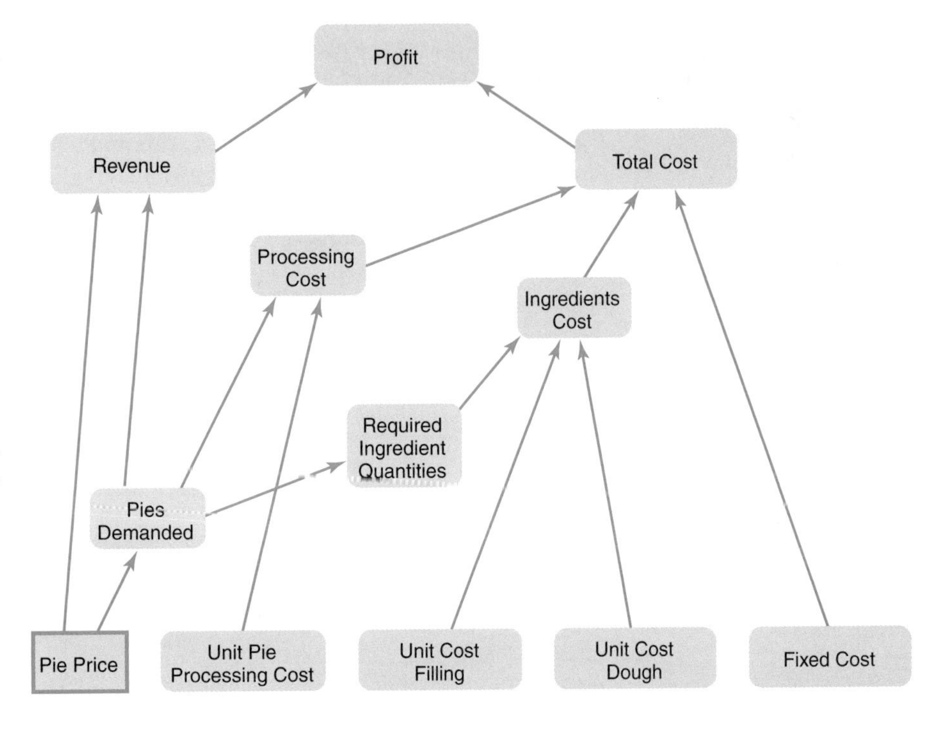

TIP: *Diagrams, such as this, are easily constructed in Excel by switching to a new worksheet, turning "grid lines" off, and displaying Excel's Drawing Toolbar. Selecting its tools, modifiers, and options allows a surprisingly rich array of drawings to be built. For example, the decision variable, Pie Price, is indicated by a square box, while all the other variables use a rounded box. You are free to adopt whatever conventions aid you in modeling and documentation.*

FIGURE 2.3

Initial Simon Pie Weekly Profit Model

	A	B	C
1	**Simon Pie Co. -- Weekly Profit Model**		
2	**Decision Variable:**		
3	Pie Price	$8.00	
4	Pies Demanded & Sold (000's per week)	16	
5			
6	**Parameters:**		
7	Unit Pie Processing Cost ($ per pie)	$2.05	
8	Unit Cost, Fruit Filling ($ per pie)	$3.48	
9	Unit Cost, Dough ($ per pie)	$0.30	
10	Fixed Cost ($000's per week)	$12	
11			
12	**Financial Results ($000's per week)**		
13	Revenue	$128	
14	Processing Cost	$33	
15	Ingredients Cost	$60	
16	Overhead Cost	$12	
17	Total Cost	$105	
18	Profit (before tax)	$23	
19			

	A	B	C
1	**Simon Pie Co. -- Weekly Pro**		
2	**Decision Variable:**		
3	Pie Price	8	
4	Pies Demanded & Sold (0(	16	
5			
6	**Parameters:**		
7	Unit Pie Processing Cost (	2.05	
8	Unit Cost, Fruit Filling ($ pe	3.48	
9	Unit Cost, Dough ($ per pie	0.3	
10	Fixed Cost ($000's per wee	12	
11			
12	**Financial Results ($000's pe**		
13	Revenue	=B4*B3	
14	Processing Cost	=B7*B4	
15	Ingredients Cost	=(B8+B9)*B4	
16	Overhead Cost	=B10	
17	Total Cost	=SUM(B14:B16)	
18	Profit (before tax)	=B13-B17	
19			

TIP: *Cell indentations are created by clicking one of the Increase/Decrease Indent tools in the Excel Formatting Toolbar:*

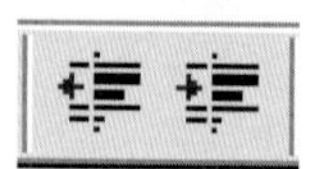

See Appendix B, Excel Features Useful for Modeling for coverage of these and other formatting options.

TIP: *Since printing the formulas for a worksheet usually requires considerable reformatting of fonts and column widths, it is easier to Copy the entire worksheet containing your model to a new sheet in the workbook via the Move or Copy Sheet item under the Edit menu. Then, display the formulas for that copied sheet (a check box in the View tab of the Options item in the Tools menu) and format for appearance. However, do this only after the model building is completed because there is no "hot link" between the two worksheets: If later you change a formula in the original worksheet, you must remember to re-copy its cells to the second formula sheet. See Appendix B for additional tips on displaying a worksheet's formulas.*

STEP 3: MODEL CONSTRUCTION

The third step, building the model, requires the equations relating the variables to be specified in the spreadsheet. If written out, most of Simon's equations would be straightforward accounting relationships:

$$\text{Profit} = \text{Revenue} - \text{Total Cost}$$

$$\text{Revenue} = \text{Pie Price} * \text{Pies Demanded}$$

$$\text{Total Cost} = \text{Processing Cost} + \text{Ingredients Cost} + \text{Fixed Cost}$$

$$\text{Processing Cost} = \text{Pies Demanded} * \text{Unit Pie Processing Cost}$$

$$\text{Ingredients Cost} = \text{Qty Filling} * \text{Unit Cost Filling} + \text{Qty Dough} * \text{Unit Cost Dough}$$

Figure 2.3 presents the Excel worksheet of Simon's weekly profit model. The results are computed for the Simon's assessment of the relevant parameter values listed in Table 2.1.

Notice how the model is represented in Excel. It is systematically organized and presented to make model interpretation easy. In general spreadsheet models should adhere to the following recommendations:

1. Input variables are presented together and labeled.
2. Model results are clearly labeled.
3. The units of measure are given where appropriate.
4. Parameters are stored in separate cells as data and referred to in formulas by cell references. Placing parameters outside of formulas that use them aids model modification, analysis, and documentation.
5. Bold fonts, cell indentations, cell underlines, and other Excel formatting options are used to facilitate interpretation.

The three steps outlined above are an example of model building discussed in Chapter 1. Next, Simon moves to stage two of modeling, analyzing the model to produce results.

Table 2.1

Simon's Initial Model Input Values

Pie Price	$8.00
Pies Demanded and Sold	16
Unit Pie Processing Cost ($ per pie)	$2.05
Unit Cost, Fruit Filling ($ per pie)	$3.48
Unit Cost, Dough ($ per pie)	$0.30
Fixed Cost ($000's per week)	$12

FIGURE 2.4

Two "What if?" Projections for Simon Pie Model

	A	B
1	**Simon Pie Co. -- Weekly Profit Model**	
2	**Decision Variable:**	
3	Pie Price	$7.00
4	Pies Demanded & Sold (000's per week)	20
5		
6	**Parameters:**	
7	Unit Pie Processing Cost ($ per pie)	$2.05
8	Unit Cost, Fruit Filling ($ per pie)	$3.48
9	Unit Cost, Dough ($ per pie)	$0.30
10	Fixed Cost ($000's per week)	$12
11		
12	**Financial Results ($000's per week)**	
13	Revenue	$140
14	Processing Cost	$41
15	Ingredients Cost	$76
16	Overhead Cost	$12
17	Total Cost	$129
18	Profit (before tax)	$11

	A	B
1	**Simon Pie Co. -- Weekly Profit Model**	
2	**Decision Variable:**	
3	Pie Price	$9.00
4	Pies Demanded & Sold (000's per week)	12
5		
6	**Parameters:**	
7	Unit Pie Processing Cost ($ per pie)	$2.05
8	Unit Cost, Fruit Filling ($ per pie)	$3.48
9	Unit Cost, Dough ($ per pie)	$0.30
10	Fixed Cost ($000's per week)	$12
11		
12	**Financial Results ($000's per week)**	
13	Revenue	$108
14	Processing Cost	$25
15	Ingredients Cost	$45
16	Overhead Cost	$12
17	Total Cost	$82
18	Profit (before tax)	$26

"WHAT IF?" PROJECTION

The simplest analysis applied to spreadsheet models is to project the consequences of alternative inputs, called **"What if?" projection.**[1] A "What if?" projection is exactly what the name suggests. Simon wants to know what happens to some endogenous output variable of interest if some characteristic of his environment (a parameter) or his decision variable changes in a specified way. Obviously, such questions are fundamental to any management task, and hence, "What if?" projection is by far the most popular use made of spreadsheet models. Using "What if?" projection, Simon may examine the Profit consequences of changes in his assumptions and/or decisions. Figure 2.4 shows different snapshot results of two of Simon's "What if?" questions, the Profit for Pie Price amounts of $7.00 and $9.00, and Pies Demanded of 20 and 12 thousand, respectively.

REFINING THE MODEL

In reviewing the model as it compares to the influence diagram of Figure 2.2, Simon notices that his model treats Pie Price and Pies Demanded as if they were independent of each other. He realizes this is unrealistic, as all else equal, high Pie Price should be coupled to low Pies Demanded. Thus, he has not linked Pies Demanded to Pie Price as indicated in his influence diagram. Linking Pies Demanded to Pie Price via an equation requires some thought, as this is not just an obvious accounting relationship. The simplest equation relating two variables is a linear one, in this case one that must have an inverse relationship. That is, the demand for pies should be a function of pie price with higher prices producing lower demand (sales). After some reflection, Simon concludes that at a Pie Price of $12 there would be no demand for his pies and that below a $12 price he would gain an additional 4,000 pies sold per week for each $1.00 reduction in price. So, for simplicity, he assumes that the demand relationship is expressed by a linear equation, producing the following equation for Simon's weekly pie demand in thousands of pies:

$$\text{Pies Demanded} = 48 - 4 * \text{Pie Price, valid for Pie Price between \$0 and \$12.}$$

Figure 2.5 shows the refined Simon Pie model incorporating the endogenous variable Pies Demanded as a linear function of Pie Price. The same rules 1 to 5 above have been followed for consistency and clarity in the Excel model, except a sixth recommendation is now added:

6. The physical results should be separated from the financial or economic results.

[1] Some modelers call this "forecasting," but we prefer to reserve that term for use with probabilistic models.

FIGURE 2.5

Simon Pie Model with Pies Demanded Related to Pie Price

	A	B
1	**Simon Pie Co. -- Weekly Profit Model**	
2	**Decision Variable:**	
3	Pie Price	$8.00
4	**Parameters:**	
5	Unit Pie Processing Cost ($ per pie)	$2.05
6	Unit Cost, Fruit Filling ($ per pie)	$3.48
7	Unit Cost, Dough ($ per pie)	$0.30
8	Fixed Cost ($000's)	$12
9	Equation Coefficients	
10	Pie Demand Equation	
11	Intercept	48
12	Slope (Linear Coefficient)	-4
13	**Physical Results (000's per week)**	
14	Pies Demanded & Sold	16.0
15	**Financial Results ($000's per week)**	
16	Revenue	$128
17	Processing Cost	$33
18	Ingredients Cost	$60
19	Overhead Cost	$12
20	Total Cost	$105
21	Profit (before tax)	$22.7
22		

	A	B
1	**Simon Pie Co. -- Weekly Profi**	
2	**Decision Variable:**	
3	Pie Price	8
4	**Parameters:**	
5	Unit Pie Processing Cost ($	2.05
6	Unit Cost, Fruit Filling ($ per	3.48
7	Unit Cost, Dough ($ per pie)	0.3
8	Fixed Cost ($000's)	12
9	Equation Coefficients	
10	Pie Demand Equation	
11	Intercept	48
12	Slope (Linear Coefficient	-4
13	**Physical Results (000's per w**	
14	Pies Demanded & Sold	=B11+B12*B3
15	**Financial Results ($000's per**	
16	Revenue	=B14*B3
17	Processing Cost	=B5*B14
18	Ingredients Cost	=(B6+B7)*B14
19	Overhead Cost	=B8
20	Total Cost	=SUM(B17:B19)
21	Profit (before tax)	=B16-B20
22		

As before Simon can now perform "What if?" projections on his revised model. Although straightforward, "What if?" projection in Excel suffers from several shortcomings:

- Unless separate snapshot printouts are made, the results of a new "What if?" question overwrites the results of any previous one when the worksheet recalculates for the new input, thereby making comparisons difficult;
- It is hard to "see" or "get a feel" for the sensitivity of any change in one variable upon another while reviewing only one "What if?" result at a time; and
- Analysis of the model by repeated "What if?" projections is somewhat haphazard.

Fortunately, Simon has conserved his use of worksheet columns in his Excel model. In the case that the model is contained in a single column, the most general way to tabulate multiple "What if?" projections is by copying the model into adjacent columns, one column for each "What if?" projection.[2] In effect, each column becomes a copy of the original model, allowing the consequences of multiple changes in data values to be compared and contrasted, as illustrated in Figure 2.6. Also, in the case of a systematic change in a single variable, this layout of the model is suited for using Excel's Chart Wizard to produce insightful graphs of results for sensitivity analysis and for communicating Simon's results to others. In this example, from the graph it is easy to verify that the performance measure, Profit, is largest at a Pie Price of about $9.00[3] and that the **break-even point** of zero Profit occurs at a Pie Price of about $6.25. It also appears to Simon from the chart that Profit is not very sensitive to Pie Price in the neighborhood around Pie Price of $9.00.

To explore this further, Simon copies the original model to a new worksheet for further analysis. First, he decides that the Pie Price of $9.00 will be his base case for doing sensitivity analysis. Recall that **sensitivity analysis** examines the effect (small) changes in a given input variable has upon another variable, usually a performance measure. In this case Simon is interested in the effect of small Pie Price changes upon his Profit performance measure. To avoid getting lost in the numbers, he elects to examine the effect a given percentage change in Pie Price has upon the percentage change in Profit, an approach familiar

---

[2] If the model already occupies several columns, then Excel's report generator, the Scenario Manager, is an alternative way to generate multiple scenarios.

[3] Further analysis reveals that Profit is about $.07 thousand higher if Pie Price is closer to $8.90, but such precision is often not appropriate.

FIGURE 2.6

Alternative Pie Price Projections, Simon Pie Model

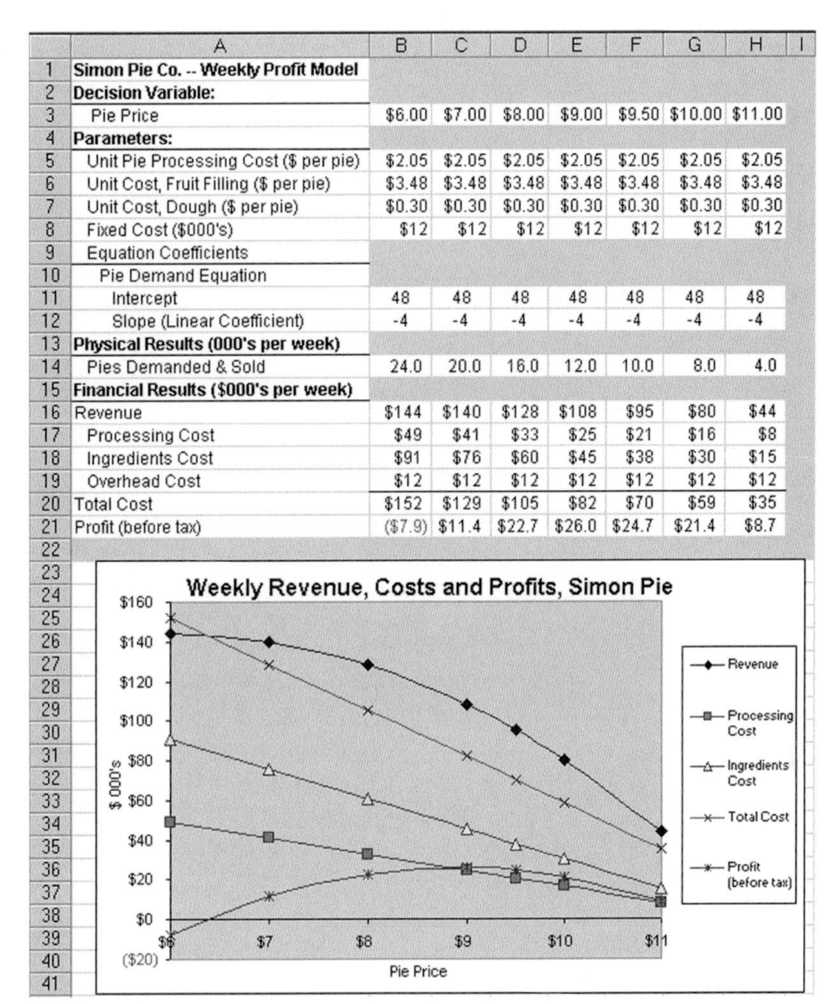

	A	B	C	D	E	F	G	H
1	**Simon Pie Co. -- Weekly Profit Model**							
2	**Decision Variable:**							
3	Pie Price	$6.00	$7.00	$8.00	$9.00	$9.50	$10.00	$11.00
4	**Parameters:**							
5	Unit Pie Processing Cost ($ per pie)	$2.05	$2.05	$2.05	$2.05	$2.05	$2.05	$2.05
6	Unit Cost, Fruit Filling ($ per pie)	$3.48	$3.48	$3.48	$3.48	$3.48	$3.48	$3.48
7	Unit Cost, Dough ($ per pie)	$0.30	$0.30	$0.30	$0.30	$0.30	$0.30	$0.30
8	Fixed Cost ($000's)	$12	$12	$12	$12	$12	$12	$12
9	Equation Coefficients							
10	Pie Demand Equation							
11	Intercept	48	48	48	48	48	48	48
12	Slope (Linear Coefficient)	-4	-4	-4	-4	-4	-4	-4
13	**Physical Results (000's per week)**							
14	Pies Demanded & Sold	24.0	20.0	16.0	12.0	10.0	8.0	4.0
15	**Financial Results ($000's per week)**							
16	Revenue	$144	$140	$128	$108	$95	$80	$44
17	Processing Cost	$49	$41	$33	$25	$21	$16	$8
18	Ingredients Cost	$91	$76	$60	$45	$38	$30	$15
19	Overhead Cost	$12	$12	$12	$12	$12	$12	$12
20	Total Cost	$152	$129	$105	$82	$70	$59	$35
21	Profit (before tax)	($7.9)	$11.4	$22.7	$26.0	$24.7	$21.4	$8.7

TIP: *For modeling purposes it is recommended that you use Chart Wizard's XY (Scatter) chart type for graphing, as it is the only chart that actually plots Y versus X according to their respective values. For example, other chart types will distort the chart's true appearance if X-axis data are not evenly spaced. See Appendix B for additional information on using Excel's Chart Wizard.*

to students of elasticity analysis in Economics. He inserts additional rows into the original model to allow calculating the percentages as shown in Figure 2.7 in which the Split command in Excel's Window menu has been used to hide unnecessary detail in the original model. Be sure to note Simon's use of Absolute Addressing in his percentage formulas so that his formulas always refer to the base case cells when he copies the percentage change formula to new cells.

The sensitivity analysis in Figure 2.7 reveals an important insight to Simon: A small 5% decrease in Pie Price from the base case produces a substantial increase in Pies Demanded and Sold (15%) with very little sacrifice in weekly profit (less than 2% Profit loss). Indeed, Simon might prefer to set Pie Price at $8.10 or 10% less than the base case, thereby sacrificing about 10% in Profit in order to achieve a 30% increase in weekly volume of Pies Sold. This might be especially attractive to him because of his company's start-up status, which suggests he might want to build market volume and thus customer awareness quickly. Such considerations are often called **trade-off analysis** because they reflect how much of one performance measure (Profit) must be sacrificed to achieve a given improvement in another performance measure (Pies Demanded and Sold).

In summary, Simon started this example deductively from simple relationships suggested by his Influence Diagram, and after some analysis, he enriched it to include a

FIGURE 2.7

Sensitivity Analysis of the Simon Pie Model

	A	B	C	D	E	F	G	H
1	**Simon Pie Co. -- Weekly Profit Model**							
2	**Decision Variable:**				Base Case			
3	% Change from $9.00 Base Price	85%	90%	95%	100%	105%	110%	115%
4	Pie Price	$7.65	$8.10	$8.55	$9.00	$9.45	$9.90	$10.35
14	**Physical Results (000's per week)**							
15	Pies Demanded & Sold	17.4	15.6	13.8	12.0	10.2	8.4	6.6
16	% Change from Base Demand	45.0%	30.0%	15.0%	100%	-15.0%	-30.0%	-45.0%
17	**Financial Results ($000's)**							
18	Revenue	$133	$126	$118	$108	$96	$83	$68
19	Processing Cost	$36	$32	$28	$25	$21	$17	$14
20	Ingredients Cost	$66	$59	$52	$45	$39	$32	$25
21	Overhead Cost	$12	$12	$12	$12	$12	$12	$12
22	Total Cost	$113.4	$102.9	$92.5	$82.0	$71.5	$61.0	$50.5
23	Profit (before tax)	$19.67	$23.41	$25.54	$26.04	$24.92	$22.19	$17.83
24	% Change from Base Profit	-24.5%	-10.1%	-1.9%	100%	-4.3%	-14.8%	-31.5%
25								

	A	B	C	E	F	G
1	**Simon Pie Co. -- Weekly Pı**					
2	**Decision Variable:**			Base Price		
3	% Change from $9.00 Base Pr	0.85	0.9	1	1.05	1.1
4	Pie Price	=B3*$E$4	=C3*$E$4	9	=F3*$E$4	=G3*$E$4
14	**Physical Results (000's pei**					
15	Pies Demanded & Sold	=B12+B13*B4	=C12+C13*C4	=E12+E13*E4	=F12+F13*F4	=G12+G13*G4
16	% Change from Base Demand	=(B15-$E$15)/$E$15	=(C15-$E$15)/$E$15	1	=(F15-$E$15)/$E$15	=(G15-$E$15)/$E$15
17	**Financial Results ($000's p**					
18	Revenue	=B15*B4	=C15*C4	=E15*E4	=F15*F4	=G15*G4
19	Processing Cost	=B6*B15	=C6*C15	=E6*E15	=F6*F15	=G6*G15
20	Ingredients Cost	=(B7+B8)*B15	=(C7+C8)*C15	=(E7+E8)*E15	=(F7+F8)*F15	=(G7+G8)*G15
21	Overhead Cost	=B9	=C9	=E9	=F9	=G9
22	Total Cost	=SUM(B19:B21)	=SUM(C19:C21)	=SUM(E19:E21)	=SUM(F19:F21)	=SUM(G19:G21)
23	Profit (before tax)	=B18-B22	=C18-C22	=E18-E22	=F18-F22	=G18-G22
24	% Change from Base Profit	=(B23-$E$23)/$E$23	=(C23-$E$23)/$E$23	1	=(F23-$E$23)/$E$23	=(G23-$E$23)/$E$23
25						

TIP: *The Split command in the Window menu can divide the worksheet window horizontally and/or vertically as a way to focus attention of certain groups of cells in the model. See Appendix B for additional information on how to insert and manipulate Window Splits.*

hypothesized relationship inversely linking Pie Price and Pies Demanded. From this he examined the model by doing "What if?" projection, break-even analysis, sensitivity analysis, and finally, trade-off analysis. All of these analyses contributed to the important insights Simon was able to glean from the modeling process.

2.3 EXAMPLE 2—SIMON PIE REVISITED

Although Simon is happy with his initial model from the previous section, he has become troubled. As often happens with an initial model, it appears that his actual weekly pie profits are somewhat less than projected from it. In reviewing the model's behavior for lower pie prices, Simon suspects that the model's Processing Cost formula produces the correct historical cost for the base case of 12,000 Pies Demanded, but not for other values of Pies Demanded. To explore this further, Simon begins to validate this part of his model by collecting actual Processing Cost data from his company for different levels of pie production. This data plus the projected Processing Cost from his initial model (= 2.05 * Pies Demanded) are tabulated and XY (Scatter) charted in Figure 2.8. Clearly, his model's

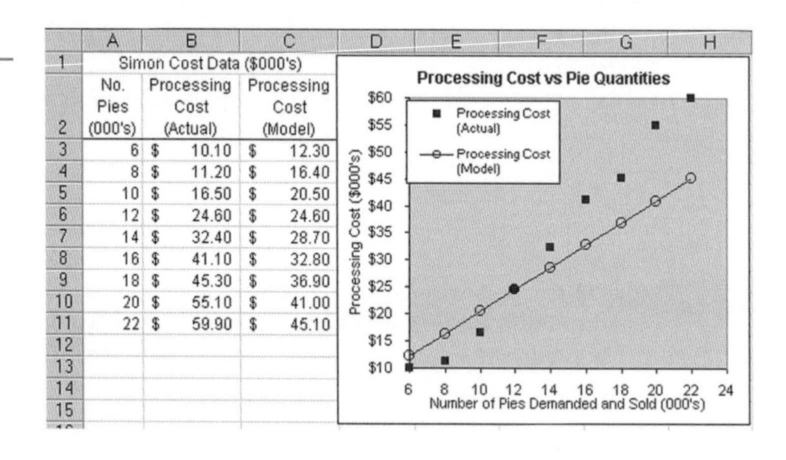

	A	B	C
1	Simon Cost Data ($000's)		
2	No. Pies (000's)	Processing Cost (Actual)	Processing Cost (Model)
3	6	$ 10.10	$ 12.30
4	8	$ 11.20	$ 16.40
5	10	$ 16.50	$ 20.50
6	12	$ 24.60	$ 24.60
7	14	$ 32.40	$ 28.70
8	16	$ 41.10	$ 32.80
9	18	$ 45.30	$ 36.90
10	20	$ 55.10	$ 41.00
11	22	$ 59.90	$ 45.10

FIGURE 2.8

Simon Pie Actual Versus Projected Processing Cost

Processing Cost formula provides a poor fit to the actual Processing Cost data, and this in turn could lead Simon to make poor decisions.

While mathematical deduction or trial-and-error guesswork can be used to develop the logic of a better Processing Cost equation, a simpler way to develop an equation representing the Processing Cost is to use Excel's Trendline capability to fit an equation directly to the actual cost data. To do this Simon selects the Processing Cost (Actual) data points on the XY (Scatter) chart, and clicks the right mouse button to produce the Trendline menu item from the pop-up menu as shown in Figure 2.9.

For simplicity Simon chooses a linear relationship, and before clicking OK, clicks Options to have the Trendline equation display on the chart, as shown in Figure 2.10.

The final equation is presented in Figure 2.11. Of course, a nonlinear Trendline type could have been selected for a better fit to all the data, but Simon wants to keep his model simple for now. By inspection, the new linear trend line is a much better fit to the actual Processing Cost data, at least in the range of Pies Demanded above 8,000, which is the production range Simon learned to focus upon from the sensitivity analysis in Section 2.1.[4]

FIGURE 2.9

Fitting a Trendline to Actual Processing Cost Data

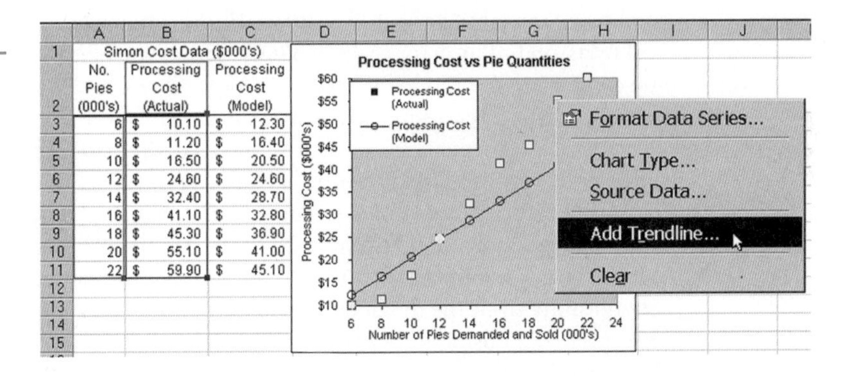

No. Pies (000's)	Processing Cost (Actual)	Processing Cost (Model)
6	$ 10.10	$ 12.30
8	$ 11.20	$ 16.40
10	$ 16.50	$ 20.50
12	$ 24.60	$ 24.60
14	$ 32.40	$ 28.70
16	$ 41.10	$ 32.80
18	$ 45.30	$ 36.90
20	$ 55.10	$ 41.00
22	$ 59.90	$ 45.10

FIGURE 2.10

A Linear Equation Fit to Actual Pie Processing Cost Data

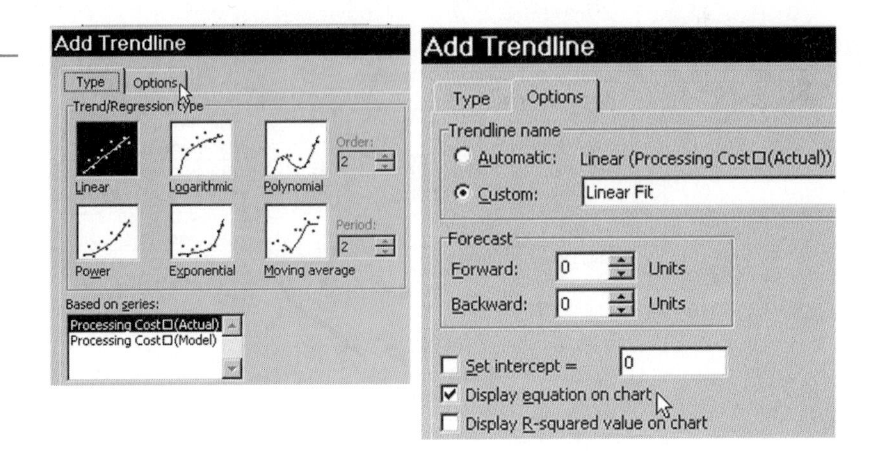

[4] This modeling with data approach for reckoning an equation is appropriate for determining hypothetical relationships or for curves that closely fit the data. In the case of real data, if the fitted curve is not close to all data points, subtle issues of dealing with "noise" in data require use of a probabilistic model for interpreting the fit. This case is postponed until the chapter on Forecasting.

FIGURE 2.11

New Processing Cost Equation

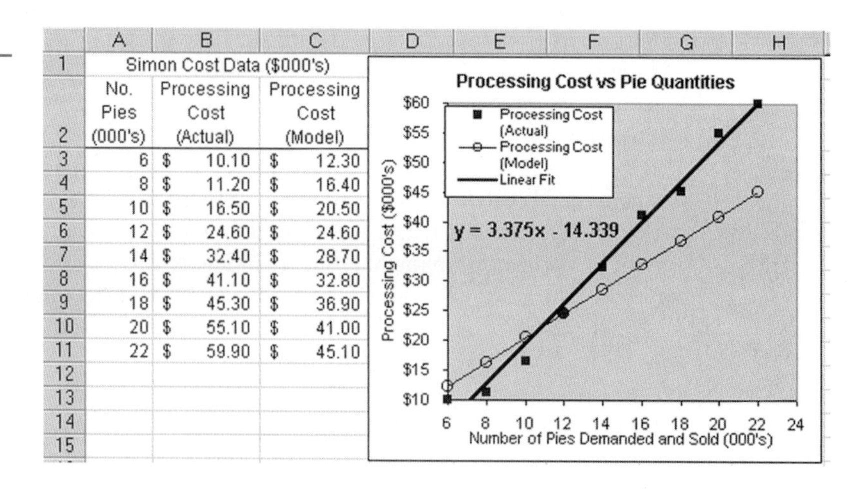

	A	B	C
1	Simon Cost Data ($000's)		
2	No. Pies (000's)	Processing Cost (Actual)	Processing Cost (Model)
3	6	$ 10.10	$ 12.30
4	8	$ 11.20	$ 16.40
5	10	$ 16.50	$ 20.50
6	12	$ 24.60	$ 24.60
7	14	$ 32.40	$ 28.70
8	16	$ 41.10	$ 32.80
9	18	$ 45.30	$ 36.90
10	20	$ 55.10	$ 41.00
11	22	$ 59.90	$ 45.10

Figure 2.12 presents Simon's revised model incorporating the more accurate Processing Cost equation.

As previously in Section 2.1, Simon's revised model is contained in a single column, and so, he can tabulate multiple "What if?" projections by copying the model into adjacent columns, one column for each "What if?" scenario, as shown in Figure 2.13. As can be seen by comparing the results of Figure 2.13 to the sensitivity analysis in Figure 2.7, Simon's more realistic Processing Cost equation has substantially changed his model's results. Surprisingly, the higher costs of this more accurate model have not produced very much change in Simon's weekly Profit, a slight decrease from the earlier maximal Profit of $26.04 to $25.79. In percentage terms, this is a change of only (26.04 – 25.79)/26.04, or less than 1%. But to maintain this revised Profit, Simon must raise his Pie Price (from the previous price of about $9.00 to $9.50, and thus, cut his volume of Pies Demanded and Sold significantly from the previous 12,000 amount to about 10,000, a drop of nearly 17% in his volume of business. Of course, evaluating these less fortunate consequences and gaining such insights is what modeling is all about. Clearly, in this case Simon would benefit if

FIGURE 2.12

Revised Simon Pie Model

	A	B
1	**Simon Pie Co. -- Weekly Profit Model**	
2	**Decision Variable:**	
3	Pie Price	$8.50
4	**Parameters:**	
5	Unit Cost, Fruit Filling ($ per pie)	$3.48
6	Unit Cost, Dough ($ per pie)	$0.30
7	Fixed Cost ($000's)	$12
8	Equation Coefficients	
9	Pie Demand Equation	
10	Intercept	48
11	Slope (Linear Coefficient)	-4
12	Processing Cost Equation	
13	Intercept	-14.339
14	Slope (Linear Coefficient)	3.375
15	**Physical Results (000's per week)**	
16	Pies Demanded & Sold	14.0
17	**Financial Results ($000's per week)**	
18	Revenue	$119
19	Processing Cost	$33
20	Ingredients Cost	$53
21	Overhead Cost	$12
22	Total Cost	$98
23	Profit (before tax)	$21.17

	A	B
1	**Simon Pie Co. -- Weekly Profit**	
2	**Decision Variable:**	
3	Pie Price	8.5
4	**Parameters:**	
5	Unit Cost, Fruit Filling ($ per p	3.48
6	Unit Cost, Dough ($ per pie)	0.3
7	Fixed Cost ($000's)	12
8	Equation Coefficients	
9	Pie Demand Equation	
10	Intercept	48
11	Slope (Linear Coefficient)	-4
12	Processing Cost Equation	
13	Intercept	-14.339
14	Slope (Linear Coefficient)	3.375
15	**Physical Results (000's per we**	
16	Pies Demanded & Sold	=B10+B11*B3
17	**Financial Results ($000's per**	
18	Revenue	=B16*B3
19	Processing Cost	=B13+B14*B16
20	Ingredients Cost	=(B5+B6)*B16
21	Overhead Cost	=B7
22	Total Cost	=SUM(B19:B21)
23	Profit (before tax)	=B18-B22

FIGURE 2.13

Alternative Pie Price Projections, Revised Simon Pie Model

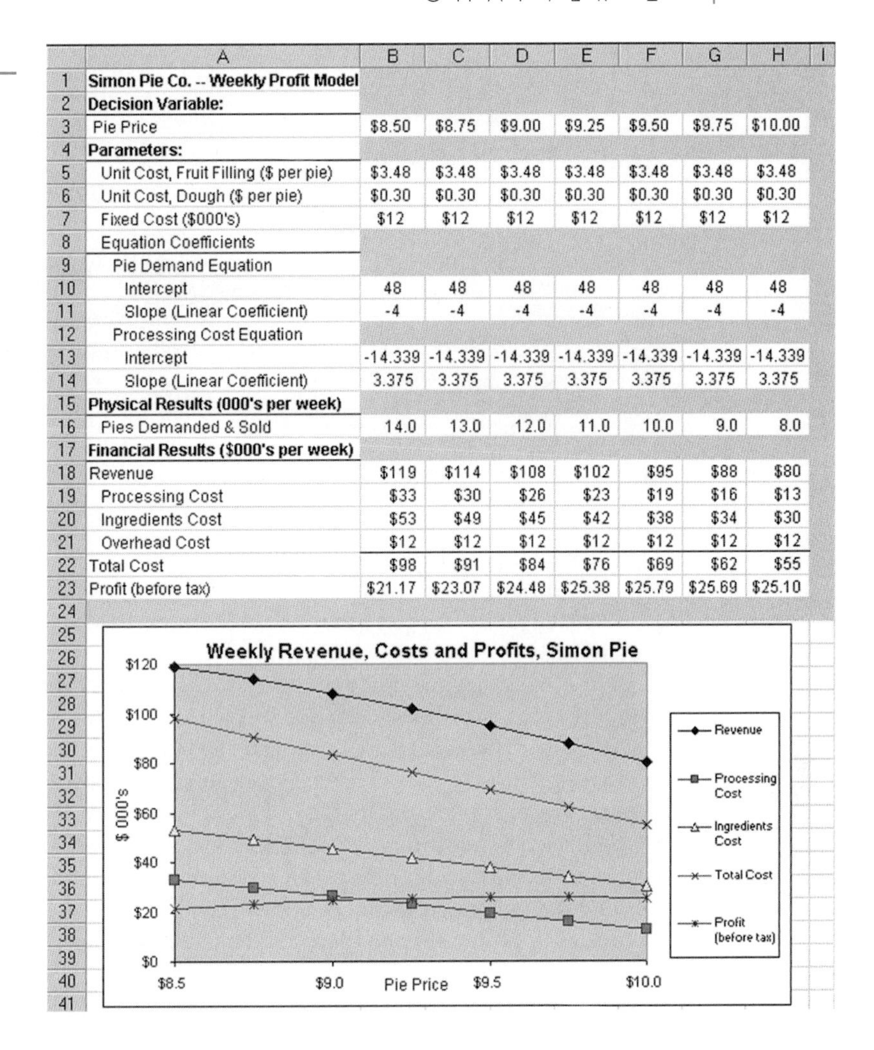

	A	B	C	D	E	F	G	H
1	**Simon Pie Co. -- Weekly Profit Model**							
2	**Decision Variable:**							
3	Pie Price	$8.50	$8.75	$9.00	$9.25	$9.50	$9.75	$10.00
4	**Parameters:**							
5	Unit Cost, Fruit Filling ($ per pie)	$3.48	$3.48	$3.48	$3.48	$3.48	$3.48	$3.48
6	Unit Cost, Dough ($ per pie)	$0.30	$0.30	$0.30	$0.30	$0.30	$0.30	$0.30
7	Fixed Cost ($000's)	$12	$12	$12	$12	$12	$12	$12
8	Equation Coefficients							
9	Pie Demand Equation							
10	Intercept	48	48	48	48	48	48	48
11	Slope (Linear Coefficient)	-4	-4	-4	-4	-4	-4	-4
12	Processing Cost Equation							
13	Intercept	-14.339	-14.339	-14.339	-14.339	-14.339	-14.339	-14.339
14	Slope (Linear Coefficient)	3.375	3.375	3.375	3.375	3.375	3.375	3.375
15	**Physical Results (000's per week)**							
16	Pies Demanded & Sold	14.0	13.0	12.0	11.0	10.0	9.0	8.0
17	**Financial Results ($000's per week)**							
18	Revenue	$119	$114	$108	$102	$95	$88	$80
19	Processing Cost	$33	$30	$26	$23	$19	$16	$13
20	Ingredients Cost	$53	$49	$45	$42	$38	$34	$30
21	Overhead Cost	$12	$12	$12	$12	$12	$12	$12
22	Total Cost	$98	$91	$84	$76	$69	$62	$55
23	Profit (before tax)	$21.17	$23.07	$24.48	$25.38	$25.79	$25.69	$25.10

he could reduce his actual Pie Processing Costs to be closer to his original assumed relationship. Similar analyses could be applied to examine the accuracy of other assumed relationships in his model, such as for ingredients cost or the Pies Demanded and Sold equations.

One consequence of refining a model to include revised equations is the appearance of more technically oriented coefficients in the Excel worksheet. That is, technically oriented parameters begin to appear in the model, which have no counterpart in typical higher-level management reports. To avoid this excessive detail in reporting, many modeler's elect to "bury" these technical coefficient parameters into the worksheet's cell formulas. But this is a violation of the earlier recommendations for good spreadsheet modeling, and moreover, makes it extremely cumbersome to do sensitivity analysis on those parameters. A suggested remedy is use of Excel's little-known Group and Outline options. Group and Outline can be used to suppress technical details by, in effect, temporarily hiding rows or columns containing model details when printing the model for reporting while preserving them in the Excel worksheet for model documentation and analysis. In the revised Simon Pie model the technical coefficient parameters of the two equations, Pie Demand and Processing Cost, can be suppressed for printing reports by selecting their rows and choosing the Group menu item, as shown in Figure 2.14.

FIGURE 2.14

Grouping Rows for Outlining in the Simon Pie Model

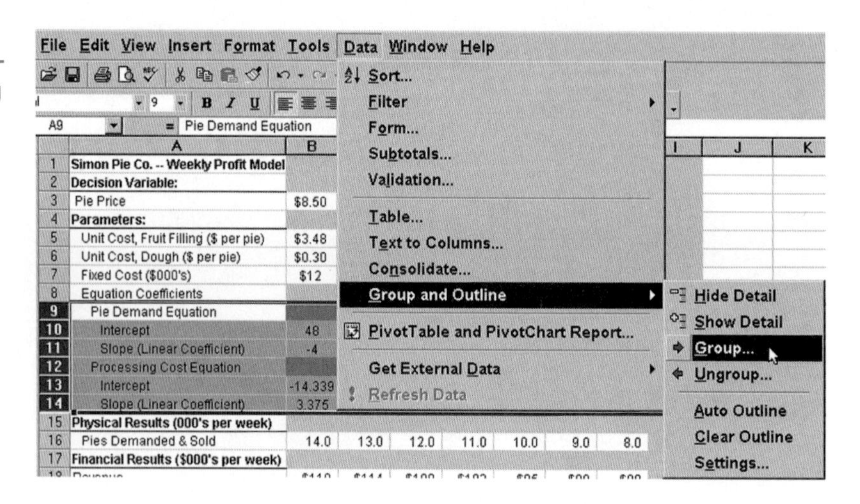

Clicking the "–" button in the outline in Figure 2.15 will collapse, that is, hide, those rows for printing and display.

Clicking the "+" button will reveal the rows again for modeling and analysis, as shown in Figure 2.16.

TIP: *If you group cells comprising a data series that appears in an Excel chart, collapsing the group will also temporarily remove that series from the chart, a handy way to toggle more-detailed data series plots in and out of a chart.*

The Simon Pie model in Figure 2.13 uses columns for replicating the model to allow multiple "What if" projections to be tabulated together for seeing interrelationships and for sensitivity analysis, in this case for several candidate pie prices. In other versions of Simon's model, columns may be designated as time intervals, as shown in Figure 2.17 in which four identical weekly models, except for variations in Pie Price, have been aggregated to produce a consolidated monthly model. For Simon Pie the monthly Total column is created by summation of variables from four nearly identical weekly models. In other settings, however, consolidation is more complicated than simple summations. For example, quantities of interrelated inventories might have to be tracked over time.

FIGURE 2.15

Outlining in Simon Pie Model

	A	B	C	D	E	F	G	H
1	Simon Pie Co. -- Weekly Profit Model							
2	Decision Variable:							
3	Pie Price	$8.50	$8.75	$9.00	$9.25	$9.50	$9.75	$10.00
4	Parameters:							
5	Unit Cost, Fruit Filling ($ per pie)	$3.48	$3.48	$3.48	$3.48	$3.48	$3.48	$3.48
6	Unit Cost, Dough ($ per pie)	$0.30	$0.30	$0.30	$0.30	$0.30	$0.30	$0.30
7	Fixed Cost ($000's)	$12	$12	$12	$12	$12	$12	$12
8	Equation Coefficients							
9	Pie Demand Equation							
10	Intercept	48	48	48	48	48	48	48
11	Slope (Linear Coefficient)	-4	-4	-4	-4	-4	-4	-4
12	Processing Cost Equation							
13	Intercept	-14.339	-14.339	-14.339	-14.339	-14.339	-14.339	-14.339
14	Slope (Linear Coefficient)	3.375	3.375	3.375	3.375	3.375	3.375	3.375
15	Physical Results (000's per week)							
16	Pies Demanded & Sold	14.0	13.0	12.0	11.0	10.0	9.0	8.0

FIGURE 2.16

Collapsed Outline in Simon Pie Example

	A	B	C	D	E	F	G	H
1	Simon Pie Co. -- Weekly Profit Model							
2	Decision Variable:							
3	Pie Price	$8.50	$8.75	$9.00	$9.25	$9.50	$9.75	$10.00
4	Parameters:							
5	Unit Cost, Fruit Filling ($ per pie)	$3.48	$3.48	$3.48	$3.48	$3.48	$3.48	$3.48
6	Unit Cost, Dough ($ per pie)	$0.30	$0.30	$0.30	$0.30	$0.30	$0.30	$0.30
7	Fixed Cost ($000's)	$12	$12	$12	$12	$12	$12	$12
8	Equation Coefficients							
15	Physical Results (000's per week)							
16	Pies Demanded & Sold	14.0	13.0	12.0	11.0	10.0	9.0	8.0

FIGURE 2.17

Simon Pie Monthly Model

	A	B	C	D	E	F
1	**Simon Pie Co. -- Monthly Profit Model**					
2		**Week 1**	**Week 2**	**Week 3**	**Week 4**	**Total**
3	**Decision Variable:**					
4	Pie Price	$9.00	$9.40	$9.10	$9.20	
5	**Parameters:**					
6	Unit Cost, Fruit Filling ($ per pie)	$3.48	$3.43	$3.52	$3.47	
7	Unit Cost, Dough ($ per pie)	$0.30	$0.28	$0.31	$0.30	
8	Fixed Cost ($000's)	$12	$12	$12	$12	
9	Equation Coefficients					
16	**Physical Results (000's per week)**					
17	Pies Demanded & Sold	12.0	10.4	11.6	11.2	45.2
18	**Financial Results ($000's per week)**					
19	Revenue	$108.00	$97.76	$105.56	$103.04	$414.36
20	Processing Cost	$ 26.16	$20.76	$ 24.81	$ 23.46	$ 95.19
21	Ingredients Cost	$ 45.36	$38.58	$ 44.43	$ 42.22	$170.60
22	Overhead Cost	$ 12.00	$12.00	$ 12.00	$ 12.00	$ 48.00
23	Total Cost	$ 83.52	$71.35	$ 81.24	$ 77.69	$313.79
24	Profit (before tax)	$ 24.48	$26.42	$ 24.32	$ 25.36	$100.57
25						

In summary, this example started from the simple Simon Pie deductive model of Example 1 and examined the behavior of an important equation, Processing Cost, against actual data. In general, if actual data are not available, you can substitute hypothetical data that reflect your judgments. From this, Simon was able to apply Excel's Trendline to revise his Processing Cost equation to a different one that was a more accurate representation of his environment. Given additional data, each equation in his original model could be examined in a similar fashion. Next, the revised model can be reanalyzed to do "What if?" projection, sensitivity analysis, or trade-off analysis, as appropriate. In the Simon Pie example, similar iterative procedures would govern Simon's review of other hypothesized relationships in the model, such as for determining ingredients cost equations, or possibly, a more realistic nonlinear pie demand equation.

2.4 EXAMPLE 3—SIMON PIES

Simon's business has become a success, and he is considering the expansion of his business to begin producing and selling additional fruit-based pie types: lemon, strawberry, and cherry. Extending Simon's model to include additional similar products is almost as straightforward as converting his single weekly model to become the four-week monthly model of Figure 2.17. This is because Simon's basic pie products share the same model form, differing only in each pie type's particular parameter values. Thus, it is conceptually no more difficult to model many similar products, or even many similar products over many time periods, because the model form is merely replicated many times followed by a particularization step in which product-specific or time-dependent parameter values are chosen. Often, this is how large (successful) models are built: by replicating the same successful small model into many products and time periods.

Exceptions to this replication of simple models to expand their scope do occur, however. For example, additional cells in a multi-time period model will be devoted to overall consolidation calculations, such as totaling up Simon's weekly results for a monthly summary. In the case of multiple products, in addition to consolidations, sometimes there will be stipulations that apply to all of the products as a group, for example, when they compete for a common scarce resource, such as capital or labor. Fortunately, it is usually straightforward to modify the replicated models to accommodate these new considerations. This will be illustrated by extending Simon's Apple Pie model to include his planned new fruit pie types.

Figure 2.18 shows the results of Simon's modification of his original Apple Pie model to extend it to three additional pie types. In this case each column is devoted to a different pie type, but they differ only in parameter values. To create the model Simon merely copied

FIGURE 2.18

Simon Multiple Pie Types Model

	A	B	C	D	E	F
1	**Simon Pie Co. -- Weekly Profit Model**					
2	**Pie Type**	Apple	Lemon	Strawbry.	Cherry	Total
3	**Decision Variable:**					
4	Pie Price	$9.32	$8.32	$9.57	$9.32	
5	**Parameters:**					
6	Price difference from Apple Pie Price		($1.00)	$0.25	$0.00	
7	Unit Cost, Fruit Filling ($ per pie)	$3.48	$2.20	$3.90	$3.10	
8	Unit Cost, Dough ($ per pie)	$0.30	$0.28	$0.35	$0.33	
9	Fixed Cost ($000's)					$33
10	Equation Coefficients					
11	Pie Demand Equation					
12	Intercept	48	43	50	49	
13	Slope (Linear Coefficient)	-4	-4.4	-4.3	-4.5	
14	Processing Cost Equation					
15	Intercept	-14.34	-11.66	-13.28	-12.30	
16	Slope (Linear Coefficient)	3.38	4.45	3.62	3.25	
17	**Physical Results (000's per week)**					
18	Pies Demanded & Sold	10.7	6.4	8.8	7.1	33.0
19	**Financial Results ($000's per week)**					
20	Revenue	$100	$53	$85	$66	$304
21	Processing Cost	$22	$17	$19	$11	$68
22	Ingredients Cost	$41	$16	$38	$24	$118
23	Total Variable Cost	$62	$33	$56	$35	$186
24	Contribution	$37.5	$20.5	$28.3	$30.9	$117
25	Overhead Cost					$33
26	Profit (before tax)					$84
27						

	A	B	C	D	E	F
1	**Simon Pie Co. -- Weekly F**					
2	**Pie Type**	Apple	Lemon	Strawbry.	Cherry	Total
3	**Decision Variable:**					
4	Pie Price	9.32	=$B$4+C6	=$B$4+D6	=$B$4+E6	
5	**Parameters:**					
6	Price difference from App		-1	0.25	0	
7	Unit Cost, Fruit Filling ($ per p	3.48	2.2	3.9	3.1	
8	Unit Cost, Dough ($ per pie)	0.3	0.28	0.35	0.33	
9	Fixed Cost ($000's)					33
16	Slope (Linear Coefficient)	3.375	4.45	3.62	3.25	
17	**Physical Results (000's pe**					
18	Pies Demanded & Sold	=B12+B13*B4	=C12+C13*C4	=D12+D13*D4	=E12+E13*E4	=SUM(B18:E18)
19	**Financial Results ($000'**					
20	Revenue	=B18*B4	=C18*C4	=D18*D4	=E18*E4	=SUM(B20:E20)
21	Processing Cost	=B15+B16*B18	=C15+C16*C18	=D15+D16*D18	=E15+E16*E18	=SUM(B21:E21)
22	Ingredients Cost	=(B7+B8)*B18	=(C7+C8)*C18	=(D7+D8)*D18	=(E7+E8)*E18	=SUM(B22:E22)
23	Total Variable Cost	=SUM(B21:B22)	=SUM(C21:C22)	=SUM(D21:D22)	=SUM(E21:E22)	=SUM(B23:E23)
24	Contribution	=B20-B23	=C20-C23	=D20-D23	=E20-E23	=SUM(B24:E24)
25	Overhead Cost					=F9
26	Profit (before tax)					=F24-F25
27						

his original Apple Pie model to the new columns. Since he has no operating experience with producing these new pie types, he cannot use data to assess their parameter values, and Simon was thus forced to use his judgment in determining their values. Of course, later when data become available, he can revise parameter values, as was illustrated in Example 2.

Note that a modification was needed to account for his, now higher, fixed overhead costs for rent, interest expense, and so on, estimated to become $33,000 per week. Since this is a fixed cost common to his entire operation and not attributable to the making of any one pie type, Simon has moved it to the right-hand consolidated Totals column.[5] As a con-

[5] Warning: Although common in Financial Accounting reports, one must be very careful in attempting to apportion common fixed costs to individual products for fear of creating a model in which these fixed costs are then mistakenly treated as variable costs. Doing so may lead to irrational decisions. This important topic will receive in-depth coverage in Chapter 3.

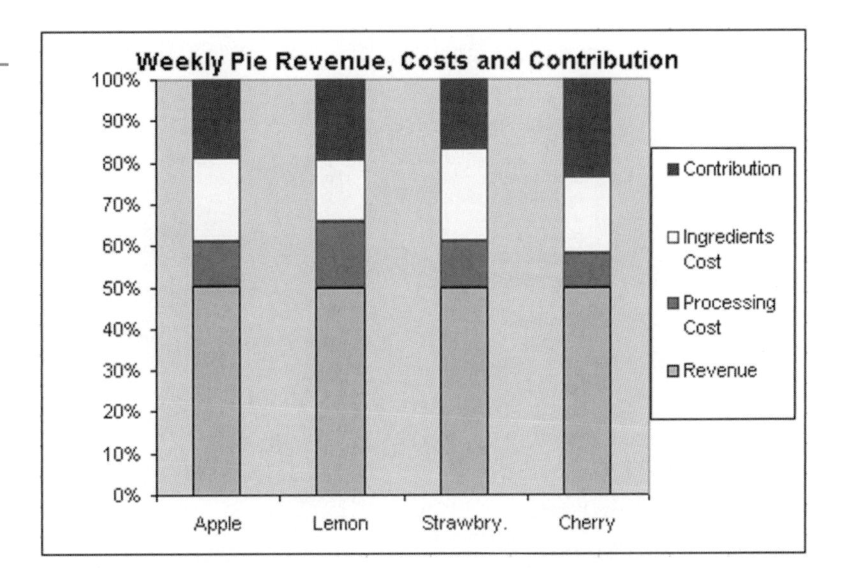

FIGURE 2.19

Stacked Column Plot of Simon's Pie Types Model

sequence, he has had to relabel some of the descriptive labels in the cells of column A. For example, Revenue minus Total Variable Costs is labeled Contribution to conform with Accounting parlance.

Another difference is Simon's treatment of his Pie Price decision variable. Simon knows that Cherry pies sell for the same price as Apple pies, and that Lemon pies sell for $1.00 less, while Strawberry pies sell for $.25 more. Rather than typing these prices individually, he has recorded these price differences as parameters and computed the other pie prices as a function of his Apple Pie price. The reason for this is to simplify sensitivity analysis of the multi-product model, as will become clear later.

While Excel offers many chart types to display results in which the X-axis data are categories, some of them in a "3-D" format that is visually appealing, often the more prosaic column or stacked column chart is most useful for analysis. An example of a Stacked Column chart is given in Figure 2.19 that gives the percentage breakdown of the important costs, and contribution of each pie type in the model of Figure 2.18.

In looking at the model results Simon realizes that he will not have sufficient capacity to produce the projected volume of 33,000 pies per week without introducing a second shift into his plant's weekly schedule. But this will add overtime payments to his Processing Cost and to assess this development, he needs to modify the model. After consulting with his plant manager, Simon concludes that if he introduces the new pie types, he will have capacity to produce a total of 25,000 pies of any type per week. Any total production above that capacity limit will incur second-shift overtime costs that Simon believes will add $.80 to the Processing Cost of any pies produced during a second shift. Since the trigger for a second shift is based upon total pie volume, he reflects this change in the right-hand Total column, as shown in the modified model of Figure 2.20. Note that he has created two new parameters, the capacity limit of 25,000 pies and the overtime processing cost increment of $.80 per pie processed on overtime. For clarity in reporting, he tabulates the Normal Processing Cost as before, and adds a new calculation for the Overtime Processing Cost. This last formula requires an IF() statement to test for Total Pies Demanded and Sold being greater than the capacity limit of 25,000, and if so, applies the $.80 additional unit cost to each pie produced beyond the capacity limit. Finally, this new cost is included in a modified Total Variable Cost formula. As can be seen, the 8,000 pies produced on overtime incur a $6.4 thousand Overtime Processing Cost. Since the Overtime Processing Cost is a variable

FIGURE 2.20

Simon's Pie Types Model with Capacity Limit

	A	B	C	D	E	F
1	**Simon Pie Co. -- Weekly Profit Model**					
2	**Pie Type**	Apple	Lemon	Strawbry.	Cherry	Total
3	**Decision Variable:**					
4	Apple Pie Price	$9.32	$8.32	$9.57	$9.32	
5	**Parameters:**					
6	Price difference from Apple Pie Price		($1.00)	$0.25	$0.00	
7	Unit Cost, Fruit Filling ($ per pie)	$3.48	$2.20	$3.90	$3.10	
8	Unit Cost, Dough ($ per pie)	$0.30	$0.28	$0.35	$0.33	
9	Normal Pie Processing Capicity					25
10	Overtime Pie Processing Cost					$0.8
11	Fixed Cost ($000's)					$33
12	Equation Coefficients					
19	**Physical Results (000's per week)**					
20	Pies Demanded & Sold	10.7	6.4	8.8	7.1	33.0
21	**Financial Results ($000's per weel**					
22	Revenue	$100	$53	$85	$66	$304
23	Normal Processing Cost	$22	$17	$19	$11	$68
24	Overtime Processing Cost					$6.4
25	Ingredients Cost	$41	$16	$38	$24	$118
26	Total Variable Cost	$62	$33	$56	$35	$193
27	Contribution	$37.55	$20.54	$28.32	$30.94	$111
28	Overhead Cost					$33
29	Profit (before tax)					$78
30						

	A	B	C	D	E	F
1	**Simon Pie Co. -- Weekly Profit M**					
2	**Pie Type**	Apple	Lemon	Strawbry.	Cherry	Total
3	**Decision Variable:**					
4	Apple Pie Price	9.32	=$B$4+C6	=$B$4+D6	=$B$4+E6	
5	**Parameters:**					
6	Price difference from Apple Pie Price		-1	0.25	0	
7	Unit Cost, Fruit Filling ($ per pie)	3.48	2.2	3.9	3.1	
8	Unit Cost, Dough ($ per pie)	0.3	0.28	0.35	0.33	
9	Normal Pie Processing Capicity					25
10	Overtime Pie Processing Cost					0.8
11	Fixed Cost ($000's)					33
12	Equation Coefficients					
19	**Physical Results (000's per week**					
20	Pies Demanded & Sold	=B14+B15*B4	=C14+C15*C4	=D14+D15*D4	=E14+E15*E4	=SUM(B20:E20)
21	**Financial Results ($000's per w**					
22	Revenue	=B20*B4	=C20*C4	=D20*D4	=E20*E4	=SUM(B22:E22)
23	Normal Processing Cost	=B17+B18*B20	=C17+C18*C20	=D17+D18*D20	=E17+E18*E20	=SUM(B23:E23)
24	Overtime Processing Cost					=IF(F20>F9,F10*(F20-F9),0)
25	Ingredients Cost	=(B7+B8)*B20	=(C7+C8)*C20	=(D7+D8)*D20	=(E7+E8)*E20	=SUM(B25:E25)
26	Total Variable Cost	=SUM(B23:B25)	=SUM(C23:C25)	=SUM(D23:D25)	=SUM(E23:E25)	=SUM(F23:F25)
27	Contribution	=B22-B26	=C22-C26	=D22-D26	=E22-E26	=F22-F26
28	Overhead Cost					=F11
29	Profit (before tax)					=F27-F28
30						

TIP: *There are other ways to specify conditional expressions than via an IF() statement. For example the formula in cell F24 could equally well have been either of "=MAX(F10*(F20-F9),0)" or "=(F20>F9)*F10*(F20-F9)."*

cost, Simon could have apportioned it to the individual pie type columns, for example, based upon their individual production volumes, but this is not necessary for his aggregate planning purposes.

While Simon is happy with the pie prices, volumes of pies sold, and the contributions of the individual four pie types, he is not satisfied with the profit sacrifice of $6.4 thousand per week, or more than $300,000 per year, that the Processing Overtime Cost extracts. So, he elects to pursue this issue further with sensitivity analysis. In this case Simon is interested (1) to see if some of the overtime cost penalty can be mitigated by raising pie prices, and thus reducing pie demand and also (2) what the profit benefit might be if he could find a way to raise Normal Production Capacity above the 25,000 limit. Since columns of his worksheet are now occupied by the four models of the four pie types, he cannot do sensitivity analysis by copying a single-column model, as was done in Examples 1 and 2. Instead, Simon will use Excel's Data Table command to exercise his model to get the same result.

The **Data Table** command in Excel can be thought of as having Excel systematically batch process whole collections of "What if?" projections at once and then tabulate their results into a rectangular array of cells suitable for charting and sensitivity analysis. In particular, the so-called Data Table 2 option allows two exogenous variables to be varied over specified ranges but tabulates the results only for a single endogenous variable, usually a performance measure. Simon is primarily interested in Total Profit as his performance measure, and so, opts for Data Table 2 analysis, varying one decision variable, Apple Pie Price, and one parameter, Normal Processing Capacity. Since Simon previously related all the other pie prices to Apple Pie Price, this means that varying Apple Pie Price will affect the other pie prices according to their (predetermined) market price differences from Apple Pie Price.

Before evoking Data Table, the ranges of values for the two exogenous variables must be defined in some empty area on the Excel Simon Pies worksheet, as shown in Figure 2.21. Simon has selected Apple Pie prices ranging from $9.30 to $9.90 in increments of $.05 and Normal Processing capacity ranging from 25,000 to 30,000 in increments of 1 thousand. The set of prices is entered as a column of values and the set of capacities as row of values. As documentation, Simon labeled each series with Text Box objects (from Excel's Drawing Toolbar) for future reference.

In the upper-left corner cell, at the intersection of each series, a reference to the single performance measure cell is entered, in this case to F29, Total Profit in the Simon Pies model of Figure 2.20. Next, selecting all the cells in the rectangular range, I3:O16, Simon chooses the Table item in the Data menu. The Table dialog is then displayed, as shown in Figure 2.22. At this point Simon must connect each of the table's two data series to their respective exogenous input variable cells in the Simon Pies model. Since the Normal Processing Capacity series is the "row" series in the table, it is linked to cell F9 in the Simon Pies model of Figure 2.20 via the "Row input cell" in the dialog. Similarly, Apple Pie Price is the "column" series in the table and is linked to cell B4 in the Simon Pies model. Clicking OK causes Excel to take each pair of inputs, place those two values into the two specified input cells in the Simon Pies model, recalculate the worksheet, and place the resulting Profit value into the corresponding cell in the table, as shown in Figure 2.23.

The compact representation of the table allows (1) convenient inspection of the results for finding high profit cells. However, the Data Table 2 representation allows for two other important analyses: (2) examining for possible independence between the two model input variables, and (3) sensitivity analysis. Because of their importance to model analysis in general, each of the three will be discussed separately.

The obvious utility of a Data Table is the ease of inspecting the results in Figure 2.23 looking for high profit combinations of the two input series. That is, for a given column,

FIGURE 2.21

Layout for Simon Pies' Data Table 2 Command

TIP: *The use of Excel's Text Box tool in the Drawing Toolbar is especially useful for documenting the meaning of Data Tables without having to allocate additional rows and columns in the worksheet for that purpose. Also, to save typing, you can use Excel's Fill Series item from the Edit menu or Autofill to enter each range of values. See Appendix B for details on setting up a Data Table for sensitivity analysis, including use of Excel's Text Box tool.*

	H	I	J	K	L	M	N	O
1								
2					Normal Processing Capacity			
3		=F29	25	26	27	28	29	30
4		$9.30						
5		$9.35						
6		$9.40						
7		$9.45						
8	Apple Pie Price	$9.50						
9		$9.55						
10		$9.60						
11		$9.65						
12		$9.70						
13		$9.75						
14		$9.80						
15		$9.85						
16		$9.90						

FIGURE 2.22

Relating Table Row and Column Inputs to Simon's Model

TIP: *The cells specified in the Table dialog must be input variable cells in the worksheet containing numbers, and not intermediate or output cells containing formulas. Also, specifying cell references in Excel dialogs by clicking the worksheet cells produces absolute cell reference addresses in the dialog box. In all cases the use of either absolute or relative cell references in dialogs produces the same results.*

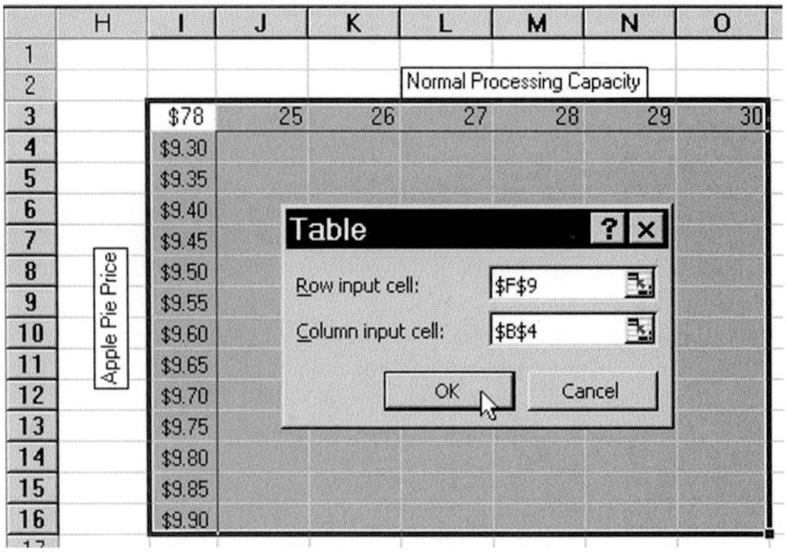

	H	I	J	K	L	M	N	O
1								
2					Normal Processing Capacity			
3		$78	25	26	27	28	29	30
4		$9.30						
5		$9.35						
6		$9.40						
7		$9.45						
8	Apple Pie Price	$9.50						
9		$9.55						
10		$9.60						
11		$9.65						
12		$9.70						
13		$9.75						
14		$9.80						
15		$9.85						
16		$9.90						

Table ? ×

Row input cell: $F$9

Column input cell: $B$4

OK Cancel

examining cells in the data table reveals the profit maximizing Apple Pie Price. Inspection also reveals that in the Simon Pies model for any given Normal Processing Capacity, there is a single Apple Pie Price that maximizes Profit.

A less obvious, but important, second analysis focuses upon what, if any, pattern exists in the set of maximal Profits. That is, Simon is interested to see if the profit maximizing Apple Pie Price is dependent or independent of Normal Processing Capacity.

Fortunately, a graph can "speak a thousand words" regarding such insights by use of a well-designed Excel chart. The Data Table 2 tabulation of Figure 2.23 is complemented by Excel's Chart Wizard for presenting the sensitivity information visually. Selecting the range I3:O16 in Figure 2.23 and choosing Chart Wizard's 3-D Surface chart type produces, after some additional formatting, the plot in Figure 2.24.[6]

FIGURE 2.23

Profit Data Table for Simon Pies' Model

	H	I	J	K	L	M	N	O
1								
2					Normal Processing Capacity			
3		$78	25	26	27	28	29	30
4		$9.30	$77.67	$78.47	$79.27	$80.07	$80.87	$81.67
5		$9.35	$78.31	$79.11	$79.91	$80.71	$81.51	$82.31
6		$9.40	$78.85	$79.65	$80.45	$81.25	$82.05	$82.85
7		$9.45	$79.31	$80.11	$80.91	$81.71	$82.51	$83.31
8	Apple Pie Price	$9.50	$79.69	$80.49	$81.29	$82.09	$82.89	$83.63
9		$9.55	$79.98	$80.78	$81.58	$82.38	$83.18	$83.23
10		$9.60	$80.18	$80.98	$81.78	$82.58	$82.74	$82.74
11		$9.65	$80.29	$81.09	$81.89	$82.17	$82.17	$82.17
12		$9.70	$80.32	$81.12	$81.51	$81.51	$81.51	$81.51
13		$9.75	$80.27	$80.77	$80.77	$80.77	$80.77	$80.77
14		$9.80	$79.94	$79.94	$79.94	$79.94	$79.94	$79.94
15		$9.85	$79.02	$79.02	$79.02	$79.02	$79.02	$79.02
16		$9.90	$78.02	$78.02	$78.02	$78.02	$78.02	$78.02

[6] As with 2-D charts, 3-D charts treat as categorical the data values for the independent variable axes in all non-XY Scatter plot charts. Thus, each input series must have evenly spaced intervals to avoid distortion in the dependent variable plot.

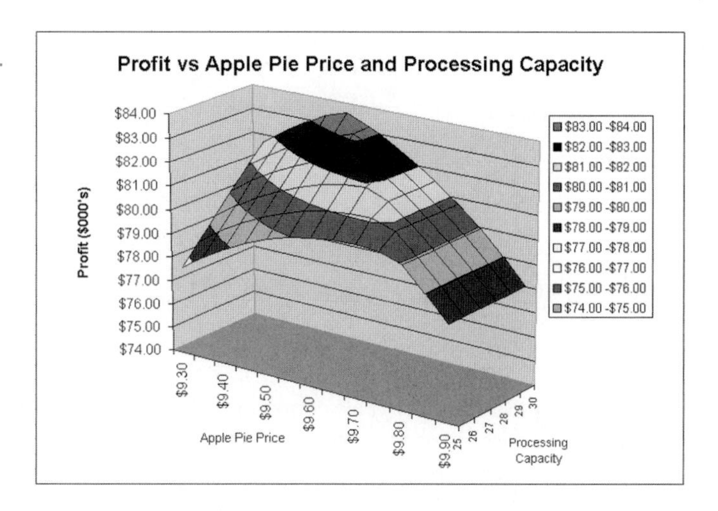

FIGURE 2.24

3-D Surface Chart of Simon Pies' Profit

TIP: *The performance measure cell reference in the upper left-hand corner of the Data Table 2 layout is not a part of either of the data series, Apple Pie Price nor Processing Capacity. Unfortunately, removing this unwanted cell from each of the data series in the chart is troublesome.*

Although Figure 2.24 is visually appealing, sensitivity analysis is difficult to see from 3-D chart contours, and the more prosaic XY Scatter chart is often more valuable for seeing relationships. Figure 2.25 presents an XY Scatter chart of the same data, using one series for each Normal Processing Capacity value. This figure suggests Simon should consider raising his Apple Pie Price from the previous value of $9.38 to at least $9.50 if Normal Processing Capacity is fixed at 25,000 pies. Also as can be seen, for any given Normal Processing Capacity value above about 27,000, Profit is relatively insensitive to Apple Pie Price for prices between $9.50 and about $9.70.

To explore other output consequences of alternative inputs, a Data Table 1 can be used. A Data Table 1 permits only one input variable to vary, but allows tabulating many output consequence variables, not just the one output variable of the Data Table 2. Before evoking Data Table 1, the values of the one exogenous variable must be defined in an empty area on a worksheet. The values may be given in a column or in a row; this example, shown in Figure 2.26, will present the values of Apple Pie Price in a row. Next, each of the endogenous consequence variables of interest is presented in a separate row below the first one. There is no limit to the number of these rows. The column immediately to the left of the exogenous variable row (column I in Figure 2.26) is special. It must contain an empty cell (I22 in this case) for the row containing the values of the exogenous variable. For the remaining rows (I23:I26), a cell reference to a formula cell in the worksheet must be given that computes that row's endogenous output quantity. Optionally, the next column to the left (column H in Figure 2.26) may contain labels. (These labels are for documentation and

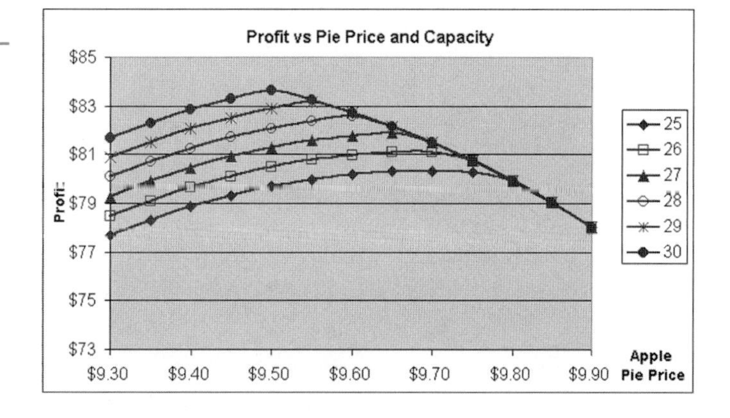

FIGURE 2.25

XY Scatter Chart of Simon Pies' Profit

FIGURE 2.26

Data Table 1 Layout for Simon Pies' Model

	H	I	J	K	L	M	N	O	P	Q	R	S
20												
21							Apple Pie Price					
22			$9.35	$9.40	$9.45	$9.50	$9.55	$9.60	$9.65	$9.70	$9.75	$9.80
23	Pies Demanded and Sold	33.0										
24	Revenue	$304										
25	Overtime Processing Cost	$6										
26	Profit (before tax)	$78										

	H	I	J	K	L	M	N	O	P	Q	R	S
20												
21							Apple Pie Price					
22			9.35	9.4	9.45	9.5	9.55	9.6	9.65	9.7	9.75	9.8
23	Pies Demanded and Sold	=F20										
24	Revenue	=F22										
25	Overtime Processing Cost	=F24										
26	Profit (before tax)	=F29										

are not a part of the Data Table command.) The final layout of the Data Table (called Data Table 1 because only one exogenous input variable is allowed to vary) and its cell formulas is given in Figure 2.26.

Next, select the cells I22:S26, which includes of all the table's rows and the left column cell references to the model, but not the labels in column H, if present, and select the "Table . . ." item from the Data menu as before. Since the exogenous variable's values are given in the first row, the cell reference in the worksheet into which those values are to be placed is indicated in the Table dialog in the "Row input cell:" field, as shown in Figure 2.27. (Conversely, had they been listed in a column, the "Column input cell" field would have been used instead.) Since for Data Table 1, only one input series has been specified, the other input cell dialog box is left empty.

Clicking OK causes the worksheet to be evaluated for each input value of the exogenous input variable, tabulating each of the listed endogenous output variable values from the model for that input value, as shown in Figure 2.28. Thus, the table gives Total Pies Demanded, Total Revenue, Overtime Processing Cost, and Profit for various Apple Pie Prices. Not shown in Figure 2.28 is the Normal Processing Capacity, which on the worksheet was set to the original 25,000 limit. From this table Simon can see that, unless he can raise Normal Processing Capacity, he must raise Apple Pie Price (and thus, other pie prices) if he wishes to reduce his overtime processing costs. In particular, raising the Apple Pie Price to the profit maximizing value of about $9.65 reduces the Overtime Processing Time cost from the original $6.4 thousand per week at an Apple Pie Price of $9.32, to less than $2,000 per week. However, to achieve this, he must reduce the volume of pies sold from 33,000 to about 27,000, approximately a 20% trade-off in reduced business volume.

FIGURE 2.27

Completing the Data Table 1 Dialog for the Simon Pies' Model

	H	I	J	K	L	M	N	O	P	Q	R	S
20												
21							Apple Pie Price					
22			$9.35	$9.40	$9.45	$9.50	$9.55	$9.60	$9.65	$9.70	$9.75	$9.80
23	Pies Demanded and Sold	33.0										
24	Revenue	$304										
25	Overtime Processing Cost	$6										
26	Profit (before tax)	$78										
27												
28												
29												
30												

Table ? X
Row input cell: $B$4
Column input cell:
OK Cancel

FIGURE 2.28

Completed Data Table 1 for the Simon Pies' Model

	G	H	I	J	K	L	M	N	O	P	Q	R
20												
21							Apple Pie Price					
22			$9.35	$9.40	$9.45	$9.50	$9.55	$9.60	$9.65	$9.70	$9.75	$9.80
23	Pies Demanded and Sold	33.0	32.5	31.6	30.8	29.9	29.1	28.2	27.3	26.5	25.6	24.8
24	Revenue	$304	$299.8	$293.5	$287.2	$280.7	$274.2	$267.5	$260.8	$254.0	$247.1	$240.1
25	Overtime Processing Cost	$6	$6.0	$5.3	$4.6	$3.9	$3.3	$2.6	$1.9	$1.2	$0.5	$0.0
26	Profit (before tax)	$78	$78.3	$78.9	$79.3	$79.7	$80.0	$80.2	$80.3	$80.3	$80.3	$79.9

2.5 EXAMPLE 4—XERTECH COPY, INC.

Emily and Bill Peterson have decided to start a company, XerTech Copy, that will place self-service copy machines onto customer premises in libraries, universities, high schools, shopping malls, etc. They plan to keep capital costs to a minimum by leasing heavy-duty copiers that have a self-service coin and smart card reader device attached. In addition to the lease cost and other expenses of the copier, XerTech would pay a fee to the customer organization providing the space for the copier. This fee would consist of a fixed monthly space rent plus, optionally, some incentive payments. As part of their business plan for XerTech, Emily and Bill have made the following assumptions:

Number of Copiers Leased (decision variable)	40
Copies per Month per Copier (decision variable)	30,000
Price Charged per Copy (decision variable)	$.05
Variable Cost per Copy (supplies, repair allowance, etc.)	$.03
Monthly Copier Space Rental Rate (decision variable)	$150
Other Monthly Expenses:	
Lease Cost of Each Copier	$250
Coin Collection Labor per Copier	$35
Miscellaneous Fixed Costs per Copier	$50

They developed the spreadsheet model in Figure 2.29 for analyzing the profitability of their new venture. Similar to the Simon Pie example, the layout of the Petersons' Excel worksheet is in a form we recommend for ease of building, debugging, and interpretation of models. They have (1) placed text labels in many of the rows and columns and (2) included the units of measure for each quantity. Also, the first seven rows present (3) the important exogenous inputs (parameters) to the model. All the formulas use cell references to these parameter cells instead of using the parameter data directly as numbers in the formula equations. The remaining rows constitute (4) the input variable of interest (Copies per Month per Copier), and (5) the main logic of the model, in this case an income statement that produces the output performance measure calculation, Monthly Net Income.

The Petersons are considering several alternative arrangements for copier space rental payments. In addition to offering the option of a fixed monthly space rent of $150 per copier per month, they might prefer to offer their customers a lower space rent plus a per-copy commission payment for each copy made. For example, the customer organization might prefer to receive a space rent of only $50 per month per copier but receive a commission of one-half cent per copy made. A third option being considered is a fixed monthly rent of $75 plus a per copy commission payment of one cent, paid only for that portion of the monthly volume that exceeds a predetermined cutoff, such as 20,000 copies per month. Before announcing these alternative rental schemes, the Petersons are interested in knowing how the break-even volumes for their new venture compare among the three alternatives.

Rather than writing and analyzing each alternative as a separate model in different worksheets, presenting three models, one alternative per column, in a single worksheet is the preferred formulation. This allows immediate managerial comparisons across the major alternatives, as shown in Figure 2.30.

More precise estimates of interesting model outputs can be found by use of Excel's Goal Seek command. **Goal Seek** searches for a value of a single model input variable that yields a given desired value of a single endogenous output variable, typically a performance measure. For example, Goal Seek can be used to find the break-even value for Copies per Month per Copier. First, select the "Goal Seek . . ." item from Excel's Tools menu, as shown in Figure 2.31.

FIGURE 2.29

The First XerTech Spreadsheet

	A	B	C	D	E
1	XerTech Copy Inc.				
2	Average Monthly Expense/Copier		No. of Copiers Leased	40	
3	Monthly Lease Cost	$250.00			
4	Copier Service Cost	$35.00	Price Charged/Copy	$0.05	
5	Other Fixed Costs	$50.00	Variable Cost/Copy	$0.03	
6	Fixed Expense/Copier	$335.00	Contribution Margin	$0.02	
7	Space Rental Rate	$150.00			
8					
9	Copies/Month/Copier	30,000			
10	Monthly Income				
11	Revenue	$60,000			
12	Cost of Goods Sold	$36,000			
13	Contribution Margin	$24,000			
14	General & Admin. Costs	$19,400			
15	Net Income	$4,600			
16					

	A	B	C	D	E
1	XerTech Copy Inc.				
2	Average Monthly		No. of Copiers Leased	40	
3	Monthly Lease Cost	250			
4	Copier Service Cost	35	Price Charged/Copy	0.05	
5	Other Fixed Costs	50	Variable Cost/Copy	0.03	
6	Fixed Expense/Copier	=SUM(B3:B5)	Contribution Margin	=D4-D5	
7	Space Rental Rate	150			
8					
9	Copies/Month/Copier	30000			
10	Monthly Income				
11	Revenue	=$D$2*B9*$D$4			
12	Cost of Goods Sold	=$D$2*B9*$D$5			
13	Contribution Margin	=B11-B12			
14	General & Admin. Co:	=$D$2*($B$6+$B$7)			
15	Net Income	=B13-B14			
16					

By typing the cell references or by clicking the worksheet cell, specify the endogenous output variable cell ("Set cell") as being Net Income, specify the ("To value") cell as the break-even value of zero, select the ("By changing cell") as being monthly copier volume, and click OK, as shown in Figure 2.32.

Excel will systematically iterate the model of Alternative 1 for different Changing Cell input values to achieve the desired output Set Cell result, if possible, as shown in Figure 2.33.[7] In this case, the break-even volume for Alternative 1 is found to be 24,250 copies per month per copier.

Two more applications of Goal Seek to each of the two remaining Net Income cells in C20:D20 produces the required break-even comparisons for the three models, as shown in Figure 2.34.

The Petersons are also interested in the points of indifference in Net Income across the three alternatives. For example, assuming 30,000 copies per month per copier, the original Alternative 1 of fixed rental payment of $150 per month per copier, and the alternative commission rates and cutoff shown in Figure 2.34, what fixed rental rates for each of the

[7] A systematic search is performed, starting from the cell's initial value. If more than one changing cell value produces the desired target value of the output cell, the first one found will stop the Goal Seek search. Discontinuities in the set of values taken on by the Set Cell output variable, caused by, for example, IF() statements or other conditional expressions in a model, may cause Goal Seek to fail to find the answer. Repeated Goal Seeks each with differing initial cell values is the only alternative in this case.

FIGURE 2.30

The Second XerTech Spreadsheet: Three Rental Payment Alternatives

	A	B	C	D
1	**XerTech Copy Inc.**			
2	Average Monthly Expense/Copier		No. of Copiers Rented	40
3	Monthly Lease Cost	$250.00		
4	Copier Service Cost	$35.00	Price Charged/Copy	$0.05
5	Other Fixed Costs	$50.00	Variable Cost/Copy	$0.03
6	Fixed Expense/Copier	$335.00	Contribution Margin	$0.02
7				
8		**Alternative 1**	**Alternative 2**	**Alternative 3**
9		**Fixed Rental Fee**	**Rental Fee + Commission**	**Rental Fee + Commission above Cut Off**
10	Copies/Month/Copier	30,000	30,000	30,000
11	Space Rental Rate	$150.00	$50.00	$75.00
12	Commission Rate		$0.005	$0.01
13	Commission cuts in at			20,000
14	Monthly Income	With No Commission	With Commission	With Commission on Sales>Cut Off
15	Revenue	$60,000	$60,000	$60,000
16	Cost of Copies	$36,000	$36,000	$36,000
17	Commissions Paid		$6,000	$4,000
18	Gross Margin	$24,000	$18,000	$20,000
19	General & Admin. Costs	$19,400	$15,400	$16,400
20	Net Income	$4,600	$2,600	$3,600
21				

TIP: *An IF() statement is another way to implement the conditional expression for calculating Commissions Paid in cell D17.*

TIP: *Formatting a cell to enable Cell Wrapping (under the Alignment tab in the Format Cells dialog) allows long text labels to more efficiently fill a cell without having to resort to over-wide columns. Also, when editing the contents of a wrapped cell text label, you can force a line break by typing Alt-Enter at the point of the break. See Appendix B for more tips on cell formatting.*

	A	B	C	D
1	**XerTech Copy Inc.**			
2	Average Monthly Expense/C		No. of Copiers Rented	40
3	Monthly Lease Cost	250		
4	Copier Service Cost	35	Price Charged/Copy	0.05
5	Other Fixed Costs	50	Variable Cost/Copy	0.03
6	Fixed Expense/Copier	=SUM(B3:B5)	Contribution Margin	=D4-D5
7				
8		**Alternative 1**	**Alternative 2**	**Alternative 3**
9		**Fixed Rental Fee**	**Rental Fee + Commission**	**Rental Fee + Commission above Cut Off**
10	Copies/Month/Copier	30000	30000	30000
11	Space Rental Rate	150	50	75
12	Commission Rate		0.005	0.01
13	Commission cuts in at			20000
14	Monthly Income	With No Commission	With Commission	With Commission on Sales>Cut Off
15	Revenue	=$D$2*B10*$D$4	=$D$2*C10*$D$4	=$D$2*D10*$D$4
16	Cost of Copies	=$D$2*B10*$D$5	=$D$2*C10*$D$5	=$D$2*D10*$D$5
17	Commissions Paid		=$D$2*C10*C12	=(D10>D13)*(D10-D13)*$D$2*D12
18	Gross Margin	=B15-B16-B17	=C15-C16-C17	=D15-D16-D17
19	General & Admin. Costs	=$D$2*($B$6+B11)	=$D$2*($B$6+C11)	=$D$2*($B$6+D11)
20	Net Income	=B18-B19	=C18-C19	=D18-D19
21				

FIGURE 2.31

Goal Seek

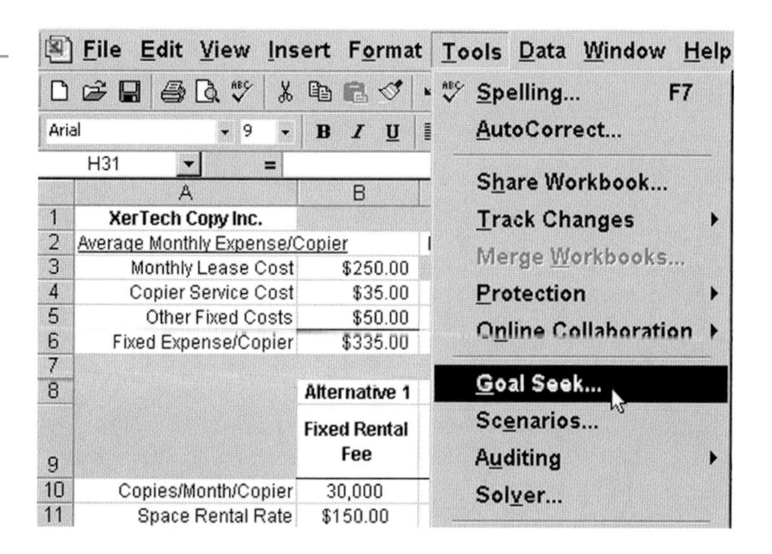

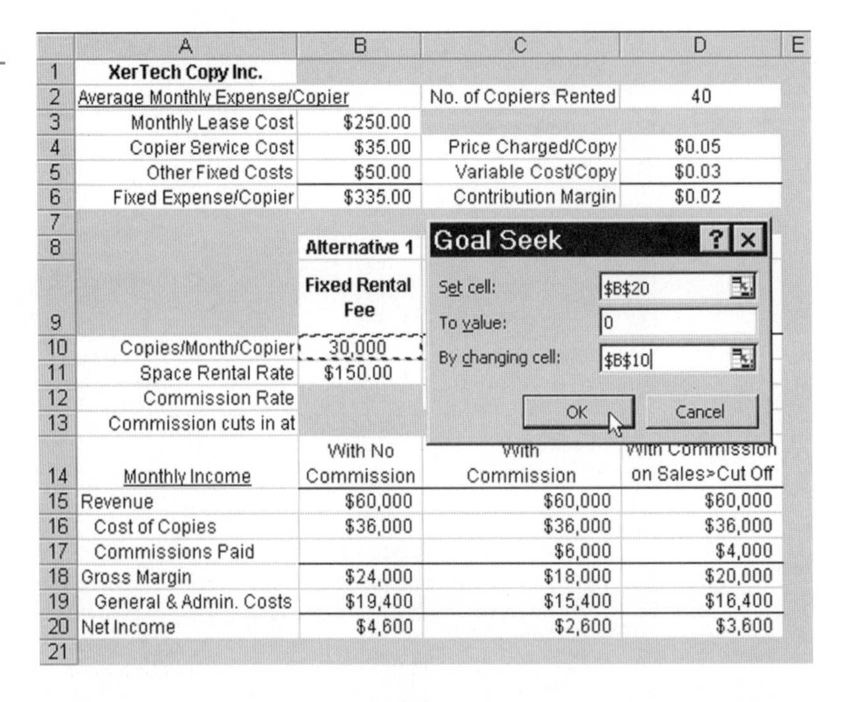

	A	B	C	D
1	XerTech Copy Inc.			
2	Average Monthly Expense/Copier		No. of Copiers Rented	40
3	Monthly Lease Cost	$250.00		
4	Copier Service Cost	$35.00	Price Charged/Copy	$0.05
5	Other Fixed Costs	$50.00	Variable Cost/Copy	$0.03
6	Fixed Expense/Copier	$335.00	Contribution Margin	$0.02
7				
8		Alternative 1		
9		Fixed Rental Fee		
10	Copies/Month/Copier	30,000		
11	Space Rental Rate	$150.00		
12	Commission Rate			
13	Commission cuts in at			
14	Monthly Income	With No Commission	With Commission	With Commission on Sales>Cut Off
15	Revenue	$60,000	$60,000	$60,000
16	Cost of Copies	$36,000	$36,000	$36,000
17	Commissions Paid		$6,000	$4,000
18	Gross Margin	$24,000	$18,000	$20,000
19	General & Admin. Costs	$19,400	$15,400	$16,400
20	Net Income	$4,600	$2,600	$3,600
21				

FIGURE 2.32

Goal Seek Dialog

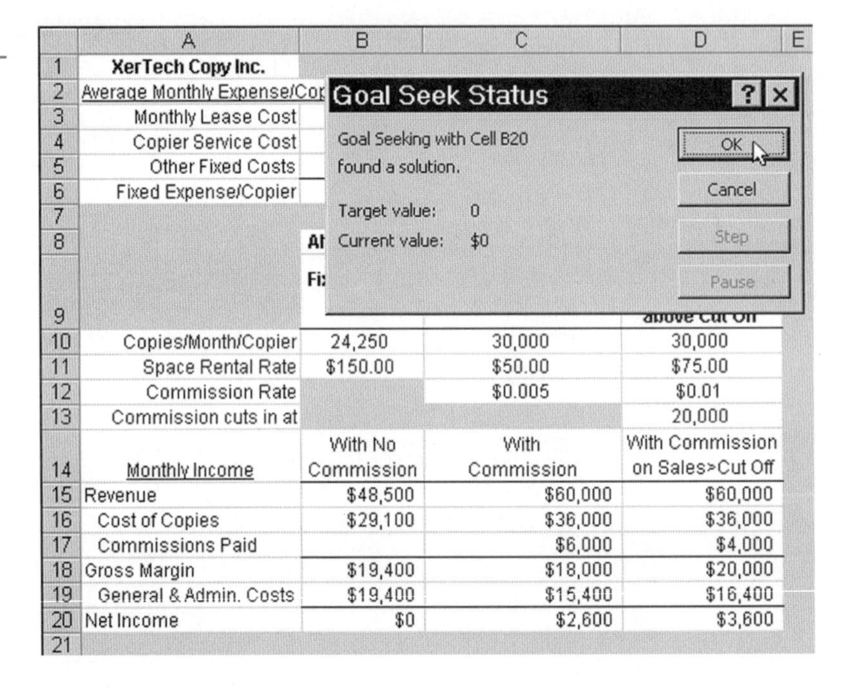

	A	B	C	D
1	XerTech Copy Inc.			
2	Average Monthly Expense/Cop			
3	Monthly Lease Cost			
4	Copier Service Cost			
5	Other Fixed Costs			
6	Fixed Expense/Copier			
7				
8		Al		
9		Fi		above Cut Off
10	Copies/Month/Copier	24,250	30,000	30,000
11	Space Rental Rate	$150.00	$50.00	$75.00
12	Commission Rate		$0.005	$0.01
13	Commission cuts in at			20,000
14	Monthly Income	With No Commission	With Commission	With Commission on Sales>Cut Off
15	Revenue	$48,500	$60,000	$60,000
16	Cost of Copies	$29,100	$36,000	$36,000
17	Commissions Paid		$6,000	$4,000
18	Gross Margin	$19,400	$18,000	$20,000
19	General & Admin. Costs	$19,400	$15,400	$16,400
20	Net Income	$0	$2,600	$3,600
21				

FIGURE 2.33

Monthly Break-Even Volume, Alternative 1

two new alternatives produce indifference in terms of Net Income in comparison to Alternative 1? To answer this question, the Petersons add formulas to the worksheet of Figure 2.30 to subtract the Net Income of Alternative 2 and the Net Income of Alternative 3 from that of Alternative 1, respectively, as shown in Figure 2.35.

This allows reapplication of Goal Seek to find the point of indifference, that is, the point where the difference in Net Income of Alternative 2 compared to Alternative 1 are zero, as shown in Figure 2.36. Goal Seek would be repeated to do the same for finding the point of indifference for Alternative 3 compared to Alternative 1; in this case the Set Cell

FIGURE 2.34

Break-Even Comparisons

	A	B	C	D	E
1	XerTech Copy Inc.				
8		Alternative 1	Alternative 2	Alternative 3	
9		Fixed Rental Fee	Rental Fee + Commission	Rental Fee + Commission above Cut Off	
10	Copies/Month/Copier	24,250	25,667	21,000	
11	Space Rental Rate	$150.00	$50.00	$75.00	
12	Commission Rate		$0.005	$0.01	
13	Commission cuts in at			20,000	
14	Monthly Income	With No Commission	With Commission	With Commission on Sales>Cut Off	
15	Revenue	$48,500	$51,334	$42,000	
16	Cost of Copies	$29,100	$30,800	$25,200	
17	Commissions Paid		$5,133	$400	
18	Gross Margin	$19,400	$15,400	$16,400	
19	General & Admin. Costs	$19,400	$15,400	$16,400	
20	Net Income	$0	$0	$0	
21					

FIGURE 2.35

Calculating Alternatives' Net Income Differences

	A	B	C	D	E
1	XerTech Copy Inc				
14	Monthly Income	With No Commission	With Commission	With Commission on Sales>Cut Off	
15	Revenue	=$D$2*B10*$D$4	=$D$2*C10*$D$4	=$D$2*D10*$D$4	
16	Cost of Copies	=$D$2*B10*$D$5	=$D$2*C10*$D$5	=$D$2*D10*$D$5	
17	Commissions P		=$D$2*C10*C12	=(D10>D13)*(D10-D13)*$D$2*D12	
18	Gross Margin	=B15-B16-B17	=C15-C16-C17	=D15-D16-D17	
19	General & Admir	=$D$2*($B$6+B11)	=$D$2*($B$6+C11)	=$D$2*($B$6+D11)	
20	Net Income	=B18-B19	=C18-C19	=D18-D19	
21		Net Income., Altern.1 - Altern.2	=B20-C20		
22			Net Income., Altern.1 - Altern.3	=B20-D20	
23					

FIGURE 2.36

Finding Space Rent Indifference, Alternative 2 versus Alternative 1

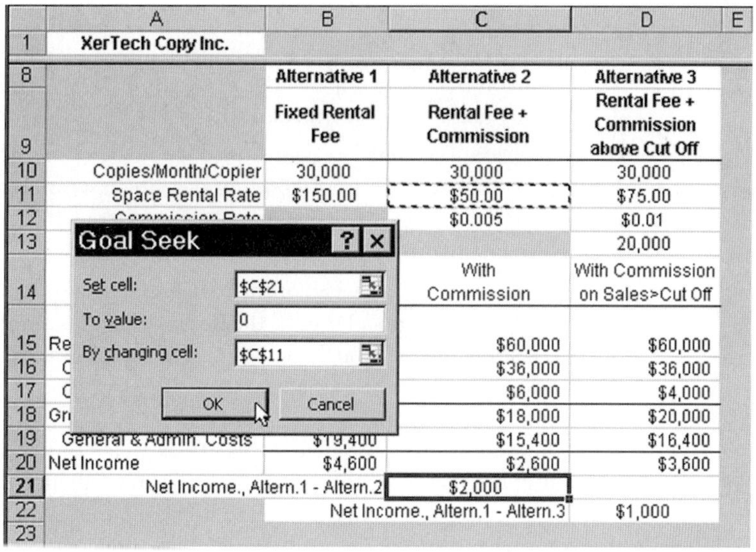

	A	B	C	D	E
1	XerTech Copy Inc.				
8		Alternative 1	Alternative 2	Alternative 3	
9		Fixed Rental Fee	Rental Fee + Commission	Rental Fee + Commission above Cut Off	
10	Copies/Month/Copier	30,000	30,000	30,000	
11	Space Rental Rate	$150.00	$50.00	$75.00	
12	Commission Rate		$0.005	$0.01	
13				20,000	
14			With Commission	With Commission on Sales>Cut Off	
15	Re		$60,000	$60,000	
16	C		$36,000	$36,000	
17	C		$6,000	$4,000	
18	Gr		$18,000	$20,000	
19	General & Admin. Costs	$19,400	$15,400	$16,400	
20	Net Income	$4,600	$2,600	$3,600	
21	Net Income., Altern.1 - Altern.2		$2,000		
22		Net Income., Altern.1 - Altern.3		$1,000	
23					

Goal Seek

Set cell: $C$21

To value: 0

By changing cell: $C$11

OK Cancel

would be D22 and the Changing Cell would be D11. The final result indifference points are shown in Figure 2.37.

While the results in Figure 2.37 would be easy for the Petersons to deduce algebraically for their initial XerTech model, the Goal Seek approach works for more complicated models where the algebra would be much more difficult and error-prone for them to work out.

FIGURE 2.37

Indifference Points for Alternatives 2 and 3

	A	B	C	D
1	**XerTech Copy Inc.**			
8		**Alternative 1**	**Alternative 2**	**Alternative 3**
9		**Fixed Rental Fee**	**Rental Fee + Commission**	**Rental Fee + Commission above Cut Off**
10	Copies/Month/Copier	30,000	30,000	30,000
11	Space Rental Rate	$150.00	$0.00	$50.00
12	Commission Rate		$0.005	$0.01
13	Commission cuts in at			20,000
14	Monthly Income	With No Commission	With Commission	With Commission on Sales>Cut Off
15	Revenue	$60,000	$60,000	$60,000
16	Cost of Copies	$36,000	$36,000	$36,000
17	Commissions Paid		$6,000	$4,000
18	Gross Margin	$24,000	$18,000	$20,000
19	General & Admin. Costs	$19,400	$13,400	$15,400
20	Net Income	$4,600	$4,600	$4,600
21	Net Income., Altern.1 - Altern.2		$0	
22		Net Income., Altern.1 - Altern.3		$0
23				

2.6 THE ART OF MODELING

As you can see from the four examples we have covered thus far, modeling with spreadsheets involves much more than simply reckoning the equations that relate variables. In setting up the model, you must anticipate the kinds of analyses you intend to do and pay a great deal of attention to the layout of the model on the Excel worksheet in order to produce a model that

1. Is logically correct,
2. Presents major alternatives for comparisons,
3. Is suitable for the manipulations necessary to do analyses,
4. Is easily understood by others, and
5. Is pleasing to the eye.

While many of the features of good models are easy to document and describe, as in the four examples, others involve elements of aesthetics that are learned with practice. The basic rules for creating a good spreadsheet model are:

1. Clearly define and label all of the variables;
2. Clearly identify model inputs, the decisions, and parameters;
3. Clearly identify the model outputs, performance measure(s), and consequence variables;
4. Do not "hard wire" parameter values into formulas; store them in separate cells to facilitate documentation and analyses;
5. Where convenient, separate the variables giving physical quantities from those that reflect them into accounting or financial consequences, and
6. Use formatting options of Excel to highlight and indent headings and cell labels to improve the appearance of the model.

We also reviewed the dilemma faced by the modeler who strives for complete documentation of the model's every parameter with the conflicting desire to keep the Excel worksheet representation small and uncluttered with technical details. Two features of Excel were presented to assist in resolving this dilemma: the use of Grouping and Outlining to allow collapsing rows and columns containing unnecessary detail and the use of Split Window to perform a similar function.

Although the dominant analysis of spreadsheet models is for "What if?" projection, the case was made for the inadequacy of this approach for serious model analysis: "What if?" projections overwrite previous results with the new ones, thus making it difficult to see the results of many scenarios simultaneously, and is not very systematic. An alternative approach was given in Example 1 by restricting the initial model to a single column, thereby preserving other columns for replicating the model to allow many completely different "What if?" scenarios to be viewed simultaneously. This provides an easy form of sensitivity analysis and is applicable for graphing the results for visual representations. It also permits you to systematically examine a range of input values looking for the more favorable, if not the optimal, values of some performance measure. We will have much more to say about optimal searches in subsequent chapters.

Unfortunately, as was seen at the end of Example 2, expanding a model to include multiple time periods or as was seen in Example 3, expanding the model to include multiple products has two attributes, one favorable and one unfavorable. The favorable attribute is that a well-designed model will have its basic structure replicated in subsequent time periods or for subsequent similar products so that the conceptual underpinnings are preserved. One simply tailors the replicated models by changing parameter values to particularize the replicated models to the new products or new time periods. This is by far how successful big models evolve from successful small models. Once you understand the basic structure of a small model it is easy to understand the structure of a much larger model made up of replicated small models.

An unfortunate consequence of such replication to produce bigger models is that both rows and columns get used up quickly, which makes further replications of the model for sensitivity analysis very cumbersome, if not impossible. Although not discussed in these examples, one solution is to copy or replicate the model into subsequent worksheets of an Excel workbook and then develop a single worksheet that consolidates important variables from each worksheet into an overall model.

The salvation when there is no room to replicate the model for purposes of sensitivity analysis is to use in the Data Table commands as documented in Example 3. Data Table comes into flavors, Data Table 2 which allows two input variables to be varied systematically and calculates a single output, usually a performance measure. The Data Table 1, on the other hand, allows only one input variable to be manipulated but will tabulate an unlimited number of output variables. Clearly both flavors of Data Table are somewhat restrictive, but creative combinations of multiple Data Tables can often be an acceptable substitute. Moreover, creating an array of tabulated values in a Data Table is ideally suited for sensitivity analysis and the visual representation of relationships via charts.

Finally, in Example 4, the Goal Seek command was introduced. Goal Seek incorporates the common orientation of managers who focus on a desirable outcome and then ask what model input value produced that outcome. Also, another use for Goal Seek is the easy identification of break-even points, and the identification of indifference points between alternative models, that is, where the performance measure has the same value for one or more major alternatives. While Goal Seek is a powerful tool, it does have its limitations: It will only manipulate a single input variable, it cannot adjust for more than one output condition, and it cannot optimize by searching for the highest or lowest value of an output variable, a common desire of management modeling.

One shortcoming of all of the examples, thus far, is that there has been little consideration of constraints. Example 3 included one constraint on processing capacity, but many business situations have many scarce resources reflected in multiple constraints. This topic will be further addressed in Example 5 below. Beginning in Chapter 3 we will see how to combine constraints, Goal Seek, and optimization into a single analytic tool. While this example group of models is hardly exhaustive, we hope that they have produced enough ideas at this juncture so that you can begin serious modeling of your own.

2.7 EXAMPLE 5—PRODUCTION AT OAK PRODUCTS, INC.

Oak Products, Inc. (OP) produces a line of high-quality solid oak chairs. There are six chairs in the product line: Captain, Mate, American High, American Low, Spanish King, and Spanish Queen. These chairs have been designed to use a number of interchangeable component parts—long and short dowels, heavy and light seats, and heavy and light rungs. In addition, each type of chair has a distinguishing rail that caps the back. The interchangeable parts help protect OP against sudden shifts in demand. It is November 15, and Tom Burr, the plant manager, is set to meet Jim White from production control to finalize the production plan for the next week. At OP, the finishing activity (i.e., sanding, spraying, and drying of the component parts) requires one week. For this reason, only components that are already on hand and finished can be used in chairs that will be produced in the next week. Jim White has developed a **production model**, or **product mix model**, and the result is the spreadsheet model shown in Figure 2.38.

As in the other examples, Jim's spreadsheet is used to represent his model in a layout we recommend for ease of building, analysis, and interpretation. In Jim's spreadsheet, columns are devoted to representing decision "activities," in this case, the act of producing a given chair type, including production level and consumption of chair parts. To make this clear Jim has placed text labels in the rows and columns to assist in understanding the

FIGURE 2.38

The First OP Spreadsheet

	A	B	C	D	E	F	G	H	I	J
1	**Oak Products Weekly Product Mix Model**									
2	Chair Style	Capt.	Mate	AmerHi	AmerLo	SpainK	SpainQ			
3	Profit/Chair	$ 36	$ 40	$ 45	$ 38	$ 35	$ 25	Profit		
4	Qty.Produced	40	40	40	40	40	40	$ 8,760		
5		Chair Component Requirements						Total Usage	Starting Inventory	End. Inv.
6	Long Dowels	8	0	12	0	8	4	1280	1280	0
7	Short Dowels	4	12	0	12	4	8	1600	1900	300
8	Legs	4	4	4	4	4	4	960	1090	130
9	Heavy Seats	1	0	0	0	1	1	120	190	70
10	Light Seats	0	1	1	1	0	0	120	170	50
11	Heavy Rungs	6	0	4	0	5	0	600	1000	400
12	Light Rungs	0	4	0	5	0	6	600	1000	400
13	Capt. Rails	1	0	0	0	0	0	40	110	70
14	Mate Rails	0	1	0	0	0	0	40	72	32
15	Amer. Rails	0	0	1	1	0	0	80	93	13
16	Span. Rails	0	0	0	0	1	1	80	85	5

	A	B	C	D	E	F	G	H	I	J
1	**Oak Product**									
2	Chair Style	Capt.	Mate	AmerHi	AmerLo	SpainK	SpainQ			
3	Profit/Chair	36	40	45	38	35	25	Profit		
4	Qty.Produced	40	40	40	40	40	40	=SUMPRODUCT($B$4:$G$4,B3:G3)		
5		Ch						Total Usage	Starting Inventory	End. Inv.
6	Long Dowels	8	0	12	0	8	4	=SUMPRODUCT($B$4:$G$4,B6:G6)	1280	=I6-H6
7	Short Dowels	4	12	0	12	4	8	=SUMPRODUCT($B$4:$G$4,B7:G7)	1900	=I7-H7
8	Legs	4	4	4	4	4	4	=SUMPRODUCT($B$4:$G$4,B8:G8)	1090	=I8-H8
9	Heavy Seats	1	0	0	0	1	1	=SUMPRODUCT($B$4:$G$4,B9:G9)	190	=I9-H9
10	Light Seats	0	1	1	1	0	0	=SUMPRODUCT($B$4:$G$4,B10:G10)	170	=I10-H10
11	Heavy Rungs	6	0	4	0	5	0	=SUMPRODUCT($B$4:$G$4,B11:G11)	1000	=I11-H11
12	Light Rungs	0	4	0	5	0	6	=SUMPRODUCT($B$4:$G$4,B12:G12)	1000	=I12-H12
13	Capt. Rails	1	0	0	0	0	0	=SUMPRODUCT($B$4:$G$4,B13:G13)	110	=I13-H13
14	Mate Rails	0	1	0	0	0	0	=SUMPRODUCT($B$4:$G$4,B14:G14)	72	=I14-H14
15	Amer. Rails	0	0	1	1	0	0	=SUMPRODUCT($B$4:$G$4,B15:G15)	93	=I15-H15
16	Span. Rails	0	0	0	0	1	1	=SUMPRODUCT($B$4:$G$4,B16:G16)	85	=I16-H16

TIP: *The worksheet in Figure 2.38 conserves column width using the Alignment tab in the Format Cells dialog to rotate the Orientation of the chair-type labels by 90 degrees. In addition, the Total Usage formulas in column H use the SUMPRODUCT() function. This function multiplies each pair of the corresponding cells in its arguments and then adds up all the resulting products. This function is used frequently in spreadsheet models. If formatting cells or the SUMPRODUCT function is unfamiliar to you, review their operation in Appendix B.*

FIGURE 2.39

Use of Range Names to Improve Formula Documentation

TIP: *Named variables are global within an Excel workbook. That is, they are available to all worksheets within it. This allows a cell in one worksheet model to reference a variable in any other worksheet by its name. For details of creating range names, see Appendix B.*

	H	I	J
3	Profit		
4	=SUMPRODUCT(Qty.Produced,Profit_Chair)		
5	Total Usage	Starting Inventory	End. Inv.
6	=SUMPRODUCT(Qty.Produced,Long_Dowels)	1280	=Starting_Inventory-Total_Usage
7	=SUMPRODUCT(Qty.Produced,Short_Dowels)	1900	=Starting_Inventory-Total_Usage
8	=SUMPRODUCT(Qty.Produced,Legs)	1090	=Starting_Inventory-Total_Usage
9	=SUMPRODUCT(Qty.Produced,Heavy_Seats)	190	=Starting_Inventory-Total_Usage
10	=SUMPRODUCT(Qty.Produced,Light_Seats)	170	=Starting_Inventory-Total_Usage
11	=SUMPRODUCT(Qty.Produced,Heavy_Rungs)	1000	=Starting_Inventory-Total_Usage
12	=SUMPRODUCT(Qty.Produced,Light_Rungs)	1000	=Starting_Inventory-Total_Usage
13	=SUMPRODUCT(Qty.Produced,Capt._Rails)	110	=Starting_Inventory-Total_Usage
14	=SUMPRODUCT(Qty.Produced,Mate_Rails)	72	=Starting_Inventory-Total_Usage
15	=SUMPRODUCT(Qty.Produced,Amer._Rails)	93	=Starting_Inventory-Total_Usage
16	=SUMPRODUCT(Qty.Produced,Span._Rails)	85	=Starting_Inventory-Total_Usage

meaning of the numbers. For example, the "4" in B7 indicates that four short dowels are used in producing one Captain chair. Also, Jim has placed his suggested production plan in the cells B4:G4. Thus, Jim's proposal is to produce 40 chairs of each type, yielding a total weekly profit of $8,760. The entries in the cells H7:J7 indicate that

1. Jim's production plan will use a total of 1,600 short dowels;
2. The starting inventory of short dowels, a parameter, is at 1,900; and
3. Jim's plan will leave a final, end-of-week inventory of 300 short dowels.

Figure 2.39 illustrates the use of Excel's Naming capability to create names for ranges of cells in Jim's model. This improves readability of worksheet formulas in comparison to the formulas shown in Figure 2.38. Names can be used in any spreadsheet model to improve documentation, but are particularly useful when referring to collections of adjacent cells, as in the Oak Production model.

Using Jim's model, the production-planning session proceeds as follows:

JIM: I've used the usual procedure to determine production—that is, to make the same quantity of each product and maximize the total amount produced. This time we run out of long dowels first, but we do pretty well. We produce 40 of each chair and make $8,760.

TOM: I know that we've always produced equal quantities of each chair, but this time things are different. The president tells me that solid wood products are a hot item now, and we will sell out no matter what we produce. He says to make as much profit as possible. What should we do?

JIM: I don't know the complete answer, but I do have an idea. American Highs are clearly our most profitable item, but notice that they also use the most long dowels and we're short of long dowels. If I give up two American Highs, I lose $90 of profit, but I gain 24 long dowels. I can use those dowels to make three Captains, in which case, I'll gain $108. So what if we make 100 Captains and no American Highs?

(Jim enters this new proposal into the cells B4:G4, yielding the result shown in Figure 2.40.)

TOM: Jim, that's great! You've increased weekly profits by $360. I wonder if we can do better? I'm sure we can. In fact, I think we can use your idea again. Spanish Kings require 8 long dowels, while Spanish Queens require only 4. I should be able to give up a King and lose $35, but make two Queens and gain $50. So, what if I make no Kings and a total of 120 Queens? (The result is shown in Figure 2.41.)

JIM: There's some good news and some bad news. The good news is that your economics was right. Weekly profits increased by $600. The bad news is that we don't have the inventory to support your plan. I had included IF() statements in column K to test for any negative ending inventories and generate messages signaling a stock out whenever a plan causes a stock

FIGURE 2.40

Jim's Revised Spreadsheet

	A	B	C	D	E	F	G	H	I	J
1	**Oak Products Weekly Product Mix Model**									
2	Chair Style	Capt.	Mate	AmerHi	AmerLo	SpainK	SpainQ			
3	Profit/Chair	$ 36	$ 40	$ 45	$ 38	$ 35	$ 25	Profit		
4	Qty.Produced	100	40	0	40	40	40	$ 9,120		
5		Chair Component Requirements						Total Usage	Starting Inventory	End. Inv.
6	Long Dowels	8	0	12	0	8	4	1280	1280	0
7	Short Dowels	4	12	0	12	4	8	1840	1900	60
8	Legs	4	4	4	4	4	4	1040	1090	50
9	Heavy Seats	1	0	0	0	1	1	180	190	10
10	Light Seats	0	1	1	1	0	0	80	170	90
11	Heavy Rungs	6	0	4	0	5	0	800	1000	200
12	Light Rungs	0	4	0	5	0	6	600	1000	400
13	Capt. Rails	1	0	0	0	0	0	100	110	10
14	Mate Rails	0	1	0	0	0	0	40	72	32
15	Amer. Rails	0	0	1	1	0	0	40	93	53
16	Span. Rails	0	0	0	0	1	1	80	85	5

FIGURE 2.41

Tom's Revised Spreadsheet

	A	B	C	D	E	F	G	H	I	J	K
1	**Oak Products Weekly Product Mix Model**										
2	Chair Style	Capt.	Mate	AmerHi	AmerLo	SpainK	SpainQ				
3	Profit/Chair	$ 36	$ 40	$ 45	$ 38	$ 35	$ 25	Profit			
4	Qty.Produced	100	40	0	40	0	120	$ 9,720			
5		Chair Component Requirements						Total Usage	Starting Inventory	End. Inv.	
6	Long Dowels	8	0	12	0	8	4	1280	1280	0	
7	Short Dowels	4	12	0	12	4	8	2320	1900	-420	Short Dowels Stockout
8	Legs	4	4	4	4	4	4	1200	1090	-110	Legs Stockout
9	Heavy Seats	1	0	0	0	1	1	220	190	-30	Heavy Seats Stockout
10	Light Seats	0	1	1	1	0	0	80	170	90	
11	Heavy Rungs	6	0	4	0	5	0	600	1000	400	
12	Light Rungs	0	4	0	5	0	6	1080	1000	-80	Light Rungs Stockout
13	Capt. Rails	1	0	0	0	0	0	100	110	10	
14	Mate Rails	0	1	0	0	0	0	40	72	32	
15	Amer. Rails	0	0	1	1	0	0	40	93	53	
16	Span. Rails	0	0	0	0	1	1	120	85	-35	Span. Rails Stockout

	A	I	J	K
1	**Oak Product**			
2	Chair Style			
3	Profit/Chair			
4	Qty.Produced			
5		Starting Inventory	End. Inv.	
6	Long Dowels	1280	=I6-H6	=IF(J6<0,A6&" Stockout","")
7	Short Dowels	1900	=I7-H7	=IF(J7<0,A7&" Stockout","")
8	Legs	1090	=I8-H8	=IF(J8<0,A8&" Stockout","")
9	Heavy Seats	190	=I9-H9	=IF(J9<0,A9&" Stockout","")
10	Light Seats	170	=I10-H10	=IF(J10<0,A10&" Stockout","")
11	Heavy Rungs	1000	=I11-H11	=IF(J11<0,A11&" Stockout","")
12	Light Rungs	1000	=I12-H12	=IF(J12<0,A12&" Stockout","")
13	Capt. Rails	110	=I13-H13	=IF(J13<0,A13&" Stockout","")
14	Mate Rails	72	=I14-H14	=IF(J14<0,A14&" Stockout","")
15	Amer. Rails	93	=I15-H15	=IF(J15<0,A15&" Stockout","")
16	Span. Rails	85	=I16-H16	=IF(J16<0,A16&" Stockout","")

TIP: *The IF() statements in column K test cells in column J and display a message if a negative value occurs; otherwise an empty string is displayed. The & character concatenates character strings, in this case, the row labels in column A.*

out. This means, for example, that your plan would have to use more Short Dowels, Legs, and so on than we have. It's just not possible.

TOM: I see what you mean. Clearly I overshot the mark. I understand that we could decrease the production of Spanish Kings and increase the production of Spanish Queens somewhat and increase profits. With enough effort, I guess we could figure out how much we can push this trade-off before running out of inventory. But even so, how do we know it's a good solution? I really wonder what's best.

OPTIMIZATION MODELS

Like the other examples, the Oak Products model is certainly a quantitative decision model. It specifies the relationship between the decision variables (the quantity of each chair to produce) and the parameters (the number of parts used in each chair and the supplies of parts) and computes a performance measure (profit) and other consequence variables (ending inventories). It does not, however, tell us how many chairs to produce. When you think about it, that is a funny question. How many chairs to produce to do what? We might want to know how many chairs to produce to use up as much of our parts inventory as possible. Or how many chairs to produce to satisfy normal customer demand for each model. As with the previous examples, it is more likely that we would want to know how many chairs to produce in order to maximize OP's weekly profit. Unfortunately, none of the analytical techniques we have covered in the examples of this chapter permit "What if" projections, including Data Tables, Goal Seek, and charts, while simultaneously adhering to specified constraints. You might, for example, want to make sales or profits large in one model and costs or delivery times small in another while honoring constraints on capacities, resources, and time.

2.8 CONSTRAINTS AND CONSTRAINED OPTIMIZATION

If Tom and Jim decide that they want to make their weekly profit as large as possible, then the Oak Products model becomes an **optimization model**. The Oak Products model is an example of a constrained optimization problem: a model in which we wish to maximize (or minimize) some performance measure function of the decision variables subject to a set of constraints. A constraint is ultimately a limitation on the range of allowable decisions. In this particular case the constraints are the quantities of various parts available to produce chairs, but there are many different types of constraints. Indeed, managers make most of their personal and professional decisions in situations where the allowable decisions have been restricted in some way. In our private lives we are nearly always dealing with limitations of some sort—of time, of money, of space, of energy. In business, the kinds of constraints encountered are even more numerous. A manager must often take into account capital requirements, personnel availability, delivery schedules, import quotas, union work rules, factory capacities, environmental regulations, inventory costs, legal requirements, and a host of other factors. It is perhaps not surprising, therefore, that constrained optimization—achieving the best possible result given the restrictions that apply—is one of the most active areas of management research.

The Oak Products formulation is a standard type of managerial planning optimization model, and the best alternative, or **optimal solution** is easily obtained. There are several spreadsheet "add-in" application packages that take a model with constraints like Oak Products and then **optimize** it. Two such packages are Solver and What's Best. Excel includes a restricted version of Solver that produced the optimized result for the Oak Products model shown in Figure 2.42. It is interesting to note that the Solver solution projects that weekly profit would be increased by $1,174 over Jim's revised plan and that no Spanish style chairs are part of the optimal solution, that is, the **optimal decision** is to produce zero Spanish style chairs.

The use of Solver to optimize models will be covered extensively in Part 2.

FIGURE 2.42

The Optimal Solution to OP's Model

	A	B	C	D	E	F	G	H	I	J
1	**Oak Products Weekly Product Mix Model**									
2	Chair Style	Capt.	Mate	AmerHi	AmerLo	SpainK	SpainQ			
3	Profit/Chair	$ 36	$ 40	$ 45	$ 38	$ 35	$ 25	Profit		
4	Qty.Produced	100	72	40	53	0	0	$ 10,294		
5		Chair Component Requirements						Total Usage	Starting Inventory	End. Inv.
6	Long Dowels	8	0	12	0	8	4	1280	1280	0
7	Short Dowels	4	12	0	12	4	8	1900	1900	0
8	Legs	4	4	4	4	4	4	1060	1090	30
9	Heavy Seats	1	0	0	0	1	1	100	190	90
10	Light Seats	0	1	1	1	0	0	165	170	5
11	Heavy Rungs	6	0	4	0	5	0	760	1000	240
12	Light Rungs	0	4	0	5	0	6	553	1000	447
13	Capt. Rails	1	0	0	0	0	0	100	110	10
14	Mate Rails	0	1	0	0	0	0	72	72	0
15	Amer. Rails	0	0	1	1	0	0	93	93	0
16	Span. Rails	0	0	0	0	1	1	0	85	85

2.9 SUMMARY

This chapter has introduced you to spreadsheet modeling, primarily by a series of short examples. We have suggested ways to translate a black box representation into a spreadsheet model, given recommendations for good spreadsheet model design and layout, offered suggestions for documenting your models, and introduced you to useful features of Excel for modeling and analysis.

Influence Diagrams facilitate the building of models and provide model documentation. Model equations are built iteratively by revising relationships to conform to hypothesized relationships contained in data. "What if?" projections are the primary analysis tool for exercising spreadsheet models. Replicating the model, Data Table, and charting are all useful in evaluating collections of "What if?" projections for purposes of sensitivity analysis and trade-off analysis. In addition, Goal Seek is useful for break-even analysis and for finding points of (performance measure) indifference between major alternatives.

In constructing Excel models we emphasized that a good Excel model adheres to the following attributes:

1. All of the variables are clearly defined and labeled,
2. The inputs including decision and parameters are clearly identified as such,
3. The performance measure(s) and consequence variables of interest are similarly easily found and well labeled,
4. Parameter values are stored in separate cells and not "hard wired" into formulas to facilitate documentation and analyses,
5. Where convenient, the variables giving physical quantities are separated from those that reflect them into accounting or financial consequences, and
6. Formatting options of Excel are used to highlight headings, cell labels, and otherwise improve the appearance of the model.

The layout of the model in the spreadsheet is critically important in developing models that are understandable, free of logic bugs, easy to maintain and document, pleasing to the eye, and easy to communicate to others. Making the logic clear, avoiding parameters in formulas, labeling variables, and use of variable names all contribute to good spreadsheet modeling practice. Finally, Excel conditional tests, such as IF() statements, can be included in a model to signal unusual conditions by displaying message alerts when, for example, a candidate set of inputs produce undesirable or infeasible outcomes.

Key Terms

Influence Diagram. A hierarchical flowchart drawing beginning with a performance measure and using arrows to clarify the relationships of it to the variables and parameters of a model.

Intermediate Variable. Endogenous variables within a model created for convenience that combine mathematically with other variables to produce a model's outputs: performance measure(s) or consequence variables.

"What if?" Projection. Substituting decision and/or parameter values into a symbolic model to calculate their effect upon performance measure(s) and consequence variables.

Break-Even Point. The set of values for model input variables that produces a payoff performance measure equal to zero.

Trade-Off Analysis. The amount of one performance measure that must be sacrificed to achieve a given improvement in another performance measure.

Data Table. The systematic tabulation of a performance measure and/or consequence variable values for a range of values of one or two exogenous variables.

Goal Seek. Finding the value of a single exogenous variable that produces a given value of a single endogenous variable.

Sensitivity Analysis. Calculating, often in percentage terms, the effect a given percentage change in an exogenous variable has upon another variable.

Production Model. A decision model in which decision variable(s) specify the quantities of one or more items to manufacture.

Product Mix Model. A production model with more than one item to manufacture.

Optimization Model. A deterministic decision model consisting of a single performance measure (objective function) to be optimized subject to satisfaction of given set of constraints.

Optimize. To maximize or minimize an objective function.

Optimal Decision. A feasible set of values for the decisions that optimizes the objective function of an optimization model.

Optimal Solution. Alternative term for optimal decision.

Self-Review Exercises

True-False

1. **T F** It doesn't make much difference how a model is presented on a spreadsheet, as long as the calculations are correct.
2. **T F** Putting numbers into formulas improves spreadsheet documentation.
3. **T F** Units of measure are important to include in spreadsheet models.
4. **T F** Given hypothetical data on two variables, Excel's Trendline is useful for investigating alternative algebraic formulas that relate them.
5. **T F** There is usually no single correct way to draw an Influence Diagram.
6. **T F** Columns in an Excel model are always used to represent time.
7. **T F** The analysis of spreadsheet models requires that profit be the performance measure.
8. **T F** Goal Seek is a procedure for optimizing spreadsheet models.
9. **T F** Managers have no need to concern themselves with the formulas in a spreadsheet model, only the results of the model.
10. **T F** Groups and Outlines can be used to conceal important details of the model in spreadsheet printouts.
11. **T F** It is a good idea to separate calculations to create intermediate variables for physical quantities from those related to accounting for their costs.
12. **T F** "What if" projections are only useful for examining changes in the values of decision variables.
13. **T F** Data Tables are useful for creating tabulations of "What if?" projections.
14. **T F** Data Tables have no use other than for calculating numbers to be input to the Chart Wizard.
15. **T F** The Goal Seek command is useful for finding values of an exogenous variable that produce the same performance measure value as that of another alternative model.

Multiple Choice

16. A good spreadsheet model will
  a. have model results clearly labeled
  b. give units of measure for its variables
  c. separate input variables from endogenous variables
  d. make it clear how endogenous variables are calculated from input variables
  e. all of the above

17. Optimization models contain
a. decision variables
b. an objective function
c. both of the above

18. An optimization model
a. provides the best decision in a mathematical sense
b. provides the best decision within the limited context of the model
c. can provide a consistent tool for evaluating different policies
d. all of the above

19. With a "What if?" projection, we are sure to find
a. an optimal solution
b. a good solution
c. a feasible solution (if one exists)
d. none of the above

20. An optimal decision in the Oak Products problem is one that
a. uses all available component parts
b. uses as many as possible of the least-expensive parts
c. maximizes contribution margin (revenue minus costs)
d. maximizes weekly profit
e. maximizes the total number of chairs produced

21. A Data Table 1 command
a. requires a range of values for one exogenous variable
b. allows specification of multiple endogenous variables
c. both of the above
d. none of the above

22. A Data Table 2 command
a. requires a range of values for two exogenous variables
b. allows specification of multiple endogenous variables
c. both of the above
d. none of the above

23. Sensitivity analysis
a. compares the changes in an endogenous variable to changes in an exogenous variable
b. cannot be applied to decision variables
c. cannot be applied to comparing two parameter values
d. a) and b) above
e. a) and c) above
f. all of the above

24. Named cells and named ranges
a. make formulas easier to interpret
b. assist documenting the spreadsheet model
c. hide the underlying structure of formulas
d. a) and b) above
e. a) and c) above
f. all of the above

25. Excel features that can be used to aid model interpretation and documentation are
a. use of bold fonts
b. cell indentations for labels and results
c. underlining and shading cells
d. borders on cells
e. all of the above

Answers

1. F, **2.** F, **3.** T, **4.** T, **5.** T, **6.** F, **7.** F, **8.** F, **9.** F, **10.** T, **11.** T, **12.** F, **13.** T, **14.** F, **15.** T, **16.** e, **17.** c, **18.** d, **19.** d, **20.** d, **21.** c, **22.** a, **23.** a, **24.** d, **25.** e

Problems

2-1. Simon does not consider his Simon Pie model to be valid for pie price outside of the range $6 to $11. Use IF() statements and/or Excel's conditional formatting to modify the model of Example 1 to produce warnings if a price outside of this range is input to the model.

2-2. The Petersons decide that the Variable Cost per Copy is more complicated than in the current XerTech model in which supplies cost $.02 per copy and the average repair cost per copy is $.01. They now believe that the average repair cost per copy is more than proportional to the monthly number of copies made per copier. They estimate the relationship as below. Modify the XerTech model to incorporate this new information and prepare a report for the Petersons with these new results.

MONTHLY DATA	
# of Copies/Copier (000's)	**Repair Cost/Copier**
20	$ 50
30	150
40	400
50	1,000

2-3. Use Data Table to examine the profit sensitivity of the Example 2 Simon Pie model to changes in the following parameters: Unit cost of pie filling, Unit cost of dough, fixed cost, slope of the pie demand equation, intercept of the pie demand equation.

2-4. Bartel Job Shop Co. has received an offer to assemble approximately 15,000 electronic "portasols" for $26.50 each. Using its existing manufacturing facility, Bartel estimates their variable cost of assembling each portasol is $21. Alternatively, Bartel can subcontract some of the assembly steps to Wizard Fabrication Co., thereby reducing Bartel's assembly cost to $18 each. Wizard will charge Bartel a fixed fee of $42,000 for their contract. Another option for Bartel is to lease a parts insertion robot for $150,000. If leased, the robot will reduce Bartel's variable assembly cost to $11. Prepare a model to project the total profit from accepting this offer for each of the three alternative production options. At what level of portasol production would Bartel be indifferent between using its existing facility and subcontracting or between subcontracting and leasing the robot? Prepare a managerial report summarizing your recommendations for different possible quantities of portasols.

2-5. You have founded a company to sell thin client computers to the food processing industry for Internet e-commerce transaction processing. Before investing in your new company, a venture capitalist has asked for a five year pro-forma income statement showing unit sales, revenue, total variable cost, marketing expense, fixed cost, and profit before tax. You expect to sell 1,600 units of the thin client computers in the first year for a price of $1,800 each. Swept along by Internet growth, you expect to double unit sales each year for the next five years. However, competition will force a 15% decline in price each year. Fortunately, technical progress allows initial variable manufacturing costs of $1,000 for each unit to decline by 6% per year. Fixed costs are estimated to be $1,000,000 per year. Marketing expense is projected to be 14% of annual revenue. When it becomes profitable to do so, you will lease an automated assembly machine that reduces variable manufacturing costs by 20% but doubles annual fixed cost; the new variable manufacturing cost will also decline by 6% per year. Net Present Value (NPV) will be used to aggregate the stream of annual profits, discounted at 15% per year. Ignoring tax considerations, build a spreadsheet model for the venture capitalist. How many units will you need to sell in the first year (1) to break even in the first year or (2) to break even in the second year? To what parameters is NPV most sensitive? Prepare a managerial report summarizing your findings.

2-6. Simon has decided that his model (Simon Pie Example 2 model) needs to be modified for the slow winter selling season. During this season, he can achieve the weekly quantity of pies demanded given in the model only if he advertises his pies very heavily. With less advertising, pies demanded will be a percentage of the pie quantity given by the model. He estimates the relationship by the following data, where a 100% Market Potential means that the quantity of pies projected by the original model will be sold and a 50% Market Potential means that only one-half of that projected quantity will be sold. He will pick a weekly advertising amount between $5,000 and $12,000. Modify the Example 2 Pie model to incorporate this new information and recommend pricing and advertising decisions to Simon. Examine the sensitivity of weekly profit to advertising amount.

ADVERTISING ($000'S PER WEEK)	% OF MARKET POTENTIAL
$ 5	40
7	65
10	78
12	88

2-7. Surfing USA, an Internet service provider, is considering to offer a service in Laramie County, WY, that connects a device directly to televisions and allows customers to either watch TV or access the Internet. The expected price of the service per customer is $26 per month and the variable cost per customer to provide the service is expected to be $17 per month. The number of customers in Laramie County that are expected to subscribe to the service at that price is 20,000 per month.

1. Develop an Excel model to find the maximum monthly fixed cost that Surfing USA would pay to offer the service in Laramie County and not operate at a loss.
2. Assume that Surfing USA's monthly fixed costs are $100,000 and monthly service cost per customer is $17. The price per customer will affect the monthly demand for the service. Assume that for a monthly price of $26 per customer, the demand will be 20,000 customers and for each $1 increase in price demand will fall by 2,700 customers. Develop an Excel model to recommend a monthly price to Surfing USA and examine the sensitivity of monthly profit to changes in price for prices from $20 to $30.

"It's the profit per customer that counts in this business," says Ron Sperry, president of Surfing USA. ". . . and to make the most money we want to make that as big as possible," he continues. If Surfing USA were to set its price to maximize the average profit per customer (monthly profits divided by monthly number of customers), does Ron achieve his objective of making "the most money"? Modify your model and use it to explain to Ron the consequences of his business policy.

3. Surfing USA can increase its customer base in Laramie County by advertising. The variable monthly service cost is $17 per customer, assuming 20,000 customers and no advertising. With advertising the variable monthly service cost per customer would rise $1 for every 1,000 customers that are added to the service above the base of 20,000. Assuming the monthly price of the service is $26 per customer and the monthly fixed cost is $100,000, develop an Excel model to recommend a monthly advertising amount to Surfing USA and examine the sensitivity of monthly profit to advertising.

2-8. The Evermore Beauty Parlor employs seven beauticians, each of whom is paid a wage of $18 per hour. In addition, fixed annual expenses for Evermore are $48,000 per year for rent, loan interest expense, and so on. All hairstyling offered by Evermore is the same and each hairstyle is priced at $32. Assume each beautician works 2,000 hours per year and that all seven beauticians work the entire year. Build an Excel model to answer the following questions.

1. What is Evermore's break-even point in number of hairstyles?
2. What is Evermore's profit if 15,000 hairstyles are given per year?
3. If Evermore were to change to paying its beauticians a wage of $10 per hour plus a commission of $12 per hairstyle, what would be the new break-even point in number of hairstyles?
4. If Evermore were to change to paying its beauticians no wages with a commission of $25 per hairstyle, what would be the new break-even point in number of hairstyles?
5. At an annual volume of hairstyles of 15,000, which of the three beautician remuneration schemes—2, 3, or 4 above—would the beauticians prefer? Which one would the owner of Evermore prefer?
6. Given an annual volume of 15,000 hairstyles per year and assuming the Evermore owner opted to pay only a commission to beauticians, as in 4 above, what would the commission rate have to be for the owner to be indifferent to the commission-only scheme or paying only a wage of $18 per hour?

Case Study Kayo Computer[1]

Kayo Computer assembles and sells personal computers. Each computer needs one custom-designed printed circuit board (PCB). Kayo has contracted to buy the PCBs from an outside PCB manufacturer, Apex Manufacturing. The one-year contract stipulates that Kayo pays $200 per board to Apex for up to 2,000 PCBs. If the annual order quantity exceeds 2,000 PCBs, then Apex is obligated to give a discount of $40 per board for the portion beyond 2,000, thus selling them at $160.

Kayo can also buy the same PCBs from another manufacturer, TCI Electronics, that offers a lower price of $120 per PCB but asks a one time payment of $100,000 as a nonrefundable design and engineering fee. Kayo's engineers have determined that Kayo may use PCBs from either of the two manufacturers, or from both in any mixture without any manufacturing cost or compatibility problems.

The PCB along with other components are assembled by Kayo into its personal computer. The variable assembly cost of the Kayo personal computer is $450 each with an annual fixed cost of $1,500,000. Kayo sells the assembled computer for $1,000 each. At the moment no one is sure how many Kayo computers the company can sell for the next year. Jenny Silk, VP of Finance at Kayo Computer, informs you that this model of Kayo computer will be discontinued after next year and so any one-time fee that might be paid to TCI must be justified based on next year's sales alone. She has asked you to help her evaluate certain economic and legal issues as part of her financial plan for the next year.

Questions

1. Build a spreadsheet model that captures the profitability of the Kayo personal computer for next year. As a start, assume that 5,000 computers can be sold next year and only 1,000 of the PCBs are purchased from Apex (the balance being supplied by TCI).
2. If total sales were 5,000 units, how many PCBs would you recommend Kayo buy from Apex and how many from TCI to maximize next year's profits? (Use a Data Table to help you search for your preferred recommendation.)
3. In reviewing the Apex contract, you note that it requires Kayo to purchase at least 20% of the PCBs used in the

Kayo computers sold (and not less than 1,000 PCBs) from Apex. The contract also contains a liquidated damages clause in the event of Kayo's default in the amount of $100,000. What would be the economic effect if unforeseen changes caused Kayo to default on the 20%/1,000 minimum contracted purchase provision (by substituting more TCI boards) in the event that 5,000 Kayo computers can be sold next year? Assuming that Apex would be open to renegotiating the contract, what new terms and/or maximum settlement amount would you recommend to Silk for her consideration in the discussions with Apex. Justify your recommendation with relevant spreadsheet exhibits.

4. A market analysis reveals that unit sales will depend on the price of the computer. At the price of $1,000, about 5,000 units will be sold, but for every increase (or decrease) of $100, sales will decrease (or increase, respectively) by 1,000 units. Use Data Table 2 to maximize Kayo's profit next year, by finding (a) the optimal price, and (b) the optimal number of boards to buy from Apex while still honoring the original contract.

Case Study Watson Truck Rental Company[1]

Consisting of 50 large trucks rented by industrial contractors, the Watson Truck Rental Company is for sale for $1,000,000. Eric Watson, the seller, wants you to develop a three-year economic analysis to assist buyers in evaluating the company.

Watson pays property taxes of $35,000 per year and it costs $4,800 per truck per year to administer and maintain the fleet. The property taxes are expected to grow at a rate of 4% per year, and the maintenance costs are estimated to grow 7% per year.

Truck rental rate is currently $1,000 per month each. At this rental rate on average 60% of the trucks are rented each month. Watson believes that if he lowered the rent by $100 per truck per month, he would increase the average rental percentage by seven percentage points and that this increment would apply to each additional reduction in rent rate of $100. For example, at a $600 truck rental rate 88% of the trucks would be rented each month. Whatever truck rental rate is set for the first year will be increased by 9% per year for years 2 and 3. Average percent of trucks rented in years 2 and 3 will be the same as determined in the first year, regardless of the increased rental rate in those years.

At the end of three years, Watson assumes the buyer will resell the truck business for cash at a profit. The selling price at that time is assumed to be three times the revenue in year 3.

Cash flow in each year is assumed to be the same as the net income (revenue minus expenses) for that year. Effects of depreciation and other factors relating to income taxes can be ignored. Cash flow in year 3 includes in addition the cash from the resale of the business. Overall investment profit is defined to be the Net Present Value of the annual cash flows (discount rate = 10%) including the purchase price at the *beginning* of year 1. Assume no trucks are bought or sold during the three years.

Questions

1. Identify the decision variables, the exogenous variables, the performance measure, the intermediate variables, and any constraints in this problem and use these to build an Excel model.
2. Use a Data Table to find the initial truck rental rate that achieves the highest overall investment profit after the property is sold in three years.
3. Investigate the sensitivity of overall investment profit to the following variables: purchase price, maintenance cost per truck, annual property taxes, and sales multiplication factor. (Use the rental rate found in question 2 above for this analysis.) To which factor is profit most sensitive?
4. Prepare a managerial report for Eric Watson summarizing your findings and recommendations.

Case Study Personal Financial Plan[1]

You recently received a $100,000 inheritance from your great uncle Wilberforce. You and your spouse are concerned with what to do with the money.

 Written by Professor Evan L. Porteus.

Salary

You and your spouse's salaries amount to $80,000 and you confidently expect that total to grow at 15% per year. You have decided to keep a tight budget and peg your family expenditures to a fixed percent, tentatively set at 75%, of your salaries. Of course, since your salaries will grow, so will these expenditures. Note that these are based on gross salaries (not net after taxes).

Taxes

The Congress has just passed a new tax bill—one with a flat-tax rate. Under this law, a couple (such as you and your spouse) have a deduction of $15,000, and the combined state and federal tax rate is 35% for all income above this base of $15,000. Also a capital gains tax has been instituted: 40% of all capital gains are taxed as regular income.

Tax Shelter Investment

You have the option of investing any amount of your funds in a real estate venture. One advantage of this investment is that it will incur accounting losses (tax losses due to depreciation) in each of the next five years while simultaneously returning a small (nontaxable) cash payment. At the end of the five years the property will be sold, you will share in the profits, and you will pay capital gain taxes on these profits. For each $1,000 invested in the project, the following are the various factors:

Annual Tax Loss	$200
Annual Cash Payment to You	$40 (not taxable)
Amount Returned at End of Year 5	$1,800
Capital Gain Tax Liability in Year 5	$2,300

Mutual Fund Investment

The only other investment you are considering is a money market fund. This fund pays interest at a rate of 14% per year and this interest income is taxable. You can invest any amount in this fund at any time.

For convenience, assume the interest is paid in any year on the balance at the beginning of that year (the end of the prior year). The $100,000 inheritance has been tentatively placed in the money market fund but can be withdrawn immediately if needed.

You and your spouse wish to build a personal financial model that will allow you to see how your wealth (market fund balance) will grow by the end of five years. You wish to use this model to decide how much to invest in the tax shelter investment, and to examine how sensitive your plan is to some of the assumptions made.

Questions

Use your model to answer the following questions:

1. How much should you invest in the tax shelter plan?
2. Suppose your salary growth rate is only 10%, how does this affect your wealth at the end of five years? Explain this result.
3. Increase each of the tax shelter investment parameters by 10%. (Do each separately.) Which has the greatest impact on your five-year wealth?
4. What is the maximum percentage of your salaries that you can consume (spend) without running into debt (so that your money market fund balance is never negative)?
5. What would the yield on the money market fund have to be for you to be indifferent between investing fully in the real estate investment and investing nothing in it?

Case Study Santa Rosa Raisins

Located in California's Napa Wine Country, Santa Rosa Raisins (SRR) is a food-processing company that purchases surplus grapes in the autumn from grape growers, dries them into raisins, applies a layer of sugar, and sells the sugar-coated raisins to major cereal and candy companies. In the spring, at the beginning of the grape growing season, SRR has several interrelated decisions to make. The first involves how many grapes to buy under an existing grower supply contract, and the second relates to the price to charge for the sugar-coated raisins SRR sells.

SRR has an option contract with a grower who, if asked in the spring, must supply a given amount of grapes in the autumn at a fixed cost of $.25 per pound. The balance between SRR's grape requirements and any supplied by the grower must be purchased by SRR in the autumn from the open market at a price that could vary from a historical low of $.15 per pound to a high of $.35 per pound.

The other major decision facing SRR is the price to charge for sugar-coated raisins. SRR has several customers—large breakfast cereal and candy processors—who, together, buy all SRR's output of sugar-coated raisins. SRR negotiates with these processors as a group to arrive at a price for the sugar-coated raisins and the quantity of sugar-coated raisins the processors will buy at that negotiated price. The negotiations with these processors take place in the spring (before the autumn open market price of grapes is known) and SRR's management is considering its alternatives.

SRR's management concludes that the following represents their best judgment about the raisin price-quantity negotiations with the processors. Based upon prior years' experience, SRR's management believe that (1) if they price the sugar-coated raisins at $2.15 per pound, the processors as a group will demand, that is, order, 700,000 pounds of sugar-coated raisins and (2) the total demand for sugar-coated raisins will increase by 15,000 pounds for each penny reduction in sugar-coated raisin price below $2.15.

Sugar-coated raisins are made by washing and drying grapes into raisins, followed by spraying the raisins with a sugar coating that SRR buys for $.30 per pound. It takes 2.5 pounds of grapes plus .05 pound of sugar coating to make one pound of sugar-coated raisins, the balance being water that evaporates during grape drying. In addition to the raw materials cost of the grapes and sugar coating, SRR's processing plant incurs a variable cost of $.20 to process one pound of grapes into raisins up to its capacity of 3,500,000 pounds of grapes. Processing more than 3,500,000 pounds of grapes requires SRR to outsource the processing of those grapes to a competitor, who charges SRR $.60 to process a pound of grapes into raisins. SRR also incurs other fixed (overhead) costs in the grape-processing plant of $200,000 per year.

Jan Thurston, SRR's chief negotiator, has asked you to build an Excel model to analyze the situation in order to guide her in the upcoming raisin price-quantity negotiations. Her goal is to examine the effect of various "What if?" projection scenarios upon SRR's profits. Thurston is primarily interested in evaluating annual pre-tax profit as a function of sugar-coated raisin prices, and the uncertain open market grape price, under the assumption that contract grapes purchased is fixed at 1,000,000 pounds.

It is important to Thurston what, if any, pattern exists in the set of maximal pre-tax profits for alternative open market grape prices. That is, Thurston is interested to see how dependent the profit maximizing raisin price is upon open market grape price. To do this she asks you to do a sensitivity analysis to see in profit percentage change terms how different open market grape prices would affect pre-tax profit once she commits to a particular raisin price, assuming SRR commits to buying 1,000,000 pounds of grapes at the contract price of $.25. In particular, assume Thurston has decided that the base case to start from will be an open market grape price equal to last year's value of $.25 and contract grapes purchased is fixed at 1,000,000 pounds. Of course, she is interested in what would happen if the contract grapes purchased amount were to be different than the base case of 1,000,000 pounds.

Develop a clear and well-documented Excel model to assist Thurston in her analysis of this management situation. Your model should recommend specific raisin price decisions under various assumptions of open market grape price and amount of contract grapes purchased. In addition relevant sensitivity analyses should accompany your report in the form of charts or easily understood tables to assist Thurston in understanding and gaining insights to this important business opportunity. Summarize your findings into a concise executive summary with supporting tables and charts.

Case Study Ebel Mining (A)[1]

Ebel Mining Company owns two different mines that produce a given kind of ore. The mines are located in different parts of the country and hence have different production capacities and ore quality. After crushing, the ore is graded into three quality classes, depending on the concentration of a critical mineral: high-grade, medium-grade, and low-grade ores. At the end of each five-day workweek, Ebel has contracted to provide its parent company's smelting plant with at least 12 tons of high-grade ore, at least 8 tons of medium-grade ore, and at least 24 tons of low-grade ore per week. It costs the Ebel $20,000 per day to run the first mine and $16,000 per day to run the second. However, in a day's operation the first mine produces 6 tons of high-grade ore, 2 tons of medium-grade ore, and 4 tons of low-grade ore, while the second mine produces daily 2 tons of high-grade ore, 2 tons of medium-grade ore, and 12 tons of low-grade ore.

Questions

1. Develop an Excel model to answer the following question: How many days a week should each mine be operated in order to fulfill the Ebel's commitments most economically? (It is acceptable to schedule a mine to operate for a fraction of a day.)
2. How sensitive is Ebel's total weekly cost to the contracted amounts of high-, medium-, and low-grade ore?

 This is the first of several cases you will see based upon Ebel Mining in future chapters. Each version of Ebel will elaborate on this setting and be used to illustrate different modeling approaches and techniques.

Case Study Benson Appliance Corporation[1]

The Benson Appliance Corporation manufactures two kinds of small appliances at its single plant in Aurora, Illinois. Both of the company's products, electric knives and electric can openers, are marketed exclusively through manufacturing representatives, who service the retail appliance dealers. Representatives are paid a fixed salary, plus a commission on each unit sold. Most retailers add a standard markup to Benson's wholesale price.

Throughout the 1980s industry sales grew steadily at about 10% annually, and everybody followed the price leadership of the large appliance manufacturers. However, this cozy situation eventually attracted numerous small competitors. Total industry sales continued to expand, but no individual manufacturer could expect his sales to expand after 1997. During 1998 and early 1999, many of Benson's competitors engaged actively in price cutting. Benson had established an image of quality for both products, so it elected to maintain prices and to initiate a modest advertising campaign instead. This occurred in 1999, along with some experimental price manipulations to determine the sales sensitivity of each product to price. By the end of 1999, prices had stabilized throughout the industry, leaving Benson's products with both a price and a quality image somewhat above average. Benson's 1999 income statement appears in Exhibit 1.

The manufacture of small appliances is such that Benson can expand production of either product to almost any reasonable level on short notice. However, the unit variable manufacturing cost of either product increases by 25%, if the total annual production volume of that product exceeds 400,000 units. Thus, if knife production were 450,000 units, the first 400,000 units would cost $8 each in variable manufacturing cost, and the remaining 50,000 units would cost $10 each. Similarly, the first 400,000 openers would cost $16 each, and any excess over 400,000 units would cost $20 each. Variable manufacturing costs are mostly direct materials and relatively unskilled direct labor. Fixed manufacturing costs are allocated equally to the two products regardless of production volumes, since their facilities take up about the same plant space. Variable marketing costs are mostly sales commissions and freight expenses. Further details of Benson's costs appear in Exhibit 2.

Maximilian Benson, president, founder, and sole stockholder of the Benson Appliance Corporation, is in the process of formulating his 2000 budget and operating plan. This had been an easy task throughout the late 1980s and 1990s, when he simply charged the market price and projected a 10% annual sales growth. Now, however, Mr. Benson was not sure what to do. He asked his marketing manager, Clare Voyance, to report whatever conclusions she had drawn from the price and advertising experiments conducted during 1999 and to recommend prices and advertising budgets for 2000.

Ms. Voyance reported that sales of each product were influenced by both price and advertising, although in somewhat different ways. As long as both prices and advertising expenditures remained within certain reasonable operating limits, Ms. Voyance believed that she could project 2000 sales results fairly accurately.

"At every level of advertising expenditure, our unit knife sales appear to vary approximately linearly with knife price, so long as we keep the price between $12 and $23," Ms. Voyance reported. "I chose these limits because we would fail to recover even our variable costs at a price below $12, and our sales would vanish at prices much above $23. Within this range, an extra 100,000 units are sold every time we cut the knife price by an extra dollar. This is true regardless of whether or not we advertise. To see the effect of advertising on sales, I plotted unit knife sales (on the vertical axis) against price charged per knife (on the horizontal axis). Then, if we advertise, the effect of advertising is to shift the unit sales line upward at every price by an amount directly proportional to how much we spend. We sell an extra 4,000 knives for every extra $10,000 we spend on knife advertising, at least up to the $300,000 you authorized last year, Max. Actually, we only spent $100,000 on knife advertising in 1999, and we charged an average price of $20 per unit. This resulted in sales of 400,000 knives. Had we done no advertising at all, as in all years before 1999, we still would have sold 360,000 knives."

"At every level of advertising expenditure, our unit opener sales also vary approximately linearly with opener

EXHIBIT 1 1999 Income Statement for Benson Appliance Corporation (All figures in thousands of dollars)

Total Sales	$18,000
Total Manufacturing Costs	11,100
Gross Margin	6,900
Total Marketing Costs	3,600
Total General and Administrative Costs	860
Total Advertising Costs	200
Profit Before Taxes	2,240

Note: 400,000 electric knives were sold during 1999 at an average unit price of $20, and 400,000 electric can openers were sold at an average unit price of $25.

EXHIBIT 2 Cost Analysis for Benson Appliance Corporation (All figures in dollars based on 1999 results)

		PRODUCT TYPE	
		Electric Knives	Electric Can Openers
Variable Costs			
Unit Variable Manufacturing Cost			
Volume =< 400,000 Units		$ 8	$16
Volume > 400,000 Units		10	20
Unit Variable Marketing Cost		2	2
Fixed Costs			
Fixed Manufacturing Cost	$1,500,000		
Fixed Marketing Cost	2,000,000		
Fixed General and Administrative Cost	500,000		
Budgeted Costs			
Advertising	$200,000		

Note: In addition, 2% of total dollar sales revenue is required to cover partially variable general and administrative costs.
Note: The 2000 advertising budget has yet to be set.

price, so long as we keep the price between $20 and $30," Ms. Voyance continued. "I chose these limits for the same reasons as before. However, the effect of advertising openers depends on the price we charge, which is different from advertising's effect on knife sales. As with knives, unit sales are increased in direct proportion to advertising expenditures, but the proportionality factor is different at different opener prices. In fact, the proportionality factor appears to be a linear function of the opener price. At the 1999 average price of $25 per unit, we could sell an extra 1,500 openers for every extra $10,000 spent on advertising, at least up to your maximum authorization of $200,000. As it was, we spent $100,000 advertising openers, and we sold 400,000 units. Had we increased the price to $30, advertising would have had no impact on opener sales, no matter how heavily we advertised. Sales would have remained steady at 100,000 openers. Once again, I plotted unit opener sales (on the vertical axis) against price charged per opener (on the horizontal axis), and the effect of advertising openers is to rotate the unit sales line in a clockwise direction around the pivot price of $30, with the effect always being proportional to advertising expenditures, but increasingly so as the opener price falls."

"Clare," Mr. Benson asked, "why did you choose to spend $100,000 each last year advertising knives and openers? I authorized up to $300,000 for knives and up to $200,000 for openers, and I am willing to spend up to the same amounts (for each product, separately) in 2000. Furthermore, it's OK with me if you charge any price within your reasonable operating limits for each product next year."

"Well, Max," Ms. Voyance replied, "we sort of fell into it by accident. Truman Hardy, the production manager, was very anxious to keep average unit manufacturing costs down. After all, the annual bonus you pay him depends on his success in doing just that. Since the average unit manufacturing cost of each product is half of the fixed manufacturing cost plus variable manufacturing cost for that product, all divided by the number of units produced, and since you had already decided not to alter the 1999 price on either product by more than one dollar compared to the previous year's price, Truman reasoned that we should stick with exactly the same prices we charged in the previous year and advertise just enough to drive the sales of each product up to 400,000 units. That would minimize average costs, according to Truman. It also suggested an equal division of the advertising budget between the two products, which seemed fine, because we had no basis for doing otherwise. Last year was our first experience with advertising."

"One other thing, Clare," Mr. Benson continued, "do last year's results suggest any cross-impact between the two products?"

"Fortunately, not," Ms. Voyance replied. "The two products have different brand names. As far as we can tell, changing the price or the advertising on either one has negligible impact on the other product's sales."

"OK, Clare, what do you recommend for 2000?" asked Mr. Benson.

"I suggest we push for increased sales volume, greater revenue, and more market share," she replied. "We can do this by cutting both prices and by advertising both products more heavily than last year. Since the market has stabilized and there is very little inflation, I believe that 2000 will be virtually a repeat of 1999. Hence, all of my conclusions about last year apply equally to next year. I feel that now is just the time to build market share, since we have higher than average prices, and we have slack in the advertising budget. Reducing our prices to the industry average will not be seen as an aggressive move. Building market share will not be difficult, if we act now, and this will contribute to long-term profitability. On the other hand, we can certainly maintain last year's somewhat high prices without any damage, if that is what you want, Max."

"That sounds fine for you, Clare," retorted Mr. Benson. "Your bonus depends on Benson's sales revenue. But what does it do to 2000 profits? I care about company profits, and I don't want to wait forever to receive them."

Questions

1. Create a spreadsheet model for 2000 that projects for both knives and can openers: average unit manufacturing cost, unit sales, dollar sales revenues, and overall dollar profit.
2. Use Data Table(s) to find the optimal value of the dollar profit for 2000 (within the operating limits specified in the case) and the optimal value of average unit manufacturing cost for 2000.
3. Truman Hardy did not use a computer for his analysis, bute did succeed in minimizing the average unit manufacturing cost for 1999. His argument was: "*To minimize average unit manufacturing cost: 400,000 units should be produced so as to spread the fixed manufacturing costs over as large a production volume as possible, without incurring the increased variable manufacturing costs that apply to higher volumes.*" Do you accept Mr. Hardy's argument in general? Why or why not?
4. For 2000, recommend a pair of prices and a pair of advertising expenditures to Mr. Benson. Explain why you are making these recommendations. Tell Mr. Benson whether your recommendations are apt to be resisted by any of his employees. If such resistance is likely, explain to Mr. Benson how he might go about soliciting their approval and obtaining their cooperation.

Reference

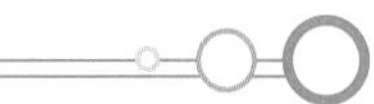

Mark Bucciarelli and Kip Brown, "A Desktop-OR Success: Modeling Coast Guard Buoy Tender Operations," *Interfaces* 25, no. 4 (1995): 1–11.

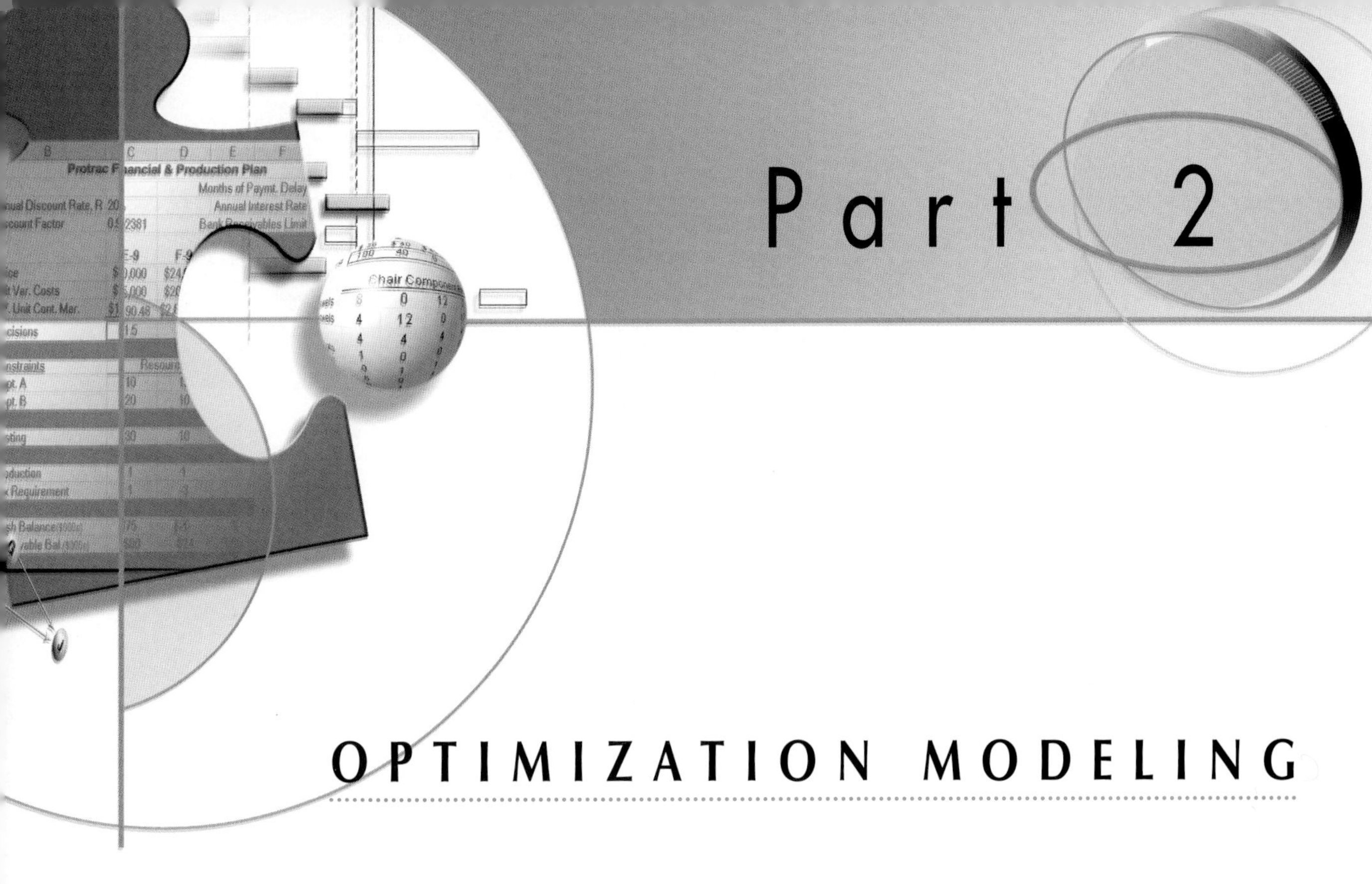

Part 2

OPTIMIZATION MODELING

As evident in the discussion at the end of Chapter 2, finding an optimal solution to a model is of great interest. Excel's Goal Seek command is highly suggestive as an efficient search technique for finding decision values that produce desirable results. However, Goal Seek has shortcomings:

1. Goal Seek cannot honor any constraints on variables in its search.
2. Goal Seek allows adjustment of only a single exogenous variable.
3. Goal Seek must have the desired performance measure value specified in advance, that is, you must know the optimal payoff value before Goal Seek can search for the decision that produces that payoff.

Chapters 3 and 4 will introduce Solver, an Excel tool that generalizes Goal Seek to remove the three shortcomings above. Solver is almost as easy to apply to a given model as Goal Seek. However, Solver is a powerful tool and its use requires care to avoid the pitfalls that can entrap the unwary modeler. For example, using Solver on some models may produce a solution that is in fact not optimal, while for others it is easy to misinterpret Solver's results. Avoiding these pitfalls requires us to understand some concepts for optimizing models. Initially, our approach will be to restrict attention to models having linear relationships among all the variables. Linear models are much easier to understand, work with, and optimize with Solver. Chapter 5 will present applications to illustrate the wide applicability of linear optimization to management situations. In addition, the theory we develop for understanding how linear models are optimized provides the basis for the integer and nonlinear models developed in Chapters 6 and 7. Chapter 12 on the CD concludes this part by considering optimization given multiple performance measures.

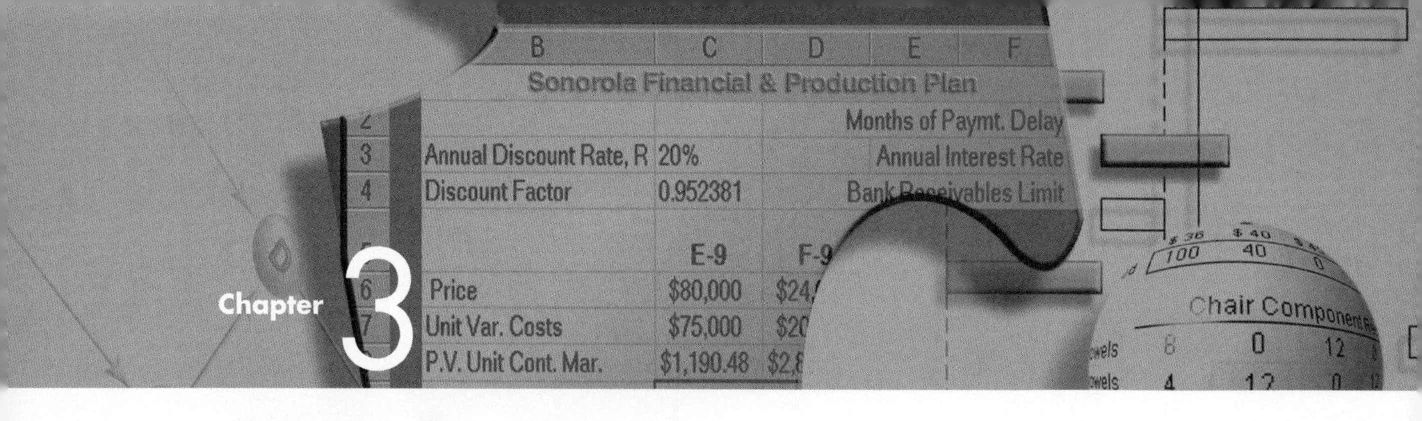

Chapter 3

LINEAR OPTIMIZATION

CHAPTER OUTLINE

APPLICATION CAPSULE Fleet Assignment at Delta Air Lines

Delta Air Lines flies over 2,500 domestic flight legs every day, using about 450 aircraft from 10 different fleets that vary by speed, capacity, amount of noise generated, and so forth. A flight leg might consist of a Boeing 757 flying from Atlanta (leaving at 6:21 A.M.) to Boston (arriving at 8:45 A.M.). The fleet assignment problem is to match aircraft (e.g., Boeing 747, 757, DC-10, or MD80) to flight legs so that seats are filled with paying passengers. The pattern that the aircraft fly along the route system is called the schedule. The schedule is the heartbeat of an airline. Delta is one of the first airlines to solve to completion this fleet assignment problem—one of the largest and most difficult problems in the airline industry.

An airline seat is the most perishable commodity in the world. Each time an aircraft takes off with an empty seat, a revenue opportunity is lost forever. So the schedule must be designed to capture as much business as possible, maximizing revenues with as little direct operating cost as possible. The airline industry combines the worst of two worlds—it has the capital-intensive quality of the manufacturing sector and the low profit margin quality of the retail sector. Airlines are capital, fuel, and labor intensive. Survival and success depend on the ability to operate flights along the schedule as efficiently as possible.

Both the size of the fleet and the number of different types of aircraft have a significant impact on schedule planning. The basic trade-off is that if the airline assigns too small a plane to a particular market, it will leave potential passengers behind, while if it assigns too large a plane, it will suffer the expense of the larger plane transporting empty seats. The goal is to have the right plane at the right place at the right time, but the many constraints on the way that planes can actually be operated make this difficult to accomplish.

Delta implemented a large-scale linear program (LP) to assign fleet types to flight legs so as to minimize a combination of operating and passenger "spill" costs, subject to a variety of operational constraints. The most important operational constraint is the number of aircraft available in each fleet. Some of the complicating factors include planning for scheduled maintenance (e.g., which is the best city to do the maintenance?), matching which pilots have the skills to fly which aircraft, providing sufficient opportunity for pilot rest time, as well as other factors such as the range and speed capability of the aircraft and airport restrictions (e.g., noise levels).

The typical size of the LP model Delta has to optimize daily is 40,000 constraints and 60,000 decision variables. Use of this LP model is expected to save Delta $300 million over the next three years. American Airlines has also reported using such LP models to help them save millions of dollars. (See Subramanian et. al.)

3.1 INTRODUCTION TO LINEAR PROGRAMMING

As we saw in the Oak Products example at the end of Chapter 2, constrained optimization models are important because they capture the essence of many important management situations. Recall from the Oak Products example, a constrained optimization model takes the form of a performance measure to be optimized over a range of feasible values of the decision variables. The feasible values of the decision variables are determined by a set of inequality constraints. That is, we must choose the values of the decision variables in such a way as to satisfy the inequality constraints while making the performance measure as large (maximization model) or as small (minimization model) as possible. For Oak Products, this was the task of finding the values of six quantity-to-produce decision variables, one for each chair type, while satisfying eleven constraints on the resources available.

Of course, "What if?" projections with the Oak Products model is one way to investigate the consequences of alternative product mixes, that is, the values of each of the six chair production quantities. Our goal is now more ambitious. In this chapter, we want to move beyond "What if?" projections to address the question of "What's best?" by finding optimal decisions. In so doing, we must avoid random or unsystematic search over a range of decision alternatives for fear of missing the optimal decision values. However, a systematic "What if?" search over the range of decision alternatives for a typical constrained optimization model would quickly become tedious even if you are the most obsessive spreadsheet user. Moreover, you cannot appeal to the Data Table command to help automate the search, as it handles at most two decision variables at a time.

Even if you could utilize an extended (more than two variables) Data Table, consider the time it would take you to do a "What if?" investigation for the Oak Products production model assuming each of the six decision variables could take on, say, 100 different candidate production quantity values. Exhaustive "What if?" investigation of all the combinations of the first decision variable (quantity of Captain Chairs to produce) for each of its 100 candidate values with each of the other five decision variables over each of their 100 values in order to tally the profit implications of each combination is practically impossible—no matter how extended the Data Table command becomes or how fast your computer:

Each of the 100 values of the first decision variable would need to be paired with the 100 values of the second decision variable (quantity of Mate chairs to produce). This yields 10,000 "What if?" inputs to give to the spreadsheet model, which in turn would compute the model's profit numbers and constraints for these 10,000 input values. But for each of these 10,000 input values there are 100 values of the third decision variable to examine, yielding 1,000,000 "What if?" inputs into the spreadsheet for tabulation for the first three decision variables. Do you see the pattern developing? Each added decision variable *multiplies* the previous number of "What if?" input combinations by 100. Since there are altogether six decision variables for the Oak Products model, the total number of "What if?" inputs for the spreadsheet model to tally is 100 times itself 6 times yielding 100^6 or 10^{12} possible alternatives to investigate. That is a thousand billion "What if?" alternatives to examine for feasibility (no constraints violated) and profitability!

(For fun, consider a slightly larger version of the Oak Products model having 20 chair types to produce instead of six. Again, assume each chair-type decision variable could take on 100 candidate production quantities. As before, the task is to completely enumerate all possible combinations of the 100 input values for each of the 20 chair types to ascertain the profit maximizing combination. To make it interesting, assume you were given simultaneous use of the computing capacity all the 150 million or so computers connected to the Internet and each of them would be dedicated to running the Oak Products spreadsheet model at the rate of, say, 100,000 or even 1,000,000 "What if?" projections per second. Use Excel to compute how many days tallying all the alternative "What if?" projections would occupy all the computers connected to Internet for this 20 decision variable example. The answer might surprise you.)

Of course, the vast majority of chair production combinations in the Oak Products example are uninteresting because they would violate one or more constraints in the model or have low profitability. But which combinations of alternatives are those? It is difficult to know in advance without first "What if?" testing each of them in Excel—a "catch-22" situation. In short, optimization models are a breed apart from the more simple "What if?" models we developed earlier. We must find a faster and more efficient way to "What if?" search over the set of decision alternatives. To do this we must, in effect, "turn the table around" by taking the spreadsheet model *inputs* normally used for "What if?" projection—the decision variables in this case—and make them into model *outputs*. This allows us to bypass exhaustive enumeration of many thousands of "What if?" input alternatives in favor of more efficient search procedures.

The Oak Products example involved six decisions (the quantity of chairs of each of six types to manufacture) and eleven constraints. Some optimization models in use today involve thousands or even tens of thousands of decision variables and constraints requiring special software and large-scale computers. However, many interesting management-oriented optimization models involve tens or hundreds of decision variables and constraints. For models in this latter range of size, a modern spreadsheet package is frequently the preferred vehicle for optimization models, such as the Oak Products one we developed in Chapter 2. For models of this size, the spreadsheet provides a near-perfect combination of flexibility, convenience of modeling, ease of use, and computational power for optimization.

Very efficient search techniques exist to optimize constrained linear models. For historical reasons a constrained linear model is called a linear program (LP). However, the flexibility of a spreadsheet requires some attention to LP model representation in it before we can proceed with the details of the optimization process itself. Our goals in this chapter are (1) to develop some techniques for formulating LP models, (2) to give some recommended rules for expressing LP models in a spreadsheet that facilitates application of Solver, the optimizer package built into Excel (and several other spreadsheet packages), and (3) to use Solver to optimize spreadsheet LP models far more efficiently than an exhaustive search.

3.2 FORMULATING LP MODELS

CONSTRAINTS

For our purposes, a first step in model formulation will be the recognition of **constraints**. In Chapter 2's Oak Products model we saw numerous causes for the appearance of constraints. Constraints can be thought of as *restrictions* on the set of allowable decisions. Specific illustrations of such restrictions are particularly evident when dealing with the problems of management. For example:

1. A portfolio manager has a certain amount of capital at his or her discretion. Investment decisions are restricted by the amount of that capital and government regulations, such as those of the Security and Exchange Commission.
2. The decisions of a plant manager are restricted by the capacity of the plant and the availability of resources.
3. The staffing and flight plans of an airline are restricted by the maintenance needs of the planes and the number of employees on hand.
4. An oil company's decision to use a certain type of crude oil in producing gasoline is restricted by the characteristics of the gasoline (e.g., the octane rating and the anti-knock capabilities).

In the context of modeling, a restriction, or constraint, on the allowable decisions is a concept of special importance. Constraints are often in one of two forms: *limitations* or *requirements*. The constraints may be further classified to reflect physical limitations or requirements, economic limitations or requirements, or policy limitations or requirements. In the examples listed above:

1. The portfolio manager is constrained by limitations of capital (economic limitation) and the stipulations of the Security and Exchange Commission (policy limitations or requirements).
2. Production decisions are constrained by limitations on capacity (physical limitations) and resource availability (physical and economic limitations).
3. The airlines are constrained by the requirement that a crew must spend at least 24 hours on the ground between flights (policy requirement).
4. The oil company is constrained by the limitation of the types of crude oil that are available (physical limitation) and the requirement that the gasoline have at least a specified octane rating (policy requirement).

THE OBJECTIVE FUNCTION

All linear programming models have two important features in common. The first feature, illustrated in the examples above, is the existence of constraints. The second feature is that in every linear programming model there is a single performance measure to be maximized or minimized.[1]

To show this, let us consider again the same four examples. The portfolio manager may want to maximize the return on the portfolio, and the production manager may want to

[1] In many situations it is not easy to develop a single performance measure acceptable to everyone. Optimization is still possible in these cases and will be treated in Chapter 12.

satisfy the demand at minimum production cost. Similarly, the airline wants to meet a given schedule at the minimum cost, and the oil company wants to use the available crude oil in such a way as to maximize profit.

Thus, you can see that in each of these examples there is some performance measure that the decision maker desires either to maximize (typically profit, return, efficiency, or effectiveness) or to minimize (typically cost or time). In the language of optimization, a performance measure to be optimized is called the **objective function**.

Every linear programming model has two important features: an *objective function* to be maximized or minimized, and *constraints*.

Linear programming provides an example of what is more generally called a *constrained decision-making model*, also called a **constrained optimization model**. One common way of describing such a model is:

A constrained optimization model represents the problem of allocating scarce resources in such a way as to optimize an objective of interest.

In this description, the phrase "scarce resources" means resources that are subject to constraints.

Although different and more general types of constrained decision-making models exist, it is nevertheless true that in many applications linear programming is most useful. It has been successfully applied to literally thousands of different types of managerial decision-making problems, and it is for this reason that we give considerable attention to the topic. We shall begin by presenting a specific numerical example of a linear programming formulation for a version of the Oak Products model introduced in Section 2.7 of Chapter 2. The Oak Products model will be simplified here to allow focusing on the mechanics of optimization; later we will show how to optimize the full Oak Products model. First, however, we will show how Solver can be used to solve the simplified decision-making model.

For ease of exposition in this simplified model Oak Products produces only two lines of chairs, Captain and Mate, instead of six lines of chairs, and will include only six constraints instead of eleven. Note that the simplified model has slightly different parameter values than the larger model of Chapter 2, but otherwise is of the same form. Using economic forecasts for next week, Jim White has judged that during that period it will be possible to sell as many Captains or Mates as the firm can produce. Jim must now recommend a production target for next week. That is, how many Captains and Mates should be produced if Oak Product's management wishes to maximize next week's profit contribution (i.e., contribution margin, defined as revenue minus variable costs)?

OAK PRODUCT DATA

Making this decision requires that the following major factors be considered:

1. Oak Product's chairs are produced and sold in the same week and the unit contribution margin (price minus unit variable cost) next week is $56 on each Captain that is sold and $40 on each Mate.
2. Assembling a chair requires long dowels, short dowels, legs, and one of two types of seats, which are available in limited inventories that cannot be increased.
3. For next week's production, the inventory of long and short dowels is 1,280 and 1,600, respectively. Each Captain produced uses 8 long dowels and 4 short dowels, whereas each Mate produced uses 4 long dowels and 12 short dowels, as summarized in Table 3.1.

Table 3.1

Dowel Data

Type	per Captain	per Mate	Total Available
	DOWELS		
Long Dowels	8	4	1280
Short Dowels	4	12	1600

Table 3.2

Legs Data

Type	per Captain	per Mate	Total Available
	LEGS		
Legs	4	4	760

Table 3.3

Seat Data

Type	per Captain	per Mate	Total Available
	SEAT		
Heavy Seat	1	0	140
Light Seat	0	1	120

4. For next week's production, the inventory of legs is 760. Each chair produced of either type uses 4 legs, as summarized in Table 3.2.
5. For next week's production, the inventory of heavy seats and light seats is 140 and 120, respectively. Each Captain produced uses a heavy seat and each Mate produced uses a light seat, as summarized in Table 3.3.
6. In order for management to honor an agreement with the union, the total number of chairs produced of both types cannot fall below 100.

Given these considerations, Jim's problem is to decide how many Captains and how many Mates to produce next week. In modeling terms, he seeks to determine the **optimal product mix**, also called the **optimal production plan**. Let us now show how this situation can be expressed first as an optimization formulation, in particular as a linear program, and then as an Excel optimization model. To do so, we must identify the constraints and the objective function.

THE CONSTRAINTS

We have stated that for each chair part there is a limitation on the amount of inventory available for producing Captains and Mates. These limitations are constraints on total chair production. To formulate the constraints concisely, let us begin by determining the number of long dowels that will be required. Recall that both Captains and Mates require long dowels. We know that each Captain produced will use 8 long dowels while each Mate produced will use 4. Hence, for any particular production plan

8(no. Captains produced) + 4(no. Mates produced) = total long dowels required.

This can be expressed more easily if we introduce some simple notation. Let

C = number of Captains to be produced

M = number of Mates to be produced

Then the expression for the total long dowels required becomes

$8C + 4M$ = total long dowels required

But, as already stated, at most 1,280 long dowels are available. It follows that the decision variables C and M must satisfy the condition (i.e., the restriction)

$$8C + 4M \leq 1280 \tag{3.1}$$

This is the constraint on total long dowels required. The symbol $\leq$ means *less than or equal to* and condition (3.1) is called an **inequality constraint**. The number 1,280 is called the **right-hand side** (RHS) of the inequality. The left-hand side (LHS) of the inequality clearly depends on the unknowns C and M, and is called a **constraint function**. The inequality (3.1) is a concise symbolic way of stating the constraint that the total long dowels required to produce C units of Captain and M units of Mate must not exceed the 1,280 long dowels available.

We also see that each Captain produced will use 4 short dowels and each Mate produced will use 12 short dowels. Since there are at most 1,600 short dowels available, it follows that the values of C and M must also satisfy

$$4C + 12M \leq 1600 \tag{3.2}$$

Inequalities (3.1) and (3.2) represent two of the constraints in the current model. Are there any others? The foregoing discussion of major considerations indicates that there is also a union agreement to be honored (i.e., major consideration 6 above). Since the requirement is on the total number of chairs,

$$C + M = \text{total number of chairs}$$

This total cannot fall below 100 chairs. Hence, we obtain the constraint

$$C + M \geq 100 \tag{3.3}$$

The symbol $\geq$ means *greater than or equal to*, and condition (3.3) is also called an inequality constraint. Note that condition (3.3) is an inequality of the $\geq$ type (a requirement), as opposed to conditions (3.1) and (3.2), which are inequalities of the $\leq$ type (limitations).

Another constraint is that each Captain and each Mate must have 4 legs and there are only 760 legs available. This is stated in symbols as

$$4C + 4M \leq 760 \tag{3.4}$$

The fourth major consideration states that at each Captain chair requires a heavy seat and each Mate requires a light seat. Since there are two types of seats involved, this translates into two constraints stated as

$$C \leq 140 \quad \text{and} \quad M \leq 120 \tag{3.5}$$

We have now specified in concise symbolic form six inequality constraints associated with Oak Product's simplified production model. Since it does not make physical sense to produce a negative number of Captains or Mates, we must include the two additional conditions

$$C \geq 0 \quad \text{and} \quad M \geq 0 \tag{3.6}$$

Conditions such as (3.6), which require C and M to be nonnegative, are called **nonnegativity conditions**. It is important to bear in mind that the term *nonnegative* is not the same as the term *positive*. The difference is that "nonnegative" allows for the possibility of the value zero, whereas the term "positive" forbids this value.

In summary, here are the constraints and the nonnegativity conditions for the simplified Oak Product, Inc., model:

$$8C + 4M \leq 1280 \tag{3.1}$$

$$4C + 12M \leq 1600 \tag{3.2}$$

$$C + M \geq 100 \tag{3.3}$$

$$4C + 4M \leq 760 \tag{3.4}$$

$$C \leq 140 \tag{3.5}$$

$$M \leq 120 \quad (3.5)$$

$$C \geq 0, \quad \text{and} \quad M \geq 0 \tag{3.6}$$

EVALUATING VARIOUS DECISIONS

In the previous model, the choice of values for the pair of variables (C, M) is called a decision; C and M are called **decision variables** because these are quantities that Jim controls. Clearly, in this problem a decision is a production mix. For example, $C = 6, M = 5$ is a decision to make six Captains and five Mates. Some nonnegative decisions will satisfy all of the constraints (3.1) through (3.5) of our model and some will not. For example, the decision $C = 6, M = 5$ can be seen to satisfy constraints (3.1), (3.2), (3.4), (3.5), and (3.6) and to violate constraint (3.3).

The mix, or decision, $C = 6$, $M = 5$ is not allowable because it has violated one of the constraints. Of the infinitely many nonnegative pairs of numbers (C, M), including fraction values, some pairs, or decisions, will violate at least one of the constraints, and some will satisfy all the constraints. In our model, only nonnegative decisions that satisfy *all* the constraints are allowable. Such decisions are called **feasible decisions.**[2]

The Objective Function Of all the allowable, or feasible, decisions, which one should be made? As we have noted earlier, every linear programming model has a specific objective as well as constraints. Jim would like to maximize next week's profit, so this is his objective. Oak Product's profit clearly comes from two sources.

1. There is profit contribution from the sale of Captains.
2. There is profit contribution from the sale of Mates.

In our earlier discussion of major factors to be considered it was stated that the unit contribution margin is \$56 for each Captain and \$40 for each Mate. Since Oak Product makes \$56 for each Captain produced, and since C denotes the number of Captains to be produced, we see that

$$56C = \text{profit contribution from producing } C \text{ units of Captain.}$$

Similarly,

$$40M = \text{profit contribution from producing } M \text{ units of Mate.}$$

Thus, the decision to produce C units of Captains and M units of Mates results in a total profit contribution given by

$$\text{total profit contribution} = 56C + 40M \tag{3.7}$$

Note, in general, that when only revenue data are given (or available) the only thing that can be done is to maximize revenue subject to the constraints. If only variable cost data are available, then all that can be done is to minimize the cost of having to produce a certain product mix. However, if variable cost and revenue data are available, it is usually more advantageous to maximize profit contribution rather than revenue.

An Optimal Solution Of all the infinitely many decisions that satisfy all the constraints (i.e., of all feasible decisions), one that gives the largest total profit contribution will be called a *solution* to the Oak Product model, or, as often referred to, an **optimal solution.** Thus, we seek a decision that will *maximize* total weekly profit contribution relative to the set of all possible feasible decisions. Such a decision is called an **optimal decision.** Since total profit contribution is a *function* of the variables C, M, we refer to the expression $56C + 40M$ as the *payoff* or *objective function*, and we want to find feasible values of C and M

---

[2] Obviously, a fractional production quantity may be feasible for the model, but not necessarily feasible in practice because Jim cannot sell a fraction of a chair. We will discuss this decision implementation issue at the end of this section.

that **optimize** (which in this case means maximize) the objective function. Our objective, then, in symbolic terms, is stated concisely as

$$\text{maximize } 56C + 40M$$

or, even more simply, this is usually written as

$$\text{Max } 56C + 40M \tag{3.8}$$

The objective function is to be maximized *only* over the set of feasible decisions.

OBSERVATIONS ON THE OAK PRODUCT MODEL

In the following section we shall see how to rigorously (i.e., without guesswork) optimize this model and many others like it from their spreadsheet representation. Also, we shall see how Solver is used to do much of the work for us. Let us first, however, take a moment to review the complete symbolic formulation of the Oak Product, Inc., model and to make several observations on the form of this model.

In the preceding discussion we translated a verbal description of a real-world situation into a complete symbolic model with an objective function and constraints. This model, which we call the **symbolic LP model**, is

$$
\begin{aligned}
&\text{Max } 56C + 40M \text{ (objective function)}\\
&\text{subject to (s.t.)}\\
&\qquad 8C + 4M \leq 1280 \quad \text{(long dowels restriction)}\\
&\qquad 4C + 12M \leq 1600 \quad \text{(short dowels restriction)}\\
&\qquad C + M \geq 100 \quad \text{(minimum production)}\\
&\qquad 4C + 4M \leq 760 \quad \text{(legs restriction)}\\
&\qquad C \leq 140 \quad \text{(heavy seats restriction)}\\
&\qquad M \leq 120 \quad \text{(light seats restriction)}\\
&\qquad C \geq 0 \text{ and } M \geq 0 \quad \text{(nonnegativity conditions)}
\end{aligned}
$$

Linear Functions Notice that in the model above, all the constraint functions (recall that the constraint functions are the left-hand sides of the inequality constraints) and the objective function are **linear functions** of the two decision variables. As you may recall, the graph of a linear function of two variables is a straight line. In general, a linear function is one where each variable appears in a separate term together with its coefficient (i.e., there are no products or quotients of variables, no exponents other than 1, no logarithmic, exponential, or trigonometric terms, and in Excel no IF() statements). As you can see, this is true of each function in the model above. By contrast, $14C + 12CM$ is a nonlinear function because of the term $12CM$ involving a product of the variables. Also, $9C^2 + 8M$ is nonlinear because the variable C is raised to the power 2. Other examples of nonlinear functions are $6\sqrt{C} + M$ and $19Log\ C + 12C^2M$. Examples of Excel functions that frequently introduce nonlinearity into models are IF( ), MAX( ), MIN( ), LN( ), and ABS( ).

As you might imagine, from the mathematical point of view, nonlinear functions are more difficult to deal with. The power of linear programming, in applications, stems from the simplicity of linear relationships (equalities and inequalities) and from the fact that linear models can be readily used in real applications by managers and analysts with little or even no training in the underlying mathematics. For our purposes at this time the important facts to be remembered are

1. A linear program always has an objective function (to be either maximized or minimized) and constraints.
2. All functions in the problem (objective and constraints) are *linear functions.*

Integrality Considerations In making a final observation, let us take another look at the complete formulation of the Oak Product model. It should be pointed out that unless we put in specific additional constraints, which force the decision variables to be integers, we must be prepared to accept fractional solutions. In many LP models, such as in the Oak Product model, it will be true that fractional values for the decision variables do not have meaningful physical interpretations. For example, a solution that says "produce 3.12 Captains and 6.88 Mates" may not be directly implementable. On the other hand, there are many problems for which fractions obviously have meaning (e.g., "produce 98.65 gallons of gasoline"). In those cases where fractional answers are not directly meaningful, there are four possible recourses:

1. Add a so-called **integrality condition** to the LP model, which forces one or more decision variables to take on only integer values. This changes the model to what is called an integer optimization model or **integer program**. Integer programming models involve many additional considerations beyond the usual linear program that are best postponed for now. Integer programs are discussed at length in Chapter 6.
2. Solve the model as an ordinary LP and then round (e.g., to the nearest integer) any decision variable for which a fractional answer cannot be implemented. In many cases this simple and plausible tactic produces solutions that may not be feasible or may not be optimal. The pitfalls of this approach are also discussed in Chapter 6.
3. Consider the one-week Oak Product model results to be an *average* week's production for an ongoing multiple week situation. For example, a solution that says "produce 70.5 Captains and 80.25 Mates" can be implemented as "follow a production plan that produces 70.5 Captains every week but (1) sells 70 Captains in one week leaving one half a Captain as 'work-in-process' inventory that is carried over to be finished the next week, and (2) sells 71 Captains every other week. Similarly, produce 80.25 Mates every week but (1) sell only 80 Mates each week carrying any fractional Mate as work-in-process inventory into the next week, except (2) sell 81 Mates in every fourth week." Clearly, such a rule results in production and sales averaged over each four-week interval of 70.5 Captains and 80.25 Mates per week, as stipulated by the LP solution. The advantages and disadvantages of using an average week model as a surrogate for production decisions across several weeks are discussed in Chapter 5 on formulating "dynamic models," also called "multi-time period" or "multi-period" models.
4. Consider the one-week Oak Product model results to be for planning purposes only and not operational decisions to be implemented *per se.* That is, the model results will serve only as a guide for final decision making, which necessarily will involve many other real-world considerations not captured by the more abstract LP model. Such considerations may very likely force the final management decisions to deviate from the fractional-valued LP decisions anyway. In this case, the LP model solution provides a starting point for such considerations or the basis for managerial insight, which you recall was the original rationale for modeling developed in Chapter 1.

In practice, all of these approaches are adopted. For the present it will suffice to assume that either fractional solutions are meaningful in the sense that they are average production rates—option 3 above—or that the model is the basis for planning and insight—option 4 above.

3.3 THE ART OF LP MODEL FORMULATION

In translating a managerial situation into a symbolic model, you may find it helpful first to create a verbal model. That is, you might proceed as follows:

1. Express the objective and its performance measure objective function in words.
2. Express each constraint in words; in doing this, pay careful attention to whether the constraint is a requirement of the form $\geq$ (at least as large as), a limitation of the form $\leq$ (no larger than), or $=$ (exactly equal to).

   Steps 1 and 2 should then allow you to

3. Verbally identify the decision variables.

It is usually of great importance that your decision variables be correctly defined. Sometimes you may feel that there are several possible choices. For example, should they represent pounds of finished product or pounds of raw material? One guideline that is often useful is to ask yourself the question, *What decisions must be made in order to optimize the objective function*? The answer to this question will help lead you to identify the decision variables correctly.

Having accomplished steps 1 through 3, invent symbolic notation or names for the decision variables. Then

4. Express each constraint in symbols (i.e., in terms of the decision variables).
5. Express the objective function in symbols (in terms of the decision variables).

At this stage it is advisable to check your work for consistency of units of measurement. For example, if the coefficients in the objective function are in dollars per *pound*, the decision variables that appear in the objective function should be in pounds, not tons or ounces. Similarly, check that for each constraint the units on the right-hand side and the units on the left-hand side are the same. For example, if one of the constraints is a limitation of $\leq$ form on labor hours, the right-hand side will be labor hours. Then if, as above, the decision variables are pounds, the data for this constraint function (i.e., the numerical coefficients for each decision variable on the left-hand side of the constraint) should be in labor hours per pound. To put it quite simply, you do not want to end up with hours on one side of any equality or inequality and minutes or seconds or pounds or tons on the other.

At this point it would be a good idea to comment on one other aspect of model formulation. We have seen that inequality constraints may be of the form $\leq$ or $\geq$. Students often ask whether a linear programming model can have a *strict inequality* constraint, such as $<$ or $>$. The answer is a resounding *no*. The reason for this is mathematical in nature. It is to assure that a well-formulated model will have a solution. The mathematical details required to justify this assertion lie outside our scope of interest. However, this is not a costly prohibition, for in just about any real-world situation you can imagine involving inequality constraints, it is true that the $\leq$ or $\geq$ representation entirely captures the real-world meaning. For example, if a variable X must be < 15, then using $X \leq 14.9999999999$ in the model will be adequate for management purposes.

Let us now discuss one critical aspect of model formulation. This deals with the nature of the cost data to be employed.

3.4 SUNK VERSUS VARIABLE COST

In many real-world problems there are often two types of costs: **sunk costs** and **variable costs**. Contrary to the first impressions that students sometimes have, sunk costs play no part in optimization.

> Only the variable costs are relevant in optimization models.

The sunk costs have already been paid, which means that no future decisions can affect these expenditures. For example, suppose that 800 pounds and 500 pounds of two grades of aluminum (grade 1 and grade 2) have been purchased for future delivery, at specified prices, \$5 and \$10 per pound, respectively, and that the contract has been signed. Management's problem is, in part, to determine the optimal use of these 1,300 pounds of aluminum so as, perhaps, to maximize profit obtained from producing aluminum knuckles and conduits. Associated with these two products there will be revenues and variable costs incurred in their production (costs of machining, stamping, and so on). In formulations of this type of model, the sunk costs of \$9,000 associated with the contracted purchase are irrelevant. This amount has already been spent and hence the *quantities to be purchased* are no longer decision variables. The variables will be how much product should be produced, and the relevant cost in this determination is only the variable cost. More specifically, the formulation corresponding to the description above might be as follows. Let

K = number of knuckles to be produced (decision variable)

C = number of conduits to be produced (decision variable)

\$10 = revenue per knuckle

\$30 = revenue per conduit

\$4 = cost of producing a knuckle (variable cost)

\$12 = cost of producing a conduit (variable cost)

For each product we must calculate what accountants call the *unit contribution margin*, that is, the difference between per unit revenue and per unit variable cost. The unit contribution margins are

for knuckles: \$10 – \$4 = \$6

for conduits: \$30 – \$12 = \$18

Suppose that each knuckle uses 1 unit of grade 1 aluminum and 2 units of grade 2 aluminum. Each conduit uses 3 units of grade 1 and 5 units of grade 2. Then we obtain the following symbolic linear programming model:

$$\text{Max } 6K + 18C$$
$$\text{s.t. } K + 3C \leq 800 \text{ (grade 1 limitation)}$$
$$2K + 5C \leq 500 \text{ (grade 2 limitation)}$$
$$K \geq 0, \qquad C \geq 0$$

One way to see the irrelevance of the sunk cost is to note that the objective function in the formulation is the total profit contribution. The income, or net profit, would be

$$\text{net profit} = \text{profit contribution} - \text{sunk cost}$$
$$= 6K + 18C - 9000$$

Finding feasible values of K and C that maximize $6K + 18C - 9000$ is the same as finding feasible values that maximize $6K + 18C$. The constant term of 9,000 can therefore be ignored. The bottom line here is that maximizing a function plus a constant, or even a positive constant times a function, gives in either case the same result, in terms of optimal values of decision variables, that you would obtain without the constant. However, adding (or subtracting) the same constant to (or from) each decision variable *coefficient* in the objective function may change the result.

To summarize, sunk costs affect only the accounting report of income or net profit in financial statements. Sunk costs play no part in decision making because by definition they are unrelated to future decisions, the subject of the modeling activity. Of course, there is no harm in subtracting the sunk cost from the objective function in the model—the same optimal decisions will be found when the model is optimized. However, there is great harm in attempting to allocate the sunk costs to the production activities if that allocation involves adjusting the variable cost coefficients in the model instead of just subtracting the total allocated costs from total cost.

A common mistake made by managers is to confuse an organization's accounting policies for allocating sunk costs to activities with the proper (short run) decision making involving those activities. For example, suppose the company above has a policy to split the \$9,000 sunk cost, say, in half, charging the Knuckle Department \$4,500 and the Conduit Department \$4,500. This would have no effect upon departmental decision making—reported profit from each department would be reduced by \$4,500 and reported overall corporate profit would reflect the same \$9,000 cost. But if the Knuckle Department revises the knuckle production cost coefficient in its LP production model from the variable cost of \$4 used originally to $\$4 + \$4500/K$, where the $\$4500/K$ term is the average of the apportioned sunk cost per knuckle produced, then nonoptimal decisions will occur when the model is optimized. Why is this? Because the actual incremental cost of producing an additional knuckle is \$4, no more and no less. Adding the additional term to the knuckle variable cost to reflect an averaging of the sunk costs, therefore, misstates the incremental (marginal) cost of knuckle production, and it is the behavior of the marginal costs that is important in optimizing decisions.

To see this, assume that $K = 1{,}000$ knuckles were being produced when the allocation of the sunk costs occurred. Under the "averaging-of-sunk-costs" scheme, the Knuckle Department will record that its average cost of knuckle production was $\$4 + \$4500/1000 = \$8.50$ per knuckle. We know that producing the $K + 1$st knuckle will cost the department an additional \$4, its variable cost of production. However, substituting \$8.50 as the knuckle production cost in the LP model misstates the cost dynamics by forcing the model to use \$8.50 as the incremental cost of that knuckle. This, in turn, will lead to much smaller than optimal quantities of knuckle production when the model is optimized. In short, calculating an average cost quantity from an apportioned sunk cost and then treating it as if it were a marginal or variable cost is a common management mistake to avoid in formulating an LP (or any other) model.

Treatment of sunk and variable costs is nicely illustrated in the Red Brand Canners case at this chapter's end. This case is a good illustration of how both sunk and variable costs arise in real-world situations.

3.5 THE OAK PRODUCT SPREADSHEET MODEL

CREATING THE OAK PRODUCT SPREADSHEET

Recall, the simplified LP model for Oak Product weekly production in terms of the decision variables C (= the number of Captains to produce) and M (= the number of Mates to produce) is given by:

$$\text{Max } 56C + 40M \text{ (objective function)}$$

subject to (s.t.)

$$\begin{aligned}
8C + 4M &\leq 1280 && \text{(long dowels restriction)}\\
4C + 12M &\leq 1600 && \text{(short dowels restriction)}\\
4C + 4M &\leq 760 && \text{(legs restriction)}\\
C &\leq 140 && \text{(heavy seats restriction)}\\
M &\leq 120 && \text{(light seats restriction)}\\
C + M &\geq 100 && \text{(minimum production)}\\
C \geq 0 \quad \text{and} \quad M &\geq 0 && \text{(nonnegativity conditions)}
\end{aligned}$$

Note that the constraints have been regrouped to put all constraints of a like-type of inequality together. The reason for grouping constraints will become clear when Solver is introduced. A spreadsheet version of the simplified Oak Product model, available as SimpleOakProduct.xls, is shown in Figure 3.1. The figure shows the model results for the Captain production of 110 and Mate production of 90. Notice that these production quantities violate the legs inventory constraint, requiring more legs than available in inventory.

FIGURE 3.1

The Simplified Oak Product Production LP Model

TIP: *The easiest way to produce inequality symbols, such as the ≤ in cell E6, is to type the < character into the cell and then click Excel's Underline tool to underline it.*

	A	B	C	D	E	F	G
1		**Simplified Oak Products Model**					
2	Chair Style	Captain	Mate				
3	Profit / Chair	$ 56	$ 40	Profit			
4	Production Qty.	110	90	$9,760			
5		Chair Component Requirements		Total Usage		Start. Inventory	End. Inv.
6	Long Dowels	8	4	1240	≤	1280	40
7	Short Dowels	4	12	1520	≤	1600	80
8	Legs	4	4	800	≤	760	-40
9	Heavy Seats	1	0	110	≤	140	30
10	Light Seats	0	1	90	≤	120	30
11				Chairs		Min. Prod.	Slack
12	Chair Production	1	1	200	≥	100	100

	A	B	C	D	E	F	G
1		**Simpl**					
2	Chair Style	Captain	Mate				
3	Profit / Chair	56	40	Profit			
4	Production Qty.	110	90	=SUMPRODUCT($B$4:$C$4,B3:C3)			
5		Chair Comp		Total Usage		Start. Inventory	End. Inv.
6	Long Dowels	8	4	=SUMPRODUCT($B$4:$C$4,B6:C6)	≤	1280	=F6-D6
7	Short Dowels	4	12	=SUMPRODUCT($B$4:$C$4,B7:C7)	≤	1600	=F7-D7
8	Legs	4	4	=SUMPRODUCT($B$4:$C$4,B8:C8)	≤	760	=F8-D8
9	Heavy Seats	1	0	=SUMPRODUCT($B$4:$C$4,B9:C9)	≤	140	=F9-D9
10	Light Seats	0	1	=SUMPRODUCT($B$4:$C$4,B10:C10	≤	120	=F10-D10
11				Chairs		Min. Prod.	Slack
12	Chair Production	1	1	=SUMPRODUCT($B$4:$C$4,B12:C12	≥	100	=D12-F12

Although most of the entries in the spreadsheet are self-explanatory, you should consult the formulas for the spreadsheet to verify that the spreadsheet has faithfully captured the symbolic model for Oak Product production. (As usual, consult Appendix B for additional information on any Excel spreadsheet items you do not understand.)

Also, pay close attention in Figure 3.1 to the layout of the spreadsheet model and how labels, coefficients, and decision variables are used, and how "slack" is computed.

Labels In particular, some cells contain labels. The labels are used in the same way that you would use labels to help read a table of data. Their purpose is to clarify the meaning of other entries in the spreadsheet. Notice how additional labels were added in row 11 to clarify the last constraint that doesn't relate to inventories.

Coefficients and Decision Variables Other cells contain numbers. Generally these numbers will represent

a. The numeric value of the coefficients and right-hand sides, which are the **parameters** for the given LP model.
b. Numeric values for the two decision variables. These numeric values are called **decision values** or just **decisions** for short.

Formulas Excel formulas are required to represent the objective function and the constraint functions (left-hand sides) in column D. In some instances, there may be underlying formulas that determine the numeric value of various coefficients in the model. Thus, for some coefficients numeric values will be entered directly. Other coefficients might be computed from formulas.

Computing Slack With the exception of G11:G12 the other entries in the spreadsheet should be self-explanatory. It remains to explain the entry, termed **slack**, that appears in G12.

In spreadsheet LP models *slack* is the generic term used to describe the difference between the constraint function and the right-hand side computed so that it is nonnegative.

Often more meaningful terminology than "slack" is preferable, such as "Ending Inventory" used in cell G5, and furthermore, the calculations in column G are optional. Their purpose is to give an indication of how close any given constraint is to **binding**, that is, evaluated as an equality; zero slack indicates a binding constraint. For example, look at the ending inventory formula in cell G6. This value corresponds to the long dowels limitation constraint , which is $8C + 4M \leq 1280$. The spreadsheet shows the formula =F6-D6 for the ending inventory value, which is the "right-hand side of the first constraint minus the left-hand side." Thus, the ending inventory or "slack" value for this constraint is unused long dowel capacity. Now consider the minimum chair production constraint $C + M \geq 100$. The entry in cell G12 of the spreadsheet shows that the slack formula is the "left-hand side minus the right-hand side," which is the order of subtraction required to make this slack value nonnegative. What we have just illustrated is the following rule:

For a ≤ constraint, slack is the right-hand side minus the left-hand side.
For a ≥ constraint, slack is the left-hand side minus the right-hand side.

Although optional, calculating slack is very useful. For example, it is immediately obvious that the production plan in Figure 3.1 is infeasible, as signaled by the negative ending inventory in cell G8.

As with Ending Inventory, often more descriptive labels can be used in place of the generic term "Slack." For ≤ constraints labels such as Unused, Remainder, Residue, or Balance may be preferable. For ≥ constraints, the generic term **surplus** is frequently substituted and labels such as Surplus, Oversupply, Excess, or Overage may be preferable.

One obvious use of the Oak Product spreadsheet model is to perform "What if?" projections for different production decisions, that is, values of Captain and Mate, by typing values into cells B4 and C4, respectively, and observing cell D4, the resulting weekly profit contribution, while keeping the slack cells G6 through G12 nonnegative. This is what Jim and Tom did for the original Oak Products model in Chapter 2. If, for example, we enter the value 20 into cell B4 and 80 into cell C4 (meaning $C = 20$ and $M = 80$), then the spreadsheet will display the result shown in Figure 3.2.

Using SimpleOakProd.xls from the CD-ROM, see if you can find a high profit by interactively trying out different decision values for C and M in a "What if?" fashion, as Jim and Tom did earlier. You'll quickly see that finding a high profit while not violating any constraints (avoiding negative slack) is not so easy, even for the simplified Oak Product LP model.

Optimizing the Spreadsheet With Solver you can transform any spreadsheet LP model into an optimized model with a few clicks of the mouse. Figure 3.3 shows the optimized spreadsheet for the simplified Oak Product LP model.

3.6 THE LP MODEL AND SPREADSHEET MODELING

You have now seen how to capture the Oak Product production model in two forms, the symbolic LP model and the spreadsheet representation of the LP model

You may well be wondering, "Do I need to write both the symbolic LP model and the Excel model for every managerial situation I wish to model? Also, why did you lay out the spreadsheet model of Oak Product as you did? Finally, how did you get Solver to produce the optimal solution in Figure 3.3?"

FIGURE 3.2

The Oak Product Production LP Model for $C = 20$ and $M = 80$

	A	B	C	D	E	F	G
1		Simplified Oak Products Model					
2	Chair Style	Captain	Mate				
3	Profit / Chair	$ 56	$ 40	Profit			
4	Production Qty.	20	80	$4,320			
5		Chair Component Requirements		Total Usage		Start. Inventory	End. Inv.
6	Long Dowels	8	4	480	≤	1280	800
7	Short Dowels	4	12	1040	≤	1600	560
8	Legs	4	4	400	≤	760	360
9	Heavy Seats	1	0	20	≤	140	120
10	Light Seats	0	1	80	≤	120	40
11				Chairs		Min. Prod.	Slack
12	Chair Production	1	1	100	≥	100	0

TIP: *As you will see later, the inequality symbols in column E separating the LHS and RHS values are* not *used by Solver, and thus, are optional. However, using them greatly facilitates model documentation.*

Although we will elaborate on this below, the best answer to your first question is "Yes, until you become more proficient, you should write both the symbolic (algebraic) LP model and the spreadsheet version of it." A spreadsheet is very useful for representing managerial LP models, and is especially useful for subsequent "What if?" manipulations. However, for novices, modeling directly on a spreadsheet is not always the best approach to your early LP model formulations. Experience has shown that until you become more proficient with LP modeling directly in Excel, the preferred approach to quickly producing a bug-free Excel LP model is to break down the process into three steps:

1. **Writing and debugging the symbolic LP model**: Write out the model on paper as a symbolic LP; this will only take a few minutes and it pays off in faster debugging of your final Excel model. Proceed to debug it, which means examine your written formulation and look for errors in the logic of the formulation.
2. **Translating and debugging the spreadsheet representation of the symbolic LP model**: Use the symbolic LP model as a guide in creating the Excel representation.

FIGURE 3.3

Profit Maximizing Values of C and M

	A	B	C	D	E	F	G
1		Simplified Oak Products Model					
2	Chair Style	Captain	Mate				
3	Profit / Chair	$ 56	$ 40	Profit			
4	Production Qty.	130	60	$9,680			
5		Chair Component Requirements		Total Usage		Start. Inventory	End. Inv.
6	Long Dowels	8	4	1280	≤	1280	0
7	Short Dowels	4	12	1240	≤	1600	360
8	Legs	4	4	760	≤	760	0
9	Heavy Seats	1	0	130	≤	140	10
10	Light Seats	0	1	60	≤	120	60
11				Chairs		Min. Prod.	Slack
12	Chair Production	1	1	190	≥	100	90

Then further debug the Excel representation of the model by trying out several candidate sets of values for the decision variables to see if any obvious errors occur (constraint violations for decisions known to be feasible, nonsense values for LHS or performance measure cells, etc.).

3. **Try to optimize the model with Solver**: An incorrectly formulated model will often trigger a Solver error message. Again, you must now debug your work, possibly by returning to Step 1 above.

The symbolic model in Step 1 is useful for documentation, allows you to "see" the entire model, and guides you in laying out a clean and easily understood Excel spreadsheet representation. Spreadsheet formulas are often a poor substitute for this global perspective of the LP model and how it relates to the original real-world situation. For a rather complicated model it is easier to examine and mentally analyze the structure of the symbolic LP model first. In fact, elucidating the structure of the underlying LP model will occupy much of our attention for the next few chapters after we address your last two questions.

In answer to your second question ("Why was the Oak Product LP model laid out in the spreadsheet this way?"), the layout of the Oak Product production model reflects a style of spreadsheet model formulation that we recommend you follow in the beginning for Excel representations of LP models. Haphazard construction of the Excel version of the LP model is *by far* the most frequent reason for student frustration and lack of results in the optimization phase with Solver that we cover next. Detecting subtle errors in the interrelationships among cells in formulas and avoiding certain interpretation problems for Solver-generated reports is greatly facilitated if initially you follow the style evident in the Oak Product production model and the examples that follow it. Later, as you become more proficient with spreadsheet LP formulations, you will be able to skip the symbolic modeling step. Until then, if you are new to LP modeling, here are a few recommendations for laying out an Excel LP model.

- Each decision variable is allocated to a separate cell, often grouped together across columns and/or rows, and each constraint is allocated to a separate row and/or column in the spreadsheet. (Usually, decision variables go into columns and constraints go into rows.)
- Except for optional labels, the decision variables are grouped into a contiguous block of columns/rows and, except for optional labels, the constraints are grouped into a contiguous block of rows/columns.
- Each decision variable cell and the objective function cell has a label at the top of its column, and each constraint has a label in the leftmost cell of its row. (Do not break a label by putting pieces of it into multiple cells. If a label cannot fit into a single cell, widen the cell width or use the "Wrap Text" option under the Alignment tab in the Format Cells menu to vertically expand the size of the cell.)
- The unit payoff (e.g., contribution margin or cost) coefficients are contained in a separate row of cells immediately above or below their respective decision variables, and the objective function formula appears in a nearby cell.
- The decision variable cells and the objective function cell (payoff) are formatted with cell borders and/or cell shading—to facilitate readability.
- For each constraint the coefficient involving a given decision variable is placed as a datum in the cell at the intersection of the column or row containing that decision variable and that constraint's row or column.

- Following the coefficients in each constraint row is a cell computing the constraint function value (left-hand side totals), followed by a cell indicating the direction of the inequality, followed by the right-hand side proviso cell. Optionally a "slack" cell formula may be included giving the difference between the LHS and RHS quantities computed so that the cell's value is always nonnegative when the constraint is satisfied:

  Slack cell is = RHS – LHS for ≤ (limitation) constraints, and

  Slack cell is = LHS – RHS for ≥ (requirement) constraints.

- For the constraint rows the right-hand side cells should contain constants or formulas not involving the decision variables. To avoid Solver Report interpretation problems later, any constraint right-hand side formula related directly or indirectly to the decision variables should be algebraically moved to the left-hand side of that constraint.
- Use *no* IF(), ABS(), MAX(), MIN(), and so forth, functions or other nonlinear functions within the cells of your LP model formulation. Such functions are acceptable in cells elsewhere in the spreadsheet, but *only* if their evaluation cannot affect the objective function cell's calculation directly or indirectly during the Solver optimization process in which alternative decision values are tested.
- Including any nonnegativity constraints on the decision variables into the Excel model itself is optional, and typically, they are omitted in favor of specifying them directly in Solver's dialog box.

One consequence of this recommended method of laying out the spreadsheet model is that all the important coefficients in the model are contained in cells that can be easily changed without editing any spreadsheet formulas. Also, the grouping of decision variables and constraints allows convenient use of the spreadsheet Copy command to easily replicate formulas across cells, such as for the LHS constraint function totals. It also makes filling in Solver's dialogs more convenient by allowing use of cell ranges to specify a group of decision variables or constraints.

3.7 OVERVIEW OF SOLVER

Solver is an add-in package to Excel that numerically optimizes constrained models, such as an LP model. In doing this, Solver uses a technique called a mathematical programming algorithm to efficiently find the optimal decisions for a given spreadsheet model. An algorithm is simply a computer code that follows an iterative recipe for finding the optimal decisions. For LP's Solver uses a very efficient optimization algorithm—that works only on LP models—called for historical reasons the "Simplex Method." Not surprisingly, to benefit from this powerful capability there are some prices to pay. As discussed previously, you must set up the spreadsheet model in the appropriate form so that Solver can optimize it; you must adhere to certain technical restrictions imposed on your spreadsheet model by Solver; and most importantly, you must understand the limitations of optimization models to properly interpret Solver's results.

Solver can optimize both linear and nonlinear models. For now, we will focus only upon linear models because they are far less prone to technical difficulties. Remember: for LP optimization *every* formula in your model that includes the decision variables directly (or indirectly via a chain of cell references) and that directly or indirectly affects the objective function cell *must* be linear. The restriction (linearity) is imposed by Solver's Simplex linear programming algorithm that works correctly only for spreadsheet formulas involving linear relationships. Do not forget that many built-in Excel functions—those operations preceded by *function-name*()—involve nonlinear relationships and are not usable in your spreadsheet LP model if you intend to use the linear optimization option of Solver. In particular, the occurrence of

- Exponentiation in Excel equations,
- The use of Excel's IF(), ABS(), and LOG() functions, to name three, and
- Forming ratios (X/Y) or products (X*Y) of (decision) variables

directly or indirectly in Excel formulas, will very likely cause your model to violate linearity if these affect values of your objective function directly or indirectly via the constraints.

All Excel formulas used in your spreadsheet LP model must involve strictly linear relationships among the (decision) variables, either directly or indirectly, as they pertain to calculation of the objective function cell and the specification of any constraints.

Note that it is OK to have nonlinear formulas in your spreadsheet, even if they employ use of decision variable cells, if those formulas do not relate to determining the value of the objective function cell directly or indirectly through any constraints. An example of this is the calculation of a nonlinear statistic used only for management reporting purposes and not used elsewhere in your model's LP formulas.

USING SOLVER

The Solver add-in package consists essentially of two computer programs. The first is an Excel Visual Basic program that translates your spreadsheet model to an internal representation used by the second program. The second program, residing in memory outside of Excel as a separate software module, carries out the actual optimization and returns the solution to the first program for updating of the spreadsheet. The two communicate by means of an internal application programming interface, the details of which need not concern us. Upon choosing the Solver . . . item from the Excel Tools menu, you evoke the first Solver program that prepares your spreadsheet for optimization and calls the second optimizer program.

Your use of Solver, therefore, consists of several steps:

1. Start Excel and perform spreadsheet modeling operations normally. You can develop your Excel model, perform "What if?" and debugging analyses, and print the results in the usual way.
2. Once the model is developed and debugged (and saved to disk!), you optimize it by choosing the Solver . . . item from the Tools menu.
3. The Solver add-in and its optimization module will be loaded into memory.[3] When the loading is finished, Solver brings up a dialog box to collect information for the optimization process.
4. After specifying certain housekeeping details, such as which cell contains the objective function formula to be optimized and which cells contain decision variables, you click the "Solve" button.
5. Solver will then translate your model and carry out the optimization process. For small LP models this takes only few seconds on a modern personal computer, but for big models, it may take several minutes or longer.
6. Assuming there are no errors in your spreadsheet LP model, Solver will bring up a Solver Results dialog box in which you can request reports and have Solver update

[3] Macintosh users of Solver should increase Excel's default memory allocation by about 1Mbyte to accommodate Solver (and other add-ins). Otherwise, inadequate memory will slow Excel drastically.

your original model with the optimal decision cell values. Solver creates each requested report on a separate worksheet in your Excel workbook that you can save or print.

7. At this point, you are now in a position to continue "What If" projections to, for example, perform sensitivity analyses in the neighborhood of the optimum decisions.

A diagrammatic view of the steps in using Solver is given in Figure 3.4.

SOLVER TERMINOLOGY

Now that you have the "big picture" of how Solver works, we turn to details of how to instruct Solver to optimize your LP model. First, we need to clarify the terminology Solver uses to view your LP model. This change in terminology is necessary because Solver views the world only through the cells of a spreadsheet and not as the symbolic representation we use in LP models. Otherwise, the differences are nominal. Table 3.4 summarizes the differences in nomenclature between that used for our LP models and Solver.

FIGURE 3.4

Solver Flowchart

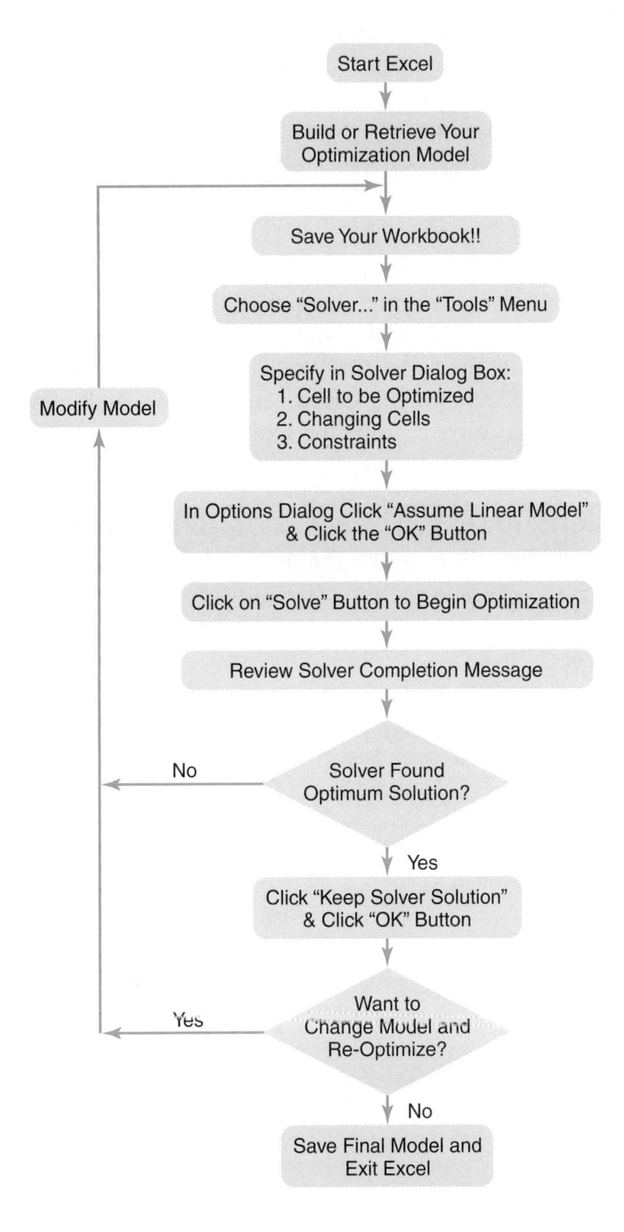

Table 3.4

Solver Terminology

LP MODELING TERMINOLOGY	SOLVER TERMINOLOGY
Objective Function	Set Cell
Decision Variables	Changing Variable Cells
Constraints	Constraints
Constraint Function (LHS)	Constraint Cell Reference
RHS	Constraint or Bound
LP Model	Assume Linear Model or Standard Simplex LP

There is one additional consideration that is important to remember for LP models. Often, negative decisions have no meaning, such as negative production of chairs in Oak Products, and so, in these cases, there should be a nonnegativity constraint on the LP's decision variables. Because they are so obvious, these nonnegativity constraints are rarely listed explicitly on the Excel spreadsheet version of the LP model. However, overlooking this nonnegativity specification on the decision variables is a common oversight when using Solver for optimizing LP models:

> If negative decisions have no meaning, remember to specify the nonnegativity constraints on your LP model's decision variables before optimizing it with Solver.

3.8 OPTIMIZING THE OAK PRODUCT MODEL WITH SOLVER

Learning to use Solver is best if you follow along the steps below while sitting at your computer. (If in the process you run into technical difficulties with Solver, consult Appendix C.) As outlined in the steps of the flowchart in Figure 3.4, if you haven't done so already, launch Excel and open the SimpleOakProd.xls workbook from the book's CD-ROM containing the simplified Oak Product spreadsheet model we built previously. Invoke the Solver add-in by selecting Solver . . . from the Tools menu, as shown in Figure 3.5.[4]

FIGURE 3.5

Invoking Solver

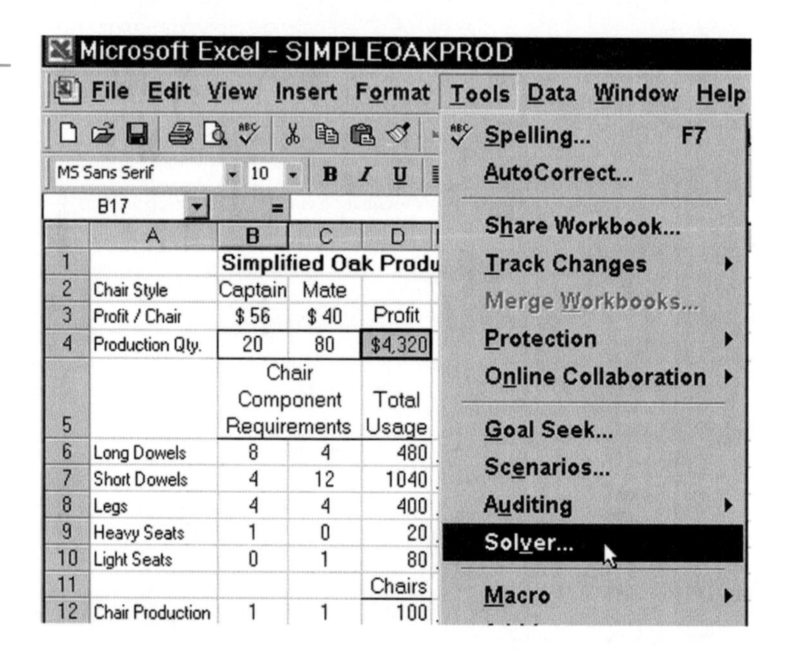

[4] Usually, the Solver add-in is *not* automatically installed for Excel during Microsoft's Setup procedure. If Solver is missing from the Tools menu, rerun Setup from your Microsoft Office or Excel CD-ROM and use the Custom option in Setup to install Solver itself. See the Add-In topic in Appendix B for details.

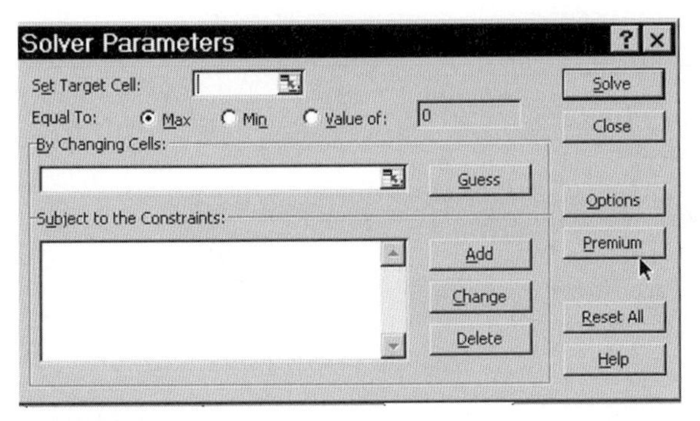

FIGURE 3.6

Solver Parameters Default Dialog

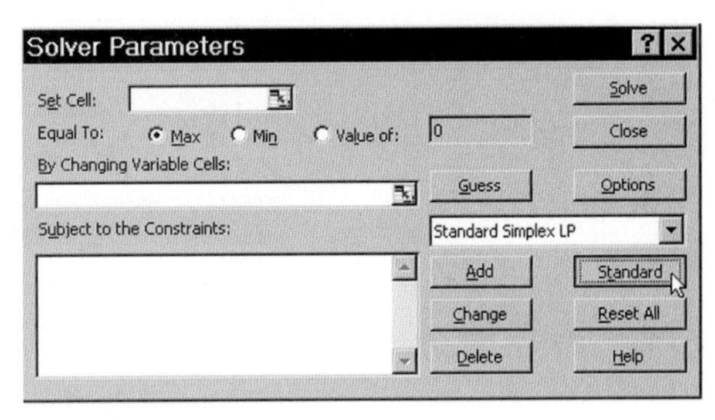

FIGURE 3.7

Solver Parameters Alternative Dialog

After the Solver add-in loads into memory, which may take a few seconds, the Solver Parameters dialog box should appear, as shown in Figure 3.6. Note that Solver defaults to a "Max"-imization model and the dialog cursor is in the first field: "Set Target Cell."

If you do not see the button marked Premium, shown above the cursor in Figure 3.6, then you have not installed Premium Solver for Education, the version of Solver contained on the CD-ROM with this book. We strongly urge you to install it before continuing.[5] Premium Solver for Education corrects several bugs in Microsoft's version of Solver bundled with Excel, has two very useful debugging reports, and has several advanced settings and optimization features we will exploit in later chapters of this book.

Premium Solver for Education allows you to customize the Solver Parameters dialog to change its appearance. If you click the Premium button, it will always show the type of optimization it will perform, as shown in Figure 3.7.

TIP: *For an LP model, it makes no difference which version of the Solver Parameters dialog you use. The two options only affect the appearance of the dialog itself. In either case the underlying optimization procedure used is the same LP Simplex optimizer.*

Your choice of the Solver Parameters dialog appearance is a matter of personal taste; we will stick with the default version in Figure 3.6 until later chapters when we will use some of the other optimizers listed under the "Standard Simplex LP" drop-down menu.

You can move the Solver Parameters dialog box around on the screen by click-dragging its title bar so that you can see all parts of your Oak Product spreadsheet. This is very useful because the easiest way to specify cells in the dialog box is to click the cell directly on your underlying spreadsheet model. Clicking on the desired cell(s) eliminates the chance of typographical errors and is usually faster, as well.

The first field, labeled "Set Target Cell:," is asking for the cell to be optimized, that is, your model's performance measure. In the Oak Product model, you could type D4 directly into the "Set Target Cell" box, or better yet, click on cell D4 in the spreadsheet to enter it automatically. This latter approach was used in Figure 3.8. Notice the marquee around cell

FIGURE 3.8

Specifying Solver's Target Cell

	A	B	C	D	E	F
1		Simplified Oak Products Model				
2	Chair Style	Captain	Mate			
3	Profit / Chair	$ 56	$ 40	Profit		
4	Production Qty.	20	80	$4,320		

Solver Parameters

5 Set Target Cell: $D$4

6 Equal To: Max Min Value of: 0

[5] Instructions for installing it are contained in Appendix C. Also, you must have Microsoft's version of Solver already installed in Excel in order to install Premium Solver for Education. (Macintosh users must use Microsoft's version of Solver, or install a Windows emulator program, such as Virtual PC.)

FIGURE 3.9

Minimizing the Solver Parameters Dialog

	A	B	C	D	E	F	G	H	I
1		Simplified Oak Products Model							
2	Chair Style	Captain	Mate						
3	Profit / Chair	$ 56	$ 40	Profit					
4	Production Qty.	20	80	$4,320					
5	Solver Parameters $D$4								
6	Long Dowels	8	4	480	≤	1280	800		
7	Short Dowels	4	12	1040	≤	1600	560		
8	Legs	4	4	400	≤	760	360		

TIP: *If you click on the icon at the right of any Solver Parameters field, the dialog will minimize to show only that field, as shown in Figure 3.9. This reveals more of the worksheet to facilitate cell selection. To maximize the dialog back to its full size after cell clicking, press the Enter key or click the icon at the right of the field in Figure 3.9.*

D4 as confirmation. (When you click on the spreadsheet to enter cell references, Excel inserts $'s that signify absolute references. You may use either absolute references—from cell clicking—or relative references—from direct typing of cell references. Either will produce the same result.)

The next field in the dialog box, labeled "Equal to:," allows you to define the type of optimization. In this case, you want to maximize the Oak Product's Profit performance measure cell. To select this option, click on the radio button next to "Max." Alternatively, you could click another radio button to "Min"-imize the cell value (for example, if a model's performance measure were Total Cost) or click "Value of:" to cause the Target Cell to become equal to a value of your choosing. (This last option allows Solver to perform goal seeking for constrained models with multiple decision variables, an option that cannot be handled by the "unconstrained, single decision variable" Goal Seek command we covered in Chapter 2.)

The next field, labeled "By Changing Cells," allows you to specify the Oak Product model's decision variables, consisting in this case of cells B4:C4. So, click in the "By Changing Cells" box, and then on the Oak Product spreadsheet click-drag over the two cells B4:C4. That will copy the correct range of decision variable cells into the dialog box, as shown in Figure 3.10—again, note the marquee around the Oak Product decision variable cells as confirmation. (You can try Solver Parameter's "Guess" button as a shortcut, but that option frequently guesses the wrong decision variable cell references.)

TIP: *If you cannot arrange your spreadsheet model into the recommended layout with all your decision variable cells clustered together thus allowing range click-dragging, you can specify each decision variable individually by clicking on its cell, typing a comma into the Changing Cells dialog, and clicking on the next decision variable cell, and so forth.*

Next you must define the Oak Product model's constraints for Solver. Clicking on the button labeled "Add . . ." that is to the right of the box labeled "Subject to the Constraints:" will bring up the Add Constraint dialog that allows you to enter a constraint, as shown in Figure 3.11. Note that Add Constraint defaults to a less than or equal to constraint, shown as "<=."

If groups of contiguous constraint rows in your spreadsheet model are reordered to cluster together those of the same type of inequality, that is, all are "≤" or "≥," you can specify them all at once by using cell ranges. Otherwise, you must enter each constraint individually, by repeatedly clicking the "Add" button in the Add Constraint dialog.

FIGURE 3.10

Specifying Solver's Changing Cells

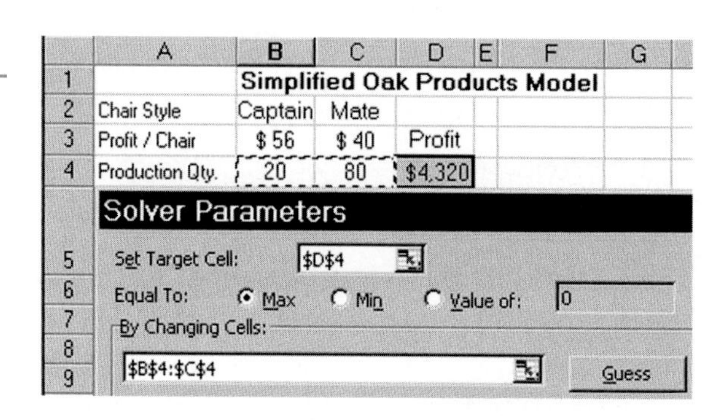

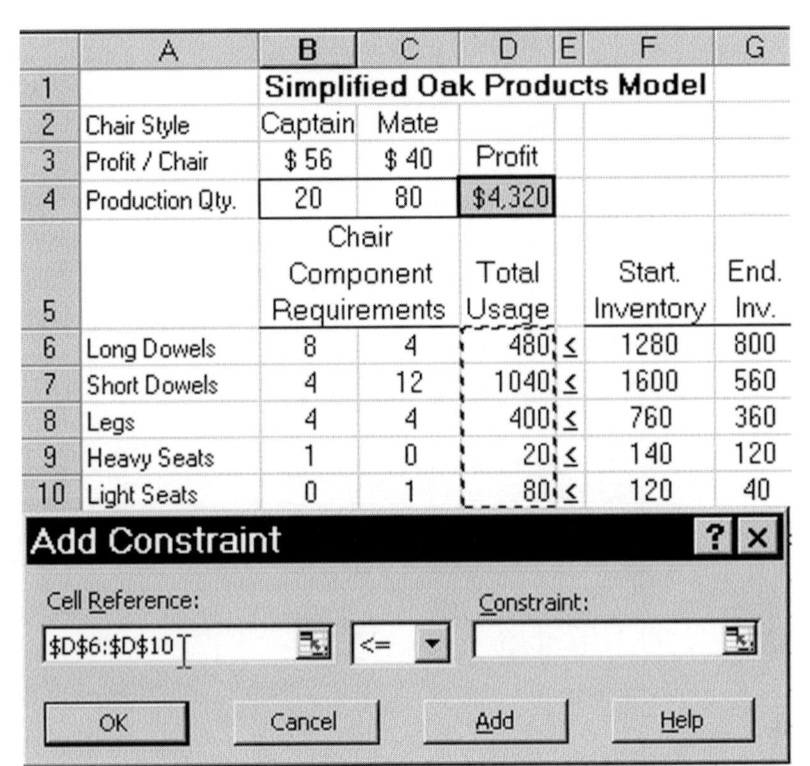

	A	B	C	D	E	F	G
1		Simplified Oak Products Model					
2	Chair Style	Captain	Mate				
3	Profit / Chair	$ 56	$ 40	Profit			
4	Production Qty.	20	80	$4,320			
5		Chair Component Requirements		Total Usage		Start. Inventory	End. Inv.
6	Long Dowels	8	4	480	≤	1280	800
7	Short Dowels	4	12	1040	≤	1600	560
8	Legs	4	4	400	≤	760	360
9	Heavy Seats	1	0	20	≤	140	120
10	Light Seats	0	1	80	≤	120	40

FIGURE 3.11

Specifying the LHS of Oak Product's "≤" Constraints

TIP: *If you have an older version of Excel, sometimes Solver's Add Constraint dialog complains by beeping when you attempt this click-dragging and refuses to respond. You can "unlock" this condition by repeatedly pressing the "Tab" key to cycle through all of the options in the Add Constraint dialog until you return to the original field in the dialog. Then, you can click-drag to complete your cell range specification.*

With the cursor in the left "Cell Reference:" field of the Add Constraint dialog, click-drag on the Oak Product spreadsheet the cells comprising the Total LHS for the five "≤" constraints, that is, D6:D10, as shown in Figure 3.11. Note: Solver will not accept formulas in the "Cell Reference" field; all entries must be references to spreadsheet cells—which, of course, commonly do contain formulas.

Next, place the cursor in the right-hand box of the Add Constraint dialog and click-drag over the corresponding five RHS cells, F6:F10. Your five inventory resource limitations or "upper bound" constraints should look as in Figure 3.12. Although filled out as a single dialog, the specification of cell ranges in the Add Constraint dialog actually creates five constraints. Of course, you must be careful that the number of cells referenced in the LHS range must equal the number of cells referenced in the RHS range. Click the Add Constraint dialog's "Add" button to add these five constraints to Solver's specification, and clear the Add Constraint dialog box for more constraints.

Next, we are ready to specify Oak Product's "≥" constraints. The procedure is the same as above. With the cursor in the left "Cell Reference:" field, click on the cell comprising the Chairs LHS for the "≥" constraint, D12. In the center of the Add Constraint dialog, choose the "greater than or equal to" (">=") sign, as shown in Figure 3.13. Note that all three inequality options ("<=," "=," and ">=") are available in the center constraint drop-down list. (Ignore the fourth and fifth options in the list labeled "int" and "bin"; they are used for models that require some of the decision variable cells to have integer values, a topic we will cover in Chapter 6.)

Next, place the cursor in the right-hand box of the Add Constraint dialog and click on cell F12. Your one requirement or "lower bound" constraint should look as in Figure 3.14.

This completes the specification of the one explicit ≥ constraint on the Oak Product model. However, you're not done with specifying the Oak Product model's ≥ constraints. You must remember to specify the nonnegativity constraints on cells B4 and C4. We do that in a later step below.

FIGURE 3.12

Specifying the RHS of Oak Product's "≤" Constraints

	A	B	C	D	E	F	G
1		Simplified Oak Products Model					
2	Chair Style	Captain	Mate				
3	Profit / Chair	\$ 56	\$ 40	Profit			
4	Production Qty.	20	80	\$4,320			
5		Chair Component Requirements		Total Usage		Start. Inventory	End. Inv.
6	Long Dowels	8	4	480	≤	1280	800
7	Short Dowels	4	12	1040	≤	1600	560
8	Legs	4	4	400	≤	760	360
9	Heavy Seats	1	0	20	≤	140	120
10	Light Seats	0	1	80	≤	120	40

Add Constraint

Cell Reference: \$D\$6:\$D\$10 <= Constraint: =\$F\$6:\$F\$10

OK Cancel Add Help

Now you can click on the Add Constraint dialog's "OK" button to finish the adding of constraints and return to the Solver Parameters dialog box. (If you ever inadvertently click "Add," simply click "Cancel" and you will be returned to the Solver Parameters dialog box.)

Your Solver specification for the Oak Product model should look as in Figure 3.15. (Although we did not need to use them, the "Change" and "Delete" constraint buttons, listed below the "Add" button in the Solver Parameters dialog, work in a manner similar to

FIGURE 3.13

Specifying the LHS of Oak Product's "≥" Constraint

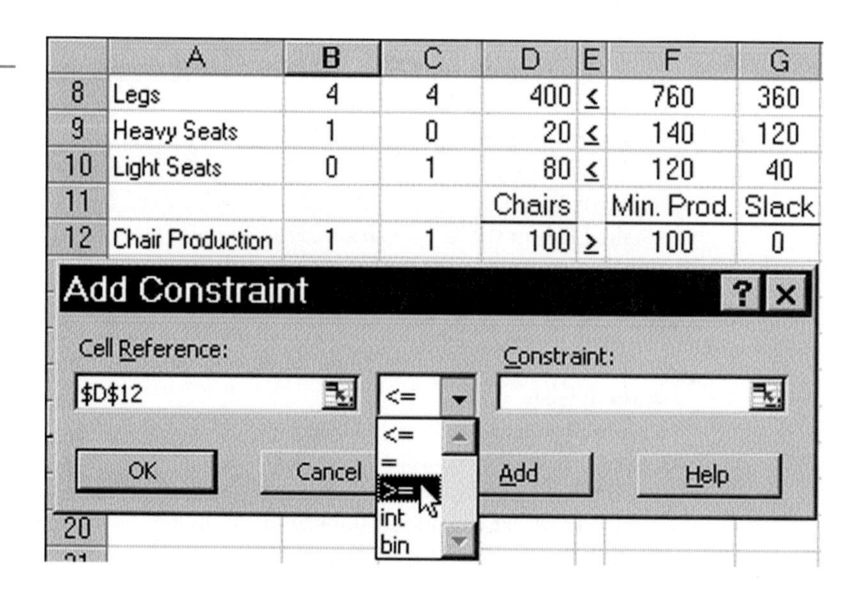

FIGURE 3.14

Specifying the RHS of Oak Product's "≥" Constraint

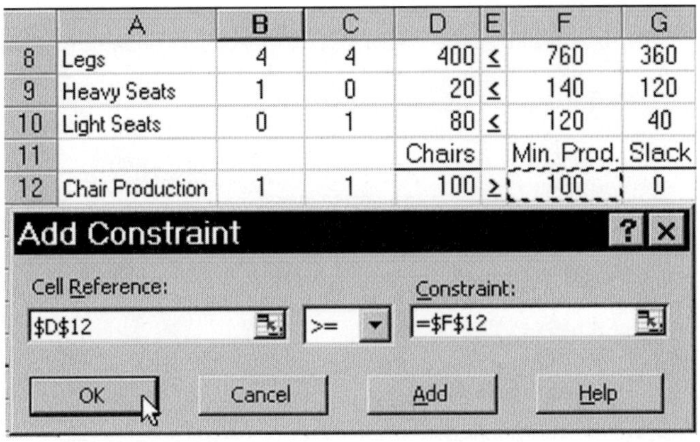

	A	B	C	D	E	F	G
8	Legs	4	4	400	≤	760	360
9	Heavy Seats	1	0	20	≤	140	120
10	Light Seats	0	1	80	≤	120	40
11				Chairs		Min. Prod.	Slack
12	Chair Production	1	1	100	≥	100	0

Add Constraint

Cell Reference: $D$12 >= Constraint: =$F$12

OK Cancel Add Help

"Add." First, highlight the constraint you wish to change or delete and then click on either of these buttons. Then, follow a procedure similar to the steps for "Add." Note: the "Reset All" button clears all entries in the Solver Parameters dialog in the case that you wish to start your Solver specification process all over again.)

Finally, since we are working with an LP model that has strictly linear relationships, you *must* click the "Options" button in the Solver Parameters dialog box, as shown under

FIGURE 3.15

Oak Product's Solver Parameters Specification

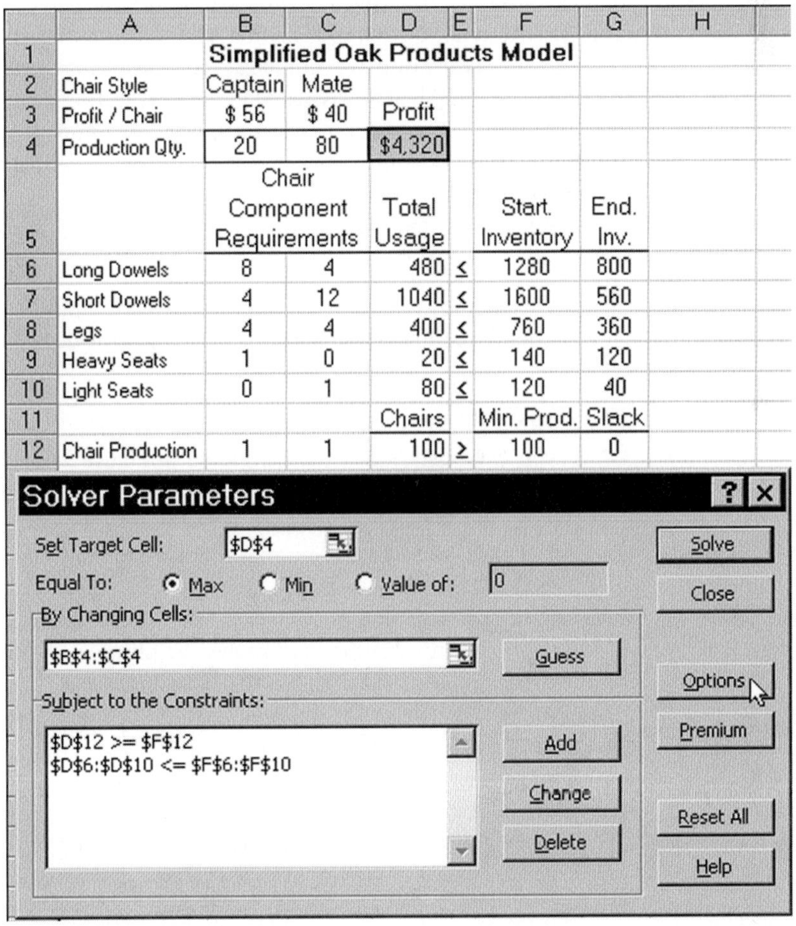

	A	B	C	D	E	F	G	H
1		Simplified Oak Products Model						
2	Chair Style	Captain	Mate					
3	Profit / Chair	$ 56	$ 40	Profit				
4	Production Qty.	20	80	$4,320				
5		Chair Component Requirements		Total Usage		Start. Inventory	End. Inv.	
6	Long Dowels	8	4	480	≤	1280	800	
7	Short Dowels	4	12	1040	≤	1600	560	
8	Legs	4	4	400	≤	760	360	
9	Heavy Seats	1	0	20	≤	140	120	
10	Light Seats	0	1	80	≤	120	40	
11				Chairs		Min. Prod.	Slack	
12	Chair Production	1	1	100	≥	100	0	

Solver Parameters

Set Target Cell: $D$4

Equal To: (•) Max ( ) Min ( ) Value of: 0

By Changing Cells: $B$4:$C$4

Subject to the Constraints:

$D$12 >= $F$12

$D$6:$D$10 <= $F$6:$F$10

Solve Close Guess Options Premium Add Change Delete Reset All Help

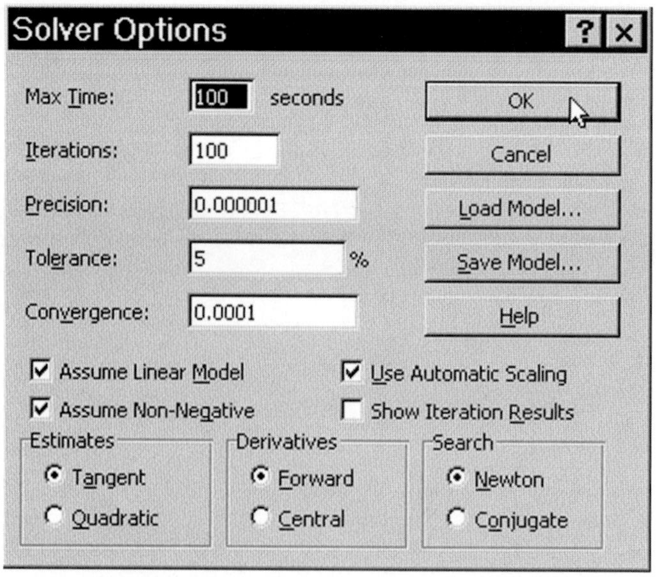

FIGURE 3.16

Specifying Model Linearity and Nonnegativity Constraints

the cursor arrow in Figure 3.15. The Solver Options dialog box will then appear, as shown in Figure 3.16.

Click the check boxes next to "Assume Linear Model" and "Assume Non-Negative," and "Use Automatic Scaling." The first specifies to Solver that the model is an LP and the second applies the last two ≥ nonnegativity constraints to the two decision variables. "Use Automatic Scaling" will be discussed in the next section. (Ignore the other options for now; they relate to optimizing integer and nonlinear models, to displaying of intermediate results, to saving/loading more than one Solver model formulation per worksheet, etc.) Click "OK" to return to the Solver Parameters dialog.

TIP: *If earlier you opted to use the alternative Solver Parameters dialog by clicking the "Premium" button, the equivalent to "Assume Linear" is selecting "Standard Simplex LP" on its main Solver Parameters dialog. However, you still must remember to click "Options" and check the other two options for "Assume Non-Negative," and "Use Automatic Scaling."*

You have now specified the optimization model completely by telling Solver about:

- The cell containing the objective function to optimize (the cell to be maximized in this case),
- The range of cells that Solver is to change (the decision variables),
- The constraints, and
- That your model is an LP.

Lastly, click the "Solve" button shown in Figure 3.15. You can follow the progress of Solver's iterative "Simplex" search in Excel's Message Box in the Status Bar at the lower left-hand corner of the Excel window. However, optimization will happen very fast for so small a model as Oak Products. So, you might not see the messages from Solver this time.

In general, Solver will display "Setting up problem . . ." while the Solver Visual Basic program translates your spreadsheet model. Then Solver passes control to the optimizer module. The optimizer module displays the number of "iterations" and the value of the objective function cell as it explores Oak Product's set of feasible decisions during the optimization process. This information is useful to monitor Solver's progress for large models that might take many seconds or minutes to optimize.

If you have made no mistakes to this point, after a second or two, the Solver Results dialog should display a completion message, as shown in Figure 3.17. *Always, be sure to read the top sentences in this dialog*! Solver may stop short of optimality. Unfortunately, the Solver Results dialog always looks the same except for the top sentence(s). If, in your haste to click the "OK" button to dismiss the Solver Results dialog, you don't read the message, you may miss important information about your solution. For example, just because Solver

FIGURE 3.17

The Solver Results Dialog Box

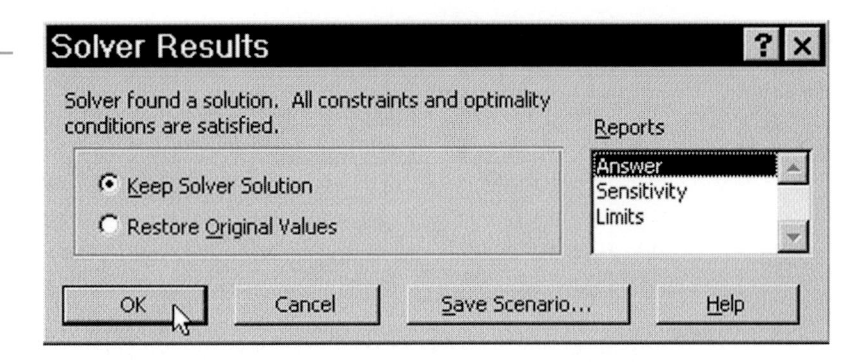

finished, it doesn't mean it found the optimum solution. So, read the message—each and every time. The two key sentences to look for in the Solver Results dialog are:

- Solver found a solution, and
- All constraints and optimality conditions are satisfied.

If you do not see *both* of these two sentences, Solver has failed to optimize your LP model. In that eventuality, (1) click the "Help" button for additional—but usually inadequate—information about the Solver Results dialog or (2) consult Appendix C for additional tips and hints on how to proceed.

TIP: *If the Solver completion message complains about an infeasible model or a nonlinear relationship in your model, the Solver Results dialog for the Premium Solver Educational Edition will list one or two optional troubleshooting reports, an Infeasibility Report and a Non-Linear Report. If selected, these reports will be added to your workbook. Examine them, as they are valuable debugging aids.*

If you got the successful completion message, as shown in Figure 3.17, you have the option to "Keep the Solver Solution" or to throw it away by "Restore (-ing the) Original Values" for the Oak Product decision variable cells before Solver started. You also have the option of receiving up to three reports on the solution, each formatted as a new worksheet added to your SimpleOakProd.xls workbook.

Select the Answer Report, accept the default of "Keep Solver Solution" and click OK. Ignore the Sensitivity Report and the Limits Report for now. We will address them later.[6] Figure 3.18 shows the Answer Report for the Oak Product model. The Answer Report should appear in your workbook under the worksheet tab named "Answer Report 1" if that name isn't already used for another worksheet in the workbook. As a result, you may freely reformat, print, or copy the cells of any Solver report in the normal way for any worksheet. For example, superfluous rows were deleted and several columns had their contents centered in the Answer Report shown in Figure 3.18.

FIGURE 3.18

The Solver Answer Report for Oak Product

Microsoft Excel 9.0 Answer Report

Target Cell (Max)

Cell	Name	Original Value	Final Value
$D$4	Production Qty. Profit	$4,320	$9,680

Adjustable Cells

Cell	Name	Original Value	Final Value
$B$4	Production Qty. Captain	20	130
$C$4	Production Qty. Mate	80	60

Constraints

Cell	Name	Cell Value	Formula	Status	Slack
$D$12	Chair Production Chairs	190	$D$12>=$F$12	Not Binding	90
$D$6	Long Dowels Total Usage	1280	$D$6<=$F$6	Binding	0
$D$7	Short Dowels Total Usage	1240	$D$7<=$F$7	Not Binding	360
$D$8	Legs Total Usage	760	$D$8<=$F$8	Binding	0
$D$9	Heavy Seats Total Usage	130	$D$9<=$F$9	Not Binding	10
$D$10	Light Seats Total Usage	60	$D$10<=$F$10	Not Binding	60

[6] For future reference: In versions prior to Excel 97, more than one report can be selected by holding down the Control key (Windows Excel) or the Command key (Macintosh Excel) and then clicking on each of the desired reports.

FIGURE 3.19

The Profit Maximizing Decisions

	A	B	C	D	E	F	G
1		**Simplified Oak Products Model**					
2	Chair Style	Captain	Mate				
3	Profit / Chair	$ 56	$ 40	Profit			
4	Production Qty.	130	60	$9,680			
5		Chair Component Requirements		Total Usage		Start. Inventory	End. Inv.
6	Long Dowels	8	4	1280	≤	1280	0
7	Short Dowels	4	12	1240	≤	1600	360
8	Legs	4	4	760	≤	760	0
9	Heavy Seats	1	0	130	≤	140	10
10	Light Seats	0	1	60	≤	120	60
11				Chairs		Min. Prod.	Slack
12	Chair Production	1	1	190	≥	100	90

TIP: *Remember: The Answer Report (and also any of the other reports) is just another Excel worksheet that happens to have its grid lines turned off. You may turn them back on by setting the proper check marks in the View tab dialog evoked from the Options . . . item in the Tools menu. Also, if you forget to select a report and dismiss the Solver Results dialog, there is no way to re-create the report without re-optimizing the model to get back to the Solver Results dialog.*

Your original Oak Product spreadsheet should now appear as in Figure 3.19 in which Solver has recorded the optimal decision values for Captain and Mate production, 130 and 60, respectively. The spreadsheet then recalculates one last time to produce the Profit maximizing payoff of $9,680.

Note that the cells in the column G have changed to reflect the inventory consequences of the optimal production decisions. If the slack cell for a constraint shows 0 slack, then that constraint is said to be "binding at optimality" or "binding" for short. Binding constraints prevent Solver from producing more profit. That is, increasing profit by additional Captain and/or Mate production would drive one or more slack cells below 0, violating one or more constraints. Constraints having nonzero (and, therefore by design, have positive) slack are not binding at optimality. Nonbinding constraints cannot hamper Solver's ability to produce additional payoff, at least initially. This is true regardless of whether you optimize a maximization model or a minimization model. As a result, it is the binding constraints that are of interest to you in any LP model. The occurrence of zero Ending Inventory in the Long Dowels and Legs resource limitation constraints means that these are the two binding constraints, that is, "bottlenecks" that prevent further improvement in Oak Product payoff by making and selling more chairs.

If you compare Figure 3.19 to the Answer Report in Figure 3.18, you will see that the layout we have chosen for the Oak Product spreadsheet directly presents all the information contained in the Answer Report. That is, except for formatting differences, the Answer Report information is completely duplicated on the original Oak Product spreadsheet. As a result, the Answer Report is largely redundant, and we will omit it in future Solver optimizations. However, it can become useful if you must deviate from our modeling recommendations in setting up your Excel LP model.

You are free at this point to explore alternatives in the neighborhood of optimality by doing additional "What if?" projections for Oak Product's Captain and/or Mate production quantities around their optimum values.

TIP: *All the Solver Parameters dialog settings for each worksheet model are preserved when you save your Excel workbook to disk.*

Alternatively, you can see the immediate effect on profit of adding additional inventory by changing the proper right-hand side cell, and then running Solver again to re-optimize the model with the new right-hand side value(s). In this way, you can explore how much profit is helped or hurt by such a change. Of course, you can change the contribution margin coefficients and/or the technical coefficients in the constraints to examine their effect on profit, as well. Remember, for each change you must evoke the Solver dialog again and click the Solve button to get a new optimum.

3.9 RECOMMENDATIONS FOR SOLVER LP MODELS

To facilitate your use of Solver, there are three LP modeling habits you should develop.

First, make sure your LP model's numbers are scaled so that the difference between the smallest and largest numbers in the spreadsheet to be optimized is no more than six or seven digits of precision. For example, a model with one of its decision variables defined as an interest rate (having a value of 5%, for example) along with a payoff measure in dollars may produce incorrect Solver solutions, if the dollar performance measure cell grows to, say, eight digits (tens of millions of dollars). This causes a span in your spreadsheet model of ten orders of magnitude between the smallest valued cell (.05) and the largest ($10,000,000, for example). The resulting internal round-off and truncation errors, which get compounded as Solver manipulates the model during optimization, may cause so great a loss of internal precision that Solver will not be able to reliably finish the process. This situation may result in nonoptimal solutions and/or bogus Solver Results completion messages ("The conditions for Assume Linear are not satisfied"—when, in fact, they are).

In this case, and in similar cases, the remedy is simple: change the scale of measure of the very large or very small numbers in your spreadsheet model. In the above example, we could rescale money in the LP model to be defined as millions of dollars instead of dollars. This causes no loss of the model's generality and will keep the range of its numbers small—in this revised example the difference between the smallest number (.05) and the largest number ($10) is now only four orders of magnitude.

Other than forgetting any nonnegativity constraints, poorly scaled models cause the *most* trouble in optimizing LP models with Solver.

TIP: *Beginning with Excel 97, checking the "Use Automatic Scaling" item in the Solver Options dialog (see Figure 3.16) helps with most scaling problems, but this cannot be guaranteed to successfully eliminate all problems with scaling. (This option does not work for LP models in Solver versions prior to Excel 97.)*

The less insidious causes of Solver failures are usually easier to track down, especially with the help of the additional troubleshooting reports in Premium Solver Educational Edition, such as an overconstrained model ("Solver could not find a feasible solution" completion message).

Second, Solver accepts RHS entries in the Solver Parameters dialog showing numeric constants or cell references or formulas, and doing this in your modeling does not harm the optimization process. Nevertheless, good Solver modeling practice should avoid their use. That is, you should never place any constants or the cell address of variables whose values could change during optimization into the RHS of a constraint in the Solver Parameters dialog itself. In other words, all RHS's in the Constraints section of the Solver Parameters dialog should contain cell references pointing to constraint RHS cells in your spreadsheet that contain either (1) constants or (2) formulas whose evaluation will never change during Solver optimization, that is, formulas that are *not* related to the values of the decision variables directly or indirectly.

If it is acceptable to Solver, why avoid such practices? Let us illustrate this recommendation with an example—in this case a modification to the original Oak Product model. Suppose Jim decides for policy reasons that no more than 80 Captains and no more than 60 Mates should be produced next week. Clearly the optimal decisions from the Oak Product LP model just optimized by Solver violate these new policy constraints, and so, the Oak Product model must be revised to include two new constraints and then re-optimized. One way to do this is shown in Figure 3.20. Note the two new upper bound constraints in the Solver Parameters dialog.

When the "Solve" button is clicked, Solver correctly optimizes this revised model, with a new solution as shown in Figure 3.21.

Note the disadvantage of this revised Oak Product model formulation: There is no clue on the spreadsheet regarding two of the revised model's constraints; from the spreadsheet in Figure 3.21, it appears no constraints are binding. As a result, you would have to (1) generate and consult the Answer Report after every optimization and (2) translate that report's

FIGURE 3.20

Revised Oak Product Model's Solver Parameters Specification

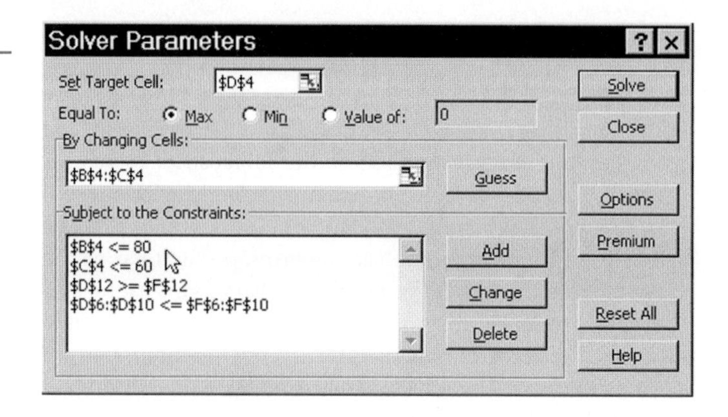

information back to the spreadsheet model for interpretation, a cumbersome procedure. In addition, this style of modeling with Solver is another form of "hard-wiring" of data, in this case into the Solver Parameters dialog instead of into a formula, but with the same effect: The complete structure of the model is not obvious, and any model changes require "editing," in this case, of the Solver Parameters dialog. The recommended approach would be for Jim to add the two new constraints to the Oak Product model on the worksheet itself as two additional constraint rows, and then modify the Solver Parameters dialog to include their specification along with the original Oak Product constraints.

Since there is no loss of generality in laying out the spreadsheet this way, we recommend, therefore, that

1. RHSs in the constraints specified in the Solver Parameter dialog should always contain cell references (to the RHS cells in the spreadsheet model itself), and
2. The RHS cells on the spreadsheet model itself should contain constants and not formulas (or more precisely: no formulas that involve decision variables directly or indirectly).

FIGURE 3.21

Optimal Solution to the Revised Oak Product Model

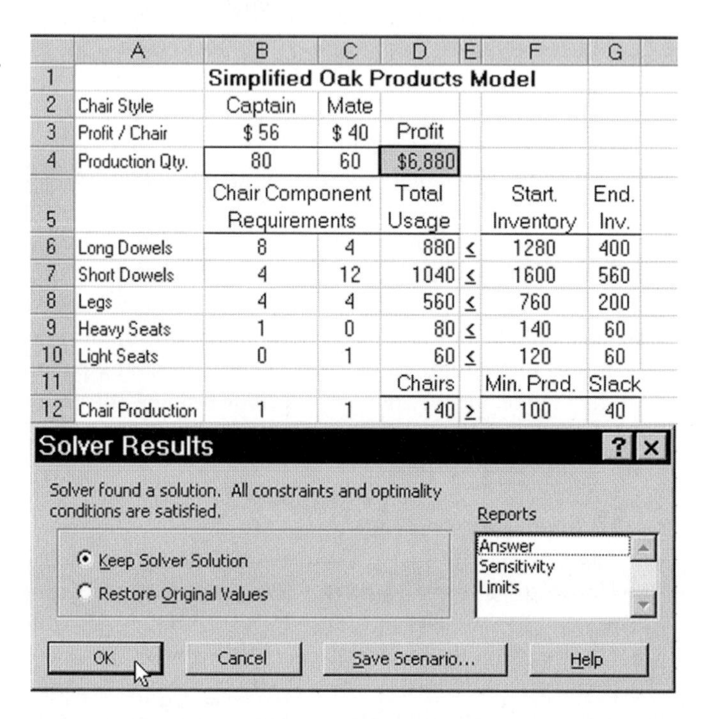

	A	B	C	D	E	F	G
1		Simplified Oak Products Model					
2	Chair Style	Captain	Mate				
3	Profit / Chair	$ 56	$ 40	Profit			
4	Production Qty.	80	60	$6,880			
5		Chair Component Requirements		Total Usage		Start. Inventory	End. Inv.
6	Long Dowels	8	4	880	≤	1280	400
7	Short Dowels	4	12	1040	≤	1600	560
8	Legs	4	4	560	≤	760	200
9	Heavy Seats	1	0	80	≤	140	60
10	Light Seats	0	1	60	≤	120	60
11				Chairs		Min. Prod.	Slack
12	Chair Production	1	1	140	≥	100	40

FIGURE 3.22

Original Oak Products Production Model from Chapter 2

	A	B	C	D	E	F	G	H	I	J	K
1		**Oak Products Model**									
2	Chair Style	Capt.	Mate	AmerHi	AmerLo	SpainK	SpainQ				
3	Profit / Chair	$ 36	$ 40	$ 45	$ 38	$ 35	$ 25	PROFIT			
4	Qty.Produced	100	72	40	53	0	0	$10,294			
5		Chair Component Requirements						Total Usage		Starting Inventory	End. Inv.
6	Long Dowels	8	0	12	0	8	4	1280	≤	1280	0
7	Short Dowels	4	12	0	12	4	8	1900	≤	1900	0
8	Legs	4	4	4	4	4	4	1060	≤	1090	30
9	Heavy Seats	1	0	0	0	1	1	100	≤	190	90
10	Light Seats	0	1	1	1	0	0	165	≤	170	5
11	Heavy Rungs	6	0	4	0	5	0	760	≤	1000	240
12	Light Rungs	0	4	0	5	0	6	553	≤	1000	447
13	Capt. Rails	1	0	0	0	0	0	100	≤	110	10
14	Mate Rails	0	1	0	0	0	0	72	≤	72	0
15	Amer. Rails	0	0	1	1	0	0	93	≤	93	0
16	Span. Rails	0	0	0	0	1	1	0	≤	85	85

Solver Parameters

Set Target Cell: $H$4

Equal To: (•) Max ( ) Min ( ) Value of: 0

By Changing Cells: $B$4:$G$4

Subject to the Constraints: $H$6:$H$16 <= $J$6:$J$16

Solve | Close | Guess | Options | Premium | Add | Change | Delete | Reset All | Help

Solver Options

☑ Assume Linear Model ☑ Use Automatic Scaling

☑ Assume Non-Negative ☐ Show Iteration Results

TIP: *Pressing the PrintScreen key will copy a picture of your display screen onto the Clipboard. Pressing Alt-PrintScreen will copy a picture of the frontmost window or a Solver dialog onto the Clipboard. From the Clipboard, you can paste the picture into an Excel worksheet or another application's document as a picture for model documentation.*

Third, for larger LP models it facilitates documentation if you use Excel's Range Naming commands, illustrated earlier in Chapter 2, to range name the model's performance measure cell, its decision cells, its constraint function (Total LHS) cells, and its RHS cells. If you do this, Solver will automatically substitute the range names for the corresponding cell ranges in the Solver Parameters dialog.

This completes our detailed overview of Solver. At this point you should save your Oak Product workbook to disk to preserve the LP's optimal decisions and the Answer Report.

Now that you see how the simplified Oak Products LP model was constructed in Excel and optimized with Solver, we can reveal how the much larger original Oak Products model of Chapter 2 was optimized, as shown slightly reformatted in Figure 3.22, and giving the optimal solution found by Solver. Below it are the Solver Parameters dialog and relevant pieces from the Solver Options dialog. Since you have seen the simplified Oak Products model being built, you can almost certainly deduce the underlying Excel formulas in the original Oak Products model given in Figure 3.22. You can refer to Figure 2.38 to confirm your formula deductions.

3.10 A TRANSPORTATION EXAMPLE

A company has two plants and three warehouse outlet stores. The first plant can supply at most 100 units and the second at most 200 units of the same product. The maximum sales quantities of the product at the first warehouse outlet is 150, at the second warehouse outlet 200, and at the third 350. The price per unit sold at the three warehouse outlets are $12 at the first, $14 at the second, and $15 at the third. The cost of manufacturing one unit at plant i and shipping it to warehouse outlet j is given in Table 3.5. The company wishes to determine how many units should be shipped from each plant to each warehouse so as to maximize profit.

Table 3.5

Per Unit Manufacturing and Shipping Costs

	TO WAREHOUSE ($)		
From Plant	1	2	3
1	8	10	12
2	7	9	11

Note that the proper choice of the decision variables is given to you in the example statement itself. Models of this sort are often formulated with decision variables having two rather than a single subscript, and in turn, this translates to using blocks of adjacent cells in Excel to contain the decision variables, rather than having the decision variables in a single row, as was used in the Oak Products model. Using this device, the decision variables are:

X_{ij} = number of units manufactured and sent from plant i to warehouse outlet j

For each decision variable, X_{ij}, the corresponding unit profit is the sales price per unit sold at warehouse outlet j minus the cost of making and shipping a unit from plant i to warehouse outlet j. Thus, for items shipped from plant 1 to warehouse outlet 1, for example, the profit is $12/unit sales revenue – $8/unit shipping = $4/unit. Similar calculations for each plant-warehouse outlet combination provide the coefficients for the terms of the objective function. The symbolic model is therefore

$$\text{Max } 4X_{11} + 5X_{21} + 4X_{12} + 5X_{22} + 3X_{13} + 4X_{23}$$

$$\text{st.} \quad X_{11} + X_{12} + X_{13} \leq 100 \text{ (supply capacity for plant 1)}$$

$$X_{21} + X_{22} + X_{23} \leq 200 \text{ (supply capacity for plant 2)}$$

$$X_{11} + X_{21} \leq 150 \text{ (sales limit for warehouse outlet 1)}$$

$$X_{12} + X_{22} \leq 200 \text{ (sales limit for warehouse outlet 2)}$$

$$X_{13} + X_{23} \leq 350 \text{ (sales limit for warehouse outlet 3)}$$

$$X_{ij} \geq 0 \quad \text{for all } i, j$$

From the formulation above you can see that a transportation model has a very special form. For example, all the given X_{ij} coefficients in the constraints above are 1. In fact, a transportation model is an example of an entire class of linear programs called *network models*. Other important examples of network models appear in Chapter 5.

The Excel representation can take advantage of the row/column spreadsheet framework to match the X_{ij} decision variables that connect shipments from plants to warehouse outlets, thus producing a very compact spreadsheet model. In this case the decision variables will occupy a block of cells rather than a single row of cells as was the case for the Oak Products model. Figure 3.23 shows the Excel LP model. The decision variables are given by the range B3:D4 specifying the quantities to be manufactured by a given plant and shipped to a given outlet for sale. G3:G4 gives the plant production limits and B7:D7 gives the outlet sales limits. The remaining formulas are self-explanatory, reflecting usual accounting definitions. Figure 3.24 gives the optimal solution to the transportation model along with the Solver Parameters settings that produced it.

3.11 EASTERN STEEL: A BLENDING EXAMPLE

Although the Oak Product and Transportation examples turned out to be maximization models, many real-world problems occur in a minimization context. When profit is the objective, then clearly maximization is called for; but if, for example, cost is the objective, then minimization is called for. As an example of a minimization model, we consider the following model.

Iron ore from four different mines will be blended to make a metal alloy for a new product at Eastern Steel. Analysis has shown that in order to produce a blend with suitable tensile qualities, minimum requirements must be met on three basic elements, denoted for

FIGURE 3.23

Transportation Model

	A	B	C	D	E	F	G
1		Transportation Model					
2	Shipments From\To	Outlet1	Outlet2	Outlet3	Total		Capacity
3	Plant1	20	0	5	25	≤	100
4	Plant2	10	10	0	20	≤	200
5	Total	30	10	5			
6		≤	≤	≤			
7	Sales Limit	150	200	350			
8	Sales Price	$12	$14	$15			
9	Sales Rev.	$360	$140	$75			
10	Unit Cost From\To	Outlet1	Outlet2	Outlet3			
11	Plant1	$8	$10	$12			
12	Plant2	$7	$9	$11			
13	Total Cost	$230	$90	$60	Total		
14	Profit	$130	$50	$15	$195		

	A	B	C	D	E	F	G
1		Transportation M					
2	Shipments From\To	Outlet1	Outlet2	Outlet3	Total		Cap
3	Plant1	20	0	5	=SUM(B3:D3)	≤	100
4	Plant2	10	10	0	=SUM(B4:D4)	≤	200
5	Total	=SUM(B3:B4)	=SUM(C3:C4)	=SUM(D3:D4)			
6		≤	≤	≤			
7	Sales Limit	150	200	350			
8	Sales Price	12	14	15			
9	Sales Rev.	=B5*B8	=C5*C8	=D5*D8			
10	Unit Cost From\To	Outlet1	Outlet2	Outlet3			
11	Plant1	8	10	12			
12	Plant2	7	9	11			
13	Total Cost	=B3*B11+B4*B12	=C3*C11+C4*C12	=D3*D11+D4*D12	Total		
14	Profit	=B9-B13	=C9-C13	=D9-D13	=SUM(B14:D14)		

FIGURE 3.24

Transportation Model Solution

	A	B	C	D	E	F	G
1		Transportation Model					
2	Shipments From\To	Outlet1	Outlet2	Outlet3	Total		Capacity
3	Plant1	100	0	0	100	≤	100
4	Plant2	50	150	0	200	≤	200
5	Total	150	150	0			
6		≤	≤	≤			
7	Sales Limit	150	200	350			
8	Sales Price	$12	$14	$15			
9	Sales Rev.	$1,800	$2,100	$0			
10	Unit Cost From\To	Outlet1	Outlet2	Outlet3			
11	Plant1	$8	$10	$12			
12	Plant2	$7	$9	$11			
13	Total Cost	$1,150	$1,350	$0	Total		
14	Profit	$650	$750	$0	$1,400		

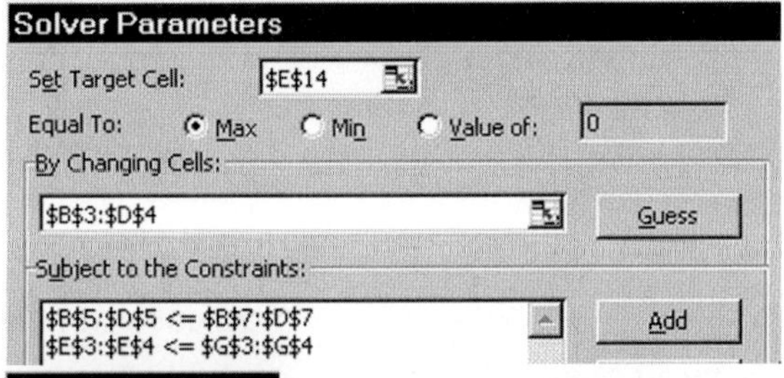

simplicity as A, B, and C. In particular, each ton of ore must contain at least 5 pounds of basic element A, at least 100 pounds of basic element B, and at least 30 pounds of basic element C. These data are summarized in Table 3.6.

The ore from each of the four different mines possesses each of the three basic elements, but in different amounts. These compositions, in pounds per ton, are given in Table 3.7.

Notice that a ton of ore from the first mine contains 10 pounds of basic element A and hence satisfies the minimum requirement on this element of 5 pounds per ton. Similarly, this same ton of ore contains 90 pounds of basic element B and 45 pounds of basic element C, hence satisfying the requirement on basic element C but not on basic element B. Similarly, you can verify that a single ton of ore from the second mine will not satisfy the requirement on A or C. A single ton of ore from mine 3 will not satisfy requirements on B and C, and a single ton from mine 4 will not satisfy the requirement on A. However, many different blends can easily be found that will indeed satisfy the minimal requirements on all three basic elements. An example of such a blend would be a mixture composed of one-half ton from mine 1 and one-half ton from mine 4. The amount of basic element A in this blended ton is computed as follows:

$$\begin{aligned}\text{pounds of } A = &(\text{pounds of } A \text{ in 1 ton from mine 1})(1/2)\\ &+ (\text{pounds of } A \text{ in 1 ton from mine 4})(1/2)\end{aligned}$$

Hence

$$\text{pounds of } A = 10(1/2) + 2(1/2) = 5 + 1 = 6$$

Since $6 \geq 5$, the minimal requirement on basic element A is satisfied by this blend. Similarly, for the same blended ton, we can compute

$$\begin{aligned}\text{pounds of } B = &(\text{pounds of } B \text{ in 1 ton from mine 1})(1/2)\\ &+ (\text{pounds of } B \text{ in 1 ton from mine 4})(1/2)\end{aligned}$$

Hence

$$\text{pounds of } B = 90(1/2) + 175(1/2) = 132.5$$

In a similar fashion

$$= 45(1/2) + 37(1/2) = 41$$

Comparing 132.5 with the requirement of 100 pounds of B, and 41 with the requirement of 30 pounds of C, it is seen that this blend of one-half ton from mine 1 and one-half ton from mine 4 easily satisfies all the minimal requirements, and hence this is said to be a *feasible blend*. There are many other possible blends of 1 ton that satisfy all the minimal

Table 3.6

Requirements of Basic Elements

BASIC ELEMENT	MINIMUM REQUIREMENT PER TON OF BLEND (POUNDS OF EACH ELEMENT)
A	5
B	100
C	30

Table 3.7

Compositions from Each Mine

	MINE (POUNDS PER TON OF EACH ELEMENT)			
Basic Elements	**1**	**2**	**3**	**4**
A	10	3	8	2
B	90	150	75	175
C	45	25	20	37

Table 3.8

Cost of Ore from Each Mine

MINE	DOLLAR COST PER TON OF ORE
1	800
2	400
3	600
4	500

requirements and hence also feasible. However, since the ore from each mine has a different cost, different blends will also have different costs. The cost data are given in Table 3.8

For example, the cost of the feasible blend one-half ton from mine 1 and one-half ton from mine 4 is

$$\begin{array}{ccccc} (\text{cost per ton from mine 1})(1/2) & + & (\text{cost per ton from mine 4})(1/2) & = & \\ 800(1/2) & + & 500(1/2) & = & \$650. \end{array}$$

Compare this cost with the cost of some of the other feasible blends that you may have discovered. The objective of Eastern Steel's management is to discover a *least-cost feasible blend.* Let us see how this can be formulated as an LP model.

Since we are interested in finding an *optimal* 1-ton blend, we set up the *decision variables* as follows:

$$T_1 = \text{fraction of a ton to be chosen from mine 1}$$

$$T_2 = \text{fraction of a ton to be chosen from mine 2}$$

$$T_3 = \text{fraction of a ton to be chosen from mine 3}$$

$$T_4 = \text{fraction of a ton to be chosen from mine 4}$$

Then, using the data from Table 3.5, the amounts of the basic elements in 1 ton of blend are calculated as follows:

$$\text{pounds of basic element } A \text{ in 1 ton of blend}$$
$$= 10T_1 + 3T_2 + 8T_3 + 2T_4 \tag{3.9}$$

$$\text{pounds of basic element } B \text{ in 1 ton of blend}$$
$$= 90T_1 + 150T_2 + 75T_3 + 175T_4 \tag{3.10}$$

$$\text{pounds of basic element } C \text{ in 1 ton of blend}$$
$$= 45T_1 + 25T_2 + 20T_3 + 37T_4 \tag{3.11}$$

We can now combine expressions (3.9), (3.10), and (3.11) with the minimal requirements designated in Table 3.4 to obtain the three (requirement) constraints:

$$10T_1 + 3T_2 + 8T_3 + 2T_4 \geq 5 \tag{3.12}$$

$$90T_1 + 150T_2 + 75T_3 + 175T_4 \geq 100 \tag{3.13}$$

$$45T_1 + 25T_2 + 20T_3 + 37T_4 \geq 30 \tag{3.14}$$

Are there any other constraints in this model? Of course, we must include the usual nonnegativity conditions $T_1, T_2, T_3, T_4, \geq 0$, but there is still another important constraint that must be included. Since there are no other contributions to the 1 ton aside from the four mines, the fractional contributions from each mine must add up to 1. That is, we must include the constraint

$$T_1 + T_2 + T_3 + T_4 = 1 \tag{3.15}$$

The latter constraint, sometimes called a *material balance condition,* is an **equality constraint**, and it restricts the values of the decision variables in such a way that the left-hand side *exactly* equals the right-hand side. This illustrates an important principle:

The constraints in a linear programming model can be equalities as well as inequalities.

Using the data in Table 3.7, it is easy to see that the cost of any blend is given by:

$$\text{cost of 1 ton of blend} = 800T_1 + 400T_2 + 600T_3 + 500T_4$$

Noting that the objective is to minimize cost, we can now write the complete symbolic model:

$$\begin{aligned} \text{Min } & 800T_1 + 400T_2 + 600T_3 + 500T_4 \\ \text{s.t. } & 10T_1 + 3T_2 + 8T_3 + 2T_4 \geq 5 \\ & 90T_1 + 150T_2 + 75T_3 + 175T_4 \geq 100 \\ & 45T_1 + 25T_2 + 20T_3 + 37T_4 \geq 30 \\ & T_1 + T_2 + T_3 + T_4 = 1 \\ & T_1, T_2, T_3, T_4 \geq 0 \end{aligned}$$

You should verify that all functions in this model are linear and consequently it is a LP model.

This completes our introduction to LP formulations with Solver. Next, we return to the major theme of this book, formulating useful models to aid decision making. Before starting the next section, however, test your abilities with spreadsheet modeling and Solver: Take the symbolic LP model for the Eastern Steel Ore Blending example and implement it as a Excel LP model using the spreadsheet formulation style of this chapter. Then, optimize it with Solver. Our version of the Ore Blending example appears at the end of this chapter, but don't ruin the opportunity to test your understanding by peeking at it. Build the spreadsheet LP model and try to solve it first. After doing it and a few of the more structured problems in the next section, developing Excel LP models with Solver will begin to come naturally.

3.12 LEARNING TO FORMULATE LP MODELS

The remainder of this chapter contains examples of some formulations that you can use to cement your ability to make the transition between the real-world managerial situation and the symbolic LP model and then to the Solver-ready Excel model. This transition—the way in which the model has been set up, the way the constraints and the objectives have been formulated—is of prime importance.

To get formulation experience try to model the following problems on your own. Develop the symbolic LP model as quickly as possible and *do not read more into a problem than precisely what is given.* At this stage do not introduce additional constraints or logical nuances or flights of imagination of your own that might in your opinion make the model more realistic. Do not, for example, worry about "what happens next week" if the problem never refers to "next week." The problems that we pose are chosen to help you develop a facility for model formulation assuming the abstraction step from the real-world situation is completed. In order to do this, and so that you may check your work and gauge your progress, it must be true that within the described context the correct formulation should be unambiguous. In other words, contrary to real-world situations, for this restricted set of example problems there is a "right answer." Later, when you have more experience, the latitude for shades of interpretation and real-world subtleties will be broader. Because the topic of formulation is so important, and because practice is the only way to master this topic, a long list of problems appears at the end of this chapter.

Again, we repeat our advice: Do not simply read the problem and then immediately read the formulation given at the end of the chapter. That would be the best way to deceive yourself about what you understand. Do not read the solution until either (1) you are certain you have correctly modeled the problem on your own or (2) you are absolutely convinced that you have hit an impasse. Peeking ahead at the solution before you have struggled with model formulation robs you of learning how to formulate LP models in Excel.

Table 3.9

Astro and Cosmo Data

	DAILY CAPACITY	LABOR UTILIZATION PER SET (HRS)		PROFIT PER SET ($)
		Dept. A	Dept. B	
Astro	70	1	1	20
Cosmo	50	2	1	10
Total Availability		120	90	

3.13 EXAMPLE 1: ASTRO AND COSMO (A PRODUCT MIX PROBLEM)

A TV company produces two types of TV sets, the Astro and the Cosmo. There are two production lines, one for each set, and there are two departments, both of which are used in the production of each set. The capacity of the Astro production line is 70 TV sets per day. The capacity of the Cosmo line is 50 TV sets per day. In department A picture tubes are produced. In this department the Astro set requires 1 labor hour and the Cosmo set requires 2 labor hours. Presently in department A a maximum of 120 labor hours per day can be assigned to production of the two types of sets. In department B the chassis is constructed. In this department the Astro set requires 1 labor hour and the Cosmo also requires 1 labor hour. Presently, in department B a maximum of 90 labor hours per day can be assigned to production of the two types of sets. The profit contributions are 20 and 10 dollars, respectively, for each Astro and Cosmo set. These data are summarized in Table 3.9.

If the company can sell as many Astro and Cosmo sets as it produces, what should be the daily production plan (i.e., the daily production) for each set? Review the Oak Product model and then try to formulate Astro and Cosmo as an LP model. Write the symbolic LP model, develop the Excel LP model, and optimize it with Solver.

3.14 EXAMPLE 2: BLENDING GRUEL (A BLENDING PROBLEM)

A 16-ounce can of dog food must contain protein, carbohydrate, and fat in at least the following amounts: protein, 3 ounces; carbohydrate, 5 ounces; fat, 4 ounces. Four types of gruel are to be blended together in various proportions to produce a least-cost can of dog food satisfying these requirements. The contents and prices for 16 ounces of each gruel are given in Table 3.10.

Review the previous ore blending model and then formulate this gruel blending problem as a linear program. Write the symbolic LP model, develop the Excel LP model, and optimize it with Solver. HINT: Let X_i denote the proportion of gruel i in a 16-ounce can of dog food, $i = 1, 2, 3, 4$.

3.15 EXAMPLE 3: SECURITY FORCE SCHEDULING

A university personnel supervisor must schedule the campus security force in such a way as to satisfy the staffing requirements shown in Table 3.11.

Officers work 8-hour shifts. There are six such shifts each day. The starting and ending times for each shift are given in Table 3.12.

Table 3.10

Gruel Blending Data

	CONTENTS AND PRICE PER 16 OZ OF GRUEL			
Gruel	Protein Content (oz)	Carbohydrate Content (oz)	Fat Content (oz)	Price ($)
1	3	7	5	4
2	5	4	6	6
3	2	2	6	3
4	3	8	2	2

Table 3.11

Security Staffing Requirements

TIME	MINIMUM NUMBER OF OFFICERS REQUIRED
Midnight–4 A.M.	5
4 A.M.–8 A.M.	7
8 A.M.–Noon	15
Noon–4 P.M.	7
4 P.M.–8 P.M.	12
8 P.M.–Midnight	9

Table 3.12

Shift Schedule

SHIFT	STARTING TIME	ENDING TIME
1	Midnight	8:00 A.M.
2	4:00 A.M.	Noon
3	8:00 A.M.	4:00 P.M.
4	Noon	8:00 P.M.
5	4:00 P.M.	Midnight
6	8:00 P.M.	4:00 A.M.

The personnel supervisor wants to determine how many officers should work each shift in order to minimize the total number of active officers, while still satisfying the staffing requirements. We can define the decision variables as follows:

$$X_1 = \text{number of officers working shift 1}$$
$$X_2 = \text{number of officers working shift 2}$$
$$\vdots$$
$$X_6 = \text{number of officers working shift 6}$$

In formulating the objective function, note that the total number of officers is the sum of the number of officers assigned to each shift. Now write out the objective function, noting that the personnel supervisor wants to minimize this sum. The objective function is

$$X_1 + X_2 + X_3 + X_4 + X_5 + X_6$$

In formulating the constraints, you want to be sure that a particular set of values for $X_1, \ldots, X_6$ satisfies the staffing requirements. Some device is needed to see which officers are on duty during each of the 4-hour intervals prescribed. A tabular arrangement, such as in Table 3.13, is helpful in making this determination. Here we see that the officers who

Table 3.13

Officers on Duty in Each Interval

	TIME INTERVAL					
SHIFT	Midnight to 4:00 A.M.	4:00 A.M. to 8:00 A.M.	8:00 A.M. to Noon	Noon to 4:00 P.M.	4:00 P.M. to 8:00 P.M.	8:00 P.M. to Midnight
1	x_1	x_1				
2		x_2	x_2			
3			x_3	x_3		
4				x_4	x_4	
5					x_5	x_5
6	x_6					x_6
Requirements	5	7	15	7	12	9

Table 3.14

Longer Boats Data

SLOOP	SELLING PRICE PER UNIT ($)	VARIABLE COST PER UNIT ($)	FIXED COST ($)
Sting	10,000	5,000	5,000,000
Ray	7,500	3,600	3,000,000
Breaker	15,000	8,000	10,000,000

work shift 1 are on duty during each of the first two time intervals, and so on. The table also shows (adding down columns) how many officers work in each time interval (e.g., in the first time interval $X_1 + X_6$ officers are on duty; thus we write the first constraint $X_1 + X_6 \geq 5$).

Now try to write out the remaining constraints for this model. Write the symbolic LP model, develop the Excel LP model, and optimize it with Solver.

The examples thus far have shown a product mix model (Astro/Cosmo), a blending model (gruel), and a scheduling model (security force). These are all illustrations of *types* of LPs that you encounter in real-world problem solving. Here is another important type of LP, called a *break-even model.*

3.16 EXAMPLE 4: LONGER BOATS YACHT COMPANY—A VIGNETTE IN CONSTRAINED BREAK-EVEN ANALYSIS

The Longer Boats Yacht Company produces three high-performance racing sloops. These three boats are called the Sting, the Ray, and the Breaker. Pertinent revenue and cost data for the next planning period are given in Table 3.14.

As you can see from these data, the *fixed cost* of each of these activities is considerable. A fixed cost is a lump cost that is paid regardless of the quantity to be produced. Thus, the same fixed cost of $3,000,000 for Rays will occur whether the production run consists of 0 boats, 1 boat, or 40 boats. The high fixed costs include the costs of design modification, mold reconstruction, and yacht basin testing.

Figure 3.25 shows a break-even analysis of the production of Stings. We see that if Longer Boats were to produce only Stings, it would have to produce at least 1,000 boats to break even.

Longer Boats' problem is more complicated, however. First, for the next planning period management has already contracted to produce 700 Stings. Another customer has requested 400 Breakers, a request that management would like to honor. Longer Boats' marketing surveys have convinced management that at most 300 Rays should be produced. Management is still interested in how much it must sell to break even, but now there are three products as well as previous commitments or restrictions to take into consideration. Starting from basic principles, management notes that at break-even

$$\text{total revenue} = \text{total cost.}$$

Since Longer Boats is a relatively new company and is experiencing the cash flow problems associated with rapid growth, management would like to minimize the capital outflow. The fixed costs are, of necessity, incurred in their totality, and thus the goal becomes one of minimizing total variable costs. Management's goal is to find the production plan

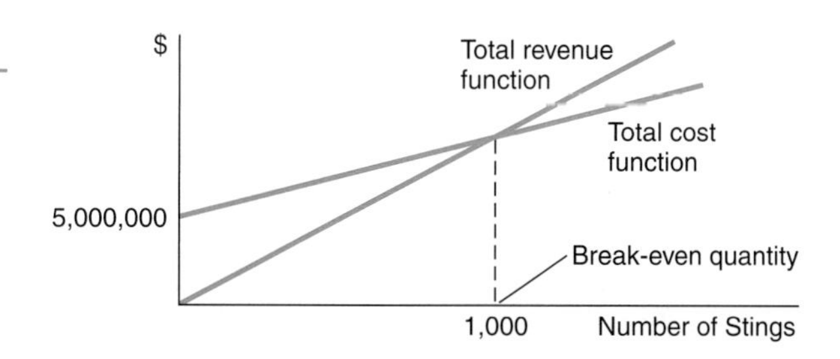

FIGURE 3.25

Break-Even Analysis for Stings

with the lowest total variable cost that honors the constraints and yields total revenue equal to total cost. Write the symbolic LP model, develop the spreadsheet LP model, and optimize it with Solver.

3.17 FURTHER HINTS FOR DEVELOPING LP MODELS

As you can see from the models formulated thus far in this chapter, LP modeling is hardly the black art it has been considered historically. Rather, it is simply the reasoned and careful specification of the model ingredients (decision variables, constraints, objective function, etc.) appropriate to a symbolic linear optimization model. However, like the "sunk costs" issue discussed previously, there are other pitfalls to avoid in formulating LP models. Let us identify a few of the common ones followed by a brief discussion of each.

- Like all else in modeling, avoid putting too much detail into your model or you will never get the model completely and consistently formulated. Later, your Excel formulation of the (overcomplicated) model will carry over these inconsistencies, which will appear as difficult-to-detect "bugs" in the spreadsheet. It is better to formulate a minimally sufficient set of decision variables and constraints, just to get started. It is much, much easier to add complexity in the form of more variables and constraints later to a simple model that you have come to understand thoroughly.
- Avoid nonlinear relationships, at least initially, in your modeling. Instead, use linear equations, possibly with bounds on the values of its variables via added constraints, as approximations in the region of interest for the more realistic, but complex nonlinear relationships. Although we will cover important nonlinear models in Chapter 7, nonlinear optimization is much more difficult to achieve and is fraught with pitfalls of its own. Even if you need to include some nonlinear relationships in your model, it is best to develop a simpler linear model first and then add the nonlinear relationships later.

  Be aware that just like P^2 ($= P*P$) produces a nonlinearity in a model if P is a decision variable, so does $P*Q$ produce a nonlinearity, if P and Q are *both* decision variables. In other words, you cannot multiply (or divide) two decision variables without introducing nonlinearity into the model.

  Note that some nonlinear relationships can be converted to linear ones easily without any loss of generality in the model. For example, assume Jim wanted to add a "product mix" blending constraint in the Oak Product model that required at least 1 Mate chair be produced for every 3 Captains. Expressing this constraint as $C/M \leq 3$ is algebraically correct, but is a nonlinear function of one of the decision variables, M, in the denominator of the ratio. However, standard manipulations of the equation produces the equivalent constraint, $C - 3M \leq 0$, which is linear in both of the decision variables.

TIP: *All the standard algebraic manipulations applied to both sides of an equation also work identically if applied to both sides of an inequality constraint with one exception: Multiplying or dividing both sides of an inequality by a negative number* reverses *the direction of the inequality. (For example, if $C - 3M \leq 0$, then multiplying both sides by -1 produces the equivalent inequality $-C + 3M \geq 0$.)*

- Don't become concerned too early with the real-world consequences of noninteger values of decision variables that might occur when the model is optimized. We will also cover models that require the decision variables to be integer-valued in Chapter 6. However, like nonlinear relationships, the requirement of integer values for decision variables introduces additional complexity in optimization that is best ignored at first.
- Many interesting LP models involve decision making over multiple time periods, such as choosing weekly production quantities for each of several weeks in cases where the weeks are not independent of each other. Although of great managerial interest, it is best to model the situation for a single time period (one week in this case) first and then modify it later to add the more complicated multi-week formulation. We will examine these models in detail in Chapter 5.

- Be sure the LP model has some "tension" built into it that forces nonobvious trade-offs to be made when it is optimized by Solver. For example, a cost-minimization model without any ≥ (requirements) constraints will very likely produce the real-world nonsense result of setting all decision variables to zero when it is optimized, that is, costs are minimized by going out of business. Similarly, a profit-maximization model without any ≤ (resource) constraints will very likely produce the pleasant, but impractical result of infinite profit, as one or more decision variables is increased toward infinity during the model optimization process. This latter outcome is called an "unbounded solution" in LP parlance.

- Be very suspicious of equality constraints—limit them in your LP modeling, if possible, to those cases where a definitional relationship must be maintained. For example, it is acceptable to include a constraint that Profit = SalesRevenue – TotalCost, an accounting identity, or a constraint that Ending Inventory = Beginning Inventory + Production – Shipments, a material balance constraint. However, even these equations bear managerial scrutiny. Inventories may "shrink" because of spoilage or theft, and Revenues booked may not be collected, and so forth. Hence, the proper formulation may be given by inequality constraints, "Profit ≤ . . ." and "Ending Inventory ≤ . . . ," respectively. In general, try to write relationships as inequalities, even if you believe they should be equalities at optimality. Later, when the model is optimized by Solver you can check to see if the inequality constraint is binding, that is, satisfied as an equality, as you expected. If not, then you can search for the reason why, thereby learning in the process.

  The major difficulty with including equality constraints is the risk of overconstraining your model, producing low payoff decisions when it is optimized, or in the worst case, no feasible decisions at all. Be especially sensitive to the inclusion of implied "organizational" policy constraints that manifest themselves as equalities in your model. For example, an unwritten policy in a company might be stated as "We have always followed the practice of assigning one supervisor (S) to every 10 workers (W) here at XYZ Corporation. Therefore, we must impose the constraint $W = 10\ S$." If there is no compelling reason for including this policy, payoff may be improved by leaving such constraints out of the model. On the other hand, if policy constraints are important to include in the model, then consider including them as inequalities instead of equalities. For example, the above constraint might be relaxed to ". . . no more than 10 workers are to be assigned to a supervisor," which produces $W \le 10S$ as a constraint. This lowers the chance of the "no-feasible-decisions" result when the model is optimized, and moreover, allows for the possibility that the best strategy is to abandon the exact "10-to-1" historical policy.

- Do *not* add constraints unless they are actually required by the situation being modeled. This commonly occurs when you allow your (often wrong) intuition about the nature of the optimal solution to force stipulations onto the LP model from the beginning. That is, you create a self-fulfilling prophesy by predetermining the model's solution before the model is optimized! As a result, you will never learn whether your intuition was correct, and worse, if your intuition is wrong, you risk the "no-feasible-decisions" result when the model is optimized. For example, a manager states "It is obvious to me that in this situation it would never be cost effective to have Ending Inventory be other than zero. So, I'll add Ending Inventory = 0 as a constraint to the model just to be sure." Not only does this risk overconstraining the model, as above, but the manager loses the opportunity to gain insight if the optimal solution of his/her model without that constraint would result in a positive ending inventory.

Subsequent chapters contain additional examples of formulations that you can use to cement your ability to make the transition between the real-world situation and the LP model of it. This transition—the way in which the LP model has been set up, the way the constraints and the objectives have been formulated—is of prime importance. As you develop your skills in LP model formulation, you will add your own "tips" to the list above.

3.18 SUMMARY

Constraints were defined to be mathematical conditions that rule out certain combinations of values for the decision variables, and feasible or allowable decisions were defined to be values of the variables that satisfy *all* the constraints. Linear programming was seen to involve a search for a feasible decision that optimizes an objective function. More specifically, linear programming was defined to be a mathematical model with the following properties:

1. There is a linear objective function that is to be maximized or minimized.
2. There are linear constraints, each a mathematical inequality (either $\leq$ or $\geq$) or an equality.

The flexibility of spreadsheet modeling requires some discipline be followed to facilitate building a spreadsheet representation that is (1) faithful to the LP model, (2) self-documenting, (3) suitable for optimization by Solver, and (4) does not cause problems later with interpretation of Solver's reports. There are four things to keep in mind to avoid pitfalls in using Solver.

1. Any formula affecting the objective function cell or the constraints must be linear if it involves the decision variables either directly or indirectly via other cell formulas.
2. Algebraically, a linear model is just a special case of a nonlinear model. However, this is not true for Solver's optimization software; it uses different software for optimizing the two classes of models. If you mistakenly forget to set the "Assume Linear" option and optimize an LP model via Solver's nonlinear optimizer, you may not get the optimal solution, and even if you do, Solver's reports, covered later, are different for the two types of procedures.
3. The right-hand side field of each constraint in the Solver Parameters dialog box should reference spreadsheet cells that are constants or evaluate to constants that will not change during optimization. Moreover, you may not put any formula into the *left*-hand side field of a constraint in the Solver Constraint dialog box. Therefore, it is best to avoid confusion by not putting formulas or constants explicitly into either the LHS or RHS fields in the Solver Add Constraint dialog. It is recommended that you put formulas or constants in spreadsheet cells and specify the corresponding worksheet cell references in the Add Constraint dialog box fields.
4. Range naming of the decision variable cells, the performance measure cell, groups of like-type-inequality constraint LHS cells, and groups of like-type-inequality RHS cells is a useful documentation step for larger LP models.

Completing the Solver Parameters dialog entails specifying the Target cell, the Changing Cells, the constraints, and setting the Assume Linear option, before Solving the model. In addition, the Assume Non-Negativity option may have to be set if negative values of the decisions have no meaning. After optimization completes, Solver displays the Solver Results dialog containing important completion messages and allowing one or more Solver reports to be generated. Upon completion the spreadsheet displays the optimal solution generated by Solver.

Several examples were given to show how a real-world situation can be translated into a symbolic LP model. The examples illustrated that a profit objective leads to a maximization (Max) model, whereas a cost objective gives a minimization (Min) model. We also saw that a constraint of the "limitation" type is usually translated into a mathematical inequality of the ≤ form, and a constraint of the "requirement" type is usually translated into a ≥ inequality. In some situations, such as in blending problems, logical considerations will require the presence of equality constraints. Guidelines were also given on how to proceed with developing the LP model and its spreadsheet formulation.

3.19 SOLUTIONS TO EXAMPLE PROBLEMS

SOLUTION TO THE EASTERN STEEL ORE BLENDING MODEL

The spreadsheet model, showing the optimal solution, is given in Figure 3.26 along with the Solver Parameters, relevant portions of Solver Options, and formulas.

SOLUTION TO EXAMPLE 1: ASTRO AND COSMO

The symbolic LP model for Astro and Cosmo is given by:

A = daily production of Astros (TV sets/day)

C = daily production of Cosmos (TV sets/day)

$$\text{Max } 20A + 10C$$

$$\text{s.t. } A \leq 70$$

$$C \leq 50$$

$$A + 2C \leq 120$$

$$A + C \leq 90$$

$$A, C, \geq 0$$

FIGURE 3.26

Ore Blending Model

	A	B	C	D	E	F	G	H	I
1	Ore Blending Production Plan								
2	Mine	T1	T2	T3	T4				
3	Ton Fractions	0.259	0.704	0.037	0	Total			
4	Cost/Ton	$800	$400	$600	$500	$511.11			
5	Constraints	Composition per Ton				Total Elements		Requirements	Surplus
6	A	10	3	8	2	5.00	≥	5	0
7	B	90	150	75	175	131.67	≥	100	31.67
8	C	45	25	20	37	30.00	≥	30	0
9	Balance	1	1	1	1	1.00	=	1	0

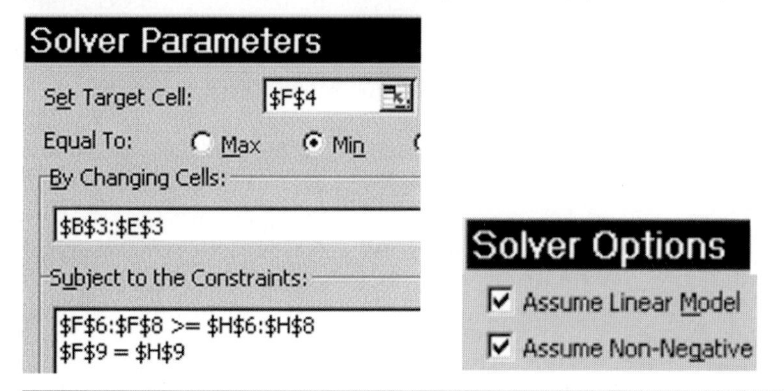

	A	B	C	D	E	F	G	H	I
1									
2	Mine	T1	T2	T3	T4				
3	Ton Fra	0.2592	0.7037	0.0370	0	Total			
4	Cost/To	800	400	600	500	=SUMPRODUCT($B$3:$E$3,B4:E4)			
5	Constrai	Com				Total Elements		Rec	Surplus
6	A	10	3	8	2	=SUMPRODUCT($B$3:$E$3,B6:E6)	≥	5	=F6-H6
7	B	90	150	75	175	=SUMPRODUCT($B$3:$E$3,B7:E7)	≥	100	=F7-H7
8	C	45	25	20	37	=SUMPRODUCT($B$3:$E$3,B8:E8)	≥	30	=F8-H8
9	Balance	1	1	1	1	=SUMPRODUCT($B$3:$E$3,B9:E9)	=	1	=F9-H9

FIGURE 3.27

Astro Cosmo Model

	A	B	C	D	E	F	G
1	Astro and Cosmo						
2		Astro	Cosmo				
3	Production Quantities	70.0	20.0	Profit			
4	Contribution Margins	$ 20	$ 10	$ 1,600			
5	Constraints	Resource Usage		Total		Avail.	Slack
6	Labor Dept. A	1	2	110	≤	120	10
7	Labor Dept. B	1	1	90	≤	90	-1.6E-10
8	Prod. Capacity, Astro	1		70	≤	70	-7.6E-12
9	Prod. Capacity, Cosmo		1	20	≤	50	30

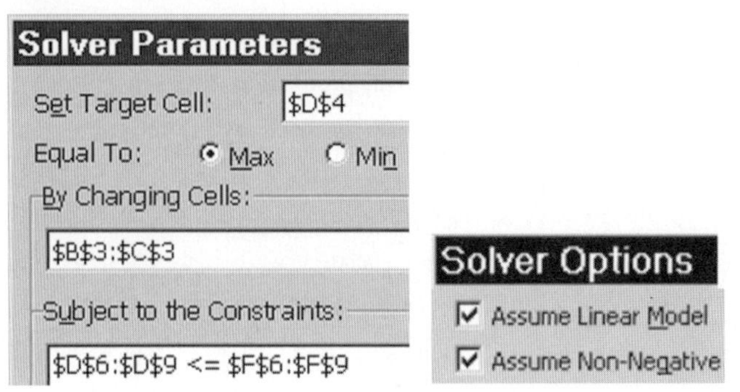

Note that like the Oak Products model not all the decision variables appear in all the constraints. For example, the variable C does not appear in the constraint $A \leq 70$. In general, not all the decision variables have to appear explicitly in every constraint.[7] The Excel model is given in Figure 3.27 along with the Solver Parameters and the optimal solution. The SUMPRODUCT() formulas for Profit and Total LHS cells are similar to that of the Eastern Steel Ore Blending example above and are omitted for this and later examples. The binding constraints for "Labor Dept. B" and "Prod. Capacity, Astro" do not show exactly a zero Slack. Very small negative or positive numbers occur in many Solver solutions because of Excel's finite arithmetic precision. In this and similar cases, the values represent extremely small numbers at the limit of Excel's computational precision and can be assumed to be zero for practical purposes.

SOLUTION TO EXAMPLE 2: BLENDING GRUEL

The LP model for blending gruel is given by:

$$
\begin{aligned}
\text{Min} \quad & 4x_1 + 6x_2 + 3x_3 + 2x_4 \\
\text{s.t.} \quad & 3x_1 + 5x_2 + 2x_3 + 3x_4 \geq 3 \\
& 7x_1 + 4x_2 + 2x_3 + 8x_4 \geq 5 \\
& 5x_1 + 6x_2 + 6x_3 + 2x_4 \geq 4 \\
& x_1 + x_2 + x_3 + x_4 = 1 \\
& x_1, x_2, x_3, x_4 \geq 0
\end{aligned}
$$

The spreadsheet model is shown in Figure 3.28 along with the Solver Parameters and the optimal solution.

Note that in Example 1, from the point of view of implementation, fractional values for the decision variables would probably be unacceptable unless one adopted the rationale of the decisions being daily average production rates. In Example 2, however, fractional values would be expected and acceptable.

[7] You may think of all decision variables being included, but with zero coefficients in places. Thus, the constraint $A \leq 70$ is the same as $A + 0 * C \leq 70$.

FIGURE 3.28

Blending Gruel Model

	A	B	C	D	E	F	G	H	I
1	Blending Gruel							Requirements	
2	Gruel	#1	#2	#3	#4				
3	Proportion of Gruel	0	0.167	0.333	0.5	Cost			
4	Cost/16 oz.	$4	$ 6	$ 3	$2	$3.00			
5	Constraints	Resource Provided				Total			Excess
6	Protein	3	5	2	3	3	≥	3	1.3E-15
7	Carbohydrate	7	4	2	8	5.333	≥	5	0.333
8	Fat	5	6	6	2	4	≥	4	1.8E-15
9	Total Proportion	1	1	1	1	1	=	1	2.2E-16

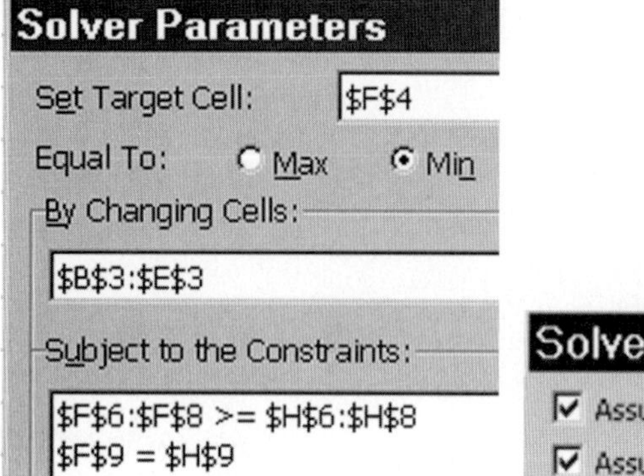

SOLUTION TO EXAMPLE 3: SECURITY FORCE SCHEDULING

The security force scheduling model is given by:

$$\begin{aligned} &\text{Min } x_1 + x_2 + x_3 + x_4 + x_5 + x_6 \\ &\text{s.t. } x_6 + x_1 \geq 5 \\ &\quad x_1 + x_2 \geq 7 \\ &\quad x_2 + x_3 \geq 15 \\ &\quad x_3 + x_4 \geq 7 \\ &\quad x_4 + x_5 \geq 12 \\ &\quad x_5 + x_6 \geq 9 \\ &\quad x_i \geq 0, \qquad i = 1, 2, \ldots, 6 \end{aligned}$$

Example 3 illustrates another setting where integer values would be needed. The spreadsheet model is shown in Figure 3.29 along with the Solver Parameters and the optimal solution. (You may get a different schedule from Solver, but it will have the same minimum Total #. This is because this model has several alternative optimal schedules.)

This type of problem has been used to schedule operators for several telephone companies, as well as for companies that have "800" numbers. Typically, each hour is broken into 15-minute segments; thus each 24-hour day has 96 constraints. The number of variables is determined by the different possible shifts allowed.

SOLUTION TO EXAMPLE 4: LONGER BOATS YACHT COMPANY

To obtain an expression of the break-even in terms of the production quantities, the following decision variables are defined:

S = number of Stings to produce

R = number of Rays to produce

B = number of Breakers to produce

FIGURE 3.29

Security Force Scheduling Model

	A	B	C	D	E	F	G	H	I	J	K
1	Security Force Schedulting										
2	Shift	#1	#2	#3	#4	#5	#6	Total #			
3	# on Shift	0	7	8	0	12	5	32			
4	Constraints	Resource Available						Total		Requiremts	Excess
5	Mid. - 4am	1					1	5	≥	5	0
6	4am - 8 am	1	1					7	≥	7	0
7	8am - Noon		1	1				15	≥	15	-7E-13
8	Noon - 4pm			1	1			8	≥	7	1
9	4pm - 8pm				1	1		12	≥	12	1E-12
10	8pm - Mid.					1	1	17	≥	9	8

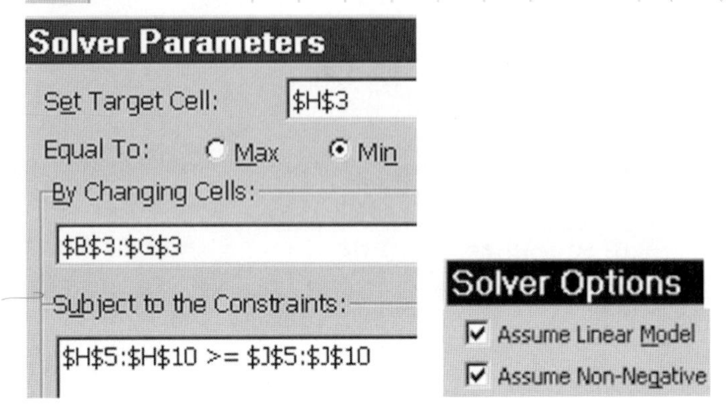

The break-even constraint, then, is

$$10{,}000S + 7500R + 15{,}000B = 5000S + 3600R + 8000B + 18{,}000{,}000$$

or

$$5000S + 3900R + 7000B = 18{,}000{,}000.$$

We note that there is an infinite number of sets of values for S, R, and B that satisfy this constraint. Thus, in the multiproduct case, there are many break-even points, whereas in the single-product case, there is only one. In the multiproduct case, then, management must specify an additional restriction in order to identify a particular break-even point of interest. The fixed costs are of necessity incurred in their totality, and thus the goal of minimizing capital outlay becomes one of minimizing total variable costs. The total variable cost (the objective function) is

$$5000S + 3600R + 8000B$$

The complete model reflecting the break-even constraint, as well as the preestablished requirements and limits on demand, is as follows:

$$\text{Min } 5000S + 3600R + 8000B$$
$$5000S + 3900R + 7000B = 18{,}000{,}000$$
$$S \geq 700$$
$$B \geq 400$$
$$R \leq 300$$
$$S \geq 0, \qquad R \geq 0, \qquad B \geq 0$$

The spreadsheet model is shown in Figure 3.30 along with the Solver Parameters and the optimal solution. Note that the original data disaggregations are preserved with formulas performing the aggregations to allow flexibility in data editing for "What if?" projections.

FIGURE 3.30

Longer Boats Constrained Break-Even Model

	A	B	C	D	E	F	G	H
1	Longer Boats							
2	($ 000s)	Stings	Breakers	Rays				
3	Selling Price	$ 10.0	$ 15.0	$ 7.5				
4	Variable Cost	$ 5.0	$ 8.0	$ 3.6			Total Fixed Cost	
5	Fixed Cost	$5,000	$ 3,000	$10,000			$ 18,000	
6								
7	Break Even Model ($ in 000's)							
8		Stings	Breakers	Rays				
9	# to Produce	2806	400	300	Var. Cost			
10	Unit Cost	$5.00	$8.00	$3.60	$ 18,310			
11	Constraints		Resource Usage		Total		Requiremts	Slack
12	Break Even	$5.00	$7.00	$3.90	$ 18,000	=	$ 18,000	0
13	Min Prod. Stings	1			2806	≥	700	2106
14	Min Prod. Breakers		1		400	≥	400	0
15	Max Prod. Rays			1	300	≤	300	0

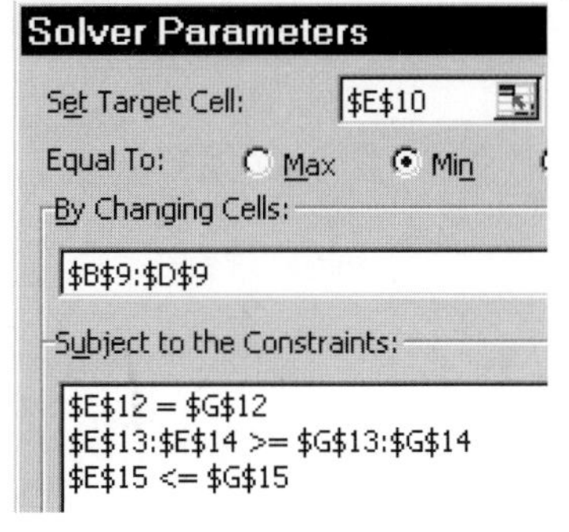

Solver Options

☑ Assume Linear Model

☑ Assume Non-Negative

Key Terms

Constraint. A mathematical inequality (an inequality constraint) or equality (an equality constraint) that must be satisfied by the variables in the model.

Binding Constraint. A constraint for which, when evaluated at optimality, the left hand side equals the right hand side.

Objective Function. Every linear program has a linear objective function that represents the performance measure to be either maximized or minimized.

Constrained Optimization Model. A model whose objective is to find values of decision variables that optimize an objective function subject to constraints.

Optimal Product Mix. Alternative term for optimal production plan.

Optimal Production Plan. The optimal decision for a production model, that is, the optimal quantities of each product to be produced.

Inequality Constraint. A constraint requiring some function of the decision variables in a model to be ≥ (greater than or equal to) or ≤ (less than or equal to) a constant.

Right-Hand Side. The number on the right-hand side (RHS) of a constraint. Abbreviated RHS.

Constraint Function. The left-hand side (LHS) of a constraint. It depends on the decision variables.

Nonnegativity Conditions. Conditions in a model that stipulate that the decision variables can have only nonnegative (*positive or zero*) values.

Decision Variables. The variables under the decision maker's control. These are the variables that appear in the models that we have formulated in this chapter.

Feasible Decision. A decision that satisfies all the constraints of a model, including the nonnegativity conditions. Feasible means allowable.

Optimal Decision. A feasible decision that optimizes the objective function.

Optimal Solution. Alternative term for optimal decision.

Optimize. To maximize or minimize.

Symbolic LP Model. The algebraic representation of an LP problem.

Linear Function. A function in which each variable appears in a separate term. There are no powers other than 1, and there are no logarithmic, exponential, IF() statements or trigonometric terms.

Integrality Condition. A requirement that one or more variables in a model have only integer values.

Integer Program. A model in which one or more variables can have only integer values.

Parameter. A number or symbol in a model that must have a numerical value supplied exogenously.

Decision Values. A set of numerical values for the decision variables.

Equality Constraint. A constraint requiring some function of the decision variables in a model to be exactly equal to a constant.

Sunk Costs. Costs whose values have already been determined, and therefore cannot be affected by subsequent decisions.

Variable Costs. Costs whose final values will be determined by decisions yet to be made.

Solver. A spreadsheet add-in program that can optimize the spreadsheet representation of an LP model.

Surplus. The amount by which the left-hand side of a ≥ constraint, when evaluated at optimality, exceeds the right-hand side. Surplus is always nonnegative.

Slack. The amount by which the left-hand side of a ≤ constraint, when evaluated at optimality, is less than the right-hand side. Slack is always nonnegative.

Self-Review Exercises

True-False Quiz

1. **T F** In the context of modeling, restrictions on allowable decisions are called constraints.
2. **T F** Not every LP has to have constraints.
3. **T F** Any model with an objective function, constraints, and decision variables is an LP.
4. **T F** A limitation is expressed as a ≥ constraint.
5. **T F** The nonnegativity conditions mean that all decision variables must be positive.
6. **T F** Since fractional values for decision variables may not be physically meaningful, in practice (for the purpose of implementation) we often round the optimal LP solution to integer values.
7. **T F** All the constraints in an LP are inequalities.
8. **T F** Properly defining the decision variables is an important step in model formulation.
9. **T F** The objective function of a cost-minimization model need only consider variable, as opposed to sunk, costs.
10. **T F** The way in which a situation has been formulated as a model is of considerable interest to the manager, who may one day have to pass judgment on the validity of the model.

Multiple Choice

11. A constraint limits the values
  a. that the objective function can assume
  b. that the decision variables can assume
  c. neither of the above
  d. both a and b

12. Constraints may represent
  a. limitations
  b. requirements
  c. balance conditions
  d. all of the above

13. Linear programming is
  a. a constrained optimization model
  b. a constrained decision-making model
  c. a mathematical programming model
  d. all of the above

14. In an LP Max model
  a. the objective function is maximized
  b. the objective function is maximized and then it is determined whether this occurs at an allowable decision
  c. the objective function is maximized over the allowable set of decisions
  d. all of the above

15. The *distinguishing* feature of an LP (as opposed to more general mathematical programming models) is that
  a. the model has an objective function and constraints
  b. all functions in the problem are linear
  c. optimal values for the decision variables are produced

16. In translating a word problem into a symbolic model, it is often helpful to
  a. express each constraint in words
  b. express the objective in words
  c. verbally identify the decision variables
  d. all of the above

17. Model formulation is important because
  a. it enables us to use algebraic techniques
  b. in a business context, most managers prefer to work with symbolic models
  c. it forces management to address a clearly defined problem
  d. it allows the manager to postpone decision making while appearing to be busy

18. The nonnegativity requirement is included in an LP because
  a. it makes the model easier to solve
  b. it makes the model correspond more closely to the real-world problem
  c. neither of the above
  d. both a and b

Questions 19 through 26 refer to the following problem:

Three itinerant industrialists, Lotta Anderson, Claire Mosley, and Finny Jones, are en route to Hollywood to seek their fortune. The flight time is 40 hours at a fuel cost of $100 per gallon. In a Hollywood deli they strike up a quick friendship with the notorious Peter Rehnberg. Peter's net income per year is $40,000—his alimony payments are $60,000. Knowing almost everyone in town, Peter is able to spin out a stairway to the stars for our three fortune seekers. They are now inspecting capsule medicine products by passing the capsules over a special lighting table where they visually check for cracked, partially filled, or improperly tainted capsules. Currently, any of our three moguls can be assigned to the visual inspection task. However, they differ in height, accuracy, and speed abilities. Consequently, their employer (Flora Sager) pays them at slightly different wage rates. The significant differences are summed up in the following table.

INSPECTORS	SPEED (UNITS/HR)	ACCURACY (%)	HOURLY WAGE ($)	HEIGHT
Lotta	300	98	11.80	5 ft 10 in
Claire	200	99	10.40	4 ft 3 in
Finny	350	96	11.00	5 ft 2 in

Operating on a full 8-hour shift, Flora needs to have at least 2,000 capsules inspected with no more than 2% of these capsules having inspection errors. In addition, because of the devastating carpal tunnel syndrome, no one inspector can be assigned this task for more than 4 hours per day. Let

X_1 = number of hours worked by Lotta

X_2 = number of hours worked by Claire

X_3 = number of hours worked by Finny

The objective is to minimize the cost of 8 hours of inspection. Assume that the inspection process must be in operation for all 8 hours. In other words, continuous production must occur during the 8-hour period. In addition, Lotta, Claire, and Finny are the only inspectors, no more than one inspector can work at a time, and the plumber works at most 4 hours per day.

19. A correct accuracy constraint is
   a. $(0.98)(300)X_1 + (0.99)(200)X_2 + (0.96)(350)X_3 \geq 2000$
   b. $(0.02)(300)X_1 + (0.01)(200)X_2 + (0.04)(350)X_3 \leq (0.02)(2000)$
   c. $-2X_2 + 7X_3 \leq 0$
   d. none of the above

20. The production requirement constraint is correctly written as $300X_1 + 200X_2 + 350X_3 = 2000$.
   a. T
   b. F

21. Excluding the nonnegativity constraints, a proper formulation for this problem will contain six constraints.
   a. T
   b. F

22. It is possible that the correct formulation for this problem will have no feasible decisions. (Answer this question for the given data.)
   a. T
   b. F

23. If it were not for the accuracy requirement and the 4-hour limitation, the optimal solution would have only Finny working.
   a. T
   b. F

24. The optimal solution will require that at least two of the three employees inspect.
   a. T
   b. F

25. A feasible policy is provided by
   a. 4 hours Claire, 4 hours Finny
   b. 4 hours Lotta, 4 hours Claire
   c. both a and b

26. Let policy A be $X_1 = 4, X_2 = 4, X_3 = 0$. Let policy B be $X_1 = 3, X_2 = 4, X_3 = 1$. Note that each policy is feasible. Since A produces 2,000 capsules and B produces 2,050, A is preferred.
   a. T
   b. F

27. A parameter in a model can be a number or a symbol.
   a. T
   b. F

28. Consider the constraint $10C + 15M \leq R$, where R is a parameter denoting hours in department A. Now suppose values of R are given by $(1 - e^{-(.05MA)})$ where MA is a new decision variable. If we substitute this into the original constraint, it becomes $10C + 15M \leq 200\ (1 - e^{-(.05MA)})$. This new constraint is linear in C, M, and the new parameter MA.
   a. T
   b. F

29. In the spreadsheet representation of an LP, a constraint function is represented as a formula in a cell.
   a. T
   b. F

30. For feasible decisions, the slack cells if present in the spreadsheet will contain nonnegative numbers.
   a. T
   b. F

31. Excel can be used to create a spreadsheet representation of an LP but without Solver it will *not* optimize the spreadsheet.
   a. T
   b. F

32. A parameter
   a. is a number in a model, or symbol that is exogenous to the model (i.e., a symbol whose numerical value must be supplied to the model)
   b. may be represented by a symbol (such as R) whose value must be determined by the model
   c. both of the above

33. A suggested way to create a spreadsheet representation of an LP is to first write out the symbolic LP model and then use this as a guideline to create a spreadsheet model.
a. T
b. F

34. A spreadsheet representation of an LP can be useful because
a. parameters representing raw data may enter into the model nonlinearly
b. it makes the model easy to debug
c. both of the above

Answers

1. T, **2.** F, **3.** F, **4.** F, **5.** F, **6.** T, **7.** F, **8.** T, **9.** T, **10.** T, **11.** d, **12.** d, **13.** d, **14.** c, **15.** b, **16.** d, **17.** c, **18.** b, **19.** c, **20.** b, **21.** a, **22.** b, **23.** b, **24.** a, **25.** b, **26.** b, **27.** a, **28.** b, **29.** a, **30.** a, **31.** a, **32.** a, **33.** a, **34.** a

Skill Problems

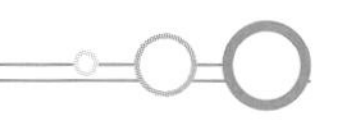

3-1. Match each of the following terms with the most appropriate description below.
(a) Linear program
(b) Requirement
(c) Variable cost
(d) Sunk cost
(e) Decision variables
(f) Constraint function
(g) Restriction
(h) Limitation
1. The unknowns in an LP that represent decisions to be made.
2. Usually, a constraint of ≥ form.
3. A concept that is proper to include in the model.
4. Usually, not relevant to the model (break-even analysis would be an exception).
5. Usually, a constraint of ≤ form.
6. The left-hand side of the constraint.
7. Synonymous with constraint.
8. A special type of constrained optimization model.

3-2. Which of the following mathematical relationships could be found in a linear programming model? For those relationships that could not be found in an LP, state the reasons.
(a) $3x_1 + x_2 \leq \sqrt{5}$
(b) $\sqrt{x_1} + x_2 \leq 10$
(c) $\sqrt{2x_1} - \pi\, x_3 \leq e$
(d) $x_1^2 + 2x_2 = 0$
(e) $x_1 + x_1x_2 + x_3 = 5$
(f) $x_1 + \log(x_2) = 5$
(g) $\log(10)\, x_1 + e^2 x_2 = 6$
(h) $e^{x_1} + x_2 = 23$
(i) the Excel formula for the RHS of a constraint in which F6 is a decision variable: =IF($F$6>=2,SUM(G1:G10),SUM(G1:G5))

Application Problems

3-3. *A Production Problem.* The Swelte Glove Company manufactures and sells two products. The company makes a profit of $12 for each unit of product 1 sold and a profit of $4 for each unit of product 2. The labor-hour requirements for the products in each of the three production departments are summarized in the following table. The supervisors of these departments have estimated that the following numbers of labor hours will be available during the next week: 800 hours in department 1, 600 hours in department 2, and 2,000 hours in department 3. Assuming that the company is interested in maximizing profits, develop the linear programming model.

DEPARTMENT	LABOR-HOUR REQUIREMENT	
	Product 1	Product 2
1	1	2
2	1	3
3	2	3

3-4. *A Production Problem.* Wood Walker owns a small furniture shop. He makes three different styles of tables: A, B, C. Each table requires a certain amount of time for cutting component parts, for assembling, and for painting. Wood can sell all the units he makes. Furthermore, model C may be sold without painting. Wood employs several individuals who work on a part-time basis, so the time available for each of these activities varies from week to week. Use the data in the following to formulate an LP model that will help Wood determine the product mix that will maximize his profit next week.

MODEL	CUTTING (HRS)	ASSEMBLING (HRS)	PAINTING (HRS)	PROFIT PER TABLE ($)
A	3	4	5	25
B	1	2	5	20
C	4	5	4	50
Unpainted C	4	5	0	30
Capacity	150	200	300	

3-5. *Financial Planning.* Willie Hanes is president of a one-person investment firm that manages stock portfolios for a number of clients. A new client has just requested the firm to manage a $100,000 portfolio. The client would like to restrict the portfolio to a mix of the three stocks shown in the following table. Formulate an LP to show how many shares of each stock Willie should purchase to maximize the estimated total annual return.

STOCK	PRICE PER SHARE $	ESTIMATED ANNUAL RETURN PER SHARE $	MAXIMUM POSSIBLE INVESTMENT $
Gofer Crude	60	7	60,000
Can Oil	25	3	25,000
Sloth Petroleum	20	3	30,000

3-6. *A Blending Problem.* Douglas E. Starr, the manager of Heavenly Hound Kennels, Inc., provides lodging for pets. The kennels' dog food is made by mixing three grain products to obtain a well-balanced dog diet. The data for the three products are shown in the following table. If Douglas wants to make sure that each of his dogs consumes at least 8 ounces of protein, 1 ounce of carbohydrate, and no more than 0.5 ounces of fat each day, how much of each grain product should each dog be fed in order to minimize Douglas's cost? (Note: 16 ounces = 1 pound.)

GRAIN PRODUCT	COST PER POUND ($)	PROTEIN (%)	CARBOHYDRATE (%)	FAT (%)
A	0.45	62	5	3
B	0.38	55	10	2
C	0.27	36	20	1

3-7. *A Blending Problem.* McNaughton, Inc., produces two steak sauces, Spicy Diablo and mild Red Baron. These sauces are both made by blending two ingredients, A and B. A certain level of flexibility is permitted in the formulas for these products. The allowable percentages, along with revenue and cost data, are given in the following table. Up to 40 quarts of A and 30 quarts of B could be purchased. McNaughton can sell as much of these sauces as it produces. Formulate an LP whose objective is to maximize the net revenue from the sale of the sauces.

SAUCE	INGREDIENT		SALES PRICE PER QUART ($)
	A	B	
Spicy Diablo	at least 25%	at least 50%	3.35
Red Baron	at most 75%	*	2.85
Cost per Quart	$1.60	$2.59	

* No explicit maximum or minimum percentage.

3-8. *A Blending Problem.* Corey Ander's Spice Company has a limited amount of three ingredients that are used in the production of seasonings. Corey uses the three ingredients—HB01, HB02, and HB03—to produce either turmeric or paprika. The marketing department reports that the firm can sell as much paprika as it can produce, but it can sell up to a maximum of 1,700 bottles of turmeric. Unused ingredients can be sold on the open market. Prices are quoted in $/ounce. The current prices are: HB01—$0.60, HB02—$0.70, HB03—$0.55. In addition, Corey has signed a contract to supply 600 bottles of paprika to Wal-Mart. Additional data are shown in the following table. Formulate Corey's problem as a revenue-maximizing LP.

	INGREDIENTS (OZ/BOTTLE)				
	HB01	HB02	HB03	DEMAND (BOTTLES)	SALES PRICE PER BOTTLE ($)
Turmeric	4	2	1	1700	3.25
Paprika	3	2	3	Unlimited	2.75
Availability (ounces)	8,000	9,000	7,000		

3-9. *A Blending Problem.* Guy Chung, superintendent of buildings and grounds at Gotham University, is planning to put fertilizer on the grass in the quadrangle area early in the spring. The grass needs nitrogen, phosphorus, and potash in at least the amounts given in the following table.

MINERAL	MINIMUM WEIGHT (LB)
Nitrogen	10
Phosphorus	7
Potash	5

Three kinds of commercial fertilizer are available; analysis and prices per 1,000 pounds are given in the following table. Guy can buy as much of each of these fertilizers as he wishes and mix them together before applying them to the grass. Formulate an LP model to determine how much of each fertilizer he should buy to satisfy the requirements at minimum cost.

FERTILIZER	NITROGEN CONTENT (LB)	PHOSPHORUS CONTENT (LB)	POTASH CONTENT (LB)	PRICE ($)
I	25	10	5	10
II	10	5	10	8
III	5	10	5	7

Fertilizer Characteristics (per 1,000 lb.)

3-10. *A Production Problem.* Two products are manufactured on each of three machines. A pound of each product requires a specified number of hours on each machine, as presented in the following table. Total hours available on machines 1, 2, and 3 are 10, 16, and 12, respectively. The profit contributions per pound of products 1 and 2 are $4 and $3, respectively. Define the decision variables and formulate this problem as a profit-maximizing linear program and solve it.

	MACHINE-HOUR REQUIREMENT	
MACHINE	Product 1	Product 2
1	3	2
2	1	4
3	5	3

3-11. Sally's Solar Car Company has a plant that can manufacture family sedans, station wagons, and sports coupes. The contribution, variable production time, and fixed cost for manufacturing these cars are given in the following table.

MODEL	PROFIT CONTRIBUTION ($)	VARIABLE PRODUCTION TIME (HOURS)	FIXED COST ($)
Sedan	6,000	12	2,000,000
Station Wagon	8,000	15	3,000,000
Coupe	11,000	24	7,000,000

Sally currently has orders for 100 sedans, 200 station wagons, and 300 coupes. She must satisfy these orders. She wants to plan production so she will break even as quickly as possible—that is, she wants to make sure that the total contribution margin will equal total fixed costs and that total variable production time is minimized. Formulate this problem as an LP and solve it.

3-12. *Break-Even Analysis.* Reese Eichler, a manufacturer of air filtration equipment, produces two units, the Umidaire and the Depollinator. Data pertaining to sales price and costs are shown in the following table. Reese's firm has already contracted to provide 500 Umidaires and would like to calculate the break-even quantities for both types of units. Formulate the cost-minimizing LP model and solve it.

PRODUCT	SELLING PRICE PER UNIT ($)	VARIABLE COST PER UNIT ($)	FIXED COST ($)
Umidaire	450	240	150,000
Depollinator	700	360	240,000

3-13. *Portfolio Planning.* An investment company currently has $10 million to invest. The goal is to maximize expected return earned over the next year. Their four investment possibilities are summarized in the following table. In addition, the company has specified that at least 30% of the funds must be placed in common stock and treasury bonds, and no more than 40% in money market funds and municipal bonds. All of the $10 million currently on hand will be invested. Formulate an LP model that tells how much money to invest in each instrument and solve it.

INVESTMENT POSSIBILITY	EXPECTED EARNED RETURN (%)	MAXIMUM ALLOWABLE INVESTMENT (MILLIONS $)
Treasury Bonds	8	5
Common Stock	6	7
Money Market	12	2
Municipal Bonds	9	4

3-14. *Farm Management.* A firm operates four farms of comparable productivity. Each farm has a certain amount of usable acreage and a supply of labor hours to plant and tend the crops. The data for the upcoming season are shown in the following table.

FARM	USABLE ACREAGE	LABOR HOURS AVAILABLE PER MONTH
1	500	1700
2	900	3000
3	300	900
4	700	2200

The organization is considering three crops for planting. These crops differ primarily in their expected profit per acre and in the amount of labor they require, as shown in the following table.

CROP	MAXIMUM ACREAGE	MONTHLY LABOR HOURS REQUIRED PER ACRE	EXPECTED PROFIT PER ACRE ($)
A	700	2	500
B	800	4	200
C	300	3	300

Furthermore, the total acreage that can be devoted to any particular crop is limited by the associated requirements for harvesting equipment. In order to maintain a roughly uniform workload among the farms, management's policy is that the percentage of usable acreage planted must be the same at each farm. However, any combination of the crops may be grown at any of the farms as long as all constraints are satisfied (including the uniform-workload requirement). Management wishes to know how many acres of each crop should be planted at the respective farms in order to maximize expected profit. Formulate this as a linear programming model and solve it.

3-15. *A Blending Problem.* A vineyard wishes to blend four different vintages to make three types of blended wine. The supply of the vintages and the sales prices of the blended wines are shown in the following table, together with certain restrictions on the percentage composition of the three blends. In particular, vintages 2 and 3 together must make up at least 75% of Blend A and at least 35% of Blend C. In addition, Blend A must contain at least 8% of vintage 4, while Blend B must contain at least 10% of vintage 2 and at most 35% of vintage 4. Any amounts of Blends A, B, and C can be sold. Formulate an LP model that will make the best use of the vintages on hand and solve it.

	VINTAGE				
BLEND	1	2	3	4	SALES PRICE PER GALLON
A	*	at least 75% 2 & 3 in any proportion		at least 8%	80
B	*	at least 10%	*	at most 35%	50
C	*	at least 35% 2 & 3 in any proportion		*	35
SUPPLY (gallons)	130	200	150	350	

* Indicates no restriction.

3-16. *A Scheduling Problem.* A certain restaurant operates 7 days a week. Waiters are hired to work 6 hours per day. The union contract specifies that each must work 5 consecutive days and then have 2 consecutive days off. All waiters hired receive the same weekly salary. Staffing requirements are shown in the following table. Assume that this cycle of requirements repeats indefinitely, and ignore the fact that the number of waiters hired must be an integer. The manager wishes to find an employment schedule that satisfies these requirements at a minimum cost. Formulate this problem as a linear program and solve it.

DAY	MINIMUM NUMBER OF WAITER HOURS REQUIRED
Monday	150
Tuesday	200
Wednesday	400
Thursday	300
Friday	700
Saturday	800
Sunday	300

3-17. *A Production Problem.* A plant can manufacture four different products (A, B, C, D) in any combination. Each product requires time on each of four machines in minutes per pound of product, as shown in the following table. Each machine is available 60 hours per week. Products A, B, C, and D may be sold at prices of $9, $7, $6, and $5 per pound, respectively. Variable labor costs are $2 per hour for machines 1 and 2 and $3 per hour for machines 3 and 4. Material cost for each pound of product A is $4. The material cost is $1 for each pound of products B, C, and D. Formulate a profit-maximizing LP model for this problem, given the maximum demands for each product below, and then solve it.

	MACHINE				
PRODUCT	1	2	3	4	MAXIMUM DEMAND
A	5	10	6	3	400
B	3	6	4	8	100
C	4	5	3	3	150
D	4	2	1	2	500

3-18. *A Production Problem.* A manufacturer has four jobs, A, B, C, and D, that must be produced this month. Each job may be handled in any of three shops. The time required for each job in each shop, the cost per hour in each shop, and the number of hours available this week in each shop are given in the following table. It is also possible to split each job among the shops in any proportion. For example, one-fourth of job A can be done in 8 hours in shop 1, and one-third of job C can be done in 19 hours in shop 3. The manufacturer wishes to determine how many hours of each job should be handled by each shop in order to minimize the total cost of completing all four jobs. Identify the decision variables, formulate an LP model for this problem, and solve it.

	TIME REQUIRED (HR)					
SHOP	A	B	C	D	COST PER HOUR OF SHOP TIME ($)	SHOP TIME AVAILABLE (HR)
1	32	151	72	118	89	160
2	39	147	61	126	81	160
3	46	155	57	121	84	160

3-19. *A Scheduling Problem.* While it is operating out of Stockholm, the aircraft carrier Mighty is on maneuvers from Monday through Friday and in port over the weekend. Next week the captain would like to give shore leave for Monday through Friday to as many of the 2,500-sailor crew as possible. However, he must carry out the maneuvers for the week and satisfy navy regulations. The regulations are

(a) Sailors work either the A.M. shift (midnight to noon) or the P.M. shift (noon to midnight) any day they work, and during a week they must remain on the same shift every day they work.

(b) Each sailor who works must be on duty exactly four days, even if there is not enough "real work" on some days.

The number of sailors required each shift of each day is shown in the following table. Formulate and solve this problem as a linear programming problem so that one would know how many sailors work on each day.

	M	TU	W	TH	F
A.M.	900	1000	450	800	700
P.M.	800	500	1000	300	750

3-20. *A Process Mix Problem.* A small firm has two processes for blending each of two products, charcoal starter fluid and lighter fluid for cigarette lighters. The firm is attempting to decide how many hours to run each process. The inputs and outputs for running the processes for one hour are given in the following table. Let x_1 and x_2 be the number of hours the company decides to use process 1 and process 2, respectively. Because of a federal allocation program, the maximum amounts of kerosene and benzene available are 300 units and 450 units, respectively. Sales commitments require that at least 600 units of starter fluid and 225 units of lighter fluid be produced. The per hour profits that accrue from process 1 and process 2 are $450 and $390, respectively. Formulate this as a profit-maximizing linear programming model and solve it.

	INPUTS		OUTPUTS	
PROCESS	**Kerosene**	**Benzene**	**Starter Fluid**	**Lighter Fluid**
1	3	9	15	6
2	12	6	9	24

3-21. *Portfolio Planning with the CAPM Model.* (*Note*: This problem will be especially interesting to students with a background in investments. Others should be cautioned that it includes terms not defined in this text.) An investment company currently has $10 million to invest. Its goal is to maximize expected return over the next year. The company wants to use the capital asset pricing model (CAPM) to determine each investment's expected return. The CAPM formula is:

$CR = Rf + b\,(Rm - Rf)$, where

CR = expected return

Rf = risk-free rate

b = investment beta (market risk)

Rm = market return

The market return and risk-free rate fluctuate, and the company wants to be able to reevaluate its decision on a weekly basis. Its four investment possibilities are summarized in the following table. In addition, the company has specified that at least 30% of the funds must be placed in treasury bonds and money markets, and no more than 40% in common stock and municipal bonds. All of the $10 million currently on hand will be invested.

(a) Formulate this problem as an LP model.

(b) Optimize the model if the market return is 12% and the risk-free rate is 6%.

INVESTMENT POSSIBILITY	BETA	MAXIMUM ALLOWABLE INVESTMENT (MILLIONS $)
Treasury Bonds	0	7
Common Stock	1	2
Money Market	$\frac{1}{3}$	5
Municipal Bonds	$\frac{1}{2}$	4

3-22. In the human diet, 16 essential nutrients have been identified. Suppose that there are 116 foods. A pound of food j contains all pounds of nutrient i. Suppose that a human being must have N_j pounds of each nutrient i in the daily diet and that a pound of food j costs C_j cents. What is the least-cost daily diet satisfying all nutritional requirements? Use summation notation to write the symbolic formulation of this model. Aside from the question of palatability, can you think of an important constraint that this problem omits?

3-23. *Waiter Scheduling.* For this problem, you will need to use Excel's VLOOKUP command. A certain restaurant operates seven days a week. Waiters are hired to work six effective hours per day. The restaurant attracts individuals and small groups, which we will call regular demand. In addition, the restaurant attracts a number of larger groups (Rotary, Lions, Quarterback Club, etc.) that schedule weekly meetings. The union contract specifies that each waiter must work five consecutive days and then have two consecutive days off. All waiters receive the same weekly salary. The minimum required waiter hours is a function of the regular daily demand plus the waiter hours needed to staff the scheduled group meetings for the day. The regular daily demands (in waiter hours) and the number of group meetings currently scheduled each day are given in the following table.

DAY	REGULAR DAILY DEMAND (WAITER HOURS)	SCHEDULED LARGER GROUP MEETINGS
Monday	125	1
Tuesday	200	0
Wednesday	350	1
Thursday	300	0
Friday	650	3
Saturday	725	4
Sunday	250	2

The manager uses the following table to determine the waiter hours required for the larger group meetings. The manager would like to find an employment schedule that satisfies required waiter hours at a minimum cost. Assume that this cycle repeats indefinitely, and ignore the fact that the number of waiters hired must be an integer. Because demand may change from time to time, the spreadsheet model should be constructed in such a way that all the data are entered directly into their own cells. The spreadsheet should represent the appropriate LP for any set of these data. Optimize the spreadsheet for the data presented.

NUMBER OF GROUP MEETINGS PER DAY	WAITER HOURS NEEDED
0	0
1	24
2	36
3	52
4	64
5	80

3-24. *Farm Management.* A firm operates four farms of comparable productivity. Each farm has a certain amount of usable acreage and a supply of labor hours to plant and tend the crops. The data for the upcoming season are shown in the following table.

FARM	USABLE ACREAGE	LABOR HOURS AVAILABLE PER MONTH
1	500	1700
2	900	3000
3	300	900
4	700	2200

The organization is considering three crops for planting. These crops differ in their expected profit per acre and in the amount of labor required, as shown in the following table. Also shown is the fact that each crop requires a different type of harvester, with a different cost. The total acreage that can be devoted to any particular crop is limited by the firm's decision as to how many hours of harvesting equipment to rent. The firm has made a fixed investment of $19,000 in a harvesting equipment cooperative. For this investment, it can use any of the three types of harvesters at the costs given below, up to the fixed \$19,000. A harvester typically works at a slower rate when it is first put into operation on a farm. Each season, as the crew once again becomes familiar with the machine and any small problems are worked out, the rate of production increases. This phenomenon is generally referred to as learning. In this case, the harvesting rate after t hours is given by the equation

$$\text{rate} = n\,(1 - e^{-\lambda t}) \text{ acres per hour where}$$

$$n = \text{long-run rate of harvesting, in acres per hour}$$

$$\lambda = \text{short-run adjustment factor}$$

The total acreage harvestable in a certain time period, say T hours, can then be found by integrating the rate with respect to time:

$$\text{total acreage harvestable in } T \text{ hours} = \int_0^T n(1 - e^{-\lambda t})\, dt$$

$$= n[T - (1/\lambda)(1 - e^{-\lambda T})].$$

The long-run rates and short-run adjustment factors for each type of equipment can be found in the table below. Management has decided to use 400, 315, and 335 harvesting machine hours for crops A, B, and C, respectively. In order to maintain a roughly uniform workload among the farms, management's policy is that the percentage of usable acreage planted must be the same at all farms. However, any combination of the crops may be grown at any of the farms as long as all constraints are satisfied (including the uniform-workload requirements). Management wishes to know how many acres of each crop should be planted at the respective farms in order to maximize expected profit.

CROP	MONTHLY LABOR HOURS REQUIRED PER ACRE	EXPECTED PROFIT PER ACRE (\$)	λ	n	HARV. MACHINE COST/HR (\$)
A	2	500	.02	2	15
B	4	200	.02	3	20
C	3	300	.03	1	20

(a) Create a spreadsheet model of this LP. The spreadsheet should be constructed in such a way that the rental hours for each of the harvesting machines are entered as parameters.

(b) Optimize this model.

(c) Suggest another choice of harvesting machine hours that the farm could select. Does your choice yield a higher profit? Can you find a choice that does?

3-25. *Producing Forestry and Earthmoving Equipment.* Suppose that forestry equipment produces a net revenue of \$802 per unit and requires 700 pounds of iron, 50 hours of labor, 30 hours of heat treatment, and 1 transmission per unit. Earthmoving equipment yields a net revenue of \$660 per unit and requires 4,200 pounds of iron, 110 hours of labor, 12 hours of heat treatment, and 1 transmission per unit. The company's capacity during this period is 680,000 pounds of iron, 21,000 hours of labor, and 6,000 hours of heat treatment. Transmissions are supplied by a wholly owned subsidiary that produces transmissions for the entire product line. The capacity for transmissions for forestry and earthmoving equipment is then determined by the number of production hours dedicated to their production at the subsidiary plant. Production of transmissions involves three phases: setup, start-up, and regular production. The duration and production rates for these phases are given in the following table.

PHASES	DURATION (HRS)	TRANSMISSION (UNITS/HR)
Setup	8	0
Start-up	120	.5
Regular Production	—	1

(a) For example, if 10 hours are available at the subsidiary, 8 of these are required for setup, during which there is no production, and 2 are in the start-up phase, during which 2(.5) = 1 transmission would be produced. If $H \geq 128$ hours are used, 120 of the hours will produce .5 transmission/hr, while $H - 128$ hours will produce one transmission/hr. Hence, the total transmissions produced would be $60 + H - 128 = H - 68$. Show the equations that determine the limit on transmissions capacity if T hours are available at the subsidiary for $T = 6$, $T = 108$, and $T = 308$.

(b) Evaluate the equations you created in (a). Your answers should be 0, 50, and 240.

(c) Define the decision variables and formulate this as a revenue-maximizing LP model. The spreadsheet should be constructed in such a way that the number of labor hours in the subsidiary plant can be entered as parameters, and the appropriate constraint will be created in the LP. HINT: In this problem, you can use nested IF()'s to determine which phase the scheduled hours will reach. Why can you use these IF()s within the LP?

(d) Find the optimal solution if 358 hours of production time are available at the subsidiary plant.

3-26. *Work Force and Production Planning.* Review the Simplified Oak Product model. Now assume that heavy and light seats are actually produced in two departments, A and B, respectively. The number of heavy seats produced per week in department A and the number of light seats produced per week in department B depend on the number of workers assigned to each department. Management decides that it is reasonable to approximate the seat production capacity in these departments with the functions shown below:

$$\text{Heavy Seat Capacity Dept. A} = 200(1 - e^{-.05(WA)})$$

$$\text{Light Seat Capacity Dept. B} = 222(1 - e^{-.06(WB)})$$

where WA and WB are the number of workers assigned to departments A and B respectively. In the original version of this problem, it was assumed that 24 workers were assigned to department A (i.e., $WA = 24$) and 13 were assigned to department B (i.e., $WB = 13$). Thus

$$\text{Heavy Seat Capacity Dept. A} = 200(1 - e^{-1.2}) = 139.8$$

$$\text{Light Seat Capacity Dept. B} = 222(1 - e^{-.78}) = 120.23$$

(The light seat production capacities were rounded to 140 and 120, respectively, for the Simplified Oak Product model.)

(a) Modify the SimpleOakProd.XLS worksheet so that number of workers in departments A and B can be entered directly as parameters and modify the heavy and light seat constraint right hand sides, as appropriate.

(b) Assume that 20 workers are assigned to department A and 6 workers are assigned to department B. Use Solver to find the optimal production policy when $WA = 20$ and $WB = 6$. Can Solver optimize this model as an LP? Why or why not?

(c) Assume $WA = 20$. Plot the optimal profit as a function of WB for WB ranging from 0 to 8 in intervals of 1. To do this, Solver will have to be run 9 times, and you must copy the optimal profit and WB value into a table of cells. After the 9 runs of data have been obtained, use the Chart Wizard to plot the data. What phenomenon does the graph of this optimal profit function illustrate? (Later in Chapter 4 we will see how to use SolverTable to automate calculations such as this.)

3-27. Slick Oil Company has three warehouses from which it can ship products to any of three retail outlets. The demand in cases for the product Gunkout is 100 at retail outlet 1, 250 at outlet 2, and 150 at outlet 3. The inventory in cases of Gunkout at warehouse 1 is 50, at warehouse 2 is 275, and at warehouse 3 is 175. The cost of transporting one case of Gunkout from each warehouse to each retail outlet is given in the table that follows. Formulate an LP to determine how many cases should be shipped from each warehouse to each retailer so the demand at each retailer is met at minimum cost.

	RETAILER		
WAREHOUSE	**1**	**2**	**3**
1	5	7	6
2	8	9	10
3	4	3	11

3-28. HiTech operates three Internet servers and each of them processes up to three types of Internet requests—Web page, Database Query, and eCommerce. Web page requests are the easiest request type to process. HiTech measures the capacity of its servers using the number of Web page requests it can process per day as the basis. The other request types are much more computer intensive and HiTech rates those types of requests as the number of Web page equivalent requests that must be sacrificed to process one request of another type. For example, Server 1 can process 230 thousand requests per day, if all of them are Web page requests, but for each eCommerce request it processes Server 1 must give up the equivalent processing of 2 Web page requests. So, if dedicated to eCommerce request processing, Server 1's capacity would be only 115 thousand requests per day. The table that follows summarizes processing capacities of the servers using Web page equivalent requests as the basis for overall capacity. (NA means a given server lacks the software to process a request of that type.)

NUMBER OF WEB EQUIVALENT REQUESTS TO PROCESS A REQUEST ON A GIVEN SERVER	SERVER 1	2	3
Web	1	1	1
Database	2.5	NA	4
eCommerce	2	5	NA
Server Capacity (thousands of Web equivalent request/day)	230	360	160

HiTech expects the maximum daily demand for requests to be given in the table that follows.

REQUEST TYPE	REQUEST DEMAND (THOUSANDS/DAY)
Web	310
Database	40
eCommerce	120

HiTech would like to process as many requests per day as possible. Develop an Excel LP model that allocates requests to servers to achieve this objective.

3-29. Candy's Fragrances makes three products at a factory located in Santa Maria, California. The factory produces the products using two shifts of laborers. The first shift has a labor cost of $15 per hour and is limited to 30,000 hours. The second shift has a shift premium of $2 per hour increasing labor cost to $17 per hour. The second shift labor hours are limited to 20,000. The three products that are manufactured by Candy's Fragrances are perfume, shampoo, and skin creme. There are three raw materials involved in the manufacture of each product. Candy pays $2 per pound of raw material A, $2.50 per pound of raw material B, and $2 per pound for raw material C. The material, labor, and demand requirements are given in the following table.

	PERFUME	SHAMPOO	SKIN CREME
Labor (hours/case)	1.5	2	2
Raw Material A (lbs./case)	5	7	4
Raw Material B (lbs./case)	2	2	5
Raw Material C (lbs./case)	3	5	3
Demand (cases)	10,000	7,000	15,000

Candy can also purchase the shampoo and skin creme from an overseas supplier. The delivered cost to import shampoo is $50 per case and skin creme will cost $60 per case. Formulate an Excel model to minimize cost to meet or exceed demand for Candy's products.

3-30. Bear Lake Electronics makes three types of DVD players for the consumer market, basic, deluxe, and laptop. Bear Lake is trying to optimize the product mix at their three factories. Assume that all the DVD players that are manufactured can be sold. The production capacities for assembly and fabrication at the three facilities are given in the following table.

FACILITY	ASSEMBLY (HOURS)	FABRICATION (HOURS)
1	20,000	100,000
2	30,000	100,000
3	10,000	70,000
Totals	60,000	270,000

The profit for a basic DVD player is $75, a deluxe model is $125, and a laptop DVD has a profit of $195. The hours required to assemble and fabricate each type of player are given in the following table.

PLAYER	ASSEMBLY (HOURS PER PLAYER)	FABRICATION (HOURS PER PLAYER)
Basic	3	8
Deluxe	4	11
Laptop	8	16

Create an Excel model and find the optimal product mix for Bear Lake.

3-31. Environmental Energy Associates (EEA) own and operate a small electric utility in southern California. The facility produces electricity by burning three fuels in a boiler, which in turn produces steam that powers a turbine generator. The boiler can burn manure, wood chips, and natural gas. Mark Vaughn, the plant manager, wants to minimize fuel cost while producing at least 7,200 megawatt-hours next month. Manure is available from local ranchers and feedlots who pay EEA $50 per ton to dispose of the manure. Wood chips are purchased from a local sawmill for $25 per ton. Natural gas is supplied through a pipeline for $120 per MMscf (million standard cubic feet). The following table gives the energy, availability, and cost to EEA for each type of fuel.

FUEL	ENERGY	AVAILABILITY	COST
Manure	10 megawatts hrs/ton	100 tons	$(50.00) per ton*
Wood Chips	7 megawatts hrs/ton	200 tons	$ 25.00 per ton
Natural Gas	40 megawatts hrs/MMscf	Unlimited	$120.00 per MMscf

* Note: Cost is negative because EEA is paid to dispose of this fuel.

Develop an Excel model to answer this question. How much fuel of each type should Mark Vaughn obtain for electrical generation next month?

Case Study Ebel Mining (A) Revisited

Revisit the Ebel Mining (A) Case at the end of Chapter 2. Reformulate that spreadsheet model as an LP and optimize it with Solver to answer its question 1.

Case Study Red Brand Canners[1]

Here is a simple but interesting case that captures several points that are important in real-world model formulation. In any real situation it is important for the manager to distinguish between those facts and data that are relevant and those that are not. Distinguishing the two may be especially difficult because on occasion confused or incorrect concepts will be strongly held by members of the management team. This case is designed to reproduce such a situation. The present task will simply involve model formulation. You will deal with this case again, however, in Chapter 4, where you will be asked to produce analyses, critiques, and interpretations.

On Monday, September 13, 1996, Mitchell Gordon, vice president of operations, asked the controller, the sales manager, and the production manager to meet with him to discuss the amount of tomato products to pack that season. The tomato crop, which had been purchased at planting, was beginning to arrive at the cannery, and packing operations would have to be started by the following Monday. Red Brand Canners was a medium-sized company that canned and distributed a variety of fruit and vegetable products under private brands in the western states.

[1] © 1996 by the Board of Trustees of the Leland Stanford Junior University. All rights reserved. Written by Professor Robert Wilson.

William Cooper, the Controller, and Charles Myers, the Sales Manager, were the first to arrive in Mr. Gordon's office. Dan Tucker, the Production Manager, came in a few minutes later and said that he had picked up Produce Inspection's latest estimate of the quality of the incoming tomatoes. According to their report, about 20% of the crop was grade "A" quality and the remaining portion of the 3,000,000-pound crop was grade "B."

Gordon asked Myers about the demand for tomato products for the coming year. Myers replied that for all practical purposes they could sell all the whole canned tomatoes they could produce. The expected demand for tomato juice and tomato paste, on the other hand, was limited. The sales manager then passed around the latest demand forecast, which is shown in Exhibit 1. He reminded the group that the selling prices had been set in light of the long-term marketing strategy of the company, and potential sales had been forecast at those prices.

Bill Cooper, after looking at Myers's estimates of demand, said that it looked like the company "should do quite well (on the tomato crop) this year." With the new accounting system that had been set up, he had been able to compute the contribution for each product, and according to this analysis the incremental profit on the whole tomatoes was greater than for any other tomato product. In May, after Red Brand had

EXHIBIT 1 Demand Forecasts

PRODUCT	SELLING PRICE PER CASE	DEMAND FORECAST (CASES)
24-2½ whole tomatoes	$12.00	800,000
24-2½ choice peach halves	$16.20	10,000
24-2½ peach nectar	$13.80	5,000
24-2½ tomato juice	$13.50	50,000
24-2½ cooking apples	$14.70	15,000
24-2½ tomato paste	$11.40	80,000

signed contracts agreeing to purchase the grower's production at an average delivered price of 18 cents per pound, Cooper had computed the tomato products' contributions (see Exhibit 2).

Dan Tucker brought to Cooper's attention that, although there was ample production capacity, it was impossible to produce all whole tomatoes, because too small a portion of the tomato crop was "A" quality. Red Brand used a numerical scale to record the quality of both raw produce and prepared products. This scale ran from zero to ten, the higher number representing better quality. Rating tomatoes according to this scale, "A" tomatoes averaged nine points per pound and "B" tomatoes averaged five points per pound. Tucker noted that the minimum average input quality for canned whole tomatoes was eight points per pound, and for juice it was six. Paste could be made entirely from "B" grade tomatoes. This meant that whole tomato production was limited to 800,000 pounds.

Gordon stated that this was not a real limitation. He had recently been solicited to purchase any amount up to 80,000 pounds of grade "A" tomatoes at 25½ cents per pound and at that time had turned down the offer. He felt, however, that the tomatoes were still available.

Myers, who had been doing some calculations, said that although he agreed that the company "should do quite well this year," it would not be by canning whole tomatoes. It seemed to him that the tomato cost should be allocated on the basis of quality and quantity rather than by quantity only, as Cooper had done. Therefore, he had recomputed the marginal profit on this basis (see Exhibit 3), and from his results, Red Brand should use 2,000,000 pounds of the "B" tomatoes for paste, and the remaining 400,000 pounds of "B" tomatoes and all the "A" tomatoes for juice. If the demand expectations were realized, a contribution of $144,000 would be made on this year's tomato crop.

EXHIBIT 2 Product Item Profitability

PRODUCT	24-2½ WHOLE TOMATOES	24-2½ CHOICE PEACH HALVES	24-2½ PEACH NECTAR	24-2½ TOMATO JUICE	24-2½ COOKING APPLES	24-2½ TOMATO PASTE
Selling Price	$12.00	$16.20	$13.80	$13.50	$14.70	$11.40
Variable Costs:						
Direct Labor	3.54	4.20	3.81	3.96	2.10	1.62
Variable OHD	.72	.96	.69	1.08	.66	.78
Variable Selling	1.20	.90	1.20	2.55	.84	1.14
Packaging Mat'l.	2.10	1.68	1.80	1.95	2.10	2.31
Fruit[1]	3.24	5.40	5.10	3.60	2.70	4.50
Total Variance Costs	10.80	13.14	12.60	13.14	8.40	10.35
Contribution	1.20	3.06	1.20	.36	6.30	1.05
Less Allocated OHD	.84	2.10	1.56	.63	2.25	.69
Net Profit	.36	.96	(.36)	(.27)	4.05	.36

[1] Product usage is as given below.

PRODUCT	POUNDS PER CASE
Whole Tomatoes	18
Peach Halves	18
Peach Nectar	17
Tomato Juice	20
Cooking Apples	27
Tomato Paste	25

EXHIBIT 3 Marginal Analysis of Tomato Products

Z = Cost per pound of A tomatoes in cents
Y = Cost per pound of B tomatoes in cents
(1) (600,000 lbs. × Z) + (2,400,000 lbs. × Y)
= (3,000,000 lbs. × 18¢)
(2) $Z/9 = Y/5$
Z = 27.96 cents per pound
Y = 15.54 cents per pound

PRODUCT	CANNED WHOLE TOMATOES	TOMATO JUICE	TOMATO PASTE
Selling Price	$12.00	$13.50	$11.40
Variable Cost (Excl. Tomato Costs)	$7.56	$9.54	$5.85
	$4.44	$3.96	$5.55
Tomato Cost	$4.47	$3.72	$3.90
Marginal Profit	($.03)	$0.24	$1.65

Questions

1. Why does Tucker state that the whole tomato production is limited to 800,000 pounds (i.e., where does the number 800,000 come from)?
2. What is wrong with Cooper's suggestion to use the entire crop for whole tomatoes?
3. How does Myers compute his tomato costs in Exhibit 3? How does he reach his conclusion that the company should use 2,000,000 pounds of "B" tomatoes for paste, the remaining 400,000 pounds of "B" tomatoes, and all of the "A" in juice? What is wrong with Myers's reasoning?
4. Without including the possibility of the additional purchases suggested by Gordon, formulate as an LP the problem of determining the optimal canning policy for this season's crop. Define your decision variables in terms of pounds of tomatoes. Express the objective function coefficients in cents per pound.
5. How should your model be modified to include the possibility of the additional purchases suggested by Gordon?

Alternate Questions for Red Brand Canners

Suppose Produce Inspection could use three grades to estimate the quality of the tomato crop.

"A" tomatoes average nine points per pound, "B" tomatoes average six points per pound, and "C" tomatoes average three points per pound. Using this system their report would indicate that 600,000 pounds are grade "A" quality, 1,600,000 pounds are grade "B," and the remaining 800,000 pounds are grade "C." Paste has no minimum average quality requirement.

6. What is the maximum production in pounds of canned whole tomatoes? Can Cooper's suggestion be implemented?

Myers extends his analysis to three grades in Exhibit 4. On the basis of Exhibit 4, Myers recommends using all grade "C" tomatoes and 1,200,000 pounds of grade "B" tomatoes for paste, and all grade "A" tomatoes and all remaining grade "B" tomatoes for juice.

7. How does Myers compute his tomato costs in Exhibit 4? How does he reach his conclusion to use 800,000 pounds of grade "C" and 1,200,000 pounds of grade "B" for paste, and the rest of the tomatoes for juice? What is wrong with Myers's reasoning?
8. Without including the possibility of the additional purchases suggested by Gordon, formulate as an LP the problem of determining the optimal canning policy for this season's crop. Define your decision variables in terms of pounds of tomatoes. Express the objective function in cents.
9. How should your model be modified to include the possibility of the additional purchases suggested by Gordon?

EXHIBIT 4 Myers's Marginal Analysis of Tomato Products

Z = Cost per pound of A tomatoes in cents
Y = Cost per pound of B tomatoes in cents
X = Cost per pound of C tomatoes in cents
(1) (800,000 lbs. × Z) + (1,600,000 lbs. × Y)
+ (800,000 lbs. × X) = (3,000,000 lbs. × 18¢)
(2) $Z/9 = Y/6$
(3) $Y/6 = X/3$
Z = 27.93 cents per pound
Y = 18.61 cents per pound
X = 9.30 cents per pound

PRODUCT	CANNED WHOLE TOMATOES	TOMATO JUICE	TOMATO PASTE
Selling Price	$12.00	$13.50	$11.40
Variable Cost (Excl. Tomato Costs)	$7.56	$9.54	$5.85
	$4.44	$3.96	$5.55
Tomato Cost	$4.47	$3.72	$2.33
Marginal Profit	($.03)	$0.24	$3.22

Case Study | Foreign Exchange at HiTech

HiTech, Inc., has manufacturing and sales operations in five major trading countries: United States, United Kingdom, France, Germany, and Japan. Due to the different cash needs in the various countries at various times, it is often necessary to move available funds from one country and denomination to another. In general, there will be numerous ways to rearrange funds to satisfy cash requirements out of availabilities. On this particular morning the divisions in France and Japan are short of cash. Specifically, the requirements are, respectively, 7 million francs and 1040 million yen. The divisions in the United States, Britain, and Germany are long on cash. They have surpluses of 2 million dollars, 5 million pounds, and 3 million marks. Since there are many possible ways of redistributing the cash to satisfy the shortages out of the surpluses, the issue to be addressed is how one compares the possible conversion strategies. Because of high short-term U.S. interest rates, the firm has decided to evaluate its final cash position by this measure: the equivalent total dollar value of its final cash holdings.

On this morning, as usual, at 7:00 A.M. Jack Walker, the corporate treasurer, and Ezra Brooks, VP for overseas operations, meet at corporate headquarters to determine what funds, if any, should be moved. Refer to Exhibits 1 and 2 as you go through the dialog. The conversation proceeds as follows:

EZRA: Good morning, Jack. I have something to show you. I've asked Fred to set this exchange model up on a spreadsheet. I think it will make our lives considerably easier.

JACK: I like the idea, but you'll have to explain the model to me.

EZRA: Sure, Jack. It contains all the usual information, but let's go through it step by step. The figures in the rectangle defined by C3 through G7 are the exchange rates. If we let a_{ij} be the rate in row *i* and column *j*, then one unit of currency *i* will exchange for a_{ij} units of currency *j*. In fact, these data reflect the bid-ask prices. For example, if we sell one British pound we get \$1.665. That is, 1.665 is the bid price, in dollars, for a pound. On the other hand, if we sell one dollar we will receive 0.591 pounds. This means we can buy a pound for 1/0.591 = \$1.692 (the asking price, in dollars, for a pound is 1.692). Hence the bid-ask spread is 1.665, 1.692. You can see that if we start with \$1 and buy as many pounds as possible and then use those pounds to buy dollars we end up with 0.591 × 1.665 = \$0.9810 dollars—we lose money.

JACK: That's the transaction cost. So obviously we want to minimize these transaction costs by not moving more money around than we have to. But where does this model say something about our cash needs today?

EZRA: Our current cash holdings are shown in column C rows 17 to 21. All figures are in millions; we have 2 million dollars, 5 million pounds, and 3 million marks. Our requirements appear in column G in the same rows. You can see that we need 7 million French francs and 1040 million yen. As you know, our policy is to satisfy requirements in such a way that the dollar value of final holdings is maximized.

EXHIBIT 1

Spreadsheet Model for Currency Trading

	A	B	C	D	E	F	G	H	I
1		Currency Trading Model							
2			Dollar	Pound	FFranc	DMark	Yen	Avg. Dollar Value	
3		Dollar	1	0.591	5.385	1.594	116.3	1.0000	
4		Pound	1.665	1	9.12	2.607	193.1	1.6785	
5		FFranc	0.1823	0.1095	1	0.2965	21.11	0.1840	
6		DMark	0.6149	0.3694	3.351	1	72.14	0.6211	
7		Yen	0.00847	0.005093	0.0465	0.01379	1	0.0085	
8									
9		Sell \ Buy	Dollar	Pound	FFranc	DMark	Yen	Total Sold	
10		Dollar	0	0	1.3	0	9	10	
11		Pound	4.3	0	0	0	0	4	
12		FFranc	0	0	0	0	0	0	
13		DMark	2	0	0	0	0	2.000	
14		Yen	0	0	0	0	0	0	
15	Total Purchased		8.389	0	7.0	0	1047		
16			Initial Holding (millions)	Amount Purchased (millions)	Amount Sold (millions)	Final Holding (millions)	Cash Required (millions)	Excess Held (Slack)	$ Value of Final Holding
17		Dollar	2	8.389	10.3	0	>=0	0.089	$ 0
18		Pound	5	-	4.3	0.700	>=0	0.700	$ 1.175
19		FFranc	0	7.001	-	7.001	>=7	0.000	$ 1.288
20		DMark	3	-	2	1	>=0	1.000	$ 1
21		Yen	0	1,047	-	1,047	>=1040	6.700	$ 8.933
22								Total	$ 12.106

EXHIBIT 2

Spreadsheet Formulas for Currency Trading Model

	A	B	C	D	E	F	G	H	I
1		Currenc							
2			Dollar	Pound	FFranc	DMark	Yen	Avg. Dollar Val	
3		Dollar	1	0.591	5.385	1.594	116.3	=(C3+1/C3)/2	
4		Pound	1.665	1	8.933	2.507	193.1	=(C4+1/D3)/2	
5		FFranc	0.1823	0.1095	1	0.2965	21.11	=(C5+1/E3)/2	
6		DMark	0.6149	0.3694	3.351	1	72.14	=(C6+1/F3)/2	
7		Yen	0.00847	0.005093	0.0465	0.01379	1	=(C7+1/G3)/2	
8									
9		Sell \ Bu	Dollar	Pound	FFranc	DMark	Yen	Total Sold	
10		Dollar	0	0	1.3	0	9	=SUM(C10:G10)	
11		Pound	4.3	0	0	0	0		
12		FFranc	0	0	0	0	0	Copy	
13		DMark	2	0	0	0	0		
14		Yen	0	0	0	0	0		
15		Total P	=SUMPRODUCT(C3:C7,C10:C14)	Copy					
16			Initial Holding (millions)	Amount Pu	Amount	Final Holding	Cash F	Excess Held ($	$ Value of Fin
17		Dollar	2	=C15	=H10	=C17-E17+D17	0	=F17-G17	=H3*F17
18		Pound	5	=D15			0		
19		FFranc	0	=E15	Copy		8	Copy	
20		DMark	3	=F15			0		
21		Yen	0	=G15			1280		
22								Total	=SUM(I17:I21)

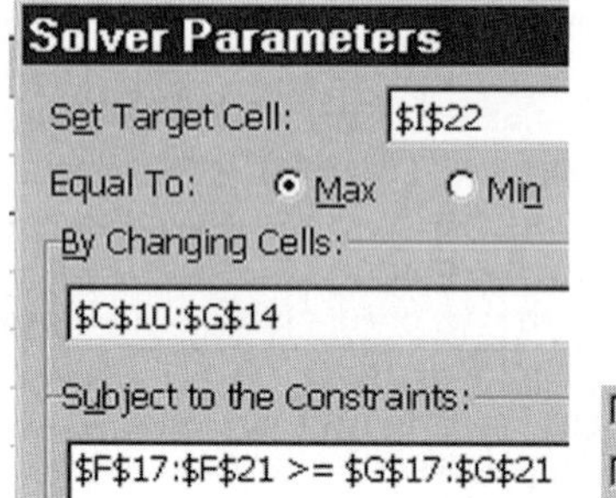

JACK: Great! So let's figure out what to do.

EZRA: That's the good part. We simply put our decisions in the appropriate cells in the currency transactions section labeled "Sell/Buy." I've already entered what I think would be our typical decisions in this set of circumstances. Cells C10 through C14 show that I've sold 2 million marks and 4.3 million pounds in return for 8.389 million dollars. I've then taken 1.3 million of those dollars and purchased 7 million francs, and with the remaining 9 million dollars I bought 1047 million yen. All of these numbers appear in cells C11, C13, C10, and G10 of the currency transactions section. For example, you see in C10 that we used 1.3 million dollars to buy francs, and C17 shows that this purchase yielded 7 million francs. You can see by comparing C17 through C21 with M17 through M21 that we have satisfied our goals. Indeed, H17 through H21 show how much additional cash we have in each denomination. As you can see, the policy I've entered gives final holdings worth 12.106 million dollars.

JACK: I see that we've met our cash requirements, but you know how I am, Ez. I'd feel that I understood better if I could see all of the formulas used to do the calculations.

EZRA: That's easy. I'll simply print out the spreadsheet formulas and you can look through it at your leisure!

JACK: (*Some time later that morning*): (All of this seems clear, Ez, but why did we follow such a complicated strategy?

EZRA: As you know, we have always run our exchange operation through Country Bank in New York, and this is their recommended strategy.

JACK: I guess that seeing the problem in the spreadsheet model makes it easier to think about the trading strategy. I sure would like to know if this really is a good approach.

EZRA: I worried about that for a while, too, but the foreign exchange market is very efficient for these major currencies, so it probably doesn't make much difference what strategy we follow.

JACK: I can't say that banal invocations of efficiency make me any more confident. As you know, I've made millions exploiting market inefficiencies. Anyway, I don't have more time this morning to look for a better approach. Let's go with what we have.

As you are already aware, the foreign exchange model presented in Exhibits 1 and 2 is a linear programming model, and the optimal solution can be easily found with Solver. The spreadsheet for the optimal solution is shown in Exhibit 3.

EXHIBIT 3

Optimized Spreadsheet for Currency Trading

	A	B	C	D	E	F	G	H	I
1		Currency Trading Model							
2			Dollar	Pound	FFranc	DMark	Yen	Avg. Dollar Value	
3		Dollar	1	0.591	5.385	1.594	116.3	1.0000	
4		Pound	1.665	1	9.12	2.607	193.1	1.6785	
5		FFranc	0.1823	0.1095	1	0.2965	21.11	0.1840	
6		DMark	0.6149	0.3694	3.351	1	72.14	0.6211	
7		Yen	0.00847	0.005093	0.0465	0.01379	1	0.0085	
8									
9		Sell \ Buy	Dollar	Pound	FFranc	DMark	Yen	Total Sold	
10		Dollar	0	0	0	0	2.000	2	
11		Pound	0	0	5.000	0	0	5	
12		FFranc	0	0	0	38.600	0	38.600	
13		DMark	0	0	0	0	11.192	11.192	
14		Yen	0	0	0	0	0	0	
15	Total Purchased		0	0	45.60	11.445	1040		
16			Initial Holding (millions)	Amount Purchased (millions)	Amount Sold (millions)	Final Holding (millions)	Cash Required (millions)	Excess Held (Slack)	$ Value of Final Holding
17		Dollar	2	-	2.0	0.0	>=0	0.000	$ 0
18		Pound	5	-	5.0	0.0	>=0	0.000	$ -
19		FFranc	0	45.600	38.600	7.0	>=7	0.000	$ 1.288
20		DMark	3	11.445	11	3.253	>=0	3.253	$ 2
21		Yen	0	1,040	-	1040	>=1040	0.000	$ 8.876
22								Total	$ 12.184

The optimal dollar value of the final cash positions is 12.184 million, as compared with the 12.106 million that was obtained with Ezra's solution. We note that in some sense Ezra is right. The difference is about .6%: (12.184 – 12.106)/12.184 = .0064. On the other hand, when large sums are being transferred, even a small percentage can be a lot of money. In this example, the difference is $78,000, a handsome quantity that can be captured with almost no effort.

Questions

1. Write out the LP model for the foreign exchange problem. In your model use the following notation for the data given in the problem description:

   a_{ij} = exchange rate from currency i into currency j (i.e., 1 unit of currency i will exchange for a_{ij} units of currency j)

   $C_i = \frac{1}{2}(a_{ij} + 1/a_{ji})$ = "average dollar value" of currency i

   b_i = initial holding in currency i

   L_i = minimum amount of currency i required as final holding

   Denote the decision variables, as follows:

   X_{ij} = amount of currency i changed into currency $j, j \neq i$

   Y_i = final holding in currency i

2. In the dialog, Jack says, "We want to minimize these transaction costs by not moving more money around than we have to." Suppose we define OV_1 = maximum "average dollar value" that can be generated from initial holdings

Note that finding the value of OV_1 requires more than simply evaluating each initial position in terms of average dollar value. For example, converting 1 pound to average dollar value gives $1.665; converting 1 pound to 9.12 francs to average dollar value gives (9.12)(.1840) = $1.67808. Thus, it is preferable to convert initial holdings of pounds into francs rather than to leave the pound position intact. In fact, in order to find OV_1 one must solve a linear program. The solution is shown in Exhibit 4, which was created by setting the final cash requirement to zero and then optimizing the value of final holdings. We see that OV_1 = 12.261. Now let OV_2 = maximum "average dollar value" of final holdings subject to the cash requirements constraints. That is, OV_2 is the optimized objective value shown in Exhibit 3 (OV_2 = 12.184).

In a case like this, a more highly constrained LP cannot have a better OV than a less highly constrained LP, so it must always be true that $OV_2 \leq OV_1$. Let us define, for the problem,

$$\text{Transactions Costs} = OV_1 - OV_2$$

Using this definition, is the statement by Jack correct? That is, does the optimized solution in Exhibit 3 minimize transaction costs?

3. Recall the spreadsheet presented in Exhibit 1. Use this spreadsheet to answer the following questions:
   - **(a)** Suppose that the exchange rates for two currencies (say the franc and the mark) are such that if we start with 1 franc and execute the trade 1 franc → marks → francs we end up with more than 1 franc. What would the optimal value of the objective function be under these circumstances? What economic term is used to describe this condition?
   - **(b)** Comment on the following statement: If HiTech has no specific cash requirements, the optimal solution would be to stand pat (i.e., in order to maximize "average dollar value" of final holdings, one should do no trading).

EXHIBIT 4

Optimized Model with Final Cash Requirements Equal Zero

	A	B	C	D	E	F	G	H	I
1		Currency Trading Model							
2			Dollar	Pound	FFranc	DMark	Yen	Avg. Dollar Value	
3		Dollar	1	0.591	5.385	1.594	116.3	1.0000	
4		Pound	1.665	1	9.12	2.607	193.1	1.6785	
5		FFranc	0.1823	0.1095	1	0.2965	21.11	0.1840	
6		DMark	0.6149	0.3694	3.351	1	72.14	0.6211	
7		Yen	0.00847	0.005093	0.0465	0.01379	1	0.0085	
8									
9		Sell \ Buy	Dollar	Pound	FFranc	DMark	Yen	Total Sold	
10		Dollar	0	0	0	0	0.000	0	
11		Pound	0	0	5.000	0	0	5	
12		FFranc	0	0	0	45.600	0	45.600	
13		DMark	0	0	0	0	0.000	0.000	
14		Yen	0	0	0	0	0	0	
15	Total Purchased		0	0	45.60	13.520	0		
16			Initial Holding (millions)	Amount Purchased (millions)	Amount Sold (millions)	Final Holding (millions)	Cash Required (millions)	Excess Held (Slack)	$ Value of Final Holding
17		Dollar	2	-	0.0	2.0	>=0	2.000	$ 2
18		Pound	5	-	5.0	0.0	>=0	0.000	$ -
19		FFranc	0	45.600	45.600	0.0	>=0	0.000	$ 0.000
20		DMark	3	13.520	-	16.520	>=0	16.520	$ 10
21		Yen	0	0	-	0	>=0	0.000	$ 0.000
22								Total	$ 12.261

(c) Comment on the following statement: Because the foreign exchange market is efficient, we have seen that the best solution isn't much better (in percentage terms) than Ezra's solution. It is also true, for the same reason, that the worst solution isn't much worse (again in percentage terms) than Ezra's. HINT: Find the solution that minimizes "average dollar value" of final holdings.

(d) Comment on the following statement: Consider a general currency trading model like the HiTech one. Such a model might include hundreds of currencies. However, those currencies for which HiTech has no initial holding or no required cash position can be dropped from the formulation without affecting the optimal value of the objective function.

References

J. Abara, "Applying Integer Linear Programming to the Fleet Assignment Problem," *Interfaces* 19, no. 4 (1989): 20–28.

Radhka Subramanian, Richard Scheff, John Quillinan, Steve Wiper, and Roy Marsten, "Coldstart: Fleet Assignment at Delta Air Lines," *Interfaces* 24, no. 1 (1994): 104–120.

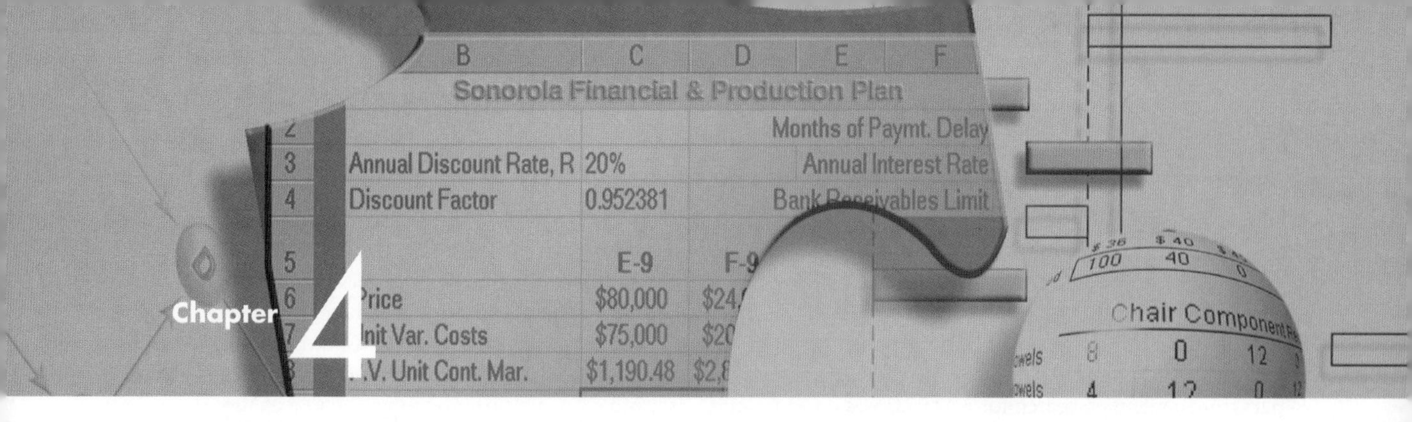

LINEAR OPTIMIZATION: SENSITIVITY ANALYSIS

CHAPTER OUTLINE

APPLICATION CAPSULE More Bang for the Buck: LP Helps the USAM Stock Its Arsenal

The United States Air Force has a distinguished record of winning important battles. Americans recall with pride the success of our pilots in the skies over Germany during World War II, and more recently in the Persian Gulf. This success results in part from a relentless search for new tactics and technology. Thus it is no surprise that in recent years the Air Force has turned to a modern approach—using LP—in the evaluation and procurement of weapon systems and in the annual battle of the budget.

Each year the Air Force must present a weapons development plan to Congress. To prepare this plan, it is necessary to decide (1) what new projects to start, (2) what current projects to continue, and (3) what projects to discontinue. The final recommendation is highly dependent on the level of funding available.

A key consideration is the effectiveness of each weapon system and its possible contribution, in a mix of weapons, to achieving a desired increase in target value destroyed. Effectiveness estimates must be made for a great many combinations of aircraft, munitions, and targets (tanks, command and communication facilities, bridges, and the like). These factors interact in complex ways. Different munitions require aircraft to fly at different altitudes for different durations, and their vulnerability to enemy antiaircraft fire will vary accordingly. Even a small change in the rate at which aircraft are lost can have a major effect on the cost-effectiveness of a system, to say nothing of the loss of human life.

The Air Force must also assess annually the consequences of a possible increase or decrease in the budget—that is, how sensitive a given proposal might be to a change in the level of funding. Budget changes can affect the mix of weapon systems purchased as well as the number of any particular weapon acquired. The number of items purchased, in turn, can drastically affect the purchase price per unit.

For analyses of this kind, the Air Force has developed a linear program that can evaluate trade-offs among both aircraft types and munitions. It can not only specify the optimal mix of weapons needed to destroy a particular target set, but also display graphically such relationships as

- The ratio of funds expended on aircraft versus munitions
- Target value destroyed as a function of expenditure on individual weapons, or on a mixture of weapons
- Target value destroyed versus expenditure as a function of conflict duration

This information is plotted out in the form of two-dimensional graphs, with axes properly scaled, so that managers and analysts can study possible trade-offs and perform "What-if" analyses. (See Might.)

4.1 INTRODUCTION

An important, even daily, challenge faced by managers in the real world is making good use of spreadsheet analysis. The Oak Products LP model was optimized by Solver at the end of Chapter 3. You may well feel that you now have a good spreadsheet solution to Oak Products production planning situation and thus are free to turn attention to other matters. In most cases this simply is not true. Often the solution to a model is only a starting point to the analysis of the situation. Remember that the model is an abstraction of the real-world situation. If you were Tom Burr, the responsible manager at Oak Products, you would need to ask numerous additional questions of Jim White's model before you would be confident enough about the Solver results to implement the decisions recommended by the model. For example, there may be rather significant considerations that because of their complexity have not been built into the model. To the extent that a model is a simplification of reality there will always be factors that are left out. These factors may, for example, be of a political or ethical nature. There may, as another example, be inexactitudes and uncertainty in some of the data that were used as parameters in the model. Such considerations are usually difficult to quantify but must be addressed. Thus, having optimized the model, you must now turn to address how well the optimal solution "fits in" with other considerations, which may not have been included. In real-world situations this is the norm rather than the exception. The motto is: "Do the best with what you have."

Recall from a similar discussion in Chapters 1 and 2 that sensitivity analysis—calculating the effect a (small) change of an exogenous variable has upon another variable—provides important additional insights that guide real-world decision making in light of these other considerations. In the case of optimization models, sensitivity analysis refers to the process of analyzing such changes in a model after the optimal solution has been found. In this chapter we look in detail at how, in practice, you can use the wealth of sensitivity information provided by Solver analysis of an LP model to do the best with what you have.

Two-dimensional geometry contained in graphs will be used as a picture to illustrate many of the important elements of LP models, how they are optimized with Solver, and from this how to interpret LP sensitivity analysis. Although two-dimensional geometry is a very special case, it is easy to work with, and many general concepts can be communicated with simple graphical pictures. In particular, two-dimensional geometry provides a simple way to solve an LP model having only two decision variables. Although most real-world models have more than two decision variables, and hence such a graphical solution method will not be practical, it nevertheless provides a good intuitive basis for much that follows. In other words, the purpose of this chapter is to introduce graphical insights into the general LP model as a vehicle to understand the rich variety of modeling insights LP sensitivity analysis provides you. In the process we will introduce two useful tools, the Solver Sensitivity Report and SolverTable, for doing sensitivity analysis on LP models. This will provide a good foundation for your interpretation of LP model results in a variety of real-world applications. Finally, in Section 4.12 we give a cautionary tale on some of the pitfalls of sensitivity analysis.

4.2 THE GRAPHICAL SOLUTION METHOD APPLIED TO OAK PRODUCTS

The **graphical solution method** provides an easy way of solving LP models with two decision variables. Since the simplified Oak Products model from Chapter 3 has only two decision variables, C and M, we can employ that model to illustrate the graphical approach. Recall the simplified Oak Products LP model:

C = number of Captain chairs to be produced and sold, and

M = number of Mate chairs to be produced and sold.

$$\text{Maximize } 56C + 40M \quad \text{(objective function)} \tag{4.1}$$

subject to

$$8C + 4M \le 1280 \quad \text{(long dowels restriction)} \tag{4.2}$$

$$4C + 12M \le 1600 \quad \text{(short dowels restriction)} \tag{4.3}$$

$$C + M \ge 100 \quad \text{(minimum production)} \tag{4.4}$$

$$4C + 4M \le 760 \quad \text{(legs restriction)} \tag{4.5}$$

$$C \le 140 \quad \text{(heavy seats restriction)} \tag{4.6}$$

$$M \le 120 \quad \text{(light seats restriction)} \tag{4.7}$$

$$C \le 0 \quad \text{and} \quad M \le 0 \quad \text{(nonnegativity conditions)} \tag{4.8}$$

The labels (4.1) through (4.8) are used in the following discussion to distinguish the objective function and the constraints. We will use the Stanford Graphic LP Optimizer, GLP.exe, available on the book's CD-ROM to graph and analyze the LP model. GLP is a stand-alone Windows program;[1] it does not require Excel. Graphical LP optimization is best understood by following along the steps below by running GLP on your PC.

PLOTTING THE OAK PRODUCTS LP MODEL

Figure 4.1 shows the top part of GLP's window; the bottom part contains a graphing pane. In GLP's dialog fields you may type labels for the X and Y axes, up to six constraints (nonnegativity constraints are always assumed by GLP thus limiting its plots to the **nonnegative**

[1] GLP works best if your display is set to a resolution of 800 by 600 (Super VGA) or higher. Being a Windows program, GLP does not run on Macintosh. Macintosh users may execute GLP by means of a Windows emulator package, such as Virtual PC by Connectix.

FIGURE 4.1

GLP's Window

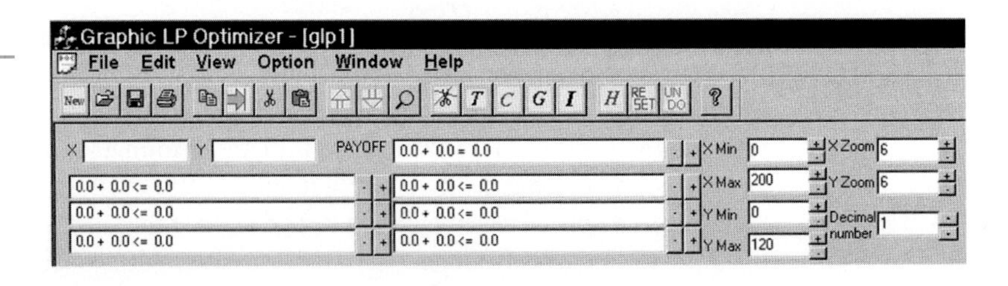

quadrant), and the objective function (PAYOFF). As you type the constraints or the objective function GLP will graph them for you in its graphing pane.

Obtaining a graphical portrayal of the constraint set is the first step in the LP graphical solution procedure. Figure 4.2 portrays the Long Dowels constraint **contour**, in which M has been assigned arbitrarily to the vertical axis. The gray area represents the set of all nonnegative points that satisfy the Long Dowels constraint given by (4.2). If you click-drag the constraint line, the feasible region gets bigger and smaller, but the slope of the constraint does not change, only its right-hand side (RHS) value, the available inventory of long dowels. This is because the constraint's slope is fixed by the ratio of the two coefficients in (4.2). You can see this by solving (4.2) for M, the variable on the vertical axis:

TIP: *As you drag the constraint line GLP continuously recomputes the constraint's RHS value for you. Also, you may move the equation label next to the constraint line by click-dragging it.*

$$2C + 4M = 1280 \qquad \text{or} \qquad 4M = 1280 - 2C \qquad \text{or } M = 320 - .5C.$$

Thus, the slope for this constraint is fixed at –.5 and changing the 1280 inventory availability of long dowels affects only the constraint's intercept on the Y axis.

Next, you can type the rest of the constraints given by (4.3) to (4.7) and GLP will plot them for you, but to save typing open the SimpleOakProd.glp file from the book's CD-ROM, which portrays the entire simplified Oak Products LP model from Chapter 3, as

FIGURE 4.2

The Long Dowels Constraint in Simplified Oak Products LP

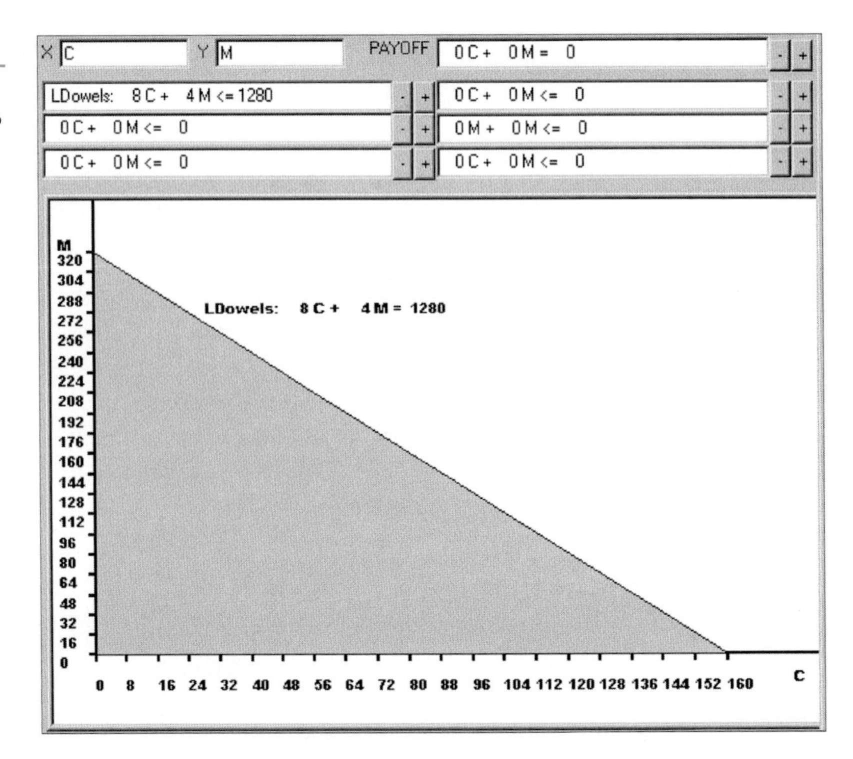

FIGURE 4.3

Simplified Oak Products LP Model

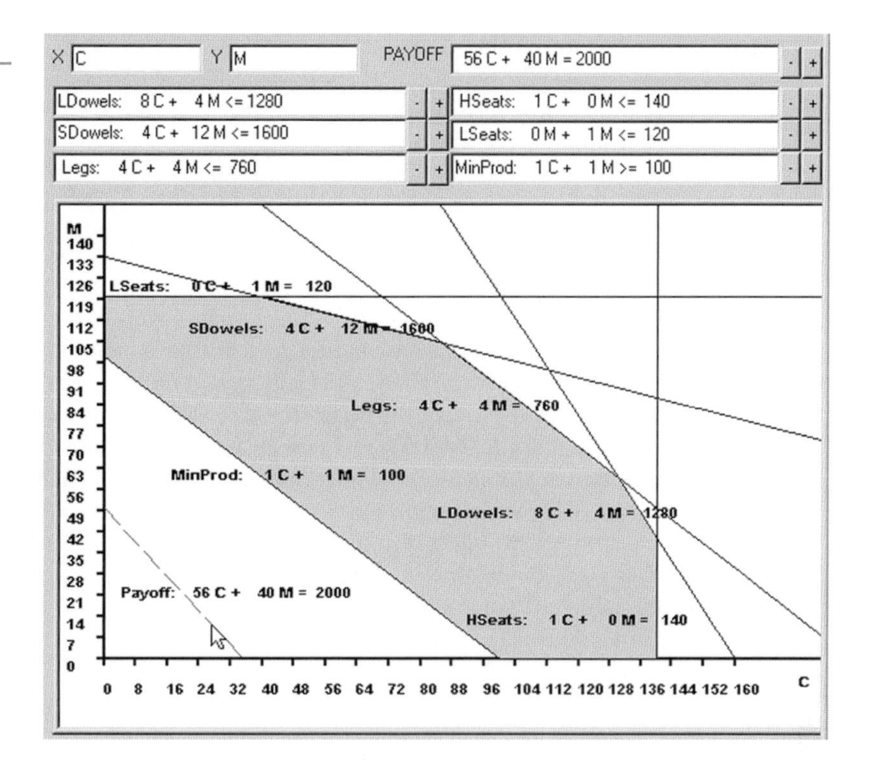

shown in Figure 4.3. The gray area gives the **constraint set** or **feasible region**, that is, the set of all possible combinations of production decisions, C and M, that simultaneously satisfy all the constraints.

The set of all values of the decision variables that satisfies all the constraints simultaneously is called the constraint set, or the feasible region.

As before, you may experiment by click-dragging any constraint line to see how changes in that constraint's RHS affect the feasible region. By visually comparing Figure 4.2 with Figure 4.3 the following general optimization principles should be obvious.

Adding additional constraints can never enlarge the feasible region, but leaves the feasible region either unchanged or smaller.

Deleting constraints leaves the feasible region either unchanged or larger.

Now we want to use the graphical portrayal to find the *optimal* solution to the simplified Oak Products model. Since the Oak Products LP is a profit-maximization model, we must find a feasible production alternative that gives the highest possible value to the objective function given by (4.1).

In keeping with our definition of feasible region, any production plan—any pair of values for C and M—that satisfies all the constraints is known as a **feasible solution** or *feasible decision.* These feasible decisions are the allowable production alternatives according to our model. Note that it is *incorrect* to speak of a feasible value of C separately, or a feasible value of M separately. Think carefully about this statement, for it is important to understand that the term "feasible," in this two-dimensional illustration, always applies to a pair of numbers, not to a single number.

Figure 4.3 also shows (4.1) as the "Payoff" equation, as the dashed line under the cursor arrow in the figure's lower left corner. The dashed line gives the set of all values of C and M production decisions that produce exactly \$2,000 profit, and is thus called the \$2,000 **isoprofit line.** Like the constraints, the Payoff's slope is determined by the ratio of the given coefficients in (4.1), which, as before, you can verify by solving it for M:

$$56C + 40M = 2000 \qquad \text{or} \qquad 40M = 2000 - 56C \qquad \text{or} \qquad M = 50 - 1.4C$$

Thus, the slope for the Payoff is fixed at −1.4 and changing the \$2,000 profitability number affects only the Payoff's intercept on the Y axis. Since Oak Products wants maximal profit, you can find this by click-dragging the Payoff line. A few seconds experimentation will convince you that moving the Payoff line "northeast" is the **optimizing direction** because it increases profit, but that you must confine your greed to those values of M and C that are feasible, that is, the points in the gray area. Because the slope of the Payoff line is fixed, the profit maximizing set of feasible points turns out to be a single point in the **uphill direction** determined by the intersection of the Long Dowels constraint and the Legs constraint, as shown in Figure 4.4.

In this LP model only one point in the feasible region lies on the maximum isoprofit line, so this point is called a **unique optimal solution** to our model. From Figure 4.4 we see the value of the **maximum isoprofit line** (i.e., the maximum attainable profit contribution) is \$9,680, the same optimal profit contribution produced by Solver for the simplified Oak Products LP model in Chapter 3.

Resorting to some easy algebra it is easy to see where this value comes from. The message in the lower right-hand corner of Figure 4.4 indicates that the optimal value of C is 130, and the optimal value of M is 60. You can also see that the optimal solution occurs at the intersection of two constraint lines, both of which are now binding:

$$8C + 4M = 1280 \qquad \text{(long dowels restriction)} \tag{4.9}$$

$$4C + 4M = 760 \qquad \text{(legs restriction)} \tag{4.10}$$

FIGURE 4.4

Solution to the Simplified Oak Products LP Model

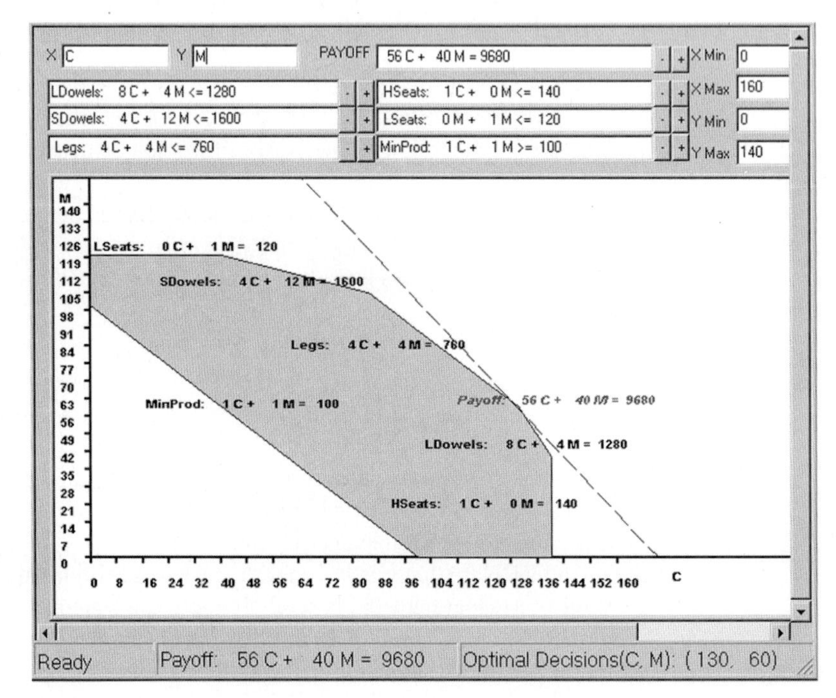

TIP: *As you drag the Payoff line GLP continuously recomputes the model's profit for you. To quickly find the maximal payoff, you may just click GLP's Auto Max Tool button, the one showing the "up arrow." Finally, as shown in Figure 4.4, you can (1) move the Payoff equation label itself to be next to the dashed line's final location, and (2) click GLP's Scissors Tool button to eliminate the clutter of superfluous line segments from the constraints.*

We thus have two linear equations, which can be algebraically solved for the two unknowns, C and M, by either elimination or substitution methods. For example, using substitution (4.10) can be rearranged to give.

$$4M = 760 - 4C \qquad \text{or} \qquad M = 190 - C$$

Substituting this expression into (4.9) and simplifying gives $C = 130$. This value for C can then be inserted into either of the original equations, yielding $M = 60$. This solution of the two binding constraints (4.9) and (4.10) for the two unknowns, C and M, is precisely what GLP (and Solver) does to evaluate the optimal values of the two decision variables.

Let us use the notation C^* and M^* to distinguish the optimal values of the decision variables, C and M, respectively. We have found the optimal production plan $C^* = 130$ and $M^* = 60$. This is the **optimal solution**, or, more simply, **the solution** to the Oak Products model. Using these optimal values we can now see how the value of the maximum profit is computed by GLP (and Solver):

$$56C^* + 40M^* = 56(130) + 40(60) = 7280 + 2400 = 9680$$

This is the value called the **optimal objective value**, or, sometimes, merely the **optimal value**. The term *solution*, or *optimal solution*, always refers to the optimal values of the decision variables. The term *optimal value* (singular), which we often call the OV or payoff, refers to the objective function evaluated at the solution. In the Oak Products model, the optimal production plan ($C^* = 130$, $M^* = 60$) is the solution; the optimal profit of $9,680 is the OV. Now we can define some important terms more precisely and develop several more general conclusions that apply to all LP solutions.

The optimal solution to any LP model will *never* occur at an interior point of the feasible region.
Geometrically, a **binding constraint** is one that passes through the optimal solution.
Geometrically, a *nonbinding constraint* is one that does not pass through the optimal solution.
Adding constraints to a model will either impair the OV or leave it unchanged.
Deleting constraints will either improve the OV or leave it unchanged.
Adding decision variables will either improve the OV or leave it unchanged.
Deleting decision variables will either impair the OV or leave it unchanged.

4.3 EXTREME POINTS AND OPTIMAL SOLUTIONS

As you have seen, the solution to the Oak Products LP model occurs at a corner of the feasible region—namely, at the corner where (what we have called) the Long Dowels inventory and Legs inventory constraints intersect. In LP jargon the corners of the feasible region are called **extreme points**. The two terms, *extreme points* and *corners*, will be used interchangeably in our discussion.

To understand the importance of the extreme points, let us take a different linear objective function, with the same constraint set, and solve the LP model again. For example, suppose that Oak Products were to change the price of Mate chairs in such a way that the profit-per-chair contribution margin is raised from $40 to $80 per unit. Let us use GLP to see how this change in the objective function affects the solution to the LP model. First, since we have changed only the objective function, leaving the constraints as they were, the feasible region remains unchanged. All that is new is that the objective function, that is, the Payoff line in GLP, will assume a new tilt. Typing 80 as the new coefficient for M in the Payoff box and clicking GLP's Auto Max Tool to re-optimize the model, gives the revised model's optimal solution shown in Figure 4.5.

FIGURE 4.5

Solution to the Oak Products LP Model for a New Objective Function

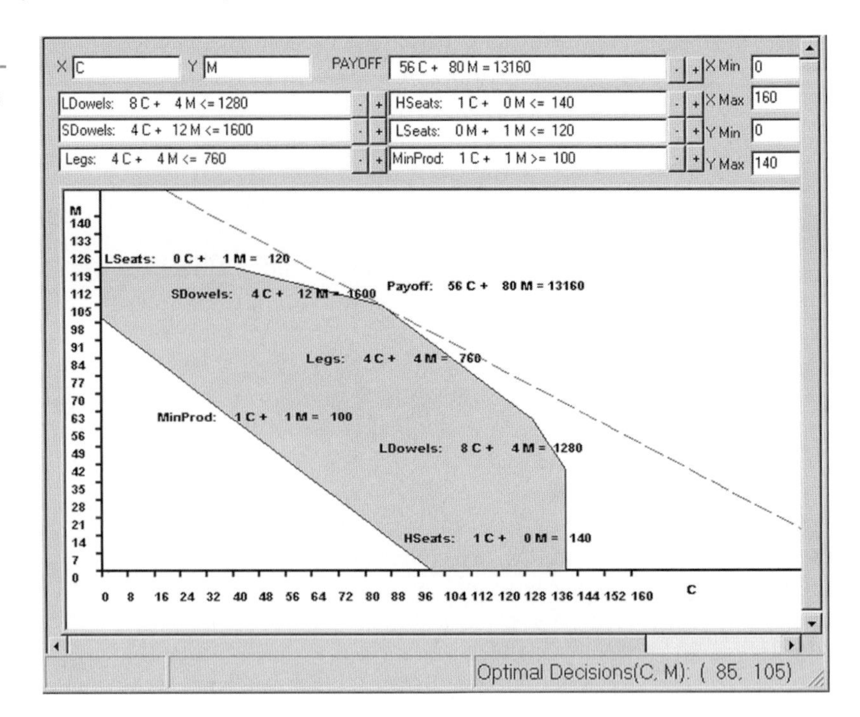

Note from Figure 4.5 that at the new optimal point the binding constraints have changed. Now the Short Dowels inventory and Legs inventory constraints are binding, whereas previously the Long Dowels inventory and Legs inventory constraints were binding. Thus, you can see that the change in the slope of the objective function has moved the optimal solution away from the previous corner, but it has moved to another *corner*, or extreme point. As you might have predicted, the new price structure, which has increased the relative profitability of Mate chairs, leads to an optimal production plan that specifies a cutback in Captains (down from 130 to 85) and an increase in Mates (up from 60 to 105).

What we have seen is that with each of two different objective functions for Oak Product's LP model we obtained an optimal corner solution. In fact, you can experiment for yourself with GLP to see that no matter how much you change the objective function, as long as it remains linear, there will always be an optimal corner solution. You can even change the constraint set and there will still always be an optimal corner solution, as long as everything is kept linear. This is a vitally important insight that warrants additional attention below.

In Figure 4.6 you see an arbitrary six-sided constraint set and contours of three *different* objective functions, denoted *f*, *g*, and *h*. For each objective function the arrow indicates the direction in which we want to slide the plotted contour to optimize the objective function. Note that in each case there is an optimal solution at a corner. The objective function *g* in Figure 4.6 illustrates the interesting case in which *the optimal objective contour coincides with one of the constraint lines on the boundary of the feasible region. This only occurs when the objective function contour has the same slope as the constraint, and in this case there will be many optimal solutions, namely the corners B and C and all the boundary points in between.* This is called a case of **multiple optima**, or **alternative optima**. However, even in this case, when there is not a *unique* optimal solution, it is still true that there is a corner solution that is optimal (in fact, there are two). Thus, the geometry illustrates an important fact about any LP model with any number of decision variables:

In an LP model, if there is an optimal solution, there is always at least one optimal corner solution.

FIGURE 4.6

You Always Get a Corner Solution

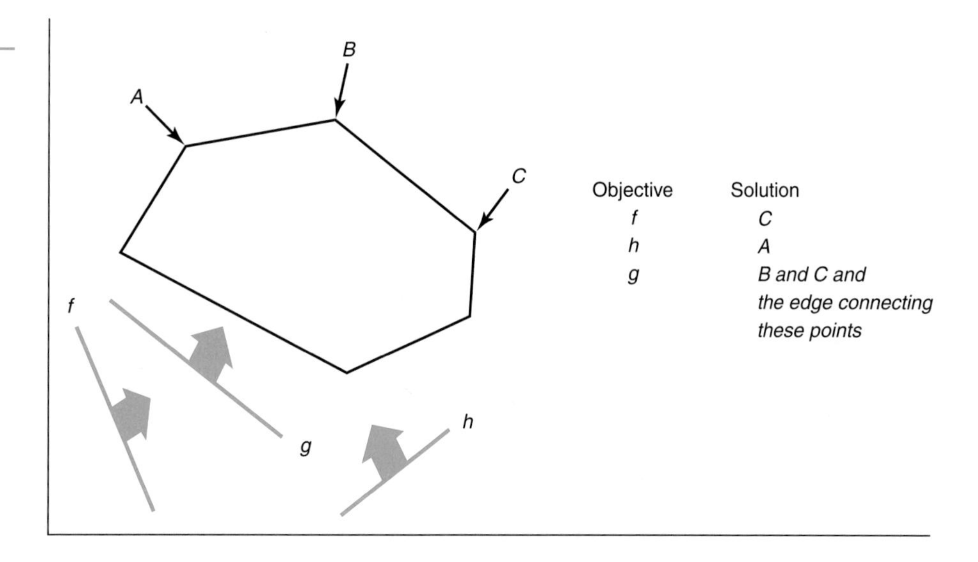

4.4 THE GRAPHICAL METHOD APPLIED TO A MIN MODEL

THE "DOWNHILL" DIRECTION

Thus far we have dealt only with the graphical representation of a Max model. As we noted in Chapter 3, many real-world models occur in a minimization context, and this was illustrated with the Eastern Steel model. The graphical method applied to a Min model is quite similar, the only difference being that *the optimizing direction of the objective function contours* is now "**downhill**" rather than "uphill." In a Max model the objective function contours are often isoprofit lines or, more simply, profit lines. In a Min model, the objective function contours are often **isocost lines** or, more simply, cost lines. Our goal, in a Min model, is to determine a corner of the feasible region that lies on the *lowest-valued* objective function contour that still intersects the feasible region. As an example, let us apply GLP to the following simple minimization model in two decision variables, which we denote as x_1 and x_2.

$$\begin{aligned} &\text{Min } x_1 + 2x_2 \\ &\text{s.t.} -3x_1 + 2x_2 \leq 6 \\ &x_1 + x_2 \leq 11 \\ &-x_1 + 3x_2 \geq 6 \\ &x_1, x_2 \geq 0 \end{aligned}$$

Figure 4.7 presents the GLP version of this example. It was optimized in GLP by dragging the Payoff line to the southwest (or clicking the "down arrow" Auto Min Tool button).

Note that the optimal solution lies on the intersection of the third constraint and the nonnegativity constraint at the x_2 axis. The equation of the x_2 axis is $x_1 = 0$. Hence, the optimal solution is given by the two equations $x_1^* = 0$ and $-x_1^* + 3x_2^* = 6$, and so, $x_1^* = 0$, and $x_2^* = 2$, as indicated in Figure 4.7. This example shows that the graphical analysis for a Min model is exactly the same as that for a Max model, as long as the objective contours are always moved in the *optimizing direction.*

One caveat here always deserves emphasis. Students on occasion fall into the trap of thinking that in a Max model the solution will always be the corner "farthest away" from the origin. And for a Min model, they instinctively feel that if the origin is feasible, it must be optimal, and if the origin is not feasible, then the corner "closest to" the origin will be optimal. *Such reasoning may be false.* The incorrect logic has to do with the false impression

FIGURE 4.7

Optimal Solution for the Min Model

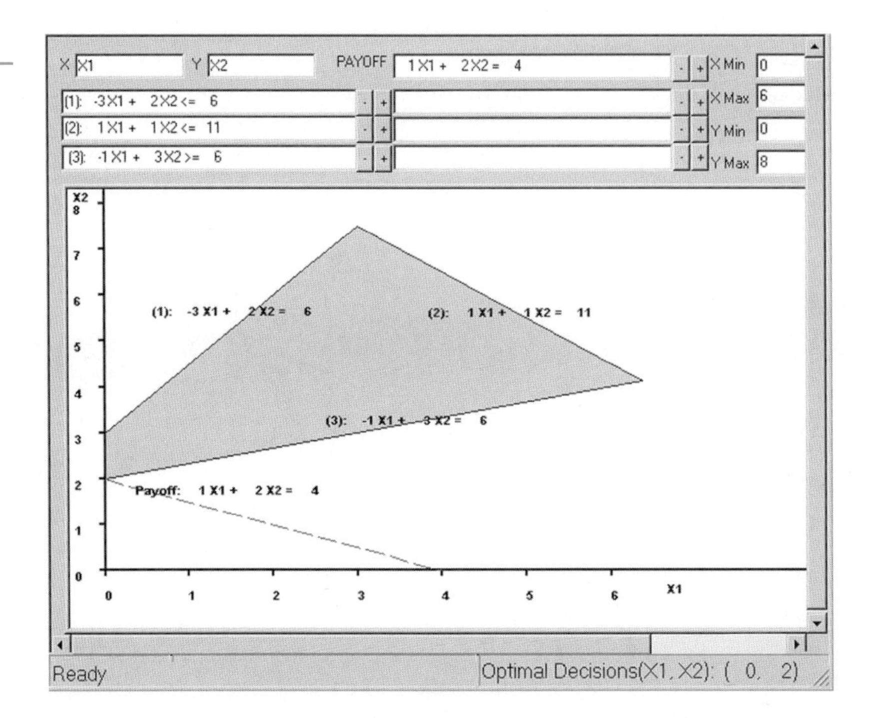

that the uphill direction is always outward from the origin strictly to the northeast, and the downhill direction is always inward toward the origin strictly to the southwest. In fact, there is no general relationship between uphill or downhill and the origin.

4.5 UNBOUNDED AND INFEASIBLE MODELS

Thus far we have developed a geometric portrayal for optimizing LP models in two decision variables. This portrayal has also illustrated the important conclusion that "*if* there is an optimal solution, there will always be at least one at a corner." But how can an LP fail to have an optimal solution? In this section we use the geometric representation to see how that can occur.

UNBOUNDED MODELS

Recall the graphical display of the Oak Products model as shown in Figure 4.3, but let us now change the model by supposing that all but constraints (4.4) and (4.7) were inadvertently omitted from the model. The GLP graphical analysis for this new model is shown in Figure 4.8. You can see that the feasible region now extends indefinitely to the "east," and it is possible to slide the profit line arbitrarily far in this direction. Clicking the Auto Max tool will produce the message given in Figure 4.8.

Since for this particular model the east is the optimizing direction, we can find allowable decisions that give arbitrarily large values to the objective function. In other words, we can obtain profits approaching infinity. Such a model has no solution, because the objective function is **unbounded**. That is, for any set of allowable values for the decision variables we can always find other allowable values that improve the objective value. Models of this type are termed **unbounded models**. Unbounded models are "pathological." They can arise, as in Figure 4.8, when one or more important constraints have been left out of the model, or possibly because of typing errors when entering a model into GLP or the spreadsheet for Solver optimization. In the real world no one has yet discovered how to obtain an infinite profit, and you can be assured that when a model is correctly formulated and cor-

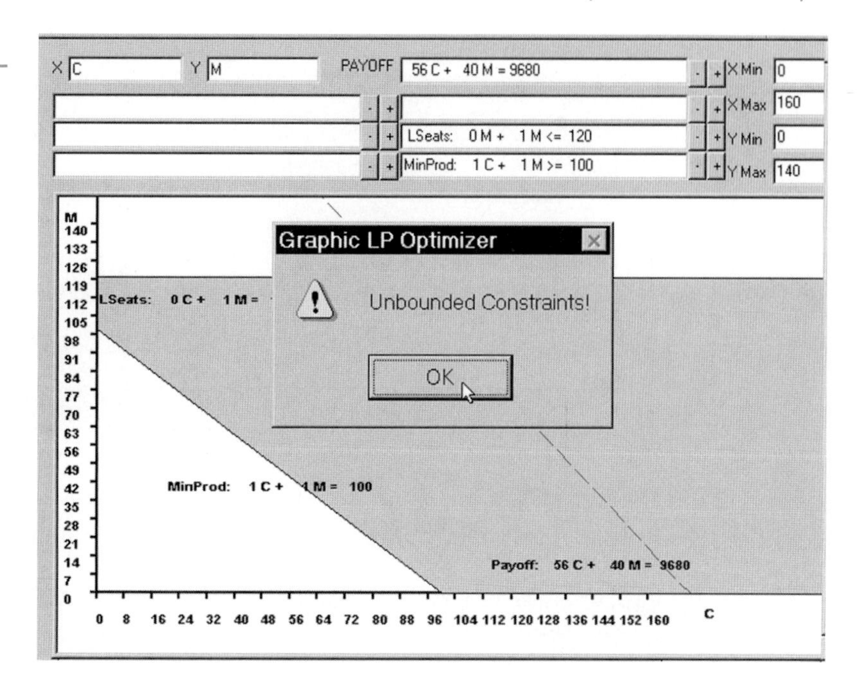

FIGURE 4.8

Unbounded Oak Products LP Model

rectly entered into the spreadsheet it will not be unbounded. Note: It is possible to have an **unbounded feasible region** and not have an unbounded model. For example, if a different objective function in Figure 4.8 produced an uphill direction to the northwest, the model would have a solution.

INFEASIBLE MODELS

As introduced in Chapter 3, there is another type of pathology to be aware of in LP. It is called **infeasibility** or, alternatively, **inconsistency**. This term refers to a model with an empty feasible region; that is, there is no combination of values for the decision variables that simultaneously satisfies all the constraints. A graphical illustration of an **infeasible model** is given by the example LP model below.

$$\text{Max } 50E + 40F$$
$$\text{s.t.} \quad E + F \leq 5 \qquad ①$$
$$E - 3F \leq 0 \qquad ②$$
$$10E + 15F \leq 150 \qquad ③$$
$$20E + 10F \leq 160 \qquad ④$$
$$30E + 10F \geq 135 \qquad ⑤$$
$$E, F \geq 0$$

Both the GLP and a graphical representation of the feasible region for this LP is presented in Figure 4.9. You can see that there is no pair of values (E, F) that satisfies *all* the constraints.

As Figure 4.9 illustrates, *infeasibility depends solely on the constraints and has nothing to do with the objective function.* Obviously, an infeasible LP has no solution, but this pathology will not appear if the model has been formulated correctly. In other words, in well-posed real models, infeasibility always means that the model has been incorrectly specified, either because of logical errors in your symbolic model or because of typing errors when

FIGURE 4.9

An Infeasible LP Model

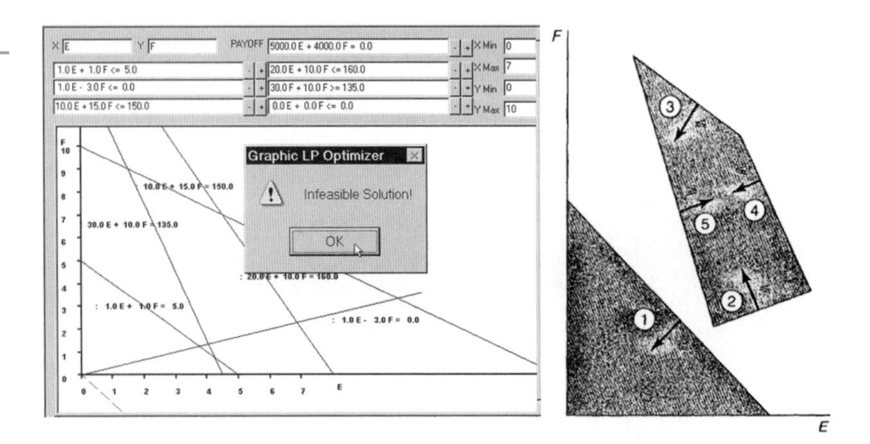

entering the model into Excel or GLP. Logical errors may mean that either too many constraints or the wrong constraints have been included. In summary:

Every linear program will fall into one of the following three mutually exclusive categories:

1. The model has an optimal solution.
2. There is no optimal solution, because the model is unbounded.
3. There is no optimal solution, because the model is infeasible.

APPLICATION CAPSULE The Diet Model

Preparing the best possible meals at the least possible cost is the objective of food-systems management for most feeding programs (e.g., hospitals, nursing homes, schools, and prisons). Menu planning is the key component since the menu determines food, equipment, and personnel requirements. Menu planning, however, deceives both nutrition experts and the public by appearing to be a simple procedure. The model must consider numerous constraints. For example, the Food and Nutrition Board identified minimum intake levels for 29 nutrients (often called recommended daily allowances). Other health-care agencies have recommended upper limits for intakes of fat, cholesterol, and sodium. All in all, it can get quite complex to plan menus that meet all the nutritional constraints.

Nutrition cannot be the only goal, however. Simple spreadsheet diet models can easily be developed that meet the nutritional constraints at a minimum cost, but nobody in his or her right mind would eat the recommended diet. The diet is generally the equivalent of a human dog biscuit. One particularly humorous story comes from the father of linear programming theory, George Dantzig. When George first created a personal diet model in the early 1950s to help him lose weight by controlling his diet, it recommended a bunch of weird stuff AND 500 gallons of vinegar. He eliminated vinegar as a possibility and the next "optimal" diet included 200 bouillon cubes per day. When he tried to drink 4 cubes dissolved in hot water for breakfast the next day, he had to spit the briny mixture out! After several more iterations of adding constraints and getting ridiculous recommendations, his wife finally took over the diet herself.

Obviously, this example, although true, is a little extreme on what can go wrong with spreadsheet formulation of a diet based on nutrition alone, but the fact is that the consumer's food preferences must be considered. Good diet models will include these additional constraints. Generally they are included in one of two ways—a separation rating or a frequency constraint. The first approach looks at how much time should pass before the item is eaten again (e.g., no more mashed potatoes for three more days). In the latter approach, you simply indicate how many times per week you'd be willing to eat the particular food item.

Institutions that have implemented these spreadsheet-generated menus have: (1) realized 10 to 30% cost savings; (2) always met the nutrient constraints, which wasn't always the case before; and (3) actually had the same acceptance by the customers in terms of taste as those meals planned with traditional methods.

The case at the end of this chapter discusses the diet problem and summarizes Dantzig's contributions to the development of the simplex method used by Solver to optimize LP models. (See Lancaster and Dantzig.)

In practice, a correctly formulated real-world LP will always have a solution. States 2 and 3 can arise only from (1) errors in model formulation or (2) errors in entering the model into Excel or GLP.

4.6 LP SENSITIVITY ANALYSIS

Thus far in this chapter we have introduced a graphical perspective to help you visualize the important role that extreme points of the feasible region play when Solver optimizes a constrained linear model. Now we turn to the question: How *sensitive* is the optimal solution to any inexact data? We may have an estimate of the expected value of a model's parameter, and the model has been run using this estimate. What happens to the optimal solution if we change the estimate by 5%, 10%, or 15%, or more? Will the optimal solution or its objective function value (OV) vary wildly, or will it remain more or less unchanged? Obviously, as was the case for sensitivity analysis examples in Chapter 2, the answer to such questions will help to determine the credibility of the model's recommendations. For example, if the OV changes very little with large changes in the value of a particular parameter, you would not be concerned about uncertainty in that value. If, on the other hand, the OV varies wildly with small changes in that parameter, you cannot tolerate much uncertainty in its value. In this case more resources might be worth committing to establish or forecast a more precise value for the parameter in question.

Although some of the foregoing considerations can be dealt with only informally, we fortunately do have some rigorous and precise tools at our disposal. These tools are in the realm of **sensitivity analysis** or **postoptimality analysis**. Both of these terms mean essentially the same thing, and the topic is of such significance that the rest of this chapter is devoted to understanding the sensitivity information contained in the Solver solution to an LP model. Extending the graphical approach will make it easy to do this. The ability to *see*, geometrically, how changes in the model affect the solution in this special two-decision-variable case makes it much easier to understand the changes that will occur in larger, more realistic models.

It is important to note that *sensitivity analysis is based on the proposition that all parameter values except for one number in the model are held fixed*, and we ask for information about the effect of changing the one piece of data that is allowed to vary. The information we might be interested in could include (1) the effect on the OV, for example, the maximum possible profit, and (2) the effect on the optimal solution, that is, the decision values. In mathematical terms, sensitivity analysis is the concept of the partial derivative, where all variables are held constant except for one. This is also known in economics as *marginal analysis.*

In order to introduce sensitivity analysis in a very specific way, let us again refer to the simplified Oak Products LP model, represented previously by (4.1) through (4.8). Recall that the purpose of this model is to recommend a production target *for a future time period.* A major application of LP involves planning models such as this, where future plans and policies are to be determined, and in such models future data are naturally required. Obviously in many real-world situations such data may not be known with complete certainty. Suppose, for example, that the stated unit contribution margins of \$56 per C and \$40 per M are only estimates based on selling prices and projected variable costs and that some of these are subject to change. Unfortunately, in order to achieve the lead time required in the planning process, the model must be run now, before the exact data are known. Thus, we must use the numbers above, which are our best current estimates, knowing full well that the future unit contribution margins could differ. We might have some fairly solid ideas about the possible ranges in which the true values will lie, and the unit contribution margins of \$56 and \$40 might be our best estimates with such ranges. But how do we deal with the fact that the data are not known with complete certainty? That is one important topic covered in sensitivity analysis applied to LP models.

Another possible concern may involve uncertainty in some of the constraint data. In LP models, this type of uncertainty usually focuses on the right-hand sides of the constraints. For example, consider the number 1280, which is the right-hand side (starting inventory) of the Long Dowels constraint. In a real-life application it is possible that such a number could also be uncertain. The actual starting inventory of long dowels could be different from 1280 for a variety of reasons. Thus, the value of 1280 is only a "best estimate." Again, Oak Products management must cope with the uncertainty in such data.

A final source of uncertainty concerns the coefficients in the constraint functions, that is, coefficients that make up the formulas for the LHS in constraint equations. Since these coefficients relate the decisions to requirements or resource limitations given by the inequalities and RHS's, they are often called the model's **technical coefficients**. Clearly, it would stretch credibility to imagine that Oak Products management would face uncertainty concerning some of its LP model's technical coefficients, for example, that a Captain chair might need more than four legs. In other LP models, however, uncertainty in technical coefficients would be more plausible. For example, a new constraint in the Oak Products LP might relate the time for sanding and finishing each chair to total available labor hours. In this case, variations in wood quality and labor productivity might make the sanding and finishing time coefficient for each chair somewhat uncertain.

The first example, in which unit contribution margins are uncertain, illustrates what we call *changes in the objective function coefficients.* The second example illustrates *changes in the right-hand sides.* The third example illustrates *changes in technical coefficients.* In the parlance of Chapter 1, the objective function coefficients, the right-hand sides, and technical coefficients are **parameters**, and for this reason the term ***parametric analysis*** is sometimes also used for the investigation of the effects of changing the values of these parameters. However, to be consistent with nomenclature from Chapter 1 and with Solver's reports, we will refer to these investigations as sensitivity analysis. Let us see how graphical analysis and the Solver Sensitivity Report can provide insight into the effects of the first two types of changes; the third type of change will be addressed later in Section 4.9.

4.7 CHANGES IN THE OBJECTIVE FUNCTION COEFFICIENTS

Suppose that the constraint data remain unchanged and only the objective coefficients are changed. Then the only effect on the model, from the geometric viewpoint, is that the slope of the isoprofit lines is changed. We have, in fact, already seen an illustration of this phenomenon in Section 4.3. In Figure 4.5 all data in the Oak Products model remained unchanged except for the fact that the contribution margin of Mate's was raised from \$40 to \$80 per unit. We saw that the effect of this change was to change the tilt of the isoprofit lines to such an extent that a new corner solution was obtained.

By experimenting with the objective function coefficients for the Oak Products model in GLP, you can also quickly see that some changes in the objective function coefficients will *not* change the optimal solution, even though the isoprofit lines will have a different slope. For example, let us replace the old objective function $56C + 40M$ with a new objective function $56C + 48M$. As we saw in Figure 4.4, the solution with the old objective function is $C^* = 130$, $M^* = 60$. The new objective function assigns a higher contribution margin to M's. You might therefore expect to obtain a new optimal solution calling for production of more than 60 of the M's because their profitability has increased. However, Figure 4.10 presents GLP analysis that shows that this is not the case. The optimal values of C and M do not change because the same corner point solution reappears.

It is evident that the negative slopes of the contours associated with each of the three objective functions in Figure 4.4, Figure 4.5, and Figure 4.10 become progressively less steep (i.e., the isoprofit contours become flatter) as the profitability of M's increases relative to C's (i.e., as the ratio $\frac{\text{coefficient of } M}{\text{coefficient of } C}$ increases). However, although the objectives $56C + 40M$ and $56C + 48M$ have contours with different slopes, *the slopes are not sufficiently dif-*

FIGURE 4.10

Oak Products Model for a Third Profit Function

TIP: *If you click on the Payoff line with the right mouse button near where it intersects one axis and then drag, GLP will rotate the Payoff line around the other axis intercept. This allows you to visually see the connections among the Payoff slope, corner points, and any movement of the optimal solution from one corner point to another, as you change the Payoff slope.*

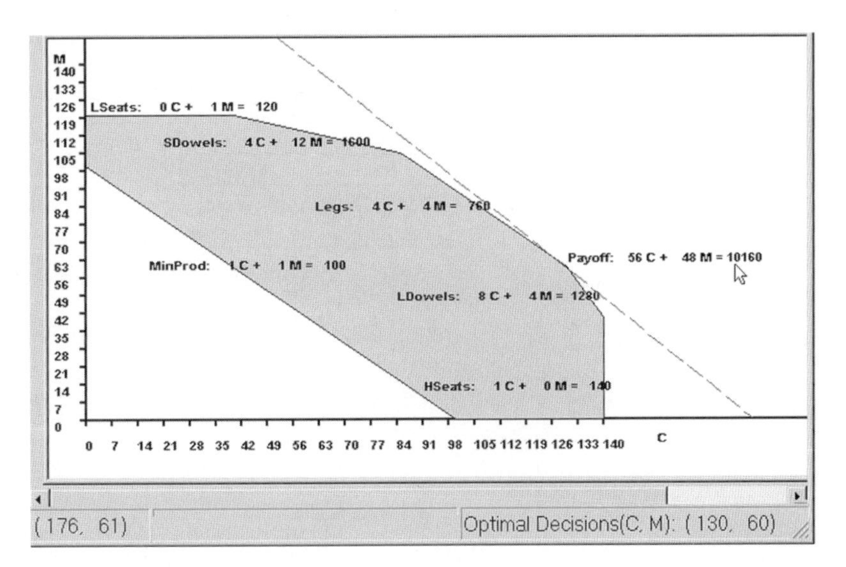

ferent to give us a new corner solution. For each of these two objectives the optimal solution is the same, namely $C^* = 130$, $M^* = 60$. On the other hand, it is important to note that because of the objective coefficient changes in this case the optimal profits (i.e., the optimal objective function values) do differ, as shown in the three figures. In conclusion, what we have just seen can be summarized thus:

Changing the objective function coefficients changes the slopes of the objective function contours. This may or may not affect the optimal solution.

Comparing the three figures should indicate to you that as soon as the ratio $\frac{\text{coefficient of } M}{\text{coefficient of } C}$ equals 1, the isoprofit line will have the same slope as the Legs constraint. Moreover, the new corner point solution of Figure 4.5 will become preferred to that of Figure 4.4 as soon as the ratio $\frac{\text{coefficient of } M}{\text{coefficient of } C}$ just exceeds 1. If the $\frac{\text{coefficient of } M}{\text{coefficient of } C}$ is exactly 1, then the isoprofit line is parallel to the Legs constraint, and GLP or Solver would be indifferent to the corner solution of Figure 4.4 compared to the corner solution of Figure 4.5, because both would yield the same optimal payoff.

Remember for a two decision variable model, when the contours of the objective function are parallel to a constraint, such as the Legs constraint, there are *two* optimal corner solutions: the current corner, at the intersection of the Legs and Long Dowels constraints, and the corner determined by the intersection of the Legs constraint and the Short Dowels constraint. Moreover, in this case all the points on the Legs constraint between these two corners are also optimal. The term **alternative optimal solutions** is used for situations such as this one, in which there is more than one set of decision variables that yield the same optimal value of the objective function. Indeed, as we have seen geometrically:

If there is more than one solution to an LP, that is, there exist alternative optimal solutions, then there are an infinite number of alternative optimal solutions.

Next, let us look at the Solver results for these three isoprofit slopes to learn how to interpret its Sensitivity Report information. Figure 4.11 presents the Oak Products Excel worksheet showing the optimal LP solution from Chapter 3, except this time instead of

FIGURE 4.11

Oak Products LP Model with Sensitivity Report

TIP: *In preparing its Sensitivity Report, for each LHS cell in a constraint, Solver scans to the left on the LP-model worksheet until it encounters a label, if any, in that constraint's row. Then it scans above the LHS cell on the LP-model worksheet until it encounters a label, if any, in that constraint's column. The two labels, if present, are concatenated to form the label for that constraint in the Sensitivity Report. A similar scanning process is done for labeling the decision variable cells in the Sensitivity Report. Wise choice and placement of labels in the LP model's Excel worksheet can produce a self-documenting set of labels in the Sensitivity Report.*

	A	B	C	D	E	F	G
1		Simplified Oak Products Model					
2	Chair Style	Captain	Mate				
3	Profit / Chair	$ 56	$ 40	Profit			
4	Production Qty.	130	60	$9,680			
5		Chair Component Requirements		Total Usage		Start. Inventory	End. Inv.
6	Long Dowels	8	4	1280	≤	1280	0
7	Short Dowels	4	12	1240	≤	1600	360
8	Legs	4	4	760	≤	760	0
9	Heavy Seats	1	0	130	≤	140	10
10	Light Seats	0	1	60	≤	120	60
11				Chairs		Min. Prod.	Slack
12	Chair Production	1	1	190	≥	100	90

Microsoft Excel 9.0 Sensitivity Report

Adjustable Cells

Cell	Name	Final Value	Reduced Cost	Objective Coefficient	Allowable Increase	Allowable Decrease
$B$4	Production Qty. Captain	130	0.0	56	24	16
$C$4	Production Qty. Mate	60	0.0	40	16	12

Constraints

Cell	Name	Final Value	Shadow Price	Constraint R.H. Side	Allowable Increase	Allowable Decrease
$D$12	Chair Production Chairs	190	0.0	100	90	1E+30
$D$6	Long Dowels Total Usage	1280	4.0	1280	40	180
$D$7	Short Dowels Total Usage	1240	0.0	1600	1E+30	360
$D$8	Legs Total Usage	760	6.0	760	72	40
$D$9	Heavy Seats Total Usage	130	0.0	140	1E+30	10
$D$10	Light Seats Total Usage	60	0.0	120	1E+30	60

requesting the Answer Report from Solver, the Sensitivity Report was requested. The Sensitivity Report is a separate worksheet with its gridlines turned off; a copy of the report is also included in Figure 4.11. Notice in the top portion of the report, labeled Adjustable Cells, row 2 contains the Objective Coefficient of 40 (for Mate's) with the Allowable Increase entry for that coefficient of 16. This means that *holding all the other data in the model constant* the Mate Objective Coefficient can increase by up to 16 additional dollars of unit profit and the original LP corner point solution will remain the same; if the increase is more than 16, then the current Solver solution is no longer optimal. Why is this?

If the increase in the Mate Objective Coefficient is:

. . . less than 16, then the ratio $\frac{\text{coefficient of } M}{\text{coefficient of } C}$ will be less than 1, which we saw in the previous GLP analysis was not enough of a change for the isoprofit line to move from the current corner solution.

. . . more than 16, then the ratio $\frac{\text{coefficient of } M}{\text{coefficient of } C}$ will be more than 1, which we saw in the previous GLP analysis was enough of a change for the isoprofit line to move from the current corner solution to a new corner solution.

. . . exactly equal to 16, then the ratio $\frac{\text{coefficient of } M}{\text{coefficient of } C}$ will be exactly $^{56}/_{56} = 1$, which we saw in the previous GLP analysis causes both corner solutions to have the same payoff, yielding alternative optimal solutions.

By a similar analysis, *holding all the other data in the model constant* the 56 Objective Coefficient for Captain's has an Allowable Decrease of up to 16 dollars before the ratio $\frac{\text{coefficient of } M}{\text{coefficient of } C}$ becomes equal to $^{40}/_{40} = 1$, meaning that a decrease of less than 16 will cause no change in the current Solver solution.

In general, for the Adjustable Cells section of the Solver Sensitivity Report, the Allowable Increase and Allowable Decrease entries indicate how much a given decision variable's Objective Coefficient may change *holding all the other data in the model constant* and still have Solver report back the same LP solution if the model were re-optimized. In other words, the **objective coefficient ranges** give the range of change for a single objective function coefficient over which *no* change in the optimal solution will occur. While we can see graphically via GLP what new corner point solution the LP will jump to for changes in an objective coefficient outside those limits, there is no information presented in the Solver Sensitivity Report as to what the new corner point solution will be. On the other hand, the Solver Sensitivity Report provides this more limited information for arbitrarily large LP models while the visual appeal of the GLP analysis is limited to only small two-variable LP models. To summarize:[2]

1. The columns "Allowable Increase" and "Allowable Decrease," in the "Adjustable Cells" part of the Sensitivity Report, tell you how much the coefficient of a given decision variable in the objective function may be increased or decreased without changing the optimal solution (the values of the decision variables), where all other data are assumed to be fixed. Of course, the total profitability varies in this range because the OV values are affected by any coefficient change.
2. When a coefficient is changed by less than the allowable amounts, the current optimal solution remains the unique optimal solution to the model.
3. When a particular coefficient is increased by its allowable amount exactly, there will be an alternative optimal corner solution with, for a Max model, a larger optimal value for the distinguished variable. (For a Min model, increasing a coefficient the allowable amount exactly will produce an alternative optimum corner with a lower optimal value for the distinguished variable.)
4. When a variable's coefficient is decreased by its allowable amount, there will be another alternative optimal corner solution with the distinguished variable having a lower (higher) optimal value for a Max (Min) model.

One other fact of interest applies to a solution:[3] *When you see, for some variable in the "Adjustable Cells" section of the Sensitivity Report, a zero entry under either of the columns "Allowable Increase" or "Allowable Decrease," you know that there is at least one alternative optimal corner point solution to the model at hand.* Moreover, whenever there are alternative optima such a signal will appear. This principle is illustrated in Figure 4.12, a hypothetical maximization LP example in two decision variables and three inequality constraints. The objective function contour is parallel to the second constraint (labeled ②), and in employing the graphical solution technique you can see that the corners labeled I and II are alternative optima for this model. Because the optimization method Solver employs to optimize an LP model considers only corner solutions taken one at a time, Solver will find only one of these two corners as an optimal solution and the Sensitivity Report applies only to that corner.[4] Let us suppose that corner I is the solution found by Solver. The geometry in Figure 4.12 shows that any increase in the coefficient of x_1 will change the objective function contour to a tilt like that of the dashed line, and corner II becomes the unique optimal solution. The Solver Sensitivity Report for the solution at corner I would have, as a signal

[2] The solution to an LP model may exhibit a technical condition known as *degeneracy*, which if it occurs makes the summary points listed to be slightly oversimplified. A more in-depth treatment of degeneracy in LP models is given in the Enrichment Topics contained on the book's CD-ROM.

[3] More precisely, a *nondegenerate* solution.

[4] When alternative optima exist for an LP model, imperceptible differences in CPU arithmetic precision will often cause Solver on one computer model to find one alternative optimal corner solution while the same worksheet will solve to another alternative optimal corner solution on another computer model. For example, Excel-Solver on a Macintosh and Excel-Solver on a Windows PC may converge to different alternative optimal corner solutions for the same LP worksheet.

FIGURE 4.12

Alternative Optima Example

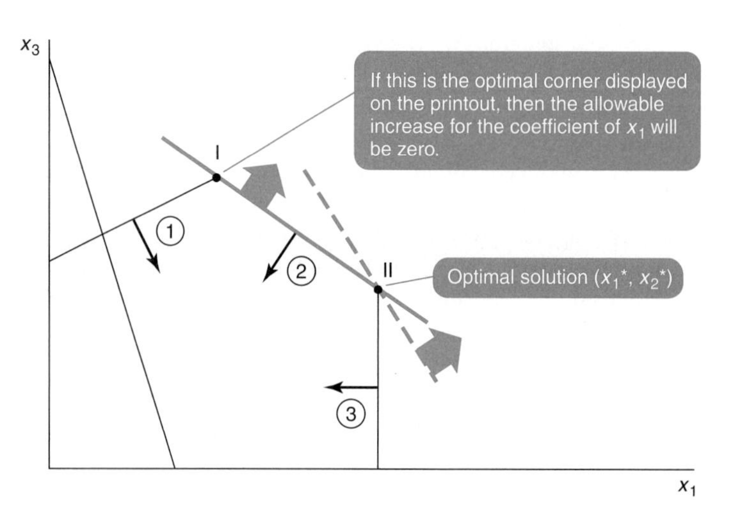

for this phenomenon, a zero value for x_1 in the "Adjustable Cells" section under the "Allowable Increase" column.

Now recall that as the coefficient of M increased (holding the coefficient of C fixed) we eventually obtained a new solution (Figure 4.5) in which the optimal value of M increased. This result agrees with your intuition since increasing the profitability of M would not cause you to prefer a lower activity level of producing fewer Mates! This case illustrates a general concept:

In a Max model, increasing the profitability of an activity associated with a decision and keeping all other data unchanged cannot reduce the optimal level of that activity.

The situation for a cost-minimization model is just reversed. Since we want to minimize total cost, we certainly would not expect that increasing the cost of an activity, while keeping all other data unchanged, could lead to a higher optimal level of that activity. This case illustrates another general concept:

In a Min model, increasing the cost of an activity associated with a decision and keeping all other data unchanged cannot increase the optimal level of that activity.

APPLICATION CAPSULE Product Planning at a Chinese Chemical Plant

The Dalian Dyestuff Plant, one of the largest chemical dye plants in China, includes 11 workshops that produce about 100 different kinds of dyes and other chemical products. The products are sold in both domestic and foreign markets. Some products are end-products while others are semifinished. For example, soda is one product that is made by an electrolytic reaction technology that generates chlorine as a by-product. To prevent air pollution, chlorine should either be disposed of properly or used as a raw material in producing other products.

With economic reform taking place in China, the government, which used to control 100% of the products that Dalian could produce, now only controls about 20% of the products made. This change means that the plant managers now have to decide which products and how much of each to produce. This is particularly challenging because the economy is growing and changing so rapidly.

An LP-based optimization model was implemented at the Dalian Dyestuff Plant. The objective is to maximize the company's profit over a one-year period. The system contains subsystems for production planning, accounting and finances, inventory, and information services. Operational results indicate that the system increased annual profits by at least 4 million RMB (about 1 million U.S. dollars at 1987 exchange rates) or an increase in profits of 10%. (See Yang.)

4.8 CHANGES IN CONSTRAINT RIGHT-HAND SIDES

Let us now ignore the objective function and focus on the right-hand sides of the constraint functions. We begin this discussion on constraint sensitivity analysis by making some general observations on the effects of right-hand-side changes for *inequality constraints*. This will lead us to several useful new terms. Again, graphical analysis will nicely explain the effects of changes in these parameters. You should experiment with moving the constraints in the Oak Product model of Figure 4.3 by assigning different values to the right-hand sides of constraints to see the variety of different-looking feasible regions that can arise from simple perturbations. You can do this in GLP by typing different RHS values for the constraints, by click-dragging the constraint lines,[5] or by clicking the +/– buttons at the right of each GLP equation box. By experimenting with moving the constraints in the Oak Product model of Figure 4.3, you should be able to conclude that increasing the RHS of a ≥ constraint **tightens the constraint**, that is, making it more difficult to satisfy. Similarly, if the RHS of a ≤ constraint is decreased, the constraint becomes more difficult to satisfy and hence is tighter.

Tightening an inequality constraint means making it more difficult to satisfy. For a ≥ constraint this means increasing the RHS. For a ≤ constraint this means decreasing the RHS.

Conversely, the process of decreasing the RHS of a ≥ constraint is called **loosening the constraint**. You should be able to see in Figure 4.3 that if the right-hand side of a ≥ constraint has become smaller, there are now *more* combinations of values for *C* and *M* that will satisfy the constraint. Thus, the constraint has become easier to satisfy. Similarly, if the RHS of a ≤ constraint is increased, the constraint becomes easier to satisfy and hence is looser.

Loosening an inequality constraint means making it easier to satisfy. For a ≥ constraint this means decreasing the RHS. For a ≤ constraint this means increasing the RHS.

We now summarize our observation on the geometric effects of tightening and loosening inequality constraints.

Tightening an inequality constraint either contracts the feasible region or leaves it unaffected. Loosening an inequality constraint either expands the feasible region or leaves it unaffected.

These results are generally true for inequality constraints and do not depend on the dimension of the model (the number of decision variables) or on whether the constraint is of ≤ or ≥ form. It should be emphasized that in this analysis we have assumed that one constraint is manipulated while all the others remain fixed. The effects of tightening (loosening) several at a time are also to contract (expand) or, possibly, to leave the feasible region unchanged. However, if some constraints are tightened and others simultaneously loosened, there is little that can be categorically stated about the result. Finally, we observe that tightening a constraint too much can produce unfeasibility.

We summarize what we have graphically seen for two-dimensional models. These results, as with the previous results for changing an objective function coefficient, are also valid for models with more than two decision variables.

[5] You must be in "un-trim" mode with all of each constraint line graphed to directly click-drag a constraint.

Changing a right-hand-side value results in a parallel shift of the changed constraint. This *may* affect both the optimal solution and the OV (the optimal objective value). The effect will depend on exactly which right-hand-side values are changed, and by how much.

Let us now move on to see how this relates to the analysis of the bottom part of the Solver Sensitivity Report, beginning with the row labeled "Constraints."

RHS SENSITIVITY AND THE SHADOW PRICE

For the Oak Products model, first consider a situation in which we hold all numbers fixed except for the inventory of Long Dowels. What if, instead of having 1280 long dowels available, we were to have 1281 dowels available? What would be the effect on the OV? Since this constraint is the ≤ form, we can say, that increasing the RHS amounts to "loosening" the constraint, which means making it easier to satisfy. Hence, you would certainly expect that the change from 1280 to 1281 will not decrease the OV. Will it, though, improve the OV; and if so, by how much?

First, let us use the tools we have already acquired, namely geometric analysis, to answer our questions. Then we shall relate this analysis to the Solver Sensitivity Report. Let the symbol L denote the value of the RHS on the Long Dowel inventory constraint. Thus, in Figure 4.4, $L = 1280$. In our experiments with the Oak Products model in Figure 4.4 we will change the Long Dowel inventory constraint by substituting the values $L = 1281$, $L = 1320$, and $L = 1350$. We know from the discussion in Section 4.2 that these three new values for L correspond, geometrically, to parallel displacements (away from the origin) of the constraint line.

Also since an increase in L means that we are loosening this constraint, the geometric interpretation is that the feasible region, if it changes at all, will expand. The new constraint sets, together with the GLP determined optimal solutions corresponding to the Long Dowel inventories of 1281, 1320, and 1350, are shown in Figure 4.13, Figure 4.14, and Figure 4.16, respectively. These figures reveal some interesting facts you can verify directly by altering the Oak Products model with GLP.

L = 1281 When $L = 1281$ (Figure 4.13), the constraints on Legs and Long Dowels continue to be binding and the new solution is $C = 130.25$, $M = 59.75$ with OV of $9,684. Notice that the OV has increased by $4 from the original model's OV of $9,680.

FIGURE 4.13

Oak Products LP with $L = 1281$

TIP: *To get this solution with GLP, you must increase the entry in GLP's Decimals field to 2.*

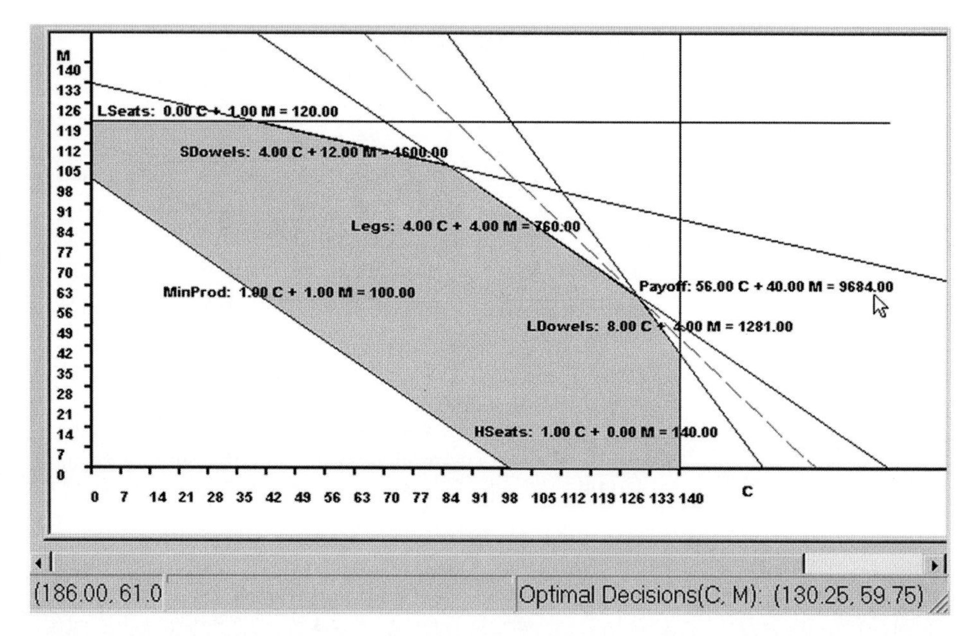

This increase of \$4 is also, as shown in Figure 4.11, the shadow price corresponding to the Long Dowels constraint. What we have just illustrated is that on the Sensitivity Report, the **shadow price** for the Long Dowels constraint shows the amount of change in the optimal objective value as the RHS of that constraint is increased a unit, with all other data held fixed. It is called a "price" because it reflects the maximum price you would be willing to pay to buy an additional Long Dowel. It is called a "shadow" price because its value is masked or shadowed until the model is optimized and sensitivity analysis is done by Solver. In economic theory the shadow price is sometimes called a *reservation price.*

> The shadow price on a given constraint can be interpreted as the rate of change in OV as the RHS of that constraint increases with all other data held fixed.

L = 1320 Figure 4.14 shows that when $L = 1320$, the optimal solution occurs for $C = 140$ and $M = 50$ and three constraints, Long Dowels, Legs, and Heavy Seats are all binding. Also, the OV = 9840.

The corresponding Solver solution and Sensitivity Report for this revised model is shown in Figure 4.15. Figure 4.15 shows zero Ending Inventory values on the three binding constraints. For the previous cases of $L = 1280$ and 1281, at optimality both decision variables were positive and only two constraints were binding. However this case, at optimality the model has both decision variables positive, but with three binding constraints. Loosely speaking, an LP solution having more binding constraints than positive variables is called **degenerate**, which can lead to some anomalies when interpreting the Sensitivity Report. For example, in Figure 4.15 note how the allowable increase or allowable decrease in some shadow prices is equal to zero.[6]

When $L = 1320$, the RHS on the Long Dowels constraint has been increased 40 units beyond the original value of 1280. Consistent with the interpretation above of the shadow price, which was given as 4, we see that the OV has increased by

$$\Delta OV = 9840 - 9680 = 160 = (4)(40)$$

FIGURE 4.14

Oak Products LP with $L = 1320$

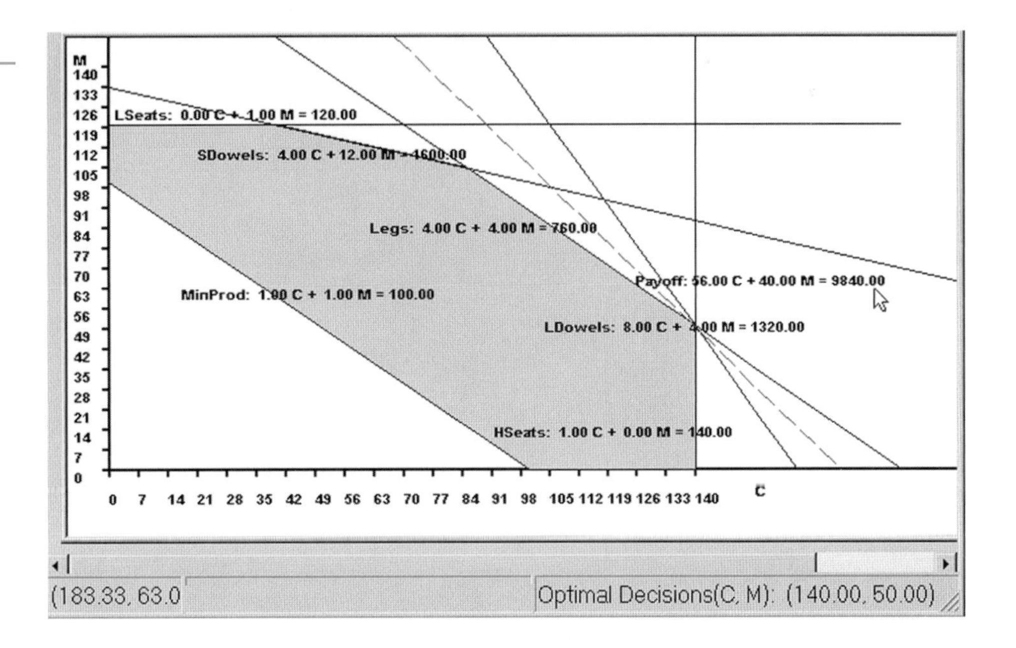

[6] The presence of degeneracy in an optimal solution is usually just a technicality. However, its presence requires more careful interpretation of the Sensitivity Report information. Readers interested in a more in-depth treatment are referred to the Degeneracy Enrichment topic on the book's CD-ROM.

FIGURE 4.15

Solver Solution and Sensitivity Report for $L = 1320$

TIP: The Sensitivity Report is just a worksheet with its gridlines turned off. You can alter the formatting of its contents for improved appearance. ***Very important:*** *The decimal formatting for each shadow price defaults to the format of the LHS cell for its constraint in the original Excel worksheet. If the LHS cell is formatted to zero or a small number of decimal places, this may produce the misleading appearance of a 0 shadow price when in fact it is a small fraction, such as 0.023. Get into the habit of cursoring over the 0 entries in the Sensitivity Report to verify whether the entry is actually a 0 or a small number requiring an increased decimal format specification.*

	A	B	C	D	E	F	G
1		**Simplified Oak Products Model**					
2	Chair Style	Captain	Mate				
3	Profit / Chair	$ 56	$ 40	Profit			
4	Production Qty.	140	50	$9,840			
5		Chair Component Requirements		Total Usage		Start. Inventory	End. Inv.
6	Long Dowels	8	4	1320	≤	1320	0
7	Short Dowels	4	12	1160	≤	1600	440
8	Legs	4	4	760	≤	760	0
9	Heavy Seats	1	0	140	≤	140	0
10	Light Seats	0	1	50	≤	120	70
11				Chairs		Min. Prod.	Slack
12	Chair Production	1	1	190	≥	100	90

Microsoft Excel 9.0 Sensitivity Report

Adjustable Cells

Cell	Name	Final Value	Reduced Cost	Objective Coefficient	Allowable Increase	Allowable Decrease
$B$4	Production Qty. Captain	140	0.0	56	1E+30	16
$C$4	Production Qty. Mate	50	0.0	40	16	40

Constraints

Cell	Name	Final Value	Shadow Price	Constraint R.H. Side	Allowable Increase	Allowable Decrease
$D$12	Chair Production Chairs	190	0.0	100	90	1E+30
$D$6	Long Dowels Total Usage	1320	0.0	1320	1E+30	0
$D$7	Short Dowels Total Usage	1160	0.0	1600	1E+30	440
$D$8	Legs Total Usage	760	10.0	760	0	200
$D$9	Heavy Seats Total Usage	140	16.0	140	0	55
$D$10	Light Seats Total Usage	50	0.0	120	1E+30	70

$L > 1320$ When L increases above the value 1320, Figure 4.14 and Figure 4.16 show that the Long Dowels inventory constraint becomes nonbinding, indeed it becomes **redundant** in that its complete removal would not affect the solution. The optimal values of C and M and the OV remain as in Figure 4.14 and Figure 4.15. For example, the Solver solution and Sensitivity Report corresponding to $L = 1350$ appears in Figure 4.17.

FIGURE 4.16

Oak Products LP with $L = 1350$

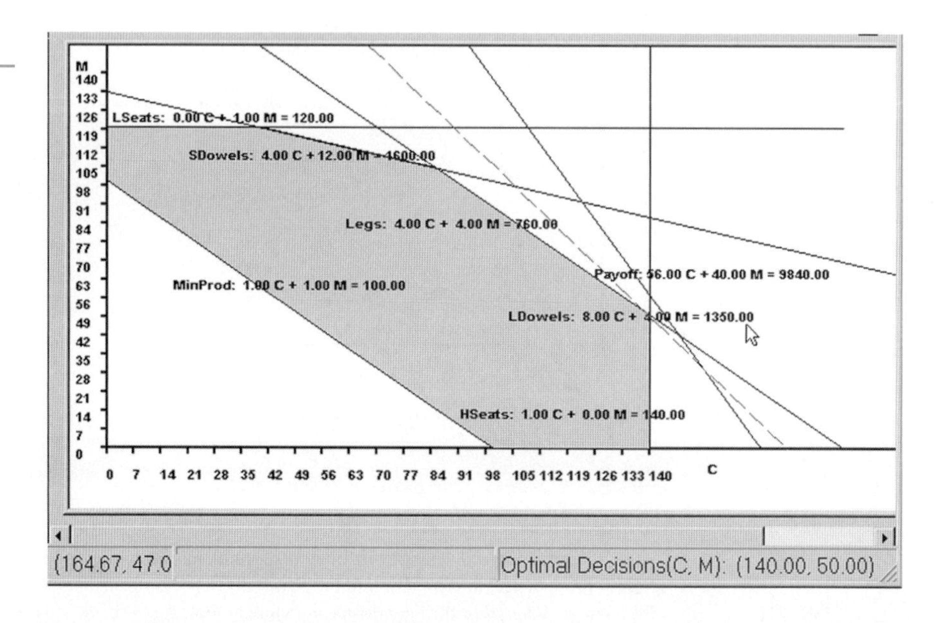

FIGURE 4.17

Solver Solution and Sensitivity Report for $L = 1350$

	A	B	C	D	E	F	G
1		Simplified Oak Products Model					
2	Chair Style	Captain	Mate				
3	Profit / Chair	$ 56	$ 40	Profit			
4	Production Qty.	140	50	$9,840			
5		Chair Component Requirements		Total Usage		Start. Inventory	End. Inv.
6	Long Dowels	8	4	1320	≤	1350	30
7	Short Dowels	4	12	1160	≤	1600	440
8	Legs	4	4	760	≤	760	0
9	Heavy Seats	1	0	140	≤	140	0
10	Light Seats	0	1	50	≤	120	70
11				Chairs		Min. Prod.	Slack
12	Chair Production	1	1	190	≥	100	90

Microsoft Excel 9.0 Sensitivity Report

Adjustable Cells

Cell	Name	Final Value	Reduced Cost	Objective Coefficient	Allowable Increase	Allowable Decrease
$B$4	Production Qty. Captain	140	0.0	56	1E+30	16
$C$4	Production Qty. Mate	50	0.0	40	16	40

Constraints

Cell	Name	Final Value	Shadow Price	Constraint R.H. Side	Allowable Increase	Allowable Decrease
$D$12	Chair Production Chairs	190	0.0	100	90	1E+30
$D$6	Long Dowels Total Usage	1320	0.0	1350	1E+30	30
$D$7	Short Dowels Total Usage	1160	0.0	1600	1E+30	440
$D$8	Legs Total Usage	760	10.0	760	30	200
$D$9	Heavy Seats Total Usage	140	16.0	140	7.5	55
$D$10	Light Seats Total Usage	50	0.0	120	1E+30	70

Note that the binding constraints (meaning ones with 0 slack or in this case 0 Ending Inventory) now are those on Legs and Heavy Seats (compare with Figure 4.16). Also note that the shadow price on the Long Dowels constraint has dropped from 4 to zero. This change in the shadow price shows that the previous interpretation of its meaning must be restricted to a specific range in RHS values. The range of RHS values for which the shadow price remains constant is the **allowable RHS range**. The appropriate range appears on the Sensitivity Report in the "Constraints" section under the "Allowable Increase" and "Allowable Decrease" columns.

Thus, the Solver Sensitivity Reports shown in Figure 4.11, Figure 4.15, and Figure 4.17 tell us that:

a. When $L = 1280$ (Figure 4.11) the shadow price of 4 is valid for an allowable increase (in L) of 40 Long Dowels and an allowable decrease of 180 Long Dowels. We see that *for* L *values between 1000 and 1320 Long Dowels, the change in the OV for each unit of RHS inventory increase, with all other data held fixed, is $4/Long Dowel.*

b. When $L = 1320$ (Figure 4.15) the shadow price remains at 4, but the allowable increase is 0, which means that the value 4 does not apply to RHS values any larger than 1320. Indeed, the geometric analysis shows that the constraint becomes nonbinding and redundant when $L > 1320$. *Small changes in the RHS of a nonbinding constraint cannot affect the OV, and hence for a nonbinding constraint the shadow price will always be zero.*

c. When $L = 1350$ (Figure 4.17) we see that now, with the relevant constraint nonbinding, the shadow price is indeed zero and the allowable increase is infinite.[7] That is, for any further increase in L the constraint will remain nonbinding and the shadow price

[7] The largest number Excel can represent is 1E + 30, that is, a 1 followed by 30 zeros. For practical purposes this is considered infinitely big by the scale of numbers used in most LP models.

will remain at the value 0. In Figure 4.17 the allowable decrease of 30 will take the RHS back to 1320. For values of L less than 1320 we have seen in Figure 4.15 that the shadow price is 4, not zero.

In summary,

1. The shadow price on a given constraint can be interpreted as the rate of change in OV as the RHS of that constraint increases (i.e., the change per unit increase in RHS) with all other data held fixed.[8] The interpretation of the shadow price is valid only within a range for the given RHS. This range is specified by the "Allowable Increase" and "Allowable Decrease" columns in the "Constraints" section of the Sensitivity Report. It is a range in which the shadow price is constant. Outside this allowable range the shadow price may change to a different value.
2. According to the interpretation above, the shadow price of a nonbinding constraint will always be zero. A nonbinding constraint means that at optimality the constraint has slack or surplus.
3. The RHS sensitivity information that the Sensitivity Report provides does *not* tell us how the optimal decisions for C and M change. It merely explains the way in which the OV will change as the RHS changes.

APPLICATION CAPSULE — Against the Grain: LP Modeling Helps a Cabinet Company Save on Its Raw Materials

Wellborn Cabinet, Inc., owns a cabinet manufacturing facility in Alabama. The operation consists of a sawmill, four dry kilns, and a wood cabinet assembly plant with a rough mill for making blanks (cabinet components). Wellborn obtains the lumber used for manufacturing the cabinets in two ways: (1) buying logs that are processed by its sawmill to make lumber, which is then used in the assembly plant; (2) buying lumber that has been sawed elsewhere. Currently, about 73% of the input comes from the company's own sawmill.

Both logs and lumber are graded #1 or #2; #1 is of better quality and more expensive. About two-thirds of the total volume of logs that Wellborn had been buying were #1. Purchased lumber, accounting for about 27% of the lumber used, was of two types: green (18%), which had to be dried in the company's kilns, and dry (9%). Nearly all of the dry lumber was also grade #1.

The cost of wood makes up about 45% of the total material cost of making cabinets. Management thus wanted to know if its approach to buying wood for the cabinet assembly plant was the most economical. To help answer this question, Auburn University's Technical Assistance Center, in cooperation with the School of Forestry, analyzed the company's operation. An LP model of blank production was created, with constraints that included the capacities of the sawmill and kilns, the required output of blanks, and the available supply of raw materials.

Optimizing revealed that the company could minimize the cost of producing blanks by purchasing only two kinds of wood: #2 grade logs with small-end diameters of 9 to 15 inches (88% by volume) and #2 common green lumber (12%). This purchasing policy would reduce Wellborn's raw materials costs by nearly one-third, an annual savings of about $412,000. Also, the model provided managers with much additional useful information:

- Shadow prices associated with the purchase of logs of various sizes enabled management to make the most cost-effective selection from among the logs available at any given time.
- Sensitivity analysis revealed the price ranges for which the solution prescribed by the model would remain optimal. In particular, it indicated that reductions of up to 20% in the price of dry lumber or #1 grade logs would not affect the optimal purchase policy.
- A slack value of zero for the operation of the dry kilns indicated that this operation represented a bottleneck—kiln capacity was the only factor limiting increased production. A 22% increase in kiln capacity would permit an increase of 29% in blank output without any additional changes. (See Carino, et al.)

[8] Indeed, the Allowable Increase/Allowable Decrease information in the Sensitivity Report will not apply when more than one parameter is being changed.

4.9 SENSITIVITY ANALYSIS WITH SOLVERTABLE

Shortcomings of the Sensitivity Report are that it (1) gives sensitivity information for perturbations of parameters only in the immediate neighborhood of the solution, and only for changing one parameter at a time, (2) gives sensitivity only for effects upon the OV, and (3) gives no sensitivity information for changes in the model's technical coefficients. Behavior of the model for larger parameter changes outside the range of Allowable Increase or Decrease or for changing more than one parameter at a time or for changes in technical coefficients requires cumbersome manual solving and re-solving the model for the parameter changes, followed after each run by a manual tabulation of the results. Previously in Chapter 2, we used the Excel Data Table command to batch process multiple "What if?" runs for sensitivity analysis. Unfortunately, the Data Table is inadequate to accomplish this for LP models because after each change the Data Table instructs Excel merely to recalculate the worksheet and not to rerun Solver. Included on the book's CD-ROM, SolverTable.xla is a Data Table-like macro to re-optimize and tabulate an LP model after each change in its parameters.

The use of SolverTable is exactly like Data Table as covered in Chapter 2 with the single exception that SolverTable knows how to re-solve the LP model for each change before tabulating any results. Moreover, SolverTable knows about the Solver Sensitivity Report and can tabulate its information, as well. Finally, SolverTable is not restricted to two-variable models as GLP is, but can work with any sized optimization model acceptable to Excel's built-in Solver or the Premium Edition Solver for Education.[9] We will illustrate SolverTable using once again the simplified Oak Products model of this chapter.

To begin, open your copy of the SimpleOakProd.xls workbook from the book's CD-ROM, if it is not already open. Next, open the add-in file SolverTable.xla via Excel's File menu Open command. Excel will ask permission to install the extended macros; as shown in Figure 4.18, click the Enable Macros button. SolverTable will install itself as a menu item that you can verify by clicking the Tools menu. However, as with the Data Table, you must set up your results table first.

RHS RANGING WITH SOLVERTABLE

To illustrate SolverTable, the equivalent of a Data Table 1 analysis will be done on the RHS parameter of the Long Dowels Starting Inventory constraint. Recall a Data Table 1 ranges only one parameter, but tabulates an unlimited number of model outputs. First, a range of RHS parameter values for the constraint is entered as data in a column (or a row); Figure 4.19 shows a range from 399 to 1350 entered in I7:I17. Next, like a Data Table 1, a row of references to model output cells is entered at the top of the table in cells J6:P6 (the formula references in those cells are indicated by callouts in the figure). The first four references in cells J6:M6 are to the LHS of the Long Dowels constraint (the demand for Long Dowels), the two decision variables, and the Profit payoff, respectively. The remaining three references in cells N6:P6 are to the Solver Sensitivity Report entries corresponding to the constraint's Shadow Price, Allowable Increase, and Allowable Decrease, respectively (the cells referred to can be seen in the Sensitivity Report contained in Figure 4.11). The labels in cells I5:P5 are optional documentation.

Next, the table is highlighted by click-dragging and SolverTable is evoked from the Tools menu, as shown in Figure 4.20.

Like Data Table, SolverTable presents a two-field dialog in which the parameter location in the model to place the input quantities is entered. Since only one RHS parameter was varied and the table definition of it placed the values in a column, the location in the

[9] SolverTable also works with Excel 98 on Macintosh computers.

FIGURE 4.18

Installing SolverTable

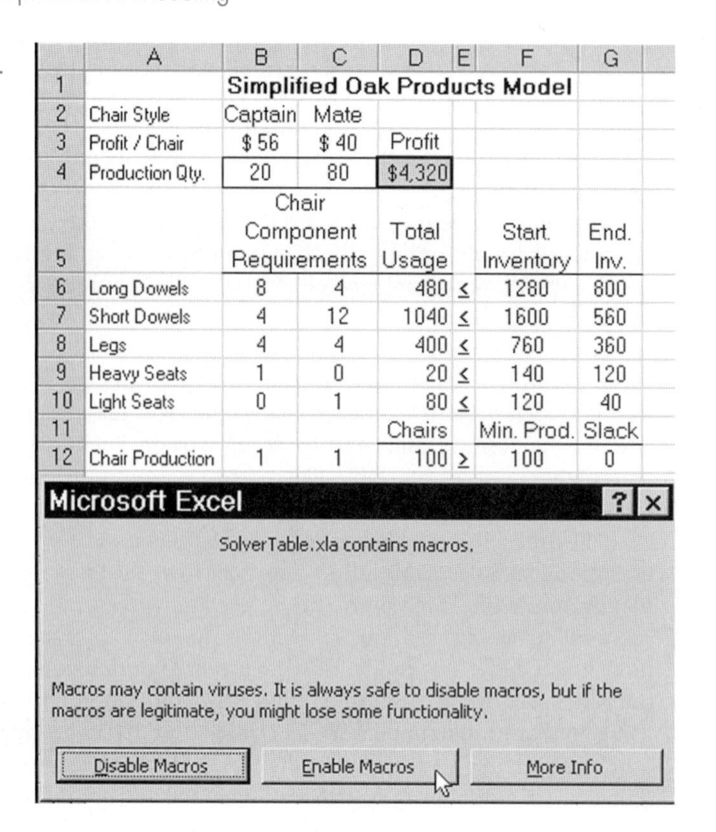

	A	B	C	D	E	F	G
1		**Simplified Oak Products Model**					
2	Chair Style	Captain	Mate				
3	Profit / Chair	$ 56	$ 40	Profit			
4	Production Qty.	20	80	$4,320			
5		Chair Component Requirements		Total Usage		Start. Inventory	End. Inv.
6	Long Dowels	8	4	480	≤	1280	800
7	Short Dowels	4	12	1040	≤	1600	560
8	Legs	4	4	400	≤	760	360
9	Heavy Seats	1	0	20	≤	140	120
10	Light Seats	0	1	80	≤	120	40
11				Chairs		Min. Prod.	Slack
12	Chair Production	1	1	100	≥	100	0

TIP: *Use of SolverTable requires that the LP model be correctly optimized with Solver first. This ensures that Solver is loaded into memory by Excel and that the Solver specifications in its Parameters dialog are correctly given. Also, if any Sensitivity Report entries are to be tabulated by SolverTable, then an* unaltered *standard Solver Sensitivity Report worksheet for that LP model must be present in the workbook.*

model of the Long Dowel constraint's RHS is entered into the "Input Column Cell" field of the dialog, leaving the other field empty, as shown in Figure 4.21.

SolverTable will then run Solver on the model for each Long Dowels constraint RHS value, in this case for 11 optimizations, and for each run tabulate the requested model results referenced in the table's columns, as shown in Figure 4.22.

Figure 4.23 displays the GLP pictures of the Oak Products model for the Long Dowels Starting Inventory amounts, L, tabulated in Figure 4.22. As can be seen, sweeping the values of L from 400 to 1350 causes the feasible region to expand until the Long Dowels constraint becomes redundant. Moreover, comparing the two figures indicates that the shadow price

FIGURE 4.19

SolverTable 1 Table Set Up for Long Dowels RHS Analysis

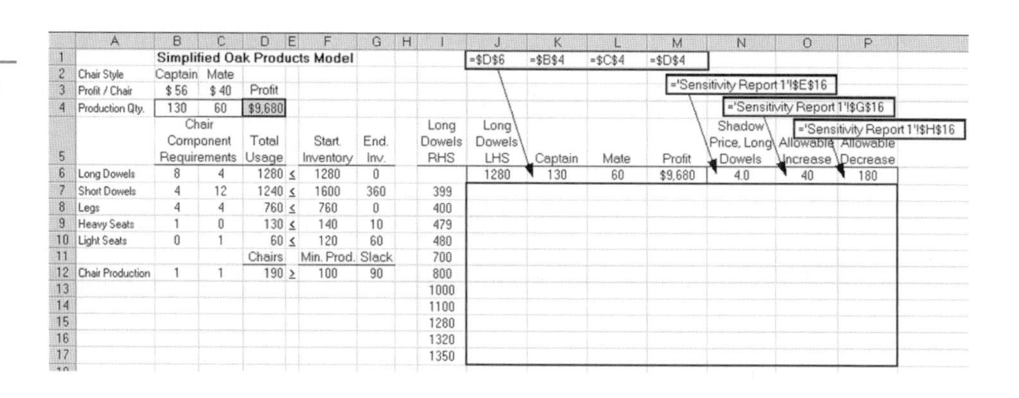

	A	B	C	D	E	F	G	H	I	J	K	L	M	N	O	P
1		**Simplified Oak Products Model**								=$D$6	=$B$4	=$C$4	=$D$4			
2	Chair Style	Captain	Mate											='Sensitivity Report 1'!$E$16		
3	Profit / Chair	$ 56	$ 40	Profit											='Sensitivity Report 1'!$G$16	
4	Production Qty.	130	60	$9,680												='Sensitivity Report 1'!$H$16
5		Chair Component Requirements		Total Usage		Start. Inventory	End. Inv.		Long Dowels RHS	Long Dowels LHS	Captain	Mate	Profit	Shadow Price, Long Dowels	Allowable Increase	Allowable Decrease
6	Long Dowels	8	4	1280	≤	1280	0			1280	130	60	$9,680	4.0	40	180
7	Short Dowels	4	12	1240	≤	1600	360		399							
8	Legs	4	4	760	≤	760	0		400							
9	Heavy Seats	1	0	130	≤	140	10		479							
10	Light Seats	0	1	60	≤	120	60		480							
11				Chairs		Min. Prod.	Slack		700							
12	Chair Production	1	1	190	≥	100	90		800							
13									1000							
14									1100							
15									1280							
16									1320							
17									1350							

FIGURE 4.20

Starting SolverTable for Long Dowels RHS Analysis

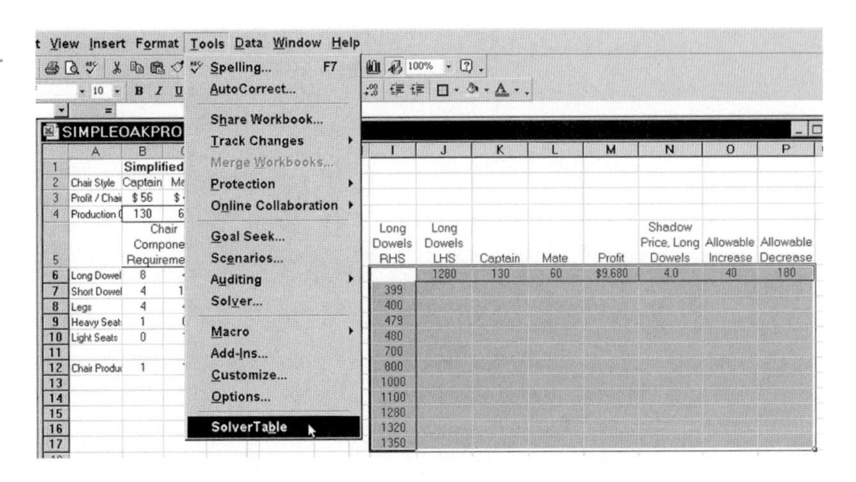

FIGURE 4.21

SolverTable 1 Dialog for Long Dowels RHS Analysis

	A	B	C	D	E	F	G	H	I	J	K
5		Chair Component Requirements		Total Usage		Start. Inventory	End. Inv.		Long Dowels RHS	Long Dowels LHS	Capt
6	Long Dowels	8	4	1280	≤	1280	0			1280	130
7	Short Dowels	4	12	1240	≤	1600	360		399		
8	Legs	4	4	760	≤	760	0		400		
9	Heavy Seats								479		
10	Light Seats								480		
11									700		
12	Chair Production								800		
13									1000		
14									1100		
15									1280		
16									1320		
17									1350		

SolverTable

Input Row Cell

Input Column Cell $F$6

OK Cancel Help

FIGURE 4.22

SolverTable 1 Results for Long Dowels RHS Analysis

Long Dowels RHS	Long Dowels LHS	Captain	Mate	Profit	Shadow Price, Long Dowels	Allowable Increase	Allowable Decrease
	1280	130	60	$9,680	4.0	40	180
399	Infeasible	Infeasible	Infeasible	Infeasible	Infeasible	Infeasible	Infeasible
400	400	0	100	$4,000	10.0	80	0
479	479	0	119.75	$4,790	10.0	1	79
480	480	0	120	$4,800	7.0	320	0
700	700	27.5	120	$6,340	7.0	100	220
800	800	40	120	$7,040	6.4	300	0
1000	1000	70	110	$8,320	6.4	100	200
1100	1100	85	105	$8,960	4.0	220	0
1280	1280	130	60	$9,680	4.0	40	180
1320	1320	140	50	$9,840	0.0	1E+30	0
1350	1320	140	50	$9,840	0.0	1E+30	30

changes abruptly each time a different set of constraints combine to determine the optimal corner point solution. Finally, since the shadow prices are stepping down to lower values as L is increased in Figure 4.22, the OV is increasing at a decreasing rate, a common occurrence in a Max model as a single ≤ constraint is loosened.

The Sensitivity Report is limited to single parameter changes holding all other data constant. SolverTable can mimic Data Table 2 to tabulate simultaneous variations in two parameters, but as in Data Table 2, with the restriction that only one output cell can be tab-

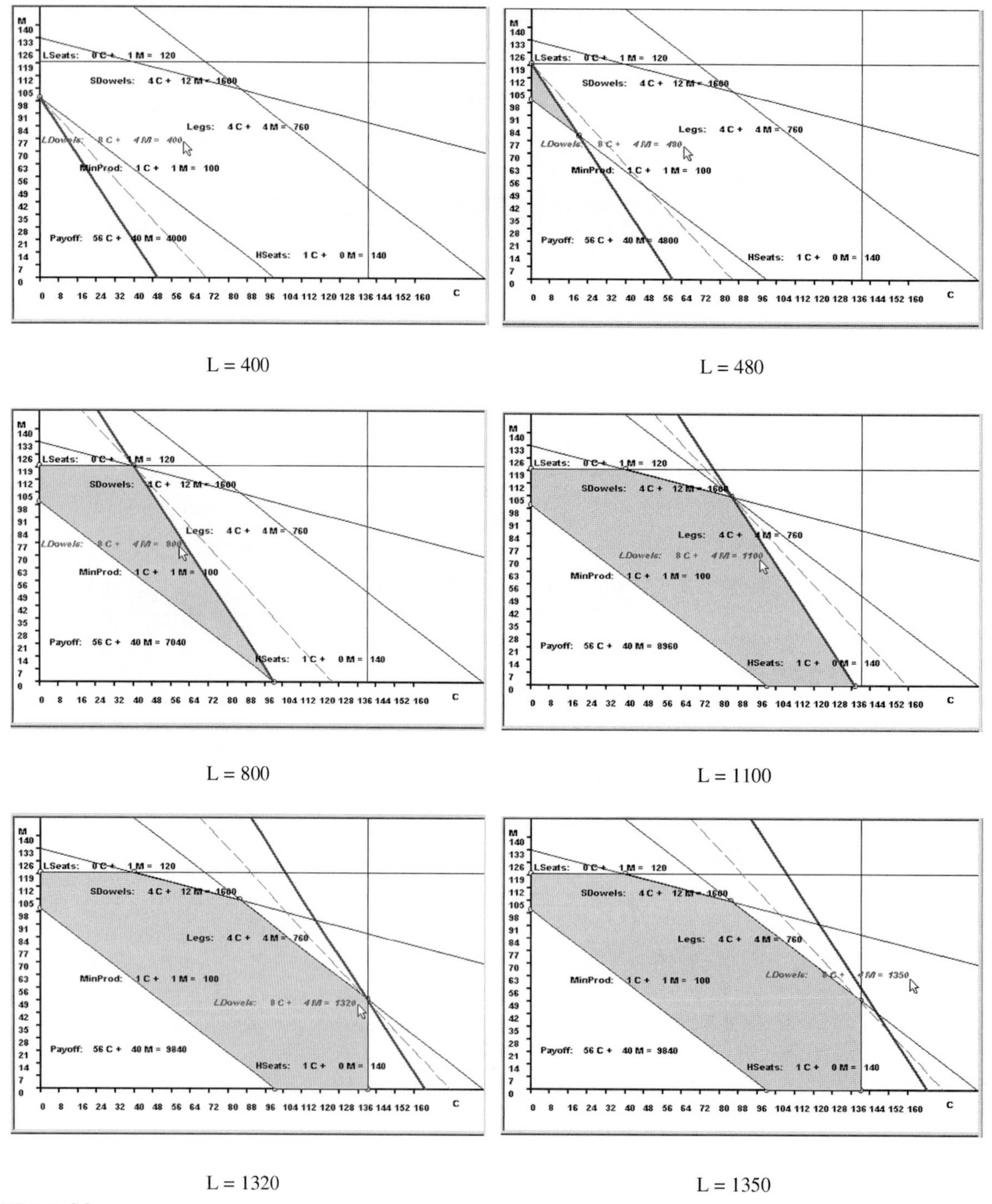

FIGURE 4.23

GLP Results for Long Dowels RHS Analysis

ulated. To illustrate this, a range of parameter values for the Inventory constraint RHS values for both Long and Short Dowels will be done. As before, a table is set up first, in this case with a range of parameter values for both parameters, as shown in Figure 4.24.

SolverTable will then run Solver on the model for each paired combination of Long Dowels constraint and Short Dowels constraint RHS values, in this case for 108 optimiza-

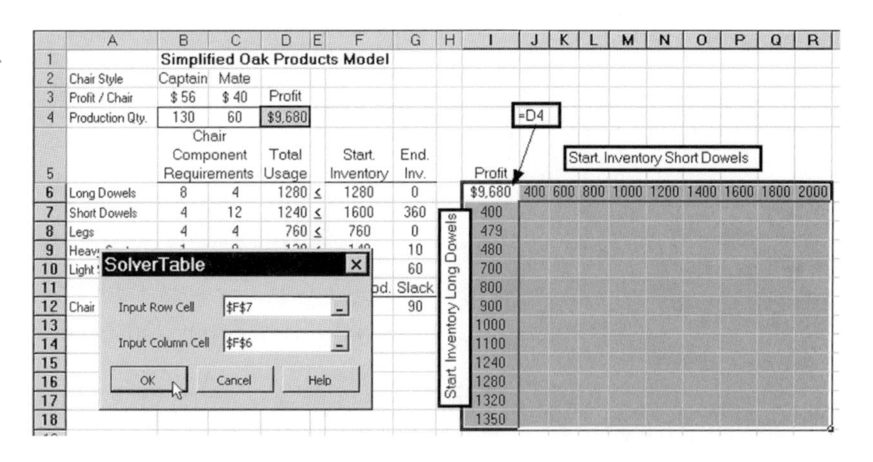

FIGURE 4.24

SolverTable 2 Dialog for Long and Short Dowels RHS Analysis

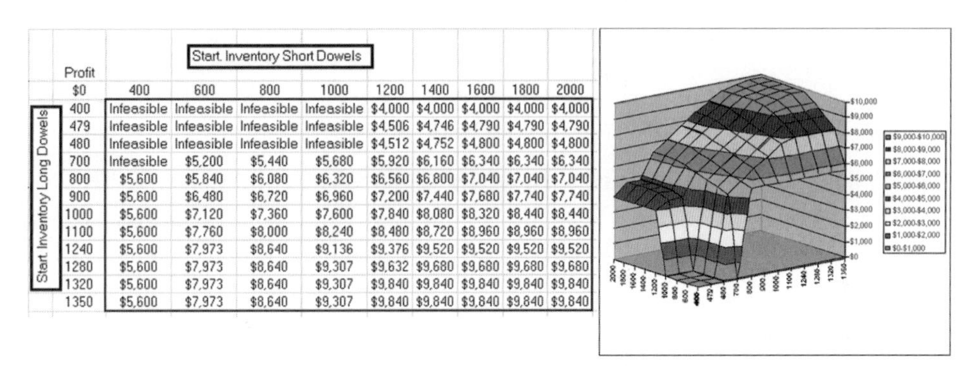

Start. Inventory Short Dowels (columns); Start. Inventory Long Dowels (rows)

Profit $0	400	600	800	1000	1200	1400	1600	1800	2000
400	Infeasible	Infeasible	Infeasible	Infeasible	$4,000	$4,000	$4,000	$4,000	$4,000
479	Infeasible	Infeasible	Infeasible	Infeasible	$4,506	$4,746	$4,790	$4,790	$4,790
480	Infeasible	Infeasible	Infeasible	Infeasible	$4,512	$4,752	$4,800	$4,800	$4,800
700	Infeasible	$5,200	$5,440	$5,680	$5,920	$6,160	$6,340	$6,340	$6,340
800	$5,600	$5,840	$6,080	$6,320	$6,560	$6,800	$7,040	$7,040	$7,040
900	$5,600	$6,480	$6,720	$6,960	$7,200	$7,440	$7,680	$7,740	$7,740
1000	$5,600	$7,120	$7,360	$7,600	$7,840	$8,080	$8,320	$8,440	$8,440
1100	$5,600	$7,760	$8,000	$8,240	$8,480	$8,720	$8,960	$8,960	$8,960
1240	$5,600	$7,973	$8,640	$9,136	$9,376	$9,520	$9,520	$9,520	$9,520
1280	$5,600	$7,973	$8,640	$9,307	$9,632	$9,680	$9,680	$9,680	$9,680
1320	$5,600	$7,973	$8,640	$9,307	$9,840	$9,840	$9,840	$9,840	$9,840
1350	$5,600	$7,973	$8,640	$9,307	$9,840	$9,840	$9,840	$9,840	$9,840

FIGURE 4.25

SolverTable 2 Results for Long and Short Dowels RHS Analysis

tions, and for each run tabulate the single Profit result referenced in the table's upper left corner, as shown in Figure 4.25. Not surprisingly, the OV increases as either or both RHS values are increased. As with Data Table 2, a graph of the results using the Chart Wizard is easy to produce, in this case illustrating the joint diminishing returns in OV as the constraints are loosened. The flat faces on the Surface Chart reflect ranges of the LP in which the same set of constraints are binding, yielding constant shadow price(s).

OBJECTIVE FUNCTION COEFFICIENT RANGING WITH SOLVERTABLE

Ranging an objective function coefficient with SolverTable is similar to ranging a RHS. First, set up a table with values of the objective function coefficient in a column or row; Figure 4.26 shows the setup for the coefficient values in a column, selected model outputs, key formula callouts, and the SolverTable dialog.

Figure 4.27 shows the results from the SolverTable analysis of the different objective function coefficients for profit per Captain chair and makes clear why those particular coefficient values were chosen in this case: They are the coefficient values at which the LP

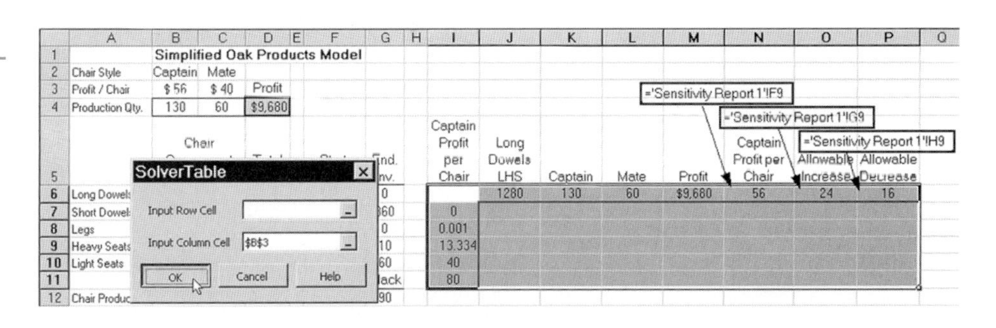

FIGURE 4.26

SolverTable 1 Table Set Up for Captain Profit per Chair Analysis

FIGURE 4.27

SolverTable Results for Captain Profit per Chair Analysis

Captain Profit per Chair	Long Dowels LHS	Captain	Mate	Profit	Captain Profit per Chair	Allowable Increase	Allowable Decrease
	1280	130	60	$9,680	56	24	16
0	480	0	120	$4,800	0.0	0	1E+30
0.001	800	40	120	$4,800	0.001	13.332	0.001
13.334	1100	85	105	$5,333	13.334	26.666	0.001
40	1280	130	60	$7,600	40.0	40	0
80	1280	140	40	$12,800	80.0	1E+30	0

solution changes. This can be seen from study of the Allowable Increase column in Figure 4.27.

Figure 4.28 displays the GLP pictures of the Oak Products model for the Captain objective function coefficient values, V, tabulated in Figure 4.27. As can be seen, sweeping the values of V from 0 to 99999 causes the objective function to rotate from horizontal to nearly vertical slope. Moreover, comparing the two figures indicates that the corner point solution changes abruptly for critical values of V. Finally, the presence of the zero's in the Allowable Increase or Decrease at these critical values of V indicates the occurrence of alternative optimal solutions.

TECHNICAL COEFFICIENT RANGING WITH SOLVERTABLE

Investigation of alternative production technologies is also straightforward with SolverTable. Recall, the constraint function equations with their coefficients determine the LHS calculations for resource demands, and thus, reflect a given technology. Suppose that Oak Products were to consider the option of strengthening or slightly weakening a Mate chair by increasing or decreasing the number of long dowels it uses. In addition to the engineering and safety evaluations of such a change, Tom would like to examine the economic effects of reducing the number of long dowels per Mate from the current 4 to 2, and increasing the number above 4. On reflection the economic analysis is not so obvious because aside from the immediate effect of such a change on Mate chair costs, the change would also affect the production demand for the tightly constrained inventory of long dowels. This would affect the production possibilities not only for Mate chairs but possibly also for Captain chairs, which in turn could lead to different production plans for both chair types. So, his investigation requires repeated re-optimization of the model with SolverTable.

The procedure to apply SolverTable for this analysis is similar to the RHS analysis of Starting Inventory values done previously: Set up a SovlerTable 1 table layout with a range of alternative technical coefficient values around the base case value of 4, and run SolverTable to tabulate the model outputs of interest. The results of doing this are shown in Figure 4.29, which presents the final tabulated outcomes for ranging the number of long dowels per Mate chair from 2 to 10, along with the SolverTable dialog that produced it.[10] As Tom expected, increasing the number of long dowels per Mate chair from 4 to 6 reduces the optimal number of Mates to produce, compensated by an increase in Captains to produce, with a net reduction in Profit of about $570. Surprisingly, however, reducing the number of long dowels per Mate chair from 4 to 2 *also reduces* the optimal number of Mates, increases the number of Captains, but with a net increase in Profit. Review of the other results in Figure 4.29, such as the Long Dowels Shadow Price, reveals similar nonsystematic changes.

[10] For comparative purposes Tom has assumed that the objective function coefficient, Profit per Mate chair, was the same as before, in effect assuming that the number of long dowels used has a negligible impact upon variable costs.

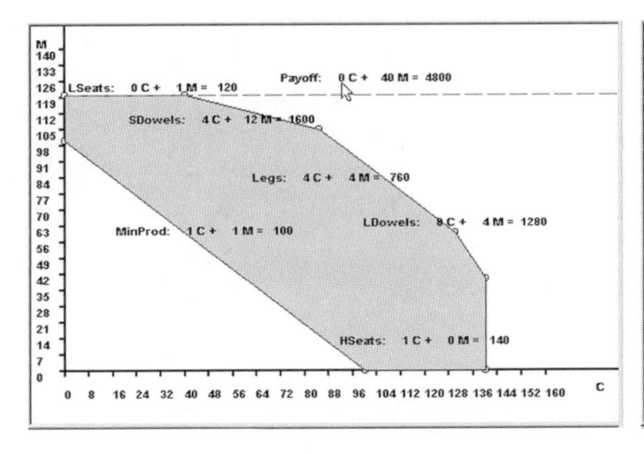

V = 0

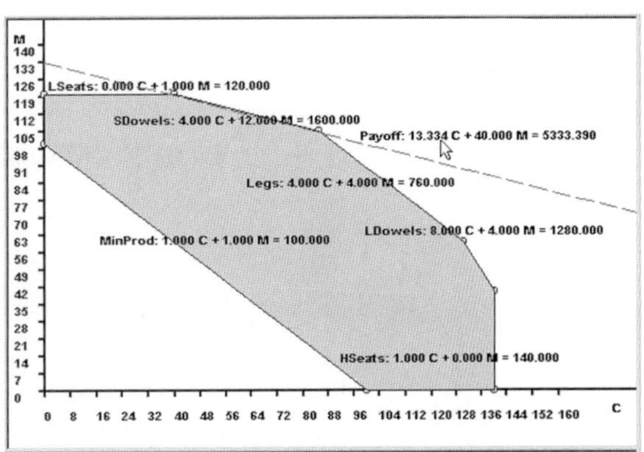

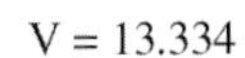
V = 13.334

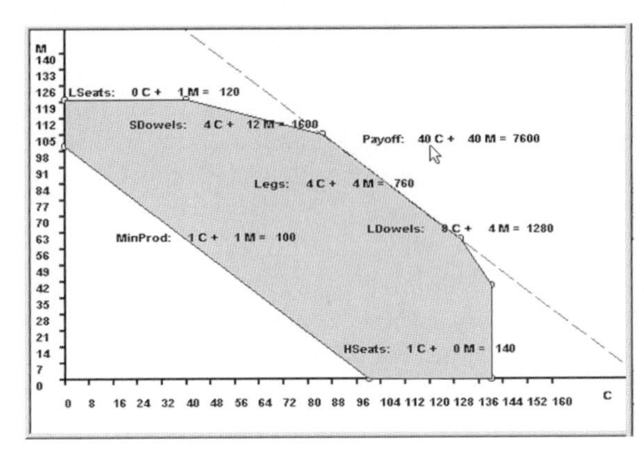

V = 40

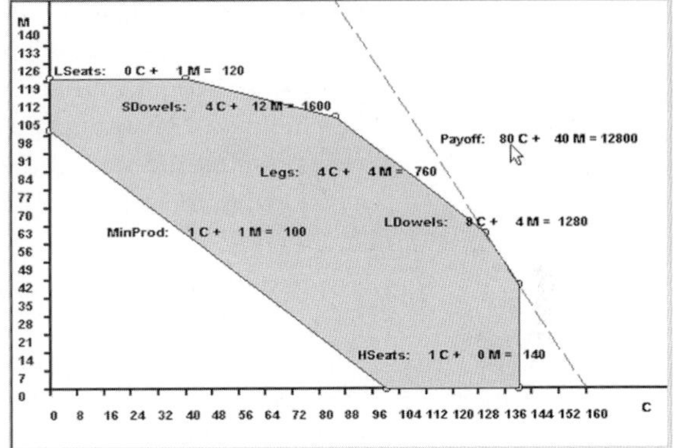

V = 80

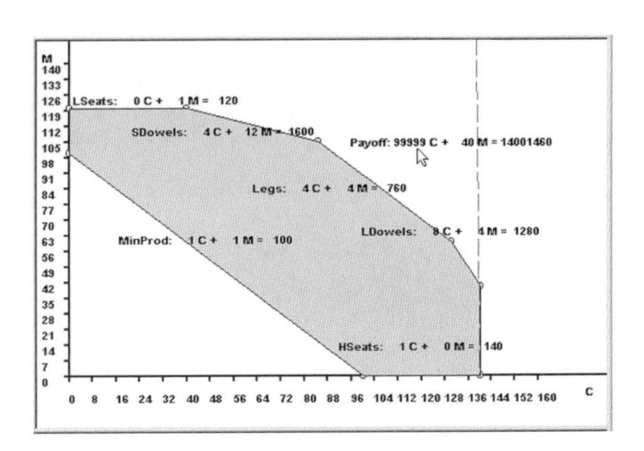

V = 99999

FIGURE 4.28

GLP Results for Captain Profit-per-Chair Analysis

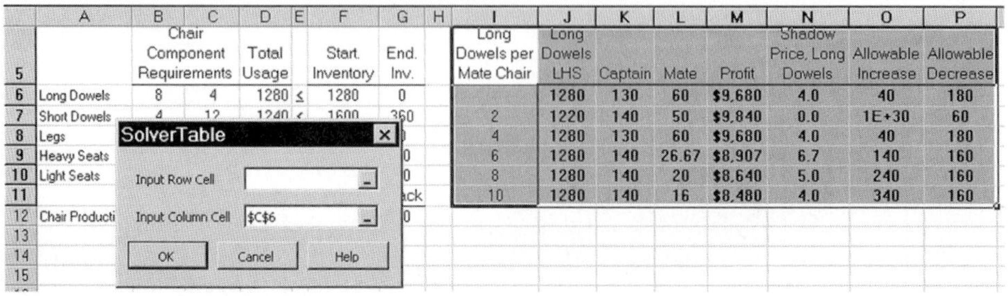

FIGURE 4.29

SolverTable 1 Results for Alternative Mate Technical Coefficients

	A	B	C	D	E	F	G
5		Chair Component Requirements		Total Usage		Start. Inventory	End. Inv.
6	Long Dowels	8	4	1280	≤	1280	0
7	Short Dowels	4	12	1240	≤	1600	360
8	Legs						
9	Heavy Seats						0
10	Light Seats						0
11							ack
12	Chair Producti						0

SolverTable

Input Row Cell

Input Column Cell $C$6

OK Cancel Help

Long Dowels per Mate Chair	Long Dowels LHS	Captain	Mate	Profit	Shadow Price, Long Dowels	Allowable Increase	Allowable Decrease
	1280	130	60	$9,680	4.0	40	180
2	1220	140	50	$9,840	0.0	1E+30	60
4	1280	130	60	$9,680	4.0	40	180
6	1280	140	26.67	$8,907	6.7	140	160
8	1280	140	20	$8,640	5.0	240	160
10	1280	140	16	$8,480	4.0	340	160

Considering that all the relationships in the model are linear, such counterintuitive results for LP are often surprising because they reflect subtle and often unpredictable interactions among the constraints of even a simple LP model.

This almost completes our exploration of the meaning of each entry in the Sensitivity Report. Although our discussion has been introductory, if you have mastered the material presented from Chapter 3 up to this point, you should now be able to use LP in practical situations—to formulate models, optimize them with Solver, correctly interpret the Sensitivity Report, and use SolverTable for broader parametric analysis.[11] However, we have not given an example of Sensitivity Analysis for a Minimization LP model, nor have we explained the Reduced Cost entry in the Sensitivity Report. Both of these will be addressed in the next example.

4.10 EASTERN STEEL: A DIALOG WITH MANAGEMENT (SENSITIVITY ANALYSIS IN ACTION)

The Eastern Steel model was introduced in Section 3.10. Recall that the ore from four different locations is blended to make a steel alloy. Each ore contains three essential elements, denoted for simplicity as *A*, *B*, and *C*, that must appear in the final blend at minimum threshold levels. Eastern pays a different price per ton for the ore from each location. The cost-minimizing blend is obtained by solving the following LP model, where T_i = the fraction of a ton of ore from location *i* in one ton of the blend. The Solver solution to this LP model is given in Figure 4.30 along with its Sensitivity Report.

$$
\begin{aligned}
\text{Min } & 800T_1 + 400T_2 + 600T_3 + 500T_4 && \text{(total cost)} \\
\text{s.t. } & 10T_1 + 3T_2 + 8T_3 + 2T_4 \geq 5 && \text{(requirement on } A\text{)} \\
& 90T_1 + 150T_2 + 75T_3 + 175T_4 \geq 100 && \text{(requirement on } B\text{)} \\
& 45T_1 + 25T_2 + 20T_3 + 37T_4 \geq 30 && \text{(requirement on } C\text{)} \\
& T_1 + T_2 + T_3 + T_4 = 1 && \text{(blend condition)} \\
& T_i \geq 0, i = 1, 2, 3, 4
\end{aligned}
$$

REDUCED COST

We explained previously everything in the Sensitivity Report except for the entries under the column "Reduced Cost." The following facts pertain to these entries.[12]

1. The reduced cost of any particular decision variable is defined to be *the amount the coefficient of that variable in the objective function would have to change in order to have a positive optimal value for that variable.*[13] Thus, if a decision variable is already posi-

[11] The Solver Limits Report is of limited practical importance and will not be covered.

[12] This is another instance where, in order to give a completely correct interpretation, you must first observe whether the optimal solution is nondegenerate.

[13] This is the standard definition for Reduced Cost for the case of a nondegenerate solution. Unfortunately, even in the case of a nondegenerate solution, the Solver Sensitivity Report sometimes presents other information in the Reduced Cost column, which can cause confusion. An example of this is covered in Section 4.12.

tive at optimality, its reduced cost is zero (as is the case for both Oak Products decision variables in Figure 4.5, Figure 4.15, and Figure 4.17). If the optimal value of a decision variable is zero, then from the definition of reduced cost you can see that the reduced cost is either the "Allowable Increase" or "Allowable Decrease" that corresponds to the given variable (one of these values will be infinite; the other will be the reduced cost). For example, the decision variable *T4* in the Ore Blending Model in Figure 4.30 is zero at optimality. Then the reduced cost of *T4* is the amount its unit cost (the coefficient of *T4* in the objective function) would have to be *decreased* in order to have an optimal solution with $T4 > 0$. This is precisely the entry that you would find corresponding to *T4* in the "Allowable Decrease" column. In this case, for any increase in the coefficient of *T4* (making *T4* more costly) the value optimal *T4* will remain at zero. Hence, the corresponding "Allowable Increase" would be infinite.

2. Another equivalent interpretation of the reduced cost of a decision variable (whose optimal value is currently zero) is the rate (per unit amount) at which the objective value is hurt as that variable is "forced into" a previously optimal solution, that is, if Solver's optimal value of zero is overridden and that variable is forced to assume positive values. With $T4 = 0$, the original OV cost would increase if we forced ourselves to find an optimal solution with the *additional* constraint that, for example, $T4 = .1$. (To see that the OV would *increase* you need merely recognize that in the current model the optimal value of *T4* is zero. Forcing *T4* to be .1, then, can only yield us higher cost.) This *rate of increase in optimal cost* as *T4* is initially forced to be positive would be given by the reduced cost of *T4*.

   Recall that a constraint's shadow price gives the rate of change in the OV as that constraint's RHS is increased. Since in this model $T4 = 0$, the nonnegativity constraint on *T4* is therefore binding. If *T4* is then forced to be positive, that is the same as raising the RHS on its nonnegativity constraint. Thus this equivalent interpretation is easily articulated: For models having nonnegativity constraints, the reduced cost is simply the shadow price on that decision variable's nonnegativity constraint.

FIGURE 4.30

Solver Solution and Sensitivity Report for Eastern Steel Model

	A	B	C	D	E	F	G	H	I
1	Ore Blending Production Plan								
2	Mine	T1	T2	T3	T4				
3	Ton Fractions	0.259	0.704	0.037	0	Total			
4	Cost/Ton	$800	$400	$600	$500	$511.11			
5	Constraints	Composition per Ton				Total Elements		Requirements	Surplus
6	A	10	3	8	2	5.00	≥	5	0
7	B	90	150	75	175	131.67	≥	100	31.67
8	C	45	25	20	37	30.00	≥	30	0
9	Balance	1	1	1	1	1.00	=	1	0

Microsoft Excel 9.0 Sensitivity Report

Adjustable Cells

Cell	Name	Final Value	Reduced Cost	Objective Coefficient	Allowable Increase	Allowable Decrease
$B$3	Ton Fractions T1	0.259	0.00	800	223.64	120
$C$3	Ton Fractions T2	0.704	0.00	400	66.85	300
$D$3	Ton Fractions T3	0.037	0.00	600	85.71	118.27
$E$3	Ton Fractions T4	0	91.11	500	1E+30	91.11

Constraints

Cell	Name	Final Value	Shadow Price	Constraint R.H. Side	Allowable Increase	Allowable Decrease
$F$6	A Total Elements	5.00	44.44	5	2.375	0.25
$F$7	B Total Elements	131.67	0.00	100	31.67	1E+30
$F$8	C Total Elements	30.00	4.44	30	0.71	7
$F$9	Balance Total Elements	1.00	155.56	1	0.25	0.043

Additional examples of the two interpretations will appear in the management discussion to follow. The management discussion that follows is intended to increase your familiarity with model interpretation by showing you how the Sensitivity Report might be employed in a realistic scenario. The orientation is managerial, with an emphasis on the sensitivity information and its use. Place yourself in the position of the manager at Eastern Steel who is responsible for planning future production. A number of questions are on your mind. The modeler responds.

MANAGER: First of all, what is the solution to our LP model?

By "solution" I take it you mean the optimal values of the decision variables. You can see that the rounded optimal values (cells B3:E3) are T1 = 0.26, T2 = 0.70, T3 = 0.04, T4, = 0.00. You can also see that the minimum cost is $511.11 (cell F4).

MANAGER: I'd like to keep my costs under $500 per ton. Isn't there any way I can do this? I see a column labeled Surplus.

If it were possible to find a lower-cost mixture that satisfies the constraints you have imposed, Solver would have found it. For convenience the column is labeled "Surplus," but in general it means "slack or surplus," whichever is appropriate. In this case the Surplus column lists the amounts by which you have exceeded your requirements.

MANAGER: Well, maybe I can modify those requirements. The surplus for constraint A is zero (cell I6) and the requirement on A was 5 pounds. This means that exactly 5 pounds of A is produced per ton. And since the surplus in cell I8 is zero, the optimal mix must contain exactly 30 pounds of C. However, for B in cell I7, I see a surplus of 31.67, and so, it must be that the constraint is not binding and we are overproducing B.

That's correct, this means that in the optimal mix the minimum B *requirement of 100 pounds is actually exceeded by 31.67. That is, there are 131.67 pounds of* B *actually included, as shown in cell F7.*

MANAGER: Isn't that odd? You'd think I could make a cheaper blend by using less B. Why should I use more than 100 pounds if I need only 100?

That is a very good question. You see, the combination of ores that satisfies the requirements on A *and* C *at a minimum cost just happens to contain more than 100 pounds of* B*. Any combination of ores that includes less* B *will either not have enough of* A *and/or* C*, or, if it does have enough, it will cost more than $511.11 per ton. In other words, forcing yourself to include less of the excess amount of* B *while still satisfying the requirements on* A *and* C *will end up costing you more. You may have to think about that assertion, but it is exactly what Solver's solution to the model is telling us.*

MANAGER: I see your point; but how can I get my total cost down to $500 or less?

You will have to loosen your constraints. This means loosening the requirements on A *or* C.

MANAGER: Why not on B?

Because, in order to satisfy the requirements on A *and* C *at minimum cost, you're already including over 100 pounds of* B*, which is more than your minimal threshold. In other words, the requirement on* B *is not binding. You could loosen this requirement to a smaller number, such as 98, and the optimal mix would still contain the same composition and cost. Thus, loosening the requirement on* B *to a smaller number won't get us anywhere. You have to loosen one of the binding requirements to affect total cost.*

MANAGER: Okay. So I have to relax the requirement on *A* or *C*. But which one? And how much?

We can use the information under the "Shadow Price" heading of the Sensitivity Report to analyze these questions. It means rate of change in the OV as we increase the right-hand side. Since we are interested in loosening a ≥ constraint, we will be decreasing the right-hand side. Now let's look at the shadow price on constraint A. *It is +44.44. The positive sign means that as the right-hand side is increased the OV cost is increased or hurt. Thus, as the right-hand side is loosened, or decreased, the OV is improved. What all of this boils down to is the common-sense idea that, as your requirement for* A *is loosened, your minimum cost will go down. The shadow price tells us it goes down at the rate of $44.44 per decreased pound of* A.

MANAGER: Loosening the requirement for *A* must mean reducing it from 5 pounds to something less. And the shadow price of +44.44 says that for each pound of reduction that total cost goes down $44.44. So, if I require only 4 pounds per ton of *A*, instead of 5, the cost goes down to about $466.67 and I'm well under $500. If I cut the requirement to just 4.5 pounds, I'd save ($^1/_2$)(44.44), which is over $22, and my final cost would still be under $500! Right?

Well, you're right in spirit. You have the correct rate of change, but this rate applies only to some interval of values around the original value of 5, but the appropriate interval may not allow you to analyze the decrease of a whole unit—or even half a unit.

MANAGER: I see. In the Allowable Decrease column for constraint *A* we have 0.25. That must mean I can analyze a change from 5 down to only 4.75. So my saving would be (0.25) (44.44), which is $ 11.11, and this gets me down exactly to $500. But what if I relaxed the requirement a little more, like to 4.5. Wouldn't that reduce the cost further?

Probably, but I can't tell you exactly how much because the rate of change may be different after a decrease of 0.25; in other words, the shadow price may change.

MANAGER: Now just to see if I have it all straight, let me analyze the potential savings if I relax the requirement on *C*. The original right-hand side is 30. The Sensitivity Report shows an allowable decrease of 7, so I can go down to 23. The corresponding shadow price is +4.44. This is my rate of savings as I decrease the right-hand side from 30. Hence, if I decrease the requirement to 23, I save (7)(4.44) = $31.08. This also gets me well under $500. In fact, if I cut down the requirement only 2.5 pounds, I can apply the same rate of change, and consequently I should save (2.5)(4.44) = $11.10, and this just about gets me down to a cost of $500. How am I doing?

Very well.

MANAGER: Okay. I see that I can get the cost per ton down to $500 if I relax the requirement on *A* to 4.75 pounds per ton *or* the requirement on *C* to 27.5 pounds per ton. But what if I relax both requirements on *A* and *C*, perhaps a little less but both at the same time? Then what?

Sorry, but again we don't have precise information on the Sensitivity Report to answer that. When you interpret the shadow price on one of the right-hand-side values, it's important to keep the others unchanged. The only way to tackle the question of what happens when you simultaneously change several right-hand sides would be to re-solve the model numerous times, using a tool like SolverTable, with different right-hand sides for A *and* C.

MANAGER: So let me review this. I know that I can get my cost per ton down to $500 if I relax the requirement on *A* to 4.75 pounds per ton *or* the requirement on *C* to 27.5 pounds per ton. Which should I do?

The Sensitivity Report alone cannot give you a guideline on that. The point is that you, as the manager, have to decide on which change would do more harm to the properties of the final blend, and that is really an engineering question.

MANAGER: Right. By the way, I assume the column that says "Allowable Increase" pertains to increases in the right-hand side. Would you just run through the analysis on the increase side to make sure that I'm with you?

Let's take the requirement on A. *Suppose that you want to tighten this requirement.*

MANAGER: Since we are dealing with a greater than or equal to constraint, tightening would mean an increase in the right-hand side, which is the required amount of *A*.

Correct. Tightening a requirement can never help the OV and may hurt. In this case the shadow price of +44.44 tells us that increasing the right-hand side will hurt by driving the optimal total cost up. The allowable increase of 2.375 tells us that if we increase the original amount, 5, by any amount up to 2.375, the increase in cost is given by 44.44 times that amount.

MANAGER: In other words, the same shadow price pertains to both increases and decreases in the right-hand side. So, the shadow price is the rate of change in the objective value as the right-hand side increases over that entire allowable range.

Right. And loosening a constraint will always mean that the OV cannot be hurt and may be improved. Tightening means that the OV cannot be improved and may be hurt.

MANAGER: I notice that the shadow price on *B* is zero, which means that any within range changes in the value of 100 don't have any effect. Since it doesn't affect the solution, could the constraint on *B* be discarded?

I would think not. If later you would ever want to change some of the data and then re-solve the model, the constraint on B *could become binding. In particular, we can see from the Allowable Increase of 31.67 that if the RHS were to exceed 131.67, this constraint would become binding. So I don't really want to say that it can be removed from the model.*

MANAGER: Could you be a little more explicit?

All right. Just as an example, suppose that the cost of ore from location 2 might increase.

MANAGER: Well, I must admit that such a possibility is something I'm concerned about. But I don't see how we can take that kind of uncertainty into account.

This relates to your question. The cost of ore from location 2 is the coefficient of T2 in the objective function, namely 400. If this cost is increased, we would expect our optimal minimum cost to increase. If the cost of ore from location 2 goes up enough, we might even expect that less of it, or maybe even none of it, would be used in the optimal blend. This means more of the others must be used because the total amount used has to sum up to 1 ton. This means that the relative importance of the constraints could change. Previous constraints that had been binding might not be, and vice versa. A lot of things can happen when you start playing with the data.

MANAGER: Fine. But I'm still confused. What does all this have to do with the cost of ore from location 2?

Let's look at the cost of ore from location 2. We can actually determine the range over which this cost can vary without influencing the optimal blend. In particular, look at the portion of the Sensitivity Report labeled "Adjustable Cells." In the row corresponding to T2 there are items called Allowable Increase and Allowable Decrease. This gives the range in which the cost of T2 can vary without changing the optimal mix.

MANAGER: Okay. In other words, the cost of T2 is now \$400 in our model, and the Sensitivity Report says it could be anywhere between \$100 and \$466.85 and the optimal mix stays the same. So if the cost increases from \$400 to, say, \$450, we have nothing to worry about.

Well, I don't know about that. We know that the optimal mix will stay the same. This means that the optimal values of all the variables stay the same. But our total cost will increase by \$50 times the amount of T2 being used in the current solution.

MANAGER: I see. The OV will go from the old value, \$511.11, to the new value 511.11 + (50)(0.704) = \$546.31, because within the range everything stays the same except the total cost. By the way, what happens if the cost of *T2* increases by more than the allowable amount?

Well, since we have a Min model I know that increasing the cost of an input cannot increase its use. Therefore, as the cost of T2 increases I know that the optimal value of T2 can never increase.

MANAGER: So, if the per unit cost of ore from mine 2 increases by more than its allowable amount, we will get an optimal solution with the same or a smaller value of T2.

Yes. And not only that. The optimal values of some of the other variables may also change, but it isn't possible to say exactly which ones or how much. This means that a surplus that was positive could become zero, and hence a constraint that was nonbinding could become binding, and vice versa.

MANAGER: You're talking about a cost change that *exceeds* the allowable limit. What if it actually hits the limit?

Then we know that there will be alternative optimal solutions, the current solution together with a new one that has less T2 in it.

MANAGER: Well, it seems to me that we have considerable information about the influence of uncertainty. That strikes me as remarkable. In fact, I'm amazed at how much we can learn about the actual model, above and beyond the solution.

Right. That is because of the ease of computing sensitivity information for linear models. By the way, do you mind if I ask you just one question to more or less check you out?

You have already noticed on the output that the optimal value of T4 is zero, and I happen to know that it isn't unreasonable to renegotiate the cost of T4 periodically. How much would the cost of T4 have to decrease before you're willing to buy some?

MANAGER: Let's see. The current cost of *T4* is \$500 per ton. I think what you're trying to ask is: How much must this cost decrease before we obtain an optimal solution that uses *T4*? To find the answer I look at the Sensitivity Report, where I see that if the cost of *T4* decreases by less than \$91.11 per ton, then, according to what you just said, the optimal value of this variable remains unchanged at zero. Consequently, I know that if its cost is negotiated down to 408.89 or less, there will be an optimal solution with *T4* positive. But what happens if the reduction exactly equals 91.11? You've told me that in this case the optimal value of *T4* will become positive. Is that right?

Not quite. There will be two optimal extreme point or corner solutions: the current one, and another one that has a positive optimal value of T4 *and some new values for some of the other variables. But I don't know exactly how the others will change.*

MANAGER: Okay, but does this mean that when the cost of *T4* is reduced by exactly $91.11, the total cost suddenly drops down from $511.11?

No, since these are alternative optima the OV equals 511.11 at each.

MANAGER: Can we tell how much of *T4* will be used in the alternative optimum?

I'm afraid not from the Sensitivity Report. All we know is that there will be some positive value for this variable. To find out its precise value we would have to re-solve the model for a reduction in the cost of T4 *just barely more than $91.11.*

MANAGER: I have to ask one final question. What about that column under the heading "Reduced Cost"? What does Reduced Cost mean?

A decision variable's reduced cost entry is really meaningful only when the reduced cost is nonzero. For a decision variable whose optimal value is zero, there are two equivalent interpretations of its reduced cost. For a minimization model like this one, reduced cost (1) tells how much the objective function unit cost entry for that decision variable can be reduced before the optimal value of the variable will become nonzero, or equivalently, reduced cost (2) is the shadow price on that decision variable's ≥0 nonnegativity constraint. To elaborate on (2), recall that if the decision variable is zero, then that variable's negativity constraint is binding, and consistent with shadow price interpretation, the reduced cost is thus also the rate at which OV would be hurt if we overruled the Solver solution and forced that decision variable to increase above zero by raising the RHS of the ≥0 nonnegativity constraint above zero.

Interpretation (1) is sometimes called a "reward" interpretation—how much the unit cost must improve before Solver will increase that decision variable above zero to lower total costs. Interpretation (2) is sometimes called a "penalty" interpretation—how much the solution would be hurt if you forced Solver to increase that decision variable above zero.

MANAGER: Well, interpretation (1) refers to changes in objective function coefficients, and we just answered that question about *T4*. In fact, looking at the "Allowable Decrease" part of the Sensitivity Report, I see that exactly the same value, 91.11, appears in both places. So why bother with the reduced-cost entry if the same value appears under the "Allowable Decrease" column?

You are correct, interpretation (1) of reduced cost refers to changes in objective function coefficients, and so, the identical information will always appear under one or the other of the Allowable change columns of the report. However, putting the reduced cost information in the same Sensitivity Report column as the other shadow prices reminds you of the equivalent interpretation (2), the penalty interpretation that regards reduced cost as a shadow price. You are free to choose whichever interpretation you feel most comfortable with. That's all there is to it.

MANAGER: Thank you. It's been very instructive!

4.11 A SYNOPSIS OF THE SOLVER SENSITIVITY REPORT

When an LP model built according to our recommendations is optimized, the Solver-optimized worksheet and Sensitivity Report contain the following information:

1. Optimal values are given for the decision variables, the slack and surplus variables, and the objective function. From the total LHS amounts you can quickly deduce the values of the constraint functions (the amount of resources used, the levels of requirements satisfied, and so on) at an optimal solution. The constraints with zero slack or surplus are called *binding*, and thus prevent further payoff improvement. Those with positive slack or surplus are called *nonbinding*.
2. In the Sensitivity Report the Shadow Price tells you the rate of change in the OV (optimal value of the objective function) as the right-hand side (RHS) of a constraint increases. Allowable Increase and Decrease give you an allowable range in RHS changes over which the given shadow price is valid.
3. The Allowable Increase and Decrease of Objective Coefficients tell you the allowable changes that can be made in the objective function coefficients without changing the optimal solution (the optimal values of the variables). If an objective function coefficient is changed by an amount that *equals* an allowable change, there will be an alternative optimal corner point solution with new values for the variables (assuming nondegeneracy). If the coefficient is changed by an amount that *exceeds* the allowable change, there will be a new optimal solution (assuming nondegeneracy).
4. Strictly speaking, "Reduced Cost" applies only to a decision variable whose optimal value is zero. In this case, it can be interpreted as the shadow price on the nonnegativity constraint for that variable, if present, and provides the same information as deduced from the Allowable Increase or Decrease information for this variable. If the Reduced Cost value *and* the decision variable are both nonzero, then some given upper or lower bound constraint directly that decision variable is binding and the Reduced Cost is the shadow price on that binding constraint instead of on the nonnegativity constraint.[14]
5. Investigation of changes in technical coefficients or for model behavior outside of the Allowable Increase or Decrease limits involves changes beyond the scope of the Sensitivity Report thus requiring use of SolverTable to tabulate such data from a sequence of re-optimized models.

4.12 SENSITIVITY REPORT INTERPRETATION FOR ALTERNATIVE LP MODELS, A CAUTIONARY TALE

The recommendations for laying out the spreadsheet LP models that we have been using since Chapter 3 are a bit restrictive and sometimes lead to a worksheet layout that is not compact and not managerially pleasing. Like the Transportation example in Chapter 3, and beginning with the next chapter on applications of LP modeling, we want to expose you to several more compact and appealing worksheet layouts of LP models. As you might guess, there are some prices to pay for using an appealing model representation: You must exercise a bit more care in model building, and especially, in interpreting the Sensitivity Report provided by Solver to avoid some nasty pitfalls. However, by now you should be somewhat comfortable with the steps for LP spreadsheet model formulation and Sensitivity Report interpretation and can accommodate to these added demands. The new modeling and interpretation pitfalls are best illustrated by a simple example.

Wayne Foley, recently promoted to manager of the newest branch of the Friendly Loan Company, is eager to please his new boss by loaning his annual $15 million budget prof-

[14] This confusing wrinkle pertaining to Reduced Cost entries is given additional coverage in Section 4.12.

itably. Each local branch office at Friendly generates profit by the interest income from three types of loans, First Mortgage loans on real estate at 7% annual interest, Furniture loans collateralized by liens on home furnishings at 12% annual interest, and Signature loans with no collateral at 15% annual interest. Having the highest risk, Signature loans carry the highest loan interest rate.

Friendly's home office has set loan limits to guide branch managers and to protect the company from excessive amounts of high-risk loans. Friendly requires each branch manager to place at least 60% of its loans into First Mortgages and no more than 10% of its loans in risky Signature loans. Using these loan interest rates, loan policy limitations, and the $15 million loan budget allocated to him for the upcoming year, Wayne has built the LP model in Figure 4.31, which displays his model, its formulas, the Solver dialog, and the optimal allocation of his loan budget.

Notice several features of Wayne's model. First, it is compact; there are no unnecessary calculations for LHS values, and for readability, the constraints are immediately adjacent to the quantities they affect. Next Wayne has shaded all the empty cells in his spreadsheet to help focus your attention on the relevant parts of his model, a nice aesthetic. Finally, Wayne is cleverly making some cells do double duty, both as a RHS value and as an inequality symbol. For example, cell G5 actually contains the $15 million budget datum, as is clear from the formulas printout in Figure 4.31. The "<=" appearing in G5 is *not* in the cell, but is part of that cell's formatting specification, called a "format dressing." Format dressing allows user-defined strings of characters to be displayed just like currency symbols, for example. Similar formatting was applied to the formula cells, C6 and E6. (See Appendix B for details on cell format dressing.) He has also included a side calculation for the average return of

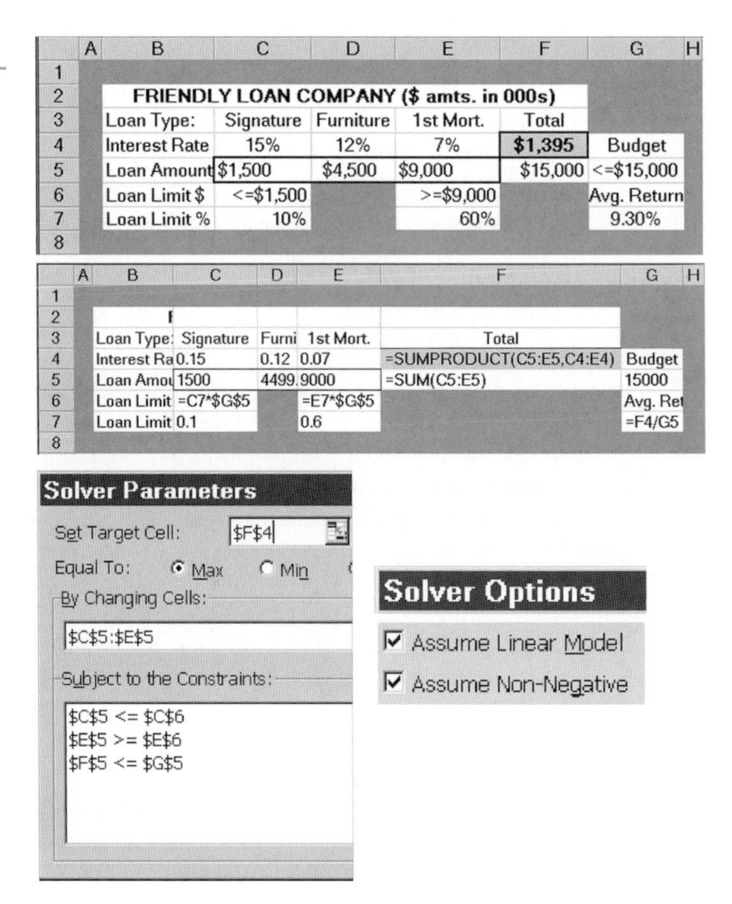

	A	B	C	D	E	F	G	H
1								
2		FRIENDLY LOAN COMPANY ($ amts. in 000s)						
3		Loan Type:	Signature	Furniture	1st Mort.	Total		
4		Interest Rate	15%	12%	7%	$1,395	Budget	
5		Loan Amount	$1,500	$4,500	$9,000	$15,000	<=$15,000	
6		Loan Limit $	<=$1,500		>=$9,000		Avg. Return	
7		Loan Limit %	10%		60%		9.30%	
8								

	A	B	C	D	E	F	G	H
1								
2		F						
3		Loan Type:	Signature	Furni	1st Mort.	Total		
4		Interest Ra	0.15	0.12	0.07	=SUMPRODUCT(C5:E5,C4:E4)	Budget	
5		Loan Amou	1500	4499.	9000	=SUM(C5:E5)	15000	
6		Loan Limit	=C7*$G$5		=E7*$G$5		Avg. Ret	
7		Loan Limit	0.1		0.6		=F4/G5	
8								

FIGURE 4.31

Wayne's Loan Portfolio Model

his loan portfolio in cell G7 (=F4/G5). Before proceeding, verify for yourself that Wayne's model correctly captures the three mandated constraint limits on Budget, Signature, and First Mortgage loan amounts.

Not surprisingly, the Solver solution to Wayne's LP model loans out all $15 million, placing $9 million into First Mortgages, $1.5 million into Signature loans, and the balance into Furniture loans to yield annual Total interest income of $1,395,000. Wayne's side calculation in cell G7 shows an average return of 9.3% for his loan portfolio. Wayne also notes that all three constraints in the model are binding (two policy constraints on loan types and one budget constraint).

Eager to apply his new-found LP modeling knowledge, Wayne reviews the model's Solver Sensitivity Report in Figure 4.32 and, seeing the shadow price on his budget constraint, immediately reaches for the phone to call his boss to ask for a bigger loan budget. Surprised by Wayne's claim that he can produce a 12% return on any additional budget allocation, Wayne's boss comments that no other branch manager can produce more than about $9\frac{1}{3}$% overall return. "That's because they don't understand optimization, marginal analysis, and the power of shadow prices," Wayne retorts. Not wanting to dampen the enthusiasm of his new strange-talking branch manager, the boss asks if Wayne can generate this 12% return for another $5,000,000. Quickly checking the Allowable Increase amount on the budget constraint, Wayne confidently tells his boss to "send all $5,000,000 and more" to the branch.

As he hangs up the phone, however, Wayne begins to feel a bit uneasy. "There certainly are three constraints listed in my model's Solver dialog box in addition to the required non-negativity condition. What happened to the two binding loan-type constraints in the Sensitivity Report? Instead of one, shouldn't there be three constraints listed along with their shadow prices in the Sensitivity Report?" he asks himself. As his uneasiness turns to fear, he elects to verify Solver's Sensitivity Report information by typing his new budget limit, 20,000, into cell G5. He runs Solver again for this new RHS limit, producing the results in Figure 4.33. Fear turns to shock as Wayne notices that the Average Return in cell G7 for the re-optimized model is unchanged at 9.3%. Since the marginal return on the extra $5 million is 12%, he reasons that the average return for his new portfolio should have gone up.

No longer trusting either Solver or Excel, Wayne grabs his calculator and taps out (1860–1395)/5000, the difference in Total interest income from the two Solver solutions divided by the incremental budget amount, verifying what he already suspects—that the marginal return for the extra $5 million is actually 9.3% and not 12%. Looking skeptically at the budget constraint's shadow price and range information in the new model's Sensitivity Report in Figure 4.33, Wayne concludes that, unbelievably, Solver has lied to him twice. Sheepishly, Wayne reaches for the phone to offer his boss a mea culpa.

What happened? Are the data poorly scaled, producing erroneous Solver reports? If not, does Solver indeed lie or mislead for some models? If it doesn't, how do you explain the .120 budgetary shadow prices in Figure 4.32 and Figure 4.33, given the results Wayne

FIGURE 4.32

Sensitivity Report for Wayne's Loan Portfolio Model

Microsoft Excel 8.0 Sensitivity Report

Adjustable Cells

Cell	Name	Final Value	Reduced Cost	Objective Coefficient	Allowable Increase	Allowable Decrease
$C$5	Loan Amount Signature	$1,500	0.030	15%	1E+30	0.03
$D$5	Loan Amount Furniture	$4,500	0.000	12%	0.03	0.05
$E$5	Loan Amount 1st Mort.	$9,000	-0.050	7%	0.05	1E+30

Constraints

Cell	Name	Final Value	Shadow Price	Constraint R.H. Side	Allowable Increase	Allowable Decrease
$F$5	Loan Amount Total	$15,000	0.120	$15,000	1E+30	4500

FIGURE 4.33

Wayne's Loan Portfolio Model for $20 million Budget

	A	B	C	D	E	F	G	H
1								
2		FRIENDLY LOAN COMPANY ($ amts. in 000s)						
3		Loan Type:	Signature	Furniture	1st Mort.	Total		
4		Interest Rate	15%	12%	7%	$1,860	Budget	
5		Loan Amount	$2,000	$6,000	$12,000	$20,000	<=$20,000	
6		Loan Limit $	<=$2,000		>=$12,000		Avg. Return	
7		Loan Limit %	10%		60%		9.30%	
8								

Microsoft Excel 8.0 Sensitivity Report

Adjustable Cells

Cell	Name	Final Value	Reduced Cost	Objective Coefficient	Allowable Increase	Allowable Decrease
$C$5	Loan Amount Signature	$2,000	0.03	15%	1E+30	0.03
$D$5	Loan Amount Furniture	$6,000	0.00	12%	0.03	0.05
$E$5	Loan Amount 1st Mort.	$12,000	-0.05	7%	0.05	1E+30

Constraints

Cell	Name	Final Value	Shadow Price	Constraint R.H. Side	Allowable Increase	Allowable Decrease
$F$5	Loan Amount Total	$20,000	0.120	$20,000	1E+30	6000

produced by re-solving? And what did happen to the shadow price information for the other two loan-type constraints missing from Wayne's Solver Sensitivity Report?

Although always worthy of suspicion, in this case the range of data in Wayne's model is not wide enough to cause numerical problems within Solver, as checking the Use Automatic Scaling box in Solver's Options dialog and re-solving will verify. To understand more clearly what happened to poor Wayne, let us reformulate the model using the recommended formulation rules from Chapter 3, as shown in Figure 4.34, which displays the optimal solution and its Sensitivity Report.

Clearly the two LP formulations produce the same optimal loan decisions and total interest income as shown in Figure 4.31 and Figure 4.34. The differences pertain to the models' Sensitivity Report and its interpretation. To answer the other questions above note the following for the results of the LP model built by the rules of Chapter 3. First, immediately apparent in Figure 4.34 is the presence of all three constraints in the Sensitivity Report and their associated shadow prices and ranges of RHS changes. Second, the shadow price for the Wayne's budget constraint in Figure 4.34 is the correct marginal value (9.3%). Third, for those of you who have mastered the optional Enrichment Topics on degeneracy on the book's CD-ROM, the solution to either formulation is not degenerate, as easily verified by counting the total non-zero decision variables and slacks (=3) in Figure 4.34 and comparing that to the number of constraints (=3). And fourth, in contrast to the Sensitivity Report of Wayne's model, the Reduced Cost column in Figure 4.34 correctly lists zeros for all three decision variables, because none of the decision variables are zero, that is, none of their nonnegativity constraints are binding.

Of course, all this implies that Wayne's original Sensitivity Report in Figure 4.32 is misleadingly bad—with its missing shadow prices and ranges, incorrect reduced cost numbers, and an erroneous budgetary shadow price—and that the recommended LP formulation of Figure 4.34 is good. On the other hand, Wayne's spreadsheet model layout in Figure 4.31 is certainly managerially easier to understand and interpret than the recommended spreadsheet formulation of Figure 4.34. It would seem that you must make a Hobson's choice: a pleasing and compact managerial layout of the LP model coupled with confusing or erroneous sensitivity results, or a rigid layout of the model coupled with correct sensitivity results. Paradoxically, this is not the case; both models are completely correct, and *neither*

FIGURE 4.34

Wayne's Loan Portfolio Model Using Rules from Chapter 3

	A	B	C	D	E	F	G	H	I	J
1										
2		FRIENDLY LOAN COMPANY ($ amts. in 000's)								
3		Loan Type:	Signature	Furniture	1st Mort.	Budget	Total			
4		Interest Rate	15%	12%	7%		$1,395			
5		Loan Amount	$1,500	$4,500	$9,000	$15,000				
6		Constraints					Total	RHS	Slack	
7		Budget				1	$15,000	<=$15,000	0.0	
8		Sign. Limit	1			-10%	0.0	<=0	0.0	
9		Mortg. Min.			1	-60%	0.0	>=0	0.0	
10										

	A	B	C	D	E	F	G	H	I	J
1										
2		FRIEN								
3		Loan T	Signatu	Furniture	1st Mo	Budget	Total			
4		Interes	0.15	0.12	0.07		=SUMPRODUCT($C$5:$E$5,C4:E4)			
5		Loan A	1500	4500	9000	=SUM(C5:E5)				
6		Constr					Total	RHS	Slack	
7		Budge				1	=SUMPRODUCT($C$5:$F$5,C7:F7)	15000	=H7-G7	
8		Sign. L	1			-0.1	=SUMPRODUCT($C$5:$F$5,C8:F8)	0	=H8-G8	
9		Mortg.			1	-0.6	=SUMPRODUCT($C$5:$F$5,C9:F9)	0	=G9-H9	
10										

Microsoft Excel 8.0 Sensitivity Report

Adjustable Cells

Cell	Name	Final Value	Reduced Cost	Objective Coefficient	Allowable Increase	Allowable Decrease
$C$5	Loan Amount Signature	$1,500	0.00	15%	1E+30	0.03
$D$5	Loan Amount Furniture	$4,500	0.00	12%	0.03	0.05
$E$5	Loan Amount 1st Mort.	$9,000	0.00	7%	0.05	0.155

Constraints

Cell	Name	Final Value	Shadow Price	Constraint R.H. Side	Allowable Increase	Allowable Decrease
$G$7	Budget Total	$15,000	0.093	$15,000	1E+30	15000
$G$8	Sign. Limit Total	0	0.030	0	4500	1500
$G$9	Mortg. Min. Total	0	-0.050	0	4500	9000

Sensitivity Report contains any errors whatsoever. That is, you can have the benefits of a more managerially appealing model layout in the spreadsheet without producing any Solver-related errors in the Sensitivity Report. But this requires a bit more understanding of Solver that, unfortunately, Wayne lacked. So, to resolve the paradox let us delve a little more into Solver's workings.

SIMPLE UPPER AND LOWER BOUNDS

The time and memory requirements for Solver to optimize a model are determined primarily by the size of the coefficient matrix of cells making up the LHS of the set of constraints, for example, C7:F9 in Figure 4.34. The size of this constraint coefficient matrix is proportional to the product of the number of decision variables (columns) and the number of constraints (rows). Anything that can be done to reduce either of these numbers will have a multiplicitive effect in reducing the overall matrix size, and hence, the speed of optimization. Solver incorporates an advanced procedure that allows any upper or lower constraint bounds directly on the decision variables (in addition to the nonnegativity bounds) to be honored without actually considering them as constraints. This treatment of decision variable bounds, called "simple upper and lower bounds," keeps the coefficient matrix smaller, producing faster Solver optimization times while consuming less RAM memory on the PC, or equivalently, allowing larger LP models to be optimized on a given PC. The price paid for the use of this simple upper and lower bounds feature is the loss of some

Sensitivity Report information produced after optimization. The only sensitivity information available for any simple upper and lower bound constraints are their shadow prices, but without the associated range-of-applicability information produced for shadow prices on a normal constraint.

Since, at most, only one upper or lower bound constraint can be binding on a given decision variable at optimality, and no range information is available, a compact Sensitivity Report results if the relevant non-zero shadow price on a simple upper or lower bound constraint, if any, is listed next to its associated decision variable. The Reduced Cost column in the Sensitivity Report always has one cell per decision variable, and so, Solver places any non-zero shadow price on an upper or lower bound constraint into the Reduced Cost column next to the relevant decision variable. For example, the shadow prices on the two loan-type constraints are given in the conventional way in Figure 4.34 as 3% and –5% on the Signature and First Mortgage constraints, respectively. Those values are presented in Figure 4.32 for Wayne's model in the Reduced Cost column next to the Signature and First Mortgage decision variables, respectively. Since each of these two decision variables has two constraints given in the LP model, it is not immediately clear which bound is the binding one producing that variable's non-zero shadow price entry in the Reduced Cost column for Wayne's model.

The Signature loan amount has both a simple lower bound constraint (the "≥ 0" nonnegativity constraint) and a simple upper bound constraint ("≤ $1500"). However, both bounds on the Signature decision cannot be binding simultaneously. Inspection reveals that the upper bound is binding; and so, the 0.03 number in the Reduced Cost column of Wayne's model must be the shadow price on the "Signature ≤ $15000" constraint. Because it is not binding, the "Signature ≥ 0" constraint, therefore, must have a shadow price of zero.

Similarly, there are two lower bound constraints on the First Mortgage decision ("1st Mortgage ≥ 0" and "1st Mortgage ≥ 9000"), both of which cannot be binding. Since the First Mortgage decision is $9,000, the shadow price entry in the Reduced Cost column of Wayne's model must be for the binding "1st Mortgage ≥ 9000" simple lower bound constraint. Because it is not binding, the "1st Mortgage ≥ 0" constraint, therefore, must have a shadow price of zero.

Thus, there is no loss of shadow price information from utilizing simple upper and lower bounds in LP formulations once you know where to look for them and how to deduce the bound to which any non-zero shadow price refers. Since simple lower and upper bounds on decisions leads to a more appealing spreadsheet layout and faster solution times (noticeable for large models) their use is common in spreadsheet LP model formulations. Be aware, however, that their use produces Sensitivity Reports that violate the standard definition for "Reduced Cost" given in Section 4.10.

Recall one interpretation for the reduced cost on a decision variable represents it as the shadow price on that variable's nonnegativity constraint. Instead, the reduced cost numbers for Solver LP models containing simple upper and lower bounds are the shadow prices for whichever bound, if any, is binding on that decision variable. The table below gives a more complete picture of the values the Reduced Cost shadow price entry may have in Solver models containing simple upper and lower bounds.

VALUE OF DECISION VARIABLE AT OPTIMALITY	REDUCED COST ENTRY, MAXIMIZATION MODEL	REDUCED COST ENTRY, MINIMIZATION MODEL
Lower Bound (≥) Binding	Zero or Negative Shadow Price	Zero or Positive Shadow Price
Upper Bound (≤) Binding	Zero or Positive Shadow Price	Zero or Negative Shadow Price
Neither Bound Binding	Zero Shadow Price	Zero Shadow Price

Is there a way to deduce the RHS range information present in the Sensitivity Report of Figure 4.34 under the Allowable Increase and Decrease columns, but missing when simple upper and lower bounds are used? Unfortunately, the answer is "No." If that were possible, Solver would always present a Sensitivity Report like Figure 4.34. If the RHS range information for simple upper and lower bounds is important, then you must reformulate the spreadsheet representation of the LP model in Figure 4.31 to avoid Solver's detecting the presence of simple upper and lower bounds and re-optimize the model. Solver will not evoke its simple upper and lower bounding procedure if the upper or lower bound on any decision variable is specified indirectly on the worksheet. This "indirect reference" can be achieved by use of some intervening formula, such as the SUMPRODUCT formulas in Figure 4.34, which relate each decision variable to its bound via a third LHS cell. Otherwise, if Solver sees any "Changing Cells" cell references in the "Subject to the Constraints:" box of the Solver Parameters dialog (other than any nonnegativity ones), then it will evoke its special bounding procedure. For example, Wayne's model in Figure 4.31 references the Changing Cells, C5 and E5, in the first two constraints listed in the "Subject to the Constraints:" box of the Solver Parameters dialog, and that triggered Solver's upper and lower bounding procedure.

SHADOW PRICE INTERPRETATION

As mentioned earlier, the Solver shadow price on Wayne's budget constraint of .120 is *not* incorrect; rather, it was Wayne's interpretation of that shadow price that got him into trouble. Note that Wayne's model in Figure 4.34 has formulas on the right-hand side of the Loan Limit constraints for Signature and First Mortgage loans, a violation of one of the recommended spreadsheet formulation rules in Chapter 3. Recall the definition of a shadow price is the change in the LP's OV per unit of change in a given constraint's RHS value *holding all other data, including the other RHS's, constant.* Therefore, the shadow price of .120 reported in Wayne's Figure 4.32 Sensitivity Report should be interpreted as follows: Holding the Loan Limit RHS's for Signature and First Mortgage loans at their original dollar amount bounds of $1500 and $9000, respectively, the improvement in the objective function value is .12 for each additional budget dollar.

Holding Signature and First Mortgage loans at their original RHS dollar values allows the incremental budget dollar only one option in Wayne's model, to be allocated as a Furniture loan returning 12%. Thus, Solver is correctly reporting the shadow price for Wayne's model. Of course, holding the Signature and First Mortgage loans at their original RHS dollar values is inconsistent with the results of a re-optimized solution in which all *three* RHS's will be adjusted to reflect the revised RHS limits implied by an additional budget dollar. Wayne's mistake was assuming that Friendly's percentage policy constraints on loans would be maintained in his model's Sensitivity Report, but that is not true in his model because of the formulas appearing on two of his RHSs.

The LP formulation in Figure 4.34 avoids this mistaken interpretation by placing all formulas on the LHS of constraints leaving constants for all RHSs. Having the budget-related formulas on the LHS of constraints forces Solver to make the necessary adjustments in all three LHSs when evaluating an incremental budget dollar's contribution. This adjustment of the LHSs produces a Sensitivity Report yielding the correct .093 shadow price in Figure 4.34. Clearly, the formulation of Figure 4.34 reflects Wayne's intended model for Friendly's policy constraints.

The conclusion from this example is that the use of simple upper and lower bounds and the use of formulas on RHSs of LP formulations can lead to more compact and managerially appealing spreadsheet formulations of LP's. For these reasons, we will use such LP model formulations extensively in the applications of LP in the next three chapters. Keep in mind, however, that such formulations often require additional care in interpreting the managerially valuable information in Solver's Sensitivity Report.

4.13 SUMMARY

The powerful role of two-dimensional geometry in illustrating certain important concepts has been explained in this chapter. In particular, we used the geometric approach to solve LP models in two decision variables, to illustrate the meaning of binding and nonbinding constraints, to show the important connection between optimal solutions and corners to the feasible region, and finally, to illustrate pathological properties.

Using the GLP graphic optimizer we saw that the graphical solution method involves two main steps: determining the set of feasible decisions and then selecting the best of the decisions. We saw in Section 4.3 that if an LP has an optimal solution, there will always be at least one optimal corner solution, also called an extreme point solution.

The graphical solution method also demonstrated that it is only necessary to identify the binding constraints of the solution to an LP. Then, the optimal values of the decision variables are obtained by simultaneously solving these equations. From the geometric point of view, binding constraints were defined as those that pass through the optimal corner of the feasible region. Algebraically, a binding constraint is one for which the left-hand side, when evaluated at optimality, is equal to the right-hand side. *Surplus* and *slack* are terms used to denote the nonnegative difference between the two sides of an inequality constraint. The term *surplus* is often used for a ≥ constraint, and *slack* for a ≤ constraint.

Section 4.2 is devoted to a summary of the graphical solution method for a Max model, and in Section 4.4 we saw that the technique was easily extended to Min models. The only necessary modification for a Min model is to make sure that the contours of the objective contour are displaced in a downhill direction in the process of finding the best feasible decision.

Section 4.5 considered two pathological cases in which an LP model does not have an optimal solution. In an unbounded Max model the objective function can assume arbitrarily large values (arbitrarily negative values in an unbounded Min model). This typically implies that one or more important constraints have been omitted in formulating the model. An infeasible model is one in which there are no feasible solutions: that is, the set of decision variable values that satisfies all the constraints is empty. Such a result may occur because of incorrect formulation, such as insisting that two or more contradictory conditions must hold. Unbounded and infeasible models can also occur as a result of transcription errors made when entering the LP model into GLP, or in general, into the worksheet for Solver.

This chapter also used graphical analysis to introduce the topic of sensitivity analysis, which is also called postoptimality analysis. The general approach in sensitivity analysis is to assume that an LP model has been solved and then to investigate the effect of making various changes in the model. Typically, one is interested in the effect of the changes on the optimal solution and on the optimal value of the objective function.

In Section 4.7 we saw that changing the objective function coefficients changes the slope of the objective function contours. This may or may not affect the optimal solution. Section 4.8 dealt with changes in the right-hand side of the constraints. We first observed that changing a right-hand-side value results in a parallel shift of the changed constraint. This may effect both the optimal solution and the optimal objective value. The effect will depend on exactly which right-hand-side values are changed.

Changes in the right-hand side of an inequality constraint can be thought of as tightening or loosening the constraint. Tightening a constraint means making it more difficult to satisfy. For a ≥ constraint this means increasing the RHS. For a ≤ constraint this means decreasing the RHS. Similarly, loosening a constraint means making it easier to satisfy. For a ≥ constraint this means decreasing the RHS. For a ≤ constraint this means increasing the RHS. From a geometric point of view, tightening an inequality constraint either contracts the feasible region or leaves it unaffected. Loosening an inequality constraint either expands the feasible region or leaves it unaffected. From a practical point of view, these operations can further limit, further augment, or leave unchanged the options available to the manager.

The emphasis in this chapter was also on the interpretation of the Solver Sensitivity Report for an LP model. We stressed the wealth of information available through sensitivity analysis on the right-hand sides and on the objective function coefficients. In Section 4.9 we investigated the use of a powerful new tool, SolverTable, to allow more in-depth sensitivity analysis than that available from just the Sensitivity Report.

In Section 4.12 we explored the confusing Sensitivity Report results generated by Solver when upper or lower bounds are placed directly upon decision variables and the pitfalls in shadow price interpretation that may occur when placing Excel formulas on the RHS of constraints.

Key Terms

Contour. A contour of the function $f(x_1, x_2)$ is the set of all combinations of values for the variables (x_1, x_2) such that the function f takes on a specified constant value.

Isoprofit Line. A contour of a profit function.

Isocost Line. A contour of a cost function.

Graphical Solution Method. A two-dimensional geometric analysis of LP models with two decision variables.

Nonnegative Quadrant. The northeast sector of the two-dimensional coordinate system in which both variables have nonnegative values.

Feasible Region. The set of combinations of values for the decision variables that satisfies any nonnegativity conditions and *all* the constraints simultaneously, that is, the allowable decisions.

Constraint Set. A synonym for feasible region.

Feasible Solution. One that satisfies all the constraints. Graphically, the feasible solutions are in one-to-one correspondence with the points in the feasible region.

Optimizing Direction. The direction in which decisions with better objective function values lie.

Uphill Direction. The optimizing direction for a Max model.

Optimal Solution. A point in the feasible region that maximizes the objective function.

Solution. Same as optimal solution.

Unique Optimal Solution. Refers to the case in which an LP has one and only one optimal solution.

Maximum Isoprofit Line. The optimal contour of the objective function in a two-dimensional graphical analysis.

Optimal Objective Value (Optimal Value). The optimal value of the objective function: that is, the value of the objective function when evaluated at the optimal solution. Abbreviated as OV.

Binding Constraint. A constraint for which, when evaluated at optimality, the left-hand side equals the right-hand side. Geometrically, this corresponds to a constraint line on which the optimal solution lies.

Surplus. The amount by which the left-hand side of a $\geq$ constraint, when evaluated at optimality, exceeds the right-hand side. Surplus is always nonnegative.

Slack. The amount by which the left-hand side of a $\leq$ constraint, when evaluated at optimality, is less than the right-hand side. Slack is always nonnegative.

Extreme Point. Corner of the feasible region. If an LP has a solution, there is always at least one extreme point solution.

Alternative Optima. Refers to the case in which an optimization model has more than one optimal solution.

Multiple Optima. A synonym for alternative optima.

Downhill Direction. The optimizing direction for a Min model.

Unbounded Objective Function. An objective function that, over the feasible region, can be made arbitrarily large (positive) for a Max model, or arbitrarily negative for a Min model.

Unbounded Model. An LP model for which the optimal value can be increased without limit. Such a model has no solution.

Unbounded Feasible Region. Feasible region in which at least one decision variable can be made arbitrarily large in value.

Infeasibility. A term referring to an infeasible model.

Inconsistency. A synonym for infeasibility.

Infeasible Model. An LP model with an empty feasible region. Such a model has no solution.

Sensitivity Analysis. Analyzing the effect on the model, in particular the effect on the optimal solution and the optimal value of the objective function, of changes in various parameters.

Parametric Analysis. A synonym for sensitivity analysis.

Postoptimality Analysis. Another synonym for sensitivity analysis.

Technical Coefficients. Cofficients that multiply the decision variables to create the formulas for the left hand sides in constraint equations.

Parameters. Refers to the numerical data in an LP model. The values of the parameters may change, and the model may be re-solved with these changed values.

Tightening a Constraint. Refers to changes in the RHS of an inequality constraint that make the constraint more difficult to satisfy. This is accomplished by increasing the RHS of a ≥ constraint and decreasing the RHS of a ≤ constraint.

Loosening a Constraint. Refers to changes in the RHS of an inequality constraint that make the constraint easier to satisfy. This is accomplished by decreasing the RHS of a ≥ constraint and increasing the RHS of a ≤ constraint.

Redundant Constraint. A constraint whose removal does not change the feasible region.

Slack or Surplus Variable. Used to convert an inequality constraint to an equality constraint.

Degenerate Solution. An LP solution for which the number of positive-valued variables (counting both the decision variables plus the slack or surplus variables) is less than the number of constraints. A degenerate solution is usually signaled by shadow price(s) with zero allowable increase or decrease.

Nondegenerate Solution. An LP solution for which the number of positive-valued variables (counting both the decision variables plus the slack or surplus variables) is equal to the number of constraints. A nondegenerate solution is usually signaled by having all shadow price(s) with non-zero allowable increase and decrease values.

Shadow Price. The *i*th shadow price on the Solver Sensitivity Report is the rate of change in OV as the *i*th RHS is increased.

Allowable RHS Range. Range of RHS values for which the shadow price remains constant.

Alternative Optimal Solutions. The existence of more than one optimal solution, a synonym for alternative optima or multiple optima.

Objective Coefficient Ranges. Gives ranges of objective function coefficients over which no change in the optimal solution will occur.

Self-Review Exercises

True-False

1. **T F** The feasible region is the set of all points that satisfy at least one constraint.
2. **T F** In two-dimensional models, the intersection of any two constraints gives an extreme point of the feasible region.
3. **T F** An optimal solution uses up all of the limited resources available.
4. **T F** A well-formulated model will be neither unbounded nor infeasible.
5. **T F** Infeasibility, as opposed to unboundedness, has nothing to do with the objective function.
6. **T F** If an LP is not infeasible, it will have an optimal solution.
7. **T F** Consider any point on the boundary of the feasible region. Such a point satisfies all the constraints.
8. **T F** A binding inequality constraint has zero slack or surplus, which means that the optimal solution satisfies the constraint with equality.
9. **T F** Sensitivity analysis greatly increases the possibility that a model can be useful to management.
10. **T F** Consider a model in which, for some of the data, we know there is error. For example, some of the data represent estimates of future values for certain parameters. Suppose sensitivity analysis reveals that the OV is highly sensitive to these parameters. Such information provides more confidence in the recommendations of the model.
11. **T F** Sensitivity analysis is a precise tool.
12. **T F** Changing the RHS of a constraint changes its slope.
13. **T F** Changing an RHS cannot affect the set of nonbinding constraints.
14. **T F** Loosening an inequality constraint means changing the RHS to make it easier to satisfy.
15. **T F** A ≥ constraint is tightened by increasing the RHS.
16. **T F** Tightening a redundant inequality constraint cannot affect the feasible region.
17. **T F** For a given set of data, the nonbinding constraints are less important than the binding ones.
18. **T F** Adding constraints to a model may help (i.e., improve) the OV.
19. **T F** If a ≤ constraint is nonbinding, the associated slack is negative.
20. **T F** The occurrence of alternative optima in a solution is important because we must give more restrictive interpretations to the Solver Sensitivity Report.
21. **T F** The shadow price for a given constraint is the rate of change in OV as its RHS increases.
22. **T F** The shadow price on the *i*th constraint is a nonconstant linear function of the *i*th RHS value over the range given by allowable decrease and allowable increase.
23. **T F** Nonzero slack for a constraint at optimality indicates it is redundant.
24. **T F** A ≤ constraint with positive optimal slack will always have an infinite allowable increase for the RHS.

The following two questions refer to the spreadsheet output shown in Figure 4.30:

25. **T F** If the requirements on *A* and *C* are each increased by 0.5 pound, sensitivity analysis tells us that the optimal cost will increase by $24.44.
26. **T F** The fact that the shadow prices are all ≥ 0 is exclusively explained by the fact that we are dealing with a Min model.

Answers

1. F, **2.** F, **3.** F, **4.** T, **5.** T, **6.** F, **7.** T, **8.** T, **9.** T, **10.** F, **11.** T, **12.** F, **13.** F, **14.** T, **15.** T, **16.** F, **17.** T, **18.** F, **19.** F, **20.** F, **21.** T, **22.** F, **23.** T, **24.** T, **25.** F, **26.** F

Multiple Choice

27. The graphical method is useful because
a. it provides a general way to solve LP models
b. it gives geometric insight into the model and the meaning of optimality
c. both a and b

28. The phrase unbounded LP means that
a. all decision variables can be made arbitrarily large without leaving the feasible region
b. the objective contours can be moved as far as desired in the optimizing direction and still touch at least one point in the feasible region
c. not all of the constraints can be satisfied

29. Consider an optimal solution to an LP. Which of the following must be true?
a. At least one constraint (not including nonnegativity conditions) is binding at the point.
b. Exactly one constraint (not including nonnegativity conditions) is binding at the point.
c. Neither of the above.

30. Binding constraints
a. are those on which the optimal solution lies
b. are those which, at optimality, do not use up all the available resources
c. both a and b

31. An isoprofit contour represents
a. an infinite number of feasible points, all of which yield the same profit
b. an infinite number of optimal solutions
c. an infinite number of decisions, all of which yield the same profit

32. Which of the following assertions is true of an optimal solution to an LP?
a. Every LP has an optimal solution.
b. The optimal solution always occurs at an extreme point.
c. The optimal solution uses up all resources.
d. If an optimal solution exists, there will always be at least one at a corner.
e. All of the above.

33. Every corner of the feasible region is defined by
a. the intersection of two constraint lines
b. some subset of constraint lines and nonnegativity conditions
c. neither of the above

34. An unbounded feasible region
a. arises from an incorrect formulation
b. means the objective function is unbounded
c. neither of the above
d. a and b

35. Sensitivity analysis
a. allows us to more meaningfully interpret the spreadsheet solution
b. is done after the optimal solution is obtained, and is therefore called postoptimality analysis
c. is sometimes called parametric analysis
d. all of the above

36. Sensitivity analysis
a. can be done graphically in two dimensions
b. can increase our confidence in a model
c. can weaken our confidence in the recommendations of a model
d. all of the above
e. a and b

37. The value of the geometric approach, in two dimensions, is
a. to solve the model quickly
b. to understand what is happening in higher dimensions
c. to better understand two-dimensional algebra

38. In LP, sensitivity analysis
a. can deal with changes in the objective function coefficients
b. can deal with changes in RHS
c. both of the above

39. Changing an objective function coefficient
a. produces a new optimal solution
b. changes the tilt of the objective function contours
c. gives a new OV
d. all of the above

40. Tightening an inequality constraint
a. improves the OV
b. cannot improve the OV
c. hurts the OV

41. A redundant constraint
a. may not be easy to recognize in advance of model optimization
b. should always be dropped from the model
c. may not be redundant if the data are changed
d. all of the above

e. a and c
f. a and b
g. b and c

42. A degenerate optimal solution
a. has fewer than m positive variables (where m is the number of binding constraints)
b. provides no information on alternative optima
c. may not provide information on the full range of allowable increase and allowable decrease in objective coefficients
d. all of the above

43. "Improvement" in an LP model means
a. the OV is increased for a Max model
b. the OV is decreased for a Min model
c. both a and b

44. For a nondegenerate optimal solution to a Max model, if the objective function coefficient c_1 increases by (exactly) the allowable increase
a. the OV may change
b. the previous optimal solution remains optimal
c. there will be a new optimal solution with a larger optimal value of x_1
d. all of the above

45. We have just solved a cost Min model with nonnegativity constraints and $x_1^* = 0$. Management wants to know: "How much does the cost of x_1 have to be reduced before we will begin to use it at a positive level in an optimal solution?" The answer appears in which portion of the worksheet or Solver Sensitivity Report?
a. values of variables
b. allowable changes in RHS of first constraint
c. allowable increase in the coefficient of x_1
d. reduced cost

46. Suppose that the first constraint of an LP, evaluated at a given point P_0, has a zero value for its slack. Then
a. P_0 lies on the boundary of the feasible region
b. P_0 lies on the first constraint line
c. both a and b

47. A correct relationship is
a. a constraint with zero shadow price must be nonbinding
b. a constraint with positive shadow price must be binding
c. both a and b

The following four questions refer to the spreadsheet output shown in Figure 4.30:

48. If the requirement on A is changed from 5 to 6.5
a. the OV will decrease by $66.66
b. the OV will improve by $66.66
c. the OV will increase by $66.66
d. the OV will not change

49. If the requirement on C is reduced from 30 to 20
a. the OV will decrease by $44.44
b. the OV will increase by $44.44
c. the OV will improve by at least $31.00

50. If the cost of ore from location 2 is decreased to $300 per ton
a. the OV will not change
b. the optimal solution will not change
c. neither a nor b
d. both a and b

51. If the cost of ore from location 1 is reduced to $680 per ton
a. there will be a new optimal solution with T1* > 0.259
b. there will be alternative optima
c. the optimal solution above remains optimal
d. all of the above

Answers

27. b, **28.** b, **29.** c, **30.** a, **31.** c, **32.** d, **33.** b, **34.** c, **35.** d, **36.** d, **37.** b, **38.** c, **39.** b, **40.** b, **41.** e, **42.** d, **43.** c, **44.** d, **45.** d, **46.** b, **47.** b, **48.** c, **49.** c, **50.** b, **51.** d

Skill Problems

4-1. Claire Archer, a colorful dealer in stereo equipment, puts together amps and preamps. An amp takes 12 hours to assemble and 4 hours for a high-performance check. A preamp takes 4 hours to assemble and 8 hours for a high-performance check. In the next month Claire will have 60 hours of assembly time available and 40 hours of high-performance check time available. Use GLP to plot the combinations of amps and preamps that will satisfy:
(a) The constraint on assembly time.
(b) The constraint on performance check time.
(c) Both constraints simultaneously.

4-2. One can of grade A dog food contains 12 mg of protein and 4 mg of fat, while one can of grade B dog food contains 3 mg of protein and 8 mg of fat. Del Matthews manages a small kennel that boards dogs. To feed his boarders tomorrow he would like to obtain a blend of dog foods that contains at least 30 mg of protein and 24 mg of fat. Use GLP to plot the combination of cans of grade A and grade B that Del can buy to satisfy:

(a) The constraint on the amount of protein.
(b) The constraint on the amount of fat.
(c) Both constraints simultaneously.

4-3. In Problem 4-1, suppose that Claire makes a profit of $10 on each amp and $5 on each preamp. Use GLP to plot the $10, $20, and $60 profit contours.

4-4. In Problem 4-2, assume that one can of grade A food costs $0.80 and one can of grade B food costs $0.60. Use GLP to plot the combinations of the two grades that Del can buy for
(a) $4.80
(b) $2.40

4-5. Consider Claire's activity as described in Problems 4-1 and 4-3. Suppose that because of limitations, she has determined that there are two additional constraints in her model. Namely, she can produce a maximum of 4 preamps and 6 amps in the next month. Taking all constraints into account,
(a) Find Claire's optimal (profit-maximizing) production plan using graphical analysis with GLP.
(b) What is the OV?
(c) Which constraints are binding?
(d) Which constraints are nonbinding and what are their slack values?

4-6. Assuming the costs presented in Problem 4-4, find how many cans of each grade of dog food Del should buy to satisfy the requirements from Problem 4-2 at minimum total cost.

4-7. Could the omission of any two constraints make Claire's model (Problem 4-5) unbounded?

4-8. Suppose that when Del arrives at the store there is only one can of grade A dog food available and that he cannot buy the dog food anywhere else. Does this change the minimum cost solution you found in Problem 4-6? If so, how?

4-9. Suppose that Claire's constraint on amps, $A \le 6$, is replaced by $A \ge 6$. How does this affect the model?

4-10. If Del must buy at least three cans of grade B dog food, does this affect the minimum cost solution you found in Problem 4-6? If so, how? (Note: For the purposes of this problem it is assumed that Del can buy fractional cans of dog food.)

4-11. Consider the following LP:

$$\begin{aligned} \text{Max } & x_1 + x_2 \\ \text{s.t. } & x_1 + 2x_2 \le 6 \\ & 3x_1 + 2x_2 \le 12 \\ & x_1, x_2 \ge 0 \end{aligned}$$

(a) Use GLP to find the optimal solution and the OV.
(b) Change the objective function to $2x_1 + 6x_2$ and find the optimal solution.
(c) How many extreme points does the feasible region have? Find the values of (x_1, x_2) at each extreme point.

4-12. Consider the following LP:

$$\begin{aligned} \text{Max } & 2x_1 + 3x_2 \\ \text{s.t. } & 3x_1 + x_2 \ge 6 \\ & x_1 + 7x_2 \ge 7 \\ & x_1 + x_2 \le 4 \\ & x_1, x_2 \ge 0 \end{aligned}$$

(a) Use GLP to find the optimal solution and the OV.
(b) Change the objective function to $3x_1 + 2x_2$ and find the optimal solution.
(c) How many extreme points does the feasible region have? Find (x_1, x_2) at each extreme point.

4-13. Consider the following LP:

$$\begin{aligned} \text{Max } & 3x_1 + 4x_2 \\ \text{s.t. } & -2x_1 + 4x_2 \le 16 \\ & 2x_1 + 4x_2 \le 24 \\ & -6x_1 - 3x_2 \ge -48 \\ & x_1, x_2 \ge 0 \end{aligned}$$

(a) Use GLP to find the optimal solution and the OV.
(b) Find the slack and surplus values for each constraint.

4-14. Consider the following LP:

$$\begin{aligned} &\text{Max } 6x_1 + 2x_2 \\ &\text{s.t.} \quad 2x_1 + 4x_2 \le 20 \\ &\qquad 3x_1 + 5x_2 \ge 15 \\ &\qquad x_1 \ge 3 \\ &\qquad x_2 \ge 0 \end{aligned}$$

(a) Use GLP to find the optimal solution and the OV.
(b) Find the slack and surplus values for each constraint.

4-15. Consider the following LP:

$$\begin{aligned} &\text{Min } 5x_1 + 2x_2 \\ &\text{s.t.} \quad 3x_1 + 6x_2 \ge 18 \\ &\qquad 5x_1 + 4x_2 \ge 20 \\ &\qquad 8x_1 + 2x_2 \ge 16 \\ &\qquad 7x_1 + 6x_2 \le 42 \\ &\qquad x_1, x_2 \ge 0 \end{aligned}$$

(a) Use GLP to find the optimal solution and the OV.
(b) Which constraints are binding? Which are nonbinding?
(c) What are the slack and surplus values associated with each constraint?
(d) How many extreme points does the feasible region have?
(e) Change the objective function to $15x_1 + 12x_2$. What are the alternative optimal corner solutions?

4-16. In Problem 4-14 change the objective function to $x_1 + 3x_2$. Answer parts (a) and (b) for the new model.

4-17. Consider the following LP:

$$\begin{aligned} &\text{Max } 600E + 1000F \\ &\text{s.t.} \quad 100E + 60F \le 21{,}000 \\ &\qquad 4000E + 800F \le 680{,}000 \\ &\qquad E + F \le 290 \\ &\qquad 12E + 30F \le 6000 \\ &\qquad E, F \ge 0 \end{aligned}$$

(a) Let E be the horizontal axis and F the vertical axis, and use GLP to find the optimal solution to this model and the OV.
(b) One of the constraints is redundant in the sense that it plays no role in determining the feasible region. Which one is it?
(c) What is the minimum change in the RHS of this constraint that would cause the constraint to become binding?
(d) The coefficient of E in the third constraint is currently 1. What is the minimum increase in this coefficient that would cause the constraint to become binding?
(e) Suppose that the coefficient of E, say C_E, in the objective function is increased, whereas the coefficient of F, say C_F, remains fixed. At what value for the coefficient of E would alternative optima first become encountered?

4-18. Consider the following LP:

$$\begin{aligned} &\text{Max } 3x_1 + x_2 \\ &\text{s.t.} \quad 6x_1 + 3x_2 \ge 12 \\ &\qquad 4x_1 + 8x_2 \ge 16 \\ &\qquad 6x_1 + 5x_2 \le 30 \\ &\qquad 6x_1 + 7x_2 \le 36 \\ &\qquad x_1, x_2 \ge 0 \end{aligned}$$

(a) Use GLP to find the optimal solution and the OV.
(b) Consider a Min model with the feasible region above. Assume that the objective function is $x_1 + Bx_2$. What is the largest value of B so that the optimal solution lies at the intersection of the lines $6x_1 + 3x_2 = 12$ and $4x_1 + 8x_2 = 16$? Find the optimal solution and the OV.

(c) In a Max model, assume that the objective function is $Ax_1 + Bx_2$. Determine the set of values for A and B for which the optimal solution lies at the intersection of $6x_1 + 5x_2 = 30$ and $6x_1 + 7x_2 = 36$. Use a graph to show the set of values.

4-19. In the simplified Oak Products model, suppose that the objective function is changed to $58C + 20M$.
(a) Use GLP to determine the effect on the optimal solution.
(b) What is the effect on the OV?

4-20. In the simplified Oak Products model, suppose that the objective function is changed to $25C + 50M$.
(a) Use GLP to determine the effect on the optimal solution.
(b) What is the effect on the OV?

4-21. Consider the two objective functions for the simplified Oak Products model in Figure 4.5

$$56C + 40M$$

$$56C + 80M$$

The figure indicates that when the per unit contribution margin of M is increased from 40 to 80, without changing the per unit contribution margin of C, the optimal value of C decreases. Why should the optimal value of C depend on the coefficient of M? Try to answer this question in words.

4-22. In the simplified Oak Products model, suppose that the objective function is changed to $10C + 100M$.
(a) Use GLP to decide whether there will be a new optimal solution.
(b) What is the effect on the OV?

4-23. Consider the LP

$$\begin{aligned} \text{Max } & 30x_1 + 10x_2 \\ \text{s.t. } & 2x_1 + x_2 \le 4 \\ & 2x_1 + 2x_2 \le 6 \\ & x_1, x_2 \ge 0 \end{aligned}$$

(a) Solve it with GLP and state the optimal solution.
(b) Keeping all other data as is, what per unit contribution margin should the product, whose current optimal value is zero, have in order that this product enter the optimal solution at a positive level?
(c) How many optimal corner solutions exist after making the change described in part (b)? What are they?
(d) In the original model, how much can the RHS of the second constraint be increased (decreased) before the optimal solution is changed?
(e) Answer part (d) for the RHS of the first constraint.
(f) How do you explain the difference between parts (d) and (e)?
(g) What will be the impact of adding the constraint $4x_1 + x_2 = 4$ to the original model?
(h) What is the impact (on the optimal solution) of adding the constraint $3x_1 + 3x_2 \le 15$ to the original model?
(i) Fill in the blanks: The difference between parts (g) and (h) is that the original optimal solution already ________ the constraint in (h) but does not ________ the constraint in (g).

4-24. Consider the LP

$$\begin{aligned} \text{Max } & 2x_1 + x_2 \\ \text{s.t. } & 3x_1 + 3x_2 \le 12 \\ & x_1 + 3x_2 \le 6 \\ & x_1, x_2 \ge 0 \end{aligned}$$

In terms of this model, answer questions (a–g) in Problem 4-23.
(h) What will be the impact of adding the constraint $x_1 + x_2 \le 1$ to the original model?

4-25. Of the two constraints

$$-3x_1 + 2x_2 \ge -6$$
$$-3x_1 + 2x_2 \ge -10$$

(a) Which is tighter?
(b) Which of the constraints, if either, does the point $(x_1 = 2, x_2 = 1)$ satisfy?
(c) What about the point $(x_1 = 3, x_2 = 0)$?

4-26. Of the constraints

$$4x_1 - 3x_2 \leq 12$$
$$4x_1 - 3x_2 \leq -12$$

(a) Which is tighter?
(b) Which of the constraints, if either, does the point ($x_1 = -2, x_2 = 3$) satisfy?
(c) What about the point ($x_1 = 2, x_2 = 3$)?

4-27. Which of the two constraints in Problem 4-25 is looser?

4-28. Which of the two constraints in Problem 4-26 is looser?

4-29. Fill in the blanks: Increasing the RHS of a $\leq$ constraint means that there will be __________ combinations of decision-variable values that satisfy the constraint. This means that one is __________ the constraint.

4-30. Fill in the blanks: Increasing the RHS of a $\geq$ constraint means that there will be __________ combinations of decision-variable values that satisfy the constraint. This means that one is __________ the constraint.

4-31. Using the words *enlarge, diminish, smaller, larger, unchanged,* fill in the blanks: Tightening a constraint cannot __________ the feasible region and may leave it or __________.

4-32. Using the words supplied in Problem 4-31, fill in the blanks: Loosening a constraint cannot __________ the feasible region and may leave it __________ or __________.

4-33. Suppose that you have created a model and that by some means you are able to identify a redundant constraint. Would you say it is generally true that such a constraint should be dropped from the model? Why (or why not)?

4-34. How would your answer to Problem 4-33 differ if the model is to be run one and only one time?

4-35. Suppose you know that in a given run of a model a particular constraint will be redundant. Does it follow that this constraint will also be nonbinding?

4-36. Match up the phrases in the two columns. (Note: Some phrases may have more than one match.)

(a) Adding constraints	1. May enlarge the feasible region
(b) Deleting constraints	2. May make the feasible region smaller
(c) Important constraints	3. Depend on the data set
(d) Tightening constraints	4. May improve the OV
(e) Loosening constraints	5. May hurt the OV

4-37. The shadow price on a nonbinding constraint always has what value? What can you say about the shadow price on a binding constraint?

4-38. Consider a constraint with a positive optimal slack value. What must the shadow price be?

4-39. You have just solved an LP model. You observe that you have a nondegenerate solution and for some objective function coefficient you see a zero entry under the "Allowable Increase" column. What does this tell you?

4-40. Explain how to use the reduced costs to know if there are alternative optimal solutions.

4-41. Employing the terms *rate* and *OV*, give the correct interpretation of shadow price in the Solver Sensitivity Report.

Application Problems

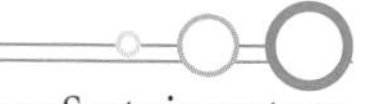

4-42. In the simplified Oak Products model, replace the RHS of the fifth constraint Heavy Seats inventory, which is currently 140, with the value 170. State the effect on the feasible region.

4-43. In the simplified Oak Products model, how much can you increase the RHS of the Legs constraint before it becomes redundant? How small can the RHS be made without destroying feasibility?

4-44. In the simplified Oak Products model, which constraint(s) are redundant? Will each such constraint remain redundant if its RHS value is increased by 10%, all other data held fixed?

4-45. In the simplified Oak Products model, for what values of the RHS will the Legs constraint become redundant, assuming all other data are held fixed?

4-46. A manufacturer of tires produces two kinds of tires. The premium tire, The Last-Forever, is a steel belted, puncture resistant, long-wear tire that holds all records for quality within the industry. The other tire, Lane-Handler, is a simple low-cost 40,000-mile warranty unbranded tire. The Last-Forever contributes \$50 per tire to the profit for the company, while the Lane-Handler contributes only \$10 to profit. Both tires are manufactured at the same factory and require the same machines to be produced. Machine A and machine B are both used in the two-step process used to make the tires. The time consumed in hours on each machine to fabricate a tire is given below.

	LANE-HANDLER	LAST-FOREVER	TOTAL HOURS AVAILABLE
Machine A	1	4	120
Machine B	2	2	100

Twenty Lane-Handlers have been promised to a valued dealer and four Last-Forevers have been promised to the owner's son.

(a) Use GLP to find the product mix that maximizes profit.
(b) What is the OV?
(c) If machine *B* hours could be increased to 120, then what would be the change in the OV?
(d) What would be the impact if a maintenance problem reduced available machine *A* hours to 100?

4-47. A printing company produces two free publications, LinksLetter and Ragged Edge, that consumers can pick up at local retailers and restaurants. The company makes money through the sale of advertising space within the publications. The cost of the LinksLetter is $50 per thousand copies. The cost of the Ragged Edge is $100 per thousand copies. Both publications are produced on the same printing press. The LinksLetter requires 1 hour per thousand copies to print, while the Ragged Edge requires only half an hour of printing press time per thousand copies. The total printing press time available next week is 120 hours. Both publications are folded in a folding machine, available for 200 hours, that folds both publications at a rate of 1000 per hour. The printing company wants to use all the time available for the printing press while minimizing the cost of the publications produced. Use GLP to determine the mix of publications to be printed and the minimum cost to print them.

4-48. The manager at the printing company in the previous problem has decided that profit for the publications should be maximized. He has determined that the profit per thousand copies of LinksLetter is $25. The profit per thousand copies for the publication of the Ragged Edge is $45. He has to print at least 60,000 copies of the LinksLetter and 30,000 copies of the Ragged Edge. Assume that the constraints of the printing press time and folding machine time are the same as the previous problem.

(a) Use GLP and plot the model.
(b) What is the publication mix with this new objective function?
(c) Which constraints are binding?

4-49. Karma Computers produces two computer models, Standard and Deluxe. A Standard model is produced by assembling a single disk drive with a Standard Chassis. A Deluxe model is produced by assembling two disk drives with a Deluxe Chassis. The Standard model has a net profit per unit of $300 while the Deluxe model has a net profit per unit of $400. The current inventory of Karma consists of 60 Standard Chassis, 50 Deluxe Chassis, and 120 Disk Drives.

(a) Formulate the Karma LP model and use GLP to plot a geometric representation of it.
(b) Optimize the Karma model with GLP and use that result to fill in the missing values in the blank cells of the worksheet in Figure 4.35.
(c) Use the results from the worksheet to fill in the missing values for Final Value and Constraint R.H. Side in the blank cells of the Karma model Sensitivity Report in Figure 4.36. Next, use the

FIGURE 4.35

LP Model for Problem 4-49

	A	B	C	D	E	F	G
1	KARMA COMPUTER						
2	Decision Variables	S	D				
3	Quantity			PROFIT			
4	Contrib. Margin	$300	$400				
5	Subject To:			LHS		RHS	Slack
6	Schas Constr	1			≤	60	
7	Dchas Constr		1		≤	50	
8	Ddrive Constr				≤		

FIGURE 4.36

Sensitivity Report for Problem 4-49

Microsoft Excel 8.0 Sensitivity Report
Adjustable Cells

Cell	Name	Final Value	Reduced Cost	Objective Coefficient	Allowable Increase	Allowable Decrease
$B$3	Quantity S			300		
$C$3	Quantity D			400	200	400

Constraints

Cell	Name	Final Value	Shadow Price	Constraint R.H. Side	Allowable Increase	Allowable Decrease
$D$6	Schas Constr LHS			60	60	
$D$7	Dchas Constr LHS			50		20
$D$8	Ddrive Constr LHS					60

GLP Karma model to determine the values of the remaining missing cells in the Sensitivity Report in Figure 4.36.

4-50. Refer to the Solver output in Figure 4.11.
 (a) Suppose that 30 more Short Dowels are made available. What will be the change in the OV?
 (b) Suppose that there are 300 fewer Short Dowels. What will be the change in the OV?
 (c) The shadow price on Short Dowels is valid for what range of values of the RHS?

4-51. Refer to the Solver output shown in Figure 4.11.
 (a) Suppose that the right-hand side of the Legs constraint is changed to 750. What is the effect on the OV?
 (b) By how much can the total chair production constraint be tightened before the shadow price could possibly change?
 (c) Suppose that 50 more Legs are available. By how much will the OV change?

4-52. Note that in Figure 4.15 there is an allowable decrease of zero for Long Dowels. What anomaly is responsible for this?

4-53. Refer to Figure 4.15. Is the exhibited solution degenerate or nondegenerate? Support your answer.

4-54. Refer to Figure 4.11. Suppose that the contribution margin of Mate chairs is reduced to 30 per unit.
 (a) What is the resulting optimal solution?
 (b) What is the *change* in the OV?

4-55. Refer to Figure 4.11. Suppose that the contribution margin of Captain chairs is increased to 80 per unit.
 (a) What is the resulting optimal solution?
 (b) What is the *change* in the OV?

4-56. Refer to Figure 4.30.
 (a) How much would the price per ton of ore from location 4 have to decrease in order for it to become attractive to purchase it?
 (b) Suppose that the price of ore from location 1 decreases by $80 per ton. Is there any change in the optimal solution or in the OV?
 (c) Suppose that the price of ore from location 1 increases by $100 per ton. Is there any change in the optimal solution? What, if any, is the associated change in the cost of an optimally blended ton?

4-57. Refer to Figure 4.30.
 (a) Suppose that the price of ore from location 3 increases by $50 per ton. Is there any change in the optimal solution? What, if any, is the associated change in the OV?
 (b) Analyze the effect on the optimal solution of decreasing the cost of ore from location 3 by exactly $118.269 per ton. (For example, does the present solution remain optimal? Is there an additional optimal solution, and if so how can it be characterized?)
 (c) For the change described above in part (b), what is the new OV?

4-58. Buster Sod operates an 800-acre irrigated farm in the Red River Valley of Arizona. Sod's principal activities are raising wheat, alfalfa, and beef. The Red River Valley Water Authority has just given its water allotments for next year (Sod was allotted 1000 acre-feet), and Sod is busy preparing his production plan for next year. He figures that beef prices will hold at around $500 per ton and that wheat will sell at $2 per bushel. Best guesses are that he will be able to sell alfalfa at $22 per ton, but if he needs more alfalfa to feed his beef than he can raise, he will have to pay $28 per ton to get the alfalfa to his feedlot.

Some technological features of Sod's operation are wheat yield, 70 bushels per acre; alfalfa yield, 4 tons per acre. Other features are given in the table below.

ACTIVITY	LABOR, MACHINERY, AND OTHER COSTS ($)	WATER REQUIREMENTS (ACRE-FT)	LAND REQUIREMENTS (ACRES)	ALFALFA REQUIREMENTS (TONS)
1 acre of wheat	20	2	1	
1 acre of alfalfa	28	3	1	
1 ton of beef	50	0.05	0.1	5

Define the variables:
Wheat = wheat raised and sold (acres)
Alfalfa Tons = alfalfa raised (tons)
Beef = beef raised and sold (tons)
Alfalfa Bought = alfalfa bought (tons)
Alfalfa Sold = alfalfa sold (tons)

An LP formulation and solution to Buster Sod's model are shown in Figure 4.37. Using this information, answer the following questions.

(a) Show calculations that explain the values of the coefficient of *Wheat Acres* and *Alfalfa Tons* in the objective function and the coefficients of *Alfalfa Tons* in the first and second constraints.
(b) How much water is being used?
(c) How much beef is being produced?
(d) Does Sod buy or sell alfalfa?
(e) How much should Sod pay to acquire another acre-ft of water?
(f) Interpret the shadow price on "Acres Limit" of 800.
(g) What happens to the optimal planting policy if the price of wheat triples? What happens to the OV?

FIGURE 4.37

LP Solution and Sensitivity Report for Problem 4-58

	A	B	C	D	E	F	G	H	I	J
1		Wheat	Alfalfa	Beef	Alfalfa Bought	Alfalfa Sold				
2	Yield	70 Bu/Ac	4Tons/Ac							
3	Price	$2 /Bu		$500/Ton		$22/Ton				
4	Costs	$20/Ac	$28/Ac	$50/Ton	$28/Ton					
5		Wheat Acres	Alfalfa Tons	Beef Tons	Alfalfa Bought Tons	Alfalfa Sold Tons				
6		0	0	8,000	40,000	0	Profit			
7	Contribution	$120/Ac	$(7)/Ton	$450/Ton	$(28)/Ton	$22/Ton	$2,480,000			
8							Total		Avail.	Slack
9	Acres Limit	1	0.25	0.1			800	≤	800	0
10	Water Limit	2	0.75	0.05			400	≤	1000	600
11	Balance		-1	5	-1	1	0.000	=	0	0
12										

Microsoft Excel 9.0 Sensitivity Report

Adjustable Cells

Cell	Name	Final Value	Reduced Cost	Objective Coefficient	Allowable Increase	Allowable Decrease
$B$6	Wheat Acres	0	-2980	120	2980	1E+30
$C$6	Alfalfa Tons	0	-754	-7	754	1E+30
$D$6	Beef Tons	8,000	0	450	1E+30	298
$E$6	Alfalfa Bought Tons	40,000	0	-28	6	55.85
$F$6	Alfalfa Sold Tons	0	-6	22	6	1E+30

Constraints

Cell	Name	Final Value	Shadow Price	Constraint R.H. Side	Allowable Increase	Allowable Decrease
$G$11	Balance Total	0.0	28	0	40000	1E+30
$G$9	Acres Limit Total	800	3100	800	1200	800
$G$10	Water Limit Total	400	0	1000	1E+30	600

(h) How much profit will Sod receive from the optimal operation of his farm?

(i) What happens to the optimal value of the objective function if the cost of alfalfa purchased increases from $28 to $29?

NOTE: The coefficient of *Alfalfa Bought* is currently –$28 and it will become –$29. Thus, the coefficient will *decrease* by $1.

(j) How much can the cost of buying alfalfa decrease before the current optimal planting policy will change?

4-59. A plant in a developing country can manufacture five different products in any combination. Each product requires time on each of three machines, as shown in the table below. All figures are in minutes per pound of product.

Product	MACHINE-TIME (MIN/LB)		
	1	2	3
A	12	8	5
B	7	9	10
C	8	4	7
D	10	0	3
E	7	11	2

Each machine is available 128 hours per week. Products A, B, C, D, and E are purely competitive, and any amounts made may be sold at per pound prices of $5, $4, $5, $4, and $4, respectively. Variable labor costs are $4 per hour for machines 1 and 2, and $3 per hour for machine 3. Material costs are $2 for each pound of products A and C, and $1 for each pound of products B, D, and E. The management wishes to maximize profit to the firm. The Solver LP solution and Sensitivity Report are shown in Figure 4.38.

(a) What is the Excel formula in B9 giving the first value of the coefficient in the objective function?

(b) How many hours are spent on each of the three machines and what are the units of the shadow prices on the constraints that control machine capacity?

(c) How much should the firm be willing to spend to obtain another hour of time on machine 2?

(d) How much can the sales price of product A increase before the optimal production plan changes? State your answer in the proper units.

FIGURE 4.38

LP Solution and Sensitivity Report for Problem 4-59

	A	B	C	D	E	F	G	H	I	J
1	Product	A	B	C	D	E				
2	Price/Lb.	$5	$4	$5	$4	$4				
3	Cost/Hr Mach. 1	$4	$4	$4	$4	$4				
4	Cost/Hr Mach. 2	$4	$4	$4	$4	$4				
5	Cost/Hr Mach. 3	$3	$3	$3	$3	$3				
6	Matrl.Costs/Lb	$2	$1	$2	$1	$1			Mach. Hours	
7	Product	A	B	C	D	E			Avail/Week	
8	Pounds Prod.	0	0	512	0	512	Profit		128	
9	Contr. Mar./Lb	$1.417	$1.433	$1.850	$2.183	$1.700	$ 1,817.60			
10							Total		MinutesAvail./Wk.	Slack
11	Mach. 1 Min.	12	7	8	10	7	7680	≤	7680	0.00
12	Mach. 2 Min.	8	9	4	0	11	7680	≤	7680	0.00
13	Mach. 3 Min.	5	10	7	3	2	4608	≤	7680	3072
14										

Microsoft Excel 9.0 Sensitivity Report

Adjustable Cells

Cell	Name	Final Value	Reduced Cost	Objective Coefficient	Allowable Increase	Allowable Decrease
$B$8	Pounds Prod. A	0	-1.38	1.417	1.38	1E+30
$C$8	Pounds Prod. B	0	-0.245	1.433	0.245	1E+30
$D$8	Pounds Prod. C	512	0	1.85	0.093	0.041
$E$8	Pounds Prod. D	0	-0.075	2.183	0.075	1E+30
$F$8	Pounds Prod. E	512	0	1.7	0.1125	0.08125

Constraints

Cell	Name	Final Value	Shadow Price	Constraint R.H. Side	Allowable Increase	Allowable Decrease
$G$11	Mach. 1 Min. Total	7680	0.226	7680	2671.304	2792.727
$G$12	Mach. 2 Min. Total	7680	0.011	7680	4388.571	3840
$G$13	Mach. 3 Min. Total	4608	0	7680	1E+30	3072

4-60. *A Product Mix/Process Selection Model.* Two products, A and B, are processed on three machines. Both products have two possible routings. Routing 1 processes the product on machines 1 and 2 while routing 2 processes the product on machines 1 and 3. Processing times in hours per unit are given in the table below.

		MACHINE-TIME (HR/UNIT)		
Product	**Routing**	**1**	**2**	**3**
A	1	2	1	
A	2	2		1.5
B	1	1	2	
B	2	1		3

The costs per hour on machines 1, 2, and 3 are \$20, \$30, and \$18, respectively. Each machine is available for 40 hours per week. Any amount of products A and B may be sold at \$110 and \$150 per unit, respectively. The Solver LP solution and Sensitivity Report are shown in Figure 4.39 where

$$A_i = \text{units of A produced by routing } i(i = 1, 2)$$
$$B_i = \text{units of B produced by routing } i(i = 1, 2)$$

(a) What is the Excel formula in B8 giving the first value of the coefficient in the objective function?

(b) How much product B is being produced? How much by the first routing? (Interpret the numbers as production rates. Thus 4.44 would represent 4.44 units per week. This could be accomplished by producing 4 units and starting the 5th in the first week, finishing the 5th through the 8th units, and starting the 9th in the second week, etc.)

(c) How many hours are used on each of the three machines?

(d) What are the units of the shadow prices on the machine capacity constraints?

(e) Suppose that there is an opportunity to work up to 8 hours of overtime on machine 2 at a cost of \$45 per hour (50% more than the regular time cost of \$30 per hour). Should machine 2 be scheduled for 8 hours of overtime?

FIGURE 4.39

LP Solution and Sensitivity Report for Problem 4-60

	A	B	C	D	E	F	G	H	I	J
1	Product	A1	A2	B1	B2					
2	Price	$ 110	$ 110	$ 150	$ 150					
3	Cost/Hr Mach. 1	$ 20	$ 20	$ 20	$ 20					
4	Cost/Hr Mach. 2	$ 30	$ 30	$ 30	$ 30					
5	Cost/Hr Mach. 3	$ 18	$ 18	$ 18	$ 18					
6	Product	A1	A2	B1	B2					
7	Qty. Produced	4.444	0.000	17.778	13.333	Profit				
8	Contr. Margin	$ 40	$ 43	$ 70	$ 76	$ 2,435.56				
9						Total		Hrs.Avail.	Slack	
10	Machine 1 Hrs.	2	2	1	1	40	≤	40	-0	
11	Machine 2 Hrs.	1		2		40	≤	40	-0	
12	Machine 3 Hrs.		1.5		3	40	≤	40	0	
13										

Microsoft Excel 9.0 Sensitivity Report

Adjustable Cells

Cell	Name	Final Value	Reduced Cost	Objective Coefficient	Allowable Increase	Allowable Decrease
$B$7	Qty. Produced A1	4.444	0.00	40	100	0
$C$7	Qty. Produced A2	0.000	0.00	43	0	1E+30
$D$7	Qty. Produced B1	17.778	0.00	70	0	50
$E$7	Qty. Produced B2	13.333	0.00	76	1E+30	0

Constraints

Cell	Name	Final Value	Shadow Price	Constraint R.H. Side	Allowable Increase	Allowable Decrease
$F$10	Machine 1 Hrs. Total	40	3.333	40	53.33	6.67
$F$11	Machine 2 Hrs. Total	40	33.333	40	13.33	26.67
$F$12	Machine 3 Hrs. Total	40	24.222	40	20	40

4-61. *A Blending Model.* A vineyard wishes to blend four different vintages to make three types of blended wine. Restrictions are placed on the percentage composition of the blends (see table below).

BLEND	VINTAGE 1	2	3	4	SALES PRICE PER GALLON ($)
A	at least 75% 1 & 2		*	at most 5%	70
B	*	at least 35% 2 & 3		*	40
C	at least 50% 1 & 3, no restriction on 2			at most 40%	30
Supply (gallons)	180	250	200	400	

*Indicates no restriction.

The LP solution is shown in Figure 4.40 and the Sensitivity Report is shown in Figure 4.41.

(a) What is the purpose of the constraints in F2:G5?

(b) What is the purpose of the constraints in C16:E17 and C25:E26?

(c) Explain why the LHS and RHS of the constraint C16:C17 have the values they do. What restriction does it represent?

(d) What is the maximum revenue that can be achieved by blending the four vintages?

(e) How much of each blend should be produced? What is the composition of each blend?

(f) What is the minimum amount by which the selling price of blend *C* would have to change, and in what direction, before it would become optimal to produce blend *C*?

(g) What are the shadow prices of the four vintages? What are the units of these shadow prices?

(h) Suppose an earthquake destroys half of the available vintage 3. What can you say about the impact on the optimal solution and the optimal revenue?

FIGURE 4.40

LP Model and Solution for Problem 4-61

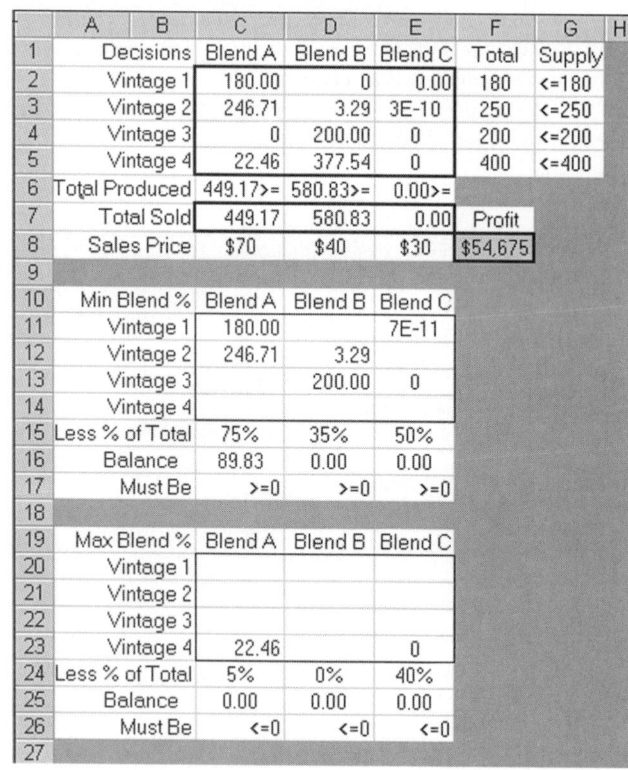

	A / B	C	D	E	F	G
1	Decisions	Blend A	Blend B	Blend C	Total	Supply
2	Vintage 1	180.00	0	0.00	180	<=180
3	Vintage 2	246.71	3.29	3E-10	250	<=250
4	Vintage 3	0	200.00	0	200	<=200
5	Vintage 4	22.46	377.54	0	400	<=400
6	Total Produced	449.17>=	580.83>=	0.00>=		
7	Total Sold	449.17	580.83	0.00	Profit	
8	Sales Price	$70	$40	$30	$54,675	
9						
10	Min Blend %	Blend A	Blend B	Blend C		
11	Vintage 1	180.00		7E-11		
12	Vintage 2	246.71	3.29			
13	Vintage 3		200.00	0		
14	Vintage 4					
15	Less % of Total	75%	35%	50%		
16	Balance	89.83	0.00	0.00		
17	Must Be	>=0	>=0	>=0		
18						
19	Max Blend %	Blend A	Blend B	Blend C		
20	Vintage 1					
21	Vintage 2					
22	Vintage 3					
23	Vintage 4	22.46		0		
24	Less % of Total	5%	0%	40%		
25	Balance	0.00	0.00	0.00		
26	Must Be	<=0	<=0	<=0		
27						

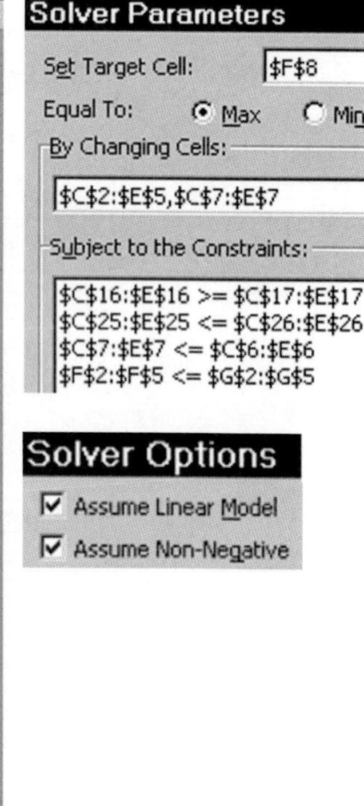

Cell	Formula	Copy To
C6	= SUM(C2:C5)	D6:E6
C11	= C2	C12, D12, D13, E11, E13
C16	= SUM(C11:C14)–C$6*C15	D16:E16, C25:E25

FIGURE 4.41

Sensitivity Report for Problem 4-61

Microsoft Excel 9.0 Sensitivity Report

Adjustable Cells

Cell	Name	Final Value	Reduced Cost	Objective Coefficient	Allowable Increase	Allowable Decrease
$C$2	Vintage 1 Blend A	180.00	0.00	0	0	0
$D$2	Vintage 1 Blend B	0.00	-50.000	0	50.000	1E+30
$E$2	Vintage 1 Blend C	0.00	0.00	0	0	0
$C$3	Vintage 2 Blend A	246.71	0.00	0	0	0
$D$3	Vintage 2 Blend B	3.29	0.00	0	0	40.602
$E$3	Vintage 2 Blend C	0.00	0.00	0	85.000	0
$C$4	Vintage 3 Blend A	0.00	0.00	0	0	1E+30
$D$4	Vintage 3 Blend B	200.00	0.00	0	1E+30	0
$E$4	Vintage 3 Blend C	0.00	0.00	0	0	1E+30
$C$5	Vintage 4 Blend A	22.46	0.00	0	771.429	46.154
$D$5	Vintage 4 Blend B	377.54	0.00	0	46.154	21.862
$E$5	Vintage 4 Blend C	0.00	-56.250	0	56.250	1E+30
$C$7	Total Sold Blend A	449.17	0.00	70	38.571	30.000
$D$7	Total Sold Blend B	580.83	0.00	40	30.000	14.211
$E$7	Total Sold Blend C	0.00	0.00	30	22.500	30

Constraints

Cell	Name	Final Value	Shadow Price	Constraint R.H. Side	Allowable Increase	Allowable Decrease
$C$16	Balance Blend A	89.83	0.00	0	89.833	1E+30
$D$16	Balance Blend B	0.00	-50.00	0	155.816	2.079
$E$16	Balance Blend C	0.00	0.00	0	0	0
$C$25	Balance Blend A	0.00	50.00	0	5.643	20.731
$D$25	Balance Blend B	0.00	0.00	0	1E+30	0
$E$25	Balance Blend C	0.00	106.25	0	0	144.000
$F$2	Vintage 1 Total	180	72.5	180	112.857	180
$F$3	Vintage 2 Total	250	72.5	250	112.857	239.717
$F$4	Vintage 3 Total	200	72.5	200	3.198	200
$F$5	Vintage 4 Total	400	22.5	400	445.188	5.940
$C$7	Total Sold Blend A	449.17	70.00	0	1E+30	449.167
$D$7	Total Sold Blend B	580.83	40.00	0	1E+30	580.833
$E$7	Total Sold Blend C	0.00	30.00	0	1E+30	0

4-62. The Party Nut Company has on hand 550 pounds of peanuts, 150 pounds of cashews, 90 pounds of brazil nuts, and 70 pounds of hazelnuts. It packages and sells four varieties of mixed nuts in standard 8-ounce (half-pound) cans. The mix requirements and the contribution margin per can are shown in the table below. The firm can sell all that it can produce. What mixes of products should it produce to maximize profit contribution?

MIX	CONTENTS	CONTR. MARGIN PER CAN
1 (peanuts)	Peanuts only	$0.26
2 (party mix)	No more than 50% peanuts; at least 15% cashews; at least 10% brazil nuts	0.40
3 (cashews)	Cashews only	0.51
4 (luxury mix)	at least 30% cashews; at least 20% brazil nuts; at least 30% hazelnuts	0.52

The model can be formulated as the linear program shown in Figure 4.42. Note that in Figure 4.42 the coefficient for Peanut Mix in the objective function is $.52 rather than $.26 because there are two 8-ounce cans for each pound of peanuts sold as peanuts only. In the Sensitivity Report (see Figure 4.43) we have purposely deleted several of the shadow prices and reduced costs. Use this output to answer the questions. If it is impossible to answer the question, state why.

(a) Explain the calculation that justifies $1.02 as the coefficient of Cashew Mix in the objective function.

(b) How many cans of Party Mix are produced in the optimal solution?

(c) Is the shadow price on the G3:H3 constraint ≥ 0 or ≤ 0? Explain why.

(d) What is the value of the shadow price on the constraint D18 ≥ 0? How do you know?

FIGURE 4.42

LP Model and Solution for Problem 4-62

	A–B	C	D	E	F	G	H
1	Decisions	Peanut Mix	Party Mix	Cashew Mix	Luxury Mix	Total	Supply
2	Peanuts	380.00	123.333		46.667	550	<=550
3	Cashews		80.00	0.00	70	150	<=150
4	Brazils		43.33		46.667	90	<=90
5	Hazelnuts		0.00		70	70	<=70
6	Total	380.00	246.667	0.00	233.333	Profit	
7	Contr. Margin	$0.52	$0.80	$1.02	$1.04	$637.60	
8							
9	Blend %	Peanut Mix	Party Mix	Cashew Mix	Luxury Mix		
10	Peanuts	=100% of Total	<=50% of Total				
11	Cashews		>=15% of Total	=100% of Total	>=30% of Total		
12	Brazils		>=10% of Total		>=20% of Total		
13	Hazelnuts				>=30% of Total		
14							
15	Balance >= 0	Peanut Mix	Party Mix	Cashew Mix	Luxury Mix		
16	Peanuts	0	0				
17	Cashews		43.000	0	0		
18	Brazils		18.667		0		
19	Hazelnuts				0		
20							

	B	C	D	E	F	G
6	Total	=SUM(C2:C5)	=SUM(D2:D5)	=SUM(E2:E5)	=SUM(F2:F5)	Profit
7	Contr. Margin	0.52	0.8	1.02	1.04	=SUMPRODUCT($C$6:$F$6,C7:F7)
8						
9	Blend %	Peanut Mix	Party Mix	Cashew Mix	Luxury Mix	
10	Peanuts	1	0.5			
11	Cashews		0.15	1	0.3	
12	Brazils		0.1		0.2	
13	Hazelnuts				0.3	
14						
15	Balance >= 0	Peanut Mix	Party Mix	Cashew Mix	Luxury Mix	
16	Peanuts	=C2-C10*C$6	=-(D2-D10*D$6)			
17	Cashews		=D3-D11*D$6	=E3-E11*E$6	=F3-F11*F$6	
18	Brazils		=D4-D12*D$6		=F4-F12*F$6	
19	Hazelnuts				=F5-F13*F$6	

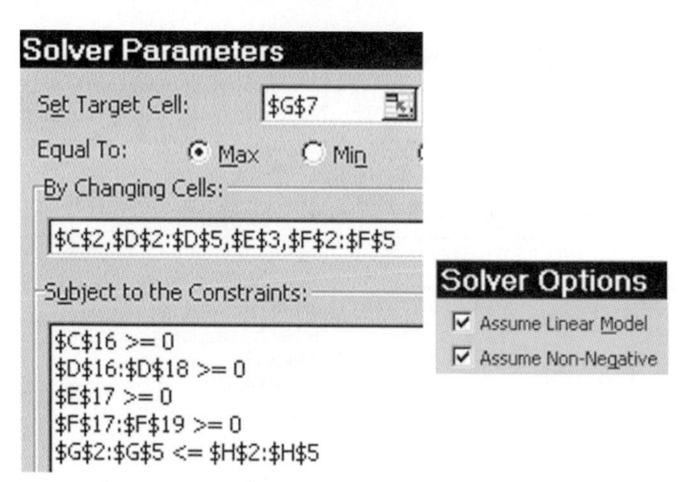

(e) What is the meaning of the fact that the content of cell D17 is positive? Explain (not using LP jargon).

(f) What is the effect on the optimal solution and the OV if the sales price of the Peanut Mix increases to $0.27 per 8-ounce can?

(g) What is the numerical value of the shadow price on the G2:H2 constraint? (Hint: What would you do with another pound of peanuts if you had them?)

FIGURE 4.43

Sensitivity Report for Problem 4-62

Microsoft Excel 9.0 Sensitivity Report

Adjustable Cells

Cell	Name	Final Value	Reduced Cost	Objective Coefficient	Allowable Increase	Allowable Decrease
$C$2	Peanuts Peanut Mix	380.00	0	0.52	0.06	0.12
$D$2	Peanuts Party Mix	123.33		0.8	0.09	0.06
$D$3	Cashews Party Mix	80.00	0	0.8	0.24	0.06
$D$4	Brazils Party Mix	43.33	0	0.8	0.36	0.56
$D$5	Hazelnuts Party Mix	0	-0.24	0.80	0.24	1E+30
$E$3	Cashews Cashew Mix	0		1.02	0.06	1E+30
$F$2	Peanuts Luxury Mix	46.67	0	1.04	1E+30	0.36
$F$3	Cashews Luxury Mix	70	0	1.04	0.56	0.24
$F$4	Brazils Luxury Mix	46.67	0	1.04	0.56	0.36
$F$5	Hazelnuts Luxury Mix	70	0	1.04	1E+30	0.24

Constraints

Cell	Name	Final Value	Shadow Price	Constraint R.H. Side	Allowable Increase	Allowable Decrease
$G$2	Peanuts Total	550		550	1E+30	380
$G$3	Cashews Total	150		150	93.33	61.43
$G$4	Brazils Total	90	1.08	90	143.33	23.33
$G$5	Hazelnuts Total	70	1.32	70	56	70
$C$16	Peanuts Peanut Mix	0	0	0	0	1E+30
$D$16	Peanuts Party Mix	0	-0.56	0	61.67	93.33
$D$17	Cashews Party Mix	43.00	0	0	43	1E+30
$D$18	Brazils Party Mix	18.67		0	18.67	1E+30
$E$17	Cashews Cashew Mix	0	0	0	0	1E+30
$F$17	Cashews Luxury Mix	0	-0.56	0	46.67	70
$F$18	Brazils Luxury Mix	0	-0.56	0	23.33	46.67
$F$19	Hazelnuts Luxury Mix	0	-0.80	0	28	56

(h) Why is the allowable increase for the RHS of the G2:H2 constraint infinity? (Hint: The answer to part (g) provides the basis for the rationale.)

(i) Provide an explanation as to why it is possible to have an optimal solution even though there is a positive surplus on the D11 constraint.

(j) What are the numerical values for the reduced costs for Peanuts in the Party Mix and Cashews in the Cashew Mix?

4-63. Why is the allowable decrease on the objective function coefficient of *M*, Mate chairs, equal to 12 in Figure 4.11 and 40 in Figure 4.15?

4-64. Note that the RHS of the Heavy Seats constraint has an allowable increase of 1E + 30 in Figure 4.11 and 7.5 in Figure 4.17. Explain this difference in the values of allowable increase.

4-65. Encorporation is a manufacturer of networked power control devices. These networked controls are used for energy management in large facilities like department stores or office buildings. The control devices are produced using three processes. Electrical Assembly builds the electronic boards, Sheet Metal Fabrication builds the package, and Final Assembly installs the boards into the package. Encorporation would like to minimize the cost of producing the three networked control products they manufacture. The three control products are affectionately known by the production workers as A, B, and C. Electrical Assembly requires 3, 2, and 1 hours for A, B, and C, respectively. Sheet Metal Fabrication requires 6, 3, and 2 hours for A, B, and C, respectively. Final Assembly requires 5 hours to complete each product. The cost for each A is $10. The cost for each B is $20. And the cost for each C is $30. Encorporation has promised five A, six B, and five C networked controls to a large discount retailer to be delivered next week. There is 80 hours available in each process. Create the spreadsheet model to minimize the cost to Encorporation and create a sensitivity report.

(a) Explain the Allowable Decrease column in the Adjustable Cells section of the report.

(b) Why is the Reduced Cost for each product zero?

(c) Explain the significance of the Allowable Decrease column for the constraints of Electrical Assembly, Sheet Metal Fabrication, and Final Assembly.

(d) How many binding constraints exist in this model?

(e) (Optional.) Is this model degenerate?

Case Study The Simplex Method

Today we take for granted the ability to solve linear programming problems. Students who are new to modeling quickly learn to develop an LP spreadsheet model in a form suitable for Solver optimization. But it hasn't always been this way.

In 1982 George Stigler won the Nobel Prize in economics for his "seminal studies of industrial structures, functioning of markets, and causes and effects of public regulation." You may be surprised to learn that earlier in his career he was working on what we would now call the diet problem. He had set out to find the least expensive diet that would satisfy the nine nutritional requirements determined by the National Research Council in 1943. Stigler had 77 foods, ranging from wheat flour to strawberry jam, to choose from. His formulation of the problem was the same as the one we saw for the Gruel example in Chapter 3.

In a 1945 paper reporting his results, titled "The Cost of Subsistence," Stigler wrote that "there does not appear to be any direct method of finding the minimum of a linear function subject to linear conditions." George Dantzig changed all that when he developed the simplex method in the late 1940s. Without the simplex method to help him, Stigler "solved" his diet problem by a combination of clever insights and brute force. At the time, he could not prove that he had a good to say nothing of optimal solution. Later, when the problem was solved with the simplex method, it turned out that his methods had produced a solution that was very close to (though not quite) optimal.

The cost-minimizing diet suggested in Stigler's paper and its annual cost (based on 1939 prices) are shown below. (Obviously, there was not a constraint for taste in this model.)

Commodity	Quantity	Annual Cost ($)
Wheat Flour	370 lbs	13.33
Evaporated Milk	57 cans	3.84
Cabbage	111 lbs	4.11
Spinach	23 lbs	1.85
Dried Navy Beans	285 lbs	16.80
Total Cost		$39.93

It is interesting to think that in less than 60 years the diet model has gone from a problem that challenged one of the finest economic scholars of all time to a simple exercise for beginning students.

The simplex method used by Solver is essentially a hill-climbing method. Once it has found a corner solution, Solver looks at all of its immediate neighboring corners and asks, "If I move to one of these corners, will the value of the objective function be improved?" If the answer is yes, the Solver moves to one such corner and then again asks whether or not a move to a neighbor will improve things further. If the answer is no, the Solver proclaims victory and quits.

Questions

1. Consider Figure 4.3 and assume that Solver started at the corner created by the intersection of constraints $C + M \geq 100$ and $C \geq 0$. Show how a hill-climbing method is guaranteed to arrive at the optimal solution.
2. On paper create a diagram like Figure 4.3 with a different feasible region for which a hill-climbing method is *not* guaranteed to yield an optimal or even a good solution. Can a feasible region like the one you have created occur in a linear programming model; that is, could you create such a region in GLP?
3. On paper use a diagram like Figure 4.3 to show a situation in which a hill-climbing method might take many or a few steps in its route to find an optimal solution.
4. Consider a new diagram for a nonlinear model with only one decision variable. With the value of a decision variable on the X axis and the value of the objective function on the Y axis, use such a diagram to illustrate the fact that in general a hill-climbing method, as described above, will not always lead to an optimal solution.

Case Study Ebel Mining (B)

Should Ebel wish to do so, its customers for lower grades of ore will gladly accept a higher-quality ore than that specified in the delivery contracts. [See Ebel Mining (A) Case in Chapter 2 and the Ebel Mining (A) Revisited Case in Chapter 3.]

"Why in the world would I want to consider such an option?" asks Truman Hardy, Ebel's on site chief mining supervisor. "You must understand that I cannot risk any activities that might increase the number of days in each mine's weekly schedule, which I must run at the minimum costs necessary to meet our delivery commitments. And we certainly don't want to spend good money producing a higher grade ore than that needed to satisfy our lower grade ore customers!" he exclaims dismissively.

"Besides," he continues, "I need to worry about ore disposal. It seems we are overproducing ore in excess of our commitments, and it now looks like Ebel will have to pay an outrageous cost of at least $15 per ton to get rid of the excess ore in an environmentally safe way. Let's see, there has just got to be a way to reduce total mining costs by eliminating this overproduction at the mines, and thus, avoiding any disposal costs. . . ."

Questions

1. Is Truman correct that Ebel can reduce costs by eliminating overproduced ore in excess of its commitments? Explain your answer to him in nontechnical language.
2. Modify your LP model from Ebel (A) Revisited to include disposal of overproduced ore and re-optimize it. As before, assume a mine can be operated for a fraction of a day. What is the recommended mining schedule for this new situation of costly disposal? Why, if at all, is it different from the previous schedule?
3. Could the option of reclassifying some tons of higher grade ores and shipping them to lower grade customers help Truman to further lower Ebel's mining costs? To investigate this, run Solver on the original model from Ebel (A) Revisited and examine its Sensitivity Report. Using only the information in the Sensitivity Report, prepare a brief rejoinder to Truman's rationale for rejecting the reclassify option. Next, do the same for the model in 2 above. Do the conclusions also hold for this model? Why or why not?
4. To more completely answer the reclassify question in 3 above, the concept of a Network Flow diagram is introduced. A Network Flow diagram documents *physical* variables in a model by means of connected arcs and nodes. The arcs represent physical movements of things, such as tons of low grade ore delivered a customer, and the nodes represent accumulations of things, such as tons of work-in-process inventory of low grade ore produced. A Network Flow diagram is a particularly useful tool in helping you build correct LP models in which physical flows of things occur. For example, material balance constraints are often needed, and this can be checked by verifying in your LP model that the sum of flows of material into a node equals the sum of material flowing out of it plus any remaining inventory. A Network Flow diagram for Ebel (A) is presented in Exhibit 1.

   Modify the flow diagram to incorporate new arcs to indicate the activities of reclassifying amounts of higher grade ores to lower grade ores.
5. Using your modified diagram from 4 above, define additional decision variables for the revised Ebel LP model of 3 above to reflect the amount of any ore type reclassified. Provide a new spreadsheet formulation of the problem, reflecting the new arcs representing the substitutability of higher grade ores for lower grades. Use the diagram to help verify that the revised constraints in your new LP model correctly accounts for material balance of ores in and out of a node. Obtain the solution to your new formulation using Solver.

   Provide an executive summary giving a managerial explanation of the optimal solution, including a discussion of the savings, if any, obtained, compared to the original solution from Ebel (A) Revisited. What is your managerial interpretation of any new shadow prices? Explain in economic terms. In your summary, comment on your recommendation for Ebel's response to the high environmental costs of disposing of any nondelivered ore. Based only on the results of your model in 5 above should Ebel lobby to try to reduce those costs?

EXHIBIT 1

Network Flow Diagram for Ebel Mining

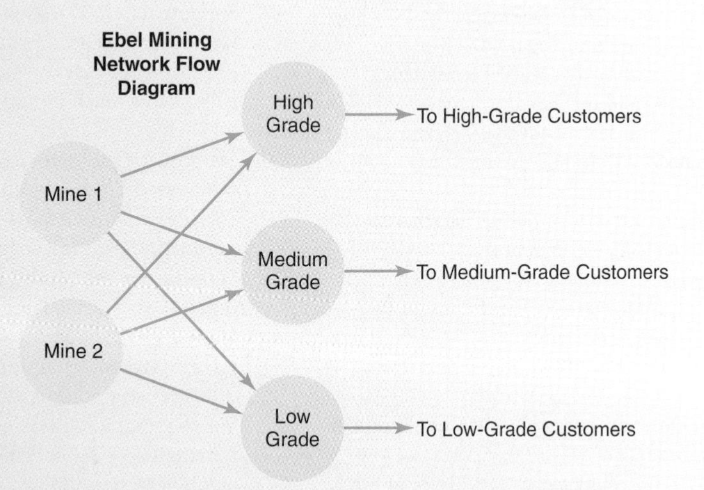

Case Study Questions Based on the Red Brand Canners Case

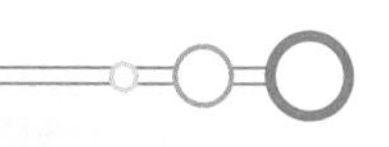

We first saw the Red Brand Canners (RBC) case in Chapter 3, where the model was formulated and assumptions were discussed. In the following questions, the analysis continues. You are asked to solve several formulations in Excel and then analyze the Solver Sensitivity Reports.

Questions

1. Use Solver to optimize your LP formulation of the Red Brand Canners production model. Do not include the option of purchasing up to 80,000 additional pounds of grade A tomatoes.
2. What is the net profit obtained after netting out the cost of the crop?
3. Myers has proposed that the net profit obtained from his policy would be $144,000. Is this true? If not, what is his net profit (taking into account, as in Question 2 the cost of the crop)?
4. Suppose Cooper suggests that, in keeping with his accounting scheme as advanced in Exhibit 2 of the original case, the crop cost of 18 cents per pound should be subtracted from each coefficient in the objective function. Change your formulation accordingly, and again solve the model. You should obtain an optimal objective value that is greater than that obtained in Question 2. Explain this apparent discrepancy (assume that unused tomatoes will spoil).
5. Suppose that unused tomatoes could be resold at 18 cents per pound. Which solution would be preferred under these conditions? How much can the resale price be lowered without affecting this preference?
6. Use the Sensitivity Report from Question 1 to determine whether the additional purchase of up to 80,000 pounds of grade A tomatoes should be undertaken. Can you tell how much should be purchased?
7. Use a reformulated model to obtain an optimal product mix using the additional purchase option. The solution to your reformulated model should explicitly show how the additional purchase should be used.
8. Suppose that in Question 1 the Market Research Department feels it could increase the demand for juice by 25,000 cases by means of an advertising campaign. How much should Red Brand be willing to pay for such a campaign?
9. Suppose in Question 1 that the price of juice increased 30 cents per case. Does your Solver Sensitivity Report tell you whether the optimal production plan will change?
10. Suppose that RBC is forced to reduce the size of the product line in tomato-based products to 2. Would you need to rerun the Solver to tell which product should be dropped from the line?
11. Suppose that in Question 1 an additional lot of grade B tomatoes is available. The lot is 50,000 pounds. How much should RBC be willing to pay for this lot of grade B tomatoes?

Alternate Questions on Red Brand Canners

For the following questions assume three grades of tomatoes, as in the alternate questions in Chapter 3.

12. Use Solver to optimize your LP formulation of Question 8 of the Alternate Questions for Red Brand Canners from Chapter 3.
13. What is the net profit obtained after netting out the cost of the crop?
14. Myers claims the net profit from his policy of producing 2,000,000 lb. paste and 1,000,000 lb. juice is $268,800. Is this correct? If not, what is his net profit (taking into account, as in Question 13, the cost of the crop)?
15. Suppose Cooper suggests that, in keeping with his accounting scheme as advanced in Exhibit 2 of the original case, the crop cost per pound should be subtracted from each coefficient in the objective function. Change your formulation accordingly, and again solve the model, assuming a crop cost of 21 cents per pound. You should obtain a solution that is different from that obtained in Question 12. Which solution has a higher net profit (assume unused tomatoes will spoil)? Is it correct to include tomato costs in the objective function?
16. If in Question 15 unused tomatoes could be resold for 21 cents a pound, which solution would be preferred? How much can the resale price be lowered without affecting this preference?
17. Use the Solver Sensitivity Report from Question 12 to determine whether the additional purchase of up to 80,000 pounds of grade A tomatoes should be undertaken. Can you tell how much should be purchased?
18. Use a reformulated model to obtain an optimal product mix using the additional purchase option. The solution to your reformulated model should explicitly show how the additional purchase should be used.
19. Suppose that in Question 12 the Market Research Department feels they could increase the demand for paste by 3,000 cases by means of an advertising campaign. How much should Red Brand be willing to pay for such a campaign?
20. Suppose in Question 12 that the price of canned whole tomatoes decreased by 48 cents per case. Does your Solver Sensitivity Report tell you whether the optimal production plan will change?
21. Suppose that the Market Research Department suggests that if the average quality of paste is below 4 the product will not be acceptable to customers. Would you need to rerun Solver to determine the optimal production plan if this constraint were added to the model?
22. Suppose that in Question 12 an additional lot of grade C tomatoes is available. The lot is 200,000 lb. How much would RBC be willing to pay for this lot of grade C tomatoes?

Case Study **Eastern Steel and a New Angle**

In important respects, part of a manager's task invokes analysis and evaluation of the work of others as opposed to producing "from rock bottom" his or her own formulation and analysis. In this diagnostic role the manager will judge someone else's model. Have the correct questions been asked? Has a correct analysis been performed? The following vignette captures the spirit of such a situation. You are asked to comment on the analysis of a new opportunity.

Ralph Hanson has been the chief metallurgist at Eastern Steel's cast iron foundry for the last five years. He brings several important qualities to this position. First, he has an excellent background. He graduated with a Master of Material Science degree and had five years' experience with another foundry before joining Eastern. He has used this training and experience to implement several changes that have contributed to product quality and process efficiency. In addition, he has become an effective manager. Through a combination of formal coursework and self-education, he has become familiar with many modern management techniques and approaches and has worked to see that these new methods are exploited whenever it is appropriate. Indeed, Ralph is responsible for introducing the use of LP models into the ore-blending and scrap-recycling activities at Eastern.

Ralph was the chief metallurgist when first ore-blending application was completed. By now both Ralph and Sam Togas, the plant manager, are comfortable with the use of LP models in the ore-blending area. Ralph typically formulates, solves, and interprets the output himself. Currently, he is facing a new problem. The recession has seriously affected the demand for steel alloys, and Eastern has excess capacity in most departments, including the foundry. However, the housing industries are booming. A fabricator of skyscraper buildings requires a high-grade ore for producing beams. Indeed, the requirements are exactly the same as Eastern used in the blending model of Section 4.10. The fabricator is willing to pay Eastern $850 per ton of ore for up to 150,000 tons to be delivered within the next month. Ralph learns that he can have up to 98,000 tons of ore available. This is made up of 21,000 tons from mine 1; 40,000 from mine 2; 15,000 from mine 3; and 22,000 from mine 4.

On the basis of these data, Ralph formulates a new LP model. In this model, T_i is the thousands of tons of ore from mine i (for $i = 1, 2, 3, 4$) that are used in the blend, and B is the thousands of tons of blended ore. He carefully annotates the formulation so that he can easily explain his analysis to Sam, the plant manager. The formulation and solution that Ralph used in his presentation are shown in Exhibit 1.

Sam was delighted with the project. It yielded a contribution margin of $30,500,000 and occupied resources (labor and machinery) that otherwise would have been idle. He immediately had the legal department draw up a contract for the sale of 98,000 tons of ore.

When Ralph arrived the next morning, Sam was waiting for him. The following discussion took place:

SAM: The contract is ready and I was about to call and confirm the arrangement, but there is a new development. We've just received an e-mail message from mine 1. Due to the cancellation of another order, we can have up to another 3,000 tons of ore at the standard price of $800 per ton if we want it. What should we do? Why don't you go back and re-solve your model including the possibility of the additional 3,000 tons from mine 1 and draw up a new contract if the new solution is better. Obviously, we can't do worse than we are doing now, and that's not bad.

RALPH: Actually, we don't have to do that. One of the great things about LP is that we can answer many questions involving changes from the original model. In particular, the shadow price on the amount of T1 available provides an upper bound on how much more we should pay to have the opportunity of buying an additional ton of ore from mine 1. If the shadow price is positive, say $10, we should be willing to pay up to $10 more for the opportunity to buy another ton of ore (i.e., up to $810 for a ton of ore from mine 1). If it is zero, increasing the amount of ore that is available from mine 1 will not enable us to increase profit.

A quick inspection of the solution reveals that the shadow price on this constraint is zero.

RALPH: Since we can't increase our contribution margin, let's just leave the contract as it is and get back to work.

SAM: Darn it, Ralph, I don't understand this. We can buy the ore for $800 a ton and sell it for $850 a ton and you tell me we shouldn't do it.

RALPH: I know it's hard to see, but I know that if the right-hand side of the constraint (cell I7) is increased, the optimal value of the objective function will remain the same. This implies that additional tons of ore from mine 1 won't help us. I suppose it's because we can't add this additional ore to our blend and still satisfy the minimum element requirements. Remember that the ore from mine 1 has only 90 pounds of element B per ton, and the blend must have at least 100.

SAM: Look, Ralph, I have to meet with the grievance committee now. I just can't spend any more time on this project. I can't say I understand your answer, but you're the expert. Let's go with the current contract.

EXHIBIT 1

Ralph's LP Model

	A	B	C	D	E	F	G	H	I	J
1	Product	Blend	T1	T2	T3	T4				
2	Qty. Prod. (000s)	98.0	21.0	40.0	15.0	22.0	Profit			
3	Contr. Mar.	$850	$(800)	$(400)	$(600)	$(500)	$30,500			
4							Total		RHS	Slack
5	Blended Ore	1	-1	-1	-1	-1	0	=	0	0
6	Blended Limit	1					98	≤	150	52
7	Ore Limit Mine 1		1				21	≤	21	1E-04
8	Ore Limit Mine 2			1			40	≤	40	0
9	Ore Limit Mine 3				1		15	≤	15	0
10	Ore Limit Mine 4					1	22	≤	22	0
11	Total Ore Avail.		1	1	1	1	98	≤	98	0
12	Minimum A		5	-2	3	-3	4	≥	0	4
13	Minimum B		-10	50	-25	75	3065	≥	0	3065
14	Minimum C		15	-5	-10	7	119	≥	0	119

Microsoft Excel 8.0 Sensitivity Report

Adjustable Cells

Cell	Name	Final Value	Reduced Cost	Objective Coefficient	Allowable Increase	Allowable Decrease
$B$2	Qty. Prod. (000s) Blend	98.0	0.0	850	1E+30	50
$C$2	Qty. Prod. (000s) T1	21.0	0.0	-800	200	50
$D$2	Qty. Prod. (000s) T2	40.0	0.0	-400	1E+30	400
$E$2	Qty. Prod. (000s) T3	15.0	0.0	-600	1E+30	200
$F$2	Qty. Prod. (000s) T4	22.0	0.0	-500	1E+30	300

Constraints

Cell	Name	Final Value	Shadow Price	Constraint R.H. Side	Allowable Increase	Allowable Decrease
$G$1:	Minimum A Total	4	0	0	4	1E+30
$G$1:	Minimum B Total	3065	0	0	3065	1E+30
$G$1·	Minimum C Total	119	0	0	119	1E+30
$G$5	Blended Ore Total	0	850	0	52	98
$G$6	Blended Limit Total	98	0	150	1E+30	52
$G$7	Ore Limit Mine 1 Total	21	0	21	1E+30	0
$G$8	Ore Limit Mine 2 Total	40	400	40	0.5714	0
$G$9	Ore Limit Mine 3 Total	15	200	15	2	0
$G$1	Ore Limit Mine 4 Total	22	300	22	0.5	0
$G$1	Total Ore Avail. Total	98	50	98	0	0.8

Questions

1. Is Ralph's interpretation of the numbers on the Sensitivity Report correct?
2. Is Ralph's response to the additional purchase opportunity correct? If you believe he has erred, where is the flaw?
3. Suppose row 11 (Total Ore Avail. constraint) were dropped from the model. What would be the shadow price on the Ore Limit Mine 1 constraint? The Ore Limit Mine 2 constraint?
4. Can you figure out what will happen to the OV if the RHS of the Mine 2 constraint (cell I8) is changed to 39.999?
5. Suppose the RHS of this constraint (cell I8) is increased to 40.001. What are the new optimal values of $T1$, $T2$, $T3$, and $T4$?
6. Figure out why the Allowable Increase on this constraint (cell I8) is 0.5714.
7. Is the solution to Ralph's model degenerate? If so, can you tell which constraint(s) causes the degeneracy in his model?
8. Exhibit 2 presents an attempt by Ralph to reformulate the LP into a more compact form similar to Wayne Foley's model in Section 4.12. Its optimal solution is the same, but the Sensitivity Report looks different from the one in Exhibit 1. How do you explain the Objective Coefficients and Reduced Costs listed in Exhibit 2's Sensitivity Report as compared to the same in Exhibit 1's Sensitivity Report? Can you answer Questions 4 and 5 using Exhibit 2?

EXHIBIT 2

Ralph's Second LP Model

	A	B	C	D	E	F	G	H
1	Product	T1	T2	T3	T4	Blend	Profit	
2	Contr. Mar.	$(800)	$(400)	$(600)	$(500)	$850	$ 30,500	
3	Qty. Prod. (000s)	21.0	40.0	15.0	22.0	98.0	<=98	
4	Supply or Demand Limit	<=21	<=40	<=15	<=22	<=150		
5	Element Constraints					Total	RHS	Slack
6	Minimum A	5	-2	3	-3	4	>=0	4
7	Minimum B	-10	50	-25	75	3065	>=0	3065
8	Minimum C	15	-5	-10	7	119	>=0	119

	A	B	C	D	E	F	G	H
1	Product	T1	T2	T3	T4	Blend	Profit	
2	Contr. Mar.	-800	-400	-600	-500	850	=SUMPRODUCT($B$3:$F$3,B2:F2)	
3	Qty. Prod. (000s)	21	40	15	22	=SUM(B3:E3)	98	
4	ly or Demand Limit	21	40	15	22	150		
5	Element Constrain					Total	RHS	Slack
6	Minimum A	5	-2	3	-3	=SUMPRODUCT($B$3:$E$3,B6:E6)	0	=F6-G6
7	Minimum B	-10	50	-25	75	=SUMPRODUCT($B$3:$E$3,B7:E7)	0	=F7-G7
8	Minimum C	15	-5	-10	7	=SUMPRODUCT($B$3:$E$3,B8:E8)	0	=F8-G8

Microsoft Excel 8.0 Sensitivity Report

Adjustable Cells

Cell	Name	Final Value	Reduced Cost	Objective Coefficient	Allowable Increase	Allowable Decrease
$B$3	Qty. Prod. (000s) T1	21	50	50	1E+30	50
$C$3	Qty. Prod. (000s) T2	40	450	450	1E+30	450
$D$3	Qty. Prod. (000s) T3	15	250	250	1E+30	250
$E$3	Qty. Prod. (000s) T4	22	350	350	1E+30	350

Constraints

Cell	Name	Final Value	Shadow Price	Constraint R.H. Side	Allowable Increase	Allowable Decrease
$F$6	Minimum A Total	4	0	0	4	1E+30
$F$7	Minimum B Total	3065	0	0	3065	1E+30
$F$8	Minimum C Total	119	0	0	119	1E+30
$F$3	Qty. Prod. (000s) Blend	98	0	150	1E+30	52
$F$3	Qty. Prod. (000s) Blend	98	0	98	1E+30	0

Case Study Saw Mill River Feed and Grain Company[1]

The purpose of this case is to exercise both judgmental and technical skills. You will have to decide, on the basis of Mr. Overton's objectives, just what information you should provide him. You will then have to formulate an LP model (or models), optimize it (or them), and present, in a summary report, the relevant results.

On Monday, August 28, 2000, Mr. Overton called in his sales manager and purchasing manager to discuss the company's policy for the coming month. Saw Mill had accepted orders from Turnbull Co. and McClean Bros. and had the option of accepting an order from Blue River, Inc. It also had the option of buying some additional grain from Cochrane Farm. Mr. Overton, managing director of Saw Mill, had to decide by the end of the week what action to take.

Usually all purchases of grain are completed by the end of August. However, Saw Mill still has the possibility of an extra purchase of grain from Cochrane Farm. This commitment has to be made by September 1. The grain would be delivered to the Midwest Grain Elevator by the 15th of the month. This elevator acts simply as a storage facility for Saw Mill.

It is immutable company policy to charge a markup of 15% on the cost of the grain supplied to customers. Payments to the Midwest Grain Elevator are treated as an overhead, and this policy is not to be challenged. Turnbull, McClean, and Blue River have agreed to pay, for their current orders, whatever price Saw Mill charges. However, Saw Mill realizes that if its price becomes too high, future business will be lost.

The details of the Turnbull, McClean, and Blue River orders are presented in Exhibit 1. The quantity, as well as the maximum moisture content, minimum weight per bushel,

[1] From an idea by Jonathan Kornbluth, based upon data originally published in Thomas H. Naylor, Eugene T. Byrne, and John M. Vernon, *Introduction of Linear Programming: Methods & Cases*, (1971) Wadsworth Publishing Co., Inc.

EXHIBIT 1 Data on Grain Orders

ORDERING COMPANY	QUANTITY (BUSHELS)	MAXIMUM PERCENT MOISTURE (PER LB)	MINIMUM WEIGHT PER BUSHEL (LB)	MAXIMUM PERCENT DAMAGE (PER LB)	MAXIMUM PERCENT FOREIGN MATERIAL (PER LB)	DELIVERY DATE
Turnbull	40,000–45,000	13	56	2	2	9/20
McClean	32,000–36,000	15.5	54	5	3	9/22
Blue River	50,000–54,000	15	56	2	4	9/26

EXHIBIT 2 Characteristics of Corn Types

TYPE OF CORN	QUANTITY (BUSHELS)	COST PER BUSHEL ($)	PERCENT MOISTURE CONTENT	WEIGHT PER BUSHEL (LB)	PERCENT TOTAL DAMAGE (PER LB)	PERCENT FOREIGN MATERIAL (PER LB)
1	30,000	1.45	12	57	2	1.5
2	45,000	1.44	15	57	2	1
3	25,000	1.45	12	58	3	3
4	40,000	1.42	13	56	4	2
5	20,000	1.38	15	54	4	2
6	30,000	1.37	15	55	5	3
7	75,000	1.37	18	57	5	1
8	15,000	1.39	14	58	2	4
9	16,000	1.27	17	53	7	5
10	20,000	1.28	15	55	8	3
11	10,000	1.17	22	56	9	5

maximum percentage damaged, and maximum percentage foreign material, is presented.

The company has the option to supply any amount of grain that it wishes, within the specified range. It must, of course, satisfy the requirements. By September 4, Saw Mill must inform Turnbull and McClean how much grain they will receive. By the same date it must inform Blue River if it will accept its order and how much grain will be delivered if it accepts.

Saw Mill blends the grains that it owns to satisfy customer orders. On August 28 the company had 326,000 bushels of corn stored in the elevator. Obviously, it would be impossible to identify the exact composition of each kernel of corn that the Saw Mill River Feed and Grain Company delivered to the elevator. Hence, Exhibit 2 represents aggregated amounts of characteristics of different types of corn credited to Saw Mill River's account with the elevator. The 326,000 bushels are segregated into 11 types of corn, which differ according to (1) quantity available, (2) cost per bushel, (3) percentage moisture content, (4) weight per bushel, (5) percentage damaged, and (6) percentage foreign material.

The grain on offer from Cochrane Farm is one load of up to 50,000 bushels, with an average of 15% moisture, 3% damage, and 2% foreign material. The load has a density of 57 pounds per bushel, and Straddle (the purchasing manager) is convinced that the order can be obtained at a cost of $1.41 per bushel.

Develop an LP model to help analyze Mr. Overton's model. (Use notation T_i = bushels of corn type i to be sent to Turnbull. Similarly for M_i and B_i. Also let corn type 12 denote the corn from Cochrane Farm.) In no more than one page, labeled "Executive Summary," provide as concisely as possible information that will help Overton answer his questions. His main objectives are to maximize profit and to keep prices to the customers sufficiently low to attract future business. He can be expected to use his judgment to make the eventual decision; your job is to provide information that will enable him to look at the important trade-offs. You should also make your own recommendations.

Your presentation will be judged on the readability of your formulation as well as the insights in your Executive Summary and on your recommendations concerning

(a) to buy or not buy from Cochrane;

(b) to accept or not to accept the Blue River option;

(c) how much corn to supply to Blue River, Turnbull, and McClean.

Case Study Kiwi Computer

Kiwi Computer of Australia manufactures two types of personal computers: a portable "laptop" model and a deluxe desktop model. Kiwi assembles the cases and printed circuit boards at its only plant, which also manufactures the cases and stuffs the circuit boards with components. Monthly production is limited by the capacities in Exhibit 1.

For example, 4,000 portable cases can be produced in a month and no desktop cases, or no portable cases and 2,000 desktop cases, or if equal time is devoted to both, 2,000 portable and 1,000 desktop cases can be produced. In order to be feasible, production of portable and desktop computers for a month must satisfy all the constraints simultaneously. The set of feasible production plans is shown in Exhibit 2.

The wholesale prices charged by Kiwi to retail computer stores are $1500 for the desktop and $1400 for the portable. The entry of a large and well known computer manufacturer has caused a boom in the industry as the market has shifted from one aimed primarily at business professionals alone to business and home computer users. Because of this shift, the market was now a "seller's market," and currently, Kiwi sells as many computers of either model as it produces. During the first quarter of the year Kiwi produced 2,000 portables a month and 600 desktops. Both board stuffing and portable assembly were operating at capacity, but there was slack in case production and desktop assembly. Kiwi's cost accountants determined standard costs and fixed overhead as shown in Exhibits 3 and 4. The fixed overhead data in Exhibit 3 are derived from the fixed overhead totals in Exhibit 4.

At a quarterly meeting of the company's executives great dissatisfaction was expressed at Kiwi's recent profit performance. The president expected much better profits as a result of the seller's market. In response, the sales manager pointed out that it was impossible to sell the desktop computer at a profit. Therefore, to improve profitability, he suggested that it be dropped from the company's product line.

The controller objected to this suggestion. He maintained that the real problem faced by desktop computers was that they had to absorb the entire fixed overhead of the desktop assembly department with only a small number of units being produced. He claimed that the production and sale of desktop computers were in fact making a positive contribution to overhead and profits. This contribution was just insufficient to cover the fixed costs. He concluded, "If we produce more desktop computers, we can lower the fixed final assembly cost of $415. It's high now because we are producing so few units."

The sales manager was appalled to hear this. It was the controller's job to provide all Kiwi executives with accounting

EXHIBIT 1 Monthly Capacity

OPERATION	PORTABLE	DESKTOP
Case Production	4000	2000
Board Stuffing	2500	3000
Portable Assembly	2000	—
Desktop Assembly	—	1800

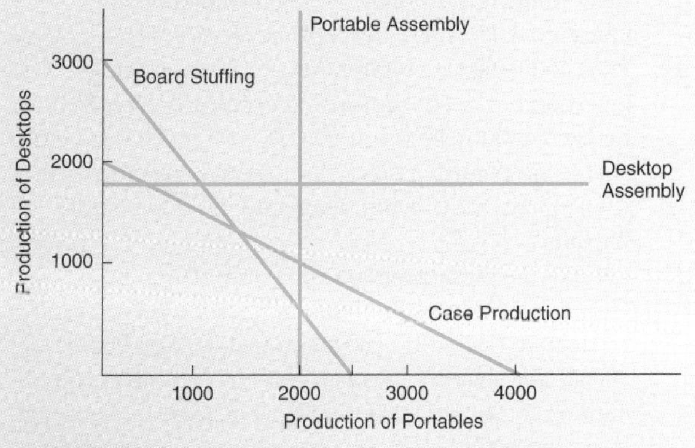

EXHIBIT 2

EXHIBIT 3

	DESKTOPS		PORTABLES	
Direct Materials		$ 800		$ 690
Direct Labor				
Case Production	$ 20		$ 15	
Board Stuffing	100		90	
Final Assembly	5	125	10	115
Fixed Overhead				
Case Production	$ 95		$ 95	
Board Stuffing	205		205	
Final Assembly	415	715	115	415
Total		$1640		$1220

EXHIBIT 4

	TOTAL FIXED OVERHEAD ($000)*	FIXED OVERHEAD PER UNIT ($)
Case Production	247	95
Board Stuffing	533	205
Desktop Assembly	249	415
Portable Assembly	230	115
Total	1259	

* Based on production of 600 desktop and 2,000 portable computers per month.

information that would help them make appropriate business decisions. If the controller's surmise were really correct, then cost figures in Exhibit 4 were quite misleading—and had been for some time.

Following up on the controller's surmise, the production manager suggested a way to increase production, "We can increase production if we outsourced some of the board stuffing to a subcontractor. We could supply the boards and components and pay the subcontractor some negotiated price to stuff each desktop board and a (probably different) negotiated price to stuff each portable board."

At this point, the president entered the discussion. He concluded the meeting by asking the sales manager, the controller, and the production manager to get together and come up with a recommendation concerning the company's product mix and subcontracting. He told them to assume that demand would remain high and current capacity would remain fixed. Specifically, he asked them to consider jointly two questions raised by their comments. His questions were as follows:

A. Assuming no change in capacity, prices charged for computers, and assuming no outsourcing of board stuffing, what would be Kiwi's most profitable mix of desktop and portable computers and would that mix involve fewer desktop computers as suggested by the sales manager?

B. What would be the maximum price per stuffed board that Kiwi should be willing to pay the subcontractor to stuff desktop boards, and what would be the maximum price per stuffed board that Kiwi should be willing to pay the subcontractor to stuff portable boards and still make as much profit as could be made by stuffing all boards of both model computers entirely within Kiwi's plant?

Prepare an executive summary memo based upon an LP analysis of the situation. In it provide specific answers to the two questions A and B.

Optional Additional Questions

Part A. Subcontracting not allowed.

1. In Exhibit 3 the standard overhead cost assigned to desktop computers for final assembly is $415. Clearly indicate how this figure was derived.
2. **(a)** Do the desktop units make a contribution to profit? In other words, given that the overhead costs are fixed in the short run, is the company's profit higher than it would be if no desktop units were produced?
   (b) A correct computation of per unit profitability's will show that the portable is more profitable than the desktop. Does this mean that more (or only) portables should be produced? Why?
3. In answering this question assume that boards cannot be stuffed by a subcontractor. Formulate an LP model for determining the optimal product mix.
4. Answer the president's first question by optimizing your model using Solver and indicate the optimal mix of desktop and portable computers. Noninteger answers are acceptable for this problem.
5. Find the best feasible integer answer that can be achieved by rounding to adjacent integers your answers from Question 4.
6. **(a)** Go back and recalculate the company's "standard costs" using your integer answers from Question 5 and compare with those in Exhibit 3.
   (b) How much larger is the profit using the new mix (using the integer answers from Question 5) than the old (i.e., 600 desktops, 2000 portables)?

Part B. Subcontracting allowed.

We now allow some boards to be stuffed by a subcontractor. Assume that production of a computer with a board stuffed by the subcontractor requires the same amount of time in case production and final assembly as production of a computer with a board stuffed at the factory.

7. Assume that the subcontractor is going to charge $110 for each desktop board stuffed and $100 for each portable board stuffed. Kiwi provides the subcontractor with the necessary materials. Should Kiwi employ the subcontractor to stuff boards? Argue why or why not without formulating and solving a new LP model.
8. Now formulate an LP model that includes subcontracting. In your formulation, distinguish between computers produced with internally and externally stuffed boards.
9. Assume that in addition to the per board charge the subcontractor is now going to include a fixed charge for stuffing a batch of boards (same charge regardless of the number of boards or their type). For what fixed charge will Kiwi be indifferent between subcontracting and stuffing all boards internally?

Part C. Sensitivity analysis.

10. Refer to the linear programming formulation in Question 8. Is the optimal solution degenerate? Explain.
11. Refer to the linear programming formulation in Question 8. Do alternative optima exist? Explain.
12. Refer to the linear programming formulation in Question 8. The subcontractor currently charges $110 for each desktop board stuffed. By how much would this charge have to decrease so that it would be optimal for Kiwi to have the subcontractor stuff desktop boards? Explain.
13. Refer to the linear programming formulation in Question 3. Assume Kiwi can increase the board-stuffing capacity so that either 600 additional desktop boards or 500 additional portable boards or any equivalent combination can be stuffed. Should Kiwi increase the capacity if the cost would be $175,000 per month? Answer *without* re-solving the LP model.

14. Refer to the linear programming formulation in Question 3. Suppose a redesign of the desktop unit to use fewer chips reduces the cost of direct materials by $200. Does your Sensitivity Report tell you whether the optimal production plan will change? Explain.
15. Answer the president's second question.

Alternative Questions on Kiwi Computer

Kiwi is considering consolidating desktop assembly and portable assembly into one department. The new department would be capable of assembling 3000 portable in a month and no desktops, or no portables and 2200 desktops, or if equal time were devoted to both, 1500 portables and 1100 desktops could be assembled. It estimates that the monthly fixed overhead for this department would be less than $479,000, the current combined overhead for the desktop and portable assembly departments. In answering the following questions assume the departments will be combined.

Part A. Subcontracting not allowed.

1. Let *D* and *P* equal the monthly production rate of desktops and portables, respectively, and *F* the fixed overhead of the new unified assembly department. Express total profit as a function of *D*, *P*, and *F*.
2. Must the value of *F* be known in order to determine the optimal product mix? Assume that fixed overhead is not affected by the values of *D* and *P*.
3. In answering this question assume that boards cannot be stuffed by a subcontractor. Formulate a linear program for determining the optimal product mix.
4. Optimize your model using Solver and indicate the optimal mix of desktop and portable computers. Noninteger answers are acceptable.
5. Find the best feasible integer answer that can be achieved by rounding to adjacent integers your answers from Question 4.
6. Suppose that the optimal profit (revenue minus *all* costs) is $330,286 if the two assembly departments are not combined. What is the largest that the fixed overhead of a combined assembly department could be and Kiwi still prefer to combine the departments?

Part B. Subcontracting allowed.

7. Assume that the subcontractor is going to charge $150 for each desktop board stuffed and $135 for each portable board stuffed. Kiwi provides the subcontractor with the necessary materials. Should Kiwi employ the subcontractor to stuff boards? Argue why or why not without formulating and solving a new linear program.
8. Now formulate a linear program that includes subcontracting. In your formulation, distinguish between computers produced with internally and externally stuffed boards.
9. Assume that in addition to the per board charge the subcontractor is now going to include a fixed charge for stuffing a batch of boards (same charge regardless of the number of boards or their type). For what fixed charge will Kiwi be indifferent between subcontracting and stuffing all boards internally?

Part C. Sensitivity analysis.

10. Refer to the linear programming formulation in Question 8. Is the optimal solution degenerate? Explain.
11. Refer to the linear programming formulation in Question 8. Do alternative optima exist? Explain.
12. Refer to the linear programming formulation in Question 8. The subcontractor currently charges $150 for each desktop board stuffed. Could the subcontractor lower his price enough so that it would be optimal for Kiwi to have him stuff desktop boards? Explain.
13. Refer to the linear programming formulation in Question 3. Assume Kiwi can increase the board stuffing capacity so that either 600 additional desktop boards or 500 portable boards or any equivalent combination can be stuffed. Should Kiwi increase the capacity if the cost would be $175,000 per month? Answer *without* resolving the linear program.
14. Refer to the linear programming formulation in Question 3. Suppose a redesign of the desktop unit to use fewer chips reduces the cost of direct materials by $200. Does your Sensitivity Report tell you whether the optimal production plan will change? Explain.

Case Study Valley Chassis Company[1]

Valley Chassis produces fine-quality polished steel and aluminum sheeting and two lines of industrial chassis for the rack mounting of Internet routers, modems, and other telecommunications equipment into six-foot high bays. For the metal sheeting sold the company earns in contribution to fixed costs and profit $0.40 per pound for steel and $0.60 per pound for aluminum. For example, the $.40 per pound for steel sheeting consists of the sales price (per pound) less direct labor and materials, including the cost of the raw unfinished steel. On the sale of a Standard chassis rack $12.00 contribution is earned while a Deluxe chassis rack yields $15.00.

 Based upon a case originally written by Evan Porteus.

For the month of January the company can buy and use up to 25,800 pounds of raw unfinished steel either in sheeting or in chassis. (Recall that the contribution margins of the various products represent the results after the direct cost of the raw materials and labor has been subtracted from the unit sales price.) Similarly, 20,400 pounds of aluminum are available. One Standard chassis rack requires 16 pounds of steel and 8 pounds of aluminum. A Deluxe chassis rack requires 12 pounds of each metal.

The output of metal sheeting is restricted only by the capacity of the polisher. For January the polisher can handle any mix of the two metals up to 4,000 pounds of metal sheeting.

Chassis manufacture can be restricted by either metal stamping or assembly operations; no polishing is required. During the month no more than 2,500 total chassis can be stamped. There are 920 hours of assembly time available each month. Valley's efficient MBA operations managers have reduced assembly time to 24 minutes for the Standard chassis rack and 36 minutes for the Deluxe chassis rack.

Market conditions limit the number of Standard chassis racks sold to no more than 1,200 Standard and no more than 1,000 Deluxe. Any quantities of metal sheeting can be sold.

Use only the following decision variables to formulate this model in Excel as an LP:

SS = pounds of steel sheeting produced and sold

AS = pounds of aluminum sheeting produced and sold

SC = number of Standard chassis racks produced and sold

DC = number of Deluxe chassis racks produced and sold

Optimize your model with Solver and answer the following questions using the output and results from the Solver Sensitivity Report. Treat each question as if it were an independent inquiry about the original optimal solution.

Questions

1. What is the incremental contribution associated with adding an hour of assembly time? Over what range of increase is this marginal value valid?
2. What is the value of additional capacity on the polisher? How much increase and decrease in this capacity is possible before a basis change occurs, that is, movement to a new corner point solution?
3. Suppose that the Standard Manufacturing Company is interested in purchasing some of Valley's available assembly time. What is the least amount of dollars per hour that Valley should be willing to accept for letting Standard purchase assembly time? Why? Over what range of time is this value valid?
4. It is forecasted that contribution per pound of steel sheeting will increase from \$0.40 to \$0.43. What effect will this have on the current solution? Briefly explain why.
5. How low can contribution per Deluxe chassis be before fewer Deluxe chassis should be built? When the contribution drops just below that critical point, how many Deluxe chassis should be produced? Explain what else is happening to the optimal plan at this point.
6. The advertising agency of Phillips, West, and Thornton has devised a marketing plan for the Valley Chassis Company that will increase the market for Deluxe chassis. The plan will increase demand by 100 Deluxe chassis per month at a cost of \$200 per month. Should Valley adopt the plan? What if the plan costs only \$120 (per month)? \$160? Answer each case as best as you can without resolving the LP.
7. Suppose that four more hours of chassis assembly time could be made available. What specific effect would this have on the production of metal sheeting and chassis products? How much would profit change?
8. A third type of chassis rack has been proposed as a very lightweight, "top-of-the-line" item. Such a chassis would contribute \$16.00 and require 8 pounds of steel and 16 pounds of aluminum. In addition, one unit of stamping capacity and 48 minutes of assembly time would be required. Should any of this type of chassis be produced? Briefly explain why or why not, *without* incorporating the change into the LP model and re-solving. (Hint: Compute the rate of profitability of this new chassis assuming that any resources needed to produce one unit of it are acquired from the existing model's constrained resources using their shadow prices as transfer prices.) Now, reformulate your Excel LP model to include the new chassis, re-solve, and compare its results to your analysis above.

Case Study Advanced Semiconductor Devices

Advanced Semiconductor Devices (ASD) is a small component parts manufacturer supplying the consumer electronics industry with high-quality Indium-Phosphide microchips. ASD has a new opportunity to supply a cellular phone manufacturer with chips that will allow the cellular phone manufacturer to build innovative lightweight phones that the user can wear in a fashion similar to earrings. These phones would use digital signal processing (DSP) to gather voice

EXHIBIT 1

	Product		
	B wafer	I wafer	Total Hours
SM	2	2	120
LIM	2	4	120
PKG	3	4	110

commands from the user and process the commands to place and receive calls with no hands or microphones required. The manufacturer will offer another product with a heads-up display screen that the user could use for Internet access also incorporating voice-activated command features so that device would be hands-free. ASD has decided that this market could be the future of the company and has spent millions in the development of these high-speed extremely small chips. ASD's process for producing the chips starts with wafer substrate manufacture (SM). A wafer will contain 100 component parts. The wafer is then sent to lithography and ion milling (LIM). This process builds the circuits for the chip on the wafer. The wafers then go to packaging (PKG) where they are broken into the individual chips. The chips have leads soldered to them and are placed in machines that package them in heat-conducting plastic packages. ASD can sell the basic cellular chip (B) for $100 each. The Internet capable chip (I) can be sold for $150. ASD is planning the next week's production. The customer will buy all the chips that can be manufactured. The total hours in each process and the hours to process each type of wafer are given in Exhibit 1.

Form the linear program and optimize it using Solver using an objective of maximizing revenue. Generate a Sensitivity Report and answer the following questions concerning the decisions or adjustable cells portion of the report. Ignore the fact that only integer numbers of wafers can be manufactured, and treat each question as if it were an independent inquiry about the original optimal solution.

Questions

1. What is the optimum production plan in numbers of wafers of (B) and (I) chips?
2. If ASD's customer will not pay more than $130 for the (I) chips, would the production plan change?
3. If the plan does not change, what would the OV be? If the plan changes, how would you find the OV?
4. If ASD could renegotiate a higher price of $115 per (B) chip, would the production plan change?
5. If the customer required 1,000 (B) chips, how would ASD's revenues be affected and what would be the OV?
6. Explain the cell indicating the allowable increase for the decision of number of (I) wafers.
7. If the ion milling process is disrupted by a mechanical failure causing the available hours to drop to 90, what will be the OV?
8. If a production engineer can find a way to improve the substrate manufacturing process so that the number of hours available can be increased to 130, what will be the resulting OV?
9. The packaging process hours are limited by the number of hours a highly trained operator is willing to work. Each hour he works increases the available time in packaging by one hour. How much would you be willing to pay the worker for 5 hours of overtime?
10. That valuable worker is now motivated by your offer to pay overtime and wants to work 20 hours more. What would be the impact of allowing the worker to work 20 hours of overtime?
11. A process-reengineering consultant has recommended that ASD can improve his revenue by attacking problems in critical processes. Use the sensitivity report to create a priority list for reengineering ASD's chip manufacturing processes. In a short executive summary memo to ASD's president present your priority list and explain the reasoning used in developing the list.

Case Study Yeltsin Farms

Igor Yeltsin operated a farm under the former Russian collective farm system. The collective farm raised hogs for distribution by the central government as its main activity. Previously, Igor was told how many hogs to raise each year by Moscow's central planning agency and was allocated the necessary animal feed to raise the hogs. With the new market-driven economy, Igor receives no instructions on how to operate his hog farm and must survive as best he can on his own by buying animal feed, raising hogs, and selling them to any buyers he can find. Hogs were fed a combination of corn and potatoes, mixed to assure that minimum amounts of two primary nutrients were met: crude protein and calories. Corn and potato supplies have become less certain, and Igor has contracted to buy waste food scraps from a nearby food processing plant to supplement the previous hog diet of corn and potatoes. Igor has turned to you, a recently arrived United Nations consultant, for help in managing his farm in the new and very uncertain Russian market economy. On his own, Igor contracted to sell up to 100 hogs to a Moscow butcher in the next month for a fixed price of 450 rubles per hog. In addition, Igor contracted to buy up to 800 kilograms of waste food from the processing plant for a price of 10 rubles per kilogram. He believes he can buy any amount of corn for 19 rubles per kilogram and can purchase up to 600 kilograms of potatoes from a nearby potato farm for 15 rubles per kilogram. The table below presents the monthly requirements per hog in units of protein and thousands of calories, and the supply per kilogram of the same for the three sources of animal feed.

NUTRIENT	MINIMUM REQUIREMENT PER HOG PER MONTH	AMT. SUPPLIED PER KILOGRAM OF CORN	AMT. SUPPLIED PER KILOGRAM OF FOOD WASTE	AMT. SUPPLIED PER KILOGRAM OF POTATOES
Crude Protein	174	18	9	15
Kilo-calories	1400	30	120	80

EXHIBIT 1

Yeltsin Farm Model

	A	B	C	D	E	F	G	H	I
1	Yeltsin Model	Hogs Sold	Corn Purchased	Food Scraps Purchased	Potatoes Purchased	Operating Income			
2	Decisions	100.00	95.24	742.86	600.00	26761.90			
3	Price	450	-19	-10	-15	Supply Limit			
4	Hogs	1				100.00	≤	100	
5	Food Scraps			1		742.86	≤	800	
6	Potatoes				1	600.00	≤	600	
7	Nutrient	Unit Nutrient Demand	Unit Nutrient Supply			Net Excess Nutrients			
8	Crude Protein	-174	18	9	15	0.00	≥	0	
9	Kilo-Calories	-1400	30	120	80	0.00	≥	0	
10		=SUMPRODUCT($B$2:$E$2,B3:E3); Copied to F4:F6 & F8:F9							
11									

Microsoft Excel 9.0 Sensitivity Report

Adjustable Cells

Cell	Name	Final Value	Reduced Cost	Objective Coefficient	Allowable Increase	Allowable Decrease
$B$3	Decisions Hogs Sold	100.00	0.00	450	1E+30	261.05
$C$3	Decisions Corn Purchased	95.24	0.00	-19	1.92	1
$D$3	Decisions Food Scraps Purchased	742.86	0.00	-10	0.5	24.69
$E$3	Decisions Potatoes Purchased	600.00	0.00	-15	1E+30	1.10

Constraints

Cell	Name	Final Value	Shadow Price	Constraint R.H. Side	Allowable Increase	Allowable Decrease
$F$4	Hogs Supply Limit	100.00	261.05	100	5.41	21.74
$F$5	Food Scraps Supply Limit	742.86	0.00	800	1E+30	57.14
$F$6	Potatoes Supply Limit	600.00	1.10	600	166.67	109.09
$F$8	Crude Protein Net Excess Nutrients	0.00	-1.048	0	46800	1500
$F$9	Kilo-Calories Net Excess Nutrients	0.00	-0.005	0	6000	78000

To help Igor understand how to run his farm, another United Nations consultant has built the Excel model, Yeltsin.xls, in Exhibit 1 in a form suitable for Solver. The Excel model shown shows the main Solver dialog and already displays the optimum answer to maximize Igor's operating income. The corresponding Solver Sensitivity Report is also presented. Igor has many questions to ask about operating his farm, which you will expertly answer by examining your Solver model results.

Some of Igor's questions cannot be answered from the Solver information given in Exhibit 1. If so, answer as best you can from the information, state why a more detailed answer is not available, and if appropriate, modify the Yeltsin.xls model from the book's CD-ROM, and rerun Solver to produce the answers he seeks.

Questions

1. "If I follow your recommended approach to managing my farm so as to maximize my operating income next month, how much will I earn from selling the 100 hogs?" asks Igor. "How many hogs will I sell, and how much corn, food scraps, and potatoes should I now purchase in that case?"
2. "I am confused," laments Igor. "You are telling me to buy fractional kilograms of corn and food scraps for my hogs. I have to make my purchases in whole kilograms. What should I do?"
3. "I think I can persuade the butcher to buy another 5 hogs from me at the same 450 ruble price. Would it improve my situation for me to try to sell him 105 hogs instead of 100? By how much would my operating income be improved, if at all?" asks Igor.
4. "You have to understand that everything is very volatile just now." Igor comments. "For example, it could easily happen that the cost of the corn that I buy might suddenly change. How much could the cost of corn increase before I would have to change my plans?"
5. "Business relationships are really uncertain in Russia just now. I am nervous that the farm manager selling me the potatoes will not honor his promise to deliver the 600 kilograms. If he delivers only 500 kilograms of potatoes, how much will I be hurt and what changes do I need to make in my decisions?"
6. "Are there any alternate ways for me to achieve the same optimal operating income, involving, for example, different purchases of corn, food, or potatoes? If so, what are they?" asks Igor.
7. "An international salesman from the Ralston-Purina Company stopped by the farm and wants to sell me prepackaged dry hog feed imported from Poland. He wants to charge me 16 rubles per kilogram for the packaged hog food, which includes transportation from Poland. He says each kilogram of his product provides 16 units of crude protein and 150 kilocalories. Should I start importing hog feed from Poland? And how much should I buy, if any, and what would be the impact of this opportunity on my optimal operating income?" asks Igor, sounding more and more like a capitalist farmer.

References

George Dantzig, "The Diet Problem," *Interfaces*, 20, no. 4 (1990): 43–47.

Lily Lancaster, "The Evolution of the Diet Model in Managing Food Systems," *Interfaces*, 22, no. 5 (1992): 59–68.

Robert J. Might, "Decision Support for Aircraft and Munitions Procurement," *Interfaces*, 17, no. 5 (1987): 55–63.

De-Li Yang and Weiqin Mou, "An Integrated Decision Support System in a Chinese Chemical Plant," *Interfaces*, 23, no. 6 (1993): 93–100.

Honorio Carino and Clinton LeNoir, "Optimizing Wood Procurement in Cabinet Manufacturing," *Interfaces*, 18, 2, (1988): 101–19.

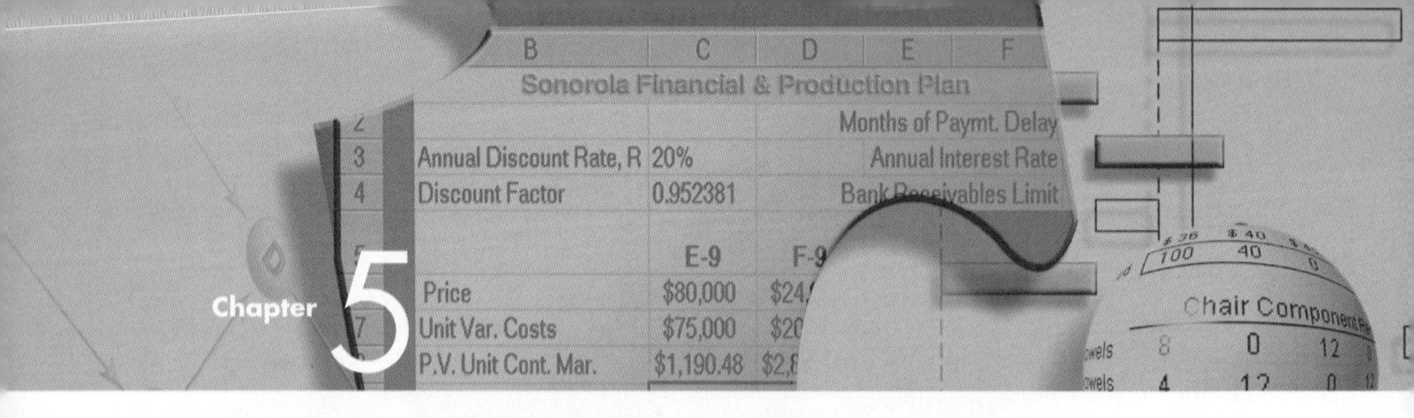

Chapter 5

LINEAR OPTIMIZATION: APPLICATIONS

CHAPTER OUTLINE

APPLICATION CAPSULE

Ici on parle HASTUS: Montréal Streamlines Its Transportation Scheduling with LP

Controlling the costs of public transportation is a problem that knows no national boundaries. One highly successful approach was developed by Société de la Communauté urbaine de Montreal (S.T.C.U.M.) in Canada. This organization, with a staff of 8,000 and an annual budget of more than $575 million, provides close to 400 million passenger trips per year. To do so, it runs 1,700 buses and 750 subway cars, for which it must schedule 3,000 drivers and other personnel daily.

Efficient scheduling is extremely important—it improves service and working conditions and can have a dramatic impact on operating costs. Such scheduling is difficult because of the large variation in service levels required during the course of the day. During peak demand hours, nearly 1,500 vehicles may be needed, compared to a fifth that number during slack periods. Scheduling must take into account vehicle frequencies on each route during the day, as well as the effect on average vehicle speed of traffic conditions (such as rush-hour congestion) at different times.

Transit-system scheduling is done in two successive operations. Vehicle scheduling is done first. The aim is to provide the number of buses and subway trains required to maintain desired service frequencies on each route. Crew scheduling then assigns drivers to the vehicles. To facilitate these tasks S.T.C.U.M., in cooperation with the Center for Research on Transportation of the University of Montreal, developed the HASTUS system. The program consists of three main software modules:

- One module is used to provide optimum vehicle scheduling, using network methods.
- A second module uses the LP models to obtain a "good" initial solution for crew scheduling. Carefully chosen simplifications reduce the enormous number of variables to 3,000, so that the model can be solved very rapidly.
- The final module refines the solution to produce detailed driver scheduling assignments, using assignment and shortest-route techniques.

The scheduling department has carefully compared the costs of parallel manual and computer-generated solutions. HASTUS was found to reduce manual scheduling errors, saving at least $100,000 per year in unnecessary wages. The system thus paid for itself in less than three months. In addition, HASTUS has been shown to reduce unproductive paid time of drivers and other employees by 20% compared to existing manual solutions. The total annual savings amount to some $4 million: $3 million in manpower scheduling and an additional $1 million in vehicle scheduling.

The system also permits managers to perform sensitivity and "What-if?" analysis. Simulations that would have required weeks using manual techniques can now be done in minutes. Such analyses have helped management to tailor the most cost-effective proposals in negotiations with its labor unions.

HASTUS is easy to learn and use, and has proved popular with schedulers because it makes their jobs more interesting and challenging. The success of the program has been so great that today versions of HASTUS in several languages are helping planners in 40 cities around the world. (See Blaise et al.)

5.1 INTRODUCTION

Linear optimization is *the* workhorse in the world of optimization models. The ability of an LP model to scale from simple models involving dozens to complex models involving tens of thousands of decision variables and constraints, and the incredible number of interactions that these numbers imply makes LP an important tool in a wide variety of business situations.

In this chapter we concentrate on some applications of linear optimization. In particular, we consider eleven specific models in a variety of settings that can serve as templates for larger, more realistic applications in practice. Section 5.2 is devoted to one of the most popular applications of linear optimization, the *transportation model.* In this model, management must determine how to send products from various sources (e.g., warehouses) to various destinations (e.g., customers) in order to satisfy requirements at the lowest possible cost. Section 5.3 is devoted to the *assignment model.* This model enables management to investigate allocating fixed-sized resources, for example, to determine the optimal assignment of salespeople to districts, jobs to machines, tasks to computers, or editors to manuscripts. The model itself is a special type of transportation model.

Section 5.4 considers an important marketing model. Called the *media selection model,* it is concerned with designing an effective advertising campaign. More precisely, management must decide how many ads to place in each of several possible advertising media. The decision is constrained by an overall budget allocation, the number of openings for ads in the various media, and rules of thumb insisted on by management. The media selection model is a specific example of an important class of management models. These are models in which either decreasing returns to scale occur, in this case declining marginal returns to advertising, or blending occurs, in this case a required proportional mix of advertising media employed.

Next, in Sections 5.5 through 5.8 we investigate the important case of multiperiod or *dynamic* models in which coordinated decision making must occur over more than one time period. We illustrate dynamic models with three examples in which management of a physical inventory plays a role in production, in production scheduling, and in cash management over time.

A financial and production planning model is presented in Section 5.9. Although it is relatively simple by the standards of actual applications, it illustrates how business models involving the joint optimization of both production and financial resources can be constructed.

The transportation and assignment models are special cases of a more general class of logistics models called *network models* involving the movement or assignment of physical entities (products, people, money, Internet packets, etc.). The balance of the chapter is devoted to several popular examples of network models for transshipment, finding the shortest route, and maximizing the flow of entities in a network.

5.2 THE TRANSPORTATION MODEL

The AutoPower company makes a variety of battery and motorized uninterruptible electric power supplies (UPSs) to provide backup electric power to hospitals, Internet service providers, chemical and semiconductor fabrication plants, and so forth, that cannot tolerate an interruption in their electric power service. AutoPower has four final assembly plants for their large diesel motor-generator UPSs in Europe. They are located in Leipzig, Germany (1); Nancy, France (2); Liege, Belgium (3); and Tilburg, the Netherlands (4). As part of AutoPower's supply chain, the diesel motors used by these UPSs are produced in the United States, shipped to harbors in Amsterdam (A), Antwerp (B), and Le Havre (C) and are then sent to the assembly plants.

Production plans for the third quarter, July through September, have been set. The *requirements* (the *demand* at **destinations**) for motors are as shown in Table 5.1.

The *available* number of motors at harbors (the *supply* at **origins**) in time to be used in the third quarter are shown in Table 5.2.

Table 5.1

Demand for Motors

ASSEMBLY PLANT	NUMBER OF MOTORS REQUIRED
(1) Leipzig	400
(2) Nancy	900
(3) Liege	200
(4) Tilburg	500
	2000

Table 5.2

Supply of Motors

HARBOR	NUMBER OF MOTORS AVAILABLE
(A) Amsterdam	500
(B) Antwerp	700
(C) Le Havre	800
	2000

FIGURE 5.1

AutoPower's Transportation Problem

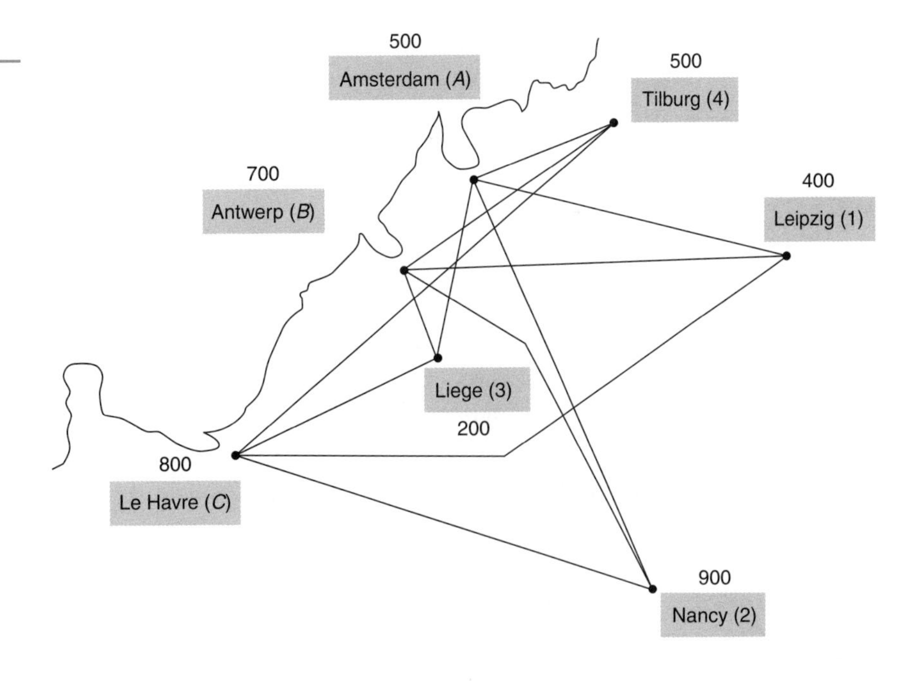

Table 5.3

Cost to Transport a Motor from an Origin to a Destination ($)

From Origin	Leipzig (1)	Nancy (2)	Liege (3)	Tilburg (4)
	TO DESTINATION			
(A) Amsterdam	120	130	41	59.50
(B) Antwerp	61	40	100	110
(C) Le Havre	102.50	90	122	42

Note that this is a *balanced* model in the sense that the total supply of motors available equals the total number required. Figure 5.1 illustrates the model. In this figure the number above the harbors indicates the supply available; and the number above the assembly plants indicates the quantity demanded. The lines indicate the possible delivery routes.

AutoPower must decide how many motors to send from each harbor to each plant. The motors are transported by common carrier trucks, and charges are on a per motor basis. The relevant costs are given in Table 5.3. For ease of presentation, we will refer to the harbors with letters and the plants with numbers, as indicated in the supply and demand information above.

THE LP FORMULATION AND SOLUTION

AutoPower's goal is to minimize the total cost of transporting the motors from the harbors to the plants. Since the transportation cost for any specific harbor-plant combination (e.g., Antwerp-Nancy) is directly proportional to the number of motors sent from the harbor to the plant ($40 per motor in the Antwerp-Nancy example), we can formulate this situation as an LP model. To do so, we let

$$x_{ij} = \text{number of motors sent from harbor } i \text{ to plant } j;\ i = \text{A, B, C};\ j = 1, 2, 3, 4$$

Thus, x_{C4} is the number of motors sent from C, Le Havre, to 4, Tilburg. With this definition, the total transportation cost, which is our objective function, becomes

$$120x_{A1} + 130x_{A2} + \cdots + 42x_{C4}$$

The model has two general types of constraints:

1. The number of items shipped from a harbor cannot exceed the number that are available. For example, $x_{A1} + x_{A2} + x_{A3} + x_{A4}$ is the total number of motors shipped from A, Amsterdam. Since only 500 motors are available at A, the constraint is

$$x_{A1} + x_{A2} + x_{A3} + x_{A4} \leq 500$$

   A similar constraint is required for each origin. Note that equality constraints could be used instead of the $\leq$ inequalities in expressing these supply restrictions. Since the supply and demand are balanced for this model, the supply inequality constraints will be binding at optimality giving the same effect.

2. Demand at each plant must be satisfied. For example, $x_{A1} + x_{B1} + x_{C1}$ is the total number of motors sent to plant 1, Leipzig. Since 400 motors are demanded at plant 1, the constraint is

$$x_{A1} + x_{B1} + x_{C1} \geq 400$$

A similar constraint is required for each plant. As with the supply constraints, equalities could be used for the demand constraints because supply and demand are balanced.

The Excel formulation showing the optimal solution to AutoPower's transportation model is presented in Figure 5.2. Note how the model's layout takes advantage of the

FIGURE 5.2

The Optimal Solution for AutoPower's Transportation Model

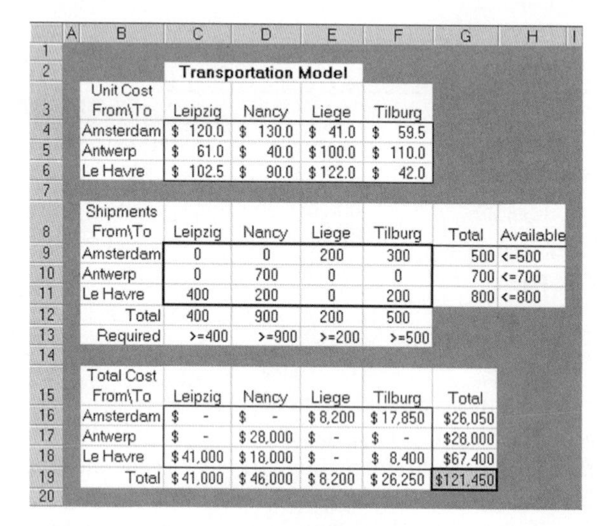

Transportation Model

Unit Cost From\To	Leipzig	Nancy	Liege	Tilburg
Amsterdam	$ 120.0	$ 130.0	$ 41.0	$ 59.5
Antwerp	$ 61.0	$ 40.0	$ 100.0	$ 110.0
Le Havre	$ 102.5	$ 90.0	$ 122.0	$ 42.0

Shipments From\To	Leipzig	Nancy	Liege	Tilburg	Total	Available
Amsterdam	0	0	200	300	500	<=500
Antwerp	0	700	0	0	700	<=700
Le Havre	400	200	0	200	800	<=800
Total	400	900	200	500		
Required	>=400	>=900	>=200	>=500		

Total Cost From\To	Leipzig	Nancy	Liege	Tilburg	Total
Amsterdam	$ -	$ -	$ 8,200	$ 17,850	$26,050
Antwerp	$ -	$ 28,000	$ -	$ -	$28,000
Le Havre	$ 41,000	$ 18,000	$ -	$ 8,400	$67,400
Total	$ 41,000	$ 46,000	$ 8,200	$ 26,250	$121,450

Cell	Formula	Copy To
C16	= C4*C9	C16:F18
G9	= SUM(C9:F9)	G10:G11
C12	= SUM(C9:C11)	D12:F12

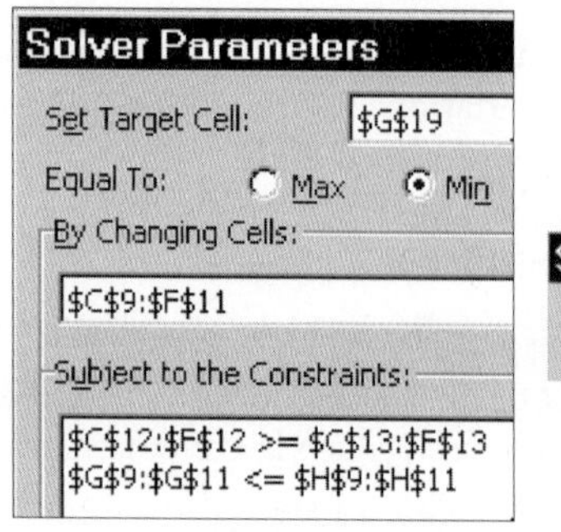

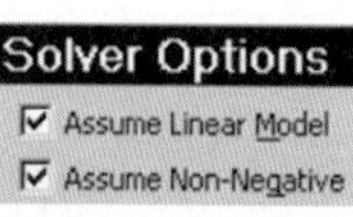

TIP: *Consistent with the recommendations of Chapter 3, models in this chapter (1) isolate cost/contribution parameters, decision variables, and total costs/profits into blocks of cells surrounded by shaded cells, and (2) outline the decision variables with a border and the OV cell with a dark border and shaded background. Using these or similar conventions will improve your model's readability. Also, as described in Section 4.12, format dressing is used to display each RHS parameter along with its constraint symbol in the same cell. For example the contents of cell H9 is the datum 500, but its cell format is a Custom setting of "<="0 that allows the cell to also document the constraint. Details on format dressing are contained in Appendix B.*

Microsoft Excel 9.0 Sensitivity Report

Adjustable Cells

Cell	Name	Final Value	Reduced Cost	Objective Coefficient	Allowable Increase	Allowable Decrease
$C$9	Amsterdam Leipzig	0	0	120	1E+30	0
$D$9	Amsterdam Nancy	0	22.5	130	1E+30	22.5
$E$9	Amsterdam Liege	200	0	41	98.5	41
$F$9	Amsterdam Tilburg	300	0	59.5	0	17.5
$C$10	Antwerp Leipzig	0	8.5	61	1E+30	8.5
$D$10	Antwerp Nancy	700	0	40	8.5	1E+30
$E$10	Antwerp Liege	0	126.5	100	1E+30	126.5
$F$10	Antwerp Tilburg	0	118	110	1E+30	118
$C$11	Le Havre Leipzig	400	0	102.5	0	120
$D$11	Le Havre Nancy	200	0	90	22.5	8.5
$E$11	Le Havre Liege	0	98.5	122	1E+30	98.5
$F$11	Le Havre Tilburg	200	0	42	17.5	0

Constraints

Cell	Name	Final Value	Shadow Price	Constraint R.H. Side	Allowable Increase	Allowable Decrease
$C$12	Total Leipzig	400	120	400	0	300
$D$12	Total Nancy	900	107.5	900	0	200
$E$12	Total Liege	200	41	200	0	200
$F$12	Total Tilburg	500	59.5	500	0	300
$G$9	Amsterdam Total	500	0	500	1E+30	0
$G$10	Antwerp Total	700	-68	700	200	0
$G$11	Le Havre Total	800	-18	800	300	0

FIGURE 5.3

The Sensitivity Report for AutoPower's Transportation Model

"from-to" organization of a transportation model and the use of three blocks of cells to isolate the model's major modules: cost parameters, decision variables, and total costs. In Figure 5.2 we see that 6 of the 12 possible routes are used, and that the minimum possible transportation cost is $121,450. Moreover, Solver's Sensitivity Report for this solution in Figure 5.3 indicates that, for example, total costs would fall at the rate of $107.5 per motor if Nancy's requirements were reduced, and total costs would fall at the rate of $67.50 per motor if Antwerp's supply of motors were increased. (Movement in the opposite directions—increased demand or reduced supply—is not allowable because it would cause infeasibility.)

5.3 VARIATIONS ON THE TRANSPORTATION MODEL

In general, the term **transportation model** is an LP model to find the least expensive way of satisfying demands at n destinations with supplies from m origins.

SOLVING MAX TRANSPORTATION MODELS

Suppose that in the example your goal was to maximize the value of the objective function rather than minimize it. You could use the same model with one small, but fundamental, change. Define the objective function coefficients as contribution margins, that is, unit returns, rather than unit costs. The Solver formulation is then modified to be a Maximization instead of a Minimization model. Interpretation of Solver's Sensitivity Report information is similarly modified.

WHEN SUPPLY AND DEMAND DIFFER

Suppose that in the example model the supply at harbor A was 600 motors rather than 500. Then, when all demand is satisfied, the sum, over the three origins, of the motors left over will be 100. Because inequalities were used in the Solver model in Figure 5.2, this causes no special problems. The supply that was not allocated at each origin would appear as slack in the supply constraint for that origin.

If total demand exceeds total supply, the LP model has no feasible solution. AutoPower management might, however, be interested in supplying as much demand as possible at minimum cost. There are two approaches to model this situation. We can rewrite the harbor supply constraints to be equalities, thereby forcing all available supply of motors to be shipped to some plant, and rewrite the demand constraint to be a ≤ inequality for each destination plant's demand, that is, shipments of motors to a plant will not exceed its demand. Unfilled demand will appear as slack on each of these demand constraints upon Solver optimization. Alternatively, we can revise the model to append a placeholder origin, called a **dummy origin**, with supply equal to the difference between total demand and total supply. This dummy origin is an imaginary source that is added to a transportation model so that total supply equals total demand. The cost of supplying any destination from this origin is zero. Any supply allocated by Solver from the dummy origin to a destination is interpreted as unfilled demand. An advantage of this second approach is that you can assign unit costs to each of the dummy-origin-to-destination decision variable links. If these costs accurately reflect the opportunity costs of unmet demand at that destination, then Solver will account for these costs in concert with the transportation costs in its optimization and Sensitivity Report information.

ELIMINATING UNACCEPTABLE ROUTES

Assume that certain routes in a transportation model are unacceptable. Organizational constraints such as regional restrictions or delivery time could indicate that certain origins could not serve certain destinations. For example, assume that the Amsterdam-to-Liege route could not be used. This restriction is handled in formulating transportation models by assigning an arbitrarily large unit cost number, identified as M, to that route. M is chosen to be much, much larger than any other unit cost number in the model. This would then force Solver to eliminate the use of that route since the cost of doing so would be very much larger than that of any other feasible alternative. In the case of this example, assigning a unit transportation cost coefficient to cell E4 in Figure 5.2 of, say, \$1,000,000 would effectively eliminate that route from consideration by Solver.

INTEGER-VALUED SOLUTIONS

From earlier chapters we know that, in general, LP models do *not* produce integer solutions. Even general LP models in which all of the parameters (unit payoffs, constraint technical coefficients, and RHSs) are integer do not necessarily produce integer solutions. The transportation model is an exception and has integer solutions under quite general conditions.

If all of the supplies and demands in a transportation model have integer values, the optimal values of the decision variables will also have integer values.

USING ALTERNATIVE OPTIMA TO ACHIEVE MULTIPLE OBJECTIVES

The zeros in the Allowable change for objective coefficients in the Sensitivity Report of Figure 5.3 signal alternative optimal solutions.[1] This provides us an opportunity to illustrate how to exploit such occurrences that happen often in LP models, especially transportation models. Suppose AutoPower Europe's president is concerned about the risk of higher costs to its supply chain caused by a potential trucker's strike at Le Havre. She tells you to "find a cheaper transportation schedule that also minimizes the costs of shipping those motors out

[1] More precisely, they indicate alternative optima if the solution is nondegenerate.

TIP: *Users of Excel 2000 should be aware of a serious Excel bug that is triggered by Solver optimization and that generates bogus "Out of Memory" error messages during Solver optimization. As of this book's printing, Microsoft has no plans to release a fix for it. However, it is triggered by the use of any Merged Cells in a worksheet. To avoid problems do not merge any cells of a worksheet. A common use of merged cells is to center descriptive titles over columns. The same effect can be obtained by using the Center Across Selection in the Horizontal Text Alignment field under the Alignment tab of Format Cells dialog. This was done to center the title in C2:E2 of Figure 5.4. See Appendix B for information on Center Across Selection. Also consult the book's Web Page at Prentice-Hall for any more recent information on the Excel 2000 bug.*

of Le Havre." Of course, if there were a cheaper schedule Solver would have found it, but the prospect of shifting costs away from Le Havre to reduce AutoPower Europe's risk is potentially a good idea even if total costs were to increase somewhat. In this case the presence of alternative optima may allow the president to avoid some of the risk without increasing total costs. To explore this further note that we want to investigate those alternative optimal solutions that in addition minimize Le Havre's transportation costs. But we already have a minimization tool in Solver; the trick is how to tell Solver to reduce Le Havre's total transportation costs without it raising total costs. From the discussion in Section 4.7 on alternative optima, we know that for this model there are an infinite number of alternative optima that produce a minimal cost of $121,450. So, the original objective can then be recast as an additional total cost constraint thereby allowing Solver to be given a new OV to minimize. Figure 5.4 shows the solution to a revised model to minimize Le Havre's total costs with the added constraint that total costs in G19 be no higher than the previous minimum cost of $121,450. This forces Solver to consider only alternatives no more costly than that found originally, and thus known to be feasible, while minimizing Le Havre's total costs, in this case producing a shift of more than $18,000 in costs to other routes.

This process of moving the original optimal OV to become a constraint allowing a new objective to be specified to Solver can be continued so long as each resulting Sensitivity Report signals alternative optima. This approach can also be applied in cases of no alternative optima by loosening the added total cost constraint, for example, to find the minimal Le Havre costs subject to the added constraint that total costs be no more than a given total cost number, such as, say, no more than 5% higher than the previous minimum. Of course, this multi-objective approach to optimization by constraints on original payoff can be applied to any LP model, not just to a transportation model.

Let us now turn to an important special case of the transportation model, called the *assignment model.*

FIGURE 5.4

Minimizing Le Havre's Transportation Costs

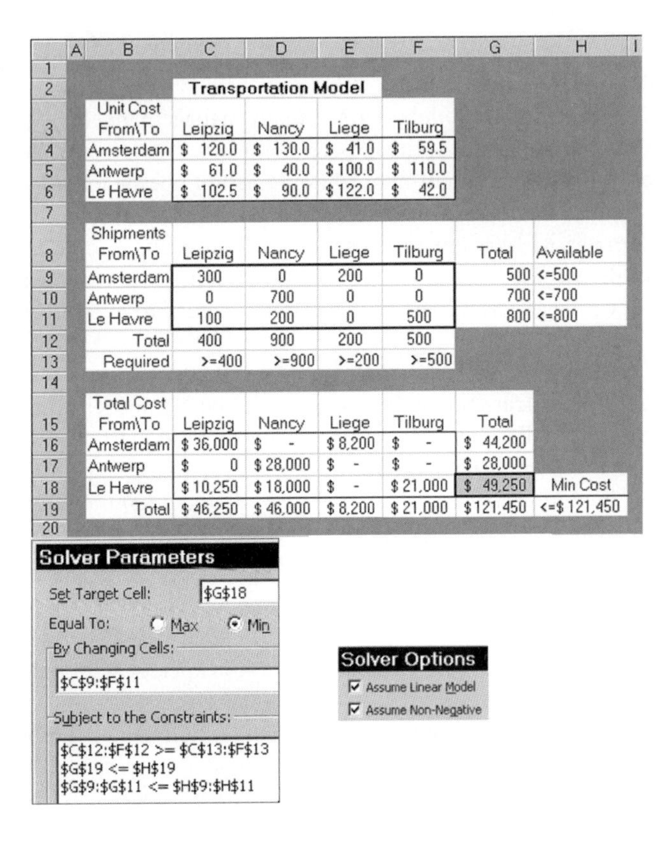

Transportation Model

Unit Cost From\To	Leipzig	Nancy	Liege	Tilburg
Amsterdam	$ 120.0	$ 130.0	$ 41.0	$ 59.5
Antwerp	$ 61.0	$ 40.0	$ 100.0	$ 110.0
Le Havre	$ 102.5	$ 90.0	$ 122.0	$ 42.0

Shipments From\To	Leipzig	Nancy	Liege	Tilburg	Total	Available
Amsterdam	300	0	200	0	500	<=500
Antwerp	0	700	0	0	700	<=700
Le Havre	100	200	0	500	800	<=800
Total	400	900	200	500		
Required	>=400	>=900	>=200	>=500		

Total Cost From\To	Leipzig	Nancy	Liege	Tilburg	Total	
Amsterdam	$ 36,000	$ -	$ 8,200	$ -	$ 44,200	
Antwerp	$ 0	$ 28,000	$ -	$ -	$ 28,000	
Le Havre	$ 10,250	$ 18,000	$ -	$ 21,000	$ 49,250	Min Cost
Total	$ 46,250	$ 46,000	$ 8,200	$ 21,000	$121,450	<=$ 121,450

Solver Parameters
Set Target Cell: $G$18
Equal To: Max Min
By Changing Cells:
$C$9:$F$11
Subject to the Constraints:
$C$12:$F$12 >= $C$13:$F$13
$G$19 <= $H$19
$G$9:$G$11 <= $H$9:$H$11

Solver Options
Assume Linear Model
Assume Non-Negative

APPLICATION CAPSULE **Play Ball! The American League Uses an LP Assignment Model to Schedule Umpiring Crews**

Each year, the American League, after the difficult task of scheduling 162 games for its 14 teams, must assign the umpiring crews that will work each game. Typically, teams play one another in series consisting of 2, 3, or 4 games, with each team playing a total of 52 series in the course of the 26-week season. One of the League's seven umpiring crews must be assigned to each series.

Not surprisingly, with teams in cities across the entire North American continent, from Baltimore to Seattle and from Texas to Toronto, minimizing total travel costs is one of the principal goals of the schedulers. However, it is not the only factor that must be taken into consideration. To guarantee fairness, there are limits to the number of times each crew is exposed to each team, for both its home and its away games. Moreover, every effort is made to avoid a crew being assigned to the same team for more than two consecutive series.

Travel restrictions impose additional constraints on the schedule. Some of the more important examples include:

- A crew cannot work a night game in one city and an afternoon game in another city the next day.
- Because of time changes, a crew cannot travel from a West Coast city to Chicago or any eastern city without a day off between series.
- Because of limited airline flight schedules, a crew traveling into or out of Toronto must have a day off if it is coming from or going to any city other than New York, Boston, Detroit, or Cleveland.

While the total number of possible crew assignments is far too large for each one to be evaluated individually, the scheduling of umpires can be formulated as a relatively simple assignment model. The League now uses a PC-based decision support system, developed by Dr. Jim Evans of the University of Cincinnati, that produces a better schedule in less than half the time previously required.

The program color-codes each crew in the screen display of schedule assignments. This makes it easy for the user to follow a particular crew and examine the flow of its assignments. In addition to the assignment scheduling algorithm, the system includes a statistical computation and database program that makes it easy to keep track of crew/team combinations. As a result, the balance of crew exposures has improved since the system came into use. In its first year of use, the system saved the American League some $30,000 in travel costs. (See Blaise et al.)

5.4 THE ASSIGNMENT MODEL

The **assignment model** occurs in many management contexts. In general, it is the problem of determining the optimal assignment of n "*indivisible*" agents or objects to n tasks. For example, management might have to assign salespeople to sales territories, service representatives to service calls, consultants to clients, lawyers to cases, computers to networks, or commercial artists to advertising copy. The agents or objects to be assigned are indivisible in the sense that no agent can be divided among several tasks. The important constraint, for each agent, is that he or she or it be assigned to *one and only one task.*

AUTOPOWER EUROPE'S AUDITING PROBLEM

Let us illustrate the assignment model with another situation facing the president of AutoPower Europe. AutoPower's European headquarters is in Brussels. This year, as part of her annual management audit, AutoPower Europe's president has decided to have each of the four corporate vice presidents visit and audit one of the assembly plants during the first two weeks in June. As you recall, the assembly plants are located in Leipzig, Germany; Nancy, France; Liege, Belgium; and Tilburg, the Netherlands.

There are a number of advantages and disadvantages to various assignments of the vice presidents to the plants. Among the issues to consider are:

1. Matching the vice presidents' areas of expertise with the importance of specific problem areas in a plant.
2. The time the management audit will require and the other demands on each vice president during the two-week interval.
3. Matching the language ability of a vice president with the dominant language used in the plant.

Table 5.4

Assignment Costs in $000s for Every Vice President–Plant Combination

	PLANT			
V. P.	Leipzig (1)	Nancy (2)	Liege (3)	Tilburg (4)
Finance (F)	24	10	21	11
Marketing (M)	14	22	10	15
Operations (O)	15	17	20	19
Personnel (P)	11	19	14	13

Table 5.5

One Assignment Scenario

ASSIGNMENT		
V. P.	Plant	COST
F	1	24
M	2	22
O	3	20
P	4	13
Total Cost		79

Attempting to keep all these factors in mind and arrive at a good assignment of vice presidents to plants is a challenging problem. The president decides to start by estimating the (opportunity) cost to AutoPower Europe of sending each vice president to each plant. The data are shown in Table 5.4.

With these costs, the president can evaluate any particular assignment of vice presidents to plants. For example, if she chooses the assignment in Table 5.5 she incurs a total cost of $79,000.

SOLVING BY COMPLETE ENUMERATION

Since there are so few vice presidents and plants, and only a finite number of ways to make the vice president assignments, she might try *complete enumeration*, that is, calculate the cost of each feasible assignment pattern, and pick the lowest. However, similar to the Oak Products example of Chapter 3, complete enumeration of all alternatives quickly becomes burdensome. Let us see how many alternatives there are to this vice president assignment model. Consider assigning the vice presidents in the order F, M, O, P. We have the following steps:

1. F can be assigned to any of the four plants.
2. Once F is assigned, M can be assigned to any of the three remaining plants.
3. Similarly, O can be assigned to any of the two remaining plants.
4. P must be assigned to the only available plant.

There are, thus, $4 \times 3 \times 2 \times 1 = 24$ possible solutions. In general, if there were n vice presidents and n plants, there would be $n(n-1)(n-2)(n-3)\cdots(2)(1)$ solutions, which is n factorial, $n!$. As n increases, $n!$ increases *extremely* rapidly. Here is the relation between n and $n!$ for values of n between 1 and 20:

n	1	2	3	4	5	6	7	8	9	10	20
$n!$	1	2	6	24	120	720	5040	40,320	362,880	3,628,800	2.4×10^{18}

Thus, if the president were currently worrying about which of her 15 salespeople to assign to each of AutoPower Europe's 15 sales districts, it is clear that complete enumeration would be extremely difficult or impossible to enumerate even in Excel. This shows how quickly combinatorial problems can grow. While it may be easy to solve smaller models by inspection, insight, or intuition, when they grow even moderately larger, a sure, and efficient optimization method is needed.

THE LP FORMULATION AND SOLUTION

To create the model we use the same definition of variables as we used for the transportation model. In particular, we let

x_{ij} = number of vice presidents of type i assigned to plant j; i = F, M, O, P; j = 1, 2, 3, 4

AutoPower Europe's assignment model is shown in Figure 5.5, which also displays the cost-minimizing assignment. In this figure we note that there is only one of each type of vice president available (the supply), and one vice president is required at each plant (the demand). Also, it is a balanced model in the sense that the total number of vice presidents available equals the total number required. Hence, equality constraints could have been used instead of the inequality ones. Each of the numbers in cells C18:F21 is AutoPower Europe's cost for that assignment.

In this formulation the first constraint in Figure 5.5 states that the number of vice presidents "sent" from Finance, F, must be no more than 1. Similar restrictions are placed

FIGURE 5.5

The Optimal Solution for the AutoPower Assignment Model

Assignment Model

Unit Cost

VP\To	Leipzig	Nancy	Liege	Tilburg
Finance	$ 24	$ 10	$ 21	$ 11
Marketing	$ 14	$ 22	$ 10	$ 15
Operations	$ 15	$ 17	$ 20	$ 19
Personnel	$ 11	$ 19	$ 14	$ 13

Assignment

VP\To	Leipzig	Nancy	Liege	Tilburg	Total	Available
Finance	0	1	0	0	1	<=1
Marketing	0	0	1	0	1	<=1
Operations	1	0	0	0	1	<=1
Personnel	0	0	0	1	1	<=1
Total	1	1	1	1		
Required	>=1	>=1	>=1	>=1		

Total Cost

VP\To	Leipzig	Nancy	Liege	Tilburg	Total
Finance	-	$ 10	-	-	$ 10
Marketing	-	-	$ 10	-	$ 10
Operations	$ 15	-	-	-	$ 15
Personnel	-	-	-	$ 13	$ 13
Total	$ 15	$ 10	$ 10	$ 13	$ 48

Cell	Formula	Copy To
C18	= C4*C10	C18:F21
G10	= SUM(C10:F10)	G11:G13
C14	= SUM(C10:C13)	D14:F14

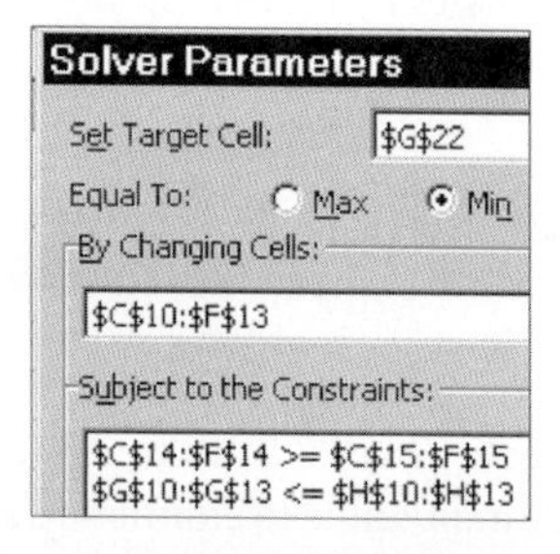

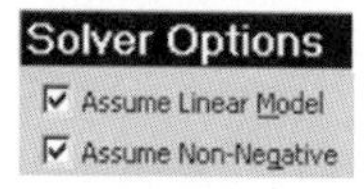

TIP: *The layout of the Solver Options dialog is different if The Premium Edition Solver for Education is installed and the "Premium" button is clicked on the Solver Parameters dialog, but its functions are the same. An exception is the "Bypass Solver Reports," which if clicked will prevent you from selecting any post-optimality reports in exchange for some time savings in Solver's optimization. The rest of the Solver Options can be ignored for properly scaled LP models, but are covered in the Solver Tips and Messages in Appendix C.*

Table 5.6

The Optimal Assignment

ASSIGNMENT		
V. P.	Plant	COST
F	2	10
M	3	10
0	1	15
P	4	13
Total Cost ($000s)		48

on vice presidents M, O, and P, respectively. Thus, each decision variable cell in C10:F13 is constrained to be between 0 and 1 by these upper-bound constraints and the nonnegativity specification in the Solver Options dialog. The "Required" constraint on Plant1 stipulates that at least 1 vice president be assigned to plant 1. The remaining constraints place a similar requirement on plants 2, 3, and 4, respectively.

Since Figure 5.5 also gives the optimal solution, we see that all decision variables are 0 or 1, and the optimal assignment is as summarized in Table 5.6.

RELATION TO THE TRANSPORTATION MODEL

This hauntingly familiar representation is, of course, reminiscent of the standard transportation model introduced in Section 5.2. There is only one difference. In the assignment model, we must respect the additional requirement that supply cannot be distributed to more than one destination. That is, as previously mentioned, each unit of supply (each vice president) must go to one and only one destination. An answer that sent three-fourths of a vice president to Leipzig and the remaining one-fourth to Liege would not be meaningful in this context and is, therefore, prohibited.[2] Recall for transportation models that, if all the supplies and demands are integers, the optimal allocations will also be integers. In the assignment model, all supplies and demands are one, and hence integer. Thus, we can be assured that Solver will not produce fractional allocations. As a result, in the solution of AutoPower Europe's assignment model, each decision variable cell in C10:F13 will contain either a 0 or a 1 where a 1 represents the assignment of a specific vice president to a specific plant.[3] In general, we can see that:

> The assignment model can be formulated as a transportation model in which the supply at each origin and the demand at each destination is equal to 1.

THE ASSIGNMENT MODEL: OTHER CONSIDERATIONS

AutoPower Europe's assignment model is a minimization model in which the number of vice presidents equals the number of plants, and every possible assignment is acceptable. Next we consider assignment-like models in which all these conditions do not hold. In particular, we consider situations where

1. There are an unequal number of "persons" to assign and "destinations" needing assignees.
2. There is a maximization model.
3. There are unacceptable assignments.

---

[2] Of course, if fractional assignments were meaningful, then the situation can be modeled as a transportation model, using the available total supply constraint of a given vice president as a RHS of 100 to indicate 100%. Fractional assignments would only appear in the solution, however, if the total demand at some plant for vice presidents is more or less than 100, that is, 100%.

[3] Decision variables constrained by a model to be either a 0 or 1 value, as in this example, are often called "indicator" or "binary" variables.

Table 5.7

Assignment Costs in $000s, Supply Exceeds Demand

V. P.	PLANT 1	PLANT 2	PLANT 3	NUMBER OF V. P.s AVAILABLE
F	24	10	21	1
M	14	22	10	1
O	15	17	20	1
P	11	19	14	1
Number of V. P.s Required	1	1	1	3 \ 4

UNEQUAL SUPPLY AND DEMAND: THE AUDITING PROBLEM RECONSIDERED

We wish to consider two cases. First, assume that supply exceeds demand. In particular, assume that the president herself decides to audit the plant in Tilburg. She must then decide which of the four vice presidents to assign to each of the three remaining plants, as given in the cost matrix in Table 5.7.

To formulate this revised model we would simply drop the constraint that required a vice president at plant 4 in Figure 5.5. The result of this change is that the slack in one of the four vice president supply constraints would be 1 in the optimal solution, that is, one vice president would not be assigned to a plant.

We now consider the case where demand exceeds supply. For example, assume that the vice president of personnel had to visit AutoPower's International Headquarters in the United States during the first two weeks in June and is thus unable to participate in the European audit. The president's problem is then represented by the cost matrix in Table 5.8.

Demand > Supply: Adding a Dummy Vice President In this form the model is infeasible. It is clearly impossible to satisfy the demand for four vice presidents with a supply of three. If the president wanted to find which three plants to audit in order to minimize her cost, she could (1) modify the inequalities in the constraints in a way similar to that done for the transportation example in Section 5.3 when demand exceeded supply or (2) add a dummy vice president as a placeholder to the cost matrix as shown in Table 5.9. In the solution, the dummy vice president would be assigned to a plant. In reality, this plant would not be audited. Like the earlier transportation example, an advantage of the second approach, however, is that it might make more sense to think that AutoPower Europe would incur some (opportunity) cost if a plant were not audited by a vice president and that this cost could vary from plant to plant. Under these assumptions the new row of the model could be labeled "Not Audited" in the Excel model and the appropriate opportunity cost should be entered in each cell.

Table 5.8

Assignment Costs in $000s, Demand Exceeds Supply

V. P.	PLANT 1	PLANT 2	PLANT 3	PLANT 4	NUMBER OF V. P.s AVAILABLE
F	24	10	21	11	1
M	14	22	10	15	1
O	15	17	20	19	1
Number of V. P.s Required	1	1	1	1	4 \ 3

Table 5.9

Adding a Dummy Vice President

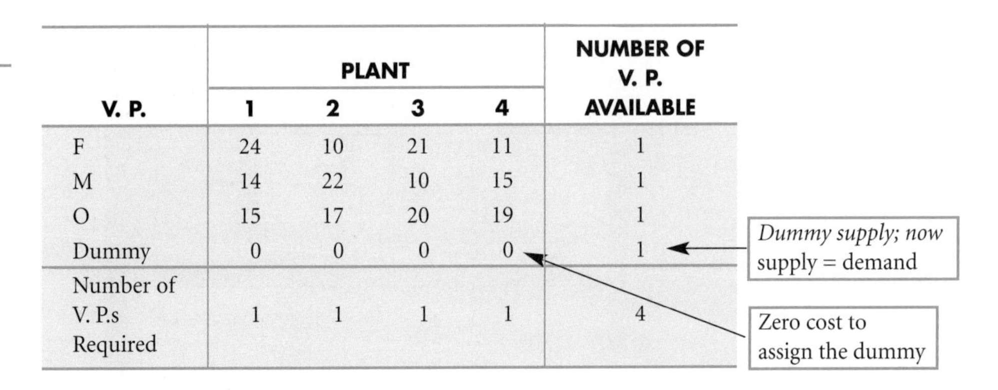

V. P.	PLANT 1	2	3	4	NUMBER OF V. P. AVAILABLE
F	24	10	21	11	1
M	14	22	10	15	1
O	15	17	20	19	1
Dummy	0	0	0	0	1
Number of V. P.s Required	1	1	1	1	4

Dummy supply; now supply = demand

Zero cost to assign the dummy

The optimal solution is the solution that minimizes the cost of the audits undertaken by F, M, and O. At any rate, when demand exceeds supply, one or more new rows of supply, with costs if appropriate, can be appended to the model to allow a feasible solution to be found.

MAXIMIZATION MODELS

Consider an assignment model in which the response from each assignment is a profit rather than a cost. For example, suppose that AutoPower Europe must assign new salespeople to sales territories. Four trainees are ready to be assigned and three territories require a new salesperson. One of the salespeople will have to wait until another territory becomes available before he or she can be assigned.

The effect of assigning any salesperson to a territory is measured by the anticipated marginal increase in profit contribution due to the assignment. Naturally, AutoPower Europe is interested in maximizing total profit contribution. The *profit* matrix for this model is presented in Table 5.10. The only new feature of this figure is that the number in each cell represents a profit contribution rather than a cost.

The Excel formulation and optimal solution for this model is shown in Figure 5.6.

SITUATIONS WITH UNACCEPTABLE ASSIGNMENTS

Suppose that you are building an assignment model and you know that certain assignments are simply unacceptable. For example, assume that because of a strong personality conflict the president of AutoPower Europe is sure that she does not want to have the vice president of operations (O) audit the assembly plant at Nancy (2). To achieve this goal, simply assign a unit cost number to cell D6 in Figure 5.5 that is very much larger than the model's other cost numbers. Such an assignment will automatically eliminate the assignment of vice president O to plant 2. This is, of course, the same general approach used to

Table 5.10

Assignment Costs in $000s, Demand Exceeds Supply

SALESPERSON	TERRITORY 1	2	3	NUMBER OF SALESPEOPLE AVAILABLE
A	40	30	20	1
B	18	28	22	1
C	12	16	20	1
D	25	24	27	1
Number of Salespeople Required	1	1	1	3 / 4

Profit if A is assigned to 3

FIGURE 5.6

The LP for the Maximization Assignment Model

Assignment Model

Contribution Salesperson\To	Territory 1	Territory 2	Territory 3
A	$ 40	$ 30	$ 20
B	$ 18	$ 28	$ 22
C	$ 12	$ 16	$ 20
D	$ 25	$ 24	$ 27

Assignment Salesperson\To	Territory 1	Territory 2	Territory 3	Total	Available
A	1	0	0	1	<=1
B	0	1	0	1	<=1
C	0	0	0	0	<=1
D	0	0	1	1	<=1
Total	1	1	1		
Required	<=1	<=1	<=1		

Total Contribution Salesperson\To	Territory 1	Territory 2	Territory 3	Total
A	$ 40	-	-	$ 40
B	-	$ 28	-	$ 28
C	-	-	-	$ 0
D	-	-	$ 27	$ 27
Total	$ 40	$ 28	$ 27	$ 95

Cell	Formula	Copy To
C18	= C4*C10	C18:E21
F10	= SUM(C10:E10)	F11:F13
C14	= SUM(C10:C13)	D14:E14

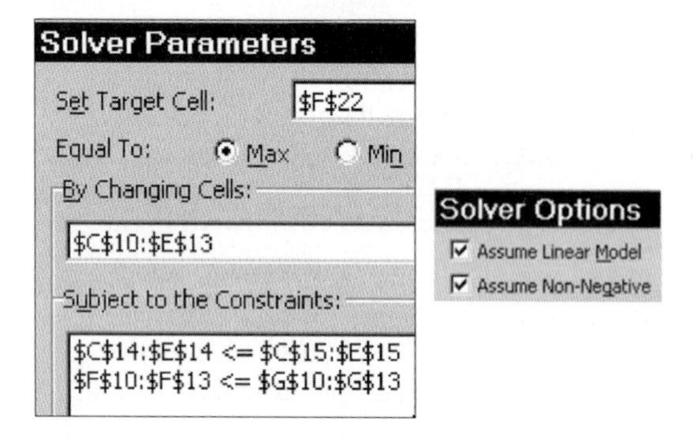

ensure that unacceptable routes are not part of the optimal solution in a transportation model covered in Section 5.3.

Next we turn to the important case of modeling a situation having both blending requirements and diminishing returns without abandoning the simplicity of linear relationships.

5.5 THE MEDIA SELECTION MODEL

The media selection model is faced by a firm or advertising agency as they try to develop an effective advertising campaign. Basically, the question is how many "insertions" (ads) the firm should purchase in each of several possible media (e.g., radio, TV, newspapers, magazines, and Internet Web pages). The goal, in a not very specific sense, is to have the advertising campaign be as effective as possible. As we shall see, the explicit objective we will adopt is subjective. Constraints on the decision maker are typically provided by the total advertising budget and the number of opportunities to place an ad that are available in each of the media. Management may further constrain the decision by insisting on various rules of thumb. For example, it might be insisted that at least a certain dollar amount be spent on a specific medium (e.g., at least $10,000 must be spent on newspaper advertising). Alternatively, it might be stipulated that no more than a certain percentage of the budget (say 50%) be spent on any one medium.

Finally, the decision may be influenced by "the law of diminishing returns"; that is, management may believe that the effectiveness of an ad decreases as the number of exposures in a medium increases during a specified period of time. For example, the tenth exposure of a TV ad in a given week would typically not have the same impact on the audience as the first or second exposure.

We will present a media selection example in detail. It is at first, however, interesting to point out that the model has an unusual objective function. Clearly, management would like to select its advertising campaign to maximize demand for the product being advertised. Conceptually, then, the model should find the advertising campaign that maximizes demand and satisfies the budget and other constraints. Unfortunately, the link between product demand and the advertising campaign is sufficiently vague so that it is difficult to construct a useful model based on this approach. The approach commonly used is to measure the response to a particular ad in a particular medium in terms of what are called **exposure units**. This is a subjective measure based on management's assessment of the quality of the particular ad, the desirability of the potential market, and so on. In other words, it is an arbitrary measure of the "goodness" of a particular ad. An exposure unit can be thought of as a kind of economic utility function. Management's goal then becomes one of maximizing total exposure units, taking into account other properties of the model (e.g., cost per number of potential customers reached, and so on). A specific example follows.

PROMOTING A NEW PRODUCT

The RollOn company has decided to enter the recreational vehicle market with a motorcycle-like machine with three oversized tires. Since this is a new product line, an advertising campaign is planned during the introductory month, and a budget of $72,000 is set up to fund the campaign. RollOn decides to use daytime radio, evening TV, and daily newspaper ads in its advertising campaign. Data concerning the cost per ad in each of these media and the number of purchasing units reached by each ad are provided by RollOn's advertising agency. The data are summarized in Table 5.11.

We have already mentioned that the effectiveness of an ad is measured in exposures. RollOn management arbitrarily selects a scale from 0 to 100 for each offering of an ad. In particular, it is assumed that each of the first 10 radio ads has a value of 60 exposure units, and each radio ad after the first 10 is rated as having 40 exposures. Figure 5.7 shows a plot of total exposures as a function of the number of daytime radio ads during the month.

Note that in this figure, since each of the first 10 radio ads is rated as having 60 exposures, the slope of the first line segment is 60. After the first 10 ads, since each radio ad is rated as having 40 exposures, the slope of the second line segment is 40. Radio ads, then, suffer from diminishing returns. It is RollOn management's subjective evaluation that the first ads are more effective than later ones. This evaluation is based primarily on the assumption that a large proportion of those who see/hear the later ads in a given medium will also have seen/heard the earlier ones.

Table 5.11

Media Data

ADVERTISING MEDIUM	NUMBER OF PURCHASING UNITS REACHED PER AD	COST PER AD ($)
Daytime Radio	30,000	1700
Evening TV	60,000	2800
Daily Newspaper	45,000	1200

FIGURE 5.7

Total Exposures vs. Number of Radio Ads

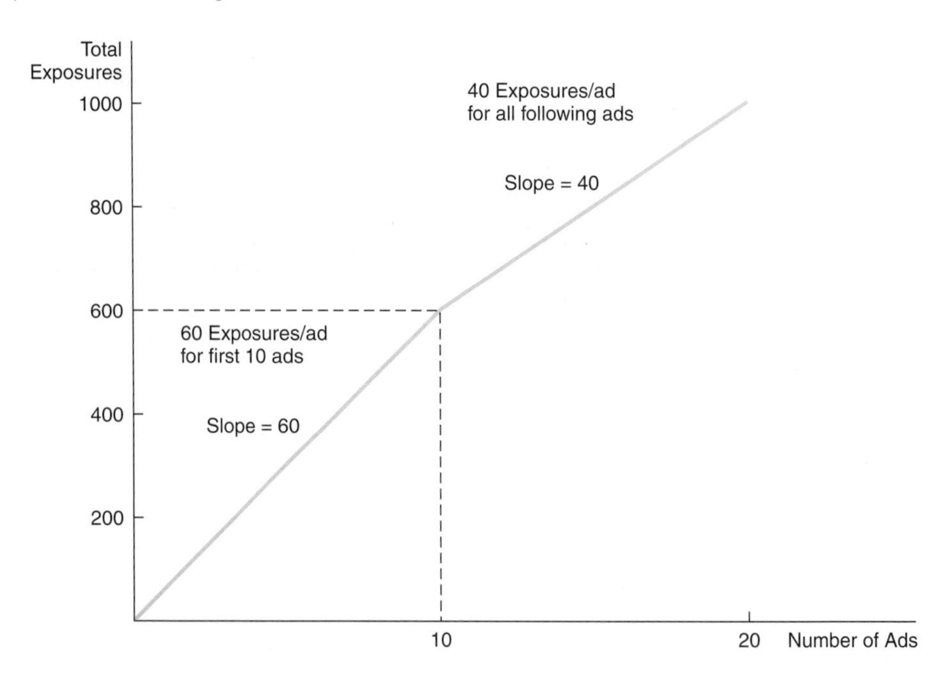

RollOn's analysts feel that the same situation will occur with TV and newspaper ads; that is, they, too, will suffer from diminishing returns. For simplicity, they assume that in all three cases the slope (i.e., the exposures per ad) will change at the tenth ad. The exposures per ad (i.e., the slope of the two line segments), however, vary with the particular medium. These data are summarized in Table 5.12. The total exposures as a function of the number of ads in each medium are plotted in Figure 5.8.

RollOn management wants to ensure that the advertising campaign will satisfy certain criteria that it feels are important. In particular: (1) no more than 25 ads should appear in a single medium, (2) a total number of 1,800,000 purchasing units must be reached across all media, and (3) a blending requirement that at least one-fourth of the ads must appear on evening TV. To model RollOn's media selection model as an LP model, we let

x_1 = number of daytime radio ads up to the first 10

y_1 = number of daytime radio ads after the first 10

x_2 = number of evening TV ads up to the first 10

y_2 = number of evening TV ads after the first 10

x_3 = number of newspaper ads up to the first 10

y_3 = number of newspaper ads after the first 10

With this notation we note that $60x_1$ is the total exposures from the number of "first 10" radio ads and $40y_1$ is the total exposures from the remaining radio ads. Thus, the objective function is

$$\text{Max } 60x_1 + 40y_1 + 80x_2 + 55y_2 + 70x_3 + 35y_3$$

Table 5.12

Exposures per Ad

ADVERTISING MEDIUM	FIRST 10 ADS	ALL FOLLOWING ADS
Daytime Radio	60	40
Evening TV	80	55
Daily Newspaper	70	35

FIGURE 5.8

Total Exposures Versus Number of Ads

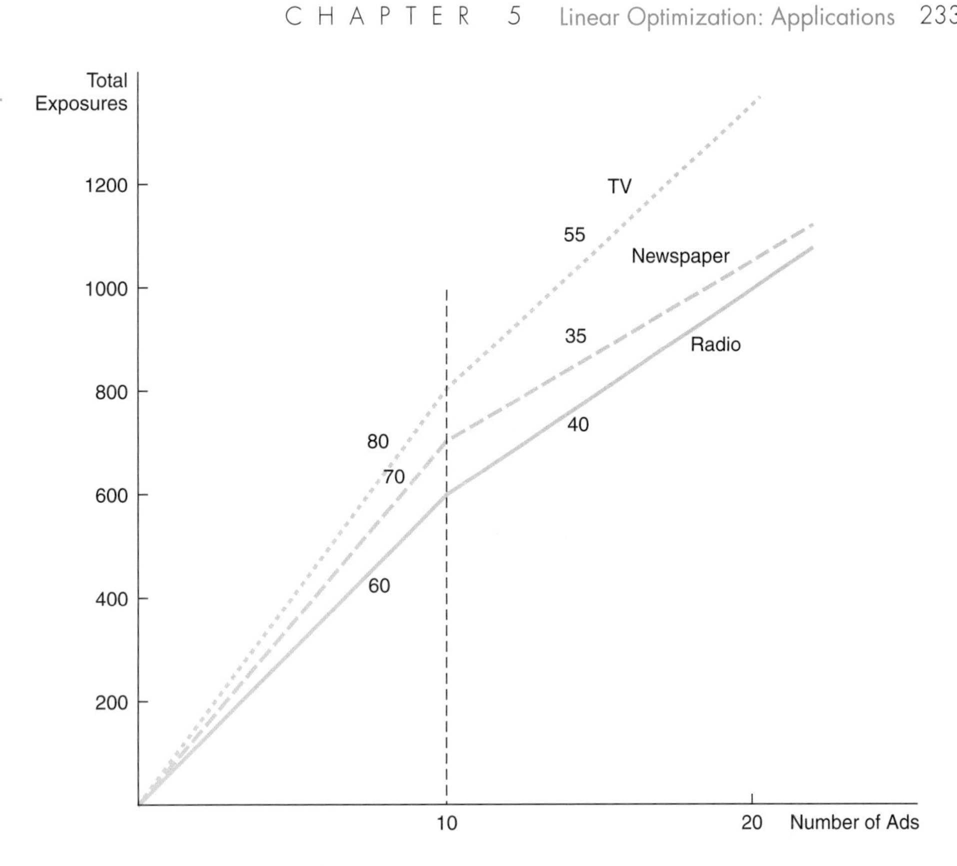

TIP: *This trick of representing a percentage-of-total requirement as a linear constraint is commonly used in this and other LP modeling situations involving blending, such as blending petroleum, blending wines, mixing animal feed or paint or chemicals, and so forth. It is recommended that you write out each blending constraint symbolically as a nonlinear fraction first, and then rewrite the constraint as a linear one when creating the Excel model. Otherwise, it is very likely you will get the direction of the inequality wrong. This happens so commonly in blending models, that if Solver generates the error message "The linearity conditions required by this LP Solver are not satisfied" or "Solver could not find a feasible solution," then immediately suspect that you forgot to linearize some blending constraint or got its direction of the inequality wrong, respectively.*

Turning to the constraints, we note that

$$x_1 + y_1 = \text{total radio ads}$$
$$x_2 + y_2 = \text{total TV ads}$$
$$x_3 + y_3 = \text{total newspaper ads}$$

Referring to Table 5.11, we see that each radio ad costs \$1700. The expression for the total spent on radio ads is $1700(x_1 + y_1)$. Since TV ads cost \$2800 each and newspaper ads cost \$1200 each, the total advertising expenditure is $1700(x_1 + y_1) + 2800(x_2 + y_2) + 1200(x_3 + y_3)$. RollOn has allocated \$72,000 for the promotional campaign. This constraint is enforced by the following inequality:

$$1700x_1 + 1700y_1 + 2800x_2 + 2800y_2 + 1200x_3 + 1200y_3 \le 72{,}000$$

The constraint that no more than 25 ads appear on daytime radio is imposed by the inequality $x_1 + y_1 \le 25$. A similar constraint is required for each other medium.

Referring again to Table 5.11, we see that each radio ad reaches 30,000 purchasing units. Thus, the total number of purchasing units reached by radio ads is $30{,}000(x_1 + y_1)$. The requirement that the entire campaign reach at least 1,800,000 purchasing units is imposed by the inequality

$$30{,}000x_1 + 30{,}000y_1 + 60{,}000x_2 + 60{,}000y_2 + 45{,}000x_3 + 45{,}000y_3 \ge 1{,}800{,}000$$

Finally, the blending constraint that at least one-fourth of the ads must appear on evening TV is guaranteed by the constraint

$$\frac{x_2 + y_2}{x_1 + y_1 + x_2 + y_2 + x_3 + y_3} \ge \frac{1}{4}$$

Unfortunately, the appeal of this constraint is offset by the presence of decision variables in the fraction's denominator for the left-hand side. Creating this constraint in Excel will produce "The linearity conditions required by this LP Solver are not satisfied" error message when it is optimized. Although a nonlinear optimization could be done, a topic we cover in Chapter 7, a simpler trick is simply to make the constraint linear by multiplying out the denominator as follows.

$$x_2 + y_2 \geq .25(x_1 + y_1 + x_2 + y_2 + x_3 + y_3)$$

The complete formulation with its optimal solution is presented in the Excel model of Figure 5.9. Note that the three constraints in cells I3:K3 enforce the 10-ad upper bound on the variables x_1, x_2, and x_3, while the three constraints in cells I4:K4 impose a very large 1000 upper bound on the variables y_1, y_2, and y_3. There is, however, one additional point to be noted. According to the definitions x_1 is the number of radio ads up to the first 10 and y_1 is the number of radio ads after the first 10. Let x_1^* and y_1^* be the optimal values of these variables. Clearly it would not make sense to have an optimal solution with $x_1^* < 10$ and $y_1^* > 0$; that is, it does not make sense to have placed ads after the first 10 when not all of the first 10 have been placed. Nothing in the constraints prevents this. However, it will not occur. The reason is that the marginal contribution of x_1, in the objective function, is larger than that of y_1. If $x_1 < 10$ and $y_1 > 0$ is feasible, you can see from the constraints that the values $x_1 + \varepsilon$ and $y_1 - \varepsilon$ will also be feasible, where ε is a very small positive number. Moreover,

TIP: *Do not forget the recommendations from Chapter 3 to avoid having both very large and very small numbers in your Excel models when using Solver. Otherwise, you risk getting bogus Solver error messages caused by numerical inaccuracies in your microprocessor's binary arithmetic. Either check "Use Automatic Scaling" (operative only in Excel 97 or later versions for LP models) in Solver Options dialog, or manually rescale your parameters, or both. The latter is recommended, as "Use Automatic Scaling" is insufficient in some situations. In this example cost parameters were scaled to be in thousands of dollars instead of dollars. Details on Solver's difficulties handling a model with a wide range of numbers are contained in the Solver Tips and Messages in Appendix C.*

	A	B	C	D	E	F	G	H	I	J	K	L	M	N
1		Media Selection Model												
2		No. Ads	Radio Ads	TV Ads	Newsp. Ads	Total		Segment Limits	Radio Ads	TV Ads	Newsp. Ads		TV % Limit	
3		Segmt. 1	10	10	10	30		Segmt. 1	<=10	<=10	<=10		25%	
4		Segmt. 2	0	0.47	11.41	11.87		Segmt. 2	<=1000	<=1000	<=1000			
5		Total	10	10.47	21.41	41.87		Purch. Units/Ad	30	60	45	Tot.Units	Required	
6		Media Limit	<=25	<=25	<=25			Tot. Purch. Units	300	628.13	963.281	1891.41	>=1800	
7		TV % Limit		>=10.47										
8		Exposures Per Ad	Radio Ads	TV Ads	Newsp. Ads			Unit Cost/Ad	Radio Ads	TV Ads	Newsp. Ads			
9		Segmt. 1	60	80	70			Segmt. 1	$ 1.70	$ 2.80	$ 1.20			
10		Segmt. 2	40	55	35			Segmt. 2	$ 1.70	$ 2.80	$ 1.20			
11														
12		Total Exposures	Radio Ads	TV Ads	Newsp. Ads	Total		Total Cost (000s)	Radio Ads	TV Ads	Newsp. Ads	Total		
13		Segmt. 1	600	800.0	700	2,100		Segmt. 1	$17.00	$28.00	$12.00	$57.00		
14		Segmt. 2	0	25.78	399.2	425		Segmt. 2	$0.00	$1.31	$13.69	$15.00	Budget	
15		Total	600	825.78	1099.2	2,525		Total	$17.00	$29.31	$25.69	$72.00	<=$72	
16														

Cell	Formula	Copy To
D7	= M3*F5	—
I6	= C5*I5	J6:K6
C13	= C3*C9	C13:E14
I13	= C3*I9	I13:K14

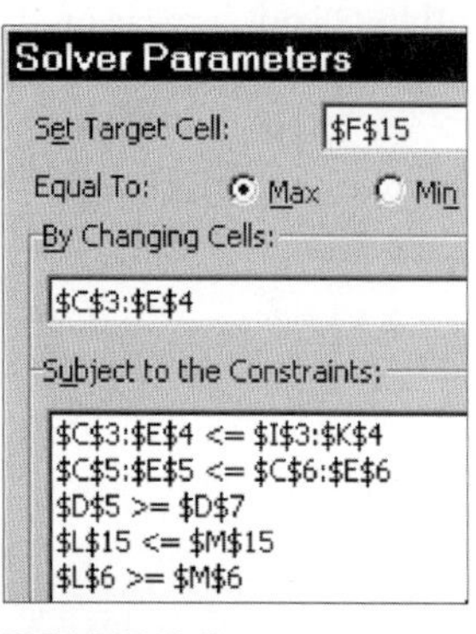

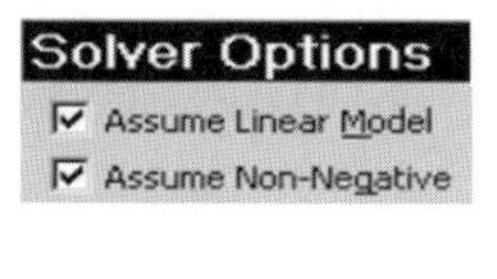

FIGURE 5.9

Spreadsheet for the Media Selection Model

FIGURE 5.10

Diagram of Inventory Relationships

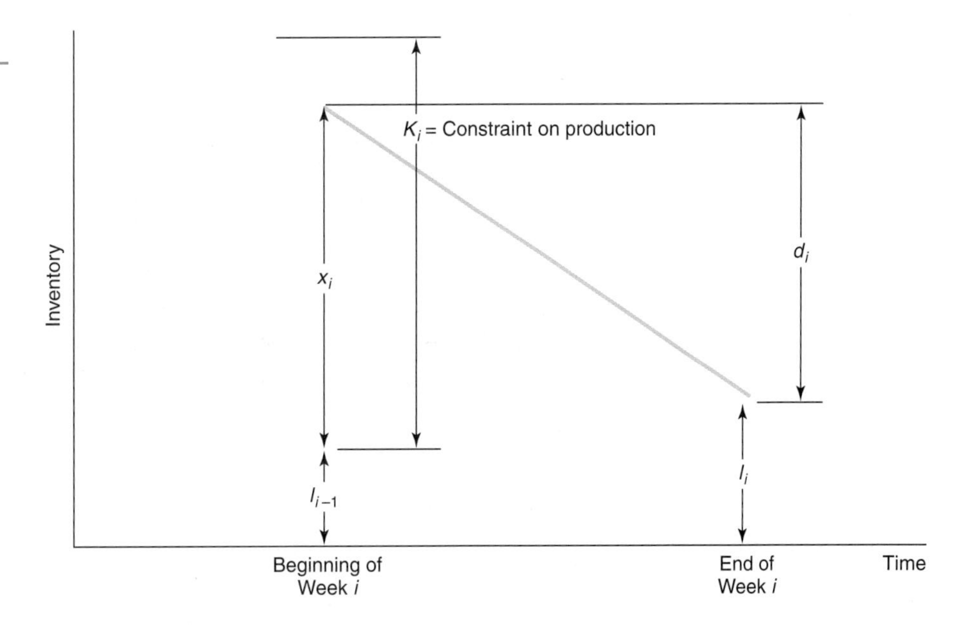

> The condition that demand in a time period t must be satisfied is equivalent to the condition that inventory I_t at the end of the time period t must be nonnegative.

This is illustrated in the diagram of Figure 5.10.

VERBAL MODEL

Minimize production costs + inventory costs

subject to

inventory at the end of week $t \geq 0$	$t = 1, 2, \ldots, 6$
production in week $t \leq K_t$	$t = 1, 2, \ldots, 6$
production in week $t \geq 0$	$t = 1, 2, \ldots, 6$

THE SYMBOLIC MODEL

x_t = production in week t

$$\text{Min} \sum_{t=1}^{6} C_t x_t + \sum_{t=1}^{6} h_t I_t$$

$$\text{s.t.} \quad \left.\begin{array}{l} I_t = I_{t-1} + x_t - d_t \\ x_t \leq K_t \\ x_t \geq 0, \qquad I_t \geq 0 \end{array}\right\} \quad t = 1, 2, \ldots, 6$$

In general, finding good solutions of such models is fairly complex. That is, interactions are occurring between large numbers of variables. For example, inventory at the end of a given time period t is determined by all production decisions in time periods 1 through t. This is seen from the inventory equation.

$$I_t = I_0 + \sum_{i=1}^{t} (x_i - d_i)$$

Therefore, the cost in time period t is also determined by all production decisions in time periods 1 through t. Next, we present a practical example of a dynamic inventory model, the situation faced by Andrew Tan.

A DYNAMIC INVENTORY MODEL

Andrew Tan is responsible for the final assembly and delivery of AutoPower's diesel-powered UPS electric generators in Singapore. The generators are assembled from imported parts, tested in Singapore, and exported to AutoPower's Asian customers needing uninterrupted electric power. Table 5.13 gives the number of generators that have been sold and must be delivered in each of the next four months along with Andrew's estimates of monthly production capacity and variable costs of generator production. These capacities and costs differ because of the logistics of inbound shipping of parts and variability in the cost of commodity materials, particularly copper wire. Also listed in Table 5.13 are the holding costs of storing a completed generator in a commercial warehouse from one month to the next. Commercial storage costs for large diesel-powered generators are a significant factor for Andrew because of Singapore's extremely limited land area. Note that it is the possibility of holding inventory from one month to the next that makes Andrew's model a dynamic inventory model as opposed to a collection of four static models if there were no inventory options.

Andrew's task is to produce and deliver the required number of generators over the four month interval at the lowest total four month cost, given that he begins January with 15 generators in inventory. Figure 5.11 presents Andrew's Excel model. It follows a common convention for dynamic models in spreadsheets in which one column is devoted to each time period. In this model, the Ending Inventory values in cells C10:F10 are consequential (definitional) variables, in this case, calculated for each month as

= Production + Beginning Inventory – Delivery Requirements.

Each month's Beginning Inventory (cells D8:F8) is set equal to the previous month's Ending Inventory (cells C10:E10).[4] As developed previously, a nonnegative ending inventory requirement for each month must be added in the Solver Parameters dialog. This will prevent Solver from artificially lowering costs by shipping more generators in a month than are on hand.

Implicit in Andrew's model are two fundamental decisions that must be addressed in every dynamic model: the overall time interval covered by the model, called the model's "planning horizon," and the number of discrete time epochs to include within that interval. For Andrew's model the planning horizon is four months, and time is divided into four month-long epochs. Both of these decisions can have profound effects upon the relevance of the model for Andrew's situation. For example, by definition, the four-month planning horizon means the model cannot take account of production and delivery requirements beyond April, that is, Andrew's ongoing business of generator production and deliveries comes to an end after April, as far as the model is concerned.

Also, the discrete monthly time scale requires that Andrew approximate all of the many day-to-day activities within a month by a *single* set of numbers applied to the whole

Table 5.13

Monthly Data for Generator Production

	JAN.	FEB.	MAR.	APR.
Delivery Requirements	58	36	34	59
Production Capacity	60	62	64	66
Unit Production Costs (000s)	$28	$27	$27.8	$29
Unit Inventory Holding Cost	$300	$300	$300	$300

[4] In this example no generators are lost, damaged, or stolen in inventory. In other inventory models inventory losses or "shrinkage" can be accommodated by multiplying the ending inventory in a given month by a fraction, such as .99, to produce the next month's beginning inventory. This would then model an average 1% inventory shrinkage for that month.

FIGURE 5.11

Andrew's Dynamic Production and Inventory Model

	A	B	C	D	E	F	G	H
1		Singapore Electric Generator Production						
2		Unit Costs	Jan.	Feb.	Mar.	Apr.	May	
3		Production	$28.0	$27.0	$27.8	$29.0		
4		Inventory	$0.3	$0.3	$0.3	$0.3		
5								
6		Production Qty.	53	62	64	0		
7		Production Limits	<=60	<=62	<=64	<=66		
8		Begining Inventory	15	10	36	66		
9		Delivery Reqmts.	58	36	34	59		
10		Ending Inventory	10	36	66	7	>=7	
11								
12		Production Cost	$1,484.00	$1,674.00	$1,779.20	$ -		
13		Inventory Cost	$ 3.75	$ 6.90	$ 15.30	$ 10.95	Total (000s)	
14		Total	$1,487.75	$1,680.90	$1,794.50	$ 10.95	$ 4,974.10	
15								

Cell	Formula	Copy To
C10	= C6+C8–C9	D10:F10
C12	= C3*C6	D12:F12
C13	= C4*(C8+C10)/2	D13:F13
D8	= C10	E8:F8

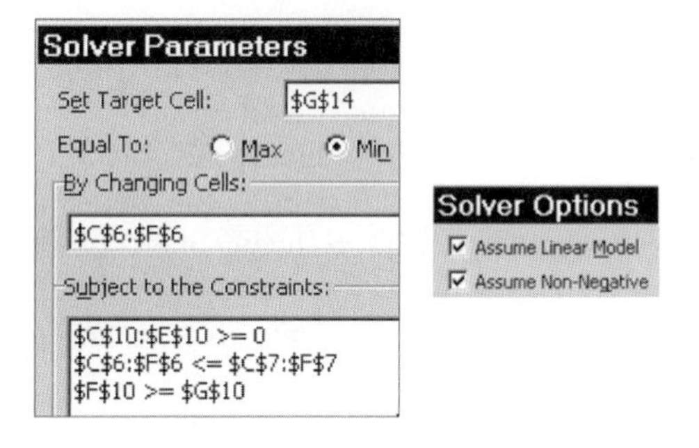

month. For example, January's ending inventory is the difference between January production plus beginning inventory and January deliveries, a single number, even though the actual inventory amount will vary each day of each week within the month as generators are produced and delivered. To make this clear, consider the extreme case where all production occurs on the first working day of January and all deliveries occur on the last working day of January. In that extreme case the January holding cost of inventory is determined by the production amount plus beginning inventory and not their sum less deliveries. At the other extreme, if all production and deliveries occurred on the last working day of January, then inventory holding costs for completed generators would be applied only to the January beginning inventory. Assuming for simplicity that production and deliveries occurs uniformly over the month, Andrew elected to approximate inventory holding costs based upon the average inventory for each month—(beginning inventory + ending inventory)/2. This is equivalent to assuming that all production and deliveries occur at mid-month. Obviously, capturing the movement of generators more accurately within a month would require breaking up the model into more time epochs, such as weekly or daily or even hourly. Finer time grids allow more precise measurements of actual movements of generators in and out of inventory, producing more accurate inventory cost tracking within the model.

In addition to using a finer time grid for more accurate within-month cost tracking, Andrew's costs associated with activities for the missing months beyond April can be accommodated by extending the model's planning horizon. Unfortunately, the realism of long planning horizons and fine time grids produces an exponential growth in the size of the dynamic model. For example, a daily model with a one-year planning horizon would have hundreds of time-epoch columns, quickly exceeding Excel's 256 column limit and Solver's limit of 200 decision variables.[5] Moreover, even if these technical barriers could be relaxed, Andrew would be faced with the need to estimate many more hundreds of parameter values, such as the daily shipping requirements for generators, the daily cost of materials, and the daily production capacity for generators. The temptation to add realism by finer time grids and longer planning horizons in dynamic models is called the "curse of dimensionality," because adding each new column adds a new dimension to the model in terms of new decision variables, decision and consequential variable linkages across time, and parameters to be considered.

Finally, every dynamic model must also pay attention to what are called its "edge conditions." These refer to the set of parameters that must be specified at the beginning and the end of time in the model. In Andrew's model this becomes the values of initial inventory in January and ending inventory in April. As in Andrew's case of January initial inventory of 15 generators, the beginning parameter values are usually given or easily estimated. However, the ending edge condition is more troublesome because it must stand as a reasonable starting condition or proxy for all of time beyond the planning horizon. In his model, Andrew judges that 7 generators for the ending inventory in April would constitute a "good" initial inventory condition for subsequent months.

Figure 5.12 shows the result of optimizing Andrew's model four times, separately for each of the four months. That is, Solver was run for January alone using January production as the decision variable and January total cost as the objective function. Then the same was done for February and so on through April, a total of four Solver runs. Note that no inventories are maintained to carry over from one month to the next because each month is treated as a separate static model;[6] producing in excess of required shipments in a month raises total cost and in a static model there are no offsetting savings. It is for this reason that static models are often referred to as **myopic** because they ignore any consequences of current decisions upon future payoff. The advantages of a four-month dynamic model in contrast to four static monthly models is illustrated by comparing the total four-month cost

FIGURE 5.12

Andrew's Model Optimized as Four Static Models

	A	B	C	D	E	F	G	H
1		Singapore Electric Generator Production						
2		Unit Costs	Jan.	Feb.	Mar.	Apr.	May	
3		Production	$28.0	$27.0	$27.8	$29.0		
4		Inventory	$0.3	$0.3	$0.3	$0.3		
5								
6		Production Qty.	43	36	34	66		
7		Production Limits	<=60	<=62	<=64	<=66		
8		Begining Inventory	15	0	0	0		
9		Delivery Reqmts.	58	36	34	59		
10		Ending Inventory	0	0	0	7	>=7	
11								
12		Production Cost	$ 1,204.00	$ 972.00	$ 945.20	$1,914.00		
13		Inventory Cost	$ 2.25	$ -	$ -	$ 1.05	Total (000s)	
14		Total	$ 1,206.25	$ 972.00	$ 945.20	$1,915.05	$ 5,038.50	
15								

[5] Commercial upgrades that expand this limitation to Excel's Solver are available from Solver's developer, Frontline Systems, *www.frontsys.com*, but dynamic models that exceed even the commercial limits are easily-created.

[6] The two Inventory Cost numbers appearing in January and April in Figure 5.12 represent the half-month cost of holding the beginning inventory for January and the required ending inventory for April.

FIGURE 5.13

Sensitivity Report for Andrew's Four-Month Inventory Model

Microsoft Excel 9.0 Sensitivity Report

Adjustable Cells

Cell	Name	Final Value	Reduced Cost	Objective Coefficient	Allowable Increase	Allowable Decrease
$C$6	Production Qty. Jan.	53	0	29.05	0.1	0.8
$D$6	Production Qty. Feb.	62	-1.3	27.75	1.3	1E+30
$E$6	Production Qty. Mar.	64	-0.8	28.25	0.8	1E+30
$F$6	Production Qty. Apr.	0	0.1	29.15	1E+30	0.1

Constraints

Cell	Name	Final Value	Shadow Price	Constraint R.H. Side	Allowable Increase	Allowable Decrease
$C$10	Ending Inventory Jan.	10	0	0	10	1E+30
$D$10	Ending Inventory Feb.	36	0	0	36	1E+30
$E$10	Ending Inventory Mar.	66	0	0	66	1E+30
$F$10	Ending Inventory Apr.	7	29.05	7	7	10

difference between Figure 5.11 and Figure 5.12, a savings of more than $64,000 in this case. A little thought should convince you that the dynamic model of Andrew's four-month decision-making situation could *never* do worse than running four static models for the same situation and often would do much better.

Figure 5.13 shows the Solver Sensitivity Report for the four-month dynamic model of Figure 5.11. Note that because the four production limits were specified as simple upper bounds on the production decision variables, those constraint's shadow prices appear in the Reduced Cost column of the Sensitivity Report, and hence, no range information is given for those shadow prices.[7] Also, at first glance the objective function coefficients for the model in the Sensitivity Report appear to be incorrect. For example, the objective function coefficient for January production is shown as $29,050 while the variable production cost of a generator in January is clearly specified as $28,000 in Figure 5.11.

Many users of Solver presume that Solver somehow "reads" each objective function coefficient from the appropriate cell within the active Excel worksheet. In fact, Solver does not do this because the calculation of that coefficient might be spread among formulas in several cells within the original Excel model. Instead, Solver perturbs the Excel worksheet for each of the decision variables individually, substituting trial values, and tabulating the effect that each such change has upon the objective function value after Excel recalculates the worksheet. From that information Solver estimates the objective coefficients.[8] Of course, this does not answer the question as to why there is a discrepancy between the variable cost of production in January and the objective coefficient for January production estimated by Solver and tabulated in the Sensitivity Report.

It should be easy to see that the $29.05 thousand represents the $28 thousand cost of producing a generator in January plus the $1.05 thousand inventory holding cost for $3\frac{1}{2}$ months to carry that generator to the end of April. (Recall, Andrew's use of average inventory levels is equivalent to assuming that production occurs in the middle of a month.) You can convince yourself that the $29.05 value is in fact the correct objective coefficient by taking the worksheet of Figure 5.11—AndrewEx.xls on the book's CD-ROM—typing in a candidate production decision for January, noting the total four-month cost number, and then adding 1 to that candidate January production decision. You will observe that the incremental generator produced in January will be added to all the future month's inven-

[7] See Section 4.12 for a discussion of Solver's penchant for putting shadow prices relating to constrained decision variables into the Reduced Cost column of the Sensitivity Report.

[8] This coefficient estimation process is what is happening during Solver's "Setting up problem . . ." activity, displayed as a message after you click the Solve button. (For those of you with a mathematical inclination, Solver is developing a Tailor Series for the objective function from this information and uses that series in its optimization process.)

tory levels and will increase the ending inventory in April by one, thereby producing a $29.05 increase in four-month total cost.

To understand why $29.05 is the correct coefficient for January, recall that everything else (generators produced and delivered in other months) is being held constant, and so, there is no place for that incremental January generator to go except into ending April inventory. However, during Solver optimization of the model, that incremental January generator creates an opportunity for Solver to reduce another month's production decision by one. For example, if the incremental generator in January allowed Solver to reduce February's production by one, then the net effect would be the difference between the two objective coefficients for January and February, $29.05 – $27.75 = $1.30 thousand. This difference is the correct incremental cost impact of these two simultaneous changes, that is, shifting production of a generator from February to January incurs the $28,000 – $27,000 = $1000 higher January production cost plus the $300 cost to carry the mid-January-produced generator into mid-February. Thus, the confusing objective coefficients listed in the Sensitivity Report are correct and are a result of the more complex interactions among the decision variables of a dynamic model.

A second version of Andrew's model appears in Figure 5.14. This model differs from Andrew's original model in Figure 5.11 in that each month's Beginning Inventory (cells D8:F8) is not modeled as a consequential variable but as a decision variable. Of course, for this approach to make sense, constraints must be added to prevent Solver from treating

FIGURE 5.14

Andrew's Production Model with Beginning Inventory as Additional Decisions

TIP: *Note that discontiguous ranges of decision variables can be entered into Solver's Changing Cells box separated by a comma. Be careful, however, as versions of Excel prior to Excel 2000 limit each field entry of all dialog boxes, Solver included, to no more than 256 characters.*

	A	B	C	D	E	F	G	H
1		Singapore Electric Generator Production						
2		Unit Costs	Jan.	Feb.	Mar.	Apr.	May	
3		Production	$28.0	$27.0	$27.8	$29.0		
4		Inventory	$0.3	$0.3	$0.3	$0.3		
5								
6		Production Qty.	53	62	64	0		
7		Production Limits	<=60	<=62	<=64	<=66		
8		Begining Inventory	15	10	36	66		
9		Delivery Reqmts.	58	36	34	59		
10		Ending Inventory	10	36	66	7	>=7	
11								
12		Production Cost	$1,484.00	$1,674.00	$1,779.20	$ -		
13		Inventory Cost	$ 3.75	$ 6.90	$ 15.30	$ 10.95	Total (000s)	
14		Total	$1,487.75	$1,680.90	$1,794.50	$ 10.95	$ 4,974.10	
15								

Cell	Formula	Copy To
C10	= C6+C8–C9	D10:F10
C12	= C3*C6	D12:F12
C13	= C4*(C8+C10)/2	D13:F13

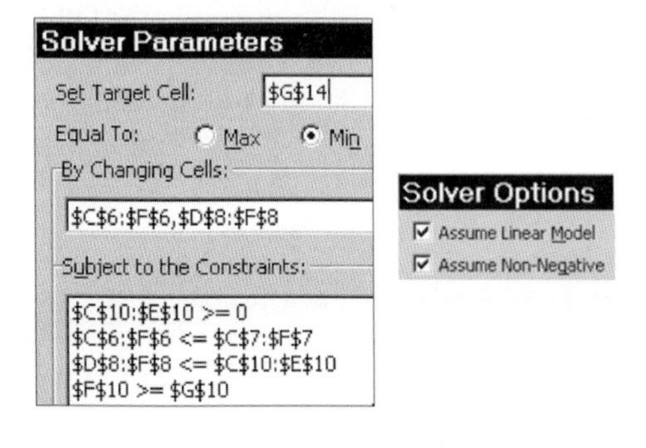

FIGURE 5.15

Sensitivity Report for Andrew's Revised Model

Microsoft Excel 9.0 Sensitivity Report

Adjustable Cells

Cell	Name	Final Value	Reduced Cost	Objective Coefficient	Allowable Increase	Allowable Decrease
$C$6	Production Qty. Jan.	53	0	28.15	0.1	0.8
$D$6	Production Qty. Feb.	62	-1.3	27.15	1.3	1E+30
$E$6	Production Qty. Mar.	64	-0.8	27.95	0.8	1E+30
$F$6	Production Qty. Apr.	0	0.1	29.15	1E+30	0.1
$D$8	Begining Inventory Feb.	10	0	0.3	0.1	0.8
$E$8	Begining Inventory Mar.	36	0	0.3	0.1	0.8
$F$8	Begining Inventory Apr.	66	0	0.3	0.1	29.05

Constraints

Cell	Name	Final Value	Shadow Price	Constraint R.H. Side	Allowable Increase	Allowable Decrease
$C$10	Ending Inventory Jan.	10	0	0	10	1E+30
$D$10	Ending Inventory Feb.	36	0	0	36	1E+30
$E$10	Ending Inventory Mar.	66	0	0	66	1E+30
$D$8	Begining Inventory Feb.	10	-28.15	0	10	7
$E$8	Begining Inventory Mar.	36	-28.45	0	10	7
$F$8	Begining Inventory Apr.	66	-28.75	0	10	7
$F$10	Ending Inventory Apr.	7	29.05	7	7	10

Beginning Inventory as a decision independent of the production decisions. In this case Beginning Inventory in D8:F8 is constrained to be no more than the previous month's Ending Inventory C10:E10. Other than this additional complication, the model of Figure 5.14 is logically equivalent to Andrew's original model in Figure 5.11. However, the benefit of this formulation is apparent in looking at its Sensitivity Report in Figure 5.15.

Note that additional information of managerial interest is displayed in this model's Solver Sensitivity Report. For example, the sensitivity of total cost to changes in inventory holding cost is now immediately apparent because the structure of the model in Figure 5.15 introduces additional inventory decision variables and constraints, and hence, their shadow prices and coefficient ranging, missing when inventory was modeled simply as a consequential variable. Note also in Figure 5.15, a side benefit of the new model: Modeling inventory as a decision variable isolates the unit costs into separate production coefficients (unit cost plus half-month holding cost) and inventory coefficients, thereby making the objective function coefficients to appear as originally specified in the spreadsheet model.

THE DYNAMIC INVENTORY MODEL RECASTED AS A TRANSPORTATION MODEL

Often a dynamic model like Andrew's can be modeled as a transportation model with the sources (From) representing decisions in a given time period and the destinations (To) representing one or more time periods affected, either in the current time period or a later one. A recast of Andrew's original model of Figure 5.11 into the transportation framework is given in Figure 5.16, which also shows the optimal decisions from Solver. As with the previous transportation example in Figure 5.2, the three blocks of cells in Figure 5.16 represent Unit Costs, Decisions, and Total Costs, respectively.

The non-gray cells in rows 4 through 7 of the model represent the unit cost of producing a UPS generator in a given month (From) and delivering it to a customer in a future month (To), including the $300 inventory holding cost for each additional month. A similar rationale applies to row 8 for calculating total unit holding costs of January's beginning inventory held for shipment in a future month. The corresponding decisions in the "Shipments" block of cells represent total production in a given month (row total) with the cells within a row being the number of generators for that production month to ship to customers in the current or future months. Similarly, row 15 represents the apportioning of the initial inventory of 15 generators into shipments in future months. Contents of the Shipments block of cells C11:G15 are the decision variables adjusted by Solver to minimize total costs.

FIGURE 5.16

Andrew's Dynamic Production and Inventory Formulation as a Transportation Model

Transportation Model	Hold.Cost	$ 0.3			
Unit Cost From\To	Jan.	Feb.	Mar.	Apr.	May
Production Qty. Jan	$ 28.0	$ 28.3	$ 28.6	$ 28.9	$ 29.1
Production Qty. Feb	1000.0	$ 27.0	$ 27.3	$ 27.6	$ 27.8
Production Qty. Mar	1000.0	1000.0	$ 27.8	$ 28.1	$ 28.3
Production Qty. Apr	1000.0	1000.0	1000.0	$ 29.0	$ 29.2
Begining Inventory	$ 0.15	$ 0.45	$ 0.75	$ 1.05	$ 1.20

"Shipments" From\To	Jan.	Feb.	Mar.	Apr.	May	Total	Available Capacity
Production Qty. Jan	43	0	0	3	7	53	<=60
Production Qty. Feb	0	36	0	26	0	62	<=62
Production Qty. Mar	0	0	34	30	0	64	<=64
Production Qty. Apr	0	0	0	0	0	0	<=66
Begining Inventory	15	0	0	0	0	15	=15
Total	58	36	34	59	7		
Required	>=58	>=36	>=34	>=59	>=7		

Total Cost From\To	Jan.	Feb.	Mar.	Apr.	May	Total
Production Qty. Jan	$1,204.0	$ -	$ -	$ 86.7	$203.4	$1,494.1
Production Qty. Feb	$ -	$ 972.0	$ -	$ 717.6	$ -	$1,689.6
Production Qty. Mar	$ -	$ -	$945.2	$ 843.0	$ -	$1,788.2
Production Qty. Apr	$ -	$ -	$ -	$ -	$ -	$0.0
Begining Inventory	$ 2.3	$ -	$ -	$ -	$ -	$2.3
Total	$1,206.3	$ 972.0	$945.2	$1,647.3	$203.4	$4,974.1

Cell	Formula	Copy To
D4	= C4+$E$2	E4:F4, E5:F5, F6, D8:F8
G4	= F4+$E$2/2	G5:G8
C8	= $E$2/2	
C16	= SUM(C11:C15)	D16:G16
H11	= SUM(C11:G11)	H12:H15
C20	= C4*C11	C20:G24

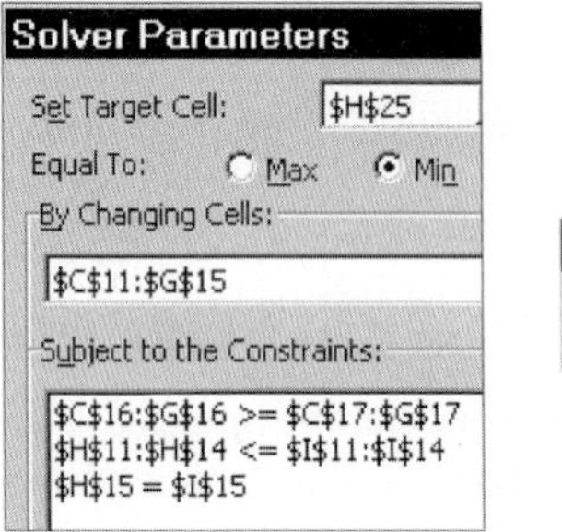

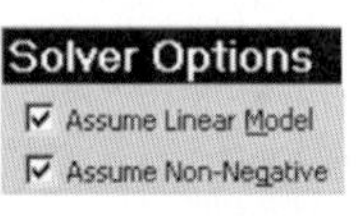

New in Figure 5.16 are the gray cells in the Unit Cost block, rows 5 through 7. Following the "large-M" penalty technique discussed in Section 5.3, setting those cells to contain huge unit costs ($1 million), forces Solver to avoid assigning any positive amounts in the corresponding gray cells in the Shipments decisions block in rows 12 through 14. In Andrew's case, these gray cells represent time reversal decisions—for example, producing generators in March for shipment in the previous January—that are impossible (as far as we know!), and so, must be avoided by Solver.[9] In a different context, however, the gray decision cells could be employed to represent the more complicated case of allowing *back-ordering*, for example, the filling of January generator orders by shipping two months late

[9] Alternatively, you could leave the gray unit cost cells blank, place zeros into C12, C13:D13, and C14:E14, and remove those cells from Solver Parameters "By Changing Cells" field to produce the same effect.

out of March production. In such cases the unit cost parameters for the (gray) cells representing backordered shipments are set to reflect any additional (opportunity) costs of customer ill-will or inconvenience, and costs of special communications or substitute arrangements caused by the delay.

The formulas in C8:F8 and G4:G8 reflect the special treatments to handle the dynamic model's edge conditions, in this case the extra one-half month of unit holding costs for the beginning inventory in the first half of January and the ending inventory for the last half of April, respectively.

We have developed three logically equivalent models for Andrew's situation, each successive one having increasing detail of more decision variables and constraints. All produce the same optimal solution, and you might ask why take the trouble to create a more detailed model than that minimally needed to get the solution. Although matters of creativity and personal taste in modeling often play a role in selecting a particular formulation, usually models with more decision variables and constraints have the advantage of providing additional information that may be of value to managers. This was already illustrated in the previous example involving making monthly inventories into decision variables that increased the information in the Sensitivity Report.

This advantage can also be seen in the current transportation formulation of Figure 5.16, as compared to the first model of Figure 5.11. For example, in Figure 5.11 Andrew knows to produce 53 generators in January and to ship 58 carrying the ending inventory of 10 generators into future months' inventory, but what exactly happens to those unshipped generators: How long are they kept and when do they ship? That information is not readily available in Figure 5.11, but is easily seen in Figure 5.16: Three are carried in inventory and shipped in April and the remaining ones become the seven left in inventory at model's end in May. In addition, the structure of the first model in Figure 5.11 forces inventory holding costs to be paid monthly, while the model of Figure 5.16 tracks inventory holding costs by each generator and pays them in the month when a given generator ships. This results in a different monthly profile of cost allocations that is more consistent with principles of accrual accounting. Finally, Figure 5.17 presents a portion of the much more detailed Sensitivity Report for the model of Figure 5.16. In addition to the signals of alternative optima, the report makes it easy to see the cost consequences of a given small change in the required shipping amount for a given month, an increased or decreased beginning inventory in January, and so on.

FIGURE 5.17

A Portion of the Sensitivity Report for Andrew's Transportation Formulation

Microsoft Excel 9.0 Sensitivity Report

Adjustable Cells

Cell	Name	Final Value	Reduced Cost	Objective Coefficient	Allowable Increase	Allowable Decrease
$C$1	Production Qty. Jan Jan.	43	0	28	972	0
D	Production Qty. Jan Feb.	0	0	28.3	1E+30	0
$E$1	Production Qty. Jan Mar.	0	2.3E-13	28.6	1E+30	2.3E-13
$F$1	Production Qty. Jan Apr.	3	0	28.9	0	1.1E-13
G	Production Qty. Jan May	7	0	29.05	1.1E-13	29.05
$C$1	Production Qty. Feb Jan.	0	973.3	1000	1E+30	973.3
D	Production Qty. Feb Feb.	36	0	27	0	28.3
$E$1	Production Qty. Feb Mar.	0	4.5E-13	27.3	1E+30	4.5E-13
$F$1	Production Qty. Feb Apr.	26	0	27.6	1.1E-13	0

Constraints

Cell	Name	Final Value	Shadow Price	Constraint R.H. Side	Allowable Increase	Allowable Decrease
$C$1	Total Jan.	58	28.00	58	7	43
D	Total Feb.	36	28.30	36	7	3
$E$1	Total Mar.	34	28.60	34	7	3
$F$1	Total Apr.	59	28.90	59	7	3
G	Total May	7	29.05	7	7	7
H	Production Qty. Jan Total	53	0	60	1E+30	7
H	Production Qty. Feb Total	62	-1.30	62	3	7
H	Production Qty. Mar Total	64	-0.80	64	3	7
H	Production Qty. Apr Total	0	0	66	1E+30	66
H	Begining Inventory Total	15	-27.85	15	43	7

In general, thought should be given in advance when creating a dynamic model as to what should be a consequential variable and what should be a decision variable, and how finely decomposed over time those decision variables should be. Often, valuable additional managerial information can be created by a well-designed model formulation.

The next section will present two more examples of dynamic models to illustrate the range of situations that can be modeled. The first, Bumles, presents a more complicated dynamic inventory model involving simultaneous production and labor scheduling.

5.7 A DYNAMIC PRODUCTION SCHEDULING AND INVENTORY CONTROL MODEL

Bumles, Inc., uses part of its capacity in its Mexican plant to make custom hand-painted teapots sold in that local market. One teapot takes 0.5 hours of a painter's time. Bumles has 30 painters available. The plant is used to make the teapots on Thursday, Friday, and Saturday each week. During the remainder of the week the productive capacity is devoted to another product line. Not all of the 30 painters will necessarily be engaged, but each painter who is engaged is available to work any part of an 8-hour day, 2 days a week. A painter can be assigned to any 2-day schedule and is paid for a total of 16 hours of regular-time work, no matter what part of that time he or she actually spends producing teapots. If there is not enough production to keep all the workers assigned to a particular day busy for the entire day, the slack time is spent on cleaning the plant and similar activities.

If labor costs are not taken into account, the revenue, net of other costs, from selling a teapot is \$15. Demand must be satisfied on the day on which it occurs or it is lost. Production on a given day can be used to satisfy demand that day or demand later in the week (i.e., teapots produced on Thursday can be inventoried and used to satisfy demand on Friday or Saturday). However, because of the change of operations to hand-painted statues on Monday, Tuesday, and Wednesday, all teapots produced in a week must be shipped that week (i.e., there are edge conditions of no initial teapot inventory on Thursday morning and no final teapot inventory on Saturday evening). Because of increased handling costs, it costs \$0.50 to carry a teapot in ending inventory from one day to the next. A unit of lost demand results in an all-inclusive penalty cost of \$1 for a unit on Thursday, \$3 on Friday, and \$5 on Saturday. Painters are paid the peso equivalent of \$8 per hour. Weekly demand for the teapots is 100 on Thursday, 300 on Friday, and 600 on Saturday.

Figure 5.18 presents the Solver-optimized Bumbles model that schedules painters and production in such a way as to maximize revenue minus cost, where cost equals labor plus inventory holding and any penalty costs reflecting unfilled demand. Since sales may be less than demand, the model relates sales, demand, and lost sales any particular day by:

$$\text{lost sales on day } x = \text{demand on day } x - \text{sales on day } x$$

In addition to the above relation between demand, sales, and lost sales, the model also includes the following material balance relationship between production, inventory, and sales:

$$\text{inventory at end of day } x = \text{inventory at beginning of day } x + \text{production on day } x - \text{sales on day } x$$

Finally, as with Andrew's model earlier, the material balance across time periods is included by requiring beginning inventory on each day to be equal to ending inventory of the previous day. These relationships are captured in the formulas of cells I3:K7 in which the decision variables for each day in I4:K5 are the number of teapots to produce and the number to sell. Thus, the lost sales on each day and ending inventory on each day are consequential variables. Another way of saying this is that the inventory and lost sales are dependent variables.

The other decisions for the Bumles model are the number of painters to schedule for each of the three two-day shifts in cells C9:C11. Cells D9:F11 contain references to assign

FIGURE 5.18

The Bumles Production Model

	A	B	C	D	E	F	G	H	I	J	K	L
1		Bumles Model		Thurs.	Fri.	Sat.			Thurs.	Fri.	Sat.	
2		Teapot Price		$15	$15	$15		Demand	100	300	600	
3		Wage Rate/Hour		$8	$8	$8		Beg. Inventory	0	0	120	
4		Inventory Carrying Cost		$0.5	$0.5	$0.5		Production	60	420	480	
5		Unit Cost of Lost Sales		$1	$3	$5		Sales	60	300	600	
6		Hours/Teapot		0.5	0.5	0.5		End. Inventory	0	120	0	
7		Hours/Day		8	8	8		Lost Sales	40	0	0	
8												
9		No. Paint. TF Sched	0	0	0			Revenue	$900	$4,500	$9,000	
10		No. Paint. TS Sched	3.75	3.75		3.75		Labor Cost	$240	$1,680	$1,920	
11		No. Paint. FS Sched	26.3		26.25	26.25		Inv. Carry Cost	$0	$60	$0	
12		Total Painters Used	30	3.75	26.25	30		Lost Sales Cost	$40	$0	$0	
13		Painters Available	<=30					Contribution	$620	$2,760	$7,080	
14		Labor Hrs Required		30	210	240			Total Contribution		$10,460	
15		Labor Hrs Available		<=30	<=210	<=240						
16												

Cell	Formula	Copy To
D14	= I4*D6	E14:F14
D15	= D12*D7	E15:F15
I6	= I3–I5+I4	J6:K6
I7	= I2–I5	J7:K7
I10	= D12*D3*D7	J10:K10
I11	= D4*I6	I11:K12

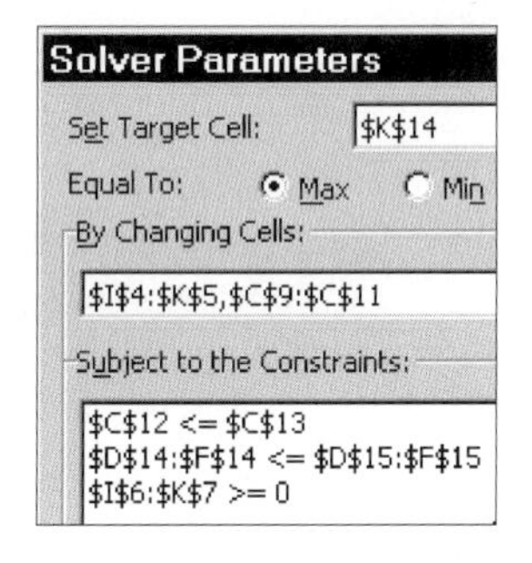

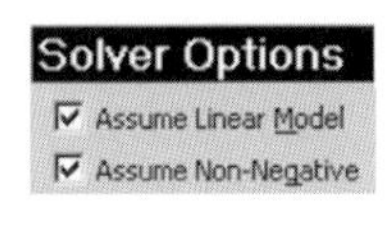

the painters for each schedule to the appropriate days. The Solver Parameters contains the constraints I6:K7 >= 0. Since backordering is not feasible for Bumles' customers, this stipulates that neither negative inventories nor negative lost sales occur on any day. The latter is required to assure that sales cannot exceed demand in any day.

Extending the Bumles model to accommodate more production days and labor schedule options is easily done. More production days can be added by inserting a new column after each of columns F and K for each additional day of production. Additional scheduling options are accommodated by inserting new cells in the left half of the model above row 12 to represent new work day assignment options. Next, the various totaling formulas would be modified accordingly, and the additional parameter data entered for the new cells. Finally, editing the Solver Parameters dialog to add the new decision variables and constraints would complete the model expansion.

The dynamic models thus far have included inventories of products, but the same principles apply in financial planning situations in which cash becomes the inventory to be managed over time, as shown in the next example.

5.8 A DYNAMIC CASH MANAGEMENT MODEL

Winston-Salem Development Corporation (WSDC) is trying to complete its investment plans for the next two years. Currently, WSDC has $2,000,000 on hand and available for investment. In 6 months, 12 months, and 18 months, WSDC expects to receive a cash income stream from previous investments. The data are presented in Table 5.14. There are

Table 5.14 Cash Income from Previous Investments

	6 MONTHS	12 MONTHS	18 MONTHS
Income	$500,000	$400,000	$380,000

Table 5.15 Foster City Cash Flow

	INITIAL	6 MONTHS	12 MONTHS	18 MONTHS	24 MONTHS
Income	$–1,000,000	$–700,000	$1,800,000	$400,000	$600,000

Table 5.16 Middle-Income Housing Cash Flow

	INITIAL	6 MONTHS	12 MONTHS	18 MONTHS	24 MONTHS
Income	$–800,000	$500,000	$–200,000	$–700,000	$2,000,000

two development projects in which WSDC is considering participation along with other non-WSDC investors.

1. The Foster City Development would, if WSDC participated at a 100% level, have the projected cash flow shown in Table 5.15 (negative numbers are investment, positive numbers are income). Thus, in order to participate in Foster City at the 100% level, WSDC would immediately have to lay out $1,000,000. In 6 months there would be another outlay of $700,000, followed later by a receipt of $1,800,000, and so on.
2. A second project involves taking over the operation of some old Middle-Income Housing on the condition that certain initial repairs be made. The cash flow stream for this project, at a 100% level of participation, would be as shown in Table 5.16.

WSDC can participate in either project at a level less than 100%, in which case other investors would make up the difference, and all of the cash flows of that project are reduced proportionately for WSDC. For example, if WSDC were to opt for participation in Foster City at the 30% level, the cash flows associated with this decision would be 0.3 times the data given in the Foster City table. Because of company policy WSDC is not permitted to borrow money. However, at the beginning of each 6-month period any surplus funds (those not allocated to either Foster City or Middle-Income Housing) can be invested into a certificate of deposit (CD) for a return of 7% for that 6-month period. The task currently facing WSDC is to decide how much of the $2,000,000 on hand should be invested in each of the projects and how much should simply be invested for the 7% semiannual return. WSDC management's goal is to maximize the cash on hand at the end of 24 months. To build the symbolic model we first must define the decision variables

F = fractional participation in the Foster City project

M = fractional participation in the Middle-Income Housing project

S_1 = surplus funds (not invested in F or M initially) to be invested in a CD at 7%

S_2 = surplus funds after 6 months to be invested in a CD at 7%

S_3 = surplus funds after 12 months to be invested in a CD at 7%

S_4 = surplus funds after 18 months to be invested in a CD at 7%

The constraints in this model must say that at the beginning of each of the four 6-month periods: cash invested ≤ cash on hand. Then the first constraint must say

$$\text{initial investment} \le \text{initial funds on hand} \quad \text{or}$$

$$1{,}000{,}000F + 800{,}000M + S_1 \le 2{,}000{,}000$$

Because of the interest paid, S_1 becomes 1.07S1 after 6 months, and similarly for S_2, S_3, and S_4, the remaining three constraints are

$$700{,}000F + S_2 \le 500{,}000M + 1.07S_1 + 500{,}000$$
$$200{,}000M + S_3 \le 1{,}800{,}000F + 1.07S_2 + 400{,}000$$
$$700{,}000M + S_4 \le 400{,}000F + 1.07S_3 + 380{,}000$$

The constraints above provide material balance of the cash flows from one time period to another. Note that equalities could have been used in the constraints instead of inequalities, because uninvested cash earns no return. However, good modeling practice suggests avoiding equalities unless necessary. Formulating models like this as inequalities allows Solver to confirm this belief about idle cash for you when, as expected, it makes the inequality constraints binding during optimization.

The objective function is to maximize the (undiscounted in this case) cash on hand at the end of 24 months, which is

$$600{,}000F + 2{,}000{,}000M + 1.07S_4$$

We have thus derived the following LP dynamic cash management model:

$$\begin{aligned}
\text{Max } & 600{,}000F + 2{,}000{,}000M + 1.07S_4 \\
\text{s.t. } & 1{,}000{,}000F + 800{,}000M + S_1 \le 2{,}000{,}000 \\
& 700{,}000F - 500{,}000M - 1.07S_1 + S_2 \le 500{,}000 \\
& -1{,}800{,}000F + 200{,}000M - 1.07S_2 + S_3 \le 400{,}000 \\
& -400{,}000F + 700{,}000M - 1.07S_3 + S_4 \le 380{,}000 \\
& F \le 1 \quad \text{and} \quad M \le 1 \\
& F \ge 0,\ M \ge 0,\ S_i \ge 0,\ i = 1, 2, 3, 4
\end{aligned}$$

The model with optimal solution and a portion of the Sensitivity Report is given in Figure 5.19. The decision variables are the amount of surplus cash to invest in CDs (cells D12:G12) and the percentage participation in the two projects (cells C7:C8). The investment amounts in cells D7:G8 are given by multiplying the Project Participation percentage by the project cash flow requirements in cells D3:I4. For convenience and to conform with the constraints in the symbolic model above, the sign convention on investments is reversed in the Cash Outlays portion of the model. As can be seen, both investment projects are attractive with WSDC participating fully, and from the Sensitivity Report, the marginal or incremental return to WSDC's initial funds is 31% over 24 months.

This model considered only the financial aspects of cash management while previous models considered only production without regard to cash management. The next example illustrates combining both concepts into an integrated production and cash management model.

5.9 A FINANCIAL AND PRODUCTION PLANNING MODEL

The AutoPower Europe production model for its diesel-powered UPS generators is a product-mix model for deciding how many of its two models, BigGen and SmallGen, to produce and sell in each of the coming months in view of a number of constraints. The relevant data for the production process is given below.

1. The financial data on each BigGen and SmallGen that is sold is given by Table 5.17.
2. Each product is put through machining and assembly operations in two production departments, called A and B. These two departments have 150 and 160 hours of available time each month, respectively.
3. Each BigGen produced uses 10 hours of machining and assembly in department A and 20 hours of machining and assembly in department B, whereas each SmallGen produced uses 15 hours in department A and 10 hours in department B.
4. Testing is performed in a third department and has nothing to do with the activities in departments A and B. Each BigGen is given 30 hours of testing and each SmallGen is given 10. AutoPower Europe's labor contract mandates that the total labor hours devoted to testing cannot fall below 135 hours each month.

FIGURE 5.19

Winston-Salem Development Model

	A	B	C	D	E	F	G	H	I
1			Winston Salem Development Project						
2		CD Int. Rate	7%	Initial	6 Mo.	12 Mo.	18 Mo.		24 Mo.
3			Foster City Cash Flow	$ (1,000)	$ (700)	$ 1,800	$ 400		$ 600
4			Middle Income Cash Flow	$ (800)	$ 500	$ (200)	$ (700)		$ 2,000
5				Cash Outlays					
6		Funds Invested	Project Participation	Initial Investment	6 Months	12 Months	18 Months		Cash Returned (24 Months)
7		Foster City	100%	$ 1,000	$ 700	$ (1,800)	$ (400)		$ 600
8		Middle Incom	100%	$ 800	$ (500)	$ 200	$ 700		$ 2,000
9			Maturing CD's		$ (200)	$ (514)	$ (2,550)		$ 2,808
10			CD Interest Income		$ (14)	$ (36)	$ (178)		$ 197
11			Total Cash Requirements	$ 1,800	$ (14)	$ (2,150)	$ (2,428)		$ 5,605
12			Surplus Cash into CD's	$ 200	$ 514	$ 2,550	$ 2,808		
13			Invested New Cash	$ 2,000	$ 500	$ 400	$ 380		
14			Available New Cash	<=$2000	<=$500	<=$400	<=$380		
15									

	A	B	C	D	E	F	G	H	I
6		Funds Investe	Project Particip	Initial Investment	6 Months	12 Months	18 Months		Cash Returned
7		Foster (		=-$C7*D3	=-$C7*E3	=-$C7*F3	=-$C7*G3		=C7*I3
8		Middle		=-$C8*D4	=-$C8*E4	=-$C8*F4	=-$C8*G4		=C8*I4
9			Maturir		=-D12	=-E12	=-F12		=G12
10			CD Inte		=-D12*$C$2	=-E12*$C$2	=-F12*$C$2		=G12*C2
11			Total (	=SUM(D7:D10)	=SUM(E7:E10)	=SUM(F7:F10)	=SUM(G7:G10)		=SUM(I7:I10)
12			Surplu						
13			Investe	=D11+D12	=E11+E12	=F11+F12	=G11+G12		
14			Availa	2000	500	400	380		

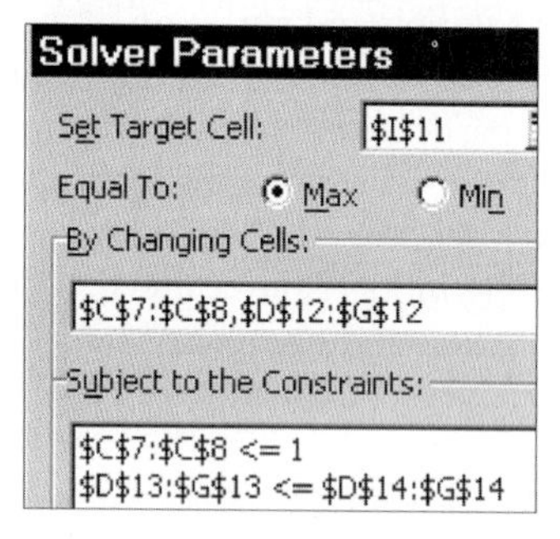

Solver Options

☑ Assume Linear Model

☑ Assume Non-Negative

Microsoft Excel 9.0 Sensitivity Report

Constraints

Cell	Name	Final Value	Shadow Price	Constraint R.H. Side	Allowable Increase	Allowable Decrease
$D$13	Invested New Cash Initial Investment	$ 2,000	1.311	2000	1E+30	200
$E$13	Invested New Cash 6 Months	$ 500	1.225	500	1E+30	514
$F$13	Invested New Cash 12 Months	$ 400	1.145	400	1E+30	2550.0
$G$13	Invested New Cash 18 Months	$ 380	1.070	380	1E+30	2808.5

Table 5.17

AutoPower Europe's UPS Generator Financial Data

PRODUCT	SALES PRICE $000	PER UNIT MATERIAL AND LABOR COSTS $000	CONTRIBUTION MARGIN $000
BigGen	80	75	5
SmallGen	24	20	4

Defining B as the number of BigGen's and S as the number of SmallGen's to produce each month, the symbolic model for this simple product-mix model is given by

$$\begin{array}{lll} & \text{Max } 5B + 4S & \text{(Profit in \$000's)} \\ \text{s.t.} & 10B + 15S \leq 150 & \text{(hours in department A)} \\ & 20B + 10S \leq 160 & \text{(hours in department B)} \\ & 30B + 10S \geq 135 & \text{(testing hours)} \\ & B, S \geq 0 & \end{array}$$

The Excel model is given in Figure 5.20, which has already been optimized by Solver. (Recall from the discussion in Chapter 3 that the fractional production number for BigGen can be interpreted as an average month's production and sales; actual BigGen's sales would alternate between 4 and 5 UPS generators every other month.)

FIGURE 5.20

AutoPower Europe's Product Mix Model

	A	B	C	D	E	F	G	H
1		AutoPower Production Model						
2			BigGen	SmallGen				
3		Price ($000s)	$80	$24				
4		Unit Variable Costs ($000s)	$75	$20				
5		Unit Contribution Margin ($000s)	$5	$4	Profit ($000s)			
6		Decisions	4.5	7	$50.5			
7								
8		Constraints	Resource Usage		Total Hours	Hrs Avail.	Slack	
9		Department A	10	15	150	<=150	0	
10		Department B	20	10	160	<=160	0	
11					Total Hours	Hrs Req.	Surplus	
12		Testing	30	10	205	>=135	70	
13								

Cell	Formula	Copy To
E6	= SUMPRODUCT($C$6:$D$6,C5:D5)	
E9	= SUMPRODUCT($C$6:$D$6,C9:D9)	E10,E12

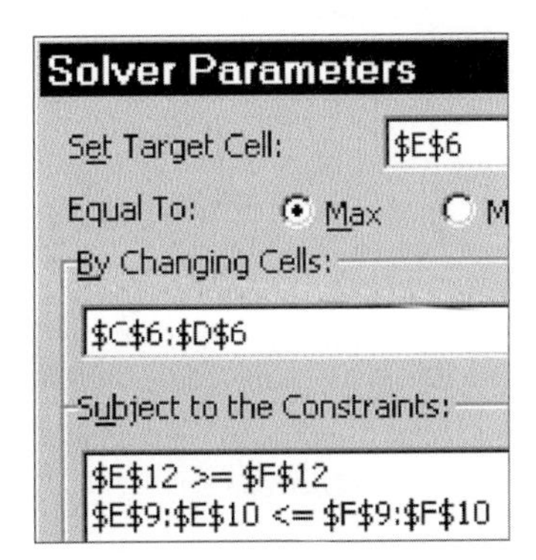

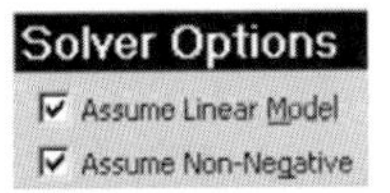

The production manager is satisfied that from his perspective this model captures the essence of the situation. He sends to the AutoPower Europe management committee a proposal that the recommendations of the model be considered for implementation. When the management committee reviews the activities that are proposed for the coming month, it soon becomes clear that the AutoPower production model captures only a part of AutoPower Europe's real situation. In particular, certain important financial considerations have been ignored. Specifically, AutoPower must incur the material and direct labor costs in the next month, whereas payments from the eventual customers will not be forthcoming for another three months. The current formulation ignores the fact that AutoPower Europe will have to borrow funds to cover at least part of the current expenditures.

FINANCIAL CONSIDERATIONS

AutoPower Europe has budgeted \$100,000 of cash on hand to cover the current material and labor costs and plans to borrow any additional funds for these material and labor costs. AutoPower Europe can borrow money at an annual interest rate of 16%, but in order to hedge against downside risks, the bank has limited the total due to the bank (principal plus interest) to be no more than two-thirds of the sum of AutoPower's cash on hand and accounts receivable. The management committee is concerned that the time value of money has been ignored in calculating the profit contributions. It feels that if present value of net cash flow is maximized fewer BigGen's and more SmallGen's should be produced, because of the relatively high material and labor costs of the BigGen's. The committee cannot agree, however, on what the proper discount rate should be. Some members argue for a 12% annual discount rate, others for a 16% rate, and a few for a 20% rate.

AutoPower Europe's problem is to formulate a new objective function, determine how much to borrow (if any), and devise a production plan incorporating this new information. To model this situation, it is convenient to introduce a variable to the symbolic model. Let D = debt (i.e., total dollars borrowed), in thousands of dollars. The net cash flow next month in dollars will be $D - 75B - 20S$, while (since payments will not be forthcoming for another three months) the net cash flow three months later will be $80B + 24S - 1.040D$. The coefficient 1.040 is derived from the above statement that AutoPower can borrow at 16% per annum, and hence at 4% for three months. Define the discount factor, α, based on the annual discount rate, R, as $\alpha = \frac{1}{1 + R/4}$. The objective is to maximize present value of net cash flow, so the objective function becomes in thousands of dollars

$$\text{Max } 1D - 75B - 20S + \alpha(80B + 24S - 1.040D)$$

For example, if $R = 20\%$ and thus $\alpha = 0.952381$, the objective function becomes

$$\text{Max } 1.19048B + 2.85714S + .00952381D$$

Note that D actually has a positive coefficient here, because AutoPower Europe is assuming it can earn 20% on its investments, but has to pay only 16% interest on borrowed funds. If $R = 16\%$ or $R < 16\%$, then the coefficient of D would be zero or negative, respectively. Additional constraints are also required:

1. AutoPower Europe must borrow enough so that it is able to cover the material and labor costs associated with production. Since the total uses of funds cannot exceed the total sources of funds, the appropriate inequality is

$$\text{material and labor costs} \le \text{debt} + \text{cash on hand}$$

To expand this expression, we note that AutoPower Europe has \$100,000 of cash on hand. In addition, from Table 5.17 total material and labor costs are \$75 for each B and \$20 for each S. Thus, our equation becomes

$$75B + 20S \le D + 100$$

2. The bank requires that the total amount due the bank (i.e., debt plus interest) must be no greater than two-thirds of AutoPower Europe's cash on hand plus the accounts receivable. In other words

$$\text{debt} + \text{interest} \leq \frac{2}{3}(\text{cash on hand} + \text{accounts receivable})$$

From Table 5.17 we see that each B sells for \$80 and each S sells for \$24. Thus, the total accounts receivable is $80B + 24S$ and the constraint becomes

$$D + .04D \leq \frac{2}{3}(100 + 80B + 24S)$$

$$1.5(1.04D) \leq 100 + 80B + 24S$$

Note that the lower bound on the value of D (implicit in the constraint from 1 above) depends upon the cost of labor and materials, whereas the upper limit of D (implicit in the last of the above constraints) is based on the generator sales prices.

The revised AutoPower Europe production and financial model with selected formulas and its optimal solution for the case $R = 20\%$ is shown in Figure 5.21. In the solu-

FIGURE 5.21

AutoPower Europe Financial and Production Planning Model

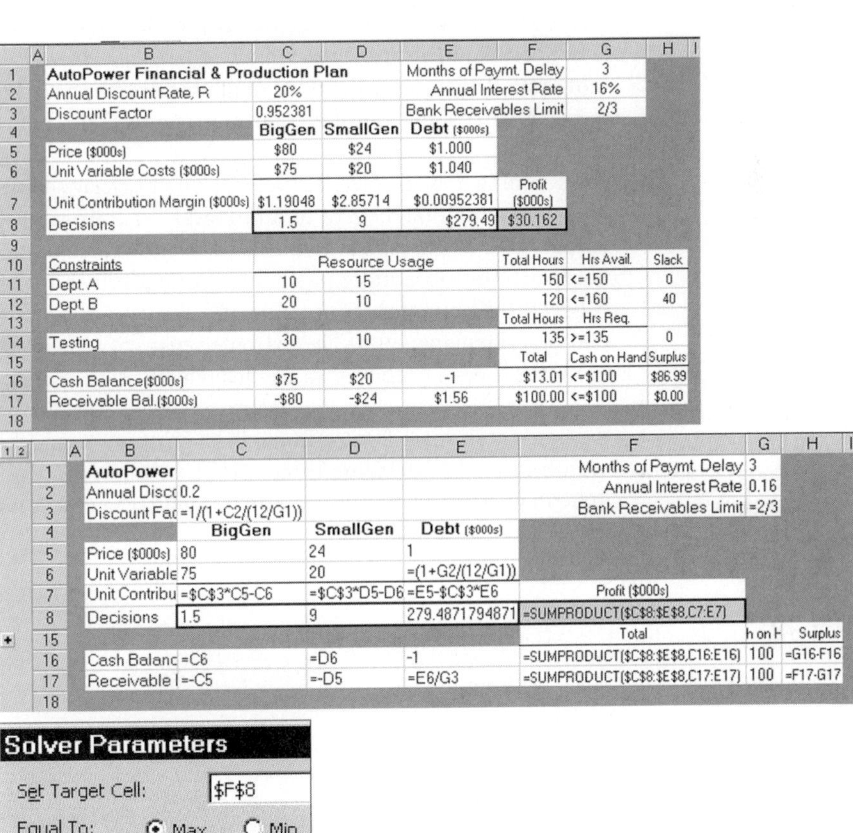

	A	B	C	D	E	F	G	H
1		AutoPower Financial & Production Plan			Months of Paymt. Delay		3	
2		Annual Discount Rate, R	20%		Annual Interest Rate		16%	
3		Discount Factor	0.952381		Bank Receivables Limit		2/3	
4			BigGen	SmallGen	Debt ($000s)			
5		Price ($000s)	$80	$24	$1.000			
6		Unit Variable Costs ($000s)	$75	$20	$1.040			
7		Unit Contribution Margin ($000s)	$1.19048	$2.85714	$0.00952381	Profit ($000s)		
8		Decisions	1.5	9	$279.49	$30.162		
9								
10		Constraints		Resource Usage		Total Hours	Hrs Avail.	Slack
11		Dept. A	10	15		150	<=150	0
12		Dept. B	20	10		120	<=160	40
13						Total Hours	Hrs Req.	
14		Testing	30	10		135	>=135	0
15						Total	Cash on Hand	Surplus
16		Cash Balance($000s)	$75	$20	-1	$13.01	<=$100	$86.99
17		Receivable Bal.($000s)	-$80	-$24	$1.56	$100.00	<=$100	$0.00
18								

	A	B	C	D	E	F	G	H
1		AutoPower				Months of Paymt. Delay	3	
2		Annual Discc	0.2			Annual Interest Rate	0.16	
3		Discount Fac	=1/(1+C2/(12/G1))			Bank Receivables Limit	=2/3	
4			BigGen	SmallGen	Debt ($000s)			
5		Price ($000s)	80	24	1			
6		Unit Variable	75	20	=(1+G2/(12/G1))			
7		Unit Contribu	=$C$3*C5-C6	=$C$3*D5-D6	=E5-$C$3*E6	Profit ($000s)		
8		Decisions	1.5	9	279.4871794871	=SUMPRODUCT($C$8:$E$8,C7:E7)		
15						Total	h on H	Surplus
16		Cash Balanc	=C6	=D6	-1	=SUMPRODUCT($C$8:$E$8,C16:E16)	100	=G16-F16
17		Receivable I	=-C5	=-D5	=E6/G3	=SUMPRODUCT($C$8:$E$8,C17:E17)	100	=F17-G17
18								

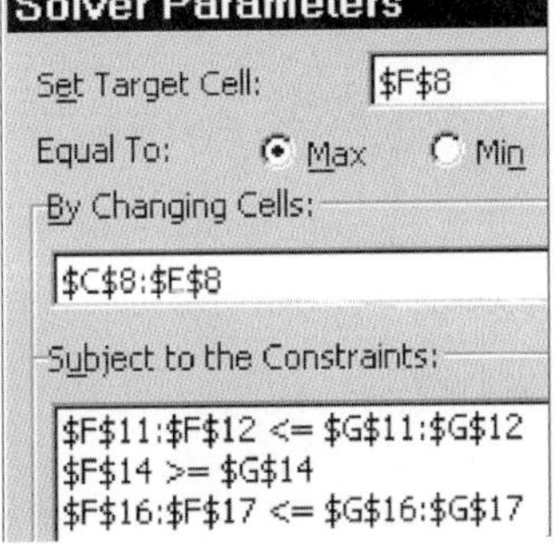

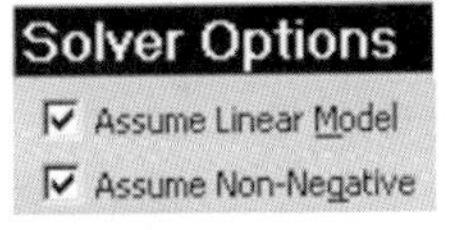

tion we also see that AutoPower Europe should borrow approximately $279.49 thousand, and as expected, reduce production of BigGen UPS generators in favor of the SmallGen model. The surplus variables for the cash constraints in rows 16 and 17 indicate that (since the Receivables Balance constraint is binding) AutoPower Europe will borrow as much as possible, which (since the Cash Balance has positive surplus) is more than is required to finance material and labor costs. This occurs because the model assumes that excess funds can be invested to earn 20% interest, while the cost of those funds is only 16%.

EFFECT OF FINANCIAL CONSIDERATIONS

We note that inserting the financial considerations in the original production mix model leads to quite a different plan, yielding a substantially smaller profit, from the one determined on the basis of only the production constraints. The optimal value of the objective function is less in the production and finance model because future cash flows are discounted and interest costs of borrowing are included. Running SolverTable 1 on the production and finance model of Figure 5.21 for different values of the discount rate, *R*, between 12% and 20% yields the results shown in Figure 5.22. In the production and finance model the optimal production plan does not depend on the value of the discount rate within the observed range of 12% to 20% and is thus insensitive to *R*. The optimal debt does, but in a simple manner. If $R < 16\%$, borrow as little as possible, namely $192.5 thousand. If $R > 16\%$, borrow as much as possible, namely $279.49 thousand. If $R = 16\%$, there are alternative optimal solutions where *D* lies between $192.5 and $279.49 thousand.

TIP: *It often happens that substituting a given parameter value into a model will cause Excel to generate an error message, which in turn will cause Solver to report an infeasible solution. Substituting a payment delay value of 0 into cell G1 of the model in Figure 5.21 causes a "#DIV/0" error in the formula in cell C3. The trick of using a parameter value close to zero and small by the scale of numbers in the rest of the model, such as a payment delay of .000001 in this case, will usually avoid this problem satisfactorily.*

Running SolverTable 1 again for Payment Delays between zero and four months illustrates the substantial benefit to AutoPower Europe of improving its accounts receivable by encouraging its customers to pay invoices promptly. Not only does this allow AutoPower Europe to shift to a more profitable product mix, but depending upon the relationship between the annual discount rate and the cost of borrowing, can improve AutoPower Europe's financing costs. The extreme sensitivity of Profit to shortening Payment Delay below the three month base case is given by the side calculation to the SolverTable of Figure 5.23 where the formula for "% Improvement" is (Profit – 30.162)/30.162, where 30.162 is the base case profit. For example, if its customers paid for their UPS generators in one month instead of delaying three months, AutoPower Europe's profit would increase by more than 40% per month while an immediate payment would increase monthly profit by more than two-thirds!

FIGURE 5.22

Running SolverTable 1 for *R* Between 12% and 20%

	BigGen	SmallGen	Debt	Profit
R	1.5	9	279.49	$30.162
12%	1.5	9	192.50	$31.845
14%	1.5	9	192.50	$31.208
16%	1.5	9	192.50	$30.577
18%	1.5	9	279.49	$30.368
20%	1.5	9	279.49	$30.162

FIGURE 5.23

Running SolverTable 1 for Payment Delays from 0 to 4 Months

	BigGen	SmallGen	Debt	Profit	
Paymt.Delay	1.5	9	279.4872	$30.162	% Improvement
0.000001	4.5	7	377.50	$50.500	67.4%
1	4.5	7	413.16	$43.199	43.2%
2	4.5	7	407.79	$36.099	19.7%
3	1.5	9	279.49	$30.162	0.0%
4	1.5	9	275.95	$25.949	-14.0%

APPLICATION CAPSULE

New Merchandise Arriving Daily: Network Models Help a Discount Chain Keep Shipping Costs at Bargain-Basement Levels

Finding the most economical way of routing merchandise from suppliers to warehouses and from warehouses to retail stores is a complex problem for many retailing chains. The problem is particularly difficult when the company is growing at a rate of 30% per year. This was the case with Marshall's, the off-price clothing retailer. Adding new stores at a rapid rate, Marshall's needed to be able to alter shipping patterns quickly to accommodate its expansion, as well as decide where new distribution centers should be located. To help accomplish these objectives, Marshall's adopted a computerized logistics planning system.

One part of this system, Network Optimization, consists of three software modules designed to minimize shipping costs.

- An "inbound" module deals with the flow of merchandise from suppliers to warehouses and processing centers.
- An "outbound" module deals with shipments from warehouses and processing centers to retail outlets.
- A third module analyzes the placement of new warehouses, a decision that strongly affects the first two modules.

Each module has four components:

1. A network generator that builds network links and nodes
2. A network editor that allows users to modify the network by directly changing costs, demands, and constraints
3. An optimization program
4. A post-processor for downloading the optimization results into readable format for use by management.

Each of the three modules required a separate modeling approach to capture important economic trade-offs of the particular situation and still ensure computational feasibility. Size was a real challenge with both the inbound and outbound models, each of which initially required the solution of a network with 350,000 links. Use of a heuristic method and other ingenious simplifications reduced that number to around 20,000. Thus streamlined, the models could be run on a PC rather than a mainframe, allowing them to incorporate such user-friendly features as interactive graphics. Now the workhorses of the entire system, they have enabled managers to examine a variety of scenarios, changing such factors as the number of trucks used and their capacities, costs, and warehouse locations, and then quickly reoptimizing. The speed of the process allows interactive feedback for sensitivity analysis.

Use of these models enabled Marshall's to evaluate both costs and service levels of its delivery network, producing estimated savings of $250,000 per year. In addition, the model helped determine the site for a new distribution center, expected to save the company $1.4 million in shipping costs. (See Carlisle et al.)

5.10 NETWORK MODELS

The transportation and assignment models covered in the Sections 5.2 and 5.3 are members of a more general class of models involving from-to sources and destinations, called *network models.* Network models are often applied to management logistics and distribution, and also have wide applicability in engineering and computer science. Network models are important for several reasons. First, a wide variety of real-world models can be cast as network models. The flows may represent physical quantities, Internet data packets, cash, airplanes, container ships, products, and so on. The type of business situation amenable to the network approach is often very large in scale. One can imagine, for example, a network model of an international enterprise involved in paper production. The network might depict the overall multiperiod distribution system from the forest through lumber storage, a variety of paper mills, widely distributed warehouses, transportation alternatives, and wholesalers in numerous countries and marketing districts. A dynamic supply chain model for such a vast operation offers the potential of creating considerable efficiency gains in the firm's global operations.

Recent years have seen the development of extensive supply chain and materials resource planning software based upon network applications. The main emphasis of such software is often on strategic planning from the point of view of supply chain and distribution studies, where the terms *supply chain* and *distribution* are taken in a quite general sense: flow of physical product, data, transportation vehicles, international currencies, and so on. State-of-the-art software for efficiently optimizing very large-scale network applications involving tens of thousands of decisions and constraints—models much too large for Solver—can be purchased from specialized software vendors.

The application of network models to real situations involves considerable skill and experience in casting models, which initially may not appear to be network models, into a network representation. To capitalize on the large-scale advantages of the network structure, it is often worth the price of rethinking the initial formulation to cast it into a network representation, such as was done with Andrew Tan's dynamic production model in Figure 5.16. Often the crucial element in network modeling is the modeler's ingenuity in being able to cast the original complex model into the network format. Usually, this is far from a trivial exercise in model formulation, and considerable on-site experience inside the operation being modeled is often a prerequisite. As a final note, many real modeling situations contain submodels that may have a network form.

The very large number of different applications of network models can be nicely illustrated by a few popular examples. We begin by illustrating a more general form of the transportation model, called a *transshipment* model used widely in transportation logistics.

5.11 A CAPACITATED TRANSSHIPMENT MODEL

Seymour Miles is the distribution manager for Zigwell Inc., AutoPower's largest U.S. distributor of UPS generators in five midwestern states. Currently, Seymour has ten BigGen's at what we shall designate as site ①. These generators must be delivered to construction sites in two cities denoted as sites ③ and ④. Three BigGen's are required at site ③, and seven are required at site ④. Because of prearranged schedules concerning driver availability, these generators may be distributed only according to any of the alternative routes shown in Figure 5.24.

NETWORK TERMINOLOGY

Figure 5.24 is an example of a **network diagram** or **network flow diagram**. Each of the arrows between sites is termed an **arc** or **branch** of the network. The arc from ② to ④ is sometimes denoted symbolically by the pair (2, 4). Each site is termed a **node** of the network.

Figure 5.24 shows a +10 identified with site ①. This means that ten BigGen's (items of *supply*) are available at this site. The identifiers –3 and –7 attached to sites ③ and ④, respectively, denote the *requirements*, or *demands*, at these two sites. The figure also indicates that BigGen's may be delivered to site ③ via any of the alternative routings ①→②→③, ①→②→④→③, ①→②→⑤→④→③, or ①→②→⑤→③.

Which of the allowable routes is ultimately selected and will be determined by the associated *costs* of traversing the routes and *capacities* along the routes. These additional data are shown symbolically as the costs, c_{ij} and capacities, u_{ij}, in Figure 5.25. The costs c_{ij} are *per unit costs.* For example, the cost of traversing arc (5, 3) is c_{53} per generator. These costs are primarily due to fuel, tolls, and the cost of the driver for the average time it takes to traverse the arc. Because of pre-established agreements with the teamsters, Zigwell must

FIGURE 5.24

Network Diagram for Seymour's Model

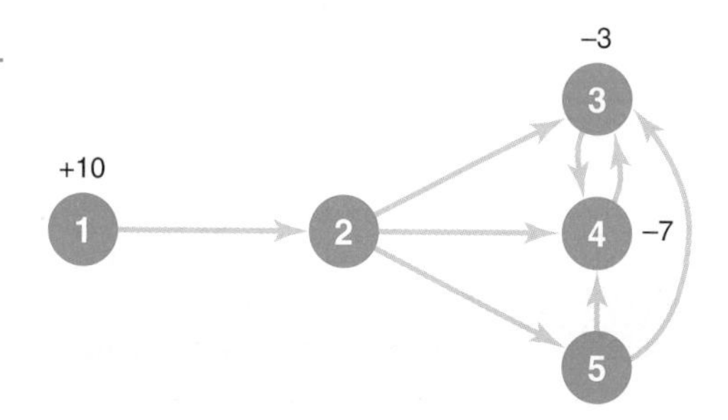

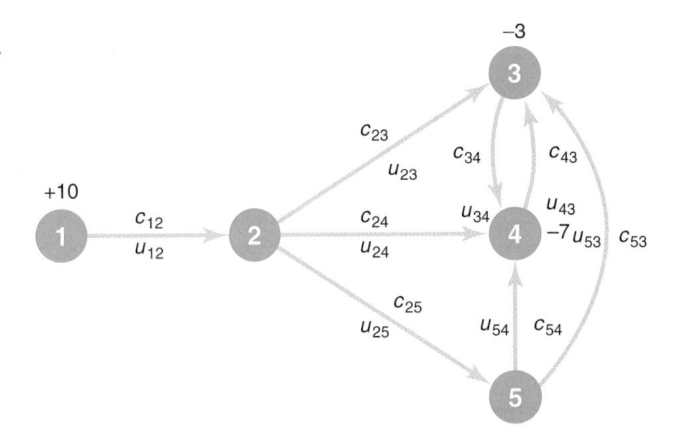

FIGURE 5.25

Arc Capacities and Costs Appended

change drivers at each site it encounters on a route. Because of limitations on the current availability of drivers, there is an upper bound, u_{ij}, on the number of generators that may traverse any given arc. Thus, as an example, u_{53} is the upper bound or capacity on arc (5, 3).

LP FORMULATION OF THE MODEL

Seymour's problem is to find a shipment plan that satisfies the demands at minimum cost, subject to the capacity constraints. You can now appreciate the trade-offs facing Seymour. For example, if $(c_{25} + c_{53})$ less than c_{23}, the route ①→②→⑤→③ will have a total cost that is less than the total cost of route ①→②→③, and hence ①→②→⑤→③ is preferred to ①→②→③. However, the maximum number of BigGen's that can be sent across the preferred route is MIN (u_{12}, u_{25}, u_{53}). If this number is less than 3, the number of BigGen's required at 3, all of the shipment cannot be accomplished via ①→②→⑤→③. This is a model in only five nodes and eight arcs, and even in a simplified example such as this, the optimal solution may not be obvious. Imagine such a model with 300 or 400 nodes and many thousands of arcs, and you begin to see what the challenge of transportation logistics is all about.

This model is basically identical to the transportation model covered earlier except that:

1. Any plant or warehouse can ship to any other plant or warehouse, and
2. There can be upper and/or lower bounds (capacities) on each shipment (branch).

Because these capacities can be added to the model, and shipments can cross (trans) from warehouse to warehouse (or plant to plant), it is called the **capacitated transshipment model**. We now show that this model can easily be expressed as an LP model. First, define the decision variables

$$\begin{aligned} x_{ij} &= \text{total number of BigGen's sent on arc } (i, j) \\ &= \text{flow from node } i \text{ to node } j \end{aligned}$$

Then Seymour's model is

$$\begin{aligned} \text{Min } & c_{12}x_{12} + c_{23}x_{23} + c_{24}x_{24} + c_{25}x_{25} + c_{34}x_{34} + c_{43}x_{43} + c_{53}x_{53} + c_{54}x_{54} \\ \text{s.t. } & +x_{12} = 10 \\ & -x_{12} + x_{23} + x_{24} + x_{25} = 0 \\ & -x_{23} - x_{43} - x_{53} + x_{34} = -3 \\ & -x_{24} + x_{43} - x_{34} - x_{54} - -7 \\ & -x_{25} + x_{53} + x_{54} = 0 \\ & 0 \le x_{ij} \le u_{ij}, \text{ all arcs } (i, j) \text{ in the network} \end{aligned}$$

PROPERTIES OF THE MODEL

There are several observations to be made about this model.

1. The model is indeed an LP. There is one variable x_{ij} associated with each arc in the network of Figure 5.25. There are eight arcs in this network and thus eight corresponding variables, x_{12}, x_{23}, x_{24}, x_{25}, x_{43}, x_{53}, x_{34}, and x_{54}. The objective is to minimize total cost.
2. There is one material **flow balance equation** associated with each node in the network. The first equation says that the total flow *out of* node ① is ten units. Recall that this is the total supply at node ①. The second equation says that the total flow *out of* node ② (namely, $x_{23} + x_{24} + x_{25}$) minus the total flow *into* node ② (namely, x_{12}) is zero. In other words, the total flow out of node ② must equal the total flow into node ②. The third equation says that the total flow *out of* node ③ (namely, x_{34}) must be 3 units less than the total flow *into* node ③ (namely, $x_{23}+ x_{43} + x_{53}$). This is the mathematical way of expressing the requirement for a *net delivery* of 3 units to node ③. The equations for nodes ④ and⑤, respectively, have similar interpretations. Thus, the equation for each node expresses a flow balance and takes into account the fact that the node may be either a supply point or a demand point or neither. Intermediate nodes (such as ② and ⑤ in Figure 5.24) that are neither supply points nor demand points are often termed **transshipment nodes**.

   In general, flow balance for a given node, *j*, is given by

   $$\text{total flow out of node } j - \text{total flow into node } j = \text{supply at node } j$$

   where negative supply represents a requirement. Nodes with negative supply are often called *destinations, sinks*, or *demand points*. Nodes with positive supply are often called *origins, sources*, or *supply points*. Nodes with zero supply are often called *transshipment points*.
3. The positive right-hand sides correspond to nodes that are net suppliers (origins). The negative right-hand sides correspond to nodes that are net destinations. The zero right-hand sides correspond to transshipment nodes that have neither supply nor demand. The sum of all right-hand-side terms is zero, which means that the total supply in the network equals the total demand.

Figure 5.26 gives the Excel formulation for Seymour's transshipment model and shows the optimal solution. For Seymour's data, the shipping capacity matrix giving the arc capacity values, u_{ij} is given in cells C3:G7, and the unit cost matrix giving the arc unit cost values, c_{ij}, is given in cells J3:N7. The RHS specification of Seymour's net requirement's constraints is given in cells C17:G17. The decision variables are in cells C10:G14 and the total cost matrix is calculated by formulas in cells J10:N14. The "Shipped-Received" cells in C16:G16 are computed by subtracting the Total Received quantities in C15:G15 from the corresponding Total Shipped quantities in H10:H14.

The capacitated transshipment model (often called the **network model**) is important because several important management decision models are special cases. In particular the transportation model, assignment model, and shortest-route model, described next, are special cases of the capacitated transshipment model, and the maximal-flow model, described in Section 5.14, is closely related.

INTEGER OPTIMAL SOLUTIONS

There are two advantages in being able to identify a model as a special case of the network (or capacitated transshipment) model. First, theoretical results that are established for the general model apply automatically to the specific cases. The outstanding example of this phenomenon is the integer property of the network model. The integer property can be stated thus:

> If all the RHS terms and arc capacities, u_{ij}, are integers in the capacitated transshipment model, there will always be an integer-valued optimal solution to this model.

FIGURE 5.26

Seymour's Transshipment Model

TIP: *The only way to calculate the quantities in cells C16:G16 of Figure 5.26 in Excel by a single formula requires array operations using the TRANSPOSE function. Highlight cells C16:G16 and enter the array formula {=TRANSPOSE(H10:H14)-C15:G15} into C16. See Appendix B for details on array operations and entering array formulas. Otherwise, separate formulas must be entered for each cell: C16 contains "=H10–C15," D16 contains "H11–D15," and so forth.*

Capacited Transshipment Model

Capacity From\To	Site 1	Site 2	Site 3	Site 4	Site 5
Site 1		10			
Site 2			4	3	3
Site 3				2	
Site 4			4		
Site 5			3	5	

Unit Cost From\To	Site 1	Site 2	Site 3	Site 4	Site 5
Site 1		$100			
Site 2			$45	$50	$20
Site 3				$60	
Site 4			$85		
Site 5			$10	$55	

Shipments From\To	Site 1	Site 2	Site 3	Site 4	Site 5	Total Shipped
Site 1		10				10
Site 2			4	3	3	10
Site 3				1		1
Site 4						0
Site 5				3		3
Total Received	0	10	4	7	3	
Shipped - Received	10	0	-3	-7	0	
Required Net	=10	=0	=-3	=-7	=0	

Total Cost	Site 1	Site 2	Site 3	Site 4	Site 5	Total
Site 1		$1,000				$1,000
Site 2			$180	$150	$ 60	$ 390
Site 3				$ 60		$ 60
Site 4						
Site 5				$165		$ 165
Total		$1,000	$180	$375	$ 60	$1,615

Cell	Formula	Copy To
J10	= C10*J3	J10:N14
H10	= SUM(C10:G10)	H11:H14
C15	= SUM(C10:C14)	D15:G15

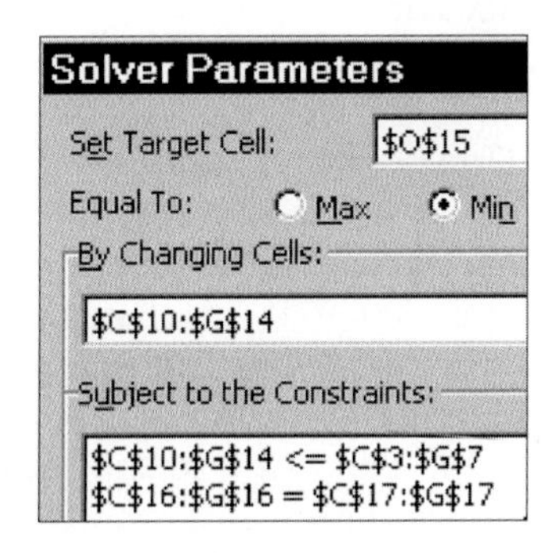

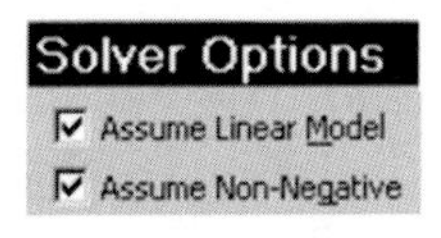

From earlier chapters you know that LP models do not in general yield optimal solutions that have integer-valued variables. The network model with integer values for all RHS's and u_{ij} does. This has an important implication on the usefulness of the various special versions of the network model.

EFFICIENT SOLUTION PROCEDURES

The second reason it is useful to identify a model as a special case of the capacitated transshipment model is that the *structure* of this model typically makes it possible to apply special solution methods and software that optimize the model much more quickly than the more general simplex method used by Solver. This makes it possible to optimize very large-scale network models quickly and cheaply. The impact of some of the super efficient solution methods derived from the special structure of the network model is rather amazing. For example, the Internal Revenue Service constructed a network model with 50,000 constraints and 600 million variables! Only one hour of a mainframe computer's time was required to optimize this model.

The next two sections cover two other variations on the network model, the shortest-route model and the maximal-flow model, respectively. In each case the model is represented with a network diagram, and an Excel formulation for solving the model is presented. The shortest-route model is another special case of the capacitated transshipment model.

FIGURE 5.27

Aaron's Network of Sites

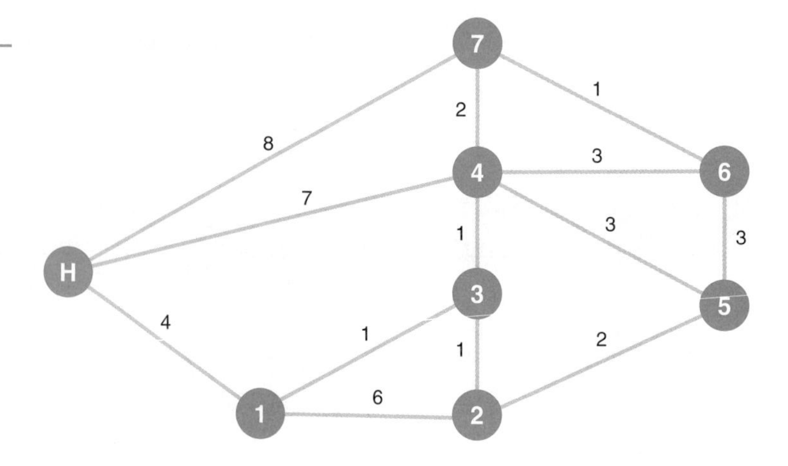

5.12 A SHORTEST-ROUTE MODEL

The **shortest-route model** refers to a network for which each arc (i,j) has an associated number, c_{ij}, which is interpreted as the distance (or possibly the cost, or time) from node i to node j. A *route*, or a *path*, between two nodes is any sequence of arcs connecting the two nodes. The objective is to find the shortest (or least-cost or least-time) routes from a specific node to each of the other nodes in the network. The applicability of finding the shortest route for product shipments, data packets in a computer network, and so forth are obvious.

As an illustration, Aaron Drunner makes frequent wine deliveries to seven different sites. Figure 5.27 shows the seven sites together with the possible travel routes between sites. Note that here, unlike in the transshipment model, the arcs are *nondirected.* That is, on each arc, flow is permitted in either direction. It is certainly possible to have directed arcs between the nodes, with the cost from node 1 to 2 different than from 2 to 1. This might be the case when there is rush-hour traffic in one direction but not in the other, or to be able to go from 1 to 2 but not from 2 to 1 (one-way street). Each arc in Figure 5.27 has been labeled with the distance between the nodes the arc connects. The home base is denoted H. Aaron feels that his overall costs will be minimized by making sure that any future delivery to any given site is made along the shortest route to that site. Thus, his objective is to specify the shortest routes from node H to any of the other seven nodes. Note that in this model, as stated, the task is not to find optimal x_{ij}'s. The task is to find an optimal route.

Figure 5.28 gives Aaron's Excel model and its optimal solution for finding the shortest path between any two nodes, in this case from Home to Site 5. The starting node, Home, and the ending node, Site 5, are specified in row 23 by a 1 and –1, respectively. Cells M3:T10 specify the arc distances as parameters. Other than the use of indicator variables to signify the node-arc connectivity in cells C3:J10, the model is the same form and uses the same formulas as the general transshipment model illustrated in Figure 5.26. The decision variables are constrained to be between 0 and 1, as in the assignment model, and the objective function in U21 to be minimized is the total distance.

5.13 AN EQUIPMENT REPLACEMENT MODEL

A novel application of the shortest-route model is for optimizing the financing or costs of equipment over time. Michael Carr is responsible for obtaining a high-speed printing press for his newspaper company. In a given year he must choose between acquiring a new printing press at high annual acquisition cost but low initial maintenance cost or continuing to use a previously acquired printing press with no further annual acquisition cost but higher annual maintenance costs. For simplicity, assume Michael has a four-year time horizon to

FIGURE 5.28

Aaron's Model for Shortest Path from H to Node 5

Shortest Route Model

Connectivity From\To	Home	Site 1	Site 2	Site 3	Site 4	Site 5	Site 6	Site 7
Home		1			1			1
Site 1	1		1	1				
Site 2		1		1		1		
Site 3		1	1		1			
Site 4	1			1		1	1	1
Site 5			1		1		1	
Site 6					1	1		1
Site 7	1				1		1	

Distance From\To	Home	Site 1	Site 2	Site 3	Site 4	Site 5	Site 6	Site 7
Home		4			7			8
Site 1	4		6	1				
Site 2		6		1		2		
Site 3		1	1		1			
Site 4	7			1		3	3	2
Site 5			2		3		3	
Site 6					3	3		1
Site 7	8				2		1	

Route From\To	Home	Site 1	Site 2	Site 3	Site 4	Site 5	Site 6	Site 7	Total From
Home		1							1
Site 1				1					1
Site 2						1			1
Site 3			1						1
Site 4									0
Site 5									0
Site 6									0
Site 7									0
Total To	0	1	1	1	0	1	0	0	
Total From - Total To	1	0	0	0	0	-1	-0	0	
Required Net	=1	=0	=0	=0	=0	=-1	=0	=0	

Total Distance	Home	Site 1	Site 2	Site 3	Site 4	Site 5	Site 6	Site 7	Total
Home		4						0	4
Site 1				1					1
Site 2						2			2
Site 3			1						1
Site 4									
Site 5									
Site 6									
Site 7							0		0
Total		4	1	1		2	0	0	8

Solver Parameters

Set Target Cell: $U$21

Equal To: ○ Max ◉ Min

By Changing Cells:

$C$13:$J$20

Subject to the Constraints:

$C$13:$J$20 <= $C$3:$J$10
$C$22:$J$22 = $C$23:$J$23

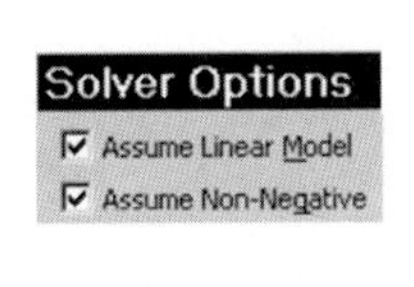

consider. Let c_{ij} denote the cost of acquiring new equipment at the beginning of year i, $i = 1, 2, 3, 4$, and maintaining it to the beginning of year j, where j can take on the values 2, 3, 4, 5. If the equipment is maintained only to the beginning of year j, for $j < 5$, additional equipment must again be acquired at the beginning of j. For example, three alternative feasible policies are:

1. Acquiring new equipment at the beginning of each year. Presumably, such a policy would involve the highest total acquisition costs and the minimum total maintenance charges. The total (acquisition + maintenance) cost of this policy would be $c_{12} + c_{23} + c_{34} + c_{45}$.
2. Acquire new equipment only at the beginning of year 1 and maintain it through all successive years. This would undoubtedly be a policy of minimum total acquisition costs but maximum total maintenance costs. The total (acquisition + maintenance) cost of this policy would be c_{15}.
3. Acquire new equipment at the beginning of years 1 and 4. The total cost would be $c_{14} + c_{45}$.

Of all feasible policies, Michael desires one with a minimum total cost. The solution to this model is obtained by finding the shortest (i.e., in this case, minimum-cost) route from node 1 to node 5 of the network shown in Figure 5.29. Each node on the shortest route denotes a replacement, that is, a year at which new equipment should be acquired.

Using the same general layout and formulas as in Figure 5.26, Figure 5.30 gives Michael's equipment replacement model. The cost parameters are given in cells H2:H7,

FIGURE 5.29

Network for Michael's Equipment Replacement Decision

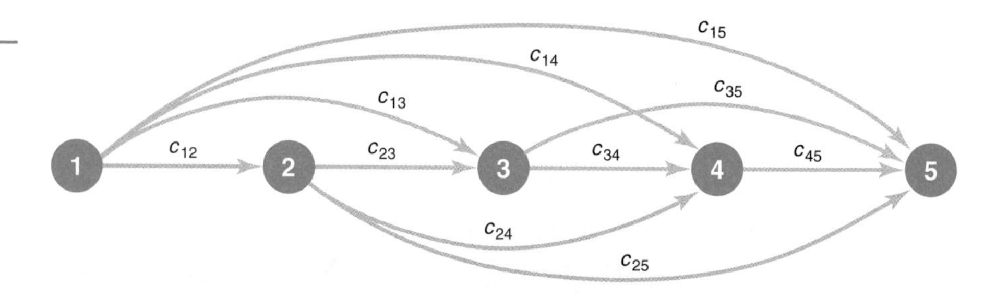

FIGURE 5.30

Michael's Equipment Replacement Model

	B	C	D	E	F	G	H
1	Equipment Leasing Model						Lease
2	Capacity From\To	Year 1	Year 2	Year 3	Year 4	Year 5	$1.6
3	Year 1		1	1	1	1	Maint.
4	Year 2			1	1	1	$0.5
5	Year 3				1	1	$1.0
6	Year 4					1	$1.5
7	Year 5						$2.2
8							
9	Acquire From\To	Year 1	Year 2	Year 3	Year 4	Year 5	Total From
10	Year 1			1			1
11	Year 2						0
12	Year 3					1	1
13	Year 4						0
14	Year 5						0
15	Total To	0	0	1	0	1	
16	Total From - Total To	1	0	0	0	-1	
17	Required Net	=1	=0	=0	=0	=-1	
18							

	I	J	K	L	M	N	O
2	Unit Cost From\To	Year 1	Year 2	Year 3	Year 4	Year 5	
3	Year 1		$2.1	$3.1	$4.6	$6.8	
4	Year 2			$2.1	$3.1	$4.6	
5	Year 3				$2.1	$3.1	
6	Year 4					$2.1	
7	Year 5						
9	Cost From\To	Year 1	Year 2	Year 3	Year 4	Year 5	Total
10	Year 1			$3.1			$3.1
11	Year 2						
12	Year 3					$3.1	$3.1
13	Year 4						
14	Year 5						
15	Total			$3.1		$3.1	$6.2

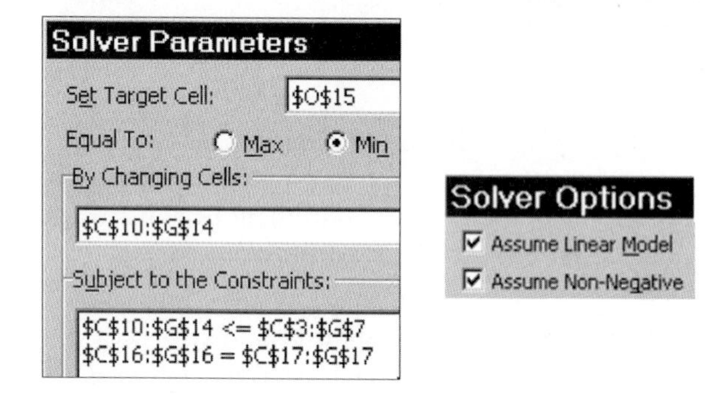

assuming an acquisition cost of $1,600,000 plus maintenance of $500,000 in the year the equipment is acquired and annual maintenance costs of $1,000,000, $1,500,000, and $2,200,000 for each additional year the equipment is kept thereafter. Cells J3:N6 compute the cost consequences of acquiring and maintaining a printing press beginning in one year and continuing to a terminal year. For example, the formula in M3 is "= H2 + H4 + H5 + H6." As with the impossible decisions covered earlier in Figure 5.16, the light gray decision cells in C10:G14 represent time reversals that have no meaning, for example, acquiring a printing press in Year 3 for use in Year 1. The beginning year and the ending year for Michael's equipment needs are specified in row 17 by a 1 and –1, respectively. As before with the shortest-path model, indicator variables are used to signify the node-arc connectivity in cells C3:G7, and cells J10:N14 compute the costs of the decisions in cells C10:G14. In this case Michael's optimal strategy is to acquire a printing press at the beginning of year 1 and keep it for two years, replacing it at the beginning of year 3 with a new printing press, which he keeps until the beginning of year 5 for a total four-year cost of $6.2 million.

APPLICATION CAPSULE Japan's Hanshin Expressway

The Hanshin Expressway started with only a 2.3 kilometer (km) stretch in 1964. This was the first urban toll expressway in Osaka. Two years later, an expressway was opened in Kobe that connected that city to Osaka. About 5000 cars per day used the expressway in the mid-1960s. This area of Japan, on the main island of Honshu, is the second most populated area of Japan (Tokyo is first). In 1992, the expressway operated a network of 200 km with an average of 828,000 cars flowing onto the expressway each day.

The average number of cars per unit of arable land in Japan is much more than that in the United States. Almost all cities and towns in Japan suffer from severe traffic congestion. Because land is scarce, it is estimated that the capacity of the road networks will never catch up with demand. Thus, the importance of finding ways to maximize utilization of the road networks will continue into the foreseeable future.

In 1970, the expressway started operating an automated traffic-control system to maximize the total traffic flowing into its expressway network. The maximum flow idea is somewhat tricky. One might think that in order to maximize flow you would let all the cars enter that wanted to and may even lower the toll to stimulate demand. But, if too many cars are allowed to enter, major congestion can occur, thus greatly decreasing the total flow on the system.

One of the controls used by the Hanshin Expressway is to limit the cars coming onto the expressway at each entrance ramp to avoid congestion. This is done by calculating maximum allowable inflows by solving an LP model once every five minutes using data from detectors installed every 500 meters along the expressway and at all ramps. The linear program has the objective of maximizing the flow on the expressway, which will automatically maximize the income. From the LP solution, the expressway management decides how many new cars to allow onto the expressway at each on-ramp. Management can also use the LP model if there is an accident to determine how many cars should be forced to exit upstream from the accident. In order to reduce congestion and bottlenecks, the expressway authority also analyzed the number of accidents, disabled cars, and road maintenance that could be expected. A second method of control that is used is to give drivers the most recent and accurate traffic information about the expressway and its vicinity, including expected travel times and accidents.

Management has been able to keep the cost of this traffic-control system to about 1% of the total toll revenue. The greatest benefit has been the travel time saved by the drivers. The total time saved over the decade of the 1970s was estimated at 17,850,000 hours. Based on the average hourly benefit of the citizens of Osaka, this is worth some 27,300,000,000 Yen (U.S. $260 million at 1994 exchange rates)! Hanshin's LP model has also been a prototype to the rest of Japan and Taiwan as they have tried to implement automatic traffic control to gain the same benefits. (See Yoshino et al.)

5.14 A MAXIMAL-FLOW MODEL

In the **maximal-flow model** there is a single *source* node (the input node) and a single *sink* node (the output node). The goal is to find the maximum amount of total flow (petroleum, cash, Internet packets, traffic) that can be routed through a physical network (from source to sink) in a unit of time. The amount of flow per unit time on *each arc* is limited by *capacity restrictions.* For example, pipeline diameters limit the flow of crude oil on the links of a pipeline distribution system. Flow capacities for nodes are not specified. The only requirement here is that for each node (other than the source or the sink) the material flow balance relation, flow out of the node = flow into the node, must be satisfied.

This model, together with the shortest-path model, is of interest in its own right. It also appears as a submodel in solving other, more complicated, models. For such reasons, as well as because of some of the theoretic underpinnings (which go beyond our present scope of interest), it is sometimes stated that these two models (shortest-path and maximal-flow) are of central importance in network theory development in transportation logistics, computer networking, and so on.

AN APPLICATION OF MAXIMAL FLOW: THE URBAN DEVELOPMENT PLANNING COMMISSION

Gloria Stime is in charge of the UDPC (Urban Development Planning Commission) *ad hoc* special-interest study group. This group's current responsibility is to coordinate the construction of the new subway system with the state's highway maintenance department.

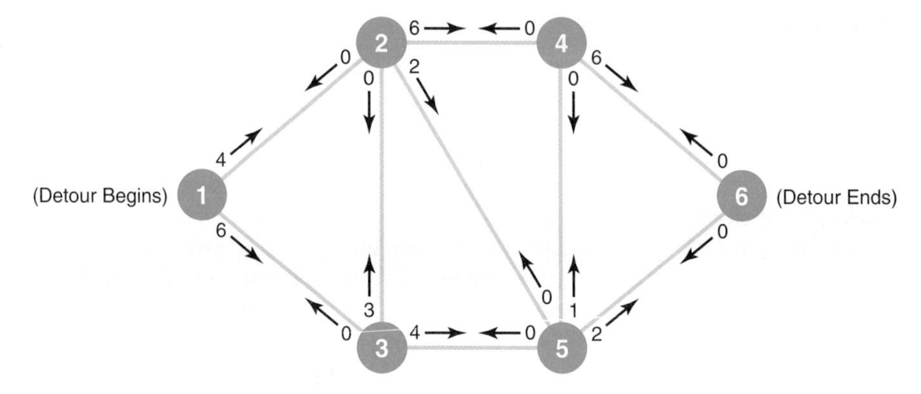

FIGURE 5.31

Proposed Network and Flow Capacities (000s of Vehicles/Hour)

Because the new subway system is being built near the city's beltway, the eastbound traffic on the beltway must be detoured. The planned detour actually involves a network of alternative routes that have been proposed by the highway maintenance department. Different speed limits and traffic patterns produce different flow capacities on the various arcs of the proposed network, as shown in Figure 5.31.

Node ① denotes the beginning of the detour, that is, the point at which the eastbound traffic leaves the beltway. Node ⑥ is the point at which the detoured traffic reenters the beltway. Also, in Figure 5.31, the flow capacities depend on the direction of the flow. The symbol 6 on arc (1, 3) denotes a capacity of 6000 vehicles per hour in the ① → ③ direction.

FIGURE 5.32

Maximal-Flow Model for Gloria's Network

	A	B	C	D	E	F	G	H	I	J
1		Max Flow Model								
2		Capacity From\To	Node 1	Node 2	Node 3	Node 4	Node 5	Node 6		
3		Node 1		4	6					
4		Node 2				6	2			
5		Node 3		3			4			
6		Node 4						6		
7		Node 5						2		
8										
9		Flow From\To	Node 1	Node 2	Node 3	Node 4	Node 5	Node 6	Total From	
10		Node 1		4	4				8	
11		Node 2				6			6	
12		Node 3		2			2		4	
13		Node 4						6	6	
14		Node 5						2	2	
15		Total To		6	4	6	2	8		
16		Total From - Total To		0	0	0	0			
17		Required Net		=0	=0	=0	=0			
18										

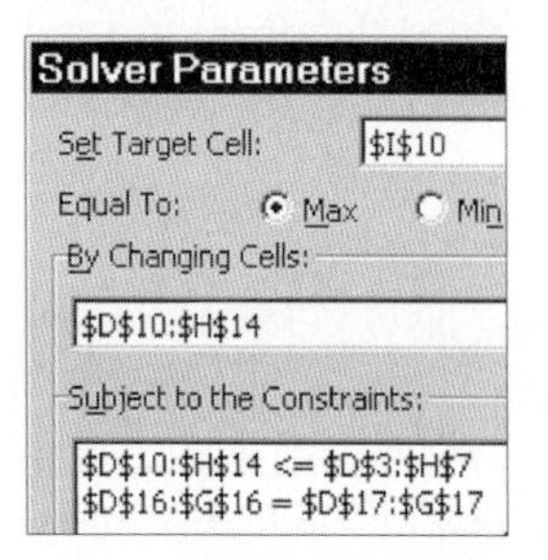

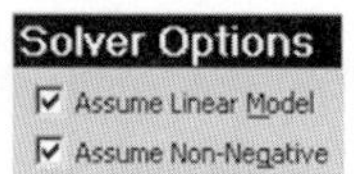

FIGURE 5.33

A Maximal-Flow Pattern for Gloria's Network

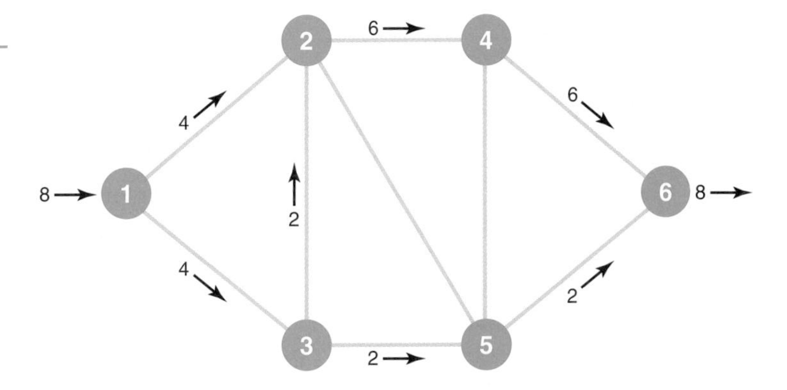

The symbol 0 on the same arc means that a zero capacity exists in the ③ → ① direction. This is because the indicated arc (1, 3) denotes a one-way street from ① to ③. In this example it is seen that each of the other arcs denotes one-way travel. (The Excel model to be presented also applies to models with arcs permitting positive levels of flow in each direction.)

The Excel model for Gloria's network giving the optimal solution for finding the maximal flow is given in Figure 5.32. Except for the absence of cost data the model is similar in form to the other network models we have seen. The (nonnegative) decision variables in cells C10:H14 are the flows from node to node constrained to be no greater than the given arc capacity parameters in cells C3:H7. This model maximizes flow out of Node 1 as its objective function in cell I10. (Equivalently, we could have maximized the flow into Node 6 in cell H15 as the objective function.) The constraints in cells C17:G17 specify that the net flow at each intermediate node must sum to zero, that is, flow into each intermediate node equals flow out of the node.

From the optimal solution the maximal flow is 8000 vehicles per hour. Translating the Excel solution to Gloria's original network diagram gives a traffic pattern as shown in Figure 5.33.

As is common in network models, there are alternative optimal solutions to Gloria's model, as illustrated in Figure 5.34.

FIGURE 5.34

Alternative Optimal Solution for Gloria's Network Model

	A	B	C	D	E	F	G	H	I	J
1				Max Flow Model						
2		Capacity From\To	Node 1	Node 2	Node 3	Node 4	Node 5	Node 6		
3		Node 1		4	6					
4		Node 2				6	2			
5		Node 3		3			4			
6		Node 4						6		
7		Node 5						2		
8										
9		Flow From\To	Node 1	Node 2	Node 3	Node 4	Node 5	Node 6	Total From	
10		Node 1		4	4				8	
11		Node 2				6	1		7	
12		Node 3		3			1		4	
13		Node 4						6	6	
14		Node 5						2	2	
15		Total To		7	4	6	2	8		
16		Total From - Total To		0	0	0	0			
17		Required Net		=0	=0	=0	=0			
18										

5.15 SUMMARY

This chapter was devoted to applications of linear optimization. Section 5.2 covered the transportation model. The generic model is one of determining the least-cost method of satisfying demands at a number of destinations by shipping materials from supplies available at several origins. This model is motivated by a specific problem faced by AutoPower Europe. We also discussed the adaptations that are necessary in order to solve the transportation model when the models differ from the original model. Next, using the transportation model as an example, we investigated how to pursue multiple objectives when alternative optima occur. Finally, we saw that the transportation model has a special property. If all supplies and demands are integer quantities, there is an optimal integer solution.

Section 5.3 treated the assignment model following the pattern of the transportation model. The generic assignment model is one of assigning n persons to n tasks in order to minimize the total cost of the assignments. This model was again motivated by a specific problem faced by AutoPower Europe. In this process we noted that the assignment model is a special type of transportation model in which all supplies and demands equal 1.

Section 5.4 discussed and formulated an example of an LP model used for media selection in the marketing context. An important attribute of this model was the modeling of situations with blending requirements and also diminishing returns, which were approximated by piece-wise linear segments.

Dynamic models were covered in some detail beginning in Section 5.5. The distinction was made between static (one time period) models and dynamic models. The observation was made that, in terms of payoff, a dynamic model for a given planning horizon can always do as well as a collection of static models covering the same time horizon and may do much better. Correctly formulating dynamic models requires attention to definitions of variables within a time period and timing of activities and material flow balances across time periods. Edge conditions must be determined for the starting and ending time periods. A dynamic production and inventory situation was modeled in Section 5.6. Three logically equivalent versions of the model of Section 5.6 were presented, each with increasing different levels of detail and correspondingly greater management information. Section 5.7 presented a dynamic production model in which labor scheduling was included. Section 5.8 presented a dynamic inventory model involving cash management. Section 5.9 presented an integrated financial and production planning model to illustrate the interactions among production, financing decisions, and delays in customer payments.

Sections 5.10 through 5.14 covered four illustrative examples of the broad topic of network models, a class of models applicable to extremely large-scale logistics situations. It was shown that under mild restrictions on the data it will always be true that integral-valued optimal solutions exist.

Key Terms

Transportation Model. An LP model to find the least expensive way of satisfying demands at n destinations with supplies from m origins.

Dummy Origin. An imaginary source that is added to a transportation model so that total supply equals total demand.

Assignment Model. The model of determining the optimal assignment of n "indivisible" agents or objects to n tasks.

Network Diagram. A schematic representation consisting of nodes and arcs over which flows may occur.

Arc. A connection between two nodes in a network.

Branch. A synonym for arc.

Node. An element in a network.

Capacitated Transshipment Model. A network model with supplies at specified origins, demands at specified destinations, and shipment alternatives through intermediate nodes on capacitated routes from origins to destinations.

Destination. A node in a network with positive demand.

Origin. A node in a network with positive supply.

Network Model. Generally refers to the capacitated transshipment model or one of its special forms.

Flow Balance Equation. A material balance constraint in a network model that stipulates the supply plus total flow into a node must equal demand plus flow out of the node.

Shortest-Route Model. The model of finding shortest routes from a specified node (the origin) to each of the other nodes in a network.

Transshipment Node. An intermediate node in a capacitated transshipment model that is neither a supply nor a demand node.

Maximal-Flow Model. The model of routing the maximal amount of flow through a network.

Exposure Units. An arbitrary measure of the "goodness" of an ad used in solving media selection models.

Dynamic Model. A model of interrelated decision making across multiple time periods in which the possibility set of allowable decisions in later time periods is affected by decisions in earlier time periods.

Static Model. A model in which decisions are made in a single time period without regard to their effects in future periods.

Dynamic Inventory Model. A dynamic model of decision making affecting inventories of things across multiple time periods.

Multiperiod Inventory Model. Same as Dynamic Inventory Model.

Myopic Model. A static model that ignores consequences of its decisions upon payoffs in future time periods.

Self-Review Exercises

True-False

1. **T F** The coefficient of x_{ij} in the objective function of a transportation model is the cost of sending a unit from *i* to *j*.
2. **T F** If total supply exceeds total demand in a transportation model, to find a solution one option is to add a dummy destination with a transportation cost of zero from every origin.
3. **T F** A transportation model cannot have an optimal integer solution unless all of the supplies, demands, and transportation costs are integers.
4. **T F** A capacitated transshipment model has one variable for each node.
5. **T F** A transportation model is a special case of the capacitated transshipment model.
6. **T F** If the right-hand side of any arc capacity inequality in a capacitated transshipment model is zero, the model is infeasible.
7. **T F** A collection of static models for each of the time periods over a planning horizon will always do at least as well as a single dynamic model defined over the entire planning horizon.

Multiple Choice

8. A transportation model can be used only when
   a. demand exceeds supply
   b. supply exceeds demand
   c. demand and supply are equal
   d. all of the above

9. The assignment model
   a. is a special case of the transportation model
   b. can be solved with Solver's LP optimizer
   c. always has an optimal integer solution
   d. all of the above

10. A positive right-hand side in a flow balance equation of a capacitated transshipment model indicates that
   a. the node is an origin
   b. the node is a destination
   c. the node is a transshipment node
   d. none of the above

11. Which of the following is a condition that assures that there is an optimal integer solution to a capacitated transshipment model?
   a. the right-hand side of all flow equations must be integer
   b. the arc capacities (the u_{ij}'s) must be integer
   c. either a or b
   d. both a and b

12. The shortest-path
   a. connects every node
   b. is the set of all arcs used in tracing the shortest path from a base node H to a given destination node
   c. both a and b

Questions 13 through 17 refer to the following model: A company has two plants and three warehouses. The first plant can supply at most 500 pounds of a particular product, and the second plant at most 200 pounds. The demand at the first warehouse is 150, at the second warehouse 200, and at the third warehouse 350. The cost of manufacturing one pound at plant i and shipping it to warehouse j is given below:

From Plant	TO WAREHOUSE 1	2	3
1	8	10.2	12.6
2	7	9	11.8

Suppose the model is to determine a shipping schedule that satisfies demand at minimum cost.

13. The model is
a. a network model
b. a transportation model
c. a dynamic model
d. all of the above
e. a and b

14. Let x_{ij} denote the amount sent from plant i to warehouse j. The demand constraint for the first warehouse is properly written as
a. $x_{11} + x_{21} = 150$
b. $x_{11} + x_{21} \geq 150$
c. both a and b are correct (i.e., it does not matter whether = or ≥ is used)

15. Let x_{ij} denote the amount sent from plant i to warehouse j. In symbols, the supply constraints can be written as
a. $\sum_{i=1}^{3} x_{ij} \leq s_j, j = 1, 2$
b. $\sum_{i=1}^{3} x_{ij} = s_j, i = 1, 2$
c. $\sum_{j=1}^{3} x_{ij} = s_j, i = 1, 2$
d. none of the above
e. both a and b are correct (i.e., it does not matter whether = or ≥ is used)

16. Solver will always find an integer solution to this model.
a. T
b. F

17. Since total supply = total demand, all constraints (supply and demand) must be written as equalities.
a. T
b. F

Answers

1. T, **2.** T, **3.** F, **4.** F, **5.** T, **6.** F, **7.** F, **8.** d, **9.** d, **10.** a, **11.** d, **12.** c, **13.** e, **14.** c, **15.** d, **16.** a, **17.** b

Skill Problems

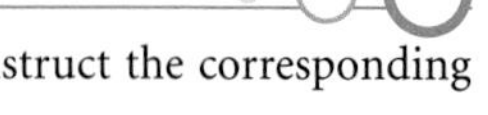

5-1. Consider the following linear constraints of a transshipment model. Construct the corresponding network diagram, labeling each node with its supply or demand.

$$
\begin{aligned}
x_{13} + x_{12} + x_{14} &= 2 \\
-x_{12} + x_{24} &= 1 \\
-x_{13} + x_{35} &= 0 \\
-x_{24} - x_{14} + x_{46} + x_{45} &= 0 \\
-x_{35} + x_{56} - x_{45} &= 0 \\
-x_{46} - x_{56} &= -3 \\
x_{ij} \geq 0, \quad & \text{all } (i, j)
\end{aligned}
$$

5-2. Consider the following constraints:

$$
\begin{aligned}
x_{12} + x_{13} &= 2 \\
-x_{12} + x_{24} + x_{25} &= 0 \\
-x_{13} + x_{34} &= 0 \\
-x_{24} - x_{34} + x_{45} &= -1 \\
-x_{25} - x_{45} &= -1
\end{aligned}
$$

Construct the corresponding network diagram.

5-3. Write the linear constraints corresponding to the transshipment network of Figure 5.35.

5-4. Write the linear constraints corresponding to the transshipment network of Figure 5.36.

5-5. Consider the distribution network shown in Figure 5.37. Find the shortest path from node ① to node ⑦.

5-6. In Figure 5.37, by how much does the distance on the arc from ① to ③ have to decrease before it can become part of the shortest path from node ① to node ⑦.

FIGURE 5.35

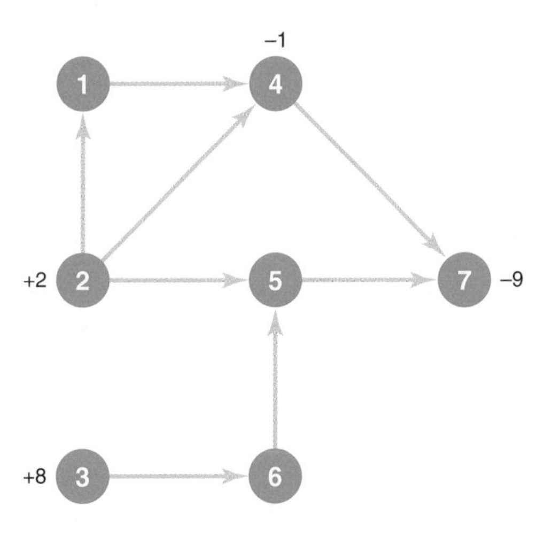

FIGURE 5.36

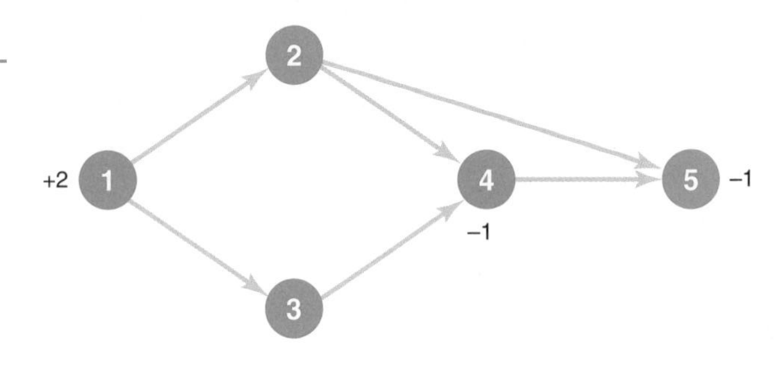

FIGURE 5.37

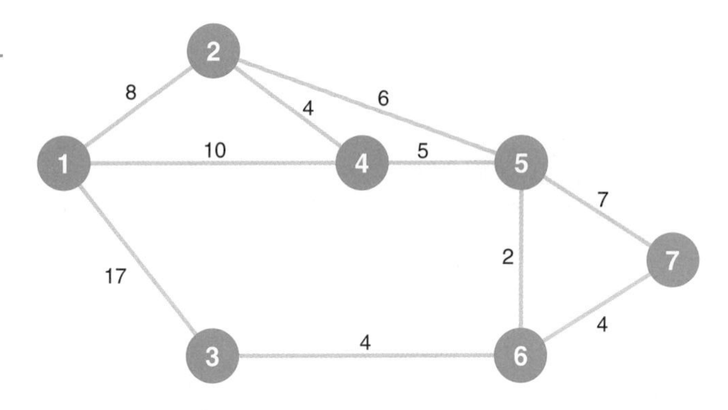

5-7. Consider the distribution network shown in Figure 5.38. Find the shortest route from node ① to node ⑧ in the network.

5-8. In Figure 5.38, by how much does the distance on the arc from ④ to ⑦ have to decrease before it can become part of the shortest path from node ① to node ⑧?

5-9. Consider the transshipment network of Figure 5.39. Nodes ① and ⑤ are the plant sites. The plants produce 200 and 150 truckloads, respectively. Nodes ③, ⑥, and ⑨ are the outlet sites. The outlets demand 50, 250, and 50 truckloads, respectively. The number on arc (i, j) indicates costs of transporting one truckload from i to j. Assume the cost from i to j is the same as the cost from j to i.

(a) Find the least costs of moving one truckload from ① to ③, ⑥ and ⑨.

(b) Find the least costs of moving one truckload from ⑤ to ③, ⑥, and ⑨.

(c) Formulate and solve the transshipment model. What is the minimum total cost?

FIGURE 5.38

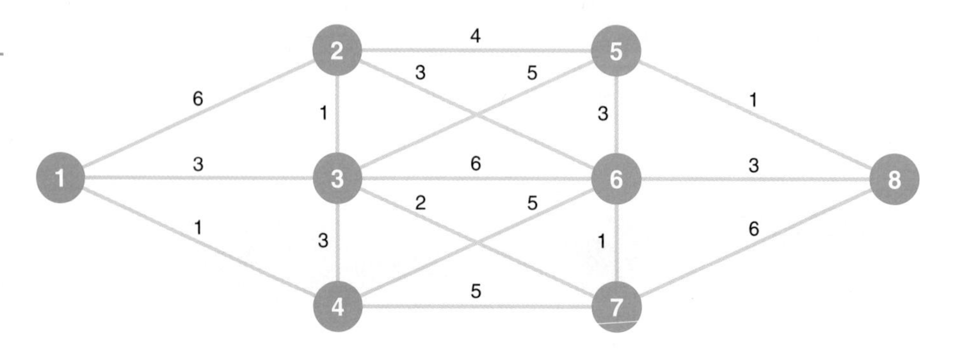

FIGURE 5.39

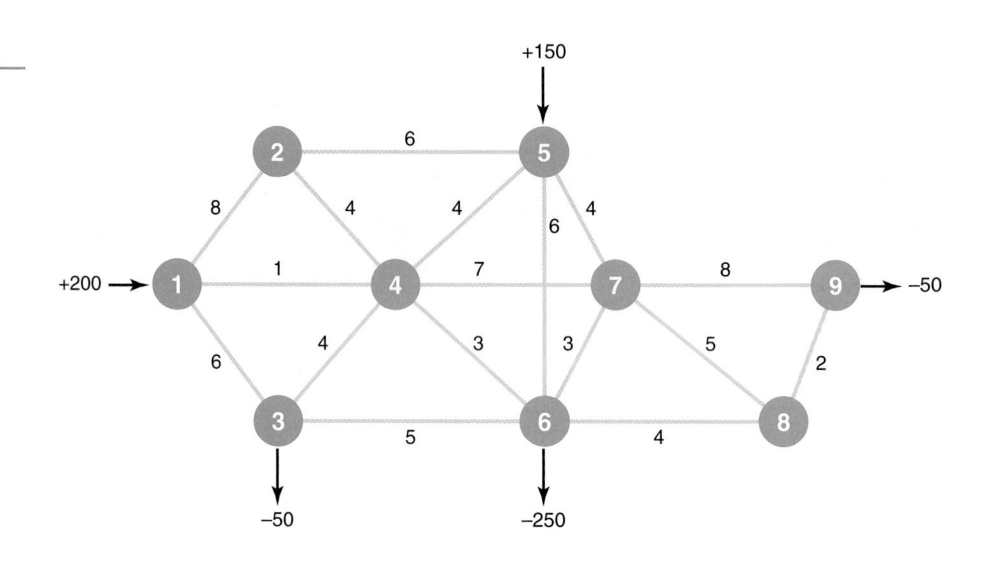

FIGURE 5.40

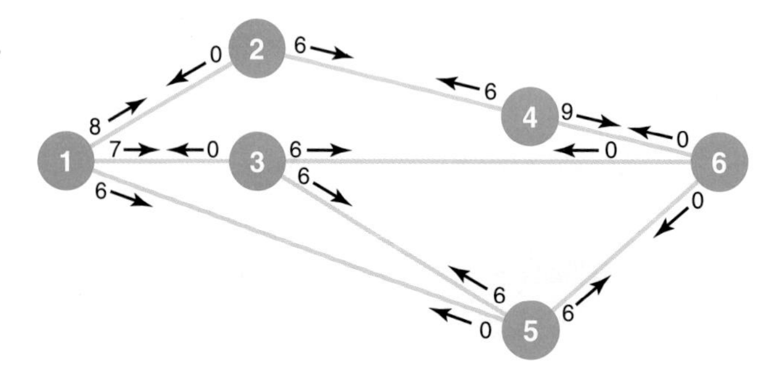

5-10. Determine the maximal flow from node ① to node ⑥ across the highway network shown in Figure 5.40.

5-11. Consider the network shown in Figure 5.41. Find the maximal flow. Assume ① is the source and ⑦ the sink.

5-12. Demonstrate that the transportation model with *S* origins and *D* destinations is a special case of the capacitated transshipment model.

5-13. Demonstrate that the assignment model is a special case of the capacitated transshipment model.

5-14. Demonstrate that the model for determining the minimum-cost route from one node to another specific node can be expressed as a special case of the capacitated transshipment model.

FIGURE 5.41

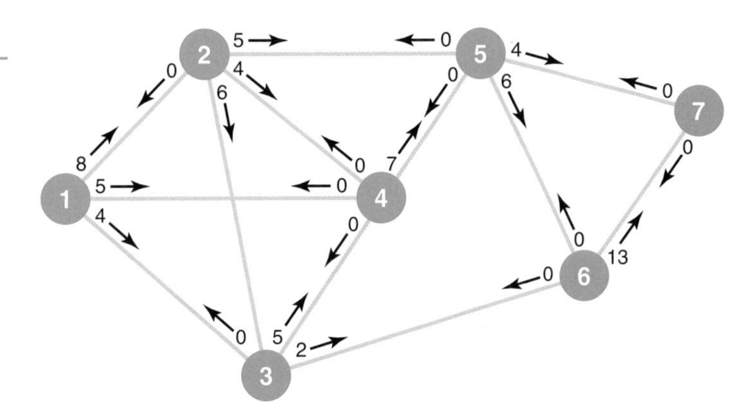

Application Problems

5-15. *Crude Distribution.* Lindsay Doyle is responsible for the transport of crude oil to several storage tanks. A portion of the pipeline network is shown in Figure 5.42. What is the maximal flow from node ① to node ⑦?

••5-16. Mr. Crimmage is operating the Chicago Health Club with leased equipment and space. Recently, his landlord suggested long-term leasing. Based on the long-term lease plan, Mr. Crimmage obtained the following table, which displays the expected net cost if he leases from the beginning of year *i* to the beginning of year *j* (in thousands of dollars).

	i			
i	**2**	**3**	**4**	**5**
1	13	25	37	45
2		12	21	30
3			10	20
4				9

Mr. Crimmage wishes to know when and how long to lease so as to minimize the cost over the next four years. Formulate his model and solve it. Are there alternative optimal solutions?

5-17. Moebius Products, Inc. faces the following situation. It has to deliver 1000 Klein bottles per month for the next four months. The production cost per bottle is \$5 during month 1, \$9 during month 2, \$10 during month 3, and \$14 during month 4. The inventory holding cost is \$3 per bottle per month. The manager of the company would like to determine the most cost-efficient production schedule, that is, how many bottles to make at one time, and when. Assume that production is in multiples of 1,000 bottles. That is, production in month *i* covers demand for months *i* through *j*, for some $j \geq i$. Formulate this model as a network representation and solve it.

5-18. Slick Oil Company has three warehouses from which it can ship products to any of three retail outlets. The demand in cans for the product Gunkout is 100 at retail outlet 1; 250 at outlet 2; and 150 at outlet 3. The inventory of Gunkout at warehouse 1 is 50; at warehouse 2 is 275; and at warehouse 3 is

FIGURE 5.42

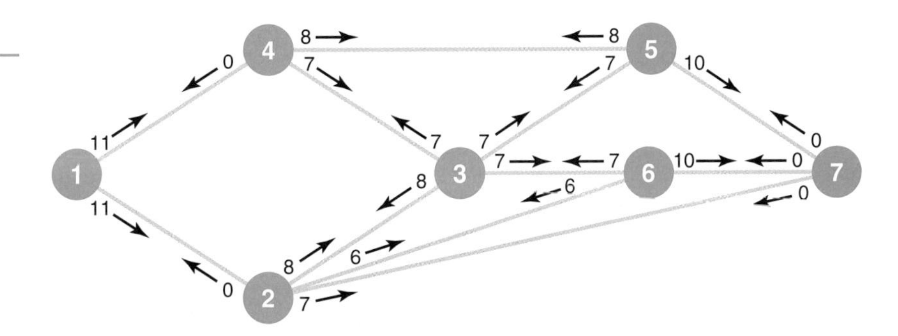

175. The cost of transporting one unit of Gunkout from each warehouse to each retail outlet is given in the following table.

	RETAILER		
Warehouse	**1**	**2**	**3**
1	5	7	6
2	8	9	10
3	4	3	11

Formulate an LP to determine how many units should be shipped from each warehouse to each retailer so the demand at each retailer is met at minimum cost.

5-19. Bob Frapes packages holiday gift-wrapped exotic fruits. His packages are wrapped at two locations from which they are sent to five wholesalers. The costs of packaging at locations 1 and 2 are \$5.25 and \$5.70, respectively. Bob's forecasts indicate demand for shipments as in the following table.

WHOLESALER	1	2	3	4	5
Shipment Required	4000	6000	2000	10,000	8000

Wrapping capacity at location 1 is 20,000 packages and at location 2 is 12,000 packages. The distribution costs in dollars from the two locations to the five wholesalers are given in the following table. Formulate an LP model to determine how many packages Bob should send from each location to each wholesaler.

	WHOLESALER				
From Location	**1**	**2**	**3**	**4**	**5**
1	.60	.40	1.20	.90	.50
2	1.50	.90	.50	.80	.80

5-20. Wonka Widget, Inc. faces a three-period inventory model. The manufacturing cost per widget varies from period to period. These costs are \$2, \$4, and \$3 for periods, 1, 2, and 3, respectively. A cost of \$1 is incurred for each unit of inventory that is carried from one period to the next. Demand is 10,000, 20,000, and 30,000 units in periods 1, 2, and 3, respectively. The initial and final inventories are zero. Formulate an LP to determine how much the manufacturer should produce during each period to satisfy demand at minimum cost.

••5-21. *Purchasing.* Jack Biensaulk is responsible for purchasing canned goods for GAGA food service at a large university. He knows what the demand will be over the course of the school year, and he has estimated purchase prices as well. These data are shown in the following table.

	SEP.	OCT.	NOV.	DEC.	JAN.	FEB.	MAR.	APR.	MAY
Demand (cases)	1000	900	850	500	600	1000	1000	1000	500
Cost per Case \$	20	20	20	21	21	21	22	22	22

He may purchase ahead of demand to avoid price increases, but there is a cost of holding inventory of \$0.20 per case per month applied to inventory on hand at the end of a month. The initial and final case inventories are zero. Formulate and solve a cost-minimizing LP that will help Jack determine the timing of his purchases. HINT: Let P_t be the number of cases purchased in month t and I_t be the number of cases in inventory at the end of month t.

5-22. A manufacturer faces a three-period inventory situation for an item sale priced at \$4. The manufacturing cost is \$4 during the first period and \$3 during the other two periods. The demand and inventory costs are the same as in Problem 5-20. The manufacturer does not have to meet the demand. However, each unit of lost sales costs them \$1.50. The production is restricted to 40,000 units during the first period and to 10,000 units during the other two periods. The initial and final inventories are zero. Formulate an LP to determine the production schedule that maximizes their profit.

5-23. Johnson Electric produces small electric motors for four appliance manufacturers in each of its three plants. The unit production costs vary with the locations because of differences in the production equipment and labor productivity. The customer orders that must be produced next month are shown in the following table.

CUSTOMER	DEMAND
1	300
2	500
3	400
4	600

The unit production costs and monthly capacities (supplies) are shown in the following table.

PLANT	UNIT PRODUCTION COST ($)	MONTHLY PRODUCTION CAPACITY
A	17	800
B	20	600
C	24	700

The cost of supplying these customers varies from plant to plant. The unit transportation costs in dollars are given in the following table.

	TO			
From	1	2	3	4
A	3	2	5	7
B	6	4	8	3
C	9	1	5	4

Johnson must decide how many units to produce in each plant and how much of each customer's demand to supply from each plant. It wishes to minimize total production and transportation costs. Formulate Johnson's problem as a transportation model and solve for the optimal solution.

5-24. *A Scheduling Model.* In a calculated financial maneuver, AutoPower has acquired a new manufacturing facility for producing UPSs. You have been asked to provide an answer to the following question: How many new personnel should be hired and trained over the next six months? The requirements for trained manufacturing employees and monthly wage rates for the next six months are given in the following table.

	MONTH					
	Jan.	Feb.	Mar.	Apr.	May	June
Labor Requirements (hr)	7800	7500	7500	9200	10,000	9000
Monthly Wage Rates ($)	3600	3600	3900	3900	4200	4200

Trainees are hired at the beginning of each month. One consideration to take into account is the union rule that workers must have one month of classroom instruction before they can work in manufacturing. Therefore, a trainee must be hired at least a month before a worker is actually needed. Each classroom student uses 80 hours of a trained manufacturing employee's time, so the employee has 80 less hours for work in manufacturing. Also, by contractual agreement, each trained employee can work up to 195 hours a month (total time, instructing plus in manufacturing). If the maximum total time available from trained employees exceeds a month's requirements, management may lay off at most 15% of the trained employees at the beginning of the month. All employees are paid a full month's salary even if they are laid off. A trainee costs $1,800 a month in salary and other benefits. There are 40 trained employees available at the beginning of January. Formulate the hiring-and-training model as a linear programming model. HINT: Let x_t denote the number of trained employees on hand at the beginning of the month t before any layoffs, let y_t denote the number of trainees hired in month t, and let z_t denote the number of trained employees laid off at the beginning of month t.

5-25. A partner at Foot, Thompson and McGrath, an advertising agency, is trying to decide which of four account executives to assign to each of four major clients. The estimated costs in \$000s of each assignment for each executive are presented below. Formulate a model and solve for the optimal solution.

	ACCOUNT			
Exec.	1	2	3	4
A	15	19	20	18
B	14	15	17	14
C	11	15	15	14
D	21	24	26	24

5-26. *Financial Planning.* An investor has two money-making activities, coded Alpha and Beta, available at the beginning of each of the next four years. Each dollar invested in Alpha at the beginning of a year yields a return two years later (in time for immediate reinvestment). Each dollar invested in Beta at the beginning of a year yields a return three years later. A third investment possibility, construction projects, will become available at the beginning of the second year. Each dollar invested in construction yields a return one year later. (This option will be available at the beginning of the third and fourth years also.) The investor starts with \$50,000 at the beginning of the first year and wants to maximize the total amount of money available at the end of the fourth year. The returns on investments are given below.

ACTIVITY	RETURN PER DOLLAR INVESTED (\$)
Alpha	1.50
Beta	1.80
Construction	1.20

(a) Identify the decision variables and formulate a symbolic LP model. HINT: Let M_i be the money available at the beginning of year i and maximize M_5 subject to the appropriate constraints.
(b) Develop an Excel version of your symbolic LP model and solve it.
(c) Can you determine the solution of the symbolic LP model by direct analysis without Solver?

5-27. AutoPower is deciding which of four salespeople to assign to each of four sales districts. Each salesperson is apt to achieve a different sales volume in \$000s in each district. The estimates are given in the following table.

	DISTRICT			
Salesperson	1	2	3	4
A	65	73	55	58
B	90	67	87	75
C	106	86	96	89
D	84	69	79	77

AutoPower would like to maximize total sales volume. However, it is impossible to assign salesperson B to district 1 or salesperson A to district 2 since these assignments would violate personnel rotation policies. Model this situation and find the optimal solution.

5-28. *An Arbitrage Model.* A speculator operates a silo with a capacity of 6,000 bushels for storing corn. At the beginning of month 1, the silo contains 5,000 bushels. Estimates of the selling and purchase prices of corn during the next four months are given in the following table.

MONTH	PURCHASE PRICE PER 1000 BUSHELS (\$)	SELLING PRICE PER 1000 BUSHELS (\$)
1	45	40
2	50	45
3	60	56
4	70	65

Corn sold during any given month is removed from the silo at the beginning of that month. Thus, 5,000 bushels are available for sale in month 1. Corn bought during any given month is put into the silo, but it cannot be sold until the following month. Assume that the cost of storing the corn is based on average inventory and that it costs $0.01 to store one bushel for one month. The storage cost for a month must be paid at the end of the month. All purchases must be paid for with cash by the delivery time. The speculator has $100 to invest and has no intention of borrowing to buy corn or pay storage costs. Therefore, if he has no cash at the beginning of a month, he must sell some of his stock to pay the storage charge at the end of the month and to pay for the corn if he purchases any. Given the sales and purchase prices and the storage cost, the speculator wishes to know how much corn to buy and sell each month so as to maximize total profits shortly after the beginning of the fourth month (which means after any sale that may occur in that month). Formulate and solve the LP model. HINT: Let A_t denote bushels in the silo immediately after delivering the quantity sold in month t (x_t), and B_t bushels in the silo immediately after receiving the quantity purchased in month t (u_t), and P_t the cash position at the end of month t.

5-29. Sam has four repair bays in the maintenance shop and three jobs to assign to them. Because of differences in the equipment available, the people assigned to each bay, and the characteristics of the job, each job requires a different amount of time in each bay. The estimated times for each job in each bay are given in the following table.

	JOB		
Bay	1	2	3
A	27	48	30
B	38	51	28
C	27	55	23
D	35	59	24

Sam would like to minimize the total time required. Formulate the model and obtain the optimal solution. Are there alternative optimal solutions?

5-30. Fernwood Lumber produces plywood. The cost to produce 1,000 board feet of plywood varies from month to month because of the variation in handling costs, energy consumption, and raw materials costs. The production cost per 1,000 board feet in each of the next six months is shown in the following table.

MONTH	1	2	3	4	5	6
Production Cost ($)	900	950	1250	1050	900	850

Demand for the next six months is shown in the following table.

MONTH	1	2	3	4	5	6	TOTAL
Demand (000s)	60	70	110	80	70	60	450

Fernwood can produce up to 90,000 board feet per month. It also has the option of holding inventory from one month to the next for a holding cost of $25 per 1,000 board feet per month. For example, 1,000 board feet produced in month 1 for demand in month 2 incurs a holding charge of $25. Furthermore, unsatisfied demand in one month can be filled in later periods at the cost of $40 per 1,000 board feet per month-delay. Initial and final inventories are zero. Fernwood would like to know how much to produce each month and how much inventory to carry in order to satisfy demand at minimum cost. Formulate Fernwood's problem as a transportation model and solve for the optimal solution.

5-31. A realtor plans to sell four plots of land and has received individual bids from each of five developers. Because of the amount of capital required, these bids were made with the understanding that no developer would purchase more than one plot. The bids in $000s are shown in the following table. The realtor wants to maximize total income from these bids. Formulate the model and optimize it.

	DEVELOPER				
Plot	1	2	3	4	5
A	19	19	29	23	24
B	23	21	27	19	25
C	19	19	22	0	20
D	23	0	19	21	18

Case Study Trans World Oil Company[1]

The Trans World Oil Company is an international producer, refiner, transporter, and distributor of oil, gasoline, and petrochemicals. Trans World is a holding company with subsidiary operating companies that are wholly or partially owned. A major problem for Trans World is to coordinate the actions of these various subsidiaries into an overall corporate plan, while at the same time maintaining a reasonable amount of operating autonomy for the subsidiary companies.

To deal with this dilemma, an annual corporate-wide plan that detailed the pattern of shipments among the various subsidiaries was developed. This plan was not rigid but provided general guidelines and the plan was revised periodically to reflect changing conditions. Within the framework of this plan, the operating companies could make their own decisions and plans.

This corporate plan was originally done on a trial-and-error basis. There were two problems with this approach. First, the management of the subsidiaries complained that the planners did not take into account the operating conditions under which the subsidiary had to operate. The plan might call for operations or distribution plans that were impossible to accomplish. Second, the corporate management was concerned that the plan did not optimize for the total company.

The technique of linear programming seemed a possible approach to aid in the annual planning process that would be able to answer, at least in part, the two objections above. In addition, the building of such a model would make it possible to make changes in plans quickly when the need arose.

Far Eastern Operations

The details of the 1996 planning model for the Far Eastern Operations are now described.

There are two sources of crude oil, Iran and Borneo. The Iranian crude is relatively heavier (24° API), and the Far Eastern sector could obtain as much as 60,000 barrels per day (b/d) at a cost of $18.50 per barrel at Abadan during 1996. A second source of crude is from the Brunei fields in Borneo. This is a lighter crude oil (36° API). Under the terms of an agreement with the Netherlands Petroleum Company in Borneo, a fixed quantity of 40,000 b/d of Brunei crude, at a cost of $20.50 per barrel is to be supplied during 1996.

There are two subsidiaries that have refining operations. The first is in Australia, operating a refinery in Sydney with a capacity of 50,000 b/d throughout. The company also marketed its products throughout Australia, as well as having a surplus of refined products available for shipment to other subsidiaries.

The second subsidiary is in Japan, which operates a 30,000 b/d capacity refinery. Marketing operations are conducted in Japan, and excess production is available for shipment to their Far Eastern subsidiaries.

In addition, there are two marketing subsidiaries without refining capacity of their own. One of these is in New Zealand and the other in the Philippines. Their needs can be supplied by shipments from Australia, Japan, or the Trans World Oil subsidiary in the United States. The latter is not a regular part of the Far Eastern Operations, but may be used as a source of refined products.

Finally, the company has a fleet of tankers that move the crude oil and products among the subsidiaries.

Refinery Operations

The operation of a refinery is a complex process. The characteristics of the crudes available, the desired output, the specific technology of the refinery, and so on make it difficult to use a simple model to describe the process. In fact, management at both Australia and Japan have complex linear programming models involving approximately 300 variables and 100 constraints for making detailed decisions on a daily or weekly basis.

For annual planning purposes the refinery model is greatly simplified. The two crudes (Iranian and Brunei) are input. Two general products are output—(a) gasoline products; and (b) other products known collectively as distillate. In addition, although the refinery had processing flexibility that permitted a wide range of yields, for planning purposes it was decided to include only the use of the values at highest and lowest conversion rates (process intensity). Each refinery could use any combination of the two extreme intensities. These yields are shown in Table 1.

The incremental costs of operating the refinery depended somewhat upon the type of crude and process intensity. These costs are shown in Table 1. Also shown are the incremental transportation costs from either Borneo or Iran.

Marketing Operations

Marketing is conducted in two home areas (Australia and Japan) as well as in the Philippines and New Zealand. Demand for gasoline and distillate in all areas has been estimated for 1996 and is shown in the following table.

	1996 DEMAND (THOUSANDS OF B/D)	
Area	**Gasoline**	**Distillate**
Australia	9.0	21.0
Japan	3.0	12.0
Philippines	5.0	8.0
New Zealand	5.4	8.7
Total	22.4	49.7

[1] An earlier version of this case is in *Computer Models for Decision Analysis* (Scientific Press, 1980) by Charles P. Bonini.

TABLE 1 Refinery Costs and Yields

LOCATION, CRUDE, PROCESS INTENSITY	Cost of Crude/bbl.	Incremental Shipping Costs/bbl.	Incremental Refining Costs/bbl.	Total Costs	YIELDS (BBL. OUTPUT PER BBL. CRUDE INPUT)	
					Gasoline	Distillate
Australia:						
Brunei Crude, Low (BLA)	$20.50	$.78	$.36	$21.64	.259	.688
Brunei Crude, High (BHA)	20.50	.78	.84	22.12	.365	.573
Iran Crude, Low (ILA)	18.50	1.86	.45	20.81	.186	.732
Iran Crude, High (IHA)	18.50	1.86	.90	21.26	.312	.608
Japan:						
Brunei Crude, Low (BLJ)	$20.50	.72	.48	21.70	.259	.688
Brunei Crude, High (BHJ)	20.50	.72	1.02	22.24	.350	.588
Iran Crude, Low (ILJ)	18.50	1.77	.60	20.87	.186	.732
Iran Crude, High (IHJ)	18.50	1.77	1.17	21.44	.300	.620

Variable costs of supplying gasoline or distillate to New Zealand and the Philippines are shown in the following table.

	VARIABLE COSTS OF SHIPMENT OF GASOLINE/DISTILLATE IN $/BBL.	
From/To:	New Zealand	Philippines
Australia	.30	.45
Japan	.30	.60

Tanker Operations

Tankers are used to bring crude from Iran and Borneo to Australia and Japan and to transport refined products from Australia and Japan to the Philippines and New Zealand. The variable costs of these operations are included in the previous shipment table. However, there is a limited capacity of tankers available. The fleet had a capacity of 6.9 equivalent (standard-sized) tankers.

The amount of capacity needed to deliver one barrel from one destination to another depends upon the distance traveled, port time, and other factors. The table below lists the fraction of one standard-sized tanker needed to deliver 1,000 b/d over the indicated routes. It is also possible to charter independent tankers. The rate for this was $8,600 per day for a standard-sized tanker.

TANKER USAGE FACTORS (FRACTION OF STANDARD-SIZED TANKER NEEDED TO DELIVER 1000 B/D)

Between	Australia	Japan
Iran	.12	.11
Borneo	.05	.045
Philippines	.02	.01
New Zealand	.01	.06

United States Supply

United States operations on the West Coast expected a surplus of 12,000 b/d of distillate during 1996. The cost of distillate at the loading port of Los Angeles is $19.80 per barrel. There is no excess gasoline capacity. The estimated variable shipping costs and tanker requirements of distillate shipments from the United States are:

	Variable Cost of shipments ($ per bbl.)	Tanker Requirements (Fraction of standard-sized tanker needed to deliver 1000 b/d)
New Zealand	2.10	.18
Philippines	1.65	.15

Required

1. Formulate and optimize a linear program that could be used to generate a comprehensive plan for the whole Far Eastern Operations.
2. Use the model to respond to the following four new requests.

Memo To: Trans World Oil Headquarters

From: Australian Affiliate

Re: Supplements to Annual Plan

Since submitting data for annual planning purposes, two additional opportunities have arisen. We would like to include them in the plans.

A. *Bid on Gasoline Contract with Australian Government*

The government of Australia will submit to bid a contract for buying 1.5 thousand b/d of gasoline for 1996. We expect we could win this contract and still make a profit at a bid price of $29.20 per barrel. We would like permission to submit this bid for the contract.

B. *Expansion of Australian Refinery*

For the past two years, the Australian refinery has been operating at full capacity. We request authorization for capital expenditures to increase the refinery capacity to 65 thousand b/d. There are several reasons for the need for this expansion:

1. Australia can supply the current requirements in New Zealand and the Philippines more cheaply than can Japan.
2. The proposed bid on Australian government gasoline contract (above).
3. We understand the New Zealand affiliate is considering increasing its requirements by 4.8 thousand b/d. [See below.]

The cost of this expansion is $6,000,000. To recover this investment, we need an annual savings of $1,053,000.

This assumes a cost of capital rate of 20%. Depreciation tax effects are included. With these considerations, the $1,053,000 savings per year is equivalent to the $6 million investment.)

Memo To: Trans World Oil Headquarters

From: New Zealand Affiliate

Re: Supplement to Annual Plan

Negotiations have begun with the NOZO Oil Company in New Zealand. This company is a distributor, with sales of 1.6 thousand b/d of gasoline and 3.2 thousand b/d of distillate. If negotiations are successfully completed, these requirements would be added to current requirements for New Zealand, making total requirements of:

Gasoline: 7.0 thousand b/d

Distillate: 11.9 thousand b/d

The anticipated revenue (after subtracting variable marketing costs) for this acquisition are $34.30 per barrel for gasoline and $25.90 per barrel for distillate. The purchase cost of NOZO oil is expected to be about $31.0 million. On an annual basis, this would require $5.2 million per year incremental profit to justify the purchase.

Memo To: Trans World Oil Headquarters

From: Tanker Affiliate

Re: Supplement to Annual Plan

We are currently operating the tanker fleet at capacity. Any additional requirements will increase the transport requirements both for crude and refined products. This will necessitate spot chartering unless additional tanker capacity is added.

We can lease additional tankers at a rate of $4.8 thousand dollars per day per 1 unit tanker equivalent. We propose a lease of 0.5 equivalent taker units giving us a total capacity of 7.4 equivalent units. The cost of this would be $3.5 thousand per day or $1,278,000 per year.

Memo To: Trans World Oil Headquarters

From: Borneo Office

Re: Supplement to Annual Plan

We have just been offered the opportunity to increase our contract with our supplier of Brunei crude. They are willing to supply us an additional 5 thousand b/d at a cost of $21.50 per barrel. Should we accept the offer?

Case Study Production Planning at Bumles

(Before attacking this case you will want to review the solution to the Bumles example in this chapter, for the correct formulation of this model will be similar.) Bumles, Inc. uses part of its capacity to make two types of hand-painted statues. The finished products can reasonably be grouped into two categories, A and B. A requires 0.5 hours of a painter's time and B requires 0.75 hours. Bumles has 45 painters available, but not all of these painters need to be used. The plant is used for hand-painted statues on Monday, Tuesday, and Wednesday each week. During the remainder of the week the productive capacity is devoted to another product line. Each painter who is engaged is available to work painting statues any part of an eight-hour day, two days a week. A painter can be assigned to any two-day schedule and is paid for 16 hours of regular-time work, no matter what part of that time he actually spends producing statues. If there is not enough production to keep all the workers assigned to a particular day busy for the entire day, the slack time is spent on cleaning the plant and similar activities. In addition, on any day, Bumles can request each working painter to work up to four hours of overtime (i.e., if a painter normally works on Tuesday, Bumles can have him work 2, 3, or any other number between 0 and 4, hours of overtime on that day).

Revenue from selling an A is $21 and a B is $30. Demand must either be satisfied on the day on which it occurs or it is lost. Production on a given day can be used to satisfy demand that day or demand later in the week; that is, statues produced on Monday can be used to satisfy demand on Monday, Tuesday, or Wednesday, and statues produced on Tuesday can be used to satisfy demand on Tuesday or Wednesday. However, because of the change of operations in production, all statues produced in a week must be shipped that week; that is, there is never inventory on hand Monday morning. Because of increased handling costs, it costs $0.25 to carry an A and $0.30 to carry a B in inventory from one day to the next. A unit of lost demand results in an all-inclusive penalty cost of $2 for a unit of A on Monday, $4 on Tuesday, and $5 on Wednesday. The per unit penalty costs for B are $5 on Monday, $10 on Tuesday, and $11 on Wednesday. Painters are paid $10 per hour of regular time and $15 per hour of overtime.

Demand varies significantly at Bumles. Management is considering two generic demand patterns, Pre-Christmas Rush and After-Christmas Slump, shown in the following tables.

PRE-CHRISTMAS RUSH

	M	T	W
A	1500	1000	150
B	240	90	1100

AFTER-CHRISTMAS SLUMP

	M	T	W
A	240	48	64
B	160	32	64

Bill Bumles, the Executive VP, notes that A's yield a contribution of 21/0.5 = $42 per labor hour, whereas B's yield a contribution of 30/0.75 = $40 per labor hour. He also notes that the penalty for lost sales increases as the week goes on. He concludes that Bumles should first satisfy all demand for A's starting with Wednesday, then Tuesday, then Monday, and then used any leftover capacity to produce B's.

Specific Questions

1. Comment on the approach suggested by Bill Bumles.
2. Ignoring integrality conditions (i.e., allowing the possibility of fractional values of all decision variables), create an Excel LP model that will schedule painters and production in such a way as to maximize revenue minus cost, where cost equals labor plus penalty and inventory-holding costs. The model should be correct for any set of demands. In your formulation the first six constraints should reflect the demand for A on Mondays, Tuesdays, and Wednesdays, and the demand for B on Mondays, Tuesdays, and Wednesdays. Thus, to solve the model for any set of demands one must provide only the RHSs for these constraints. In your formulation of the model, pay attention to relationships between production, sales, lost sales, demand, and inventory on any particular day. For example,

   demand on day t = sales on t + lost sales on t

3. What are the decision variables? Define them carefully.
4. For each of the above two specific demand patterns, optimize the model.

Then, for both demand patterns summarize the following into a report for a general manager:

5. How many items of what to produce each day.
6. How to schedule as many of the painters as you use, for example, schedule 14.3 painters to work a Monday/Tuesday schedule, and so forth.
7. How many hours of overtime to use each day.
8. How much inventory of each product to carry each day.
9. How many units of lost sales to have each day.
10. Use your model to answer the following question: Assume that a year consists of 32 weeks of pre-Christmas rush demand and 18 weeks of after-Christmas slump demand. If Bumles wants each of the 45 painters to work an equal number of weeks, how many weeks will each painter work?

Additional Considerations

[The questions in this section should be answered by using the model created in Question 2 above, with new parameters and performing additional analysis as needed.]

The painters' union has suggested a contract with a guaranteed annual wage (GAW) provision. In particular, this agreement specifies that a painter must be paid at least $11,500 per year for work on hand-painted statues. If, at the end of the year, the amount earned is less than $11,500, the firm simply gives the painter a check to make up the difference. Bumles plans to use all 45 painters even if the GAW provision is not accepted; but, if it is, all 45 painters will earn at least $11,500 per year.

To estimate the effect of this proposal on the Bumles operation, Bill assumes that 30 weeks of the 50-week year will have pre-Christmas rush demands, and the other 20 weeks will have the demand schedule shown in the following table.

	M	T	W
A	240	48	300
B	160	32	200

He also assumes that a detailed schedule can be worked out so that each painter earns the same pay during a year. Based on your LP model and Bill's assumptions

11. What is Bumles' total annual profit without the GAW provision?
12. Does your solution to Question 11 satisfy the GAW provision? What effect will accepting the GAW provision have on Bumles' profitability (increase, decrease, or no

effect)? Show the spreadsheet calculations to support your answers.

13. How much would average wages have to be in the low-demand weeks for the annual wage to be $11,500? For the low-demand weeks, formulate an LP model that Bumles could use to find a production plan that would meet the GAW provision. Present a justification for your model and optimize it.
14. Suppose the GAW provision is accepted. How much would Bumles save per year by using the plan found in Question 13 compared with the plan of Question 11 where additional payments would have to be made to the painters at the end of the year?

Sensitivity Questions

[These questions refer to the Sensitivity Reports for the models you created to answer Questions 1–10.]

15. In the current solution to the pre-Christmas version of the model, if we combine regular and overtime pay then each painter is paid $280/week. If another painter should become available, what is the maximum weekly amount that Bumles should pay him or her?
16. Suppose that, in the pre-Christmas model, the demand for A on Monday increases by 10 units. What happens to the OV?
17. Answer Question 16 for the after-Christmas model.
18. What is responsible for the major difference in the answers to Questions 16 and 17?
19. Suppose that, in the pre-Christmas model, management's recent experience calls for an adjustment in the penalty cost for unsatisfied demand for A on Monday. The new value is set at $3. What happens to the optimal solution and the OV?
20. In Question 19, suppose the new value is reset to $4. What is the effect on the optimal solution and the OV? (Give the best answer you can based on the Sensitivity Report.)
21. Suppose that, in the pre-Christmas problem, the selling price of A is reduced to $15 and B is reduced to $20. Can you give a bound on the new OV?

Case Study | Biglow Toy Company[1]

In late August 1997, Jean Biglow, treasurer of Biglow Toy Company, was concerned with financing its sales operations during the upcoming Christmas selling season. To cope with the Christmas sales peak, Jean planned to build up Biglow's toy inventory throughout the fall. This would generate substantial cash deficits in October, November, and December. Some means of short-term financing had to be found to cover these deficits. On the other hand, Jean anticipated a cash surplus in January and February, when Biglow's retailers paid their Christmas invoices. A small cash surplus was also anticipated in September as a result of over-the-summer toy purchases.

Jean tried to maintain a minimum balance in Biglow's cash account throughout the year. This was to protect against errors in estimating both the size and timing of future cash flows. The planned minimum balance was normally set as a fixed percentage of each month's anticipated dollar sales volume. This procedure had proven adequate in the past against virtually all contingencies.

Except for deciding how to finance the fall buildup in inventory, Jean had already completed a six-month financial plan. This covered the period September 1997 through February 1998. Selected portions of the plan are shown in the table below.

SIX-MONTH FINANCIAL PLAN
(ALL FIGURES IN THOUSANDS OF DOLLARS)

	SEP	OCT	NOV	DEC	JAN	FEB
Accounts Receivable Balance	$700	$500	$700	$1200	$1000	$500
Planned Payments for Purchases	$800	$900	$1000	$600	$400	$500
Cash Surplus From Operations	$200	—	—	—	$300	$1500
Cash Deficit From Operations	—	$300	$600	$900	—	—

[1] Inspired by a Stanford case developed originally by Professor Charles P. Bonini.

The accounts receivable balances shown in the table refer to the beginning of each month. Thus, Jean anticipates \$700,000 in accounts receivable at the beginning of September, \$500,000 at the beginning of October, and so forth.

On the average, Biglow receives a 3% discount from its toy suppliers for prompt payment of purchases. Jean normally takes advantage of such discounts, whenever possible, and so, the planned payments shown in the table assume prompt payment and realization of the 3% average discount. If Biglow's payments are delayed, the discount will be lost, and actual payments will exceed planned payments, accordingly.

The cash surplus and deficit figures shown in the table are net of all other operations, including anticipated sales receipts, planned payments for purchases, and all other planned receipts and payments. These figures are also net of the standard provision for each month's minimum cash balance. Thus, Jean expects a surplus of \$200,000 from operations during September, a deficit of \$300,000 from operations during October, and so forth. Each of the surplus and deficit figures shown in the table represents the incremental (not cumulative) surplus or deficit anticipated during that month.

As indicated in Exhibit 1, Jean has three sources of short-term borrowing to meet Biglow's monthly cash needs. These are:

1. Pledging accounts receivable balances, that is, factoring;
2. Delaying payments of purchases; and
3. Obtaining a six-month bank loan.

A local bank has agreed to loan Biglow funds at the beginning of any month against a pledge of its accounts receivable balance. The maximum loan that Biglow can obtain from this source is 75% of the accounts receivable balance outstanding at the beginning of that month. Whatever is borrowed, if anything, must be returned to the bank at the beginning of the next month, plus an interest payment of 1.5% of the amount actually borrowed.

Payments to suppliers for purchases may be delayed for a maximum of one month. Thus, up to \$1,000,000 in payments currently scheduled for November may be delayed until December. Whatever portion, if any, of these planned payments is delayed would become available to finance the anticipated deficit from operations during November. However, Jean's own policy strictly forbids delaying payments more than one month beyond the month when they are supposed to be paid. Also, the average 3% discount is lost on all payments that are actually delayed. For example, if Jean delays the planned payment of \$1,000,000 for November, then the payment in December for this delayed amount will be 1,000,000/.97 = 1,000,000 * 1.031 = \$1,031,000 approximately.

The local bank is also willing to make a one-time loan to Biglow of any amount from a minimum of \$400,000 to a maximum of \$1,000,000 for six months. If such a loan is taken, the entire loan will be received by Biglow at the beginning of September and repaid at the end of February. In addition, Biglow must pay the bank a 1% monthly interest charge at the end of each month. Once taken, it is not possible to increase the loan nor to repay any portion of it during the six-month

EXHIBIT 1

Sources and Uses of Funds for Biglow Toy Company

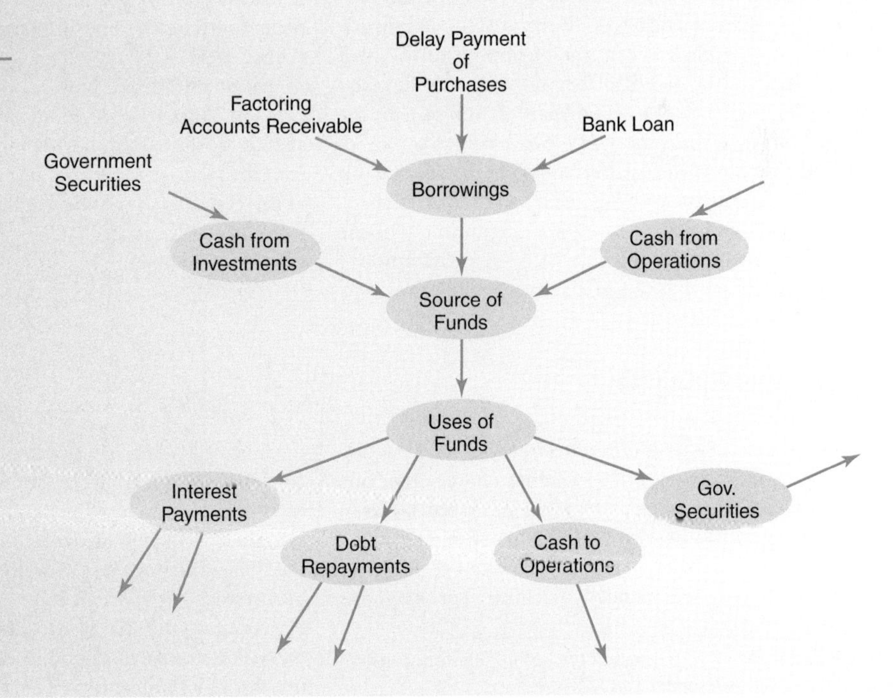

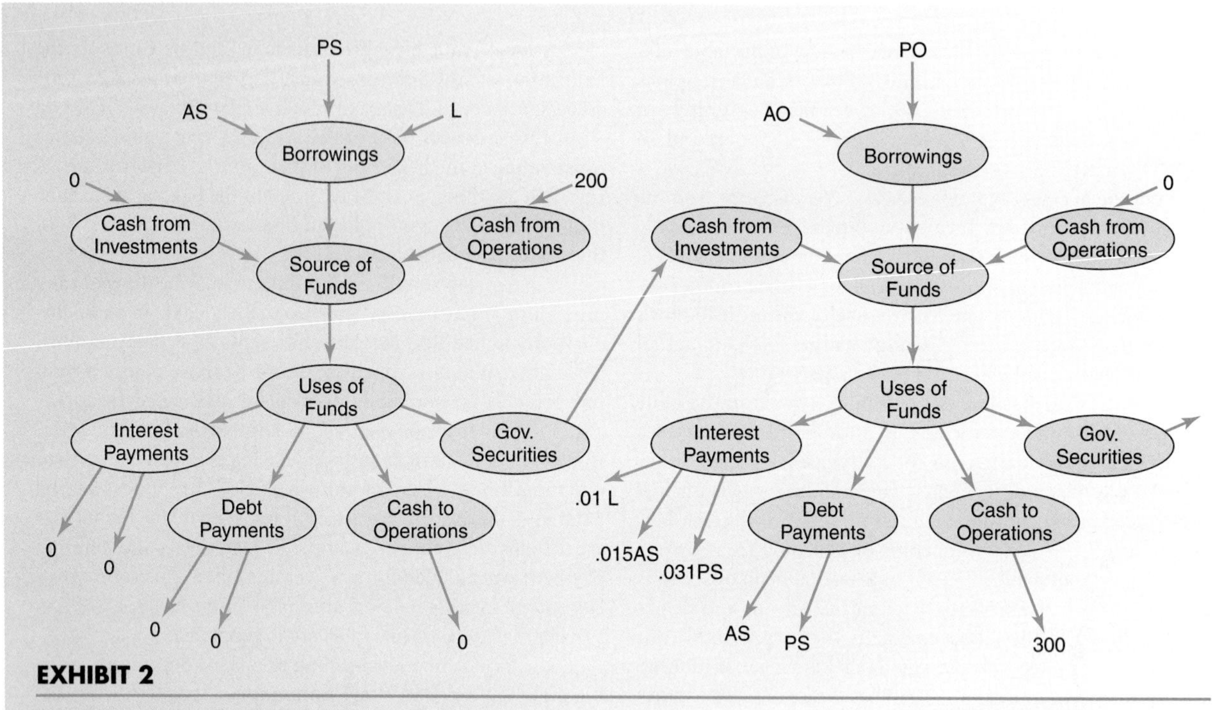

EXHIBIT 2

Sources and Uses of Funds for September and October

period. The 1% monthly interest charge therefore applies to the entire amount, if any, actually borrowed.

At the end of every month, Jean inspects the current balance in Biglow's cash account. Whatever excess funds remain over and above the minimum balance planned for the next month are invested immediately in 30-day government securities. Securities are purchased at the beginning of the next month and sold at the end of that month. Upon selling the securities, Biglow receives one-half percent interest on the excess funds, if any, actually invested. No excess funds are anticipated for the month of August, but Jean plans to continue this investment procedure between September and February.

The sources and uses of funds are diagrammed for the first two months in Exhibit 2 in which **AS** is the amount borrowed by pledging **A**ccounts Receivable in **S**eptember, **AO** is the amount borrowed by pledging **A**ccounts Receivable in **O**ctober, **PS** is the amount made available by postponing **P**ayments in **S**eptember, **PO** is the amount made available by postponing **P**ayments in **O**ctober, and **L** is the amount of the (one-time) six month **L**oan in September, if any.

Jean must decide how to cover the operating deficits indicated in Table 1 by utilizing some combination of the three sources of short-term borrowing. Jean expects to maintain at least the planned minimum balances in Biglow's cash account at the end of each month as a reserve for contingencies while minimizing the net dollar cost of whatever six-month financing plan is adopted.

Case Study **Ebel Mining (C)**[1]

"That was very clever—your idea of reclassifying higher-quality ore and sending it to customers wanting a lower-grade ore. Looks like it will save us some money after all." Truman Hardy, Ebel's chief mining supervisor, comments admiringly. "Of course, we had considered a similar idea long ago when we acquired a special ore blender machine. For example, medium-grade ore is just a lower percentage of the minerals needed than high grade. In fact, we could blend low-grade and high-grade ore in a .6 to .4 combination (1.5 times as much low grade as high grade in each blended ton) and ship that as medium-grade ore just as well. The blender has capacity of processing 8 tons of ore per week, which seemed ample. However, we decided not to pursue blending ore because it turned out to cost us an additional $100 per ton for processing ore through the blender and doing quality assurance on the blending process, which obviously would raise our total weekly costs. . . ."

Questions

1. Revise the Network Flow Diagram [See Ebel (B) Case] to include the added Blending option in addition to any reclassification activities. Include that option in addition to the Reclassify version of the Ebel (B) flow diagram.
2. Reformulate the Ebel (B) model to include a new decision variable, amount of medium-grade ore coming out of the blender, and optimize the new model to minimize total weekly cost. Be sure to account for material balance of all the ores into and out of nodes represented by your constraints. Are total costs higher as claimed by Truman?
3. Explain your model changes, the resulting mine schedule, blending and reclassify decisions, and shadow price information in an executive summary memo to Ebel management. In it include a brief discussion commenting on Hardy's rationale for dropping the option of blending ore. Also, comment on the effect this new plan will have on disposal of any overproduced ores.

Case Study Ebel Mining (D)[1]

"Look here, you haven't been very realistic in your modeling," says Truman Hardy, Ebel's chief mining supervisor. "First of all, we operate on a monthly production schedule with shipments at the end of each week. And, we typically have to build up inventory of the three ore types (high, medium, and low grade) to carry over from one week to the next (up to our total storage capacity of 75 tons for all ores taken together in any week). We have to do that because each 'day' a mine runs is actually a 24-hour day and we are limited by union contracts to no more than a five day per week operation. You can appreciate that we need to tell everyone in advance, if we will be running a mine for less than five days in any week."

"Because of these factors we must plan an entire month's production, storage, and deliveries at a time. So, to be realistic, you should revise your earlier weekly model, including the reclassify and blending options, to become a four-week model for the month. Our weekly delivery requirements in tons of ore for the next month are given in the following schedule."

TONS OF ORE TO DELIVER EACH WEEK

	Week 1	Week 2	Week 3	Week 4
High Grade	12	20	30	44
Medium Grade	8	22	38	35
Low Grade	24	40	44	60

"Our mining costs also vary each week, because of maintenance activities and use of temporary workers to replace those on vacation. I have summarized them in the table below."

MINING COST PER DAY OF OPERATION ($ 000'S PER DAY)

	Week 1	Week 2	Week 3	Week 4
Mine 1	20	20.5	20.5	21
Mine 2	16	16.4	16.4	16.4

"I would guess that the blender is still limited to processing no more than eight tons of ore per week, and the cost of operating it is the same as before, $100 per ton processed, and that wouldn't vary over the month," says Truman. "Also, I figure it costs us nothing to reclassify a higher-grade ore to a lower grade and ship that instead, assuming we wanted to continue to do such a silly thing."

"By the way, the monthly inspection by the Environmental Protection Agency (EPA) cannot be conducted if there is any ore stored on the premises. Therefore, we must schedule everything to have no month-end inventory of ore," Truman continues. "I know you have been very creative in looking at my problems. But, I am sure you now can see that my situation is much too complicated for your little toy spreadsheet model. Besides, my controller wants me to use the net present value of costs in decision making, discounting the costs at 1% per month (=.25% per week), and that alone destroys your simplistic linearity assumption. You see the real world of mining is very complicated and we have to do the best we can. Let's see, looking at the delivery requirements, I'd better build up inventories in the early weeks. . . ."

Questions

1. Is Truman correct in his last statement that his net present value calculation destroys linearity? Why or why not?
2. Adapt your LP model from Ebel Mining (C) to handle his more realistic dynamic situation and provide him a production schedule. HINT: Make four copies of your Ebel (C) model onto a single worksheet and link them up where necessary, adding any new constraints as appropriate.
3. Explain your model changes, the resulting mine schedule, blending, reclassify and inventory decisions for each week, and any relevant shadow price information in a brief executive summary memo to Ebel management.

References

Jean-Yves Blais, Jacques Lamont, and Jean-Marc Rousseau, "The HASTUS Vehicle and Manpower Scheduling System at the Société de la Communauté urbaine de Montréal," *Interfaces*, 20, no. 1 (Jan.–Feb. 1990).

James Evans, "A Microcomputer-Based Decision Support System Scheduling Umpires in the American Baseball League," *Interfaces*, 18, no. 6 (Nov.–Dec., 1988).

David Carlisle, Kenneth Nickerson, Stephen Porbst, Denise Rudolph, Yosef Sheffi, and Warren Powell, "A Turnkey Microcomputer-Based Logistics Planning System," *Interfaces*, 17, no. 4 (July–Aug. 1987).

Tsuyoshi Yoshino, Tsuna Sasaki, and Toshiharu Hasegawa, "The Traffic-Control System on the Hanshin Expressway," *Interfaces*, 25, no. 1 (1995): 94–108.

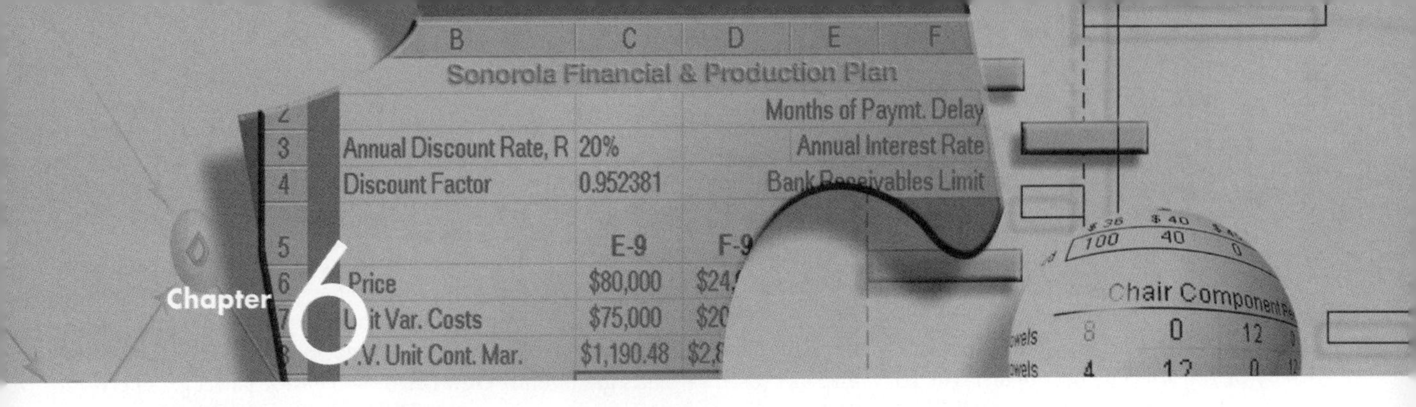

INTEGER OPTIMIZATION

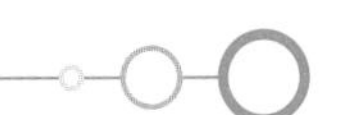

CHAPTER OUTLINE

APPLICATION CAPSULE **American Airlines Uses Integer Program for Crew-Pairing Optimization**

American Airlines (AA) employs more than 8,300 pilots and 16,200 flight attendants to fly one of the largest fleets in the United States, with over 510 aircraft. Total crew cost, which includes salaries, benefits, and expenses, exceeds $1.3 billion per year and is second only to fuel cost. But unlike fuel costs, a large part of crew costs are controllable. Therefore, a priority of the crew resources department at AA is to develop crew assignment plans that achieve high levels of crew utilization. To meet this goal, the crew resources department has come to rely heavily on an integer program.

AA schedules its flights once every month. Each flight must be assigned a crew (pilots and flight attendants). Crews reside in 12 different cities called crew bases; therefore, the assignment of a crew to flights must be such that the crew works a sequence of flights that starts and ends at the same crew base. This sequence of flights is called a pairing and typically lasts three days. A crew works four to five pairings each month.

The construction of crew pairings is complicated by a complex array of union and Federal Aviation Authority (FAA) work rules. These rules vary by crew type (pilot or flight attendant), crew size, aircraft type and type of operation (domestic or international). Work rules concern duty periods and rests. A stringent union rule specifies maximum duty length of between 14 and 16 hours during the day. In the actual model, a shorter duty length is imposed at the planning stage in anticipation of delays during actual operations. The FAA imposes rules to minimize crew fatigue and ensure passenger safety.

The cost of a pairing includes a complex formula for pay involving the guaranteed hours of pay and the actual hours flown, as well as more straightforward items like hotel, per-diem and ground transportation costs. Of course, the goal is to come up with an assignment of crews to all flights for the next month that minimizes this total cost. The model can also be used on a more strategic basis to recommend whether an existing crew base should be closed or a new base should be opened.

Crew pairing optimization is an enormously complex combinatorial problem. It has been the subject of intense research since the 1950s because small improvements leverage into large dollar savings. In fact, a 1% increase in AA's crew utilization translates into $13 million worth of savings each year. AA estimates that the model generates annual savings in excess of $20 million. The model has been so successful that it has also been sold to 11 other major airlines and one railroad company. (See Ranga et al.)

6.1 INTRODUCTION

This chapter is devoted to models that could be formulated and optimized as linear programming models except for the complication that some or all of the variables are required to assume integer values. Such models are called **integer linear programming (ILP)** models.[1] Like the network models covered in Chapter 6, integer linear programming has become an important specialized area of optimization modeling. In this introductory section, it will be possible only to scratch the surface—to illustrate the importance of the topic, as well as introduce several important ILP modeling examples.

At the outset, let us recall from previous chapters that in a linear programming model the variables are permitted to take on fractional values, such as 6.394, and in keeping with the principle that "whatever is allowed will occur," fractional answers must be expected.[2] In spite of this, actual (real-world) decision variables often must be integer valued. For example, a firm produces bags of cattle feed. A solution that requires them to produce and sell 3000.472 bags does not make sense. In such situations a noninteger solution is often adapted to the integer requirement by simply rounding the results to a neighboring integer. This method produces what we call a **rounded solution**. Using such a solution is acceptable

[1] Not all integer programming models are necessarily linear, and many of the things we say in this section about ILPs apply to both linear and nonlinear integer programs in general. However, since we deal only with linear models in this section, we will use the abbreviation ILP throughout to avoid the need for additional terminology and minimize the possibility of confusion.

[2] An exception to this is described in Chapter 5. In general, network models, including transportation and assignment models, with integral supplies and demands will always produce integer-valued solutions when optimized as an LP. In fact, this remarkable property is true of the more general class of network models.

to management in situations where, in a significant practical sense, the rounding does not matter. For example, there is no significant difference either in the profit objective function or in the constraints between producing 19,283.64 and 19,283 bags of cattle feed. Indeed, there are probably enough approximations used in assembling the data for the model that management would likely be content with any production figure near the 19,200-bag level. Generally, the larger the scale of the decision variables, that is, the larger the LP solution decision variable values, the more likely that a rounded integer answer will be acceptable in practice.

WHEN INTEGER SOLUTIONS MATTER

There are, however, a number of important models where this rather cavalier attitude toward the integer requirements of the real world does not work. This complication can be caused by a small scale of the decision variables under consideration. For example, if the solution to an LP model suggested that Boeing should build 3.6 747 airplanes and 4.8 777 airplanes next quarter, its management probably would not be comfortable just going ahead and deciding to build four 747s and five 777s, or, for that matter any other rounded combination. For one thing, rounding up in this case may introduce infeasibilities as resource constraints are violated. Moreover, even if infeasibilities from rounding did not occur, the magnitude of the financial return and the commitment of scarce resources associated with each airplane produced make it advisable to determine the best possible *integer solution.*

As another example, it will be seen that many models must use integer variables to indicate logical decisions. For example, we will see models where we want X to equal 1 if we should build a warehouse in Kansas City and X to equal 0 if we should not. Suppose that the solution to an LP version of this model yielded a noninteger value (e.g., $X_7 = 0.38$). We shall see that this value contains no useful information about the solution to the real model. Clearly, we cannot build 0.38 of a warehouse. We certainly could select warehouses of different sizes, but nevertheless, either we have a warehouse in Kansas City or we do not. You might guess that, in a case such as this, rounding to the nearest integer (0 in this case) would be a way to approach this difficulty. Unfortunately, that is not guaranteed to give a good (to say nothing of optimal) solution. Indeed, we shall see that rounding may not even lead to a feasible solution in cases such as these.

There are many important management models that would be LPs except for the requirement of integer values for some of the decision variables, where you *cannot* find a good solution by using straight LP optimization in Solver and then rounding off the resulting optimal values of the decision variables. These models must be solved with methods designed especially to solve large integer programming models.

Integer linear programming models have been important for years, and a great deal of time and effort has been devoted to research on the optimization of these models. These efforts are returning dividends, and marked progress has been made in this area. The great strides in computer technology have also made a crucial contribution to the increased ability to solve large integer linear programming models that would have been impossible to optimize a decade ago.

LP VERSUS ILP

In spite of the impressive improvement in our ability to optimize integer programming models, the technology is still quite different from what we have available to attack models in which the decision variables need not be integer. Many models that can be solved easily as LP formulations become unsolvable for practical purposes if the decision variables are required to be integers (i.e., the time and cost needed to compute an optimal solution are too large). This seems counterintuitive because adding the integer restriction reduces the number of feasible alternatives to consider, and reducing the set of feasible alternatives should make the search for the optimum alternative easier. In practice, however, integer programming models often take at least ten times longer and frequently hundreds, thousands, or millions of times longer to optimize than when not using integer restrictions.

In the following sections we first describe two general classes of integer linear programming models and use graphical analysis to illustrate the relationship between linear programming, integer linear programming, and the process of rounding LP solutions to obtain a possible solution to the ILP. This graphical approach will provide an intuitive feeling for the nature of the integer model, and why your intuition that ILP models should be easier to optimize is wrong. We then turn our attention to a special variety of integer models in which the integer variables are restricted to the binary values of 0 or 1. Using such "indicator" or "Boolean" variables allows us to *formulate* a variety of true/false logical conditions that are not otherwise easily captured. A number of important practical models involve such conditions, and several of these formulations are discussed. Then our attention turns to the topic of integer linear programming in practice, emphasizing strategic considerations as well as discussing possibilities for sensitivity analysis.

6.2 TYPES OF INTEGER OPTIMIZATION MODELS

Integer programming is a general term for creating optimization models with *integrality conditions* (conditions stipulating that some or all of the decision variables must have integer values). We have already pointed out that integer linear programming (ILP) models are linear programming models with the additional characteristic that some or all of the decision variables are required to take on integer values. There are several classifications within this category of models.

An **all-integer linear program** is, as the name suggests, a model in which *all* of the decision variables are required to be integers. For example

$$\begin{aligned} \text{Min} \quad & 6x_1 + 5x_2 + 4x_3 \\ \text{s.t.} \quad & 108x_1 + 92x_2 + 58x_3 \geq 576 \\ & 7x_1 + 18x_2 + 22x_3 \geq 83 \\ & x_1, x_2, x_3 \geq 0 \text{ and } \textit{integer} \end{aligned} \tag{6.1}$$

TIP: *Creative use of binary variables permits many conditional or logical tests to be successfully incorporated into an optimization model, thus providing an acceptable substitute for the otherwise banned Excel IF() function in worksheet formulas. Recall, if the objective function or constraints are related to the decision variables directly or indirectly by means of a worksheet IF() function, or a similar nonsmooth function, such as ABS(), MAX(), MIN(), VLOOKUP(), and so on, then Solver's internal optimization methods are likely to fail to converge to an optimum.*

is an all-integer model. Without the additional constraints x_1, x_2, x_3 integer (i.e., the integrality conditions), this model is an LP model.

A model in which *only some* of the variables are restricted to integer values and others can assume any number (i.e., *any continuous value*) is referred to as a **mixed integer linear program (MILP)**. Suppose that in the previous model (6.1) only x_1 and x_2 were required to be integer and x_3 was not, and thus, could assume fractional values. This would be an example of a MILP model.

In some models the integer variables are restricted to the values 0 or 1. Such models are called **binary, or 0–1, integer linear programs**. These models are particularly important because the 0–1 variables may be used to represent dichotomous decisions (true/false decisions). A variety of scheduling, plant location, production planning, and financial portfolio models are 0–1 integer linear programming models. They are discussed in some detail in Section 6.4. As we shall see, 0–1 variables can be found in all-integer models and in MILPs.

We will often consider the linear programming (LP) model that results if we start with an ILP formulation but then ignore the integer restrictions. This LP model is referred to as the **LP relaxation** of the ILP. For example, if we remove the phrase "and *integer*" from the ILP presented in model (6.1), the resulting LP is the LP relaxation of the original integer program.

6.3 GRAPHICAL INTERPRETATION OF INTEGER MODELS

In Chapter 3 we saw that it is possible to gain substantial insight into the nature and the solution of LP models by examining the graphical analysis of a problem with two decision variables. The same approach is useful for an ILP model, and we now turn our attention to that topic.

OPTIMIZING A TWO VARIABLE ILP MODEL

Consider the following two variable ILP product mix model in which E and F might represent the quantities of two products to make and sell for a profit. For discussion, assume the $\leq$ constraints represent resource limitations and the $\geq$ constraints represent certain minimum commitments.

$$
\begin{aligned}
\text{Max} \quad & 18E + 6F \\
\text{s.t.} \quad & E - 3F \leq 0 \quad (1) \\
& 42.8E + 100F \leq 800 \quad (2) \\
& 20E + 6F \leq 142 \quad (3) \\
& 30E + 10F \geq 135 \quad (4) \\
& E, F \geq 0 \text{ and integer}
\end{aligned}
\tag{6.2}
$$

The only important change between (6.2) and the LP product mix models in previous chapters is the word *integer*. As we shall see shortly, the impact of this single word is profound.

To optimize this model with a graphical approach, we prescribe three steps:

1. Find the feasible set for the LP relaxation of the ILP model.
2. Identify the integer points inside the set determined in step 1.
3. Find, among those points determined in step 2, one that optimizes the objective function.

In the top part of Figure 6.1 the first two steps have been accomplished by the GLP application software covered in Chapter 4 while the bottom part of the figure gives the formulation and Solver solution to the LP relaxation of the ILP. The shaded region in the GLP window is the feasible set for the LP relaxation, and the dark dots, enabled by clicking "I" tool on GLP's Toolbar, are the integer points contained within the LP feasible region. This set of integer points is the set of feasible solutions to the ILP. In other words, there are only 13 feasible solutions to the ILP model. They are the points (3, 6), (4, 6), (3, 5), (4, 5), (5, 5), (4, 4), (5, 4), (4, 3), (5, 3), (6, 3), (4, 2), (5, 2), and (6, 2).

TIP: *The integer condition is specified as a constraint in Solver and is selected by choosing the "int" condition in the constraint dialog's drop-down list. Do not type the word "integer" in the dialog's "Constraint:" RHS field; it will be entered for you by the dialog. (In contrast, Macintosh Excel users may have to type "integer" in the RH field after choosing "int.") Note that Solver allows the integer condition to be applied only to decision variables and not to any consequence variables, such as left-hand side cells in constraints. Also, you must manually change the Tolerance setting in the Solver Options dialog to zero. Otherwise, the Solver solution to the ILP may not be the optimal one. See the discussion in Section 6.4 for details.*

To optimize the model, we must now determine which of the ILP feasible points yields the largest value of the objective function. We proceed as in an LP model; that is, by moving a contour of the objective function in an *uphill direction* (since we are dealing with a Max model) until it is not possible to move it farther and still intersect an integer feasible point.

The result of this process is shown in Figure 6.2 in which the Auto Max or "Up Arrow" tool on GLP's Toolbar was clicked while the bottom part of the figure gives the formulation and Solver solution to the ILP. We see that the optimal solution to the ILP is the point $E = 6$ and $F = 3$. Since the objective function is $18E + 6F$, this solution yields an optimal value of the objective function of $18(6) + 6(3) = 126$, as shown in Figure 6.2.

THE LP RELAXATION

Figure 6.3 sketches the GLP solution and labels several nearby points. We can use Figure 6.3 to illustrate some important facts about the LP relaxation. We first note that the optimal solution to the LP relaxation occurs at the intersection of the two constraint lines (2) $42.8E + 100F = 800$ and (3) $20E + 6F = 142$, as shown in Figure 6.1. This result is obtained by pushing, uphill, the contour of the objective function as far as possible and still have it intersect the feasible set for the LP relaxation. Since the intersection of the two constraints does not occur at an integer point, the optimal solution to the LP relaxation is not feasible for the ILP. As shown in Figure 6.1, the optimal values of the decision variables for the LP relaxation yields $E^* = 5.39$, $F^* = 5.69$. Also shown in Figure 6.1, the **optimal value** of the objective function, termed the **OV**, for the LP relaxation is 131.21.

FIGURE 6.1

LP Optimum and Feasible Set for ILP Example Model (6.2)

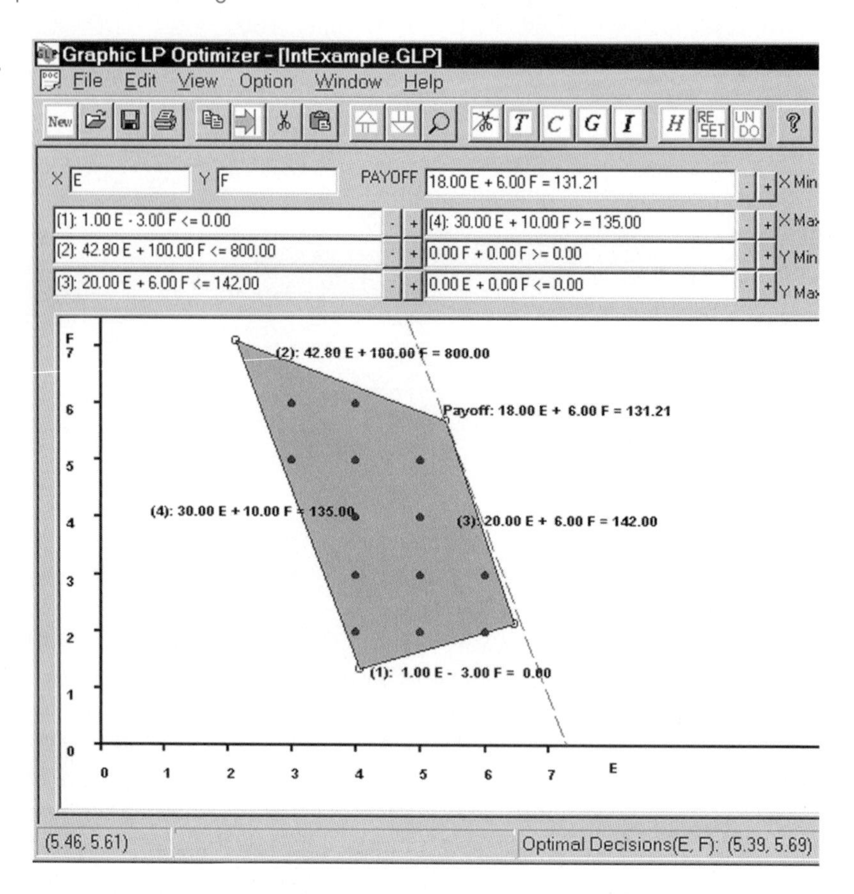

	A	B	C	D	E	F	G
1	Product:	E	F				
2	Production Qty.	5.39	5.69	Profit			
3	Unit Contri. Mar.	$18	$6	$131.2			
4	Constraints			Total LHS		RHS	Slack
5		1	-3	-11.68	≤	0	11.68
6		42.8	100	800	≤	800	0
7		20	6	142	≤	142	0
8		30	10	218.69	≥	135	83.69

Cell	Formula	Copy To
D3	= SUMPRODUCT($B$2:$C$2,B3:C3)	D5:D8
G5	= F5–D5	
G8	= D8–F8	

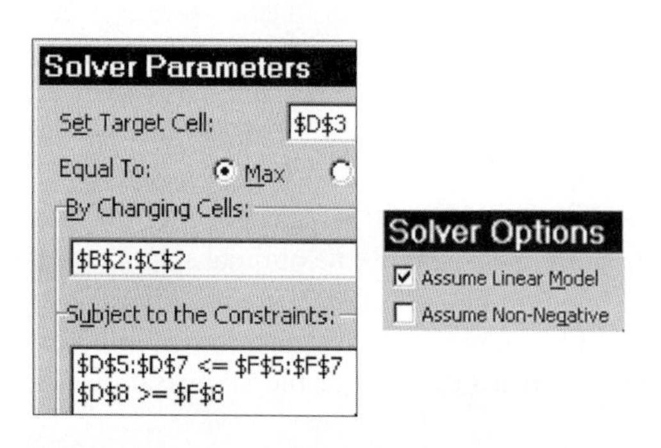

FIGURE 6.2

Optimal Integer Solution to the ILP Example Model (6.2)

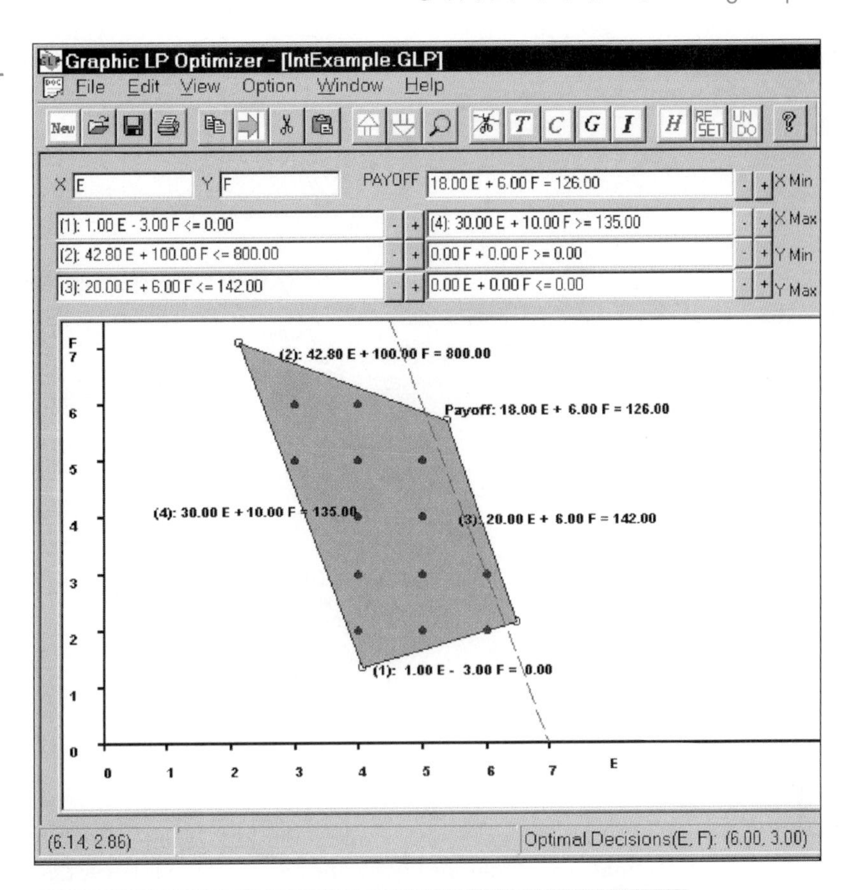

	A	B	C	D	E	F	G
1	Product:	E	F				
2	Production Qty.	6.00	3.00	Profit			
3	Unit Contri. Mar.	$18	$6	$126.0			
4	Constraints			Total LHS		RHS	Slack
5		1	-3	-3.00	≤	0	3.00
6		42.8	100	556.8	≤	800	243
7		20	6	138	≤	142	4
8		30	10	210.00	≥	135	75

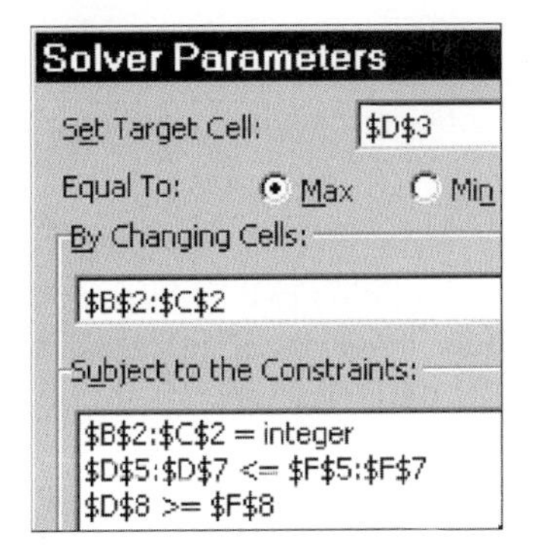

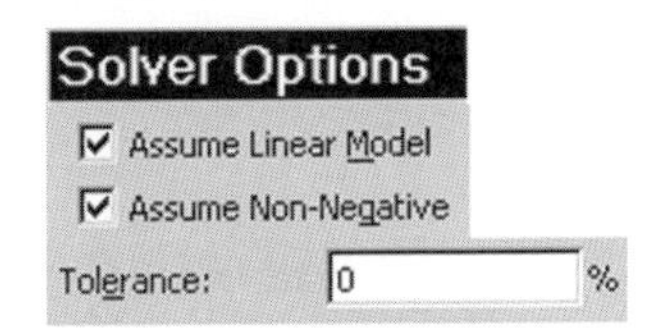

FIGURE 6.3

Graphical Solution to the ILP Example Model (6.2)

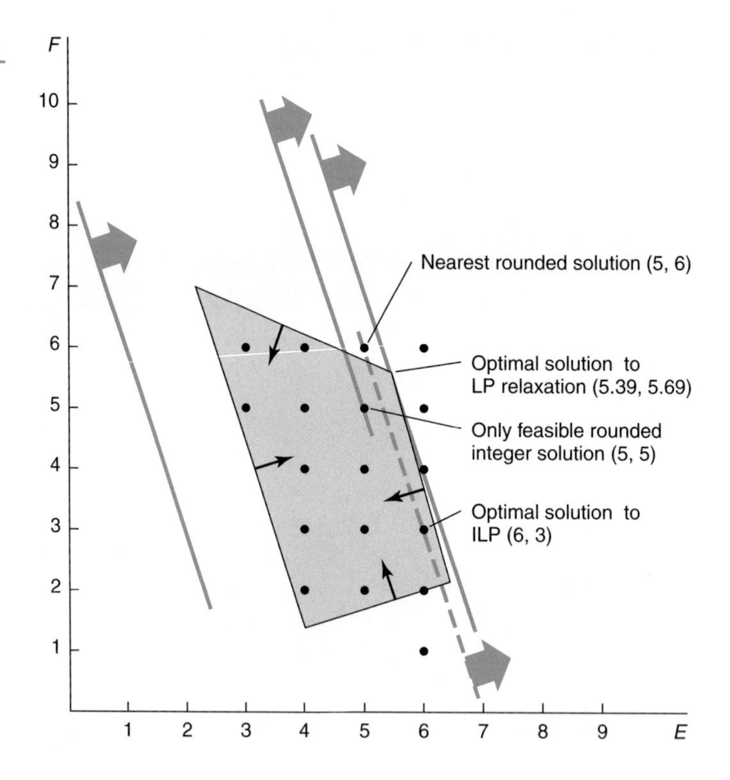

Comparing these two optimal values (126 for the ILP and 131.21 for the LP relaxation), we see that the OV for the LP relaxation is larger than for the original ILP. This fact is a special case of a phenomenon that we observed in our earlier discussions of linear optimization in Chapter 4. Think of creating an ILP or an MILP by starting with the LP relaxation and adding the integer restrictions. We know that *in any optimization model, adding constraints cannot help and may hurt the optimal value of the objective function.* Thus, our optimal value for the solution of (6.2) decreases with the addition of the integer constraint. With this observation we are prepared to make the following more general comments:

1. In a *Max* model the OV of the LP relaxation always provides an *upper bound* on the OV of the original ILP. Adding the integer constraints either hurts or leaves unchanged the OV for the LP. In a Max model, hurting the OV means making it smaller.
2. In a *Min* model the OV of the LP relaxation always provides a *lower bound* on the OV of the original ILP. Again, adding the integer constraints either hurts or leaves unchanged the OV for the LP. In a Min model, hurting the OV means making it larger.

ROUNDED SOLUTIONS

We have observed that the optimal solution to the LP relaxation is $E^* = 5.39$, $F^* = 5.69$. Each of these variables could be rounded up or down and hence there are four rounded solutions ([5, 5], [5, 6], [6, 5], [6, 6]) near the optimal solution to the LP relaxation. In general, with two decision variables there are four rounded neighbor solutions. Note that with n decision variables there would be 2^n such points to consider, growing to a very large number as n grows.

Let us now examine in more detail some of the potential problems that can arise when using a rounded solution. Refer to Figure 6.3. If we solve the LP relaxation and round each variable to the nearest integer, we obtain (5, 6), which is infeasible. In this case the point (5, 5) is the only feasible point that can be obtained by rounding (5.39, 5.69). The other candidates, (5, 6), (6, 6), and (6, 5), are all infeasible. This model illustrates two important facts about rounded solutions:

1. ***A rounded solution need not be optimal.*** In this case the value of the objective function at the only feasible rounded solution is

$$18(5) + 6(5) = 120.$$

   This compares with a value of 126 for the optimal value of the ILP. We see, then, that a proportional loss of $^6/_{126}$, or almost 5%, is incurred by using this rounded solution rather than the optimal solution. In other models the loss could be much larger.
2. ***A rounded solution need not be near the optimal ILP solution.*** Students often have an intuitive idea that even though a rounded solution may not be optimal, it should be "near" the optimal ILP solution. Referring again to Figure 6.3, we see that the rounded solution is not one of the immediate integer neighbors of the optimal ILP solution. Indeed, only four points in the feasible set ([3, 6], [4, 6], [3, 5], and [4, 5]) are farther from the optimal solution than the rounded solution. It seems hard to claim that in this example the rounded solution is near the optimal ILP solution.

In Figure 6.4 we sketch another ILP example that illustrates an additional and even more drastic problem associated with rounded solutions. In this figure the shaded area is the feasible set for the LP relaxation, the dots are integer points, and the circled dot is the only feasible solution to the ILP. The optimal solution to the LP relaxation is indicated at the tip of the wedge-shaped feasible set. Notice that if we start with the optimal solution to the LP (roughly [3.3, 4.7]) and then round this to any of the four neighboring integer points, we obtain an infeasible point. That is, for this example, *no manner of rounding can produce feasibility.*

In summary, we have noted that an intuitively appealing way of attacking an ILP is to solve the LP relaxation of the original model and then round the solution to a neighboring integer point. We have seen that this approach can have certain problems.

1. None of the neighboring integer points may be feasible.
2. Even if one or more of the neighboring integer points is feasible
   a. Such a point need not be optimal for the ILP.
   b. Such a point need not even be near the optimal ILP solution.

FIGURE 6.4

All Rounded Solutions Are Infeasible

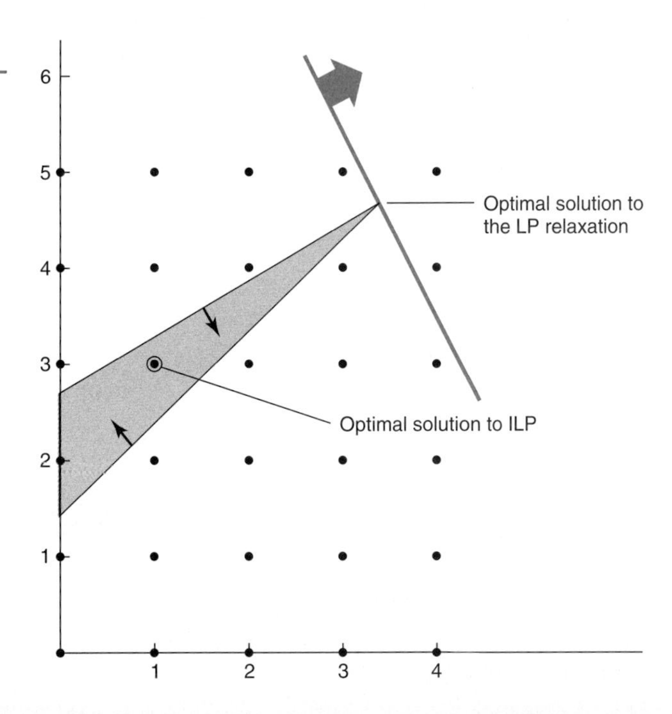

ENUMERATION

Looking at the ILP solution in Figure 6.2 should make clear why adding the *integer* constraint and thus drastically reducing the feasible region from the shaded region to just the integer dots within the shaded region does not make solution-finding easier for Solver as intuition would suggest. Recall Solver's LP simplex method makes use of the fact that the solution to an LP always lies on the boundary of the feasible region. Thus, Solver never has to consider any interior points of the feasible region. But for an ILP optimization Solver might have to visit many integer points strictly within the interior of the feasible region, and thus, the LP simplex method alone cannot be employed.

Of course, since there are only 13 feasible integer points in Figure 6.1 for the ILP example model, you may get the also-mistaken impression that you or Solver can reasonably list all the integer feasible points, evaluate the objective function at each of them, and select the best one; that is, solve the model by **complete enumeration** of the feasible integer points. For this example, one could do that. Unfortunately, however, as with LPs, complete enumeration of all the feasible integer points is not a reasonable procedure for most ILPs. Suppose, for example, that we had an ILP with only 20 decision variables, each of which could take on an integer value between 1 and 50. In this case there would be 50^{20} or more than 9.5×10^{33} points to enumerate and test for feasibility! Even with the fastest supercomputer, it would take many lifetimes to enumerate all of these points.

It is interesting to compare the enumeration method for ILPs with the simplex optimization method used by Solver for LPs. As we have seen, the simplex method can be viewed as a way of visiting corners of the constraint set and evaluating the objective function at the corner points visited. It is also true that there can be many billions of corners on the constraint set of a large LP model. The important point, however, is that *not all corners are visited.* Indeed, the simplex method is very efficient. It proceeds in such a way as to always improve the value of the objective function at each successive corner point it visits. Once no improvement is possible, Solver stops and indicates that an optimal solution has been reached. This typically occurs after visiting only a very, very small subset of all the corners. At this time there is no comparable method for ILPs. The methods (discussed in the Branch and Bound Enrichment Topic on the book's CD-ROM) do much better than complete enumeration, but they are not able to eliminate the large numbers of alternative solutions as quickly and efficiently as the simplex method does for LPs.

6.4 APPLICATIONS OF BINARY VARIABLES

Binary, or 0–1, variables play an especially important role in the applications of ILPs. These variables make it possible to incorporate Excel-like IF() statement yes-or-no decisions, sometimes called dichotomous decisions, into an optimization model. Two quick examples will illustrate what we mean:

1. In a plant location model we let $x_j = 1$ if we choose to have a plant at location *j* and $x_j = 0$ if we do not.
2. In a routing model we let $x_{ijk} = 1$ if truck *k* goes from city *i* to city *j* and $x_{ijk} = 0$ if it does not.

You can see from these examples that the use of 0–1 variables provides us with a new formulational tool. Importantly, this formulation tool allows many variations of logical conditions in an optimization model without resorting to any of Excel's "IF()" statements whose use would otherwise likely defeat Solver optimization of the model. In this section we will see some examples of how 0–1 variables are used to make dichotomous decisions in several applications. We will also see how they can be manipulated to enforce various types of logical conditions.

CAPITAL BUDGETING: AN EXPANSION DECISION

Many firms make decisions on capital investments on an annual basis. In large firms the decisions are often the culmination of a long process that starts with recommendations

Table 6.1 AutoPower's Capital Budgeting Alternatives

ALTERNATIVE	PRESENT VALUE OF NET RETURN ($000s)	CAPITAL REQUIRED IN YEAR BY ALTERNATIVE ($000s)				
		1	2	3	4	5
Expand Belgian Plant	400	100	50	200	100	0
Expand Small Machine Capacity in U.S.	700	300	200	100	100	100
Establish New Plant in Chile	800	100	200	270	200	100
Expand Large Machine Capacity in U.S.	1000	200	100	400	200	200
	Capital Available	500	450	700	400	300

from individual departments and continues through various firm-wide and division-wide competitions. It is not unusual for the final selection to rest with the board of directors. In smaller firms the process is not so elaborate, but the capital budgeting decision is still a fundamental part of an annual evaluation of the firm's future.

In its simplest form, the capital budgeting decision is a matter of choosing among n investment alternatives in order to maximize the return subject to constraints on the amount of capital invested over time. As a particular example, suppose that AutoPower's board of directors faces the data summarized in Table 6.1. The board must select one or more of the alternatives. If they decide to expand the Belgian plant, the present value of the net return to the firm is $400,000. This project requires $100,000 of capital in the first year, $50,000 in the second, and so on. The board has previously budgeted up to $500,000 for all capital investments in year 1, up to $450,000 in year 2, and so on.

An ILP Model for Capital Budgeting at AutoPower This model can be modeled as an ILP in which all the variables are binary variables. This is called a binary or 0–1 ILP. In particular, let $x_i = 1$ if project i is accepted and $x_i = 0$ if project i is not accepted. The model then becomes

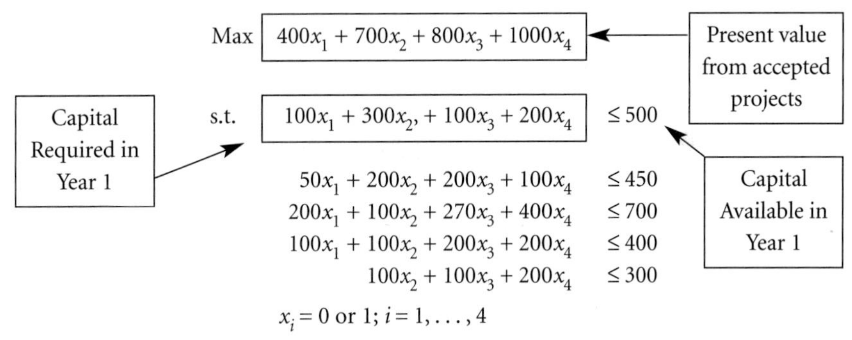

Here the objective function is the total present value of the net returns and each constraint assures that the amount of capital used in each of the five years does not exceed the capital available for that year.

The LP Relaxation Let us approach this model by first solving the LP relaxation. The formulation and solution are shown in Figure 6.5 in which defined names have been used for cell ranges. Note that in working with the LP relaxation to a binary ILP, we ignore the constraints $x_i = 0$ or 1. Instead, we add the constraints $x_i \leq 1$, $i = 1, 2, 3, 4$ in addition to the nonnegativity constraints, as shown in Figure 6.5. Thus, in the relaxation, instead of $x_i = 0$ or 1, we have x_i constrained to the interval, $0 \leq x_i \leq 1$. It would be nice if in the optimal solution each x_i were, fortuitously, to take one extreme or the other of these allowable values (either 0 or 1), for then the original ILP would be solved. Unfortunately, as Figure 6.5

FIGURE 6.5

LP Relaxation of the Capital Budgeting Model

	A	B	C	D	E	F	G	H	I
1			Capital Budget Model ($000s)						
2		Alternative Investment	Expand Belgian Plant	Expand Small Machine Cap. in U.S.	Estab. New Plant in Chile	Expand Large Machine Cap. in U.S.			
3		Symbol	X1	X2	X3	X4			
4		Decisions	0.67	0.67	0.33	1.00	Total PV		
5		PV, Net Return	$400	$700	$800	$1000	$ 2,000.00		
6		Capital Constraints					Capital Req.	Capital Avail.	Slack
7		Capital Req. Yr. 1	$100	$300	$100	$200	500.00	<=$500	0
8		Capital Req. Yr. 2	$50	$200	$200	$100	333.33	<=$450	117
9		Capital Req. Yr. 3	$200	$100	$270	$400	690.00	<=$700	10
10		Capital Req. Yr. 4	$100	$100	$200	$200	400.00	<=$400	0
11		Capital Req. Yr. 5		$100	$100	$200	300.00	<=$300	0
12									

TIP: *As discussed in Chapter 2, use of Excel Defined Names can improve the readability of models. If present, Solver will also use them in its dialogs. To document Names definitions use the Insert>Name>Paste . . . option on the Excel Insert menu to paste the name definitions onto the worksheet, as shown in Figure 6.5. Be aware that deleting a Name may produce errors in the Solver Parameters dialog. See Appendix B and C for details on using Names and recovering from errors.*

Cell	Formula	Copy To
G5	= SUMPRODUCT(Decisions,C5:F5)	G7:G11
I7	= H7–G7	I8:I11

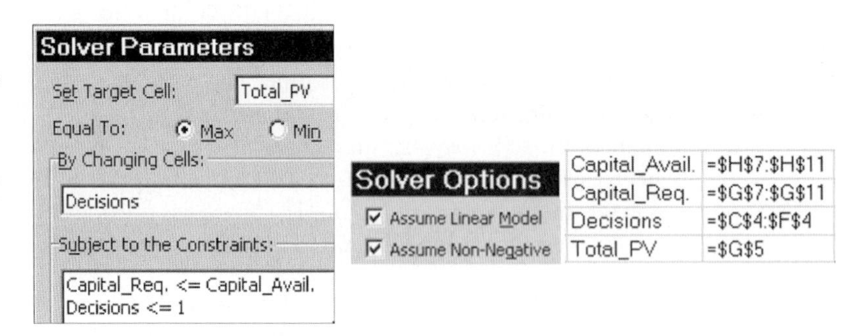

shows, this happened only with x_4; the values of x_1, x_2, and x_3 are fractional.[3] Since x_3 should equal 1 if AutoPower establishes a plant in Chile and 0 if it does not, the result $x_3 = 0.33$ is not meaningful. We also note that attempting to find a solution to the ILP model by solving the LP relaxation and then rounding does not work very well. Standard nearest-integer rounding rules (i.e., round numbers ≤ 0.499 to 0 and numbers ≥ 0.500 to 1) yield the solution $x_1 = 1, x_2 = 1, x_3 = 0, x_4 = 1$. A quick spreadsheet check for these values reveals that this solution is infeasible since it grossly violates the first constraint.

The Optimal ILP Solution To obtain the optimal ILP solution for the AutoPower capital budgeting model, we must use Solver's *binary* option. The formulation and solution of the ILP are shown in Figure 6.6. Note that the four constraints that require the x_i's to be ≤ 1 have been dropped. In Solver, the constraint "Decisions = binary," that is "C4:F4 = binary," indicates that all four of the decision variables are 0–1 variables.[4]

The solution in Figure 6.6 shows that AutoPower management should accept the first three alternatives; x_4 is now zero, whereas in the LP relaxation of Figure 6.5 it was 1. Note also that the objective function value (OV) is now 1900. This is a reduction of 100 (5%) from the optimal value of the objective function for the LP relaxation. In practice, one may well be interested in solving integer programs with hundreds of 0–1 variables. After seeing

[3] Your solution may differ; the model has alternative optimal solutions.

[4] Remember, the designations "binary" or "integer" in the Solver constraints dialog can be applied only to decision variables, that is, Solver's "Changing Cells."

FIGURE 6.6

ILP Model of AutoPower's Capital Budgeting Problem

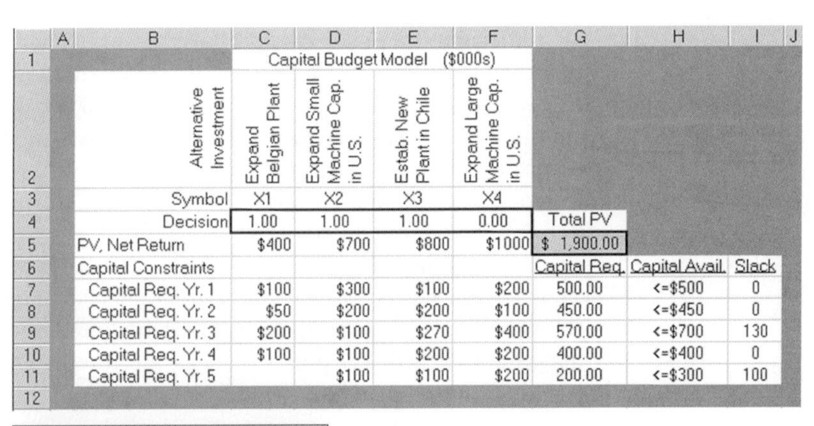

Capital Budget Model ($000s)							
Alternative Investment	Expand Belgian Plant	Expand Small Machine Cap. in U.S.	Estab. New Plant in Chile	Expand Large Machine Cap. in U.S.			
Symbol	X1	X2	X3	X4			
Decision	1.00	1.00	1.00	0.00	Total PV		
PV, Net Return	$400	$700	$800	$1000	$ 1,900.00		
Capital Constraints					Capital Req.	Capital Avail.	Slack
Capital Req. Yr. 1	$100	$300	$100	$200	500.00	<=$500	0
Capital Req. Yr. 2	$50	$200	$200	$100	450.00	<=$450	0
Capital Req. Yr. 3	$200	$100	$270	$400	570.00	<=$700	130
Capital Req. Yr. 4	$100	$100	$200	$200	400.00	<=$400	0
Capital Req. Yr. 5		$100	$100	$200	200.00	<=$300	100

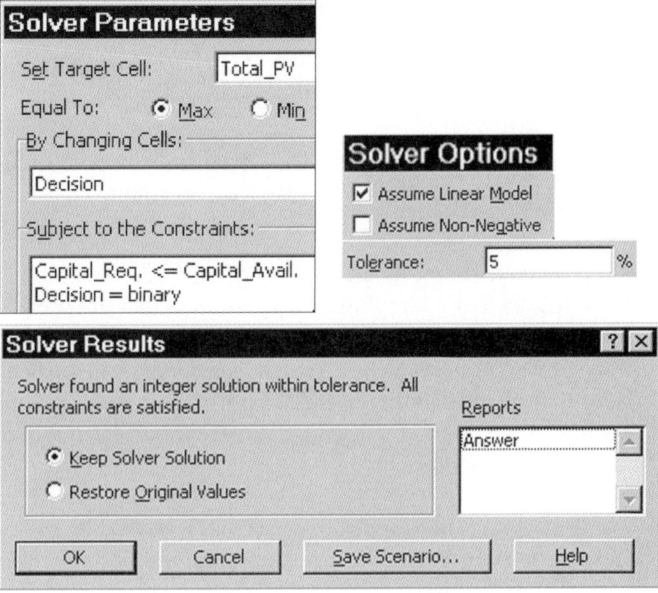

TIP: *The Premium Edition Solver for Education produces a different Solver Results completion message for ILPs, as shown in Figure 6.6, to remind you that the ILP solution may not be optimal. Versions of Solver prior to Excel 2000 always display the less informative "Solver found a solution. All constraints and optimality conditions are satisfied." Solver Results message, which is not always true for ILPs. In particular, unless you manually change the Tolerance setting to zero, the solution may not be the optimal one, but instead one that is within Tolerance's default of 5% of the optimum.*

the analysis of this small example and the problems associated with the relaxation approach, you can well appreciate the even greater importance, in larger and more complex applications, of using Solver's special methods to solve the ILP model.

Tolerance Explained Because reasonably sized ILPs are often very time-consuming to optimize, even on a fast personal computer, Solver defaults to possibly stopping short of optimality for ILP models to save time. The Solver Options dialog includes a Tolerance field—relevant only for IP models. The default Tolerance value of 5% means that the Solver ILP optimization procedure is continued only until the ILP solution OV is within 5% of the ILP's optimum OV. This is the reason for the more informative Solver Results completion message in Figure 6.6 produced by the Solver Premium Edition for Education included in the book's CD-ROM.[5] A higher Tolerance value speeds up Solver on ILPs at the risk of a reported solution further from the true ILP optimum. Setting Tolerance to 0% forces Solver to find the true ILP optimum at the cost of potentially much longer solution times. How does Solver know it is within a given percentage of the optimum? First, Solver

[5] It turns out that the solution reported in Figure 6.6 is the ILP optimum, as re-optimizing with Tolerance = 0% will verify.

drops the integer restriction and solves the relaxed LP. Since the ILP solution OV can never do better than that of the relaxed LP, the relaxed LP solution OV provides an upper bound on the ILP payoff. In addition, during optimization Solver keeps track of the best solution it has found thus far in its search, and this provides a lower bound on the ILP's optimal OV. Because these bounds bracket the OV of the optimum ILP solution, Solver continues its search until the two bounds are Tolerance% apart and this guarantees that the ILP solution is within Tolerance% of the optimum.

The layout of the Solver Options dialog is different if The Premium Edition Solver for Education is installed and the "Premium" button is clicked on the Solver Parameters dialog, but its functions are the same. An exception is the "Integer Options," which appear as a button that when clicked will present a separate Integer Options dialog containing the Tolerance field. See Appendix C for additional details on the other items in this dialog.

LOGICAL CONDITIONS

An important use of binary variables is to impose constraints that arise from logical (true/false) conditions. Several examples are cited below.

No More Than *k* of *n* Alternatives Suppose k is a given integer and x_i is binary, that is, $x_i = 0$ or 1, for $i = 1, \ldots, n$. The constraint

$$x_1 + x_2 + \cdots + x_n \leq k$$

implies that, at most, k alternatives of n possibilities can be selected. That is, since each x_i can be only 0 or 1, the above constraint says that not more than k of them can equal 1. For the data given in Table 6.1, assume that AutoPower's management feels that not more than one foreign project can be accepted. For this reason, the board wants to rule out an alternative that includes both the Belgian expansion and a new plant in Chile. Adding the constraint $x_1 + x_3 \leq 1$ to the ILP in Figure 6.6 implies that the solution can contain at most one of the overseas alternatives.

Dependent Decisions You can use 0–1 variables to force a dependent relationship on two or more decisions. Suppose, for example, that AutoPower's management does not want to select alternative k unless it first selects alternative m. The constraint

$$x_k \leq x_m \quad \text{or, equivalently,} \quad x_k - x_m \leq 0 \tag{6.3}$$

enforces this condition. Note that if alternative m is *not* selected, then $x_m = 0$. Condition (6.3) then forces x_k to be 0 (i.e., alternative k cannot be selected either). Alternatively, if m is selected, $x_m = 1$; then (6.3) becomes $x_k \leq 1$. This leaves Solver free to select $x_k = 1$ or $x_k = 0$.

As an example, again consider Figure 6.6, and suppose that AutoPower's management feels that, if they are going to expand within the United States, their competitive position implies that they must definitely expand the large machine capacity. Adding the constraint $x_2 \leq x_4$ or equivalently $x_2 - x_4 \leq 0$ to the ILP in Figure 6.6 assures that the model cannot select "expand small machine capacity" unless "expand large machine capacity" is also selected.

Similarly, suppose the board decided, "If we're going to expand our domestic capacity, we're going to expand both large and small lines." Adding the constraint $x_4 = x_2$ or equivalently $x_4 - x_2 = 0$ to the ILP in Figure 6.6 would enforce this condition since it requires that x_4 and x_2 must take the same values.

Lot Size Constraints Consider a portfolio manager with the following constraints: (1) If he purchases security *j*, he must purchase at least 200 shares; and (2) he may not purchase more than 1,000 shares of security *j*. Let x_j be the number of shares of security *j* purchased. The constraint that if *j* is purchased, then at least 200 shares must be purchased, is called a "minimum lot size" or "batch size" constraint. Note that we cannot create such a constraint in an LP model. The constraints

$$200 \le x_j \le 1000$$

do not do the job since they insist that x_j always be at least 200. We want the conditions either $x_j = 0$ or $200 \le x_j \le 1000$. To achieve this we will make use of a binary variable, say y_j, for security j. The variable y_j has the following interpretation:

- If $y_j = 1$, then purchase security j.
- If $y_j = 0$, do not purchase security j.

Now consider the two constraints

$$x_j \le 1000y_j \tag{6.4}$$

$$x_j \ge 200y_j \tag{6.5}$$

We see that if $y_j = 1$, then (6.4) and (6.5) imply that $200 \le x_j \le 1000$. On the other hand, if $y_j = 0$, then (6.4) implies that $x_j \le 0$. Similarly, (6.5) implies $x_j \ge 0$. These two inequalities together imply that $x_j = 0$. Thus, if $y_j = 1$ when we purchase j, and 0 when we do not, we have the proper conditions on x_j.

How can we be sure that $y_j = 1$ if we purchase security j? The (6.4) inequality, $x_j \le 1000y_j$, guarantees it. We see that in this inequality you cannot have both $x_j > 0$, and $y_j = 0$. Thus, if $x_j > 0$, y_j must equal 1. We see then that inequalities (6.4) and (6.5) together guarantee the "minimum lot size" constraint.

***k* of *m* Constraints** Mischa Gaas, an exchange student from the Middle East, came to the university for graduate work in world history. He was told by his adviser that anyone intending to earn a Ph.D. degree to teach world history had to satisfy at least two of the following criteria: "You must be single, rich, or crazy." Unfortunately Mischa was destitute and married. In fact, before entering into matrimony, he spent years looking for a bride who was tall, dark, beautiful, and rich. Finally in frustration he said to himself, "Three out of four ain't bad;" and the woman he chose (who chose him) was not rich. These are examples of models in which k of m constraints must be satisfied. In general notation, let the "superset" of m constraints on a model's n (nonbinary) decision variables, x, be

$$g_i(x_1, \ldots, x_n) \le b_t, \qquad i = 1, \ldots, m$$

where each g_i is a given constraint function on the n decision variables, x. Now introduce m additional 0–1 decision variables y_i to the model, and let M be chosen as a very large number, so large that, for each i, $g_i(x_i, \ldots, x_n) \le M$ for every x satisfying any set of k inequalities taken from the above m. Then the following $m + 1$ constraints express the desired condition:

$$\sum_{i=1}^{m} y_i = k$$

$$g_i(x_i, \ldots, x_n) \le b_i y_i + M(1 - y_i), \qquad i = 1, \ldots, m$$

Note that the constraint $\sum_{i=1}^{m} y_i = k$ forces exactly k of the new y_i decision variables to have the value 1. This means that exactly k of the above inequality constraints are equivalent to

$$g_i(x_1, \ldots, x_n) \le b_i$$

The remaining $m - k$ inequality constraints are equivalent to

$$g_i(x_1, \ldots, x_n) \le M$$

and by the assumption of the very large number choice for M, each such constraint is redundant and cannot affect the model's optimal solution.

As an example of this, assume that a company must find production quantities of three products, x_1, x_2, and x_3, as part of a large LP model, but within the LP formulation may also choose one or the other of two different production technologies for the three products, each of which is specified by a constraint. That is, the company must choose one or the other technology, as illustrated by the two constraints below, but not both.

$$30x_1 + 20x_2 + 10x_3 \le 100 \qquad \text{(Technology 1)}$$
$$10x_1 + 30x_2 + 5x_3 \le 110 \qquad \text{(Technology 2)}$$

You cannot simply specify both constraints to the LP model because that implies both constraints must be satisfied during production rather than one or the other. In this case, the trick is to add two new binary decision variables to the LP model, y_1 and y_2, thus converting it to an ILP model.[6] The interpretation of the binary variables, y_1 and y_2, is

$y_1 = 1$ means "Choose Technology 1,"

$y_1 = 0$ means "Do not choose Technology 1,"

$y_2 = 1$ means "Choose Technology 2,"

$y_2 = 0$ means "Do not choose Technology 2."

Then modify the original LP constraint formulation as below in which the first constraint forces Solver to choose exactly one technology option, and the large number, arbitrarily set to 999999 in this example, must be carefully chosen to guarantee that one or the other constraint will be redundant for the whole LP model, depending on Solver's choice of the values for y_1 and y_2 for *any* feasible set of production quantities Solver might also choose for x_1, x_2, and x_3.

$$y_1 + y_2 = 1$$
$$30x_1 + 20x_2 + 10x_3 \le 100\, y_1 + 999999(1 - y_1) \qquad \text{(Technology 1)}$$
$$10x_1 + 30x_2 + 5x_3 \le 110\, y_2 + 999999(1 - y_2) \qquad \text{(Technology 2)}$$

We now turn to one of the most important applications of ILP, modeling a situation in which a fixed fee must be paid before an economic activity can be started, called the **fixed charge** model.

6.5 A FIXED CHARGE MODEL

In order to conserve capital, STECO, an electronic parts wholesaler, leases regional warehouses for its use. It currently has a candidate list of three warehouses it can lease. The cost per month to lease warehouse i is F_i. Also, warehouse i can load a maximum of T_i trucks per month.

There are four sales districts, and the typical monthly demand in district j is d_j truckloads. The average cost of sending a truck from warehouse i to district j is c_{ij}. STECO wants to know which warehouses to lease and how many trucks to send from each warehouse to each district. Note that STECO pays no lease cost for a given warehouse unless it plans to dispatch at least one truck from it. If any trucks are sent from a warehouse, then its entire monthly lease amount must be paid. Lot size models incorporating this cost behavior are common and are called *fixed charge models*. A network flow diagram representation of STECO's fixed charge model is illustrated in Figure 6.7.

The data for this model are presented in Table 6.2. We see, for example, that it costs $7,750 to lease warehouse A for a month and that up to 200 trucks can be loaded and dispatched from this warehouse. Also, the monthly demand in sales district 1 is 100 trucks. The numbers in the body of the table are the variable costs of sending a truck from warehouse i to sales district j (e.g., the variable cost of sending a truck from B to 3 is $100).

[6] This example formulation illustrates the general formulation case. An equivalent and more compact formulation for this particular example could use only one binary decision variable, y.

FIGURE 6.7

Warehouse Location Problem

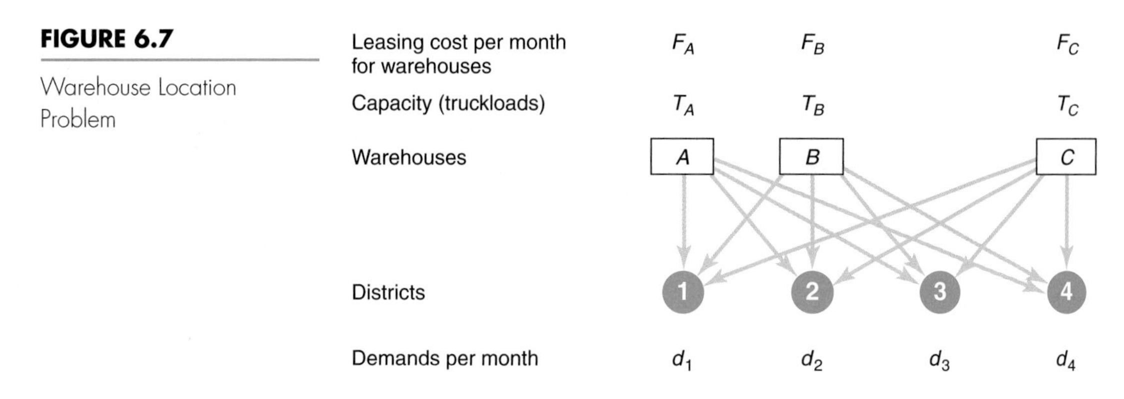

Table 6.2 Warehouse Location Data

WAREHOUSE	COST PER TRUCK SALES DISTRICT ($) 1	2	3	4	MONTHLY CAPACITY (NUMBER OF TRUCKS)	MONTHLY LEASING COSTS ($)
A	170	40	70	160	200	7750
B	150	195	100	10	250	4000
C	100	240	140	60	300	5500
Monthly Demand (truck loads)	100	90	110	60		

MODELING CONSIDERATIONS

If you want to attack this model with a mixed integer linear programming (MILP) model, you must first decide which variables (if any) you will treat as integers and which (if any) you will treat as continuous variables. The decision to lease a particular warehouse or not seems to require a binary variable since the cost of leasing warehouse i does not vary with the level of activity (i.e., with the number of trucks sent from it). We will thus define y_i as a binary decision variable and let $y_i = 1$ if we lease warehouse i, and $y_i = 0$ if we do not.

At first glance it also seems appropriate to treat the number of trucks sent from a warehouse to a district as an integer variable. Trucks are, after all, integer entities, and it does not make sense to talk about sending one-third of a truck from here to there. However, several factors could persuade us to treat the number of trucks as a continuous variable.

1. This is a planning model, not a detailed operating model. In actual operation the demands in the districts will vary. STECO management will have to devise methods of handling this uncertainty. Trucks assigned to a specific warehouse might be allocated among adjacent districts on a daily-as-needed basis, or STECO might use common carriers to satisfy excess demand. At any rate, the number of trucks that the solution to our optimization model says should go from warehouse i to district j is only an *approximation* of what will actually happen on any given day. Thus, treating these entities as continuous variables and rounding to the nearest integer to determine how many trucks to assign to each warehouse should provide a useful answer and a good approximation of the *average* monthly operating cost.
2. Treating the number of trucks as integer variables may make the model much more difficult to optimize. This is simply a reflection of the general fact that the greater the number of integer variables and the greater the number of integer values each can take on, the more difficult it is to solve an ILP.
3. It certainly costs much more to lease one of the warehouses than to send a truck from a warehouse to a sales district. The relative magnitude of these costs again implies

that it is relatively more important to treat the "lease or not lease" decision as an integer variable, as opposed to the trucks. To illustrate this point, note that it costs $5,500 per month to lease warehouse C and $60 to send a truck from warehouse C to sales district 4. Suppose that we modeled the problem as an LP. If $y_c = 0.4$ in the optimal solution, rounding to 0 causes a $2,200 change in the OV (optimal value of the objective function), whereas if $x_{c4} = 57.8$, rounding either up or down has less than a $60 effect.

In summary, there are, in this example, arguments that suggest little advantage to treating the number of trucks as integers. We thus proceed to formulate STECO's warehouse location model as an MILP, and we will have a pleasant surprise.

THE MILP MODEL

To model STECO's model as an MILP, we will let

$y_i = 1$ if lease warehouse i, $\quad y_i = 0$ if not; $\quad i = \text{A, B, C}$

$x_{ij} =$ the number of trucks sent from warehouse i to district j; $i = \text{A, B, C}$; $\quad j = 1, \ldots, 4$

We shall now construct the model by developing each of its component parts. First consider the objective function. The expression

$$170x_{A1} + 40x_{A2} + 70x_{A3} + \cdots + 60x_{C4}$$

is the total cost associated with the trucks, and

$$7750y_A + 4000y_B + 5500y_C$$

is the total leasing cost. Thus, the total cost minimizing objective function is

$$\text{Min } 7750y_A + 4000y_B + 5500y_C + 170x_{A1} + \cdots + 60x_{C4}$$

Now consider the constraints. We must consider both demand and capacity. The following constraint guarantees that demand will be satisfied at sales district 1:

$$x_{A1} + x_{B1} + x_{C1} \geq 100$$

Four constraints like this (one for each district) are required to guarantee that demand is satisfied. The constraint

$$x_{A2} + x_{A2} + x_{A3} + x_{A4} \leq 200y_A \qquad \text{or} \qquad x_{A1} + x_{A2} + x_{A3} + x_{A4} - 200y_A \leq 0$$

serves two purposes. It guarantees that capacity at warehouse A is not exceeded, and it forces us to lease warehouse A if we want to send anything out of this warehouse. To see this, recall that y_i, or in this case y_A, must equal 0 or 1. First, assume that $y_A = 1$. The inequality above then becomes

$$x_{A1} + x_{A2} + x_{A3} + x_{A4} \leq 200$$

that is, no more than a total of 200 trucks can be sent out of warehouse A. You have previously seen this type of capacity constraint in transportation models. Now consider the case when y_A is 0. Then the inequality becomes

$$x_{A1} + x_{A2} + x_{A3} + x_{A4} \leq 0$$

that is, no items can be sent out of warehouse A. This constraint then guarantees that nothing can be sent out of warehouse A unless $y_A = 1$. Note that when $y_A = 1$, the term $7750y_A$ in the objective function equals 7750. Thus, we see that nothing is sent out of warehouse A unless we incur the monthly (fixed charge) leasing cost for that particular warehouse. Three such constraints, one for each warehouse, are needed in the model. The complete model and its solution are shown in Figure 6.8.

Solution Analysis A quick glance at the solution shows that the optimal values of all truck allocations are integer, even though we decided in the formulation to allow these variables to be continuous. Was this just fortuitous? The answer is no. Here is the reason. We started with a warehouse location model. Note that once we have decided which warehouses to lease, the problem of finding the optimal allocation of trucks is an LP trans-

FIGURE 6.8

STECO's Warehouse Location Problem

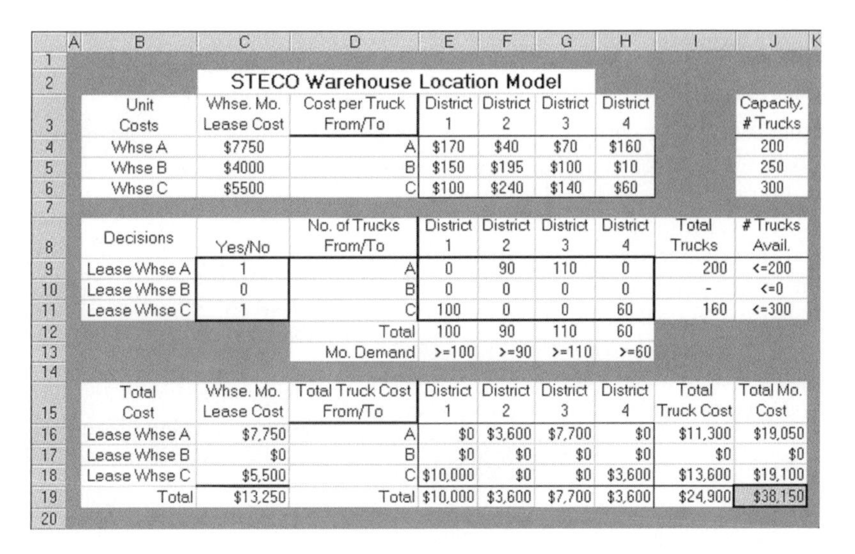

	B	C	D	E	F	G	H	I	J
2		STECO Warehouse Location Model							
3	Unit Costs	Whse. Mo. Lease Cost	Cost per Truck From/To	District 1	District 2	District 3	District 4		Capacity, # Trucks
4	Whse A	$7750	A	$170	$40	$70	$160		200
5	Whse B	$4000	B	$150	$195	$100	$10		250
6	Whse C	$5500	C	$100	$240	$140	$60		300
7									
8	Decisions	Yes/No	No. of Trucks From/To	District 1	District 2	District 3	District 4	Total Trucks	# Trucks Avail.
9	Lease Whse A	1	A	0	90	110	0	200	<=200
10	Lease Whse B	0	B	0	0	0	0	-	<=0
11	Lease Whse C	1	C	100	0	0	60	160	<=300
12			Total	100	90	110	60		
13			Mo. Demand	>=100	>=90	>=110	>=60		
14									
15	Total Cost	Whse. Mo. Lease Cost	Total Truck Cost From/To	District 1	District 2	District 3	District 4	Total Truck Cost	Total Mo. Cost
16	Lease Whse A	$7,750	A	$0	$3,600	$7,700	$0	$11,300	$19,050
17	Lease Whse B	$0	B	$0	$0	$0	$0	$0	$0
18	Lease Whse C	$5,500	C	$10,000	$0	$0	$3,600	$13,600	$19,100
19	Total	$13,250	Total	$10,000	$3,600	$7,700	$3,600	$24,900	$38,150
20									

Cell	Formula	Copy To
J9	= J4*C9	J10:J11
C16	= C9*C4	C17:C18
E16	= E4*E9	E16:H18
J16	= C16+I16	J17:J19

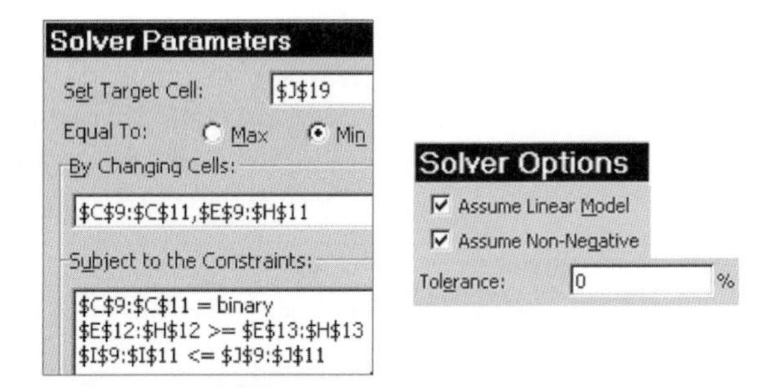

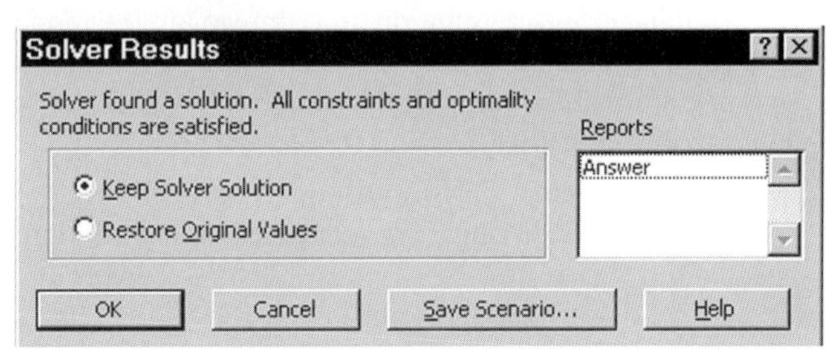

portation model. In Chapter 5 we saw that if the supply available at each warehouse and the demand at each district are integers, then the optimal solution to the transportation model will be all integers.

We now have enough information to conclude that the optimal solution to the above warehouse location model with integer supplies and demands will always include an integer allocation of trucks. The argument involves two steps: (1) the optimal solution must lease some set of warehouses, and (2) every possible set of leased warehouses yields an integer allocation of trucks. For this model, then, we now see that it would have been naive and costly to require as additional constraints that the x_{ij}'s be integer. The word is "Never pay for a free good."

APPLICATION CAPSULE

How Can I Help You? AT&T Woos Customers by Saving Them Money with the Aid of a Mixed Integer Program

AT&T, a major supplier of services to the telemarketing industry, is always looking for ways of helping its customers expand their operations. One of the models facing companies that do a large volume of telemarketing (using toll-free 800 numbers to take customer orders) is deciding on the number and location of sites for telemarketing offices. It was therefore in AT&T's best interests to develop a set of programs that would aid their customers in this process.

AT&T researchers soon found that, contrary to the general perception, the location of telemarketing offices was not always dictated primarily by real estate or communications costs. Rather, political or psychological considerations often played a major role. Thus, an office might be located in the same city as the regional headquarters or in a city where upper management wanted to have a presence, even though these might not be cost-efficient choices.

AT&T developed a model that analyzes the costs of plausible candidate sites and allows users to evaluate various site configurations on the basis of both quantitative and qualitative factors. The model, a mixed integer program similar to a facility-location planning model, is solved by means of a branch-and-bound code. It answers four questions:

1. How many telemarketing centers should be opened?
2. Where should centers be located?
3. What geographic regions should be served by each center?
4. How many attendant positions are required at each location?

Originally developed on a mainframe, the model was adapted for use on a PC, with more graphic display and user interaction added. It provides not only an optimal solution that minimizes the three operational cost factors (communications, labor, and real estate) but alternative solutions as well, so that the user can take factors other than costs into account. To this end, an analytical hierarchy process, described in Chapter 12, has been added to the model, allowing users to include qualitative or subjective factors in the decision process.

The AT&T model has greatly accelerated the siting of telemarketing offices while saving customers many hours of research and consulting costs—savings that some companies estimated at up to $240,000. Moreover, a number of customers have reported savings averaging $1 million per year from use of the locations identified by the model rather than ones they had previously considered.

From AT&T's point of view, the model has proven its worth in terms of enhanced customer relations and sales of services. At least 46 AT&T customers made decisions on site locations with the aid of the model, in the process committing themselves to $375 million per year in network services and $31 million in new equipment purchases. As a result of business generated by the model, AT&T's share of this market has risen from 30% to 40%. (See Spencer et al.)

6.6 INTEGER OPTIMIZATION METHODS

Very simplified, Solver's solution procedure for an ILP model, called **branch-and-bound**, is as follows for a maximization model. (A more complete treatment of branch and bound with a graphical and numerical example is found as the Branch and Bound Enrichment topic on the book's CD-ROM.)

1. Solve the original ILP formulation as a relaxed LP. The OV for the relaxation is the value of the ILP's upper bound. If the optimal solution is all-integer, it is optimal for the ILP, and so, quit.
2. If the LP relaxation has some integer variable at a fractional value, form two submodels from this parent *branch* so as to create two new unsolved LP submodels (the successors) with the property that the optimal solution to one of the successor ILPs will be the optimal solution to the parent ILP. The branching may be accomplished by taking any fractional variable, say x_i^*, of the optimal solution to the parent's relaxation. Let $[x_i^*]$ be the truncation of x_i^* to its integer part. Then $[x_i^*] + 1$ is the next integer larger than x_i^*. One successor submodel will be the parent's LP model augmented by the constraint in $x_i \leq [x_i^*]$. The other successor submodel is formed by augmenting the parent's LP model with $x_i \geq [x_i^*] + 1$.
3. Commence with any unsolved submodel in step 2 and optimize it as a relaxed LP submodel. If the optimal solution is all-integer, evaluate its objective function at this point. Compare the OV of the best ILP model's solution found so far with this

relaxed submodel's OV. If the relaxed submodel's OV is worse than the best ILP solution found so far, don't continue to eliminate any remaining fractional variables in the submodel, as it is already an inferior candidate; instead, throw that submodel away and continue with another one. If the relaxed submodel is better than the best ILP so far, then proceed to eliminate any other fractional variables it may have using the constraint augmentation procedure by going back to step 2. If all remaining relaxed submodels have integer solutions, go to step 4; otherwise go back to step 2.

4. The optimal solution to the original ILP is the all-integer solution of some submodel that produced the best value of the OV found so far.

It should be clear from this cryptic summary that the original ILP is decomposed into a growing sequence of LP submodels, each augmented with additional constraints on any fractional decision variables, which are then in turn re-optimized. Hence, the method used by Solver uses *numerous* optimizations of increasingly augmented LP submodel formulations to solve a given ILP. For this reason it is, in general, much more time-consuming to optimize ILPs than LPs.

The operation of the branch-and-bound procedure can be observed during optimization of an ILP model by Solver as illustrated in Figure 6.9. Solver displays the progress of the branching sequence by showing a message in Excel's lower left corner containing a "Branch:" iteration count that reflects the number of separate LP optimizations carried out thus far during the branch-and-bound procedure. The "Trial Solution:" is the count of the number of corner points visited during the currently augmented LP submodel's simplex optimization and the "Set Cell:" is the value of the objective function cell during the current LP submodel's optimization. In the example of Figure 6.9, 1421 LP submodels have been optimized thus far; Solver is evaluating the eleventh corner point of the 1422nd LP submodel being optimized; and that LP submodel's OV is currently $39,366.

Finally, let us comment on the application of the branch-and-bound technique to special ILPs with binary variables. In this case, suppose that one is branching on the binary variable y_1. Then one successor will have $y_1 = 0$. The other will have $y_1 = 1$. For the special case of very large ILP models in binary variables another type of branch-and-bound method not used by Solver, sometimes called *partial enumeration*, has enjoyed considerable success. Also, for general ILP and MILP modes is other optimization methods have been applied. These include *cutting-plane methods* and *Lagrangian relaxation*. As stated at the outset of this chapter, our introductory discussion covers only the ILP technique used by Solver and merely touches the surface of this intricate and important topic.

SENSITIVITY ANALYSIS FOR ILPS

We have seen that the branch-and-bound method used by Solver is, in general, much more time-consuming to solve ILPs than LPs. Unfortunately, it is also true that the solution to an ILP contains much less information than the solution to an LP. As shown in the Solver Results completion dialog in Figure 6.8 following the successful optimization of STECO's ILP, there is no option to request a Sensitivity Report! That is because *the Solver solution to an ILP does not contain any sensitivity information.* No information concerning the sensitivity of the OV (i.e., the optimal value of the objective function) to changes in the RHS of a constraint or to changes in the value of an objective function coefficient is produced. In other words, *an ILP solution does not include information that is equivalent to the shadow price, reduced cost and objective coefficient sensitivity information in an LP.* This does not

Branch: 1422 Trial Solution: 11 Set Cell: $39,366

FIGURE 6.9

Solver Messages During ILP Optimization

imply that changes in a RHS or in an objective coefficient do not affect the solution to an ILP. They do. Indeed, the solutions to ILPs can be *extremely* sensitive to changes in parameter values.

The following somewhat unrealistic, but for the present purpose illustrative, capital budgeting example will illustrate these points:

$$\begin{aligned} \text{Max} \quad & 10x_1 + 100x_2 + 1000x_3 \\ \text{s.t.} \quad & 29x_1 + 30x_2 + 31x_3 \le b_1 \\ & x_1, x_2, x_3 \text{ are binary: either 0 or 1} \end{aligned} \tag{6.6}$$

The model is easily solved by inspection for given values of b_1. Table 6.3 shows the optimal solution of the model and the optimal value of the objective function (OV) for various values of the RHS parameter b_1. From this data we note that a change in 1 unit in the right-hand side of the constraint (say from 29 to 30) increases the OV by a factor of 1000% (from 10 to 100). Clearly, if you were aware of such an opportunity, you would be anxious to make such a change.

Unfortunately, no such sensitivity information is produced when you solve this or any ILP model with Solver. You receive from Solver only the optimal solution and the OV. Sensitivity information, such as that shown in Table 6.3, can be determined only by repeatedly optimizing the Solver ILP model with new parameter values and tabulating the results. Of course, the SolverTable add-in introduced in Section 4.9 can be a big help in grinding through such analyses. However, the absence of a Sensitivity Report leaves you with no guidance as to which parameters to focus upon for tabulating sensitivities. So, even with SolverTable, when the model has a number of constraints and decision variables, using this approach to generate useful sensitivity data for an ILP can require you to run a large number of SolverTable tabulations, each requiring a number of alternative Solver ILP solutions, each of which in turn may be slow to optimize. Thus, sensitivity analysis for ILPs can be a very expensive and time-consuming activity, but it is the price you must pay for the convenience of including integer-valued conditions in your models.

HEURISTIC METHODS

Because of the importance of the applications, integer optimization is currently an active area of research. Much of this research is in the area of *heuristic methods.* These are methods designed to efficiently produce "good," although not necessarily optimal, solutions. We will see one important example of a heuristic approach using Solver Premium Edition for Education's Evolutionary method, an approach based surprisingly upon concepts of biologic reproduction, in Chapter 7.

From the viewpoint of the manager, a heuristic procedure may certainly be as acceptable as, and possibly even preferable to, a "more exact" ILP method that produces an optimal solution. The dominant considerations should be the amount of insight and guidance the model can provide and the cost of obtaining these.

Table 6.3

ILP Sensitivity Data for the Example Model (6.6)

	OPTIMAL SOLUTION			
b_1	x_1	x_2	x_3	OV
29	1	0	0	10
30	0	1	0	100
31	0	0	1	1000

6.7 NOTES ON IMPLEMENTATION OF INTEGER OPTIMIZATION MODELS

Integer solutions are an important, indeed essential, condition for the application of optimization models to many important real-world situations. Recent advances in research and computer technology have made it possible to make real progress on models that involve variables that must be treated as integers. Two examples appear in the Application Capsules in this chapter. Other examples follow.

KELLY-SPRINGFIELD

The Kelly-Springfield Tire Company has a model-based system to coordinate sales forecasting, inventory control, production planning, and distribution decisions. One crucial link in this system is the production planning model. Central to this model is the effect of setup time. In the manufacture of each particular line of tires a machine is set up by installing a piece of equipment (called a die) particular to that line. It takes a fixed amount of time (and thus a fixed cost) to remove one die from a machine and insert another. In other words, there is a fixed changeover or setup cost of moving from the production of one line of tires to another, no matter how many tires you decide to produce after the machine is set up. The decision to set up (i.e., to produce a particular line in a given production period) or not is treated as a 0–1 variable in the MILP used to attack this model. The total integrated system (including the production planning system) is credited with impressive results. The system is estimated to have yielded savings of $500,000 a year. After an improved system was installed, average unit inventory decreased by 19%, customer service improved, productivity increased, and additional savings totaling $7.9 million annually resulted.

FLYING TIGER LINE

Another interesting application concerns the use of integer programming by the Flying Tiger Line (an all-cargo airline owned by Federal Express) in approaching two strategic questions: the design of their service network and the selection and deployment of their aircraft fleet. One model for 33 cities, 8 hubs (locations where cargo can be interchanged), and 10 aircraft types included 843 constraints, 3,807 continuous variables, and 156 integer (aircraft selector) variables. No explicit cost savings are included in the presentation of this application. Management's satisfaction with the project, however, is obvious from the ongoing nature of the investigation.

HUNT-WESSON FOODS

A third application is a major distribution-system model for Hunt-Wesson Foods, Inc. The model is to select sites for regional distribution centers and to determine what customer zones each distribution center should serve, as well as which of several plants should supply the distribution centers. The model is an MILP with the quantities of material shipped as continuous variables and two types of integer variables:

$y_k = 1$ if site k is used for a distribution center, and $y_k = 0$ if it is not

$y_{kl} = 1$ if customer district l is served by the warehouse at site k, and $y_{kl} = 0$ if it is not

The model involved 17 commodity classes, 14 plants, 45 possible distribution center sites, and 121 customer zones. The size of the MILP used to attack this model and the cost of solving it are staggering when your primary exposure has been to small spreadsheet models. The MILP model had 11,854 constraints, 727 0–1 integer variables, and 23,513 continuous variables, and a special optimization method had to be developed to solve the model. The realizable annual cost savings produced by the study were estimated to be in the low-seven figures.

The three studies briefly cited here have a number of features in common:

1. Each attacked a major model of strategic importance to a firm.
2. Each made a significant contribution to successfully dealing with the situation.
3. Each included a large-scale MILP.
4. Clever modeling and/or special solution methods were required in each application.
5. Each project required a major commitment of funds and managerial talent.

The examples illustrate that a good model may enable management to achieve a level of analysis and performance that might otherwise be impossible, but such models may be costly to develop and often require an ongoing and time-consuming input from management. All of the examples required a close working relationship between the modelers and management. For example, the Kelly-Springfield model evolved over a 15-year interval with two major modeling efforts. We see, then, that the use of models to address important management challenges may well entail a serious commitment to a long process. Small models may be successfully subdued with a quick spreadsheet optimization. Fundamental large scale strategic models are seldom that obliging. We treat these issues in more detail in Chapter 11.

6.8 SUMMARY

The introduction pointed out that integer linear programming (ILP) is an important and developing area of constrained optimization. Section 6.2 identified all-integer models and mixed integer models (MILP) as the two main types of integer linear programs. In MILPs only some of the decision variables are restricted to integer values. Further, the importance of models involving binary integer variables that are restricted to the values 0 or 1 was discussed. Finally, the LP relaxation was defined. Section 6.3 used a graphical approach to solve an ILP with two decision variables. This approach was then used to investigate the conceptual relationships between an ILP and its LP relaxation. We saw that:

1. In a *Max* model the OV of the LP relaxation always provides an *upper bound* on the OV of the original ILP.
2. In a *Min* model the OV of the LP relaxation always provides a *lower bound* on the OV of the original ILP.

In Section 6.3 we also discussed *rounded solutions.* These are any rounding of the optimal solution to the LP relaxation. Thus, there are many rounded solutions. For n variables that have fractional answers, there are 2^n possible rounded solutions. Thus, for Flying Tigers there could be $2^{156} = 9.1344 \times 10^{46}$ rounded solutions! If only 50 of these variables had fractional answers in the relaxed LP, there would be 1.1259×10^{15} (over a quadrillion) solutions to investigate just to find the best rounded feasible solution. In some applications, as discussed in Section 6.1, any rounded solution may be an acceptable substitute for the true ILP solution. In other cases, no rounded solution will be acceptable. We saw in Section 6.3 that, in general:

3. It may be that no rounded solution is near the ILP optimum, or
4. It may be that no rounded solution is feasible (i.e., satisfies the constraints of the LP relaxation).

Section 6.4 considered the use of binary or 0–1 variables in a variety of applications. In particular, models for capital budgeting and warehouse location were considered in some detail. Section 6.5 contained an application of the fact that certain LPs always have all-integer solutions. Section 6.6 briefly summarized the branch-and-bound approach used by Solver to optimize ILPs. Section 6.6 dealt with two important topics concerning the real-world use of ILPs. First, we pointed out the inherent slowness of any ILP optimization method, including Solver's branch-and-bound approach. Second, we saw that sensitivity data are not produced as a natural by-product of the solution to an ILP. Further, it was illustrated that ILPs may be inconsistent and erratic in their sensitivity to changes in parameter values. These two facts combine to establish the necessity of using SolverTable to make multiple optimization runs with different parameters and parameter values to extensively tabulate sensitivity information in the ILP setting. This process is often an important part of attacking a real model with an ILP model. In Section 6.7 several additional major applications of integer programming were cited.

Key Terms

Integer Linear Program (ILP). A model that satisfies all the conditions of an optimization model except that some or all of the variables are required to be integers.

Integer Programming. The process of creating an ILP.

Rounded Solution. A feasible solution to an ILP found by solving the LP relaxation and rounding each of the integer variables either up or down.

All-Integer Linear Program. An integer linear program in which all the decision variables are required to be integers.

Mixed Integer Linear Program (MILP). An integer linear program in which only some of the variables are required to be integers.

Binary (0–1) Integer Linear Program. An integer linear program in which all the decision variables are required to be either 0 or 1.

LP Relaxation. An LP model that is derived from an ILP by ignoring the integrality constraints.

Optimal Value (OV). Short for the optimal value of the objective function.

Complete Enumeration. Solving an ILP by listing all the feasible points, evaluating the objective function at each of them, and selecting the best solution.

Branch and Bound. An optimization technique for ILPs based on dividing the original model into mutually exclusive parts and employing the OV from the LP relaxations to obtain bounds that force decision variables to be integer valued.

Fixed Charge Model. A model in which a given decision variable may become different from zero only if a fixed payment is made.

Heuristic Method. An approach to optimization using a search procedure that efficiently finds good, but not necessarily optimal, solutions to a model.

Self-Review Exercises

True-False

1. **T F** Rounding LP solutions to meet the real-world requirement for integer decision variables is a common practice.
2. **T F** In general, it is no more difficult to solve an ILP than an LP.
3. **T F** The binary variable in an ILP may be used to represent the dichotomous true-false decisions of an Excel IF() function.
4. **T F** In a *Max* model, the OV of the LP relaxation always provides a *lower bound* on the OV of the original ILP or MILP.
5. **T F** The first step in obtaining a rounded solution to an MILP is to solve its LP relaxation.
6. **T F** Solving an ILP by complete enumeration involves evaluating the objective function at all corners of the feasible set of the LP relaxation.
7. **T F** In the LP relaxation of the ILP capital budgeting model there are as many constraints as there are time periods.
8. **T F** In an ILP with *n* binary decision variables, each of which indicates the selection (or not) of an alternative, the condition that no more than *k* alternatives be selected can be imposed with the constraint $x_1 + x_2 + \cdots + x_n \leq k$.
9. **T F** In STECO's warehouse location model, the optimal number of trucks to send from each warehouse to each plant was an integer because after the warehouses are selected the model is a transportation model with integer supplies and demands.
10. **T F** Suppose x_1 and x_2 are both binary variables where $x_i = 1$ has the interpretation of building a plant in location *i*. The condition "a plant can be built in location 2 only if the plant in location 1 is also built" is captured with the constraint $x_1 \leq x_2$.
11. **T F** Consider a transportation model with integer supplies and demands and where in addition, integrality conditions are imposed on the x_{ij}'s. Since this makes the model an integer program, it must be solved by specifying Solver's changing cells to be integer.

Multiple Choice

12. In an ILP
- **a.** ignoring integrality restrictions, all constraint functions are linear
- **b.** all decision variables must be integers
- **c.** all decision variables must be nonnegative
- **d.** a and b above

13. In an MILP
- **a.** the objective function is linear
- **b.** all decision variables must be integers
- **c.** some coefficients are restricted to be integers, others are not
- **d.** all of the above

14. The LP relaxation of an ILP
- **a.** permits a nonlinear objective function
- **b.** ignores the integrality restrictions on the decision variables
- **c.** relaxes the nonnegativity restrictions on the decision variables
- **d.** all of the above

15. A rounded solution to a Max ILP may not be feasible because
- **a.** it violates the integrality constraints
- **b.** it violates the nonnegativity constraints
- **c.** its OV is smaller than the OV of the LP relaxation
- **d.** none of the above

16. If x_k and x_m and are 0–1 variables (the value 1 meaning select) for projects k and m, respectively, the constraint, $x_k + x_m \leq 0$ implies that
- **a.** k cannot be selected unless m is selected
- **b.** k must be selected if m is selected
- **c.** m cannot be selected unless k is selected
- **d.** none of the above

17. Suppose a product can be manufactured either not at all or else in lot sizes $\geq L$, and let x be the quantity of the product produced. The following two constraints are appropriate:
- **a.** $x + My \leq 0$; $x - Ly \geq 0$
- **b.** $x - My \geq 0$; $x - Ly \geq 0$
- **c.** $x - My \leq 0$; $x - Ly \geq 0$
- **d.** $x - My \leq 0$; $x - Ly \leq 0$

where M is an arbitrarily large number and y is a 0–1 variable.

18. In solving a Max ILP a lower bound for the OV of the original model can always be found by
- **a.** solving the LP relaxation of the ILP and using the OV of the LP
- **b.** finding a feasible solution to the ILP by any available means and evaluating the objective function
- **c.** solving the LP relaxation and then rounding fractions <0.5 down, those ≥0.5 up, and evaluating the objective function at this point
- **d.** none of the above

19. In the branch-and-bound approach to optimizing an ILP,
- **a.** starts by solving a relaxed LP of the model
- **b.** requires multiple LPs to be optimized if the initial relaxed LP solution has fractional values of integer variables
- **c.** the occurrence of any fractional value of an integer variable requires adding constraints to the original relaxed LP model
- **d.** all of the above

20. The Solver solution to an MILP
- **a.** contains no sensitivity information
- **b.** contains sensitivity information on only the noninteger variables
- **c.** contains sensitivity information on only right-hand sides
- **d.** contains sensitivity information on only the objective function

More-Challenging Questions

The next ten questions are based on the following model:

A firm has ten outlets that must be supplied with a certain product. The demands (all positive) at the outlets are $d_1, d_2, \ldots, d_{10}$, and these demands must be *exactly* satisfied (i.e., d_i units must be distributed to outlet i). The firm may supply these demands by having a supplier deliver directly to each outlet. The supplier charges \$50 for each unit delivered, independent of the outlet location. The supplier would charge only \$35 per unit for any location if the location would order at least D units. Since each of the $d_j < D$, the firm can make no use of the discount. The firm is considering leasing a centrally located warehouse for $K >$ 0 dollars and using this warehouse as an intermediary depot. The depot could order any quantity and could distribute to any number of outlets. It has been agreed that the depot would pay the same as the outlets (\$50 per unit if <D units are ordered; \$35 per unit if the total order is at least D units).

The cost of sending a unit from the warehouse to outlet i is $C_i > 0$, $i = 1, 2, \ldots, 10$. Assume that $D < \sum_{i=1}^{n} d_i$. Management would like to know

1. Should the warehouse be leased?
2. If so, which outlets should be served by the warehouse and which should be supplied directly by the supplier?

In formulating a model to answer these questions, let

x_i = quantity sent directly from supplier to location i

y_i = quantity sent from warehouse to location i

z = quantity sent from supplier to warehouse

A correct set of constraints for this model is

$$x_i + y_i = d_i, \quad i = 1, 2, \ldots 10$$

$$\sum_{i=1}^{10} y_i \leq z$$

$$z \geq tD$$

$$z \leq t\sum_{i=1}^{10} d_i$$

$$x_i, y_i \geq 0 \quad (i = 1, 2, \ldots, 10); \quad z \geq 0; \quad t = 0 \text{ or } 1$$

21. The correct objective function is

a. Min $\sum_{i=1}^{10} 50x_i + \sum_{i=1}^{10} C_i y_i$

b. Min $\sum_{i=1}^{10} 50x_i + \sum_{i=1}^{10} (C_i + 35)y_i + tK$

c. Min $\sum_{i=1}^{10} 50x_i + 35z + \sum_{i=1}^{10} C_i y_i + tK$

d. Min $\sum_{i=1}^{10} (50x_i + C_i y_i) + 35D$

e. none of the above

22. For the model as stated, there will never be an optimal solution in which the depot orders a positive amount that is less than D units.

a. T
b. F

23. Management should lease the warehouse if

a. the optimal value of D is positive
b. the optimal value of t is positive
c. the optimal value of z is positive
d. all of the above
e. b and c

24. Consider location k such that $35 + C_k > 50$. Since the marginal cost of shipping directly to k from the supplier is less than the marginal cost of going through the warehouse, there will be no optimal solution in which this outlet (the kth) receives products both from the warehouse and directly from the supplier.

a. T
b. F

25. There always will exist an optimal solution in which no outlet receives deliveries from both the supplier (directly) and the warehouse.

a. T
b. F

26. Suppose $35 + C_i = 50, i = 1, \ldots, 10$. Then $t^* = 0$ in any optimal solution.

a. T
b. F

27. This model may have an optimal solution in which the total quantity ordered from the supplier exceeds $\sum_{i=1}^{10} d_i$.

a. T
b. F

28. If the optimal value $z^* = \sum_{i=1}^{10} d_i$, then it is certain that the optimal solution will be $x_i^* = 0, (i = 1, 2, \ldots, 10), y_i^* = d_i, (i = 1, 2, \ldots, 10)$, and $t^* = 1$

a. T
b. F

29. This model will allow the possibility of having inventory left at the warehouse after all demands are satisfied.

a. T
b. F

30. Suppose each $C_i \geq 15$.

a. Then the optimal solution to the model is obviously $x_i^* = d_i, (i = 1, 2, \ldots, 10), y_i^* = 0, (i = 1, 2, \ldots, 10)$, and $z^* = t^* = 0$
b. For some values of the parameters d_i the solution may differ, and hence it is wisest to optimize the model with Solver.

Answers

1. T, **2.** F, **3.** T, **4.** F, **5.** T, **6.** F, **7.** F, **8.** T, **9.** T, **10.** F, **11.** F, **12.** d, **13.** a, **14.** b, **15.** d, **16.** d, **17.** c, **18.** b, **19.** d, **20.** a, **21.** c, **22.** a , **23.** e, **24.** b, **25.** b, **26.** a, **27.** a, **28.** a, **29.** a, **30.** a

Skill Problems

6-1. A firm produces two products, A and C. Capacity on the A line is 7 units per day. Each unit of C requires 4 hours of drying time, and a total of 22 drying hours per day is available. Also, each unit of A requires 2 hours of polishing, and each unit of C requires 3 hours of polishing. A total of 19 hours of polishing time is available each day. Each unit of A yields a profit of \$1, whereas each unit of C yields a profit of \$3. The firm wants to determine a daily production schedule to maximize profits. A and C can be produced only in integer amounts.

(a) Formulate this model as an ILP.
(b) Use GLP to find the optimal solution to the LP relaxation.
(c) Use GLP to find the optimal solution to the ILP.
(d) Find an integer solution by rounding each value in the answer to part (b) to its integer part. Is this solution feasible?
(e) How much profit would the firm lose by adopting the latter rounded solution?

6-2. Consider the following ILP:

$$\begin{aligned} &\text{Max } x_1 + 2x_2 \\ &\text{s.t.} \quad 3x_1 + x_2 \le 15 \\ &\qquad 3x_1 + 7x_2 \le 42 \\ &x_1, x_2 \ge 0 \text{ and integer} \end{aligned}$$

(a) Use GLP to find the optimal solution to the LP relaxation.
(b) How many feasible points are there?
(c) Using GLP, find the optimal solution to the ILP.
(d) Find an integer feasible solution by rounding the answer to part (a). Is the rounded solution optimal?

6-3. Consider a minimization ILP. Does the optimal value for the LP relaxation provide an upper or a lower bound for the optimal value of the ILP? Explain your answer.

6-4. Consider a minimization ILP. Does the value of the objective function at a feasible rounded solution provide an upper or a lower bound for the optimal value of the ILP? Explain your answer.

6-5. Consider a maximization ILP. Does the optimal value of the LP relaxation of this model provide an upper or a lower bound for the optimal value of the ILP? Explain your answer.

6-6. Consider a maximization ILP. Does the value of the objective function at a feasible rounded solution provide an upper or a lower bound for the optimal value of the ILP? Explain your answer.

6-7. Optimize Problem 4.60 in Chapter 4 as an ILP. By how much is the OV reduced over the LP solution?

6-8. Optimize Problem 4.61 in Chapter 4 as an LP and then as an ILP. Approximately how much longer did the ILP optimization take compared to the LP optimization? By how much is the OV reduced over the LP solution? How different is the ILP solution from the LP solution?

6-9. Optimize Problem 4.62 in Chapter 4 as an ILP. Approximately how much longer did the ILP optimization take compared to the LP optimization? By how much is the OV reduced over the LP solution? How different is the ILP solution from the LP solution?

6-10. Consider the following formulation of Problem 6-1:

$$\begin{aligned} &\text{Max } A + 3C \\ &\text{s.t.} \quad A \le 7 \\ &\qquad 4C \le 22 \\ &\qquad 2A + 3C \le 19 \\ &A \ge 0 \text{ and integer,} \quad C \ge 0 \text{ and integer} \end{aligned}$$

Plot the optimal objective value as a function of the RHS of the second constraint as the value of the RHS ranges between 0 and 24. Use GLP or SolverTable to create the data for this plot.

6-11. Consider the ILP presented in Problem 6-2. Plot the optimal objective value as a function of the RHS of the constraint $3x_1 + x_2 \le \text{RHS}$ for $0 \le \text{RHS} \le 24$. Use GLP or SolverTable to create the data for this plot.

6-12. Consider the following ILP:

$$\begin{aligned} &\text{Min } 4x_1 + 5x_2 \\ &\text{s.t.} \quad 3x_1 + 6x_2 \ge 18 \\ &\qquad 5x_1 + 4x_2 \ge 20 \\ &\qquad 8x_1 + 2x_2 \ge 16 \\ &\qquad 7x_1 + 6x_2 \le 42 \\ &x_1 \ge 0 \text{ and integer,} \quad x_2 \ge 0 \text{ and integer} \end{aligned}$$

(a) Use GLP to find the optimal solution to the LP relaxation.
(b) List all the feasible points.
(c) Use GLP to find the optimal solution to the ILP.
(d) Use GLP to find a feasible rounded solution.
(e) Is (d) optimal?
(f) How large is the cost of using the rounded solution identified above relative to the optimal solution?

Application Problems

6-13. *Investment Problem.* A portfolio manager has just been given $100,000 to invest. She will choose her investments from a list of 20 stocks. She knows that the net return from investing one dollar in stock i is r_i. Thus, if she invests x_i dollars in stock i she will end up with $(1 + r_i)x_i$ dollars. In order to maintain a balanced portfolio, she adopts the following two rules of thumb:

(a) She will not invest more than $20,000 in a single stock.

(b) *If* she invests anything in a stock, she will invest at least $5,000 in it.

The manager would like to maximize her return subject to these rules of thumb. Formulate this model as a symbolic MILP. Define your decision variables carefully.

6-14. *Airline Scheduling.* Alpha Airline wishes to schedule no more than one flight out of Chicago to each of the following cities: Columbus, Denver, Los Angeles, and New York. The available departure slots are 8 A.M., 10 A.M., and 12 noon. Alpha leases the airplanes at the cost of $5,000 before and including 10 A.M. and $3,000 after 10 A.M., and is able to lease at most two per departure slot. Also, if a flight leaves for New York in a time slot, there must be a flight leaving for Los Angeles in the same time slot. The expected profit contribution in thousands per flight before rental costs is shown in the following table. Formulate and solve a model for a profit-maximizing schedule. Define your decision variables carefully.

	TIME SLOT		
	8	10	12
Columbus	10	6	6
Denver	9	10	9
Los Angeles	14	11	10
New York	18	15	10

6-15. *A Startup Problem.* A model faced by an electrical utility each day is that of deciding which generators to start up. The utility in question has three generators with the characteristics shown in the following table. There are two periods in a day, and the number of megawatts needed in the first period is 2,900. The second period requires 3,900 megawatts. A generator started in the first period may be used in the second period without incurring an additional startup cost. All major generators (e.g., A, B, and C) are turned off at the end of each day. Formulate and solve this model as an MILP. Define your decision variables carefully.

GENERATOR	FIXED STARTUP COST ($)	COST PER PERIOD PER MEGAWATT USED ($)	MAXIMUM CAPACITY IN EACH PERIOD (MW)
A	3000	5	2100
B	2000	4	1800
C	1000	7	3000

6-16. *Production Planning.* A certain production line makes two products. Relevant data are given in Table 6.4. Total time available (for production and setup) each week is 80 hours. The firm has no inventory of either product at the start of week 1 and no inventory is allowed at the end of week 4. The cost of carrying a unit of inventory from one week to the next is $4 for each product. One unit of unsatisfied demand costs $10 for product A and $15 for product B. Demand data are given in Table 6.5. The line is shut down and cleaned each weekend. As a result, if a product is produced in a week the appropri-

Table 6.4

Product Data

	PRODUCT	
	A	B
Setup Time	5 hours	10 hours
Per Unit Production Time	0.5 hours	0.75 hour
Setup Cost	$200	$400
Per Unit Production Cost	$10	$15
Selling Price	$20	$30

Table 6.5

Demand Data

Product	WEEK 1	2	3	4
A	80	100	75	80
B	15	20	50	30

ate setup time cost is incurred. Only one product can be produced during a week. No production can take place during the time that the line is being set up. Formulate and solve this 4-week planning model as an MILP. The objective is to maximize the profit over a 4-week period.

6-17. The board of directors of a large manufacturing firm is considering the set of investments shown in the following table. Let R_i be the total revenue from investment i and C_i be the cost to make investment i. The board wishes to maximize total revenue and invest no more than a total of M dollars. Formulate this model as an ILP. Define your decision variables and write the model's equations symbolically.

INVESTMENT	CONDITION
1	None
2	Only if 1
3	Only if 2
4	Must if 1 *and* 2
5	Not if 1 *or* 2
6	Not if 2 *and* 3
7	Only if 2 *and not* 3

6-18. A distribution company wants to minimize the cost of transporting goods from its warehouses A, B, and C to the retail outlets 1, 2, and 3. The costs for transporting one unit from warehouse to retailer is given by the following table.

WAREHOUSE	RETAILER 1	2	3
A	15	32	21
B	9	7	6
C	11	18	5
Demand	200	150	175

The fixed cost of operating a warehouse is \$500 for A, \$750 for B, and \$600 for C, and at least two of them have to be open. The warehouses can be assumed to have unlimited storage capacity. Formulate and solve an ILP to decide which warehouses should be opened and the amount to be shipped from each warehouse to each retailer.

6-19. *Line Balancing.* A job requires five operations, A, B, C, D, and E, each of which can be done on either machine 1 or machine 2. The time taken for each operation on each of the given machines is given in the following table.

	A	B	C	D	E
Machine 1	5	9	2	3	4
Machine 2	3	4	7	5	4

Formulate and solve an ILP to assign the jobs to the machines so that if T1 is the total time taken on machine 1 and T2 the time taken on machine 2, then Max (T1, T2) is minimized.

6-20. Consider the STECO Warehouse Location Model in Figure 6.8. Given the optimal decisions for leasing warehouses A, B, and C, write out the transportation model symbolically that the optimal truck allocations solve.

6-21. *Site Location.* The city council found that to service the city, fire stations have to be opened at either locations A, B, and C or locations A, C, and D or locations B, C, and D. The cost of opening a fire station (in millions of \$) at location A is \$1.5, at B is \$2.3, at C is \$1.8, and at D is \$2.1. Formulate and solve an ILP that will allow the city council to decide which fire stations should be opened so as to service the city at minimum cost.

6-22. *Capacity Expansion.* An electric utility is planning the expansion of its generating capacity for the next five years. Its current capacity is 800 megawatts (MW), but based on its forecast of demand it will require additional capacity as shown in the following table.

YEAR	MINIMUM CAPACITY (MW)
1	880
2	960
3	1050
4	1160
5	1280

The utility can increase its generating capacity by installing 10-, 50-, or 100-MW generators. The cost of installing a generator depends on its size and the year it is brought on-line. See the following table.

GENERATOR SIZE	YEAR				
MW	1	2	3	4	5
10	300	250	208	173	145
50	670	558	465	387	322
100	950	791	659	549	458

Once a generator is brought on line its capacity is available to meet demand in succeeding years. Formulate and solve an ILP that minimizes the cost of bringing generators on-line while satisfying the minimum capacity requirements. HINT: Let x_t, y_t, and z_t, be the number of 10-, 50-, and 100-MW generators brought on line in year t and c_t the total capacity in year t after these generators have been brought on-line.

6-23. Norco Home Cosmetics Sales is just moving into a six-county region of southern Utah. The map below shows the location of the counties and their populations, P_i. Norco plans to assign two salespersons to this region. The company assigns two counties to each salesperson, a base county and an adjacent county. Counties are adjacent if they share a common *side*; a common corner is *not* sufficient.

P_1 1	P_2 2	P_3 3
P_4 4	P_5 5	P_6 6

For example, in the map above, counties 1 and 2 are adjacent, but 1 and 5 are not. Norco's objective is to maximize the total population of the assigned counties. A feasible solution is to make 4 a base with 1 as the assigned adjacent and also make 3 a base with 2 as the assigned adjacent. The value of the objective function for this solution is $P_1 + P_2 + P_3 + P_4$. Define

$$B_j = \begin{cases} 1 \text{ if county } j \text{ is used as a base} \\ 0 \text{ if not} \end{cases} \quad j = 1, \ldots, 6$$

$$A_{ij} = \begin{cases} 1 \text{ if county } i \text{ is used as a county adjacent to base } j \\ 0 \text{ if not} \end{cases} \quad \begin{matrix} j = 1, \ldots, 6; \\ i \text{ adjacent to } j \end{matrix}$$

Thus the variables are B_1, B_2, B_3, B_4, B_5, B_6, A_{21}, A_{41}, A_{12}, A_{52}, A_{32}, A_{23}, A_{63}, and so on.

(a) Double counting in the model must not occur (i.e., a county must not be used as both a base and an assigned adjacent). Write a constraint that assures no double counting for county 1.

(b) Write a constraint that says "if any salesperson is assigned to county 2 as a base, then a salesperson must also be assigned to an appropriate adjacent county."

(c) Write a constraint that says "if either county adjacent to 1 is scheduled (as an adjacent to 1), then 1 must be used as a base."

(d) This model can be written with 12 inequality constraints and 1 equality constraint. True or False.

(e) This model can be written with 7 equality constraints and 6 inequality constraints. True or False.

6-24. Refer to the description that precedes exercise 21 in the Self-Review Exercises. Assume in addition to the conditions described there, that there is a fixed cost of $R > 0$ dollars assigned to each shipment that leaves the supplier. This implies, for example, that if the supplier makes direct shipments to locations 3, 5, and 8 and to the warehouse, then an additional cost of $4R$ dollars is incurred. Formulate the symbolic model as an MILP, using the notation introduced earlier and whatever additional notation is required.

6-25. Bradford Electronics produces a variety of DVD drives for installation into home-use DVD players. Bradford can assemble DVD drives on any or all of five production stations, some of which are more automated than others, and thus, have lower variable costs of assembly but require higher one-time setup costs to convert to assembling a particular model of DVD drive. Bradford has received an order for assembling 2,500 DVD drives of a particular model. Given the one-time setup costs, capacities and variable assembly costs at each of the five production stations in the following table, how many DVD drives should be assembled at each of the five production stations to minimize total costs?

ASSEMBLY STATION	VARIABLE ASSEMBLY COST/DVD DRIVE	CAPACITY IN DVD DRIVES	ONE-TIME SETUP COST
1	$62	500	$12,000
2	$68	600	$6,000
3	$72	700	$3,000
4	$78	450	$1,500
5	$85	1000	$500

Case Study Assigning Sales Representatives

One of the main themes in the text is that you, the manager, play the role of the intermediary between the real world and the model. You must decide if the assumptions are appropriate and if the solution produced by the model makes sense in the context of the real world.

Sally Erickson is midwest sales director for Lady Lynn Cosmetics. Lady Lynn is a rapidly expanding company that sells cosmetics through representatives. These representatives originally contact most of their customers through house parties. At these parties, the representative demonstrates the products and takes orders. The guests have an opportunity to win some samples of the products and to order products.

Sally is in the process of assigning representatives to the seven eastern Iowa counties shown in Exhibit 1. Actually, she

EXHIBIT 1

Seven Eastern Iowa Counties

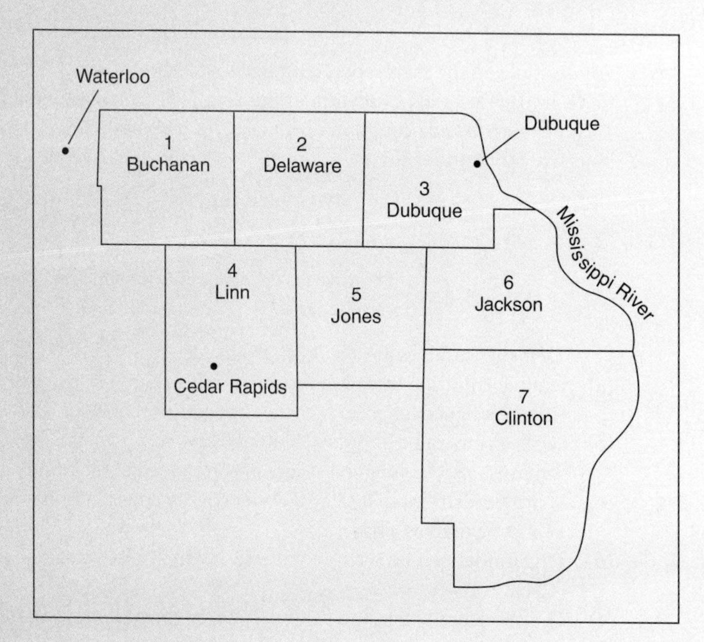

has only two trained representatives to assign at this time. The policy at Lady Lynn is to assign a representative to a base county and one adjacent county. Actual practice is based on a heuristic model that assigns representatives sequentially. The county with the largest population is selected as the base for the first representative, and the adjacent county with the largest population is also assigned to her. The unassigned county with the largest population is assigned as the next base and so on. The populations of the counties are shown below.

1.	Buchanan	16,000
2.	Delaware	15,000
3.	Dubuque	98,000
4.	Linn	109,000
5.	Jones	4,000
6.	Jackson	6,000
7.	Clinton	100,000

Using this scheme, the first representative would be assigned to Linn County as a base. As the map shows, Buchanan, Delaware, and Jones are the adjacent counties. Since Buchanan has the largest population of these three counties, it would be the assigned adjacent county. The second representative would be based in Clinton with Jackson as the assigned adjacent county. Sally realizes that the goal is to maximize the total population assigned to representatives. She is concerned that, since Dubuque County is nearly as large as Clinton, the proposed solution may not be optimal, and after a moment's thought she can see that it clearly is not: The pair Dubuque and Delaware beat Clinton and Jackson. She decides to abandon the traditional heuristic approach and to model the model as an IP. Although this particular model is quite simple, she believes that if she can create a successful model it could then be appropriately modified to assign the company's 60 midwest representatives to well over 300 counties. In formulating the model, she lets

$Y_j = 1$ if county j is a base, $j = 1, 2, \ldots, 7$
$= 0$ if not

$x_{ij} = 1$ if adjacent county i is assigned to base j, $i = 1, 2, \ldots, 7$; $j = 1, 2, \ldots, 7$
$= 0$ if not

The symbolic model is shown below. Sally developed a spreadsheet version of it and used Solver to optimize the model.

$$\begin{aligned}\text{Max } & 16Y_1 + 15Y_2 + 98Y_3 + 109Y_4 + 4Y_5 + 6Y_6 + 100Y_7 + \\ & 15X_{21} + 109X_{41} + \\ & 16X_{12} + 98X_{32} + 109X_{42} + 4X_{52} + \\ & 15X_{23} + 4X_{53} + 6X_{63} + \\ & 16X_{14} + 15X_{24} + 4X_{54} + \\ & 15X_{25} + 98X_{35} + 109X_{45} + 6X_{65} + 100X_{75} + \\ & 4X_{56} + 98X_{36} + 100X_{76} + \\ & 4X_{57} + 6X_{67}\end{aligned}$$

$$\begin{aligned}\text{s.t. } & X_{21} + X_{41} = Y_1 \\ & X_{12} + X_{32} + X_{42} + X_{52} = Y_2 \\ & X_{23} + X_{53} + X_{63} = Y_3 \\ & X_{14} + X_{24} + X_{54} = Y_4 \\ & X_{25} + X_{35} + X_{45} + X_{65} + X_{75} = Y_5 \\ & X_{56} + X_{36} + X_{76} = Y_6 \\ & X_{57} + X_{67} = Y_7 \\ & Y_1 + Y_2 + Y_3 + Y_4 + Y_5 + Y_6 + Y_7 = 2\end{aligned}$$

Her solution showed that Y_4 and $Y_1 = 1$ and X_{14} and $X_{41} = 1$ thus, Linn and Buchanan counties were selected as both base counties and adjacent counties. It also gave the optimal value of the objective function as 250, which implies that 250,000 people will be served by the two representatives. Sally thus is pleased to have discovered that the solution suggested by the standard heuristic approach was incorrect before she implemented that solution. She is a bit surprised that the optimal solution does not involve either Dubuque or Clinton county, but she feels sure that Solver provides the optimal solution to her model and thus she is determined to implement it.

Questions

1. Sally's solution is obviously wrong. Find, by inspection of the data, a correct optimal solution. How many alternative optima are there?
2. What is wrong with Sally's model? Write out the additional constraints that will give a correct formulation.
3. Develop a spreadsheet version of the reformulated model and optimize it with Solver to determine the optimal solution.

Case Study Municipal Bond Underwriting[1]

The municipal bond market is tough and aggressive, which means that a successful underwriter must be on the cutting edge in terms of competitive bidding. Bond markets often change from hour to hour. An active underwriter may bid on several issues each day with as little as 15 to 20 minutes to prepare a bid. This case has two objectives: (1) to familiarize you with some of the mechanics of an important financial market; and (2) to develop an IP model with real-world importance. A variant of this model is actually used by several banks and

[1] This case was initially formulated by Professor R. Kipp Martin, Graduate School of Business, University of Chicago.

investment bankers. In practice, bids are routinely prepared for models involving as many as 100 maturities and 35 coupon rates.

Basic Scenario

Each year billions of dollars of tax-exempt debt securities are offered for sale to the public. This is usually done through an underwriter acting as a broker between the issuer of the security and the public. The issuing of the securities to the underwriter is usually done through a competitive bid process. The issuer will notify prospective underwriters in advance of the proposed sale and invite bids that meet constraints set forth by the issuer. In constructing a proposed sale, the issuer divides the total amount to be raised (say \$10,000) into bonds of various maturities. For example, to raise \$10,000, the issuer might offer a one-year bond with face value of \$2,000, a two-year bond with face value of \$3,000, and a three-year bond with face value of \$5,000. At maturity, the face value of these bonds would be paid to the buyer. Thus in this example, the issuers would pay the buyers \$2,000 in principal at the end of year 1, and so on. A bid by an underwriter (to the issuer) has three components:

1. An agreement to pay the issuer the face value of all the bonds at the issue date (\$10,000 in our example).
2. A premium paid to the issuer at the issue date (more on this later).
3. An annual interest rate for each of the bonds cited in the proposal. These rates are called the coupon rates and determine the amount of interest the issuer must pay the buyers each year. Suppose that the underwriter proposed the following coupon rates for our example.

MATURITY DATE	RATE (%)
1 year	3
2 years	4
3 years	5

The interest to be paid by the issuer would then be calculated as follows:

$$\text{Year 1} = 2000(.03) + 3000(.04) + 5000(.05) = 430$$

$$\text{Year 2} = 3000(.04) + 5000(.05) = 370$$

$$\text{Year 3} = 5000(.05) = 250$$

Historically, the net interest cost (NIC) is the criterion most often employed by the issuer in evaluating bids. The NIC is the sum of interest payments over all years for all maturities minus any premium offered by the underwriter. The winning bid is the one with the minimum NIC. The time value of money is ignored in calculating the NIC. Even though the bid with the lowest NIC may not be best for the issuer when present values are considered, this is immaterial to the underwriter since the bid is evaluated according to the NIC.

The profit of the underwriter is the difference between what the buyer pays him and what he (the underwriter) pays the issuer. That is,

Profit = (total selling price to public) – (total face value + premium)

Thus, in preparing a bid the underwriter must

1. Determine the coupon (interest) amounts the issuer will pay on each maturity, and
2. For each maturity, estimate the selling price (i.e., the underwriter's selling price to the public) for bonds of each coupon rate. (The selling price for bonds need not be the same as the face value of the bond.)

The underwriter has two conflicting objectives. Higher coupon rates imply the bonds have a higher selling price to the public and hence more money to the underwriter, which can be used both as premium and profit. Thus the coupon rates must be set large enough so that if the bid is accepted the underwriter makes a reasonable profit. But higher coupon rates affect the interest the issuer will have to pay (higher coupon rates imply more interest) as well as the premium that the underwriter can offer the issuer. This trade-off between premium and interest may imply that lower coupon rates will decrease the cost to the issuer and hence increase the chances of winning the bid.

The approach we take is to incorporate the underwriter's profit as a constraint and then minimize NIC (the cost to the issuer) in order to maximize the chances of winning the bid.

Data for a Specific Scenario

The city of Dogpatch is going to issue municipal bonds in order to raise revenue for civic improvements. Sealed bids will be received until 5:00 P.M. on February 7, 1998 for \$5,000,000 in bonds dated March 1, 1998. The bid represents an offer from the underwriter to (1) pay \$5,000,000 to Dogpatch, (2) pay an additional (specified) premium to Dogpatch, and (3) include an interest schedule that Dogpatch will pay to the bond holders. The interest is payable on March 1, 1999, and annually thereafter.

The bonds become due (i.e., Dogpatch must pay off the face value, without option for prior payment) on March 1 in each of the maturity years in Table 1 below and in the amounts

TABLE 1 Bond Face Amounts

YEAR (MATURITY)	AMOUNT (\$000)
2000	250
2001	425
2002	1025
2003	1050
2004	1100
2005	1150

TABLE 2 Estimating Selling Price ($000)

FACE VALUE	250	425	1025	1050	1100	1150
Percent	2000	2001	2002	2003	2004	2005
3	245	418	1015	1040	1080	1130
$3\frac{1}{4}$	248	422	1016	1042	1084	1135
$3\frac{1}{2}$	250	423	1017	1044	1085	1140
$3\frac{3}{4}$	251	424	1025	1046	1090	1150
4	253	430	1029	1050	1095	1155
$4\frac{1}{4}$	255	435	1035	1055	1096	1160
$4\frac{1}{2}$	256	437	1037	1060	1105	1165
$4\frac{3}{4}$	257	440	1038	1062	1110	1170
5	258	441	1040	1065	1115	1175

indicated. That is, Table 1 indicates Dogpatch's obligation (in terms of principal) to the bondholders.

The bonds will be awarded to the bidder on the basis of the minimum NIC. No bid will be considered with an interest rate greater than 5% or less than 3% per annum. Bidders must specify interest rates in multiples of one-quarter of one percent per annum. Not more than three different interest rates will be considered (a repeated rate will not be considered a different rate). The same rate must apply to all bonds of the same maturity.

Estimating selling prices of various maturities as a function of coupon rates is a complicated process depending upon available markets and various parameters. For the sake of this example, take the data in Table 2 as given. Note that the underwriter may sell bonds to the public at more or less than the face value.

Example (A Sample Bid)

Assume an underwriter establishes the coupon rates for each maturity as in Table 3.

Given these coupon rates the bonds would be sold to the public (see estimates in Table 2) for $5,050,000. Assume the underwriter's spread or profit requirement is $8 per $1,000 of face value of bonds. For a $5,000,000 issue this will be $40,000. Thus the premium paid to Dogpatch by the underwriter for this bid is

$$\begin{aligned}\text{premium} &= \$5{,}050{,}000 - \$5{,}000{,}000 - \$40{,}000 \\ &= \$10{,}000\end{aligned}$$

TABLE 3 Example Coupon Rates

MATURITY	COUPON RATE (%)	TOTAL INTEREST ($000)
2000	3	15.00
2001	$4\frac{1}{2}$	57.375
2002	$4\frac{3}{4}$	194.75
2003	$4\frac{1}{2}$	236.25
2004	$4\frac{1}{2}$	297.00
2005	$4\frac{1}{2}$	362.25

Questions

1. Calculate Dogpatch's NIC for the example.
2. Suppose, as in Table 2, the underwriter has a choice between selling a 2000 bond at $4\frac{1}{4}$% for $255,000 or a 2000 bond at $4\frac{1}{2}$% for $256,000. Just in terms of minimizing NIC (ignoring other possible constraints), which would the underwriter prefer to offer? Suppose that the underwriter's profit is the same in both cases.
3. In Table 2, consider the 2000 maturity at 5%. Suppose that you as an investor can with certainty receive 5% interest on money invested on March 1, 1999. What compounded yearly rate of interest would you be receiving if you pay $258,000 for the 2000 bond and use the above investment opportunity with your first receipt of interest?
4. Formulate a constrained optimization symbolic model for solving the underwriter's model. This formulation should minimize the NIC of the underwriter's bid subject to the underwriter receiving an $8 margin per $1,000 of face amount and the other constraints given. Be very clear and concise in defining any notation you use, and indicate the purpose of each constraint in your formulation.
5. Develop a constrained optimization model in Excel and optimize it using Solver.
6. Bid requests often include additional constraints. Assume that one such additional restriction is that coupon rates must be nondecreasing with maturity. Add the necessary constraint(s) to the spreadsheet model to enforce this condition. You do not need to resolve with Solver.
7. Next assume that the maximum allowed difference between the highest and lowest coupon rates is 1%. Add the necessary constraint(s) to the symbolic model to enforce this condition. You do not need to resolve with Solver.
8. Refer to your formulation in Question 4. If the bonds (regardless of maturity and coupon value) could never

be sold in excess of face value, will your formulation have a feasible solution? Why or why not?

9. Assume your formulation in Question 4 has a feasible solution. Is it possible that the addition of the constraint(s) from Question 6 or the constraint(s) from Question 7 (or both taken together) make the formulation infeasible?

A Word of Advice: One danger of misformulating a rather large integer programming model, and then attempting to optimize it, is that you may waste a great deal of computer time (this of course could be true of any large model). Your solution to Question 5, using a correctly formulated model, should take no more than a few minutes on a Pentium-level PC.

Case Study Cash Flow Matching

In some applications, a stream of cash flows must be generated over a planning horizon. For example, in a personal injury lawsuit, the plaintiff must be compensated for future medical expenses or lost wages or both. Both parties often agree on an initial lump sum that is "equivalent in value" to the cash flows over time. What is an equivalent lump sum? The plaintiff, who wants to maximize the size of the payment, argues that future interest will be low so that a large lump sum is needed. The defendant argues that interest rates will be high and thus a smaller lump sum is required.

One resolution is to purchase a portfolio of bonds so that the return from the bonds satisfies the required cash flow. A bond offers a guaranteed annual payment (determined by the coupon rate) and its face value at maturity. Thus, it is clear how much each bond will contribute to meeting the cash flow. The current price of the bonds is also known and thus the "lump payment model" becomes one of finding the lowest-cost bond portfolio that will satisfy the agreed-upon cash flow.

It is reasonable to think of many pension fund planning models as cash flow matching models. In this model a corporation or a union has an obligation to meet the cash requirements of a pension fund over some planning horizon. The goal is to purchase a minimum-cost, low-risk portfolio that generates an income stream to match the cash outflow requirements of the pension plan.

Consider the following small but conceptually realistic cash flow model. The cash requirements (in millions) for the next five years are shown in Table 1.

The investment committee is considering five types of low-risk investments: an insured money market fund paying an annual rate of 5% and the four types of AAA bonds described in Table 2.

Assume that all cash transactions associated with investments occur on January 1 of each year. Table 3 shows the cash flows for each bond.

Note that in the year the bond matures the return is equal to the sum of the coupon plus the face value of the bond. Also note that bond 3 is a zero coupon bond, that is, it does not pay any interest until maturity.

There is also an opportunity for borrowing in most cash flow matching models. In this model assume that the pension fund managers have the opportunity to borrow as much cash

TABLE 1 Cash Requirements

YEAR	2000	2001	2002	2003	2004
Cash Requirement	10	11	12	14	15

TABLE 2 (Values in $000,000s)

BOND	CURRENT COST	COUPON (YEARLY)	YEARS TO MATURITY	FACE VALUE
1	.97	.04	1	1.00
2	.947	.05	2	1.00
3	.79	.00	3	1.00
4	.829	.03	4	1.00

TABLE 3 (Values in $000,000s)

BOND	2000	2001	2002	2003	2004
1	–.970	1.040			
2	–.947	.050	1.050		
3	–.790	.000	.000	1.000	
4	–.829	.030	.030	.030	1.030

as they want at an annual rate of 13%. Loans are made for one year only, that is, a loan made in 2000 must be paid off in 2001. However, another one-year loan could be taken out immediately.

In the real world, cash flows (both in and out) occur at various times during the year. In the model it is assumed that:

1. All inflows (returns from the bonds, money invested in the money market fund as well as interest earned on these funds, funds borrowed during the year under consideration, and the original lump sum) are available on the morning of January 1.
2. All cash outflows (the cash required by the pension fund, payment of debt and interest from the previous year, deposits in the money market account) occur in the afternoon of January 1.

These assumptions make it possible to keep the proper relationship between the various cash flows. For example:

1. In 2000 the cash outflow needed by the pension fund, as well as any purchases of bonds or money to deposit in the money market account, must come from the original lump sum payment or from funds borrowed in 2000.
2. Debt and interest that arise from borrowing in 2000 can be paid for by borrowing funds in 2001.

Questions

1. Plot the yield curve for the four bonds listed in Table 2. To do this you must first determine for each bond the interest rate that makes the present value of the cash flows for that bond equal to zero. This is accomplished with a financial calculator or the Excel IRR() function. Now plot the interest rate as a function of the maturity of the bond for the four bonds.
2. Comment on the general shape of the function you plotted in Question 1. What does this shape suggest about the preferences and expectations of lenders? About borrowers? Does the yield curve have to have this shape? What preferences and expectations of borrowers and lenders might cause it to look otherwise?
3. Assume your goal is to minimize the original lump-sum payment. Formulate an MILP to solve this model. Assume that only an integral number of bonds may be purchased and that these purchases are made in January 2000. In the symbolic model define the decision variables as follows:

   L = initial lump sum required

   B_i = amount borrowed in year i

   M_i = amount invested in money market fund in year i

   X_i = number of bonds of type i purchased in 2000

   C_i = cash not utilized in year i

   Assume that it is not possible to borrow funds in 2004, the fifth year. In your formulation, there should be a balance constraint in each year that sources of funds must equal uses of funds.
4. In a real world, the data in Table 1 would in fact be estimates of future requirements since these would not generally be known with certainty. What other significant assumptions were made in creating this model?
5. Will there always be a feasible answer for general models of the type constructed in Question 3? That is, consider the model in Question 3 with any set of cash demands and rates of return. Will there always be a feasible solution? Explain.
6. Use Solver to optimize the model you formulated in Question 3.
7. Solve the model using the following heuristic procedure:
   (a) Solve the model from Question 3 as an LP.
   (b) Round the number of bonds to the next largest integer.
   (c) Fix the integer variables at the levels in (b) and optimize the model as an LP.
8. Calculate the value of the following ratio: OV Question 7(c)/OV Question 6. Do you expect this ratio to be greater or less than 1? Why? What does the value of this ratio suggest about solving real (i.e., much bigger) cash flow matching models?
9. What interpretation do you give to the shadow prices produced by the LP solution in Question 7(a)?
10. Comment on the following statement: "The way to minimize the initial lump sum is to limit your purchase of bonds to only the bond with the highest rate of return."
11. Comment on the following statement: "If the rate of return on the money market fund exceeds the rate of return on all the bonds, then there is an optimal solution in which the money market fund is the only investment used."

Case Study Ebel Mining (E)[1]

"I thought I made it clear in our last meeting," exclaims Truman Hardy, Ebel's chief mining supervisor. "I told you before that each 'day' a mine runs is actually a 24-hour day and we are limited by union contracts to no more than a five day per week operation. And we need to tell everyone in advance, if we will be running a mine for less than five days in any week. But I never dreamed you would recommend we run a mine for a noninteger number of days a week. What planet are you from? Don't you know that no United Mine Workers union leader will allow us to schedule and pay workers for part of a day? And I am certainly not going to authorize the cost of a full day's operation by just rounding any fractional amounts up. That would give the miners a free ride of pay for no work, and that won't happen as long as I am running these mines!"

After catching his breadth, Truman continues, "Take that previous spreadsheet solution of yours giving the four-week plan and re-do it to (1) give me a cheaper 4-week schedule than the one you found earlier [See Ebel Mining (D) in Chapter 5.] while at the same time, (2) make sure that schedule has no fractional days of operation of any mine."

Questions

1. What is your response to Truman's request that you find a cheaper schedule than that found in Ebel (D) while at the same time eliminating fractional mine days from every weekly schedule in the month? Explain to him the rationale for your answer.
2. Adapt your four-week LP model from Ebel Mining (D) to handle his request for the number of days both mines operate each week to be an integer.
3. Finally, revisit the issue of disposing of any nondelivered ore. Are your recommendations concerning any undelivered ore disposal altered by Truman's new integer requirements?
4. Explain your model changes, the resulting mine schedule, blending, reclassify, and inventory decisions for each week, and any relevant shadow price information in a brief executive summary memo to Ebel management.

References

Ranga Anbil, Eric Gelman, Bruce Patty, and Rajan Tanga, "Recent Advances in Crew-Pairing Optimization at American Airlines," *Interfaces*, 21, no. 1 (1991): 62–74.

Thomas Spencer III, Anthony Brigandi, Dennis Dargon, and Michael Sheehan, "AT&T's Telemarketing Site Selection System Offers Customer Support," *Interfaces*, 20, no. 1 (Jan.–Feb. 1990).

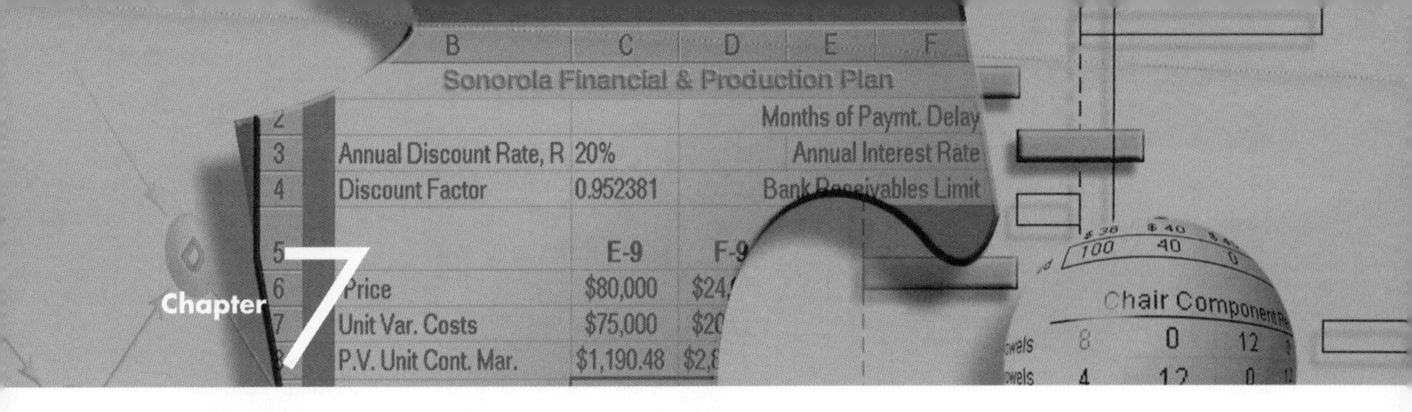

NONLINEAR OPTIMIZATION

CHAPTER OUTLINE

APPLICATION CAPSULE **Asset and Liability Management at Pacific Financial Asset Management Company**

Trying to decide what investments are desirable depends upon the particular situation of the investor. A person who is close to retirement should accept less risk than a young person who is setting aside money for her retirement in 40 years. Another difference is that investors who must pay taxes on their gains should be distinguished from institutional investors like insurance companies or pension funds who are generally tax exempt. Measuring the risks and rewards of various alternative investment strategies depends on individual circumstances.

In order to build a more customized investment portfolio model, Pacific Financial Asset Management Company (PFAMC) developed a new model that extended the traditional financial model for assets only by Markowitz and Sharpe to include both assets and liabilities. The critical issue is to balance the risk and rewards of the strategic investment decisions in concert with the movements of the projected liabilities. The model developed by PFAMC is a nonlinear optimization system. The aim of the integrative asset-liability system is the preservation of the firm's wealth as measured by the market value of the assets minus the present value of the liabilities. The model has been implemented on a personal computer so that it can be interactive with the investor and thus account for the individual circumstances and risk preference. For example, large institutional investors must decide how much money to invest in each of several broad asset categories—stocks, bonds, real estate, and so on. This decision is their most important strategic planning decision.

Although this new approach requires greater information, its recommendations are more closely tailored to the investor's needs and circumstances. Both PFAMC and its clients have been very pleased with its results. (See Mulvey.)

7.1 INTRODUCTION TO NONLINEAR OPTIMIZATION MODELS

In many business and economics problems the functions or mathematical relationships involved are not all linear. In fact, it is probably true that the real-world problems that fit the strict mold of linearity are the exception rather than the rule. As a simple illustration, in a linear model, price is usually assumed to be a given constant, say p, and sales, the quantity to be sold, is a variable x that is assumed to be independent of price. Hence, revenue is given by px, and we say that revenue is proportional to price. This linearity assumption was the cornerstone of our analysis in Chapters 3 through 6 because it leads to a simple model structure. In reality, however, price may be a variable, and quantity of sales (demand) might be dependent on price. This dependency is expressed by writing sales = $f(p)$, where f is some specified (nonconstant) function of p. Thus, revenue would be given by

$$\text{revenue} = \text{price} \times \text{sales} = p \times f(p)$$

which is nonlinear in the variable p. In this case a model to find the price level that maximizes revenue would be a nonlinear model. In general, some of the prominent (and not necessarily distinct) reasons for nonlinearity are

1. *Nonproportional relationships* (in the example above, revenue is not proportional to price, for, depending on the specific form of $f(p)$, price may increase and revenue decrease);
2. *Nonadditive relationships* (e.g., when two chemicals are added together the resulting volume need not be the sum of the two added volumes); and
3. *Efficiencies or inefficiencies of scale* (e.g., when too many workers try to work on manufacturing the same product they begin to get into each other's way and the yield per worker will decrease, rather than remain constant[1]).

In short, any number of physical, structural, biological, economic, and logical relationships may be responsible for the appearance of nonlinearity in a model. It must be repeated

[1] Note that this diseconomy of scale situation leads to a nonproportional relationship between total yield and number of workers.

at the outset that, although nonlinear phenomena are common, nonlinear models are considerably more difficult to optimize than linear models. For example, in contrast to LP, you cannot assume that Solver's nonlinear optimization procedure will always find the optimal solution for all nonlinear models. Combine this difficulty with the fact that linear models, in many contexts, provide *good approximations* to nonlinear models, and you can understand the popularity of linear models, such as LP.

As we know, a model is not the real world. It is an abstract representation of reality. The important point for the modeler is to know when a linearized version provides an *adequate* representation of the nonlinear world. The answer to such a judgmental question comes with experimentation and much experience, and even then only imperfectly and often without consensus. In this chapter we want to address those situations where nonlinear programming models are deemed to be required. Our objective is to provide some understanding of the tools and concepts necessary to deal with nonlinear programming models, and as will become apparent, some knowledge of calculus is required for complete understanding.

The chapter is organized as follows. For those of you comfortable with calculus, Section 7.2 reviews the facts concerning *unconstrained* optimization in several decision variables. Then we give a descriptive and geometric introduction to constrained nonlinear optimization. Sections 7.3 through 7.6 deal with NLP (nonlinear programming) formulation and solution using Solver. Following this, in Section 7.7 we loosely define the concept of concave and convex programs and discuss in a qualitative way the kinds of nonlinear problems that can be routinely solved and those that cannot. Next, in Section 7.8 we introduce the Evolutionary Solver, a special type of optimizer based upon principles of genetics that can be applied to otherwise intractable NLP models. We then focus in Section 7.9 upon a particular class of NLP called *quadratic* models, which turn out to be relatively easy to optimize. These models have wide application in financial decision making and we give two examples of quadratic models to portfolio optimization. In Section 7.12 we turn to inventory theory, another popular use of NLP. We develop the classic economic order quantity model (EOQ) and then extend it with two examples. Finally, in Section 7.15 we conclude with some notes on implementation of NLP.

7.2 UNCONSTRAINED OPTIMIZATION IN TWO OR MORE DECISION VARIABLES (OPTIONAL)

Let us first consider the case of two decision variables, x_1 and x_2 and a given function $f(x_1, x_2)$. For the case of two decision variables (that is, two independent variables) partial derivatives from calculus are used to describe local or global optima of f. We shall use the notation f_{x_i} for first partial derivative, $f_{x_i x_i}$ for second partial derivative, and so on. Any point (e.g., values for x_1 and x_2) at which all first partial derivatives vanish is called a **stationary point**. We have the following *necessary condition* for optimality.

> At a local max or min both partial derivatives must equal zero (i.e., $f_{x_1} = f_{x_2} = 0$). That is, a local maximizer or a local minimizer is always a stationary point.

However, not all stationary points provide maxima and minima. We can employ the so-called second-order (meaning that second derivatives are involved) sufficient condition for optimality, which is somewhat more complicated than the necessary condition. Thus, just as for functions of a single variable, there is a first-order (first derivative) and second-order (involving second derivatives) test that can be applied to locate unconstrained local optima for functions of more than one variable. These tests are called **first-order optimality conditions** and **second-order optimality conditions**. Note that the first-order conditions are necessary; the second-order conditions are sufficient. Also note that the second-order conditions subsume the first-order ones (that is, the second-order conditions assume that x_1^*, x_2^* is a stationary point).

In the absence of some additional properties of the function, such as convexity or concavity, a local (as opposed to global) optimizer is the most that one can generally hope to find. The first-derivative test (the necessary condition) says that the local optima are contained among the stationary points of the function. The second-derivative test (the sufficient condition) allows us to distinguish between local maximizers and minimizers, and points that are neither.

For a differentiable function of n variables, each local optimizer is a stationary point. In order to guarantee that a stationary point is, for example, a local maximizer, second-order sufficiency conditions must be invoked. Although these two types of optimality conditions have theoretic interest, they have, for many nonlinear models in more than two variables, limited *practical relevance.* The reasons are:

1. Setting the first partial derivatives equal to zero gives a system of n equations in n unknowns. Unless this system is linear (i.e., the original function was quadratic) it is not easy to find solutions. It may well be impossible to do by hand.
2. The second-order sufficiency conditions are quite complicated, requiring the evaluation of determinants of certain entries in the matrix of second partial derivatives. Indeed, even in the case of one or two decision variables, if the function f is sufficiently complicated, it may not be possible to hand-solve the optimality conditions, and hence, this approach is not generally viable.

The description above reveals the main role of the first-order necessary conditions in nonlinear optimizers. They are used indirectly, in the sense that they serve as a *termination criterion* for the hill-climbing optimization methods that search for local optima. The second-order sufficiency conditions, for the general problem in n variables, are mainly of theoretic interest, and go beyond the introductory nature of this chapter.

In concluding this section we mention one other important result when maximizing a *concave function.* For a concave function, any stationary point is a global maximizer (for a convex function, any stationary point is a global minimizer). Whereas in the general case an optimized solution could be a local maximizer or minimizer or neither, in the concave case we are guaranteed that any solution is a global maximizer. This fact is important in optimizing quadratic nonlinear models, a topic covered in Section 7.9.

7.3 NONLINEAR OPTIMIZATION: A DESCRIPTIVE GEOMETRIC INTRODUCTION

Specialized optimization software packages, such as Solver, have been developed to find local optima of nonlinear functions involving many decision variables. Often such packages are based on iterative hill-climbing (or hill-descent) methods.[2] In a hill-climbing method for a maximization problem, an initial point is chosen, that is, a set of numerical values for the decision variables, and then an uphill direction is determined by approximating the initial rate of change in all directions (the first partial derivative) of the objective function at that initial point. Intuitively, for unconstrained optimization, the method moves from the initial point, along a line in an **optimal value** (OV) increasing or "uphill" direction, to the highest point that can be attained on that line. Then a new uphill direction is defined, and the procedure is continued. The method terminates when the approximated rates of further OV change in all directions (the first partial derivatives) are close to zero (the first-order conditions are satisfied). Such a point, then, will always be a "local peak" or "local optimum" because in a nonlinear model there may be other, still higher, peaks that would have been reached if the initial starting point had been different. The other local maxima are searched for by initiating the optimizer package to start at a different starting point, that is, a different set of initial values for the decision variables.

[2] The hill-climbing/hill-descent method Solver uses for optimizing nonlinear models, called Generalized Reduced Gradient (GRG), is completely different from the simplex method it uses to optimize an LP model.

The analogy of this approach with mountain climbing is appropriate: depending on where you start hill climbing you may end up reaching the top of a low foothill instead of the tallest mountain. To be more precise with the analogy, you always mountain climb in a dense fog that limits visibility only to the terrain at your feet. Thus, you can detect when you have reached a peak, but have no idea if there is a taller mountain nearby that you might have climbed had you started from a different base camp. Unfortunately in the world of nonlinear hill climbing, there is no "Sherpa guide" nor map of all the terrain to tell you that you started your hill-climbing trek from the wrong spot.

Nonlinear optimization, up to this point, has focused on *unconstrained* optimization. More typically, for management-oriented decision making, we are interested in optimizing an objective function subject to constraints. These constraints are in the form of equalities and/or inequalities, just as in the case of LP modeling, except linearity of the constraints is not assumed in this case. Thus, the general NLP symbolic model can be written in the form illustrated below where f and the g_i's and the h_j's are just symbols for complicated nonlinear functions of the decision variables, x, to compute the OV and each constraint's LHS, respectively. For nonlinear models they substitute for the simpler =SUMPRODUCT() left-hand-side constraint functions that sufficed for the linear models of previous chapters.

$$\begin{aligned} &\text{Max } f(x_1, x_2, \ldots, x_n) && \text{(objective)} \\ &\text{s.t.} \quad \left.\begin{aligned} g_1(x_1, \ldots, x_n) &= b_1 \\ g_2(x_1, \ldots, x_n) &= b_2 \\ &\vdots \\ g_m(x_1, \ldots, x_n) &= b_m \end{aligned}\right\} && m \text{ equality constraints} \\ &\qquad \left.\begin{aligned} h_1(x_1, \ldots, x_n) &\le r_1 \\ h_2(x_1, \ldots, x_n) &\le r_2 \\ &\vdots \\ h_k(x_1, \ldots, x_n) &\le r_k \end{aligned}\right\} && k \text{ inequality constraints} \end{aligned}$$

GRAPHICAL ANALYSIS

Just as with LP, we can use two-dimensional geometry to gain insight into NLPs. For example, let us use graphical analysis to optimize the symbolic model

$$\begin{aligned} \text{Max } \; & x_1 - x_2 \\ \text{s.t.} \quad & -x_1^2 + x_2 \ge 1 \\ & x_1 + x_2 \le 3 \\ & -x_1 + x_2 \le 2 \\ & x_1 \ge 0, x_2 \ge 0 \end{aligned}$$

Note that everything in this model is linear except for the first constraint. A model is called nonlinear if at least one of the constraint functions or the objective function or both are nonlinear. Therefore, the model above is properly termed a **nonlinear program (NLP)**.

The Feasible Region In order to use the graphical approach to optimize this model, we proceed just as we did in LP. First we plot the set of points that simultaneously satisfy *all* the constraints. This set of points is called, just as in LP, the *constraint set*, or the *feasible*

FIGURE 7.1

Graphical Solution to Example Nonlinear Model

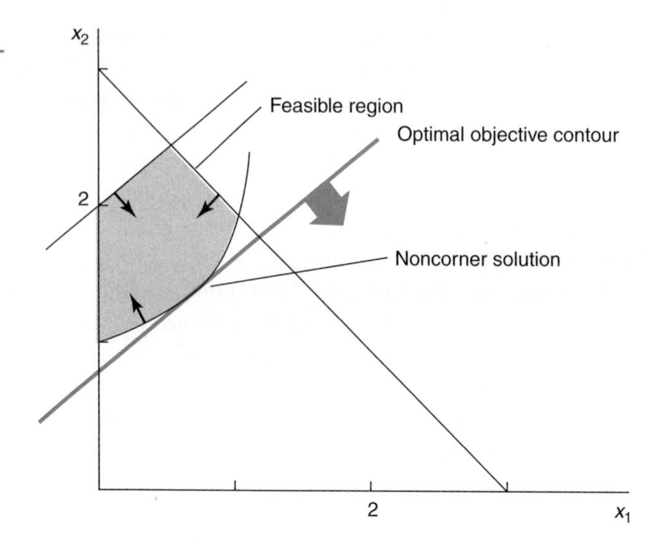

region. This set represents the allowable decisions. In order to find an allowable decision that maximizes the objective function, we find the "most uphill" (i.e., highest-valued) *contour* of the objective function that still touches the constraint set. The point at which it touches will be an optimal solution (often more simply referred to as a solution) to the model.[3] Figure 7.1 shows the graphical solution to the model presented above. Note that the negative sign on x_2 in the model's objective function makes the optimizing direction to the "southeast."

You can see in Figure 7.1 that the nonlinear constraint puts curvature into the boundary of the constraint set. The feasible set is no longer a polyhedron (i.e., the flat-sided, faceted, feasible region defined by linear inequalities) as is the case with LP models. Recall that for LP models, the graphical analysis allowed us to identify the binding constraints at an optimal corner, and then the *exact solution* was obtained by solving (in the two-decision variable case) two equations in two unknowns. In general this method does not work in the nonlinear models. As shown in Figure 7.1, there is only one binding constraint and the solution is *not* at a corner intersection of constraints.

Noncorner Optima Another example of an NLP is shown in Figure 7.2, which shows a *hypothetical* nonlinear inequality constrained maximization model. In this figure the constraints are all linear, and hence the constraint set is a standard LP polyhedron. The objective function, however, is nonlinear, and again it is seen that the solution does not occur at a corner. In fact, for some nonlinear objective functions the optimal solution may not even lie on the boundary of the feasible region but could occur in the feasible region's interior. Of course, for some NLP models a solution *could* appear on the boundary or at a corner, but the important point is that this property is not guaranteed, as it is in the linear model.

This fact has significant implications for Solver's optimization methods for NLPs. It means that in the nonlinear case, Solver cannot use a "corner-searching" method such as the simplex method it uses for finding a solution to LP models. This restriction enormously complicates Solver's optimization procedure. The substantial ramifications of this for NLP modeling will be taken up in the next three sections.

[3] Note the precision in terminology of "a" solution instead of "the" solution. This is necessary because of the potential for more than one local optima in NLP models.

FIGURE 7.2

Noncorner Solution to NLP

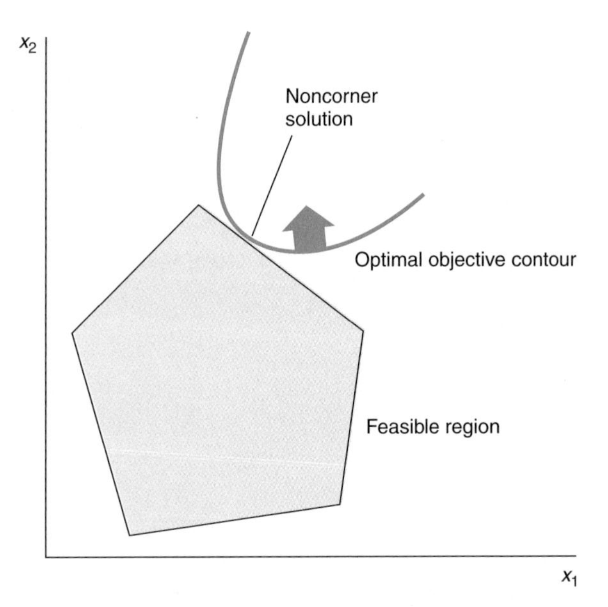

COMPARISONS BETWEEN LP AND NLP

There are several instructive parallels between LP and NLP. For example, the following four statements hold *in either type of model.*

1. Increasing (decreasing) the RHS on a $\leq$ ($\geq$) constraint loosens the constraint. This cannot contract and may expand the constraint set.
2. Increasing (decreasing) the RHS on a $\geq$ ($\leq$) constraint tightens the constraint. This cannot expand and may contract the constraint set.
3. Loosening a constraint cannot hurt and may help the optimal objective value.
4. Tightening a constraint cannot help and may hurt the optimal objective value.

Another concept that is common to both LP and NLP is the notion of changes in the objective function value (OV) as a right-hand side changes, with all other data held fixed. In LP we defined (see Chapter 4) the *shadow price* on a specified constraint to be *the rate of change in OV as the RHS of that constraint increases*, with all other data unchanged. For historical reasons, in NLP models this rate of change is called the **Lagrange multiplier** as opposed to the shadow price, but the meaning is nearly the same.

The Lagrange Multiplier There is one important property of shadow price associated with LP that a Lagrange multiplier in the NLP context will not generally share. Recall that in an LP the shadow price is constant for a range of values for the RHS parameter of interest. It can be easily illustrated that in the NLP context this property does not generally hold true. As an illustration, consider the following simple NLP:

$$\text{Max } x^2$$
$$\text{s.t.} \quad x \leq b$$
$$x \geq 0$$

In order to maximize x^2, we want to make x as large as possible. Thus, the optimal solution is $x^* = b$, and the optimal value of the objective function, OV, is $(x^*)^2 = b^2$. Thus, you can see that the OV is a function of b; that is, $\text{OV}(b) = b^2$.

Since the definition of a shadow price (Lagrange multiplier) is the rate of change in the OV as the RHS, b, is increased, from basic calculus we know that the rate of change of this

FIGURE 7.3

Local and Global Solutions

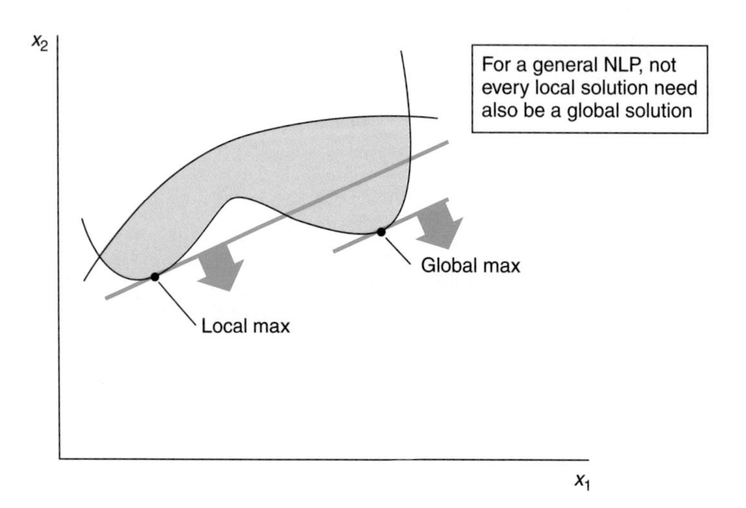

OV function as b increases is the derivative of OV(b), namely $2b$. In other words, the Lagrange multiplier is *not* constant for a range of values of the RHS, b. It varies continuously with b, as might be expected.[4]

Local Versus Global Solutions Another important difference between LP and NLP has to do with *global* versus *local solutions.* In an LP, it is always true that there cannot be a local solution that is not also global. This is not usually true for general NLP models. In other words, such models may have local as well as global solutions. This is illustrated by the hypothetical Max model in Figure 7.3 in which the uphill direction is again to the "southeast." In this figure the point identified as "Local max" is termed a *local constrained maximizer* because the value of the objective function at this point is no smaller than at its neighboring feasible points.

The point identified as "Global max" is termed a *global constrained maximizer* because the value of the objective function at this point is no smaller than at *all other* feasible points. In general for NLPs, additional conditions must be imposed upon the model, called convexity and concavity conditions, that must be satisfied to guarantee that a local constrained optimizer is also global. These properties will be defined in Section 7.7. In the absence of these properties it is generally *not* possible for you or Solver to know whether a given NLP solution is a local or a global maximizer.

EQUALITY-CONSTRAINED NLPs

Many nonlinear models in business and economics are of the following form, where again f and the m inequality g_i constraint functions are just symbols for complicated nonlinear functions of the decision variables, x, to compute the OV and each constraint's LHS, respectively.

$$\text{Maximize (or Minimize) } f(x_1, \ldots, x_n)$$
$$\text{s.t.} \quad g_i(x_1, \ldots, x_n) = b_i, \; i = 1, \ldots, m \; (m \leq n)$$

[4] It may be briefly noted that this same example also serves to illustrate that the optimal value for an NLP max problem can exhibit increasing marginal returns. This can never happen in LP (i.e., the OV for an LP max model *always* exhibits nonincreasing marginal returns).

That is, the goal is to maximize or minimize an objective function in n variables subject to a set of m *equality* constraints. Here are three examples.

Example 1 A manufacturer can make a product on either of two machines. Let x_1 denote the quantity made on machine 1, and x_2 the amount on machine 2. Let

$$a_1x_1 + b_1x_1^2 = \text{cost of producing on machine 1}$$
$$a_2x_2 + b_2x_2^2 = \text{cost of producing on machine 2}$$

Find the values of x_1 and x_2 that minimize total cost subject to the requirement that total production quantity is to be some given number, say R. The symbolic model is

$$\text{Min } a_1x_1 + b_1x_1^2 + a_2x_2 + b_2x_2^2$$
$$\text{s.t.} \quad x_1 + x_2 = R$$

Example 2 (the classic microeconomic model) Let p_1, p_2, and p_3 denote given market prices of three goods, and let B, a specified constant, denote a person's available budget. Let s_1, s_2, and s_3 be given person-specific parameters, and let $x_1^{s_1} + x_2^{s_2} + x_3^{s_3}$ denote the person's "utility" derived from consuming x_1 units of good 1, x_2 units of good 2, and x_3 units of good 3. Determine the consumption mix that maximizes that person's utility subject to his/her budget constraint. The symbolic model is

$$\text{Max } x_1^{s_1} + x_2^{s_2} + x_3^{s_3}$$
$$\text{s.t.} \quad p_1x_1 + p_2x_2 + p_3x_3 = B$$

Example 3 Consider the model

$$\text{Max } x_1 - x_2$$
$$\text{s.t.} \quad -x_1^2 + x_2 = 1$$

The geometric analysis is shown in Figure 7.4. This analysis shows that at the optimal solution the contour of the objective function is tangent to the equality constraint. It also suggests that the optimal solution is approximately $x_1^* = 0.5$ and $x_2^* = 1.25$, as confirmed by the Excel model also shown in Figure 7.4 that gives the optimal Solver solution.

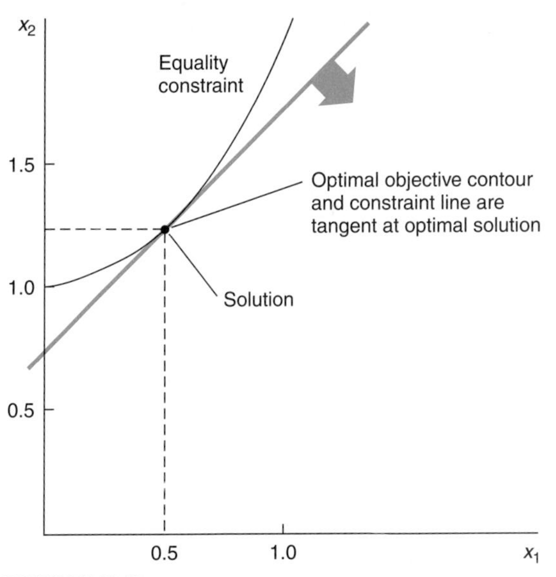

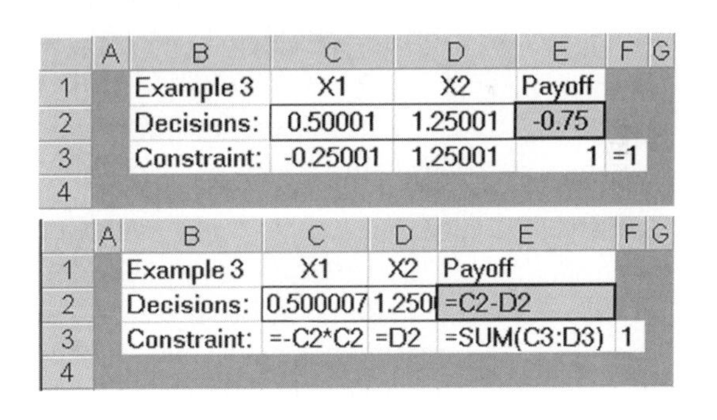

	A	B	C	D	E	F	G
1		Example 3	X1	X2	Payoff		
2		Decisions:	0.50001	1.25001	-0.75		
3		Constraint:	-0.25001	1.25001	1	=1	
4							

	A	B	C	D	E	F	G
1		Example 3	X1	X2	Payoff		
2		Decisions:	0.500007	1.250	=C2-D2		
3		Constraint:	=-C2*C2	=D2	=SUM(C3:D3)	1	
4							

FIGURE 7.4

Graphical and Solver Solution of Example 3

7.4 USING SOLVER FOR NLP MODELS

We have seen from our study of LP models that it is very natural to construct linear models with linear inequality constraints, and optimize them with Solver. Solver also allows us to easily enter and optimize a model that could contain a nonlinear objective or nonlinear constraint functions or both. Remember, however, that Solver uses completely different solution methods for LP and NLP formulations. For LP optimization, Solver uses the simplex method to move from corner to corner in the feasible region. For NLP optimization Solver uses a hill-climbing method based upon a generalized reduced gradient search procedure, called GRG. Summarized, the steps of the procedure are as follows. First, using the initial values of the decision variables specified in Solver's "Changing Cells" field, the procedure finds a feasible solution, that is, a set of decision variable values that satisfies the constraints. Then, from that initial starting point, a direction is computed that most rapidly improves the OV. Movement, that is, changes in values of decision variables, is made in that direction until a constraint boundary is encountered or until the OV no longer improves. Next, a new direction is computed from that new point, and the process is repeated. This continues until no further improvement in any direction occurs, terminating the procedure.

As discussed in Appendix C, an objective function is not even necessary; if one is not given, Solver will try to identify a feasible solution. So, Solver can be used to test for feasibility of the constraint set or to solve systems of linear or nonlinear equations. It is also not necessary to include any constraints, so that Solver can be used to do unconstrained optimization of NLP models.[5]

7.5 EXAMPLE NONLINEAR MODELS

To illustrate NLP concepts, this section will present several more examples. These examples will involve the more general case of inequality constraints.

Marketing Expenditures A restaurant's average daily expense for advertising is \$100, all of which is to be allocated to newspaper ads and radio commercials. Suppose that we let

$$x_1 = \text{average number of dollars per day spent on newspaper ads}$$

$$x_2 = \text{average number of dollars per day spent on radio commercials}$$

In terms of these quantities, the restaurant's total annual cost of running the advertising department, including the daily ad expenses, has been estimated to be the following nonlinear function

$$\text{cost} = C(x_1, x_2) = 20{,}000 - 440x_1 - 300x_2 + 20x_1^2 + 12x_2^2 + x_1x_2$$

Find the restaurant's budget allocation that will minimize this total annual cost while adhering to the desired ad expenditures of \$100 per day. The symbolic model to be optimized is

$$\text{Min } 20{,}000 - 440x_1 - 300x_2 + 20x_1^2 + 12x_2^2 + x_1x_2$$

$$\text{s.t.} \quad x_1 + x_2 = 100 \quad \text{and} \quad x_1 \geq 0, x_2 \geq 0$$

The Solver optimized version of this model is given in Figure 7.5, along with its Sensitivity Report. The Lagrange multiplier indicates that the initial rate of increase in the annual cost of the advertising department would be about \$1,195 for each additional budget dollar spent daily on advertisements.

ECONOMIC INTERPRETATION OF LAGRANGE MULTIPLIERS AND REDUCED GRADIENTS

Lagrange multipliers have an interesting and important economic interpretation. As mentioned previously, the Lagrange multipliers in NLP have almost the same interpretation as the shadow prices in LP. In other words, at optimality the value of the Lagrange multiplier

[5] Unconstrained optimization is meaningful only for nonlinear models.

FIGURE 7.5

Marketing Expenditures Model

TIP: *Solver is susceptible to numerical analysis errors caused by the finite precision of binary computer arithmetic. This is especially a problem for optimizing highly nonlinear models involving numbers spanning a wide range of values. If your model's smallest numbers and largest numbers differ by more than about six or seven orders of magnitude, then Solver's nonlinear GRG solution procedure is susceptible to these errors. Checking Solver Option's "Use Automatic Scaling" box will assist in preventing these errors in many instances. However, as with LP models, that option is not guaranteed to prevent this problem in all cases. It is better to manually rescale very large or very small numbers to avoid this problem in the first place. See Appendix C for further discussion and examples of rescaling numbers in models.*

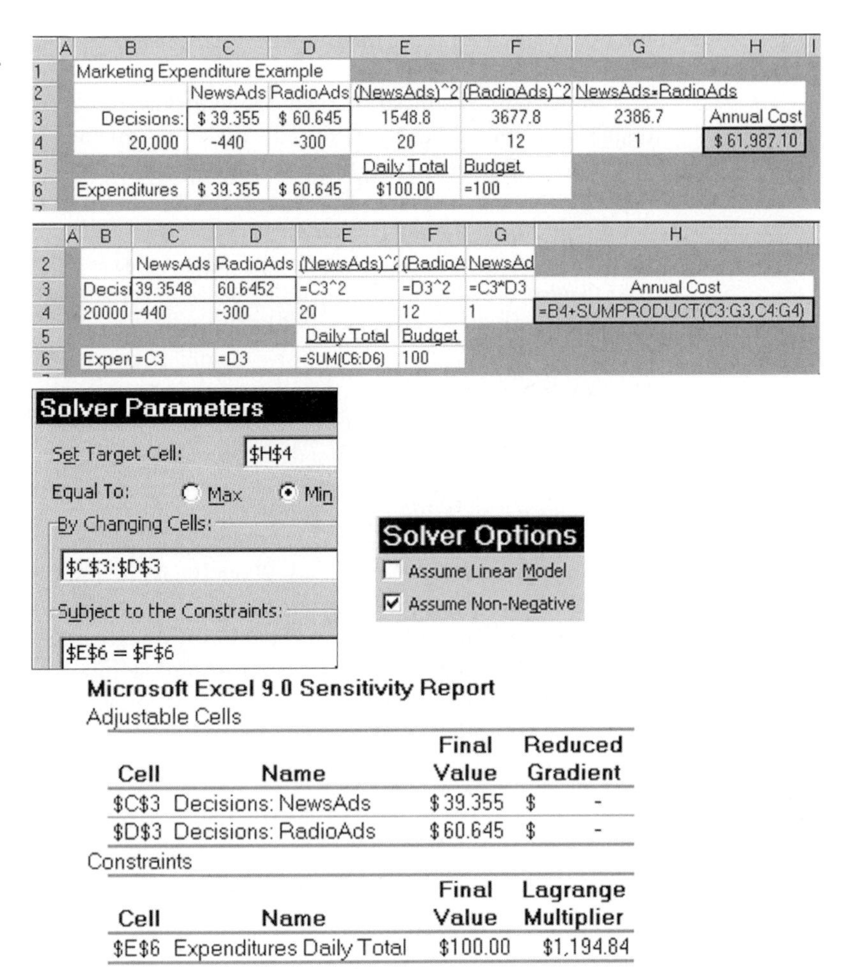

Microsoft Excel 9.0 Sensitivity Report

Adjustable Cells

Cell	Name	Final Value	Reduced Gradient
$C$3	Decisions: NewsAds	$ 39.355	$ -
$D$3	Decisions: RadioAds	$ 60.645	$ -

Constraints

Cell	Name	Final Value	Lagrange Multiplier
$E$6	Expenditures Daily Total	$100.00	$1,194.84

is the *instantaneous* rate of change in the optimal value of the objective function as the *i*th RHS, b_i, is increased, with all other data unchanged. Another way of saying this, in economic terminology, is that the *i*th Lagrange multiplier reflects the marginal value of the *i*th resource. Thus, its units are

$$\frac{\text{units of the objective function}}{\text{units of RHS of constraint } i}$$

Recall Example 1, where a manufacturer wished to minimize total product cost, the objective in dollars, subject to the restriction that the total production, say in tons, of two products had to equal R. The Lagrange multiplier for this restriction then has units of dollars per ton, and its value is the instantaneous marginal cost of producing the Rth unit.

From our earlier discussion, however, the sensitivity numbers have a somewhat more restricted meaning in the NLP Sensitivity Report. For NLP models the Lagrange multiplier of a constraint is the *initial* (i.e., instantaneous) rate of change in the optimal value of the objective function as the RHS of the constraint is increased. Like LP shadow prices, a positive Lagrange multiplier would indicate that increasing the RHS would initially increase the OV. A negative Lagrange multiplier would indicate that increasing the RHS would initially decrease the OV. In contrast to what we've learned about linear programming, it is not possible to say over what range of increase or decrease of the RHS the stated Lagrange multiplier is valid. In fact, the usual case is for the Lagrange multiplier itself to change as soon as the RHS changes, so that the allowable increase and decrease are zero. However, this does not prevent us from using the Lagrange multiplier to *estimate* what will happen to the optimal value if the RHS is changed.

Similarly, the Reduced Gradient values in Solver's NLP Sensitivity Report have an analogous interpretation as the Reduced Cost values for the LP Sensitivity Report covered in Chapter 4. Like reduced cost, the **reduced gradient** of a variable relates to the upper or lower bound constraints on decision variables. A negative reduced gradient for a decision variable indicates that increasing the variable will initially decrease the OV while a positive reduced gradient for a variable indicates that increasing the variable will initially increase the OV. Also, as with a reduced cost, if a decision variable is at its upper bound, the reduced gradient should be nonnegative for the solution to be optimal in a Max model; otherwise, decreasing the variable would improve the objective function value. If a decision variable is at its lower bound, the reduced gradient should be nonpositive in a Max model; otherwise, increasing the variable would improve the objective function. (The opposite conclusions are the case for Min models.) If a decision variable is between its upper and lower bounds, the reduced gradient, like reduced cost, should be zero for the solution to be optimal, as is the case for the model in Figure 7.5.

Astro and Cosmo Revisited When the Astro and Cosmo model was formulated in Chapter 3, it was assumed that the unit profit per TV set was constant over all feasible product mixes. Suppose that in reality more TV sets can be sold only if the selling price is reduced; that is, the company faces downward sloping demand curves for its products. Suppose further that (for relevant daily production values, A and C) these demand curves are quantified by the following equations:

$$PA = 314 - 1.9A + .01A^2$$

$$PC = 243 - .14C$$

where

$$A = \text{daily production of Astros}$$

$$PA = \text{selling price of Astros}$$

$$C = \text{daily production of Cosmos}$$

$$PC = \text{selling price of Cosmos}$$

In the preceding expression, PA is the price that the company must set for Astros in order to sell all of the Astros it produces, and PC is the price set for Cosmos to sell all Cosmos it produces. It follows that the profit per unit now depends on the total production. If the unit variable cost of an Astro is \$210 and the unit variable cost of a Cosmo is \$230, then the total profit is

$$\text{profit} = (PA - 210)A + (PC - 230)C.$$

Adding the other constraints from the original Astro and Cosmo model, the new symbolic NLP model is given below. Note that it contains two equality constraints defining the selling price of each product in terms of its production. One of these constraints is nonlinear. Since PA is a function of A and PC is a function of C, the objective function is also nonlinear.

$$\text{Max } (PA - 210)A + (PC - 230)C$$

$$\begin{aligned}
\text{s.t.} \quad PA &= .01A^2 - 1.9A + 314 && \text{(selling price of Astros)}\\
PC &= -.14C + 243 && \text{(selling price of Cosmos)}\\
A &\le 70 && \text{(capacity of Astro line)}\\
C &\le 50 && \text{(capacity of Cosmo line)}\\
A + 2C &\le 120 && \text{(department A labor hours)}\\
A + C &\le 90 && \text{(department B labor hours)}\\
A, PA, C, PC &\ge 0
\end{aligned}$$

Figure 7.6 presents the Excel model, showing the optimal solution, and the Sensitivity Report. The constraint on labor hours in department A is binding. The Lagrange multiplier on that constraint indicates that initially the OV increases at the rate of about $0.86 per unit of additional labor hours in department A. If we had 10 more hours available in department A, we might estimate that the objective function would increase by 10 × 0.85766, or about $8.58. However, such an estimate would be quite inaccurate, for actually increasing the RHS in cell F13 by 10 and reoptimizing the model gives a new objective function value of $2,061.51 (not shown), an increase of only $5.24. This illustrates the previously stated fact that in NLP models Lagrange multipliers reflect only the *initial* rate of improvement in OV, and this rate may change considerably as the RHS is changed. This is true even when the RHS change is small. The initial, or marginal, information may be useful, but the bottom line is that caution should be used in extrapolating that information. For NLP models, the only reliable way to determine the actual effect of RHS (and other changes) is to use SolverTable to tabulate the changes and use this data to calculate model sensitivities, as was done in the Chapter 5 example in Figure 5.23.

FIGURE 7.6

Solver Solution to NLP Astro and Cosmo Model

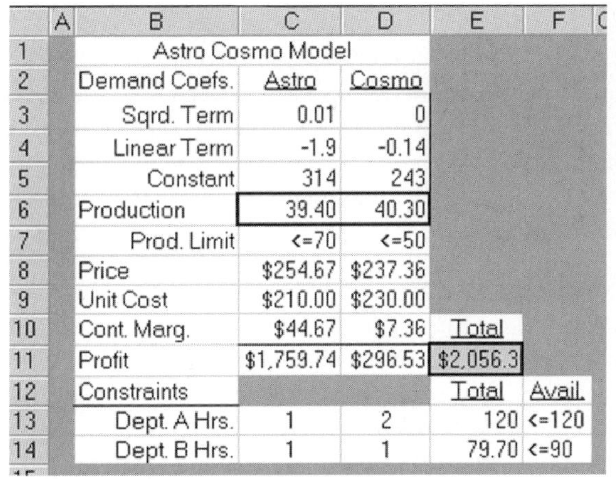

	A	B	C	D	E	F
1		Astro Cosmo Model				
2		Demand Coefs.	Astro	Cosmo		
3		Sqrd. Term	0.01	0		
4		Linear Term	-1.9	-0.14		
5		Constant	314	243		
6		Production	39.40	40.30		
7		Prod. Limit	<=70	<=50		
8		Price	$254.67	$237.36		
9		Unit Cost	$210.00	$230.00		
10		Cont. Marg.	$44.67	$7.36	Total	
11		Profit	$1,759.74	$296.53	$2,056.3	
12		Constraints			Total	Avail.
13		Dept. A Hrs.	1	2	120	<=120
14		Dept. B Hrs.	1	1	79.70	<=90

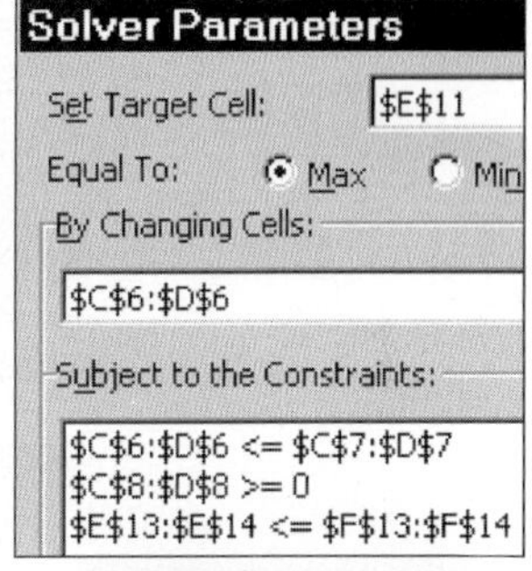

Cell	Formula	Copy To
C8	= C3*C6^2+C4*C6+C5	D8
C11	= C6*C10	D11
E13	= SUMPRODUCT($C$6:$D$6.C13:D13)	E14

Microsoft Excel 9.0 Sensitivity Report

Adjustable Cells

Cell	Name	Final Value	Reduced Gradient
$C$6	Production Astro	39.40	0.00
$D$6	Production Cosmo	40.30	0.00

Constraints

Cell	Name	Final Value	Lagrange Multiplier
$C$8	Price Astro	$254.67	$0.00
$D$8	Price Cosmo	$237.36	$0.00
$E$13	Dept. A Hrs. Total	120	0.85766
$E$14	Dept. B Hrs. Total	79.70	0.00

FIGURE 7.7

Astro/Cosmo Feasible Region

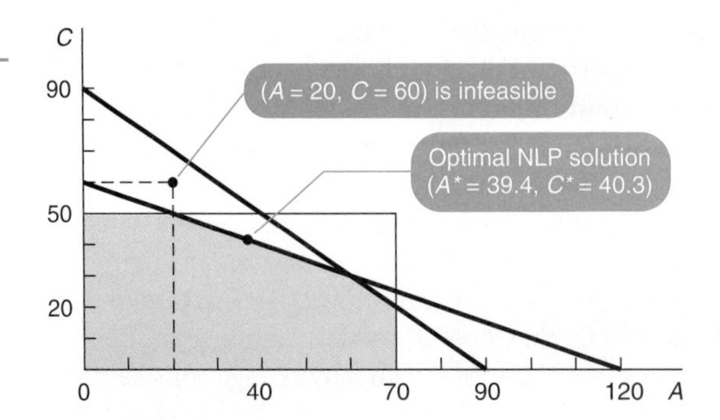

We have learned that in LP models, if an optimal solution exists, some corner of the feasible region must be optimal. Figure 7.7 shows that for the Astro and Cosmo NLP model the optimal solution does not occur at a corner of the feasible region, though it is on the boundary. In fact, for different demand curves, the optimal solution may not even be on the boundary of the feasible region.

OPTIMALITY IN NLPs

In LP models we have become accustomed to looking at the optimal solution produced by Solver and being confident that we do indeed have the optimal solution. Life is not so simple with NLPs. Solver might stop at a solution that is not optimal, or it might stop at an optimal solution that is a local rather than a global optimum. You must be aware of these possibilities and be prepared to take appropriate action. These ideas are illustrated by the following example.

Gulf Coast Oil Model Chapters 3 and 5 presented examples of a blending requirement that was formulated as an LP. Some blending requirements, however, require a nonlinear formulation. Consider the case of Gulf Coast Oil that blends gasoline from three components: Domestic Blend, Foreign Blend, and an octane Additive used only in Premium gasoline. Foreign Blend is itself a blending of two sources. Foreign Blend is transported monthly to Gulf Coast Oil in the single 8,000,000-gallon storage compartment of a large tanker. Because the oil purchased from the two sources loses its separate identities when "pooled" into the storage compartment of the tanker, the model is called a *pooling model.* As we shall see, this pooling process is responsible for introducing nonlinearities into the model. Octane numbers, refiner cost per gallon, and availability information for each component are given in Table 7.1.

Gulf Coast Oil must decide how many gallons of Regular, Midgrade, and Premium gasoline to blend each month, given that it must honor minimum supply contracts of 100,000 gallons of each type of gasoline. Each gasoline is subject to a minimum octane

Table 7.1

Component Characteristics

COMPONENT	OCTANE NO.	COST PER GALLON	AVAILABILITY (000s GAL./MONTH)
Domestic Blend	85	$0.65	10,000
Foreign Blend			
Source 1	93	$0.80	*
Source 2	97	$0.90	*
Premium Additive	900	$30	50

* Because of the way Gulf Coast Oil obtains Source 1 and Source 2, no more than 8,000,000 gallons of Source 1 *plus* Source 2 may be obtained per month.

Table 7.2

Gasoline Characteristics

	MINIMUM OCTANE NO.	WHOLESALE PRICE PER GALLON
Regular	87	$1.18
Midgrade	89	$1.25
Premium	94	$1.40

requirement. The octane number of a blend is the weighted average of the octane numbers of its components where the weights are the fraction of each component in the blend. Data on minimum octane numbers and selling prices of gasoline to wholesale dealers are given in Table 7.2. The following decision variables are used in the formulation:

R = thousand gallons of Regular gasoline produced

M = thousand gallons of Midgrade gasoline produced

P = thousand gallons of Premium gasoline produced

D = thousand gallons of Domestic Blend purchased

A = thousand gallons of Premium Additive purchased

RD = thousand gallons of Domestic Blend in Regular gasoline

RF = thousand gallons of Foreign Blend in Regular gasoline

MD = thousand gallons of Domestic Blend in Midgrade gasoline

MF = thousand gallons of Foreign Blend in Midgrade gasoline

PD = thousand gallons of Domestic Blend in Premium gasoline

PF = thousand gallons of Foreign Blend in Premium gasoline

Taking account of the pooling nature of the problem requires three additional decision variables:

$S1$ = thousand gallons purchased from Foreign Source 1

$S2$ = thousand gallons purchased from Foreign Source 2

OCT = octane number of pooled Foreign Blend

The octane number is a weighted average of the octane's from the two foreign sources determined by the following nonlinear equation:

$$OCT = \frac{93S1 + 97S2}{S1 + S2} \quad \text{or} \quad OCT(S1 + S2) = 93S1 + 97S2$$

Note that the LP trick used in previous models of multiplying both sides by the denominator to obtain a linear equation is not sufficient for this case. The expression above is still nonlinear after clearing the denominator because OCT is a decision variable, and thus, the left side is nonlinear because it contains products of decision variables.

The symbolic model is given below (gasoline is measured in thousands of gallons). Note that the true decision variables are RD, RF, MD, MF, PD, PF, A, $S1$, and $S2$. All other variables can be interpreted as consequential variables. Also note that the minimum octane constraints are nonlinear.

$$\text{Max } 1.18R + 1.25M + 1.40P - .65D - .8S1 - .9S2 - 30A$$

$$\begin{aligned}
\text{s.t.} \quad R &= RD + RF && \text{(composition of Regular gasoline)} \\
M &= MD + MF && \text{(composition of Midgrade gasoline)} \\
P &= PD + PF + A && \text{(composition of Premium gasoline)} \\
D &= RD + MD + PD && \text{(total Domestic Blend used)} \\
RF + MF + PF &= S1 + S2 && \text{(uses must equal supply of Foreign Blend)}
\end{aligned}$$

The next four constraints are the nonlinear aspects of the model.

$85RD + OCT^{*}RF \geq 87R$	(min octane number for Regular gasoline)
$85MD + OCT^{*}MF \geq 89M$	(min octane number for Midgrade gasoline)
$85PD + OCT^{*}PF + 900A \geq 94P$	(min octane number for Premium gasoline)
$OCT(S1 + S2) = 93S1 + 97S2$	(pooling constraint for foreign sources)
$S1 + S2 \leq 8{,}000$	(tanker capacity for foreign sources)
$D \leq 10{,}000$	(supply limit for Domestic Blend)
$A \leq 50$	(supply limit for Premium Additive)
R, M, and P each ≥ 100	(contract delivery minimums)

All variables are nonnegative.

The Excel model with example decision values is shown in Figure 7.8. The nine decision cells are F2:F3, C6:E7, and E8, that is, the amount of foreign purchases, amount of foreign and domestic purchases into each of the three gasolines, and amount of additive used, respectively. Note that the pooling of foreign purchased oil does not allow specific assignment of Source 1 nor Source 2 gallons to any of the three gasoline types, only the assignment of the pooled Foreign Blend. Also, the additive is used only in Premium gasoline, and this is the reason for the grayed out cells in the middle of the worksheet.

The first two sets of constraints of the Solver dialog refer to the gasoline minimum requirements for octane and quantity produced, respectively. The third constraint forces total Foreign Blend sold in all three gasolines to be equal to Foreign Blend purchased, and the last constraint set limits the gasoline components to be less than available capacities. In addition, the "Assume Non-Negative" option has been checked under Options. The values for the nine decision variables in Figure 7.8 are not feasible, but, nevertheless, Solver will find an initial starting point from them for Solver's GRG NLP optimization procedure.

The first solution found by Solver is given in Figure 7.9. Note that upon stopping Solver reports that it has "converged to the current solution."[6] This message suggests that an optimum has been found; in fact, it has not. Solver *must* state that "all optimality conditions are satisfied" in its Solver Results message for this to be true, that is, that the first-order conditions for an optimum have been satisfied.[7]

The Solver Results message actually means that Solver has stopped its search because the rate of change in the OV was below the Solver Convergence value, described in more detail below, for five iterations, that is, that the rate of improvement in the OV was too low to continue the optimization method. Since for NLPs, Solver always starts from the given initial point, if feasible, you can restart Solver to force it to begin optimization again to see if it will improve upon its solution. Evoking Solver a second time and simply clicking the Solve button will cause this to happen, producing the results in Figure 7.10, after only a small additional change in the decisions. Solver now reports the desirable completion message, ". . . All constraints and optimality conditions are satisfied," which means that the necessary first-order conditions for an optimum are satisfied. And the Solver solution looks reasonable. However, it would be prudent to explore different initial starting decision variable values, because this solution may be a local optimum and not the global optimum.

USE OF AN INITIAL GUESS

When Solver begins the optimization of an NLP, it uses the set of values stored in the decision variables' cells. As mentioned, this initial set of values, which need not be feasible (Solver will correct for that), is the starting point for its GRG hill-climbing method.

---

[6] Your results may vary, depending on your starting point decision variable values, the version of Excel you use, and your computer's central processor type.

[7] Consult Appendix C for details on Solver's conditions for termination and its completion messages.

FIGURE 7.8

Gulf Coast Oil Blending Model with Initial Decisions

	A	B	C	D	E	F	G	H	I
1		Gulf Coast Oil Model				Foreign Purchases		Octane	Unit Cost
2					Foreign Source 1	1.0		93	$0.80
3					Foreign Source 2	2.0		97	$0.90
4		Gasoline Sold (000s)	Regular	Midgrade	Premium	3.0	=Pooled Foreign Purchased		
5		Price Per Gallon	$1.18	$1.25	$1.40	Total Gal.	Capacity	Octane	Unit Cost
6		Foreign Blend Gal.	1.0	1.0	1.0	3	<=8000	95.67	$0.87
7		Domestic Gal.	0.0	0.0	0.0	0	<=10,000	85	$0.65
8		Prem. Additive Gal.			0	0	<=50	900	$30.00
9		Total Gallons Sold	1.0	1.0	1.0	3			
10		Minimum Sales	>=100	>=100	>=100				
11		Octane of Gas. Sold	95.67	95.67	95.67				
12		Min Octane	>=87	>=89	>=94	Total ($000s)			
13		Gasoline Revenue	$1.18	$1.25	$1.40	$3.83			
14		Foreign Blend Cost	$0.87	$0.87	$0.87	$2.60			
15		Domestic Cost	$0.00	$0.00	$0.00	$0.00			
16		Prem. Additive Cost			$0.00	$0.00			
17		Total Cost	$0.87	$0.87	$0.87	$2.60			
18		Profit	$0.31	$0.38	$0.53	$1.23			

Cell	Formula	Copy To
H6	= ($F$2*H2+$F$3*H3)/($F$4+1E–30)	I6
C11	= SUMPRODUCT(C6:C8,$H$6:$H$8)/(C9+1E-30)	D11:E11
C13	= C9*C5	D13:E13
C14	= C6*$I6	C14:E15, E16
F6	= SUM (C6:E6)	F7:F9, F13:F18

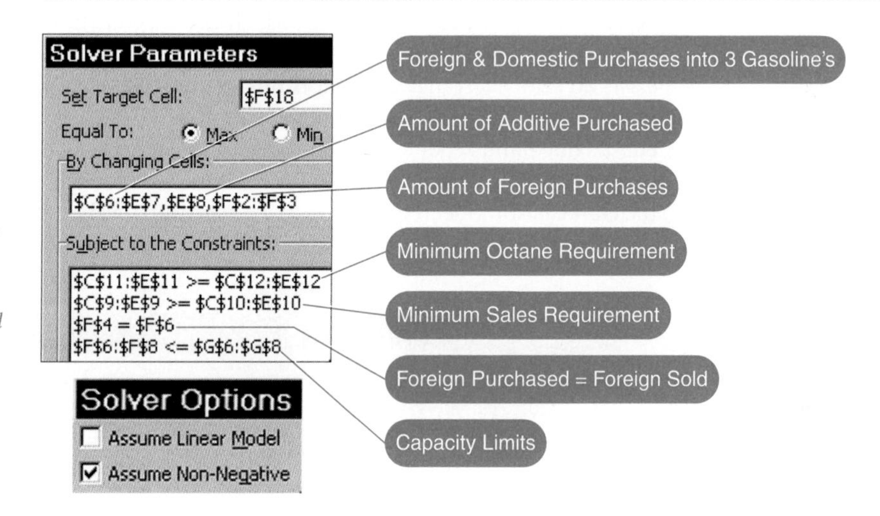

TIP: *During NLP optimization, Solver determines an "up-hill" direction, takes a step in that direction, and then evaluates the constraints (for feasibility) and the first-order conditions (for determining a new direction or to stop). It is possible that Solver will "overstep," thereby violating one or more constraints. Normally, Solver will detect this infeasibility, will back up, and then take a smaller step. But if the new point triggers an Excel error message, then Solver is forced to abort optimization before it can back up. Tricks are often needed to avoid this problem during optimization. One solution is to modify cell formulas to prevent Excel errors without affecting the model's logic. For example, the original formula for cell E11 in Figure 7.8 calculated the Premium octane number by =SUMPRODUCT(E6:E8,$H$6:$H$8)/E9. During optimization Solver may overstep and set Premium production to zero, and thus, E9 becomes zero. This will cause an Excel "#DIV/O!" error, stopping Solver before it detects that the constraint in E10 has been violated. Changing the formula's divisor to be (E9+1E–30) by adding a very small constant avoids the error, allowing Solver to continue.*

Because of the form of the nonlinear constraints, this particular Gulf Coast Oil model is called a *nonconcave model.* As we will see in the next section, the starting point for the method can be quite important for a nonconcave model, and several different starting points may be required to find a "good" solution. Guessing all zeros for the initial decisions is often a very poor choice of an initial point for nonconcave models. Much better is to guess an initial starting point near the global optimal solution to the model. Of course, this is an exquisite "Catch-22" situation: You must know the model's global optimal solution to produce a good initial guess for finding the model's global optimal solution! Nevertheless, this is an unfortunate consequence of NLP models. Particularly for nonconcave models, there is no guarantee that the Solver solution is the global optimal one. In fact, after two attempts to optimize the Gulf Coast Oil model, Solver has converged to a local optimum in

FIGURE 7.9

Solver's First Solution to Gulf Coast Oil Model

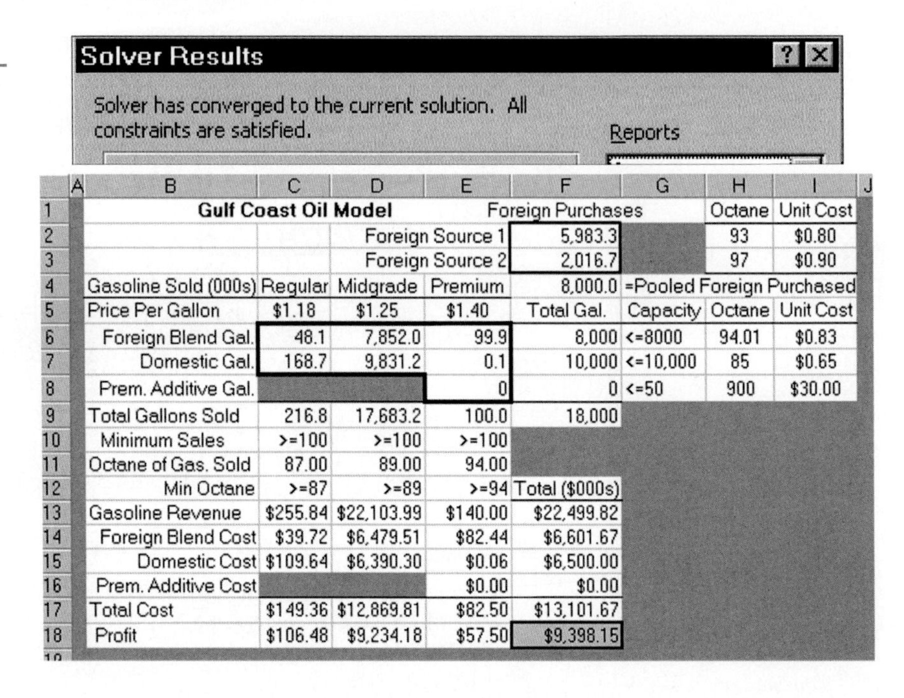

	B	C	D	E	F	G	H	I
1	Gulf Coast Oil Model			Foreign Purchases			Octane	Unit Cost
2			Foreign Source 1		5,983.3		93	$0.80
3			Foreign Source 2		2,016.7		97	$0.90
4	Gasoline Sold (000s)	Regular	Midgrade	Premium	8,000.0	=Pooled Foreign Purchased		
5	Price Per Gallon	$1.18	$1.25	$1.40	Total Gal.	Capacity	Octane	Unit Cost
6	Foreign Blend Gal.	48.1	7,852.0	99.9	8,000	<=8000	94.01	$0.83
7	Domestic Gal.	168.7	9,831.2	0.1	10,000	<=10,000	85	$0.65
8	Prem. Additive Gal.			0	0	<=50	900	$30.00
9	Total Gallons Sold	216.8	17,683.2	100.0	18,000			
10	Minimum Sales	>=100	>=100	>=100				
11	Octane of Gas. Sold	87.00	89.00	94.00				
12	Min Octane	>=87	>=89	>=94	Total ($000s)			
13	Gasoline Revenue	$255.84	$22,103.99	$140.00	$22,499.82			
14	Foreign Blend Cost	$39.72	$6,479.51	$82.44	$6,601.67			
15	Domestic Cost	$109.64	$6,390.30	$0.06	$6,500.00			
16	Prem. Additive Cost			$0.00	$0.00			
17	Total Cost	$149.36	$12,869.81	$82.50	$13,101.67			
18	Profit	$106.48	$9,234.18	$57.50	$9,398.15			

Figure 7.10 and not the global optimum. The global optimum for this model is *believed* to be the one displayed in Figure 7.11, which also displays the Sensitivity Report.

We emphasize the solution of Figure 7.11 "is believed to be" optimal because there exists no litmus test that guarantees this solution is the global optimum for the Gulf Coast model. It was found by re-optimizing the model dozens of times, each time using a different starting point set of decision cell values. Unfortunately, SolverTable is not of much help to reduce the drudgery of such re-optimizations. Specifying an initial set of decisions for the Gulf Coast model requires inputting nine initial values and SolverTable can input only two at most. All is not lost, however, as we will cover a different approach to this thorny

FIGURE 7.10

Solver's Second Solution to Gulf Coast Oil Model

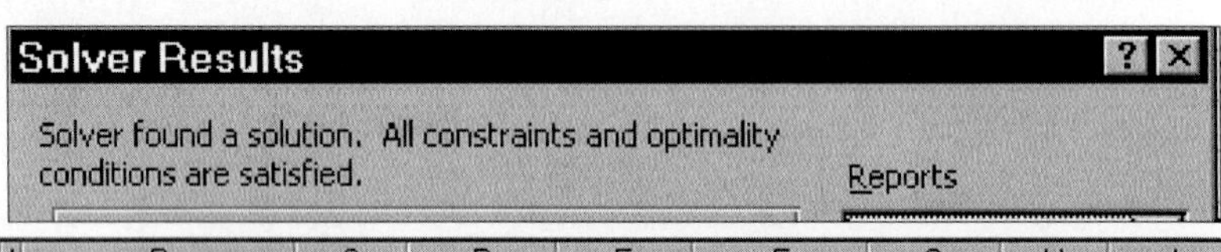

	B	C	D	E	F	G	H	I
1	Gulf Coast Oil Model			Foreign Purchases			Octane	Unit Cost
2			Foreign Source 1		5,983.4		93	$0.80
3			Foreign Source 2		2,016.6		97	$0.90
4	Gasoline Sold (000s)	Regular	Midgrade	Premium	8,000.0	=Pooled Foreign Purchased		
5	Price Per Gallon	$1.18	$1.25	$1.40	Total Gal.	Capacity	Octane	Unit Cost
6	Foreign Blend Gal.	48.1	7,852.0	99.9	8,000	<=8000	94.01	$0.83
7	Domestic Gal.	168.6	9,831.3	0.1	10,000	<=10,000	85	$0.65
8	Prem. Additive Gal.			0	0	<=50	900	$30.00
9	Total Gallons Sold	216.7	17,683.3	100.0	18,000			
10	Minimum Sales	>=100	>=100	>=100				
11	Octane of Gas. Sold	87.00	89.00	94.00				
12	Min Octane	>=87	>=89	>=94	Total ($000s)			
13	Gasoline Revenue	$255.71	$22,104.12	$140.00	$22,499.83			
14	Foreign Blend Cost	$39.70	$6,479.52	$82.44	$6,601.66			
15	Domestic Cost	$109.58	$6,390.36	$0.06	$6,500.00			
16	Prem. Additive Cost			$0.00	$0.00			
17	Total Cost	$149.29	$12,869.87	$82.50	$13,101.66			
18	Profit	$106.42	$9,234.25	$57.50	$9,398.17			

FIGURE 7.11

Optimal Solution to the Gulf Coast Oil Model

	A	B	C	D	E	F	G	H	I
1		Gulf Coast Oil Model			Foreign Purchases			Octane	Unit Cost
2				Foreign Source 1		0.0		93	$0.80
3				Foreign Source 2		8,000.0		97	$0.90
4		Gasoline Sold (000s)	Regular	Midgrade	Premium	8,000.0	=Pooled Foreign Purchased		
5		Price Per Gallon	$1.18	$1.25	$1.40	Total Gal.	Capacity	Octane	Unit Cost
6		Foreign Blend Gal.	16.7	4,353.3	3,630.0	8,000	<=8000	97.00	$0.90
7		Domestic Gal.	83.3	8,706.7	1,210.0	10,000	<=10,000	85	$0.65
8		Prem. Additive Gal.			0	0	<=50	900	$30.00
9		Total Gallons Sold	100.0	13,060.0	4,840.0	18,000			
10		Minimum Sales	>=100	>=100	>=100				
11		Octane of Gas. Sold	87.00	89.00	94.00				
12		Min Octane	>=87	>=89	>=94	Total ($000s)			
13		Gasoline Revenue	$118.00	$16,325.00	$6,776.00	$23,219.00			
14		Foreign Blend Cost	$15.00	$3,918.00	$3,267.00	$7,200.00			
15		Domestic Cost	$54.17	$5,659.33	$786.50	$6,500.00			
16		Prem. Additive Cost			$0.00	$0.00			
17		Total Cost	$69.17	$9,577.33	$4,053.50	$13,700.00			
18		Profit	$48.83	$6,747.67	$2,722.50	$9,519.00			

TIP: *Our admonition for LP Sensitivity Reports also applies to NLP Sensitivity Reports: After each report is produced by Solver, always cursor over the values in the report and adjust formatting to display increased decimal precision if the entries are small numbers.*

Microsoft Excel 9.0 Sensitivity Report

Adjustable Cells

Cell	Name	Final Value	Reduced Gradient
$C$6	Foreign Blend Gal. Regular	16.7	0.0
$D$6	Foreign Blend Gal. Midgrade	4,353.3	0.0
$E$6	Foreign Blend Gal. Premium	3,630.0	0.0
$C$7	Domestic Gal. Regular	83.3	0.0
$D$7	Domestic Gal. Midgrade	8,706.7	0.0
$E$7	Domestic Gal. Premium	1,210.0	0.0
$E$8	Prem. Additive Gal. Premium	0.0	-4.42
$F$2	Foreign Source 1 Foreign Purchases	0.0	-0.02
$F$3	Foreign Source 2 Foreign Purchases	8,000.0	0.0

Constraints

Cell	Name	Final Value	Lagrange Multiplier
$C$11	Octane of Gas. Sold Regular	87.00	-3.00
$D$11	Octane of Gas. Sold Midgrade	89.00	-391.80
$E$11	Octane of Gas. Sold Premium	94.00	-145.20
$C$9	Total Gallons Sold Regular	100.0	-0.01
$D$9	Total Gallons Sold Midgrade	13,060.0	0.00
$E$9	Total Gallons Sold Premium	4,840.0	0.00
$F$4	Premium Foreign Purchases	8,000.0	0.00
$F$6	Foreign Blend Gal. Total Gal.	8,000	0.59
$F$7	Domestic Gal. Total Gal.	10,000	0.48
$F$8	Prem. Additive Gal. Total Gal.	0	0.00

problem in Section 7.8. Also, as we will see, there is a "nice" class of NLPs, called *concave* or *convex* models, where we do not need to worry about a starting point. For this class of NLP models, Solver's GRG search method finds the desired global optimum solution, no matter where it starts.

It is a useful exercise to interpret the sensitivity information in Figure 7.11. For example, forcing purchase of Foreign Source 1 gallons would reduce profits at an initial rate of $.02 per gallon, and forcing the addition of the additive to Premium gasoline would hurt profit at the rate of $4.42 per gallon, initially (Reduced Gradient values). Also, expanding tanker capacity would help profit by $.59 per gallon initially, while increasing the octane requirement for Premium gasoline would hurt profit at the rate of $145.20 per octane point initially (Lagrange multiplier values).

7.6 SOLVER OPTIONS SETTINGS

It is worth mentioning that some of Solver's Options for NLPs, as shown in Figure 7.12, can be investigated experimentally, especially for nonconcave or highly nonlinear models, such as the Gulf Coast model, to try and improve Solver's GRG's hill-climbing tactics. The Convergence value is used to terminate Solver's search when the OV is improving very

FIGURE 7.12

Solver Options Dialog

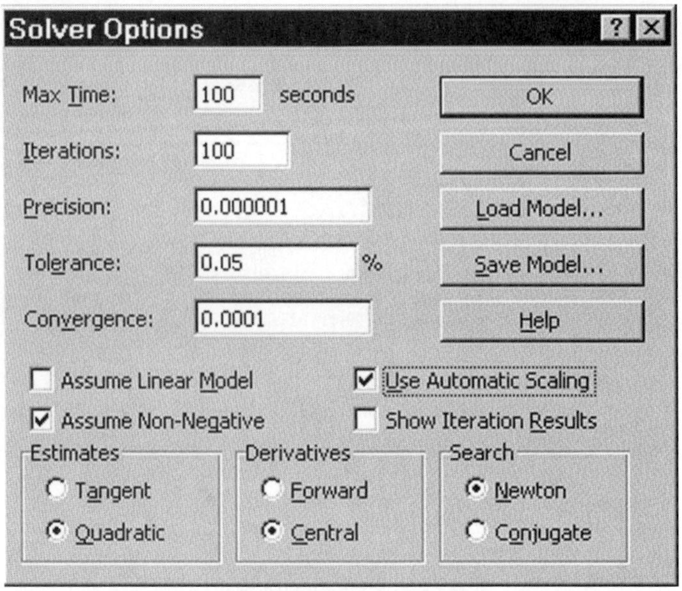

Solver Options

Max Time:	100	seconds	OK
Iterations:	100		Cancel
Precision:	0.000001		Load Model...
Tolerance:	0.05	%	Save Model...
Convergence:	0.0001		Help

☐ Assume Linear Model ☑ Use Automatic Scaling

☑ Assume Non-Negative ☐ Show Iteration Results

Estimates	Derivatives	Search
○ Tangent	○ Forward	◉ Newton
◉ Quadratic	◉ Central	○ Conjugate

slowly. If the improvement is less than or equal to the default value of .0001 for five iterations, Solver stops with the completion message of Figure 7.9. Setting Convergence smaller than its default value forces Solver to continue the optimization method even if the rate of change in OV is small.

Setting the Estimates option to "Quadratic" forces Solver to approximate its estimates of the variable equations in its one-dimensional searches by a quadratic (parabolic) function instead of a linear (tangent) one. Also, selecting "Central" instead of "Forward" for computing partial derivatives for the OV and constraints forces Solver to produce a more accurate approximation by estimating each directional derivative using two adjacent points to each iterative solution point instead of just one. Both of these changes improve Solver's numerical estimates of the functions for nonlinear models, but at the potential cost of longer solution times because of the additional calculations required at each iteration.

The search options determine how Solver chooses the search direction along which an improvement in the OV will be sought. The Conjugate Search option uses less memory during optimization but requires more Solver calculations for a given level of accuracy than the default "Newton" method. However, especially for large nonlinear models, the lower random access memory demands with this option may on balance improve Solver solution speed by reducing memory management overhead.

The Precision setting determines how closely the LHS calculations must match the RHS in order for a given constraint to be satisfied. The match cannot be exact in all cases because of numerical errors in the computer's finite binary representation of numbers. If a constraint's LHS differs from its RHS by an amount less than the Precision setting, then the two are considered equal, and thus, the constraint binding.

For highly nonlinear or nonconcave NLPs, one suggested set of Solver Options settings for experimentation might be Quadratic Estimates, Central Derivates, Newton Search, and Convergence left at the default of .0001 or no less than .000001. Also, do not forget to manually scale your model's numbers, as discussed in Chapters 3 and 5, and in addition check the "Use Automatic Scaling" option. Finally, if the NLP model involves some integer decision variables, then setting the Tolerance to 0% will force Solver to continue its search for the true integer optimum, as described in Chapter 6. Consult Appendix C for additional details on setting Solver Options.

7.7 SOLVABILITY OF NLP MODELS

The methods for solving general NLP models are markedly different from the simplex used by Solver for LPs. In LP we saw that for a model that has an optimal solution, we could always be assured that there would in fact be at least one optimal corner solution. This is a critically important characteristic of LP models, for the corners of the feasible region can be defined by linear equations in such a way that a simple algebraic operation allows us to move from one corner to any adjacent corner at which the objective value either improves or remains at the same value. Using this technique, Solver's simplex method provides a fail-safe method for attacking LP models. None of these comments apply to the general NLP model.

Moreover, there is no single preferred optimization method for optimizing NLPs. Without difficulty one can easily find 10 to 15 methods developed in the literature. However, three classes of procedures currently seem to be most useful in solving general nonlinear programs: GRG (generalized reduced gradient), SLP (successive linear programming), and SQP (successive quadratic programming). As mentioned earlier, Solver uses an NLP method in the GRG class. But nonlinear programming is a very broad topic, and many interesting special types of NLP models are identified in the literature, many of which are designed to solve special types of NLP models. For example, some methods are designed exclusively for quadratic programming models, covered in Section 7.9, others for models that are "mostly" linear with the nonlinear terms entering the objective function or constraints in special ways.

Rather than confronting you with a compendium of the numerous types of methods for solving NLP models, we shall give a brief description of a few major classes of nonlinear programs that one might encounter in practical applications. That is, we can break down this very general class of problems into more special cases, defined by the nature of the objective function and the constraint functions, and then discuss how easily solvable these special cases are. Indeed, from the managerial perspective these are important issues: to know what type of NLP one may be facing, and the prospects for finding a solution. It will be seen that these prospects are heavily dependent on the type of nonlinear model one faces.

We might begin this overview with the observation that nonlinear models are divided into two classes: (1) those that can be optimized and (2) those that one can try to optimize. The models that can be optimized must typically conform to certain qualifications of structure and size. The hierarchy of increasing computational difficulty is shown in Figure 7.13. In this figure, the increasing Roman numerals reflect increasing computational difficulty. Let us now consider these several classes of NLPs in somewhat more detail.

FIGURE 7.13

Increasing Computational Difficulty

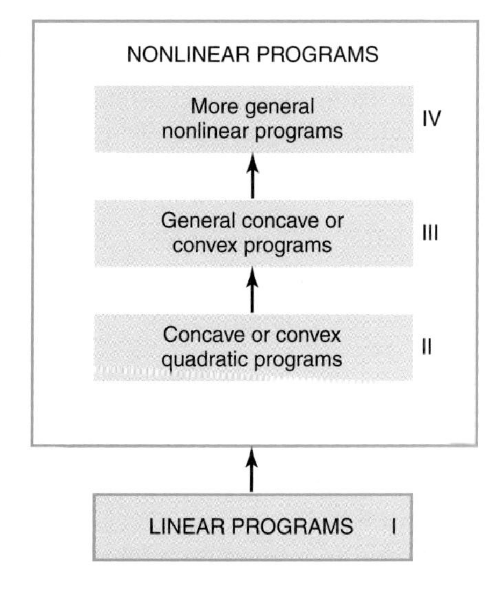

FIGURE 7.14

Convex and Nonconvex Sets of Points

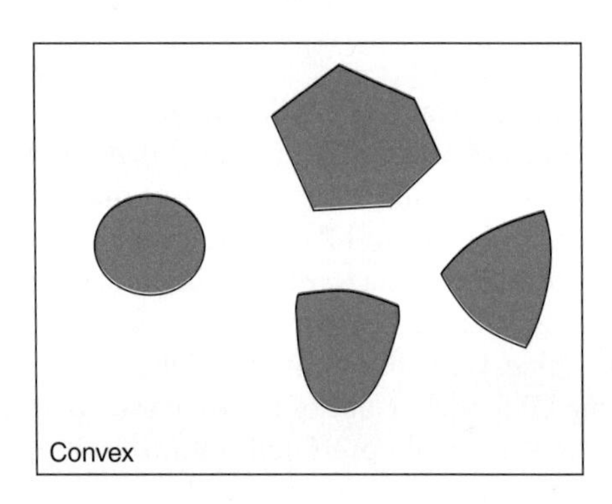

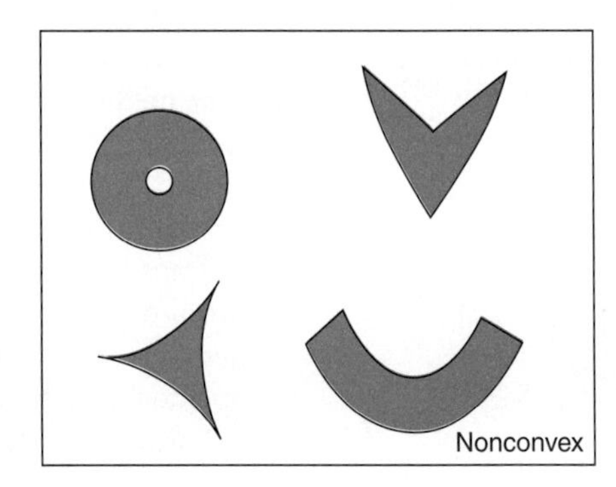

NONLINEAR PROGRAMS THAT CAN BE SOLVED: CONCAVE AND CONVEX PROGRAMS

To define these problems it is necessary to introduce a new technical term, a **convex set of points**. Loosely speaking, this is a set of points without any "holes" or "indentations." More formally, a convex set is any set that has the following property:

> Consider all possible pairs of points in the set, and consider the line segment connecting any such pair. All such line segments must lie entirely within the set.

Figure 7.14 shows two-dimensional sets of points that do not satisfy this property and hence are *not* convex sets, together with sets that are convex. The polygon in the first of these two figures may remind you of the constraint sets that occur in LP problems. This is appropriate since any constraint set for a linear program is a convex set. *The nonlinear programs that we can be reasonably sure of solving must also have convex constraint sets.*

Concave and Convex Functions The next question to be asked then is: What kinds of nonlinear programs have convex constraint sets? It is useful to be able to use the notion of concave and convex functions in answering this question. If the function has two independent variables, a *concave function* is shaped like an upside-down bowl. In general, a concave function, by definition, has the property that the line segment connecting any two points on the graph of the function never enters the space above the graph (if it always lies strictly under the graph, then the function is *strictly concave*). Similarly, if the function has two variables, a *convex function* is shaped like a bowl. In general, a convex function, by definition, has the property that the line segment connecting any two points on the graph of the function never enters the space below the graph (if it always lies strictly above the graph, then the function is *strictly convex*). The same ideas hold for functions that have a single variable, or more than two variables. It should also be remarked that a linear function is considered to be both concave and convex (the above-mentioned line segments always lie in the graph).

Now suppose that we have a nonlinear program with only inequality constraints.

> If the LHS constraint function associated with each $\leq$ constraint is convex and the LHS constraint function associated with each $\geq$ constraint is concave, the constraint set will be a convex set.

These facts are illustrated in Figure 7.15, which shows a convex function g of a single variable, given by $g(x) = x^2 + 1$. You can see that the set of x values for which $g(x) \leq 2$ is convex (i.e., this is the set $-1 \leq x \leq 1$), whereas the set of x values for which $g(x) \geq 2$ is not convex (i.e., this is the set $x \leq -1$, $x \geq 1$). This set is not convex because it is possible to find two

FIGURE 7.15

Constraint Sets $g(x) \leq 2$ and $g(x) \geq 2$

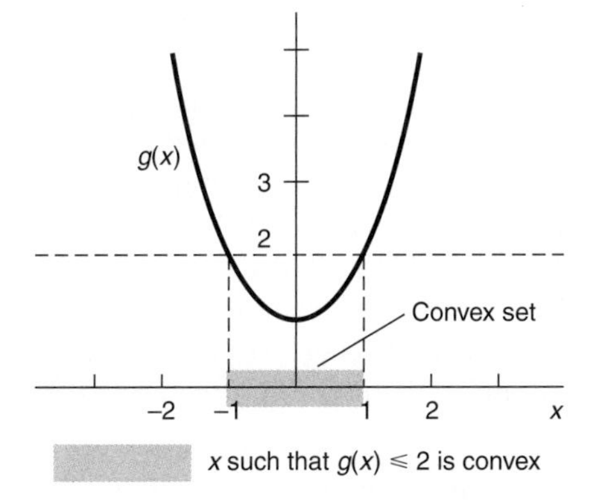

points in the set (say, $x = +2$ and $x = -2$) such that the straight line that connects them passes through points (e.g., the point $x = 0$) that are not in the set.

Thus, we see that in this example the function $g(x)$ is convex and the set defined by the inequality $g(x) \leq 2$ is convex, whereas the set defined by the inequality $g(x) \geq 2$ is not convex. A similar demonstration could be constructed to show that if the function $g(x)$ is concave, then the set defined by the inequality $g(x) \geq 2$ is convex, whereas the set defined by the inequality $g(x) \leq 2$ is not convex (this is related to the fact that the negative of a concave function is convex and vice versa). We thus have a test at our disposal that will enable us to verify that certain NLPs have a convex constraint set. This test certainly will not enable us to determine if the constraint set for *any* NLP is convex or not. In particular, in the case of models involving one or more *nonlinear equality* constraints, there is great difficulty in characterizing whether or not the constraint set is convex. Concerning the discussion in this subsection, it is worth noting that the term *concave* applies only to functions, whereas the term *convex* can apply either to a function or to a set of points, depending on the context.

Now that you understand the meaning of a convex set, it is easy, at least formally, to define a concave or convex program.

- A **concave NLP** is a Max model with a concave objective function and a convex constraint set.
- A **convex NLP** is a Min model with a convex objective function and a convex constraint set.

Note that because of linearity, an LP satisfies both of the conditions above. The rationale for this characterization has to do with the fact that in the maximization context, just as in elementary calculus with one variable, concave objective functions are very convenient to work with in terms of the mathematical properties associated with the upside-down bowl shape. Convex objective functions (bowl-shaped) are convenient in the minimization context. Finally, the convexity of the constraint set endows the model with other attractive mathematical properties that can be exploited both theoretically and computationally. A most important characteristic of concave (or convex) NLPs is that for such models *any local solution is necessarily a global solution.* This fact has obvious implications for nonlinear applications of Solver. For this reason concave (or convex) NLPs are often called **well behaved**.

Solution Procedures Figure 7.13 indicates that the easiest nonlinear programs are concave or convex quadratic programs. These models, by definition, have linear (equality or inequality) constraints. The objective function must be quadratic and concave if it is a

Max model and quadratic and convex if it is a Min model. It turns out that a variation of the simplex method can be used to solve such problems, and in practice this is reasonably efficient. It is not uncommon to solve quadratic programs with hundreds of constraints and several thousand variables. As we will see in the next section, financial models such as those used in portfolio analysis are often quadratic programs, so this class of models is of considerable applied importance.

In Figure 7.13 the next level of difficulty involves general (nonquadratic) concave or convex models. There are numerous mathematical approaches and corresponding optimization procedures for solving such models. For example, suppose that the problem to be solved is a Max model. Similar to the GRG procedure used by Solver, many NLP procedures operate as follows:

1. Find an initial feasible point "inside" the constraint set (not on the boundary).
2. Find an uphill direction (or downhill for Min models) and move along this straight line until either reaching a maximum (or minimum) along the line or hitting some boundary of the constraint set.
3. Modify the direction of motion so as to continue uphill (downhill) while remaining in the feasible region.
4. Terminate the algorithm when a point satisfying the necessary optimality conditions is found.

In this type of procedure, as well as most others that apply to nonlinear programs that are not quadratic, there is considerable use of advanced calculus, and hence it is not possible in this development to go into much detail. Suffice it to say that *for general concave or convex NLPs, as opposed to LPs, the number of nonlinear variables (i.e., those that enter into the model nonlinearly) seems to be more significant than the number of constraints as an indicator of model difficulty.*

NONLINEAR PROGRAMS THAT WE TRY TO SOLVE

Finally, we consider the highest level of difficulty in Figure 7.13, general NLPs. These models are often called *highly nonlinear,* which usually means that the convexity and concavity properties discussed above are absent. To attack such models, it is common practice to use the same optimizer, such as Solver, one would use for general concave and convex NLPs. The results are different, however. Any NLP optimizer will generally terminate at a point at which the necessary (i.e., first-order) optimality conditions are satisfied. For a concave or convex program, such a point is guaranteed to be a global optimizer (indeed, if the objective function is *strictly* concave, or *strictly* convex, we are guaranteed that such a point is a *unique* global optimizer). But for general NLPs this need not be true, as was illustrated in the Gulf Coast Oil model earlier and is illustrated for a model in one variable in Figure 7.16. From the graph the objective function that is to be maximized is neither concave nor

FIGURE 7.16

Nonconcave Constrained Max Model

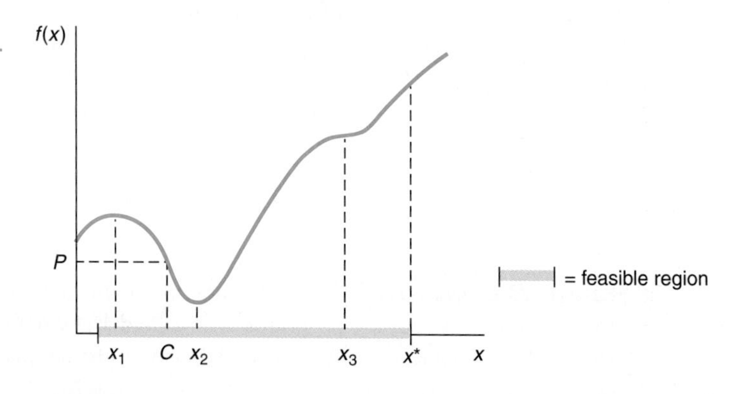

convex. The solution to the model is given by x^*, but the optimizer may terminate at any of the points or x_1, x_2, x_3 or x^* (for they will satisfy the first-order conditions). To date, no one has been smart enough to invent an optimizer that guarantees complete immunity from this possibility.

In practice, this difficulty is usually overcome by starting the optimizer at many different initial points, as was done in the Gulf Coast Oil model. For example, if the initial guess is somewhat larger than x_3 in Figure 7.16, any reasonable optimizer would converge to x^*. If x_1 had also been obtained by some other initial guess, it would now be rejected, because although we may not know with certainty that x^* is optimal, we would see that the objective value at x_1 is lower than that at x^*.

In concluding, let us address one additional practical aspect. How can we tell whether a nonlinear program in many variables is concave, convex, or neither? In other words, how do we know whether the objective function and the constraints have the right mathematical form? There are several answers to this question:

1. Sometimes, there are mathematical tests that can be applied to the model's functions to determine whether they are concave, convex, or neither.
2. Sometimes, economic intuition is used to assert that such-and-such a phenomenon reflects diminishing marginal returns or increasing marginal costs, and hence the associated function is concave or convex.
3. In many real models nothing is done to address the question. One simply attempts to optimize the model and then inquires as to the practical usefulness of the terminal point (the purported "solution" produced by Solver). As stated above, for a model that is thought or known to be nonconvex or nonconcave, one frequently restarts Solver from many different initial points, to explore the possibility of producing a better solution with higher OV.

Finally, we now have the concepts to state explicitly why we have long advised you to avoid using certain nonsmooth Excel functions that typically produce extreme nonlinear behavior. Examples of these functions are IF(), ABS(), CHOOSE(), VLOOKUP(), MIN(), and MAX(). Clearly, in most cases, these functions void the use of an LP model by destroying linearity. But they also cause problems in NLPs as well. These and similar nonsmooth functions can cause either "kinks" or discontinuities in the objective function or constraint function values for some values of the decision variables. A kink occurs when the "slope," that is, the set of first partial derivatives, of a smoothly changing function value changes abruptly for some threshold value(s) of decision variable(s), because, for example, an IF() statement triggers a different relationship. Similarly, a discontinuity occurs when the threshold value(s) trigger a completely different relationship by shifting the entire objective or constraint function to a new set of values. Although not discontinuous for the function itself, a kink causes a discontinuity in the partial derivatives to the function that are used for direction finding by Solver's hill-climbing/hill-descent procedure. The result is often lack of convergence as the Solver oscillates around the point where the discontinuity occurs in the function or its derivative, ultimately causing Solver to give up and quit, displaying one of its nonoptimal completion messages. Note that this problem is in addition to any difficulty with lack of concavity or convexity in the underlying NLP formulation that can lead to convergence to a local optimum instead of the global optimum.

7.8 INTRODUCTION TO EVOLUTIONARY SOLVER

As evident in the previous section's discussion, highly nonlinear models, like the Gulf Coast Oil model, occur frequently in business situations. Also, many existing real-world spreadsheet models make heavy use of Excel's nonsmooth functions, such as IF(), ABS(), CHOOSE(), VLOOKUP(), MIN(), and MAX(). The presence of (1) highly nonlinear Excel models often having (2) nonsmooth functions and (3) many local optima usually means that the convexity and concavity properties necessary for Solver to reliably optimize an

NLP to find a global optimum are absent. In fact, nonsmooth functions in the worksheet may prevent Solver from finding even a local optimum because its direction finding methods depend on smoothly changing topographies of the objective function.

An illustration of how easy it is to produce an NLP model that contains all three of these irregularities is shown in Figure 7.17 in which the OV is the product of two nonsmooth nonlinear functions in two decision variables X1 and X2. A Data Table 2 was used to prepare a chart of the Y Total objective function for X1 and X2 using values of each between 1 and 5 to enumerate the shape of the Y Total objective function. The chart also appears in Figure 7.17 verifying the nonconcavity of Y Total. The model can be thought of

FIGURE 7.17

A Nonconcave, Nonsmooth, Multiple Optima NLP Model

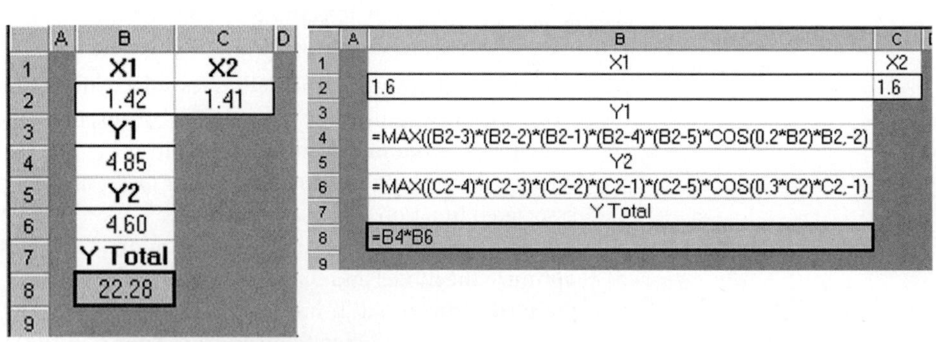

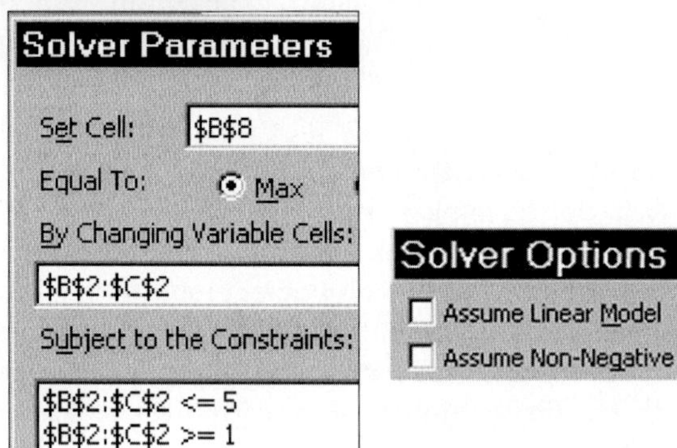

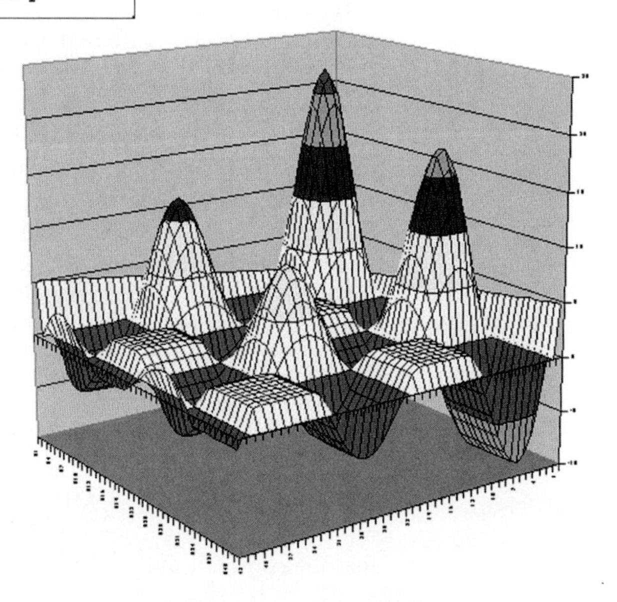

FIGURE 7.18

Two Solver NLP Optimization Runs

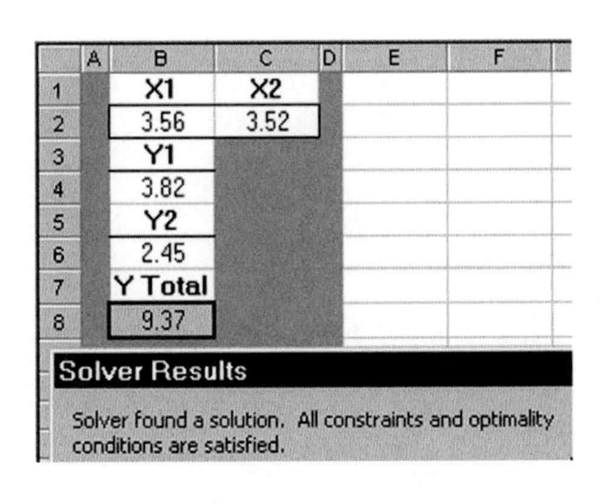

as a two decision variable business model with the goal of maximizing Y Total, a profit objective function. As can be seen in the chart, there are numerous local optima, some with very flat tops, and others with deep troughs. Starting Solver's GRG optimizer at an arbitrary pair of values for X1 and X2 will almost certainly not produce the unique global optimum, which occurs at X1 = 1.42 and X2 = 1.41, approximately, with an OV of 22.28.

Figure 7.18 illustrates the perverse nature of this simple NLP model. In the first run, X1 and X2 were each initialized to 3.3 and Solver's GRG nonlinear optimizer converged to a local optimum far below the global one. In the second run X1 and X2 were each initialized to 1, an initial point very close to the global optimum, but again, Solver failed to find it. Of course, in this simple model it is obvious what is going on, but in a bigger NLP model in many decision variables and constraints it is nearly impossible to visualize the shape of the feasible objective function surface, and thus one is likely to end up accepting a suboptimal solution with payoff potentially far removed from the optimum.

In response to this dilemma, recent research in optimization theory has focused on creating robust procedures that are more immune to the difficulties caused by the three gremlins of (1) highly nonlinear models with (2) multiple optima, and (3) nonsmooth functions. What is needed is a systematic way to select good initial starting values for the decision variables, to evaluate the model for each while tabulating the results in an organized way, and to use those results for finding better decision variable values without relying on methods based upon calculus that are often defeated by the grimlins. And that is exactly what the Evolutionary Solver optimizer does.

Based upon concepts from biology, Solver's Evolutionary search procedure for optimization is different in major ways from the LP, ILP, and NLP methods covered thus far:

1. It relies in part on randomly determined starting points. Thus, it is a nondeterministic optimizer, which may yield different solutions on different runs.
2. While most optimizers keep only the best solution found during its search, the evolutionary optimizer keeps a large set of results, called a *population of candidate solutions*, not all of which are good solutions. The population is used to help create new starting solution points not necessarily in the neighborhood of the current best solution, and thus helping to avoid Evolutionary Solver getting trapped at a local optimum.
3. Much like gene mutation in biology, Evolutionary Optimizer makes random changes in one or more members of the population at times to create new "offspring" candidate starting points that may be far removed from other members of the population.
4. Like sexual reproduction, elements of existing solutions in the population are combined with each other by a DNA-like strand crossover operation in order to create a new solution candidate with some of the features of each parent solution.

5. Any constraint violations produced by a new solution are reflected by subtracting (maximization model) or adding (minimization model) a penalty function amount to the solution's OV reflecting the degree of the violation. This modified OV becomes that solution's "fitness" measure.
6. Much like natural selection, offspring starting points that do not produce improved OV and that do not help produce other candidate starting points with improved OV are ultimately purged from the population as being "unfit."

While the details of exactly how the Solver Evolutionary procedure works are beyond the scope of the book, we can easily demonstrate its usefulness for attacking perverse NLPs that will not yield to the standard Solver optimizers. A limited version of the Solver Evolutionary procedure is contained as one of the optimizers in the Premium Edition Solver for Education contained on the book's CD-ROM. To activate it, you must click the "Premium" button on the Solver Parameters dialog to produce the drop-down list of optimizers, as shown in Figure 7.19. The default settings in the Solver Options dialog, also shown in Figure 7.19, should be adequate for most models.[8] Note, however, that the default requires that *all* the decision variables have both upper and lower bound constraints, which must be added as new constraints to the Solver Parameters dialog if they are not already present. Although, this default may be unchecked, it is not recommended because if the decision variables have no direct bounds, then the Evolutionary optimizer must consider an infinitely wide range of candidate starting points, which in turn will drastically reduce its efficiency. So, try to set a reasonable range of bounds on your decision variables, if your model does not already have them.

Clicking the Solve button will start the evolutionary search. For the illustrative model of Figure 7.17, the Evolutionary Solver found the highest peak and reported a solution very

FIGURE 7.19

Evolutionary Solver and Its Options Settings

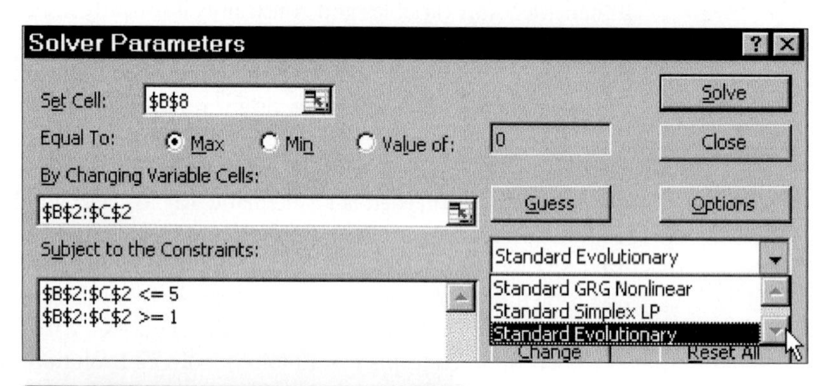

[8] Further details on the Options settings are given in Appendix C.

close to the optimum in about 10 seconds on a slow personal computer—after solving "only" about 2,000 subproblems! As shown in Figure 7.19, its progress will be marked by the message box in the lower left of Excel's window, showing the best solution found so far ("Incumbent") and a sequence of "Subproblems" and "Trial Solutions" as the optimizer performs its search, which for a moderate model may take several minutes or possibly several hours.

It should be pointed out that the Evolutionary Solver is not a panacea. In particular, Evolutionary Solver is *not an optimizer* in the sense that we have used that term because it does not claim to find the optimal solution even for well-behaved models. For example, applying it to the Gulf Coast Oil model produced no improvement after many minutes and more than 30,000 subproblems were tried when started using the initial decisions shown in Figure 7.8.[9] Running it from the final solution found by the GRG optimizer in Figure 7.10, however, produced a slight improvement shown in Figure 7.20 after about 60,000 subproblems were tried. Note that the Evolutionary Solver did not find the still better solution reported in Figure 7.11. This is because it is not a true optimizer in the classic sense we have used in earlier chapters. Instead, it can be thought of as a search engine that intelligently searches the large space of candidate model solutions looking for better solutions.

TIP: *Once the Evolutionary Solver terminates with its recommended "good" solution, run Solver again, but this time select the GRG nonlinear optimizer. If the Evolutionary Solver has gotten into the neighborhood of the global optimum, and any nonsmooth Excel functions in the model do not behave perversely in that neighborhood, using that final set of decisions as the starting point for the GRG optimizer may produce a quick convergence to a nearby optimum, which you hope might be the global optimum.*

FIGURE 7.20

Applying Evolutionary Solver to Gulf Coast Oil Model

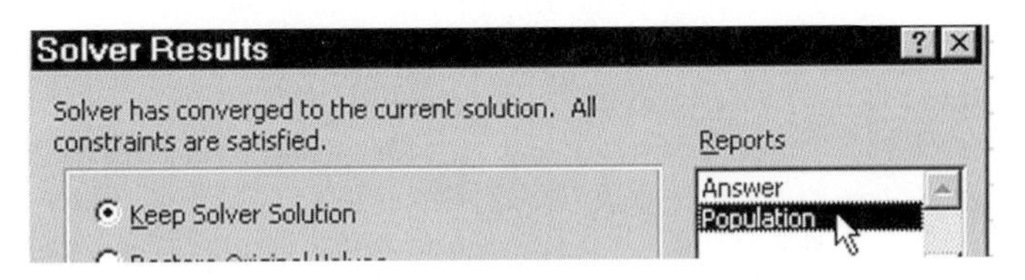

	A	B	C	D	E	F	G	H	I
1		Gulf Coast Oil Model			Foreign Purchases			Octane	Unit Cost
2				Foreign Source 1		93.9		93	$0.80
3				Foreign Source 2		7,971.1		97	$0.90
4		Gasoline Sold (000s)	Regular	Midgrade	Premium	8,065.0	=Pooled Foreign Purchased		
5		Price Per Gallon	$1.18	$1.25	$1.40	Total Gal.	Capacity	Octane	Unit Cost
6		Foreign Blend Gal.	57.6	4,303.9	3,638.5	8,000	<=8000	96.95	$0.90
7		Domestic Gal.	192.7	8,558.3	1,249.1	10,000	<=10,000	85	$0.65
8		Prem. Additive Gal.			1	1	<=50	900	$30.00
9		Total Gallons Sold	250.3	12,862.2	4,888.2	18,001			
10		Minimum Sales	>=100	>=100	>=100				
11		Octane of Gas. Sold	87.75	89.00	94.00				
12		Min Octane	>=87	>=89	>=94	Total ($000s)			
13		Gasoline Revenue	$295.32	$16,077.70	$6,843.50	$23,216.52			
14		Foreign Blend Cost	$51.76	$3,868.50	$3,270.44	$7,190.70			
15		Domestic Cost	$125.25	$5,562.87	$811.90	$6,500.01			
16		Prem. Additive Cost			$18.41	$18.41			
17		Total Cost	$177.01	$9,431.37	$4,100.75	$13,709.12			
18		Profit	$118.32	$6,646.33	$2,742.76	$9,507.40			
19									

Microsoft Excel 9.0 Population Report

Adjustable Cells

Cell	Name	Best Value	Mean Value	Standard Deviation	Maximum Value	Minimum Value
$C$6	Foreign Blend Gal. Regular	57.6	57.5	1.2	69.3	49.4
$D$6	Foreign Blend Gal. Midgrade	4,303.9	4,300.0	27.6	4380.4	4063.5
$E$6	Foreign Blend Gal. Premium	3,638.5	3,618.7	173.6	3682.4	1127.9
$C$7	Domestic Gal. Regular	192.7	192.2	2.3	197.6	170.7
$D$7	Domestic Gal. Midgrade	8,558.3	8,231.1	1198.2	8558.3	0.0
$E$7	Domestic Gal. Premium	1,249.1	1,216.4	166.2	1312.8	0.0
$E$8	Prem. Additive Gal. Premium	1	3	8.6	50.0	0.1
$F$2	Foreign Source 1 Foreign Purchases	93.9	94.7	21.3	395.6	0.0
$F$3	Foreign Source 2 Foreign Purchases	7,971.1	7,971.1	0.0	7971.1	7971.1

[9] Since the original formulation had no upper and lower bounds on the decision variables, they had to be added to the Gulf Coast Oil model to use the Evolutionary Solver.

Table 7.3 Optimizer Trade-offs

Attribute	OPTIMIZER				
	LP	**ILP**	**QP**	**NLP**	**Evolutionary**
Range of Models Supported	Narrow	Wider	Wider	Wide	Widest
Speed of Optimization	Very Fast	Slow	Fast	Slow	Extremely Slow
Finds Global Optimum	Yes	Yes	Yes	Only for Well-Behaved Models	Unlikely, Except for Well-Behaved Models
Sensitivity Report	Yes	No	Yes	Yes	No
Scales to Large Models	Yes	Only for Models with Special Structure (Network, Binary, etc.)	Yes	Only for Well-Behaved Models	No
Tolerates Nonsmooth Excel Functions in Model, =IF( ), =VLOOKUP( ), =MIN( ), etc.	No	No	No	No	Yes

TIP: *If your non-well-behaved NLP model's solution is sensitive to one or two critical model parameters or decisions, you can combine the power of SolverTable with Evolutionary Solver to batch process many Evolutionary Solver runs, tabulating its final solution for each run. Simply set up a SolverTable 1 or SolverTable 2 table with a range of parameter values or decision variable values, as before with the other Solver optimizers, and configure the settings in the Solver Parameters dialog to specify Evolutionary Solver. This can be an especially productive way to keep your PC busy all night hunting for model solutions!*

How close a "better" solution will be to a global optimum solution is *never* known. In general, one can only run the Evolutionary Solver for a sufficient amount of time and be content with the best solution it finds. Unfortunately, there is no general recipe for deciding how long a "sufficient" amount of time is, and this is usually resolved by issues of time availability and judgments about the potential improvement of still longer runs versus the opportunity costs of further delay in implementing a final decision. What can be said is that the sufficient amount of time needed is lowered for well-behaved models, models with fewer decision variables with tighter bounds on those decision variables, and for models having few nonsmooth Excel functions.

Once the Evolutionary Solver terminates, a Solver Results dialog is presented, as shown in Figure 7.20. Note that Evolutionary Solver's completion message does not make the traditional Solver claim about "All optimality conditions are satisfied." In it, however, is a new report, called the Population Report, which summarizes the characteristics of the population of solutions it created. A portion of the Population Report, shown in Figure 7.20, tabulates the best and the average values of all decision variables tried and several measures of their variability. This can give you an idea of the range of model decisions Evolutionary Solver explored.

While the procedure of trying out different decisions either manually with the GRG NLP Solver or with the help of the Evolutionary Solver does not guarantee that the global optimum will be found, it has a very practical justification. If the Solver optimization of the NLP can produce a *better* solution than is currently being used in practice, then the use of the NLP model might well be justified. This is consistent with the overall theme that in practice there is nothing so pure as a truly optimal solution. As we have said, *the goal in modeling is always to assist in the search for better decisions.* The general considerations are the cost of improvement (the cost of the modeling effort and obtaining the solution) versus the benefit rendered by the solution.

To help you understand the trade-offs involved, Table 7.3 compares some of the attributes of the Solver optimizers we have studied.

7.9 INTRODUCTION TO QUADRATIC PROGRAMMING

As indicated in Section 7.7, a quadratic programming model has the important concavity (convexity) property that avoids the optimization difficulties inherent with more generalized NLPs. In fact, a **quadratic program** (QP), like a linear integer program (ILP), is a first cousin of a linear program, possessing many of LP's desirable properties. Compare the following:

- *Linear Programming Model.* Maximize or minimize the value of *linear* objective function subject to a set of linear equality and inequality constraints as well as possible nonnegativity conditions on the values of the decision variables.
- *Quadratic Programming Model.* Maximize or minimize the value of a *quadratic* objective function subject to a set of linear equality and inequality constraints as well as possible nonnegativity conditions on the values of the decision variables.

Obviously, the only difference in these two models is in the functional form of the objective function.

Quadratic Functions We know about linear functions. Here are some examples of quadratic functions:

$$9x_1^2 + 4x_1 + 7$$

$$3x_1^2 - 4x_1x_2 + 15x_2^2 + 20x_1 - 13x_2 - 14$$

These functions are the sum of terms involving the squares of variables (e.g., $3x_1^2$), cross products (e.g., $4x_1x_2$), linear functions (e.g., $20x_1$), and constants (e.g., 14). In general, a quadratic function in N variables can be written in the form

$$\sum_{i=1}^{N} A_i x_i^2 + \sum_{i=1}^{N-1} \sum_{j=i+1}^{N} B_{ij} x_i x_j + \sum_{i=1}^{N} C_i x_i + D$$

Note that when all of the coefficients A_i and B_{ij} are zero then the function is linear. Hence, a linear function is a special case of a quadratic function.

Of course, changing from a linear to a quadratic objective function requires an NLP optimizer to solve the model. This change also implies that many of the facts we have learned about linear programming models no longer hold. The following example illustrates some of the differences between quadratic programming models and linear programming models. The symbolic QP example is

$$\begin{aligned} \text{Min } & (x_1 - 6)^2 + (x_2 - 8)^2 \\ \text{s.t. } & x_1 \leq 7 \\ & x_2 \leq 5 \\ & x_1 + 2x_2 \leq 12 \\ & x_1 + x_2 \leq 9 \\ & x_1, x_2 \geq 0 \end{aligned}$$

Geometric Representation A geometric representation of this model appears in Figure 7.21. The contraint set, of course, is the same as for an LP and thus needs no new explanation. In order to see that the objective function is a special case of our previous quadratic function, it can be rewritten in the form $x_1^2 - 12x_1 + 36 + x_2^2 - 16x_2 + 64$. You may also recognize the expression

$$(x_1 - 6)^2 + (x_2 - 8)^2 = k$$

as the equation of a circle with radius $\sqrt{k}$ and center at the point (6, 8). Thus, as shown in Figure 7.21, the contours of the objective function are concentric circles around the point (6, 8). Since these contours increase in value as the radius k increases, and since the above model is a minimization model, the optimal solution in Figure 7.21 occurs at the point (4, 4). This can be roughly described as the point where the contour "first touches" the feasible set. In this example that "touch" is a point of tangency, though in other cases a solution could occur at a corner, just as in LP. The optimal value of the objective function, that is, its value at the point (4, 4), is $(4 - 6)^2 + (4 - 8)^2 = 20$.

FIGURE 7.21

Graphical Solution for the QP Example

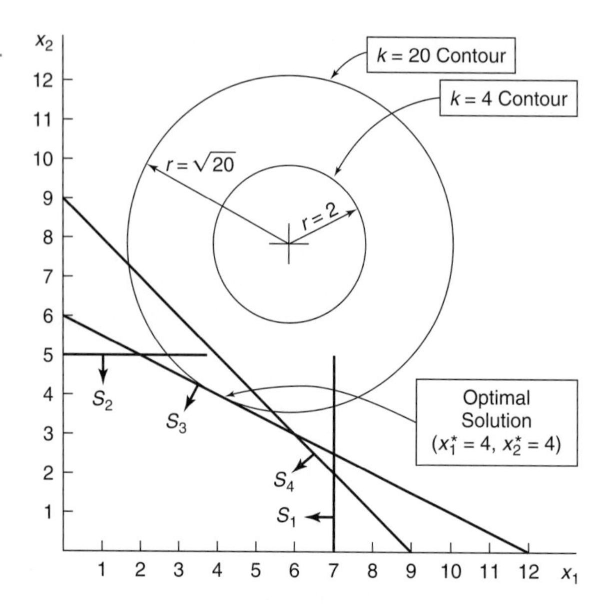

Comparison with LP This example clearly indicates that, in contrast to linear optimization:

1. Like NLP models in general, there need not be an optimal corner solution. A method like Solver's simplex, which searches for the best corner, thus cannot be used to solve this model.
2. As a direct result of 1 above, there may be more positive variables in the optimal solution than there are binding constraints. As we saw with more general NLPs, what makes solving a nonlinear model difficult is that the optimal solution does not necessarily occur at a corner of the feasible region. In this example it occurs on the edge of the feasible region, but it is possible for it to occur in the interior. In either case, there is an infinite number of possible solutions (versus LP, which has a large finite number).

SOLVER SOLUTION OF QP PROBLEMS

There are two approaches to optimizing real-world QP models: One is to use a general nonlinear programming optimizer, such as Solver, and the other is to use a specially written quadratic programming optimizer.[10] We will restrict our attention to the use of Excel's Solver.

For the previous example, Figure 7.22 shows the model, Solver dialog, optimal solution, and the Sensitivity Report. Concerning the Sensitivity Report in Figure 7.22, we simply restate the following definitions given earlier:

- Consider the number in the Lagrange multiplier column corresponding to the ith constraint. Just as in LP this represents the rate of change in OV as the ith RHS is increased, with all other data unchanged.
- In the absence of direct upper or lower bound constraints, the Reduced Gradient column applies to a nonnegative variable whose optimal value is zero. For such a variable, the reduced gradient is the rate at which the objective value is "hurt" as that variable is forced to assume positive values in an optimal solution.

This completes the general discussion of quadratic programming. In the next section we turn to a specific and important application.

[10] The commercially available version of Solver, Solver Premium Edition, contains both a NLP optimizer and a specialized quadratic optimizer.

FIGURE 7.22

Solver Solution of the QP Example

	A	B	C	D	E	F
1		QP Example				
2		X1	X2	(X1-6)^2	(X2-8)^2	Total
3		4.0	4.0	4	16	=20
4		<=7	<=5	LHS	RHS	Slack
5		1	2	12	<=12	0
6		1	1	8	<=9	1
7						

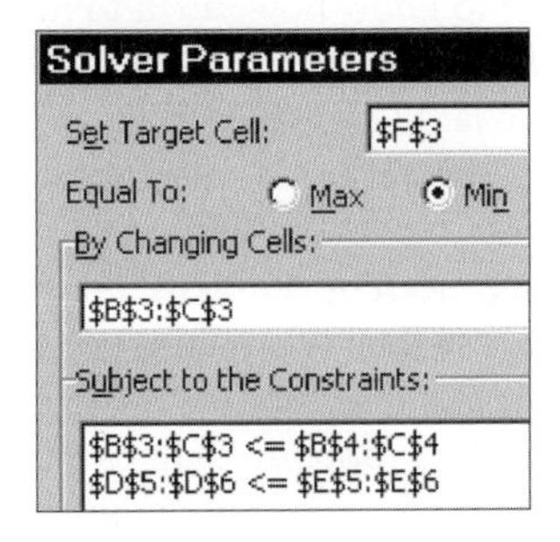

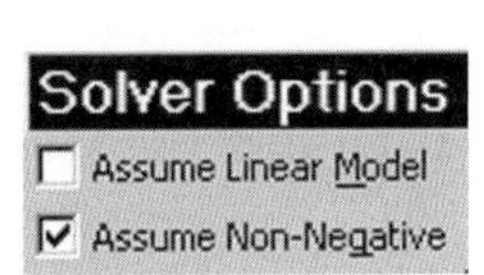

Microsoft Excel 9.0 Sensitivity Report

Adjustable Cells

Cell	Name	Final Value	Reduced Gradient
$B$3	X1	4.0	0.0
$C$3	X2	4.0	0.0

Constraints

Cell	Name	Final Value	Lagrange Multiplier
$D$5	LHS	12	-4.0
$D$6	LHS	8.0	0

APPLICATION CAPSULE Portfolio Structuring at Prudential Securities

Few financial markets in recent years have experienced the rapid growth and innovations of the secondary mortgage market. The growth has been spurred by federal agencies created to facilitate home ownership by increasing the flow of funds available for mortgage loans. These agencies include Government National Mortgage Association (GNMA), Federal National Mortgage Association (FNMA) and Federal Home Loan Mortgage Association (FHLMC). Each of these purchase mortgage loans from mortgage originators and pool them to create mortgage-backed securities (MBSs).

These securities along with those from private issuers trade in the capital markets along with other fixed-income securities such as treasury bills/bonds and their corporate equivalents. Issuance of these MBSs has reached over $1 trillion recently, with secondary market trading exceeding $5 billion per week. This secondary mortgage market is now comparable in size to the corporate bond market and has potential for considerable growth, given that only 40% of the mortgage debt has been converted into securities.

During recent years, Prudential has built a premier MBS department. Due to the complexity of these securities, standard fixed-income valuation tools are inadequate for MBSs. Prudential has used a variety of quantitative models, including LP and NLP, to allow the firm to quickly and accurately value and therefore, trade these complex MBSs.

These tools are also used to properly hedge the MBSs in their inventory, as well as to help structure their clients' portfolios to achieve given objectives (e.g., maximize expected return, minimize investment risk) while staying within specified constraints. Typical constraints include minimum and maximum percentage of the portfolio to invest in any one security, the duration of the MBSs, and the total amount to be invested. The models are used hundreds of times each day by traders, salespeople, and clients. The impact of the models is that Prudential has moved from not even being ranked in the top 10 issuers of such collateralized mortgage obligations to being consistently ranked in the top 3. (See Ben-Dove, et al.)

7.10 PORTFOLIO SELECTION

Portfolio selection is a fundamental model in modern finance. In reality there are enough aspects to portfolio analysis to fill up a book, and indeed volumes have been written on the topic. Our discussion will provide only a brief glimpse into this fascinating practice.

THE PORTFOLIO MODEL

The model of **portfolio analysis** can be stated as follows: An investor has P dollars to invest in a set of n stocks and would like to know how much to invest in each stock. The chosen collection is called the investor's portfolio. The investor has conflicting goals: He or she would like a portfolio with both a large expected return and a small risk. These goals are conflicting because most often, in the real world, portfolios with high expected return also have high risk.

Here is an example of what we mean by the term *return*. Suppose an investment of D_i dollars is put into asset i and suppose that over some specified time period this D_i dollars grows to $1.3D_i$. Then we would say that the *return* over that period is $(1.3D_i - D_i)/D_i = 0.3$. The concept of risk is more subtle and more difficult to elaborate on. For the purpose of this discussion we will assume that *risk is measured by the variance of the return on the portfolio.* Actually, this is consistent with the way that most portfolio analysts would measure risk.

Now, since the portfolio manager seeks low risk and high expected return, one way to frame the model is to minimize the variance of the return (i.e., minimize risk) subject to a given lower bound on expected return. There may also be some constraints on the proportion of the portfolio devoted to particular individual stocks.

FORMULATING THE PORTFOLIO MODEL

This model turns out to be a quadratic programming model. In formulating this model, one can let x_i be the proportion of the portfolio invested in stock i. For example, in a two-stock model if we had P dollars to invest, and if the optimal solution were $x_1 = 0.7$ and $x_2 = 0.3$, we would then invest a total of $0.7P$ dollars in stock 1, and the remaining $0.3P$ dollars would go to stock 2.

Let us now write out the general model for a two-asset model. We shall use the following notation:

σ_i^2 = variance of yearly returns from stock i, $i = 1, 2$

σ_{12} = covariance of yearly returns from stocks 1 and 2

R_i = expected yearly return from stock i, $i = 1, 2$

b = lower bound on expected yearly return from total investment

S_i = upper bound on investment in stock i, $i = 1, 2$

For the present purposes we simply accept the following facts:

1. The ***variance** of the yearly returns from stock i* is a number describing the "variability" of these returns from year to year. This will be made more precise in the next section.
2. The ***covariance** of the yearly returns from stocks 1 and 2* is a number that describes the extent to which the returns of the two stocks move up or down together. This also will be made more precise in the next section.
3. The ***expected return** of the portfolio* is defined as the number $x_1R_1 + x_2R_2$.
4. The *variance of the return of the portfolio* is defined as the number $\sigma_1^2x_1^2 + 2\sigma_{12}x_1 + \sigma_2^2x_2^2$.
5. The ***standard deviation*** of the return of the portfolio is defined as the square root of the variance.

From these definitions is follows that, for the two-stock example, the portfolio model takes the form

$$\begin{aligned}
\text{Min } & \sigma_1^2 x_1^2 + 2\sigma_{12} x_1 x_2 + \sigma_2^2 x_2^2 && \text{(variance of return)} \\
\text{s.t. } & x_1 + x_2 = 1 && \text{(all funds must be invested)} \\
& x_1 R_1 + x_2 R_2 \geq b && \text{(lower bound on the expected return of the portfolio)} \\
& x_1 \leq S_1 && \text{(upper bound on investments in stock 1)} \\
& x_2 \leq S_2 && \text{(upper bound on investments in stock 2)} \\
& x_1, x_2 \geq 0 && \text{(nonnegativity implies that "short selling" of a stock is not allowed)}
\end{aligned}$$

To create a specific numerical example let

$$\sigma_1^2 = 0.09 \quad R_1 = 0.06 \quad S_1 = 0.75 \quad b = 0.03$$

$$\sigma_2^2 = 0.06 \quad R_2 = 0.02 \quad S_2 = 0.9 \quad \sigma_{12} = 0.02$$

The feasible set for this model is shown in Figure 7.23, where for convenience the objective function and both sides of the expected return constraint have been multiplied by 100. Because of the equality constraint ($x_1 + x_2 = 1$) the feasible set is the heavy line segment connecting the points (0.25, 0.75) and (0.75, 0.25). Each contour of the objective function is an ellipse with its center at the origin and its minor axis lying on a line that forms a 26.55° angle with the x_1 axis. The 2 and 4.54 contours are shown in Figure 7.23.

Note that as the value of the contour increases, the general shape of the ellipse remains the same, but it increases in size. The challenge is to select the smallest value for the contour so that the ellipse just touches the feasible set. As indicated in Figure 7.23, the 4.54 contour touches the feasible set at the point ($x_1^* = 0.36$, $x_2^* = 0.64$), which is the optimal solution.

It is not important for you to know how to construct these contours. Real models are, after all, optimized on a computer, not graphically. The geometric representation, however, is a useful way to understand the model and is helpful in interpreting properties of the solution.

FIGURE 7.23

Graphical Solution for the Portfolio Selection Model

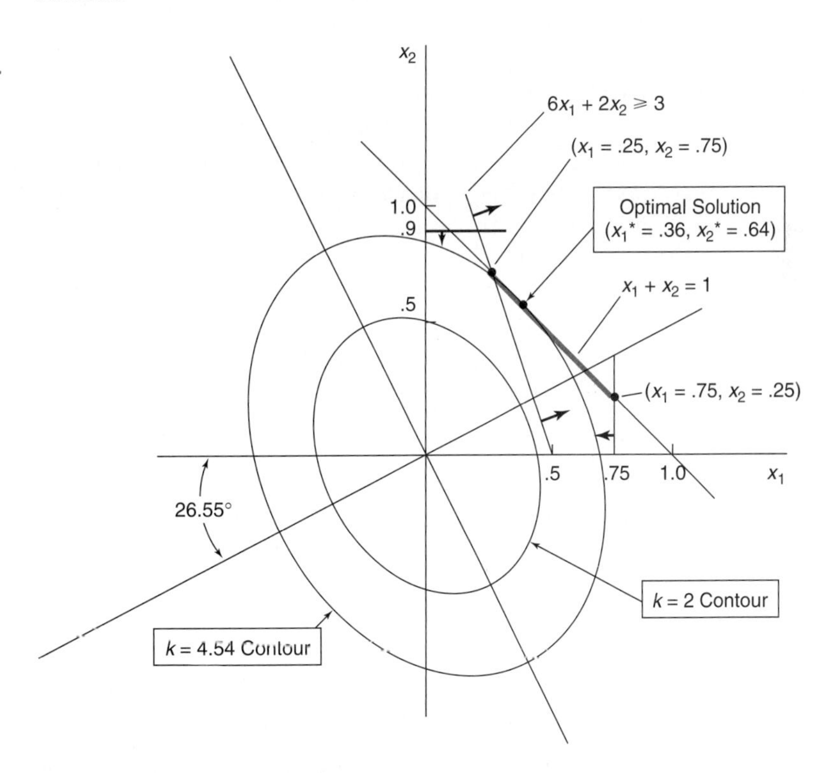

FIGURE 7.24

Solver Solution to Portfolio Example

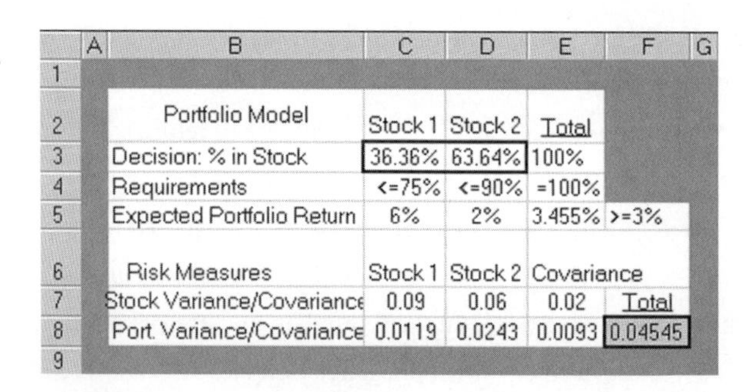

	A	B	C	D	E	F	G
1							
2		Portfolio Model	Stock 1	Stock 2	Total		
3		Decision: % in Stock	36.36%	63.64%	100%		
4		Requirements	<=75%	<=90%	=100%		
5		Expected Portfolio Return	6%	2%	3.455%	>=3%	
6		Risk Measures	Stock 1	Stock 2	Covariance		
7		Stock Variance/Covariance	0.09	0.06	0.02	Total	
8		Port. Variance/Covariance	0.0119	0.0243	0.0093	0.04545	
9							

Cell	Formula	Copy To
E5	= SUMPRODUCT(C3:D3,C5:D5)	—
C8	= C7*C3^2	D8
E8	= 2*E7*C3*D3	—

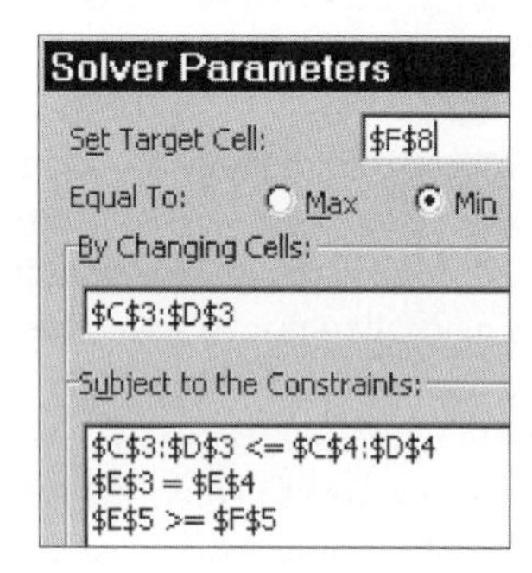

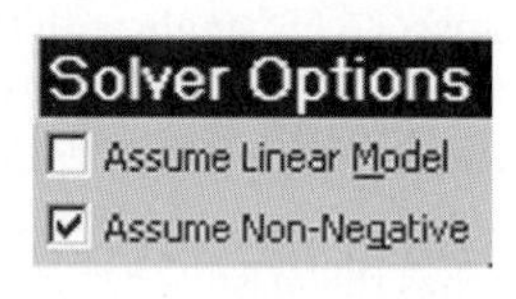

The Solver solution to the portfolio example is shown in Figure 7.24. Note that only the invest-all-funds constraint is binding. This, of course, was seen in the geometric representation in Figure 7.23. We can see from the LHS of the minimum-return constraint, that the expected return from this portfolio is 3.454%. Comparing the optimal values of x_1^* and x_2^* we see that the optimal portfolio contains more of the security with the lower expected yearly return (i.e., security 2). The reason is that the variance of security 2 is lower than that of security 1. The optimal mix is one that minimizes the portfolio variance while guaranteeing an expected portfolio return of at least 3%.

Note that Solver could equally as well been used to solve this model to maximize the portfolio return subject to a constraint that the portfolio variance not exceed a given upper bound. Since this formulation places the model's quadratic relationship as a constraint instead of as the objective function, it is not strictly speaking a quadratic model. However, such a formulation causes no difficulty with Solver's generalized gradient search procedure and many modelers prefer this latter formulation for portfolio optimization.

7.11 A PORTFOLIO EXAMPLE WITH DATA

In this section we turn to a three-asset example. In contrast to the previous example in which all the parameters were given, data will be used to estimate the parameters in this model. The model will then be optimized with Solver, and we will discuss the solution.

FORMULATING THE MODEL

In this section the three financial assets will be designated, at the outset, as x, y, and z. Let

X = fraction of asset x in the portfolio

Y = fraction of asset y in the portfolio

Z = fraction of asset z in the portfolio

The terminology "asset i" will be used to refer to asset x, or asset y, or asset z. In the previous sections the portfolio model was presented as if the parameters that describe the distribution of future returns were known, that is, it was assumed that the expected returns, variances, and covariances among the stocks were known. In the real world these parameters must be estimated with historical data. In general if n periods (years) of data are available, there will be, for each asset i, an actual historical return R_i^t associated with each period t where t ranges from 1 to n. In other words, each asset will have n historical returns. The expected periodic return from asset i is estimated with $\overline{R}_i = \frac{1}{n}\sum_{t=1}^{n} R_i^t$, which is the average of the asset's historical returns. The periodic historical returns R_i^t, are also used to estimate variances and covariances. The appropriate formulas are:[11]

$$\text{estimate of the variance of return for asset } i = \frac{1}{n}\sum_{t=1}^{n}(R_i^t - \overline{R}_i)^2$$

$$\text{estimate of the covariance of returns for assets } i \text{ and } j = \frac{1}{n}\sum_{t=1}^{n}(R_i^t - \overline{R}_i)(R_j^t - \overline{R}_j)$$

As before, we also define

b = lower bound on expected return of the portfolio

S_i = upper bound on the fraction of asset i that can be in the portfolio

In terms of the parameters, the quadratic programming formulation of the three-asset model is

$$\text{Min } \sigma_x^2X^2 + \sigma_y^2Y^2 + \sigma_z^2Z^2 + 2\sigma_{xy}XY + 2\sigma_{xz}XZ + 2\sigma_{yz}YZ$$

$$\text{s.t.} \quad \left.\begin{aligned} R_xX + R_yY + R_zZ &\geq b \\ X + Y + Z &= 1 \\ X &\leq S_x \\ Y &\leq S_y \\ Z &\leq S_z \\ X, Y, Z &\geq 0 \end{aligned}\right\} \text{Feasible region is same as in LP}$$

The objective function is the variance of the portfolio return, which, as stated in the previous section, is commonly considered to be the risk of the portfolio. (The rationale for this definition of risk, as well as the derivation of the objective function, is in the domain of statistics and is beyond our scope.)The first constraint expresses the lower bound on the expected return of the portfolio. The second constraint says that the investment fractions add to one, and the remaining constraints are upper bounds.

When a portfolio is allowed to be constructed from more than three assets the expected return is defined to be $\sum_{i=1}^{n} X_iR_i$. As before, R_i is the expected return from asset i, and X_i is the fraction of asset i in the portfolio. In this general case of N assets, the variance of the return of the portfolio is defined as[12]

$$\sum_{i=1}^{n} X_i^2\sigma_i^2 + 2\sum_{i=1}^{N-1}\sum_{j=i+1}^{N} X_iX_j\sigma_{ij}$$

[11] Readers with a statistical background will note that these estimation formulas do not account for degrees of freedom loss. We use these formulas in order to agree with Excel's COVAR() function despite the slight estimation bias they introduce.

[12] In matrix notation the variance of the portfolio return is written as X^TYX, where X is a column vector $(X_1 \ldots, X_N)$ and Y denotes the symmetric "covariance matrix" whose (i,j)th entry is σ_{ij} (and where $\sigma_{ii} = \sigma_i^2$). If X is a row vector, then the variance of the portfolio return is given by XYX^T.

Table 7.4

Historical Stock Returns

YEAR	AT&T	GM	USS
1	30.0%	22.5%	14.9%
2	10.3%	29.0%	26.0%
3	21.6%	21.6%	41.9%
4	–4.6%	–27.2%	–7.8%
5	–7.1%	14.4%	16.9%
6	5.6%	10.7%	–3.5%
7	3.8%	32.1%	13.3%
8	8.9%	30.5%	73.2%
9	9.0%	19.5%	2.1%
10	8.3%	39.0%	13.1%
11	3.5%	–7.2%	0.6%
12	17.6%	71.5%	90.8%

SOLVER SOLUTION

After numerical estimates are substituted for the parameters, this quadratic programming model can be optimized with Solver. As a specific example, let us now consider three stocks and historical returns for 12 years. The three stocks chosen were AT&T, General Motors, and USX, the holding company for US Steel. The returns for the stocks are given in Table 7.4. In this table the return in year n is defined by

$$\frac{(\text{closing price}, n) - (\text{closing price}, n-1) + (\text{dividends}, n)}{(\text{closing price}, n-1)}$$

where closing prices and dividends are expressed in dollars per share.[13]

Now suppose that you wish to minimize the variance of the return of the portfolio, subject to a 15% expected return and a restriction that no more than 75% of the portfolio can be in any individual stock. The spreadsheet model, Solver solution, and Sensitivity Report are given in Figure 7.25.[14]

The solution to the model specifies a portfolio of about 53% ATT, 35.6% GM, and 11.35% US Steel. The expected yearly return is exactly 15%. The OV indicates that the variance of portfolio yearly return is about 0.0205, which means its standard deviation is about $\sqrt{.0205} = 14.33\%$. If you had believed in the validity of this model, and if you had further assumed (in addition to the validity of the model) that the portfolio returns are Normally distributed with mean 15% and standard deviation of 14.33%, then according to statistical theory you might reasonably (to a 95% confidence level) have expected that such a portfolio, in ensuing years, would have produced returns roughly between –13.7% and +43.7% (i.e., 15% ± 2*14.33%). In fact, the returns over the ensuing three years for the three stocks were as shown in Table 7.5. Hence, using the model's optimal fractions, the actual portfolio returns would have been as shown in Table 7.5.

In concluding this section, we observe that the Lagrangian multiplier indicates that a 1% increase in expected return (an increase of 0.01 of the value in cell G21) would lead to an increase of 0.00324 in variance, approximately. Hence, the new portfolio variance would be about 0.0238 with the standard deviation equal to $\sqrt{.0238} = 15.4\%$. These numbers are

---

[13] Note the following unsatisfactory implication of this definition of averaging. Suppose there are no dividends, that in year 1 the stock goes from 1.0 to 1.5 (with a return of 0.5) and in year 2 the stock goes from 1.5 to 1 (with a return of –0.33). The average 2-year return is 0.17/2. Would you agree? This shows that estimating expected returns (and covariances) can be a delicate issue. It should be emphasized that this illustration is very introductory in nature.

[14] If "short sales" of a stock were permitted, then the nonnegativity constraints would be removed by unchecking the "Assume Non-Negative" Solver option.

FIGURE 7.25

Solver Solution to the Portfolio Example with Data

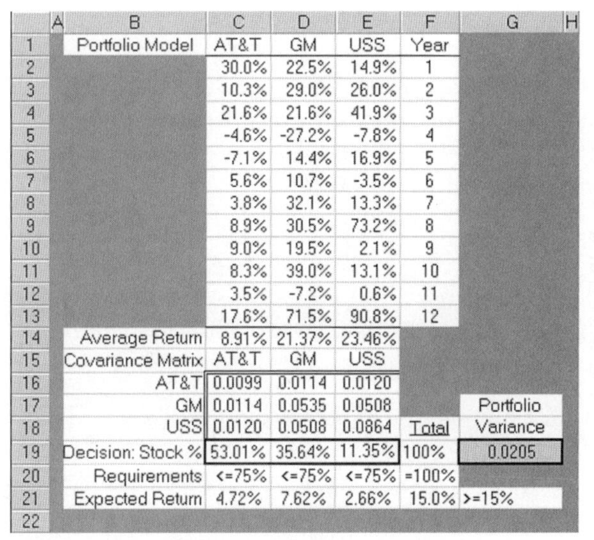

	B	C	D	E	F	G
1	Portfolio Model	AT&T	GM	USS	Year	
2		30.0%	22.5%	14.9%	1	
3		10.3%	29.0%	26.0%	2	
4		21.6%	21.6%	41.9%	3	
5		-4.6%	-27.2%	-7.8%	4	
6		-7.1%	14.4%	16.9%	5	
7		5.6%	10.7%	-3.5%	6	
8		3.8%	32.1%	13.3%	7	
9		8.9%	30.5%	73.2%	8	
10		9.0%	19.5%	2.1%	9	
11		8.3%	39.0%	13.1%	10	
12		3.5%	-7.2%	0.6%	11	
13		17.6%	71.5%	90.8%	12	
14	Average Return	8.91%	21.37%	23.46%		
15	Covariance Matrix	AT&T	GM	USS		
16	AT&T	0.0099	0.0114	0.0120		
17	GM	0.0114	0.0535	0.0508		Portfolio
18	USS	0.0120	0.0508	0.0864	Total	Variance
19	Decision: Stock %	53.01%	35.64%	11.35%	100%	0.0205
20	Requirements	<=75%	<=75%	<=75%	=100%	
21	Expected Return	4.72%	7.62%	2.66%	15.0%	>=15%
22						

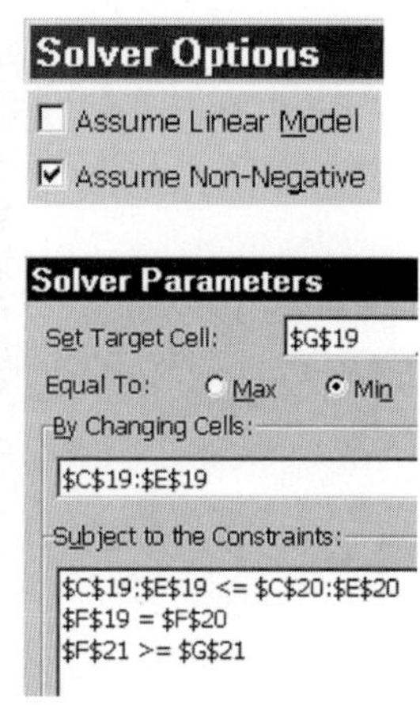

Cell	Formula	Copy To
C14	= AVERAGE(C2:C13)	D14:E14
C16	= COVAR(C2:C13,$C$2:$C$13)	D16:E16
C17	= COVAR(C2:C13,$D$2:$D$13)	D17:E17
C18	= COVAR(C2:C13,$E$2:$E$13)	D18:E18
G19	= SUMPRODUCT(MMULT(C19:E19,C16:E18),C19:E19)	—
F19	= SUM(C19:E19)	F21
C21	= C19*C14	D21:E21

Microsoft Excel 9.0 Sensitivity Report

Adjustable Cells

Cell	Name	Final Value	Reduced Gradient
$C$19	Decision: Stock % AT&T	53.01%	0.00%
$D$19	Decision: Stock % GM	35.64%	0.00%
$E$19	Decision: Stock % USS	11.35%	0.00%

Constraints

Cell	Name	Final Value	Lagrange Multiplier
$F$19	Decision: Stock % Total	100%	-0.0076
$F$21	Expected Return Total	15%	0.3244

Table 7.5

Actual Stock Returns

STOCK	YEAR 1	YEAR 2	YEAR 3
AT&T	10.3%	3.9%	3.0%
GM	51.2%	–5.0%	–20.0%
USS	64.7%	32.2%	–26.6%
Portfolio Returns	31.1%	3.9%	–8.6%

approximate because for any QP the slopes of the *OV* as a function of given RHS value are instantaneous (rather than a constant over intervals as is the case with LP). For the portfolio model, it is reflected by the general shape for the portfolio variance as a function of *b*, *OV*(*b*), as shown in Figure 7.26. To create the figure a SolverTable 1 was set up to repeatedly solve for the optimal portfolio variance using values of the expected return between 10% and 20%.

FIGURE 7.26

The Portfolio Efficient Frontier

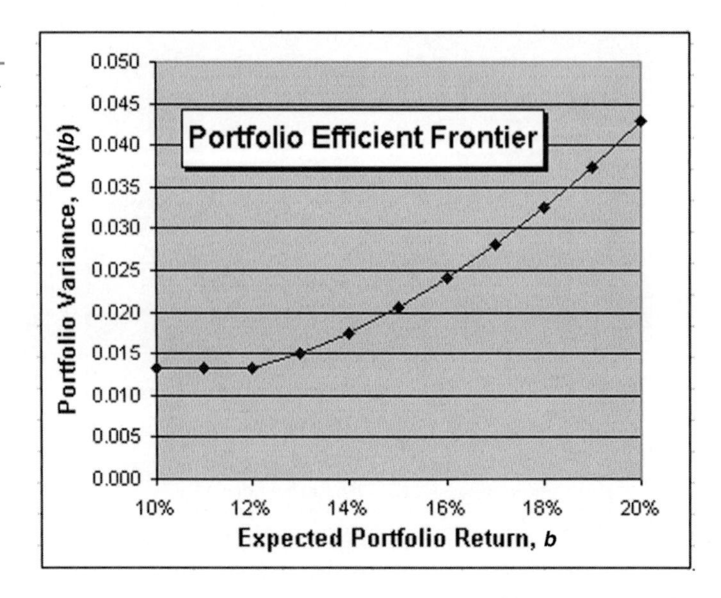

Note that the graph shows that tightening the expected return constraint—that is, increasing the expected return, *b*—hurts the OV more and more. In the language of finance, this graph is called the portfolio **efficient frontier**, and its properties are studied in finance courses. For our purposes we merely observe that it is a piecewise quadratic convex function.

7.12 THE EOQ INVENTORY MODEL

Inventories are defined as *idle goods in storage*, waiting to be used. There are many types of inventories; for example, inventories of raw materials, inventories of in-process materials, inventories of finished goods, inventories of cash, and even inventories of individuals. Inventories are held for many reasons:

1. Inventories smooth out the time gap between supply and demand. For example, the corn crop is harvested in September and October, but user demand for corn is steady throughout the year. Thus, the harvest must be stored in inventory for later use.
2. The possibility of holding inventory often contributes to lower production costs, for it is more economical to produce some items in large batches even though immediate orders for the items may not exist.
3. Inventories provide a way of storing labor. For example, the availability of labor for production may be a binding constraint in some later time period but slack in the earlier periods. The possibility of producing excess output in these earlier periods and carrying the product forward in inventory frees labor in the later periods for alternative uses.
4. Finally, inventory is a way of providing quick customer service at the time an item is needed, and customers are willing to pay for this convenience.

There are generally three types of costs associated with the inventory activity: *holding costs, ordering costs,* and *stockout costs.* These inventory costs are best explained by an example. Among other products offered for sale, STECO stocks a short-length optical fiber network cable (NC) used to connect Internet routers to local area network equipment.

Holding Costs Currently there are 3000 NCs in STECO's stock. Each NC costs STECO \$8. Thus, STECO currently has $8 \times 3000 = \$24{,}000$ tied up with the inventory of this item. Suppose that STECO were to reduce this inventory to only 1000 items. Instead of \$24,000, the investment would be reduced to \$8,000. It would then be possible to invest some of the \$16,000 that is released. In other words, by holding inventory STECO forgoes the opportunity to make other investments. This so-called **opportunity cost** is perhaps the most important contribution to inventory holding cost. The magnitude of this cost is closely tied to the market interest rate. There are other holding costs, such as breakage, pilferage, insurance, warehousing, and special handling requirements. *The larger the inventories, the larger the inventory holding costs.*

Ordering Costs Each time STECO places an order to replenish its inventories an ordering cost is incurred. *This cost is independent of the quantity ordered.* It is related to the amount of personnel time required for accounting, invoicing, order checking, and so on, when an order is placed.

Stockout Costs A **stockout** means that the firm runs out of inventory. In most technical uses, the term *stockout* refers to the specific phenomenon that orders arrive after inventory has been depleted. There are, at least in the context of a model, two ways to treat such orders. One way is to save up the orders and fill them later after the inventory has been replenished. This is called **backlogging**. The study of inventory includes models that deal with the possibility of stocking out, and in such a case some models assume backlogging; others assume no backlogging. In either case there is a cost of stocking out. This cost could include the lost profit from not making the sale (in the no-backlogging case) or from late delivery (the backlogging case), as well as discounts for a number of more intangible factors, such as the cost of possibly losing the customer, of losing goodwill, and of establishing a poor record of service. In the case of stockouts with no backlogging, we generally use the term **penalty cost**, which means the per unit cost of unsatisfied demand. In the case of stockouts with backlogging we speak of a **backlogging cost**, which means the per unit cost of backlogging demand.

For a company such as STECO, with hundreds of thousands of dollars tied up in inventory, there must be a right way and a wrong way to manage the inventory function. The main trade-offs are clear: On one hand, it is good to have inventory on hand to make sure that customers' orders can be satisfied (i.e., to avoid *stockout costs*). On the other hand, carrying inventory implies a *holding cost.* This cost can be reduced by ordering smaller quantities more often, but that approach involves increased *ordering costs.* These three cost factors must be balanced against each other.

Once the fundamental question of what items to order has been determined, the questions to be answered are the same for all inventory control systems. For every type of item held in inventory, someone must answer the two key questions of inventories: (1) *when* should a replenishment order be placed and (2) what should be the **order quantity**, or *how much* should be ordered? A multitude of factors combine to make this a difficult problem. Some of the most important considerations are

1. The extent to which future demand is known
2. The cost of stocking out and management's policy (backlogging or not)
3. The inventory holding and ordering costs
4. The possibility of long *lead times*—the period of time between when an order is placed and when the material actually arrives
5. The possibility of quantity discount purchasing plans

STECO WHOLESALING: THE CURRENT POLICY

The monthly demand for NCs during the preceding year is given in the Table 7.6. The term **demand** means "orders received." It is not necessarily the same as *sales.* For example, in January of last year 5300 items were demanded. If *at least* 5300 items were in inventory, then sales equaled demand (i.e., sales were 5300). If fewer than 5300 items were in inventory, say only 5000, then sales were 5000, which is less than the demand of 5300, and consequently a stockout occurred.

Table 7.6

Monthly NC Demand

MONTH	DEMAND (UNITS)
January	5,300
February	5,100
March	4,800
April	4,700
May	5,000
June	5,200
July	5,300
August	4,900
September	4,800
October	5,000
November	4,800
December	5,100
Total Annual Demand	60,000
Average Monthly Demand	5,000

Over a period of several years the demand has remained at a steady rate of about 5000 NCs per month. Based on this fact, STECO's policy last year was to add 5000 NCs to inventory each month. Since demand is expected to hold at about the same level in the future, this is the current policy as well. However, given this data, is this a good policy?

One way to attempt to answer this question would be to see what the policy of ordering 5000 NCs each month *would* cost in a simplified model, assuming for example that

1. Shipments always arrive on the first day of the month.
2. Demand is known and occurs at a constant rate of 5000 units per month.
3. All demand will be satisfied with no backlogging. In other words, stockouts are forbidden.

With these assumptions a plot of the inventory on hand at any time can be drawn, as in Figure 7.27. Notice how the inventory jumps up by 5000 units at the beginning of each month when a shipment arrives and decreases continuously at a constant rate of 5000 items per month (the constant monthly rate of demand). Also notice that a replenishment shipment from the producer arrives at the instant the inventory on hand hits zero. Thus, no stockouts occur. Given assumptions 1, 2, and 3, the cost of operating the system shown in Figure 7.27 depends only on *how much new stock is ordered* and on the *holding and ordering costs.* Let us see how the operating cost arises. First, note that a policy of ordering 5000 NCs each month, combined with constant demand of 5000 per month, produces an average inventory of 2500 NCs, as shown in Figure 7.27.

Figure 7.28 shows the effect of ordering 10,000 NCs every other month. Assuming demand remains constant at 5000 per month, average inventory is doubled, but the annual number of replenishment orders is halved. Thus, a policy of increasing the order quantity

FIGURE 7.27

Inventory on Hand, 5000 Order Quantity

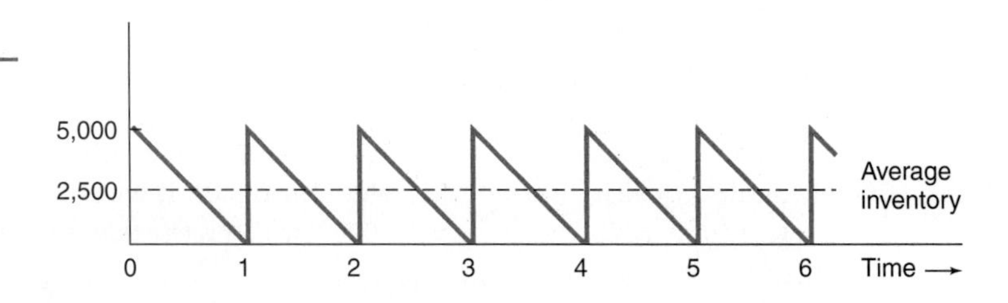

FIGURE 7.28

Inventory on Hand, 10,000 Order Quantity

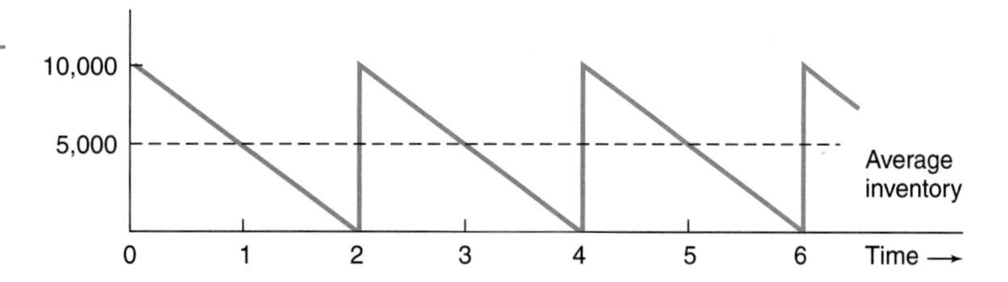

increases the holding costs, because average inventory is higher, and decreases the annual ordering cost, because fewer replenishments are required.

To answer the two questions posed above, a simple model will be used, called the **economic order quantity (EOQ) model.** The EOQ model attempts to balance the cost of placing orders with the cost of holding inventory.

DEVELOPING THE EOQ MODEL

The EOQ model in its simplest form assumes that

1. No stockouts are allowed. That is, each new order arrives (in totality) as soon as the inventory level hits zero.
2. There is a constant rate of demand.
3. The relevant costs are ordering and holding costs.

The EOQ model finds the **optimal order quantity**, which is defined to be the quantity that under the three assumptions above *minimizes the total cost per year of ordering NCs and holding them in inventory.* It is based on

1. ***Ordering cost*** = C_o: Every time an order is placed, the purchasing department must contact the supplier to determine the current price and delivery time, complete the order form, via the WWW or by e-mail, transfer the order into STECO's inventory control system, and initiate its receiving and stock-keeping records. When the order arrives, the receiver must complete the receiving and stock-keeping records and update STECO's order status data base. All of this costs money. STECO estimates the cost of placing an order for NCs, *regardless of the number of units ordered,* to be $25. This includes $20 in clerical and purchasing agent labor, plus $5 in material, and telecommunications costs.
2. ***Inventory holding cost*** = C_h: Every dollar invested in inventory could be put to use elsewhere by STECO. For example, it could be put in a bank or invested in Treasury bills to earn interest. When a dollar is tied up in inventory, STECO loses the opportunity to invest it elsewhere, thus leading to opportunity cost. Typically, the opportunity cost accounts for a large part of the cost of holding inventory. In addition, there are overhead costs such as rent, utilities, and insurance that must be allocated to the items in inventory.

The cost of holding inventory is typically expressed as the cost of holding one unit for one year and is calculated as a percentage of the cost of the item. STECO estimates that the cost of holding a NC in inventory for one year is 24% of its purchase price. The 24% figure can be subdivided into an opportunity cost of 20% plus a variable cost per item of 4%. Since each NC costs $8, the cost of holding each item in inventory for one year is $C_h = 0.24 \times \$8.00 = \$1.92$.

The Annual Holding and Ordering Cost The first step in calculating the cost-minimizing order quantity is to derive an expression for the *annual holding and ordering cost* (AHO) as a function of the order quantity. It consists of two parts, annual ordering cost and annual holding cost.

$$\text{annual ordering cost} = C_o \times (\text{number of orders per year}) \tag{7.1}$$

If the order quantity is 5000 units, STECO will place 12 orders a year, since the model assumes a total demand of 60,000, and $^{60,000}/_{5000} = 12$. The general formula is

$$N = \frac{D}{Q} \qquad (7.2)$$

where N = number of orders per year, D = annual demand, and Q = order quantity. Thus, in general

$$\text{annual ordering cost} = C_o N = C_o\left(\frac{D}{Q}\right) \qquad (7.3)$$

To compute the annual holding cost STECO makes use of two facts: (1) The annual holding cost is equal to C_h times the average inventory, and (2) the average inventory is equal to one half of the maximum inventory when demand occurs at a constant rate. Since the order quantity is also the maximum amount of inventory on hand (see Figure 7.27 and Figure 7.28), it follows that

$$\text{annual holding cost} = C_h\left(\frac{Q}{2}\right) \qquad (7.4)$$

If we add together expressions (7.3) and (7.4), we see that the assumptions of the EOQ model give the following expression for the annual holding and ordering cost as a function of the order quantity Q:

$$\text{AHO}(Q) = C_o\left(\frac{D}{Q}\right) + C_h\left(\frac{Q}{2}\right) \qquad (7.5)$$

Since demand occurs at the rate of D units per year, we know that these Q units will be depleted in Q/D years, which is precisely when the inventory level hits the value zero. For example, when $Q = 5000$ and $D = 60,000$, the order of 5000 units is depleted in $5000/60,000 = 1/12$ year = 1 month, as we have already seen (Figure 7.27). For NCs, the relevant values of C_o, D, and C_h can be plugged into expression (7.5) to give:

$$\text{AHO}(Q) = \$25\left(\frac{60,000}{Q}\right) + \$1.92\left(\frac{Q}{2}\right) = \left(\frac{1,500,000}{Q}\right) + 0.96Q \qquad (7.6)$$

When $Q = 5000$ it is seen that

$$\text{AHO}(5000) = \$300 + \$4800 = \$5100$$

Now, however, using expression (7.6), the annual holding and ordering cost for NCs can be plotted as a function of the order quantity Q, as shown in Figure 7.29. From this graph it is clear that the optimal order quantity [the one that minimizes AHO(Q)] is somewhat larger than 1000 items.

Figure 7.30 presents the spreadsheet version of STECO's inventory model. The model is nonlinear because of the Q in the denominator of the ordering cost formula. The cost for-

FIGURE 7.29

STECO Annual Holding and Ordering Costs as a Function of Order Quantity

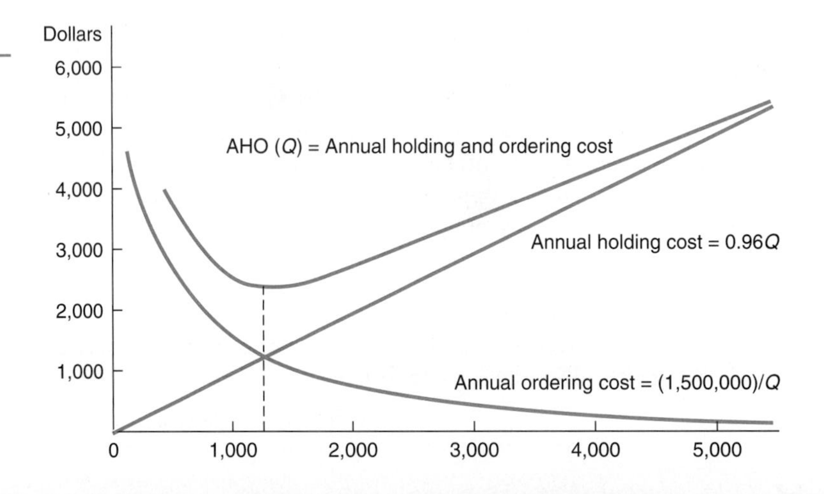

FIGURE 7.30

STECO EOQ Model

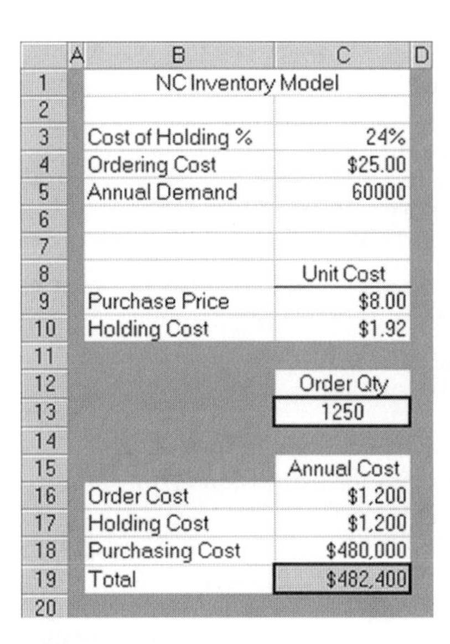

	A	B	C	D
1		NC Inventory Model		
2				
3		Cost of Holding %	24%	
4		Ordering Cost	$25.00	
5		Annual Demand	60000	
6				
7				
8			Unit Cost	
9		Purchase Price	$8.00	
10		Holding Cost	$1.92	
11				
12			Order Qty	
13			1250	
14				
15			Annual Cost	
16		Order Cost	$1,200	
17		Holding Cost	$1,200	
18		Purchasing Cost	$480,000	
19		Total	$482,400	
20				

Solver Parameters

Set Target Cell: $C$19

Equal To: Max Min

By Changing Cells:

$C$13

Subject to the Constraints:

$C$13 >= 1

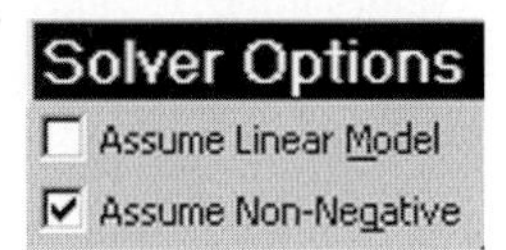

Cell	Formula
C10	= C3*C9
C16	= C4*C5/C13
C17	= C10*C13/2
C18	= C9*C5

mulas in cells C16:C17 are those of the ordering and holding costs, as given above. Because it is not a function of Q, Purchasing cost (= Purchase Price × Annual Demand) is a constant and is unnecessary for the calculation of the optimal Q. It is included for completeness of the total annual costs. The constraint that there be at least one order per year is included to prevent Solver from testing an (unreasonable) candidate $Q = 0$, thereby producing a "#DIV/0!" error in the ordering cost formula, which will abort the Solver optimization process. The optimal solution is displayed, confirming the graphical representation in Figure 7.29.

THE EOQ FORMULA: Q^*

It would obviously be useful to have an expression for Q^*, the optimal order quantity. (The asterisk indicates the value of Q that is the optimal solution to the model.) Because of its simple form, a formula can be derived to calculate its value as a function of the parameters in the problem by using calculus to minimize the function AHO(Q) presented in (7.5). A consequence of this approach is that at the optimum, the annual holding cost is equal to the annual ordering cost[15]

$$C_h\left(\frac{Q^*}{2}\right) = C_o\left(\frac{D}{Q^*}\right) \tag{7.7}$$

or

$$(Q^*)^2 = \frac{2C_oD}{C_h} \tag{7.8}$$

or

$$Q^* = \sqrt{\frac{2C_oD}{C_h}} \tag{7.9}$$

[15] That the cost minimizing quantity occurs at the point where the two terms, annual holding cost and annual ordering cost, are equal is true only for these functions. It is not true in general.

It is sometimes convenient to estimate C_h by assuming that it is some percentage (say, i) of the purchase price (P); that is, $C_h = iP$. Equation 7.9 can then be rewritten

$$Q^* = \sqrt{\frac{2C_oD}{iP}} \tag{7.10}$$

In our example, P, the purchase price for NCs, is \$8 and i, the fraction of P that is used to calculate C_h, is 0.24.

The quantity Q^* is often termed the **economic order quantity**, and it should be noted that it is expressed in terms of the input parameters C_o, C_h, and D. By substituting the NC values for D, C_o, and C_h into (7.9), the optimal order quantity for NCs is:

$$Q^* = \sqrt{\frac{2 \times 60{,}000 \times 25}{1.92}} = 1250$$

Plugging this value into the expression for the annual holding and ordering cost for NCs (equation [7.6]) yields

$$\text{AHO}(Q^*) = \text{AHO}(1250) = \frac{(1{,}500{,}000)}{1250} + (0.96)(1250)$$
$$= \$1200 + \$1200 = \$2400$$

These values are the same as found by Solver in Figure 7.30.

SENSITIVITY ANALYSIS

Whether the optimal EOQ policy should be used in the future depends on the realism of the assumptions. After all, the EOQ model, like any other model, is idealized. It is no more than a selective representation of reality: an abstraction and an approximation. In this case, as with all models, the main question is: "How sensitive are the results of the model to the assumptions and the data?"

Since the model is fairly realistic, it seems reasonable that the inventory costs obtained within the model are fairly good estimates of the costs that STECO is actually incurring. Therefore, using a policy that is optimal in the model (order quantity of 1250) seems preferable to the traditional policy of ordering 5000. However, STECO should be concerned about how sensitive the optimal order quantity and, more important, the optimal annual cost are to the data. After all, each of the parameters C_o and C_h is in itself an estimate. If STECO errs in estimating these parameters, how much effect will that error have on the difference between the calculated Q^* and AHO* and the true Q^* and AHO*? If the results are highly sensitive to the values of the estimates, it is not clear whether the optimal policy for the model should actually be implemented by STECO.

Let us therefore consider how the EOQ results might vary with changes in our estimated holding and ordering costs. Recall that STECO assumed that C_h = \$ 1.92 and C_o = \$25. We will consider four cases in which the true parameters are different from the values selected by STECO. These "true values" are shown in the first two columns in Table 7.7.

Table 7.7

Sensitivity to $C_h + C_o$

(1) TRUE PARAMETERS		(2)	(3)	(4)	(5)	(6)
C_h	C_o	OPTIMAL Q	MINIMUM COST (\$)	STECO'S DECISION*	STECO'S COST (\$)	LOSS (%)
(i) 1.72	23	1267	2179	Q = 1250	2179	0
(ii) 1.72	27	1372	2361	Q = 1250	2371	0.42
(iii) 2.12	23	1141	2419	Q = 1250	2429	0.41
(iv) 2.12	27	1236	2621	Q = 1250	2621	0

* Based on C_h = \$1.92, C_o = \$25.

In case (i) STECO has overestimated both cost parameters by about 10% each. Had STECO estimated the parameters correctly it would have ordered 1267 items and incurred an annual holding and ordering cost of \$2179. Because of STECO's parameter estimation errors, 1250 are ordered. In order to find out what costs STECO will actually incur, the AHO equation must be evaluated with its true parameter values (C_h = \$1.72 and C_o = \$23 in case [i]) and the value of Q determined by STECO estimates (1250). This calculation follows:

$$\text{AHO}(Q) = C_o\left(\frac{D}{Q}\right) + C_h\left(\frac{Q}{2}\right) = 23\left(\frac{60{,}000}{1250}\right) + 1.72\left(\frac{1250}{2}\right) = 23(48) + 1.72(625) = \$2179$$

This number is shown as STECO's Cost in column (5). We thus see that if STECO underestimates the two cost parameters as shown, it has no effect on the annual holding and ordering cost (to the nearest dollar). The other three cases show that the effect on the annual holding and ordering cost of any combination of 10% errors in the estimates of C_o and C_h is negligible. Our analysis suggests that in STECO's case the EOQ model is insensitive even to approximately 10% variations or errors in the cost estimates. It turns out that this is a property enjoyed by EOQ models in general.

7.13 INVENTORY WITH QUANTITY DISCOUNTS MODEL

The inventory model that STECO used above is the "classic" EOQ model that minimizes the annual holding and ordering cost. However, in practice there are many variations on this classic EOQ formula, each of which requires reformulation of the inventory relationships and recomputation of the EOQ quantity. In this and the next section we give two examples as illustrations.

QUANTITY DISCOUNTS AND STECO'S OVERALL OPTIMUM

Although included in the spreadsheet of Figure 7.30, there was previously no need to take into account the cost of purchasing the product, for the per item cost to STECO was assumed to be a constant independent of Q. However, STECO's NC supplier will offer a **quantity discount** as an incentive for more business. The supplier has agreed to offer a \$0.10 discount on every NC purchased if STECO orders in lots of at least 5000 items. Of course, higher-order quantities will also reduce the number of orders placed, and hence the annual ordering cost. As already discussed (compare Figures 7.27 and 7.28), a high-order quantity leads to a higher average inventory level and hence higher holding costs. Whether the discount will, on balance, be advantageous to STECO is not obvious.

Let us proceed as before, that is, to develop an annual cost curve and then find the order quantity that minimizes it. STECO's annual total cost [ATC(Q)] is the sum of the annual holding and ordering cost [AHO(Q)] and the annual purchase cost (APC), that is,

$$\text{ATC}(Q) = \text{AHO}(Q) + \text{APC}$$

From equation (7.5) and the fact that $C_h = iP$,

$$\text{AHO}(Q) = C_o\left(\frac{D}{Q}\right) + iP\left(\frac{Q}{2}\right)$$

Note that since C_h depends on the unit purchase price P, the expression for AHO also involves P. The annual purchase cost is simply the unit purchase price times annual demand. Thus, APC = PD, and it follows that

$$\text{ATC}(Q) = C_o\left(\frac{D}{Q}\right) + iP\left(\frac{Q}{2}\right) + PD$$

To see the effect of discounting, evaluate this function for two different prices, the regular price of \$8.00 per unit and the potential discounted price of \$7.90 per unit.

Regular price equation:

$$\text{ATC}(Q) = \frac{25 \times 60{,}000}{Q} + (0.24)(8.00)\left(\frac{Q}{2}\right) + (8.00)(60{,}000)$$

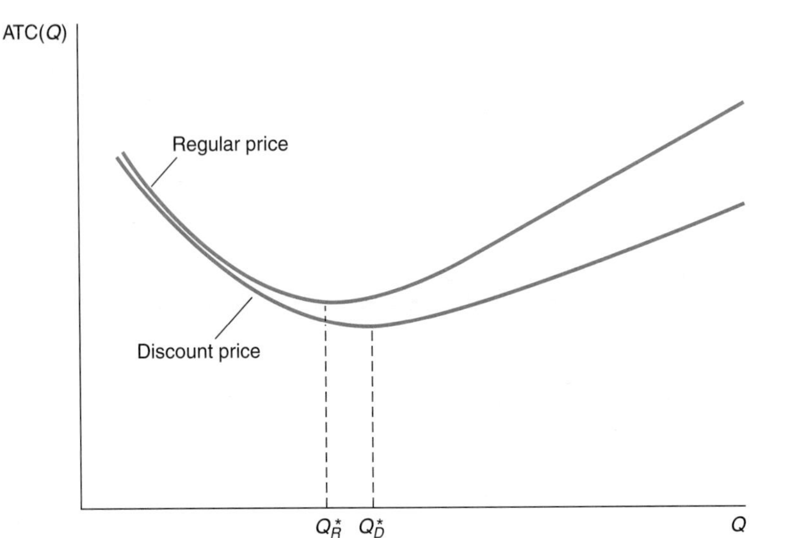

FIGURE 7.31

Annual Total Cost for Regular and Discount Prices

Discount price equation:

$$\text{ATC}(Q) = \frac{25 \times 60{,}000}{Q} + (0.24)(7.90)\left(\frac{Q}{2}\right) + (7.90)(60{,}000)$$

The general shape of these curves is shown in Figure 7.31. There are several facts to notice.

1. The discount curve lies below the regular cost curve. This is so because each term in the regular price ATC(Q) is greater than or equal to the corresponding term in the discount price ATC(Q).
2. The value of Q, say Q_D^*, that minimizes the discount price ATC(Q) is larger than the value of Q, say Q_R^*, that minimizes the regular price = ATC(Q). This is true because, using (7.10),

$$Q_D^* = \sqrt{\frac{2 \times 25 \times 60{,}000}{(0.24) \times (7.90)}} > \sqrt{\frac{2 \times 25 \times 60{,}000}{(0.24) \times (8.00)}} = Q_R^*$$

Obviously, STECO would like to minimize its annual total cost, ATC(Q). If STECO could get the discount price regardless of the order quantity, it would of course order Q_D^*. However, assume that the discount price holds only if STECO orders at least B items at a time. Two situations could arise. These are illustrated in Figure 7.32.

The dark-line portions of the curves in these figures indicate the actual cost function that STECO faces. They illustrate that the regular price curve must be used for order quantities of B or less and that the discount price curve can be used for order quantities greater than B.

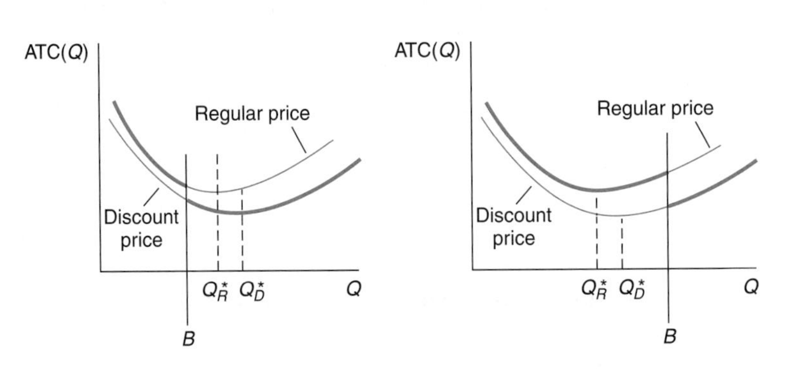

FIGURE 7.32

Effect of Minimum Order Size, B, on Order Quantity

We see that if $B \le Q_D^*$, STECO will achieve the minimum cost by ordering Q_D^*. If however, $B > Q_D^*$, the optimal decision, in general, is not immediately obvious. The best STECO can do on the regular price curve is to order Q_R^*. The best STECO can do on the discount price curve is to order B. (STECO cannot order less than B and get the discount price, and ordering more than B increases ATC.) To determine which of these is optimal STECO must calculate the ATC(Q) at these two points and compare them. The general rule then is

$$\text{If } B \le Q_D^*, \text{ order } Q_D^*.$$

$$\text{If } B > Q_D^*, \text{ order} \begin{cases} Q_R^* \text{ if regular price} \le \text{discount price} \\ \qquad \text{ATC}(Q_R^*) \quad \le \quad \text{ATC}(B) \\ B \text{ if not} \end{cases}$$

To apply this rule, STECO must order at least 5000 items to get the discount. Thus $B = 5000$. Figure 7.33 presents the Excel version of the inventory model with quantity discounts. In contrast to the symbolic approach taken above, the Excel model has been formulated to portray the annual cost as being an undiscounted Annual Cost in cells C16:C19 less a cost adjustment for the quantity discount, if any. That is, if the discount is taken, then an adjustment is made to the affected annual costs, Holding Cost and Purchasing Cost, to reflect the discount amounts. These costs are aggregated into the Total Net Cost, cells E16:E19. This approach permits treating the discount as a binary (integer) decision variable in cell D13. The formula in E13 is =D7*D13. Thus, if D13 is set by Solver to 0 (no discount), then the constraint becomes Order Quantity ≥ 0. Otherwise, if D13 is set by Solver to 1 (discount taken), then the adjustments to costs become nonzero and the constraint becomes Order Quantity ≥ 5000.

In this way Solver optimizes a mixed integer nonlinear program (MINLP) to evaluate the two EOQ functions, one with and one without the discount. Extending the model to multiple discounts (i.e., several quantity discount thresholds, each with an associated "adjustment" to total costs) requires straightforward addition of other binary variables, appropriate constraints to reflect the minimum quantities, and modifications to the Discount Adjustment formulas. For the STECO case, Figure 7.33 indicates that STECO should order 5000 items to take advantage of the quantity discount. This decision saves \$482,400 – \$479,040 = \$3360 per year over the next best decision (ordering Q_R^*). Clearly, quantity discounts can play an important role in determining an optimal inventory policy.

7.14 INVENTORY AND PRODUCTION, A LOT SIZE MODEL

Although STECO is primarily a wholesaler, it does have some productive capacity. In particular, it has an extensive and modern heat-treatment fiber cable "jacketing" facility that it uses to produce a number of specialty cable items that it then holds in inventory. The heat-treatment facility has two important characteristics: There is a large setup cost associated with producing each cable product, and once the setup is complete, production is at a steady and known rate.

The setup cost, which is analogous to the ordering cost in the EOQ model, is incurred because it is necessary to change the plastic fiber molds and the operating temperature in the heat-treatment facility to meet the specifications set forth by the cable standards specification. Also, each cable must have connectors attached and undergo testing for frequency response. Thus, an order quantity of network cables does not arrive from production into inventory all at once. Rather, it arrives steadily over a period of several days. This change requires a modification in the EOQ formula, even if the assumptions of a constant rate of demand and the inventory carrying cost being equal to C_h times the average inventory are maintained.

FIGURE 7.33

STECO EOQ Model with Quantity Discounts

	A	B	C	D	E
1		NC Inventory Model			
2			No Discount	With Discount	
3		Cost of Holding %	24%	24%	
4		Ordering Cost	$25.00	$25.00	
5		Ann. Demand	60000	60000	
6		Discount Amount		$0.10	
7		Min Order Size		5000	
8			Unit Cost	Disc. Adjustment	Net Unit Cost
9		Purchase Price	$8.00	-$0.10	$7.90
10		Holding Cost	$1.92	-$0.024	$1.896
11					
12			Order Qty	Discount Taken	Min Order Qty
13			5000	1	>=5000
14					
15			Annual Cost	Disc. Adjustment	Net Cost
16		Order Cost	$300		$300
17		Holding Cost	$4,800	-$60	$4,740
18		Purchasing Cost	$480,000	-$6,000	$474,000
19		Total Cost	$485,100	-$6,060	$479,040
20					

	A	B	C	D	E
1		NC Inventory Model			
2			No Discount	With Discount	
3		Cost of Hold	0.24	0.24	
4		Ordering Co	25	25	
5		Ann. Deman	60000	60000	
6		Discount Am		0.1	
7		Min Order Si		5000	
8			Unit Cost	Disc. Adjustment	Net Unit Cost
9		Purchase Pr	8	=-D6	=SUM(C9:D9)
10		Holding Cos	=C3*C9	=D3*D9	=SUM(C10:D10)
11					
12			Order Qty	Discount Taken	Min Order Qty
13			5000	1	=D7*D13
14					
15			Annual Cost	Disc. Adjustment	Net Cost
16		Order Cost	=C4*C5/C13		=SUM(C16:D16)
17		Holding Cos	=C10*C13/2	=D13*D10*C13/2	=SUM(C17:D17)
18		Purchasing	=C9*C5	=D13*D9*D5	=SUM(C18:D18)
19		Total Cost	=SUM(C16:C18)	=SUM(D16:D18)	=SUM(E16:E18)
20					

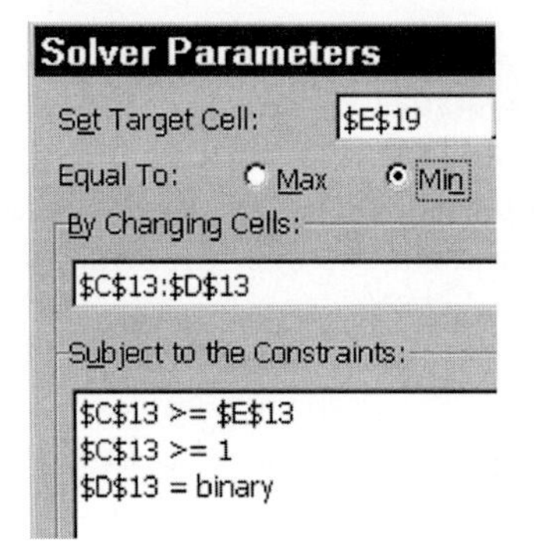

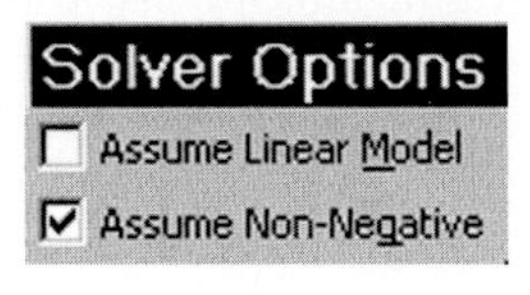

It is usually more convenient to work with this model in terms of daily production and demand rates. Thus, consider a product in which

d = number of units demanded each day

p = number of units produced each day during a production run

C_o = setup cost that is independent of the quantity produced

c_h = cost per *day* of holding inventory
(note the change in notation to emphasize holding cost per day)

It is obvious that p must be greater than d for the problem to be interesting. (If $p < d$, demand is greater than STECO's ability to produce, and holding inventory is the least of their problems.) Figure 7.34 presents a plot of what the inventory on hand would look like if STECO decided to produce in lots of Q items each. There are several aspects of this graph that must be noted in order to calculate the average holding and setup and cost per day.

1. During a production run items are added to inventory at a rate of p units per day and removed at the rate of d per day. The net effect is an increase at the rate of $p - d$ units per day.
2. At other times, items are removed from inventory at a rate of d items per day.
3. Since Q items are produced in a run, at the rate of p items per day, each production run is Q / p days long.
4. Since Q items are produced in a run, and d is the daily demand rate, each **cycle time**—that is, the interval between the start of arrivals of replenishments—is Q/d days long.

Facts 1 and 3 can be used to find the maximum amount of inventory on hand (see Figure 7.34).

$$\text{maximum inventory} = (p - d)\frac{Q}{p}$$

Since the average inventory equals one half of the maximum inventory, it follows

$$\text{average inventory} = \frac{1}{2}(p - d)\frac{Q}{p}$$

Rearranging the terms in the expression above, we obtain

$$\text{average inventory} = \frac{Q}{2}\left(1 - \frac{d}{p}\right)$$

$$\text{holding cost per day} = c_h\frac{Q}{2}\left(1 - \frac{d}{p}\right)$$

Similarly, since there is one setup every cycle and a cycle lasts Q/d days,

$$\text{setup cost per day} = \frac{C_o}{Q/d} = C_o\frac{d}{Q}$$

FIGURE 7.34

Inventory on Hand for the Production Lot Size Model

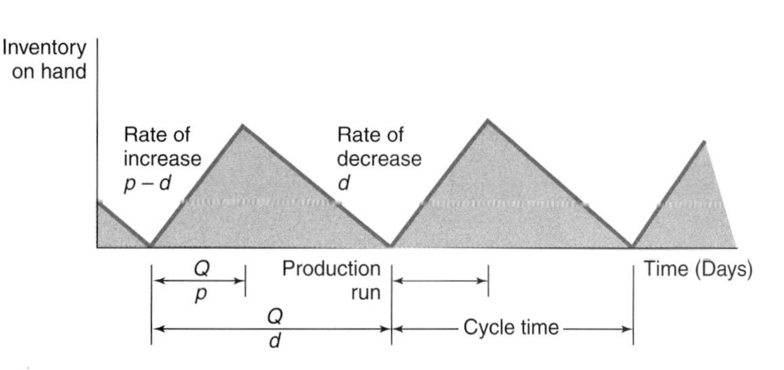

Thus, the daily holding and setup cost, denoted DHS(Q), is given by the expression

$$\text{DHS}(Q) = C_o \frac{d}{Q} + c_h \frac{Q}{2}\left(1 - \frac{d}{p}\right)$$

If you think of $c_h(1 - d/p)$ as a constant, this expression takes the same form as given by (7.5), the expression for the annual holding and ordering cost in the EOQ model.

It follows, then, that the value of Q that minimizes DHS(Q) will be given by the EOQ equation (7.9) with C_h appropriately modified. Thus, for the **production lot size model,**

$$Q^* = \sqrt{\frac{2C_o d}{c_h\left(1 - \frac{d}{p}\right)}} \qquad (7.11)$$

(This result could also have been derived with calculus.) Substituting Q^* for Q in the expression for DHS(Q) and simplifying gives us an expression for the minimum daily holding and setup cost:

$$\text{DHS}(Q^*) = \sqrt{2C_o d c_h\left(1 - \frac{d}{p}\right)}$$

Note that this expression does not depend on Q; it is valid only when the lot size is equal to the value of the expression in equation (7.11).

To apply this analysis to any particular product, STECO must estimate the various parameters for that product and then evaluate (7.11) to obtain Q^*. Thus, once the parameters are estimated, finding Q^* is reduced to a matter of evaluating the formulas.

To illustrate this model, assume the demand for this product averages 200 NCs per day. It costs \$100 to set up to jacket and heat treat the cables, and they can be produced at a rate of 400 NCs per day. STECO estimates the holding cost per day as (\$1)(0.24)/240 = \$0.001, where \$1 is the production cost of the NC, 0.24 is the annual interest rate used by STECO for all products, and 240 is the assumed number of working days per year. The optimal production lot size for this product, then, is

$$Q^* = \sqrt{\frac{2 \times 200 \times 100}{0.001\left(1 - \frac{200}{400}\right)}} = 8944$$

and the minimum daily holding and setup cost is

$$\sqrt{2 \times 200 \times 100 \times 0.001\left(1 - \frac{200}{400}\right)} = \$4.47$$

A production run of this size yields a supply of NCs large enough to satisfy demand for

$$\frac{8944}{200} = 44.72 \text{ days}$$

Alternatively, Solver can be used to perform the optimization that otherwise requires the application of calculus to determine the formulas, as above, and which may not be applicable if some of the assumptions are altered. The Excel NLP model for the production lot size problem is shown Figure 7.35. In practice, STECO might adjust this quantity to take into account the fact that a number of other products also have to make use of the cable heat-treatment facility. In addition, STECO would perhaps perform a sensitivity analysis of this model in a way similar to that done for the EOQ model in Section 7.12.

Other variations of this or the EOQ model would consider adding a safety stock to allow for the possibility that demand might run ahead of production at the beginning of a production run. Another variation would be to incorporate the concept of backlogging inventory in which the penalty costs of unavailable inventory are traded off against the savings of lowered average inventory levels.

FIGURE 7.35

Production Lot Size Model for STECO

	A	B	C	D
1		Production & Inventory Model		
2		Working Days Annually	240	
3		Annual Cost of Holding %	24%	
4		Production Setup Cost	$100	
5		Annual Demand	48000	
6		Daily Demand	200	
7		Production Rate/Day	400	
8			Unit Cost	
9		Variable Production Cost	$1.00	
10		Daily Holding Cost	$0.001	
11				
12		Production Lot Size	8944	
13			Daily Cost	
14		Order Cost	$2.24	
15		Holding Cost	$2.2361	
16		Production Cost	$400.00	
17		Total	$404.47	
18				

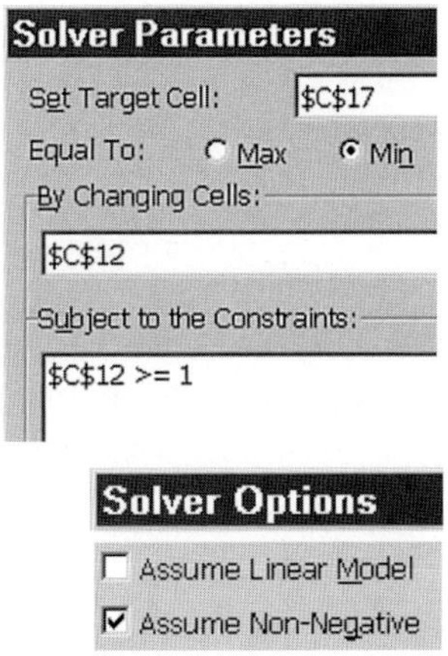

Solver Parameters

Set Target Cell: $C$17

Equal To: Max (•) Min

By Changing Cells: $C$12

Subject to the Constraints: $C$12 >= 1

Solver Options

☐ Assume Linear Model

☑ Assume Non-Negative

	A	B	C
8			Unit Cost
9		Variable Production Cost	1
10		Daily Holding Cost	=C3*C9/C2
11			
12		Production Lot Size	8944.28
13			Daily Cost
14		Order Cost	=C4*C6/C12
15		Holding Cost	=C10*C12/2*(1-C6/C7)
16		Production Cost	=C9*C7
17		Total	=SUM(C14:C16)
18			

7.15 SUMMARY AND NOTES ON NLP IMPLEMENTATION

The practice of nonlinear optimization is in some ways even more of an art than the practice of LP. Almost all LP optimizers are, in major respects, the same, since they are variants of the simplex method.[16] However, it would not be difficult to identify as many as 10 or 15 quite different procedures for solving NLP problems of which Solver uses only one. To find the best method for a given problem, indeed even to understand the differences between various approaches you, at least in this respect, must be more of an expert with mathematics. Another delicate aspect of NLP practice is the existence, from a mathematical viewpoint, of so many different types of nonlinear models with different theoretical properties (whereas there is only one type of LP). Associated with this fact is the need to reckon with the issue of local versus global solutions to the model. You must know enough about the mathematical structure of the model to have at least a feeling for the quality of the solution (e.g., local versus global) produced by Solver, and often you must experiment, either manually or with the Evolutionary Solver, in order to locate improved solutions.

While most NLP optimizers, like Solver, will compute the Lagrange multipliers (i.e., the shadow prices) and reduced gradients along with the solution, additional sensitivity analysis is generally not available without additional manual reoptimizations or use of

[16] Recent years have seen the development of new LP methods based upon approaches different from the simplex procedure used by Solver. Early evidence suggests these new methods are more efficient only for very large LP models involving thousands of variables.

TIP: *Limitations for Excel's Solver and for the Premium Edition for Education Solver NLPs are no more than 200 decision variables and no more than 100 constraints, ignoring any simple lower or upper bound constraints on the decision variables. The commercial upgrade, called Long Scale GRG Solver, optimizes larger NLP models (up to 4000 decision variables) and includes a special-purpose optimizer for QP models.*

SolverTable. Thus, from the managerial point of view, the NLP output contains less information than an LP output provides.

Although NLP applies to a wide spectrum of problems, the most common applications probably occur in situations where the model has special structure, such as for QP. For example, there may be linear constraints but a nonlinear objective function, and so on. In such cases there is hope of solving reasonably large-scale models. What do we mean by "large-scale" in NLP? Again, this is much less clearly defined than it is for LP. For a concave or convex quadratic program, we can aspire to several thousand constraints and variables. This power derives from the fact that for such a model a variant of the simplex method is often employed. However, for more general nonlinear problems, without special structure that is used to advantage, one would consider a problem with more than 2000 variables to be large even for a workstation-sized computer.

The last three sections of the chapter were devoted to applications of NLP in portfolio optimization in finance and the basic EOQ (economic order quantity) model and its various modifications in inventory management. The latter example, modifications of the basic EOQ model showed how the optimal order quantity must be modified in the face of a quantity discount and for the case in which items are not ordered from an outside source, but are produced internally.

These two classes of examples of NLP in Sections 7.10 through 7.14 satisfy the requirements of concavity and convexity that make the application of NLP models attractive. As a result, NLP is widely applied in finance and inventory management applications. Other NLP applications are clustered in such areas as engineering design, nonlinear statistical estimation, product distribution, physical applications such as oil drilling, and finally, optimal scheduling and equipment utilization when nonlinear costs are involved.

Key Terms

Optimal Value (OV). Short for the optimal value of the objective function.

Stationary Point. A point at which all first partial derivatives vanish.

First-Order Optimality Conditions. Necessary conditions for the existence of an optimum; all partial derivatives must equal zero.

Second-Order Optimality Conditions. Sufficient conditions for the existence of an optimum.

Nonlinear Program (NLP). A mathematical programming model in which at least one of the constraint functions or the objective function or both are nonlinear.

Lagrange Multiplier. Associated with a constraint, it is the rate of change in the optimal value of the objective function as the RHS of that constraint increases. Called *shadow price* in LP models (see Chapter 4).

Convex Set of Points. A set of points such that for all possible pairs of points in the set, the line segment connecting any such pair must lie entirely within the set.

Concave NLP. A Max model with a concave objective function and a convex constraint set.

Convex NLP. A Min model with a convex objective function and a convex constraint set.

Well-Behaved Model. A convex NLP or a concave NLP.

Reduced Gradient. Associated with a decision variable, it is the initial rate of change in the optimal value of the objective function as that variable is moved away from any binding upper or lower bound on its value. If a nonnegative decision variable is at zero after optimization, the reduced gradient is the rate of hurt in the objective function value as the variable is forced away from its zero value. Called a *reduced cost* in LP models (see Chapter 4).

Quadratic Programs (QP). Nonlinear models that maximize or minimize the value of a quadratic objective function subject to linear constraints and nonnegativity conditions.

Portfolio Analysis. The model of minimizing the variance of return subject to a requirement on expected return.

Variance. A statistical measure of risk.

Covariance. A statistical measure of the extent to which random quantities are correlated.

Expected Return. The weighted average of the returns of the stocks in a portfolio.

Standard Deviation. The square root of variance.

Efficient Frontier. The OV function of a portfolio analysis QP as a function of the expected return parameter.

Inventory. Units of goods, money, or individuals held in anticipation of future needs.

Holding Cost. The cost of holding inventory; it includes opportunity cost plus direct costs such as pilferage, insurance, and obsolescence.

Opportunity Cost. If taking one action (say, A) implies that another action (say, B) cannot be taken, the net return associated with action B is an opportunity cost of taking action A.

Ordering Cost. One of the cost parameters in the EOQ model. The marginal cost of placing an order.

Stockout Cost. Stated in terms of either penalty cost or backlogging cost.

Stockout. Not having enough inventory on hand to satisfy demand.

Backlogging. The practice of delivering goods to customers some time after the order has been received rather than immediately upon receipt of the order.

Penalty Cost. The loss in a no-backlogging model when it is not possible to satisfy demand; usually stated as a per unit cost of unsatisfied demand.

Backlogging Cost. One of the cost parameters in the EOQ model expanded to allow for backlogging. The cost of backlogging an item for a specified time.

Order Quantity. Part of an inventory control system. The number of items that are ordered when an order is placed.

Demand. The number of items ordered. Because of stockouts, this may be different from the number of items sold.

Economic Order Quantity Model (EOQ). An inventory control model with constant rate of demand and in which relevant costs are those of ordering and holding, and possibly those of backlogging demand.

Optimal Order Quantity. The quantity that minimizes the total annual cost of ordering and holding a particular item.

Inventory Holding Cost. One of the cost parameters in the EOQ model. The cost of holding an item in inventory for a specified time.

Economic Order Quantity. The optimal order quantity derived from the EOQ model.

Cycle Time. The interval between the arrival of the two consecutive orders.

Quantity Discount. A purchase plan under which the seller offers a special price to the buyer if he or she purchases a specified quantity or more.

Production Lot Size Model. A modification of the EOQ model that allows for a finite rate of receiving materials.

Self-Review Exercises Nonlinear Models

True-False Quiz

1. **T F** Economy of scale is a nonlinear relationship.
2. **T F** An applied problem involving a nonlinear relationship cannot be modeled as an LP.
3. **T F** If the necessary conditions for a local max occur, a local max occurs.
4. **T F** If a local min occurs, the necessary conditions for a local min occur.
5. **T F** If a local min is a global min, it is the only point where the sufficient conditions for a local min hold.
6. **T F** A straight line is neither a concave nor a convex function.
7. **T F** In an NLP or an LP, tightening a constraint cannot help and it might hurt.
8. **T F** For a max model, a Lagrange multiplier has the same interpretation as the shadow price that appears on the Solver Sensitivity Report for LP problems although in general it is not constant over an RHS interval.
9. **T F** A quadratic programming model is always a special type of concave programming model.
10. **T F** An NLP is always either a concave or a convex programming model.
11. **T F** The constraint set defined by the following inequalities is convex.

$$9x + 4y \leq 36$$
$$4x + 12y \leq 20$$

12. **T F** In practice, to find a local max of a function of several variables, one first finds all stationary points. One then applies second-order tests to these points.
13. **T F** Although nonlinear programs are more difficult than LPs, in terms of finding an optimal solution it is nevertheless true that a corner-searching technique can be applied.
14. **T F** One problem in NLP is distinguishing between local and global solutions.

Multiple Choice

In the questions below, $f'(x)$ and $f''(x)$ denote the first and second derivatives of a function of a single variable, x, and x^* is a stationary point.

15. Suppose that f is a function of a single variable. The condition $f''(x) > 0$
    - **a.** is a necessary condition for a local min
    - **b.** is a sufficient condition for a local min
    - **c.** is a sufficient condition for a local max
    - **d.** none of the above
16. Suppose that f is a function of a single variable. The condition $f'(x^*) = 0$ is
    - **a.** a necessary condition for x^* to be a local max
    - **b.** a necessary condition for x^* to be a local min
    - **c.** a necessary condition for x^* to be a global min
    - **d.** all of the above
17. In nonlinear models differential calculus is needed
    - **a.** to avoid multiple (local) solutions
    - **b.** to express optimality conditions
    - **c.** both a and b
    - **d.** neither a nor b

18. A point x^* with the property that $f'(x^*) = 0$ and $f''(x^*) > 0$ (where f is a function of a single variable) satisfies the sufficient conditions for x^* to be
- **a.** a local max
- **b.** a local min
- **c.** neither a nor b

19. Which of the following is true of a concave function?
- **a.** One can attempt to find a global maximizer by using a hill-climbing computer code such as Solver.
- **b.** Any local maximizer is also a global maximizer.
- **c.** Both a and b above.

20. Which of the following is true?
- **a.** For a general NLP, optimality conditions are directly used in solving NLP problems. That is, optimizers like Solver exist to directly solve these conditions, and this produces an NLP solution.
- **b.** For a general NLP, optimality conditions are indirectly used in solving NLP problems. That is, optimizers like Solver exist to directly attack the NLP, employing for example a hill-climbing approach. The optimality conditions provide a termination criterion for such algorithms.
- **c.** Optimality conditions are only of theoretic interest.

21. For concave programming models
- **a.** the second-order conditions are more useful
- **b.** any local optimum is a global optimum as well
- **c.** both the constraint set and the objective function must be concave

22. Convexity
- **a.** is a description that applies both to sets of points and to functions
- **b.** is an important mathematical property used to guarantee that local solutions are also global
- **c.** is useful in unconstrained as well as constrained optimization
- **d.** all of the above

23. Which of the following is *not* generally true of a Lagrange multiplier?
- **a.** It has an economic interpretation similar to that of shadow price.
- **b.** It is the rate of change of OV as the RHS of a constraint is increased.
- **c.** It is valid (i.e., constant) over an RHS range.

24. Which of the following is *not* true?
- **a.** Even when global solutions cannot be guaranteed, optimization can still be a useful tool in decision making.
- **b.** In LP, we need never worry about local solutions (i.e., every local solution is also global).
- **c.** Since we can only guarantee that local solutions are global when the appropriate convexity (or concavity) properties exist, these are the only types of NLP problems that yield useful information.

25. Which is true of corner point solutions in NLP?
- **a.** It makes no difference what objective function we have the optimal solution will always be at a corner point.
- **b.** We have to worry about corner points only if the objective function is linear.
- **c.** In general, the optimum may not be at a corner point.

26. The Evolutionary Solver
- **a.** is an intelligent search engine for finding good model solutions
- **b.** works only for convex or concave NLPs
- **c.** cannot tolerate nonsmooth functions
- **d.** can find local optima but not the global optimum

Answers

1. T, **2.** F, **3.** F, **4.** T, **5.** F, **6.** F, **7.** T, **8.** T, **9.** F, **10.** F, **11.** T, **12.** F, **13.** F, **14.** T, **15.** d, **16.** d, **17.** b, **18.** b, **19.** c, **20.** b, **21.** b, **22.** d, **23.** c, **24.** c, **25.** c, **26.** a

Self-Review Exercises Quadratic Programming

True-False

1. **T F** A quadratic programming program may have quadratic constraint functions.

2. **T F** Maximizing or minimizing any nonlinear objective function subject to a set of linear equality and inequality constraints, as well as nonnegativity conditions on the values of the decision variables, is a quadratic programming model.

3. **T F** Any LP model can be solved with a QP optimizer.

4. **T F** It is not possible to characterize extreme points of the feasible region of a QP.

5. **T F** The optimal solution to a QP model need not be a corner solution.

6. **T F** The optimal solution to a QP model must include at least as many positive variables as there are constraints.

7. **T F** Loosening a constraint in a QP either will not change or will improve the OV.

8. **T F** In a Max model the rate of improvement of OV is always the negative of the Lagrange multiplier.

9. **T F** The slope of the tangent to the graph of the function $OV(R)$ at the point $(\hat{R}, OV(\hat{R}))$ is the rate of change in the function $OV(R)$ at $R = \hat{R}$.

10. **T F** Changing a coefficient of a term in the objective function of a QP always changes the optimal solution.

11. **T F** The variance of the return from a portfolio is a linear function of the amount invested in each stock in the portfolio.

12. **T F** If there are three stocks in the portfolio, the feasible region will lie on a plane.

13. **T F** The portfolio model includes a lower bound on the expected return. In general this constraint need not be binding.

Multiple Choice

14. The definition of a QP model does not include
- **a.** quadratic constraint functions
- **b.** linear equality constraints
- **c.** nonlinear terms in the objective function

15. In a QP model in n variables, $(x_i \ldots, x_n)$, the objective function may not include terms of the form
- **a.** x_j^2
- **b.** $x_i x_j$
- **c.** $x_i^2 x_j$
- **d.** $9x_i$

16. An LP is a special case of a QP because
- **a.** the LP feasible region is a special case of a QP feasible region
- **b.** the LP constraint functions are a special case of the QP constraint functions
- **c.** nonnegativity conditions are special to an LP
- **d.** the LP objective function is a special case of the QP objective function

17. The optimal solution to a QP model with n nonnegativity constraints may not have
- **a.** negative values for all decision variables
- **b.** more than n positive decision variables
- **c.** fewer than n positive decision variables
- **d.** zero values for some decision variables

18. The optimal solution to a QP model
- **a.** must lie on a corner of the feasible set
- **b.** cannot be on a corner of the feasible set
- **c.** is always nondegenerate
- **d.** none of the above

19. In the optimal solution for a QP model, slack calculations
- **a.** have no meaning
- **b.** have the same meaning as in an LP model
- **c.** have a different meaning than in an LP model
- **d.** are unrestricted in sign

20. Solver can be used to solve
- **a.** general nonlinear programming models
- **b.** QPs
- **c.** LPs
- **d.** all of the above

21. Loosening a constraint in a variance-minimizing portfolio model
- **a.** must increase the Lagrangian multiplier on that constraint
- **b.** must decrease the Lagrangian multiplier on that constraint
- **c.** may change the sign of the Lagrangian multiplier on that constraint
- **d.** cannot increase the objective function

Answers

1. F, **2.** F, **3.** T, **4.** F, **5.** T, **6.** F, **7.** T, **8.** F, **9.** T, **10.** F, **11.** F, **12.** T, **13.** T, **14.** a, **15.** c, **16.** d, **17.** a, **18.** d, **19.** b, **20.** d, **21.** d

Self-Review Exercises Inventory Modeling

True-False

1. **T F** The opportunity cost segment of inventory holding cost is determined by factors such as breakage, pilferage, and insurance.

2. **T F** In inventory models, demand is always greater than or equal to sales.

3. **T F** In the EOQ model the annual ordering cost is directly proportional to the order quantity.

4. **T F** In the EOQ model the annual holding and ordering cost is reasonably insensitive to errors in estimating the cost parameters.

5. **T F** In the production lot size model, since production is at a steady rate, no setup cost is included in the model.

Multiple Choice

6. The following are some of the reasons inventory is held:
   a. protect against uncertainty in demand
   b. lower production costs
   c. store labor
   d. all of the above

7. Important considerations in deciding *when* and *how much* to order include all factors except
   a. the lead time
   b. the proportion of the holding cost that is due to the opportunity cost
   c. the possibility of quantity discounts
   d. the extent to which future demand is known

8. In the EOQ model
   a. each shipment arrives in a batch
   b. demand is known and occurs at a constant rate
   c. all demand must be satisfied
   d. all of the above

9. In the EOQ model if the price of the item increases and all other parameters remain the same, the optimal order quantity will typically
   a. increase
   b. decrease
   c. stay the same

10. In the EOQ model the optimal number of orders per year
    a. increases directly with
    b. increases as the square root of
    c. decreases directly with
    d. does not change with

    the annual rate of demand.

11. Consider an EOQ model with a quantity discount where a smaller per unit price applies to all units if B or more units are purchased. If Q_D^* minimizes AHO assuming the smaller price, and Q_R^* minimizes AHO assuming the regular price, and $Q_D^* > B$, the optimal order quantity is always
    a. Q_D^*
    b. either Q_R^* or B, depending on which yields the smaller annual total cost
    c. Q_R^*
    d. B

12. In the production lot size model, increasing the rate of production
    a. increases
    b. does not influence
    c. decreases

    the optimal number of orders to place each year.

13. Excel versions of EOQ models
    a. are more difficult to explain to nontechnical managers
    b. can handle more specialized situations than the EOQ analysis based upon calculus
    c. gives more insight into the underlying EOQ relationships

Answers

1. F, **2.** T, **3.** F, **4.** T, **5.** F, **6.** d, **7.** b, **8.** d, **9.** b, **10.** b, **10.** b, **11.** a, **12.** a, **13.** b

NLP Skill Problems

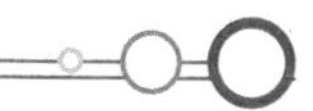

7-1. (a) Use Solver to maximize the function $f(x) = -8x^2 - 14x - 32$.
(b) Use Solver to maximize this function over the interval $1 \le x \le 10$.
(c) Can you tell whether this function is concave or convex?

7-2. (a) Use Solver to maximize the function $f(x) = -x^2 + 4x + 6$.
(b) Use Solver to maximize this function over the interval $3 \le x \le 12$.
(c) Can you tell whether this function is concave or convex?

7-3. Does the following set of constraints form a convex set? Why?

$$x + y \le 20$$
$$-2x + y \ge 10$$
$$x^2 + 2x + 1 \le 100$$
$$-x^4 - 2x^2 + 60 \ge 36$$

7-4. Use Solver to minimize $f(x, y) = x^2 + 2xy + 2y^2 - 8x - 12y + 6$. Use Data Table and Chart Wizard to plot $f(x, y)$.

7-5. We want to build a solid cylinder of volume 2π. If we would like to minimize the surface area of the cylinder (including both ends), what should be its radius and height? Hint: volume = $\pi r^2 h$, surface area = $2\pi rh + 2\pi r^2$

7-6. *Linear Regression Analysis.* In the linear regression model, historical data points (x_i, y_i), $i = 1, \ldots, n$, are given. The linear model is an estimating equation (also called the regression line) $y = ax + b$, where a and b are chosen so as to minimize the sum of squared deviations

$$S(a, b) = \sum_{i=1}^{n} [y_i - (ax_i + b)]^2$$

(a) Use this approach to determine the estimating equation for the following data:

x	8	6	12
y	6	14	–18

(b) Use the same approach to determine the estimating equation for the following data:

x	10	17.4	20.1	12.6	14.9
y	25	10	5	20	15

7-7. (a) Solve the following problem:

$$\begin{aligned} &\text{Min } 2x_1^2 + 3x_2^2 + x_1 - 9x_2 + 16 \\ &\text{s.t.} \quad x_1 + x_2 = 5 \end{aligned}$$

(b) Use the Sensitivity Report to estimate the change in OV if the RHS of the constraint were to increase from 5 to 8 and compare that estimate to the actual result for that change.

7-8. Consider the problem:

$$\begin{aligned} &\text{Max } -3x_1^2 + 42x_1 - 3x_2^2 + 48x_2 - 339 \\ &\text{s.t.} \quad 4x_1 + 6x_2 = 24 \end{aligned}$$

(a) Solve the problem.
(b) Use the Sensitivity Report to estimate the change in OV if the RHS of the constraint were to increase from 24 to 28 and compare that estimate to the actual result for that change.

NLP Applications Problems

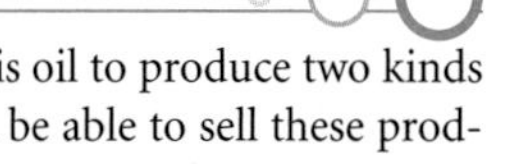

7-9. Hoot Spa imports coconut oil from his home town in Jamaica. He uses this oil to produce two kinds of tanning creme: Sear and Char. The price per kilogram at which he will be able to sell these products depends on how much of each he produces. In particular, if Hoot produces x_1, kilograms of Sear, and x_2, kilograms of Char, he will be able to sell all he produces at the following prices (in dollars):

$$\text{price per kilogram of Sear} = 120 - x_1$$

and

$$\text{price per kilogram of Char} = 150 - 2x_2$$

The cost of manufacturing x_1 kilograms of Sear and x_2 kilograms of Char is:

$$\text{cost of manufacturing the two cremes} = 1.2x_1 + 16.8x_2 + 1.3x_1x_2$$

Assuming that he can sell all he produces, Hoot wishes to determine how many kilograms of each creme should be scheduled for production so as to maximize his profit.

7-10. Ure industries gets a productivity of

$$f(x, y) = 2x^2y + 3xy^2 + 2y^3$$

from x units of labor and y units of capital. If labor costs \$50 per unit and capital costs \$100 per unit, how many units of labor and capital should Ure use, given that its budget is \$150,000? Assume Ure can either consume or supply labor or capital, that is, decision variables can be negative.
(a) Formulate the model and optimize it with Solver from an initial point of $x = 0$ and $y = 1$.
(b) Optimize as in (a) but from a starting point of $x = 1{,}000{,}000$ and $y = 1{,}000{,}000$.
(d) Explain the two answers above.

7-11. Show that the solution found in the "optimal marketing expenditures" example (Section 7.5) is actually a global (as opposed to local) optimum.

7-12. Show that the optimum solution to Problem 7-10 satisfies

$$\frac{\text{Marginal productivity of labor}}{\text{Marginal productivity of capital}} = \frac{\text{Unit price of labor}}{\text{Unit price of capital}}$$

HINT: Remove the budget constraint and substitute constraints on x and y with each being less than or equal to their optimal values in Problem 7-10.

7-13. Solve Example 2 in Section 7.3, assuming $s_i = \frac{1}{2}$ for $i = 1, 2, 3$, $p_1 = 2$, $p_2 = 2.8$, $p_3 = 4$, and budget $B = 250$. What is the Lagrange multiplier for the budget constraint?

7-14. Lenard Crumb, manager of Crumb Baking Services, is considering the offer of a distributor who sells an instant croissant mix. The total cost of x pounds of the mix is given by

$$\text{total cost} = x^3 - 50x^2 + 750x$$

What quantity of this mix will minimize *total cost per pound*?

7-15. *A Pooling Model.* Two chemical products, X and Y, are made by blending three chemical inputs, A, B, and C. The inputs are contaminated by sulfur, and the outputs must meet environmental restrictions on sulfur content. The three inputs are shipped mixed together in two tank cars. A is shipped in car 1, C is shipped in car 2, and B is shipped in car 1 and/or car 2. No more than 100 units of X and 200 units of Y may be sold. Using the data in the table below, formulate a profit-maximizing NLP model and optimize it using Solver.

CHEMICAL	COST PER UNIT ($)	SULFUR CONTENT (%)
A	6	3
B	16	1
C	10	2
	SALES PRICE PER UNIT	
X	9	no more than 2.5
Y	15	no more than 1.5

7-16. Suppose in the Gulf Coast Oil problem of Section 7.5 the octane number from Source 1 varies from month to month. Introduce a new variable, *OCTS*1, the octane number of Source 1, and replace all references to the octane number of Source 1 in the model with this variable. Add a constraint to the Solver model that sets *OCTS*1 less than or equal to 93 and then optimize the NLP. Using the Sensitivity Report, *estimate* what would happen to the optimal profit if the octane number increased to 94, to 96, and to 98, then actually change the octane number to 94, then 96, and last to 98 and re-optimize each time, comparing the actual result with your estimate. Note that what we are really doing is a sensitivity analysis on a constraint coefficient.

7-17. *Economic Substitutes.* Suppose in the Astro and Cosmo problem of Section 7.5 that Astros and Cosmos are economic substitutes. This means that an increase in price of one causes an increase in demand for the other. More specifically, suppose that the new demand equations are

$$A = 1000 - 4.7PA + PC$$
$$C = 1000 + 2PA - 6.2PC$$

Reformulate the model, and optimize it using Solver. Interpret the Sensitivity Report.

7-18. "If *at least one* of the stocks in the portfolio has an expected return greater than or equal to the required return on the entire portfolio, then this formulation will never be infeasible." Under what conditions will this statement be true?

7-19. Consider the portfolio model solved in Section 7.11. The current solution to this model is (AT&T = 0.53, GM = 0.356, USS = 0.1135). Is this point an extreme point of the feasible region? Why or why not?

7-20. Consider the portfolio model solved in Section 7.11. Assume you are considering adding the stock of the IMCRZY.com corporation to your portfolio selection model. This stock has a *negative* expected return. Under what conditions might the model select stock from IMCRZY.com to be in the portfolio?

7-21. Consider the portfolio model solved in Section 7.11. What is the allowable decrease on the constraint that limits the investment of GM stock to 75% of the portfolio?

7-22. As with pure LP analysis, there is a Sensitivity Report associated with NLP. Would you expect this NLP Sensitivity Report to include allowable increases and decreases on the RHS of constraints? Explain.

7-23. Consider the portfolio model solved in Section 7.11. Assume your objective is to maximize return subject to the constraint that the variability of the portfolio cannot exceed V. Rewrite the symbolic (algebraic) model with this modification.

7-24. Refer to Problem 7-23. Set $V = 0.0205$. If there are no alternative optima in the original model, what is the maximum expected return in your reformulated model? Explain.

7-25. Stocks x, y, and z have expected returns of 7%, 6%, and 10%, respectively, and the following variance-covariance matrix:

	x	y	z
x	.01		
y	.001	.04	
z	.001	–.04	.08

(a) Determine the fraction of the portfolio to hold in each stock so as to minimize the variance of the portfolio subject to a minimum expected return on the portfolio of 8%.
(b) Can the variance of the portfolio be smaller than the variance of any individual stock? Explain.
(c) Use the Lagrange multiplier information to estimate what would happen to the variance of the optimal portfolio if the minimum expected return were raised to 9%. Compare your estimate with the actual by resolving the model.

7-26. The demand for general books at the University Bookstore occurs at a constant rate of 18,000 books per year. The manager satisfies this demand without backlogging. She calculates the optimal order quantity based on ordering costs of $30 and an annual holding cost of $3 per book. Assume 250 days per year.

What are the values for Q^*, N^*, and AHO(Q^*)?

7-27. A local hardware store sells 364,000 pounds of nails a year. It currently orders 14,000 pounds of nails every two weeks at a price of $0.50 per pound. Assume that

1. Demand occurs at a constant rate.
2. The cost of placing an order is $50 regardless of the size of the order.
3. The annual cost of holding inventory is 12% of the value of the average inventory level.
4. These factors do not change over time.

(a) What is the average inventory level?
(b) What is the annual holding cost?
(c) What is the annual ordering cost?
(d) What is the annual holding and ordering cost?
(e) What is the annual total cost?
(f) Would it be cheaper for the owner to order in lots larger than 14,000 (and less frequently) or smaller lots (and more frequently)?

7-28. The campus ice cream store sells 180 quarts of vanilla ice cream each month. The store currently restocks its inventory at the beginning of each month. The wholesale price of ice cream is $3 per quart. Assume that

1. Demand occurs at a constant rate.
2. The annual cost of holding inventory is 25% of the value of the average inventory level.
3. Last year the annual total cost was $7,627.50.
4. These factors do not change over time.

(a) Compute average inventory level.
(b) Compute annual holding cost.
(c) Compute the ordering cost.
(d) Use Data Table 1 to graph annual holding costs, annual ordering costs, and AHO as a function of order quantity.
(e) At what point is the AHO minimized. How much can the ice cream store save if it uses the optimal order quantity?

7-29. A young entrepreneur sells pencils at a constant rate of 25 per day. Each pencil costs $0.05. If ordering costs are $5 and inventory holding costs are 20% of the cost of the average inventory, what are the optimal order quantity and the optimal number of orders that should be placed each year?

7-30. A credit card company has an annual income of $100,000,000. If the cost of sending out a billing statement is $30,000 and the prevailing interest rate is 6%, how often should the company send out bills?

7-31. Specific Electric (SE) is a giant manufacturer of electrical appliances in the United States. It uses electric motors that it purchases from another firm at a constant rate. Total purchase costs during the year are $2,400,000. Ordering costs are $100, and annual inventory holding costs are 20% of the cost of the average inventory.

(a) What is the dollar value of the optimal order quantity?
(b) How many times a year should SE order?
(c) What is the optimal cycle time in years and in days if there are 250 working days per year?

HINT: If P is the cost per unit to Specific Electric and Q^* is the optimal quantity, PQ^* is the dollar value of the optimal order quantity.

7-32. If, in Problem 7-28, the ordering cost doubles, what is the change in the optimal order quantity?

7-33. Strumm and Howell (S and H) is a local record store that specializes in country music. The store has been quite successful in recent years, with retail sales of $400,000 per year. Sales occur at a constant rate during the year. S and H buys its records from a major recording company. The retail sales price equals $5/3$ times the cost to S and H. The ordering cost for each shipment of orders is $75, independent of the size of the order. Annual inventory holding costs are 10% of the cost of the average inventory level.

(a) What is the dollar value of the optimal order quantity?
(b) How often should S and H order each year?
(c) What is the optimal cycle time in years?

HINT: If P is the cost per unit to S and H and Q^* is the optimal order quantity, PQ^* is the dollar value of the optimal order quantity.

7-34. If, in Problem 7-28, the wholesaler offers to sell ice cream at $2.43 a quart when bought in a quantity of at least 1,000 quarts, what is the campus ice cream store's optimal strategy?

7-35. The Waukon, Iowa, outlet of Cheep Chicks orders baby chickens from the firm's central incubator in Des Moines. Twenty-two-and-one-half dozen chicks are demanded each day of the 360-day year. It costs $40 to process an order independent of the number of chicks ordered and $80 to hold a dozen chicks in inventory for a year. Assume that Cheep calculates inventory holding costs on the basis of the average inventory level.

(a) What is the optimal order quantity?
(b) How many orders should be placed each year?
(c) What is the optimal cycle time in years? In working days?

7-36. The Napa Wine Company, the nation's largest distributor of California wine products, has a constant demand of 192 cases per month for its most popular product, Wino Delux. Its ordering cost is $100, annual holding costs are 25% of the average inventory, and the product costs $200 per case. Currently, it does not backlog demand and follows the optimal ordering policy. Allowing for vacations and religious holidays, there are 200 days per year.

Under the current policy (no backlogging), find Q^*, N^*, and AHO.(Q^*).

7-37. Bed Bug, a local manufacturer of orthopedic mattresses, currently satisfies its constant production requirements of 500 coiled springs per day by using an EOQ model based on an ordering cost of $90, a product cost of $1 per spring, and an inventory holding cost of 15% of the cost of average inventory. Springy Steel, its supplier, has recently offered a 0.5% discount if Bed Bug orders in quantities of at least 20,000 springs, or a 0.7% discount if it orders quarterly. Assume 240 workdays per year.

(a) Find Q^* and the annual total cost under the current cost assumptions.
(b) Calculate annual total cost for each of the discount alternatives.
(c) What should Bed Bug do?

7-38. If, in Problem 7-28, the holding cost % doubles, what is the change in the optimal order quantity?

7-39. XXX Distillery, a major producer of arthritis and nerve medicine in the Southeast, produces its stock in batches. In order to begin each run, the company owners must select a suitable location and assemble the equipment. The cost of this operation is $900. Production yields 60 gallons of product each day, each of which costs $0.025 per day to hold in inventory. Demand is constant at 1,125 gallons per month. Assume 12 months, 300 days per year, and 25 days per month.

(a) Find Q^*, N^*, and the cycle time for the optimal production lot size.
(b) Find the maximum inventory and the length (in days) of each production run for the optimal production lot size.
(c) Find DHS(Q^*).

7-40. Because of the importance of business confidentiality, XXX Distillery in Problem 7-39 decides to make three production runs per year.

(a) Find the production order quantity, Q, cycle time (in days), length of production run, and maximum inventory level.

(b) Find DHS for the policy in part (a).

7-41. Consider Problem 7-39.

(a) Suppose that XXX Distillery purchased rather than produced its product and that the cost of placing an order is $900. Find Q^* and AHO(Q^*).

(b) How does AHO(Q^*) in part (a) compare with DHS(Q^*) when there is a production rate of 60 gallons per day? Explain this relationship.

(c) Use a Data Table to plot the DHS($Q^*[p]$) as a function of the daily production rate, p.

(d) Due to the economies of scale, unit production costs decrease as p goes up. The exact relationship is $C(p) = 30/p$, where $C(p)$ is the unit production cost when the daily production rate is p. Find the minimum value of the sum of DHS and daily production costs for $p = 45$ and $p = 60$.

7-42. Due to technical obsolescence of its equipment, XXX Distillery (Problem 7-39) stops producing and functions only as a marketing organization. It now purchases its product from another producer. XXX must buy at least 1,000 gallons per order to qualify for a quantity discount. What is the smallest discount per gallon that would persuade XXX to order 1,000 gallons? Assume that now $P = \$5$, $C_h = \$2.50$, and $C_o = \$200$.

7-43. Consider a variation of the non-well-behaved model of Figure 7.17 applied to the divisions of a multiple division organization. Each division receives an allocation of capital, x, from headquarters, and returns to headquarters a payoff, y, consisting of the sum of two parts. Part one is the payoff from its own allocation of capital and part two is the payoff from its interaction with another division, assumed to be equal to one half of that division's payoff. Headquarters has a maximum of $10 (million) to allocate and its payoff is the sum of the four division's payoffs plus any unallocated capital. The minimum allocation of capital to each division is $1.1 (million). Figure 7.36 gives the model. Set up the model as an NLP and optimize it using Solver's GRG optimizer, using the minimum allocation to each division as a starting solution. Next, use Evolutionary Solver to find a recommended allocation of capital to each of the divisions. Comment on the nature of the solutions found by both optimizers.

7-44. Consider the model of Problem 7-43. Use SolverTable with Evolutionary Solver to recommend capital allocations to each division for integral amounts of capital available to allocate from headquarters ranging from $10 (million) down to $5 (million). Comment on the nature of the solutions found.

FIGURE 7.36

	A	B	C	D	E	F	G	H
1			Division					
2		1	2	3	4			
3		X1	X2	X3	X4	Total	Max	Slack
4		1.10	1.10	1.10	1.10	4.40	<=10.00	5.60
5		Y1	Y2	Y3	Y4			
6		2.08	2.08	2.08	2.08			
7		.5*Y2	.5*Y3	.5*Y4	.5*Y1			
8		1.04	1.04	1.04	1.04			
9		Y Total	Y Total	Y Total	Y Total	Grand Total		
10		3.11	3.11	3.11	3.11	18.057		
11								

Cell	Formula	Copy To
B6	= MAX((B4-3)*(B4-2)*(B4-1)*(B4-4)*(B4-5)*COS(0.2*B4)*B4,0)	C6:E6
B8	= .5*C6	C8:D8
E8	= .5*B8	—
B10	= B6+B8	C10:E10
F4	= SUM(B4:E4)	—
F10	= SUM(B10:E10)+H4	

7-45. Consider a capital allocation situation applied to four identical divisions of a multiple division organization. Each division receives an allocation of capital from headquarters, and each division returns to headquarters a payoff, according to the table below. Allocations to divisions need not be integral amounts, but because of the lumpiness of the divisional investments, the fractional part of any non-integral allocation cannot be invested for any return. For example, any allocation to a division between $2.000 (million) and 2.999 (million) will return the same $10.9 (million). Headquarters payoff is the sum of the four division's payoffs plus any unallocated capital. The minimum allocation of capital to each division is $1 (million) and headquarters has $20 (million) to allocate among the divisions. Set up the model as a NLP and optimize it using Solver's GRG optimizer using the minimum allocation to each division as a starting solution. Next, use Evolutionary Solver to find a recommended allocation of capital to each of the divisions. Comment on the nature of the solutions found by both optimizers.

ALLOCATION IN $MILLIONS	TOTAL RETURN IN $MILLIONS
1	6.1
2	10.9
3	15.1
4	18.8
5	22.2
6	25.1
7	27.8
8	28.2

7-46. Consider the model of Problem 7-45. Use SolverTable with Evolutionary Solver to recommend capital allocations to each division for integral amounts of capital available to allocate from headquarters ranging from $25 (million) down to $4 (million). Comment on the nature of the solutions found.

Case Study Just-in-Time

Just-in-time! Although the just-in-time (JIT) concept is very young, perhaps 15 years old in this country, it is so widespread in American manufacturing and service that it is almost a cliché. Perhaps this is because the idea is so simple and so appealing. In short, the JIT strategy is to have "the right product at the right place at the right time." It implies that in manufacturing or service, each stage of the process produces exactly the amount that is required for the next step in the process. This notion holds true for all steps within the system. Suppose, for example, that in our plant all products pass through a drilling operation and then a milling operation. With JIT, the drill produces only what the mill will need next. It also holds for the last step—that is, the system produces only what the customer desires.

Implementation of a JIT system typically includes emphasis on the following aspects of the production process:

1. Reduction of setup times and cost. Here the idea is to make it cost-effective to produce in very small lot sizes. The ideal is a lot size of one.
2. Emphasis on preventive maintenance. This is important because the manufacturing process must always be ready to go when you need it if you hope to be just-in-time.
3. Continuous process improvement to guarantee good quality. If you are going to make just the right number of units, you must be sure that they are of good quality—you cannot select the good items out of a larger lot with this approach. A continuous improvement process is typically based on a high level of employee involvement and empowerment.
4. Reduction of lead times through effective use of information technology and close relationships with vendors.

In many publications, JIT is placed at one end of a continuum with EOQ at the other. The EOQ model is portrayed as being old, out-of-touch, and possibly responsible for many of the problems faced by manufacturing firms in the United States. We would like to suggest an alternative interpretation. Is it possible that the concepts that form the basis for the EOQ model are consistent with the JIT philosophy, and that the problem has been in interpretation and implementation? Let's examine that possibility.

Questions

1. What is the effect of reducing setup cost on lot size in the EOQ model? Is the effect the same in a JIT system?
2. What is the role of quality and preventive maintenance in the EOQ model? Why?
3. Do you sense a difference in philosophy between the EOQ and the JIT approaches? In particular, what aspects of the production problem is it assumed we can influence in the two approaches?
4. Do you think that there are any general lessons to be learned in regard to modeling from the movement from EOQ to JIT?

Case Study Internal Revenue Service (1994–1995)[1]

Al Swanson was worried. He was looking at the costs and results of the audit program conducted by the Internal Revenue Service (IRS) in fiscal year 1992.[2] Mr. Swanson, an analyst in the Planning and Analysis Division of the IRS, had just been appointed head of an interdepartmental committee to plan and review procedures for auditing individual income tax returns for 1995. The committee included members of the Planning and Analysis Division, which had broad responsibilities for improving IRS functioning, and the audit Division, which had the specific responsibility of ensuring taxpayer compliance with existing tax laws. The formation of this committee was part of a sweeping review of IRS functioning, and its recommendations would have a direct impact on the budget-allocations made by Congress.

What made Mr. Swanson's task all the more important was the development of the IRS' Business Master Plan (BMP), released on April 1, 1994, for Fiscal years 1995–2001. The Business Master Plan would replace the existing Strategic Business Plan and the Annual Servicewide Operating Plan. The genesis of the BMP was partly due to the Government Performance and Results Act. This act requires government agencies to develop annual plans to support their strategic direction, cover all budgeted activities, provide annual performance goals and indicators, describe what is required to achieve the stated performance goals, and establish accountability throughout the process. It was hoped that the IRS, through the BMP, would be better able to present its case to the Office of Management and Budget (OMB), which helps shape the administration's budget proposals.

IRS Mission

Mr. Swanson brooded over the IRS mission statement:

- The purpose of the Internal Revenue Service is to collect the proper amount of tax revenue at the least cost; serve the public by continually improving the quality of our products and services; and perform in a manner warranting the IRS Business Vision.

  Our Business Vision is to administer a tax system for our customers that:

- Provides simple, easy-to-understand forms; simple filing procedures; alternative filing methods to suit individual needs; and optional ways to interact with the IRS to obtain forms, ask procedural questions, or resolve account-related issues, to maximize the likelihood that everyone files and pays correctly;
- Ensures access by telephone at times convenient for taxpayers and quick, accurate responses to written correspondence;
- Allows taxpayers to discuss problems or issues with employees who treat them courteously and professionally, act in an ethical manner, and have immediate access to account information and the authority to resolve problems;
- Provides employees the ability to resolve taxpayers' issues in a timely and accurate manner, with systems and processes designed for that purpose;
- Provides privacy and confidentiality of tax return information and ensures security of data and systems; and
- Provides diverse taxpayers with the ability to interact with employees or systems in ways that meet their needs.

What Mr. Swanson knew to be of great concern to the IRS was the real or perceived erosion in their effectiveness in four key areas: (a) providing information to taxpayers; (b) collecting additional taxes; (c) making refunds when appropriate; and (d) monitoring tax compliance. While improving effectiveness in the first three tasks was to be accomplished partly by investments in people and computing power (to be discussed below) and partly through improved procedures, monitoring tax compliance was more difficult. The impact of increasing the budget for auditing would be less visible and harder to evaluate, and any such proposal would have to compete with other more visible programs. Thus, the three major problems facing Mr. Swanson's committee were (*i*) to develop reasonable guidelines and performance measures for the Auditing Division; (*ii*) to make forecasts of additional taxes and penalties collected as a function of the budget allocation, to select an auditing budget to request from the OMB, and to justify that request; and (*iii*) to optimize the use of the budget eventually approved by Congress for monitoring tax compliance. Most urgent was the need to make a strong case to the OMB for an increase in the budget and to optimally use the allotted budget. While the increase in resources allocated to the IRS was not commensurate with the increase in workload over time, what Mr. Swanson wanted to investigate was whether the resources were being used optimally.

To be sure, the erosion in IRS effectiveness in certain areas reflected an overwhelming increase in workload. Since the late 1980s, the annual number of returns filed had increased significantly, largely as a result of population growth, economic expansion and added reporting requirements. In addition, the organization had not kept pace with the kinds of productivity advancements that private industry had capitalized on for years.

---

[1] This case was prepared by Krishnan Anand and Haim Mendelson of the Stanford Business School. It is intended to serve as a basis for class discussion rather than to illustrate either effective or ineffective handling of an administrative situation.

[2] In each fiscal year, the IRS collects and processes taxes for the *previous* year. Most available data are compiled on a fiscal year basis, and this case follows this convention. Sometimes we use the tax year for pedagogic reasons. All such cases will be explicitly stated. In all other cases, years are stated as *fiscal* years.

While competition had forced the private sector to be ever-mindful of the potential for technology to improve the bottom line, the IRS had been doing business in much the same way for the last 40 years. As a result, shocking anachronisms abounded. Most of the tax processing, for instance, was done manually, with returns being passed factory-style down an assembly line known in the IRS as the "pipeline."

Historically, Congress and agency officials had addressed the agency's compliance problems Washington-style—by throwing money at them. Since 1982, the IRS operating budget had nearly tripled while its workforce had grown from less than 83,000 in 1982 to a peak of about 117,000 in 1992. Although the Service was collecting record amounts, its operational productivity, in terms of the cost of collections, had plummeted. As of 1992, the IRS was spending nearly 40 percent more to collect $100 than it did in 1982 (see Table 1).

The IRS budget had grown from $4.4 billion in fiscal year 1987 to around $7 billion now, representing a real growth of 3.7 percent per annum. About one-third of this growth had gone to the $23 billion project known as Tax Systems Modernization (TSM)—a program to update its antiquated computer systems. Over the same period, the IRS workload had grown about 10 percent. Thus, under the existing organizational structure and technology base, the IRS would need to add 2,000 more employees every year just to keep up with increases in workload, officials estimate. That, however, was not what management envisioned for the IRS of the future. On the contrary, it expected to eliminate some 17,000 positions over the next decade and cut hundreds of millions of dollars from labor-intensive operations such as the "pipeline."

Mr. Swanson knew that very soon, the Cincinnati center, a sprawling low-rise building occupying a full city block on the Kentucky side of the Ohio River, would become the test site for a huge conglomeration of imaging equipment known as the Service Center Recognition/Image Processing System, or SCRIPS. A computer system costing nearly $90 million, SCRIPS was expected to pay for itself by increasing the accuracy and speed with which return information was entered into IRS computers and by reducing the center's heavy reliance on manual keyboarding of return information—number by number, line by line. The system was already in operation on a test basis, and it would pave the way for a more sophisticated $4 billion imaging package known as the Document Processing System (DPS), which was expected to be online by 2000. DPS would be able to capture tax data from nearly any document allowed for use by the IRS, eliminating much of the need for transcribers, who for years have formed the backbone of the tax processing system.

Streamlining tax processing was a wrenching aspect of the tax agency's decade-long TSM project. But the hope, as Mr. Swanson well knew, was that TSM's real breakthroughs would not be merely technological or limited to document-processing centers like Cincinnati. Sweeping changes in management and organizational structure throughout the agency were envisioned, that would redefine how, and how well, the IRS did its job.

High Stakes

There was far more riding on TSM than one agency's performance. As stated in an IRS publication,

> The purpose of the Nation's internal revenue tax system is to guarantee the fiscal soundness of the policies and programs of the United States Government.

Thus, when the IRS collects less than the full amount of tax due, this results in either less money for other public programs or more federal borrowing. The agency estimated that it had undercollected approximately $120 billion in income taxes in just the previous year. In addition, increasing the effectiveness of tax collections is a much less painful way for lawmakers to increase revenue than raising taxes. (Undercollection, by allowing people to get away with underpaying taxes, also encourages underreporting in succeeding years. Thus, it also has a serious long-term impact on collections.)

TABLE 1 Internal Revenue Service Collections, Costs, and Employees (1986–1992)

FISCAL YEAR	OPERATING COSTS ($ MILLIONS)	COLLECTIONS ($ MILLIONS)	COST OF COLLECTING $100	NUMBER OF EMPLOYEES
1982	**2,626**	**632,241**	**0.42**	**82,857**
1986	3,842	782,252	0.49	95,880
1987	4,366	886,291	0.49	102,188
1988	5,069	935,107	0.54	114,873
1989	5,199	1,013,322	0.51	114,758
1990	5,440	1,056,366	0.52	111,858
1991	6,098	1,086,851	0.56	115,628
1992	**6,536**	**1,120,800**	**0.58**	**116,673**

Data include all collections (including income, employment, excise, gift, and estate taxes).

The IRS Business Master Plan for fiscal 1995–2001 was further broken down into specific goals for the first three years of the plan, viz., fiscal years 1995–1997. The primary objective of the IRS Master Plan for 1995–1997 was improving compliance. A strong and effective auditing and tax monitoring program would increase revenues directly through additional tax collections, and it would also have an indirect but significant impact on the extent of future voluntary compliance.

Mr. Swanson sighed, and took yet another look at the data he had on IRS performance over the past couple of years, especially the numbers relating to the audit function (see Table 2).

With over 100,000 employees and nearly 30,000 in just the examination (audit) function, the IRS has many of the strengths and weaknesses of large bureaucratic organizations. Even for personnel costs within the examination function, there are significant *fixed* costs, that is, costs incurred by the agency independent of the level of examination activity or audit coverage. About 25%–30% of the personnel costs for the examination function were actually fixed, whereas the rest (slightly less than 75%) varied with the level of audit coverage.

On the collection side, there are substantial differences between individual and corporate tax returns. In terms of the relative importance of the two, Mr. Swanson observed that individual income taxes form the lion's share of total IRS receipts (Table 3). Total individual receipts had consistently been well over four times total corporate receipts for many years. Improving the functioning of the tax collection and compliance monitoring functions for individuals was therefore crucial to IRS plans for the future. In fact, individual income taxes had constituted at least 8% of the Gross

TABLE 2 Internal Revenue Service Costs and Personnel Employed (1991–1992)

		1991	1992
COSTS:	All Activities	6,098	6,536
($ millions)	Examination Function only	1,532	1,605
	Examination Function—Personnel Compensation	1,297	1,378
PERSONNEL COUNTS:	Service-Wide	117,017	117,945
	Examination Function	28,592	28,393

The table breaks down service-wide figures into those applicable to the examination (audit) function. (All costs in millions of dollars. Personnel numbers are annual averages.)

TABLE 3 Individual and Corporate Income Taxes (1986–1994)

FISCAL YEAR	INDIVIDUAL INCOME TAX RETURNS (MILLIONS)	INCOME TAX RECEIPTS ($ MILLIONS) Individual	Corporate
1986	102.4	348,959	63,143
1987	103.5	392,557	83,926
1988	107.0	401,181	94,508
1989	110.3	445,690	103,291
1990	112.5	466,884	93,507
1991	113.8	467,827	98,086
1992	115.0	475,964	100,270
1993	114.2	509,680	117,520
1994	114.5*	549,901*	130,719*
1995	—	595,048*	140,437*
1996	—	627,652*	145,790*
1997	—	664,062*	149,822*
1998	—	701,620*	152,492*
1999	—	745,120*	157,152*

* IRS estimates.

Breakdown of income taxes from corporate and individual sources, number of individual returns filed over 1986–1994, and tax receipt estimates for 1994–1999. All estimates are from the IRS Management Information System for Top Level Executives.

TABLE 4 Additional Taxes and Penalties for Individuals (1986–1992)

FISCAL YEAR	NUMBER OF AUDITS	ADDITIONAL NET TAX IN MILLIONS OF 1992 DOLLARS		
		Schedules C/P[a]	Other Individual	Total
1986	1,110,941	1,460	4,388	5,848
1987	1,109,212	1,685	4,228	5,913
1988	1,058,544	1,389	3,953	5,342
1989	982,456	1,218	3,007	4,225
1990	883,293	1,540	3,393	4,933
1991	1,099,505	1,872	4,793	6,665
1992	1,039,355	1,586	4,455	6,041

[a] **Schedule C** (Form 1040) is filed by self-employed individuals. **Schedule F** (Form 1040) is filed by individuals reporting profit or loss from farming.

Additional Taxes and penalties Recommended (ATR) by the auditing function of the IRS for individual tax returns, 1986–1992. Figures are in millions of 1992 dollars. "Schedule C/F" represents the total ATR for individuals that were self-employed or had income from farming (and, consequently, filed at least one of schedules C *or* F with their 1040 tax forms). "Other Individual" provides the ATR for all other individuals (1040 with no schedules, or the "short" forms 1040A and 1040EZ).

Domestic Product (GDP) for the past 20 years.[3] Corporate income taxes had hovered at 1–2% of GDP during that period. Due to the magnitude of the individual income tax receipts, small changes in collections have a significant impact on the federal deficit. Thus, Mr. Swanson decided to further prioritize and focus his analysis for 1995 on individual income tax returns only, which will also be the focus of the rest of this case.

Individual returns are typically far less complex than corporate returns and, therefore, their auditing costs are much lower. In the past, 56% of the total variable auditing costs had been incurred for auditing individual returns, and 44% for auditing corporate returns.

Mr. Swanson then looked at the numbers pertaining to his more immediate problem: the Additional Taxes Recommended (ATR) for collection on the basis of audits of individual filings. These had fluctuated considerably between 1986 and 1992, but did not exhibit a systematic trend (Table 4). However, considering that the number of individual *filings* had been rising more or less steadily during that period (see Table 3), Mr. Swanson was worried that the lack of a corresponding increase in the number of audits could signal weaknesses in the tax compliance and monitoring program of the IRS.

Audit Procedure: Individual Returns

For auditing purposes, income tax returns were first classified according to the type of return (e.g., individual versus corporate), then the subtypes (e.g., the types of forms filed) and finally according to the dollar amount of adjusted gross income before deductions. For individual returns,[4] this resulted in ten audit classes. To simplify his analysis, Mr. Swanson decided to categorize the individual returns into three classes based on the types of forms used: 1040A (including also 1040EZ), 1040 without schedules C/F and 1040 with schedule C or schedule F (or both). The primary result of this simplification would be that income effects within classes were ignored. However, there was considerable homogeneity *within* each such class regarding the complexity of the returns (and hence, the costs of processing and auditing returns), the types of problems observed in the filed returns, etc.

For each audit class, **audit coverage** is defined as the percentage of all returns in that class filed during a given year that are actually audited. The returns in each audit class are assigned a number known as "DIF," based on rank-ordering, prior to implementing audit coverage decisions. Starting about 1970, the DIF ranking is performed by a computer program that scores each individual return in terms of its anticipated capacity to generate additional taxes, if audited. Implementing audit coverage decisions requires auditing returns in each separate class in the rank ordering determined by the program until the desired percentage coverage for the class has been achieved. This procedure is repeated separately

[3] The year 1976 was the one exception, when individual income taxes fell to 7.8% of GDP.

[4] The regular or "long" form for individuals is known as 1040. In certain cases, to simplify work both for tax payers and the IRS, a simplified form known as 1040A is allowed (form 1040EZ is a further simplified version). When an individual earns income from businesses or professions, he or she is required to attach a form known as Schedule C to the 1040 Form. Individuals with income from farming file a form known as Schedule F instead of Schedule C. Of course, some individuals may have both business and farming incomes, and so will need to file both Schedule C and Schedule F in addition to Form 1040.

TABLE 5 1992 Auditing Record (Aggregated for Analysis)

TYPE OF RETURN	RETURNS FILED	RETURNS EXAMINED	AUDIT COVERAGE	ATR ($ MILLIONS)
1) 1040A[a]	43,430,500	300,480	0.69%	781
2) 1040 without Schedules C/F	62,977,400	575,493	0.91%	3,674
3) 1040 with Schedule C or F	7,421,300	163,382	2.20%	1,586
Overall	**113,829,200**	**1,039,355**	**0.91%**	**6,041**

[a] Including 1040EZ.
Breakdown of audit performance for the three primary audit classes, 1992. The total number of returns filed, the number of returns examined and the consequent audit coverage are shown for each class.

for each audit class. The IRS uses the term **ATR** for the "Additional Tax Recommended" as the result of an audit. The ATR may be negative (corresponding to a tax refund), zero (no change) or positive. Most cases result in a positive ATR. The audit may also result in interest charges and fines that are included in the ATR figure.

The actual audits are performed by revenue agents and tax auditors or through service centers. The most complex tax returns (with correspondingly the maximum expected additional taxes) are audited by revenue agents, who are experts on the staff of the Audit Division. Other returns are audited by IRS staff called tax auditors. Revenue agents and tax auditors conduct most of their examinations through face-to-face contacts with taxpayers and/or their representatives in the 63 district offices of the IRS. Some audits of noncomplex individual returns are handled through the mail by tax examiners in 10 service centers.

In addition to their role in determining IRS audit performance, audit coverage figures for each audit class, which are publicly released, have the role of signaling to the public the seriousness with which the Government views the underreporting of taxes. In view of this, the IRS has internal **policy constraints** on the **minimum audit coverage** it must attain for each audit class. These minimum coverages are specified both to fulfill the signaling role of the audit coverages and to ensure "fairness" to all constituencies. As seen in Tables 4 and 5, the total ATR for the 1992 audit program amounted to over 6 billion dollars, and a higher audit coverage would probably yield more revenue (even after accounting for auditing costs). However, the IRS did not audit more than around 1% of all filed returns primarily due to its budget constraints, determined by the Congressional budget allocation (Table 5 gives the 1992 audit coverages broken down by class). Even taking the budget allocation as given, the effectiveness of the audit plan *across* the different audit classes needed to be examined. Mr. Swanson's first priority was to analyze the optimal audit coverages for each class for the coming year, subject to minimum audit coverage constraints, for different Congressional budget allocation scenarios. He also wanted to evaluate how accurate the less formal (and more intuitive) methods for determining audit coverages (used so far by the IRS) were, compared to the theoretical optimum.

Planning for 1995

Mr. Swanson's first priority was planning for 1995, that is deciding on how best the auditing function could work towards achieving the objectives of the Business Master Plan. The two (not necessarily incompatible) objectives of the BMP of direct relevance to the auditing function are (*i*) maximizing revenues, and (*ii*) improving voluntary compliance, with spending limited by the Congressional budget allocation. For any budget, the auditing arm had to decide on allocations among the different audit classes. Ideally, what Mr. Swanson wanted was to develop a methodology that would take different possible budgets as inputs, and calculate as its outputs the optimal audit coverages for each class as well as estimates of the additional taxes generated, while satisfying the budget and policy constraints. To do this, he needed more data.

He first looked at estimates of the number of individual returns filed for each audit class for tax year 1993 (these were the returns that would be subject to the forthcoming audits). Since most of the returns for tax year 1993 had already been filed, he was confident that these numbers were reliable, and recorded them as Table 6.

TABLE 6 Estimated Number of Returns Filed for Tax Year 1993

	TYPE OF RETURN	RETURNS FILED (TAX YEAR 1993)
1)	1040A[a]	43,619,000
2)	1040 without Schedules	63,315,200
3)	1040 with Schedule C or F	7,609,900
	Total	**114,544,100**

[a] Including 1040EZ.
Number of individual tax returns filed for Tax Year 1993 by type of return.

When any single return is audited, the result may be no change or even a decrease in the tax due. The percentage of no changes typically varies from 10% to 20%, depending on the audit class as well as the auditor. However, the majority of audits in all audit classes result in an additional tax being recommended. Since returns are ranked for auditing based on their ATR potential—the higher the DIF score, the greater the likelihood that an audit would result in an increase in the taxpayer's tax liability—those returns chosen for an audit are more likely to yield a positive ATR.

In planning the audit program for these tax returns, Mr. Swanson considered the relationship between audit coverage and the expected additional tax recommended (ATR) resulting from an audit a key part of his analysis. The expected ATR realizable from auditing each additional return tends to decline as percentage audit coverage increases. This decline, which had been validated by the IRS's data, occurs in each separate audit class because of the rank-ordering of returns that results from the DIF ranking procedure described above.

Earlier IRS studies have confirmed that, after an appropriate normalization for the number of returns filed, the general shape of the relationship between audit coverage and ATR is consistent across the different audit classes, and hence it can be represented by similar mathematical functions. Only the *parameters* of the relationships differ from class to class, reflecting the different levels of compliance behavior associated with each class. In addition, extended multi-year statistical analyses had shown that *within* each audit class, the relationship was generally stable over time in terms of both its *shape* and its *numerical parameters* after adjusting for differences in the number of returns filed over time.

The data required for this analysis were obtained through the Tax Compliance and Monitoring Program (TCMP) of the IRS. Briefly, under TCMP, random samples of tax returns filed for each year were drawn (over all classes of returns) and these samples were audited in detail. This helped the IRS in getting a thorough understanding of the extent of tax compliance by the public. The fact that the samples drawn by the TCMP program were *random* meant that the statistical properties of the sampled returns would mirror those of the entire population. For his own analysis, Mr. Swanson acquired a sample of returns within each class (1040A, 1040 without Schedules C/F and 1040 with Schedule C or Schedule F) from the TCMP results.

Mr. Swanson simplified the data made available from the TCMP to suit his objectives (for example, he eliminated addresses and other contact information from the data). This left him with a relational database consisting of three primary tables, whose structures are given below.

(*i*) TAX RETURN Table:

Tax Return	Social Security Number	Income	Audit Class	DIF

The *Audit Class* is one of the three audit categories: '1' for 1040A/1040EZ, '2' for 1040 without Schedule C/F, and '3' for 1040 with Schedule C or Schedule F. The *DIF* for each return is the score assigned in the preliminary computerized ranking of all returns: the higher the score, the greater the audit potential. The *Social Security Number* is the nine-character taxpayer I.D.

(*ii*) AUDITOR Table:

Auditor	ID	Auditor Name	Hourly Cost

The *Auditor ID* is a five-digit code used to identify an IRS auditor. Different auditors may be paid different wages based on seniority, prior experience, and so on, and the *Hourly Cost* is the effective hourly cost of the auditor.

(*iii*) AUDIT Table:

Audit	Social Security Number	Auditor ID	ATR	Hours

This table provides the key information on audit results: the additional taxes and penalties recommended (*ATR*) and the *Hours* spent on each audit, which could be used to derive costs. The *Social Security Number* is the identifying key, and the *Auditor ID* uniquely identifies an auditor from the **Auditor** table.

The first step in Mr. Swanson's analysis was to identify the relationship between audit coverage and expected ATR. This meant (*i*) identifying the underlying mathematical function relating audit coverage to the ensuing expected ATR, and (*ii*) estimating the parameters of this function for each audit class. First and foremost was the question of what function to estimate.

For this analysis, assume that there are N tax returns from an audit class that are candidates for being audited. The most "promising" tax return in the class has the highest DIF value and should be audited first. Continuing this process, the tax returns in the class should be ranked from the highest DIF to the lowest DIF and audited in that order. Each additional audit in the class is expected to generate additional ATR. Mr. Swanson defined the **Cumulative ATR (n) function** for each class as the expected total ATR from auditing the first n returns in that class in the ranked set of N returns. As n ranges from 1 to N, there is a general tendency for Cumulative ATR (n) values to rise, but at a decreasing rate, since ever-smaller values of incremental ATR are being accumulated. The last column of Table 5 shows values of the Cumulative ATR (n) function. For example, 0.69% of the 43.4305 million ($=N$) 1040A Forms were audited, giving rise to $n = 300{,}480$ (0.69% times 43.4305 million), and the Treasury therefore realized a Cumulative ATR of 781 million dollars in the 1040A audit class.

The cumulative ATR (n) function is very sensitive to the number of returns available, N. Thus, Mr. Swanson considered

EXHIBIT 1

Shape of the Normalized Cumulative ATR as a Function of the Audit Coverage, p, for One Audit Class

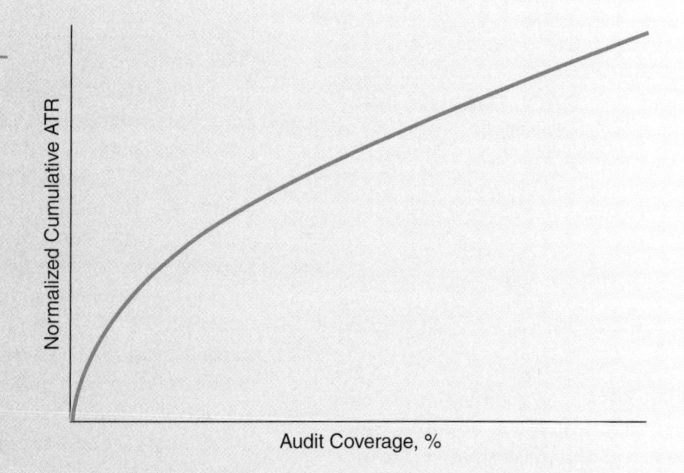

it important to use a function that was normalized for N. He decided to estimate the **Normalized Cumulative ATR (n) function**, obtained by dividing the Cumulative ATR (n) by the number of returns available in the class, N. He would then examine the relationship between the percent audit coverage and the Normalized Cumulative ATR, which should be stable for each audit class.

The Normalized Cumulative ATR function has a shape similar to that shown in Exhibit 1. Since returns are audited in descending order of their DIF scores, early audits would yield high ATR and later audits would yield progressively less ATR. The cumulative function would thus rise steeply at first and then more moderately.

The estimation of these functions was not trivial. For each audit class, Mr. Swanson asked for a random sample of $N = 2{,}000$ tax returns that participated in the TCMP program (totalling 6,000 returns across the three classes). These returns were then ranked by decreasing DIF within each audit class. To simplify matters, Mr. Swanson decided to analyze only the audit coverage range between $p = 0$ and 10%.[5] Thus, he asked the MIS personnel to provide him only the returns with the top 10% DIF values from each audit class sample. This resulted in a subsample of 600 returns, consisting of the top 200 returns from each audit class.[6] Using regression analysis, Mr. Swanson proceeded with the estimation of the three Normalized Cumulative ATR functions (one for each audit class). As indicated earlier, the mathematical form of the function should be the same across classes, with only the parameter values changing.

Mr. Swanson turned next to the estimation of the auditing costs. The auditing cost varies primarily with the complexity of the return. Thus, there are substantial cost differentials among the three audit classes. However, there was no identifiable systematic variation of the auditing costs within the three classes. He needed to estimate the auditing cost per return in each class.

Mr. Swanson reviewed all the materials he had on the problem. He decided that the tables he had put together, in addition to the TCMP data, were adequate for him to proceed to the next stage of analysis, which would be the derivation of the optimal audit coverages, and the associated total ATR values, for each audit class for fiscal 1995.

[5] Mr. Swanson considered it unlikely that the audit coverage in any class would exceed 10%, and did not want the behavior for high levels of coverage to affect his results.

[6] Recall that the returns in each class are ranked by declining DIF values from number 1 to number $N = 2{,}000$. Thus, Mr. Swanson received the data for returns 1–200 from each of these three ranked samples.

Case Study Abacus SFX

Located in Hollywood, Abacus SFX is a small high-tech start-up company specializing in creating digital special effects for science fiction movies. Abacus's costs for a given film project that it might accept are \$20,000 to set up a dedicated graphics server computer for the project plus \$25,000 for each animator assigned to that project's team. Offsetting these costs are project revenues in two forms, a "good faith" payment for Abacus accepting a given project and project billings.

As customary in the industry, when Abacus accepts a project, it receives an initial good faith cash payment from the film's producer. The good faith payment amounts vary with projects. Abacus is considering accepting up to five projects

EXHIBIT 1

PROJECT	GOOD FAITH PAYMENT ($000s)
1	$18
2	$20
3	$8
4	$26
5	$22

for the next month. Exhibit 1 gives the good faith payments for each project Abacus might accept. In addition, since assigning more animators to a given project shortens the time to complete the effects required for the project, Abacus can charge higher fees for larger project teams. Currently, Abacus charges producers a fee of $90,000 per animator assigned to each accepted project. This fee per animator assigned to an accepted project is in addition to any good faith payment Abacus receives for accepting that project.

If Abacus accepts a project, it must assign at least one animator to the project. By policy Abacus does not share animators across projects, and thus, only an integral number of animators can be assigned to a given project, if it is accepted. Abacus has a total of eight animators available next month to assign to accepted projects, and wishes to allocate the animators to projects to create high total profit for the month.

Questions

1. Develop a model to determine which projects to accept and how many animators to allocate to accepted projects. Assume no projects are accepted initially, and optimize the model with Solver's GRG Nonlinear Optimizer. Next, optimize the model with Solver's Evolutionary Optimizer using the same initial starting decision of no accepted projects. Which optimizer produces the better allocation and why?
2. Abacus would like to investigate the possibility of sharing animators across projects so that an animator would be able to split his or her time across projects. Clients would be billed for the appropriate fraction of the $90,000 animator fee and animators would receive the same appropriate fraction of their $25,000 salary. Copy your Excel worksheet from question 1 above to a new worksheet in your workbook. Modify this model to allow a noninteger number of the eight animators to be assigned to a project, subject to the continued restriction that any accepted project must have at least the equivalent of one animator assigned to it. Optimize the model with Solver's Evolutionary Optimizer using an initial starting decision of no accepted projects. Next, optimize the model with Solver's GRG Nonlinear Optimizer using as its initial starting decision the final solution just found by Solver's Evolutionary Optimizer. Does the GRG Nonlinear Optimizer improve upon the one found by the Evolutionary Optimizer and why or why not?
3. Return to the model and setting of question 1. Abacus may have as many as ten animators or as few as five animators available to assign to any of the five projects next month. Use SolverTable to produce a table giving the allocation of animators to accepted projects and the resulting profit for the number of available animators varying between ten and five, inclusive. Do this first using Solver's GRG Nonlinear Optimizer assuming a starting decision of accepting all projects and allocating one animator to each project. Next, create a second SolverTable like the first one except fill it using Solver's Evolutionary Optimizer. Which optimizer produces the better allocations? How sensitive is profit to the number of available animators to allocate?
4. Abacus has decided that the model developed for question 1 above is not realistic as to the fees it can bill for accepting a project. In particular, larger teams incur diminishing returns to productivity. All costs, any good faith payments, and the minimum of at least one animator assigned to accepted projects is the same as in question 1. However the billing for a given project team (=$90,000 × team size) is to be deflated by multiplying it by a fraction, set by Abacus management, as given in Exhibit 2. For example, a project team of three could bill only 3 × $90,000 × .63 for that project. Copy your Excel worksheet from question 1 to a new worksheet in your workbook. Modify the model to include this billing revision using the VLOOKUP () function. Assume no projects are accepted initially, eight animators are available, and optimize the model with Solver's GRG Nonlinear Optimizer. Next, optimize the model with Solver's Evolutionary Optimizer using the same initial starting

EXHIBIT 2

TEAM SIZE	FRACTION OF BILLING FEE
1	1.00
2	0.77
3	0.63
4	0.54
5	0.46
6	0.40
7	0.35
8	0.31
9	0.27
10	0.23
11	0.20
12	0.17
13	0.15
14	0.12

decision of no accepted projects. Which optimizer produces the better allocation and why?

5. Return to the model and setting of question 4. Abacus may have as many as ten animators or as few as five animators available to assign to any of the five projects next month. Use SolverTable to produce a table giving the allocation of animators to accepted projects and the resulting profit for the number of available animators varying between ten and five, inclusive. Do this first using Solver's GRG Nonlinear Optimizer assuming a starting decision of accepting all projects and allocating one animator to each project. Next, create a second SolverTable like the first one except fill it using Solver's Evolutionary Optimizer. Which optimizer produces the better allocations? How sensitive is profit to the number of available animators to allocate?

6. Summarize your findings for questions 4 and 5 into a report to Abacus management. Document your results from using Solver's GRG Nonlinear Optimizer and Solver's Evolutionary Optimizer and recommend a general procedure for using your model in future months as it concerns these two optimizers. Comment on the consequences if Abacus were to have more or fewer than eight animators for the five projects next month.

References

John Mulvey, "An Asset-Liability Investment System," *Interfaces*, 24, no. 3 (1994): 22–33.

Yosi Ben-Dov, Lakhbir Hayre, and Vincent Pica, "Mortgage Valuation Models at Prudential Securities," *Interfaces*, 22, no. 1 (1992): 55–71.

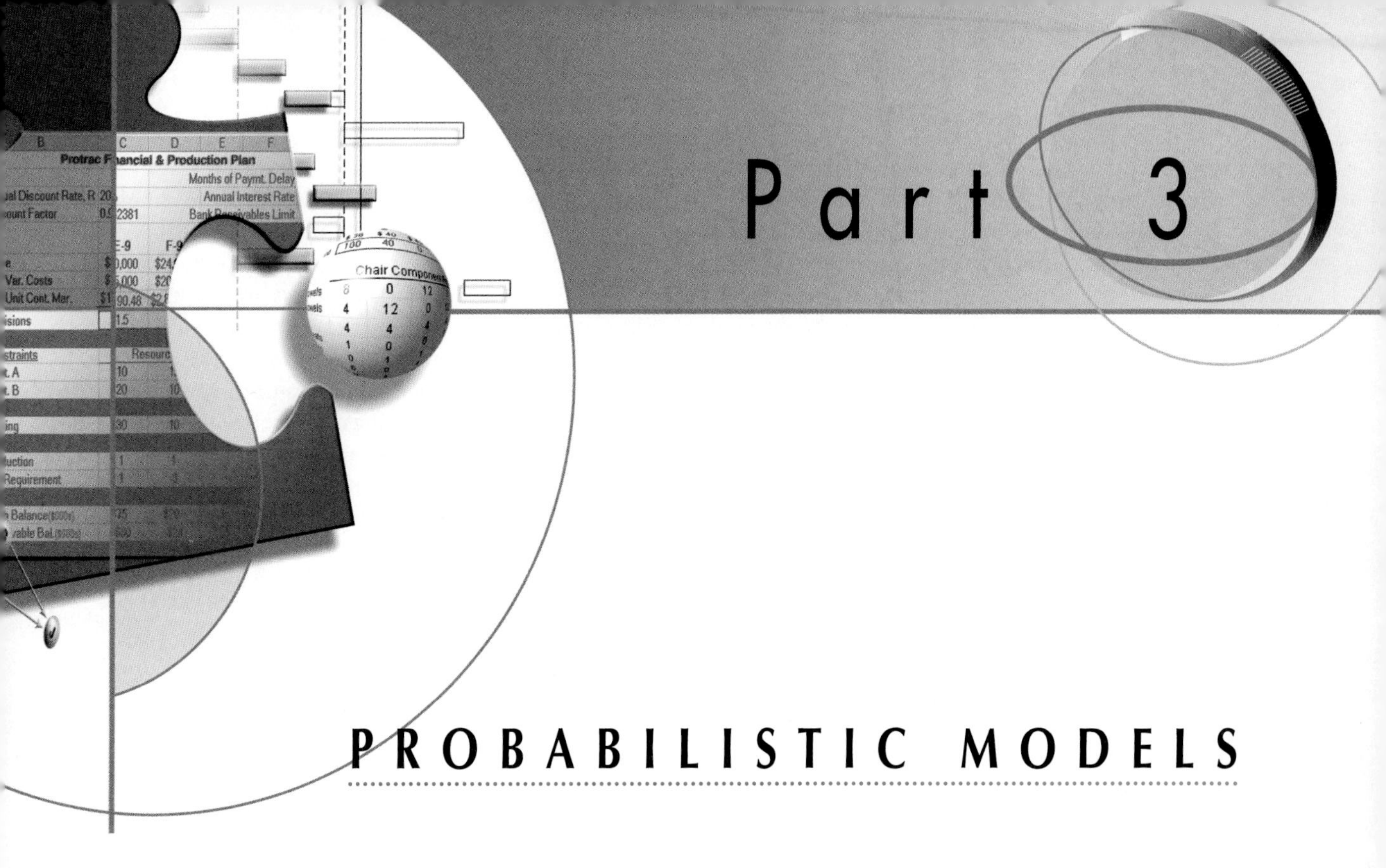

Part 3

PROBABILISTIC MODELS

We all know the saying: Only two things are sure, death and taxes. Although it can be taken as a complaint about governments, this remark also expresses a rather fundamental view of nature and human enterprise. It suggests that most earthly phenomena include some element of uncertainty and unpredictability. The biblical Book of Ecclesiastes makes the same observation about human endeavors: "Time and chance happeneth to them all."

We respond to this fact of life in various ways. In some situations we choose to ignore the uncertainty; in others we attempt to deal with it explicitly. We have spent the last seven chapters ignoring uncertainty. In the next three chapters (and three more chapters on the CD) we confront situations in which the level of uncertainty is too great to ignore, and we as managers must take this into account. There are many examples: The entire insurance industry is one. Others include investments in stocks, bonds, and real estate, as well as any business in which a product is created in anticipation of demand.

This part of the book is devoted to clarifying our way of thinking about uncertainty and developing methods for dealing with it in decision models. Our goal is to help you frame problems in which uncertainty plays a major role in a consistent and useful manner and to provide you with some helpful problem-solving techniques. The focus remains the same: We consider situations in which management has the opportunity to choose between several alternatives. But now the problem is complicated by the fact that we are not sure what the payoff will be for each of the alternatives.

Probability is the branch of mathematics that provides the foundation for the analysis in this part of the book. The language of probability is part of our everyday experience: Weather forecasts say that the *chance* of rain is 30%, *odds* on sporting events are quoted in the newspapers, and the government worries about the *probable* effects of the proposed tax law. Closer examination, however, often reveals considerable confusion about what such terms and statements really mean. To understand these chapters you will have to start with (or develop) an understanding of some concepts related to probability. Appendix A in the back of the book contains a brief introduction to the crucial concepts. The material in this appendix should provide an adequate background to enable you to master the material in this part of the text.

Probability is a difficult topic for many students. You may not find it hard to read these chapters and do the assignments; what is hard is making probability a part of your personal approach to problem solving. This will occur only when you come to think naturally about a *distribution* of profits or waiting times or demands and when you have convenient tools to use on real problems. Here again, computing plays an important role—especially in simulation. It is possible to simulate interesting problems using spreadsheets, and especially easy with the spreadsheet add-ins, Crystal Ball and @RISK. These tools are discussed in the simulation chapter of this part. We strongly encourage you to use this software and do the simulation exercises, which will greatly enhance the ultimate value of your study. The decision analysis and queuing chapters will introduce some nifty spreadsheet accessories and the discrete event simulation and project management chapters will introduce two new software packages to help you implement these tools successfully.

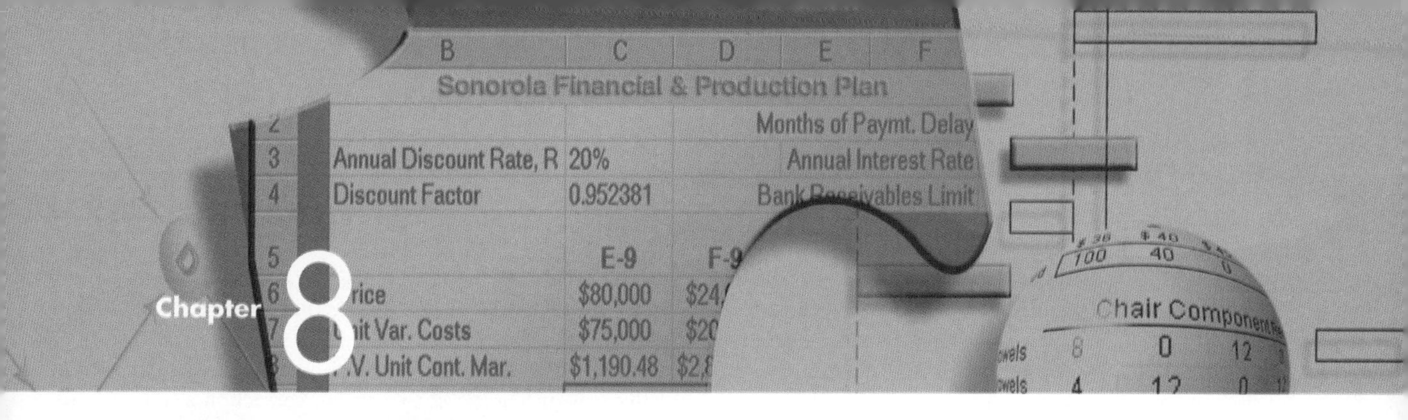

DECISION ANALYSIS

CHAPTER OUTLINE

APPLICATION CAPSULE **Vision Correction Alternatives for Myopic Adults**

Approximately 70 million Americans have myopia, commonly known as nearsightedness. Prior to 1980, myopia was treated almost exclusively with external corrective lenses, either eyeglasses or contact lenses. These corrective lenses are concave, pushing the point of focus backward onto the retina.

In the last 15 years, a surgical procedure called radial keratotomy (RK) has become a popular alternative for correcting myopia. This procedure basically involves numerous tiny incisions of the cornea. According to *Consumers Reports*, over 200,000 Americans had the operation in 1992, a 667% increase over the number in 1987. In 1995, a laser-based surgical procedure called photorefractive keratectomy (PRK) was approved by the United States Food and Drug Administration. This procedure involves using a laser to "sculpt" the entire cornea.

A potentially continuous series of vision correction decisions must be made by the typical adult. At each decision node, a myopic adult who has not had prior surgery can continue with the best available nonsurgical alternative or can elect to have surgery. If surgery is chosen, it may or may not fully correct the refractive error. Significant shifts in refractive error could also occur in subsequent years. In either case, an individual who has had prior surgery could face a subsequent decision regarding external correction of the residual refractive error.

Myopic adults have three fundamental objectives that affect his or her choice of a vision correction alternative: to maximize visual utility during their remaining lifetime, to minimize the dollar costs of vision correction during the remaining lifetime, and to minimize time costs of vision correction (e.g., time to put in your contacts and maintain them) during their remaining lifetime.

Although some of the decisions will depend on each individual's preference for such things as glasses versus contacts, several interesting insights came out of this analysis: (1) PRK is preferable to RK since it yields better expected visual utility at Year 0, has no significant risks above and beyond RK, and has future outcomes that are at least as good as RK; (2) the 40-year monetary cost of either surgical alternative is roughly equal to the 40-year monetary cost of perpetual contact lens use. The up-front monetary costs of the surgeries are approximately balanced by the expected 40-year monetary savings from a possible 20/20 surgical outcome. (See Brown.)

8.1 INTRODUCTION

Decision analysis provides a framework for analyzing a wide variety of management models. The framework establishes (1) a system of classifying decision models based on the amount of information about the model that is available and (2) a decision criterion; that is, a measure of the "goodness" of a decision for each type of model.

In the first part of this chapter we will present the decision theory framework and relate it to models previously discussed. The second half of the chapter is devoted to decision trees. Decision trees apply decision theory concepts to sequential decisions that include uncertain events. They are a pragmatic and practical aid to managerial decision making.

In general terms, decision theory treats decisions against nature. This phrase refers to a situation where the result (return) from an individual decision depends on the action of another player (nature), over which you have no control. For example, if the decision is whether or not to carry an umbrella, the return (get wet or not) depends on the state of nature that ensues. It is important to note that in this model the returns accrue only to the decision maker. Nature does not care what the outcome is. This condition distinguishes decision theory from game theory. In *game theory* both players have an economic interest in the outcome.

In decision theory models, the fundamental piece of data is a payoff table like Table 8.1. The alternative decisions are listed along the side of the table, and the possible states of nature are listed across the top.

The entries in the body of the table are the payoffs for all possible combinations of decisions and states of nature. The decision process proceeds as follows:

1. You, the decision maker, select one of the alternative decisions $d_1 \ldots d_n$. Suppose that you select d_1.
2. After your decision is made, a state of nature occurs that is beyond your control. Suppose that state 2 occurs.
3. The return you receive can now be determined from the payoff table. Since you made decision d_1 and state of nature 2 occurred, the return is r_{12}.

Table 8.1

Payoff Table

Decision	STATE OF NATURE 1	2	...	m
d_1	r_{11}	r_{12}	...	r_{1m}
d_2	r_{21}	r_{22}	...	r_{2m}
$\vdots$	$\vdots$	$\vdots$	$\vdots$	$\vdots$
d_n	r_{n1}	r_{n2}	...	r_{nm}

Again, the decision is made first, then one of the states of nature occurs. Once the decision has been made, it can't be changed after the state of nature occurs. In general terms the question is, Which of the decisions should we select? We would like as large a return as possible; that is, the largest possible value of r_{ij}, where i represents the decision made and j the state of nature that occurs. It is obvious that the decision we should select will depend on our belief concerning what nature will do, that is, which state of nature will occur. If we believe state 1 will occur, we select the decision associated with the largest number in column 1. If we believe the state of nature is more likely to be state 2, we choose the decision corresponding to the largest payoff in column 2, and so on.

In the following section we will consider different assumptions about nature's behavior. Each assumption leads to a different *criterion* for selecting the "best" decision, and hence to a different procedure.

8.2 THREE CLASSES OF DECISION MODELS

This section deals with three classes of decision models against nature. Each class is defined by an assumption about nature's behavior. The three classes are decisions under certainty, decisions under risk, and decisions under uncertainty. Of the three, we are most likely to encounter decisions under risk, but the other two classes are presented for completeness.

DECISIONS UNDER CERTAINTY

A **decision under certainty** is one in which you know which state of nature will occur. Alternatively, you can think of it as a case with a single state of nature. Suppose, for example, that in the morning you are deciding whether to take your umbrella to work and you know *for sure* that it will be raining when you leave work in the afternoon. In the payoff table for this model, Table 8.2, \$7 is the cost of having your suit cleaned if you get caught in the rain. It enters the table with a minus sign since it is a table of returns and a cost is a negative return. Obviously, the optimal decision is to take the umbrella.

All linear programming models, integer programming models, nonlinear programming models, and other deterministic models such as the EOQ model can be thought of as decisions against nature in which there is only one state of nature. This is so because we are sure (within the context of the model) what return we will get for each decision we make. For a concrete example, consider a simple linear programming model like those found in Chapter 3:

$$\begin{aligned} &\text{Max } 5000E + 4000F \\ &\text{s.t.} \quad 10E + 15F \le 150 \\ &\qquad 20E + 10F \le 160 \\ &\qquad 30E + 10F \ge 135 \\ &\qquad E - 3F \le 0 \\ &\qquad E + F \ge 5 \\ &\qquad E, F \ge 0 \end{aligned}$$

Table 8.2

Umbrella Example Payoff Table

	RAIN
Take Umbrella	0
Do Not	–7.00

Table 8.3

Payoff Table for the Simple LP Model

DECISION	STATE OF NATURE
$E = 0, F = 0$	$-\infty$
$E = 5; F = 4$	41,000
1	⋮
$E = 6, F = 3.5$	44,000
⋮	⋮

Table 8.3 presents this model in the form of a payoff table. In this table, a return of $-\infty$ is assigned to any infeasible decision. For example, since $E = 0$, $F = 0$ violates the third and fifth constraints, the associated return is defined to be $-\infty$. For any feasible pair (E, F) the return is defined to be the objective function value—namely, $5000E + 4000F$. For this model we know exactly what return we get for each decision (each choice of the pair E, F). We can thus list all returns in one column and think of it as representing one state of nature that we are sure will occur.

Conceptually, it is easy to solve a model with one state of nature. You simply select the decision that yields the highest return. In practice, as opposed to "in concept," finding such a decision may be another story. Since E and F can take on an infinite number of values, there will be an infinite number of rows for this model (see Table 8.3). Even in this simple model, enumerating the alternatives and selecting the best of them are not possible. Additional mathematical analysis (in this case, the Solver algorithm of Excel) is needed to find the optimal decision.

DECISIONS UNDER RISK

A lack of certainty about future events is a characteristic of many, if not most, management decision models. Consider how the decisions of the financial vice president of an insurance company would change if she could know exactly what changes were to occur in the bond market. Imagine the relief of the head buyer for Maxwell House if he could know exactly how large next year's crop of coffee beans would be.

It thus seems clear that numerous decision models are characterized by a lack of certainty. It is also clear that those who deal effectively with these models, through either skill or luck, are often handsomely rewarded for their accomplishments. In the first book of the Old Testament, Joseph is promoted from slave to assistant Pharaoh of Egypt by accurately forecasting seven years of feast and seven years of famine.[1]

In quantitative modeling, the lack of certainty can be dealt with in various ways. For example, in a linear programming model, some of the data may be an estimate of a future value. In the above LP model, the first constraint might represent next month's capacity (availability of hours) in department A (the right-hand side). This capacity may depend on factors that will occur next week, but the production plans, let us say, must be spelled out today. As previously described in Chapter 4 (LP sensitivity analysis), management might deal with this lack of certainty by estimating the capacity as 150 and then performing sensitivity analysis.

Definition of Risk Decision theory provides alternative approaches to models with less than complete certainty. One such approach is called **decisions under risk**. In this context, the term *risk* has a restrictive and well-defined meaning. When we speak of decisions

[1] As well as being an accurate forecaster, by virtue of his skill in successfully interpreting Pharaoh's dreams, Joseph has been called the first psychoanalyst. Less well known is the fact that Joseph was also the first management scientist. In anticipation of the famine, he advised Pharaoh to build storage facilities to hold inventories of grain. When it was all over and the famine had been survived. Joseph was asked how he had come to acquire such wisdom and knowledge. "Lean-year programming" was his reply.

under risk, we are referring to a class of decision models for which there is more than one state of nature and for which we make the assumption that *the decision maker can arrive at a probability estimate for the occurrence for each of the various states of nature.* Suppose, for example, that there are $m > 1$ states of nature, and let p_j be the probability estimate that state j will occur. Generally we will estimate the probability of state j occurring (p_j) using historical frequencies, meaning we'll look back over history and record what percentage of time that state j actually occurred out of our entire pool of observations. For example, if in the last 1,000 days, we find that it rained on 200 of those days, then we'll estimate the future probability of rain on a given day as 0.20 (=200/1000). When this historical data is not available or the manager feels that it is not relevant to the future, the manager must make subjective estimates of these probabilities. This latter approach will be covered in Section 8.10.

Recall that the expected value of any random variable is the weighted average of all possible values of the random variable, where the weights are the probabilities of the values occurring. Since different returns are associated with different states of nature, the expected return associated with decision i is the sum, over all possible states j, of terms of the form: (return in state j when decision is i) times (the probability of state j), or $r_{ij}\, p_j$. We can then use the following equation to calculate ER_i, the expected return if we make decision i:

$$ER_i = \sum_{j=1}^{m} r_{ij} \cdot p_j = r_{i1}p_1 + r_{i2}p_2 + \cdots + r_{im}p_m \qquad (8.1)$$

For this type of model, *management should then make the decision that maximizes the expected return.*[2] In other words, i^* is the optimal decision where

$$ER_{i^*} = \text{maximum over all } i \text{ of } ER_i$$

The Newsvendor Model An example of such a model is the following newsvendor model. (Similar models are treated in Chapter 9.) A newsvendor can buy the *Wall Street Journal* newspapers for 40 cents each and sell them for 75 cents. However, he must buy the papers before he knows how many he can actually sell. If he buys more papers than he can sell, he simply disposes of the excess at no additional cost. If he does not buy enough papers, he loses potential sales now and possibly in the future (disgruntled customers may no longer buy their papers from him). Suppose, for the moment, that this loss of *future* sales is captured by a cost of lost goodwill of 50 cents per unsatisfied customer. For illustrative purposes and ease of computation, also suppose that the demand distribution he faces is

$$P_0 = \text{Prob}\{\text{demand} = 0\} = 0.1$$
$$P_1 = \text{Prob}\{\text{demand} = 1\} = 0.3$$
$$P_2 = \text{Prob}\{\text{demand} = 2\} = 0.4$$
$$P_3 = \text{Prob}\{\text{demand} = 3\} = 0.2$$

In this model, each of the four different values for demand is a different state of nature, and the number of papers ordered is the decision. The returns, or payoffs, for this model are shown in Table 8.4.

The entries in this figure represent the net cash flow associated with each combination of number ordered and number demanded, less the cost of lost goodwill when the number ordered is not sufficient to meet the number demanded. These entries are calculated with the expression

$$\text{payoff} = 75\,(\text{number of papers sold}) - 40\,(\text{number of papers ordered}) - 50\,(\text{unmet demand})$$

where 75 cents is the selling price per paper, 40 cents is the cost of buying a paper, and 50 cents is the cost of disappointing a customer (cost of lost goodwill). It is important to note that in this model, sales and demand need not be identical. Indeed, sales is the minimum of

[2] It will be shown that this is equivalent to another criterion: *minimizing* expected regret.

Table 8.4

Payoff Table for the Newsvendor Model

	STATE OF NATURE (DEMAND)			
Decision	**0**	**1**	**2**	**3**
0	0	–50	–100	–150
1	–40	35	–15	–65
2	–80	–5	70	20
3	–120	–45	30	105

the two quantities (numbered ordered, number demanded). For example, when no papers are ordered, then clearly none can be sold, no matter how many are demanded, and the unmet demand will equal the demand. Thus, for all entries in the first row, the above expression for the payoff gives 75(0) – 40(0) – 50(demand) = –50(demand). If 1 paper is ordered and none are demanded, then none are sold, the unmet demand is 0, and the payoff is 75(0) – 40(1) – 50(0) = –40, which is the first entry in row 2. However, if 1 paper is ordered and 1 or more are demanded, then exactly 1 will be sold, the unmet demand will be 1 less than the demand, and the payoff becomes 75(1) – 40(1) – 50(demand – 1) = 85 – 50(demand). Can you verify that the remaining values in the body of Table 8.4 are correct? Also think about why the possible decisions of ordering 4 or more papers were ignored.

Once all the data are assembled in Table 8.4, the process of finding the optimal decision is strictly mechanical. You use equation (8.1) to evaluate the expected return for each decision (ER_i for $i = 0, 1, 2, 3$) and pick the largest. We will first demonstrate this process by hand and then we'll show how to do it in a spreadsheet. For example, if you order two papers,

$$ER_2 = -80(0.1) - 5(0.3) + 70(0.4) + 20(0.2) = 22.5$$

The first term is the return if we order 2 papers and 0 are demanded multiplied by the probability that 0 are demanded. The second term is the return if we order 2 papers and 1 is demanded (see Table 8.4) multiplied by the probability that 1 paper is demanded. The other terms are similarly defined. The expected returns for all of the other possible decisions are calculated as follows:

$$ER_0 = 0(0.1) - 50(0.3) - 100(0.4) - 150(0.2) = -85$$

$$ER_1 = -40(0.1) + 35(0.3) - 15(0.4) - 65(0.2) = -12.5$$

$$ER_3 = -120(0.1) - 45(0.3) + 30(0.4) + 105(0.2) = 7.5$$

Since ER_2 is the largest of these four values, the optimal decision is to order 2 papers.

Another way to compare the decisions is to look at a graph of their risk profiles. The **risk profile** shows all the possible outcomes with their associated probabilities for a given decision and gives the manager an idea of the range of outcomes possible. Some managers find this more helpful than simply looking at one number (e.g., expected return) that summarizes all the available information (probabilities and potential outcomes). The risk profiles for the four decisions that the newsvendor faces are shown in Figure 8.1.

We can see that all four of the possible outcomes for "Order 0" are less than or equal to zero. Seventy-five percent of the outcomes for "Order 1" are nonpositive, and 50% of the outcomes for "Order 2" and "Order 3" are nonpositive. We can also see that Order 2 has a high probability (40%) of generating the second highest payoff of all (70 cents). Of course, all of this information is available in the original payoff table, but sometimes it helps to see the data in a graph.

The Cost of Lost Goodwill: A Spreadsheet Sensitivity Analysis This decision is based on a cost, the cost of lost goodwill, whose value is much less certain than the other two parameters, the selling price and the purchase cost. What would happen to the

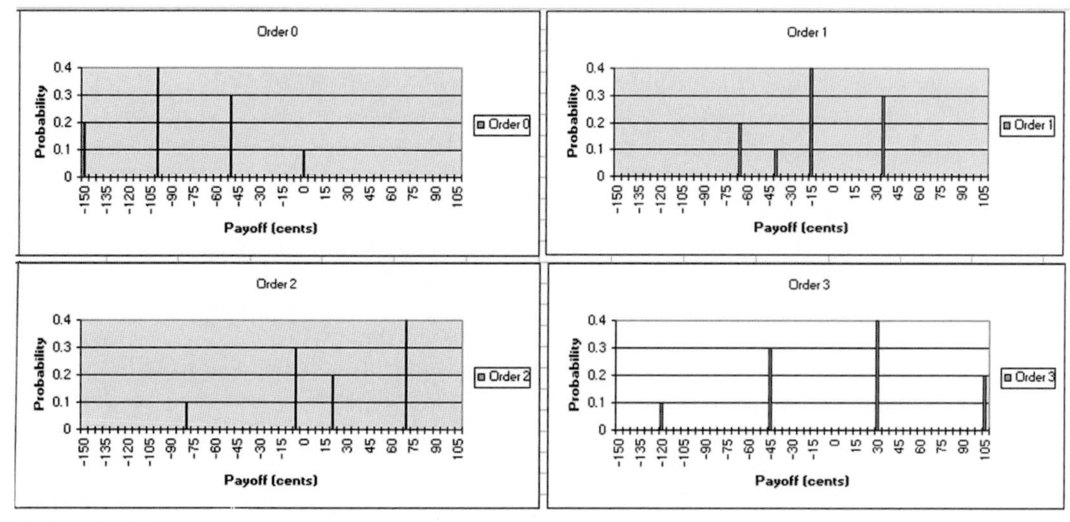

FIGURE 8.1

Risk Profiles of Four Newsvendor Decisions

optimal decision if the cost of lost goodwill were different? To answer this question we will perform a sensitivity analysis on the value of the cost of lost goodwill.

One possible way to do this would be to assume a different value for the cost of lost goodwill, recalculate the payoff matrix, recompute the expected returns, and see what happens to the optimal decision. This would be tiresome to do by hand, but is ideally suited to be done in Excel. Figure 8.2 shows the spreadsheet (NEWSVENDOR.XLS) for calculating the payoff matrix and expected returns.

The known prices and costs are entered with their labels in cells A1:B3. The payoff for any given combination of decision/state of nature is shown in the equation line of Figure 8.2 and is calculated as follows:

The first term calculates the revenue from sales: the Selling Price ($B$1) times the number sold (the smaller of the number ordered and the number demanded, =MIN($A7,B$6)). The second term subtracts the cost of the papers purchased: the

FIGURE 8.2

Newsvendor Spreadsheet

B7 = =$B$1*MIN($A7,B$6)-$B$2*$A7-$B$3*MAX(B$6-$A7,0)

	A	B	C	D	E	F	G
1	Selling Price	75					
2	Purchase Cost	40					
3	Goodwill Cost	50					
4							
5			*States of Nature*				
6	*Decision*	*0*	*1*	*2*	*3*	Expected Return	
7	*0*	0	-50	-100	-150	-85	
8	*1*	-40	35	-15	-65	-12.5	
9	*2*	-80	-5	70	20	22.5	
10	*3*	-120	-45	30	105	7.5	
11							
12	Probabilities	0.1	0.3	0.4	0.2		
13							

Cell	Formula	Copy To
B7	= $B$1*MIN($A7,B$6)–$B$2*$A7–$B$3*MAX(B$6–$A7,0)	B7:E10
F7	= SUMPRODUCT (B7:E7,$B$12:$E$12)	F8:F10

Purchase Cost ($B$2) times the number of papers purchased ($A7). The final term subtracts the lost goodwill: the Goodwill Cost ($B$3) times the unmet demand (the larger of the demand minus the quantity ordered or 0, =MAX(B$6–$A7,0)).

This formula in cell B7 has been constructed carefully using Excel's relative and absolute cell referencing so that it can be copied to obtain all the other formulas in the payoff matrix. The expected return column (column F) can be generated by using the SUMPRODUCT formula. For example, in cell F7, we enter =SUMPRODUCT(B7:E7,$B$12:$E$12), which is just the sum of the products of the probability of receiving a given payoff times the respective payoff.

Using the Data Table command, a table of expected returns can easily be generated for a range of Goodwill Costs. We've done this in a new spreadsheet "Sensitivity to Goodwill" in the same NEWSVENDOR.XLS. The data table will show the expected returns for the different order quantities for values of the Goodwill Cost between 0 and 150 in five-cent increments. In order to do this yourself, follow these steps:

1. Copy the entire "Base Case" spreadsheet over to the new spreadsheet "Sensitivity to Goodwill."
2. Enter the initial value (0) for the Goodwill costs we're going to investigate in cell A16.
3. Click back on cell A16, then click on the Edit menu, then Fill, then Series.
4. Click on "Series in Columns," enter a step value of 5 and a stop value of 150. Click on OK.
5. In cell B15 we want to enter the cell formula that gives us the expected return when we order 0 papers (=F7). In cells C15:E15 we want to do a similar thing so that the Data Table will give us the expected returns for ordering 1, 2, and 3 papers (i.e., enter=F8, =F9, =F10, respectively, in these cells).
6. Click on the Data menu, then Table. Enter the column input cell as $B$3 as shown in Figure 8.3. We're telling Excel to put the values found in column A into cell B3 (one-at-a-time) and then report back to us in columns B, C, D, and E the values it calculated in cells F7:F10.

After the Data Table does its calculations, we want to present a graph of the results to help us sort out this sea of numbers. To do this we use Excel's Chart Wizard as follows:

1. Highlight the range of data we want to graph (A16:E46).
2. Click on the Chart Wizard icon in Excel (which automatically walks us through several steps); drag and place it anywhere in the spreadsheet where you want the graph to be situated.

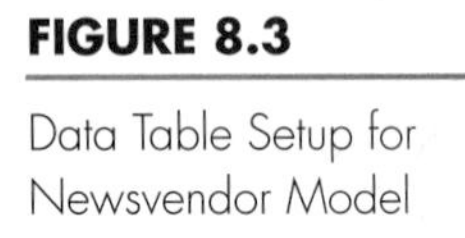

FIGURE 8.3

Data Table Setup for Newsvendor Model

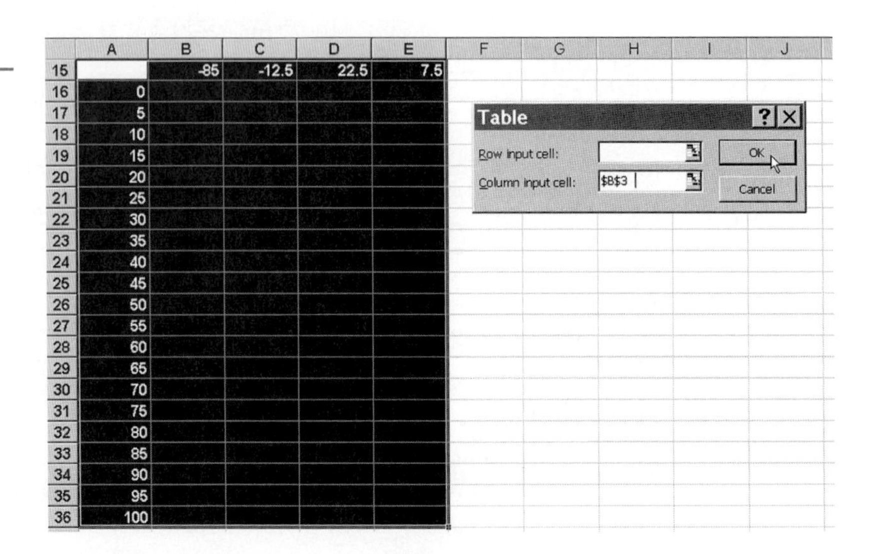

FIGURE 8.4

Chart Wizard for Newsvendor Model

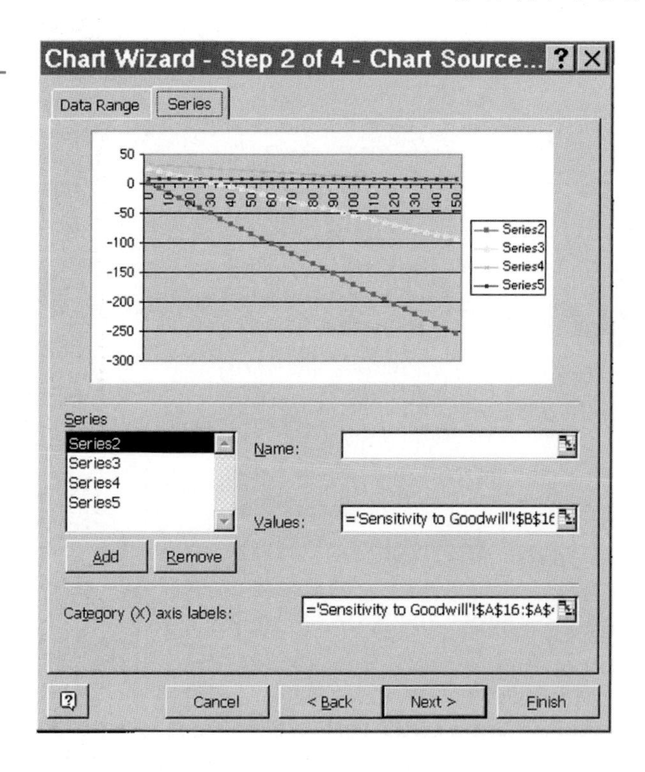

3. In the first step, you choose the kind of graph you want. Click on "Line" then click on the Chart sub-type you want (the default one [fourth] is fine) and then click on "Next>."
4. Now the Wizard shows us a sample of what the graph will look like. We only need to make one modification here. Click on the "Series" tab and then indicate that the "Category (X) axis labels" are found in A16:A46, as shown in Figure 8.4. Then we remove Series 1 from the display since it now serves as our *X*-axis label. Click on "Next>."
5. Next we have the option to enter titles for the graph or labels for the axes. We enter the appropriate values and then click on "Next>."
6. Lastly, we indicate that we want the chart placed as an object in our current worksheet (which is the default choice) and click on "Finish."
7. A graph like that shown in Figure 8.5 is displayed. (We have altered the four series legends from a generic "Series 1, Series 2, Series 3, Series 4" to "Order 0, Order 1, Order 2, Order 3" by using some of the advanced features in Excel.)

Notice that as the Goodwill Cost increases, the expected returns either decrease (when 0, 1, or 2 papers are ordered) or remain constant (when 3 papers are ordered). For Goodwill Costs less than 125 cents, the optimal decision is to order 2 papers. For a Goodwill Cost of 125 cents, alternative optima exist: order 2 or 3 papers. For a Goodwill Cost greater than 125 cents, the optimal decision is to order 3 papers. Thus, it is not necessary to know the Goodwill Cost precisely, just whether it is greater than or less than 125 cents. These results are reminiscent of the sensitivity analysis of a cost coefficient in a linear programming model where the optimal solution did not change for values of the coefficient in a given range. With this example, we have now illustrated the most important class of decision models (decisions under risk) and the associated decision criterion (maximize the expected return).

FIGURE 8.5

Graph of Sensitivity Analysis for Goodwill Cost

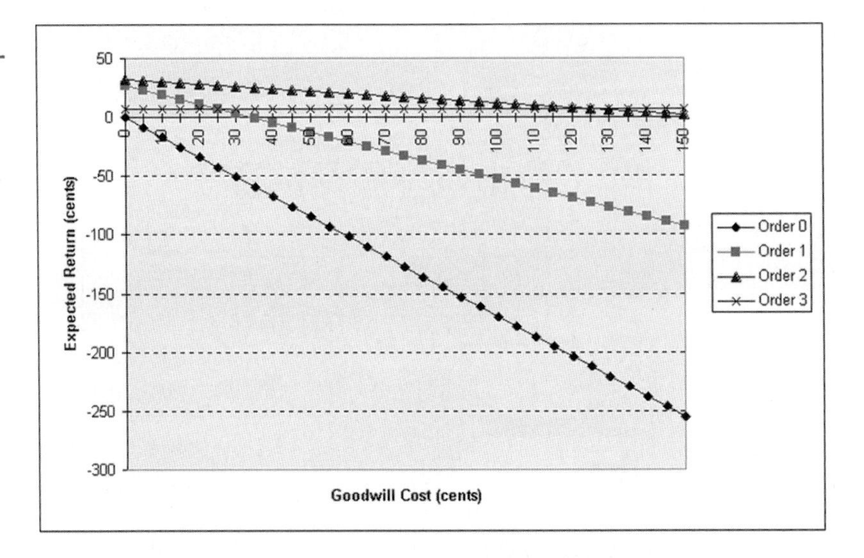

DECISIONS UNDER UNCERTAINTY (OPTIONAL)

In **decisions under uncertainty** we again have more than one possible state of nature, but now the decision maker is unwilling or unable to specify the probabilities that the various states of nature will occur. There is a long-standing debate as to whether such a situation should exist; that is, should the decision maker always be willing to at least subjectively specify the probabilities even when he or she does not know very much (anything) about what state of nature is apt to occur? Although it is hard to imagine an actual business decision being made under such a cloud, we'll leave this debate to the philosophers and turn to the various approaches suggested for this class of models for those who are interested. Notice that we have indicated that this section is optional for those who consider "Decisions Under Risk" to be the most relevant topic. For such readers, please skip ahead to Section 8.3.

Laplace Criterion The Laplace criterion approach interprets the condition of "uncertainty" as equivalent to assuming that all states of nature are equally likely. This is the point of view: "If I know nothing, then anything is equally likely." For example, in the newsvendor model, assuming all states are equally likely means that since there are four states, each state occurs with probability 0.25. Using these probabilities converts the model to a decision under risk, and one could then compute the expected return. You can easily verify that, using these probabilities, expected return would again be maximized by the decision to order 2 papers. When using the Laplace criterion, since each state has equal probability, all you need do to find the best decision is to add up all the payoffs for each decision and choose the decision with the largest sum (which will also have the largest average payoff).

Although in some situations this "equally likely" approach may produce acceptable results, in other settings it would be inappropriate. For example, consider your friend from Turkmenistan, about to watch the football game between Ohio State and Michigan in a year in which one team is experiencing a bad season and the other is thus heavily favored in the betting. Although your friend knows nothing about football and has no knowledge about the probability of either team winning, these probabilities clearly exist and are *not* equal. In other words, even though one has "no knowledge," there may be underlying probabilities on the various states of nature, and these probabilities may in no way be consistent with the "equal likelihood" assumption. With this realization, there may be contexts in which you would not wish to use the criterion of expected return based on the equal-likelihood assumption (i.e., the Laplace criterion).

For such cases, there are three different criteria that can be used to make decisions under uncertainty: *maximin*, *maximax*, and *minimax regret*. All of these criteria can be used without specifying probabilities. The discussion will be illustrated with the newsvendor model. Look at the earlier payoff table for a moment and think of what criterion you might use to make a decision. By this we mean, think of a rule that you could describe to a friend. It has to be a general rule so that your friend could apply it to any payoff table and come up with a decision. Remember, you are willing to make no assumptions about the probabilities on states of nature. Now consider the following criteria.

Maximin Criterion The **maximin criterion** is an extremely conservative, or perhaps pessimistic, approach to making decisions. It evaluates each decision by the worst thing that can happen if you make that decision. In this case, then, it evaluates each decision by the *minimum* possible return associated with the decision. In the newsvendor example the minimum possible return if 3 papers are ordered is –120; thus, this value is assigned to the decision "order 3 papers." Similarly, we can associate with each other decision the minimum value in its row. Following this rule enables the decision maker to prepare a table as shown in Table 8.5. The decision that yields the maximum value of the minimum returns (hence, maximin) is then selected. In this case, the newsvendor should order 1 paper.

Maximin is often used in situations where the planner feels he or she cannot afford to be wrong. (Defense planning might be an example, as would investing your life savings.) The planner chooses a decision that does as well as possible in the worst possible (most pessimistic) case.

It is, however, easy to create examples in which most people would not accept the decision selected with the maximin criterion. Consider, for example, the payoff table in Table 8.6. Most people would prefer decision 1. It is much better than decision 2 for all states of nature except state 3, and then it is only slightly worse. Nevertheless, the maximin criterion would select decision 2. If you are among those who strongly prefer decision 1 in this example, you must then ask yourself the following question: "If the maximin criterion provides an answer that I don't like in this simple example, would I be willing to use it on more complicated and important models?" There is no correct answer to this question. The answer depends on the taste of the decision maker, but you begin to see why we don't stress the decision rules of this section as heavily as the maximize expected value rule of the "Decisions Under Risk" section.

Maximax Criterion The **maximax criterion** is as optimistic as maximin is pessimistic. It evaluates each decision by the best thing that can happen if you make that decision. In this case, then, it evaluates each decision by the maximum possible return associated with that decision. In particular, refer again to the payoff table for the newsvendor model (Table 8.4). If the newsvendor ordered 2 papers, the best possible outcome would be

Table 8.5

Newsvendor Minimum Return Table

DECISION	MINIMUM RETURN
0	–150
1	–65
2	–80
3	–120

Table 8.6

Payoff Table: Maximin Counter Example

	STATE OF NATURE								
Decision	**1**	**2**	**3**	**4**	**5**	**6**	**7**	**8**	**9**
1	100	100	2	100	100	100	100	100	100
2	3	3	3	3	3	3	3	3	3

Table 8.7

Newsvendor Maximum Return Table

DECISION	MAXIMUM RETURN
0	0
1	35
2	70
3	105

Table 8.8

Payoff Table: Maximax Counter Example

	STATE OF NATURE								
Decision	**1**	**2**	**3**	**4**	**5**	**6**	**7**	**8**	**9**
1	100	100	100	100	100	100	100	100	100
2	3	3	101	3	3	3	3	3	3

a return of 70. This value is thus assigned to the decision "order 2 papers." In other words, for each decision we identify the maximum value in that row. Using this rule, the manager prepares a table as shown in Table 8.7. The decision that yields the maximum of these maximum returns (hence, maximax) is then selected. In this case, then, the newsvendor should order 3 papers. A point of caution is in order: Don't confuse the decision with the state of nature that produces the optimal payoff. The optimal *decision* under the maximax criterion is to "order 3 papers," not to "order 3 papers and have 3 customers."

The maximax criterion is subject to the same type of criticism as maximin; that is, it is easy to create examples where using the maximax criterion leads to a decision that most people find unacceptable. Consider the payoff table presented in Table 8.8, for example. Most people prefer decision 1 since it is much better than decision 2 for every state of nature except state 3, and then it is only slightly worse. The maximax criterion, however, selects decision 2.

Regret and Minimax Regret **Regret** introduces a new concept for measuring the desirability of an outcome; that is, it is a new way to create the payoff table. Some personnel managers believe that college graduates tend to choose between several first-job choices using the minimax regret criterion. They imagine themselves in the various jobs and decide which one would give them the least regret of being there.

So far, all the decision criteria have been used on a payoff table of dollar returns as measured by net cash flows. In particular, each entry in Table 8.4 shows the net cash flow for the newsvendor for every combination of decision (number of papers ordered) and state of nature (number of papers demanded). Table 8.9 shows the regret for each combination of decision and state of nature. It is derived from Table 8.4 by

1. Finding the maximum entry in each column of Table 8.4 (e.g., 70 is the largest entry in the third State of Nature column (i.e., the column under State of Nature "2")).
2. Calculating the new entry by subtracting the current entry from the maximum in its column. Thus, the new entry in the second row, third column is

$$70 - (-15) = 85 \text{ (new entry second row, third column)}$$

Table 8.9

Regret Table for the Newsvendor Model

	STATE OF NATURE			
Decision	**0**	**1**	**2**	**3**
0	0	85	170	255
1	40	0	(85)	170
2	80	40	0	85
3	120	80	40	0

Table 8.10

Newsvendor Maximum Regret Table

DECISION	MAXIMUM REGRET
0	255
1	170
2	85
3	120

In each column, these new entries, called regret, indicate how much better we can do. In other words, "regret" is synonymous with the "opportunity cost" of not making the best decision for a given state of nature. It follows that the manager would like to make a decision that minimizes regret, but (same old story) she does not know which state of nature will occur. If she knew a probability distribution on the state of nature, she could minimize the expected regret. (In the next section, we will see that this is equivalent to maximizing expected net cash flow.) If she does not know the probability, the typical suggestion is to use the conservative *minimax criterion*; that is, to select that decision that does the best in the worst case (the decision that has the smallest maximum regret).

For example, consider the regret table for the newsvendor model shown in Table 8.9. If 1 paper is ordered, the maximum regret of 170 occurs if 3 papers are demanded. The value 170 is thus associated with the decision, "order 1 paper." In other words, the maximum value in each row is associated with the decision in that row. Following this rule produces Table 8.10.

The manager then selects the decision that minimizes the maximum regret. In this case, the minimax regret criterion implies that the newsvendor should order 2 papers. Our newsvendor example illustrates that, when making decisions without using probabilities, the three criteria—maximin cash flow, maximax cash flow, and minimax regret—can lead to different "optimal" decisions.

8.3 THE EXPECTED VALUE OF PERFECT INFORMATION: NEWSVENDOR MODEL UNDER RISK

Let us return to the newsvendor model under risk (i.e., with the probability distribution on demand shown in row 12 of Figure 8.2). Recall that, in this case, the optimal policy was to order 2 papers and that the expected return was 22.5. It is useful to think about this model in a very stylized fashion in order to introduce the concept of the expected value of perfect information. In particular, let us assume that the sequence of events in the newsvendor's day (the "current sequence of events") proceeds as follows:

1. A genie, by drawing from the demand distribution for papers, determines the number of papers that will be demanded.
2. The newsvendor, not knowing what demand had been drawn, but knowing the distribution of demand, orders his papers.
3. The demand is then revealed to the newsvendor and he achieves an *actual* (as opposed to expected) return determined by his order-size decision and the demand.

Now consider a new scenario. The newsvendor has an opportunity to make a deal with the genie. Under the new deal the sequence of events proceeds as follows:

1. The newsvendor pays the genie a fee.
2. The genie determines the demand as above. It is important to stress that the genie can't make a certain demand come true; he simply has perfect knowledge of what will happen and is willing to sell that knowledge or information.
3. The genie tells the newsvendor what the demand will be.
4. The newsvendor orders his papers.
5. The newsvendor achieves the return determined by the demand and the number of papers he ordered.

The question is, What is the largest fee the newsvendor should be willing to pay in step 1? This fee is called the **expected value of perfect information** (EVPI): In general terms,

fee = (expected return with new deal) – (expected return with current sequence of events [no deal])

With the new deal the newsvendor, in step 4, will always order the number of papers that will give him the maximum return for the state of nature that will occur. However, the payment in step 1 must be made *before* he learns what the demand will be. Referring to Table 8.4 we see that if 0 papers will be demanded, he will order 0 papers and enjoy the maximum return of 0. Since the genie is drawing from the distribution of demand, there is a probability of 0.1 that what the newsvendor will learn from the genie is that demand will in fact be 0. Similarly, he will learn with a probability of 0.3 that 1 paper will be demanded. If this occurs, he will order 1 paper and enjoy the maximum return of 35. Following this reasoning, his expected return under the new deal is

$$ER(\text{new}) = 0(0.1) + 35(0.3) + 70(0.4) + 105(0.2) = 59.5$$

This concept could be easily implemented in Excel using the =MAX() function on the returns for each state of nature. We have already seen that in the absence of perfect information his optimal decision (order 2 papers) gives an expected return of 22.5. Thus, we can calculate the EVPI as follows:

$$EVPI = 59.5 - 22.5 = 37.0 \text{ cents}$$

This is the maximum amount our vendor should be willing to pay in step 1 for the deal with the genie. Although the story we have used to develop the concept is far-fetched, the expected value of perfect information (EVPI) has important practical significance. It is an upper bound on the amount that you should be willing to pay to improve your knowledge about what state of nature will occur. Literally millions of dollars are spent on various market research projects and other testing devices (geological tests, quality control experiments, and so on) to determine what state of nature will occur in a wide variety of applications. The expected value of perfect information indicates the expected amount to be gained from any such endeavor and thus places an upper bound on the amount that should be spent in gathering such information.

8.4 UTILITIES AND DECISIONS UNDER RISK

Utility is an alternative way of measuring the attractiveness of the result of a decision. In other words, it is an alternative way of finding the values to fill in a payoff table. Up to now we have used net dollar return (net cash flow) and regret as two measures of the "goodness" of a particular combination of a decision and state of nature.

Utility suggests another type of measure. Our treatment of this topic includes two main sections:

1. A rationale for utility (i.e., why using net cash flow can lead to unacceptable decisions)
2. Creating and using a utility function

THE RATIONALE FOR UTILITY

In the preceding section we saw that the maximin and maximax decision criteria could lead to unacceptable decisions in simple illustrative models. We now point out that the criterion of maximizing expected net cash flow in a decision under risk can also produce unacceptable results. For example, consider an urn that contains 99 white balls and 1 black ball. You are offered a chance to play a game in which a ball will be drawn from this urn. Each ball is equally likely to be drawn. If a white ball is drawn, you must pay $10,000. If the black ball is drawn, you receive $1,000,000. You must decide whether to play. The payoff table based on net cash flow is shown in Table 8.11.

Table 8.11

Payoff Table (Net Cash Flows)

	STATE OF NATURE	
Decision	**White Ball**	**Black Ball**
Play	−10,000	1,000,000
Do Not Play	0	0

We now use the information in this table, together with the facts that the probabilities of a white and a black ball are, respectively, 0.99 and 0.01, to calculate the expected return for each decision (play or do not play) in the usual way.

$$\text{ER(play)} = -10{,}000(0.99) + 1{,}000{,}000(0.01)$$
$$= -9900 + 10{,}000 = 100$$
$$\text{ER(do not play)} = 0(0.99) + 0(0.01) = 0$$

Since ER(play) > ER(do not play), we should play if we apply the criterion of maximizing the expected net cash flow.

Now step back and ask yourself if you would decide to play this game. Remember that the probability is 0.99 that you will lose $10,000. Many people simply find this large "downside risk" to be unacceptable; that is, they are unwilling to accept the decision based on the criterion of maximizing the expected net cash flow. Thus, once again we see a simple example that shows a need to take care in selecting an appropriate criterion. This is all the more true in dealing with complicated real-world models. Another example from the real world where most people don't follow the criterion of maximizing expected returns is when they choose whether or not to purchase auto insurance. Suppose you own a new sports car and can choose to purchase collision insurance or not. The insurance costs you a yearly premium for a certain deductible. In essence, you are choosing between buying insurance or taking a gamble (that you won't have a collision). Most people choose to purchase the insurance even though you can be sure that the premium you pay to the insurance company is greater than the expected cost of damage from a collision (i.e., the insurance company makes a profit).

Fortunately, it is not necessary to reject the concept of maximizing expected returns. To adapt the expected return criterion to general decisions under risk it is only necessary to recognize that net dollar returns do not always accurately reflect the "attractiveness" of the possible outcomes from our decisions. To show what this means, ask yourself if you would be willing to win or lose 10 cents depending on the flip of a fair coin. (Most people would say yes.) How about winning or losing $10,000, depending on a flip of the same coin? (Here most people would say no.) What is the difference? A 10-cent gain seems to balance a 10-cent loss. Why does a $10,000 gain not balance a $10,000 loss? The answer is that in the latter situation most people are **risk-averse**, which means they would feel that the loss of $10,000 is more painful than the benefit obtained from a $10,000 gain.

Decision analysis deals with this behavior by introducing a function that measures the "attractiveness" of money. This function is called a *utility function*, where for the sake of this discussion the word *utility* can be thought of as a measure of "satisfaction." A typical risk-averse function is shown in Figure 8.6. Two characteristics of this function are worth noting:

1. It is nondecreasing, since more money is always at least as attractive as less money.
2. It is concave. An equivalent statement is that the marginal utility of money is nonincreasing. To illustrate this phenomenon, let us examine Figure 8.6.

First suppose that you have $100 and someone gives you an additional $100. Note that your utility increases by

$$U(200) - U(100) = 0.680 - 0.524 = 0.156$$

FIGURE 8.6

Typical Risk-Averse Utility Function

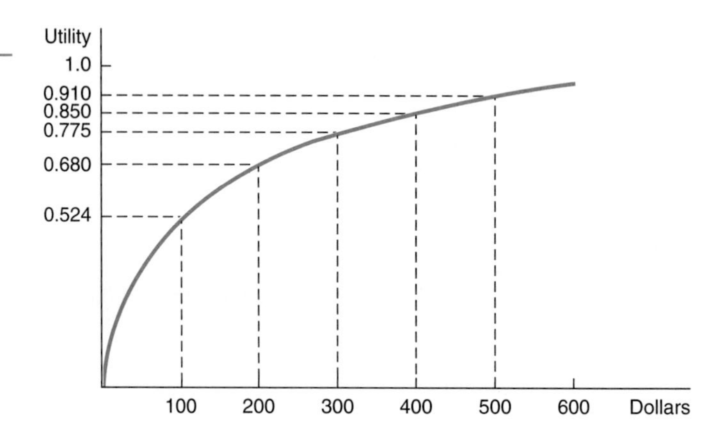

Now suppose that you start with \$400, and someone gives you an additional \$100. Now your utility increases by

$$U(500) - U(400) = 0.910 - 0.850 = 0.060$$

In other words, 100 additional dollars is less attractive to you if you have \$400 on hand than it is if you start with \$100. Another way of describing this phenomenon is that at any point, the gain of a specified number of dollars increases utility less than the loss of the same number of dollars decreases utility. For example, using the utility function in Figure 8.6, we have already calculated that the gain in utility of going from \$400 to \$500 is 0.060. The loss in utility of going from \$400 to \$300, however, is $U(400) - U(300) = 0.850 - 0.775 = 0.075$, which is greater. Another way to think about it is that for most people receiving \$1,000,000 would be tremendously exciting, but receiving \$2,000,000 would not be twice as exciting. Similarly, finding \$100 would be a nice windfall, but the difference between receiving \$1,000,000 and \$1,000,100 is negligible. Thus we see that the same increment has a decreasing utility for most people, or to get the same utility, each increment must be larger.

Figure 8.7 shows two other general types of utility functions. The first is a **risk-seeking** (convex) function, where a gain of a specified amount of dollars increases the utility more than a loss of the same amount of dollars decreases the utility. For example, if you start with \$200 and increase your holding by \$100 to \$300, your utility increases by

$$U(300) - U(200) = 0.590 - 0.260 = 0.330$$

whereas if you start with \$200 and decrease your holding by \$100 to \$100, your utility decreases by

$$U(200) - U(100) = 0.260 - 0.075 = 0.185$$

Thus, with a risk-seeking utility function an increase of \$100 increases your utility more than a decrease of \$100 decreases it. As we have seen, exactly the opposite statement holds for a risk-averse (concave) function like the one shown in Figure 8.6.

For the **risk-indifferent** function shown on the right of Figure 8.7, a gain or a loss of a specified dollar amount produces a change of the same magnitude in your utility.

CREATING AND USING A UTILITY FUNCTION

We will discuss two methods for creating the utility function. The first is a more accurate, yet tedious process, while the second method is faster because it assumes a predetermined shape. The first method of creating a utility function, like the one shown in Figure 8.6, requires the manager, in our case the newsvendor, to make a series of choices between a sure return and a lottery. In more formal language, the manager is called on to create an **equivalent lottery**. This, however, is the second step. Let us start at the beginning.

FIGURE 8.7

Some Other Utility Functions

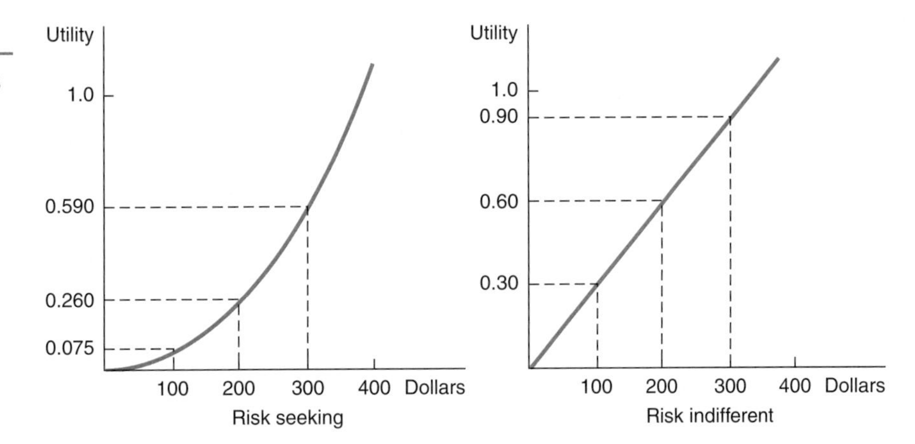

The newsvendor can arbitrarily select the endpoints of his utility function. It is a convenient convention to set the utility of the smallest net dollar return equal to 0 and the utility of the largest net return equal to 1. Since in the newsvendor example the smallest return is –150, and the largest is +105, he sets $U(-150) = 0$ and $U(105) = 1$. These two values play a fundamental role in finding the utility of any quantity of money between –150 and 105. It is perhaps easiest to proceed by example.

Assume that the decision maker starts with $U(-150) = 0$ and $U(105) = 1$ and wants to find the utility of 10 (i.e., $U[10]$). He proceeds by selecting a probability p such that he is indifferent between the following two alternatives:

1. Receive a payment of 10 for sure.
2. Participate in a lottery in which he receives a payment of 105 with probability p or a payment of –150 with probability $1 - p$.

Clearly if $p = 1$, the decision maker prefers alternative 2, since he prefers a payment of 105 to a payment of 10. Equally clear, if $p = 0$, he prefers alternative 1, since he prefers a payment of 10 to a loss of 150 (i.e., a payment of –150). It follows that somewhere between 0 and 1 there is a value for p such that the decision maker is indifferent between the two alternatives. This value will vary from person to person depending on how attractive the various alternatives are to them. We can call this value of p the utility for 10. For example, suppose that the manager chooses p to be 0.6. Then the expected value of the lottery is $0.6(105) + 0.4(-150) = 3$. In other words, she is expressing indifference between a sure payment of 10 and a gamble with a smaller expected value, 3. This means she is seeking risk, because she requires a sure payment larger than the expected return to compensate her for the loss of the possibility of making more than the expected return.

Now suppose she had chosen $p = 0.8$, the expected value of the lottery would have been $0.8(105) + 0.2\,(-150) = 54.0$. This means she is averse to risk, because she requires an expected value larger than the sure payment to compensate for the riskiness of the lottery. In some sense, the larger the value of p she chooses, the more risk-averse she is, because she requires a larger expected value of the lottery to compensate her for its riskiness. By solving the equation

$$p(105) + (1 - p)(-150) = 10$$

$$255p - 150 = 10$$

$$p = \frac{160}{255} = 0.6275$$

we find the value of p for which the expected value of the lottery is equal to the sure payment of 10. If the manager chooses a value of p greater than 0.6275, she is averse to risk;

equal to 0.6275, indifferent to risk; and less than 0.6275, seeking risk. By repeating this same procedure for all other possible dollar returns from the newsvendor example, we could completely assess the entire utility function. This is obviously a lot of work and one may wonder how many managers have the skill in probability theory and patience to do this exercise consistently and correctly. Another concern of decision analysts who work with corporations to aid in determining utility functions is that they have to be very careful that the manager uses the corporation's view of money rather than her own personal values. Individuals tend either to be afraid to risk a few thousand dollars or to get blasé about millions of dollars. Thus, there is a distinct difference between corporate utility and personal utility. Furthermore, we have not *proved* that using the probability p to define an equivalent lottery is a meaningful way to construct a utility function. An understandable discussion of why this approach works would carry us far beyond the scope of this text. We must be content to stop with the how and leave the why to other advanced courses.

Due to all the challenges mentioned above, the second, more popular way to assess utility functions is to use an exponential utility function. This function has a predetermined shape (i.e., it's concave → risk-averse) and requires the assessment of only one parameter. It has been used to analyze financial investment decisions and other business applications. The function has the following form:

$$U(x) = 1 - e^{-x/r}$$

where x is the dollar amount that we're going to convert to utility. As can be seen the only parameter to assess is r, which is a constant that measures the degree of risk aversion. That is, the *larger* the value of r, the *less* risk-averse the company or person is (i.e., the more risk he or she is willing to take). Likewise, the *smaller* value of r, the *more* risk-averse the company or person is.

There are many ways to determine the value of r. Two of the easiest are shown below. First, we must determine the dollar amount r such that the manager is indifferent between the following two choices:

1. A 50-50 gamble where the payoffs are a gain of r dollars or a loss of $r/2$ dollars
2. A payoff of zero

Let's suppose our newsvendor is indifferent between a bet where he wins $100 or loses $50 with equal probability and not betting at all, then his r is $100.

The second way to determine r comes from empirical evidence gathered by a famous decision analyst, Ron Howard. Dr. Howard has consulted with many corporations and he has found some very valuable rules of thumb (see Howard) that relate a company's net income, equity, and net sales to the degree of risk aversion, r. For example, he found that r is approximately equal to 124% of net income, 15.7% of equity, and 6.4% of net sales. In other words, a large company with net income of $1 billion would have an r of 1.24 billion, whereas a smaller company with net sales of $5 million would have an r of 320,000. Of course, these are only guidelines, but they can be very helpful and certainly indicate the trend for larger companies to have larger r values and less aversion to risk.

Now let's return to our newsvendor example and assess his utility function. Because he owns a very small business, he opts for using the predetermined exponential utility function approach and he uses the 50-50 gamble approach we discussed to determine his r value ($100). He wants to enter the utility function in a new spreadsheet called "Utility" in the same workbook (NEWSVENDOR.XLS), and assess the utility of all the dollar payoffs. Using this new exponential utility function to make decisions when the probabilities of the states of nature are known is a straightforward process. To be specific, the newsvendor creates a new payoff table where the entries are the utility of the net cash flow associated with each combination of a decision and a state of nature (i.e., he substitutes the utility of the net cash flow for that cash flow). For example, row 3 (Order 2), column 3 (Demand is 2) in Table 8.4 shows a net cash flow of 70. His spreadsheet (presented in Figure 8.8) translates

FIGURE 8.8

Newsvendor Utility Spreadsheet

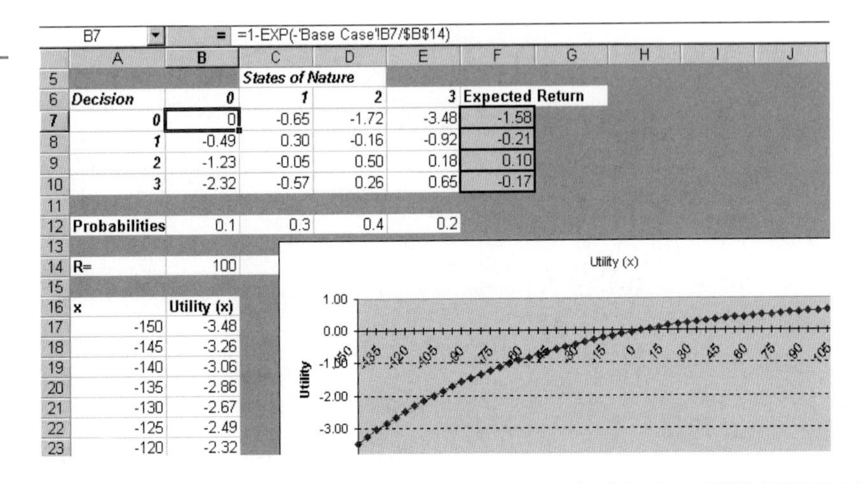

Cell	Formula	Copy To
B7	= 1 – EXP (–'Base Case' !B7/$B$14)	B7:E10
F7	= SUMPRODUCT (B7:E7,$B$12:$E$12)	F8:F10

this into a utility of about 0.50, which becomes the new entry in row 3, column 3. The newsvendor now proceeds as before; that is, he calculates the expected utility for each decision. This is shown in column F of Figure 8.8. Finally he desires to graph his utility function to see its shape, which is also shown in Figure 8.8.

To create this spreadsheet, the newsvendor does the following:

1. Create a new spreadsheet called "Utility" in the same workbook (NEWSVENDOR.XLS).
2. Copy cells A5:F12 of the "Base Case" spreadsheet into the new spreadsheet, change the formula in cell B7 to =1–exp(–'Base Case'!B7/$B$14) and then copy it to B7:E10.
3. Enter an initial value of –150 in cell A17.
4. Click back on cell A17 and click on Edit, Fill, and then Series.
5. Click on "Series in Columns" and enter a step value of 5 and a stop value of 105. Click on OK.
6. Enter the formula (shown in the equation line of Figure 8.8 to convert dollars to utility) into cell B17 and copy it down to B68.
7. Use the Graph Wizard with the data in A17:B68 to create a graph of the utility function like that shown in the lower right of Figure 8.8.

We see in column F of Figure 8.8 that, on the basis of the criterion of maximizing the expected utility, the newsvendor would order 2 papers (it has the highest expected utility of 0.10). Referring to the discussion of decisions under risk in Section 8.2, we see that if the newsvendor based his decision on maximizing the expected net cash flow, he would also order 2 papers. It is not always true, however, that the decision that has the largest expected cash flow will also have the largest expected utility. The fact that this phenomenon occurred in this particular example does not imply that it will occur in general. Let's consider a real-world example where expected utility and expected return do not generate the same decision.

Consider the following auto insurance example. Carol Lane is 10 years out of Stanford's Graduate School of Business and has just bought a beautiful new Lexus. She calls her insurance company and determines that the annual premium for collision insurance would be $1,000 with a $250 deductible. There is only a 0.5% chance she will cause a colli-

FIGURE 8.9

Auto Insurance Spreadsheet

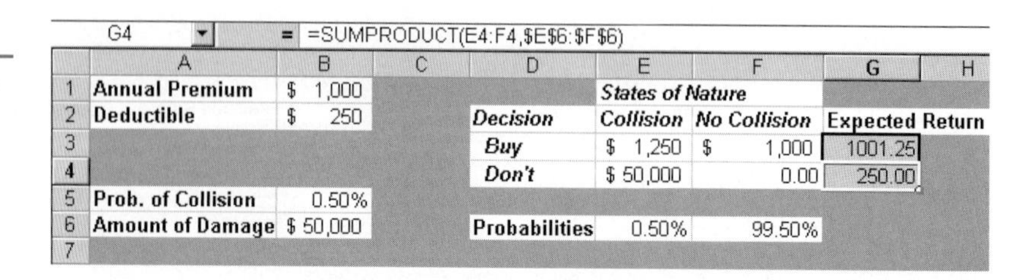
G4 = =SUMPRODUCT(E4:F4,$E$6:$F$6)

	A	B	C	D	E	F	G	H
1	Annual Premium	$ 1,000			States of Nature			
2	Deductible	$ 250		Decision	Collision	No Collision	Expected Return	
3				Buy	$ 1,250	$ 1,000	1001.25	
4				Don't	$ 50,000	0.00	250.00	
5	Prob. of Collision	0.50%						
6	Amount of Damage	$ 50,000		Probabilities	0.50%	99.50%		
7								

Cell	Formula	Copy To
E3	= B2+B1	—
F3	= B1	—
E4	= B6	—
F4	= 0	—
G3	= SUMPRODUCT(E3:F3,$E$6:$F$6)	G4
E6	= B5	—
F6	= 1−B5	—

sion in the next year, in which case she can expect about $50,000 worth of damage. Since she owns the Lexus outright (i.e., no loan), she is not required to buy the collision insurance. Should she buy the insurance or not? Carol has modeled this situation in the spreadsheet (AUTOINSU.XLS) shown in Figure 8.9.

On a "maximize expected return" basis, Carol sees that it would be less expensive for her, on average, to not buy the insurance ($250 versus $1,001.25). However, she knows the decision can't be that easy and feels somewhat uncomfortable. She remembers the concept of utility from her days at business school. She decides that she is risk-averse, and estimates her r value to be $10,000 (using the first method [50-50 gamble] taught in this section). She creates a new spreadsheet called "Utility" in the same workbook to incorporate her utility as shown below in Figure 8.10.

On this basis, she sees that the decision "Buy insurance" maximizes expected utility (–0.11 versus –0.74) because of the severe negative utility incurred in the situation created by the combination of the decision that she doesn't buy insurance with the state of nature that she has a collision. Based on her expected utility analysis, Carol feels that it is worth buying the insurance (and paying the extra $751 per year on average) to have the peace of mind that she won't have to take $50,000 out of her savings on the off-chance that she causes a collision.

FIGURE 8.10

Auto Insurance Utility Spreadsheet

F12 = =1-EXP(F3/$F$8)

	A	B	C	D	E	F	G	H
1	Annual Premium	$ 1,000		Payoffs	States of Nature			
2	Deductible	$ 250		Decision	Collision	No Collision	Expected Return	
3				Buy	$ 1,250	$ 1,000	1001.25	
4				Don't	$ 50,000	0.00	250.00	
5	Prob. of Collision	0.50%						
6	Amount of Damage	$ 50,000		Probabilities	0.50%	99.50%		
7								
8					r =	10000		
9								
10				Utilities	States of Nature			
11				Decision	Collision	No Collision	Expected Return	
12				Buy	-0.13	-0.11	-0.11	
13				Don't	-147.41	0.00	-0.74	

Cell	Formula	Copy To
E12	= 1−EXP(E3/$F$8)	E12:F13
G12	= SUMPRODUCT(E12:F12,$E$6:$F$6)	G13

8.5 A MID-CHAPTER SUMMARY

The preceding three sections provided the theoretical foundation on which the rest of the chapter is based. The ensuing sections are devoted to procedures that play an important role in solving real-world models. It is useful to summarize what we have achieved before moving ahead.

Section 8.2 provided a general framework for a class of models identified as decisions against nature. In this framework, the model can be described by a payoff table in which the returns to the decision maker depend on the decision selected and the state of nature that subsequently occurs. Three specific cases were identified:

1. ***Decisions under certainty***: The decision maker knows exactly what state of nature will occur. The "only" problem is to select the best decision. Deterministic models such as linear programming, integer programming, nonlinear programming, and the EOQ inventory model fall into this category.
2. ***Decisions under risk***: A probability distribution is specified on the states of nature. The decision maker may use the following criteria to select a "best decision":
   a. Maximize expected return as measured by net dollar return
   b. Minimize expected regret (opportunity cost)
   c. Maximize expected return as measured by utility

   We saw that criteria a and b always lead to the same decision. Most management decision models fall into this category of decisions under risk.
3. ***Decisions under uncertainty***: Here it is assumed that the decision maker has *no* knowledge about which state of nature will occur. The decision maker might apply the Laplace criterion; that is, assign equal probabilities to the various states of nature and then choose a decision that maximizes expected return. Alternatively, the decision maker may attack the model without using probabilities. In this case, we discussed three different criteria for making a "best decision":
   a. Maximize minimum net dollar return
   b. Maximize maximum net dollar return
   c. Minimize maximum regret

Each of these criteria will, in general, lead to different decisions and can produce decisions that many managers feel uncomfortable with.

Section 8.3 was devoted to the concept of the expected value of perfect information (EVPI). This entity plays an important role by establishing an upper bound on the amount you should pay to gain new information about what state of nature will occur.

Finally, in Section 8.4 we discussed utility as an alternative measure of the attractiveness of each combination of a decision and a state of nature. The desire to use a utility function is motivated by the fact that in some cases, for example, because of the magnitudes of the potential losses, the decision that maximizes the expected net dollar return is not the decision that you would want to select. A couple of methods were described for assessing the utility function.

The remaining sections in this chapter will deal with extensions of the most common model (decisions under risk). They consider decision trees, a technique of significant practical importance, via the use of a spreadsheet add-in called TreePlan and introduce two important concepts: the use of new information in decision making and the analysis of sequential decision models. Because of the sequential nature of these new, more complex models, the decision or payoff tables of previous sections will no longer work.

8.6 DECISION TREES: MARKETING CELLULAR PHONES

A **decision tree** is a graphical device for analyzing decisions under risk; that is, models in which the decisions and the probabilities on the states of nature are specified. More precisely, decision trees were created to use on models in which there is a sequence of decisions, each of which could lead to one of several uncertain outcomes. For example, a concessionaire typically has to decide how much to bid for each of several possible locations at the state fair. The result of this decision is not certain, since it depends on what the competitors decide to bid. Once the location is known, the concessionaire must decide how much food to stock. The result of this decision in terms of profits is also not certain since it depends on customer demand.

Our discussion of decision trees is organized in the following manner: In this section we introduce the basic ideas and introduce you to a spreadsheet add-in, TreePlan, that draws decision trees in a spreadsheet. This software package was developed by Michael Middleton and is made available as shareware. Check out his website at http://www.treeplan.com. (If you like the software and plan to use it beyond this class, you are expected to pay a nominal registration fee. Details are available in TreePlan's online help.) Section 8.7 examines the sensitivity of the optimal decision to the assessed values of the probabilities. Section 8.8 shows how Bayes' Theorem is used to incorporate new information into the process, and Section 8.9 considers a sequential decision model. The entire discussion is motivated by the following production and marketing model faced by the management of Sonorola.

ALTERNATE MARKETING AND PRODUCTION STRATEGIES

The design and product-testing phase has just been completed for Sonorola's new line of cellular phones. Top management is attempting to decide on the appropriate marketing and production strategy to use for this product. Three major alternatives are being considered. Each alternative is identified with a single word.

1. ***Aggressive (A)***: This strategy represents a major commitment of the firm to this product line. A major capital expenditure would be made for a new and efficient production facility. Large inventories would be built up to guarantee prompt delivery of all models. A major marketing campaign involving television commercials in all major global markets and dealer discounts would be initiated.
2. ***Basic (B)***: In this plan, production of a current cellular phone line would be moved from Tokyo to Osaka. This move would phase out a trouble-plagued department. At the same time, the current line in Tokyo would be modified to produce the new cellular phone product. Inventories would be held for only the most popular items. Headquarters would make funds available to support local or regional advertising efforts, but no global advertising campaign would be mounted.
3. ***Cautious (C)***: In this plan, excess capacity on several existing cellular phone product lines would be used to produce the new products. A minimum of new tooling would be developed. Production would be geared to satisfy demand, and advertising would be at the discretion of the local dealer.

Management decides to categorize the condition of the market (i.e., the level of demand) as either strong (S) or weak (W). In reality, the demand is characterized by a continuum of possible outcomes. For this introductory example, we will limit it to two possible states (Strong and Weak) for simplicity. For discussion of the issue on how to deal with infinite states of nature, see Section 8.11. The spreadsheet shown in Figure 8.11 (SNRLADT.XLS) presents the payoff table and management's best estimate of the probability of a strong or a weak market. The payoffs in the body are the net profits measured in millions of dollars. They were generated by carefully calculating the sales, revenues, and costs associated with each decision/state of nature combination. It is interesting to note that a cautious (C) decision yields a higher profit with a weak market than it does with a strong market. If there is a strong market and Sonorola is cautious, not only will the competition capture the new cellular phone market, but as a result of the carryover effect of these sales, the competition will seriously cut into Sonorola's current market position for accessories and other electronic products.

We are dealing here with what we have termed decisions under risk and we will calculate the expected return for each decision and select the best one (just as we did in Section

FIGURE 8.11

Sonorola's Basic Marketing Spreadsheet

D6 = =SUMPRODUCT(B6:C6,$B$1:$C$1)

	A	B	C	D	E	F	G	H
1	Probabilities	0.45	0.55					
2								
3		States of Nature						
4	DECISION	*Strong (S)*	*Weak (W)*	Expected Return				
5	*Aggresive (A)*	30	-8	9.1				
6	*Basic (B)*	20	7	12.85				
7	*Cautious (C)*	5	15	10.5				
8								

Cell	Formula	Copy To
D5	= SUMPRODUCT (B5:C5, $B$1:$C$1)	D6:D7

8.2), except that here we'll start off in a spreadsheet and skip the "by hand" approach. The formula for the expected return is shown in the equation bar of Figure 8.11 as well as the resulting expected payoffs for each of the three decisions in column D. The optimal decision if you are risk-indifferent is to select (B), the basic production and marketing strategy, which yields the highest expected payoff of $12.85 million.

CREATING A DECISION TREE

This marketing model can also be represented by a decision tree we will demonstrate below. In our exposition of decision trees, a **square node** (decision node in TreePlan) will represent a point at which a decision must be made, and each line leading from a square will represent a possible decision. The **circular nodes** (event node in TreePlan) will represent situations when the outcome is not certain. Each line leading from a circle represents a possible outcome. The term **branches** will be employed for the lines emanating from the nodes, whether square or circular. The steps to create the decision tree for the Sonorola model in TreePlan are as follows (these steps are also demonstrated by a voice-annotated tutorial [made with Lotus' Screencam software] entitled TreePlan Tutorial.exe found on the student CD):

1. Place the cursor in cell A10 and click on Tools, then TreePlan. (If TreePlan is not a choice in your menu, you'll need to add it. To do so, Click on Tools, then Add-Ins. Click on the Browse option and find TREEPLAN.XLA on your computer [either your hard drive or network]. Double click on the TREEPLAN.XLA once you find it and it should then be available on your Tools menu.) *Note*: Version 1.61 is used here.
2. Click on "New Tree" and it will draw a default tree with 2 decision nodes.
3. Because Sonorola needs 3 decision nodes, we click on the decision node (cell B14 in our case) and hit Ctrl-t. This brings up TreePlan's context-sensitive menu.
4. Click on "Add branch" (if it's not the default choice), then click OK.
5. Label the 3 branches as Aggressive, Basic, and Cautious (in cells D11, D16, D21).
6. Because we want to replace the terminal node with a random event node, click on the terminal node (cell F12) as shown in Figure 8.12, then hit Ctrl-t to bring up the menu.
7. Click on "Change to event node," indicate that we want 2 branches, then click OK.
8. TreePlan draws the resulting tree as shown in Figure 8.13. Notice that it enters default probabilities of 0.5 for each of the 2 random events, as well as default names (Events 4 and 5).
9. We change the labels from the generic "Event 4" and "Event 5" to "Strong" and "Weak" markets respectively.

Note: We want to repeat this process (steps 6–9) for the other 2 terminal nodes. Fortunately, TreePlan has a Copy feature we can take advantage of (shown in steps 10–12).

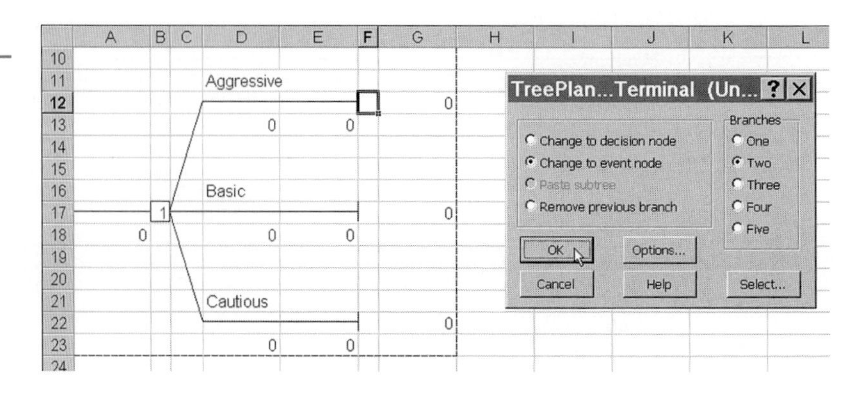

FIGURE 8.12

Adding an Event Node to the Decision Tree for the Sonorola Model

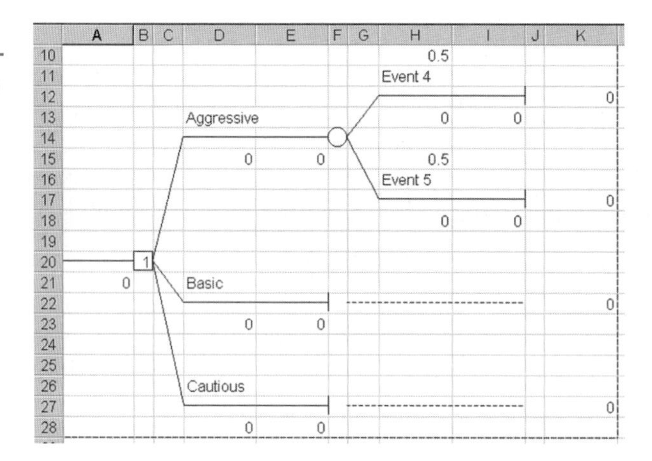

FIGURE 8.13

Partially Completed Decision Tree for the Sonorola Decision Tree

10. To copy a node (or any subtree), click on the cell you wish to copy (cell F14) and hit Ctrl-t.
11. Click on "copy subtree," then click on OK.
12. Click on the cell where you want to copy the node (cell F22), hit Ctrl-t, click on "Paste subtree," and click on OK.
13. We do the same thing (steps 10–12) for the last terminal node (cell F27 in Figure 8.13).
14. Because the tree is starting to get pretty big, we change the zoom feature to 75% and we see all the branches of the tree as shown in Figure 8.14.

Note we still need to add the endpoints or terminal values and the probabilities, but we're making good progress. For the Sonorola cellular phone model, the decision tree in Figure 8.14 shows the initial node in cell B24. Since it is square, a decision must be made. Thus, management must choose one of the strategies: Aggressive (A), Basic (B), or Cautious (C). Depending on which decision is selected, a new position will be attained on the tree. For example, selecting strategy A leads us from cell B24 to cell F14. Since this new node is a circle, the next branch that will occur is not known with certainty. If the market condition turns out to be strong, cell J12 is attained. If, instead, the market proves to be weak, cell J17 is attained. Since they represent the end of the decision process, cells such as J12 and J17 are referred to as **terminal positions.** Also, since the nodes in cells F14, F24, and F34 are not followed by other nodes, they are called **terminal nodes**.

APPENDING THE PROBABILITIES AND TERMINAL VALUES

The decision tree presented in Figure 8.14 provides an efficient way for management to visualize the interactions between decisions and less-than-certain events. However, if management wishes to use the decision tree to select an optimal decision, some additional

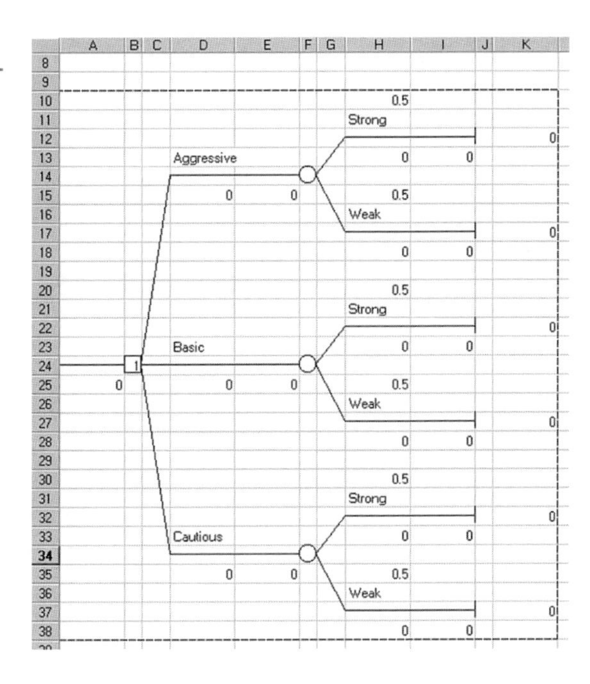

FIGURE 8.14

All Branches of the Decision Tree for the Sonorola Model

information must be appended to the diagram. In particular, one must assign the return associated with each terminal position. This is called the **terminal value**. One must also assign a probability to each branch emanating from each circular node. For the basic model this is a relatively simple task, and can be done as follows:

1. Change the default probabilities in cells H10 and H15 from 0.5 and 0.5 to the formulas =B1 (containing the value 0.45) and =C1 (containing the value 0.55), respectively. Do the same for cells H20, H25, H30, and H35. (Note that if you mistakenly enter probabilities that don't add to exactly 1.0, the expected value of the event node [cell to the left] will return a value of "#NA," which is a hint for you to go back and check your probabilities.)
2. Change the terminal values for each branch from their default values of zero. For example, in cell H13 (representing the combination of the Aggressive decision, with the state of nature "Strong market") enter the formula =B5 (representing the return of $30 million in Figure 8.11). Likewise in cell H18 (representing the combination of the Aggressive decision, with the state of nature "Weak market") enter the formula =C5 (for the return of –8). Enter the similar formulas =B6, =C6, =B7, =C7 (for the values of $20, $7, $5, and $15) in cells H23, H28, H33, and H38, respectively.

These steps yield the decision tree presented in Figure 8.15.

FOLDING BACK

Using a decision tree to find the optimal decision is called solving the tree. TreePlan does this for us automatically. To solve a decision tree one works backward (i.e., right to left) or, in the jargon of the trade, by **folding back** the tree. First, the terminal branches are *folded back* by calculating an expected value for each terminal node. For example, consider the event node in cell F14. The calculation to obtain the expected value for this node is

$$\text{expected terminal value} = 30(0.45) + (-8)(0.55) = 9.10$$

In other words, the expected value to be obtained if one arrives at cell F14 is 9.10. Now the branches emanating from that particular node are folded back (i.e., eliminated) and the expected value of 9.10 is assigned to the node, as shown in cell E15 of Figure 8.15. Performing the same calculations for nodes in cells F24 and F34 yields their expected val-

FIGURE 8.15

Complete Decision Tree for the Sonorola Model

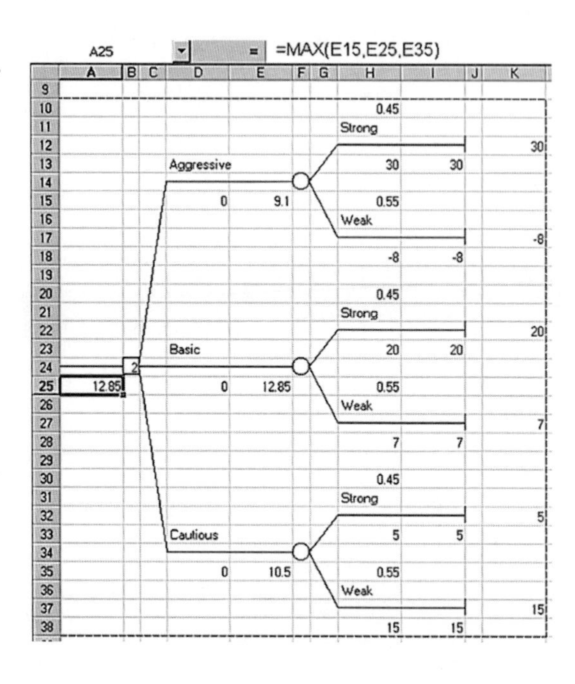

APPLICATION CAPSULE Oglethorpe Power: Invest in a Major Transmission System?

In recent years, the wholesale electric power market in the Southeastern United States has become very active. Florida's population and power needs have grown faster than the state's power generation capacity. At the same time, the availability of surplus power in neighboring states, like Georgia, has grown with large nuclear and coal-fired plants coming on line. The result is substantial power flows from Georgia and nearby states (Alabama, South Carolina) into Florida.

Oglethorpe Power Corporation (OPC) is a generation and transmission cooperative that provides wholesale power. It provides approximately 20% of the power in the state of Georgia. Late in 1990, OPC management learned that Florida Power Corporation (FPC) wanted to expand its connections to Georgia with another 500 kilovolt line capable of transmitting over 1000 MW. The key question facing OPC was whether to add this additional transmission capacity and if so, in what form. They had three choices on the decision of whether to add the line: (1) go it alone, (2) do it as a joint venture with Georgia Power, or (3) not do it. Depending on how OPC structured the investment and operated the line, the investment could be $100 million or more and the annual savings could be $20 million or more. The investment would be one of OPC's biggest and the annual savings were on the order of several percent of its annual budget.

OPC managers realized it was an extremely important decision and so formal decision analysis techniques were used. Decision analysis had become quite popular in the electric power industry in the United States because of the active encouragement provided by the Electric Power Research Institute. As the issue was studied, OPC realized there were actually three decisions, not just one as they had originally thought. It must decide whether to build the transmission line, whether to upgrade the associated transmission facilities, and the nature of the control over the new facilities.

There were five major uncertainties—the cost of building the new facilities, the demand for power in Florida, the competitive situation, OPC's market share, and the spot price for electricity. The uncertainties combined with the decisions to create nearly 8,000 branches of the decision tree. The challenge was to come up with the optimal decision that maximized expected savings. After performing some sensitivity analysis, OPC decided it should learn more about one of the uncertain factors—the competitive situation—before making a major commitment regarding the transmission line.

After doing so, the recommendation that came out of the model was that OPC should begin negotiations independently with FPC, leading to either going it alone or not doing the line. Interestingly enough, the policy that had appeared to be the leading idea going in (joint venture with Georgia Power), came out as the least attractive decision. (See Borison.)

ues as shown in cells E25 and E35 of Figure 8.15. Note that the expected terminal values on all three of these nodes are identical to the expected returns computed earlier in this section (see Figure 8.11) for decisions A, B, and C, respectively. Management now faces the simple problem of choosing the alternative that yields the highest expected terminal value. In this case, as we have seen earlier, the "optimal" choice is the Basic strategy (alternative B), and this is indicated by TreePlan in cell B24 with the "2," meaning choose the second branch or the Basic strategy.

More complex trees can be analyzed by TreePlan by following the same procedures. At each circle the software determines the sum of the expected values of each branch that emanates from it, while at each square it chooses the "best" branch (maximum value), going from right to left.

The above discussion provides a simple illustration of how the basic model can be analyzed with a decision tree. In Sections 8.8 and 8.9 you will see the use of decision trees in more complex scenarios. However, this introductory discussion illustrates an important point: *For the basic model a decision tree simply provides another, more graphic, way of viewing the same model.* Exactly the same information is utilized, and the same calculations are made whether one uses the steps described in Section 8.2 or a decision tree to solve the model.

8.7 SENSITIVITY ANALYSIS

EXPECTED RETURN AS A FUNCTION OF THE PROBABILITY FOR A STRONG MARKET

Before proceeding to the next main topic, a model in which new information becomes available concerning the likelihood of the uncertain events, it will be useful to consider again the expected return associated with each of the decisions in our previous example. We have already noted that to calculate the expected return of strategy A, one uses the relationship

$$ER(A) = (30)P(S) + (-8)P(W)$$

where $P(S)$ is the probability of a strong market and $P(W)$ is the probability of a weak market. We also know that

$$P(S) + P(W) = 1, \text{ or } P(W) = 1 - P(S)$$

Thus

$$ER(A) = 30P(S) - 8[1 - P(S)] = -8 + 38P(S)$$

This expected return, then, is a linear function of the probability that the market response is strong. A similar function can be found for alternatives B and C since

$$ER(B) = 20P(S) + 7[1 - P(S)] = 7 + 13P(S)$$

and

$$ER(C) = 5P(S) + 15[1 - P(S)] = 15 - 10P(S)$$

Plotting each of these three functions on the same set of axes is easily accomplished in Excel by using the Data Table command. To do this, we simply:

1. Copy A1:D7 from the "Base Case" spreadsheet into a new spreadsheet called "Exp. Return vs. $P(S)$." Change the entry in cell C1 from 0.55 to a formula (=1–B1). This makes it more general and allows us to do a one-way Data Table.
2. In cell A10, we enter an initial value of 0.
3. Click back on A10, then Edit, Fill, and Series.
4. Click on "Series in Columns" and enter a step value of 0.05 and a stop value of 1.0. Click on OK.
5. In cells B9:D9 we enter the quantities [ER(A), ER(B), and ER(C)] we want to track for each value of $P(S)$ that we've entered in column A. These formulas are =D5, =D6, and =D7, respectively.

6. Highlight the area A9:D30, and click on Data, then Table.
7. Enter the Column input cell as B1 and click on OK.
8. Excel automatically calculates the expected returns from the three different strategies for $P(S)$ values between 0 and 1.
9. Use the Graph Wizard to produce a chart as shown in Figure 8.16.

Let's look at Figure 8.16 more closely. The vertical axis is expected return and the horizontal axis is $P(S)$, the probability that the market is strong. Note that when $P(S) = 0$, then $ER(A) = -8$. To see that this makes sense, recall that when $P(S) = 0$, we are sure that the market will be weak; Figure 8.11 shows that if the market is weak and we make decision A, the return is –8. A similar argument shows that ER(A) should be 30 when $P(S) = 1$ since in this case we are sure that the market is strong. The fact that a straight line connects these two points follows from the fact that

$$ER(A) = -8 + 38P(S)$$

which is a linear function of $P(S)$. Since the criterion for making a decision is to select the decision with the highest expected return, Figure 8.16 shows which decision is optimal for any particular value of $P(S)$. For example, if as in Figure 8.11, the value of $P(S)$ is 0.45, then Figure 8.16 shows that $ER(B) > ER(C) > ER(A)$. Hence, as we have already computed, for this value of $P(S)$ the optimal decision is B. On the other hand, if $P(S) = 0.8$, we see that $ER(A) > ER(B) > ER(C)$ and thus A is the optimal decision.

In more general terms we see that if $P(S)$ is larger than the value of $P(S)$ at which the graphs of ER(A) and ER(B) cross, strategy A should be selected. The $P(S)$ value at which strategy A becomes optimal can be found by setting ER(A) equal to ER(B) and solving for $P(S)$; that is

$$\begin{aligned} ER(A) &= ER(B) \\ -8 + 38P(S) &= 7 + 13P(S) \\ 25P(S) &= 15 \\ P(S) &= 0.6 \end{aligned}$$

In a similar way, it is easily determined that the graphs of ER(C) and ER(B) cross when $P(S) = 0.348$. (You should try this calculation yourself.) Thus, Figure 8.16 indicates that Sonorola should select the Basic production and marketing strategy (i.e., decision B) if $P(S)$ is larger than 0.348 and smaller than 0.6. This is consistent with what we already computed under the assumption that $P(S) = 0.45$. However, the analysis of Figure 8.16 provides

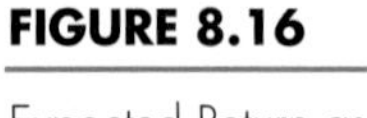

FIGURE 8.16

Expected Return as a Function of $P(S)$

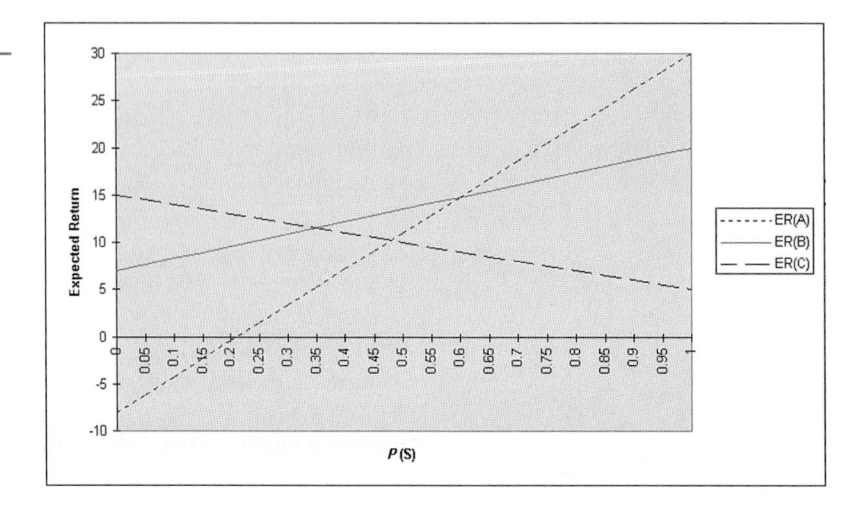

considerably more information than we had previously. It is now clear, for example, that the optimal decision in this case is not very sensitive to the precision of our estimate for *P*(S). The same strategy, B, remains optimal for an increase or decrease of more than 0.10 in the previously estimated probability of 0.45.

Similarly, it could also be important to consider how sensitive the decision is to the estimates of the cash flow returns. For example, suppose that the return of the Aggressive strategy is greater than $30 million when the market is strong. We could do a similar analysis to find out how sensitive our decision is to the estimate of a return of $30 million when the market is strong.

Although a diagram such as Figure 8.16 can be used only when there are two possible states of nature, it provides a useful pedagogical device for illustrating the sensitivity of the optimal solution to the estimates of the probabilities and returns. For higher dimensions, generalizations of this approach exist, but such a discussion would go beyond the introductory level of this chapter.

8.8 DECISION TREES: INCORPORATING NEW INFORMATION

A MARKET RESEARCH STUDY FOR CELLULAR PHONES

The management of Sonorola's cellular phone division was just on the verge of recommending the basic (B) marketing and production strategy when the board of directors insisted that a market research study had to be performed first. Only after such a study would the board be willing to approve the selection of a marketing and production strategy. As a result of the board's decision, management consulted the corporate marketing research group at Sonorola headquarters in Tokyo. It was agreed that this group would perform a market research study and would report within a month on whether the study was encouraging (E) or discouraging (D). Thus, within a month the new-product planners would have this additional information. This new information should obviously be taken into account before making a decision on the marketing and production strategy.

Management could treat the new information informally; that is, once the test results were available, management's estimate of *P*(S), the probability that the market would be strong, could be updated. If the study turned out to be encouraging (E) presumably management would want to increase the estimate of *P*(S) from 0.45 to 0.50, 0.60, or maybe more. If the study results were discouraging (D), then *P*(S) should be decreased. The question is: How should the updating be accomplished? There is a formal way to do this, based on the concept of *conditional probability*. The mathematics of why this approach works is detailed in Section 8.13. Here we will take a tabular approach that is suited to implementation in a spreadsheet program.

OBTAINING REVISED PROBABILITIES BASED ON NEW INFORMATION

The marketing research group has agreed to report within a month whether, according to their study, the test is encouraging (E) or discouraging (D). We would certainly hope their report would be perfectly reliable—that is, if their report is encouraging, then the market is absolutely guaranteed to be strong and if their report is discouraging, then the market is definitely going to be weak. This would amount to their report always revealing the true state of nature. We will see, however, that marketing's report may be useful even if it is not perfectly reliable. This raises the issues of how to quantify "reliability." We will use conditional probabilities.

Conditional Probability Suppose that A and B are two events. An informal definition of the **conditional probability**, *P*(A|B), is the probability that the event A occurs *given* that the event B occurs. For example, *P*(E|S) would be the conditional probability that marketing gives an encouraging report *given* that the market is in fact going to turn out to be strong. If marketing were perfectly reliable, this conditional probability would be 1; that is, they would always give an encouraging report when the market is in fact strong. However, marketing's track record is not perfect. In the past when the market has in fact been strong, they have issued an encouraging report only 60% of the time. Thus, $P(\text{E}|\text{S}) = 0.6$. Since marketing always issues an encouraging or discouraging report, the value of $P(\text{D}|\text{S})$ must be $1 - 0.6$, or 0.4; that is, they issued a discouraging report 40% of the time when in fact the market was strong.

What happens when the market is in fact weak? Marketing is somewhat better at predicting weak markets, but is still not perfect: $P(\text{D}|\text{W}) = 0.7$. That is, in the past when the market has in fact been weak, marketing has issued a discouraging report 70% of the time. Of course, $P(\text{E}|\text{W}) = 0.3$.

Calculating the Posterior Probabilities Suppose that marketing has come back with an encouraging report. What is the probability that the market is in fact strong? It is the conditional probability $P(\text{S}|\text{E})$. Note that this probability is in general *not* the same as $P(\text{E}|\text{S})$. We will see that it depends on the reliabilities and the initial estimates of the probabilities of a strong or weak market. These initial estimates are called **prior probabilities,** while conditional probabilities such as $P(\text{S}|\text{E})$ are called **posterior probabilities.** The division has already estimated the prior probabilities (given initially in Figure 8.11) as $P(\text{S}) = 0.45$ and $P(\text{W}) = 0.55$.

The key to obtaining the posterior probabilities is Bayes' Theorem. We will use a tabular spreadsheet approach that is justified by the argument given in Section 8.13. This process has been carried out in a new spreadsheet called "Probabilities" of the same workbook (SNRLADT.XLS) and is shown in Figure 8.17).[3] The procedure is as follows:

1. Enter the given Reliabilities (conditional probabilities) as a table (A1:C4). *Note*: The conditional probability, $P(\text{A}|\text{B})$, is found at the intersection of row A and column B. Also notice that the column sums must be 1, while the row sums may be either greater than, less than, or equal to 1.
2. Generate a new table by multiplying each column of the reliability table by the corresponding prior probability. For example, multiply each entry in the Strong column of Figure 8.17 by $P(\text{Strong})$. This table is a table of the *joint probabilities* (see Section 8.13).
3. For each row of this new table, compute the sum of the entries. In the example at hand this gives the *marginal probabilities*, $P(\text{E})$ and $P(\text{D})$ in cells D12 and D13.
4. Generate the "Posterior Probabilities" table by dividing each entry in a row of the joint probability table by its row sum (e.g., B12 would be divided by D12).

In this spreadsheet the tables labeled Reliabilities and Prior Probabilities are given and the tables labeled Joint & Marginal Probabilities and Posterior Probabilities are calculated according to the four-step procedure above. The spreadsheet makes it easy to calculate the sensitivity of the posterior probabilities to the reliabilities and the prior probabilities. For example, the Data Table command can be used to generate all posterior probabilities of a strong market [$P(\text{S}|\text{E})$ and $P(\text{S}|\text{D})$] for values of the prior probability

[3] Note that the posterior probability table in Figure 8.17 is read differently from the reliability table. For example, the probability in row D and column W of the posterior probability table is $P\{\text{W}|\text{D}\}$, whereas the probability in row D and column W of the reliability table is $P\{\text{D}|\text{W}\}$. In general, the probability $P\{\text{A}|\text{B}\}$ in the posterior probability table is found at the intersection of *column* A and *row* B. This convention is employed to simplify the copying of formulas in the spreadsheet that is used to generate the posterior probability table. If the convention for the reliability table also had to be observed in the posterior probability table, then the first *column* of the table would be the first *row* of the table in step 2 divided by its row sum, the second column of the table would be the second row of the table in step 2 divided by its row sum, and so on. These operations would be difficult to perform in one step with most spreadsheet programs.

FIGURE 8.17

Calculation of Posterior Probabilities

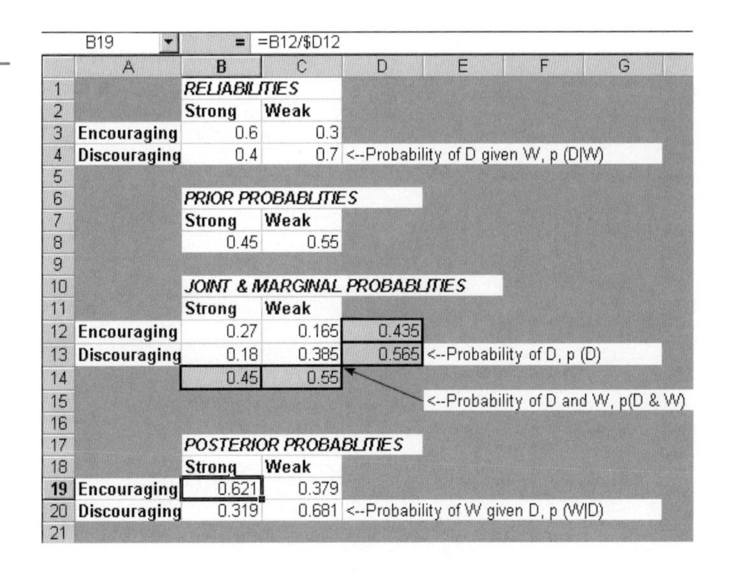

B19 = =B12/$D12

	A	B	C	D	E	F	G
1		*RELIABILITIES*					
2		**Strong**	**Weak**				
3	**Encouraging**	0.6	0.3				
4	**Discouraging**	0.4	0.7	<--Probability of D given W, p (D|W)			
5							
6		*PRIOR PROBABLITIES*					
7		**Strong**	**Weak**				
8		0.45	0.55				
9							
10		*JOINT & MARGINAL PROBABLITIES*					
11		**Strong**	**Weak**				
12	**Encouraging**	0.27	0.165	0.435			
13	**Discouraging**	0.18	0.385	0.565	<--Probability of D, p (D)		
14		0.45	0.55				
15					<--Probability of D and W, p(D & W)		
16							
17		*POSTERIOR PROBABLITIES*					
18		**Strong**	**Weak**				
19	**Encouraging**	0.621	0.379				
20	**Discouraging**	0.319	0.681	<--Probability of W given D, p (W|D)			
21							

Cell	Formula	Copy To
C8	=1 − B8	—
B12	= B3*B$8	B12:C13
D12	= SUM (B12:C12)	D13
B14	= SUM (B12:B13)	C14
B19	= B12/$D12	B19:C20

I	J	K
	P(S|E)	*P(S|D)*
Prior, P(S)	**0.621**	**0.319**
0	0	0
0.1	0.182	0.060
0.2	0.333	0.125
0.3	0.462	0.197
0.4	0.571	0.276
0.5	0.667	0.364
0.6	0.750	0.462
0.7	0.824	0.571
0.8	0.889	0.696
0.9	0.947	0.837
1	1	1

FIGURE 8.18

Sensitivity of Posterior Probabilities to Prior Probabilities

$P(S)$ between 0 and 1 increments of 0.1. The results are shown in Figure 8.18. The steps to do this in Excel are:

1. In cell I3, we enter an initial value of 0.
2. Click back on I3, then click on Edit, Fill, and then Series.
3. Click on "Series in Columns" and enter a step value of 0.1 and a stop value of 1.0. Click on OK.
4. In cells J2:K2 we enter the formulas for the quantities we want to track [$P(S|E)$ and $P(S|D)$] for each of the values for $P(S)$ that we've entered in column 1. These formulas are =B19 and =B20, respectively.
5. Highlight the area I2:K13, and click on Data, then Table.
6. Enter the Column input cell as B8 and click on OK.
7. Excel automatically calculates the two conditional probabilities for values of $P(S)$ between 0 and 1.

Note that as the prior probability of a strong market increases, so does the posterior probability of a strong market given either an encouraging or a discouraging test result. Note too that the posterior probability of a strong market is greater than the prior probability given an encouraging test result, but the posterior probability is less than the prior, given a discouraging test result (except when $P(S) = 0$ or 1, in which case the prior and posterior probabilities are equal).

INCORPORATING POSTERIOR PROBABILITIES IN THE DECISION TREE

We now represent management's model with the decision tree presented in Figure 8.19. The first node (I) corresponds to performing the marketing research. The node is circular because the outcome is not certain. There are two possible results. The test is either encour-

FIGURE 8.19

Decision Tree with Test Results

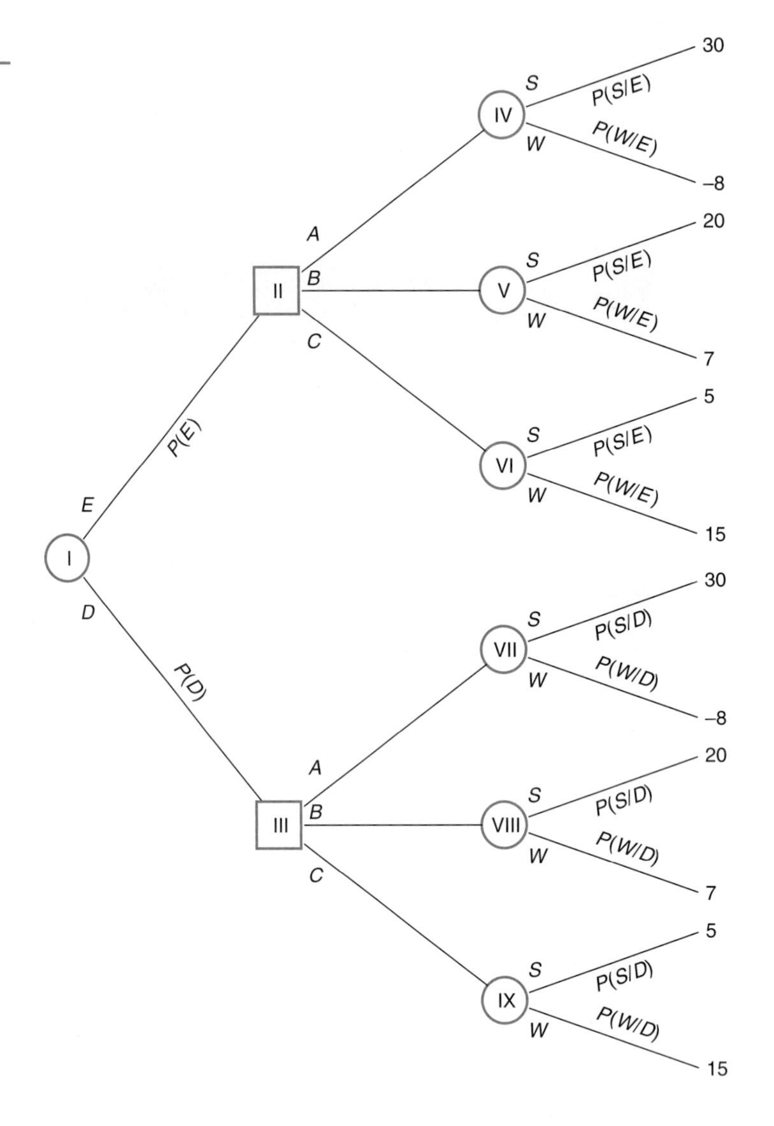

aging (E) or discouraging (D); P(E) and P(D) represent the probabilities of those two outcomes and were shown in cells D12 and D13 of Figure 8.17 previously.

If the test is encouraging, we proceed to node II, which is square because a decision must be made. Management must decide to select one of the three marketing strategies (A or B or C). Suppose that management selects A. We are then led to node IV, another situation with two possible outcomes, namely whether the market is strong (S) or weak (W). If it turns out to be strong, Sonorola will enjoy a net return of 30, which is the terminal value on the branch.

It is important to note that the tree is created in the chronological order in which information becomes available and decisions are required; that is,

1. Result of marketing research survey (Encouraging or Discouraging)
2. Make decision on which marketing strategy to pursue (Aggressive, Basic, or Cautious)
3. Market condition (Strong or Weak)

In order to solve this tree we must fill in the values for P(S|E), P(W|E), P(S|D), P(W|D), P(E), and P(D). The first four probabilities are found in the table labeled Posterior Probabilities in Figure 8.17 (cells B19:C20). For example, the probability P(W|E) is found in *column* W and *row* E of the table (again, note that this is the opposite of the convention

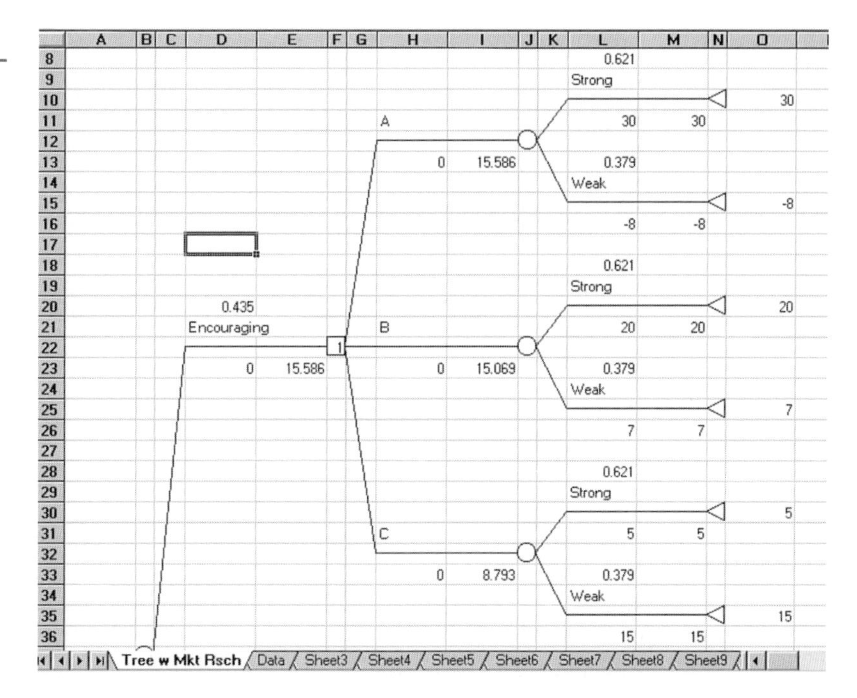

FIGURE 8.20

Upper Half of Decision Tree with New Information

used to read the Reliabilities table but is more convenient for the spreadsheet representation). So, for example, $P(W|E) = 0.379$.

Thus, the event of an encouraging test result, and the use of Bayes' Theorem allow us to update the prior value of $P(S)$, namely 0.45, to a higher value, $P(S|E) = 0.621$. Similar calculations yield $P(S|D) = 0.319$, and $P(W|D) = 0.681$. These probabilities are attached to the decision tree. TreePlan then automatically folds back the tree to solve our decision model. To do this in TreePlan we basically follow the same steps as before. The results are shown in Figures 8.20 and 8.21 (upper and lower half of the tree). Highlights are given below:

1. Hit Ctrl-t to bring up the menu and select "New Tree." (*Note*: TreePlan can't have more than one tree in a spreadsheet so we created a new spreadsheet called "SNRLADT2.XLS" for this new model.)
2. Click on the default decision node, and hit Ctrl-t. Select "Change to event" and click OK.
3. At the terminal node, hit Ctrl-t and select "Change to decision" with three branches. Click OK.
4. Repeat step 3 for the other terminal node.
5. Click on the new terminal node at the top of the tree, hit Ctrl-t, and select "Change to event" with two branches. Click OK.
6. Copy the node created in step 5 to the other two terminal values nearest it (use TreePlan's Copy subtree and Paste subtree commands, not Excel's normal Copy and Paste features).
7. Once we get the upper half of the tree done (Node II and everything to the right in Figure 8.19), we can then copy it and paste it on Node III effectively.

These figures can be used to determine the optimal decisions. We see that if the test is encouraging, E (see Figure 8.20), we arrive at cell F22. Then to maximize the expected return, we should take action A (TreePlan indicates this with a "1" in cell F22, meaning take the first branch); that is, follow the Aggressive production and marketing strategy. Similarly, if the test result is discouraging, D (see Figure 8.21), we should take action C. Why? Because 11.81 is the largest possible expected return when the test is discouraging.

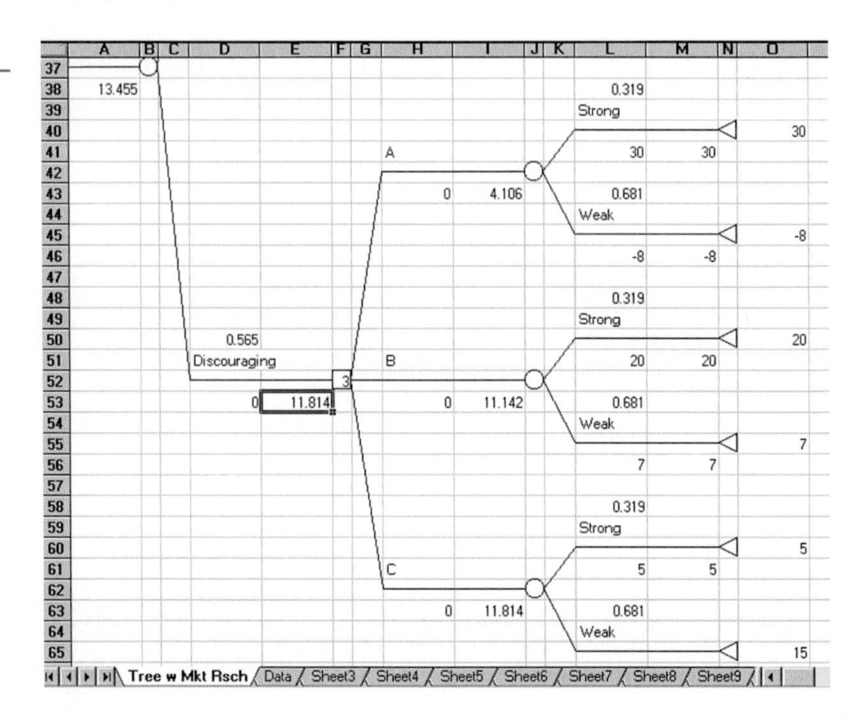

FIGURE 8.21

Lower Half of Decision Tree with New Information

THE EXPECTED VALUE OF SAMPLE INFORMATION

Suppose that we use the optimal decisions determined above to fold back the decision tree (shown in Figures 8.20 and 8.21) one more step. Cell B37 (of Figure 8.21) shows us the expected return at the initial event node is

$$\text{ER} = 15.586(0.435) + 11.814(0.565) = 13.455$$

This value is the expected return of performing the market test and making optimal decisions after determining the results.

In Section 8.6 we saw that if the market test is not performed, the optimal decision is to select B, the basic strategy, and that this decision has an expected return of 12.85. Clearly then, performing the market test increases Sonorola's expected return by \$0.61 million (=\$13.46 million – \$12.85 million). Even though the market test is not perfectly reliable, it still has some value (\$0.61 million, to be precise). Appropriately enough, this quantity is called the **expected value of sample information (EVSI)**. In general terms

$$\text{EVSI} = \begin{pmatrix} \text{maximum possible} \\ \text{expected return} \\ \text{with sample} \\ \text{information} \end{pmatrix} - \begin{pmatrix} \text{maximum possible} \\ \text{expected return} \\ \text{without sample} \\ \text{information} \end{pmatrix}$$

The EVSI is an upper bound of how much one would be willing to pay for this particular sample information.

Let us now calculate the expected value of *perfect* information. Recall from Section 8.3 that this is the amount that management would be willing to pay for perfect information. The payoff table was originally presented in Figure 8.11. If it were sure that the market would be strong, management would pick decision A and enjoy a return of 30. Similarly, if it were sure that the market would be weak, management would pick decision C and enjoy a return of 15. How much would management pay for perfect information? Since perfect information will reveal a strong market with probability 0.45, and a weak market with probability 0.55, we see that

$$\text{EVPI} = (30)(0.45) + (15)(0.55) - 12.85 = 8.90 \tag{8.2}$$

Equation (8.2) tells us that perfect information will bring us an expected increase of $8.90 million over the previous expected return. This is the maximum possible increase in the expected return that can be obtained from new information. The expected value of sample information (EVSI) is the increase in the expected return that was obtained with the information produced by the market test. Since EVPI = 8.9 and EVSI = 0.61, we see that the market test is not very effective. If it were, the value for EVSI would be much closer to EVPI. In other words, as the probabilities of correct sample information increase, EVSI approaches EVPI. In fact, when $P(E|S) = 1.00$ and $P(D|W) = 1.00$, then EVSI = EVPI.

8.9 SEQUENTIAL DECISIONS: TO TEST OR NOT TO TEST

In the preceding section, we assumed that the board of directors had decided to have a market research study done. We then considered the question of how the management of Sonorola's cellular phone division should use the information generated by the study to update the decision model. Let us step back for a moment. It seems clear that the decision to have a market study done is in essence no different from the decision to adopt one marketing and production strategy or another. Management must carefully weigh the cost of performing the study against the gain that might result from having the information that the study would produce. Suppose that the market test will cost $500,000 (or $0.5 million). It is also clear that the decision on whether to have a market research test is not an isolated decision. If the test is given, management must still select one of the marketing and production strategies. Thus, the value of performing the test depends in part on how Sonorola uses the information generated by the test. In other words, the value of an initial decision depends on a *sequence* of decisions and uncertain events that will follow the initial decision. This is called a **sequential decision model**.

ANALYZING SEQUENTIAL DECISIONS

This is an extremely common type of management model and is actually the kind of situation that decision trees are designed to handle. It is in situations where there are a number of interrelated decisions and events with more than one possible outcome that the ability to display the model graphically is especially useful.

Figures 8.22 and 8.23 show the test or no-test tree. In terms of structure and the probabilities, you see that the upper (test) branch is the tree from Figures 8.20 and 8.21 with slightly modified terminal values to account for the market test cost and the lower (no-test) branch is the tree from Figure 8.15. To do this in TreePlan we basically follow the same steps as before. We created a new spreadsheet called "SNRLADT3.XLS" for this new decision model. Highlights are given below:

1. Hit Ctrl-t to bring up the menu and select "New Tree."
2. At the first terminal node (cell F45 in Figure 8.22), hit Ctrl-t and select "Change to event" with two branches. Click OK.
3. Click on the new terminal node at the top of the tree (cell J30 in Figure 8.22), hit Ctrl-t, and select "Change to decision" with three branches. Click OK.
4. Copy the node created in step 3 to the other terminal node (cell J60 in Figure 8.22) nearest it. (Use TreePlan's Copy subtree and Paste subtree commands, not Excel's normal Copy and Paste features.)
5. To finish the upper half of the tree, click on the new terminal node at the top of the tree (cell N20 in Figure 8.22), hit Ctrl-t, and select "Change to event" with two branches. Click OK.
6. Copy the node created in step 5 to the other five terminal nodes nearest it (cells N30, N40, N50, N60, N70). This completes the upper half of the tree.
7. You can then copy the decision node with its three branches followed by event nodes of two branches (cell J30 or J60) to the node (cell F90 in Figure 8.23) at the bottom half of the tree.

FIGURE 8.22

Upper Half of Decision Tree with New Information

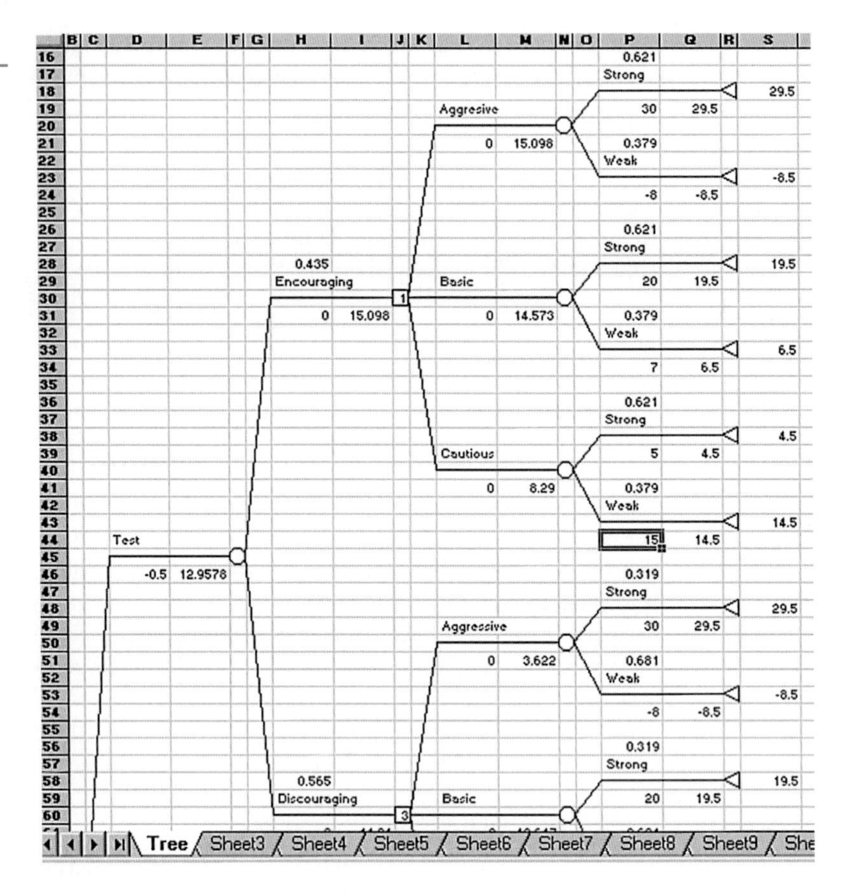

FIGURE 8.23

Lower Half of Decision Tree with New Information

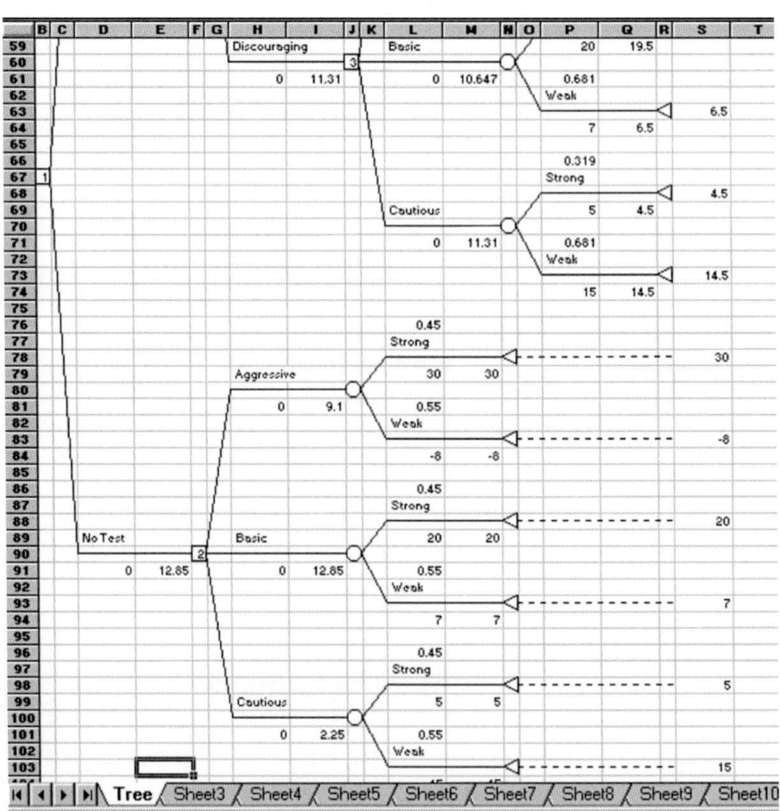

The terminal values merit some discussion. They are determined in a two-step process:

1. Assign the appropriate cash flow to each decision and uncertain event. In this model we have assumed that the market test costs $500,000. Since all costs and returns are measured in millions, a figure of –0.5 is placed by the test branch (cell D46 of Figure 8.22) and a figure of 0 is placed by the no-test branch (cell D91 of Figure 8.23). Similarly, a figure of 30 is placed on the upper branch (cell P19 in Figure 8.22) since this is the profit if Sonorola selects A and the market is strong.
2. TreePlan determines a particular terminal value by adding the cash flows on all branches between the first node and the terminal position. For example, the number 29.5 on the uppermost terminal position (cell S18 in Figure 8.22) comes from adding the costs on the path Test-Encouraging-Aggressive-Strong (i.e., returns of –0.5 + 0 + 0 + 30 = 29.5).

Again, TreePlan solves this tree by folding it back. It folds back a circular (event) node by calculating the expected returns. It folds back a square (decision) node by selecting the decision that yields the highest expected return.

The *optimal strategy* is a complete plan for the entire tree. It specifies what action to take no matter which of the uncertain events occurs. To determine the optimal strategy for the test or no-test tree, we refer to Figures 8.22 and 8.23. At the first decision node (test or no-test), we see that since 12.96 > 12.85, Sonorola should conduct the market test. If the result of the test is encouraging (E), then an Aggressive campaign (A) is the best decision since it yields the largest expected return (15.098). Similarly, if the result of the test is discouraging (D), then a Cautious campaign (C) is the best decision (with expected return of 11.31).

THE IMPACT OF UTILITIES

It is simple to incorporate utilities into a decision tree. Suppose that the utilities of all possible payoffs are given in Table 8.12 and were calculated in a manner similar to that shown in Section 8.4. A graph of utility versus payoff would show that Sonorola is risk-averse. For example, the additional utility of increasing the payoff from 20 to 30 is only 0.020 (= 0.963 – 0.943), while the additional utility of increasing the payoff from 5 to 15 is 0.205 (= 0.914 – 0.709).

To incorporate the utilities into the decision tree, all you need to do is replace the payoffs in Figure 8.22 and 8.23 with their utilities and fold back the tree as before. This is done in a new spreadsheet (SNRLADT4.XLS) and is shown in Figures 8.24 and 8.25.

It turns out that with these utilities that the optimal decision is still to test. However, if the test is encouraging, alternative B is now chosen rather than A because it has a higher

Table 8.12

Utilities of Payoffs

PAYOFF	UTILITY
–8.5	0.300
–8	0.320
4.5	0.695
5	0.709
6.5	0.748
7	0.760
14.5	0.910
15	0.914
19.5	0.941
20	0.943
29.5	0.962
30	0.963

FIGURE 8.24

Upper Half of Test or No-Test Tree with Utilities Incorporated

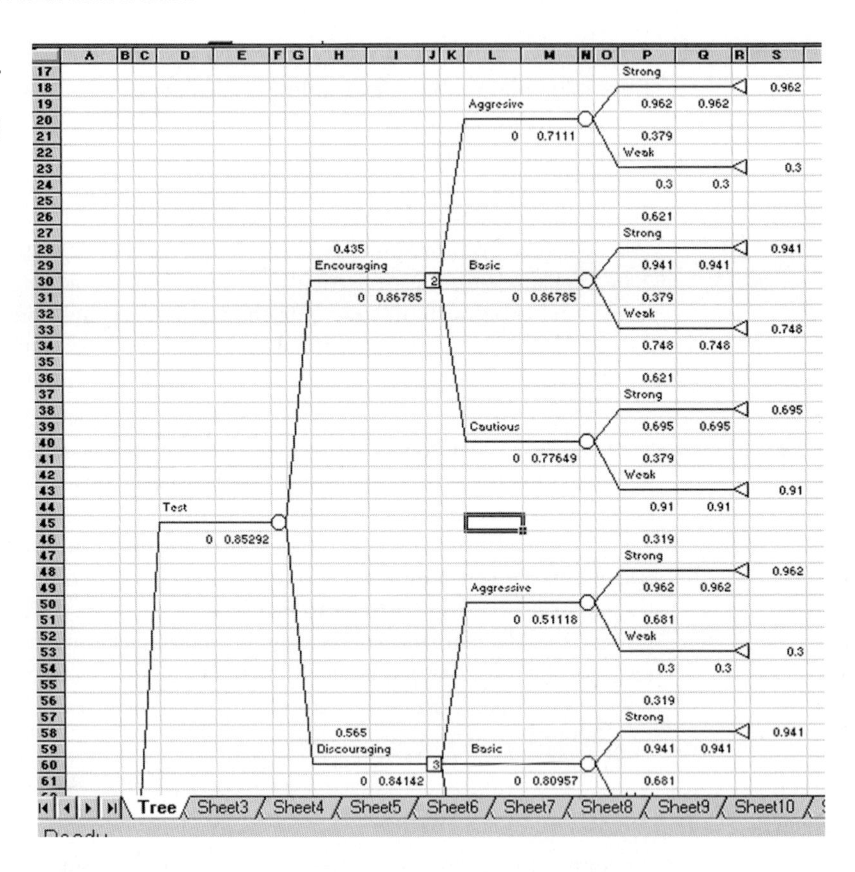

FIGURE 8.25

Lower Half of Test or No-Test Tree with Utilities Incorporated

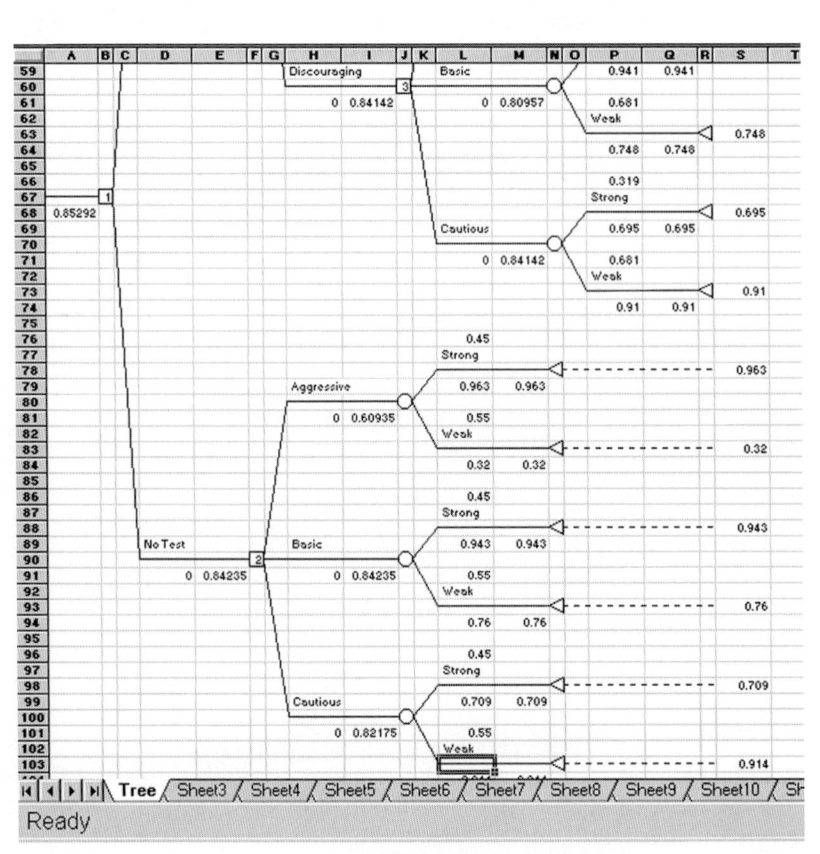

FIGURE 8.26

TreePlan Options Dialog Box

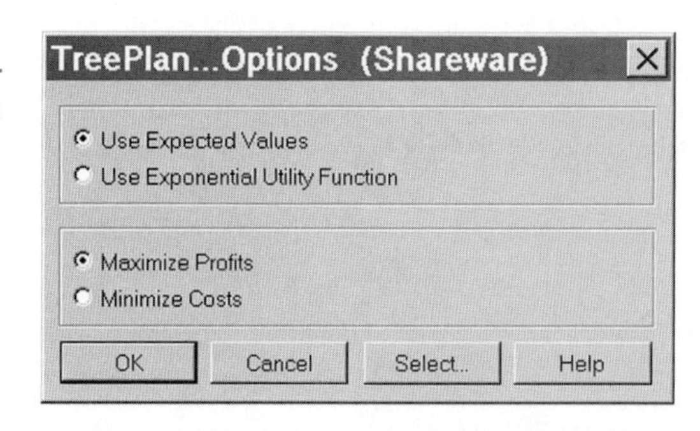

expected utility (0.868 versus 0.711). Even though A's maximum payoff ($29.5) is larger than B's ($19.5), B's minimum payoff is larger than A's ($6.5 versus –$8.5). The combination of Sonorola's utility function and the given posterior probabilities now causes the expected utility of B to be higher than that of A.

OTHER FEATURES OF TREEPLAN

If you click on the "Options" feature, you get the following dialog box (see Figure 8.26), which demonstrates two additional features of TreePlan. First note that TreePlan has a built-in exponential utility function. To activate it, click on the "Use Exponential Utility Function," and TreePlan will automatically assume a risk-averse utility function and calculate the utilities for the given cash flows already on the tree. The second feature is that TreePlan defaults to a "Maximize Profits" approach to folding back the tree (i.e., at a decision node it picks the branch with the *largest* payoff). If you want to do a cost-minimization model, you must change this to "Minimize Costs" so that it picks the branch with the *smallest* payoff at the decision nodes. It's also worth mentioning that TreePlan has online help available to those who need it.

SENSITIVITY OF THE OPTIMAL DECISION TO PRIOR PROBABILITIES

Whether cash returns or utilities are used in the decision tree, it is important to see how sensitive the optimal decision is to various parameter values. For example, how sensitive is the optimal decision to the initial estimate of a strong market, the prior probability $P(S)$? The spreadsheet shown in Figure 8.27 (SNRLADT5.XLS) reproduces the graphical analysis shown in Figures 8.24 and 8.25. The first step was to copy the "Probabilities" worksheet of SNRLADT.XLS (see Figure 8.17) over into cells A1:E20 (not shown). The rest of the spreadsheet is shown in Figure 8.27. The main advantage of the spreadsheet formulation is the ease with which various parameters can be changed and the tree effectively recalculated.

The graph of Figure 8.28 was generated by varying the value of $P(S)$ between 0 and 1 in increments of 0.01. This is done easily in Excel using the Data Table feature as follows:

1. In Cell A24, we enter an initial value of 0.
2. Click back on A24, then click on Edit, Fill, and then Series.
3. Click on "Series in Columns" and enter a step value of 0.01 and a stop value of 1.0. Click on OK.
4. In cells B23:C23 we enter the formulas for the quantities we want to track [Exp. Utility(Test) and Exp. Utility(NoTest)] for each of the values for $P(S)$ that we've entered in column A. These formulas are =G1, and =I12, respectively.
5. Highlight the area A23:C124, and click on Data, then Table.
6. Enter the Column input cell as B8 and click on OK.
7. Excel automatically calculates the two expected utilities for values of $P(S)$ between 0 and 1.

FIGURE 8.27

Spreadsheet Representation of Test/No-Test Decision Tree

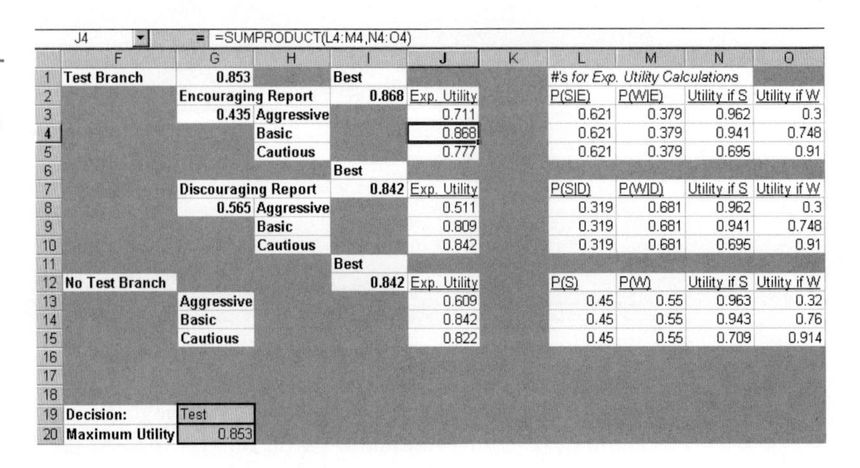

J4 = =SUMPRODUCT(L4:M4,N4:O4)

	F	G	H	I	J	K	L	M	N	O
1	Test Branch	0.853		Best			#'s for Exp. Utility Calculations			
2		Encouraging Report		0.868	Exp. Utility		P(S|E)	P(W|E)	Utility if S	Utility if W
3		0.435	Aggressive		0.711		0.621	0.379	0.962	0.3
4			Basic		0.868		0.621	0.379	0.941	0.748
5			Cautious		0.777		0.621	0.379	0.695	0.91
6				Best						
7		Discouraging Report		0.842	Exp. Utility		P(S|D)	P(W|D)	Utility if S	Utility if W
8		0.565	Aggressive		0.511		0.319	0.681	0.962	0.3
9			Basic		0.809		0.319	0.681	0.941	0.748
10			Cautious		0.842		0.319	0.681	0.695	0.91
11				Best						
12	No Test Branch			0.842	Exp. Utility		P(S)	P(W)	Utility if S	Utility if W
13		Aggressive			0.609		0.45	0.55	0.963	0.32
14		Basic			0.842		0.45	0.55	0.943	0.76
15		Cautious			0.822		0.45	0.55	0.709	0.914
16										
17										
18										
19	Decision:	Test								
20	Maximum Utility	0.853								

Cell	Formula	Copy To
G1	= G3*I2+G8*I7	—
I2	= MAX(J3:J5)	I7, I12
G3	= D12	—
J3	= SUMPRODUCT(L3:M3, N3:03)	J4:J5, J8:J10, J13:J15
L3	= B$19	L3:M5
G8	= D13	—
L8	= B$20	L8:M10
L13	= B$8	L13:M15
G19	= IF(G20=G1,"Test","NoTest")	—
G20	= MAX(G1,I12)	—

The solid line in Figure 8.28 represents the expected utility of the Test decision, while the dotted line represents the expected utility of the No-Test decision. Whenever the two curves cross, the optimal decision changes. Since the curves cross four times (although it is hard to see the last time because the curves are so close together), the optimal decision changes four times: No-Test, Test, No-Test, Test, No-Test. Test is the optimal decision for values of $P(S)$ between (approximately) 0.29 and 0.50 and between 0.94 and 0.96. No-Test is optimal for the values of $P(S)$ between 0 and 0.29, between 0.5 and 0.94, and between 0.96 and 1.

FIGURE 8.28

Expected Utility of Test and No Test

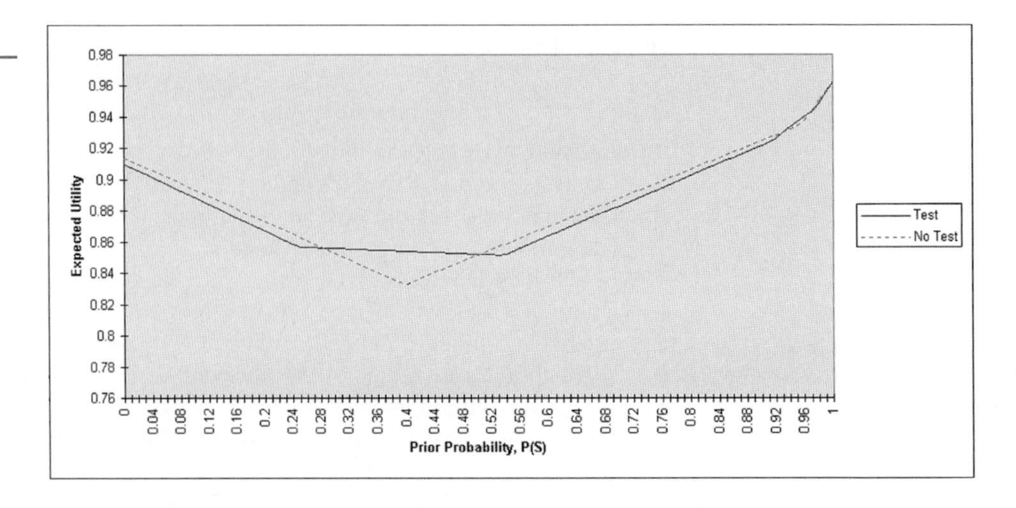

8.10 MANAGEMENT AND DECISION THEORY

A typical management decision has the following characteristics:

1. It is made once and only once (e.g., should I buy 100 shares of Intel stock today or not?).
2. The return depends on an uncertain event that will occur in the future (e.g., the price of Intel stock will go up or down), and we have no historical information about this future event.

We know about related events that may tell us something about the likelihood of the various outcomes (e.g., the behavior of the price of Intel stock last week or the last 52 weeks). But we cannot perform an experiment to provide a good, reliable estimate of the relevant probabilities (e.g., we cannot perform an experiment that tells us about the price of Intel stock next week.)

What does the material in this chapter contribute to our understanding of how to attack this model? In brief, this chapter recommends the following conceptual framework:

1. For each decision, determine the utility of each possible outcome.
2. Determine the probability of each possible outcome.
3. Calculate the expected utility of each decision.
4. Select the decision with the largest expected utility.

Once the first two steps have been completed, the next two steps are easy, at least conceptually. But how can you *know* the probabilities and the utilities?

The answer is that there are no values to *know*. These are not entities, the "true" value of which can be revealed by experimentation or further analysis. Indeed, these two quantities, *probabilities* and *utilities*, are *subjective* and represent the *best judgment and taste of the manager*. Certainly the manager's evaluation of these two quantities can be influenced by study, but there is no opportunity for direct experimentation with the underlying phenomena, as there would be, for example, in physical or biological science.

There is, nevertheless, some structure to cling to in this sea of subjectivity. The structure is provided by a logical device called an *equivalent lottery*. This concept gives one a *consistent framework* for quantifying both probabilities and utilities. We saw in Section 8.4 how a manager can use an equivalent lottery to create a utility function.

ASSESSING SUBJECTIVE PROBABILITIES

The manager can use this approach to assess a subjective probability. Suppose, for example, that on this date you wish to assess the probability that Hillary Clinton will be the Democratic candidate for President in 2004. The first step is to think of two games. In game 1 you receive \$100 if Clinton is the candidate and \$0 if she is not. In game 2 you receive \$100 with probability p and \$0 with probability $1 - p$. You now adjust the value of p until you are indifferent between the two games. The resulting value of p is *your* subjective probability that Clinton will be the Democratic candidate in 2004. It is clear that your assessment of Clinton's chances may be different from that of Hillary Clinton's assessment or anyone else's for that matter.

We have argued that the equivalent lottery allows one to quantify both subjective probability and utility. We now stress again that the values obtained through this process are personal and a matter of judgment, and thus by definition they will vary from person to person. Certainly, then, two individuals, each of whom is facing the same decision and using the recommended approach, may arrive at different decisions. And why not? The recommended approach allows the manager to incorporate personal knowledge (and experience), and surely there is no reason to believe that everyone will "know" the same things at the moment of decision.

However, a cynic might ask, "Why bother with all this machinery?" If judgment and taste play such an important role in these assessments, isn't it better to use judgment in a holistic approach and simply select the alternative that intuitively seems best? What do we gain from assessing probability and utility separately? The reply is that separating the two assessments makes it possible for a manager to concentrate attention on each of these entities (probability and utility), one at a time. The problem with a simple intuitive approach is that we humans have a hard time thinking about more than one thing at a time. While thinking about payoffs, it is hard to be thinking at the same time about likelihoods and then to combine them in one's head. In other words, the simple, intuitive approach makes it too easy to put heavy emphasis on a particularly awful outcome (or a particularly attractive outcome) and not enough weight on the fact that this outcome may be extremely unlikely. As an example, look at the number of people who won't fly in an airplane, but will drive in a car, even though the probability of being killed in an auto accident is vastly higher than that of dying in a plane crash. (Presumably, they are influenced by the thought that they *might* survive an auto accident, whereas they would be unlikely to live through a plane crash.) *Separating the assessments of probabilities and utilities forces a manager to give appropriate and separate consideration to each before combining the two to determine the final decision.*

The revolution in personal computing and the explosion in software that has accompanied it have had an impact on decision analysis. A decade ago, general-purpose decision analysis programs from commercial software suppliers were not widely available. Some companies created programs for their own purposes, but these were not available to the general public. We have demonstrated in this chapter the use of a very popular spreadsheet add-in, TreePlan, and also point out that there are other spreadsheet add-in packages available (PrecisionTree by Palisade), as well as stand-alone software packages (DPL by Applied Decision Analysis, DATA, Arborist, Riskcalc, and Supertree). Many of these packages also include the ability to draw influence diagrams, which help the manager to bring structure to all the variables involved in the model by identifying which variables influence the others.

8.11 NOTES ON IMPLEMENTATION

Ralph Keeney, a leading scholar in the field, (see Keeney and Raiffa, Keeney[B]), defines decision analysis as "a formalization of common sense for decision models which are too complex for informal use of common sense." Decision analysis, which is based on axioms originally stated by John von Neumann and Oskar Morgenstern, involves assigning probabilities and utilities to possible outcomes and maximizing expected utility. This approach is applied to highly complex models that are typically sequential in nature. It can be thought of as having four parts: (1) structuring the model, (2) assessing the probability of the possible outcomes, (3) determining the utility of the possible outcomes, and (4) evaluating alternatives and selecting a strategy.

Much of the material in this chapter concerns item (4), the technical process of evaluating alternatives and selecting a strategy. This is appropriate since this is the conceptual heart of decision analysis. In practice, however, this is the easy part of the model. A significantly greater proportion of effort is spent on the other three areas. Structuring the model, which involves generating alternatives and specifying objectives in numerically measurable terms, is a particularly unstructured task. In some of the real-world applications, objectives have been quantified in the areas of environmental impact, public health and safety, and so on.

ROLE OF PERSONAL JUDGMENT

It is important to understand that decision analysis does *not* provide a completely objective analysis of complicated models. Many aspects of a decision analysis require personal judgment—whether it be structuring the model, assessing probabilities, or assigning utilities. In many important complex models there simply are not enough empirical data to provide a basis for complete analysis. Nevertheless, experience has shown that the framework provided by decision analysis has been useful. Indeed, there are many qualitative and nonobjective factors involved in all decision making, but the important role of decision analysis is to make it consistent, not just "objective" and devoid of any subjective judgments. There is room for subjectivity, but it should not depend on how you "feel" at the moment.

In the early 1960s decision analysis began to be successfully applied to a number of models in the private sector. These included models of gas and oil exploration as well as capital investment. Although developments have continued on private-sector models, two other general modeling areas have witnessed a wide variety of applications of decision analysis. In the health-care field, decision analysis has been applied to such diverse models as the evaluation of new drugs, the analysis of treatment strategies for diseases, and the selection of medical technology for a particular facility. The second modeling area concerns applications in the government. In particular, decision analysis has been applied to everything from the seeding of hurricanes, to the negotiation of international oil tanker standards, to the choice between coal and nuclear technology for large-scale power plants (see Keeney[A]).

One final note: We can see that the decision trees can get rather large and cumbersome as the number of decision alternatives or random states of nature multiply (≥3 to 5 decisions or random outcomes per node). In decision models where the number becomes too large, we may have to make simplifying assumptions about the possible outcomes or limit the number of decision alternatives we will evaluate if we wish to press ahead with decision analysis. For example, consider the random outcome of a lawsuit or random demand for a product (one can easily see that there is a continuous range of possible outcomes [i.e., an infinite number]) and that it would be nigh impossible to model this as a decision tree in an explicit sense. There are two main options to handle such a situation: (1) approximate the continuous outcomes with a Pearson-Tukey approach (three branches [representing the 0.05 fractile, the 0.5 fractile, and the 0.95 fractile with "optimal" weights of 0.185, 0.63, and 0.185, respectively] are used to approximate the infinite number of possibilities), or (2) use the technique of Monte Carlo simulation, which is introduced in Chapter 9 and is designed to handle probability distributions of a continuous nature.

8.12 SUMMARY

The first part of this chapter dealt with the fundamentals of decision theory. A summary of that material was provided in Section 8.5.

The following four sections of the chapter expounded on the role of decision trees in facilitating the decision process. A decision tree is a graphical device for attacking models in which a sequence of decisions must be made, and these decisions are interspersed with events that have several possible outcomes. It is typically true that square nodes are used to represent decisions and circular nodes are used to represent events. The branches emanating from a square node are the possible decisions, and the branches emanating from a circular node are the possible outcomes. When a decision tree has been completed, a path from the start of the tree to a terminal node represents a specific sequence of decisions and uncertain events. The complete tree represents all possible such sequences.

Solving a decision tree is a sequential process that starts at the terminal nodes and proceeds back to the start of the tree in a process that is described as "folding back." The process includes two steps: The branches emanating from a circular node are folded back by assigning to the node the expected value of the chance events; branches emanating from a decision node are folded back by selecting the alternative with the maximum expected return and assigning this value to the decision node. This "folding back" has been greatly automated through the use of such spreadsheet add-ins as TreePlan. The solution of a decision tree yields an optimal strategy; that is, it specifies what sequence of actions should be taken for any of the possible sequences of chance events.

Bayes' Theorem plays an important role in the construction of decision trees, because this is the device that makes it possible to incorporate new information into the decision process in a formal way. Bayes' Theorem is based on the concept of conditional probability, and thus some time is devoted to that general topic.

The expected value of sample information is a measure of the value of incorporating sample information into a decision with uncertainty. The expected value of perfect information is an upper bound on the expected value of sample information.

Key Terms

Payoff Table. A table showing the returns for each possible state of nature-decision combination in a decision against nature.
Decision Under Certainty. A decision against nature in which the state of nature is known with certainty.
Decision Under Risk. A decision against nature in which a probability distribution on the states of nature is known.
Risk Profile. For a given decision, the profile shows all the possible outcomes with their associated probabilities, usually in a graphical format.
Decision Under Uncertainty. A decision against nature with no knowledge about the likelihood of the various states of nature.
Maximin Criterion. A conservative decision criterion of maximizing the minimum return.
Maximax Criterion. An optimistic decision criterion of maximizing the maximum return.
Regret. A measure of how much better the decision maker could have done had he or she known the state of nature (the opportunity cost of not making the best decision for a given state of nature).
Expected Value of Perfect Information (EVPI). An upper bound on the value of new information.
Utility. In this chapter, a measure of the "attractiveness" of an outcome to an individual.
Risk-Averse. A preference to avoid downside risks, precisely reflected in a concave utility function.
Risk-Seeking. A preference for upside returns, precisely reflected in a convex utility function.
Risk-Indifferent. Reflected by a linear utility function.
Equivalent Lottery. A device for creating a utility function.
Decision Tree. A graphical device for analyzing decisions under risk.
Square Node. A point at which a decision must be made in decision tree diagrams.
Circular Node. Indicates a nondeterministic event on a decision tree.
Branches. The lines emanating from the nodes in a decision tree.
Terminal Position. The end of a branch emanating from a terminal node.
Terminal Node. A node in a decision tree that is not succeeded by other nodes.
Terminal Value. The net return associated with a terminal position.
Folding Back. The process of solving a decision tree by working backward.
Conditional Probability. The probability of an event (say, B) given that another event (say, A) occurs; denoted $P(B|A)$ and defined $P(B|A) = P(B \text{ and } A)/P(A)$.
Prior Probabilities. The originally assessed values for probabilities.
Posterior Probabilities. An updated probability. The updating combines the prior probabilities and new information using Bayes' Theorem.
Expected Value of Sample Information (EVSI). The difference between the maximum possible expected returns with and without sample information.
Sequential Decision Model. A model in which the value of an initial decision depends on subsequent decisions and uncertain events.

Self-Review Exercises

True-False

1. **T F** Decision trees involve sequences of decisions and random outcomes.
2. **T F** In decision theory, returns are dependent on the actions of an indifferent adversary termed "nature."
3. **T F** One underlying aspect of decision theory is that, regardless of what we assume about nature, in terms of whether we know probabilities of various random states, we are led to the same criterion for selecting a "best decision."
4. **T F** Many deterministic optimization models can be thought of as decision making under certainty, where there is only one state of nature and one selects a decision that maximizes returns.
5. **T F** One way to deal with decision making in the "uncertainty" context is to treat all states of nature as equally likely and maximize expected return.
6. **T F** The computation of the value of perfect information is based on the concept that all randomness has been eliminated.
7. **T F** Maximizing expected net dollar return always yields the same optimal policy as minimizing expected regret.
8. **T F** A risk-averse utility function is convex.
9. **T F** Decision trees are solved by folding forward.
10. **T F** Bayes' Theorem provides a formula for how one can use new information to update a prior probability assessment.

Multiple Choice

11. Decision theory is concerned with
  a. the amount of information that is available
  b. criteria for measuring the "goodness" of a decision
  c. selecting optimal decisions in sequential models
  d. all of the above

12. Concerning decision making under risk, which of the following is not true?
  a. We assume that the decision maker knows the probability with which each state of nature will occur.
  b. We use the criterion of maximizing return.
  c. We use the criterion of maximizing expected return.
  d. We use the criterion of minimizing expected regret.

13. Which of the following criteria does *not* apply to decision making under uncertainty?
  a. maximin return
  b. maximax return
  c. minimax regret
  d. maximize expected return

14. Maximin return, maximax return, and minimax regret are criteria that
  a. lead to the same optimal decision
  b. can be used without probabilities
  c. both a and b

15. The expected value of perfect information (EVPI)
  a. places two-sided bounds (upper and lower) on how much should be spent in gathering information
  b. can be determined without using probabilities
  c. refers to the utility of additional information
  d. equals the expected regret of the optimal decision under risk

16. The concept of utility is a way to
  a. measure the attractiveness of money
  b. take into account aversion to risk
  c. take into account inclination to take risk
  d. both a and b
  e. a, b, and c

17. Which of the following does not apply to a decision tree?
  a. A square node is a point at which a decision must be made.
  b. A circular node represents an encounter with uncertainty.
  c. One chooses a sequence of decisions that has the greatest probability of success.
  d. One attempts to maximize expected return.

18. The expected value of perfect information (EVPI)
  a. shows the cost necessary to produce perfect information about the future
  b. shows the maximum possible increase in expected return with sample information
  c. shows the expected increase in information required to select the optimal decision
  d. all of the above

19. When computing the expected value of perfect information (EVPI), it is important that the payment is made
  a. in advance of receiving the information
  b. after receiving the information
  c. in an irrevocable way
  d. both a and c

20. When decisions are made sequentially in time
  a. decision trees cannot be employed
  b. Bayes' Theorem must be used
  c. the terminal value at the end of each sequence of branches is the net of the cash flows on that sequence
  d. the terminal value at the end of each sequence of branches is an expected net cash flow

Answers

1. T, **2.** T, **3.** F, **4.** T, **5.** T, **6.** F, **7.** T, **8.** F, **9.** F, **10.** T, **11.** d, **12.** b, **13.** d, **14.** b, **15.** d, **16.** e, **17.** c, **18.** b, **19.** d, **20.** c

Skill Problems

8-1. Consider the payoff table in Table 8.13, in which the entries are net dollar returns. Assume that this is a decision with no knowledge about the states of nature.
  (a) What is the optimal decision if the Laplace criterion is used?
  (b) What is the optimal decision if the maximin criterion is used?
  (c) What is the optimal decision if the maximax criterion is used?
  (d) Create the payoff table in which the entries are regret.
  (e) What is the optimal decision if the criterion of minimax regret is used?

Table 8.13

	STATE OF NATURE			
Decision	**1**	**2**	**3**	**4**
1	35	22	25	12
2	27	25	20	18
3	22	25	25	28
4	20	25	28	33

Table 8.14

	STATE OF NATURE		
Decision	**1**	**2**	**3**
1	5	7	8
2	6	6	6
3	3	9	1

8-2. Consider the payoff table in Table 8.14, in which the entries are net dollar returns. Assume that this is a decision with no knowledge about the states of nature.
- **(a)** What is the optimal decision if the Laplace criterion is used?
- **(b)** What is the optimal decision if the maximin criterion is used?
- **(c)** What is the optimal solution if the maximax criterion is used?
- **(d)** Create the payoff table in which the entries are regret.
- **(e)** What is the optimal decision if the criterion of minimax regret is used?

8-3. Consider the payoff table in Table 8.13. Assume that the following probabilities are specified for the states of nature:

$$P(1) = 0.1,\ P(2) = 0.4,\ P(3) = 0.3,\ P(4) = 0.2$$

- **(a)** Find the decision that maximizes the expected net dollar return.
- **(b)** Find the decision that minimizes the expected regret.
- **(c)** Comment on the relationship between the answers to parts (a) and (b).

8-4. Consider the payoff table in Table 8.14. Assume that the probabilities of the states of nature are as follows:

$$P(1) = 0.3,\ P(2) = 0.6,\ P(3) = 0.1$$

- **(a)** Find the decision that maximizes the expected net dollar return.
- **(b)** Find the decision that minimizes the expected regret. Suppose that $P(1)$ and $P(2)$ are not known, but $P(3)$ is estimated to be 0.1.
- **(c)** Plot expected net dollar return versus $P(2)$ for the three decisions in the same graph, and find the range for $P(2)$ for which each decision is optimal.
- **(d)** Plot expected regret versus $P(2)$ for the three decisions in the same graph, and find the range for $P(2)$ for which each decision is optimal.
- **(e)** What did you find in the above two answers?

8-5. Phil Johnson of Johnson's Printing in Chicago must decide to either accept a contract for a government printing job or fly to Los Angeles to bid on a brochure. Capacity constraints prohibit him from doing both jobs, and he must decide on the government contract before the bidding process starts. He estimates the payoff table in terms of net dollar return as shown in Table 8.15.
- **(a)** What is the optimal decision based on the maximin criterion?
- **(b)** If the probability that he gets the brochure job is $\frac{1}{3}$, which decision will maximize his expected net dollar return?
- **(c)** Let $P(J)$ be the probability that he gets the brochure job. Plot the expected return for each decision as a function of $P(J)$ on the same axis.
- **(d)** What is the smallest value of $P(J)$ for which Phil Johnson should decide to go to LA if he wishes to maximize his expected net dollar return?

Table 8.15

Decision	STATE OF NATURE: Do Not Get Brochure Job, NJ	Get Brochure Job, J
Accept Government Contract, G	1000	1000
Accept Brochure Job, B	−1000	4000

(e) What is the optimal decision if minimax regret is the decision criterion?
(f) What is the optimal decision if minimize expected regret is the decision criterion and $P(J) = \frac{1}{3}$?
(g) Assume that the purchasing agent for the brochure job has already decided who will receive the bid but Phil doesn't know the result. If Phil believes that $P(J) = \frac{1}{3}$, what is the maximum amount that Phil should pay to have this information?
(h) What would you call the quantity calculated in part (g)?

8-6. A souvenir vendor discovers that sales in July depend heavily on the weather. Products must be ordered in January. The wholesaler offers small, medium, and large variety packs at special prices, and the vendor must decide to buy one of them. The payoff table in terms of net dollar return is shown in Table 8.16. The utility function for money is presented in Figure 8.29. If the vendor believes that each state of nature is equally likely
(a) Which decision maximizes the expected net dollar return?
(b) Which decision maximizes the expected utility?
(c) Explain the relationship between the answers to parts (a) and (b).

Table 8.16

Decision	STATE OF NATURE: Cold	Cool	Warm	Hot
Small	0	1000	2000	3000
Medium	−1000	0	3000	6000
Large	−3000	−1000	4000	8000

FIGURE 8.29

Utility Function

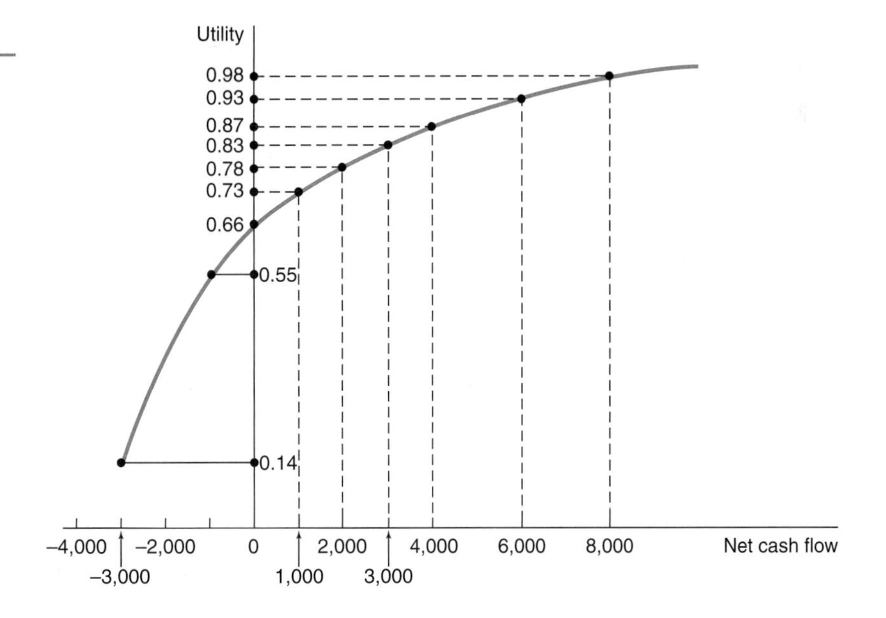

8-7. Phil Johnson of Johnson's Printing (see Problem 8-5) has decided to use the utility function shown in Figure 8.29 to determine if he should bid on the brochure job.

(a) What is the optimal decision if the decision criterion is to maximize the expected net dollar return and the probability of getting the brochure job is $\frac{1}{3}$? What is the expected net dollar return of the optimal decision?

(b) Would you expect the decision to change if the decision criterion is to maximize the expected utility? Discuss.

(c) What is the expected utility of the optimal decision?

(d) What is the utility of the expected dollar return from submitting a bid for the brochure?

(e) What is the expected utility of submitting a bid for the brochure'?

(f) Are the answers to parts (d) and (e) the same? Should they be?

8-8. Assign a utility of 0 to a net cash flow of –$20,000 and a utility of 1 to a net cash flow of $50,000. Create your own utility function by the following steps:

(a) Find equivalent lotteries for net cash flows of $0 and $20,000.

(b) Plot the four points on your utility function, and connect them with straight lines.

(c) On the basis of this utility function, are you risk-averse, risk-seeking, risk-indifferent, or none of the above?

8-9. The customer service manager for Sonorola is responsible for expediting late orders. To do the job effectively, when an order is late the manager must determine if the lateness is caused by an ordering error or a delivery error. If an order is late, one or the other of these two types of errors must have occurred. Because of the way in which this system is designed, both errors cannot occur on the same order. From experience, the manager knows that an ordering error will cause 8 out of 20 deliveries to be late, whereas a delivery error will cause 8 out of 10 deliveries to be late. Historically, out of 1,000 orders, 30 ordering errors and 10 delivery errors have occurred. Assume that an order is late. If the customer service manager wishes to look first for the type of error that has the largest probability of occurring, should it be an ordering error or a delivery error?

8-10. Walter's Dog Show is scheduled to appear in Cedar Rapids on July 10. The profits obtained are heavily dependent on the weather. In particular, if the weather is rainy, the show loses $15,000, and if sunny the show makes a profit of $10,000. (We assume that all days are either rainy or sunny.) Walter can decide to cancel the show, but if he does he forfeits a $1,000 deposit he put down when he accepted the date. The historical record shows that on July 10 it rained $\frac{1}{4}$ of the time in the last 100 years.

(a) What decision should Walter make to maximize his expected net dollar return?

(b) What is the expected value of perfect information?

8-11. Consider the model faced by Walter in Problem 8-10. Walter has the option to purchase a forecast from Victor's Weather Wonder. Victor's accuracy varies. On those occasions when it has rained, he has been correct (i.e., he predicted rain) 90% of the time. On the other hand, when it has been sunny, he has been right (i.e., he predicted sun) only 80% of the time.

(a) If Walter had the forecast, what strategy should he follow to maximize his expected net dollar return?

(b) How much should Walter be willing to pay for the forecast?

8-12. A gambler has an opportunity to play the following two-stage game. At stage 1 he pays $5 and draws a ball at random from an urn containing five white and five red balls. The balls are identical except for color. The player may now quit or move on to play stage 2 at the cost of an additional $10. In stage 2, if a white ball was drawn in stage 1, the player draws a ball at random from a white urn that contains two blue and eight green balls. If a red ball was drawn in stage 1, the player draws a ball at random from a red urn that contains six blue and four green balls. If in stage 2 the player draws a blue ball, the house pays him $35. If he draws a green ball, the house pays him $0. Use a decision tree to determine the optimal strategy for the gambler.

8-13. A certain retail firm places applicants for credit into two categories, bad risks and good risks. Statistics indicate that 10% of the population would be classified as a bad risk by the firm's standards. The firm uses a credit-scoring device to decide whether credit should be granted to an applicant. Experience suggests that if a good risk applies, the person will get credit 90% of the time. If a bad risk applies, credit will be granted 20% of the time. Management believes that it is reasonable to assume that the persons who apply for credit are selected at random from the population. What is the probability that a person granted credit will be a bad risk? (Use Bayes' Theorem.)

BILITY	OVERTIME COST TO JCM
2	$200,000
.7	100,000
.1	0

ATE OF NATURE	
dium Box Office	Large Box Office
$1,000,000	$3,000,000
900,000	900,000

same rate. Larry averages three defective parts per hun-
ne defectives per hundred, respectively.
ct out of 1,000 produced?
part selected at random was produced by Curly?
anufacturer of cellular phone casings made from one of
pting to decide whether to enter the competition to be a
rola. In order to compete, the firm must design a test fix-
e ten casings that Sonorola will test. The cost of develop-
ture and the test casings, is $50,000. If JCM gets the order,
obability 0.4, it will be possible to sell 10,000 items to
the order, the development cost is essentially lost. In order
se its current machines or purchase a new forge. Tooling
) and the per-unit production cost is $20. However, if JCM
f incurring overtime costs. The relationship between over-
business is presented in Table 8.17. The new forge costs
$260,000, including tooling costs for the cellular phone casings. However, with the new forge, JCM would certainly not incur any overtime costs, and the production cost will be only $10 per unit. Use a decision tree to determine the optimal set of actions for JCM.

8-16. Jenny Lind is a writer of romance novels. A movie company and a TV network both want exclusive rights to one of her most popular works. If she signs with the network she will receive a single lump sum, but if she signs with the movie company the amount she will receive depends on the market response to the movie. Jenny's payoffs are summarized in Table 8.18.

If the probability estimates for the states of nature are $P(\text{Small}) = 0.3$, $P(\text{Medium}) = 0.6$, $P(\text{Large}) = 0.1$, to whom should Jenny sell the rights? What is the most Jenny should be willing to pay to learn what the size of the box office would be before she decides with whom to sign?

8-17. Kelly Construction wants to get in on the boom of student condominium construction. The company must decide whether to purchase enough land to build a 100-, 200-, or 300-unit condominium complex. Many other complexes are currently under construction, so Kelly is unsure how strong demand for its complex will be. If the company is conservative and builds only a few units, it loses potential profits if the demand turns out to be high. On the other hand, many unsold units would also be costly to Kelly. Table 8.19 has been prepared, based on three levels of demand.

(a) What is the optimal decision if the maximin criterion is used?
(b) What is the optimal decision if the maximax criterion is used?
(c) What is the optimal decision if the criterion of minimax regret is used?
(d) If $P(\text{Low}) = 0.3$, $P(\text{Medium}) = 0.5$, and $P(\text{High}) = 0.2$, which decision will maximize the expected net dollar return?
(e) What is the expected value of perfect information?

8-18. Marple Manufacturing is planning the introduction of a new product. The cost to set up to manufacture one of the product's components is very high, so Marple is considering purchasing that component rather than manufacturing it. Once set up to manufacture the component, however, Marple's

Table 8.19

Decision	DEMAND Low	Medium	High
Build 50	$400,000	$400,000	$400,000
Build 100	100,000	800,000	800,000
Build 150	–200,000	500,000	1,200,000

variable cost per unit would be low in comparison to the purchase price of the component. Marple's materials manager has calculated the net profit in thousands of dollars for three different levels of demand in Table 8.20. The states of nature have probabilities $P(\text{Low}) = 0.4$, $P(\text{Medium}) = 0.3$, and $P(\text{High}) = 0.3$. Draw a decision tree and use it to decide whether Marple should make or buy the component.

8-19. Chuck drives to a consulting job in Palo Alto on Wednesdays. He returns to San Jose the same day right at the evening rush hour. If he takes Route 280 home he has observed that his travel time is highly variable from one week to the next, but if he takes El Camino his travel time is relatively constant. On the basis of his experience, Chuck has set up the payoff table shown in Table 8.21, which gives his travel time in minutes.
   - **(a)** Chuck estimates that about 90% of the time the traffic will be light. Which route should he take to minimize his expected travel time?
   - **(b)** Chuck's wife Boots gets very worried if he is even a little late in coming home. Which route would you recommend he take now? Explain.

8-20. A small hospital in rural Albemarle County buys blood each month from a distant blood bank. A certain rare blood type must be restocked each month because its shelf life is only one month long. If the order is placed one month in advance, the cost to the hospital is $10 per unit. If the demand for the rare blood type during the month exceeds the supply, it must be special-ordered at a cost of $100 per unit. The demand for the past three years is shown in Table 8.22.
   - **(a)** Develop a payoff table for the hospital.
   - **(b)** How many units should the hospital order each month?

Table 8.20

Decision	DEMAND Low	Medium	High
Make Component	11	32	53
Buy Component	15	30	45

Table 8.21

Decision	STATE OF NATURE Light Traffic	Heavy Traffic
Take 280	25	55
Take El Camino	35	40

Table 8.22

DEMAND	FREQUENCY
0	24 months
1	8
2	4
Total	36 months

8-21. Bob Davidson, head of purchasing at Marple Manufacturing, must decide from which vendor to buy a particular component. Vendor A will supply the components in lots of 1,000 for $10 a unit while Vendor B will charge only $9.50 a unit. However, 20% of the time Vendor B's lots will contain 10% defectives and 80% of the time they will contain 1% defectives, while Vendor A's lots will contain 1% defectives 99% of the time and 3% defectives 1% of the time. The cost of a defective to Marple Manufacturing is $100 due to the high cost of scrapping or reworking the assemblies containing defective components.

(a) Draw a decision tree for this model.

(b) Using the criterion of expected cost, from which vendor should Bob purchase the component?

8-22. Rick O'Shea is an independent trucker operating out of Tucson. He has the option of either hauling a shipment to Denver or hauling a different shipment to Salt Lake. If he chooses the shipment to Denver, he has a 90% chance of finding there a return shipment to Tucson. If he does not find a return shipment he will return to Tucson empty. If he chooses the shipment to Salt Lake, he has a 50% chance of finding a return shipment to Tucson. His payoffs are shown in Table 8.23.

(a) Draw the decision tree for this model.

(b) Using the criterion of expected net dollar return, to which city should Rick go?

8-23. Consider the payoff table shown in Table 8.24.

(a) Which stock would the indifferent investor choose?

(b) Which stock would the optimistic investor choose?

(c) Which stock would the pessimistic investor choose?

(d) Which stock have the highest expected return given the probability of a poor economy is 10%, a good economy is 50% and an excellent economy is 40%?

8-24. A manufacturer of disposable cameras is preparing for the holiday season. Production volumes must be determined to maximize return to the company. The company has used past demand to forecast the probability for demand this season. See Table 8.25 for this data.

If a camera is sold before the holiday, then the contribution margin is $5. If the camera is not sold before the holiday, then the contribution margin is reduced to $1 because the camera will be placed on sale.

(a) Draw the decision tree for this model.

(b) What decision should the manufacturer make?

Table 8.23

	RETURN SHIPMENT	NO RETURN
Salt Lake	$4000	$3500
Denver	3850	3350

Table 8.24

	STATE OF ECONOMY		
Stock	Poor	Good	Excellent
IBM	10	15	18
T	5	15	20
Q	−15	25	45
WFT	−15	0	15

Table 8.25

DEMAND	PROBABILITY
5,000	0.4
9,000	0.6

8-25. A photographer is preparing for a fashion photo shoot at the green sand beach near South Point, Hawaii. The schedule for the photo shoot has been set far in advance and the supermodels involved can only be there on that one day. The National Weather Service has forecasted a 40% chance of rain. Rain would prevent the event from occurring and the photographer would lose $250,000. If the weather is perfect, then the photographer will net $1,000,000.

(a) Should the photographer purchase insurance for the event?

(b) What would be the maximum price he should pay for insurance?

8-26. Fred owns a theater company on Broadway. The company is deciding on two alternative plays for production. The first play, *Dogs*, would cost much less to produce than the other alternative, *Gone with the Snow. Dogs* could be produced for $2 million, while *Gone with the Snow* would take $4 million to produce. However, *Gone with the Snow*, is an epic production that could run many times longer than *Dogs*. See Table 8.26 for all the probabilities and payoffs.

(a) Use a decision tree to determine which production Fred should pursue.

(b) What is Fred's expected return for each production?

8-27. A sculptor can sell his newly created masterpieces to an art dealer for resale at next weekend's art show. The offer from the dealer is for $10,000 for all the sculptures and is good for only a week. The sculptor could pursue selling the sculptures himself on esculpture.com, an auction site for artists. If the bidding is strong the sculptor can receive up to $15,000 for all the sculptures using the auction site. However, if the bidding is weak, then the sculptor may only get $3,000 for his masterpieces. The auction site esculpture.com charges a flat rate of $500 for promoting the sculptor's work and has some past history on the auction process. Probabilities are given in Table 8.27.

(a) Draw the decision tree for this model.

(b) What decision should the sculptor make?

8-28. Biogenetica is a small firm engaged in developing pharmaceuticals. The firm has a limited number of resources and can only develop two new products in the coming year. They have opportunities to develop four new products but must decide which ones would be the best for the firm. Typically new products in this industry have a high failure rate. Information on the payoffs is contained in Table 8.28.

(a) Choose the new products to develop using the Laplace criterion.

(b) Choose the new products to develop using the maximin criterion.

(c) Choose the new products to develop using the maximax criterion.

Table 8.26

	PROBABILITY		PAYOFF	
Level of Success	***Dogs***	***Gone with the Snow***	***Dogs***	***Gone with the Snow***
Hit	0.3	0.4	$5 million	$25 million
Moderate Success	0.3	0.3	$4 million	$15 million
Light Success	0.3	0.2	$2 million	$2 million
Flop	0.1	0.1	$0.5 million	$0.75 million

Table 8.27

BIDDING STRENGTH	PROBABILITY
Strong	0.75
Weak	0.25

Table 8.28

	PAYOFF	
DRUG	**Failure**	**Success**
Alphex	($500,000)	$7,000,000
Flubgone	($1,000,000)	$27,000,000
RidCold	($400,000)	$10,000,000
Hachoo	($700,000)	$17,000,000

Table 8.29

Decision	CARGO REVENUE		SEAT REVENUE	
	Moderate Demand	High Demand	Moderate Demand	High Demand
Cargo Space	$5,000	$7,500	N/A	N/A
Comfort Seating	N/A	N/A	($5,000)	$15,000

8-29. Biogenetica (Problem 8-28) assumes the probability for failure of each drug that it is trying to develop is 80% and the probability of success is 20%.

(a) Which two drugs should they develop to maximize expected return?

(b) Which two drugs should they develop to minimize regret?

8-30. Biogenetica (Problems 8-28 and 8-29) would like to develop RidCold but now it turns out that the product has not survived the decision-making process described in the previous problems. The company can either sell the research up to this point to a larger manufacturer or acquire the resources to continue work on the project. There is a small firm that has compatible resources nearby that could be acquired for $1 million and could be used to complete the project. The research could be sold for $500,000. The probability of a successful introduction of the product is 20% and failure is 80%. Use a decision tree to determine which alternative Biogenetica should pursue.

8-31. Possum Airlines operates in the remote regional airports of the Appalachian Mountains. The company has been struggling with revenue problems and has come up with two alternatives to improve revenue. The first alternative is to modify the seats in their aircraft to allow for more legroom and passenger comfort. The company hopes that this will improve their image and stimulate demand for their flights. The second alternative is to remove seats between the cabin and the cockpit. By removing seats and installing a bulkhead (wall) between passengers and the pilots, the airline can carry more cargo. If the comfort seating change is made, there will be no benefit to the cargo revenue. If the bulkhead is installed, then there is no benefit to seat revenue. The company will base its decision on the benefits of moderate increases or high increases in demand for cargo and seats for both alternatives, shown in Table 8.29.

(a) Which decision is favored by the Laplace criterion?

(b) Which decision is favored by the maximin criterion?

(c) Which decision is favored by the maximax criterion?

Application Problems

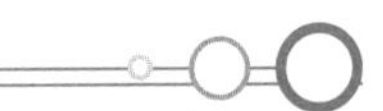

8-32. Assume you are risk-averse and have assigned the following two endpoints on your utility function:

$$U(-30) = 0$$
$$U(70) = 1$$

(a) What is a lower bound on $U(30)$?
Suppose that you are indifferent between a sure payment of 30 and a lottery with a probability of 0.7 of winning 70 and a probability of 0.3 of losing 30.

(b) What is a lower bound on your utility for a sure payment of 50?

(c) What is the smallest upper bound of your utility for a sure payment of 10? HINT: Recall that a utility function is nondecreasing and, if the decision maker is risk-averse, it is concave.

8-33. Assume that you have assigned the following two end points on your utility function:

$$U(-30) = 0$$
$$U(70) = 1$$

Suppose that you are indifferent between a sure payment of 30 and a lottery with a probability of 0.3 of winning 70 and a probability of 0.7 of losing 30. Furthermore, you feel that a sure payment of 10 is equivalent to a gamble with a probability of 0.9 of losing 30 and a probability of 0.1 of winning 30.

(a) How can you describe your utility function? Are you a "risk-taker"?

(b) What are upper and lower bounds on $U(50)$?

(c) What are upper and lower bounds on $U(25)$?

8-34. The Scrub Professional Cleaning Service receives preliminary sales contracts from two sources: (1) its own agent and (2) building managers. Historically, $\frac{1}{4}$ of the contracts have come from Scrub agents and $\frac{3}{4}$ from building managers. Unfortunately, not all preliminary contracts result in actual sales contracts. Actually, only $\frac{3}{8}$ of those preliminary contracts received from building managers result in a sale, whereas $\frac{7}{8}$ of those received from Scrub agents result in a sale. The net return to Scrub from a sale is $1,000. The cost of processing and following up on a preliminary contract that does not result in a sale is $150.

(a) What is the probability that a preliminary contract leads to a sale? What is the expected return associated with a preliminary sales contract?

(b) Which party, agents or building managers, contributes more to the expected return?

Scrub keeps all of its sales filed by the source of reference: that is, it maintains one file for sales resulting from preliminary contracts submitted by Scrub agents and another for sales resulting from preliminary contracts submitted by building managers. Scrub knows that John Jones holds one of its sales contracts, and it wishes to have more information about him.

(c) Which file should it search first to have the higher probability of finding his name?

8-35. Clyde's Coal Company sells coal by the $\frac{1}{2}$-ton, 1-ton, or 2-ton load. The probability is 0.20 that an order is from town A, 0.30 from town B, and 0.50 from town C. The relative frequency of the number of orders of each size from each town is shown in Table 8.30.

(a) What is the probability that an order will be for $\frac{1}{2}$ ton?

(b) If an order is for $\frac{1}{2}$ ton, what is the probability that it came from town A? Clyde makes a different amount of profit on each type of load of coal in each city. The profit figures are shown in Table 8.31.

(c) Find the expected profit per load for Clyde.

8-36. It is January 1 and Justin Case, chief counsel for Chemgoo, is faced with a difficult challenge. It seems that the firm has two related lawsuits for patent infringement. For each suit, the firm has the option of going to trial or settling out of court. The trial date for one of the suits, which we will cleverly identify as suit 1, is scheduled for July 15 and the second (suit 2, of course) is scheduled for January 8, next year. Preparation costs for either trial are estimated at $10,000. However, if the firm prepares for both trials, the preparation costs of the second trial will be only $6,000. These costs can be avoided by settling out of court. If the firm wins suit 1, it pays no penalty. If it loses, it pays a $200,000 penalty. Lawyers for the firm assess the probability of winning suit 1 as 0.5. The firm has the option to settle out of court for $100,000. Suit 2 can be settled out of court for a cost of $60,000. Otherwise, a trial will result in one of three possible outcomes: (1) The suit is declared invalid and the firm pays no penalty; (2) the suit is found valid but with no infringement, and the firm pays a penalty of $50,000; or (3) the suit is found valid with infringement, and the firm pays a penalty of $90,000. The likelihood of these outcomes depends in general on the result of suit 1. The judge will certainly view suit 1 as an important precedent. The lawyers' assessment of the probability of the

Table 8.30

Relative Frequencies of Number of Orders for Each Town

Town	LOAD SIZE (TONS) ½	1	2
A	0.50	0.00	0.50
B	0.00	0.50	0.50
C	0.25	0.75	0.00

Table 8.31

Profit in Dollars per Load

Town	LOAD SIZE (TONS) ½	1	2
A	100	190	370
B	90	200	360
C	70	130	270

Table 8.32

OUTCOMES	NO INFORMATION CONCERNING SUIT 1[a]	FIRM WINS SUIT 1	FIRM LOSES SUIT 1
Invalid	0.3	0.7	0.1
Valid, No infringement	0.3	0.2	0.5
Valid, Infringement	0.4	0.1	0.4

[a] That is, suit 1 is settled out of court

three possible outcomes of suit 2 under three sets of possible conditions (relating to suit 1) are presented in Table 8.32.

(a) Represent the firm's model with a decision tree.
(b) Solve the decision tree, and find the optimal strategy for the firm.
(c) What is the expected loss that the firm will incur if it follows the optimal strategy?
(d) What decisions would be made if the firm treated each suit independently, ignoring any interactions between the two? What is the expected savings from the decision analysis of this scenario?
HINT: Since all the figures are costs, you may find it easier to work with the cost figures and minimize the expected cost.

8-37. Jenny Lind's payoff table (Problem 8-16) is given in Table 8.33.
She may hire a market research firm to conduct a survey at a cost of $100,000. The result of the survey would be either a favorable (F) or unfavorable (U) public response to the movie. The firm's ability to assess the market as measured by conditional probabilities is

$P(F|\text{Small}) = .3$ $\quad$ $P(U|\text{Small}) = .7$

$P(F|\text{Medium}) = .6$ $\quad$ $P(U|\text{Medium}) = .4$

$P(F|\text{Large}) = .8$ $\quad$ $P(U|\text{Large}) = .2$

(a) Draw the decision tree for this model.
(b) Should Jenny have the survey conducted? How should she use the results of the survey?
(c) What is the EVSI? What is the most Jenny should be willing to pay for the survey?

8-38. Kelly Construction (Problem 8-17) wants to reduce the uncertainty about the number of units it should build. It has decided to conduct a survey, which will result in one of three measures of demand: M_1, weak; M_2, moderate; M_3, strong. The payoff table is shown in Table 8.34. The reliabilities are given in Table 8.35.

(a) Draw the decision tree for this model.
(b) What is Kelly's optimal strategy?
(c) What is the EVSI? Compare it with the EVPI by computing the ratio EVSI/EVPI and noting that the most this ratio could be is 1.

Table 8.33

	STATE OF NATURE		
Decision	Small Box Office	Medium Box Office	Large Box Office
Sign with Movie Company	$200,000	$1,000,000	$3,000,000
Sign with TV Network	900,000	900,000	900,000
Probability	0.3	0.6	0.1

Table 8.34

	DEMAND		
Decision	Low, D_1	Medium, D_2	High, D_3
Build 100, B_1	$500,000	$ 500,000	$ 500,000
Build 200, B_2	0	1,000,000	1,000,000
Build 300, B_3	–700,000	400,000	1,500,000
Probability	0.3	0.5	0.2

Table 8.35

	$P(M_j \mid D_i)$		
	D_1	D_2	D_3
M_1	.7	.3	.1
M_2	.2	.4	.3
M_3	.1	.3	.6

Table 8.36

	DEMAND		
Order Quantity	**0, D_1**	**1, D_2**	**2, D_3**
0, Q_1	0	100	200
1, Q_2	10	10	110
2, Q_3	20	20	20
Probability	$\frac{2}{3}$	$\frac{2}{9}$	$\frac{1}{9}$

Table 8.37

	$P(S_j \mid D_i)$		
	D_1	D_2	D_3
S_1	.95	.05	.02
S_2	.04	.8	.08
S_3	.01	.15	.9

8-39. The payoff table for the hospital in Albemarle County (Problem 8-20) is given in Table 8.36. The hospital administrator has decided to check the scheduled surgeries each month to see if there will be any operations requiring the rare blood type. He may find that there are no scheduled surgeries (S_1), one scheduled surgery (S_2), or two scheduled surgeries (S_3), requiring the rare blood type. The conditional probabilities are given in Table 8.37.
(a) Draw the decision tree for this model.
(b) What is the EVSI?
(c) How much can the administrator expect to save each month by checking the surgery schedule?

8-40. Jim, a retired geologist, has developed a software program for predicting the presence of oil based on geological surveys and seismic images. The software uses sophisticated algorithms that greatly improve the accuracy of the prediction over existing methods. Jim can sell the software rights to Dundee Software Services for \$100,000 or he can market the software himself. If he chooses to market the software himself, then his payoff will be determined by the success of the software in the marketplace. Jim has surveyed the market and has determined that there is a 15% chance of having major success, a 70% chance of moderate success, and a 15% chance of failure. If he has major success selling the software, he estimates his payoff to be \$350,000. Moderate success is estimated to have a payoff of \$80,000 and failure of the software in the marketplace would cost Jim \$110,000.
(a) Draw a decision tree for this model.
(b) What should Jim do and why?

8-41. The Riskless Insurance Company owns an office building in downtown San Francisco. The office building is presently vacant. Riskless can lease the property to the Well-Managed Property Management Corporation for a percentage of the rent that Well-Managed would receive from occupants. The present value of the revenue stream to Riskless is based on the success of Well-Managed renting office space. If Well-Managed is very successful, then the present value of the lease would be \$10,000,000. If Well-Managed is moderately successful, then the present value would be \$7,000,000. And if Well-Managed isn't successful, the present value of the lease would be

$2,000,000. Riskless has another alternative. Well-Managed has offered to purchase the property for $6,500,000. Assume all random events are equally likely to occur.

(a) Draw a decision tree for this model.
(b) Determine which alternative Riskless should take.

8-42. Pole Mountain Fly Rods manufactures high-quality fly rods for the serious angler. They presently have an old machine for making the rods. Over the next two years, the machine will probably need to be repaired. Each time it is repaired, the firm will have to pay $25,000 for the repairs. For the next two years, the manufacturing manager has estimated that the probability for the number of failures the machine might experience. An alternative to repairing the machine would be to purchase a used machine. A used machine still would have the potential for requiring repairs but the probability for error lower. Each repair of the used machine would also cost $25,000. A third alternative is to purchase a new machine for $100,000. The new machine is guaranteed to not have a failure.

(a) Draw the decision tree for this model.
(b) What is the best decision for Pole Mountain Fly Rods?
(c) What new machine cost would require Pole Mountain to change the decision?
(d) What repair cost would require Pole Mountain to change the decision?

Case Study Johnson's Composite Materials

Shirley Johnson, president of Johnson's Composite Materials (JCM), is facing the decision presented in Problem 8-19, but a new element has entered the picture. Shirley has the opportunity to hire Compal, a consulting firm that does what it calls "competitive analysis." In particular, in this situation Compal offers to do a detailed study of the other firms that will compete to supply cellular phone casings to Sonorola. After the analysis, Compal will report to JCM that conditions for JCM to get the contract are either encouraging or discouraging.

Compal states that, if conditions are encouraging, then JCM will get the Sonorola contract with probability equal to 0.5. On the other hand, Compal states that, if conditions are discouraging, the probability that JCM will get the Sonorola contract is only 0.35. At this time Compal states that the probability of encouraging and discouraging conditions are equally likely. Compal charges $1,000 for its services.

Shirley asks Linus Drawer, her assistant, to determine if JCM should hire Compal. Indeed she asks Linus to determine the optimal strategy.

Linus prepares the decision tree for the model and by working back through it, determines that the optimal strategy is

1. Hire Compal to do the study
2. If conditions are encouraging
   a. Build the test fixture
   b. If JCM gets the order, use current tools
3. If conditions are discouraging
   a. Build the test fixture
   b. If JCM gets the order, use current tools

He makes an appointment to discuss the results with Shirley. The meeting proceeds as follows:

SHIRLEY: Linus! I see the decision tree and I'm duly impressed, but the result doesn't make any sense. Why should I pay Compal $1,000 if we take the same action no matter what it says?

LINUS: Surely, Shirley, you don't mean that the analysis did not make a difference. I understand that your statement holds now that the analysis is complete, but how would you have known what strategy to follow without the decision tree?

SHIRLEY: Linus! You missed my point! No matter what costs or probabilities are involved, I say that we should build the test fixture, and then use the current tools if we get the order. This simply has to be a better strategy than to hire Compal and then do the same thing no matter what it says.

LINUS: I understand, but I know I've done the decision tree right, so I don't know what to tell you.

SHIRLEY: I don't have the time or interest to check the details of your analysis. All I know is that I want to make a decision about Compal tomorrow morning and I want to have an answer that makes sense. Your job is to provide me with that answer.

Questions

1. Is Shirley right; that is, is it impossible for Linus' strategy to be optimal?
2. Is Linus right; that is, is his analysis correct given the data at his disposal?
3. Assume Linus' role; that is, it is now your job to provide Shirley with an answer that makes sense.

Case Study | To Drill or Not to Drill

Terri Underhill has recently been assigned to the economic analysis section of Global Oil. Prescot Oil has just offered to buy the Burns Flat lease from Global for $15,000 and Terri has been assigned the task of preparing Global's response. The Burns Flat lease gives Global the right to explore for oil under 320 acres of land in western Oklahoma. Terri must recommend either to sell the lease or to drill.

If Global drills, the results are uncertain. On the basis of drilling records in western Oklahoma and current market prices, Terri prepares a table showing the possible outcomes, the probability of each outcome, and the net return to Global (Table 8.38).

Terri, however, knows that she does not have to make the decision simply on the basis of historical records. DRI, Drilling Resource, Inc., will perform a test for $6,000 to determine the underground formation of the Burns Flat terrain. The test will indicate which of three categories (plate, varied, or ridge) best describes the underground structure. The conditional probabilities of the possible outcomes vary with the underground structure. Table 8.39 shows the results of the last 50 tests.

If the test is taken, the opportunity to sell the lease is forfeited. The market for oil leases understands that a decision to sell after the test has been performed indicates that drilling does not appear to be profitable.

Questions

1. On the basis of these data, should Global drill or sell the lease?
2. What is the most that Global should pay in advance to know what the outcome of drilling would be?
3. Use a decision tree to determine the optimal strategy for Global (test or not, drill or sell lease, etc.).
4. What is the expected return associated with the optimal policy?
5. What is the maximum *additional* amount that Global should be willing to pay DRI for the test?

Table 8.38

POSSIBLE OUTCOMES	PROBABILITY	NET RETURN
Dry Well	0.2	–100,000
Gas Well	0.4	40,000
Oil and Gas	0.3	90,000
Oil Well	0.1	200,000

Table 8.39

TEST RESULT/ OUTCOME	PLATE	VARIED	RIDGE	TOTAL
Dry	8	2	0	10
Gas	2	16	2	20
Gas and Oil	0	14	1	15
Oil	0	0	5	5
	10	32	8	50

Case Study | Shumway, Horch and Sager (A)[1]

Claire Christensen was involved in a new project in her second year with the management consulting firm of Shumway, Horch, and Sager (SHS). It appeared to be another situation in which she was expected to jump quickly out of the blocks with the project and make some clever money-saving recommendation, then find the follow-on project to produce next month's billable days.

The client was an organization of magazine publishers that had become aware of the large amounts of money being wasted printing copies that were not sold. Industry practice had been always to print and deliver to newsstands more magazines than would be needed. The practice ensured that every customer requesting a copy at the newsstand could have one, thereby keeping numbers high for both newsstand circulation and advertising revenues. It also produced a phenomenal number of unsold copies. SHS was hired to look into this practice and make some recommendations for improved procedures.

Another related issue was the establishment of a rate base. This was the amount of copies that *Good Housekeeping* guaranteed selling each month and was used to determine the

[1] This case is to be used as the basis for class discussion rather than to illustrate either the effective or ineffective handling of an administrative situation. ©1990, Darden Graduate Business School Foundation. Preview Darden case abstracts on the World Wide Web at www.darden.virginia.edu/publishing.

advertising rates. If they did not meet the base value, they would refund an amount proportional to the shortage. If they exceeded the base, they were not able to go back and collect more advertising revenues.

Christensen thought saving money on production would be assured, provided she could find a way to forecast each issue's sales. She started on this task by picking the magazine *Good Housekeeping* and probing whether she could forecast January 1988 sales using previous data. She had obtained data on total circulation over the past nine years (July 1979–June 1988) from the Publisher's Statement to the Audit Bureau of Circulation (see SHSA.XLS). Without looking at this information, she tucked away the last 6 months of data to use later to test her methods of forecasting. The first $8\frac{1}{2}$ years of data (through December 1987) are shown in Table 8.40. She was aware that about 10 million copies of this magazine were generally printed.

Christensen pondered how time patterns in past sales might help her predict the sales of a future issue. (See Exhibit 1 for a graph of the circulation data.) *Good Housekeeping* was not a magazine that she read, but she had seen it while waiting for the dentist, and her aunt had it in her house. She knew that the December issue greatly increased newsstand sales because of its holiday recipes and gift-giving ideas. The January issue always seemed to be low, because people evidently felt like they had overspent and overeaten during the holidays and were trying to cut back. Changes in the interests of purchasers and in the content of the magazine were also important forces that could gradually move the sales up or down over time.

Once Christensen had the best forecast, the next question was whether to produce the forecast amount or a higher or lower amount. Unsold magazines were generally worthless when the next issue hit the newsstand. She knew this particular magazine sold for $1.95 at the newsstand, but she only had

TABLE 8.40 Shumway, Horch, and Sager (A)

DATE	OBS. #	CIRCULATION	DATE	OBS. #	CIRCULATION	DATE	OBS. #	CIRCULATION
Jul 79	1	5264165		35	5367404		69	5253739
	2	5313127		36	5316957		70	5138210
	3	5117969	Jul 82	37	5412745		71	5251664
	4	5098771		38	5387779		72	5450869
	5	5187708		39	5439224	Jul 85	73	5022522
	6	5645295		40	5341392		74	5206132
Jan 80	7	5023173		41	5396853		75	5042725
	8	5333352		42	5961612		76	5096277
	9	5224234	Jan 83	43	5335737		77	5067717
	10	5079207		44	5618540		78	5508198
	11	5167277		45	5604606	Jan 86	79	5133963
	12	5006445		46	5343116		80	5180897
Jul 80	13	5150974		47	5294990		81	5161222
	14	5180346		48	5327995		82	5174238
	15	5223467		49	5177176		83	5047775
	16	5153303	Jul 83	50	5290109		84	5152063
	17	5247109		51	5449099	Jul 86	85	5001222
	18	5789798		52	5344570		86	5232314
Jan 81	19	5350502		53	5334053		87	5235207
	20	5371371		54	5763516		88	5009584
	21	5327700	Jan 84	55	5198585		89	5352370
	22	5269993		56	5501741		90	5498755
	23	5240438		57	5329592	Jan 87	91	5159840
	24	5273266		58	5322838		92	5274075
Jul 81	25	5439920		59	5178815		93	5179002
	26	5378584		60	5247590		94	5269295
	27	5329516	Jul 84	61	5194827		95	5005048
	28	5292129		62	5118408		96	5166569
	29	5378127		63	5291564	Jul 87	97	5068848
	30	5736465		64	5047946		98	5007388
Jan 82	31	5073651		65	5105056		99	5265191
	32	5553245		66	5448542		100	5046595
	33	5439363	Jan 85	67	5023818		101	5300978
	34	5363948		68	5099829		102	5526153

Good Housekeeping Circulation Figures (July 1979–December 1987)

EXHIBIT 1

Graph of *Good Housekeeping* Total Sales over Time

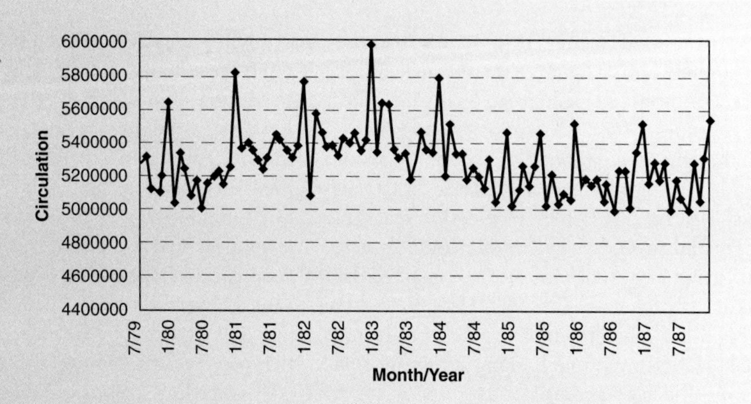

an estimate of the variable costs to produce the magazine ($.70) and the price to the wholesaler ($1.20) and the price from the wholesaler to the newsstand operator ($1.50). There was no risk to the retailer or the wholesaler, because they could return for full price any magazines not sold.

Just as Christensen was going to dive into the calculations, a representative from *Good Housekeeping* called and said they had just been given the opportunity to raise their advertising rate base from its current level of 4.78 million copies. The representative said they had already planned to use a new value effective August 1, but now he wanted to know if they should raise it one month early. The rate base was used as follows:

Advertising revenue equaled $1*the rate base, but there was a contingent penalty. If circulation was less than the rate base, they must make up the advertising in an amount equal to $1.25 in value for every impression they were off.

The new rate base talked about was 5.1 million and again the decision rested upon a forecast of circulation. Christensen knew that she would quickly have to find the best method of forecasting based on the 8.5 years of data she had, then test the method on the 6 months of data she had held out (see Table 8.41), and then hopefully apply the same method for July 1988.

TABLE 8.41 Shumway, Horch, and Sager (A)

HOLD-OUT DATA	
Obs. #	Circulation
103	5012276
104	5056537
105	5061844
106	5005226
107	5000500
108	5030805

Questions

1. Assume that the distribution of demand (circulation) for July 1988 is as follows:

Circulation	Probability
4857K	0.2
4932K	0.2
4983K	0.2
5034K	0.2
5109K	0.2

   Should Claire recommend to raise the rate base one month early? Why?

2. Assume that the forecast of demand for January 1988 is a normal distribution with mean of 5,082,329 and standard deviation of 98,324. How many copies of the magazine should be printed?

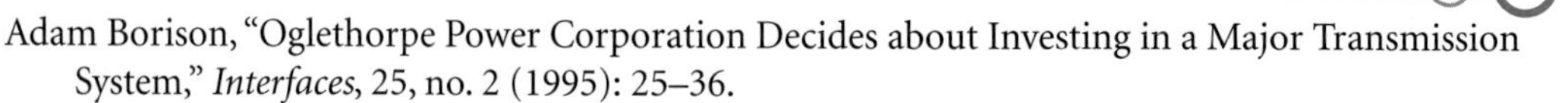

References

Adam Borison, "Oglethorpe Power Corporation Decides about Investing in a Major Transmission System," *Interfaces*, 25, no. 2 (1995): 25–36.

Mark Brown, "Evaluation of Vision Correction Alternatives for Myopic Adults," *Interfaces*, 27, no. 2 (1997): 66–84.

Ron Howard, "Heathens, Heretics, and Cults: The Religious Spectrum of Decision Aiding," *Interfaces*, 22, no. 6 (1992): 15–27.

Ralph Keeney, "Decision Analysis: An Overview," *Operations Research*, 30, no. 5 (1982): 803–838.

Ralph Keeney, *Value-Focused Thinking* (Cambridge, MA: Harvard University Press, 1992).

Ralph Keeney and Howard Raiffa, *Decisions with Multiple Objectives: Preferences and Value Tradeoffs* (New York: Wiley, 1976).

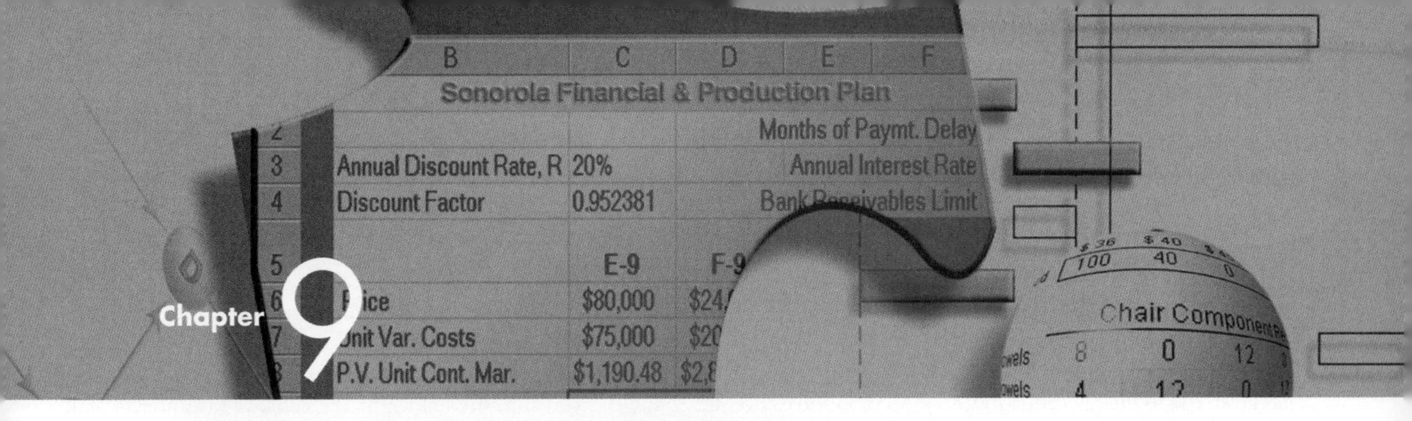

MONTE CARLO SIMULATION

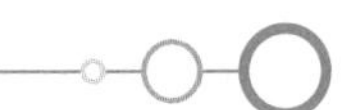

CHAPTER OUTLINE

APPLICATION CAPSULE AT&T's Call Processing Simulator

In the mid and late 1970s, there were some technology changes that made it much easier to use 1-800 phone number services for marketing purposes. It became the way America shops—it has become the front door for about $200 billion in sales. This has given rise to the call center industry. An inbound call center consists of: telecommunications lines carrying telephone calls to a specific location, switching machines to sort and allocate calls, and agents who receive the calls. The primary purpose of the inbound center would be to receive calls for catalog purchases or for airline or hotel reservations, to handle customer service questions, and so forth. There are also outbound call centers like those used for telemarketing.

The call center concept has evolved into an $8 billion service industry linking customers, businesses, and a long-distance carrier, like AT&T. In 1993, roughly 350,000 businesses employ 6.5 million people in call center environments. These centers have enjoyed 20% annual growth rates through the 1990s and are forecasted to continue double digit growth through 2000. Several factors have contributed to this trend: less discretionary time for consumer shopping, more single-head-of-household and dual-income families, increased cost of face-to-face selling, and deregulation of the telecommunications industry. A recent legislative change, called 800 portability, allows businesses to keep their same 800 number even if they switch long-distance carriers. This has greatly increased the competition in this field.

The costs of labor and communications associated with these call centers have increased and businesses are attempting to improve their call centers' ability to serve their callers. Therefore AT&T introduced a simulation model to study various operating scenarios for their existing as well as potential clients. Many factors must be considered by such a model, such as staffing, the length of the calls, the number of 800 lines, the hours of operation, and busy signals. Another reality that must be modeled is the behavior of the caller. If a caller is put on hold, some will immediately hang up, others will wait for a short period of time, and others will wait a very long time for an agent to get to them. For those that abandon the call, some will try to call again, while others will take their business to a competitor. The initial simulation model AT&T developed was for a major airline reservation center. Because of its great success, AT&T decided to develop a standard simulation model, based on a PC, that could be used as a sales-support tool.

A specific example of a success story concerns Northwest Airlines, who implemented the recommended results of such a simulation study to increase by 20% the number of calls answered, with 20% fewer agent hours and 27% less overtime, with the bottom-line result being a 5% increase in booked revenue for the airline. Over 2000 simulation studies were done in 1992, with the cumulative effect that AT&T increased or regained more than $1 billion out of the $8 billion in the 800-network market. In addition, the business customers involved in implementing these studies increased their annual profits by more than $750 million. (See Brigandi et al.)

9.1 INTRODUCTION

Many people believe that "experience is the best teacher." Unfortunately, it is often too costly (in time or money) to obtain real experience. This dilemma provides a primary motivation for the use of simulation: to find a quick, inexpensive way to acquire the knowledge that is usually gained through experience.

The basic idea of simulation is to build an experimental device, or **simulator**, that will "act like" (simulate) the system of interest in certain important aspects in a quick, cost-effective manner.

The goal is to create an environment in which information about possible alternative actions can be obtained through experimentation. The use of simulation is fundamental to many applied experiments; for example,

- Testing of medicine on laboratory animals. Here the animal responses *simulate* human responses.
- Driving automobiles on test tracks. Here the test track *simulates* the environment the auto will face.

- Testing wing designs for airplanes in wind tunnels. The wind tunnel *simulates* flight conditions.
- Training airline pilots in actual cabins with *simulated* out-of-the-window displays under *simulated* conditions.

In the context of quantitative analysis, simulation has come to mean experimentation based on a mathematical model. Although simulation and optimization (e.g., by means of LP) both use quantitative models, they are based on very different concepts. The fundamental difference lies in the role of decision variables in the two approaches.

Simulation versus optimization

- In an optimization model the values of the decision variables are *outputs.* That is, the model provides a set of values for the decision variables that maximizes (or minimizes) the value of the objective function.
- In a **simulation model** the values of the decision variables are *inputs.* The model evaluates the objective function for a particular set of values.

To see what this means, consider the following example. Suppose that a supermarket wants to decide how to assign checkout personnel (checkers and baggers) during the weekend. The goal is to minimize labor cost, subject to the restrictions imposed by the labor contract and the constraint that customers should not have to wait too long.

If we had an optimization model, we would need to supply the model parameters. Perhaps these would be quantities such as the arrival rate of customers, the distribution of time it takes to check out a customer with and without the use of a bagger, and so on. When the model was solved, the answer would include the best way to assign personnel, the corresponding value of the objective function (the total cost), and an indication as to whether there was slack in any of the constraints. We have seen this approach many times in the mathematical programming sections of this text.

In a simulation model, the inputs would include the parameters we described above (customer arrival rates and the like), an expression for the objective function (total costs), and *a possible assignment of personnel.* The model would produce a specific set of results showing how well the solution performed by various measures, such as total cost, customer waiting time, staff utilization, and so on. In general, the model measures the *quality* of the suggested solution as well as how much variability there might be in the various performance measures due to randomness in the inputs. Simulation allows for a lot of experimentation and interaction with the modeler, but it will not necessarily optimize the goal of interest. The simulator is usually a much cheaper and faster way to experiment with many factors of interest.

WHEN SHOULD SIMULATION BE USED?

From this brief description, it seems as if no one would ever want to use a simulation model. Why not use a model that always yields the best answer, that is, an optimization model? Indeed, in the past simulation was often seen as the technique of last resort, to be used only when analytical methods failed. It is true that if an analytical model is available, exact results can be obtained quickly, and often an optimizing procedure can be used to determine the optimal results. However, simulation today is one of the most frequently used tools of quantitative analysis. Why are simulation models so popular?

1. First, analytical models may be difficult or impossible to obtain, depending on complicating factors. What a complicating factor is depends on the specific model. Complicating factors for capital budgeting models include random demand. Complicating factors for queuing models are nonexponential random variables, while complicating factors for inventory models are multiple stocking points or locations.

2. Analytical models typically predict only average or "steady-state" (long-run) behavior. In real-world models, however, it is often important to understand the possible variability in the performance measures, or how the performance measures vary in the short run.
3. Simulation can be performed with a great variety of software, from spreadsheets alone (Excel, Lotus) to spreadsheet add-ins (Crystal Ball, @Risk) to general computer programming languages (PASCAL, C++) to special-purpose simulation languages (SIMAN). As simulation models can now be created and run on a PC or a workstation, the level of computing and mathematical skill required to design and run a useful simulator has been substantially reduced. It is now quite reasonable to build and use a simulator even when it is clear that an analytic (optimization) model could be constructed with more time and effort.

The ability of simulation models to deal with complexity, capture the variability of performance measures, and reproduce short-run behavior make simulation a powerful tool.

SIMULATION AND RANDOM VARIABLES

Simulation models are often used to analyze a *decision under risk*—that is, a model in which the behavior of one or more factors is not known with certainty. There are many examples: demand for a product during the next month, the return on an investment, the number of trucks that will arrive to be unloaded tomorrow between 8:00 and 9:00 A.M., and so on. In such cases the factor that is not known with certainty is thought of as a **random variable**. The behavior of a random variable is described by a **probability distribution**. (Perhaps at this point we should remind you that we assume some knowledge of probability theory in this section of the book. The basic information you will need, including the definition of a probability distribution and some examples, is contained in Appendix A.) This type of simulation is sometimes called a **Monte Carlo method**, after the roulette wheels in Monte Carlo, which can be seen as devices for generating uncertain or random events. Let us look at several examples of this approach.

Design of Docking Facilities A typical model is illustrated in Figure 9.1. Here trucks, perhaps of various sizes carrying different types of loads, arrive at a warehouse to be unloaded. The uncertainties are when a truck will arrive, what kind and size of load it will be carrying, and how long it will take to unload. In modeling these uncertainties, each

FIGURE 9.1

Truck Docking Model

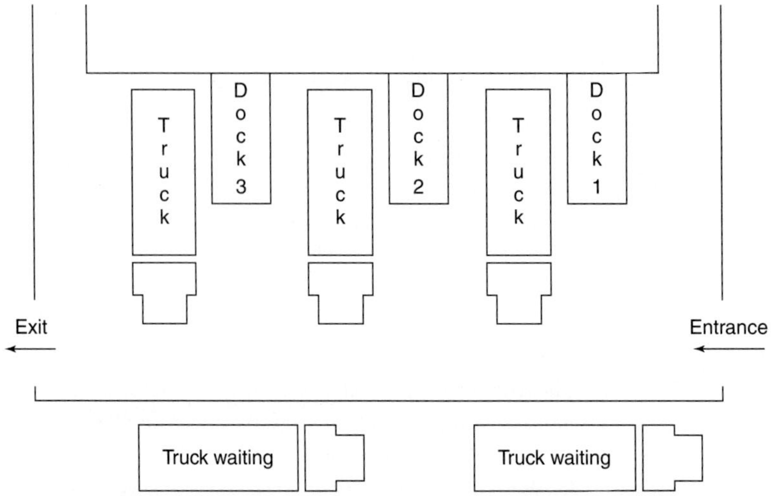

uncertain quantity would be a random variable characterized by a probability distribution. Here planners must address a variety of design questions:

- How many docks should be built?
- What type and quantity of material-handling equipment are required?
- How many workers are required over what periods of time?

The design of the unloading dock will affect its cost of construction and operation. This cost can be reduced by building fewer docks, buying less material-handling equipment, and hiring fewer personnel. However, these options will increase the amount of time it takes to unload the trucks and the amount of time a truck has to wait before unloading begins. Management must balance the cost of acquiring and using the various resources against the cost of having trucks wait to be unloaded.

A similar model of designing docking facilities for oil tankers is important to the oil companies because of the high cost of having a supertanker full of oil waiting for an open dock. Such models are in the formal domain of "queuing models" (waiting lines), described in Chapter 15. To be solved by the methods of that chapter, however, queuing models must meet certain strict assumptions. If the arrival and service times can be described by the *exponential distribution*, then the analytical results of Chapter 15 may be used to predict waiting times and other characteristics of the system. (The exponential distribution is discussed later in this chapter, as well as in Appendix A.) If, however, this distribution is not a good fit, or if there are other complexities in the model that don't fit the standard assumptions, then it may be difficult or impossible to obtain analytic results. Then simulation would have to be used.

Determination of Inventory Control Policies Simulation can be and is used to study a variety of models in the general area of inventory control. One such model is illustrated in Figure 9.2. In this system, the factory produces goods that are sent to the warehouses to satisfy customer demand. Assume that daily demand at each warehouse is a random variable. Shipping times from the factory to a warehouse may also be random. Here some of the operational questions are:

- When should a warehouse reorder from the factory and how much?
- How much stock should the factory maintain to satisfy the orders of the warehouses?

The main costs here are the cost of holding inventory, the cost of shipping goods from the factory to the warehouses, and the cost of not being able to satisfy customer demand at a warehouse. Because the demands at the warehouses are uncertain, unless a warehouse maintains an unreasonably high inventory, there will be times when it will not be able to meet all customer demand. An alternative to high inventories would be to have frequent shipments to the warehouses from the factory. This would keep inventory at the warehouse low, but now the shipping cost would be high. As in the inventory models with known demand, management's objective is to find a stocking and ordering policy that keeps the total of holding plus shipping cost low while meeting a desired fraction of the customers' demands at the warehouses. Another way simulation might be used in the inventory area is

FIGURE 9.2

Distribution System

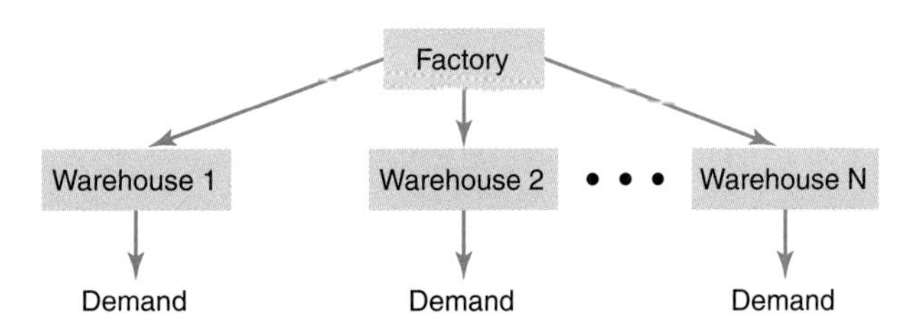

to see what the "worst case" might be in terms of stockouts and to develop a policy that will cover the company 99% of the time.

This model is in the domain of inventory theory. Most analytic results in inventory theory are for a single item stocked at a single location. Multi-item, multi-location models like the one above are much more difficult to analyze, and so are often attacked with simulation. This chapter will discuss how to perform simulation either using the spreadsheet alone or using the two most popular spreadsheet add-ins (Crystal Ball and @Risk).

To gain a fuller understanding of the nature of simulation we will next discuss how to generate the random variables (e.g., demand) and then develop a Monte Carlo simulation of a capital budgeting model. After seeing what is involved in performing this basic simulation, we will analyze by simulation the Foslins' Housewares model. In Foslins, we will be able to compare the simulation approach and the analytic approach. Next, we'll study an airline overbooking model as found in a typical service industry setting, and then a capacity balancing model as found in a typical manufacturing setting. Finally, we will tackle the interesting topic of optimization under uncertainty, combining elements of earlier chapters with the material from this chapter.

APPLICATION CAPSULE Robot Riddle: Simulation Helps GM of Canada to Automate Its Auto Assembly

General Motors of Canada has committed over $2 billion to automating its production facilities. An example of this approach is the GM assembly plant in Oshawa, Ontario. The plant is designed to produce hundreds of cars per shift, using over 600 industrial robots to perform various welding, loading, and assembly tasks. In addition, 1,200 automatic guided vehicles (AGVs) will be used to transport cars and parts through various phases of assembly.

AGVs can handle a wide variety of loads, following a path selected by the user. They are controlled by a microprocessor and receive commands through a network of antennae and receivers embedded in the floor. The use of AGVs instead of the familiar conveyer belt has enabled GM to break the assembly line into small work groups, each with the ability to control its own work speed.

The implementation of such an automated, integrated assembly system is very complex. Each component must be tested first in isolation and then as part of an integrated working unit. Any changes in such a unit tend to be costly and time-consuming. It is therefore crucial to have a fast and inexpensive way of evaluating different work configurations. Simulation provides such a tool.

GM performed a simulation study to analyze one important section of the plant—the AGV body-framing system. The basic layout of this section has 100 work stations, each capable of independent operation. Only three of the 28 work stations devoted to actual processing are operated by humans. AGVs are used to deliver heavy parts to machines at each station. The finished product is a fully welded, framed auto body lacking only doors, hood, front fenders, and trunk lid.

The computer simulation investigated such questions as

- What is the system's maximum production rate? Could a reliable throughput of 525 cars/shift be achieved?
- Where could "parking" spots for idle AGVs most effectively be located to avoid bottlenecks?
- What is the sensitivity of the system to increased equipment failure or faster machine cycle time?
- How many AGVs are needed to make production quotas?

This last question was of particular importance—too few carriers starve the system, while too many choke it. Moreover, at $50,000 each, AGVs are a major cost element.

Thirteen configurations of the framing line were modeled, with the number of AGVs ranging from 54 to 79. Each configuration was simulated in 20 separate runs of an 8.5 hour shift (including breaks and lunch). The runs took only 15 to 20 minutes each on a PC. The study found that the maximum throughput of 630 cars was obtained using 74 AGVs. However, if the aim was simply to achieve the target figure of 525 cars, this could be realized at least 99% of the time using only 42 to 44 AGVs.

The simulation model also investigated the sensitivity of the production system to an increase in the failure rate of the three most important work stations and to changes in the cycle time of the automated processes. Neither factor was found to have a very marked effect on throughput, indicating that the system was both fairly stable and robust.

This study, which required few resources, provided valuable information to help management with an important capital budgeting decision. (See Bookbinder and Kotwa.)

9.2 GENERATING RANDOM VARIABLES

In our simulation of the upcoming models, it will be necessary to generate values for random variables. In this section we will explore how to *draw a random sample* from a given probability distribution, which we take to be synonymous with generating a random variable. There are two broad categories of random variables: discrete and continuous. Discrete random variables can assume only certain, specific values (e.g., integers), and continuous random variables may take on any fractional value (an infinite number of possible outcomes).

The topic of generating random variables is dealt with at several levels. The first level shows how to use a spreadsheet to generate observations from an arbitrary discrete distribution. This is sufficient to obtain the basic view of how a simulator with random elements operates. The following section on a generalized method shows how to generate random variables from any continuous distribution. It uses the exponential and normal distributions to motivate the presentation. Finally, the method is demonstrated when using spreadsheet add-ins.

It is easy to think of a physical device that could be used to generate the demand in a given model. The game spinner shown in Figure 9.3 would work well for the upcoming omelet pan example and is equally likely to point to any point on the circumference of the circle. Therefore, the chance that the spinner lands in a sector that comprises 30% of the circumference (or, equivalently, 30% of the area) is 30%. If the areas of the sectors are made to correspond to the probabilities of different demands, the spinner can be used to simulate demand. In this omelet pan example, there is a 10% chance that demand will be 8 pans, a 20% chance that demand will be 9 pans, a 30% chance that demand will be 10 pans, a 20% chance that demand will be 11 pans, a 10% chance that demand will be 12 pans, and a 10% chance that demand will be 13 pans. For example, if the spinner stops in the sector shown in Figure 9.3, a demand of 9 would be generated. To simulate another **trial** or pass through the simulator, we would simply spin again.

USING A RANDOM NUMBER GENERATOR IN A SPREADSHEET

While the spinner is easy to understand, this method has an obvious defect if thousands of trials are necessary or if the process is to be performed on a computer. For this reason *random number generators (RNG)* have been developed in spreadsheets.

To generate demand for a given model, we first need to assign a range of random numbers to each possible demand. This assignment is arbitrary to a degree. The only require-

FIGURE 9.3

Game Spinner for Omelet Pan Demand

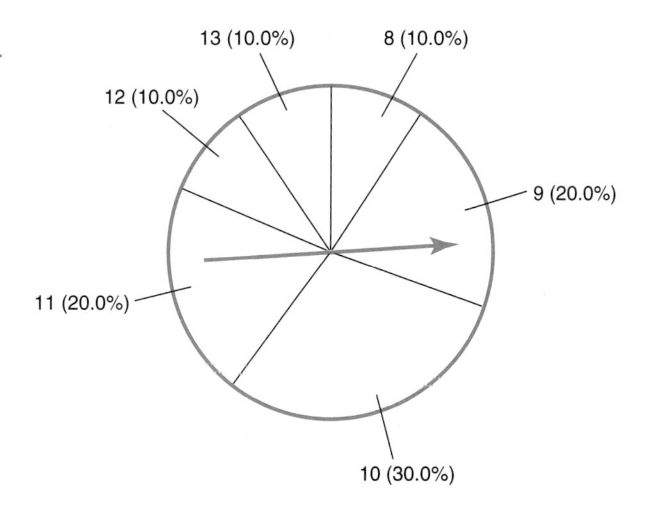

Random Number	Demand
0.0-0.09999	8
0.1-0.29999	9
0.3-0.59999	10
0.6-0.79999	11
0.8-0.89999	12
0.9-0.99999	13

FIGURE 9.4

Associating Random Numbers with Demands

ment for a correct assignment is that the proportion of total numbers assigned to a demand must equal the probability of that demand. We will assign pieces of the interval from 0 to 1 to demands from the omelet pan example. One possible assignment is shown in Figure 9.4. Note that in this example, 10% (.90–.9999) of the entire interval (0–.9999) is assigned to a demand of 13. The probability of drawing a random number in the range .90–.9999 is 1 out of 10, or 0.1, which is exactly the same as the probability that the demand is 13.

Clearly, this is not the only possible correct assignment. We could assign a demand of 13 to *any* interval of length of 10% for example, 0.1–0.19999 or 0.45–0.5499—since the probability of drawing a value in either one of these 10% intervals is also 0.1.

A GENERALIZED METHOD

The method we have just demonstrated is useful for generating discrete random variables. Many models, however, involve *continuous* random variables, which require a modification of the discrete RNG approach. Fortunately, there is a general method that can be used to generate both discrete and continuous random variables. We will develop this method and illustrate it with several examples.

To generate a discrete random variable with the RAND() function in a spreadsheet we needed two things: (1) the ability to generate discrete uniform random variables and (2) the distribution of the discrete random variable to be generated. Similarly, to generate continuous random variables we will need (1) the ability to generate continuous uniform random variables on the interval 0 to 1, and (2) the distribution (in the form of the *cumulative distribution function*) of the random variable to be generated.

Continuous Uniform Random Variables In what follows, it is important to distinguish between the uniform random variable on the interval 0 to 1, U, and a specific realization of that random variable, u. One way to generate a continuous uniform random variable would be to use a version of the game spinner introduced earlier. Figure 9.5 shows a game spinner that, conceptually at least, can be used to generate values of U. Every point on the circumference of the circle corresponds to a number between 0 and 1. For example, when the pointer is in the 3 o'clock position, it is pointing to the number 0.25.

While this device is useful for gaining an intuitive understanding of the uniform random variable, it is even more limiting in practice than the spinner for the omelet pan model, in that it requires us to be able to read the exact point at which the pointer is pointing. (For example, imagine trying to discern whether the number indicated is 0.500000 or 0.499999.) We have seen, however, that in practice we do not need to be dependent on such "analog" devices as game spinners. With the use of RAND() in the spreadsheet, we can approximate U to any number of decimal places we choose.

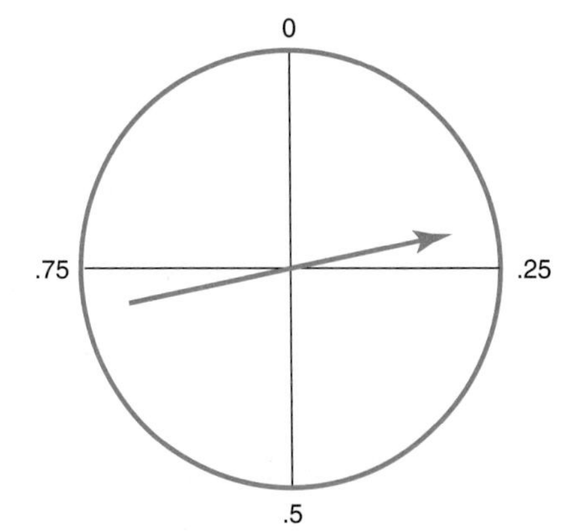

FIGURE 9.5

Game Spinner for Uniform Random Variables

The Cumulative Distribution Function The second key to generating a continuous random variable is the random variable's **cumulative distribution function (CDF)**. Consider a random variable, *D*, the demand in our omelet pan example model. The CDF for *D*, which we will designate $F(x)$, is then defined as the probability that *D* takes on a value less than or equal to x—that is, $F(x) = \text{Prob}\{D \leq x\}$. Recall that if we know the probability distribution for *D*, as we did in the omelet pan model, we can easily find the CDF. Indeed, the CDF for key values of *D* is as follows:

x	8	9	10	11	12	13
$F(x)$	0.1	0.3	0.6	0.8	0.9	1.0

We will show how to use the general approach to generate observations of the random variable *D*. You will see that it is as easy as the approach based on the probability distribution, but certainly no easier. So why adopt this general approach? The answer is a technical one. With a continuous random variable, the probability that any *specific* value occurs is, strictly speaking, 0. Thus you cannot use an approach based on the probability distribution. Indeed, continuous random variables do not have probability distributions; the density function and the CDF are the two functions used to define a continuous random variable.

A graph of the CDF is shown in Figure 9.6. To generate a demand using the graph, draw a particular value u of the random variable and locate this value on the vertical axis of the graph. From this value on the vertical axis draw a line horizontally across to the plot of the CDF, and then down vertically to the horizontal axis to obtain the value of the demand, d. For example, when $u = 0.5$, the demand is 10 (see Figure 9.6).

Why does this procedure work? It works because the probability of generating a particular demand is the probability of that demand occurring. For example, we want the probability of generating a demand of 10 to be 0.3. A demand of 10 will be generated when u lies between 0.3 and 0.6 on the vertical axis of Figure 9.6. But since U is a uniform random variable, this probability is just the length of the interval, $0.6 - 0.3 = 0.3$. Similarly, we want the probability of generating a demand of 11 to be 0.2. A demand of 11 will be generated when the value of u lies between 0.6 and 0.8, which happens with a probability of $0.8 - 0.6 = 0.2$, and so on. (You might wonder what happens if u is exactly 0.6. Should a demand of 10 or 11 be generated? The answer is that it doesn't really matter, as the probability of generating a value of u *exactly* equal to 0.6 is 0. One convention is to take the larger value. This works except when u is 1 when the larger value is not defined. In that case, just take the demand to be 13.)

FIGURE 9.6

CDF of Omelet Pan Demand

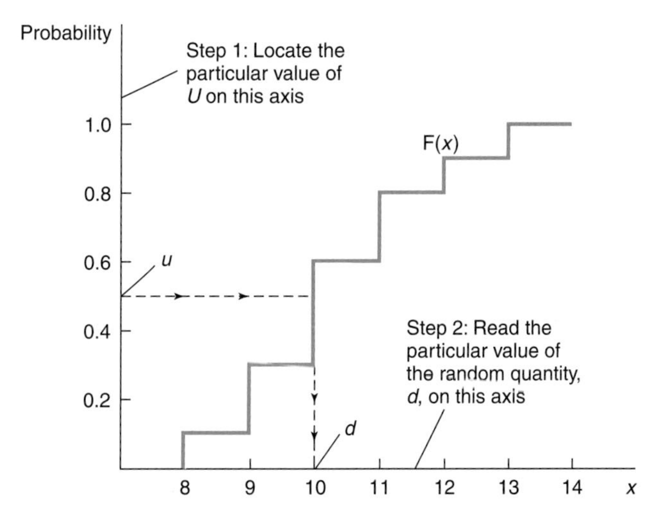

Values for RAND()	=INT(8+5*RAND())
0 <= RAND() < 0.2	8
0.2 <= RAND() < 0.4	9
0.4 <= RAND() < 0.6	10
0.6 <= RAND() < 0.8	11
0.8 <= RAND() < 1.0	12

FIGURE 9.7

Using RAND() to Generate Discrete Demands

The technique we have just illustrated with the omelet pan model can be applied back to any general discrete distribution. Now, let's suppose we want to model a **discrete uniform distribution** of demand where the values of 8 through 12 all have the same probability of occurring (uniform, because each value is equally likely). Recall that the spreadsheet has a function, =RAND(), that returns a random number between 0 and 1, all values being equally likely. RAND() is an example of a **continuous uniform distribution.** The question then is: Can we use a continuous uniform distribution to generate a discrete uniform distribution? We note that 5*RAND() will result in the creation of a continuous random number between 0 and 5, so that 8+5*RAND() will produce a continuous number between 8 and 13 (i.e., up to 12.99999 . . .). If we then make use of the INT function in Excel, which returns the integer part of the number, we can generate a discrete uniform distribution of the integers between 8 and 12 with the formula: INT(8 + 5*RAND()). Figure 9.7 shows what the value of the formula would be for different values of RAND().

Since the intervals are all of equal length (1/5), RAND() is equally likely to fall into any one of them, and thus the formula is equally likely to yield any one of the five integer values. In general, if we want a discrete uniform distribution of integer values between x and y, we can use the formula:

$$\text{INT}(x + (y - x + 1)*\text{RAND}())$$

Later, in Section 9.7, we will show how to generate a binomial random variable (which is also discrete). We shall now see how the general method can be used to generate any continuous random variable, with specific illustrations for the exponential and normal distributions.

THE GENERAL METHOD APPLIED TO CONTINUOUS DISTRIBUTIONS

The two-step process for generating a continuous random variable W is illustrated in Figure 9.8. As before, the crucial element in the graph is the cumulative distribution function of W, $F(x) = \text{Prob}\{W \leq x\}$. The figure shows a typical function of this type, namely, one that goes from 0 to 1, is nondecreasing, and is *continuous* (that is, unlike the CDF for a discrete distribution, there are no jumps in the curve). Exactly as before, the process starts by drawing a particular value u of the random variable U and locating this value on the vertical axis (0.8 in Figure 9.8). You then read horizontally across to the plot of the distribution function and then vertically down to the horizontal axis to obtain the value of the random quantity (approximately 5.1 in Figure 9.8). We should stress that Figure 9.8 motivates the

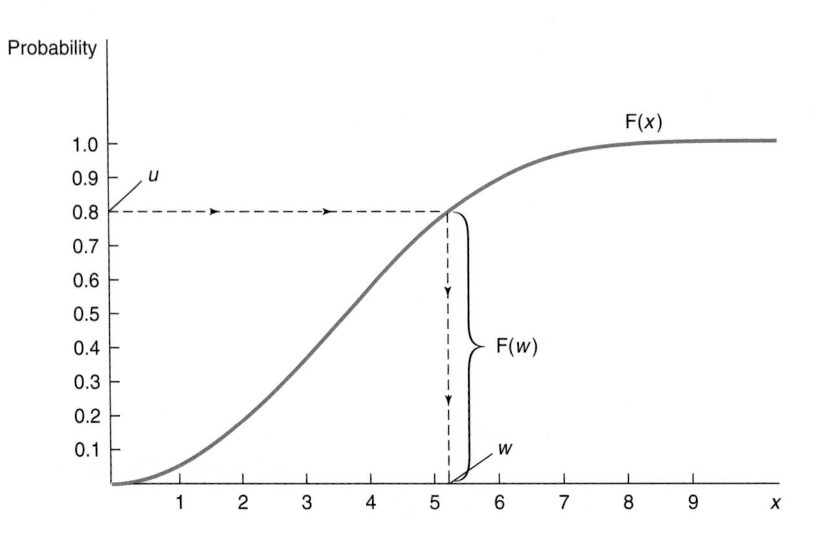

FIGURE 9.8

Generating Random Quantities

concept underlying the technique of generating an arbitrary continuous random variable. In practice, the process is typically performed in the computer with either an analytic or tabular representation of a graph like Figure 9.8. We illustrate both procedures below.

The graphical procedure illustrated is equivalent to an algebraic procedure. That procedure is to solve the equation

$$u = F(w) = \text{Prob}\{W \leq w\}$$

for w. This can be seen from Figure 9.8 where the vertical distance on the vertical axis is u and is equal to the vertical distance from w on the horizontal axis to the plot of the CDF. When the CDF has a simple enough analytic expression, it is possible to solve for w in terms of u.

Generating from the Exponential Distribution An important distribution for which this is the case is the **exponential distribution**. The exponential distribution is often used to model the time between arrivals in a queuing model (see Chapter 15). Its CDF is given by

$$F(w) = \text{Prob}\{W \leq w\} = 1 - e^{-\lambda w}$$

where $1/\lambda$ equals the mean of the exponential random variable, W. Therefore we want to solve the following equation for w:

$$u = 1 - e^{-\lambda w} \tag{9.1}$$

The solution is

$$w = -1/\lambda \ln(1 - u) \tag{9.2}$$

For example, suppose we want to draw a sample from the exponential distribution with mean equal to 20 using this equation and a random number generator. We would

1. Generate a continuous uniform random number with RAND(). For example, suppose that we obtain the number 0.75.
2. We then take the natural logarithm of 1 – 0.75 = 0.25, which is –1.386, and multiply by –20. The observation from the exponential distribution is (–20)(–1.386) = 27.72.

To summarize, we would simply put the expression = –20 *LN(1 – RAND()) in a cell in the spreadsheet and it would generate exponentially distributed random numbers with a mean of 20.

Generating from the Normal Distribution The **normal distribution** plays an important role in many simulation and analytic models. In simulation, we often assume that random quantities are normally distributed. To illustrate, we look ahead to Marie Ford and Foslins' omelet pan model (see Section 9.6). We will find Marie making the assumption that a normal distribution with a mean of 1,000 and a standard deviation of 100 described the demand that would occur.

To use simulation to estimate the expected cost of a given order size, Marie would have to draw a random demand from a normal distribution with a mean (μ) of 1,000 and a standard deviation (σ) of 100 for each iteration. It turns out that if Z is a unit normal random variable (a normal with a mean of 0 and a standard deviation 1), then $\mu + Z\sigma$ is a normal random variable with mean μ and standard deviation σ. So the problem reduces to drawing from a unit normal distribution. The difficulty here is that the CDF of the unit normal is complicated enough that it is not possible to get an analytical expression for z in terms of u. Fortunately, Excel has a built-in function that can do this for us.

So, to generate a normal random variable with mean of 1,000 and standard deviation of 100 in Excel. Marie will use this simple formula: =NORMINV(RAND(),1000,100). Excel will automatically return a normally distributed random number with mean of 1,000 and standard deviation of 100.

GENERATING RANDOM VARIABLES USING ADD-INS

The topic of generating random variables is now dealt with for both Crystal Ball and @Risk. These two software packages have different approaches. In Crystal Ball, for each cell in the spreadsheet that represents a random variable, we must go through the "Define Assumption" menu, select from a gallery of distributions, and indicate what the appropriate distribution's parameters are. In @Risk, we must actually place a formula for the random number generator (RNG) in each cell of the spreadsheet that represents a random variable. Both add-in packages offer us a number of features not available in Excel. First, add-in packages offer us numerous random distributions that are not directly available in a spreadsheet (e.g., Poisson, Binomial, Lognormal, etc.). Second, they offer easy commands to set up and run many more iterations (no limit in Crystal Ball; up to 32,767 in @Risk) than we could in Excel. Finally, they automatically gather statistical and graphical summaries of our results.

To enter the information for a particular RNG in Crystal Ball, menus are used. These menus are illustrated with examples in Sections 9.4, 9.5, 9.6, and 9.8. Table 9.1 provides the @Risk format (demonstrated in Section 9.7) for some of the most common RNG's you'll use for your simulation modeling.

@Risk also offers truncated distributions for a few of the above distributions (e.g., Exponential, Lognormal, Normal). To use Table 9.1, let's suppose that you want to gen-

Table 9.1

DISTRIBUTION	@RISK FORMULA	DESCRIPTION OF RNG
Binomial	=RiskBinomial(n, p)	Returns the number of "successes" in a sample of n trials, where p is the probability of success for an individual trial.
Chi-square	=RiskChisq(λ)	Returns a value from the chi-square distribution with mean λ. Useful when summing normally distributed random variables.
Cumulative	=RiskCumul(a, b, $\{x_1, x_2 \ldots x_n\}$, $\{p_1, p_2 \ldots p_n\}$)	Returns a value from a general distribution where a is the minimum, b is the maximum, and p_i represents the probability that a value of x_i or less will be drawn from the distribution.
Discrete (General)	=RiskDiscrete($\{x_1, x_2 \ldots x_n\}$, $\{p_1, p_2 \ldots p_n\}$)	Returns one of the n values from x_1 to x_n. The probabilities p_i represent the chance that x_i will be returned by the RNG.
Discrete (Uniform)	=RiskDuniform($\{x_1, x_2 \ldots x_n\}$)	Returns one of the n values from x_1 to x_n with equal probability.
Exponential	=RiskExp(β)	Returns value from exponential distribution with mean β. Useful for queuing models (time between arrivals).
Lognormal	=RiskLognorm(μ, σ)	Returns a value from the lognormal distribution with mean μ and standard deviation σ. Useful for such quantities as the sizes of oil fields or bank accounts.
Normal	=RiskNormal(μ, σ)	Returns a value from the normal distribution with mean μ and standard deviation σ. Useful for such quantities as the distribution of heights or weights or test scores.
Poisson	=RiskPoisson(λ)	Returns a value from the Poisson distribution with mean λ. Useful for describing the number of events that happen in a given time interval.
Triangular	=RiskTriang(a, b, c)	Returns a value from the triangular distribution with parameters (a = minimum, b = most likely, c = maximum). Useful when not much is known about the shape of the distribution other than the aforementioned parameters.
Uniform (Continuous)	=RiskUniform(a, b)	Returns a value from the uniform distribution with parameters (a = minimum, b = maximum). Useful when only the range of uncertainty is known and each value is equally likely to occur.

erate random demand in @Risk from the following distribution: 10% chance of 8 sales, 20% chance of 9 sales, 30% chance of 10 sales, 20% chance of 11 sales, 10% chance of 12 sales, and a 10% chance of 13 sales. All you need to do is type: =RiskDiscrete({8,9,10,11,12,13},{0.1,0.2,0.3,0.2,0.1,0.1}) into the cell of the spreadsheet that represents demand.

For a graph of the general shapes of these distributions, look ahead to the Crystal Ball gallery of distributions shown in Figure 9.17. You'll notice that some of the distributions listed in the preceding table are available directly in Crystal Ball (e.g., Poisson, Normal, Continuous Uniform), whereas others must be entered via the "Custom" distribution (e.g., Discrete, Cumulative), and some are not available at all (e.g., Chi-square).

The next two sections address the issue of actually doing a simulation in a spreadsheet depending on what software you have available. If you don't have any simulation add-in software available, proceed to Section 9.3, which will teach you the basics of doing a simulation with just the spreadsheet tools found in Excel, then skip Section 9.4. Otherwise (meaning you do have an add-in package available), you may choose to skip Section 9.3 and go directly to Section 9.4, unless you want to cover both topics.

9.3 SIMULATING WITH A SPREADSHEET

Most simulations are performed in a spreadsheet, because the number of calculations required soon overwhelms human capability. Simulations can be performed with spreadsheets alone (without the help of special add-in software), as this section will demonstrate. In this section we present a capital budgeting example to show the use of a spreadsheet for simulation and to establish some important facts about the output from a spreadsheet simulation.

A CAPITAL BUDGETING EXAMPLE: ADDING A NEW PRODUCT LINE

June Wilson is the manager of new-product development and is considering the financial implications of a possible addition to Airbus Industry's jet airplane product line. Startup costs for the proposed new model A3XX (which include extensive research and design, building a prototype, and so on) are estimated at $150,000 (in thousands). The new aircraft would be sold at a price of $35,000 (in thousands) per unit. Fixed costs are estimated to run at $15,000 (in thousands) per year, while variable costs should be about 75% of revenues each year.

Tax depreciation[1] on the new equipment would be $10,000 (in thousands) per year over the expected 4-year product life of the A3XX. The salvage value of the equipment at the end of the 4 years is uncertain, so June conservatively estimates it to be zero. Airbus' cost of capital is 10%, and its tax rate is 34%.

The most uncertain aspect of the proposal is the demand for the new product. If June knew the demand, she could easily calculate the *net present value* (NPV) of the proposal using a spreadsheet program. For example, if June assumes that the demand for A3XXs is 10 units for each of the next 4 years, the spreadsheet in Figure 9.9 (WILSON.XLS) shows that the NPV would be $12,455.60.

THE MODEL WITH RANDOM DEMAND

However, it is unlikely that the demand will be exactly the same every year. June feels it would be more realistic to model the demand each year not as a common constant value, but as a sequence of random variables. This model of demand is appropriate when there is a constant base level of demand that is subject to random fluctuations from year to year. When the base level demand is 10 units, actual demands for the next 4 years might turn out to be 12, 9, 8, and 10, because of the random factors affecting demand.

---

[1] Depreciation is first subtracted to determine before-tax profit and then added back to determine net cash flow.

FIGURE 9.9

Wilson's Initial Spreadsheet

B19 = =NPV($D$3,C17:F17)+B17

	A	B	C	D	E	F
1	**Assumptions**					
2	Startup Costs	$ 150,000	Variable Costs	75%	of Revenue	
3	Selling Price	$ 35,000	Cost of Capital	10%		
4	Fixed Costs	$ 15,000	Tax Rate	34%		
5	Depreciation/Yr	$ 10,000				
6			Demand/Yr	10.0	units	
7						
8		**Year 0**	1	2	3	4
9	*Demand*		10.0	10.0	10.0	10.0
10	*Revenue*		350,000	350,000	350,000	350,000
11	*Fixed Cost*		15,000	15,000	15,000	15,000
12	*Variable Cost*		262,500	262,500	262,500	262,500
13	*Depreciation*		10,000	10,000	10,000	10,000
14	*Profit before Tax*		62,500	62,500	62,500	62,500
15	*Tax*		21,250	21,250	21,250	21,250
16	*Profit after Tax*		41,250	41,250	41,250	41,250
17	*Net Cash Flow*	(150,000)	51,250	51,250	51,250	51,250
18						
19	*Net Present Value*	$12,455.60				
20						

Cell	Formula	Copy To
C10	= C9*$B$3	D10:F10
C11	= $B$4	D11:F11
C12	= C10*$D$2	D12:F12
C13	= $B$5	D13:F13
C14	= C10−SUM(C11:C13)	D14:F14
C15	= $D$4*C14	D15:F15
C16	= C14−C15	D16:F16
B17	= −$B$2	—
C17	= C16+C13	D17:F17
B19	= NPV($D$3,C17:F17)+B17	—

Sampling Demand with a Spreadsheet June decides to generate random demands for the 4 years to see what effect the variability of the demands has on the NPV. She assumes initially that demand in a year will be either 8, 9, 10, 11, or 12 units with each value being equally likely to occur. This is an example of a discrete uniform distribution. Using her new knowledge from Section 9.2, she devises the formula =INT(8+5*RAND()) to sample from the discrete uniform distribution on the five integers 8, 9, 10, 11, 12. Since the value of RAND() will change every time the spreadsheet is recalculated, June can easily perform **multiple trials**—that is, draw a new sample of demands simply by pressing the recalculation key for her spreadsheet (F9 usually). After doing this a few times, she is surprised to find that on some trials she obtains a negative NPV.

Figure 9.10 shows that the NPV corresponding to a random sequence of demands is $2,827.32, about 80% less than the NPV if demand were constant at 10 per year. If June were to hit the F9 key, she would get a different sample of demands, and hence thus possibly a different NPV. Because the demands can vary from sample to sample, the NPV can also vary. Put more technically, the demands are random variables, so the NPV is also a random variable.

EVALUATING THE PROPOSAL

June realizes that she needs to build a simulation model to help her answer two questions about the NPV distribution: (1) What is the *mean* or **expected value** of the NPV? and (2) What is the probability that the NPV assumes a negative value? The larger the mean NPV—

FIGURE 9.10

Wilson's Spreadsheet with Randomly Selected Demands

C9 = =INT(8+5*RAND())

	A	B	C	D	E	F
1	**Assumptions**					
2	Startup Costs	$ 150,000	Variable Costs	75%	of Revenue	
3	Selling Price	$ 35,000	Cost of Capital	10%		
4	Fixed Costs	$ 15,000	Tax Rate	34%		
5	Depreciation/Yr	$ 10,000				
6			Demand/Yr	10.0	units	
7						
8		**Year 0**	1	2	3	4
9	*Demand*		9.0	9.0	11.0	9.0
10	*Revenue*		315,000	315,000	385,000	315,000
11	*Fixed Cost*		15,000	15,000	15,000	15,000
12	*Variable Cost*		236,250	236,250	288,750	236,250
13	*Depreciation*		10,000	10,000	10,000	10,000
14	*Profit before Tax*		53,750	53,750	71,250	53,750
15	*Tax*		18,275	18,275	24,225	18,275
16	*Profit after Tax*		35,475	35,475	47,025	35,475
17	*Net Cash Flow*	(150,000)	45,475	45,475	57,025	45,475
18						
19	*Net Present Value*	$2,827.32				
20						

Cell	Formula	Copy to
C9	=INT(8+5*RAND())	D9:F9

and perhaps even more important—the less likely it is that the NPV is negative, the more attractive the proposal to add the A3XX to Airbus' product line.

So, the next step is to run the simulation automatically a number of times and capture the resulting NPV in a separate spreadsheet. This can be done rather easily with the spreadsheet's Data Table command as follows:

1. Click the Insert menu.
2. Select Worksheet.
3. Double click on the tab at the bottom with the name of the spreadsheet (usually some default name like "Sheet3") and rename the spreadsheet "100 Iterations."
4. Type the starting value (1) in cell A2 and hit Enter.
5. Click back on cell A2.
6. Click the Edit menu, choose Fill, then Series.
7. Select the Series in Columns option and enter a stop value of 100.
8. Click OK.

Excel will automatically fill in the column below the selected cell (A2) with values increasing by 1 (the step value) until it reaches the stop value of 100. In order to track the NPV, we enter the following formula in cell B2 of the new spreadsheet: =Random Demand!B19. We also enter labels in cells A1 and B1 for clarity. We now use the Data Table command. This is done as follows:

1. Select the range A2:B101.
2. Click the Data menu, then Table.
3. In the Table dialog box, enter cell C1 for the Column input cell.
4. Click OK.

Excel then substitutes each value in the range A2 to A101 into cell C1 (which has no real effect), recalculates the spreadsheet, and stores the resulting NPV in the adjacent cells in column B. After doing this, you should have a list of values in column B representing 100 possible values for the NPV, similar to those shown in Figure 9.11. The numbers you gen-

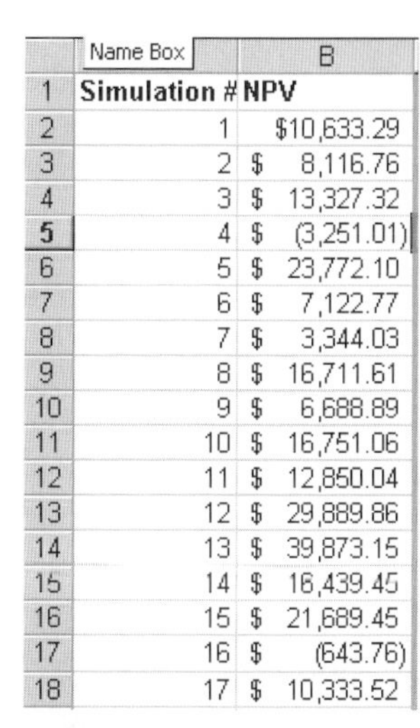

Name Box		B
1	**Simulation #**	**NPV**
2	1	$10,633.29
3	2	$ 8,116.76
4	3	$ 13,327.32
5	4	$ (3,251.01)
6	5	$ 23,772.10
7	6	$ 7,122.77
8	7	$ 3,344.03
9	8	$ 16,711.61
10	9	$ 6,688.89
11	10	$ 16,751.06
12	11	$ 12,850.04
13	12	$ 29,889.86
14	13	$ 39,873.15
15	14	$ 16,439.45
16	15	$ 21,689.45
17	16	$ (643.76)
18	17	$ 10,333.52

FIGURE 9.11

Wilson's Simulation Results

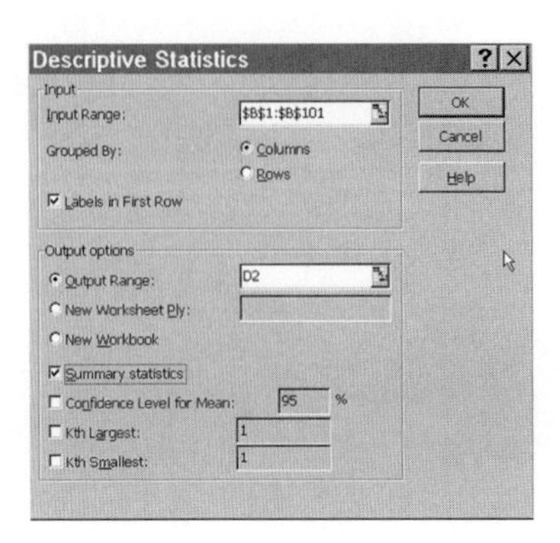

FIGURE 9.12

Descriptive Statistics Dialog Box

erate will not match those shown in Figure 9.11. Remember the procedure shown here generates a random sample of 100 trials from an infinite number of possible outcomes. Hopefully, the overall characteristics of your sample should be similar to the ones shown here.

In order to focus on these 100 observations, let's turn the formulas into values by following a simple procedure:

1. Select the range B2:B101.
2. Click on the Edit menu, then Copy.
3. Click on the Edit menu again, then Paste Special.
4. Select the Values option, then click OK.

In order to get a summary of our 100 iterations, we can use Excel's built-in data analysis tool. (If the Data Analysis option is not on your Tools menu, select the Add-ins option from the Tools menu, then select the Analysis ToolPak option.) This tool generates numerous descriptive statistics (e.g., mean, standard deviation, minimum, maximum, etc.) automatically. To use it, simply do the following:

1. Click the Tools menu, then Data Analysis.
2. Click Descriptive Statistics, and complete the dialog box as shown in Figure 9.12.
3. Click OK.

Based on this limited sample, the results are shown in Figure 9.13 and indicate that the estimated mean NPV is $12,100.37 and the standard deviation is a rather large $12,351.69.

Downside Risk and Upside Risk June also wants to know what's the best possible outcome as well as the worst possible. In this sample, we can see from Figure 9.13 that the largest NPV was $39,955.98 and the smallest was –$11,100.37. This gives her a better idea about the range of possible NPVs that could occur.

Distribution of Outcomes Although the data in Figure 9.13 offer more insight than just the base case NPV, there are other factors we should consider. How likely are these extreme outcomes (best case, worst case) to occur? In order to answer this question, we need to know something about the shape of the distribution of the NPV. Fortunately, Excel also has some built-in features to help us. To generate a histogram (a graphical distribution of the NPVs) as well as a numerical frequency table, just follow these steps:

1. Click on the Tools menu, then Data Analysis.
2. Choose Histogram and complete its dialog box as shown in Figure 9.14.
3. Click OK.

In this case, we saved the results in a separate spreadsheet called NPV Distribution. It is shown in Figure 9.15. The Frequency column shown in column B indicates the number of our 100 trials that fell into the bins defined by Excel in column A. For example, one obser-

FIGURE 9.13

Descriptive Statistics Summary

E21 = =$E$4-1.96*$E$8/SQRT($E$16)

	A	B
1	Simulation #	NPV
2	1	$10,633.29
3	2	$ 8,116.76
4	3	$ 13,327.32
5	4	$ (3,251.01)
6	5	$ 23,772.10
7	6	$ 7,122.77
8	7	$ 3,344.03
9	8	$ 16,711.61
10	9	$ 6,688.89
11	10	$ 16,751.06
12	11	$ 12,850.04
13	12	$ 29,889.86
14	13	$ 39,873.15
15	14	$ 16,439.45
16	15	$ 21,689.45
17	16	$ (643.76)
18	17	$ 10,333.52
19	18	$ 5,071.68
20	19	$ 12,104.55
21	20	$ 1,139.11
22	21	$ 21,567.17

NPV	
Mean	12100.37122
Standard Error	1235.168989
Median	10483.40277
Mode	16751.05867
Standard Deviation	12351.68989
Sample Variance	152564243.2
Kurtosis	-0.471723205
Skewness	0.35637559
Range	51056.34861
Minimum	-11100.36883
Maximum	39955.97978
Sum	1210037.122
Count	100
Confidence Level(95.0%)	2450.843684

95% Confidence Interval	
Lower Bound	$ 9,679.44
Upper Bound	$ 14,521.30

Cell	Formula
E21	=$E$4−1.96*$E$8/SQRT($E$16)
E22	=$E$4+1.96*$E$8/SQRT($E$16)

FIGURE 9.14

Histogram Dialog Box

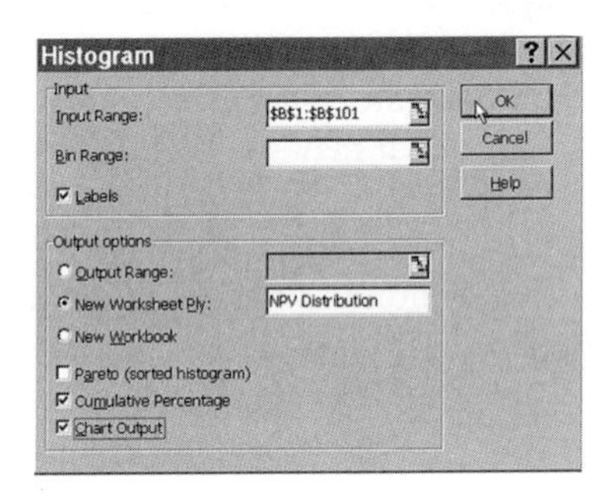

FIGURE 9.15

Historgam and Frequency Table

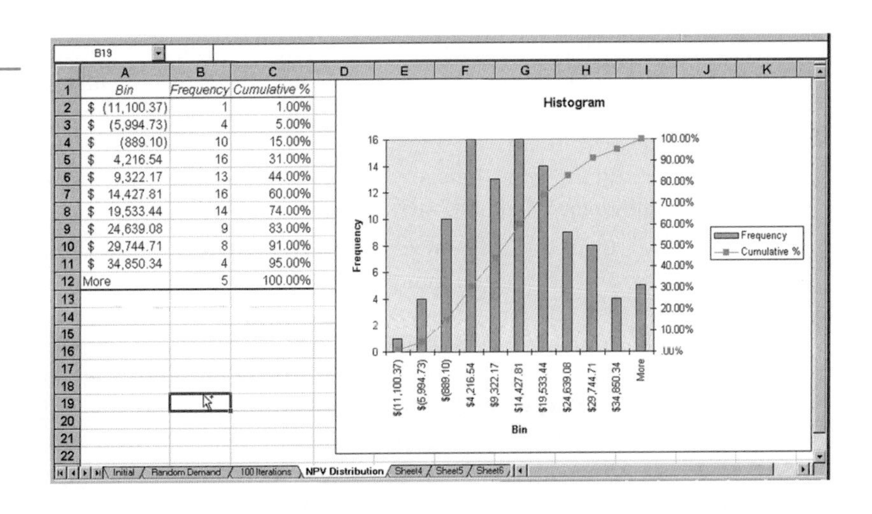

	Bin	Frequency	Cumulative %
2	$ (11,100.37)	1	1.00%
3	$ (5,994.73)	4	5.00%
4	$ (889.10)	10	15.00%
5	$ 4,216.54	16	31.00%
6	$ 9,322.17	13	44.00%
7	$ 14,427.81	16	60.00%
8	$ 19,533.44	14	74.00%
9	$ 24,639.08	9	83.00%
10	$ 29,744.71	8	91.00%
11	$ 34,850.34	4	95.00%
12	More	5	100.00%

vation was less than or equal to ($11,100.37). Ten observations were greater than ($5994.73) and less than or equal to ($889.10). The greatest number of observations (16) fell in the interval of being greater than $9,322.17 and less than or equal to $14,427.81. The histogram shown on the right of Figure 9.15 gives a visual representation of the possible outcomes for the NPV. It has somewhat of a bell shape to it.

The Cumulative % column shown (column C) indicates that more than 15% of the NPV observations were negative (less than 0). This data can be helpful in answering other questions June or her chief financial officer might come up with.

How Reliable Is the Simulation? June now has the answers to her two questions about the NPV distribution: (1) What is the *mean* value of the NPV? (A: $12,100), and (2) What is the probability that the NPV assumes a negative value? (A: >15%). We now ask some questions: How much confidence do we have in the answers June came up with? Would we have more confidence if we ran more trials?

Certainly, it is intuitive that the more trials we run, the more confidence we ought to have in our answers. But how much confidence can we have in the 100 iterations we actually sampled? From the world of statistics, we remember that we can construct confidence intervals based on the results we obtained. For example, we can have 95% confidence that the true mean NPV is contained in an interval of ±1.96 standard deviations about the estimated mean. In this case, the standard deviation of the mean is the reported standard deviation divided by the square root of the number of trials. This 95% confidence interval for the mean was calculated by June and reported in Figure 9.13 as ($9679.44; $14,521.30). Said another way, we can have 95% confidence that the true mean NPV is somewhere between $9679 and $14,521, with our current best guess that it is $12,100.

We must be careful *not* to fall in the "expected value" trap! Many students believe that the true mean NPV can always be calculated by setting all the random values to their means (set all the demands to 10 in this example). This is what June had in her initial spreadsheet (see Figure 9.9), but there is no guarantee that the NPV obtained in this manner will also be the true simulated mean. Although it may seem logical, there are some potential weaknesses in this reasoning. First of all, the way in which the demand values are used to calculate yearly cash flows and then turned into a single NPV number (or any other performance measure) could be highly nonlinear. There are other subtleties that will not be mentioned here, but be forewarned: Don't fall into the "expected value" trap!

There are cases where this "intuitive" reasoning will work, but not always. A simple example from one of life's common experiences ought to convince you that the NPV (or any other bottom-line performance measure) at the expected value of the random variables is not necessarily the same as the expected NPV. Consider a waiting line at the grocery store. Suppose the expected time to serve a customer is 0.9 minutes and the average time between customer arrivals is 1 minute. Looking at the situation using the expected values, you would predict the average waiting time to be 0 minutes (because customers are served faster than they arrive), but we all know that the *average* waiting time is greater than 0 minutes even though we sometimes get lucky and don't have to wait.

In summary, June needs more than 100 trials if she wants more accurate answers to her questions. What have we learned?

1. Increasing the number of trials is apt to give a better estimate of the expected return, but even with a large number of trials there can be some difference between the simulated *average* and the true expected return. Note that the true expected NPV in June's example turns out to be $12,455; the average NPV with 100 samples was $12,100 (a 2.85% error).
2. Simulations can provide useful information on the distribution of results. Even with a small sample of 100 trials there was an indication (a probability of greater than 0.15) that this project might yield a negative NPV. This is valuable information and something that could not have been determined with simply the base case analysis, or even Upside/Downside Risk analysis.

3. Simulation results are sensitive to assumptions affecting the input parameters. The next section shows that if June changes her assumptions about the distribution of demand (to a **Poisson distribution** with the same mean of 10), there is a significant impact on the probability of a negative NPV (it increases from about 0.15 to about 0.27).

Perhaps the most important impact of the simulation is on the decision-making process. If June had not performed any simulation analysis, she would have given an enthusiastic recommendation to proceed with the proposed addition to the heavy equipment line based on the mean NPV. However, after performing the simulation, she feels the project is too risky to recommend. While this is a qualitative judgment on her part, she can support it with the quantitative results of the simulation model. As we have noted before, models do not relieve managers from the responsibility of making decisions, but they do supply additional information for making those decisions well informed.

9.4 SIMULATING WITH SPREADSHEET ADD-INS

Spreadsheet add-ins, such as Crystal Ball and @RISK, make the task of simulation much easier than doing it alone in a spreadsheet. In particular, these programs greatly simplify the processes of generating random variables and assembling the statistical results. As we will see, both add-ins also greatly facilitate the capture and display of the output of the simulation. In this section we present a capital budgeting example to show how to use Crystal Ball [version 4.0g] for simulation and to establish some important facts about the output from a spreadsheet simulation. In other sections and their examples, we will continue to demonstrate the use of Crystal Ball, which is distributed free with this textbook in a student version. We will also briefly demonstrate @Risk [version 3.5e] in Section 9.7.

Simulation in a spreadsheet without the help of add-in packages can be time-consuming and tedious (to put it kindly) even for simple models. For more complicated models, more complicated distributions, or greater number of iterations, these characteristics are exacerbated. Fortunately, computers can be easily programmed to generate random quantities from any specific distribution in large quantities, both rapidly and accurately. As we have seen, the add-in packages have a number of different preprogrammed functions that will produce random variables automatically. For all of these reasons, almost all spreadsheet simulations are performed with the help of add-in packages.

A CAPITAL BUDGETING EXAMPLE: ADDING A NEW PRODUCT LINE

June Wilson is the manager of new-product development and is considering the financial implications of a possible addition to Airbus Industry's jet airplane product line. Startup costs for the proposed new model A3XX (which include extensive research and design, building a prototype, and so on) are estimated at $150,000 (in thousands). The new aircraft would be sold at a price of $35,000 (in thousands) per unit. Fixed costs are estimated to run at $15,000 (in thousands) per year, while variable costs should be about 75% of revenues each year.

Tax depreciation[2] on the new equipment would be $10,000 (in thousands) per year over the expected 4-year product life of the A3XX. The salvage value of the equipment at the end of the 4 years is uncertain, so June conservatively estimates it to be zero. Airbus' cost of capital is 10%, and its tax rate is 34%.

The most uncertain aspect of the proposal is the demand for the new product. If June knew the demand, she could easily calculate the *net present value* (NPV) of the proposal using a spreadsheet program. For example, if June assumes that the demand for A3XXs is 10 units for each of the next 4 years, the spreadsheet in Figure 9.16 (WILSNCB1.XLS) shows that the NPV would be $12,455.60.

[2] Depreciation is first subtracted to determine before-tax profit and then added back to determine net cash flow.

FIGURE 9.16

Wilson's Initial Spreadsheet

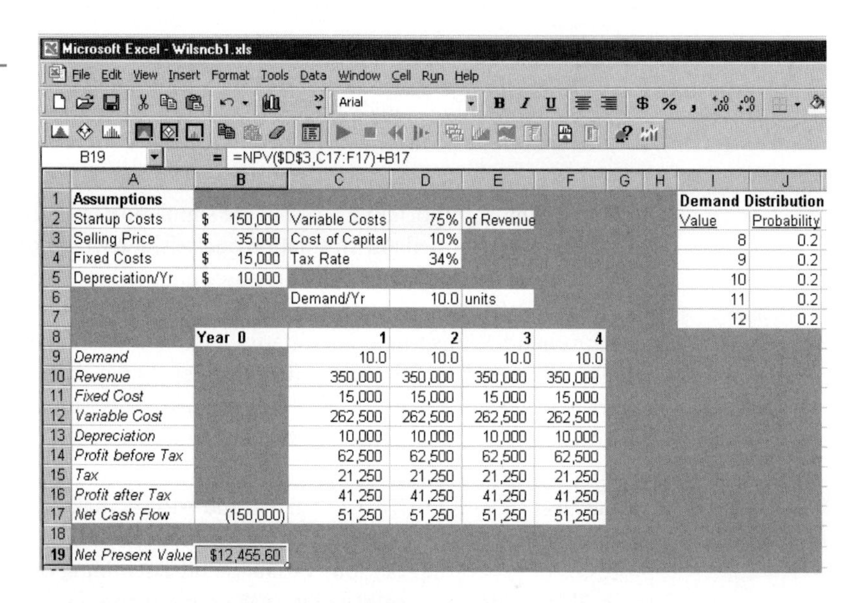
Microsoft Excel - Wilsncb1.xls

B19 = =NPV($D$3,C17:F17)+B17

	A	B	C	D	E	F	G	H	I	J
1	Assumptions								Demand Distribution	
2	Startup Costs	$ 150,000	Variable Costs	75%	of Revenue				Value	Probability
3	Selling Price	$ 35,000	Cost of Capital	10%					8	0.2
4	Fixed Costs	$ 15,000	Tax Rate	34%					9	0.2
5	Depreciation/Yr	$ 10,000							10	0.2
6			Demand/Yr	10.0	units				11	0.2
7									12	0.2
8		Year 0	1	2	3	4				
9	Demand		10.0	10.0	10.0	10.0				
10	Revenue		350,000	350,000	350,000	350,000				
11	Fixed Cost		15,000	15,000	15,000	15,000				
12	Variable Cost		262,500	262,500	262,500	262,500				
13	Depreciation		10,000	10,000	10,000	10,000				
14	Profit before Tax		62,500	62,500	62,500	62,500				
15	Tax		21,250	21,250	21,250	21,250				
16	Profit after Tax		41,250	41,250	41,250	41,250				
17	Net Cash Flow	(150,000)	51,250	51,250	51,250	51,250				
18										
19	Net Present Value	$12,455.60								

Cell	Formula	Copy To
C9	=$D$6	D9:F9
C10	=C9*$B$3	D10:F10
C11	=$B$4	D11:F11
C12	=C10*$D$2	D12:F12
C13	=$B$5	D13:F13
C14	=C10−SUM(C11:C13)	D14:F14
C15	=C14*$D$4	D15:F15
C16	=C14−C15	D16:F16
B17	=−B2	—
C17	=C16+C13	D17:F17
B19	=NPV($D$3,C17:F17)+B17	—

THE MODEL WITH RANDOM DEMAND

However, it is unlikely that the demand will be exactly the same every year. June feels it would be more realistic to model the demand each year not as a common constant value, but as a sequence of random variables. This model of demand is appropriate when there is a constant base level of demand that is subject to random fluctuations from year to year. When the base level demand is 10 units, actual demands for the next 4 years might turn out to be 12, 9, 8, and 10, because of the random factors affecting demand.

Sampling Demand with a Spreadsheet June decides to generate random demands for the 4 years to see what effect the variability of the demands has on the NPV. She assumes initially that demand in a year will be either 8, 9, 10, 11, or 12 units with each value being equally likely to occur. This is an example of a discrete uniform distribution. To "generate a random demand" for this probability distribution in Crystal Ball, June has to enter this discrete distribution in a two-column format for Crystal Ball to be able to use it. This is shown in columns I and J of Figure 9.16. To accomplish entering all this probability distribution information into Crystal Ball, June does the following:

1. Click on cell C9, which is the cell where Crystal Ball will generate random values for demand in year 1.
2. Click on the first Crystal Ball icon (Define Assumption).

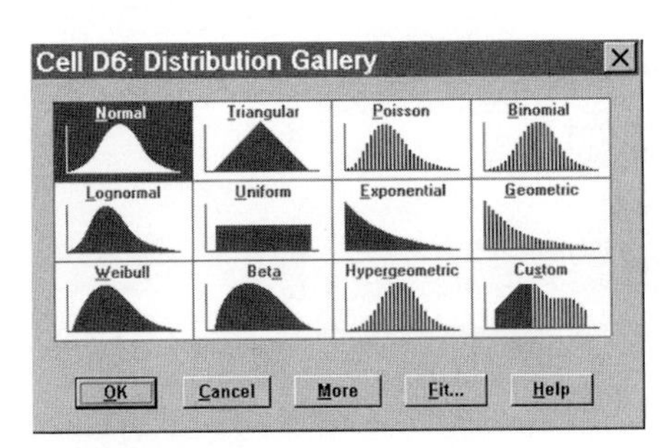

FIGURE 9.17

Crystal Ball Distribution Gallery

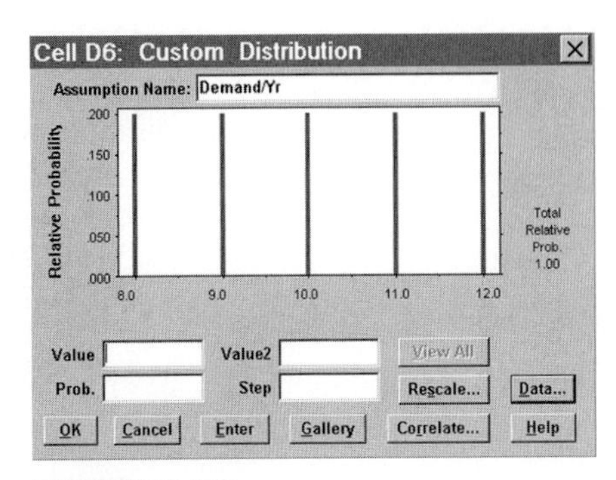

FIGURE 9.18

Airbus' Custom Random Number Generator

3. Click on the "Custom" distribution from the resulting Distribution Gallery as shown in Figure 9.17, then click on OK (or alternatively you could have double clicked on the "Custom" distribution).
4. Click on the "Data" button and enter the cell range where you entered the information on this discrete distribution (I3:J7); then click on OK.
5. Crystal Ball shows the distribution back to you as you have entered it (see Figure 9.18). Click on OK.
6. Repeat steps 1–5 for cells D9:F9 for years 2 to 4, or alternatively you can use Crystal Ball's Copy Data and Paste Data icons.

To get Crystal Ball to draw a new random sample of demands, you simply click on the twelfth icon (Single Step), which is shown in Figure 9.19. After June does this a few times, she is surprised to find that on some trials she obtains a negative NPV. Figure 9.19 shows that the NPV corresponding to a random sequence of demands is $184.57, about 98% less than the NPV if demand were constant at 10 per year. If June were to hit the Single Step icon again, she would get a different sample of demands, and hence thus possibly a different NPV. Because the demands can vary from sample to sample, the NPV can also vary. Put more technically, the demands are random variables, so the NPV is also a random variable.

EVALUATING THE PROPOSAL

June realizes that she needs to build a simulation model to help her answer two questions about the NPV distribution: (1) What is the *mean* or *expected value* of the NPV? and (2) What is the probability that the NPV assumes a negative value? The larger the mean NPV—

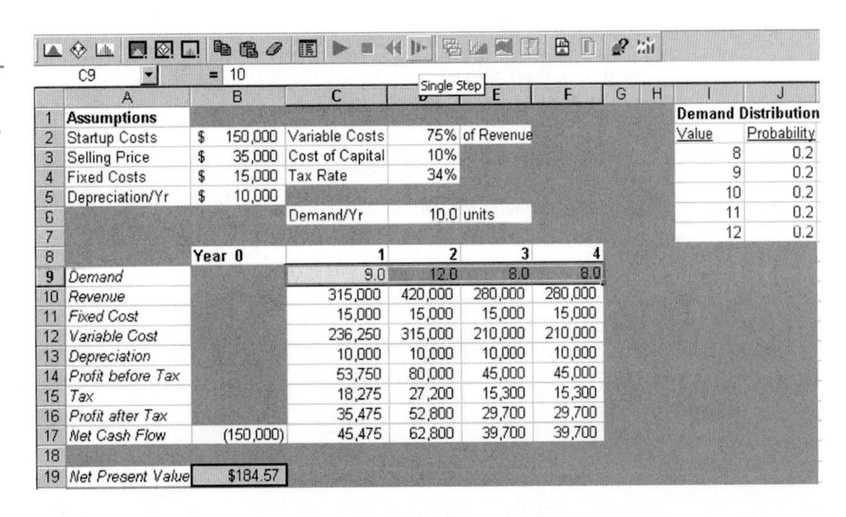

	A	B	C	D	E	F	G	H	I	J
1	Assumptions								Demand Distribution	
2	Startup Costs	$ 150,000	Variable Costs	75%	of Revenue				Value	Probability
3	Selling Price	$ 35,000	Cost of Capital	10%					8	0.2
4	Fixed Costs	$ 15,000	Tax Rate	34%					9	0.2
5	Depreciation/Yr	$ 10,000							10	0.2
6			Demand/Yr	10.0	units				11	0.2
7									12	0.2
8		Year 0	1	2	3	4				
9	Demand		9.0	12.0	8.0	8.0				
10	Revenue		315,000	420,000	280,000	280,000				
11	Fixed Cost		15,000	15,000	15,000	15,000				
12	Variable Cost		236,250	315,000	210,000	210,000				
13	Depreciation		10,000	10,000	10,000	10,000				
14	Profit before Tax		53,750	80,000	45,000	45,000				
15	Tax		18,275	27,200	15,300	15,300				
16	Profit after Tax		35,475	52,800	29,700	29,700				
17	Net Cash Flow	(150,000)	45,475	62,800	39,700	39,700				
18										
19	Net Present Value	$184.57								

FIGURE 9.19

Wilson's Spreadsheet with Randomly Selected Demands

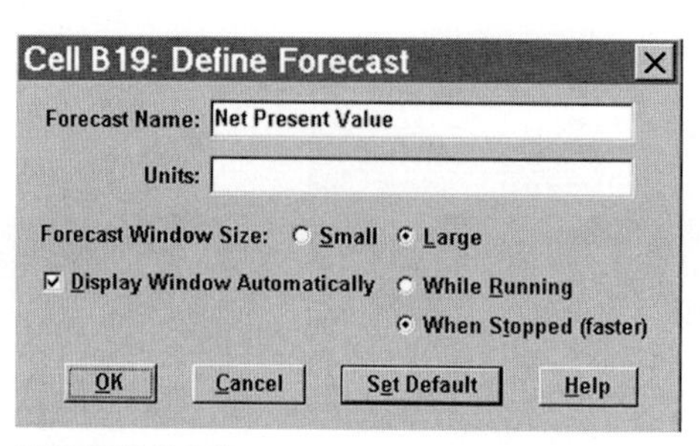

FIGURE 9.20

Crystal Ball "Define Forecast" Dialog Box

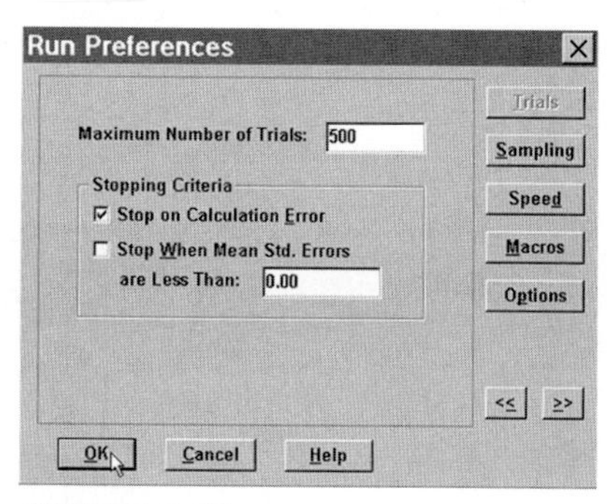

FIGURE 9.21

Crystal Ball "Run Preferences" Dialog Box

and perhaps even more important—the less likely it is that the NPV is negative, the more attractive the proposal to add the A3XX to Airbus' product line.

So, the next step is to run the simulation automatically a number of times and capture the resulting NPV. This can be done much more easily with Crystal Ball than the spreadsheet alone. After setting up the base case model as we have done, and entering the RNGs in the appropriate cells (C9:F9), all we have to do is:

1. Click on cell B19 (the NPV cell).
2. Click on the second Crystal Ball icon (Define Forecast), which brings up a dialog box.
3. Change the Window size to "Large" and change the Display to "When Stopped (faster)" in the dialog box as shown in Figure 9.20. Also click on "Set Default" if you want this to be the default choice in the future.
4. Click on OK.
5. Click on the eighth icon (Run Preferences) and change the "Maximum Number of Trials" to 500 as shown in Figure 9.21.
6. Click on OK.
7. Click on the ninth icon (Start Simulation) and after Crystal Ball has run the 500 iterations, it tells you that "Maximum number of trials reached." After clicking on OK, it automatically produces the histogram shown in Figure 9.22.
8. To look at the statistics from the simulation, click on View, then Statistics, and Crystal Ball displays a table as shown in Figure 9.23.

Notice how much faster and easier it is to run 500 iterations in Crystal Ball as opposed to 20 or 100 with the spreadsheet alone (if you covered Section 9.3), and it doesn't take up 500 rows in the spreadsheet. After doing this, you should have results similar to those shown in Figure 9.23 (representing 500 outcomes of the NPV). The numbers you generate

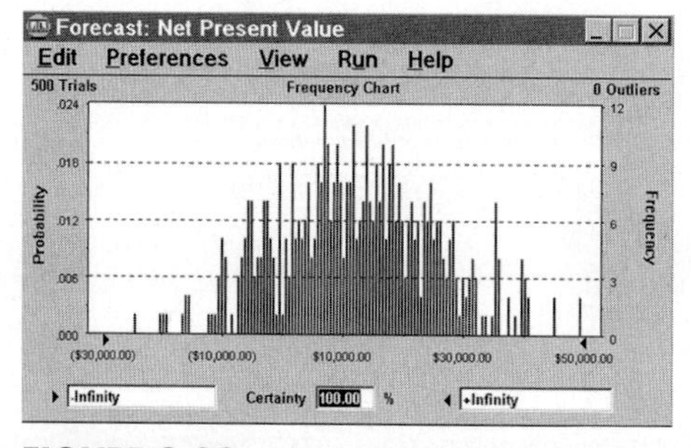

FIGURE 9.22

Airbus' Simulation Histogram of NPV

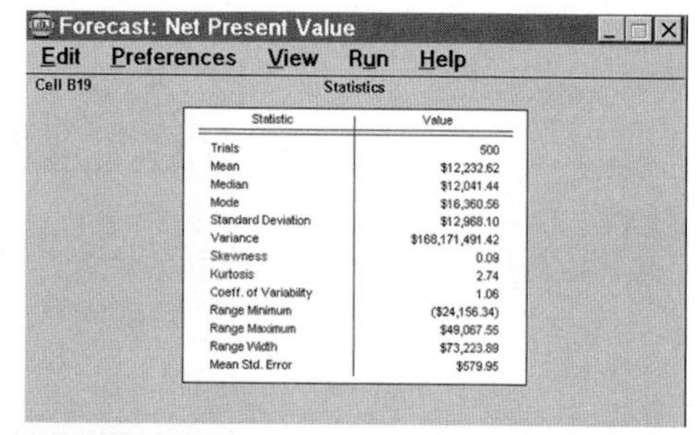
Forecast: Net Present Value

Edit Preferences View Run Help

Cell B19 Statistics

Statistic	Value
Trials	500
Mean	$12,232.62
Median	$12,041.44
Mode	$16,360.56
Standard Deviation	$12,968.10
Variance	$168,171,491.42
Skewness	0.09
Kurtosis	2.74
Coeff. of Variability	1.06
Range Minimum	($24,156.34)
Range Maximum	$49,067.55
Range Width	$73,223.89
Mean Std. Error	$579.95

FIGURE 9.23

Airbus' Simulation Statistics

will not exactly match those shown in Figure 9.23. Remember the procedure shown here generates a random sample of 500 trials from an infinite number of possible outcomes. Hopefully, the overall characteristics of your sample should be similar to the ones shown here. Based on this sample, the results indicate that the estimated mean NPV is $12,232.62 and the standard deviation is a rather large $12,968.10. Note this is much closer to the true mean NPV than we would generally get with the limited number of trials we would run with the spreadsheet alone.

Downside Risk and Upside Risk June also wants to know what's the best possible outcome as well as the worst possible. In this same display, we can see in Figure 9.23 that the largest NPV was $49,067.55 and the smallest was –$24,156.34. This gives her a better idea about the range of possible NPVs that could occur (almost $75,000).

Distribution of Outcomes Although this information offers more insight than just the base case NPV, there are other factors we should consider. How likely are these extreme outcomes (best case, worst case) to occur? In order to answer this question, we need to know something about the shape of the distribution of the NPV. Fortunately, Crystal Ball has some built-in features to help us. We already generated a histogram (a graphical distribution of the NPVs) in Figure 9.22, and it gives us a visual representation of the possible outcomes for the NPV. It has a definite bell shape to it. One of the nice features of Crystal Ball is that it has already tabulated a tremendous amount of statistical and graphical information. Some of the information is automatically displayed; other pieces of information we must ask for. As an example of some information we have to ask for, suppose we want to determine the exact probability that the NPV will be nonpositive (≤0). We can simply enter 0 in the "◀" cell shown in the lower right corner of Figure 9.24 (meaning all values to the left of 0) and hit enter, and Crystal Ball will automatically return the percentage number in the corresponding percentile cell labeled "Certainty_____%." In this case it returns 19.0%, meaning that 19.0% of the observed NPV values were less than or equal to 0. In like manner we could find out what percentage fell below or was above any arbitrary dollar amount. Also, by clicking on "View, Percentiles," Crystal Ball automatically displays the 10th, 20th, 30th, . . . , 90th percentiles of the NPV distribution. We notice that this is more precise information than we could get from Excel's Histogram feature or its Descriptive Statistics feature (which was shown in Section 9.3). This data can be helpful in answering other questions June or her chief financial officer might come up with.

How Reliable Is the Simulation? June now has the answers to her two questions about the NPV distribution: (1) What is the *mean* value of the NPV? (A: $12,232.62), and (2) What is the probability that the NPV assumes a negative value? (A: 19.0%). We now ask some questions: How much confidence do we have in the answers June came up with? Would we have more confidence if we ran more trials?

Certainly, it is intuitive that the more trials we run, the more confidence we ought to have in our answers. But how much confidence can we have in the 500 iterations we actually sampled? From the world of statistics, we remember that we can construct confidence intervals based on the results we obtained. For example, we can have 95% confidence that

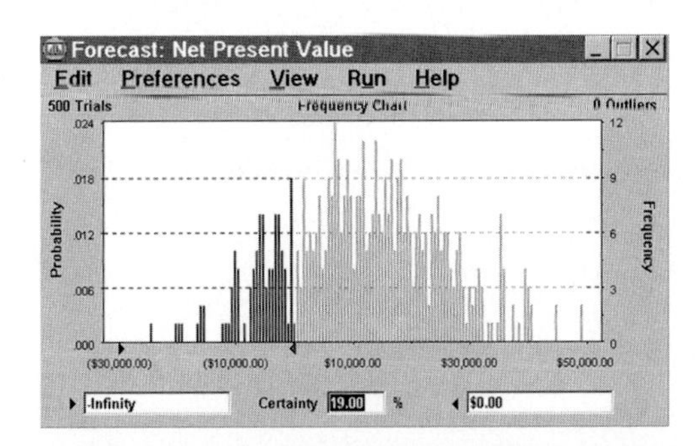

FIGURE 9.24

Wilson's Crystal Ball Percentiles

the true mean NPV is contained in an interval of ±1.96 standard deviations about the estimated mean. In this case, the standard deviation of the mean is the reported standard deviation of the sample divided by the square root of the number of trials. This 95% confidence interval for the mean was calculated by June and is reported in Figure 9.25 as ($11,095.92; $13,369.32). Said another way, we can have 95% confidence that the true mean NPV is somewhere between $11,096 and $13,369, with our current best guess that it is $12,232.62. Notice that this interval is tighter than the one we would generally develop with a spreadsheet alone where a smaller number of iterations would generally be used. The spreadsheet WILSCB1C.XLS (found on the CD distributed with the book) contains all of this completed information if you did not create it as you read along.

We must be careful *not* to fall in the "expected value" trap! Many students believe that the true mean NPV can always be calculated by setting all the random values to their means (set all the demands to 10 in this example). This is what June had in her initial spreadsheet (see Figure 9.9), but there is no guarantee that the NPV obtained in this manner will always be the true simulated mean. Although it may seem logical, there are some potential weaknesses in this reasoning. First of all, the way in which the random demand values are used to calculate yearly cash flows and then turned into a single NPV number (or any other performance measure) could be highly nonlinear. There are other subtleties that will not be mentioned here, but be forewarned: Don't fall into the "expected value" trap!

There are cases, like this model, where this "intuitive" reasoning works, but not always. A simple example from one of life's common experiences ought to convince you that the NPV (or any other bottom-line performance measure) at the expected value of the random variables is not necessarily the same as the expected NPV. Consider a waiting line at the grocery store. Suppose the expected time to serve a customer is 0.9 minutes and the average time between customer arrivals is 1 minute. Looking at the situation using the expected values, you would predict the average waiting time to be 0 minutes (because customers are served faster than they arrive), but we all know that the *average* waiting time will turn out to be greater than 0 minutes even though we sometimes get lucky and don't have to wait.

OTHER DISTRIBUTIONS OF DEMAND

June is concerned about the estimates of demand that she used in the previous simulation. In that model she assumed that the mean demand in each period would be 10 units, and then allowed for random variation in demand around that mean (between 8 and 12 units).

FIGURE 9.25

Wilson's Confidence Interval for the Mean Value of the NPV

B9 = =B3-1.96*B4/SQRT(B5)

	A	B	C
1	**Crystal Ball Results**		
2			
3	Mean	$ 12,232.62	
4	Std Dev	$ 12,968.10	
5	# Iterations	500	
6			
7	**95% Confidence Interval**		
8	Upper Limit	$ 13,369.32	
9	Lower Limit	$ 11,095.92	
10			

Cell	Formula
B8	=B3+1.96*B4/SQRT(B5)
B9	=B3−1.96*B4/SQRT(B5)

She is quite confident that the mean demand will indeed remain essentially the same in each of the next four years, but she is not at all sure that it will necessarily be 10. If the economy is slow it might be 8; if the economy continues at its current robust pace it might be 13. After some thought, June decides that the mean demand could be anywhere between 6 and 14 units a year, with all values in between being equally likely. To express this uncertainty she decides to model the mean demand as a continuous uniform distribution between 6 and 14.

She would also like to explore the impact of different demand distributions on the NPV. She has read in a probability and statistics text that when mean demand is relatively small, a distribution called the Poisson distribution is often a good fit. The Poisson is a *one-parameter* distribution, because specifying only one parameter, the mean value of the random variable, completely determines it. The Poisson is also a discrete distribution, since a Poisson random variable can take on only nonnegative integer values. June will put this new information in a new spreadsheet called WILSNCB2.XLS. To sample from a Poisson distribution with a mean of 10, June has only to call up Crystal Ball's Distribution Gallery and indicate that she wants a Poisson distribution with a mean of 10. To sample from a continuous, uniform distribution between 6 and 14, she has to call up Crystal Ball's Distribution Gallery and indicate that she wants a uniform distribution with a "min" value of 6 and a "max" value of 14. The only changes June has to make in her spreadsheet then are the following: indicate to Crystal Ball that the cell D6 will have the uniform distribution discussed above and that cells C9 through F9 will have a Poisson distribution with a mean value driven by the value in cell D6. To do this last step in Crystal Ball, we click on cell C9, then click on "Define Assumption" to bring up the Crystal Ball distribution gallery dialog box and enter the information as shown in Figure 9.26 (make sure you change to the "Dynamic" button). To get the same information from cell C9 to cells D9:F9, we can use Crystal Ball's "Copy Data" and "Paste Data" features (the fifth and sixth icons) to save us time, or we can just enter all the same information as we did for cell C9 into cells D9, E9, and F9 on an individual basis.

June decides to sample 1,000 times from the distribution of the NPV and base her estimates on the 1,000 values she obtains. She simply tells Crystal Ball to perform 1,000 iterations in the "Run Preferences" dialog box and to capture the NPV in cell B19 for each of the iterations (using the "Define Forecast" icon). She must also tell Crystal Ball to "Reset Simulation" (eleventh icon) so that it clears the results from the simulation run above. After the 1,000 iterations are completed, June can view a histogram of the results. The histogram is shown in Figure 9.27, and the related statistics reveal that the average NPV over the 1,000 iterations is $9,816.11 and that there is a large probability of a negative NPV (27.5%). The mean NPV is lower than it was with the previous distribution, and the probability of a negative outcome has increased significantly (19% to 27.5%).

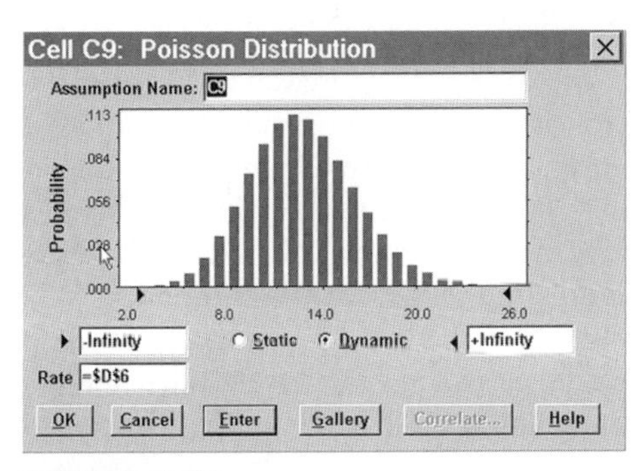

FIGURE 9.26

Wilson's Modified Distribution Dialog Box

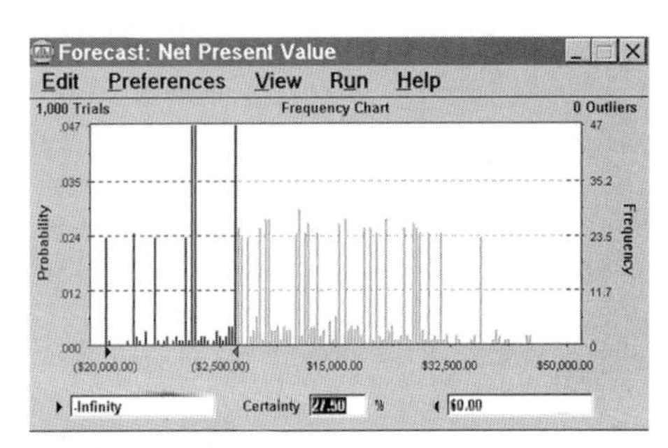

FIGURE 9.27

Wilson's NPV Histogram Using a Modified Distribution

The graph gives a qualitative impression of the distribution, but more detailed information can be obtained. Some of the other simulation statistics June could view are: the largest value observed, $44,729; and the smallest value observed, –$19,817 (a range of approximately $65,000). The completed model is found on the CD as WILSCB2C.XLS.

We have now seen three evaluations of June's A3XX capital budgeting problem: (1) a deterministic model (Figure 9.16), (2) a simulation with 500 trials but restricted assumptions about demand (Figure 9.19), and (3) a simulation with 1,000 trials, based on what June feels is a more realistic representation of demand (Figure 9.27). What have we learned?

1. Increasing the number of trials is apt to give a better estimate of the expected return, but even with a large number of trials there can sometimes be a difference between the simulated *average* and the true expected return.
2. Simulations can provide useful information on the distribution of results. With the sample of 500 trials and restricted assumptions about demand, there was an indication (a probability of 0.19) that this project might yield a negative NPV. This is valuable information and something that could not have been determined with simply the base case analysis, or even Upside/Downside Risk analysis.
3. Simulation results are sensitive to assumptions affecting the input parameters. We saw that if June changes her assumptions about the distribution of demand (from a discrete, uniform distribution to a Poisson distribution with the same mean of 10), there is a significant impact on the probability of a negative NPV (it increases from about 19% to about 27.5%).

Perhaps the most important impact of the simulation is on the decision-making process. If June had not performed any simulation analysis, she would have given an enthusiastic recommendation to proceed with the proposed addition to the heavy equipment line based on the mean NPV. However, after performing either of the simulations, she feels the project is too risky to recommend. While this is a qualitative judgment on her part, she can support it with the quantitative results of the simulation model. As we have noted before, models do not relieve managers from the responsibility of making decisions, but they do supply additional information for making those decisions well informed.

9.5 AN INVENTORY CONTROL EXAMPLE: FOSLINS HOUSEWARES

June Wilson's capital budgeting model provided an example of the use of simulation in a "yes or no" situation: June had to decide whether or not to accept the project. There are other situations, however, in which the question is, "How much of this should we do?" Simulation can be used for models of this type as well. However, there are some new concerns (or perhaps variations of old concerns) to consider when using simulation in this way. This section uses an inventory control model to provide another illustration of simulation. It will also serve to motivate a discussion of the proper interpretation of results.

THE OMELET PAN PROMOTION: HOW MANY PANS TO ORDER?

Marie Ford is the chief buyer for housewares at Foslins, one of Denver's leading retailers. The chief buyer's role is important in a retail organization like Foslins. Marie is responsible for designing the overall retailing strategy and operating procedures for her area. She also supervises a group of buyers who make specific purchase decisions.

Certain sections of the housewares department have just suffered their second consecutive bad year. Competing shops, such as Box and Barrel, which specialize in imported cooking and dining articles, have made serious inroads into Foslins' once secure position. The gourmet cooking, glassware, stainless flatware, and contemporary dishes sections of Foslins are not generating enough revenue to justify the amount of floor space currently committed to them.

Marie plans to meet this challenge head-on. She has reorganized the sections that are in trouble to create a store within a store. To achieve the same ambiance as her competitors, she has adopted display techniques that feature natural wood and modern lighting. She has essentially created a specialty shop, like her competitors, within the housewares department. With these changes, plus the store's reputation for quality and service, she feels that Foslins can effectively compete.

To introduce the new facility at Foslins, Marie decides to make the month of October "International Dining Month." This promotion will feature a sale on five special articles, each from a different country. These articles will be especially made for Foslins and include a copper omelet pan from France, a set of 12 long-stem wine glasses from Spain, and so on. Each of the items has been selected by a buyer on Marie's staff. The design and price are agreed on. The items have to be ordered at least 6 months in advance, and they will not become part of Foslins' regular product line. Any items left at the end of October will be sold to a discount chain at a reduced price. In addition, Foslins has adopted the policy that if it runs out of the special sale items, a more expensive item from its regular line of merchandise will be substituted at the sale price. It is all part of the "once-in-a-lifetime" promotion.

In the case of the omelet pans, Foslins will buy the special pans for \$22 and will sell them for \$35. Any pans left at the end of the sale will be sold to Clampton's Discount Chain for \$15 each. If Foslins runs out of the special pans, it will substitute one of its regular copper omelet pans and sell it for the sale price of \$35. Regular pans, which normally sell for \$65, cost \$32 each.

Marie's problem is that she must decide how many of the special pans to order without knowing in advance what the demand for them will be. For example, suppose she ordered 1,000 pans and the demand turned out to be 1,100 pans. Then she would have to buy 100 pans (1100 – 1000) at \$32 per pan after buying 1,000 pans at \$22 per pan and would sell all 1,100 pans at \$35 per pan. Thus her net profit would be

$$\$35(1100) - \$32(100) - \$22(1000) = \$12{,}300$$

In general, let y = number of pans ordered and D = demand. Then for $D > y$,

$$\text{Profit} = 35D - 32(D - y) - 22y = 3D + 10y$$

If, on the other hand, she ordered 1,000 pans and demand turned out only to be 200 pans, then she would sell 200 pans at \$35 and 800 pans (1000 – 200) at \$15 to Clampton's. Her net profit would be

$$\$35(200) + \$15(800) - \$22(1000) = -\$3000$$

In general, for $D < y$,

$$\text{Profit} = 35D + 15\,(y - D) - 22y = 20D - 7y$$

(You can see that for $D = y$, the two formulas become identical.)

Note that Marie's calculations assume that using regular pans to satisfy promotional demand will *not* create any unsatisfied regular demand. Because of the location of her regular pan supplier, the supply is large enough that this complication need not be considered.

Marie has modeled this in Excel as FOSLNCB1.XLS and it is shown in Figure 9.28. The spreadsheet assumes that Marie decides to order 11 omelet pans (i.e., $y = 11$). The random demand turns out to be 8 (i.e., $D = 8$), and the order quantity is greater than the demand ($y > D$). This means we have 3 extra pans leftover. Thus the profit of this single simulated promotion is \$35(8) + \$15(3) – \$22(11) = \$83.

PROFIT VERSUS ORDER QUANTITY

Marie is naturally interested in determining how the number of pans she orders affects her expected profit on the promotion and the likelihood of the promotion losing money. We will see how to attack this question with simulation, beginning with a simple illustrative example. Later, in Section 9.6, we will treat the more realistic assumption of a *normal*

FIGURE 9.28

Foslins' Base Case

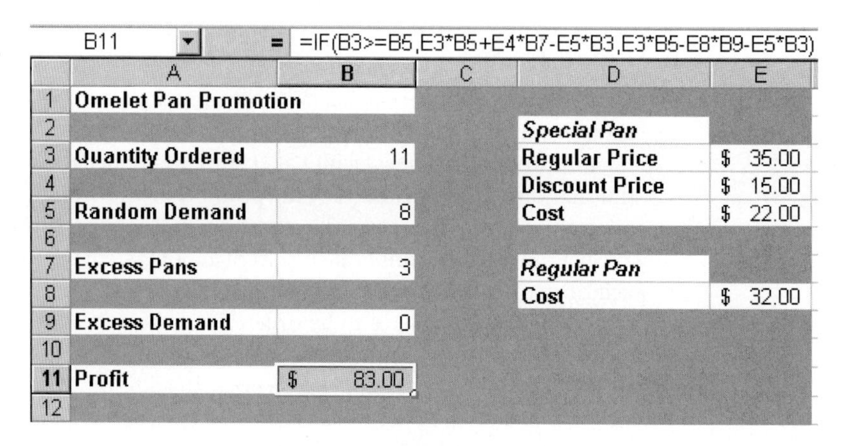

B11 = =IF(B3>=B5,E3*B5+E4*B7-E5*B3,E3*B5-E8*B9-E5*B3)

	A	B	C	D	E
1	Omelet Pan Promotion				
2				*Special Pan*	
3	Quantity Ordered	11		Regular Price	$ 35.00
4				Discount Price	$ 15.00
5	Random Demand	8		Cost	$ 22.00
6					
7	Excess Pans	3		*Regular Pan*	
8				Cost	$ 32.00
9	Excess Demand	0			
10					
11	Profit	$ 83.00			
12					

Cell	Formula
B7	=MAX(0,B3−B5)
B9	=MAX(0,B5−B3)
B11	=IF(B3≥B5,E3*B5+E4*B7−E5*B3,E3*B5−E8*B9−E5*B3)

demand distribution ($\mu = 1000$, $\sigma = 100$). Let us now assume that demand has the following probability distribution.

$$\text{Prob}\{\text{demand} = 8\} = 0.1$$
$$\text{Prob}\{\text{demand} = 9\} = 0.2$$
$$\text{Prob}\{\text{demand} = 10\} = 0.3$$
$$\text{Prob}\{\text{demand} = 11\} = 0.2$$
$$\text{Prob}\{\text{demand} = 12\} = 0.1$$
$$\text{Prob}\{\text{demand} = 13\} = 0.1$$

These demands have been chosen artificially small in order to simplify the example. To generate random demand for this probability distribution in Crystal Ball, Marie has to enter this discrete distribution in a two-column format for Crystal Ball, as shown in the previous section. This is shown in columns G and H of Figure 9.29. To accomplish entering all this probability distribution information into Crystal Ball, Marie does the following:

1. Click on cell B5, which is the cell where Crystal Ball will generate random values for demand.
2. Click on the first Crystal Ball icon (Define Assumption).

FIGURE 9.29

Foslins' Random Demand Generator

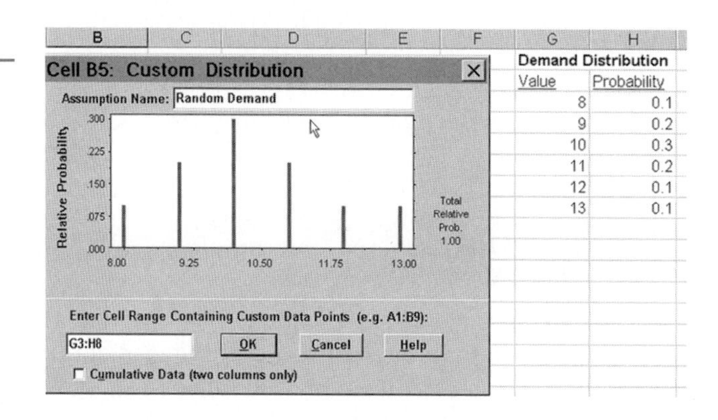

3. Click on the "Custom" distribution from the resulting Distribution Gallery (shown previously in Figure 9.17); then click on OK (or alternatively you could have double clicked on the "Custom" distribution).
4. Click on the "Data" button and enter the cell range where you entered the information on this discrete distribution (G3:H8 as shown in Figure 9.29); then click on OK.
5. Crystal Ball shows the distribution back to you as you have entered it (see Figure 9.29).

We are now prepared to use simulation to calculate the average profit. To do so, we must generate a number of trials, setting $y = 11$ and generating a new demand on each trial. The profit that results on any given trial depends, of course, on the value of demand that was generated on that particular trial. The *average profit* over all trials, then, is an estimate of the expected profit. Again, this can be done easily with Crystal Ball as follows:

1. Click on cell B11 (the Profit cell).
2. Click on the second Crystal Ball icon (Define Forecast), which brings up a dialog box.
3. Change the Window size to "Large" and change the Display to "When Stopped (faster)" in the dialog box if this is not already your default setting (shown previously in Figure 9.20). Also click on "Set Default" if you want this to be the default choice in the future.
4. Click on OK.
5. Click on the eighth icon (Run Preferences) and change the "Maximum Number of Trials" to 500 (shown previously in Figure 9.21).
6. Click on OK.
7. Click on the ninth icon (Start Simulation) and after Crystal Ball has run the 500 iterations, it tells you that "Maximum # of trials reached." After clicking on OK, it automatically produces the histogram shown in Figure 9.30.
8. To look at the statistics from the simulation, click on View, then Statistics, and Crystal Ball displays a table as shown in Figure 9.31.

The numbers you generate will not exactly match those shown in Figure 9.31. Remember the procedure shown here generates a random sample of 500 trials from an infinite number of possible outcomes. Hopefully, the overall characteristics of your sample should be similar to the ones shown here. According to Figure 9.31, the average profit for the 500 trials is \$124.30. Thus, based on these 500 trials, Marie's best estimate of the expected profit of ordering 11 pans is \$124.30. The completed spreadsheet is found on the CD as FOSLCB1C.XLS.

Marie can use the same approach to calculate the average profit associated with any order quantity. She need only place a different order size in cell B3 of the "Base Case" spreadsheet and rerun the simulation.

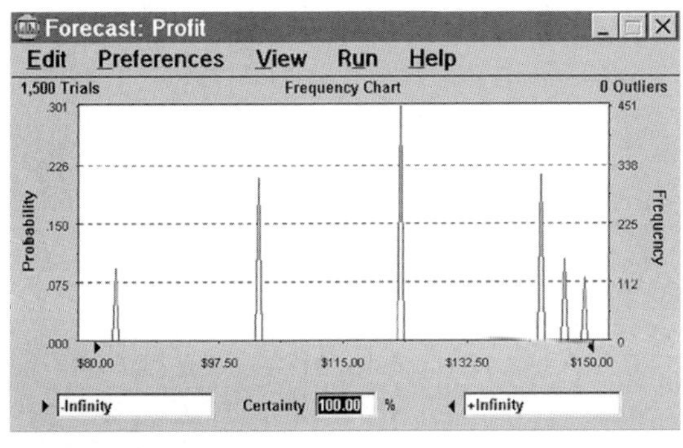

FIGURE 9.30

Foslins' Simulation Histogram of Profit

Forecast: Profit

Edit Preferences View Run Help

Cell B11 — Statistics

Statistic	Value
Trials	500
Mean	\$124.30
Median	\$123.00
Mode	\$123.00
Standard Deviation	\$20.30
Variance	\$411.99
Skewness	-0.57
Kurtosis	2.32
Coeff. of Variability	0.16
Range Minimum	\$83.00
Range Maximum	\$149.00
Range Width	\$66.00
Mean Std. Error	\$0.91

FIGURE 9.31

Foslins' Simulation Statistics

Table 9.2

Expected Profit When Ordering 11 Pans

(A) ORDER QUANTITY	(B) DEMAND	(C) PROFIT	(D) PROBABILITY OF DEMAND	(E) COLUMN (C) * (D)
11	8	\$83	.10	8.3
11	9	\$103	.20	20.6
11	10	\$123	.30	36.9
11	11	\$143	.20	28.6
11	12	\$146	.10	14.6
11	13	\$149	.10	14.9
				Expected Profit = \$123.9

But note that since the demand is random, the average profit will also be random. This means that if Marie ran another set of 500 trials with the same order size of 11 pans, the simulator could generate a different series of demands and thus would most likely obtain a different average profit.

Expected Value versus Order Quantity With this simple example, Marie can easily calculate the true *expected* profit associated with any order quantity as opposed to relying on her estimate of profit from 500 trials (this is often not the case for more realistic examples and is only done here for pedagogical reasons). This can be done by using the spreadsheet shown in Figure 9.28 to calculate the profit resulting from each of the six possible demand levels (8, 9, . . . , 13). All Marie does is place the six different possible demand values in cell B5 (one at a time) and note what profit is produced. Each of these profit values is then multiplied by the probability of that demand occurring (e.g., the profit produced when demand = 10 is multiplied by 0.3, the probability that demand will in fact be 10). Finally, the resulting terms are added. The calculation is shown in Table 9.2.

Simulated Versus Expected Profits Assuming that risk is not a factor, Marie would like to select the order quantity that yields the largest expected profit. To do so, she would calculate the expected profit for all the possible order quantities (8, 9, 10, . . . , 13), just as she did for an order quantity of 11, and select the order quantity that yields the largest profit. If she were to use simulation, she would use the same procedure that she used to determine the *average profit* with an order quantity of 11 for the other possible order quantities (8, 9, 10, 12, 13) and then select that order quantity that yielded the largest average profit.

It is no surprise that for any particular order quantity, the average profit generated by the spreadsheet simulator does not equal the true expected profit, as we have already seen that different runs will produce different values for the average profit. The implication of this fact on the process of making a decision is interesting. The computed expected profits and simulated average profits for order sizes of 9, 10, 11, and 12 pans are shown in Table 9.3. We have only shown the work behind the simulated and true expected profit for ordering 11 pans. We leave it as an exercise for the student to verify the other entries in the table (see Problems 9-8 through 9-10).

Table 9.3

NUMBER ORDERED	TRUE EXPECTED PROFIT	SIMULATED AVERAGE PROFIT (500 TRIALS)
9	\$119.2	\$118.88
10	**\$124.1**	\$124.18
11	\$123.9	**\$124.30**
12	\$120.3	\$118.81

Here we see that if Marie were to base her decision on the simulated average profit for this particular set of trials, the profit-maximizing decision would be to order 11 pans. To maximize the true expected profit, however, she should order 10 pans. This is, of course, a deliberately oversimplified example, but it is an excellent illustration of the fact that *simulation, in general, is not guaranteed to achieve optimality.*

In Marie's case, the decision to order 11 pans rather than 10 is not critical, for it reduces her true expected profit by less than 0.2%. In some instances, however, simulation can lead to results that are farther from the optimal. Marie may therefore wonder whether there is anything she can do to improve the accuracy of her simulation. Can she increase the likelihood that a simulation will in fact produce an optimal decision?

Although the nature of simulation makes it impossible to *guarantee* that an optimal decision will be identified, there is a very simple way to increase the likelihood of this outcome: *increase the number of trials.* The greater the number of trials, the more reliable the results of the simulation tend to be—just as the more often you toss a coin, the more closely the proportion of heads is likely to approach 50%. This fact leads to the following important observation:

> Suppose that, in a decision under risk, management would like to make the decision that minimizes expected cost or maximizes expected profit. With simulation, the decision may be wrongly identified if care is not taken to simulate a sufficient number of trials.

We should reemphasize that in a real problem you would not *both* calculate the true expected profit and use simulation to calculate an average profit. Simulation is used when it is computationally impractical or even not possible to calculate the expected profit associated with the alternative decisions, or when it is important to assess the variability of the performance measure for various solutions. This simple example serves to illustrate relationships between simulation and analytic models.

RECAPITULATION

Let us summarize and comment on several aspects of what we have seen so far:

1. A spreadsheet simulator takes parameters and decisions as inputs and yields a performance measure (or measures) as output.
2. Each iteration of the spreadsheet simulator (for the same parameters and decisions) will generally yield a different value for the performance measure.
3. In Marie's model the performance measure (for an order of size 11) was taken to be profit. The 500 trials taken together combine to produce another measure of the goodness of the particular order size: *average profit.*

Note that even more information is available. If we wanted to know how often a shortage occurred (demand exceeded the quantity ordered), we would need to click on cell B9, add it as a "Forecast" cell and rerun the simulation. Figure 9.32 shows that a shortage

FIGURE 9.32

Foslins' Shortage Results

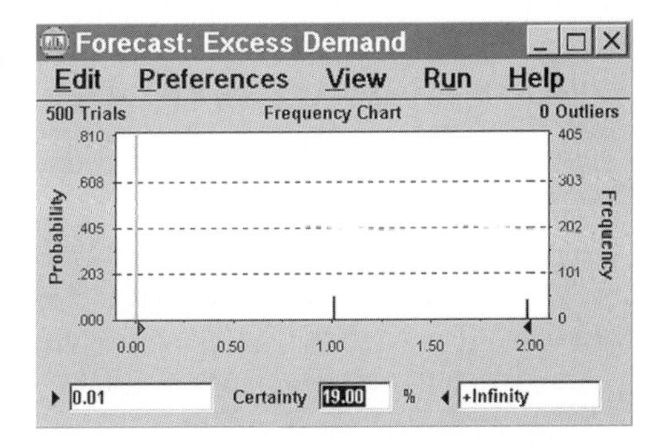

occurred in 95 of the 500 trials (19%). This is additional data with which to assess the "goodness" of ordering 11 pans, and it shows how, with simulation, numerous "performance measures" can be produced.

Yet another important property of simulation is illustrated by a previous figure (see Figure 9.31). The 500 trials have produced a distribution of profit: It varies from $83 to $149, with a mean of $124.30. We also previously generated the histogram shown in Figure 9.30. This provides some indication as to the **variability** associated with the policy being evaluated (ordering 11 pans). Indicators of variability are important products of simulation studies. *Management usually seeks policies for which the potential outcome is highly predictable, which means low variability.*

4. Increasing the number of iterations of the spreadsheet simulator (for the same parameters and decisions) will usually improve the accuracy of the estimate of the expected value of the performance measure. In other words, if Marie had used 1,000 or 5,000 trials in her simulation, the average profit for each order quantity would almost certainly be closer to the corresponding true expected profit.
5. In a simulation we can never be sure that we have found the optimal decision, although we can use our confidence interval knowledge from statistics to make sure we have performed enough trials that we have 95% or 99% confidence. This lack of 100% confidence is because a simulation can provide only an estimate of the expected effectiveness and not the exact value when randomness is present.
6. Management must assess four main factors in a simulation study:
   a. Does the model capture the essence of the real problem? (See Section 9.10 for further discussion of this point.)
   b. Are the influence of the starting and ending conditions of the simulation properly accounted for? (See Section 9.8 for a specific example.)
   c. Have enough trials been performed for each decision so that the average value of the measure (or measures) of performance is a good indication of the true expected value?
   d. Have enough decisions (and the right decisions) been evaluated so that we can believe that the best answer found is "close enough" to the optimum?

9.6 SIMULATION OF FOSLINS' MODEL WITH A MORE REALISTIC DEMAND ASSUMPTION

Although we have already analyzed the Foslins' Houseware model in Section 9.5, recall that we had assumed a simplified demand distribution when a more realistic model of demand is the normal distribution with a mean of 1,000 and a standard deviation of 100. In this section we will use a normal distribution of demand, perform 1,000 trials, and determine the optimal order quantity.

In the development of this example we will practice how to generate a normal random variable with a specific mean and standard deviation. We will also see how variability in a simulation can be reduced, allowing a better estimate of the difference in profit between two decisions. In addition, the example provides an opportunity for examining the distinction between average profit, and true expected profit, as well as a further illustration of what is meant by the distribution of profits for a specific order quantity.

THE FOSLINS' SPREADSHEET: SIMULATING DEMAND MORE REALISTICALLY

Recall our spreadsheet (FOSLNCB1.XLS) from Figure 9.28. To modify the model, we will start with a new spreadsheet (FOSLNCB2.XLS) and then change the quantity ordered to 1,020 and notify Crystal Ball that we want to change the random distribution of demand from a customized one (discrete, general) to the normal distribution with a mean value of 1,000 and a standard deviation of 100, as shown in Figure 9.33. (*Note*: To do this in Excel

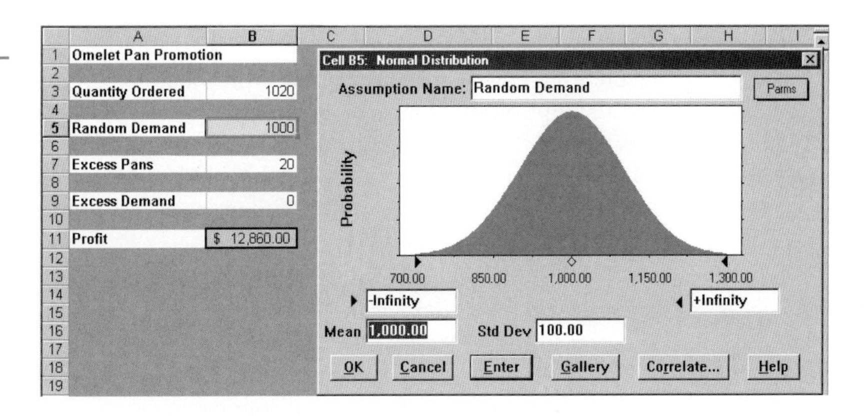

FIGURE 9.33

Foslins' Spreadsheet Assuming Normal Demand

alone, all you have to do is type the following in cell B5: NORMINV(RAND(),1000,100), or you can replace the 1,000 and 100 with appropriate cell references.)

To simulate 1,000 trials, we follow the same procedure we did before in Section 9.5 where we ran 500 trials by modifying the Run Preferences dialog box to indicate the larger number of iterations. The other change we make is to indicate that we wish to use the same 1,000 random values for demand in each of the upcoming simulations (for the different order quantities we'll compare). This is known as setting the seed value. The procedure to do this is as follows:

1. Click on "Sampling" in the Run Preferences dialog box.
2. Place a check mark in the box that says "Use Same Sequence of Random Numbers."
3. Enter an "Initial Seed Value" of 422 (or any number you like), as shown in Figure 9.34.
4. Click on OK.

It is important that the demands not change, because we want to compare the average profit for *different* order quantities but the *same* set of random demands. Then profit will differ only because of different order quantities and not because a different set of demand values had been sampled.

This process of decreasing variability in simulation results is called *variance reduction* and it is an important technique in reducing the amount of computation necessary to obtain valid simulation results. Indeed, the ability to use the *same* set of random variables to evaluate competing alternatives is a unique experimental advantage of simulation. All branches of science attempt to reduce exogenous variability in their experiments. For example, agronomists plant different varieties of corn in the same field to insure that weather and soil conditions do not vary. With simulation, using the same sequence of random variables provides us with complete control of the random elements.

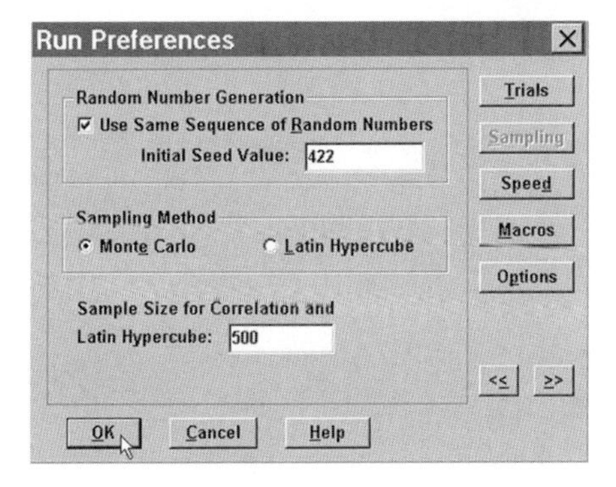

FIGURE 9.34

Foslins' New "Run Preferences" Dialog Box

THE EFFECT OF ORDER QUANTITY

Figure 9.35 shows a histogram of the profit values generated for the 1,000 iterations under the assumption of ordering 1,020 pans. The average profit of $12,270.44 is shown in Figure 9.36, along with some other statistics. By entering different order quantities in cell B3 of the spreadsheet and rerunning the simulation, we could get an idea of how the average profit varies for a range of order quantities and a *given* set of demands. To reset the simulation:

1. Place a new order quantity in cell B3.
2. Click on the eleventh icon (Reset Simulation) and click OK in response to the question asked.
3. Click on the seventh icon (Start Simulation). This simulation could take a few minutes, depending on the speed of your computer.

To search for the optimal order quantity is an iterative process. After running the simulation at an order quantity of 1,020. Marie next can check order quantities of 1,010 and 1,030. After running 1,000 iterations at each new order quantity, Marie finds that the expected profits are $12,268.95 and $12,264.60, respectively. Since the expected profit for the order quantity of 1,020 is the best so far, Marie next decides to check the order quantities on either side (e.g., 1,015 and 1,025). She finds that the expected profits are $12,270.70 and $12,268.34. At this point, an order quantity of 1,015 seems to give the highest expected profit so she checks some order quantities on either side (e.g., 1,013 and 1,017) of the best order quantity so far (i.e., 1,015). Marie finds that the expected profits are $12,270.29 and $12,270.77, respectively. The order quantity of 1,017 now seems to give the highest expected profit. Just to make sure though, Marie reruns the simulation and tries the order quantities of 1,016 and 1,018. She finds that their expected profits are $12,270.76 and $12,270.71, respectively, and is now fairly confident that an order quantity of 1,017 really is the best decision, albeit only by a few cents. The completed spreadsheet is found on the CD as FOSLCB2C.XLS.

As a result of this iterative process, Marie has found that while the order quantity of 1,017 pans maximizes the *average* profit *for the given set of 1,000 demands*, it may not maximize the true *expected* profit. As we have said before, it is nearly impossible to guarantee that the optimal solution will be found using simulation. But remember, an optimal solution is a theoretical as opposed to a real-world concept. At best, an optimal solution represents a "good decision" for the real-world problem. In this case, the average profit for order quantities between 1,015 and 1,018 only varied by a couple of pennies, and so even if we didn't get the exact optimal order quantity, we are certainly confident that we are "close enough."

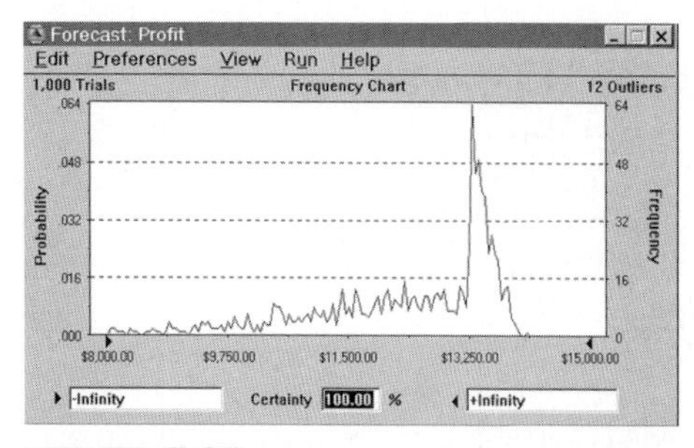

FIGURE 9.35

Foslins' Histogram of Profits when Ordering 1020 Pans

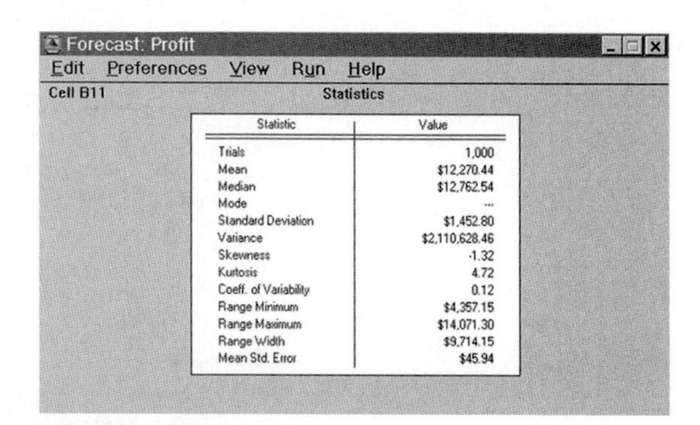
Forecast: Profit

Edit Preferences View Run Help

Cell B11 Statistics

Statistic	Value
Trials	1,000
Mean	$12,270.44
Median	$12,762.54
Mode	---
Standard Deviation	$1,452.80
Variance	$2,110,628.46
Skewness	-1.32
Kurtosis	4.72
Coeff. of Variability	0.12
Range Minimum	$4,357.15
Range Maximum	$14,071.30
Range Width	$9,714.15
Mean Std. Error	$45.94

FIGURE 9.36

Foslins' Statistical Output when Ordering 1020 Pans

FIGURE 9.37

Foslins' Histogram of Profit for Ordering 1017 Pans

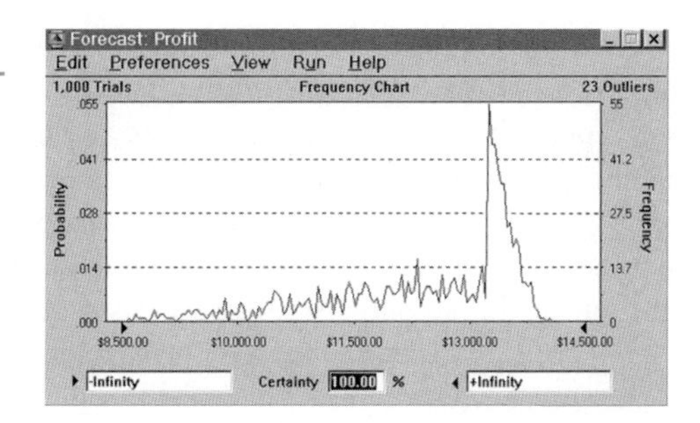

The Probability Distribution of Profit We may, however, want to know more about the solution suggested by simulation (ordering 1,017 pans). For example, how much variability can we expect around the average profit of $12,270.77? Could we make much more or much less than the average? Could this decision *lose* money? The definitive answer to these questions is given in the form of the probability distribution (or histogram) of profit as shown in Figure 9.37.

Figure 9.37 shows the distribution of profit for an order quantity of 1,017 based on a sample of 1,000 trials. This gives a nice visual picture of the range of risk that Foslins will be taking in ordering 1,017 pans, and may have more impact on Marie and her boss than just numbers and averages. The distribution appears to have somewhat of a bell shape to it, with a long left tail. The peaked distribution to the right of the expected value ($12,271) means that there is a definite probability that the profit will exceed the mean profit. The long tail to the left of the expected profit means that there is some chance of obtaining a result several thousand dollars below the expected profit. There is very little chance, however, of losing money on this promotion: In 1,000 trials, no profit was less than $4,370.

9.7 MIDWEST EXPRESS: AIRLINE OVERBOOKING MODEL

Most of the models we have discussed in this chapter so far have been from the manufacturing side of the economy (Airbus Industry and Foslins). Now that well over half of the United States' Gross Domestic Product is from the service sector, the chapter would not be complete without an example from that sector. The travel and hospitality industry is a huge, multi-billion-dollar industry. Many of the different industries (e.g., airlines, hotels, rental cars, cruise lines, etc.) within that broad group practice a set of quantitative tools called revenue management. The airlines were the first ones to pioneer the use of these tools, with American Airlines generally considered to be the leader. For example, American Airlines started the practice of auctioning off the value of a seat on a given flight when more customers showed up than it had seats available. This was a very innovative way to deal with the potential problem that exists when airlines overbook their flights. American Airlines estimates that overbooking alone adds over $200 million per year to its bottom line (see Smith et. al.) Other areas besides overbooking that are practiced in the revenue management area include forecasting, seat allocation among the various fare classes, and control of the entire network of flight legs.

This example will focus on a very successful, regional carrier (Midwest Express Airlines). Midwest Express is headquartered in Milwaukee, Wisconsin, and was started by the large consumer products company Kimberly Clark, which has large operations in nearby Appleton, Wisconsin. Laura Sorensen is the manager of revenue management. She has been reviewing the historical data on the percentage of no-shows for many of Midwest Express' flights. She is particularly interested in Flight 227 from Milwaukee to San Francisco. She has found that the average no-show rate on this flight is 15%. The aircraft (MD88) has a capacity of 112 seats in a single cabin. There is no First Class/Coach cabin distinction at Midwest Express. All service is considered to be premium service. You would believe that if you could smell the chocolate chip cookies baking as you fly along.

The question Laura wants to answer is to what level should she overbook the aircraft. Demand is strong on this primarily business route. The average fare charged on this flight is $400. If Laura accepts only 112 reservations on this flight, it is almost certain to go out with empty seats because of the no-shows that represent an opportunity cost for Midwest Express as it could have filled each seat with another customer and made an additional $400. On the other hand, if she accepts more reservations than seats, she runs the risk that even after accounting for the no-shows that more customers will show up than she has seats available. The normal procedure in the event that a customer must be denied boarding is to put the "extra" customers on the next available flight, provide them some compensation toward a flight in the future and possibly a voucher for a free meal and a hotel. This is all done to mitigate the potential ill will of the "bumped" customer. Laura figures this compensation usually costs Midwest Express around $600 on average.

To solve this challenging model, Laura built the spreadsheet shown in Figure 9.38 (MIDWSTRK.XLS). We will demonstrate the use of @Risk with this example.

In cell B12, we have modeled a binomial random variable using @Risk. For each of the reservations that Midwest Express chooses to accept, the model randomly generates the number who actually show up. Some simple calculations are then done to determine either the number of empty seats (cell B16) or the number of customers who are denied boarding (cell B14). This is essentially what Laura is trading off. The more reservations she accepts, the less likely she is to have empty seats, but she increases the likelihood that she'll have to deny boarding to a customer. She seeks to find the optimal overbooking level that maximizes her profit. This profit formula (cell B18) is shown in Excel's equation line of Figure 9.38 and takes the number of show-ups times the average fare and subtracts the costs of

FIGURE 9.38

Midwest Overbooking Model

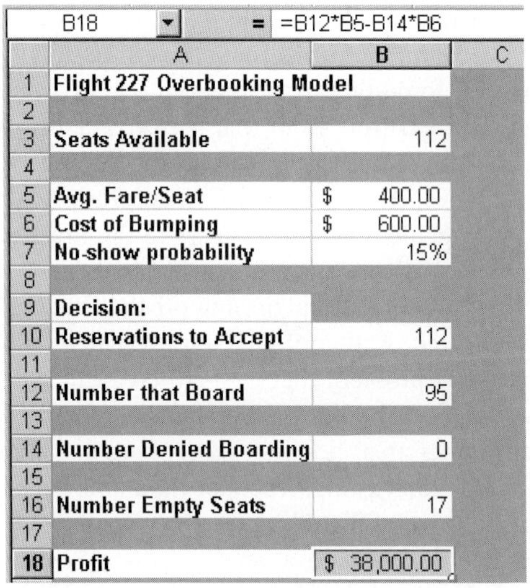

B18 = =B12*B5-B14*B6

	A	B	C
1	Flight 227 Overbooking Model		
2			
3	Seats Available	112	
4			
5	Avg. Fare/Seat	$ 400.00	
6	Cost of Bumping	$ 600.00	
7	No-show probability	15%	
8			
9	Decision:		
10	Reservations to Accept	112	
11			
12	Number that Board	95	
13			
14	Number Denied Boarding	0	
15			
16	Number Empty Seats	17	
17			
18	Profit	$ 38,000.00	

Cell	Formula
B10	=RiskSimtable ({112,114,116,118,120,. . . , 144,146})
B12	=RiskBinomial (B10,1−B7)
B14	=MAX (0,B12−B3)
B16	=MAX (0,B3−B12)
B18	=B12*B5−B14*B6

FIGURE 9.39

@Risk's Monte Carlo Display Feature

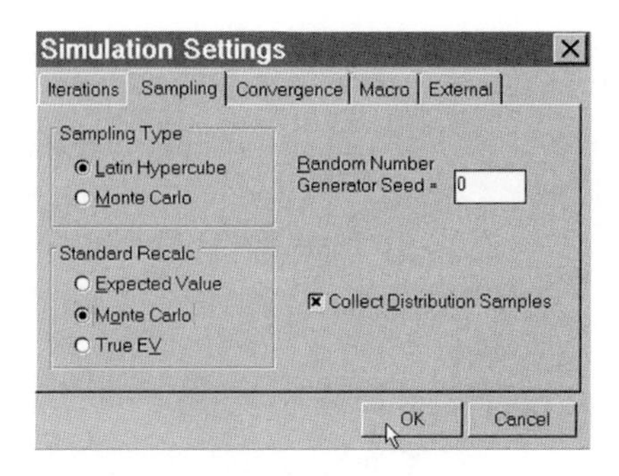

denied boarding (number of customers who are denied boarding times the cost of bumping a passenger). The model assumes that the fares are fully refundable due to the heavy percentage of business travelers on this route. That is, if a customer doesn't show up, she doesn't have to pay.

Since the value returned by @Risk will change every time the spreadsheet is recalculated, Laura can easily perform multiple trials—that is, draw a new sample of demands simply by pressing the recalculation key for her spreadsheet (F9 key usually). After doing this a few times, she is surprised to find that on some trials she obtains a profit that is several thousand dollars less than her base case. In order to see this with @Risk, you must make sure that @Risk's display is set to "Monte Carlo," as opposed to "Expected Value" in order to see the different random values returned for each iteration. To turn on this feature, simply:

1. Click on the third @Risk icon (simulation settings), then on the second tab (Sampling).
2. Indicate in the "Standard Recalc" section that you want Monte Carlo (not Expected Value), as shown in Figure 9.39.

The next step is to use simulation to help Laura determine the optimal overbooking level. She knows that if she accepts only 112 reservations, she'll never have to worry about angry customers due to denied boarding, but she'll also lose a lot of potential profit in the form of empty seats. She decides to look over the range of 112 to 146 reservations (in increments of 2) and see which value maximizes Midwest Express' profit. This ability to check numerous decisions in one grand simulation is a strength of @Risk. All Laura needs to do is:

1. Enter =RiskSimtable({112,114,116, . . . , 142,144,146}) in cell B10.
2. Click on third @Risk icon (Simulation Settings), then the "Iterations" tab and indicate that there are 18 simulations of 1,000 iterations each.
3. Click on cell B19 and then click on the fourth @Risk icon (Add Output Cell).

@Risk automatically displays the results of these 18 simulations as shown in Figure 9.40. It's much more helpful to click on the "Merge Sim#'s" button as shown in Figure 9.40 and get the display as shown in Figure 9.41.

A comment is in order on the convergence monitoring feature of @Risk. This is a very helpful feature that indicates to us when we have performed enough iterations that the output cells (performance measures) are not changing appreciably. A "frowning" face indicates we haven't done enough, whereas a "smiling" face indicates the results seem to have converged and we probably have done enough iterations. If you want to turn this feature off in order to speed up the simulation, simply click on the third icon (Simulation Settings) and then on the "Convergence" tab. Finally, click on the box that says "monitor convergence?" so that the "X" disappears.

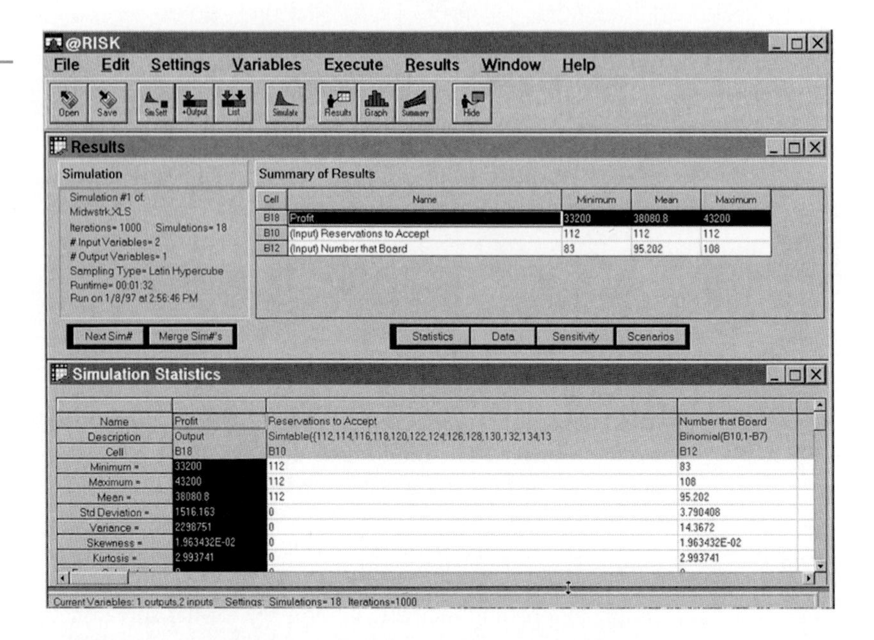

FIGURE 9.40

@Risk Initial Simulation Display

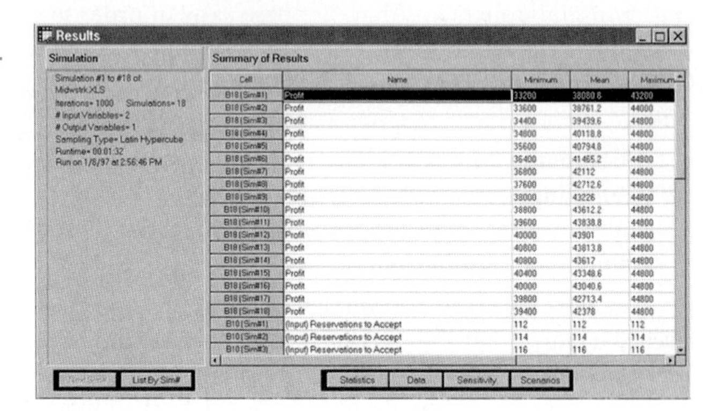

FIGURE 9.41

@Risk Display of All 18 Simulations

Looking at this @Risk output, Laura sees that if she accepted only 112 reservations (the plane's capacity), her average profit would be $38,080 (shown as Sim#1). As she increases the number of reservations accepted, the average profit climbs slowly for a while. For example, Sim#4 (accept 118 reservations) generates an average profit of $40,118.8. She finds that a value of 134 reservations (Sim#12) maximizes the average profit at $43,901, a 15.3% improvement in profit! This would represent overbooking the plane by 22 reservations, or 19.6% of its capacity. Beyond 134 reservations, the average profit starts to decline as the cost of denied boarding starts to outweigh the opportunity cost of an empty seat. Laura feels confident in her newfound answer of 134 reservations.

If we enlarge the bottom half of the statistical output shown in Figure 9.40, we can see the different fractiles of the NPV distribution (e.g., 10th, 20th, . . . , 90th). We will explore an extension of this model in Problem 9-24 by allowing for random demand. In this model, Laura has assumed that whatever number of reservations she makes available would actually be requested by customers. In reality, there is a probability distribution that describes this demand and in fact, demand may on occasion fall short of the overbooking level Laura chooses.

APPLICATION CAPSULE Simulation Model: Scheduling Drilling Rigs at a Dam in New Zealand

The Clyde Dam in the South Island of New Zealand is located in an area more unstable than was thought when it was designed. It took more than 10 years to build and is the largest concrete dam in New Zealand. Therefore the Electricity Corporation of New Zealand has taken additional precautions to ensure the stability of the hillsides surrounding it by constructing an underground curtain of 1,362 meters along the Clutha River. Such a curtain is constructed by drilling holes in the rock and injecting concrete into them. This required hiring drilling rigs and the construction company wanted to minimize the drilling time of the drilling rigs and finish the project quickly.

From the few holes the company had already drilled, the company found that the drilling rigs were often idle while it pursued interrelated activities. Since these rigs were hired from an outside company at a cost of NZ$227/hour, this idling time was a major concern. It also meant that project completion would be delayed. There were five steps to creating the grout curtain: (1) drilling the holes, (2) washing out the holes, (3) performing a water test, (4) grouting the holes, and (5) allowing the grout to set. There were five different types of holes to drill along the 1,362 meter stretch (the number of each is indicated in parentheses)—primary (228), secondary (227), tertiary (454), quaternary (908), and quinary (1816). The drilling rate at each stage varied according to the rock conditions at different depths.

Each of the steps had random times associated with them. For example, step 4 had grouting times at the different stages with right-skewed distributions. After the fifth step, there was always some probability the hole would collapse and the process would have to be repeated. Depending on the type of hole, this probability varied from 2.3% to 18.4%. The simulation model was developed to find an efficient drilling strategy. In addition to the random variables mentioned earlier, there were many decisions to analyze—the number of drilling rigs, the number of grouting machines, the distance between hole types, the number of stages and their depths for each hole type. The output measures were the total project completion time and the total idling/occupied times of the drilling rigs.

The end result of the simulation was a recommendation that allowed the project to be completed in 27 weeks (26% reduction from the original plan), total drilling hours of 34,041 (7% reduction), reduced idling time by 692 hours, and a cost savings of NZ$580,000. (See Premachandra and Gonzalez.)

9.8 CAPACITY BALANCING

Simulation is a powerful tool for gaining insights into the planning and operation of a manufacturing facility. In this section, we explore the assertion that capacity should be "balanced" throughout a manufacturing plant. We will see that variation in processing times can lead to unexpected results. This example is enlightening in several ways: (1) It shows how to use a spreadsheet to model a multiperiod problem in which results from one period are carried into the next. In this model, as in many real situations, inventory is carried from period to period. (2) It provides a graphic lesson on the risk of drawing conclusions based on relatively short simulation runs. (3) It provides useful intuitive insights into the consequences of balancing production rates in a serial manufacturing operation.

MODELING A WORK CELL

Paul Michaelson, an industrial engineer, is trying to determine the appropriate capacity to install in the small work cell shown in Figure 9.42. This cell takes a raw material, processes it at the first work station (WS1), holds it in a temporary storage area if the second work station (WS2) is busy, and then processes it at WS2. The completed part is used on one of

FIGURE 9.42

Michaelson's Work Cell

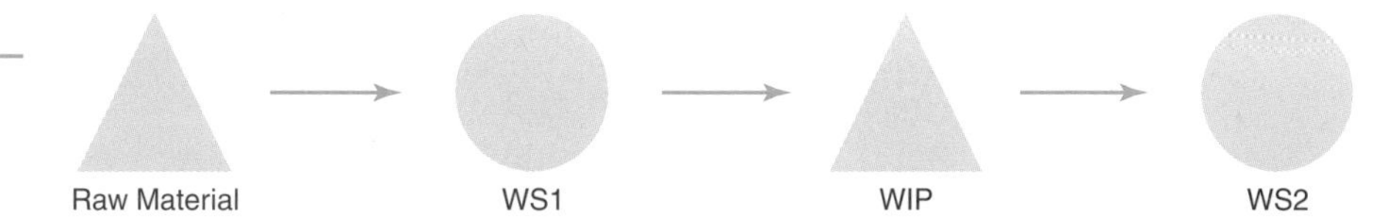

the assembly lines at the rate of 3 per hour. Consider how expensive it would be actually to set up a factory to implement and test the work cell for several days, compared to the cost of a spreadsheet simulation!

Paul has several goals in designing this work cell. He wants to meet the demand for this part on the assembly line, to keep work in process (WIP) between the two work stations down, and (in order to keep costs down) to minimize the capacity of the work stations subject to achieving the first two goals. He decides to do a simulation to help him make his capacity decisions.

SIMULATING BALANCED CAPACITY

Since the assembly area needs the part at a rate of 3 per hour, Paul initially decides to set the capacity of both work stations at 3 per hour. That is, the capacities of WS1 and WS2 are *balanced.* However, because of processing time variability, a work station might be able to process anywhere from 1 to 5 units in an hour. Suppose that during any given hour period, a work station will have the capability of processing 1, 2, 3, 4, or 5 units with equal probability (discrete, uniform distribution). Then the *average* output of that work station will be 3 units per hour *provided it always has something on which to work.* Paul assumes that sufficient raw material will always be available to WS1 so that it will never be *starved.* However, because the processing times are variable at WS1, there may be times when WS2 is idled for lack of material.

The Initial Conditions Figure 9.43 is a picture of the spreadsheet (MICHCB1.XLS) representing the first 16 simulated hours of operation of the work cell. The *initial conditions* at the beginning of the first hour of the simulation are no work in process (WIP), and WS1 and WS2 are idle. Next, Paul needs to enter discrete, uniform RNGs in cell C10 (WS1 Output) and cell D10 (Potential WS2 Output) to produce one of 5 possible values (1, 2 . . . , 5) with equal probability. This is done by typing in the data in a nice tabular

FIGURE 9.43

Michaelson's Spreadsheet

F10 = =B10+C10-E10

	A	B	C	D	E	F	G
8				Potential	Actual		
9	Hour	Initial WIP	WS1 Output	WS2 Output	WS2 Output	Final WIP	Avg WIP
10	1	0	3	3	0	3	3
11	2	3	3	3	3	3	3.00
12	3	3	3	3	3	3	3.00
13	4	3	3	3	3	3	3.00
14	5	3	3	3	3	3	3.00
15	6	3	3	3	3	3	3.00
16	7	3	3	3	3	3	3.00
17	8	3	3	3	3	3	3.00
18	9	3	3	3	3	3	3.00
19	10	3	3	3	3	3	3.00
20	11	3	3	3	3	3	3.00
21	12	3	3	3	3	3	3.00
22	13	3	3	3	3	3	3.00
23	14	3	3	3	3	3	3.00
24	15	3	3	3	3	3	3.00
25	16	3	3	3	3	3	3.00

Cell	Formula	Copy To
E10	=MIN(B10,D10)	E11:E25
F10	=B10+C10−E10	F11:F25
G10	=AVERAGE($F$10:F10)	G11:G25
B11	=F10	B12:B25

format for Crystal Ball. Paul entered the following values in cells C1:D6 for WS1 and WS2 (not shown):

OUTPUT RATE	PROBABILITY
1	0.2
2	0.2
3	0.2
4	0.2
5	0.2

Cell E10 (Actual WS2 Output) has the formula =MIN(B10,D10). For example, if the actual output of WS2 during the second hour is 1, even though there were 5 units available to work on, it would be because the random variable drawn to represent the potential WS2 Output turned out to be only 1 unit during that hour. The Final WIP (cell F10) is calculated by adding the Initial WIP (cell B10) to the WS1 Output (cell C10) and subtracting Actual WS2 Output (cell E10). The Initial WIP for a subsequent hour is simply the Final WIP for the previous hour. Average WIP at the end of any given hour is defined to be the average of the Final WIP values for all the hours observed to that point. In order to enter the discrete, uniform RNGs for WS1 Output and Potential WS2 Output in Crystal Ball, Paul must do the following:

1. Click on cell C10, which is the first cell where Crystal Ball will generate random values for the output rate. *Note*: Because the student version of Crystal Ball limits the number of Assumption cells to 6 and the number of Forecast cells to 6, we have a potential problem with this model (which has 32 Assumption cells and up to 16 Forecast cells). To get around this restriction, we will use a trick on the Assumption cells (see step #2) and limit the number of Forecast cells to 6 of the 16 hours we could possibly track.
2. Enter =CB.Custom($C$2:$D$6) in the cell. This effectively does the same thing as:
   a. Click on the first Crystal Ball icon (Define Assumption).
   b. Click on the "Custom" distribution from the Distribution Gallery; then click on OK.
   c. Click on the "Data" button and enter the cell range where you entered the information on this discrete distribution ($C$2:$D$6); then click on OK.

   but it allows us to bypass the limitation of 6 Assumption cells.
3. Crystal Ball shows the shape of the distribution you have entered. Click on OK.
4. With the cursor still on cell C10, click on Excel's "Copy" icon.
5. Highlight the range C10:D25 and then click on Excel's "Paste" icon. This copies the exact same uniform, discrete distribution to all 32 of these cells.
6. Ideally, we'd like to highlight all 16 cells that track Avg. WIP at the end of each hour (G10:G25), but since we are limited to 6 by the student version, we will limit ourselves to choosing cells G10, G13, G16, G19, G22, and G25.
7. After clicking on each cell mentioned in step 6, click on the second Crystal Ball icon (Define Forecast), which brings up a dialog box.
8. Change the Window size to "Large" and change the Display to "When Stopped (faster)" in the dialog box if this is not already the default (as shown previously). You may also modify the name to reflect which hour of the 16 it represents. Click on OK.
9. Repeat step 8 for each of the 6 forecast cells that Crystal Ball automatically prompts you with (or alternatively, you can use the Copy/Paste feature with the Forecast cells to avoid doing this 6 times).
10. Click on the eighth icon (Run Preferences) and change the "Maximum Number of Trials" to 1,000.

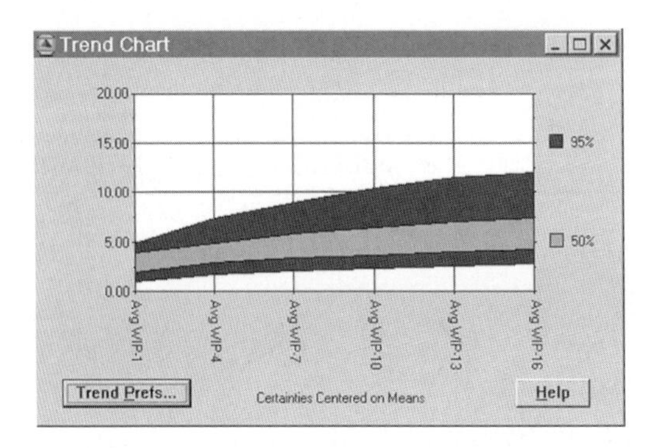

FIGURE 9.44

Michaelson's Trend Chart of Average WIP

11. Click on OK.
12. Click on the ninth icon (Start Simulation) and after Crystal Ball has run the 1,000 iterations, it automatically produces an individual histogram for each of the 6 forecast cells.
13. If you find this too cluttered, click on Run, then "Open Trend Chart," and you'll get a neater summary like that shown in Figure 9.44.

Here, Crystal Ball plots for us the distribution of Average WIP over the first 16 hours by using the six selected hours that we indicated. The centermost light-colored band indicates the mean value for average WIP ± 25% (or a 50% confidence interval), and the next darker band is a similar 95% confidence interval. We can see from this that Average WIP seems to be growing slightly over these first 16 hours and certainly the distribution is widening over time. The completed spreadsheet is found on the CD as MICHCB1C.XLS.

Beyond the Initial Conditions Paul realizes that running the simulation for only 16 hours can be very misleading, so he copies the formulas down for another 184 hours (in a new spreadsheet called MICHCB2.XLS). He reruns Crystal Ball using the same basic steps as the 16-hour simulation. Paul is quite surprised when he graphs Average WIP versus time for the first 200 hours of operation (see Figure 9.45). He knows that the initial condition of 0 WIP should lead to low values of Average WIP initially. He expects to see average WIP grow, but then to level off around some *steady-state* value. What he did not expect was the continued growth of average WIP. It appears that the longer the cell is in operation, the greater the amount of WIP that accumulates. This is somewhat counterintuitive, since it appears that with both work stations operating at an average rate of 3 units per hour there should be no tendency for WIP to grow. The completed spreadsheet is found on the CD as MICHCB2C.XLS.

A simple queuing model, however, predicts this unexpected growth. As we shall see in Chapter 15, when the average arrival rate to a queue is equal to the average service rate, the number of customers in the queue will grow without bound. Here in this model, "cus-

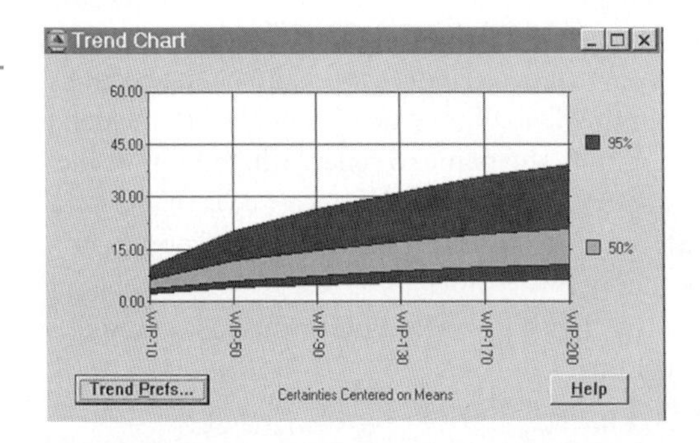

FIGURE 9.45

Average Work in Process, Balanced Capacity

tomers" are parts leaving WS1, and the queue is the temporary storage area before WS2. Because raw material is readily available, the output rate of WS1, and hence the average arrival rate to the queue, is 3 units per hour. The average service rate, the rate at which WS2 can process WIP, is also 3 units per hour. Thus, the average arrival rate and average service rate are equal when the capacities of the two work stations are balanced. Hence the continued growth of Average WIP.

SIMULATING UNBALANCED CAPACITY

On the basis of these considerations, Paul decides to add capacity to WS2 so that its average production rate is now 3.5 units per hour (using a discrete, uniform distribution between 2 and 5 units). He models this in a new spreadsheet called "Unbal. 200 Hrs" (in MICHCB3.XLS). First he copies the entire MICHCB2.XLS spreadsheet into the new one and then he adds the distribution of the potential Workstation 2 Output in cells G1:H5 as follows:

OUTPUT RATE	PROBABILITY
2	0.25
3	0.25
4	0.25
5	0.25

He then has to change the formulas in cells D10:D209 to be: =CB.Custom($G$2:$H$5). He selects six forecast cells, spread evenly across the 200 hours and then runs 1,000 iterations. The new graph of average WIP over time (Figure 9.46) now shows a much lower average WIP. His results suggest that there is no long-term growth in the Average WIP, with the steady-state value lying somewhere between 5 and 7 units.

Paul's final conclusion is that the capacity of the two work stations should not be balanced (equal output rates). If WIP is to be kept to reasonable levels, then the downstream work station (WS2) should have a somewhat greater capacity. If Paul had simulated fewer than 200 hours of operation, he would have been seriously misled about the long-term behavior of WIP in the balanced design. By running the simulation for a longer period of time, the effect of the initial conditions was overcome, and the true long-term behavior could be discerned. A general observation about simulation can be drawn from this example:

> Simulation results are useful only when care is taken in the experimental design to eliminate extraneous effects such as starting or ending conditions. Simulations that are too short may give very misleading results.

FIGURE 9.46

Average Work in Process, Unbalanced Capacity

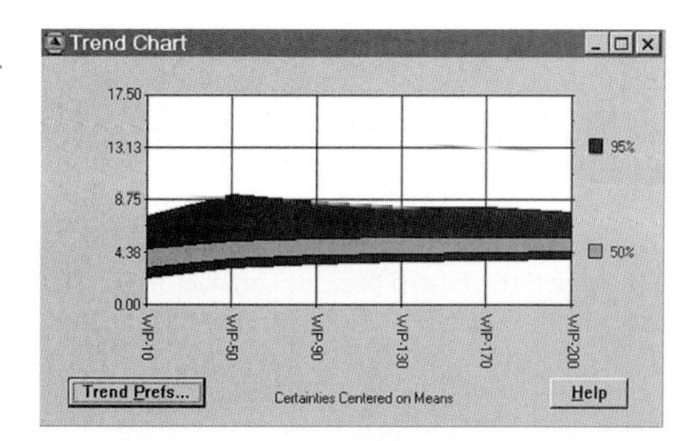

9.9 OPTIMIZATION UNDER UNCERTAINTY

For decades, students and professors have asked the question—"Wouldn't it be great if I could combine the optimization tools I've learned with the ability to do Monte Carlo simulation?" Now the answer is "You can!" As you recall from previous chapters, the Solver worked great at finding optimal solutions under conditions of certainty. That is, for example, if we could give it all the unit contribution margins, the demand, and the amount of raw materials available (with perfect certainty), then the Solver could tell us exactly how much of each kind of product to make in order to maximize the profit. But it doesn't take much additional thinking to realize that the contribution margins might fluctuate, demand is much more likely to be random than known with perfect knowledge, and even the supply of raw materials available might vary.

In fact, there are numerous fields of application for this new technique. Not only can it be used for the classic product mix example described above, but also for any problem where demand is a random function of the price charged (e.g., apartment rentals, hotel rooms, airplane seats, etc.). It also applies to any manager trying to choose how to spend his annual "capital improvements" budget between competing projects with uncertain returns or to a financial analyst trying to decide how to best allocate his client's money between many different investment opportunities, each with an uncertain return. It has bearing for a manager trying to determine the optimal inventory policy in the face of random demand. It even applies to such fields as scheduling with uncertain task times, revenue management for airlines, determining optimal levels of options purchases when hedging, groundwater cleanup, oil field development, drill bit replacement policy, and many others.

We will demonstrate the use of optimization under uncertainty with the most powerful, robust software available on the market today, OptQuest. It is available in Crystal Ball Pro and comes packaged with this textbook. We will show how it works with two very common examples—portfolio allocation and project selection. We will also compare how these results are different from the standard "optimization" results obtained from the Solver.

PORTFOLIO ALLOCATION

For this example, let's use a situation similar to the one used in Chapter 7 on Nonlinear Optimization. Let's suppose that we can choose to invest in one of three stocks—Intel, Microsoft, and Proctor & Gamble, or in a money market account. Our decision variables will be W, X, Y, and Z where:

> W represents the fraction of our portfolio invested in the Money Market account
>
> X represents the fraction of our portfolio invested in Intel stock
>
> Y represents the fraction of our portfolio invested in Microsoft stock
>
> Z represents the fraction of our portfolio invested in Proctor & Gamble stock.

Historically, based on the last nine years, we know that the average annualized return from Intel stock has been 46.6% (see www.intc.com/intel/finance/investorfacts), from Microsoft stock 62.1% (see www.microsoft.com/msft/stock.htm), from Proctor & Gamble stock 20.8% (www.pg.com/investor), and from a typical Money Market account (like Vanguard's Prime MM portfolio), the average annual return was 5.2%. As far as constraints, we don't want anymore than 50% of our portfolio to be in any one asset and obviously the sum of our decision variables must be 100%. In order to optimize this portfolio with standard optimization techniques (see Chapter 7), we really have two choices—maximize return subject to a constraint to keep the risk at some satisfactory level or to minimize risk subject to a constraint to keep the return at some satisfactory level. In this case, let's pursue the second approach (minimize risk)[3] and to do so we would simply set up a spreadsheet model

---

[3] Recall from Chapter 7 that Excel's COVAR() formula does not account for degrees of freedom lost and by thus using it here to estimate portfolio variance, we have introduced a slight estimation bias.

FIGURE 9.47

Portfolio Allocation Spreadsheet Model

H17 = =SUMPRODUCT(MMULT(C17:F17,C13:F16),C17:F17)

	A	B	C	D	E	F	G	H	I
1		Portfolio Model	Intel	Micro-soft	P&G	Money Mkt			
2				73.0%	23.3%	8.27%	1		
3				121.8%	8.4%	6.14%	2		
4				15.1%	14.2%	3.74%	3		
5			43.4%	-5.6%	6.3%	3.01%	4		
6			-48.5%	51.6%	8.8%	4.08%	5		
7			77.8%	43.6%	33.9%	5.82%	6		
8			130.7%	88.3%	29.7%	5.29%	7		
9			7.3%	56.4%	48.3%	5.44%	8		
10			68.7%	114.6%	14.4%	5.38%	9		
11		Average Return	46.6%	62.1%	20.8%	5.2%			
12		Covariance Matrix	Intel	MS	P&G	MM		Portfolio Variance	
13		Intel	0.3188	0.0704	0.0187	0.0022			
14		Microsoft	0.0704	0.1599	0.0022	0.0035			
15		Proctor&Gamble	0.0187	0.0022	0.0178	0.0007			
16		Money Market	0.0022	0.0035	0.0007	0.0002	Total		
17		Decision: Stock %	25.00%	25.00%	25.00%	25.00%	100%	0.0433	
18		Requirements	<=50%	<=50%	<=50%	<=50%	=100%		
19		Expected Return	11.64%	15.52%	5.20%	1.31%	33.7%	>=25%	
20									

Cell	Formula	Copy To
C11	= AVERAGE (C2:C10)	D11:F11
C13	= COVAR ($C$2:$C$10, C2:C10)	D13:F13
C14	= COVAR ($D2:$D$10, C2:C10)	D14:F14
C15	= COVAR ($E$2:$E10, C2:C10)	D15:F15
C16	= COVAR ($F$2:$F$10, C2:C10)	D16:F16
C19	= C17*C11	D19:F19
G17	= SUM (C17:F17)	G19
H17	= SUMPRODUCT (MMULT(C17:F17, C13:F16), C17:F17)	

(portflio.xls) like the one shown in Figure 9.47, which is very similar to the portfolio allocation model used in Chapter 7, and which shows initial selections for our decisions of 25% invested in each option available (3 stocks, 1 money market). When we set this up in Solver to optimize, we use cells C17:F17 as the decision variables, cell H17 as the objective function to minimize, and the constraints are: (1) cell G19 must be greater than or equal to cell H19 (25%), (2) the sum of the decision variables must equal 1 (i.e., cell G17 = G18), and (3) each individual decision variable must be less than or equal to 50% (i.e., C17:F17 <= C18: F18). The result from Solver comes back as shown in Figure 9.48. and selects 0.51% of Intel, 20.7% of Microsoft, 50% of Proctor & Gamble, and 28.8% in the Money Market account, with an expected return of 25.0% and minimized variance of 0.0127. Because we were trying to minimize the risk, the Solver couldn't afford to choose too much of the higher-yielding, riskier stocks like Intel and Microsoft. To enter this model into Crystal Ball with OptQuest, we do the following:

1. Because the assumption cells must be numbers rather than formulas, we must change cells C11:F11 accordingly. To do so, highlight cells C11:F11 and then click on Edit, Copy, then Edit, Paste Special. Click on "Values" and click on OK.
2. Now, define the assumption cells as cells C11:F11 (each as a normal distribution with means as given in the original spreadsheet [46.6%, 62.1%, 20.8%, 5.2%], and standard deviations as $\sqrt{.3188} = .5646$, $\sqrt{.1599} = .3999$, $\sqrt{.0178} = .1334$, $\sqrt{.0002} = .0141$). The standard procedure for entering assumption cells will be demonstrated for cell C11. To start, click on the first Crystal Ball icon ("Define Assumption"), then click on the Normal distribution from the gallery shown (which is the default choice). Click on OK. Now click in the "Std Dev" box and enter 0.5646 and click

FIGURE 9.48

Portfolio Allocation Solution from Solver

H17 = =SUMPRODUCT(MMULT(C17:F17,C13:F16),C17:F17)

	A/B	C	D	E	F	G	H
1	Portfolio Model	Intel	Micro-soft	P&G	Money Mkt		
2			73.0%	23.3%	8.27%	1	
3			121.8%	8.4%	6.14%	2	
4			15.1%	14.2%	3.74%	3	
5		43.4%	-5.6%	6.3%	3.01%	4	
6		-48.5%	51.6%	8.8%	4.08%	5	
7		77.8%	43.6%	33.9%	5.82%	6	
8		130.7%	88.3%	29.7%	5.29%	7	
9		7.3%	56.4%	48.3%	5.44%	8	
10		68.7%	114.6%	14.4%	5.38%	9	
11	Average Return	46.6%	62.1%	20.8%	5.2%		
12	Covariance Matrix	Intel	MS	P&G	MM		
13	Intel	0.3188	0.0704	0.0187	0.0022		
14	Microsoft	0.0704	0.1599	0.0022	0.0035		
15	Proctor&Gamble	0.0187	0.0022	0.0178	0.0007		
16	Money Market	0.0022	0.0035	0.0007	0.0002	Total	Portfolio Variance
17	Decision: Stock %	0.51%	20.70%	50.00%	28.80%	100%	0.0127
18	Requirements	<=50%	<=50%	<=50%	<=50%	=100%	
19	Expected Return	0.24%	12.85%	10.40%	1.51%	25.0%	>=25%
20							

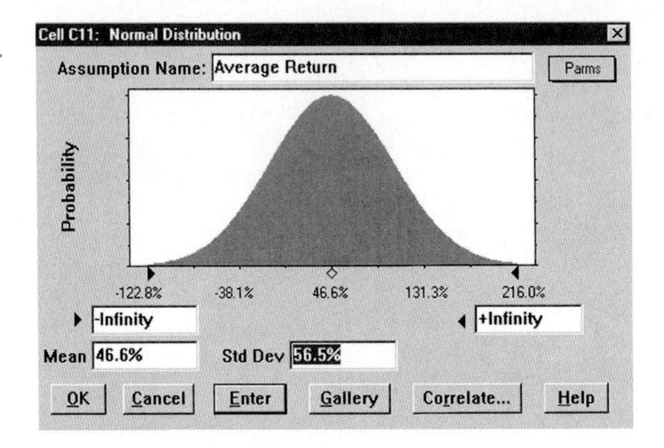

FIGURE 9.49

Assumption Cell with Normal Distribution

Enter and you should get the display as shown in Figure 9.49. Click OK. Now repeat this process for cells D11:F11 with their corresponding numbers.

3. Define the forecast cell (click on the third icon) as cell H17 with "Portfolio Variance" as the Name. Click OK.
4. Set the "run preferences" (click on the tenth icon) to—maximum number of trials equal to 1000, sampling method as Latin Hypercube, and random number generator as "Use same sequence" with initial seed value of 999 as shown in Figure 9.50. Click on OK.
5. Define the decision variables as cells C17:F17 (each as a continuous variable with lower bound of 0%, upper bound of 50%). The standard procedure for entering decision variables will be demonstrated for cell C17. To start, click on the second Crystal Ball icon ("Define Decision"), then change the name to "Intel%," enter a lower bound of 0%, an upper bound of 50%, and select the variable type as continuous as shown in Figure 9.51. Click OK. Now repeat this process for cells D17:F17 with their corresponding numbers.
6. Start OptQuest by clicking on its icon (on the far right of the CB menu) or selecting Tools, OptQuest.
7. In OptQuest, select File, New. Select Yes to optimize all decision variables (the lower and upper bounds should be ok). Check that the Type column indicates that these are continuous values. When you're done, it should look as shown in Figure 9.52. Click on OK.

FIGURE 9.50

Dialog Box for Run Preferences

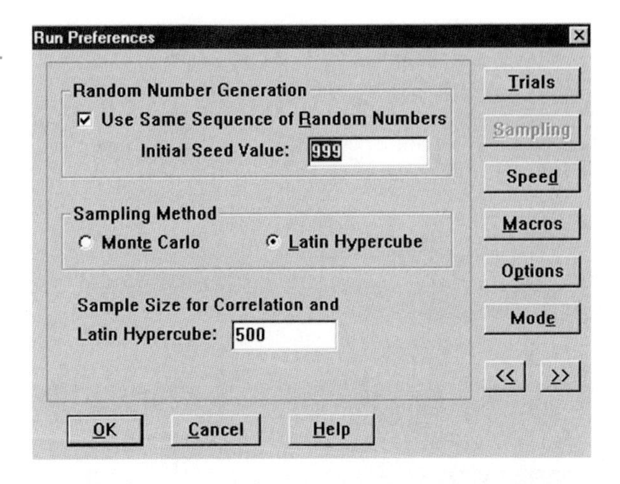

FIGURE 9.51

Dialog Box in Crystal Ball for Defining a Decision

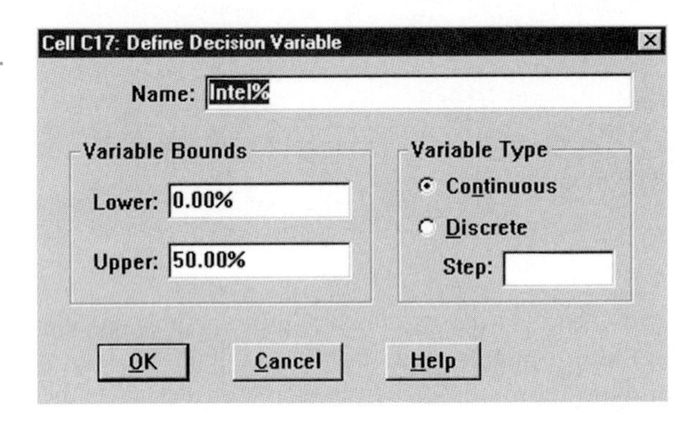

FIGURE 9.52

Dialog Box in OptQuest for Defining Decisions

Decision Variable Selection: Select variables and set bounds.

Select	Variable Name	Lower Bound	Suggested Value	Upper Bound	Type
Yes	Intel%	0	.25	.5	Continuous
Yes	Microsoft%	0	.25	.5	Continuous
Yes	P&G%	0	.25	.5	Continuous
Yes	MM%	0	.25	.5	Continuous

OK Cancel Help

8. Define the constraints as follows:
   a. Intel% + Microsoft% + P&G% + MM% = 1
   b. Intel% <= 0.5
   c. Microsoft% <= 0.5
   d. P&G% <= 0.5
   e. MM% <= 0.5
   f. 0.466*Intel% + 0.621*Microsoft% + 0.208*P&G% + 0.052*MM% >= 0.25

   When you're done, it should look as shown in Figure 9.53. Then click on OK.
9. From the "Select" drop-down menu, select Minimize Objective as shown in Figure 9.54. Click on OK.

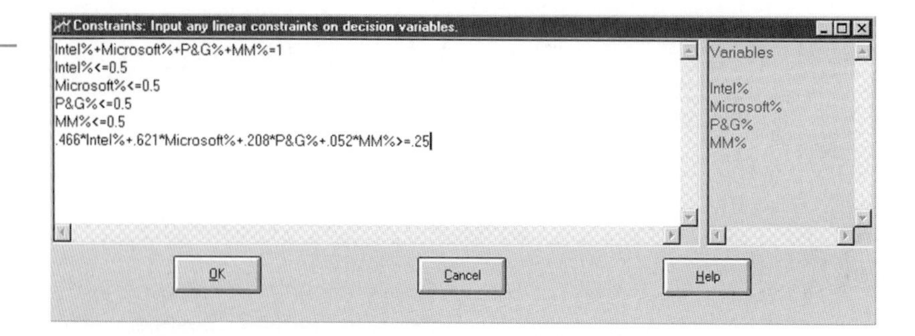

FIGURE 9.53

Dialog Box in OptQuest for Constraints

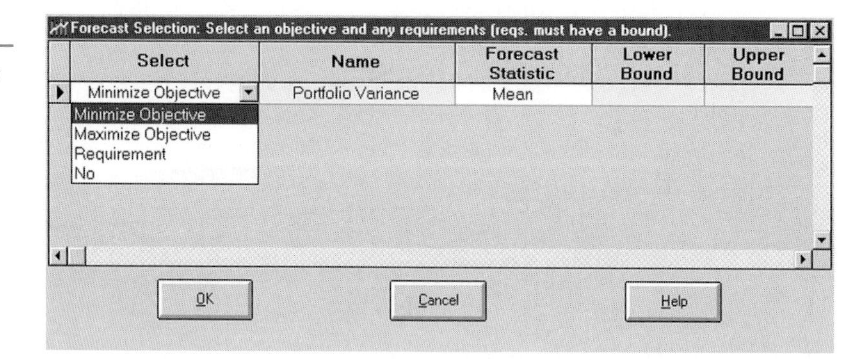

FIGURE 9.54

Dialog Box in OptQuest for the Objective

10. In the Options window, click on OK to accept the default process (ten minutes of run time). To start the Optimization under uncertainty, click on Yes. After ten minutes, you should get results that look similar to the results shown in Figure 9.55 (of course, the number of trials it will have run will vary based on how fast your processor is).
11. To interpret the results, select Edit, Copy to Excel, which will copy the resulting values for the decision variables back into your spreadsheet and automatically show you the resulting frequency diagram of your chosen statistic (in our case, the portfolio variance). In the Forecast window, you can also select View, Statistics to see some summary statistics if you so desire.

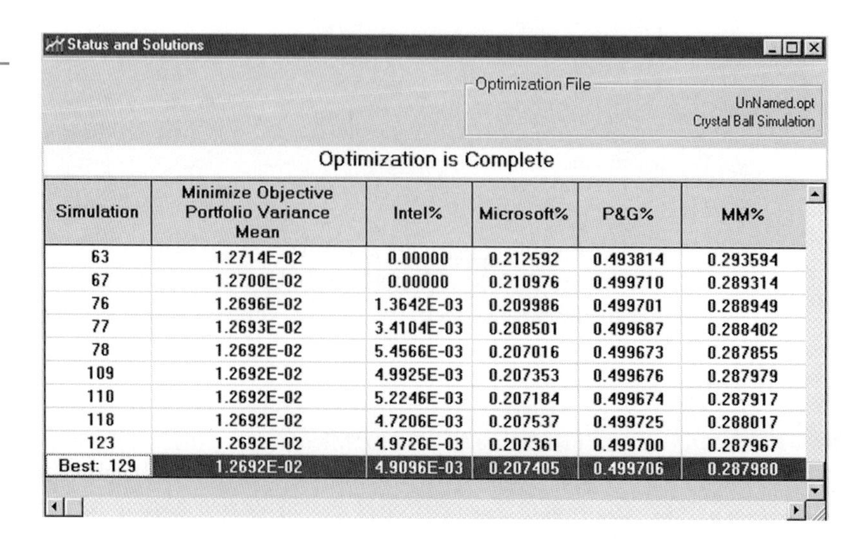

Simulation	Minimize Objective Portfolio Variance Mean	Intel%	Microsoft%	P&G%	MM%
63	1.2714E-02	0.00000	0.212592	0.493814	0.293594
67	1.2700E-02	0.00000	0.210976	0.499710	0.289314
76	1.2696E-02	1.3642E-03	0.209986	0.499701	0.288949
77	1.2693E-02	3.4104E-03	0.208501	0.499687	0.288402
78	1.2692E-02	5.4566E-03	0.207016	0.499673	0.287855
109	1.2692E-02	4.9925E-03	0.207353	0.499676	0.287979
110	1.2692E-02	5.2246E-03	0.207184	0.499674	0.287917
118	1.2692E-02	4.7206E-03	0.207537	0.499725	0.288017
123	1.2692E-02	4.9726E-03	0.207361	0.499700	0.287967
Best: 129	1.2692E-02	4.9096E-03	0.207405	0.499706	0.287980

FIGURE 9.55

Results from OptQuest for Portfolio Allocation

As we see in this example, the OptQuest engine came up with basically the same answer that we got with the Solver (in a much longer period of time), and so you might be wondering what value does this new software really add. The result from OptQuest confirmed that after running 1,000 random iterations, the average portfolio variance was indeed closely represented by the mean values used in our original spreadsheet, which Solver used to optimize. So even though this example didn't seem like it added much value, it really was helpful to confirm the value for the true expected portfolio variance. There are certainly other examples where this could have turned out differently—remember the "expected value" trap mentioned in Section 9.4. Our next example will show further strengths of the new software and demonstrate features that can't be replicated with either pure optimization or pure simulation.

PROJECT SELECTION

Consider the R&D group at a major public utility that has identified eight possible projects for the coming year. Each project has an initial investment required and the resulting NPV from a proforma cash flow analysis has also been tabulated. The CFO of the company has only authorized $2 million to be spent on R&D projects for the coming year. These eight projects (if all were implemented) would require an investment of $2.8 million, so it is necessary to choose among the eight projects those that will return the largest NPV value and yet still remain within the budget. Using the techniques of Chapter 6 (Integer Optimization), we would set up the model for optimization using binary decision variables (yes/no) for each of the eight potential projects. This spreadsheet is shown in Figure 9.56 ("initial" sheet of ProjectSelection.xls). The resulting solution from the Solver shows that projects 1, 2, 3, 4, and 7 should be chosen with the maximum NPV obtained of $3.55 million and using all $2 million of the budget. This is a straightforward application of integer programming where the NPVs are assumed to be certain. If we add some uncertainty to the success of each project as shown in the "Revised" sheet of the same spreadsheet (see Figure 9.57), what is the effect? It turns out that now, due to the uncertainty of each project succeeding, if we re-optimize with the Solver (maximize cell G15, changing cells are E5:E12,

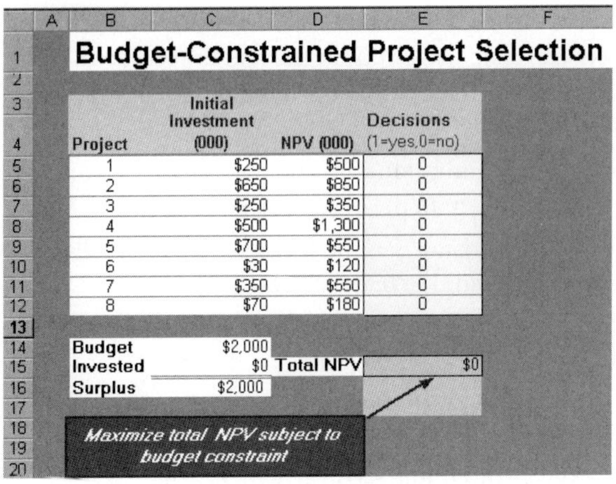

FIGURE 9.56

Project Selection Spreadsheet Model

Budget-Constrained Project Selection

Project	Initial Investment (000)	NPV (000)	Decisions (1=yes,0=no)
1	$250	$500	0
2	$650	$850	0
3	$250	$350	0
4	$500	$1,300	0
5	$700	$550	0
6	$30	$120	0
7	$350	$550	0
8	$70	$180	0

Budget	$2,000		
Invested	$0	Total NPV	$0
Surplus	$2,000		

Maximize total NPV subject to budget constraint

Cell	Formula	Copy to
C15	= SUMPRODUCT (E5:E12, C5:C12)	—
C16	= C14–C15	—
E15	= SUMPRODUCT (D5:D12, E5:E12)	—

FIGURE 9.57

Revised Project Selection Spreadsheet Model

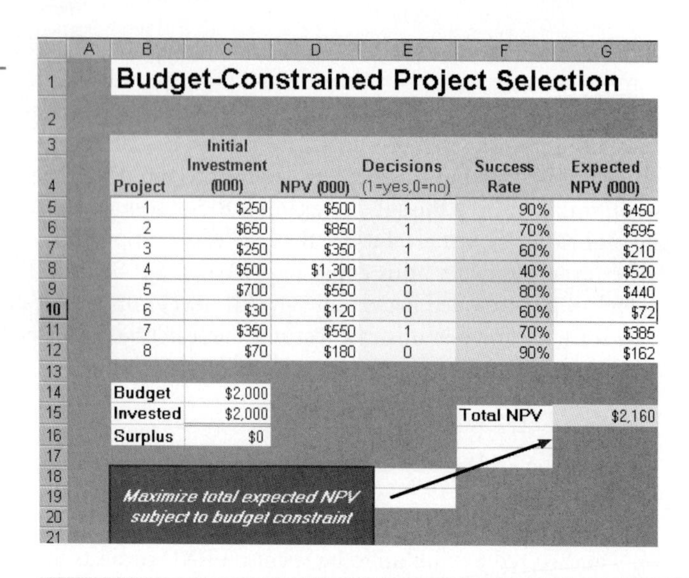

Budget-Constrained Project Selection

Project	Initial Investment (000)	NPV (000)	Decisions (1=yes,0=no)	Success Rate	Expected NPV (000)
1	$250	$500	1	90%	$450
2	$650	$850	1	70%	$595
3	$250	$350	1	60%	$210
4	$500	$1,300	1	40%	$520
5	$700	$550	0	80%	$440
6	$30	$120	0	60%	$72
7	$350	$550	1	70%	$385
8	$70	$180	0	90%	$162

Budget	$2,000
Invested	$2,000
Surplus	$0

Total NPV	$2,160

Cell	Formula	Copy to
G5	= D5*F5	G6:G12

and the single constraint is C15 <= C14), it gives us a *new* solution (i.e., it recommends that we select projects 1, 2, 4, 6, 7, 8) with an expected NPV of $2.184 million and spending only $1.85 million of the budgeted $2 million. But how can we be sure this is really the best decision, given all the uncertainty? What if our company is somewhat risk-averse and so we want to minimize the downside potential of the projects chosen? If we turn to our new tool that is available with OptQuest we can do just that—we can specify that it maximize the twenty-fifth percentile of the NPV distribution that results from a simulation of 1,000 trials. Then for each possible combination of decision variables (2^8 = 256 combinations), the software will make "intelligent" choices as it searches over all the possible decision variable combinations for the best one. Behind the scenes, some pretty sophisticated neural networks are being used to train the search routine as to where to search next in the decision variable space. To set this up in OptQuest, we follow a procedure similar to our previous example:

1. Define the assumption cells (first icon) as cells F5:F12 (each as a binomial with success rate as given in the original spreadsheet, and 1 trial).
2. Define the decision variables (second icon) as cells E5:E12 (each as a discrete variable with lower bound of 0, upper bound of 1).
3. Define the forecast cell (third icon) as cell G15 with "NPV" as Forecast name and "Dollars" as the forecast units.
4. Set the run preferences (tenth icon) to—maximum number of trials equal to 1,000, sampling method as Latin Hypercube, and random number generator as "Use same sequence" with initial seed value of 999.
5. Start OptQuest by clicking on its icon (on the far right of the CB menu) or selecting Tools, OptQuest.
6. In OptQuest, select File, New. Select Yes to optimize all decision variables (the lower and upper bounds should be ok). Check that the Type column indicates that these are discrete values.

FIGURE 9.58

Dialog Box in OptQuest for the Objective

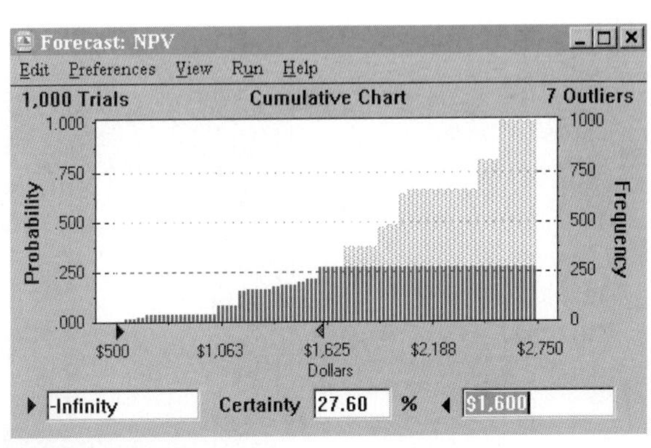

FIGURE 9.59

Cumulative Frequency Diagram from Project Selection Example

7. Define the single constraint as:

   250*Project1 + 650*Project2 + 250*Project3 + 500*Project4 + 700*Project5 +

   30*Project6 + 350*Project7 + 70*Project8 <= 2000

   Note: No commas are allowed in the numbers for OptQuest constraints, which makes it harder to debug.
8. From the "Select" drop-down menu, select Maximize Objective. Change the Forecast Statistic from the "Mean" to "percentile" and enter the number 25 as shown in Figure 9.58.
9. In the Options window, click on OK to accept the default process (ten minutes of run time). To start the Optimization under uncertainity, click on Yes in response to the question "Run Optimization Now?"
10. To interpret the results, select Edit, Copy to Excel, which will copy the resulting values for the decision variables back into your spreadsheet and automatically show you the resulting frequency diagram of your chosen statistic (in our case, the NPV). Under View, we switched to Cumulative Chart and entered the right-hand side value as $1.6 million (the value reported as the best from the OptQuest search) as shown in Figure 9.59.

In the Forecast window, you can also select View, Statistics to see some summary statistics as shown in Figure 9.60. The results from OptQuest showed that the best projects to choose are 1, 2, 5, 6, 7, which spend $1.98 million of the budget (see Figure 9.61) and generate a maximum twenty-fifth percentile value of $1.6 million. Here we were able to use OptQuest

FIGURE 9.60

Summary Statistics from Project Selection Example

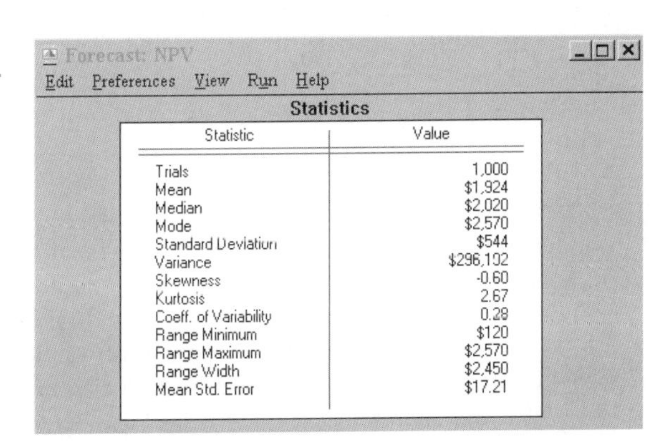

Forecast: NPV

Statistics

Statistic	Value
Trials	1,000
Mean	$1,924
Median	$2,020
Mode	$2,570
Standard Deviation	$544
Variance	$296,192
Skewness	-0.60
Kurtosis	2.67
Coeff. of Variability	0.28
Range Minimum	$120
Range Maximum	$2,570
Range Width	$2,450
Mean Std. Error	$17.21

FIGURE 9.61

Results from OptQuest for Project Selection Model

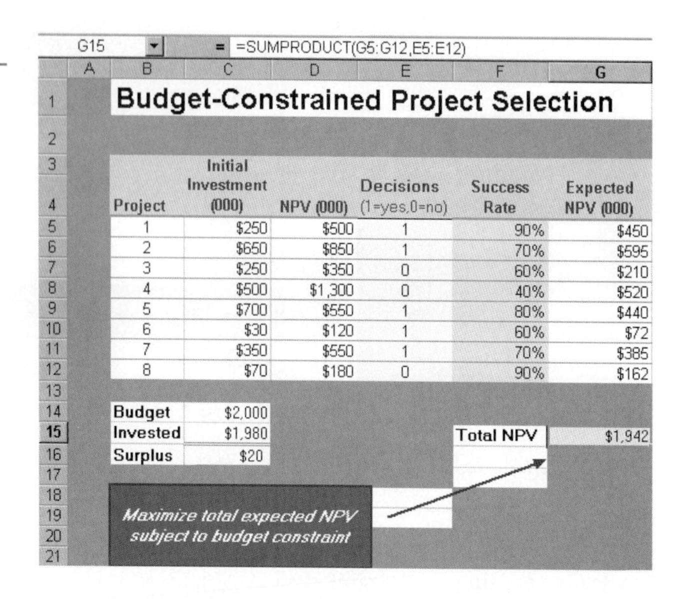

G15 = =SUMPRODUCT(G5:G12,E5:E12)

Budget-Constrained Project Selection

Project	Initial Investment (000)	NPV (000)	Decisions (1=yes,0=no)	Success Rate	Expected NPV (000)
1	$250	$500	1	90%	$450
2	$650	$850	1	70%	$595
3	$250	$350	0	60%	$210
4	$500	$1,300	0	40%	$520
5	$700	$550	1	80%	$440
6	$30	$120	1	60%	$72
7	$350	$550	1	70%	$385
8	$70	$180	0	90%	$162

Budget	$2,000
Invested	$1,980
Surplus	$20

Total NPV $1,942

to determine a *different* set of decisions that matched our risk preference better and that minimized the overall downside of our project selections. As we can see, this is a powerful new tool that allows us to optimize under uncertainty and pick those projects that will minimize our downside potential—something we couldn't do with Solver.

9.10 NOTES ON IMPLEMENTATION

Simulation is a powerful and flexible analytic tool that can be used to study a wide variety of management models. It is generally used in cases where a good analytic model either does not exist or is too complicated to solve. Simulation can also demonstrate the effects of variability and initial conditions, as well as the length of time needed to reach steady state. This description encompasses a large segment of real-world models and, as a result, surveys of the use of management science techniques typically put simulation at or near the top. However, there are a number of important factors for management to consider before making a commitment to a simulation study.

Simulation Versus Analytic Models As stated above, simulation is frequently used when no convenient analytic model is available. With an analytic model the laws of mathematics can be used, often to obtain optimal decisions and sometimes sensitivity data (provided, of course, that the analysis is not so complex as to be prohibitive). In a simulation with random events, by contrast, optimality is not guaranteed, and it may be difficult to obtain even an approximately optimal solution. Often a number of iterations are required just to get a good estimate of the "goodness" of a particular decision. However, simulation models can provide information that analytic models find it difficult or impossible to supply, such as the impact of variability, behavior before steady state is reached, and so on.

Designing a Spreadsheet Simulator The acronym KISS for "Keep It Simple, Stupid" is popular among professionals in the decision modeling area of business. The idea applies with special force to simulation. A common and often fatal error in devising simulation models is making them too complicated. This may be an overreaction to the freedom gained by moving from analytic models to simulation models. Analytic models are often quite restrictive in their assumptions. Once we depart from linear functions or very simplistic assumptions, the mathematics gets harder by an order of magnitude. The result is that many of the popular analytic models have limited applicability. Simulation can be much more permissive. Since we are typically just generating an observation from a function (rather than solving a set of equations), linear functions do not facilitate the analysis in simulation as much as they do in analytic models.

Whatever the motivation, there is typically a strong urge to include many factors in a simulation model. For example, it may not seem difficult to add a customer return feature to an inventory control model. In essence, all that is required is some additional modeling in the spreadsheet to generate this feature and incorporate it into the model. "There is no theoretical barrier, so why not do it?" This impression can be seriously wrong.

Large, complicated simulations incorporating a large number of "lifelike" features are at first blush appealing to management. However, they suffer from at least two serious problems:

1. They are often expensive to model and document.
2. Complex simulation models often produce so much data that the results are difficult to interpret.

Lean, abstract models that capture the essence of the real problem and set encumbering details aside are as important to successful simulation models as they are to good analytic models. Casual observation suggests that more simulation modeling projects have died from too grand an original conception than from any other disease.

Simulation Add-in Software The importance and widespread use of simulation has led to the creation of special simulation add-in software. Two guidelines that are useful in all quantitative studies are especially important in simulation studies:

Documentation Insist on good documentation. A new manager should be able to understand the input required, the assumptions of the model, and the meaning of the output with a reasonable amount of effort. This requires clear documentation. Too often the usefulness of a simulation model effectively ends with the tenure of the originator. The only reasonable cure for this problem is good documentation. It is difficult to overemphasize the importance of this guideline.

Group Dynamics All quantitative modeling efforts require intensive interaction and communication between modeler and end user. This is particularly true of simulation projects. The end user must understand how to enter decisions and parameters and how to analyze output. The firsthand knowledge of the user is essential in making sure that the simulation captures the essence of the real problem. Also, the fact that the user has an intimate knowledge of the real problem can be an important part of the search for good solutions.

Good documentation and group dynamics are closely interrelated and are an important part of managing any project based on quantitative modeling and analysis.

9.11 SUMMARY

Section 9.1 pointed out that the use of experimentation to evaluate alternatives is an important part of applied science and that spreadsheet-based simulation is the most common experimental approach to management decision models. It also discussed the use of simulation on decisions under risk; that is, on models in which the behavior of one or more factors can be represented by a probability distribution.

Random numbers are at the basis of the technique of simulating random events. Section 9.2 presented the procedure used to generate random variables from several different probability distributions, both in Crystal Ball and @Risk. Both discrete and continuous distributions were presented.

Section 9.3 introduced an example that dealt with capital budgeting, which involved an unpredictable element (demand). It was shown how some basic simulation could be carried out using the spreadsheet by itself. Section 9.4 was a replay of Section 9.3 with the added benefit of being able to use simulation add-in software (Crystal Ball).

Section 9.5 introduced an example dealing with inventory control, which also involved the unpredictable element of demand. All of these models were used to illustrate how random events are incorporated into a simulation model. The examples showed that simulation results will not necessarily lead to the same decision that would be derived if one could use the analytic criterion of maximizing the expected profit. By its very nature the output from a simulation with random components is random. Generally, using a large number of trials will make the simulated average profit closer to the theoretic expected profit. The examples also demonstrated how multiple measures of effectiveness can be produced and, more important, how simulation with multiple trials provides an indication of the variability with a given decision or policy.

Section 9.6 returned to the inventory model discussed in Section 9.5 to show how a much more realistic distribution of demand (i.e., normal) can be modeled. The topic of variance reduction was also addressed.

Section 9.7 turned to the service sector of the economy for an example from the airline industry. The example looked at determining the optimal overbooking level for a very successful airline, Midwest Express. A new discrete probability distribution (binomial) was introduced.

Section 9.8 turned back to an example from manufacturing to explore the question of whether balancing the production capacity of all work stations necessarily leads to an optimal result. The example illustrated the importance of designing a simulation so as to eliminate extraneous effects such as those associated with starting or ending conditions.

Section 9.9 introduced one of the newest and most exciting fields in simulation—that of optimization under uncertainty. Two examples (project selection and portfolio allocation) showed how this powerful new software can be used to find very good solutions to extremely complex situations.

The final section was devoted to the topic of implementation. The discussion took a general management point of view and considered such topics as designing a simulation, good documentation, and group dynamics.

Key Terms

Simulator. An experimental device that in important respects acts like a system of interest.

Simulation Model. A series of logical and mathematical operations that provides a measure of effectiveness for a particular set of values of the parameters and decisions.

Random Variable. An entity that will take on a numerical value; the likelihood of it assuming any particular value is given by a probability function.

Probability Distribution. A means of specifying the likelihood of an uncertain quantity.

Monte Carlo Method. A type of simulation that uses probability distributions to determine whether random events occur.

Trial. A single run of a simulation model (i.e., a single pass through the simulator).

Cumulative Distribution Function (CDF). The probability that a random variable takes on a value less than or equal to a specified number.

Discrete Uniform Distribution. A probability distribution that assigns equal probability to each member of a finite set of consecutive integers.

Continuous Uniform Distribution. A probability distribution that assigns equal likelihood to each member of an interval of real numbers. (See Appendix A for the mathematical form of this function.)

Exponential Distribution. A probability distribution typically used to describe the time between arrivals at a queuing system. (See Appendix A for the mathematical form of this function.)

Normal Distribution. A probability distribution that is a good model for many phenomena that occur in nature and business, such as fluctuating prices and demands; also, the distribution of the sample mean calculated for any random variable. (See Appendix A for details.)

Multiple Trials. Multiple passes through the simulator, each pass using the same values for decisions and parameters, but a different series of random numbers and hence possibly different outcomes for random events.

Expected Value. A statistical concept referring to the average, or mean, of some random quantity with a specified probability distribution.

Poisson Distribution. A probability distribution often used to describe the number of arrivals to a queuing system during a specified interval of time. (See Appendix A for the mathematical form of this function.)

Variability. In simulation, a reference to the amount of fluctuation in performance measures as numerous trials are performed.

Self-Review Exercises

True-False

1. **T F** The basic concept of simulation is to build an experimental device that will "act like" the system of interest in important respects.
2. **T F** A deterministic model (one with no random elements) can be used as a simulation model.
3. **T F** If a simulation includes random elements, two successive trials with the same parameter values will produce the same value for the performance measure.
4. **T F** In a simulation with random elements it is impossible to guarantee that the decision that maximizes expected profit has been selected.
5. **T F** In real-world problems, it is common practice to compare the expected cost associated with a decision with the average cost for that decision produced by a simulation.
6. **T F** In a simulation with several distinct random outcomes, a correct association of random numbers and events implies that each random number must represent one of the outcomes.
7. **T F** With small sample sizes the results of a simulation can be very sensitive to the initial conditions.
8. **T F** Simulation is sometimes described as a last resort technique since it is generally not employed until analytic approaches have been examined and rejected.
9. **T F** A common error in designing a simulation is to use such restrictive assumptions that the model fails to capture the essence of the problem.
10. **T F** Adding additional factors in a simulation model is sure to increase the simulation cost but may also improve the quality of the solution.

Multiple Choice

11. In a typical simulation model, input provided by the manager includes
    - **a.** values for the parameters
    - **b.** values for the decision variables
    - **c.** a value for the performance measure
    - **d.** all of the above
    - **e.** both a and b
12. An advantage of simulation, as opposed to optimization, is that
    - **a.** often multiple measures of goodness can be examined
    - **b.** some appreciation for the variability of outcomes of interest can be obtained
    - **c.** more complex scenarios can be studied
    - **d.** all of the above
13. Consider a simulator with random elements that uses profit as a measure of effectiveness. For a specified assignment of parameter values
    - **a.** the average profit over a number of trials is used as an estimate of the expected profit associated with a decision
    - **b.** the average profit is always closer to the expected profit as the number of trials increases
    - **c.** the average profit over ten trials is always the same
    - **d.** none of the above
14. A random number refers to
    - **a.** an observation from a set of numbers (say, the real numbers from 0–1), each of which is equally likely
    - **b.** an observation selected at random from a normal distribution
    - **c.** an observation selected at random from any distribution provided by the manager
    - **d.** none of the above
15. The random number 0.63 has been selected. The corresponding observation, v, from a *normal* distribution is determined by the relationship:
    - **a.** v is "the probability that the normally distributed quantity is ≤ 0.63"
    - **b.** v is the number such that "the probability that the normally distributed quantity is $\leq v$" equals 0.63
    - **c.** v is the number such that "the probability that the normally distributed quantity equals v" is 0.63
    - **d.** none of the above
16. Analytic results are sometimes used before a simulation study
    - **a.** to identify "good values" of the system parameters
    - **b.** to determine the optimal decision
    - **c.** to identify "good values" of the decision variables for the specific choices of system parameters
    - **d.** all of the above

17. To reduce the effect of initial conditions in a simulation study, one can
a. vary the values of the system parameters
b. increase the number of alternative decisions studied
c. increase the sample size and ignore data from a number of the first runs for each set of parameters and decisions
d. all of the above

18. If both an analytic model and a simulation model could be used to study a problem including random events, the analytic model is often preferred because
a. the simulator generally requires a number of runs just to get a good estimate of the objective value (such as expected cost) for a particular decision
b. the analytic model may produce an optimal decision
c. the simulation study may require evaluating a large number of possible decisions
d. all of the above

19. Large complicated simulation models suffer from the following problem(s):
a. average costs are not well defined
b. it is difficult to create the appropriate random events
c. they may be expensive to model
d. all of the above

20. In performing a simulation it is advisable to
a. use the results of earlier decisions to suggest the next decision to try
b. use the same number of trials for each decision
c. simulate all possible decisions
d. none of the above

Answers

1. T, **2.** T, **3.** F, **4.** T, **5.** F, **6.** F, **7.** T, **8.** T, **9.** F, **10.** T, **11.** e, **12.** d, **13.** a, **14.** a, **15.** b, **16.** c, **17.** c, **18.** d, **19.** c, **20.** a

Skill Problems

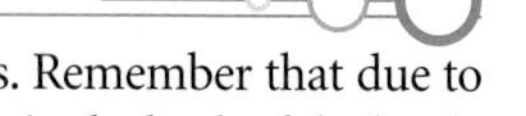

In the following problems you will be asked to perform a number of iterations. Remember that due to the nature of random numbers, your answers may vary slightly from those given in the back of the book.

9-1. Cite examples of the use of simulation (in the broad sense) by the military.

9-2. Cite examples of the use of simulation (in the broad sense) in professional sports.

9-3. Consider the following model with LP formulation:

$$\text{Max } 20A + 30C$$

s.t.

$$A \le 70$$
$$C \le 50$$
$$A + 2C \le 120$$
$$A, C \ge 0$$

(a) Construct a flowchart showing how to approach this problem as a simulation.
(b) Use the flowchart to evaluate the two potential solutions: ($A = 40, C = 30$) and ($A = 50, C = 30$).

9-4. Given in the following table are 50 weeks of historical car sales at Sally's Solar Car Co.

NUMBER OF SALES/WEEK	NUMBER OF WEEKS
0	2
1	5
2	12
3	16
4	8
5	7

(a) What probability distribution would you assign to demand so that the probability of a particular demand in the simulation is equal to the relative frequency of that demand over the last 50 weeks?
(b) Simulate 120 weeks of demand if using a spreadsheet add-in (do 12 weeks if using Excel alone).

9-5. Comment on the following statement: The simplex algorithm is a type of simulation, since it has to evaluate a number of alternative solutions en route to finding the optimal solution.

9-6. Jerry Tate is responsible for the maintenance of a fleet of vehicles used by the power company in constructing and repairing electric transmission lines. Jerry is especially concerned with the cost projections for replacing a large derrick on these vehicles.

He would like to simulate the number of derrick failures each year over the next 20 years. Jerry has looked at the last 10 years of data and compiled the following table:

NUMBER OF DERRICK FAILURES	NUMBER OF YEARS
0	4
1	3
2	1
3	1
4	1

He decides to simulate the 20-year period. Conduct the simulation for Jerry. How common is it for the total number of failures during three consecutive years to exceed 3?

9-7. SONOROLA has a cash management problem. In this model, the cash balance is determined each morning. The change in the cash balance from one morning to the next is a random variable. In particular, it increases by $10,000 with probability 0.3, decreases by $10,000 with probability 0.2, and remains the same with probability 0.5. What probability distribution would you assign to these events so as to accurately reflect the correct probability in a simulation?

9-8. In the example model in Section 9.5, we calculated the true expected profit and simulated average profit using 500 trials assuming that we ordered 11 omelet pans. Verify the same two performance measures (true expected profit, simulated average profit using 500 trials) under the assumption of ordering 9 pans.

9-9. In the example model in Section 9.5, we calculated the true expected profit and simulated average profit using 500 trials assuming that we ordered 11 omelet pans. Verify the same two performance measures (true expected profit, simulated average profit using 500 trials) under the assumption of ordering 10 pans.

9-10. In the example model in Section 9.5, we calculated the true expected profit and simulated average profit using 500 trials assuming that we ordered 11 omelet pans. Verify the same two performance measures (true expected profit, simulated average profit using 500 trials) under the assumption of ordering 12 pans.

9-11. The probability mass function of the Poisson distribution is given by

$$p = (x; \lambda) = \frac{\lambda^x}{x!} e^{-\lambda}, x = 0, 1, \ldots$$

Let $\lambda = 2$, and calculate the probability you observe x, for $x = 0, 1, \ldots, 5$.

9-12. Simulate a sample of 50 periods for the omelet pan model described in Section 9.5 (do 10 periods if using Excel alone). Assume that you have 10 pans on hand at the beginning of each period. Develop the proper probability distribution for the demand given in Section 9.5.

(a) Calculate the average profit per period.

(b) Record the number of stockouts (count a stockout as occurring when demand >10).

9-13. The weekly demand for milk for the last 50 weeks at the All-Ways-Open convenient market is shown in the following table.

(a) Assign the proper probability distribution to demands so that the probability of a particular demand in the simulation is equal to the relative frequency of that demand over the last 50 weeks.

(b) The store orders 42 cases every week. What are the average shortage and average excess inventory for 100 simulated weeks? (*Note*: Simulate 10 weeks if using Excel alone.)

(c) What are the expected shortage and the expected excess inventory?

SALES (CASES)	NUMBER OF WEEKS
40	4
41	10
42	12
43	9
44	8
45	7
Total	50

9-14. The time between arrivals at the drive-up window of the Sheridan Savings and Loan is shown in the following table. All customers form a single line and are served in the order of arrival. Assume that it takes exactly 8 minutes to serve each customer. Also assume that no one is being served or waiting to be served when the first customer arrives. Simulate the arrival of 800 customers (80 if using Excel alone), and record the number of customers who have to wait.

TIME BETWEEN ARRIVALS (MIN)	PROBABILITY
5	.25
10	.50
15	.25

9-15. Bob Ford is the new Chief Financial Officer at High Energy Electric Utility. As part of the planning for 2001 improvements, his staff has identified six potential projects that would be worthy of investment. Unfortunately, there is insufficient budget ($10 million) to fund them all.

PROJECT	INVESTMENT REQUIRED (000)	PROBABILITY OF SUCCESS	NPV (000)
1	$2,000	80%	$3,500
2	$3,000	55%	$2,700
3	$1,500	72%	$1,100
4	$2,500	90%	$2,000
5	$4,000	65%	$5,500
6	$ 750	40%	$3,000

Modify the PROJECTSELECTION.XLS file and use OptQuest to determine what combination of projects would maximize the expected NPV. Also, determine what combination would maximize the thirty-fifth percentile of the NPV. Are the solutions the same? If not, why not?

Application Problems

9-16. Consider the following brand-switching model. In this model probabilities are used to describe the behavior of a customer buying beer. Three particular beers (A, B, and C) are incorporated in the model. Customer behavior is summarized in accompanying table. Thus, we see in the first row that a customer who buys beer A in week 1 will buy the same beer in week 2 with probability 0.90, will buy beer B with probability 0.06, and will buy beer C with probability 0.04. A similar interpretation holds for the other rows. Consider a customer who buys beer A in week 1. Assume that you wish to simulate his behavior for the next 10 weeks. We know that in week 2 he would buy beers A, B, and C with probabilities 0.90. 0.06, and 0.04. If in week 2 he bought beer B, he would buy beers A, B, and C with probability 0.12, 0.78, and 0.10, respectively. Define the random events you would need to model and the appropriate random number generators for these events so as to accurately reflect the correct probabilities.

	PROBABILITY OF PURCHASE IN WEEK $i + 1$		
BEER PURCHASED IN WEEK i	A	B	C
A	0.90	0.06	0.04
B	0.12	0.78	0.10
C	0.09	0.07	0.84

9-17. The number of disk brake jobs performed by the service department of the Green Cab Company during each of the last 30 weeks is shown in the following table.

(a) Assign the proper probability distribution to the number of brake jobs performed so that the probability of a particular number of jobs in the simulation is equal to the relative frequency of that number of jobs over the last 30 weeks.

(b) Simulate 100 weeks of demand (10 weeks if using Excel alone). What is the simulated average number of brake jobs/week?

NUMBER OF BRAKE JOBS	NUMBER OF WEEKS
5	3
6	8
7	9
8	6
9	4
Total	30

9-18. STECO currently carries inventory for stainless steel sheets in two nearby cities. Los Gatos (L) and Alameda (A). Weekly demands (in trucks) and the probabilities for each city are shown in the accompanying table. Assume that the demands are independent. Los Gatos starts each week with 4 trucks of inventory on hand. Alameda starts each week with 6 trucks of inventory on hand.

(a) Simulate 500 weeks of demand at Los Gatos (20 weeks if using Excel alone), and record the number of stockouts.

(b) Simulate 500 weeks of demand at Alameda (20 weeks if using Excel alone), and record the number of stockouts.

	PROBABILITY	
DEMAND	L	A
1	0.2	
2	0.3	
3	0.3	0.1
4	0.1	0.1
5	0.1	0.3
6		0.3
7		0.2

Suppose that STECO centralized its stainless steel sheet inventory and satisfied all demand from Los Gatos and Alameda out of one new warehouse (call it LA).

(c) If LA started each week with 10 trucks of inventory on hand, would you expect the number of stockouts to increase, decrease, or remain the same as compared with when L and A operated independently? Why?

(d) Use the same random sequence of demands you used in parts (a) and (b) to simulate 500 weeks of operation for the new warehouse, LA (do 20 weeks if using Excel alone). Record the number of stockouts. Does this result agree with your answer to part (c)?

9-19. The Homeburg Volunteer Fire Department makes an annual door-to-door solicitation for funds. There are 3,000 households to solicit. The department asks households to be supporters (a $10 donation) or patrons (a $25 donation). An analysis of data from previous years indicates that

1. No one is home at 15% of the homes visited. If no one is home, the home is not revisited, and thus no donation is obtained. When someone is home, 80% of the time a woman answers the door and 20% of the time a man answers the door.
2. Of the women, 40% make a contribution: 70% of them are supporters, and 30% are patrons.
3. Of the men, 70% make a contribution: 25% of them are supporters, and 75% are patrons.

(a) What is the expected value of money received from the annual solicitation?

(b) Make a flowchart for this process. The output should be the contribution that occurs from calling on a house.

(c) Use the flowchart in part (b) to simulate 200 visits (20 visits if using Excel alone), and record the total contribution from these 200 visits. What is your estimate of the return from the annual solicitation based on this simulation?

(d) Simulate 1,000 visits (100 visits if using Excel alone) to answer the same question as in part (c).

9-20. Modify the PORTFLIO.XLS spreadsheet used in Section 9.9 to only allow selection between the 3 stocks and a new stock of your choice (e.g., Yahoo, Dell Computer, America Online). You will need to get historical stock returns from the company's web site and calculate the variance of the new stock. This time strive for at least a 30% average return and again seek to minimize the portfolio variance. Think about whether you should whether you should use Solver or OptQuest. What percent will you invest in each stock? What's the new portfolio's variance?

9-21. Laura Lene owns a flower stand near the new, beautiful Denver International Airport. She buys her flowers from a wholesaler at $0.25 per flower and sells them for $0.50 per flower. Laura wonders what is the optimal number of flowers to order each day. Based on looking at her past 3 years of history, she has found that demand can be approximated by a normal distribution with a mean of 100 and a standard deviation of 20. When she ends the day with more flowers than customers, she can sell all the leftovers for $0.05 per flower. Conversely, when she has more customers than flowers, she estimates that there is some lost goodwill in addition to the lost profit on the potential sale of $0.25. Laura estimates lost goodwill costs her the next two sales opportunities (i.e., dissatisfied customers will go to the competitor the next two times they want to buy flowers, but will then try Laura again).

(a) Use a spreadsheet simulation model with 1,000 iterations (100 iterations if using Excel alone) to determine the optimal number of flowers to order each day. Use the INT function in Excel to truncate the normal random variable values to an integer value.

(b) Construct a 95% confidence interval for the expected profit from the optimal ordering decision.

9-22. Not wanting to leave your beloved alma mater, you have come up with a scheme to stay around for 5 more years: You have decided to bid on the fast-food concession rights at the football stadium. You feel sure that a bid of $30,000 will win the concession, which gives you the right to sell food at football games for the next 5 years. You estimate that annual operating costs will be 40% of sales and annual sales will average $50,000. Your Uncle Ned has agreed to lend you the $30,000 to make your bid. You will pay him $7,700 at the end of each year. Your tax rate is 28%.

(a) Use a spreadsheet model to answer the following question. What is your average annual after-tax profit? Assume that the yearly payments of $7,700 are tax deductible.

(b) You realize that sales will probably vary from year to year. Suppose that sales can vary plus or minus 40% from the average of $50,000. You are concerned about the minimum after-tax profit you can earn in a year. You can survive if it is at least $8,000. Model annual sales for the 5 years as five continuous uniform random variables. Based on a sample of 4,000 five-year periods (400 periods if using Excel alone), estimate the probability that over any five-year period the minimum after-tax profit for a year will be at least $8,000. Will you bid for the concession?

9-23. You are the manager of Tex Electronics and are planning a promotion on a discontinued model of 27″ color TVs. The promotion will last 10 days, at the end of which any sets that you ordered but have not sold will be sold to another retailer for $250 each. You must order the sets from the manufacturer before you know what the demand during the promotion will be. Your cost is $350 per set and you will sell them for $600. You estimate that on 20% of the days you will sell 2 sets, 30% of the days you will sell 1 set, and 50% of the days you will sell no sets.

(a) What is the expected demand during the promotion? Should you necessarily order the expected demand?

(b) Estimate the optimal number of TVs to order. Simulate order quantities of 7, 8, 9, 10, and 11. In the 10 cells containing the daily demands, use a discrete, general probability distribution. Have one cell that contains the total net profit for the promotion. Based on 1,000 trials (100 trials if using Excel alone), what order quantity maximizes the average net profit? What is the simulated average net profit?

9-24. In the Midwest Express airline overbooking example in Section 9.7, it was assumed that the demand would materialize for whatever number of reservations Laura Sorensen chose to make available. In this model, we will make the model more realistic, by allowing the demand to be random according to the following discrete, general distribution:

Demand:	100	105	110	115	120	125	130	135	140	145
Probability:	0.03	0.05	0.08	0.12	0.18	0.20	0.12	0.10	0.08	0.04

Modify the MIDWSTRK.XLS file on your student CD to accommodate this new assumption.

(a) A priori, would you expect the optimal overbooking level to change with this new assumption?

(b) What is the new optimal overbooking level? What's the expected profit associated with this level?

9-25. Les Izmore, the CFO of Exxaco Oil, has a difficult problem. He wants to submit a bid for an offshore oil tract near the north shore of Alaska. Although the exact value of the tract is unknown, United States' geologists report that they expect it to be $20 million. However, there is some uncertainty in their estimates and the standard deviation is $3 million. Assume a normal distribution for the value of the tract. Les knows that his competitor, Texon, will also submit a bid for this attractive site. Both companies will contract their own individual studies on the value of the tract. Assume that the estimates obtained from these studies will have measurement errors that are normal with a mean of $0 and a standard deviation of $2 million. Modify either the EXXACOCB.XLS (if you want to use Crystal Ball) or EXXACORK.XLS (if you prefer @Risk) file on your student CD to answer the following:

(a) How many iterations should Les perform to be confident in his answer?

(b) How much should Les bid in order to maximize Exxaco's expected profit? What's the expected profit associated with this bid?

Case Study CyberLab (A)[1]

CyberLab was a new venture in the field of lab robotics. The company had a patent pending on the CyberLab system and had just finished construction of a small manufacturing facility in New Milford, Connecticut. It also had operational prototypes for all its products, but now needed a capital infusion to develop a major manufacturing facility and to provide working capital for expanded operations. CyberLab had offered 30% equity in the firm to the Precision Instrument Corporation (PRICO) in exchange for $1 million in capital and an agreement whereby PRICO would market CyberLab products through its existing international distribution system. PRICO was a major manufacturer of laboratory equipment. Some aspects of the CyberLab proposal were attractive to James Campbell, president of PRICO, but others were downright frightening. A significant new market could be harvested by his company, or the million dollar investment could vanish down a rat hole. Mr. Campbell needed to understand the financial soundness of PRICO's opportunity.

The Inception of CyberLab

Cyberlab started in 1985 as a result of the frustration of Dr. H. Meltzer, a biochemist working at the New York Psychiatric Institute. Dr. Meltzer was preparing and testing human enzymes[2] in bioassays.[3] Preparing samples was taking an inordinate amount of time and expense; human enzymes were extremely expensive, and manual sample preparation tended to waste enzyme. Dr. Meltzer was looking for an automated system that could prepare his samples, but none existed with the accuracy and reliability he needed for his tests. When he outlined his needs to his son, Walter Meltzer thought a system could be developed and the project began.

Two years later, the CyberLab system prototype was complete. Walter had designed the prototype with the idea that, eventually, all the components that needed machining could be subcontracted, and the remaining parts could be purchased from readily available sources.

[1] This case is to be used as the basis for class discussion rather than to illustrate either the effective or ineffective handling of an administrative situation. Preview Darden case abstracts on the World Wide Web at: www.darden.virginia.edu/publishing. Revised 1/90.

[2] Enzymes are complex protein substances that are essential to life. They act as catalysts in promoting reactions at cell temperatures without undergoing destruction in the process.

[3] A bioassay is the determination of the relative effective strength of a new substance by comparing its effect on a test organism with that of a standard substance.

Laboratory Robotics

Francis Zenie, president of a major lab-robot developer and manufacturer (Zymark Corporation), summed up the need for laboratory automation: "You've got 10 or 20 years of advancements in instrumental data measurements and data reduction, but our interviews revealed that people are still preparing samples like they did in the Dark Ages." Zymark personnel spent six months interviewing laboratory chemists and chemical-industry personnel by asking "What is your biggest problem?" The most common answer: sample preparation prior to analysis. Zymark correctly identified a need for new technology and introduced the first laboratory robot in 1982.

Laboratory technicians worked in the 2-D environment: dull and demanding. Preparing lab samples was tedious and required a high level of concentration. Humans could work as quickly as robots, but robots could maintain their work pace indefinitely (excluding maintenance and downtime) and were not prone to errors such as mixing up samples. The advantage of robotics lay in the increased output, enhanced consistency of preparations, and lower labor costs. Most robots currently on the market operated on a work-station principle, with the station arranged in a circle about an arm fixed in the center. The arm moved the sample to the stations for various preparations and tests. The CyberLab 800, however, worked in three dimensions and the arm was controlled by a computer such as the IBM PC. Programming involved numerous commands to control each movement. Starting and stopping the arm in the same place was the critical factor. It allowed the arm to "find" the sample and move it to the next station. Programming was essentially specific to each application and therefore took time to implement and verify.

CyberLab Products

The Cyberlab 800 System was a robot, although it certainly did not have the futuristic appearance of the more publicized of its kind (see Exhibit 1). Simply put, the Cyberlab 800 was a liquid transfer or pipetting device. It was capable of performing any repetitive laboratory liquid-preparation procedure currently done by hand. The system consisted of three separate components and a computer to execute the functions. A brief description of each component follows.

CyberLab 800 A pipette transport device that worked in three dimensions using eight independent probes (or channels) for transferring liquid into or out of the test tubes. The probes could accommodate four sizes of disposable pipette tips. (The disposable nature was essential to prevent sample contamination.) The "800" had a shaker table that mixed the samples right in the test tubes. The system also allowed hot or

EXHIBIT 1

The CyberLab 800

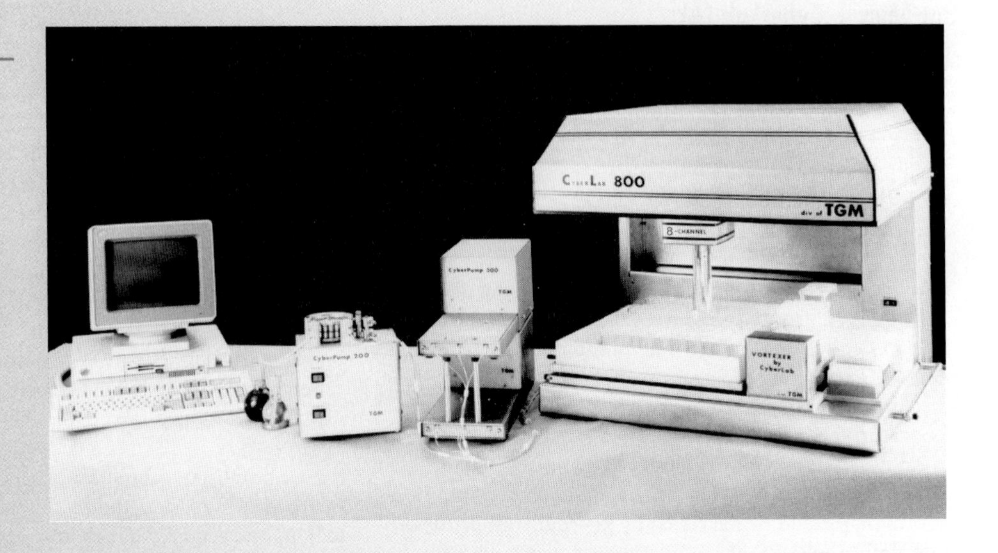

cold water to flow around the test tubes, controlling the temperature and thus the reactions taking place. The "800" was extremely accurate; it operated within an accuracy range of 1% with volumes as low as 10 microliters (a microliter is one millionth of a liter).

CyberPump 300 A precision syringe pump with three channels. Each channel was simply an individual syringe siphon pump that delivered the liquid to the pipetting system (CyberLab 800). A typical setup for the system had 2 of these "300" units.

CyberPump 200 This pump also delivered liquid to the "800" system. It differed from the "300" in that it only had two channels and was a reversible pump. The primary advantage of this pump over the "300" was its ability to move large volumes at a faster rate with no loss in accuracy. The reversible feature allowed samples that were complete to be drawn out of the test tubes and transferred to other analytical equipment for further testing.

At the end of the summer of 1987, one complete CyberLab system was at work in the New York Psychiatric Institute. Dr. Meltzer used federal grant money to pay for the machine. It replaced two lab technicians who were doing sample preparation, saving over $70,000 the first year. Dr. Meltzer's review of the new system's performance showed that less enzyme was being wasted and that the samples being prepared were more accurate.

News of the system spread within the psychiatric community, as well as without, because of the system's accuracy, associated savings in wasted material, and relatively low cost. By the end of July 1988, CyberLab had sold 4 units, and had interested buyers for 25 more.

Competition in the Laboratory Robotics Industry

An estimated 18,000 sites in the United States could use the CyberLab system. In addition, Zymark had indicated that the worldwide market was around 30,000 to 50,000 units. At the end of the second quarter of 1988, only 3,050 of those potential sites had lab robots installed. Zymark, the first entrant in the lab robot industry in 1982, had 42% of the installations to date. Two other competitors, Cetus and Micromedic, entered in 1983 and had 15% and 17% of installations, respectively. Cetus was acquired in 1986 by Perkin-Elmer, a large corporation in the analytical instruments field with $1.3 billion in sales for fiscal year 1987. Three more players entered in 1985, one of which was Beckman Instruments, a subsidiary of SmithKline Beckman, a very large corporation in the health-care and life-sciences industry with $4.3 billion in sales in fiscal year 1987. In 1987, Hewlett-Packard and Dynatech entered the market. See Exhibit 2 for a more complete description of the major competitors.

In spite of the eight other companies manufacturing lab robots, CyberLab believed its presence was needed because none of the existing players offered a machine similar to the "800" system for a similar cost. A CyberLab system cost $32,470 and would replace one chemist (average salary of $41,800 in 1987). Thus CyberLab had a payback of 0.78 years.

The Current Negotiations

In order to obtain necessary financing, Tom Friedlander, CEO of CyberLab, had approached Dean Witter and Salomon Brothers, but with no luck. He then hired a full-time consultant from a large venture capital firm to help him find the money. This consultant had interested one of the venture cap-

EXHIBIT 2

COMPANY NAME	YRS IN BSNS	# INSTLD TO DATE	% INSTLD TO DATE	GENL DESCRIPTION OF COMPANY	SALES OF COMPANY ($MM)	SALES OF LAB INSTR DIV ($MM)	COMPETING PRODUCT DESCRIPTION
Zymark	6	1000	42	First one to market, privately held.	15	15	Slow, cost 50K to 70K
Micromedic	5	400	17	Subsidiary of ICN Biomedicals, govt contract, Intl sales	43	17	Only dilutes & dispenses, cost 5K
Perkin-Elmer/ Cetus	5	350	15	Design and mfg of hi-tech analytic equip. Intl sales.	1334	416	No computer, robot arm, Cost 50K
Tecan	3	300	13	Subsidiary of Swiss corp, been in US 4 yrs	?	??	Limited use & warranty, cost 20K
Beckman	2.5	175	7	Technology intensive hlth care/life science company, Intl sales	4329	693	Moves smpl to probe, cost 26K
Hamilton	3	100	4	Been in lab equip bsns 30 years, Intl sales	25	25	One probe w/ 5 steel tip, cost 20K
HP/Genenchem	1	50	2	Established force in computers, starting in scientific equip	8090	405	Slow w/ genl purpose, only works w/ HP cmpt, cost 40–55K
Dynatech	1	4	0.2	Plan to go national	305	13	Cost 6K

Sources: Annual reports, S&P OTC reports, *Million Dollar Directory*

ital firm's partners (PRICO) in the CyberLab proposal. The terms of the possible deal were about to be negotiated between PRICO and CyberLab. CyberLab had offered 30% of its equity and the rights to market CyberLab products through PRICO's international distribution system in exchange for $1 million in capital. Under this agreement, PRICO would become the sole purchaser and marketer of the CyberLab systems. CyberLab would manufacture the machines and sell them at a prearranged transfer price to PRICO. Exhibit 3 shows the spreadsheet (CYBER.XLS), developed by CyberLab to evaluate its manufacturing-only venture under this agreement. *Note*: The assumptions used for both Exhibits 3 and 4 are shown in Exhibit 5.

The current proposal required PRICO to analyze the project as a package containing both the marketing opportunity and the equity investment. Based on the relevant costs and margins, was taking on the marketing and receiving 30% equity worth $1,000,000, or was a higher equity percentage and/or higher margin (i.e., lower transfer price) necessary to make the deal attractive?

On the marketing issue, PRICO would provide its established name, sales force, and advertising in exchange for a 23% margin. The company had been in the laboratory-equipment business for over 50 years and currently had 100 sales and service offices in the United States and 220 such offices in 60

C37 =C33-C36

	A / B	C	D	E	F
26	CYBERLAB'S PRO FORMA INCOME STATEMENT: MANUFACTURING ONLY				
27					
28	YEAR	1	2	3	
29	Selling Price/Unit	$25,000	$25,000	$25,000	
30	Matrl & Labor/Unit	$8,651	$8,651	$8,651	
31	Units Sold	29	47	51	
32					
33	Sales Revenue	$725,000	$1,175,000	$1,275,000	
34	Material,Dir Labor	250,879	406,597	441,201	
35	Overhead	138,000	196,430	207,641	
36	Cost Of Goods Sold	$388,879	$603,027	$648,842	
37	Gross Margin	$336,121	$571,973	$626,158	
38	Selling, Gen & Admin	$258,044	$343,047	$344,908	
39	Depreciation	16,000	9,600	5,760	
40	Profit before tax	$62,077	$219,326	$275,490	
41	Taxes	$24,831	$87,730	$110,196	
42	Profit after tax	$37,246	$131,596	$165,294	
43					
44	RETURN ON SALES	5.14%	11.20%	12.96%	
45	EQUITY AT	$1,000,000	$1,037,246	$1,168,842	
46	BEGINNING OF YEAR				
47	RETURN ON EQUITY	3.72%	12.69%	14.14%	
48					
49	*YEAR*	*1*	*2*	*3*	*TERM VALUE*
50	PAT	37,246	131,596	165,294	
51	DEP'N ADD-BACK	16,000	9,600	5,760	
52	CHANGE IN WORK CAP	(47,176)	(58,841)	(72,912)	
53	CASH FLOW FR. OPNS	6,070	82,355	98,142	1,635,700
54					
55	NPV	$1,141,090			
56	IRR	16.99%			
57					

EXHIBIT 3

H	I	J	K	L	M
	CYBERLAB (A)				
PRICO'S PRO FORMA INCOME STATEMENT: MARKETING ONLY					
YEAR	1	2	3		
Selling price/unit	$32,470	$32,470	$32,470		
Transfer price/unit	$25,000	$25,000	$25,000		
Margin/unit	$7,470	$7,470	$7,470		
PRICO Margin (%)	23.0%	23.0%	23.0%		
Units Sold	29	47	51		
Sales Revenue	$941,630	$1,526,090	$1,655,970		
Cost Of Goods Sold	725,000	1,175,000	1,275,000		
Gross Margin	$216,630	$351,090	$380,970		
Advertising	$51,000	$60,000	$60,000		
Sales expense	$137,400	$208,200	$210,600		
Total Sell.,Gen.& Admin	$188,400	$268,200	$270,600		
Profit before tax	$28,230	$82,890	$110,370		
Taxes	$11,292	$33,156	$44,148		
Profit after tax	$16,938	$49,734	$66,222		
RETURN ON SALES	1.80%	3.26%	4.00%		
RETURN ON INVESTMENT	11.29%	33.16%	44.15%		
YEAR	*1*	*2*	*3*	*TERM VALUE*	
PAT	16,938	49,734	66,222		
DEP'N ADD-BACK	0	0	0		
CASH FLOW	16,938	49,734	66,222	509,400	
NPV	$262,258				
IRR	51.07%				

EXHIBIT 4

H	I	J
ASSUMPTIONS		
TOTAL MARKET SIZE-YR 1	595	
CYBERLAB MKT SHARE-YR	5.00%	
TOTAL MKT GROWTH-YR 2-	7.00%	
CYBER MKT SHARE-YR 2+	7.50%	
DISCOUNT RATE	13.00%	
TAX RATE	40.00%	
INITIAL INVESTMENT	$150,000	
MATERIAL AND LABOR/UNIT	$8,651	

EXHIBIT 5

countries throughout the world. It certainly seemed reasonable to Mr. Campbell that if the patent was worth the $700,000 he was effectively paying CyberLab upfront, then his company's marketing clout was worth at least the $262,258 he had calculated as the net present value (NPV) of the marketing agreement (see Exhibit 4).

In dollar terms, PRICO would actually incur initial expenses of $150,000, for a one-time seminar and new brochures to train all the sales force on the new product, as well as ongoing expenses of $51,000 the first year and approximately $60,000 per year for the second and third years for advertising. Additional expenses included a commission of $600 per CyberLab system sold.

Another possible expense was the sales force. Frank Adams, the vice president of sales, argued there was an "opportunity" cost associated with using the sales force. He estimated the new product would take about 1% of each salesperson's schedule the first year and 1.5% for years 2 and 3. The total sales expense the previous year for PRICO was $12 million, which made the opportunity cost equal $120,000 (.01 * 12,000,000). Because the average salary for one salesperson was $24,000 a year in addition to expenses of $36,000 a year, this "cost" was the equivalent of two full-time salespeople the first year and three in years 2 and 3.

PRICO would not actually have to hire any new salespeople, but adding CyberLab products would take away some of the sales force's time spent on existing products. In a "typical" sales call to a lab director, part of the time was spent ordering routine supplies (beakers, cylinders, test tubes, pipettes, etc.), while the remainder was spent talking about new and existing nonroutine products. Mr. Campbell did not believe that there would not be any significant erosion of the standard-supply selling; Mr. Adams and his staff concurred. Even if there were some erosion, it would probably be made up by the increase in disposable pipette tip sales that would certainly accompany sales of the CyberLab system. Because PRICO would not have to pay any money out of pocket, Vince Pauli, the financial analyst for new ventures at PRICO, had argued that the sales force's time should not be included as an expense in the analysis.

The projected cash flows from PRICO's perspective, for the marketing aspect only is shown in Exhibit 4. (*Note*: This exhibit includes the opportunity cost for the sales force's time in the "sales expense" line.) The lab-instrument manufacturing industry average for return on sales (based on profit before tax) was 5.1%. Other major corporations in this industry had values for return on equity of 12% to 13%. Overall, for the million dollar investment, PRICO would get 30% of the value of CyberLab or $342,327 (.3 * $1,141,090) plus the value of the marketing agreement, $262,258 for a net of –$395,415.

Mr. Campbell thought he had some negotiating room, even though CyberLab had made it clear that it wanted both the marketing arrangement and an investment. Mr. Friedlander had just called to say that he had received an offer from a privately held company, Sperling Equipment Co., to buy a fixed number of units per year for the first three years and market them in exchange for a 30% discount from retail price. This raised the question whether PRICO would want to do the marketing alone on a nonexclusive basis without the 30% equity interest if CyberLab would let them.

This was an interesting question, but the immediate task was to evaluate the offer on the table. Is the marketing/investment opportunity attractive? If it is worth pursuing, should Campbell counter offer a higher equity position in exchange for the $1 million capital infusion? Or should they just back away from the whole idea?

Questions

1. Using the information on the uncertain quantities given in the Addendum that follows, how would you use simulation to evaluate the investment/marketing opportunity from PRICO's point of view?
2. Conduct five trials evaluating the opportunity.
3. Suppose you had available the results of many trials (think about how many you need). How could you use

these results to decide whether PRICO should take this opportunity?

4. How could you use simulation to evaluate counteroffers you may wish to carry into negotiation with CyberLab?

Cyberlab Addendum

The following information is provided for the major uncertainties for each variable including the range of possible values along with their appropriate probabilities.

Lab-Robot Market Growth

Lab robots were highly suited for any area that required repetitive testing and sample preparation on a large scale. These areas included such biotechnology industries as pharmaceuticals, agricultural products, genetic engineering, and medical technology, in addition to the research and development division of almost any company. The biotechnology market anticipated sales of $1.2 billion in 1988 and was expecting to grow to $25 billion by 2000, which would represent 28.8% annual growth. R&D expenditures were forecast by Predicasts to grow at 7% to 9% annually in the near future. Lab and analytical equipment sales were forecast to grow from $1.65 billion in 1985 to $2.35 billion in 1990—an annual growth rate of 7.3%. In the past two years, sales had grown 5% and 9%. Experts believed that the future annual growth would be as likely to fall between 6% and 8% as it would to fall outside that range, but growth rates as high as 10% and as low as 0% were possible over several years. The rates generally centered around 7%. Retention of the 20% R&D tax credit would provide continued investment incentives.

Market Size for Current Year

Based on Zymark's actual 1987 sales of $15 million and the cost of its systems of $50,000 to $70,000, Zymark sold approximately 250 units (15,000,000/$60,000) in 1987. When CyberLab combined this estimate with Zymark's estimated 42% share of installations to date, the result was an estimate of the annual market of 595 units (250/0.42).

A high-side estimate of the market was made using Zymark's average cost as $50,000 and assuming that its market share had dropped to about 35% in 1987 from the 42% share of total installations from 1982 to 1987. This approach gave an estimated market size of 809 units. Similarly, a low-side estimate was calculated of 510 units, using an average cost of $70,000 and assuming that current-year market share equaled cumulative market share.

CyberLab Market Share

Walter Meltzer estimated that first-year market share could be as low as 0 if the product completely bombed and as high as 7%, with a median value of 5%. In his mind, market share was equally likely to be between 4% and 6% as it was to be outside this range. In the second and successive years, he figured CyberLab would grab an extra 2.5% of the market over the first-year share.

Cost of Materials and Labor

Meltzer, the CyberLab-system inventor, had kept track of how long it took him to machine the 80 parts he bought and then machined, as well as what it cost to buy the other 75 parts he

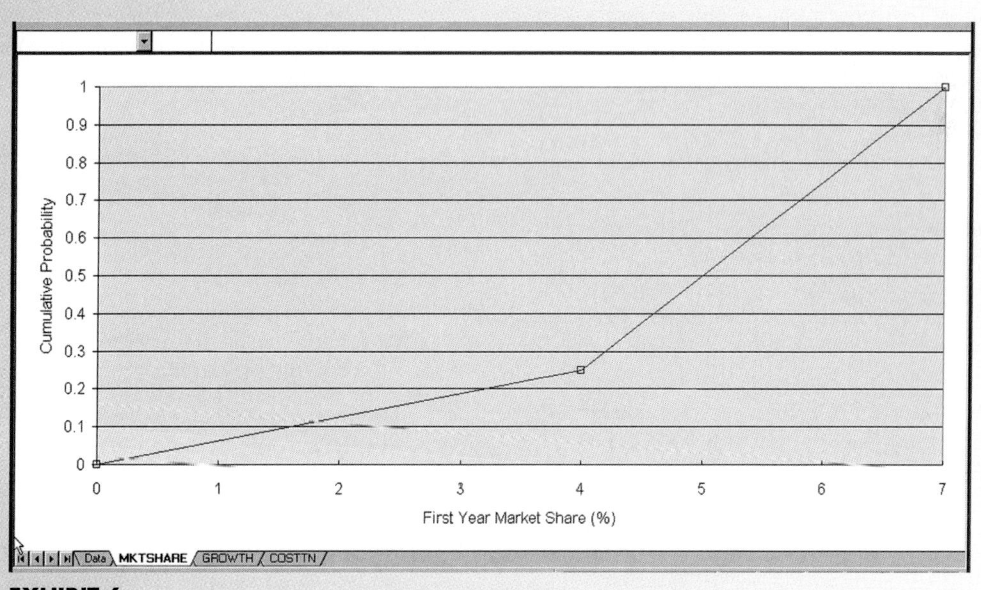

EXHIBIT 6

used unchanged in creating the system. To estimate the total cost, he added up the cost of the 75 purchased parts and his estimate of the labor and material cost for the 80 machined parts. The labor portion of the machined parts' cost was calculated by multiplying the time he took by the labor rate charged by local machine shops in New England ($100/hour). His conservative estimate of the total cost came out to be $8,651.

Both the time to do the machining and the rate charged for machined parts could vary significantly from previous estimates. Therefore, because Meltzer was very conservative when assigning the overall costs, he estimated they could vary as high as 5% above his estimate or as low as 9% below his estimate.

Tax Rate

A 35% tax rate was used as an estimate (the top federal rate was 33%; the top Connecticut rate 7%), but if the company did not do well, the tax rate would be much lower. Another factor that could change the tax rate was the fickle nature of the Congress and the president.

Of all these variables that had been estimated, the three that were believed to have the most impact on the bottom line were the following:

The first quantity was CyberLab's *first-year market share.* It could be as low as 0% and as high as 7% with it being equally likely to be greater than or less than 5%. For a graph of the cumulative probability distribution function, see Exhibit 6.

The next quantity was the *cost of materials and direct labor for the system.* The total cost could vary as much as 9% below the engineer's prediction of $8,651 to 5% above the prediction and that any percentage in this interval was possible. The following risk table was developed.

Cost Variance (Percent)	Probability of Value or Less
−10	0
−5	0.25
−2	0.50
0	0.75
+5	1.0

The last quantity was *total market growth.* The fastest the lab-robot market would grow was 10% and the slowest it would grow was 0%. It was equally likely in his mind that the actual growth would be greater than or less than 7%. He also felt that there was a 50% chance that the growth would be between 6 and 8% with the other 50% representing growth rates outside this range.

Case Study | Mountain Realty[1]

Brenda Shoots of Mountain Realty has been asked by the company president, Bill Wyth, to conduct an analysis of the Applebee Apartment complex located near the University of Wyoming. Mountain Realty maintains a diversified portfolio of commercial properties in the Laramie area for a partnership of large investors from Denver. Bill Wyth wants to assess how this new investment will fit into the current portfolio. He is, therefore, looking for an annual after-tax return in the range of 12% to 16%.

Brenda has collected the following data on the Applebee Apartments:

- The building has five units with 750 square feet each. They are currently renting at $500 per month. Therefore, the first year's gross potential income (GPI) is determined to be $30,000. GPI is expected to grow at a rate of 3% to 8% per year, but most likely will be around 5%.
- The vacancy and collection loss allowance for Laramie is 1% to 2%, but may be as high as 4% in four to five years.
- Each component of operating expenses was analyzed over the past several years and combined into a total figure as a percentage of GPI. Brenda's analysis has shown that operating expenses should be 40% of GPI. However, the standard deviation of her data was 2.5 percentage points. The building has been maintained in an acceptable fashion, therefore, no major repairs are anticipated.
- The seller is asking a fixed price of $160,000. The land is valued at $24,000 and the improvement at $136,000. With 3,750 square feet in the building, the square foot cost of the property is $42.66.
- West Interstate Bank is willing to provide a standard amortized loan for $120,000 at 12% interest with a 25-year life. Brenda has calculated the annual payment constant at $15,300.
- Improvement will be depreciated using the straight-line method over the standard 27.5 years for residential property.
- Based on market studies of the Laramie area the subject property's market value is expected to grow at 3% per year with a standard deviation of 1.5%.

[1] This case was prepared by Fred Hirsch, Ray Rogers, and Larry Weatherford, Assistant Professor. Copyright © 1993, Laramie, WY.

	A	B	C	D	E	F	G	H	I
1	*Investment Analysis - the Apartment Complex Model*								
2									
3									
4		**Year 1**	**Year 2**	**Year 3**	**Year 4**	**Year 5**		**Calculation of Gain on Sale**	
5								Tax Basis	$160,000.00
6	**Gross Potential Income**	$30,000.00	$31,500.00	$33,075.00	$34,728.75	$36,465.19		Less Depreciation	24,727.27
7	Growth in GPI		5.00%	5.00%	5.00%	5.00%		Remaining tax basis	$135,272.73
8	Less: Vacancy and								
9	Collection Allowance	300.00	472.50	661.50	694.58	729.30		Sales Price	$185,483.85
10	Vacancy Rate	1.00%	1.50%	2.00%	2.00%	2.00%		Less Selling expenses	6,000.00
11	**Effective Gross Income**	$29,700.00	$31,027.50	$32,413.50	$34,034.18	$35,735.88		**Adjusted sales price**	$179,483.85
12	Less: Operating Expenses	$12,000.00	$12,600.00	$13,230.00	$13,891.50	$14,586.08		Less: remaining tax basis	135,272.73
13	As a percentage of EGI	40%	40%	40%	40%	40%		**Total taxable gain**	44,211.12
14	Less: Major repairs							Less: tax on sale (28%)	12,379.11
15	and replacements	0.00	0.00	0.00	0.00	0.00		**After tax gain**	31,832.01
16	**Net Operating Income**	$17,700.00	$18,427.50	$19,183.50	$20,142.68	$21,149.81			
17	**Capitalization Rate**	10.74%	10.86%	10.97%	11.19%	11.40%		**Adjusted sales price**	$179,483.85
18	Less: Depreciation	4,945.45	4,945.45	4,945.45	4,945.45	4,945.45		Less: tax on sale	12,379.11
19	Less: Interest	14,400.00	14,292.00	14,171.04	14,035.57	13,883.83		Less: loan payoff	114,282.46
20	**Taxable Income**	($1,645.45)	($809.95)	$67.00	$1,161.65	$2,320.52		**Net Cash to equity from s**	$52,822.28
21	Plus: Depreciation	4,945.45	4,945.45	4,945.45	4,945.45	4,945.45		Present Value factor	0.567
22	Less: Principal Repaid	900.00	1,008.00	1,128.96	1,264.43	1,416.16		**Present Value from sale**	$29,972.78
23	**Before-tax cash flow**	2,400.00	3,127.50	3,883.50	4,842.68	5,849.81			
24	Less: taxes	0.00	0.00	18.76	325.26	649.75		**The Investment Decision**	
25	Plus: tax savings							Total present value of equity	
26	(28% x line 16 above)	460.73	226.79	0.00	0.00	0.00	Present Value	cash flow after tax	13,800.65
27	**Equity Cash Flow after tax**	2,860.73	3,354.29	3,864.74	4,517.42	5,200.07	Factor	Present value from sale	29,972.78
28	Present value factor	0.893	0.797	0.712	0.636	0.567	12.00%	**Total Present Value of Eq**	$43,773.43
29	**Present value of equity cash**							Less orginal equity	40,000.00
30	**flow after tax**	2,554.22	2,674.02	2,750.85	2,870.90	2,950.66		**Net present value**	$3,773.43
31									
32	**Mortgage Amount**	120,000	119,100	118,092	116,963	115,699			
33	Interest Rate	12%	12%	12%	12%	12%			
34	Term (years)	25	25	25	25	25			
35	Interest Payment	14,400.00	14,292.00	14,171.04	14,035.57	13,883.83			
36	Principal Payment	900.00	1,008.00	1,128.96	1,264.43	1,416.16			
37	**Debt Service**	15,300.00	15,300.00	15,300.00	15,300.00	15,300.00			
38									
39	**Depreciation Period**	27.50	Years	Project Cost	136,000	for improvements			
40	**Depreciation Per Period**	4,945.45	4,945.45	4,945.45	4,945.45	4,945.45			
41									
42	**Sales Price (End of Period)**	$164,800.00	$169,744.00	$174,836.32	$180,081.41	$185,483.85			
43	Growth Factor	3.00%	3.00%	3.00%	3.00%	3.00%			
44	Project Cost	$160,000.00							

EXHIBIT 1

- The investor partnership is currently averaging a 28% marginal tax rate.
- The partnership normally looks for a 5-year holding period. Mountain Realty offers the partnership a flat fee of $6,000 to handle the sale of this type of property.

Brenda has a standard computer spreadsheet (MTNRLTY.XLS) she has used for this type of analysis in the past (see Exhibit 1). She normally tries to vary significant values on the spreadsheet to provide a degree of sensitivity analysis to the Denver partnership. However, though generally happy with Brenda's work they have asked pointed questions on the probabilities attached to her figures. The partners are very risk-adverse not wanting to put their venture capital at significant risk.

Bill's son Jack has just taken a new decision science course at the University of Wyoming. Jack was astounded by the usefulness of some new software packages called Crystal Ball and @Risk. At Bill's suggestion, Brenda will like to use this package to present her analysis and recommendation to the partnership next week in Denver.

Questions

1. What is the expected Net Present Value (NPV) at a 12% hurdle rate? At a 16% hurdle rate?
   Note: In the spreadsheet, the term "Present Value Factor" is used as it is the commonly used word in the real estate industry. It may be more commonly known to you as "discount rate" or "hurdle rate."
2. What's the probability the NPV at 12% will be ≤0?
3. What should Brenda recommend to the Denver partnership on the feasibility of this investment?

Case Study Sprigg Lane (A)[1]

May 19, 1988, was a beautiful day in Charlottesville, Virginia. Tom Dingledine could see some cows grazing the pasture on the rolling hillside outside his window. He was grateful for the bucolic setting, which was made possible by his doing well with the projects he managed, one of which now required some concentration. Tom was the president of Sprigg Lane Natural Resources, a subsidiary of the Sprigg Lane Investment Corporation (SLIC). The decision at hand was whether to invest in the Bailey Prospect natural gas opportunity.

The Company

Sprigg Lane was a privately held investment corporation founded in 1961. It had become a diversified corporation composed of two major groups. The first was devoted to manufacturing high-quality home furnishings. Its masthead company was Virginia Metalcrafters, which produced handcrafted brass giftware. Other companies in the group included an outdoor lantern company in Maine and an antique reproduction furniture company in Maryland. With the establishment of National Legal Research Group in 1970, another major group—The Research Group—was started. Since then four other research companies had been added in the fields of consumer product marketing, computer software, tax research, and investment financial analysis.

The group's recent formation of Sprigg Lane Development Corporation, which was involved in the purchase and development of real estate, brought the total number of company subsidiaries to nine. SLIC sales for 1987 approximated $30 million and it employed over 525 people.

Drilling and Developing a Well[2]

The most common drilling rig in operation in 1988 was the rotary rig composed of five major components—the drill string and bit, the fluid-circulating system, the hoisting system, the power plant, and the blowout-prevention system. To facilitate the drilling process, generally a fluid known as drilling mud (composed of water and special chemicals) was circulated around the hole being drilled. In some cases, such as the Bailey Prospect, air was used as the "drilling mud." The major purpose of the drilling mud was to lubricate the drill bit and to carry to the surface the cuttings that could otherwise remain in the hole and clog it.

After the well was drilled, and if gas were found, the well had to be completed and prepared for production. A metal pipe of 8.625 inches diameter called casing was generally inserted about 1,300 feet into the ground. Then a pipe of 4 1/2 inches diameter called production casing was inserted into the cased hole all the way down through the production zone (about 5,400 feet) and cemented. After the cement set, the production casing was perforated so that gas could flow to the surface through it.

The cost to drill an "average" well in Doddridge County, West Virginia, location of the Bailey Prospect, was $160,000. There was some uncertainty, however, in the cost from well to well because of such factors as differing depths of wells and different types of terrain that had to be drilled. Experts in the local area said that there was a 95% chance that the cost for any given well would be within $5,400 of the average cost, assuming a normal distribution.

SLIC's Entry into Natural Gas

In January 1987, Tom, who had been working as the CFO of a private oil and gas exploration and development company, met the president of SLIC and joined the company to find some investment opportunities for it. Tom became convinced that the company could enjoy higher potential returns (30% to 40% after tax) from natural resource exploration than from other investment opportunities, including real estate, which were yielding 15% to 20%. Although natural resource exploration was clearly riskier, Tom felt the risk could be managed by drilling only sites that were surrounded on three to four sides by existing wells. Through further research, he found two other factors that helped reduce the risk: First, contracts with the pipeline distributors typically locked in the natural gas selling prices for four years, and second, well operating expenses were covered by contracts that allowed increases only every three years, with the increase capped at 15% per three-year period. Tom thought that the annual increase in the total well cost would be equivalent to one-half the rate of inflation.

The president of SLIC was so impressed with Tom's presentation on the entire subject that he offered him the job as president of a new division to be called Sprigg Lane Natural Resources (SLNR). Tom took the offer, and in his first year on the job (1987), SLNR had drilled four wells. It had not been difficult operationally to drill the four wells, but it had been challenging to find enough high-quality investment opportunities. Tom considered wells to be "good" if they met all the following criteria: (1) payback of initial cash investment in 42 months or less, (2) at least 25% internal rate of return (IRR) on an after-tax basis, and (3) at least 15% IRR on a pretax basis.

In the first five months of production, one of the wells had already paid back 52% of its initial investment—well ahead of its target 28-month payout. The other wells were also doing well, and all of them were at least on schedule for meeting their targeted return on investment. Even though things

[1] This case is to be used as the basis for class discussion rather than to illustrate either the effective or ineffective handling of an administrative situation. Preview Darden case abstracts on the World Wide Web at: www.darden.virginia.edu/publishing. Revised 10/91.

[2] U.S. Department of Energy, *The Oil and Gas Drilling Industry*, 1981, pp. 13–16.

	A	B	C	D	E	F	G	H	I	J	K	L	M
1	WELL	****ASSUMPTIONS****		ENVIRONMENT				****RESULTS****					
2													
3	TOTAL WELL COST	$160,000	!	FEDERAL TAX RATE		34.00%	!	EQUITY PAYOUT (AFTER-TAX) =				23.26	MONTHS !
4	INTANGIBLE COST(%OFTOTAL)	72.50%	!	STATE TAX RATE		9.75%	!						!
5			!	SEVERANCE TAX RATE		3.40%	!	INTERNAL RATE OF RETURN (CF AFTER-TAX) =				41.07%	!
6	MONTHLY OPERATING COSTS	$300	!	COUNTY TAX RATE		4.50%	!	INTERNAL RATE OF RETURN (PBT) =				16.65%	!
7	ANNUAL LEASE EXPENSE	$3,000	!	SECTION 29 TAX CREDIT($/MI		$0.7600	!						!
8	INFLTION FACTOR-WELL EXPENSE	1.75%	!	% QUALIFIED		100.00%	!	NET PRESENT VALUE (CFAT) @ 15%				$110,263	!
9			!				!						!
10	PRODUCTION DATA		!	GNP DEFLATOR		3.50%	!	CUMULATIVE CASH FLOW AFTER-TAX				$432,235	!
11	ENOUGH(0=NO,1=YES)?	1	!				!						!
12	1st YEAR Mcf	33,000	!	ROYALTIES		15.2344%	!						!
13	PRODUCTION DECLINE AFTER...		!				!						!
14	YEAR 1 =	22.50%	!	GAS PRICE DATA			!						!
15	YEAR 2 =	17.50%	!				!						!
16	YEAR 3-5 =	12.50%	!	CURRENTPRICE($/MMBTU)		$1.90	!						!
17	YEAR 6-14 =	10.00%	!	BTUCONTENT(BTU/FT3)		1,155	!						!
18	YEAR 15-24 =	5.00%	!	1ST YEAR OF			!						!
19			!	PRICE INCREASE		5	!						!
20													
21	YEAR	0	1	2	3	4	5	6	7	8	9	10	11
22	INITIAL INVESTMENT	($160,000)											
23	PRICE PER MCF		2.19	2.19	2.19	2.19	2.27	2.35	2.43	2.52	2.61	2.70	2.79
24	PRODUCTION(MCF)		33,000	25,575	21,099	18,462	16,154	14,135	12,721	11,449	10,304	9,274	8,347
25													
26	GROSS REVENUE		$72,419	$56,124	$46,303	$40,515	$36,691	$33,228	$30,952	$28,832	$26,857	$25,017	$23,304
27	LESS: ROYALTIES		11,033	8,550	7,054	6,172	5,590	5,062	4,715	4,392	4,092	3,811	3,550
28	NET REVENUE		$61,386	$47,574	$39,249	$34,343	$31,101	$28,166	$26,237	$24,440	$22,766	$21,206	$19,753
29	OPERATING EXPENSES		6,600	6,716	6,833	6,953	7,074	7,198	7,324	7,452	7,583	7,715	7,850
30	SEVERANCE & COUNTY TAX		5,721	4,434	3,658	3,201	2,899	2,625	2,445	2,278	2,122	1,976	1,841
31	DEPRECIATION	116,000	6,286	6,286	6,286	6,286	6,286	6,286	6,286				
32	PROFIT BEFORE TAX	($116,000)	$42,779	$30,139	$22,472	$17,904	$14,843	$12,057	$10,182	$14,710	$13,061	$11,514	$10,062
33	DEPLETION		9,208	7,136	5,887	5,151	4,665	4,225	3,936	3,666	3,415	3,181	2,963
34	STATE INC. TAX	(11,310)	2,042	1,289	830	555	369	199	83	587	484	387	296
35	FEDERAL INC. TAX	(35,595)	(18,247)	(15,853)	(14,484)	(13,821)	(12,937)	(12,141)	(11,631)	(9,231)	(8,796)	(8,393)	(8,022)
36	PROFIT AFTER TAX	($69,095)	$49,777	$37,567	$30,238	$26,018	$22,746	$19,775	$17,795	$19,688	$17,958	$16,339	$14,825
37													
38	AFTER TAX CASH FLOW	($113,095)	$65,270	$50,989	$42,411	$37,455	$33,697	$30,285	$28,016	$23,354	$21,373	$19,520	$17,788
39	CUMUL. AFT TAX CASH FLOW	($113,095)	($47,825)	$3,164	$45,575	$83,030	$116,727	$147,013	$175,029	$198,383	$219,756	$239,276	$257,064
40	NPV THROUGH YEAR N	($113,095)	($56,339)	($17,784)	$10,102	$31,518	$48,271	$61,364	$71,896	$79,531	$85,606	$90,432	$94,255

EXHIBIT 1

Bailey Prospect Base Case Spreadsheet

had gone favorably for Tom so far, he knew the pressure was still on him to make good decisions because SLNR was planning to drill 20 more wells in 1988.

Investment Strategy

SLNR acted as the managing general partner in the gas drilling ventures it formed, which gave it full responsibility for choosing sites and managing the well if gas were found. SLNR gathered information from the state of West Virginia and from other companies drilling in the vicinity of a well (if they were willing to engage in "information trading"). Tom would then put together a package of 10 wells that he considered good investments based on all the information he had gathered. The total initial investment for a typical package would be around \$1.6 million. SLNR would retain about 25% ownership and sell the rest to several other general partners.

As managing general partner, SLNR was responsible for hiring a general contractor who would actually hire a firm to do the drilling, and SLNR's geologist, Brad Thomas, would determine whether there really was enough gas to make it worth completing a well. If the decision was to go ahead, the general contractor would also be in charge of the day-to-day operations of a well. SLNR had entered into a joint venture with Excel Energy of Bridgeport, West Virginia, in which they agreed that Excel would act as the general contractor for all the wells on which SLNR acted as managing general partner.

The first-year production level varied significantly from well to well. Tom found the uncertainty could be described with a lognormal probability distribution with a mean of 33 million cubic feet and a standard deviation of 4.93 million cubic feet.

The Bailey Prospect

Exhibit 1 is a copy of the spreadsheet (SPRIGG.XLS) Tom had developed to analyze one well, called the Bailey Prospect, as a potential member of the package of 10 wells he was currently putting together (years 12 to 25 are not shown). As Tom thought about the realization of this one well, he knew the Bailey Prospect was surrounded by producing wells from the target gas-producing formation. It was virtually certain, therefore, that SLNR would hit the formation and decide to complete the well, but there was a 10% chance that either an operational failure would cause zero production or that the gas formation would be depleted because of the surrounding wells, resulting in essentially zero production. In either of these cases, the pretax loss would be \$160,000. In the more likely case, there would be gas produced and Tom would then find out how much the well would produce in the first and subsequent years. He would also learn what the BTU content (see Exhibit 2 for an explanation of the more commonly used abbreviations and terms in the well-drilling business) was for the gas, which would affect the total revenue generated by the well.

Revenues and Expenses The spreadsheet was basically an income statement over the well's life. The price per mcf was calculated by multiplying the contracted price per MMBTU times the BTU content divided by 1000. The production in mcf was then estimated for the first year and calcu-

EXHIBIT 2 Explanation of Commonly Used Terms

BTU	British Thermal Unit—amount of heat required to raise the temperature of 1 pound of water by 1° Fahrenheit.
MMBTU	1 million BTUs.
Decatherm	1 MMBTU.
FT^3	1 cubic foot.
mcf	1000 cubic feet.
Intangible well costs	Any expense for something which could not be used again (e.g., fees to the drilling crew, cement costs). A purchase of metal pipe, on the other hand, would represent a tangible cost.
Severance	Sales tax to state on gas or oil withdrawn and sold.
Depletion	Generally the concept is similar to depreciation. It compensated the company for the money spent to acquire the right to drill. Generally accepted accounting principles recognized only cost depletion, which amortized the cost on a unit of production basis (e.g., # of mcf produced this year divided by the total mcf in the ground times the cost). The IRS, however, allowed the company to calculate depletion under the more favorable of two methods. One of these being cost depletion, the other is called percentage depletion. The latter was in the spreadsheet and was almost always more favorable.

lated for each succeeding year based on the percentage decline values given in the assumptions. The gross revenue was just the product of the price per mcf times the mcf of gas produced in a given year. Out of the gross revenue came a 15.23% royalty payment to the owner of the mineral rights, leaving net revenue. Several expenses were deducted from net revenue to arrive at the profit before tax:

1. Monthly operating costs of $300 were paid to Excel Energy in addition to a budgeted amount of $3,000 for other operating expenses that might occur on an annual basis. These costs were increased annually by the well-expense inflation factor.
2. Local taxes of 4.5% times the gross revenue were paid to the county and a severance tax (see Exhibit 2) of 3.4% times the gross revenue was paid to the state of West Virginia.
3. Depreciation expense for year 0 equaled the intangible drilling cost, which was 72.5% of the total well cost. The remainder of the initial drilling cost was depreciated on a straight-line basis over seven years.

To compute profits after tax, the following equations applied:

Profit after tax = Profit before tax – Depletion – State Income Tax – Federal Income Tax

Where: Depletion = minimum of .5 * (Profit before tax) *or* .15 * (Net revenue)

State Income Tax = State tax rate * (Profit before tax – Depletion) – 1/2 * (Severance tax)

Federal Income Tax = Federal tax rate * (Profit before tax – Depletion – State income tax) – Section 29 credit

Section 29 of the Federal tax code had been passed by Congress in 1978 in order to stimulate drilling for a particular kind of natural gas that was especially difficult to extract from the ground, namely, that found in rock called devonian shale, which composed the Bailey Prospect. This rock consists of many very small pockets where the gas resides until it is ferreted out. It provided, in 1988, a tax credit of $0.76 per decatherm. This tax credit rate was increased each year with inflation, but its future value was in the hands of Congress and thus far from certain.

Initial Results and Investment Considerations

To find the net present value (NPV). Tom added back the depreciation and depletion to the profit after tax to come up with the yearly cash flows. These flows were then discounted at the company's hurdle rate of 15% for projects of this risk (see Exhibit 3 for a listing of rates of return for investments of varying maturities and degrees of risk) to calculate the NPV through any given year of the well's life. His pro forma analysis indicated the project had an IRR of 41.1% and an NPV of $110,263.

Tom was feeling good about the Bailey Prospect, even though he knew he had made many assumptions. He'd used 1155 BTU/FT^3 to estimate the heat content of the gas because it was the expected (mean) value, when in reality he knew it could be as low as 1055 or as high as 1250, with the most likely value (mode) being 1160. He also guessed that inflation, as measured by the Gross National Product (GNP) Deflator (a measure similar to the Consumer Price Index or CPI), would average 3.5% over the 25-year project life, but he thought he ought to check a couple of forecasts and look at the historical trends. See Exhibit 4 for both forecasts of GNP Deflator values as well as historical GNP Deflator values and historical natural gas prices. Tom's idea was to use the GNP Deflator to forecast natural gas prices after the four-year contract expired and to increase the value of the natural gas tax credit on an annual basis.

Further Questions and Uncertainties When Tom showed the results to Henry Ostberg, a potential partner, Henry was impressed with the "expected" scenario but asked, "What is the downside on an investment such as this?" Tom had done his homework and produced Exhibits 5 and 6 together (again years 12 to 25 are not shown). Exhibit 5 showed the results if there was not enough gas to develop. Exhibit 6 showed what would happen if there was enough gas, but all other uncertain quantities were set at their 1 chance in 100 worst levels. Henry was somewhat disturbed by what he saw but said, "Hey, Tom, we're businessmen. We're here to take risks; that's how we make money. What we really want to know is the likelihood of this sort of outcome."

EXHIBIT 3 Interest Rates and Yields

		TREASURIES							
		Bills		Notes and Bonds				Moody's[a]	
		1-Yr	3-Yr	5-Yr	7-Yr	10-Yr	30-Yr	Aaa	Baa
1985		7.81	9.64	10.12	10.5	10.62	10.79	11.37	12.72
1986		6.08	7.06	7.30	7.54	7.68	7.78	9.02	10.39
1987		6.33	7.68	7.94	8.23	8.39	8.59	9.38	10.58
1988	Jan	6.52	7.87	8.18	8.48	8.67	8.83	9.88	11.07
	Feb	6.21	7.38	7.71	8.02	8.21	8.43	9.40	10.62
	Mar	6.28	7.50	7.83	8.19	8.37	8.63	9.39	10.57
	May 18	7.34	8.23	8.66	8.90	9.20	9.30	10.22	11.45

[a]Based on yields to maturity on selected long-term corporate bonds.
Sources: *Federal Reserve Bulletin*, June 1988, and *Wall Street Journal*, May 19, 1988.

EXHIBIT 4 Historical and Forecast Data

HISTORICAL NATURAL GAS PRICES

Year	Wellhead Price($/MCF)	Year	Wellhead Price($/MCF)	Year	Wellhead Price($/MCF)	Year	Wellhead Price($/MCF)
1987	1.78	1981	1.98	1975	0.44	1969	0.17
1986	1.94	1980	1.59	1974	0.30	1968	0.16
1985	2.51	1979	1.18	1973	0.22	1967	0.16
1984	2.66	1978	0.91	1972	0.19	1966	0.16
1983	2.59	1977	0.79	1971	0.18	1965	0.16
1982	2.46	1976	0.58	1970	0.17	1964	0.15

ALL YEARS: MEAN = $0.976 STD DEV = $0.922
LAST 8 YEARS: MEAN = $2.189 STD DEV = $0.412

Source: *Basic Petroleum Data Book*, January 1988, Section VI, Table 2.

PERCENTAGE CHANGE FROM PREVIOUS PERIOD IN GNP DEFLATOR

Year	% Chg	Year	% Chg	Year	% Chg	Year	% Chg
1987	3.0	1978	7.3	1969	5.6	1960	1.6
1986	2.6	1977	6.7	1968	5.0	1959	2.4
1985	3.2	1976	6.4	1967	2.6	1958	2.1
1984	3.7	1975	9.8	1966	3.6	1957	3.6
1983	3.9	1974	9.1	1965	2.7	1956	3.4
1982	6.4	1973	6.5	1964	1.5	1955	3.2
1981	9.7	1972	4.7	1963	1.6	1954	1.6
1980	9.0	1971	5.7	1962	2.2	1953	1.6
1979	8.9	1970	5.5	1961	1.0		

LAST 16 YEARS: ARITHMETIC MEAN = 6.31%, STD DEV = 2.45%
LAST 25 YEARS: ARITHMETIC MEAN = 5.39%, STD DEV = 2.51%
LAST 35 YEARS: ARITHMETIC MEAN = 4.5%, STD DEV = 2.59%
25 YEAR MOVING AVERAGE: MEAN = 4.91%, STD DEV = 0.46%

Source: *Economic Report of the President*, 1988, p. 253.

FORECASTS FOR PERCENTAGE CHANGE IN GNP DEFLATOR

	1988	1989	1990	AVG 1988–90
Data Resources[a]	3.1	3.8	4.5	3.8
Wharton[b]	3.8	4.5	4.5	4.3
UCLA[c]	2.7	2.8	3.9	3.1

[a]*Data Resources, Inc.*, November 1987, p. 99.
[b]*Wharton Econometrics*, September 1987, pp. 9.7–9.8.
[c]*UCLA National Business Forecast*, December 1987, p. 47.

	A	B	D	F	H	L	M
1	WELL	****ASSUMPTIONS****	ENVIRONMENT		****RESULTS****		
2							
3	TOTAL WELL COST	$160,000	FEDERAL TAX RATE	34.00%	EQUITY PAYOUT (AFTER-TAX) =	#DIV/0!	MONTHS
4	INTANGIBLE COST(%OFTOTAL)	72.50%	STATE TAX RATE	9.75%			
5			SEVERANCE TAX RATE	3.40%	INTERNAL RATE OF RETURN (CF AFTER-TAX) =	#NUM!	
6	MONTHLY OPERATING COSTS	$300	COUNTY TAX RATE	4.50%	INTERNAL RATE OF RETURN (PBT) =	#NUM!	
7	ANNUAL LEASE EXPENSE	$3,000	SECTION 29 TAX CREDIT($/MI	$0.7600			
8	INFLTION FACTOR-WELL EXPENSE	1.75%	% QUALIFIED	100.00%	NET PRESENT VALUE (CFAT) @ 15%	($95,304)	
9							
10	PRODUCTION DATA		GNP DEFLATOR	3.50%	CUMULATIVE CASH FLOW AFTER-TAX	($95,304)	
11	ENOUGH(0=NO,1=YES)?	0					
12	1st YEAR Mcf	33,000	ROYALTIES	15.2344%			
13	PRODUCTION DECLINE AFTER...						
14	YEAR 1 =	22.50%	GAS PRICE DATA				
15	YEAR 2 =	17.50%					
16	YEAR 3-5 =	12.50%	CURRENTPRICE($/MMBTU)	$1.90			
17	YEAR 6-14 =	10.00%	BTUCONTENT(BTU/FT3)	1,155			
18	YEAR 15-24 =	5.00%	1ST YEAR OF				
19			PRICE INCREASE	5			
20							

	A	B	C	D	E	F	G	H	I	J	K	L	M
21	YEAR	0	1	2	3	4	5	6	7	8	9	10	11
22	INITIAL INVESTMENT	($160,000)											
23	PRICE PER MCF		2.19	2.19	2.19	2.19	2.27	2.35	2.43	2.52	2.61	2.70	2.79
24	PRODUCTION(MCF)		0	0	0	0	0	0	0	0	0	0	0
25													
26	GROSS REVENUE		$0	$0	$0	$0	$0	$0	$0	$0	$0	$0	$0
27	LESS: ROYALTIES		0	0	0	0	0	0	0	0	0	0	0
28	NET REVENUE		$0	$0	$0	$0	$0	$0	$0	$0	$0	$0	$0
29	OPERATING EXPENSES		0	0	0	0	0	0	0	0	0	0	0
30	SEVERANCE & COUNTY TAX		0	0	0	0	0	0	0	0	0	0	0
31	DEPRECIATION	160,000	0	0	0	0	0	0	0				
32	PROFIT BEFORE TAX	($160,000)	$0	$0	$0	$0	$0	$0	$0	$0	$0	$0	$0
33	DEPLETION		0	0	0	0	0	0	0	0	0	0	0
34	STATE INC. TAX	(15,600)	0	0	0	0	0	0	0	0	0	0	0
35	FEDERAL INC. TAX	(49,096)	0	0	0	0	0	0	0	0	0	0	0
36	PROFIT AFTER TAX	($95,304)	$0	$0	$0	$0	$0	$0	$0	$0	$0	$0	$0
37													
38	AFTER TAX CASH FLOW	($95,304)	$0	$0	$0	$0	$0	$0	$0	$0	$0	$0	$0
39	CUMUL. AFT TAX CASH FLOW	($95,304)	($95,304)	($95,304)	($95,304)	($95,304)	($95,304)	($95,304)	($95,304)	($95,304)	($95,304)	($95,304)	($95,304)
40	NPV THROUGH YEAR N	($95,304)	($95,304)	($95,304)	($95,304)	($95,304)	($95,304)	($95,304)	($95,304)	($95,304)	($95,304)	($95,304)	($95,304)

EXHIBIT 5

Spreadsheet with No Gas Produced

	A	B	D	F	H	L	M
1	WELL	****ASSUMPTIONS****	ENVIRONMENT		****RESULTS****		
2							
3	TOTAL WELL COST	$166,237	FEDERAL TAX RATE	34.00%	EQUITY PAYOUT (AFTER-TAX) =	65.09	MONTHS
4	INTANGIBLE COST(%OFTOTAL)	72.50%	STATE TAX RATE	9.75%			
5			SEVERANCE TAX RATE	3.40%	INTERNAL RATE OF RETURN (CF AFTER-TAX) =	#NUM!	
6	MONTHLY OPERATING COSTS	$300	COUNTY TAX RATE	4.50%	INTERNAL RATE OF RETURN (PBT) =	#DIV/0!	
7	ANNUAL LEASE EXPENSE	$3,000	SECTION 29 TAX CREDIT($/MI	$0.7600			
8	INFLTION FACTOR-WELL EXPENSE	1.34%	% QUALIFIED	100.00%	NET PRESENT VALUE (CFAT) @ 15%	($30,202)	
9							
10	PRODUCTION DATA		GNP DEFLATOR	2.67%	CUMULATIVE CASH FLOW AFTER-TAX	($18,138)	
11	ENOUGH(0=NO,1=YES)?	1					
12	1st YEAR Mcf	24,000	ROYALTIES	15.2344%			
13	PRODUCTION DECLINE AFTER...						
14	YEAR 1 =	37.20%	GAS PRICE DATA				
15	YEAR 2 =	28.93%					
16	YEAR 3-5 =	20.67%	CURRENTPRICE($/MMBTU)	$1.90			
17	YEAR 6-14 =	16.53%	BTUCONTENT(BTU/FT3)	1,060			
18	YEAR 15-24 =	8.27%	1ST YEAR OF				
19			PRICE INCREASE	5			
20							

	A	B	C	D	E	F	G	H	I	J	K	L	M
21	YEAR	0	1	2	3	4	5	6	7	8	9	10	11
22	INITIAL INVESTMENT	($166,237)											
23	PRICE PER MCF		2.01	2.01	2.01	2.01	2.07	2.12	2.18	2.24	2.30	2.36	2.42
24	PRODUCTION(MCF)		24,000	15,072	10,712	8,498	6,741	5,348	4,464	3,726	3,110	2,596	2,167
25													
26	GROSS REVENUE		$48,336	$30,355	$21,573	$17,114	$13,939	$11,353	$9,729	$8,338	$7,146	$6,124	$5,248
27	LESS: ROYALTIES		7,364	4,624	3,287	2,607	2,124	1,730	1,482	1,270	1,089	933	799
28	NET REVENUE		$40,972	$25,731	$18,287	$14,507	$11,816	$9,624	$8,247	$7,068	$6,057	$5,191	$4,448
29	OPERATING EXPENSES		6,600	6,688	6,778	6,868	6,960	7,053	7,147	7,243	7,340	7,438	7,537
30	SEVERANCE & COUNTY TAX		3,819	2,398	1,704	1,352	1,101	897	769	659	565	484	415
31	DEPRECIATION	120,522	6,531	6,531	6,531	6,531	6,531	6,531	6,531				
32	PROFIT BEFORE TAX	($120,522)	$24,023	$10,114	$3,274	($244)	($2,776)	($4,857)	($6,199)	($834)	($1,847)	($2,731)	($3,503)
33	DEPLETION		6,146	3,860	1,637	(122)	(1,388)	(2,429)	(3,100)	(417)	(924)	(1,365)	(1,752)
34	STATE INC. TAX	(11,751)	921	94	(207)	(303)	(372)	(430)	(468)	(182)	(212)	(237)	(260)
35	FEDERAL INC. TAX	(36,982)	(13,569)	(10,372)	(8,469)	(7,347)	(6,380)	(5,594)	(5,107)	(3,689)	(3,335)	(3,035)	(2,779)
36	PROFIT AFTER TAX	($71,789)	$30,525	$16,532	$10,313	$7,528	$5,364	$3,596	$2,475	$3,455	$2,623	$1,906	$1,287
37													
38	AFTER TAX CASH FLOW	($117,504)	$43,202	$26,922	$18,481	$13,937	$10,506	$7,698	$5,906	$3,038	$1,700	$541	($464)
39	CUMUL. AFT TAX CASH FLOW	($117,504)	($74,302)	($47,380)	($28,899)	($14,962)	($4,456)	$3,242	$9,148	$12,186	$13,886	$14,427	$13,962
40	NPV THROUGH YEAR N	($117,504)	($79,937)	($59,580)	($47,428)	($39,460)	($34,236)	($30,908)	($28,688)	($27,695)	($27,212)	($27,078)	($27,178)

EXHIBIT 6

Spreadsheet with Gas Found but All Other Uncertainties Set at 1 Chance in 100 Worst Level

Tom realized he had not thought enough about the probabilities associated with potential risks that a project of this kind involved. He also put his mind to work thinking about whether he had considered all the things he had seen that could change significantly from one project to another. The only additional uncertainty he generated was the yearly production decline, which could vary significantly for a given well. He had used what he considered the expected values in this case, but now he realized he ought to multiply each one by some uncertain quantity, with a most likely value of 1.0, a low of 0.5, and a high of 1.75, to allow for the kind of fluctuation he had seen.

Tom wondered what would be the most effective way to incorporate all six of the uncertainties (total well cost, whether the well produced gas or not, first-year production of gas, the BTU content, rate of production decline, and the average inflation over the next 25 years) into his investment analysis. He remembered doing "what if" tables with Lotus back in business school, but he had never heard of a six-way table. As he skimmed back through his quantitative methods book, he saw a chapter on Monte Carlo simulation and read enough to be convinced that this method was ideally suited to his current situation.

When Tom told Henry about this new method of evaluation he was contemplating, his partner laughed and said, "Come on, Tom, it can't be that hard. What you're talking about sounds like something they'd teach brand-new MBAs. You and I have been doing this type of investing for years. Can't we just figure it out on the back of an envelope?" When Tom tried to estimate the probability of his worst-case scenario, it came out to .00000001%—not very likely! There was no way he was going to waste any more time trying to figure out the expected NPV by hand based on all the uncertainties, regardless of how intuitive his friend thought it should be. Consequently, Tom thought a little more about how Monte Carlo simulation would work with this decision.

In his current method of evaluating projects, he had used the three criteria mentioned earlier (<42-month payback of initial cash investment, >15% IRR on pretax basis, and >25% IRR on after-tax basis). He could see that calculating the average IRR after several Monte Carlo trials wouldn't be very meaningful, especially since there was a 10% chance that you would spend $160K on a pretax basis and get no return! It would be impossible to find an IRR on that particular scenario. He did feel he could calculate an average NPV after several trials and even find out how many years it would take until the NPV became positive. As he settled into his chair to finish reading the chapter, which looked vaguely familiar, he looked up briefly at the verdant hillside and wondered for a moment what resources were under the hill.

Questions

1. Based on the base case scenario and the two alternative downside possibilities, is this investment economically attractive?
2. What benefit can Monte Carlo simulation add to Tom's understanding of the economic benefits of the Bailey Prospect?
3. Incorporate uncertainties into the spreadsheet using @Risk or Crystal Ball. What do the Monte Carlo results reveal? What is the probability that the NPV will be greater than zero? Should Tom invest?

References

Anthony Brigandi, Dennis Dargon, Michael Sheehan, and Thomas Spencer, "AT&T's Call Processing Simulator (CAPS) Operational Design for Inbound Call Centers," *Interfaces*, 24, no. 1 (1994): 6–28.

James Bookbinder and Terrence Kotwa, "Modeling an AGV Automobile Body-Framing System," *Interfaces*, 17, no. 6 (1987): 41–50.

I.M. Premachandra and Liliana Gonzalez "A Simulation Model Solved the Problem of Scheduling Drilling Rigs at Clyde Dam," *Interfaces*, 26, no. 2 (1996): 80–91.

Barry Smith, John Leimkuhler, and Ross Darrow, "Yield Management at American Airlines," *Interfaces*, 22, no. 1 (1992): 8–31.

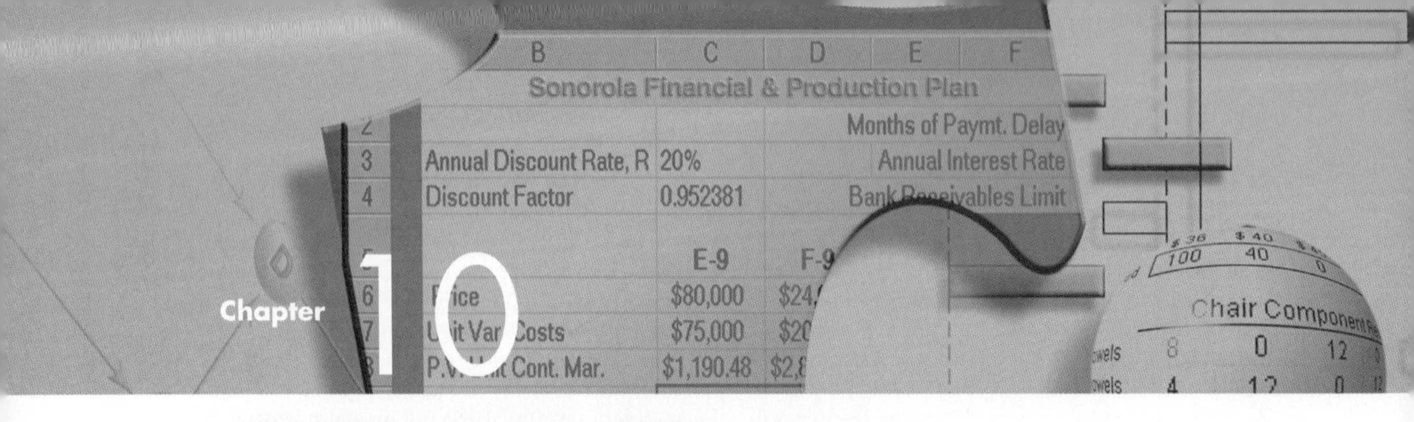

Chapter 10

DISCRETE EVENT SIMULATION

CHAPTER OUTLINE

APPLICATION CAPSULE US WEST's DS1 Line Installation Request Process

Historically, discrete event simulation was used to model industrial and manufacturing processes. Now, discrete event simulation is used in a variety of ways to model both service and product-oriented industries. Currently, there is a growing demand for DS1 networks by long distance carriers. These networks have very high capacity and high speed, and US WEST wants their handling of requests for DS1 lines to be just as high capacity and high speed as the lines themselves. US WEST turned to discrete event simulation to determine the best form for processing requests for DS1 lines.

The approval process for a DS1 line begins with a request from a long distance carrier, business, or government entity. This request is accepted by the *interexchange carrier service center* or at a *market unit service center*, which generates a work order. The work order is routed to the *high-capacity provisioning center*. At this point, any errors in the original submission are identified and a request with errors is sent back to the *interexchange service center* or *market unit service center* for correction. If the request is free of errors the *high-capacity provisioning center* produces a *work order record details* (*WORD*). This WORD can be sent to one of three places. If all of the necessary materials and conduits are in place to act on the WORD, it is sent directly to the *digital services operations center* for immediate implementation. The WORD may also be sent to either the *interoffice facilities current planning center* or the *construction management center* if the necessary materials or conduits are not present. Once these centers have procured the needed materials or conduits, the request is forwarded to the *digital services operations center* for completion.

A model was developed that reflected this process using different queues to reflect different stages of the DS1 request procedure. Using data gathered from actual operations, definitions and parameters were added to the model. Also, the processing rule of giving highest priority to requests requiring the least amount of service time was adopted. This model and its parameters were computerized using EXTEND to enhance communication of the model to US WEST managers. The predications resulting from the simulations were to be applied in Des Moines, Iowa. At first, managers in Des Moines were hesitant to act upon the results of these simulations. However, when they began to experience the exact bottlenecks in their service process that had been predicted by the simulated model, managers adopted suggestions drawn from the discrete model to hire the appropriate number of personnel in each area of the request sequence, thus eliminating bottlenecks and improving customer service. (See Lee and Elcan.)

10.1 INTRODUCTION

In a sense, all models are simulations of real-world phenomena. Typically, however, the term **simulation** refers to a specific class of dynamic models involving the detailed observation of a complex probabilistic system over time. If you have not done so already, reading Section 9.1 in the previous chapter on Monte Carlo simulation provides a good introduction to the general concepts of simulation modeling.

The simulation models covered in Chapter 9 are limited to those models involving aggregate variables that change more or less continuously with time and are thus called **continuous simulation** models. In contrast, this chapter focuses upon discrete event simulation. **Discrete event simulation** is applied most commonly whenever individual items are tracked and in which abrupt or nonsmooth changes in the timing of events is the norm. For example, a model that tracked the prime interest rate over time as a function of other macroeconomic variables, such as foreign exchange rates, unemployment, government spending, and business capital investments could be modeled either as a simple deterministic model or, given uncertainty, as a continuous simulation. Such macroeconomic models usually employ variables representing highly aggregate measures that act as surrogates for the activities in a wide class of underlying microeconomic markets involving many transaction events that are simply too cumbersome to model in fine detail. In contrast, discrete event simulation is usually employed when one desires to model those very detailed events.

As another example, a linear programming or decision analysis model might be very useful in the planning needed to decide the number and quantity of products to build in the upcoming time period and to determine the aggregate resources that would be required. However, those models cannot easily incorporate the detailed tactical decisions to actually effect those plans in the upcoming time period. Examples of the detailed tactical decisions might include scheduling of employees, setup and take down of many pieces of production machinery, the detailed provisioning of raw materials, work in process and final goods inventories, and decisions relating to unexpected equipment repair and employee absences. Discrete event simulation models can be used to delve into these fine details of complex systems with many interactions. Of course, there is a price to pay for such realism: Discrete event simulation models can become extremely complex to build and analyze properly, especially in a spreadsheet format.

The most common use of discrete event simulation modeling is to create detailed operational systems representing the contentious demands among activities requiring scarce resources over time. Examples of discrete event simulation models include **queuing simulations** of customers or jobs awaiting service, such as people in a bank's teller queue, Internet packets traversing routers, or the inventory of parts on a factory work floor. Of course, once built, a detailed discrete event simulation model is often far more convenient and risk-free to manipulate than the real-world system itself. Moreover, it is easy to repeatedly "rewind time" in a discrete event simulation model to replay scenarios while manipulating key variables to observe experimentally their effect upon important performance measures.

We begin the analysis of a discrete event simulation model by building an Excel simulation of a simple single server queuing situation. As will be seen, discrete event simulation models are not easily represented in the row and column framework of a spreadsheet and are surprisingly difficult to manipulate in spreadsheet form. This in turn will motivate the use of a special-purpose application more attuned to the detailed study of complex systems. We will illustrate the ease of building such models with a non-spreadsheet simulation application called **Extend**, a limited version of which, Extend LT, is included on the book's CD-ROM. Extend can be used for both continuous simulation and discrete event simulation. We have already examined continuous simulation in Chapter 9, and thus, will only cover Extend's discrete event simulation capabilities.

10.2 EXAMPLE 1—A SIMULATION MODEL IN EXCEL

Henry Hervis has started an airport car rental business. He believes his lower overhead costs and more efficient service will enable him to attract customers and compete with the other large established airport car rental firms. To investigate the relative efficiency of his operation, Hervis elects to model the movement of customers through his rental office. Customers arrive in an airport van and queue up, first come-first serve, for service at the rental counter. Eventually, a given customer moves to the head of the queue and, when the rental clerk is free, will receive service that consists of filling out the rental forms, choosing the rental options, receiving some driving instructions, and the like. Customers then depart the rental office to collect their rental car and drive away. Hervis has collected data on the arrival of customers to his rental office, who tend to arrive in small groups from the airport vans as airplanes land at the airport. Table 10.1 documents his data on the relative frequency distribution of customer arrivals in any given 5-minute block of time throughout a typical 24-hour day. The table also computes the cumulative probabilities of 1 or fewer, 2 or fewer, and 3 or fewer arrivals.

Table 10.1

NUMBER OF ARRIVING CUSTOMERS	PROBABILITY	CUMULATIVE PROBABILITY
0	70%	70%
1	12%	82%
2	16%	98%
3	2%	100%

FIGURE 10.1

Fill Series to Label Time Blocks

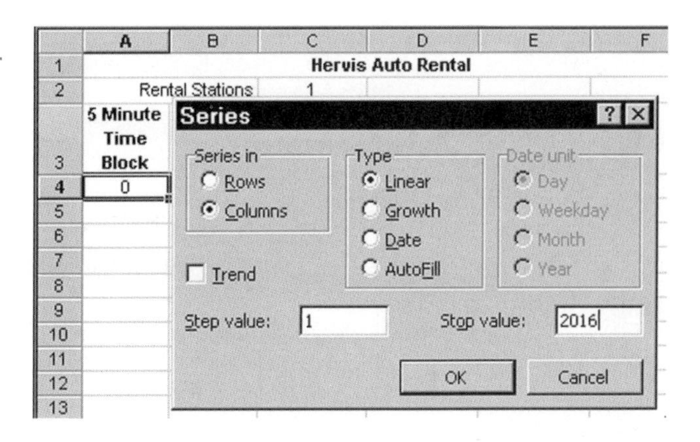

Hervis has decided to simulate a week of 24-hour operations and to segment time into 5-minute blocks. He has done this because for simplicity he assumes that it always takes *exactly* 5 minutes to serve a waiting customer. This leads to 7 * 24 * 60/5 = 2016 time blocks in his Excel queuing model, thus requiring that he model time blocks in rows to avoid exceeding Excel's 256-column limitation. The detailed simulation model will track all customer movements within each 5-minute time block and then summarize these movements into performance statistics. To build the Hervis model in Excel, first label the time blocks by using the Fill Series dialog from the Edit menu, as shown in Figure 10.1.

Next, create a probability distribution table as shown in J4:K7 in Figure 10.2. Note that the only formula is contained in K8, which computes the expected number of customer arrivals (equal to one half a customer arriving in each 5-minute block on average) via a SUMPRODUCT of the arrival counts with the corresponding probabilities.

The simulation will be driven by randomly drawn probabilities, which in turn will determine the number of customers arriving in any 5-minute time block.

To do this for the Hervis model, the RAND() function will draw a random fraction greater than or equal to 0 and less than 1, one for each of the 2016 time blocks. RAND() is a volatile Excel function, meaning that a new random number is drawn for each of the 2016 cells each time the worksheet is changed. This leads to constantly changing worksheet values as you develop the model, which becomes quite time-consuming. To avoid this

TIP: *Reviewing Section 9.2 in Chapter 9 will clarify this concept of using random probabilities in a simulation model.*

FIGURE 10.2

Probability Distribution for the Queuing Simulation

K8 = =SUMPRODUCT(J4:J7,K4:K7)

	A	B	C	J	K
1			Hervis Auto Rental		
2		Rental Stations	1	Historical Data	
3	5 Minute Time Block			Number of Arriving Customers	Probability
4	0			0	70%
5	1			1	12%
6	2			2	16%
7	3			3	2%
8	4			Exp. No. Arivals	0.5
9	5				
10	6				
2014	2010				
2015	2011				
2016	2012				
2017	2013				
2018	2014				
2019	2015				
2020	2016				

FIGURE 10.3

Changing Excel's Calculation Option to Manual

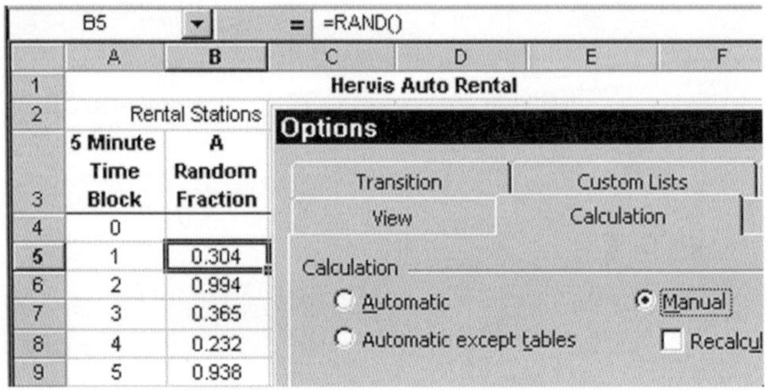

B5 = =RAND()

Hervis Auto Rental

5 Minute Time Block	A Random Fraction
	Rental Stations
0	
1	0.304
2	0.994
3	0.365
4	0.232
5	0.938

Options

Transition | Custom Lists | View | Calculation

Calculation

Automatic | Manual

Automatic except tables | Recalcul

TIP: *Do not forget that the worksheet must be manually recalculated to update its cells once the Manual Calculation option is set. Excel will flag the inconsistencies in its worksheet cells' values by displaying the word "Calculate" in the message box to remind you to do this. A worksheet is manually recalculated by pressing the F9 function key.*

TIP: *The operation of VLOOKUP is covered in Appendix B.*

annoyance, you can set Excel's Calculation in the Options dialog in the Tools menu to Manual, as shown in Figure 10.3.

After placing the "=RAND()" formula in B5, copy it down to B2020 to create all 2016 random fractions, and note how they change each time you press F9. Next, create a modified cumulative probability table, as shown in M4:N7 of Figure 10.4. This table reverses the original probability distribution in J4:K7 because probabilities from the =RAND() formulas are now the inputs and the corresponding number of customer arrivals, as outputs, will be computed by =VLOOKUP() formulas, as illustrated in C5 of the figure. Note that a modification of the original cumulative probability table from Table 10.1 to shift the cumulative probabilities down a row is needed in order to conform to the syntax of the VLOOKUP function. The mapping of the 2016 RAND() random fractions into arrival numbers is done by copying the =VLOOKUP() function in C5 to C6:C2020, as shown in Figure 10.4. Be sure to examine the specific values in column C in the figure to verify your understanding of how the VLOOKUP works in this simulation context.

Next, complete the model by typing the formulas in D5:F2020, as shown in Figure 10.5. To understand the operation of the model, note particularly the formulas in columns D, E, and F, rows 5:2020. Column D formulas in this region compute the number of customers in line, including the one receiving service at the rental counter, by adding the number of new arrivals in the current 5-minute time block to the unserved customers, if any, from the previous 5-minute time block. Column E formulas in this region compute the number of customers receiving rental counter service as being the minimum of the number in line (which could be zero) and the number of rental counter stations in C2. The number of customers remaining unserved at the end of the 5-minute time block is the difference between the entries in column D and column E.

The performance measure formulas compute interesting statistics for Hervis to evaluate his measures of operational efficiency. The formulas in C2021:F2023 compute the

FIGURE 10.4

Modified Cumulative Probability Table for VLOOKUP

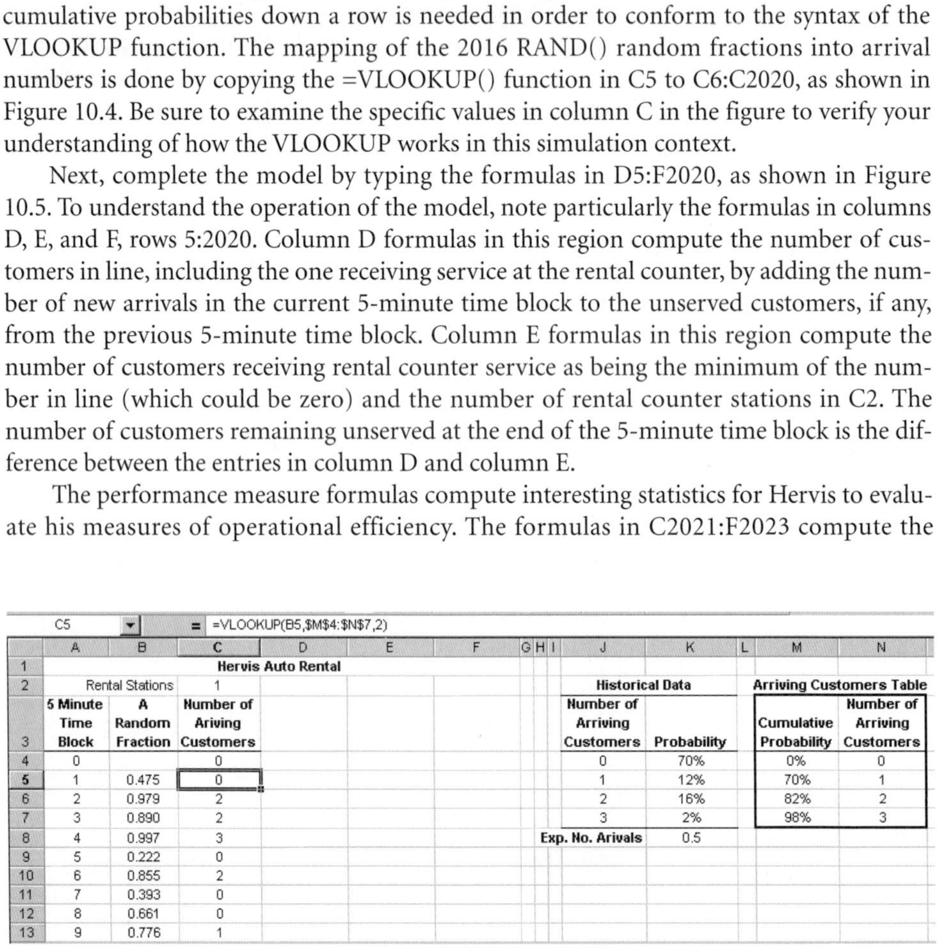

C5 = =VLOOKUP(B5,$M$4:$N$7,2)

Hervis Auto Rental

5 Minute Time Block	A Random Fraction	Number of Ariving Customers
Rental Stations		1
0		0
1	0.475	0
2	0.979	2
3	0.890	2
4	0.997	3
5	0.222	0
6	0.855	2
7	0.393	0
8	0.661	0
9	0.776	1

Historical Data

Number of Arriving Customers	Probability
0	70%
1	12%
2	16%
3	2%
Exp. No. Arivals	0.5

Arriving Customers Table

Cumulative Probability	Number of Arriving Customers
0%	0
70%	1
82%	2
98%	3

FIGURE 10.5

Completed Hervis Queuing Model in Excel

TIP: *Excel's Split Window, as shown in Figure 10.5, is helpful for copying formulas in large worksheets and viewing two different areas of a worksheet model.*

	A	B	C	D	E	F
1			Hervis Auto Rental			
2	Rental Stations		1			
3	5 Minute Time Block	A Random Fraction	Number of Ariving Customers	Number of Customers in Line	Number of Customers Served	Number of Customers Delayed
4	0		0	0	0	0
5	1	0.475	0	0	0	0
6	2	0.979	2	2	1	1
7	3	0.890	2	3	1	2
8	4	0.997	3	5	1	4
9	5	0.222	0	4	1	3
2018	2014	0.231	0	2	1	1
2019	2015	0.658	0	1	1	0
2020	2016	0.991	3	3	1	2
2021		Maximum	3	10	1	9
2022		Total	934	1937	932	1005
2023		Average	0.463	0.961	0.462	0.499

	A	B	C	D	E	F
3	5 Minute Time	A Random Fraction	Number of Ariving Customers	Number of Customers in Line	Number of Customers Served	Number of Customers Delayed
4	0		0	0	0	0
5	1	=RAND()	=VLOOKUP(B5,$M$4:$N$7,2)	=C5+F4	=MIN(D5,$C$2)	=D5-E5
6	2	=RAND()	=VLOOKUP(B6,$M$4:$N$7,2)	=C6+F5	=MIN(D6,$C$2)	=D6-E6
7	3	=RAND()	=VLOOKUP(B7,$M$4:$N$7,2)	=C7+F6	=MIN(D7,$C$2)	=D7-E7
8	4	=RAND()	=VLOOKUP(B8,$M$4:$N$7,2)	=C8+F7	=MIN(D8,$C$2)	=D8-E8
9	5	=RAND()	=VLOOKUP(B9,$M$4:$N$7,2)	=C9+F8	=MIN(D9,$C$2)	=D9-E9
2018	2014	=RAND()	=VLOOKUP(B2018,$M$4:$N$7,2)	=C2018+F2017	=MIN(D2018,$C$2)	=D2018-E2018
2019	2015	=RAND()	=VLOOKUP(B2019,$M$4:$N$7,2)	=C2019+F2018	=MIN(D2019,$C$2)	=D2019-E2019
2020	2016	=RAND()	=VLOOKUP(B2020,$M$4:$N$7,2)	=C2020+F2019	=MIN(D2020,$C$2)	=D2020-E2020
2021		Maximum	=MAX(C$5:C$2020)	=MAX(D$5:D$2020)	=MAX(E$5:E$2020)	=MAX(F$5:F$2020)
2022		Total	=SUM(C$5:C$2020)	=SUM(D$5:D$2020)	=SUM(E$5:E$2020)	=SUM(F$5:F$2020)
2023		Average	=AVERAGE(C$5:C$2020)	=AVERAGE(D$5:D$2020)	=AVERAGE(E$5:E$2020)	=AVERAGE(F$5:F$2020)

Maximum, Total, and Average values for each column, respectively. Note that these statistical indicators reflect the randomness inherent in the simulation. Your numbers will certainly be somewhat different. Indeed, pressing the F9 key will redraw another 2016 random numbers for another week's simulation. Pressing F9 repeatedly will give you a feel for their weekly variability.

Results of queuing simulations are almost always surprising, as human intuition is unreliable in the highly nonlinear situations characterized by congestion leading to queues. For example, we computed in K8 that an average of only one half a customer arrives in each 5-minute time block, or equivalently, one customer arrives every 10 minutes on average. And it always takes only one 5-minute interval to serve that customer. Thus, the rental counter is busy only one half the time on average, leading to substantial slack in Hervis's rental counter operation. Yet peak loads still occur during the week, leading to at least one case where 9 customers were awaiting service. Since it takes 5 minutes to serve a customer, that last customer must await the 8 ahead of her for a delay of 45 minutes until she receives a car. This is hardly a way for Hervis to build customer satisfaction based on rental counter efficiency, at least during peak demand.

An obvious use of this model by Hervis is to evaluate the effect of adding another rental station, thus allowing up to two waiting customers to receive service simultaneously. This should lead to about a halving of the delay one would surmise, of course, at the expense of doubling the Hervis rental office's operating costs. In fact, intuition fails again as rerunning the model for two rental stations confirms. In Figure 10.6 the revised statistics for doubling the number of stations indicate that the maximum number of customers receiving delayed service falls by almost an order of magnitude and the average number of customers delayed falls by nearly twenty-fold, a dramatic change!

FIGURE 10.6

Simulating Hervis's with Two Rental Counter Stations

	A	B	C	D	E	F
1			Hervis Auto Rental			
2	Rental Stations		2			
3	5 Minute Time Block	A Random Fraction	Number of Ariving Customers	Number of Customers in Line	Number of Customers Served	Number of Customers Delayed
4	0		0	0	0	0
5	1	0.009	0	0	0	0
6	2	0.209	0	0	0	0
7	3	0.245	0	0	0	0
8	4	0.347	0	0	0	0
9	5	0.976	2	2	2	0
2018	2014	0.939	2	2	2	0
2019	2015	0.954	2	2	2	0
2020	2016	0.028	0	0	0	0
2021		Maximum	3	3	2	1
2022		Total	1059	1112	1059	53
2023		Average	0.525	0.551	0.525	0.026

10.3 EXAMPLE 2—A SIMULATION MODEL IN EXTEND

As shown in the previous section, the use of Excel for discrete event simulation suffers from two primary shortcomings in most operational situations. First, for reasonably sized models, the resulting Excel spreadsheet quickly fills up with cells occupied with formulas. In the case of the previous Hervis model, what if customers did not arrive at the beginning of each 5-minute time block, but instead, arrived at any random minute? This would immediately expand the size of the required model by a factor of 5, because in order to capture this realism, the time grid must be in minutes and not in 5-minute blocks. Also, simulating a single week may not be a sufficient gauge for a typical month's operation. Incorporating a month's simulation would expand the model by another factor of 4 (from one week to four weeks). This expansion of the planning horizon along with ever finer time grids was first referred in Chapter 5 as the "curse of dimensionality" for dynamic models. Simulation models are almost always the extreme case of this curse, because managers often use simulation to track detailed operational performance rather than highly aggregate abstractions.

Second, discrete event simulation models in Excel do not scale well. For example, it was relatively easy to expand the number of Hervis rental stations from 1 to 2, but the entire model must be redone for an increase in the planning horizon or a finer time grid. That is, one cannot specify these factors as parameters but must redo the model by copying formulas, inserting cells, etc. To illustrate this difficulty, consider what would have to be done if the service time for a Hervis customer were not exactly 5 minutes but was a random delay varying between, say, 4.5 minutes and 5.3 minutes. To capture this realism, unfortunately, the curse of dimensionality reasserts itself with a vengeance: The time grid must be scaled in units of a tenth of a minute, leading to a tenfold expansion in the size of the model, requiring massive insertions, copying of formulas across cells, etc., which could quickly overwhelm even Excel's generous worksheet size limitations. Note that in this expanded model many of the cells would compute to zero, reflecting no customer arrivals nor service events. The presence of these empty cells takes up considerable space in the Excel model that cannot be eliminated easily, given the fixed row and column orientation of Excel.

What is needed is a modeling capability that scales well to finer time grids and long planning horizons without respecifying portions of the model, and without wasting space and effort representing time intervals in which nothing of interest occurs. Second, the model representation must be compact to avoid generating gargantuan spreadsheets that are cumbersome to manipulate and debug. Third, the models should be easy to manipulate and generate results without cumbersome programming. Fourth, the development environment should embody the latest in graphic user interfaces to facilitate easy model building and self-documentation. This is precisely what a modern discrete event simulation

TIP: *Although not included on the book's CD-ROM, large scale and Macintosh, versions of Extend are available from Extend's developer at www.imaginethatinc.com.*

application like Extend does.[1] The price paid, of course, is that one must abandon the use of Excel for such situations in favor of a dedicated simulation application.

We will illustrate the application of Extend by rewriting the Hervis model as a discrete event queuing simulation. As you will see, with Extend it is much easier to model complex, time-dependent systems than in Excel. Moreover, Extend has many self-documenting features and provides an attractive graphic user interface for visually building, observing, debugging, and analyzing your discrete event simulation models. It even provides a simple animation capability to allow you to literally see movements of customers or jobs through a simulated system. Finally, it can export its results in the form of tables of values for subsequent post-simulation analysis in Excel.

Extend's models for discrete event simulation are object oriented and are built using predefined building blocks. A **block** is Extend's object for specifying an action, process, accumulation, statistical summary, or other object for creating the simulation. If you are familiar with traditional programming either in Excel or with a typical computer language, you will need to re-orient your thinking to follow the logic of the building blocks in an Extend model.

Extend's blocks are linked together literally by drawing lines to form a network of interrelated activities. The items, such as customers or rental cars whose time varying behavior is of interest, flow through the connected network of blocks, much like packets among nodes of the Internet, while Extend gathers statistics on their movements. As items move through the network of blocks, Extend keeps track of any waiting or delay times the items experience. Extend also has special-purpose blocks to tabulate or plot important statistics such as queue length and waiting time within a block. Extend keeps its predefined blocks in libraries as part of its library folder. When starting to build a new model in Extend the required libraries must be open so that you can access the blocks to copy them into your model.

There are four types of **links** that connect blocks: two accommodate item input and output, and two accommodate value input and output. The item input and output links provide the paths that allow items to flow through the model's blocks. The links to do this appear as small connectors on the edge of each block. Value input and output links pass data and parameters about items between blocks and also appear as connectors on each block. Accessed by double clicking, each block in Extend has a dialog window for specifying parameter values and for reviewing its results after a simulation run. For example, Figure 10.7 shows an Extend *Activity, Delay* block typically used to hold an item for an amount of time and then release it to the next block.[2] For the Hervis model this delay time would represent the 5 minutes a customer is held at the rental counter. Items (customers) enter the block at the left connector and the rightmost connector is where they exit after the delay. Once an item (a single customer) enters the block, it is held for exactly 5 minutes, as shown in the Delay field in the block's dialog window. As with all blocks, this dialog is evoked by double clicking the block. As shown in the figure, the block may be labeled by filling in the field at its bottom, labeled "Service Delay" in this example. Also, the dialog's Help button was clicked to evoke the detailed documentation for the *Activity, Delay* block. In the Help dialog, you can see the purposes served by the remaining three value connectors on the block. The D tab is a value input that, if used, overrides the fixed delay time setting in the block's dialog. It could be used to specify a random delay for each customer during the simulation run instead of the fixed 5-minute delay. The T and U connectors are value outputs,

---

[1] Extend also can be used for building continuous simulation models, including Monte Carlo simulations. In Chapter 9, we used Crystal Ball to illustrate Monte Carlo simulation applications.

[2] For readability, names of Extend's predefined blocks will be *italicized*.

FIGURE 10.7

Extend's *Activity, Delay* Block with Dialog and Help Windows

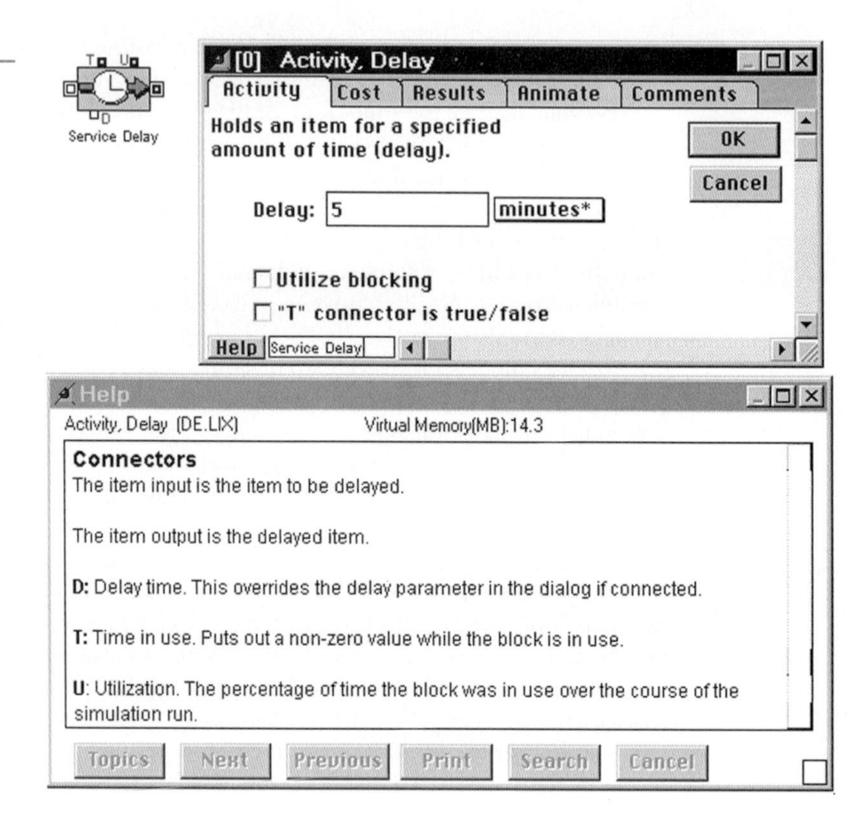

and can be used to provide information to other blocks in the model during the simulation run on whether the block is busy and its utilization percentage, respectively.

When the simulation run is finished, double clicking the block to evoke its dialog again and clicking its Results tab will reveal information recorded within the block during the simulation, such as average utilization (percentage of time the server was busy) and number of items that exited the block (i.e., number of customers served) during the simulation. All Extend blocks have this same basic structure: input and output connectors used for routing items in the model, block dialog windows for parameter settings and tabulating block statistics, and value connectors for inputting or outputting data during the simulation run.

BUILDING THE HERVIS SIMULATION MODEL

To begin, launch Extend and choose Simulation Setup from the Run menu, producing the dialog box in Figure 10.8. The Simulation Setup dialog lets you specify how the simulation will run and for how long. Normally, the only settings to be set in the dialog are global time units and the simulation's end time. For most purposes, the simulation should start at the beginning, with the default start time of 0. The "Number of runs" option can be left at 1 unless you want to look at how results vary because of the model's randomness over many runs. Because Hervis will model his rental car operations minute-by-minute for a week, click the "Global time units" button and select the "minutes" option. As with the earlier Excel model, Hervis will run the simulation for a week of simulated time, 10,080 minutes $(=24 * 7 * 60)$. So, enter 10080 into the "End simulation at time" field, as shown in Figure 10.8, and click OK. For each simulation run, Extend reuses the dialog values last specified in the Simulation Setup dialog. Thus, this dialog need only be filled in the first time a model is run.

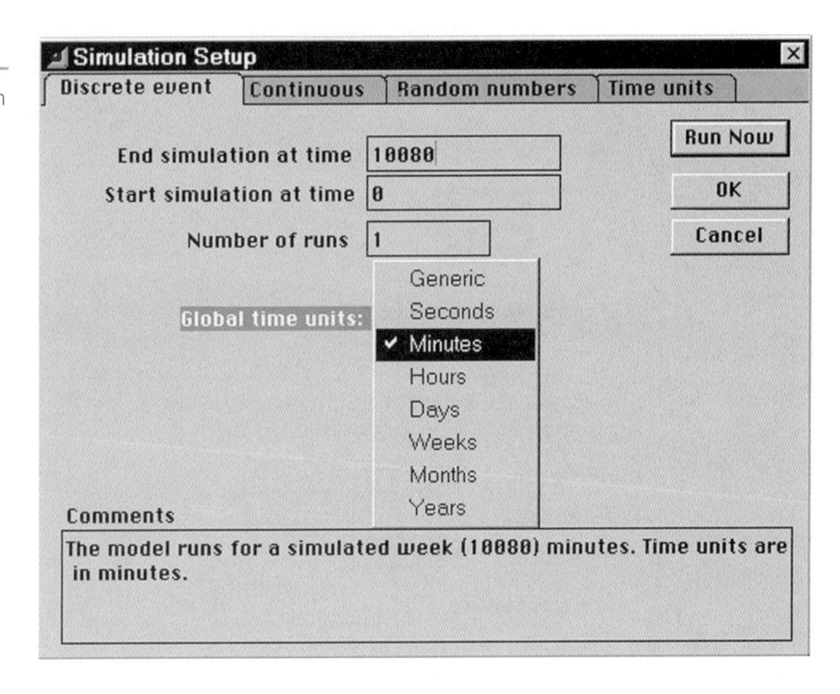

FIGURE 10.8

Simulation Setup Dialog with Settings for Hervis' Model

To start building a new model, choose New Model from Extend's File menu; Extend will open a new model window. To add a block to the model window, you always follow four steps:

1. Open the library containing Extend's predefined blocks, if necessary.
2. Add the desired block to the model by selecting it from the library.
3. Click-drag to move the block to its desired position in the model window.
4. Connect its input and output connectors to other blocks.

TIP: *Selecting the "Preferences . . ." item from the Edit menu and clicking the Libraries tab presents a dialog in which you can enter the names of these libraries in a "Preload libraries" list. This will tell Extend to automatically open these libraries each time you start Extend.*

In order to copy a predefined Extend block into a model, the library in which that block resides must be open. For the Hervis modeling in this chapter you need to open the Generic, Discrete Event, Plotter, and Stats libraries. To open the Discrete Event library, choose "Open Library . . ." from Extend's Library menu, locate the Libs subdirectory, select the Discrete Event library (DE.lix), and click "Open." Use the same steps to open the Generic (GENERIC.lix), Plotter library (PLOTTER.lix), and Stats library (STATS.lrx). Note the different ".lrx" extension on the STATS library.

To add a block to a model, click on the Library menu and select the name of the library that holds the desired block. When the library is selected, you will see a hierarchical menu of the different types of blocks in the library, and to the right of each, a list of the names of the blocks of that type in the library. Selecting a block from the list puts a copy of the block in the Extend window and selects it.

For discrete event simulation modeling, Extend **always** requires an *Executive* block from the Discrete Event library (DE.lix) to be placed as the leftmost block in the model window. This block, with an icon of a wall clock, determines the duration of the simulation, determines its stopping conditions and handles the details of event scheduling. Normally, there is no connection to the *Executive* block, and once placed in the upper left corner of the model window, it can be ignored.

The Hervis model begins with the arrival of an airport van carrying rental-car customers. The arrival of a van is represented in the model by Extend's *Generator* block. Using the same steps you followed above, add a *Generator* block from the Generators submenu of the Discrete Event library, as shown in Figure 10.9. After adding it, double click the block to evoke its dialog window, also shown in Figure 10.9. Since airport vans arrive at 5-minute

FIGURE 10.9

Using the *Generator* Block to Create Customers

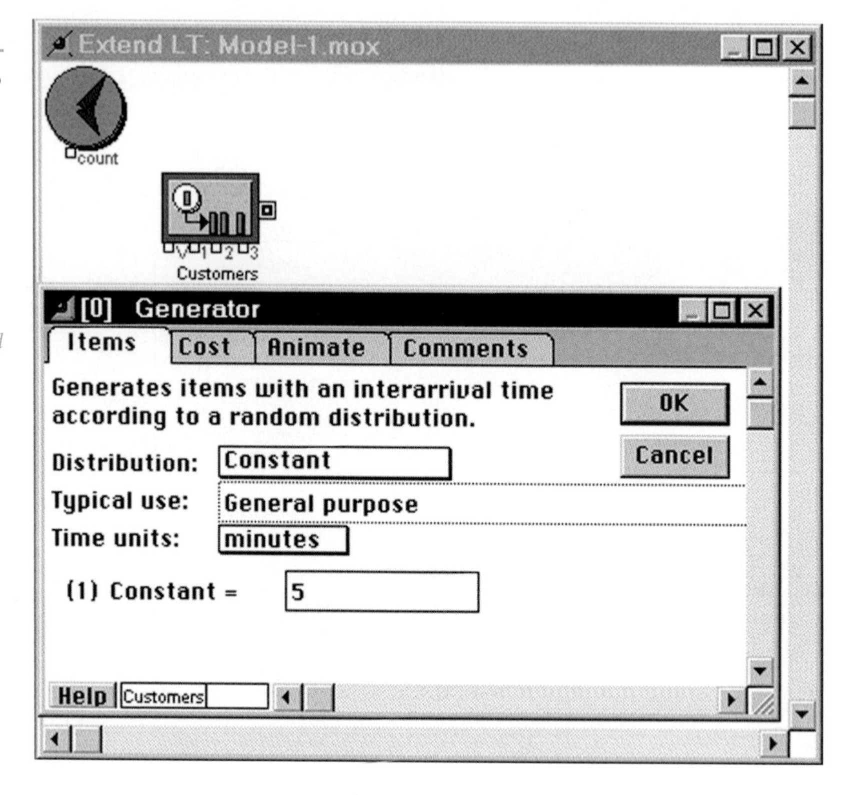

TIP: *Since Extend always puts new blocks at the last place you clicked in the model window, click where you would like the block to be placed before you add the block. Then move the block by click-dragging it. Fine adjustments are made by clicking the block to select it and using the keyboard arrow keys.*

TIP: *Text boxes provide useful model documentation. After creating it by clicking in the window and typing, a text box may be moved by click-dragging and edited by double clicking at the point in the text to be edited.*

TIP: *Non-straight connector lines can be straightened later by clicking one of the blocks and moving it via the mouse or the keyboard arrow keys. If the connection fails or the line is composed of extraneous segments, it will appear as a dotted line. Any line or line segment, dotted or solid, may be removed by clicking to select it and pressing the Delete key.*

intervals, the dialog is filled by selecting the Distribution to be "Constant" with its only parameter being 5, and Time Units to be "minutes." Finally, label the block "Customers" for documentation.

Each time a van arrives, it contains a variable number of customers, called a batch in queuing parlance, as originally specified by Hervis in Table 10.1. By default Extend's *Generator* block creates a "batch" of size one, but this can be overridden by providing another number via the V value input connector. In this case, we want the batch size to be a random number of customers between 0 and 3, according to Table 10.1. This random number of customers is created by Extend's *Input Random Number* block, found in the Inputs/Outputs menu in the GENERIC.lix library. After adding the *Input Random Number* block, its dialog is opened by double clicking it, and the data from Table 10.1 can be entered by selecting "Empirical Table" and "Discrete" in the dialog and entering the Table 10.1 data, as shown in Figure 10.10. The label "# of Customers" also can be added to the dialog to label the block in the model. In addition, a text box containing "Customers Come from Airport Van" can be added to the model's window to document this section of the model. A text box is created by simply double clicking an empty area in the model's window and typing. The properties of the text can be changed via items in Extend's Text menu (Bold, Center, etc.) in the usual way.

Although they are not needed in this model, the numbered connectors on *Input Random Number* block are used to specify external input parameter values for other probability distributions, such as Normal, Exponential, Uniform, and so on, available by clicking the "Distribution" selector in the dialog. The remaining connector on the right of the block is its output value, which we want to connect to the V input connector of the *Generator* block. Blocks are hooked together through their connectors by connection lines. In this case, the line will allow information to flow from the output of the *Input Random Number*

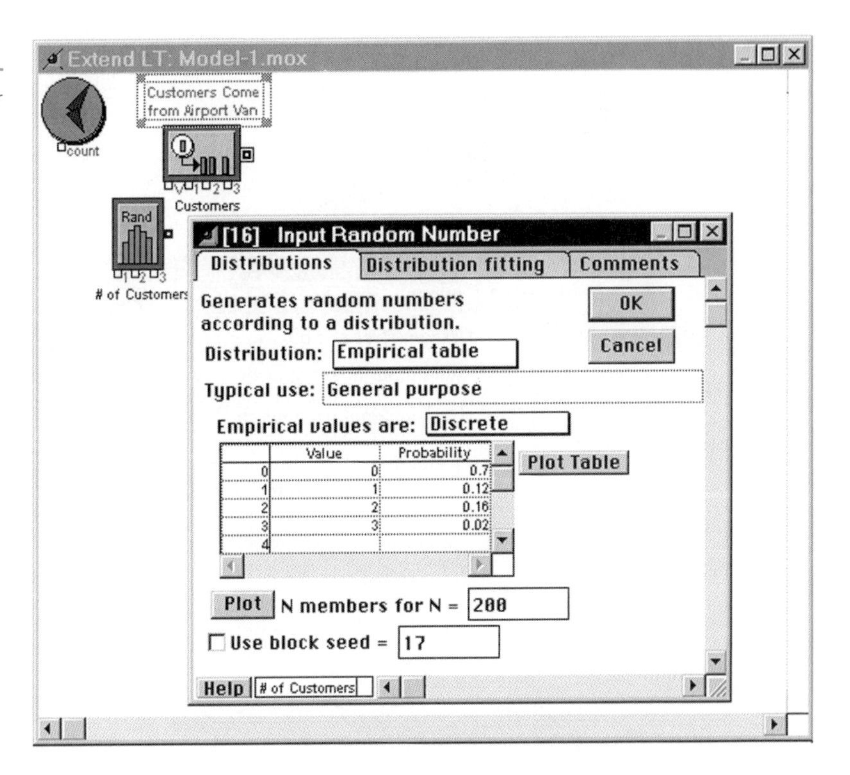

FIGURE 10.10

Using *Input Random Number* to Generate Random Number of Customers

TIP: *Usually, connections are made by drawing a straight line between two connectors. Extend also lets you connect through multisegment connections and through named connections. These two methods allow you to make your model more attractive and easy to follow. Multisegment connections involve drawing a connection using one or more anchor points at each bend in the connection line. An anchor point is created by releasing and click-ing the left mouse button while click-dragging the drawing pen.*

block to the V input connector of the *Generator* block. To connect them, position the mouse cursor over either connector; it will change to the icon of a technical drawing pen. Then click-drag the pen to the other tab. The connection is complete when the thin connector line drawn under the drawing pen changes to a thick line, as shown in Figure 10.11. Releasing the mouse button after a successful connection will leave the two connected by a thin solid line. This connected pair of blocks now will generate an arrival of a batch of items (customers), varying from 0 to 3 in size according to the Table 10.1 probabilities, every 5 minutes.

Next we want the batch of customers to queue First In, First Out (FIFO) in front of the rental station to complete their car rental contracts. This is done by adding a *Queue, FIFO* block from the Queues menu of the DE.lix library. After adding the *Queue, FIFO* block, its input connector is linked to the output connector of the *Generator* block, using the pen as before, thereby allowing the customers in the batch to join the queue. This connection is shown in Figure 10.12 in which the *Queue, FIFO* block's dialog has been opened to show its default parameter of no more than 1000 customers, effectively an unlimited queue in this model. The L and W value connectors in this block provide information during the simulation of the number of items in the queue and the waiting time for items exiting the queue, respectively.

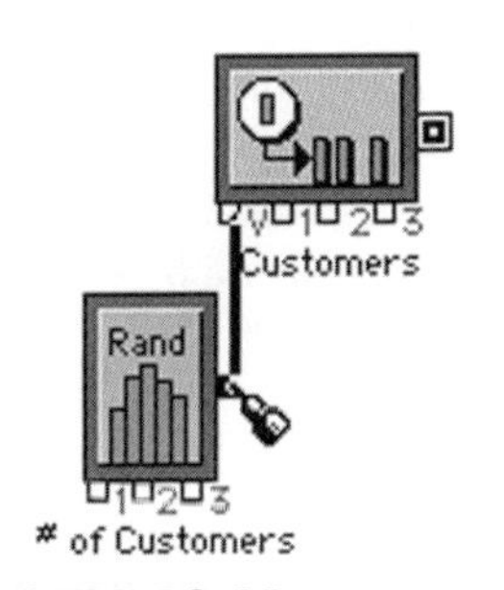

FIGURE 10.11

Connecting the Tabs of Two Extend Blocks

Note that the connecting lines over which items (customers) flow among blocks are hollow while the connection lines among blocks providing information (values) are thin solid lines.

Important: Items (customers in this case) produced by a *Generator* block are pushed out immediately and must have someplace to go in the model. This usually requires a direct connection from a *Generator* block to one of Extend's *Queue* blocks or *Resource* blocks (described later). Otherwise the *Generator* block may lose items, thereby producing incorrect simulation statistics.

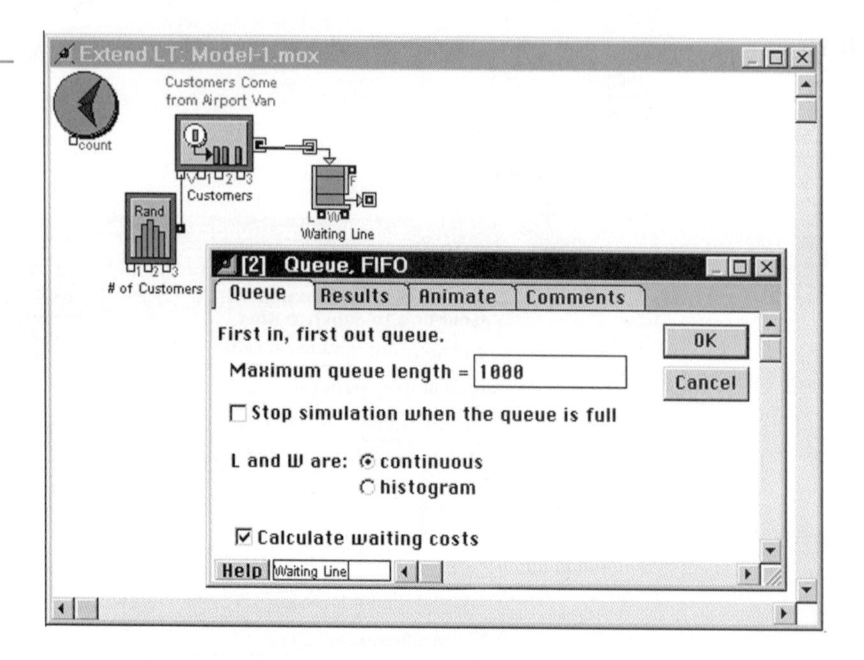

FIGURE 10.12

Customers Join a FIFO Queue

Completing the car rental contract takes time. In the original Hervis model, the rental clerk will delay each customer for 5 minutes to complete the car rental transaction. The *Activity, Delay* block described earlier can be used for introducing this delay. However, the *Activity, Delay* block accommodates at most only one item. As with the original Excel model, Hervis would also like to investigate the effects of adding additional rental clerks. The *Activity, Multiple* block, found on the Activities menu of the DE.lix library, is used instead because it allows multiple items to be delayed, that is, receiving service simultaneously, as would be the case if there were multiple rental clerks. After customers complete their car rental contracts, they exit the service center to receive their cars. Items leave the simulation model via Extend's *Exit* block found on the Routing menu of the DE.lix library.

Figure 10.13 shows the *Activity, Multiple* block with its dialog and Help windows open and the *Exit* block along with additional text blocks for documentation. Also shown in the figure, the blocks' item input connectors and output connectors have been linked, as appropriate. The *Activity, Multiple* block's dialog window correctly reflects Hervis's original model of a single rental clerk taking exactly 5 minutes to complete each customer's rental contract. The purposes of the other connectors are given in the figure's Help window for the *Activity, Multiple* block.

This completes the basic Hervis model. However, Extend offers additional data capture and graphic display blocks that can be added for preserving relevant managerial information from the simulation. The most useful of these is the *Plotter, Discrete Event* block found in the PLOTTER.lix library. The *Plotter, Discrete Event* block captures data and plots up to four variables during the simulation run. It also can be instructed to preserve these and other data into multiple pages of output over many simulation runs for further analysis. The variables to be collected and plotted are determined by connecting the *Plotter, Discrete Event* block's connectors to appropriate value connectors of other blocks in the model. As shown in Figure 10.14, the *Plotter, Discrete Event* block will capture the Utilization of the Rental Station (% of time it is busy), and the customer waiting time, W, from the *Queue, FIFO* block. Figure 10.14 also shows a simple *Help* block (found on the Inputs/Outputs menu in the GENERIC.lix library) that allows inputting some text to describe the model when it is double clicked.

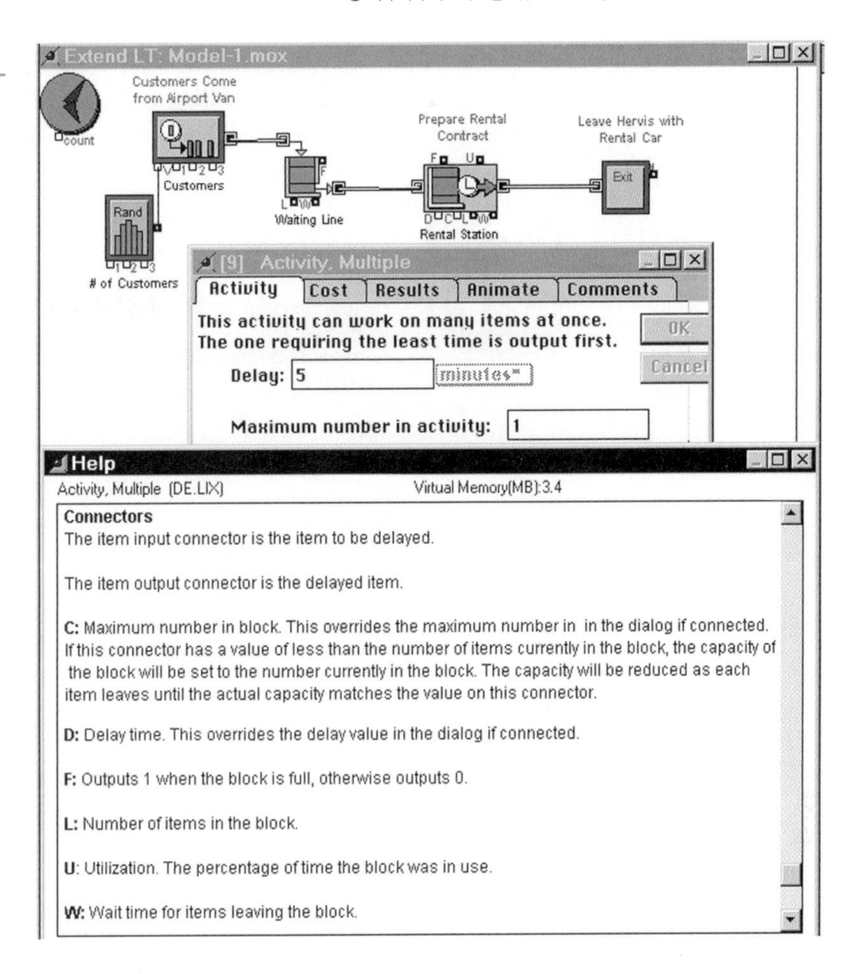

FIGURE 10.13

Adding Service Delay and Exit Blocks to the Model

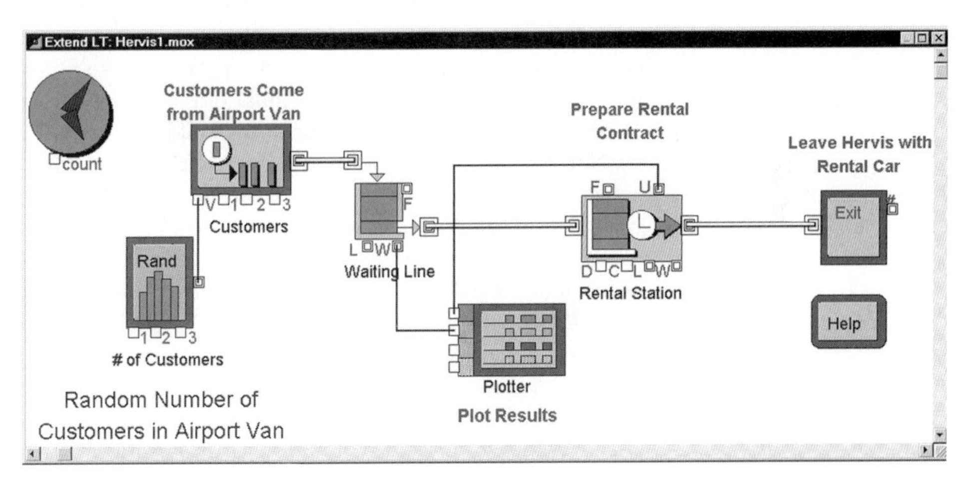

FIGURE 10.14

The Completed Hervis Simulation Model

RUNNING THE MODEL

To begin the simulation, click the Run Simulation item on the Run menu, or the right arrow button, ➡, on Extend's toolbar. As shown in Figure 10.15, when the simulation begins, Extend (1) will display a Status bar at the bottom of the screen based on the settings you designated in the Simulation Setup dialog, and (2) will open a window for the plotter

FIGURE 10.15

Simulation Results for the Hervis Model

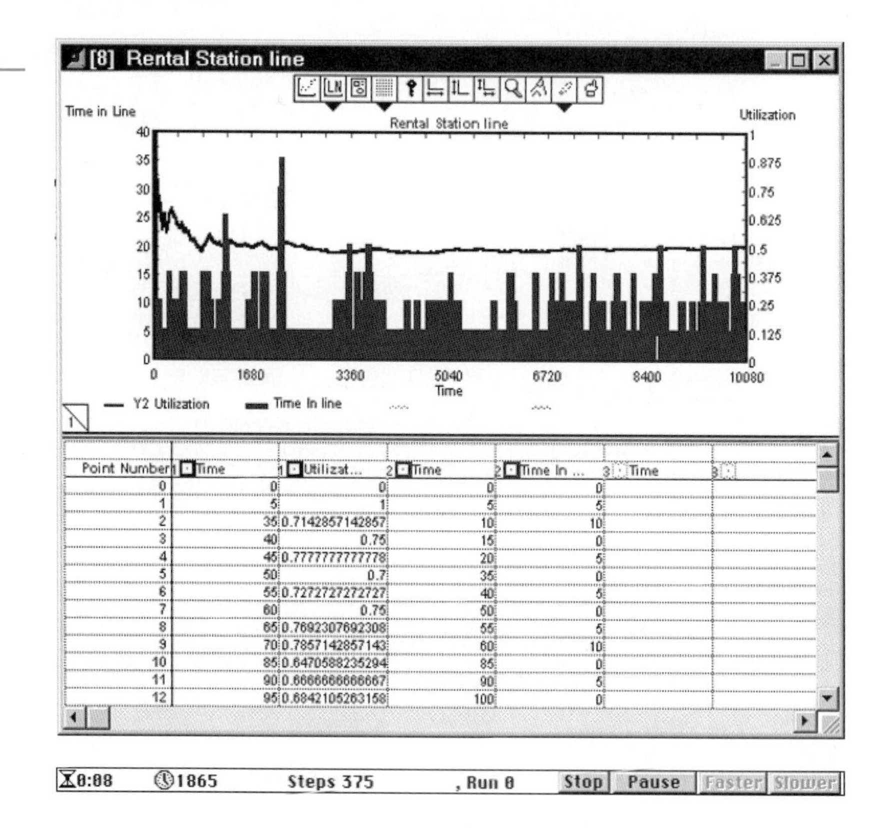

to dynamically report its variables, server utilization and waiting time in this case. Looking at the trace lines of the plot reveals results similar to the previous Excel models. In the Extend run, note how the time customers wait in line jumps up and down in discrete units of 5 minutes, that the maximum wait of a customer was 35 minutes, and the average utilization of the rental counter trended to 50%—one half customer arriving every 5 minutes (on average) implies that the Rental Station will be busy half the time (on average). Your results for customer waiting will differ, because of the randomness in the simulation data for customer batch size. Indeed, multiple runs should be made to see how variable the results can be. Note also in this and future runs, that the average rental station utilization is erratic in early time periods and takes more than a day (1440 minutes) to settle to its long run average value. This is because the system starts empty of customers as its initial edge condition.

After the simulation run finishes, you can scroll through the data table at the bottom of the plotter window to see the values that correspond to the lines in the plot. You can also move the cursor over the plot trace lines. As you do, Extend will display the coordinates where the cursor crosses the trace.

To duplicate exactly the appearance of the trace lines in Figure 10.15, you will need to work with the tool bar presented at the top of the plotter window for varying its default effects, auto rescaling the axes, and so forth. The most useful of these is the plot properties tool, [icon], the leftmost icon in the plotter toolbar. Clicking this tool will bring up a Trace Lines Properties window, as shown in Figure 10.16. Each of the (up to four) plotter variables occupies two rows, the properties of the variable's time stamp and the properties of the variable. From left to right the columns in this window govern the label, color, line weight, pattern, type of line, symbol, numerical format of the data, use of left or right vertical axis, and whether to show the trace of that variable, respectively. Note that a variable's time stamp can have only its numerical format changed.

TIP: *The Plotter Discrete Event block always uses the model's simulated time as its X axis variable. The best way to learn about all the formatting tools shown in the plotter window is to experiment with their settings.*

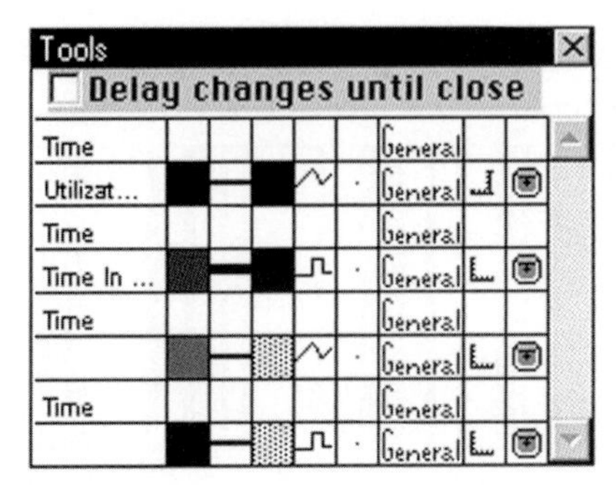

FIGURE 10.16

Properties of Plotter Trace Lines Window

TIP: *Since utilizations are usually less than 1, it is best to plot them on the second axis, as shown in Figure 10.16. Otherwise, they may not be seen with the other plots whose values are often much larger.*

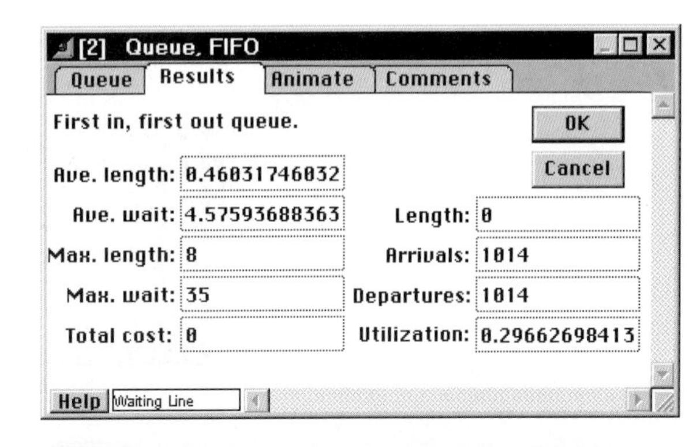

FIGURE 10.17

Results for the *Queue, FIFO* and *Activity, Multiple* Blocks

TIP: *The results of the simulation run are saved when you save the model to disk. They can be redisplayed later by double clicking the appropriate block. Also, you should always use Excel to calculate important check figures, such as the long run average server utilization, to help debug and validate your Extend model results. For example, the Rental Station utilization of .5029 in Figure 10.17 closely agrees with the long-run average utilization of .5.*

Clicking on the model's *Queue, FIFO* block and the *Activity, Multiple* block to open their dialog windows and clicking each window's Results tab will reveal the simulation run statistics for each block, as shown in Figure 10.17. For example, in this run the average wait by a customer was less than 5 minutes (4.576 minutes), but the maximum was 35 minutes for at least one customer; the queue length averaged less than half a customer (.46 items), but grew on at least one occasion to have 8 customers in it.[3] The rental station was busy about 50.29% of the time in this run, the .29% deviation from the long-run average utilization being caused by the randomness of the simulation.

As with the earlier Excel model, Hervis wants to see the effect of adding another rental station to see if an additional clerk produces the same dramatic reduction in maximum customer queue length. To do this, he need only double click the *Activity, Multiple* block and change the "Maximum Number in Activity" from 1 to 2 in the dialog shown in Figure 10.13. Rerunning the simulation produces the results shown in Figure 10.18 with results similar to the earlier Excel model: As expected, the average utilization of the two servers trends to 25%. The maximum queue length drops to four with the maximum customer waiting time of 5 minutes, a sevenfold reduction from the previous simulation result.[4]

[3] In the worst case the eighth customer arrives as service is started on the first customer, leaving 7 customers to wait while one is being serviced. Service takes 5 minutes, and so, the seventh customer in line waiting for service waits a maximum of 35 minutes to begin receiving service.

[4] In the worst case the fourth customer arrives as service is started on the first two customers, leaving two customers to wait while two are being serviced. Service takes 5 minutes, and so, the two waiting in line for service wait a maximum of 5 minutes for each to begin receiving service.

FIGURE 10.18

Hervis Simulation with Two Rental Stations

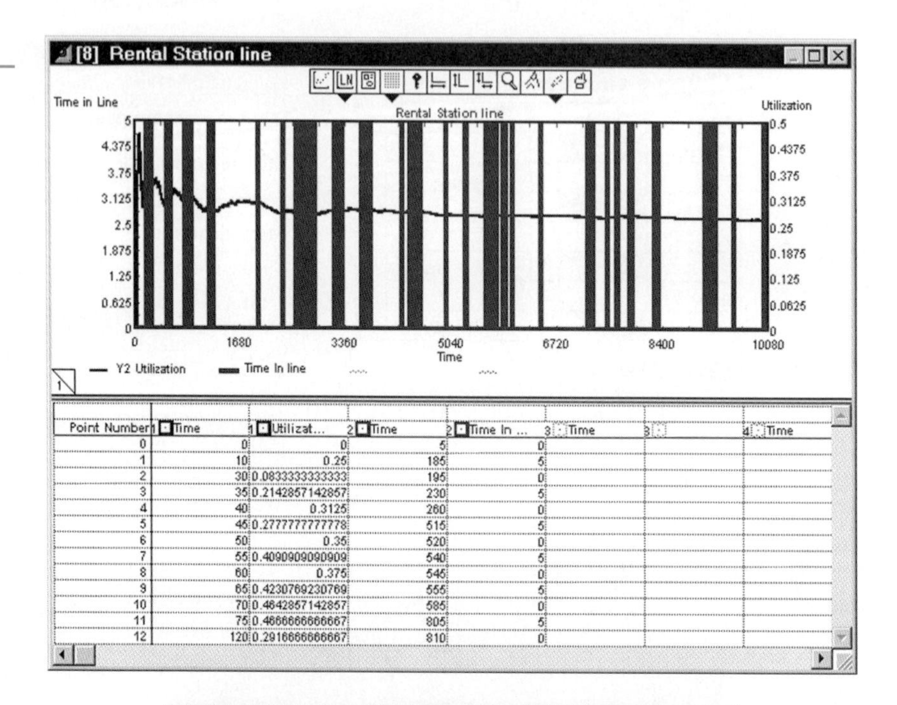

Point Number	1 Time	1 Utilizat...	2 Time	2 Time In ...	3 Time	3	4 Time
0	0	0	5	0			
1	10	0.25	185	5			
2	30	0.0833333333333	195	0			
3	35	0.2142857142857	230	5			
4	40	0.3125	260	0			
5	45	0.2777777777778	515	5			
6	50	0.35	520	0			
7	55	0.4090909090909	540	5			
8	60	0.375	545	0			
9	65	0.4230769230769	565	5			
10	70	0.4642857142857	585	0			
11	75	0.4666666666667	805	5			
12	120	0.2916666666667	810	0			

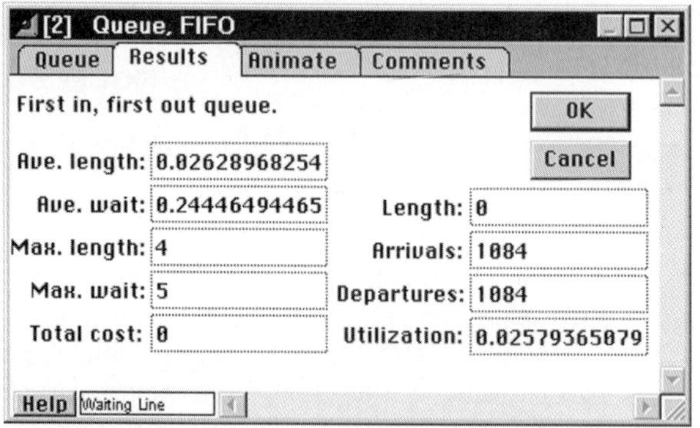

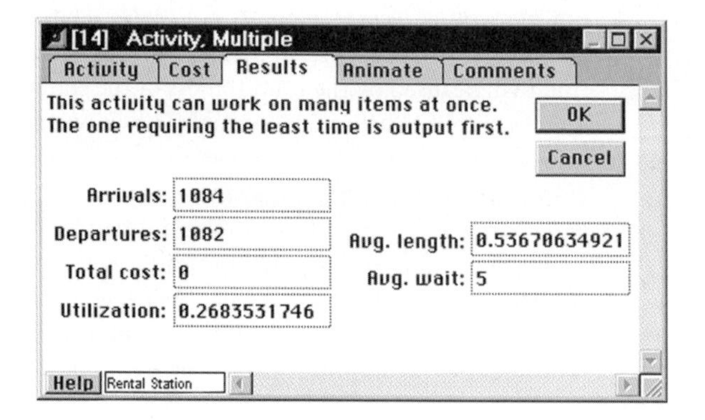

10.4 EXAMPLE 3—HERVIS CAR RENTAL MODEL EXPANDED

The ease of modifying and analyzing the Extend version of a discrete event model in comparison to the Excel version becomes apparent as Hervis investigates other aspects of his situation. For example, Hervis knows the airport vans experience traffic delays and don't always arrive exactly every 5 minutes. Modifying the model to accommodate this requires him only to specify the nature of this added variability. Figure 10.19 shows how to modify the original Extend model to allow a range of interarrival times for airport vans from 3 minutes to 7 minutes with the most likely interarrival time being 5 minutes, as before. Somewhat arbitrarily, Hervis uses a Triangular probability distribution over these values for simplicity.[5] Hervis need only select the Distribution type (from the nearly 20 predefined types provided by Extend) and specify its parameters in the *Generator* block's dialog window.

Before running the model, Hervis reflects on the reasonableness of continuing to assume that it always takes exactly 5 minutes for his clerks to complete the car rental contract. He elects to add some variability to this aspect of his model as well. However, the *Activity, Multiple* block does not have a built-in source of variability, as the *Generator* block does. But from the D connector documentation in Figure 10.13, we see that we can add another *Input Random Number* block (from the Inputs/Outputs menu in the GENERIC.lix library), specifying the variability via a Distribution, and connecting the block's output connector to the D connector of the *Activity, Multiple* block, thus overriding its fixed delay time parameter. This is shown in Figure 10.20, in which the chosen Distribution is Exponential, a common service time distribution assumption, with mean delay time of 5 minutes, as before.[6]

FIGURE 10.19

Uncertainty in Airport Van Arrival Times

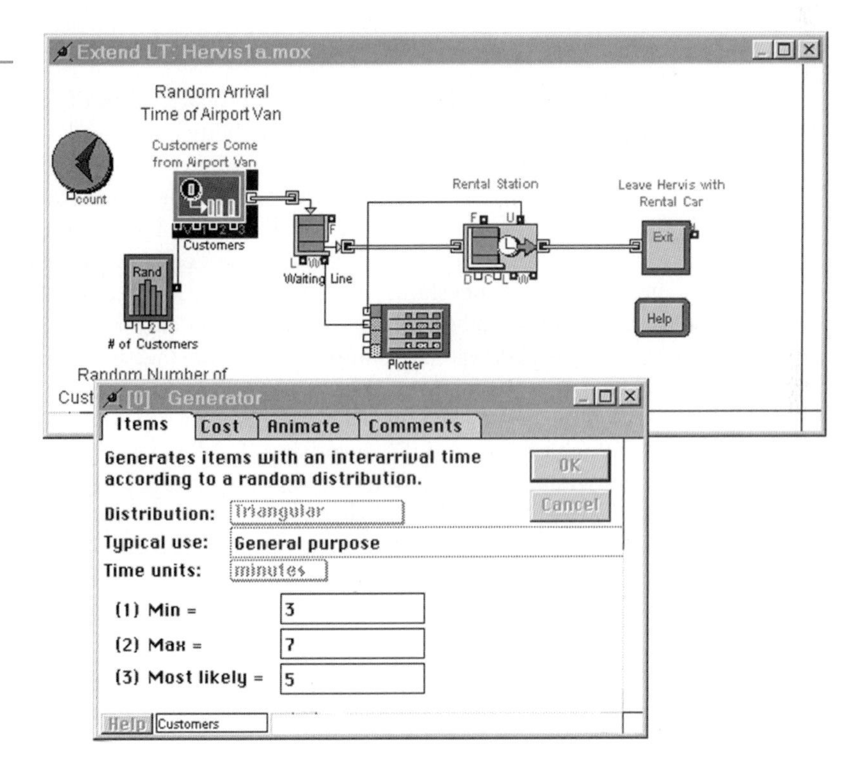

[5] To be more precise, Hervis should gather actual interarrival times for a sample of airport van arrivals and see if its distribution fits a Triangle distribution.

[6] Again, Hervis should gather empirical data on the times to prepare a car rental contract to verify the Exponential distribution assumption.

FIGURE 10.20

Adding Uncertainty to the Rental Station Service Times

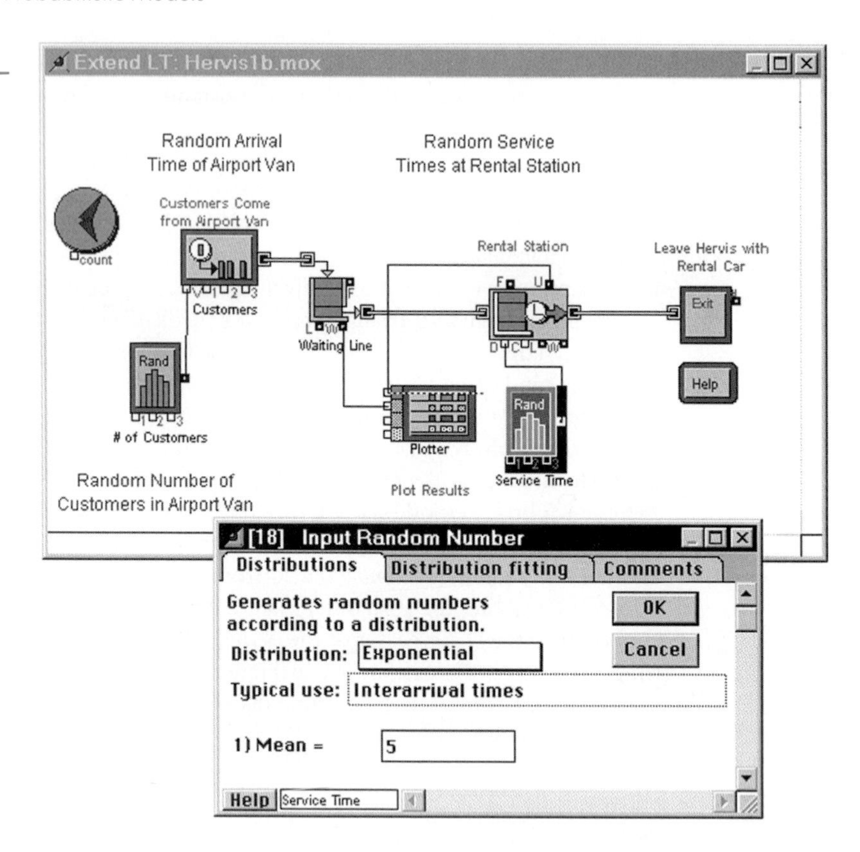

Hervis reasons that adding the additional realism of variability in interarrival times and in service times will cause more variability in the resulting customer waiting times and queue lengths, but since he has kept the means of both distributions the same as in his original model of Figure 10.14, the average queue length and waiting time will not be affected.

He tests his supposition by rerunning the model in Figure 10.20 for variable airport van interarrival times and rental station service times, using a single rental station, which produces the results shown in Figure 10.21. As expected, the added variability increased maximum wait substantially (66.6 minutes) and maximum queue length slightly (9). However, despite his maintaining the same average interarrival and service time parameters as in his original model of Figure 10.14, the simulation results in Figure 10.21 also show a much worse average wait (8.12) and average queue length (.817), nearly doubling over those of Figure 10.17. Surprisingly, adding variability alone to the distributions for interarrivals and service times worsens the average performance as well as increasing performance variability. Some thought should convince you why this should be true in general and why Hervis's original reasoning is faulty. Such insights from investigating simple simulation models are important to developing generalizations about more complex systems.

Feeling desperate that his simulations are suggesting unacceptable operational performance of his new venture, Hervis tries another run to see if adding another rental clerk to the model of Figure 10.20 will have as dramatic an improvement as before. So, he double clicks the *Activity, Multiple* block in this model with added uncertainty, changes the "Maximum Number in Activity" from 1 to 2 in its dialog window, and runs the simulation again, producing the results in Figure 10.22. Fortunately, the new average and maximum wait results look reasonable, and Hervis concludes that the average wait of only about .7 minutes and maximum wait of less than 17 minutes are acceptable. Of course, more simulation runs by Hervis are needed to confirm that these results are representative and not just a chance outcome.

FIGURE 10.21

Results of Model with Uncertain Interarrival and Service Times

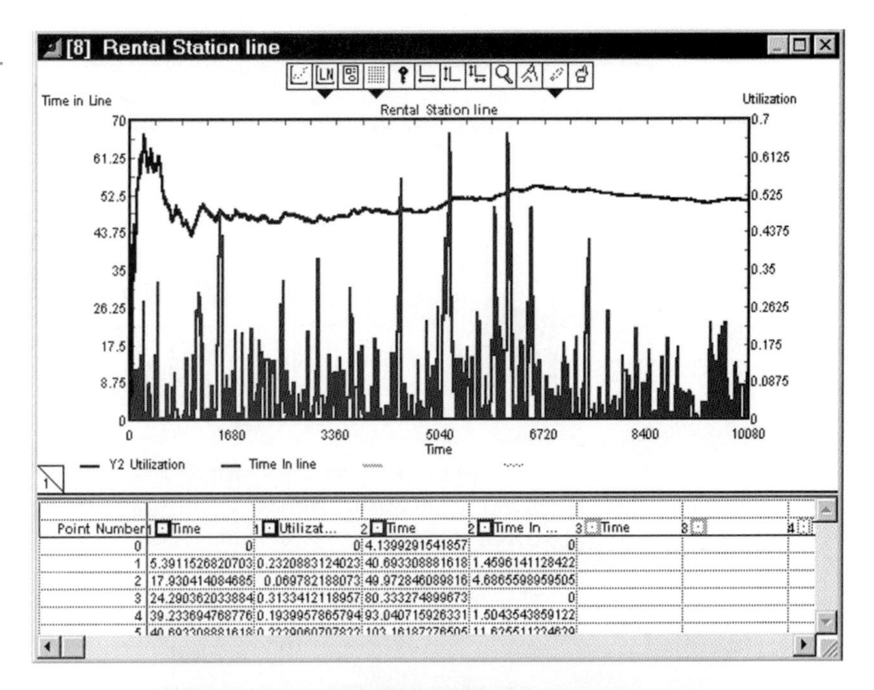

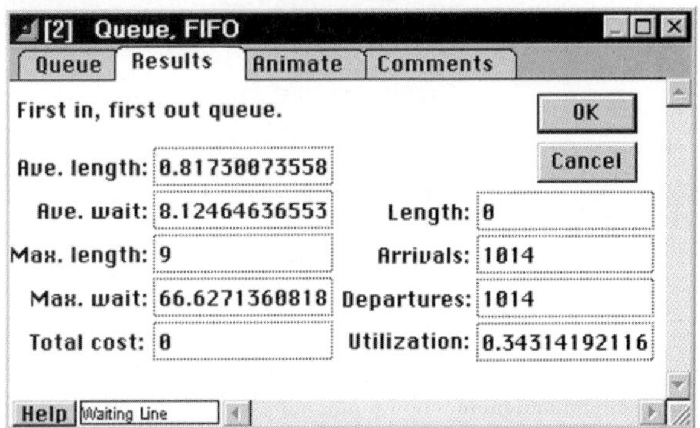

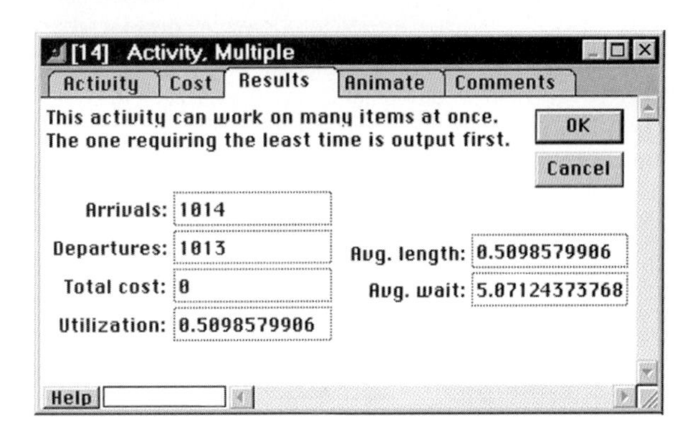

FIGURE 10.22

Results of Model with Uncertain Interarrival and Service Times and Two Rental Stations

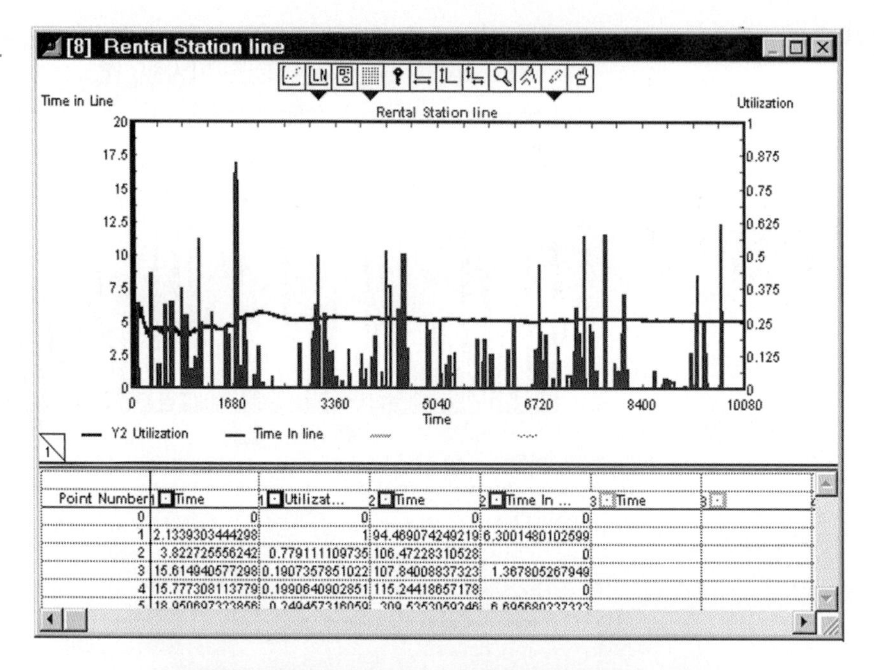

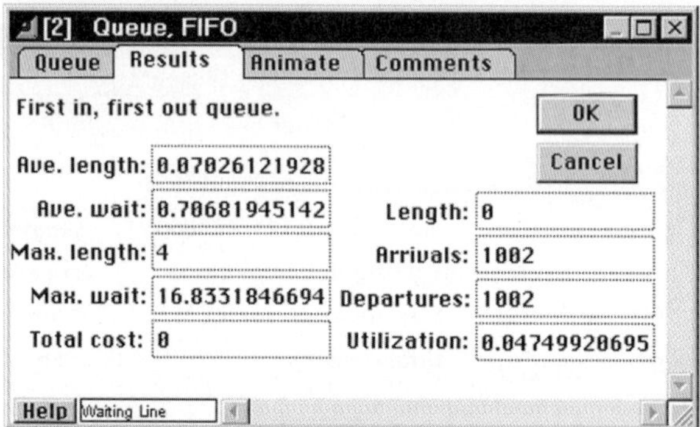

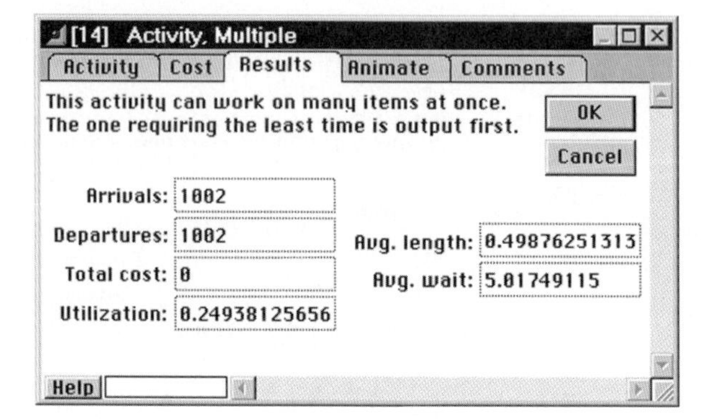

APPLICATION CAPSULE **The Chemical Industry**

In the chemical industry, plants can choose to manufacture chemicals in one of two ways. First, they can use a continuous process in which they produce one type of chemical in different strengths. Pipes feed the raw materials in, and the whole system must be flushed and inspected before any new product can be made. Switching products is costly, thus most continuous chemical process plants make only one type of chemical output. On the other hand, batch processes can produce a wide variety of products by adding raw materials in a recipe fashion, then turning out several different chemical compounds using the following method:

Raw materials are added to premix vats. These are transferred to main mix tanks. Main mix tanks must be reserved before raw materials are started into the premix process. These main tanks, as well as the pipes leading to and from the tanks, are readied and cleaned before they are used. After being mixed, chemicals are sent to one of three places: rework tanks, manifold tanks, or holding tanks. Rework tanks hold chemicals that do not meet standards after being mixed. In these tanks, chemicals are reworked in an effort to improve their quality enough so that they can be sold. Should this fail, chemicals are sent to a dump. If the rework is successful, chemicals are sent to the manifold and then to a finished product storage tank. Chemicals that are sent to the manifold tank directly are then routed to a product storage tank until the batch is sold. If chemicals are transferred to a holding tank, they are later routed through the manifold tank and then to a finished product storage tank to await purchase. Pipelines between these different types of tanks must be carefully selected and cleansed to ensure that products will not be contaminated en route. Large chemical plants can radically improve their batch processing techniques by designing plants effectively. This is especially true when designers simulate the ratio of different types of equipment and holding tanks versus products to troubleshoot for floating bottlenecks, ensure product quality, and analyze the stages of production in a plant.

Edward F. Watson, of Louisiana State University, used a simulation model to help a large chemical manufacturer design a new plant through discrete event simulation. Watson designed a system of vats and pipelines (service areas and queues) to model the processes in a chemical plant. Using data from an existing plant, he analyzed factors such as the main-mix-tank resource-selection policy, quality assurance policy, batch transfer policy, production order prioritization, and product flow. He introduced simulation to make recommendations for the efficient and effective design of a new plant. Watson explained the overall goal of the company was to minimize inventory levels, and improve product quality while never allowing a stock-out. Before using models and simulations to analyze different parameters within their production process, this chemical company had little ability to evaluate the many complex variables in that process and how to fit those variables together most effectively. By using the simulation model, the company was able to identify throughput issues related to new plant designs and to evaluate proposed improvements prior to implementation, thus saving considerable cost and time. (See Watson.)

10.5 EXAMPLE 4—HERVIS CAR RENTAL MODEL REVISITED

While waiting in a supermarket checkout line, Hervis was mulling his most recent simulation model results. Certainly with Extend he was able to quickly build a simulation model of his new car rental venture and to glean significant insights to its proposed operation. Most surprising to him was the pernicious effect on customer waiting time of adding variability to the interarrival and service time distributions, even though their mean values were unchanged from his earlier model runs. This suggests to him that reducing variability in the scheduled arrivals of his airport vans and in the car rental contracting times at the rental stations would improve average customer waiting time performance.

While thinking this over, he noticed that the supermarket manager had begun to open more checkout stations because the queues of customers with groceries were growing longer. This gave Hervis another idea for his car rental venture: He could pull some of his car service people off the car lot to staff more rental stations whenever the queue of customers became large. This would permit him to cut back on the requirement of staffing two rental stations with clerks during periods of low demand, while at the same time increasing the number of rental clerks to three or even four whenever a peak in customer demand occurred.

Intrigued by this idea, Hervis wondered how to instruct his Extend model to dynamically change its behavior by monitoring its own performance statistics during the simulation. What is needed is some way to have Extend alter the value in the "Maximum Number in Activity" field of the *Activity, Multiple* block dialog during the simulation to higher or lower numbers of rental stations as the queue length rises and falls. Looking at his model in Figure 10.13, Hervis notices the two "hooks" needed to implement his idea in the simulation model are already there.

First, he double clicks the *Queue, FIFO* block to display its dialog window, and clicks its Help button to confirm that (1) the L value output connector reads out the queue length throughout the simulation run. Next, he notices in the Help window of Figure 10.13 that (2) the C connector can be used to input a capacity value that overrides the number recorded in the "Maximum Number in Activity" field. What Hervis needs is a way to convert the L value from the *Queue, FIFO* block (Waiting Line) into the desired number of rental stations and feed that dynamic number into the C connector of the *Activity, Multiple* block (Rental Station) during the simulation run.

Extend has a block similar to Excel's VLOOKUP to do the mapping of input L values to the output C values Hervis requires. It is called the *Conversion Table* block, located in the Math menu of the GENERIC.lix library. Figure 10.23 shows the addition of the *Conversion Table* block to the Hervis model, taking its input from the L value output connector of the *Queue, FIFQ* block and sending its result to the C value input connector of the *Activity, Multiple* block. Hervis' proposed decision rule for increasing the number of rental station clerks is also shown in a text box together with the implementation of that rule in the

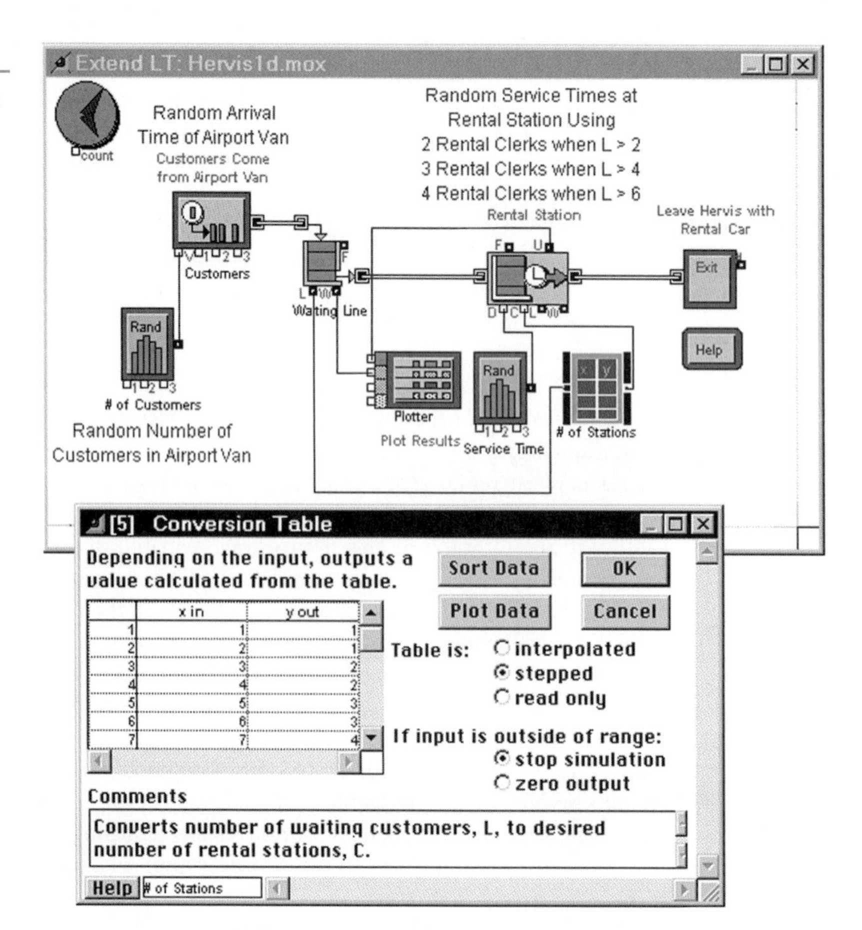

	x in	y out
1	1	1
2	2	1
3	3	2
4	4	2
5	5	3
6	6	3
7	7	4

FIGURE 10.23

Hervis Model with Dynamic Number of Rental Station Clerks

Conversion Table block's dialog window. Not shown in that window is the continued specification of 4 in the "*y* out" cells for all reasonable values of "*x* in" greater than 7, in effect capping the maximum number of rental clerks at 4. Hervis's reasoning is that the maximum number of customers in any arriving airport van is a batch of 3, and this rule provides for one more rental clerk as a hedge for those rare cases when multiple vans full of customers arrive faster than the waiting customers can be serviced. Moreover, the peak load maximum of 4 rental clerks is double the two-clerk processing capacity that led to the acceptable performance given for the prior model run in Figure 10.22.

Eager to see the improvement his new flexible rental station staffing policy will have upon customer waiting performance, Hervis clicks the right arrow Run Simulation tool on Extend's toolbar to run the new version of his simulation model. The customer queuing and waiting time performance results of his simulation run are presented in Figure 10.24.

Looking at the results, Hervis is flabbergasted at how poorly his new dynamic staffing scheme performs. It appears that increasing rental station staffing by up to a doubling of clerks during periods of peak customer arrivals will dramatically *hurt* customer waiting statistics. Comparing the results of Figure 10.24 with those of Figure 10.22 (the two full-time clerks case), the average customer wait has increased more than five-fold from about .71 minutes to 3.96 minutes and the maximum queuing wait by customers has almost doubled to more than 32 minutes! This worsening must be related to the six-fold growth in the average number of waiting customers from .07 to more than .42. But how can this be?

After verifying his Extend model's logic, Hervis concludes this was just a chance outcome caused by an unfavorable sequence of random numbers in the simulation run. But is he correct in this conclusion? One way to test this is to click the Run Simulation tool several more times and visually examine the results to see if the Figure 10.24 results are atypical. However, this approach is somewhat haphazard, as it depends on human memory to assess subjectively the results of many simulation runs. Fortunately, Extend has a queue tabulation block, *Queue Stats* in the STATS.lrx library, that collects queuing statistics from multiple runs of a simulation model to help systematically assess the influence of the model's inherent randomness on a performance measure. The *Queue Stats* block may be placed anywhere in the Extend model's window, as shown in Figure 10.25 along with the block's dialog window, opened by double clicking the block. To tabulate results of multiple runs, select the "Append new updates" option, selecting the "Update at end of simulation" option to speed up the tabulations. Next, evoke the Simulation Setup dialog, first seen in Figure 10.8, from the Run menu and change the "Number of runs" entry from 1 to, say, 20. This will instruct Extend to make 20 independent runs of the Hervis model, tabulating the queuing statistics from each run into the *Queue Stats* block.

TIP: *Remember the STATS.lrx has a different extension than the "lix" used by other libraries.*

Clicking the Run Simulation tool will run the simulation 20 times. As this will take a while, you can monitor its progress by observing Extend's Status Bar, first shown in Figure 10.15, at the bottom of the Extend window. When the runs finish, double clicking the *Queue Stats* block produces the tabular results shown in Figure 10.26 (the results for runs 11 through 20 require scrolling to be seen). For those readers with a statistical background, clicking the Confidence Interval button in the *Queue Stats* dialog window will further summarize the tabulated statistics into 95% confidence intervals, producing the intervals shown at the bottom of the figure.

Examining Figure 10.26 confirms that the results that so surprised Hervis were not atypical and that his proposed flexible staffing policy for the rental station appears to be a bad idea after all, consistently leading to longer average and maximum waits by customers than the two-clerk policy case of Figure 10.21. Clearly, simulation is a powerful tool to augment one's intuition, which otherwise is often wrong in predicting the behavior of systems subject to congestion. As confirmation of this, do you now have any insights to help you explain the shortcoming of Hervis's dynamic staffing policy after seeing these simulation results?

FIGURE 10.24

Results of Model with Dynamic Number of Rental Station Clerks

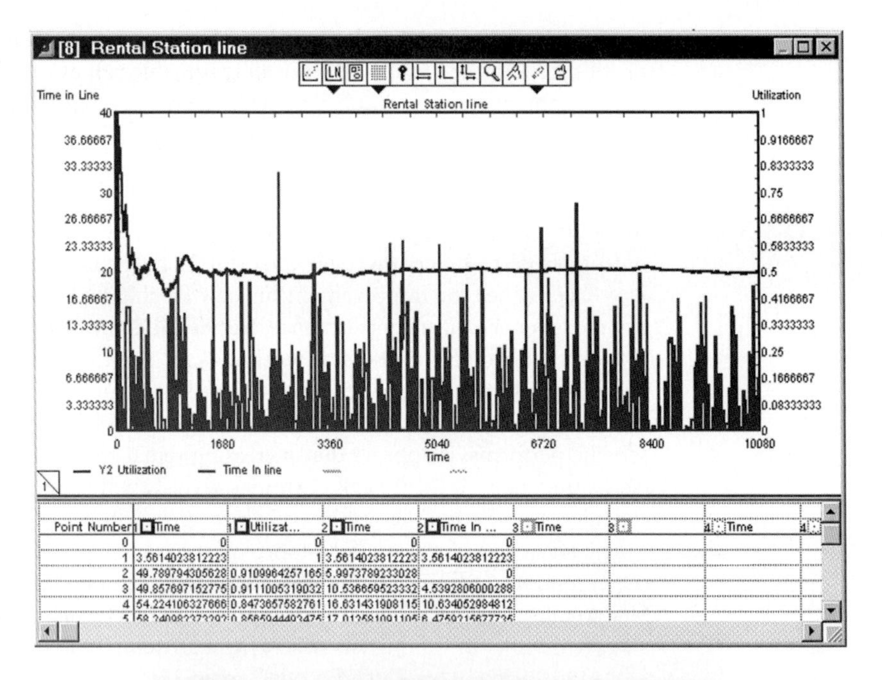

[2] Queue, FIFO

Queue | Results | Animate | Comments

First in, first out queue.

OK | Cancel

Ave. length:	0.42561656852		
Ave. wait:	3.96141736901	Length:	0
Max. length:	5	Arrivals:	1083
Max. wait:	32.4259235149	Departures:	1083
Total cost:	0	Utilization:	0.29238114101

Help | Waiting Line

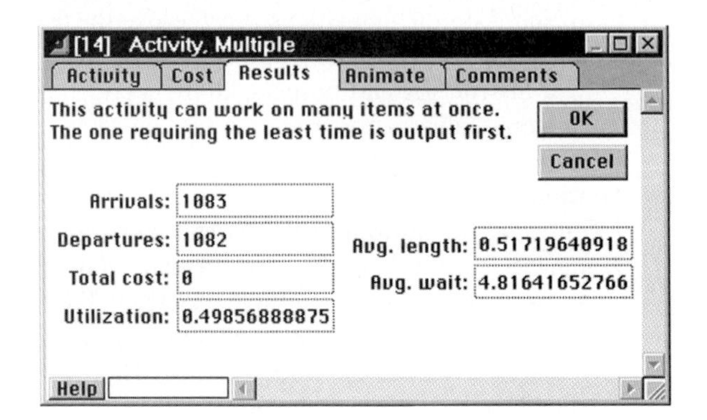

FIGURE 10.25

Tabulating Queuing Statistics via the *Queue Stats* Block

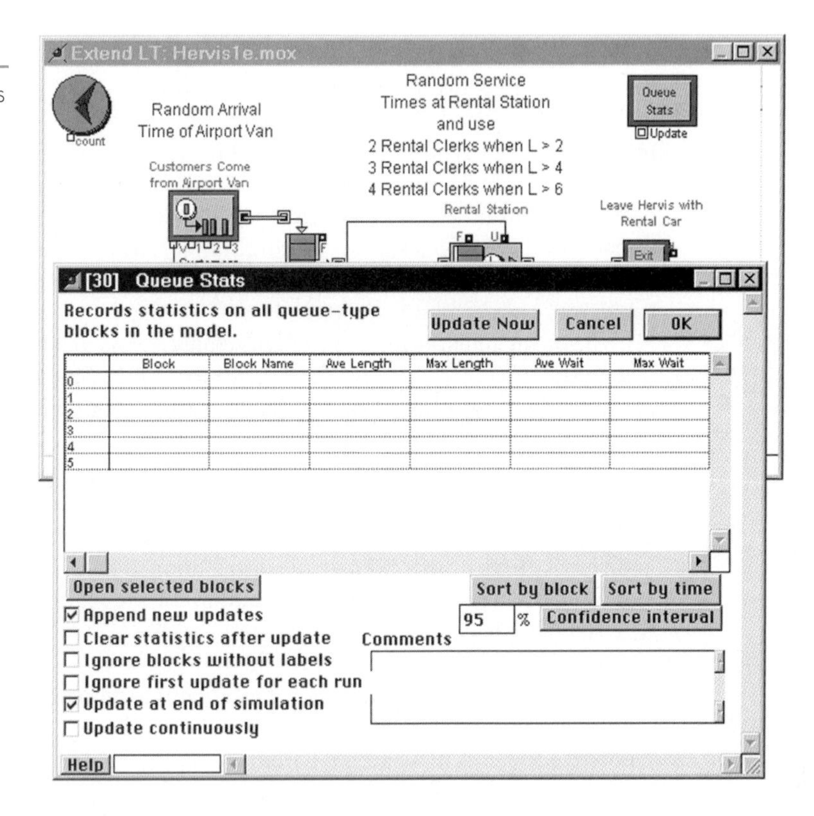

FIGURE 10.26

Queue Statistics for Individual Runs and Confidence Intervals

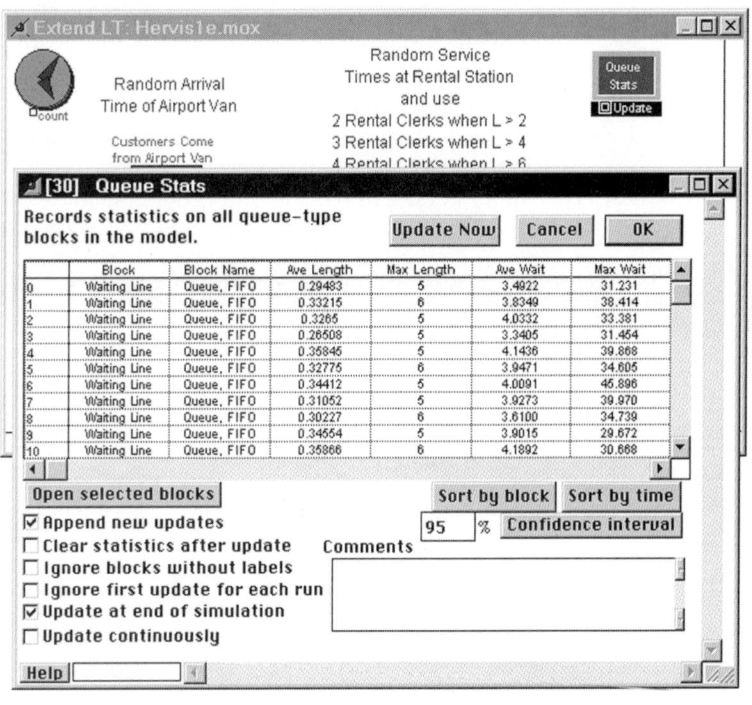

	Block	Block Name	Ave Length	Max Length	Ave Wait	Max Wait
0	Waiting Line	Queue, FIFO	0.29483	5	3.4922	31.231
1	Waiting Line	Queue, FIFO	0.33215	6	3.8349	38.414
2	Waiting Line	Queue, FIFO	0.3265	5	4.0332	33.381
3	Waiting Line	Queue, FIFO	0.26508	5	3.3405	31.454
4	Waiting Line	Queue, FIFO	0.35845	5	4.1436	39.868
5	Waiting Line	Queue, FIFO	0.32775	6	3.9471	34.605
6	Waiting Line	Queue, FIFO	0.34412	5	4.0091	45.896
7	Waiting Line	Queue, FIFO	0.31052	5	3.9273	39.970
8	Waiting Line	Queue, FIFO	0.30227	6	3.6100	34.739
9	Waiting Line	Queue, FIFO	0.34554	5	3.9015	29.672
10	Waiting Line	Queue, FIFO	0.35866	6	4.1892	30.668

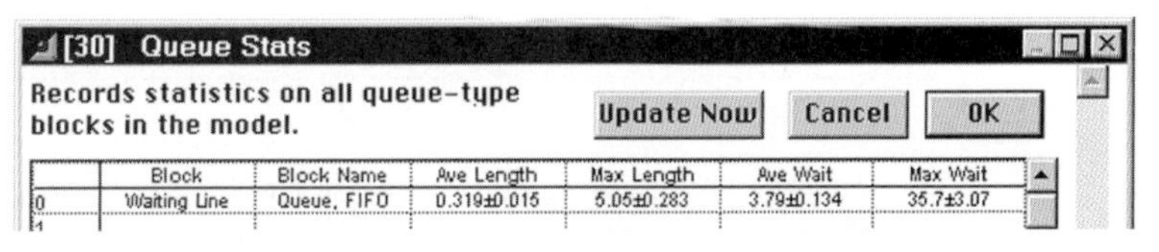

	Block	Block Name	Ave Length	Max Length	Ave Wait	Max Wait
0	Waiting Line	Queue, FIFO	0.319±0.015	5.05±0.283	3.79±0.134	35.7±3.07
1						

10.6 EXAMPLE 5—FINAL HERVIS CAR RENTAL MODEL

Concluding how fortunate he is to have discovered potential customer waiting problems with simulation modeling instead of in the real world, Hervis reverts his original two-clerk rental station policy, as shown in his final Rental Office model in Figure 10.27.

However, Hervis now realizes that quickly serving customers in completing their rental contracts in his office is not sufficient for his new venture: He must also supply them with rental cars. To keep his startup venture simple, Hervis intends to serve only two types of customers, those desiring smaller compact cars, called Economy, and those desiring to rent larger, more powerful cars, called Deluxe. Believing that most of the customers attracted to his type of car rental firm are price conscious, Hervis assumes that 70% of his customers will opt for economy cars and the balance for deluxe cars. His challenge is to decide how many of each type of car to have available at the beginning of a week to avoid car shortages during the week and the resulting customer dissatisfaction. Data on past rentals has convinced him that economy-car customers rent their car for between one and two days. Deluxe-car customers rent their cars slightly longer, typically for two days plus or minus a half day. The time interval for economy-car rentals is fairly evenly distributed in the data, and Hervis elects to approximate the distribution as being Uniform. For deluxe-car renters Hervis's data suggests a Normal distribution for the rental times is a good fit to the data, with standard deviation of half a day.

TIP: *A better choice for the Rental Time distribution might have been Lognormal instead of Normal. The Lognormal distribution can never generate a negative Rental Time, as the Normal might.*

To minimize visual complexity in this more advanced model, Hervis elects to take advantage of Extend's **Hierarchical blocks**. This allows creation of models made up of **submodels**, each of which is a logical grouping of Extend blocks. In effect, this permits you to create "super-blocks," each of which is a submodel comprised of many Extend blocks. To do this you need only open a model, select a group of connected blocks, and choose the Make Selection Hierarchical item on Extend's Model menu. Extend will encapsulate the selected blocks into a super-block, which you can label and connect in turn to other blocks or other super-blocks, leading to a very compact model appearance. For example, now that Hervis is turning his modeling attention to the operation of his car lot, he would like to suppress detail by creating a single new block that submodels the entire operation of the rental office in Figure 10.27.

To do this, select all the blocks except the *Executive* block and the *Exit* block by shift-clicking all but these two blocks,[7] and choose the Make Selection Hierarchical item from

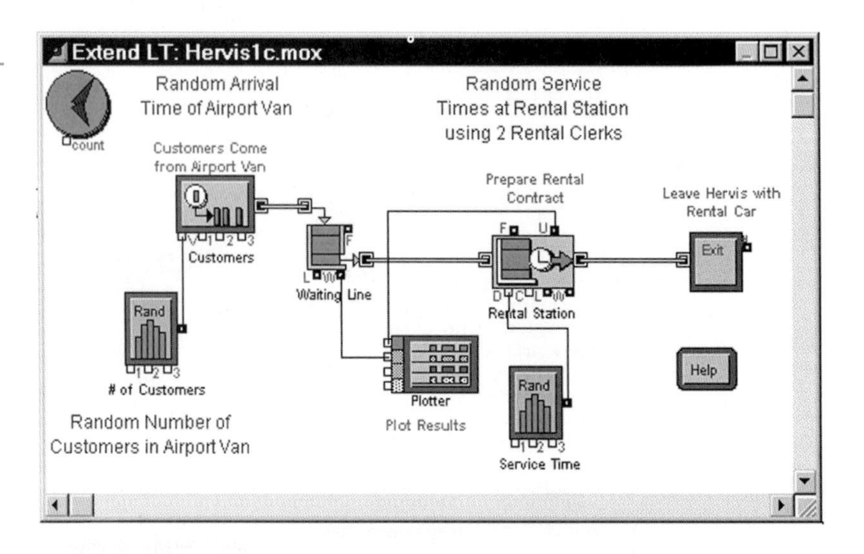

FIGURE 10.27

Final Hervis Rental Office Model

[7] Holding down the Shift key and clicking on a block will add it to any blocks already selected. A block is selected when its colors change and its background color is black. To drop a block from the selected group, click it again while continuing to hold down the Shift key.

FIGURE 10.28

Converting the Rental Office Model to a Hierarchical Block

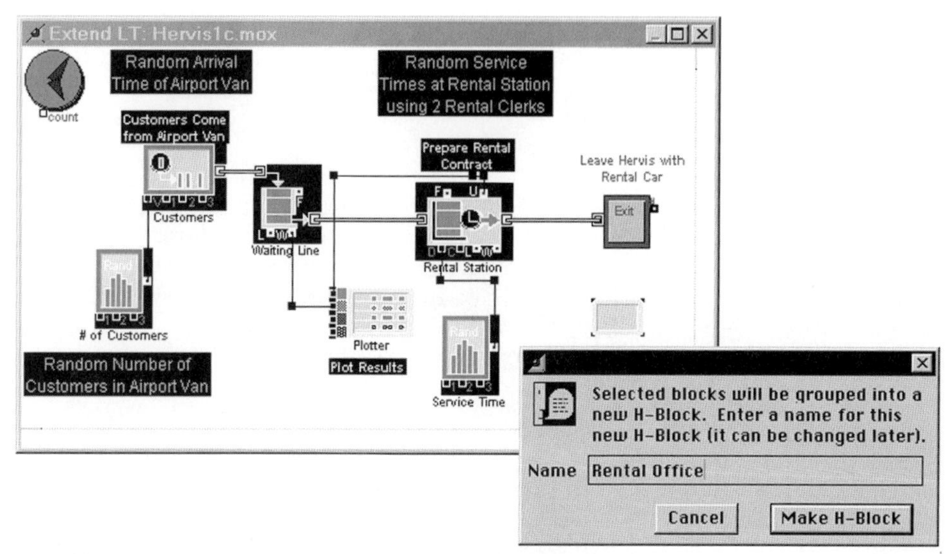

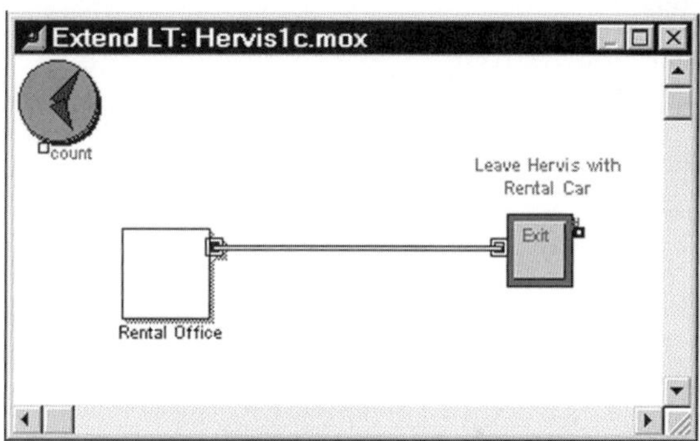

the Model menu. A dialog for naming the new super-block will be evoked as shown in Figure 10.28. Name it "Rental Office," as shown, and click Make H-Block. All of the selected blocks will be made part of a submodel connected to the *Exit* block. This can be verified by double clicking the new block. A new window with all the originally selected blocks will open, which you can label by typing "Rental Office" again in the field next to its Help button. Closing the submodel window will produce the window shown at the bottom of Figure 10.28. Now Hervis may begin to build his rental car lot's operation in his expanded model in place of the original *Exit* block, so that customers flowing out of the Rental Office submodel will enter the rental car lot of his simulation model.

To model the assignment of rental cars to customers, Hervis must distinguish those customers wanting to rent economy cars from those wanting deluxe cars. To do this, he first deletes the *Exit* block by selecting it and pressing the Delete key and begins to model his car lot by adding two new blocks, as shown in Figure 10.29. A portion of the dialog window for the new *Input Random Number* block (from Input/Output menu in the GENERIC.lix library) is at the bottom of the figure. Note that it uses an Empirical Table to assign a 0 value (to signify an economy car is wanted) with probability .7 and a 1 value (deluxe car wanted) with probability .3, as required. The output of this block is attached to the Select input connector of a new *Select DE Output* block (from Routing menu in the DE.lix library). The *Select DE Output* block splits the stream of items (customers) to one of two output connectors based upon the value present at its Select connector. The dialog window for the *Select DE Output* block is at the right of the figure. As can be seen in this dialog window, the incoming customer is directed to the top ("a" connector) output if the random number at its Select connector is 0 and is directed to the bottom ("b" connector) output if

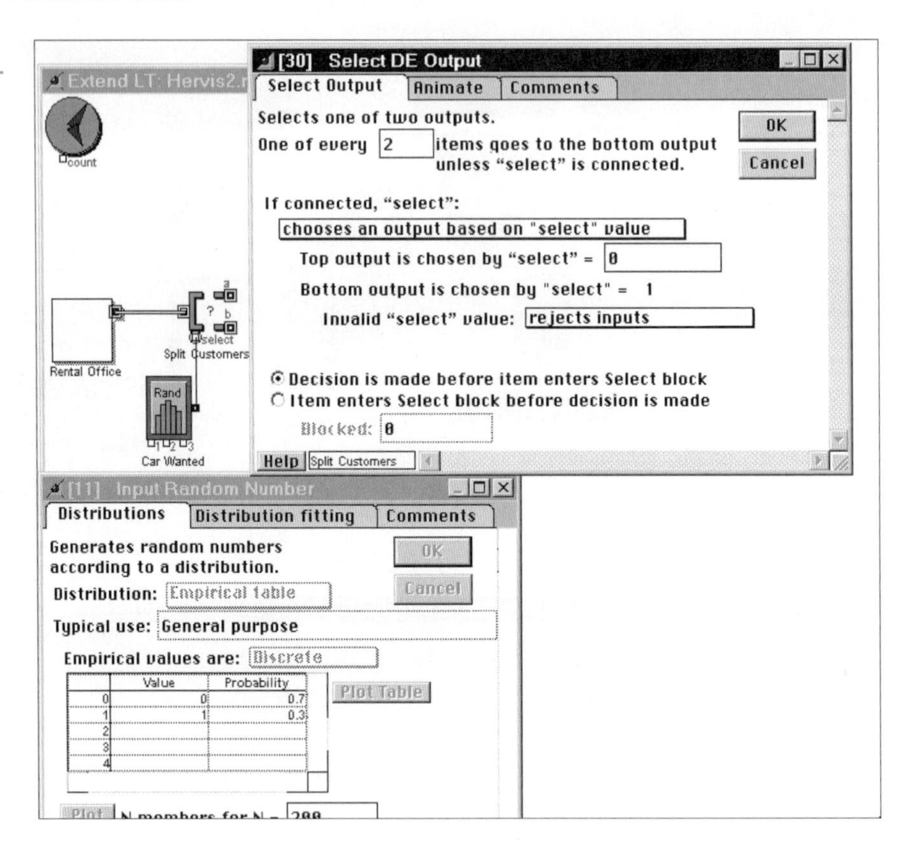

FIGURE 10.29

Splitting Customers Randomly by Car Type Wanted

the random number at its Select connector is 1. Together, these two new blocks direct a customer coming from the Rental Office to the *Select DE Output* block's top output connector (economy car) with probability .7 and to the bottom output connector (deluxe car) with probability of .3.

Once the customers are split by car type, Hervis can model the assignment of cars to customers. He begins by focusing upon the deluxe car customers and introduces two more blocks. The lower block and part of its dialog window shown in Figure 10.30 is a *Resource Pool* block (from Resources menu in the DE.lix library). A Resource Pool is a variable that indicates how many of a named constrained resource, Deluxe Cars in this case, are available. In the dialog window Hervis has initialized the resource pool of Deluxe Cars to 100, based upon his "gut feel" of the weekly maximum demand for deluxe cars. The second block and part of its dialog window is a special form of a queuing block, called a *Queue, Resource Pool* block (from Queues menu in the DE.lix library). This block holds items (deluxe-car customers) until the specified number of Resource Pool units from the Deluxe Cars pool are available, one in this case, and then releases the item and decrements the count in the pool, thus in effect, assigning a deluxe car to the customer. Note that the Resource Pool block is a globally accessible variable, tracking the number of deluxe cars on hand in this case, and has no drawn connections to other blocks.

Now that a deluxe customer has received a deluxe car, Hervis must model the rental interval until it is returned. As shown in Figure 10.31, a now-familiar *Activity, Multiple* block (from Activities menu of the DE.lix library) accomplishes this delay using a new *Input Random Number* block (from Inputs/Outputs menu in the GENERIC.lix library) to specify a Normally distributed random delay with mean of 2 days (2880 minutes) and standard deviation of .5 day (720 minutes). Not shown is the capacity of the *Activity, Multiple* block, which defaults to a large number, 1000, to assure that no items would be stopped from entering this block. After the rental time random delay, the car is returned to the

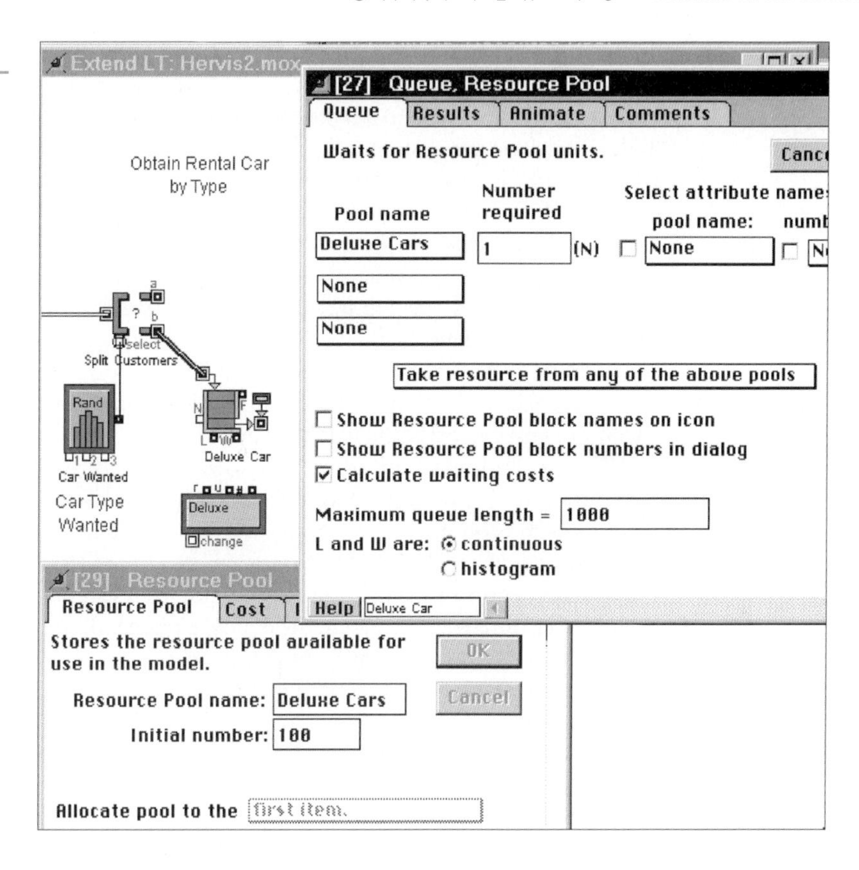

FIGURE 10.30

Assigning Deluxe Cars to Customers from a Resource Pool

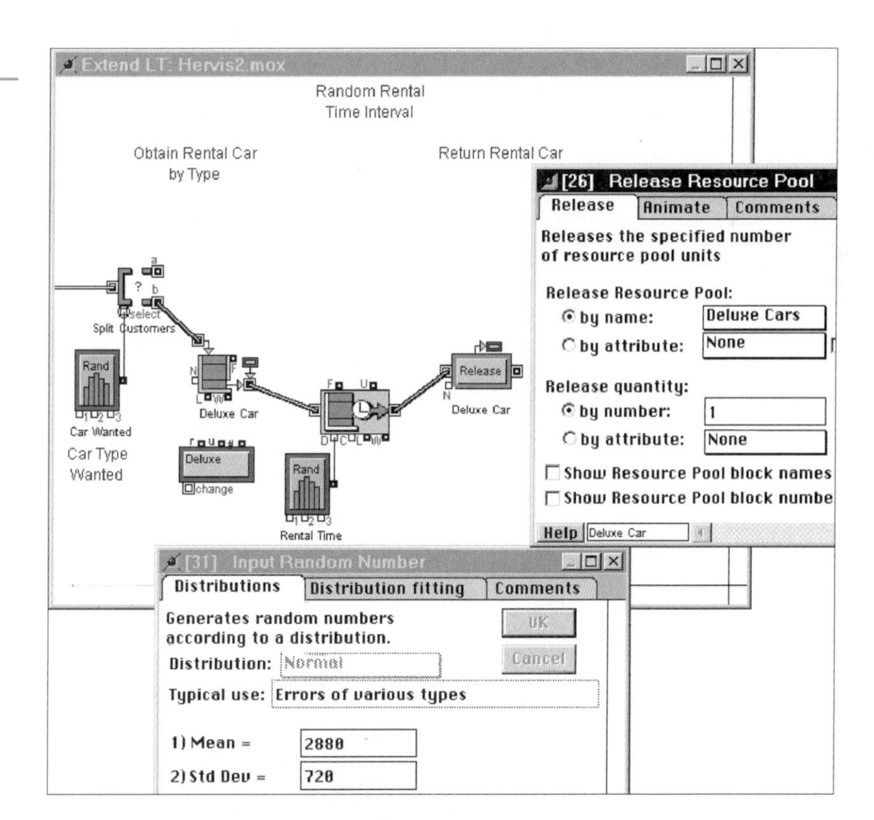

FIGURE 10.31

Rental Delay and Return to Resource Pool of Deluxe Cars

deluxe-car pool to be available for re-renting by the *Release Resource Pool* block (from Resources menu in the DE.lix library) and its dialog window at the right of Figure 10.31.

As shown in Figure 10.32, the modeling of economy-car customers is nearly identical to that of deluxe-car customers. Another *Resource Pool* block (from Resources menu in the DE.lix library) is added for economy cars. Again, based upon his "gut feel" for economy-car demand, Hervis set its initial capacity to 140 (not shown). This is followed by another *Queue, Resource Pool* block (from Queues menu in the DE.lix library) to assign economy cars from the pool, if available, followed in turn by an *Activity, Multiple* block (from Activities menu of the DE.lix library) and its *Input Random Number* block (from Inputs/Outputs menu in the GENERIC.lix library), and another *Release Resource Pool* block (from Resources menu in the DE.lix library) to return the economy car to its pool. Finally, there is an *Exit (4)* block (from Routing menu in the DE.lix library) to allow both streams of customer types to exit the model.

There is an important difference, however, when renting to a customer wanting an economy car. To preserve customer goodwill, Hervis wants to implement a policy of upgrading an economy-car customer to receive a deluxe car, if possible, in the event no economy cars are available. This is implemented in the *Queue, Resource Pool* block's (from the Queue menu in the DE.lix library) dialog window shown in Figure 10.32. Note that both pool resources are named in the dialog. Extend will start at the top of the "Pool name" list and attempt to assign a car from the "Econ. Car" pool. If that pool is empty, it will go to the "Deluxe Car" pool and assign a deluxe car if available. Otherwise, it will hold the customer until one of either car type becomes available, exactly as Hervis desires. However, there is a bookkeeping problem introduced by this approach. The model needs to know what type of car was rented in order to properly credit the correct resource pool later when the car is returned from rental.

The dialog window in Figure 10.32 allows the creation of an "attribute." In Extend, an attribute is a datum attached to an item (customer) that follows it through the blocks of a model. In this case, an attribute called "Car Type" was created by clicking the "pool name" button and creating that name in a pop-up dialog (not shown). During the simulation run, economy-car customers assigned a car from one of the two pools will have the name of that pool carried with them as a Car Type attribute for later reference.

FIGURE 10.32

Assigning Economy Cars to Customers from a Resource Pool

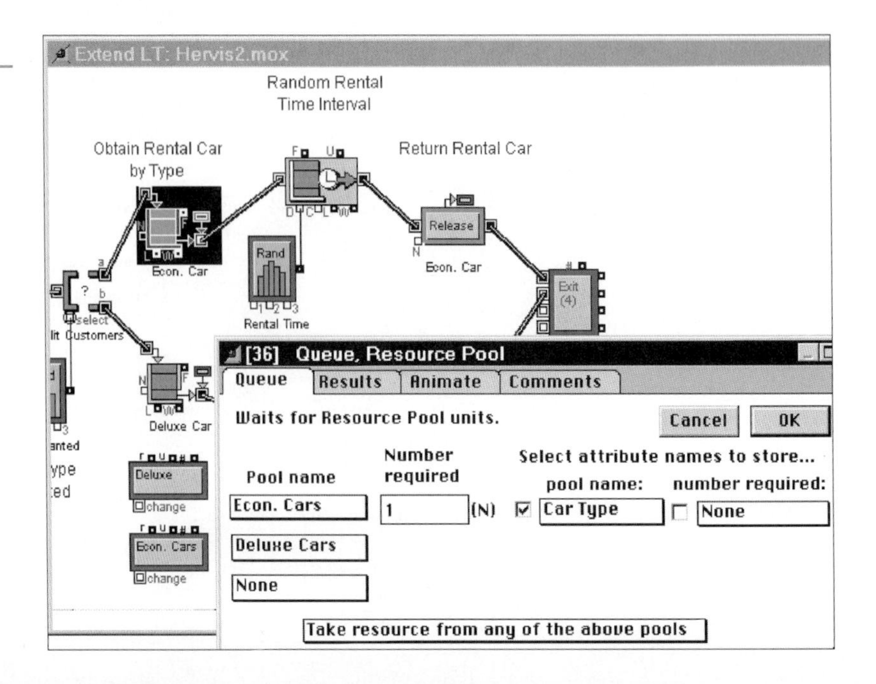

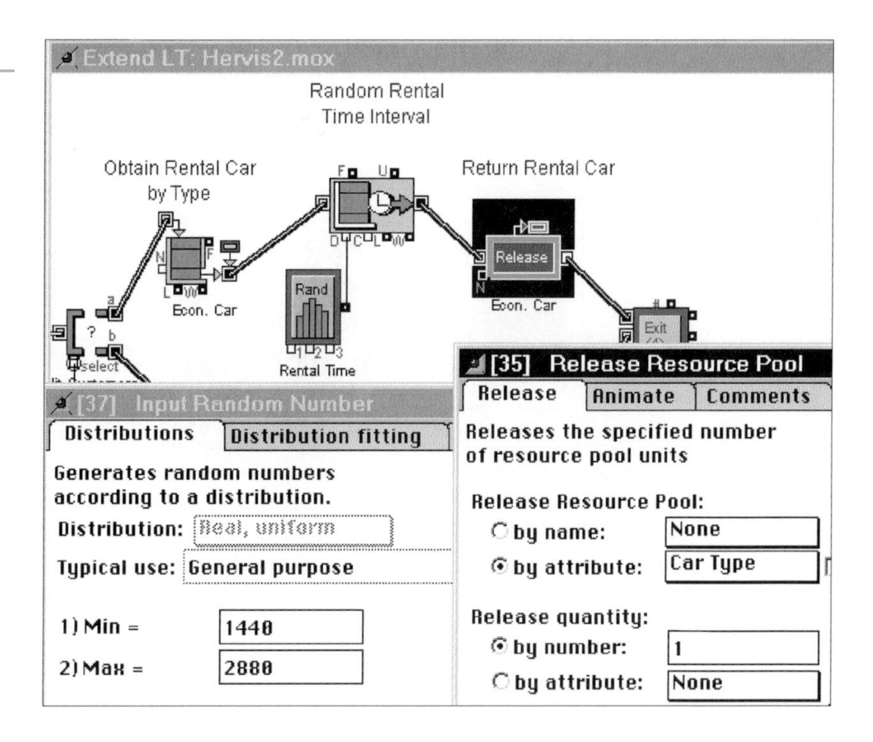

FIGURE 10.33

Rental Delay and Return to Resource Pool of Economy-Car Customers

As shown in the *Release Resource Pool* block's dialog window in Figure 10.33, the returned rental car is credited to whatever pool name was used earlier and carried by the attribute Car Type. Also shown in the figure is the *Input Random Number* block's random rental time, which for an economy-car customer is drawn from a Uniform distribution with range of 1440 to 2880 minutes, that is, one to two days, as Hervis specified.

Figure 10.34 presents the completed model with the addition of *Queue Stats* (from STATS.lrx library), *Help* (from Inputs/Outputs menu in GENERIC.lix library), and *Plotter,*

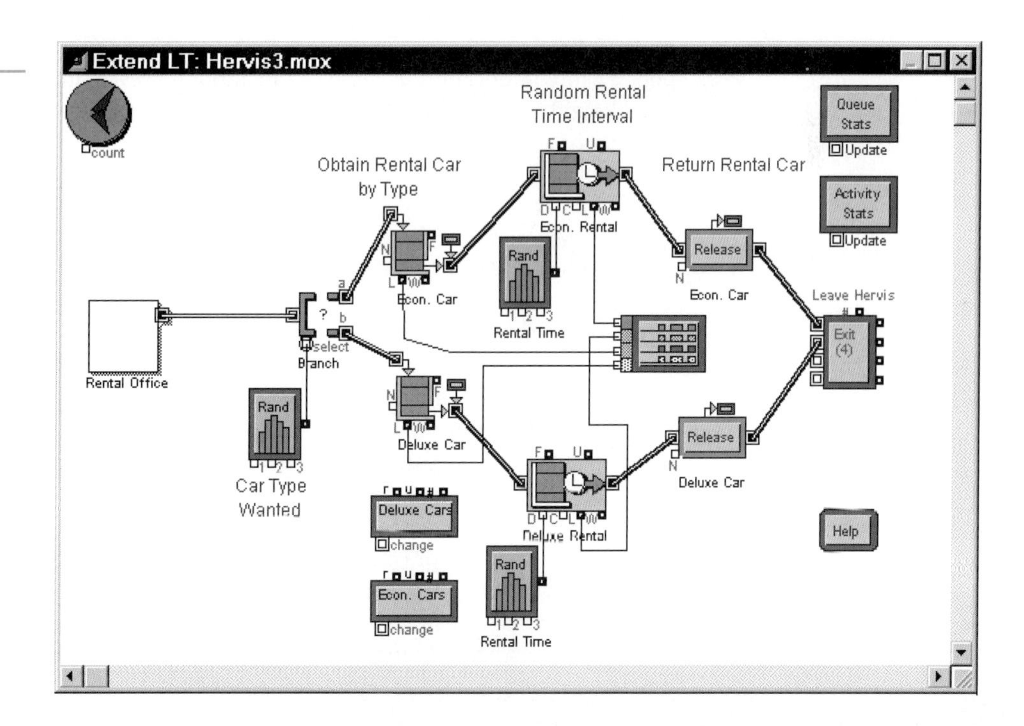

FIGURE 10.34

Final Hervis Car Rental Model

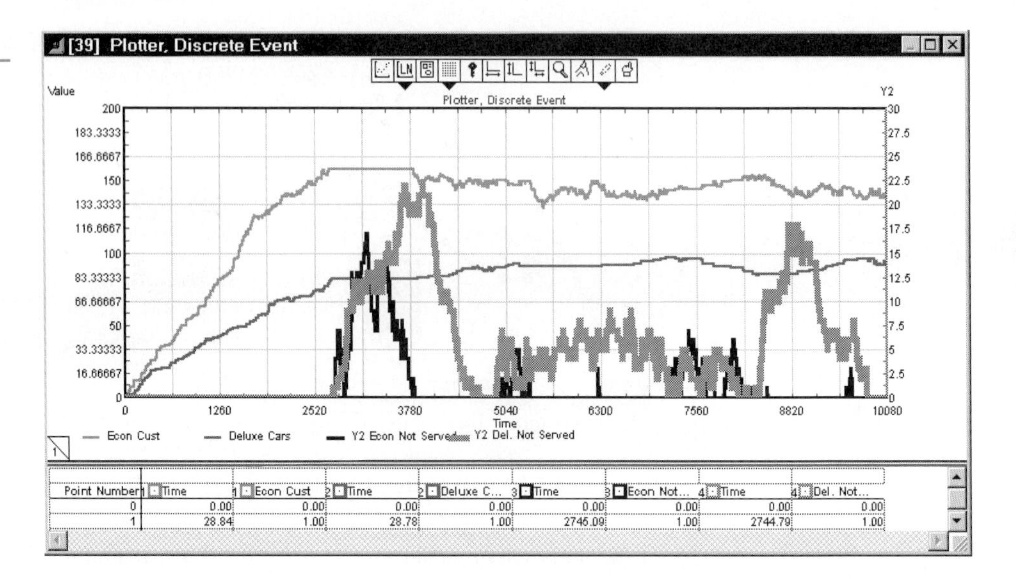

FIGURE 10.35

First Run of Hervis's Car Rental Model

Discrete Event (from PLOTTER.lix library) blocks. A new block has been added, *Activity Stats* (from STATS.lrx library). This block records statistics for the Activity delay blocks just as the *Queue Stats* block does for the Queue blocks, and as with *Queue Stats*, it may be placed anywhere in the model's window. Interpretation of its results is facilitated if all the *Activity, Multiple* blocks are named (by double clicking each to produce its dialog window and typing a name next to the window's Help button). As shown in Figure 10.34, the two *Activity, Multiple* blocks were named Econ. Rental and Deluxe Rental. As was done earlier in Figure 10.25 with the *Queue Stats* block, select the "Append new updates" and "Update at end of simulation" options in the *Activity Stats* dialog window (not shown) to force it to accumulate results across multiple simulation runs.

Figure 10.35 gives the plots of a simulation run with initial resource pools of 140 economy cars and 100 deluxe cars, the values Hervis felt would be sufficient. Using the left scale, the two thin lines give the number of cars of each type being rented during the week, the topmost line being Econ. Cars, which sometimes includes deluxe cars by Hervis' upgrade policy. More important for Hervis' evaluation, however, are the two thick line traces that use the right scale. The dark thick line is for Econ. Car customers arriving on the lot to find it empty of any car to rent, and the shaded thick line is for Deluxe Car customers arriving on the lot to find it empty of a deluxe car to rent.

Clearly, as evidenced by the thick line traces, Hervis's initial car pool sizes are grossly inadequate for his customer demands. This is confirmed as not being a chance outcome by the *Queue Stats* and *Activity Stats* windows shown in Figure 10.36, which give the 95% confidence intervals for the queue and activity delay statistics for 20 simulation runs of the model. For example, the average wait by a deluxe-car customer for a car was 140 ± 49 minutes across the 20 simulation runs, with economy-car customers waiting on average about half as long for any type of car. Worse yet are the maximum waits of 513 ± 96 minutes by a deluxe-car customer and 316 ± 90 minutes by an economy-car customer. Because no customer would tolerate waiting an average of one to two hours or more (or a maximum wait of up to ten hours) to receive a rental car, Hervis must increase his pool sizes. But by how much? Should they be doubled or tripled in size, which, of course, would double or triple Hervis's capital outlay for cars, or increased to something less?

Recalling how sensitive waiting times often are to moderate capacity increases, Hervis elects to experimentally increase each pool's initial size by about 15%, increasing the

FIGURE 10.36

Confidence Interval Statistics for First Run

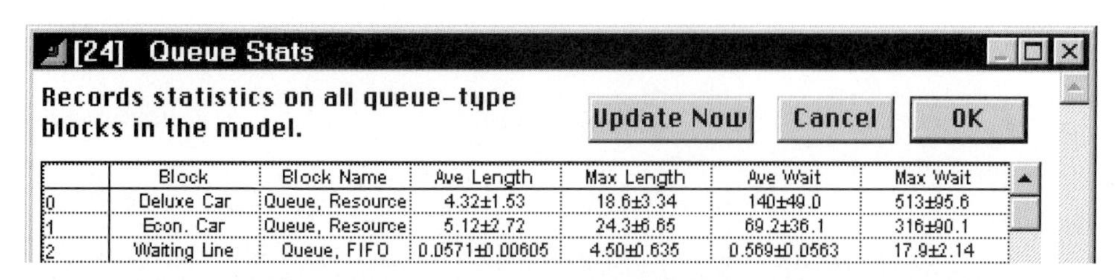

[24] Queue Stats

Records statistics on all queue-type blocks in the model.

Update Now | Cancel | OK

	Block	Block Name	Ave Length	Max Length	Ave Wait	Max Wait
0	Deluxe Car	Queue, Resource	4.32±1.53	18.6±3.34	140±49.0	513±95.6
1	Econ. Car	Queue, Resource	5.12±2.72	24.3±6.65	69.2±36.1	316±90.1
2	Waiting Line	Queue, FIFO	0.0571±0.00605	4.50±0.635	0.569±0.0563	17.9±2.14

[55] Activity Stats

Records statistics on all activity-type blocks in the model.

Update Now | Cancel | OK

	Block	Block Name	Arrivals	Departures	Utilization	Time (min)
0	Deluxe Rental	Activity, Multi	296.1±5.235	210.2±4.909	0.07165±0.00140	
1	Econ. Rental	Activity, Multi	692.0±9.611	541.6±9.664	0.1317±0.002012	
2	Rental Station	Activity, Multi	1009±17.04	1008±16.88	0.2478±0.005509	

FIGURE 10.37

Results for Resource Pools of 160 Economy and 115 Deluxe Cars

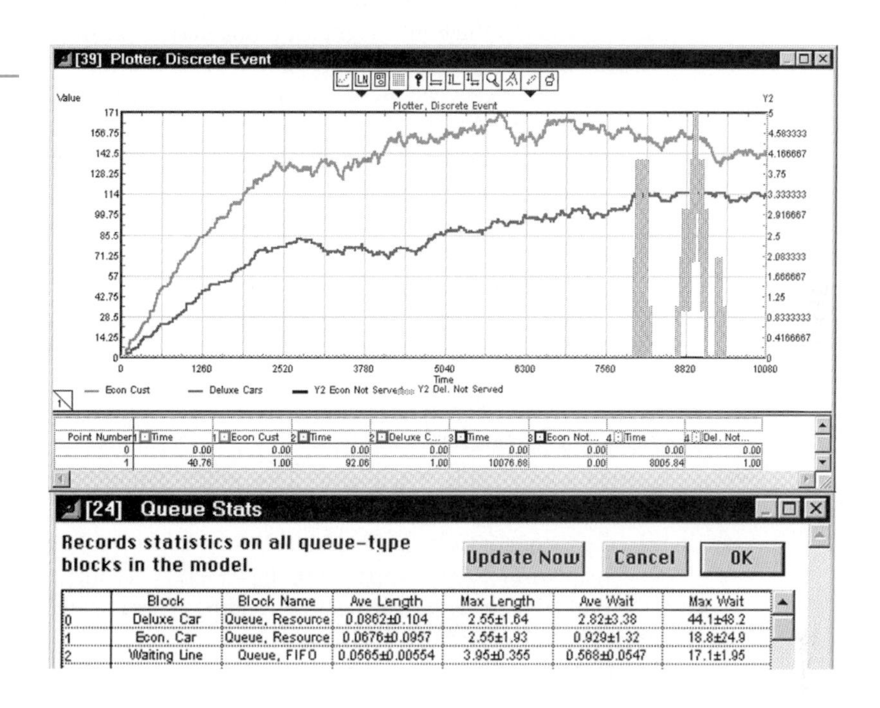

[24] Queue Stats

Records statistics on all queue-type blocks in the model.

Update Now | Cancel | OK

	Block	Block Name	Ave Length	Max Length	Ave Wait	Max Wait
0	Deluxe Car	Queue, Resource	0.0862±0.104	2.55±1.64	2.82±3.38	44.1±48.2
1	Econ. Car	Queue, Resource	0.0676±0.0957	2.55±1.93	0.929±1.32	18.8±24.9
2	Waiting Line	Queue, FIFO	0.0565±0.00554	3.95±0.355	0.568±0.0547	17.1±1.95

TIP: *Extend supports animation that can be turned on in its blocks. Although animation drastically slows execution, it is useful in debugging and demonstrating the simulation to others. Several Extend blocks also allow specifying cost parameters, thus allowing aggregate cost information to be gathered. Finally, the full version of Extend implements optimization. For example, this feature would permit Hervis to construct a model to search for the car resource pool sizes that minimize total cost.*

Deluxe Cars pool to 115 and the Econ. Cars pool to 160. To his relief, a single run shows much improvement, as shown in Figure 10.37. The figure also gives the *Queue Stats* 95% confidence intervals for 20 simulation runs of the model. The dramatic improvement in both average and maximum waiting times, with average waits centered on 2.8 ± 3.3 minutes for deluxe-car customers and centered on .93 ± 1.3 minutes for economy-car customers, suggests to Hervis that his original intuition on pool sizes was just a little too low, but that waiting times for his situation are very sensitive to initial pool sizes.

Although the average waits in Figure 10.37 are acceptable to Hervis, the maximum waits are still too long. Hervis elects to execute another batch of simulation runs using still larger initial resource pools of 170 Econ. Cars and 125 Deluxe Cars. Figure 10.38 gives the *Queue Stats* 95% confidence intervals for 20 simulation runs of the model.

Happy with the waiting results given in Figure 10.38, Hervis decides that further analysis on the effects of initial pool size should await better data on the assumptions he made earlier on the car rental time distributions and on customer arrival rates. He suspects that

FIGURE 10.38

Results for Resource Pools of 170 Economy and 125 Deluxe Cars

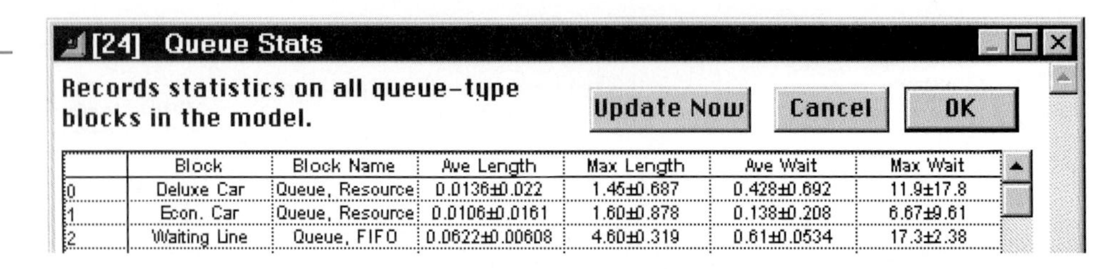

	Block	Block Name	Ave Length	Max Length	Ave Wait	Max Wait
0	Deluxe Car	Queue, Resource	0.0136±0.022	1.45±0.687	0.428±0.692	11.9±17.8
1	Econ. Car	Queue, Resource	0.0106±0.0161	1.60±0.878	0.138±0.208	6.67±9.61
2	Waiting Line	Queue, FIFO	0.0622±0.00608	4.60±0.319	0.61±0.0534	17.3±2.38

waiting times also may be sensitive to small underestimates in those distributions' parameter assumptions and that much more simulation analysis is needed before finalizing decisions on his venture.

10.7 SUMMARY

This chapter was devoted to an introduction of discrete event simulation modeling. Discrete event simulation modeling refers to those models which track the detailed movement of items throughout a complex probabilistic system over time, in order to assess the performance associated with those movements. The concept of discrete event simulation was first illustrated by means of an Excel model for serving customers who must queue for service. Since detailed tracking of individual items (customers) is required, much of the spreadsheet becomes devoted to clerical bookkeeping details for tracking the items as they flow through the system. This quickly leads to very large spreadsheet models that are cumbersome to build, document, and manipulate. Moreover, the representations for tracking items in Excel do not scale well in the sense that changing planning horizons, time grids, or the attributes of resources in the system requires changing the entire spreadsheet model, in effect, rebuilding much of it from scratch for each change.

The shortcomings of discrete event simulation modeling in Excel are overcome by the use of a special-purpose simulation application, such as Extend. A requirement for this approach is a reorientation of thinking away from the row-column orientation of a spreadsheet to the building block structure of an Extend simulation model. The building block orientation is essential to visualize the flow of items and of information among the blocks of the model. Although only a dozen or so of Extend's simulation blocks were introduced in this chapter, out of the more than 100 blocks available, it should be apparent that simulation models are easily built and analyzed using Extend once this orientation is understood.

Simulation provides a vehicle for creating an analogous representation of a real physical system for purposes of observation and experimentation. Like any other modeling endeavor, proper use of simulation places a premium on the accuracy of the model's many assumptions. This is especially true for simulation because the performance of the system often is quite sensitive to the accurate assessment of system randomness into specified probability distributions with given parameters. Moreover, the randomness inherent in any performance measure calculation for a discrete event simulation raises statistical issues that must be addressed when assessing performance: A single simulation run provides only one of many time paths that could have been observed, and assessing the likelihoods of paths requires analysis of multiple simulation runs. In addition, like any dynamic model, discrete event simulation models are influenced by edge conditions.

First introduced in Chapter 5, edge conditions refer to the initial and terminal conditions that influence the starting and ending of dynamic models. For example, in the Hervis rental car models of this chapter it was assumed that there were no outstanding rented cars and no customers in the system at the beginning of each simulation run for a week's operation. If, as is certainly the case for Hervis, these initial conditions are not realistic, then the resulting statistics used as performance measures are affected adversely. In the cases where these initial conditions quickly disappear and in which the performance measure of interest is more long term, then the tactic of making each simulation run very long relative to the time taken for the model to eliminate effects of the initial conditions is the usual approach. This was exemplified in the Hervis models in which it took more than a day of simulated time for the Activity Delay block utilizations to trend toward their theoretical average utilizations. Of course, in other situations the performance of the system immediately after the start of the simulation may be of primary interest. In those cases, properly setting the initial conditions to realistic values is critical for accurate assessments.

The approach to discrete event simulation modeling illustrated in this chapter underscores the basic philosophy of modeling in this book: Start with a simple model of the situation and add complexity in the form of more enhanced models as the situation warrants. The use of Extend's hierarchical blocks to create submodels is a useful way to maintain modularity of the simulator and preserve self-documentation while adding additional complexity to the simulation model.

Readers interested in pursuing the topic of discrete event simulation with Extend should consult the additional documentation topics present on the book's CD-ROM. In addition to an Extend user manual, these topics include additional example models that illustrate many of the other blocks available in building discrete event simulators, and examples of continuous simulation, a feature of Extend not covered in this chapter.

Key Terms

Simulation. The detailed observation of a model of a complex probabilistic system over time.

Continuous Simulation. A simulation involving aggregate variables that change more or less continuously with time.

Discrete Event Simulation. A simulation in which individual items are tracked and in which abrupt or nonsmooth changes in the timing of events is the norm.

Queuing Simulation. A discrete event simulation involving the waiting of items in lines.

Extend. A commercially available graphical application for building discrete event (and continuous) simulation models.

Block. A unit for specifying an action, process, accumulation, statistical summary, or other object describing one part of a simulation model in Extend.

Links. Connections for item flow or data communication among the blocks of a simulation in Extend.

Hierarchical Block. Same as a submodel.

Submodel. A logical grouping of blocks and links in Extend that can be named and used as a new block.

Self-Review Exercises

True-False

1. **T F** Simulation is a substitute for analysis.
2. **T F** The output of a discrete event simulation is a collection of observations on its behavior over time.
3. **T F** Re-running a simulation involving probabilistic distributions will always produce the same set of observations.
4. **T F** Discrete event simulations of queuing models can produce observations that are very sensitive to the assumed probability distributions and their parameters.
5. **T F** Complex discrete event simulation models are very easy to build in Excel.
6. **T F** Complex discrete event simulation models are essentially self-documenting when built in Extend.
7. **T F** Complex discrete event simulation models scale easily to finer time grids and longer time horizons when built in Excel.
8. **T F** Discrete event simulation models are easier to build and analyze in Extend than in Excel.
9. **T F** A discrete event simulation model is a good substitute for executive judgment and experience.
10. **T F** Extend makes it easy to decide which probability distributions are appropriate to use for a discrete event simulation model.
11. **T F** Summarizing the observations across multiple discrete event simulation runs of the same model is always preferred to using the observations from a single simulation run.
12. **T F** Incorporating additional complexity into a discrete event simulation model by adding blocks is easy to do in Extend.

Answers

1. F, **2.** T, **3.** F, **4.** T, **5.** F, **6.** T, **7.** F, **8.** T, **9.** F, **10.** F, **11.** T, **12.** T

Skill Problems

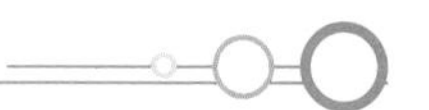

10-1. A discrete event simulation model in Extend is an example of
- **(a)** a physical model
- **(b)** an analog model
- **(c)** a symbolic model

10-2. Assume Hervis's airport van schedule changes. Vans now arrive half as often, that is, every 10 minutes instead of every 5 minutes, but each van delivers twice the frequency count of customers on each trip (0 with probability .7, 2 with probability .12, 4 with probability .16, and 6 with probability .02). The expected batch size of customers is now 1 per van load arriving every 10 minutes. Thus, this new average arrival rate is equivalent to the previous average arrival rate of .5 customers per van load every 5 minutes. Does this change increase, decrease, or have no effect upon rental station waiting times compared to the results of Figure 10.17 for the case when there is only one rental clerk? Use the file Hervis1.mox from Figure 10.14, implement the changes, and simulate to verify your answer.

10-3. A consultant has recommended to Hervis that he use an exponential distribution for airport van interarrival times with the same mean arrival rate of one van every 5 minutes. Does this change increase, decrease, or have no effect upon rental station waiting times compared to the results of Figure 10.21 for the case when there is only one rental clerk? Using the file Hervis1b.mox from Figure 10.20 change the assumed distribution of van arrivals to exponential with mean interarrival time of 5 minutes. Simulate to verify your answer.

10-4. Give a verbal managerial explanation as to why Hervis's variable staffing policy described in Section 10.5 performed worse in terms of customers' waiting times than a policy of always using the two clerks at the rental station.

10-5. All of Hervis's statistics in, for example, Figure 10.37 are misleading because he assumes that both resource pools of cars start out at the beginning of each week at their initial values. As shown in the figure, this initial condition produces short waits early in the week because it assumes that in effect all outstanding rental cars immediately return back to their resource pools at the end of the previous week. How can Hervis reduce this bias in his average waiting time statistics caused by this initial condition of resource pools?

Application Problems

10-6. In the Rental Office model in Figure 10.20, which included uncertainty in airport van interarrival times and rental station service times, customers were assumed to exit to the car lot after completing their rental contracts at the rental station. This is actually how it works for 95% of Hervis's customers. The remaining 5% of customers instead of exiting, return to the rental office because their rental contract contained an error. Assume that upon returning they join the end of any waiting queue of customers and in effect will repeat their rental contracting process, as if starting over again as a new customer. Using the file Hervis1b.mox from Figure 10.20, modify the model to accommodate this recycling of 5% of customers. Simulate and compare the effects of this change upon the results reported in Figure 10.21. HINT: Investigate the *Combine* block (from the Routing menu in the DE.lix library).

10-7. Model the same situation as in Problem 10-6 involving 5% of customers recycling back through the rental office, except recycled customers go to the head of any queue of waiting customers. Simulate and compare the effects of this change upon the results reported in Figure 10.21. *Hint*: Investigate the *Set Priority* block (from Attributes menu in the DE.lix library) and the *Queue Priority* block (from Queues menu in the DE.lix library).

10-8. Hervis's variable staffing policy described in Section 10.5 performed worse in terms of customers' waiting times than a policy of always using the two-clerk rental station policy. To investigate why in more detail, modify the queue lengths conversion table for changing the number of rental station clerks given in Figure 10.23 to new values you think superior to Hervis's rule and simulate to see the results. Does your new policy outperform the simple two-clerk rental station staffing policy? If so, does your new policy increase the average number of rental clerks at the rental station to greater than two? HINT: investigate the *Mean and Variance* block (from Statistics menu in the GENERIC.lix library) to summarize the number of clerks your policy uses.

10-9. Hervis has decided to revise the Rental Office model in Figure 10.20. It turns out a competitor car rental company is located just across the street from Hervis. Called reneging, customers waiting in line more than 15 minutes to receive service at the rental station become impatient, exit the queue, and leave Hervis taking their car rental business to the competitor. Using the file Hervis1b.mox from Figure 10.20, modify the model to accommodate this reneging of customers. Simulate and compare the effects of this change upon the results reported in Figure 10.21. On average, how many customers renege as a function of the number of rental station clerks? *Hint*: Investigate the *Queue, Reneging* block from the Queues menu in the MFG.1rx library.

10-10. Hervis has decided to further revise the Rental Office model in Figure 10.20. It turns out a competitor car rental company is located just across the street from Hervis. Called balking, 10% of Hervis's arriving customers will refuse to even join the Rental Office queue if they observe it to be longer than six waiting customers, and leave Hervis taking their car rental business to the competitor. The other 90% of Hervis customers will join the Rental Office queue no matter how long it is. Using the file Hervis1b.mox from Figure 10.20, modify the model to accommodate this balking of 10% of customers. Simulate and compare the effects of this change upon the results reported in Figure 10.21. On average, how many customers balk as a function of the number of rental station clerks?

10-11. Hervis has issued Premium Gold rental cards to 10% of his customers. Such "Gold" customers have their contracts already in Hervis's computers and simply bypass the Rental Office upon exiting the airport van. Instead, they proceed directly from the airport van to the car lot to claim a rental car by having their Premium Gold customer number swiped by a smart card reader. Gold customers have a stronger preference for deluxe cars: 50% prefer to rent deluxe cars and 50% prefer to rent economy cars. Hervis extends the same upgrade policy to Gold economy-car customers as regular economy-car customers: If an economy-car is not available, they receive a deluxe car if available. Also, Gold customers tend to keep their rental cars out for longer times: Deluxe cars for three days ± half day, and economy cars for two to three days. (Hervis assumes the underlying distributions of rental times are the same as for regular customers, Normal for deluxe cars and Uniform for economy cars.) Using the file Hervis3.mox from Figure 10.34, modify the model to accommodate both Gold and non-Gold customers. Simulate and compare the effects of this change upon the results reported in Figure 10.38. How does this change affect the recommended initial pool sizes of economy and deluxe cars?

10-12. Hervis realizes he has been unrealistic in his assumptions of the demand for his rental cars. First, Hervis has decided to use an exponential distribution for airport van interarrival times as being a better fit to the timing of his airport van interarrivals. Second, he had assumed that the level of airport activity that generated the stream of customers delivered by the airport van was constant throughout every 24-hour day. In fact the airport passenger traffic slows down in the evening hours and declines substantially after midnight until picking up again in the late morning. Hervis has altered the daily schedule of his airport vans to reflect this variation in customer traffic. Thus, Hervis would like to modify his model to shift the airport van interarrival times to an exponential distribution, but whose mean interarrival times change throughout the day, as given by the table below.

TIME INTERVAL	AIRPORT VAN MEAN INTERARRIVAL TIMES
Midnight–5:59 A.M.	30
6 A.M.–8:59 A.M.	15
9 A.M.–11:59 A.M.	10
Noon–6:59 P.M.	5
7 P.M.–8:59 P.M.	10
9 P.M.–11:59 P.M.	15

Although the arrival rate of airport vans will now vary throughout the day, Hervis believes that the distribution of the number of customers per airport van load should remain as in his original model. Using the file Hervis3.mox from Figure 10.34, modify the model to accommodate this varying parameter change in airport van interarrivals. Simulate and compare the effects of this change upon the results reported in Figure 10.38. How does this change affect the recommended initial pool sizes of economy and deluxe cars? Assume the simulation start time of 0 minutes corresponds to midnight of the first day. Thus, the simulation run begins on midnight of day 1 and continues up to just before midnight of day 7. HINT: Investigate the *Input data* block from the Input/Output menu in the GENERIC.lix library.

10-13. Recently, Dairy Burger, a fast food restaurant, ran a major ad campaign to attract noon hour customers using its drive-through service. They guaranteed that between 12-1 P.M. their customers would average no more than four minutes from the time they entered the Dairy Burger drive through until the time they received their food. To ensure the success of their new campaign, Dairy Burger must determine how many employees they need over the noon hour and where they work so that customers get their food in an average of four minutes or less. The following factors must be considered:

(a) Drive through customers queue up first-in, first-out before three service stations to get their food, the ordering window where the food order is placed, the pay window where the order is paid for, and the pickup window where the food is received.

(b) Normal staff at Dairy Burger during lunch is three to five employees, at least one of which must be assigned to each window.

(c) Assume that customer interarrival times during the noon hour are exponentially distributed with a mean of 3 minutes and that the drive through window is empty of customers at the start of the noon hour.

(d) Assume the window service times are given by the following probability distributions.

ORDERING SERVICE TIME (MIN.)	PROBABILITY	PAY WINDOW SERVICE TIME (MIN.)	PROBABILITY	PICKUP WINDOW SERVICE TIME (MIN.)	PROBABILITY
.60	0.07	.1	0.05	.4	0.05
.65	0.10	.2	0.11	.5	0.11
.70	0.14	.3	0.13	.6	0.13
.75	0.26	.4	0.23	.7	0.23
.80	0.22	.5	0.18	.8	0.18
.85	0.16	.6	0.21	.9	0.21
.90	0.05	.7	0.09	1.0	0.09

(a) What will the average customer throughput time be at Dairy Burger with three lunch-time workers, one at each window? Throughput time is the total time a customer spends in the Dairy Burger drive-through from entering the drive-through until receiving their food. HINT: In Extend the time of system entry for a customer can be gotten from the "current time" in the *System Variable* block (Generic.lix) and stored in a named attribute for each customer via a *Set Attribute* block (DE.lix). Just before the customer exits that stored entry time can be retrieved via a *Get Attribute* block (DE.lix) and subtracted via a *Subtract* block (Generic.lix) from the current time just before his exit, gotten from a second System Variable block (Generic.lix). The difference is that customer's throughput time which can be averaged over all customers via the *Mean and Variance* block (Generic.lix).

(b) What percentage of customers will not receive their food within four minutes? HINT: A histogram of the customer throughput times calculated in part a. can be created via the *Histogram Plotter* block (Plotter.lix).

(c) If Dairy Burger can allocate a total of five workers to the drive through process, which window(s) should the two additional workers be assigned to and what will be the effect upon the average customer throughput time and the percentage of customers who will not receive service in four minutes?

(d) Dairy Burger has limited space to allow for queued cars in front of the Pay and Pickup windows. There is space for only two cars in front of the Pay Window and space for only two cars in front of the Pickup Window. If the queue ahead is full, upstream cars cannot advance until a departure from that queue occurs even if their service at the upstream window is completed. How would your staffing recommendations change, if at all, for part c. under this new condition and what will be the effect upon the average customer throughput time and the percentage of customers who will not receive service in four minutes?

(e) Assume that Dairy Burger could reconfigure its space to allow up to three cars to queue for the Pay Window, but leaving only one space for cars to queue for the Pickup window. Alternatively, Dairy Burger could reconfigure its space to allow up to three cars to queue for the Pickup Window, but this would leave only one space for cars to queue for the Pay window. Which of the three queue configurations, one in d. and two in this part do you recommend Dairy Burger adopt and how would your staffing recommendations change, if at all, under this new condition and what will be the effect upon the average customer throughput time and the percentage of customers who will not receive service in four minutes?

(f) Instead of reconfiguring the queues for the Pay and the Pickup windows, as in part e., assume that Dairy Burger could pool the latter two operations of paying and food pickup. In this scheme the Pay Window would be closed and both payment and food pickup would be done at the Pickup Window. The time to complete the combined payment and pickup activities is assumed to be the sum of the times for each probability category in the original Pay and Pickup service time tables. The space for cars to queue in front of the combined window is four cars. How would your staffing recommendations change under this new alternative and what will be the effect upon the average customer throughput time and the percentage of customers who will not receive service in four minutes?

Develop a summary report to Burger Dairy management with your noon-time drive through staffing, queuing space, and window configuration recommendations.

10-14. Speed-of-Light Lube is a quick lube shop managed by Sue Cruz. Recently a competitor opened up shop down the street from Speed-of-Light Lube, making Sue re-examine her operation's efficiency. Speed-of-Light has a total of four bays for changing oil, thus accommodating at most four cars at a time. When all four bays are occupied customers queue up outside the facility in their cars for an available bay on a first-in, first-out basis. Speed-of-Light Lube has the following times between arrivals and oil change times:

TIME BETWEEN ARRIVALS (MIN.)	PROBABILITY
3	0.45
4	0.23
5	0.15
6	0.11
7	0.06

TIME TO CHANGE OIL (MIN.)	PROBABILITY
8	0.22
10	0.19
12	0.32
14	0.27

During the oil-change process, mechanics attempt to "up-sell" customers having worn out air filters into buying new air filters for their vehicles. Customers not wanting their car's air filter changed depart immediately from their bay after completion of the oil-change. Customers electing to change their car's air-filter continue to occupy an oil-change bay during the additional time it takes to change the air filter. Currently, up-sells take place 10% of the time and the time to install the new filter is as follows:

TIME TO CHANGE FILTER (MIN.)	PROBABILITY
5	0.07
6	0.25
7	0.43
8	0.25

An air filter replacement is not started on a car until after the oil change is completed. Sue's staffing allows at most three oil-changes to be done simultaneously and at most two air-filter changes to be done simultaneously, provided that the total of oil changes and filter replacements being done at the same time never exceeds the four available bays. She has decided that an average wait time in the queue outside the facility greater than four minutes will be bad for her business. Build an Extend model to simulate Sue's business. Assume Sue's facility is open for 16 hours a day and is empty of cars when it opens.

(a) What is the average waiting time for a customer to enter one of Sue's four bays?

(b) How much can Sue increase the proportion of up-sells without causing the average waiting time for a customer to enter one of Sue's four bays to exceed four minutes?

(c) What would be the effect on the average waiting time for a customer to enter one of Sue's four bays if Sue were to increase her staffing to allow more than three oil-changes simultaneously?

Develop a report to Sue summarizing your results with recommendations for staffing and up sell proportions, assuming she is limited to no more than four bays in her facility.

10-15. Pat West runs a small copy center in Eastville. Because Eastville is a small out-of-the-way destination, it takes two weeks to receive new toner cartridges for his copiers. Toner cartridges last for 10,000 copies each (10K). The copy center has the following information on weekly averages for copies made:

COPIES PER WEEK	PROBABILITY
10,000	0.12
20,000	0.25
30,000	0.41
40,000	0.17
50,000	0.05

Pat loses $7,000 per week that he cannot make copies. Each toner cartridge order costs $10 to place and toner cartridges cost $100 each. Develop an Excel simulation model to answer the questions below.

(a) Simulate 52 weeks of operation assuming he reorders 10 cartridges whenever his inventory drops to a reorder point of 6 or less at the end of each week. What percent of the time does he stockout? Is this acceptable?

(b) Add the further uncertainty that lead time for receiving new toner cartridges is also random and is distributed as follows: 25% chance for 1 week; 50% chance for 2 weeks; 25% chance for 3 weeks. Now, what do you recommend as an inventory policy (reorder quantity and reorder point)?

(c) Add the further uncertainty that cartridge duration is also random and is distributed as follows: 10% chance it lasts for 8K copies; 15% chance it lasts for 9K copies; 50% chance for 10K copies; 15% chance for 11K copies; 10% chance for 12K copies. Now, what do you recommend as an inventory policy (reorder quantity and reorder point)?

Case Study | Snowy Range Hardware[1]

Snowy Range Hardware (SRH) sells the Ace model electric drill. Daily demand for the drill is relatively low, but subject to some variability. Over the past 300 days, SRH has observed the sales shown in column 2 of Exhibit 1. This historical frequency is converted into a probability distribution for the variable daily demand (column 3). A cumulative probability distribution is formed in column 4 of Exhibit 1. Finally, SRH establishes an interval of random numbers to represent each possible daily demand (column 5).

When SRH places an order to replenish the inventory of drills, there is a delivery lag of from 1 to 3 days. This means that lead time may also be considered a probabilistic variable. The number of days that it took to receive the past 50 orders is presented in Exhibit 2. In a fashion similar to the creation of the demand variable, SRH establishes a probability distribution for the lead time variable (column 3 of Exhibit 2), computes the cumulative distribution (column 4), and assigns random-number intervals for each possible time (column 5).

The first inventory policy that SRH wants to simulate is an order quantity of 10 with a reorder point of 5. That is, every time the on-hand inventory level at the end of the day is 5 or less, SRH will call the supplier that evening and place an order for 10 more drills. Note that if the lead time is 1 day, the order will not arrive the next morning, but rather at the beginning of the following workday.

The entire process is simulated in Exhibit 3 for a 10-day period. We assume that beginning inventory (column 3) is 10 units on day 1. The random numbers (column 4) were generated in Excel.

Exhibit 3 was filled in by proceeding 1 day (or line) at a time, working from left to right. It is a four-step process:

1. Begin each simulated day by checking to see whether any ordered inventory has just arrived. If it has, increase current inventory by the quantity ordered (10 units, in this case).
2. Generate a daily demand from the demand probability distribution by generating a random number.

[1] *Note:* This case was adapted from Heizer and Render's *Operations Management*, 1999 (5th edition), Prentice Hall.

EXHIBIT 1 Probabilities and Random-Number Intervals for Daily Ace Drill Demand

(1) DEMAND FOR ACE DRILL	(2) FREQUENCY	(3) PROBABILITY	(4) CUMULATIVE PROBABILITY	(5) INTERVAL OF RANDOM NUMBERS
0	15	.05	.05	.00 through .0499
1	30	.10	.15	.05 through .1499
2	60	.20	.35	.15 through .3499
3	120	.40	.75	.35 through .7499
4	45	.15	.90	.75 through .8999
5	30	.10	1.00	.90 through .9999
	300 days	1.00		

Theoretical mean = 0 * 0.05 + 1 * 0.10 + 2 * 0.20 + 3 * 0.40 + 4 * 0.15 + 5 * 0.10 = 2.80

EXHIBIT 2 Probabilities and Random-Number Intervals for Lead Time Distribution

(1) LEAD TIME (DAYS)	(2) FREQUENCY	(3) PROBABILITY	(4) CUMULATIVE PROBABILITY	(5) RANDOM-NUMBER INTERVAL
1	10	.20	.20	.00 through .1999
2	25	.50	.70	.20 through .6999
3	15	.30	1.00	.70 through .9999
	50 orders	1.00		

Theoretical mean = 1 * 0.20 + 2 * 0.50 + 3 * 0.30 = 2.10

EXHIBIT 3 Queuing Simulation (10 Days) for Snowy Range Hardware

(1) DAY	(2) UNITS RECEIVED	(3) BEGINNING INVENTORY	(4) RANDOM NUMBER	(5) DEMAND	(6) ENDING INVENTORY	(7) LOST SALES	(8) ORDER?	(9) RANDOM NUMBER	(10) LEAD TIME
1		10	.06	1	9	0	No		
2	0	9	.63	3	6	0	No		
3	0	6	.57	3	3[1]	0	Yes	.02	1
4	0	3	.94	5	0	2	No[2]		
5	10[3]	10	.52	3	7	0	No		
6	0	7	.69	3	4	0	Yes	.33	2
7	0	4	.32	2	2	0	No		
8	0	2	.30	2	0	0	No		
9	10[4]	10	.48	3	7	0	No		
10	0	7	.88	4	3	0	Yes	.14	1
					Total 41	2			

[1] This is the first time inventory dropped to (or below) the reorder point of 5 drills. Because no prior order was outstanding, an order is placed.
[2] No order is placed on day 4 because there is an order outstanding from the previous day that has not yet arrived.
[3] The lead time for the first order placed is 1 day, but as noted in the text, an order does not arrive the next morning, but rather the beginning of the following day. Thus, the first order arrives at the start of day 5.
[4] This is the arrival of the order placed at the close of business on day 6. Fortunately for SRH, no lost sales occurred during the 2-day lead time before the order arrived.

3. Compute ending inventory = beginning inventory minus demand. If on-hand inventory is insufficient to meet the day's demand, satisfy as much as possible and note the number of lost sales.
4. Determine whether the day's ending inventory has reached the reorder point (5 units). If it has, and if there are no outstanding orders, place an order. Lead time for a new order is simulated by choosing a random number and using the distribution in Exhibit 2.

SRH's first inventory simulation yields some interesting results. The average daily ending inventory is:

$$\text{Average ending inventory} = \frac{41 \text{ total units}}{10 \text{ days}} = 4.1 \text{ units/day}$$

We also note the average lost sales and number of orders placed per day:

$$\text{Average lost sales} = \frac{2 \text{ sales lost}}{10 \text{ days}} = .2 \text{ unit/day}$$

$$\text{Average number of orders placed} = \frac{3 \text{ orders}}{10 \text{ days}} = .3 \text{ order/day}$$

Questions

1. Create this situation as a simulation in Excel and run it for 20 different 10-day periods.
2. What changes would you suggest to SRH's inventory policy (reorder point and reorder quantity) in order to decrease the number of lost sales? What is the corresponding increase in average ending inventory?

Case Study Mississippi Barges[1]

Following long trips down the Mississippi River from industrial midwestern cities, fully loaded barges arrive at night in New Orleans. The number of barges docking on any given night ranges from 0 to 5. The probability of 0, 1, 2, 3, 4, and 5 arrivals is displayed in Exhibit 1. In the same table, we establish cumulative probabilities and corresponding random-number intervals for each possible value.

A study by the dock superintendent reveals that the number of barges unloaded also tends to vary from day to day. In Exhibit 2, the superintendent provides information from which

EXHIBIT 1 Overnight Barge Arrival Rates and Random-Number Intervals

NUMBER OF ARRIVALS	PROBABILITY	CUMULATIVE PROBABILITY	RANDOM-NUMBER INTERVAL
0	.13	.13	.00 through .1299
1	.17	.30	.13 through .2999
2	.15	.45	.30 through .4499
3	.25	.70	.45 through .6999
4	.20	.90	.70 through .8999
5	.10	1.00	.90 through .9999
	1.00		

Theoretical mean = 0 * 0.13 + 1 * 0.17 + 2 * 0.15 + 3 * 0.25 + 4 * 0.20 + 5 * 0.10 = 2.52

EXHIBIT 2 Unloading Rates and Random-Number Intervals

DAILY UNLOADING RATES	PROBABILITY	CUMULATIVE PROBABILITY	RANDOM-NUMBER INTERVAL
1	.05	.05	.00 through .0499
2	.15	.20	.05 through .1999
3	.50	.70	.20 through .6999
4	.20	.90	.70 through .8999
5	.10	1.00	.90 through .9999
	1.00		

Theoretical mean = 1 * 0.05 + 2 * 0.15 + 3 * 0.50 + 4 * 0.20 + 5 * 0.10 = 3.15

[1] *Note:* This case was adapted from Heizer and Render's *Operations Management*, 1999 (5th edition), Prentice Hall.

EXHIBIT 3 Queuing Simulation of Mississippi Barge Unloadings

(1) DAY	(2) NUMBER DELAYED FROM PREVIOUS DAY	(3) RANDOM NUMBER	(4) NUMBER OF NIGHTLY ARRIVALS	(5) TOTAL TO BE UNLOADED	(6) RANDOM NUMBER	(7) NUMBER UNLOADED
1	—[1]	.52	3	3	.37	3
2	0	.06	0	0	.63	0[2]
3	0	.50	3	3	.28	3
4	0	.88	4	4	.02	1
5	3	.53	3	6	.74	4
6	2	.29	1	3	.35	3
7	0	.10	0	0	.24	0[3]
8	0	.47	3	3	.03	1
9	2	.99	5	7	.29	3
10	4	.37	2	6	.60	3
11	3	.66	3	6	.74	4
12	2	.91	5	7	.85	4
13	3	.35	2	5	.89	4
14	1	.32	2	3	.73	3[4]
15	0	.94	5	5	.59	3
	20 Total delays		41 Total arrivals			39 Tot. unloadings

[1] We can begin with no delays from the previous day. In a long simulation, even if we started with 5 overnight delays, that initial condition would be averaged out.
[2] There barges could have been unloaded on day 2. Yet because there were no arrivals and no backlog existed, zero unloadings took place.
[3] The same situation as noted in footnote 2 takes place.
[4] This time, 4 barges could have been unloaded, but because only 3 were in queue, the number unloaded is recorded as 3.

we can create a probability distribution for the variable *daily unloading rate.* As we just did for the arrival variable, we can set up an interval of random numbers for the unloading rates.

Barges are unloaded on a first-in, first-out basis. Any barges not unloaded on the day of arrival must wait until the following day. However, tying up barges in dock is an expensive proposition, and the superintendent cannot ignore the angry phone calls from barge owners reminding him that "time is money!" He decides that, before going to the Port of New Orleans controller to request additional unloading crews, he should conduct a simulation study of arrivals, unloading, and delays. A 100-day simulation would be ideal, but for purposes of illustration, the superintendent begins with a shorter 15-day analysis. Random numbers are generated in Excel for the daily arrival rates and the daily unloading rates. Exhibit 3 shows the day-to-day port simulation.

The superintendent will likely be interested in at least three useful and important pieces of information:

$$\left(\begin{array}{c}\text{Average number of barges}\\ \text{delayed to the next day}\end{array}\right) = \frac{20 \text{ delays}}{15 \text{ days}}$$
$$= 1.33 \text{ barges delayed per day}$$

$$\begin{array}{c}\text{Average number of}\\ \text{nightly arrivals}\end{array} = \frac{41 \text{ arrivals}}{15 \text{ days}}$$
$$= 2.73 \text{ arrivals per night}$$

$$\begin{array}{c}\text{Average number of barges}\\ \text{unloaded each day}\end{array} = \frac{39 \text{ unloadings}}{15 \text{ days}}$$
$$= 2.60 \text{ unloadings per day}$$

Questions

1. Create this situation as an Excel model and simulate 100 days of operation.
2. Create this situation as an Extend model and simulate 100 days operation. HINT: The average number of barges delayed to the next day is approximately equal to the number of departures from the arrivals queue multiplied by the average queue wait divided by the simulation run time.
3. What can the superintendent do to decrease the number of barges delayed per day? What is the trade-off of such a move?

Case Study California Cooperative Bank[1]

As part of a business process re-engineering project, your consulting team at the California Cooperative Bank has been analyzing videotapes from the bank's security cameras. Based on two weeks of tapes, you have estimated that:

a. The interarrival times for customers appear to have an average value of 40 seconds, with no particular pattern during the 8-hour business day. The statistics expert on your team suggests that the exponential distribution "is always used to model arrivals."

b. Ninety percent of the customers visit the tellers while 10% of the customers must see one of two branch managers. At this preliminary stage of your analysis, you can assume that the same customer will not visit both a teller and a manager. (Alternatively, you could assume that a customer who needs to see the tellers and the managers can be considered a new customer each time.)

c. The floor plan of the bank is laid out to encourage customers to enter a single line for teller service. The queue extends across the center of the bank, and funnels customers to the next available teller. A separate, somewhat more informal line tends to form in front of the managers' desks, and most customers move to whichever manager is available.

e. The average service encounter with a teller lasts 5 minutes. Your statistics expert suggests that it looks normally distributed to him, but that you should use a Log Normal Distribution to avoid negative values. His "eyeball estimate" of the standard deviation is about 2.5 minutes. You have less data on the customer discussions with the managers. The average value is 12 minutes, but the encounters vary from the quick drop-off of a document to long sessions involving opening new accounts. Your Excel worksheet shows a computed standard deviation of 10 minutes.

A competing bank has begun to advertise that their customers' average wait for teller service is less than 90 seconds, and one of your tasks is to determine whether California Cooperative can meet that challenge. While no standard for the managers' customers has been set, your team thinks that 5 minutes is a reasonable average waiting period. The Information Technology expert on your team views the situation as ripe for a Web-based-banking campaign and the installation of three new ATMs (automated teller machine), but your client is tired of hearing her competitor's ads on the car radio every morning, and wants to equal their performance standard right now. What staffing levels will be necessary for California Cooperative Bank to offer competitive service?

[1] Written by Professor James Patell.

References

Youngho Lee and Amie Elcan, "Simulation Modeling for Process Reengineering in the Telecommunications Industry," *Interfaces*, 26, no. 3 (1996): 1–9.

Edward Watson, "An Application of Discrete-Event Simulation for Batch-Process Chemical-Plant Design," *Interfaces*, 27, no. 6 (1997): 35–50.

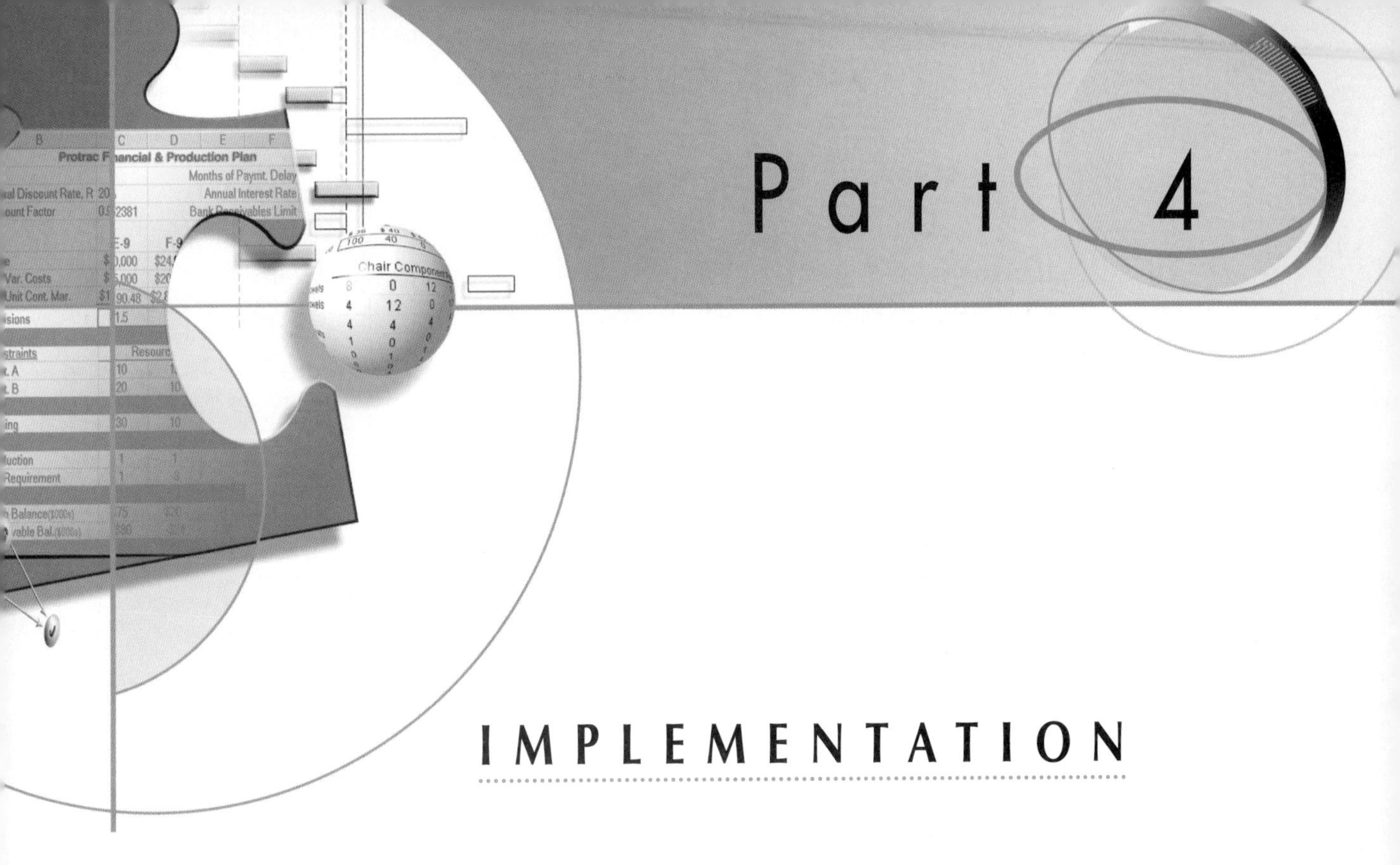

Part 4

IMPLEMENTATION

It is fair to assume that you have become much more comfortable with the prospect of using spreadsheet-based modeling techniques to improve decision making. The purpose of this part, however, is to point out that, just as knowledge of Excel is insufficient without modeling concepts, your knowledge of spreadsheet modeling alone is insufficient for truly affecting decision making in organizations. Long experience with the application of modeling by many practitioners in real organizations has confirmed the observation that creating the model itself, although an important first step, is far from sufficient in the process of systematically improving decision making in the real world of business enterprise. There are many reasons why decision-makers in real situations do not make good decisions. This part presents three conceptual frameworks for understanding how failure of modeling in organizations comes about and a list of the most common reasons why modeling fails to improve the process of decision making. We conclude with a large case concerning a real company in which a promising modeling effort ran into trouble.

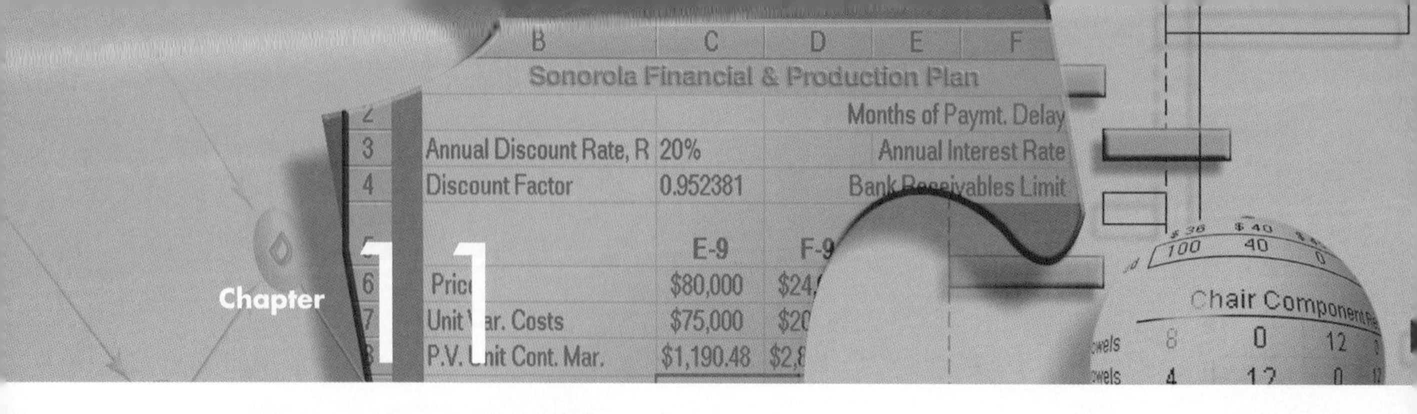

Chapter 11

IMPLEMENTATION

CHAPTER OUTLINE

11.1 INTRODUCTION

Thus far in your reading of this book, it is fair to assume that you have become much more comfortable with the prospect of using spreadsheet-based modeling techniques to improve decision making. Certainly, spreadsheet know-how and modeling concepts are a potent combination for improving your understanding of complex decision-making situations and applying that understanding in the real world. And we hope we have achieved our objective of augmenting your knowledge of Excel with important concepts of modeling in a variety of situations, including those circumstances such as discrete event simulation, where Excel is not the best choice of modeling technology. The purpose of this chapter, however, is to point out that, just as knowledge of Excel is insufficient without modeling concepts, your knowledge of spreadsheet modeling alone is insufficient for truly affecting decision making in organizations.

This last observation is sometimes received with surprise by students new to the use of spreadsheet modeling to support decision making. Certainly, the work that is involved in mastering spreadsheet modeling concepts is challenging, especially at first. In spite of this, long experience with the application of modeling by many practitioners in real organizations has confirmed the observation that creating the model itself, although an important first step, is far from sufficient in the process of systematically improving decision making in the real world of business enterprise. That is, there are many reasons why decision-makers in real situations do not make good decisions, and inadequate modeling is one of them. However, it does not follow that improving the quality of modeling alone necessarily leads to improved real-world decisions. There are many reasons for this, and purpose of this chapter is to help you identify and understand many common ones.

Of course, it is beyond the scope of this book to take on the Herculean task of summarizing all that is necessary to improve decision making in organizations. Our purpose is more limited—to highlight the critical oversights that users new to the concepts of modeling make in attempting to move forward to apply those ideas in actual decision-making situations. While we make no claim that the oversights that we cover here are sufficient, the ones we do cover have been reported as the root causes of a failure in many anecdotal "war story" applications of modeling in business and in a few research studies.

After presenting three conceptual frameworks for understanding how failure of modeling in organizations comes about, we present a list of the most common reasons why modeling fails to improve, or in some cases hurts, the process of decision making in organizations. We do not want to leave you with the impression, however, that all modeling efforts run into trouble or even lead to failure. On the contrary, like the "good news" that never gets reported, spreadsheet modeling is having an increasingly pervasive impact upon better decision making. Indeed, the many Application Capsules that have accompanied the chapters of this book attest to be upside potential for applying the modeling concepts we have covered. It is just a fact of life, however, that we learn best from the "bad news" of failed modeling projects. It is our intention in this chapter to balance the upside potential with a discussion of the potential downside risks of applying modeling, so that you will come away with a balanced perspective of the pros and cons of applying modeling concepts in practical business situations.

We conclude with a large case concerning a real company whose identity is disguised in which a promising modeling effort ran into trouble. Your efforts at trying to understand why this company had difficulty will bode well for successful applications of modeling in your career.

11.2 WHAT, AFTER ALL, IS A MODEL?

You would think that everyone in business would know what a model is. Certainly, by now you can answer that question for yourself (without peaking at the definitions from Chapter 1), right? You might offer a definition like "a model is an abstraction of a business situation suitable for spreadsheet analysis to support decision making and provide managerial insights." While this is more than acceptable as a definition for purposes of this book, you would be surprised at the variety of answers you would get by asking this question of business colleagues. In particular, the word "model" is nebulous enough that many people ascribe a variety of meanings to it that, unless addressed, could interfere with the successful pursuit of the modeling process described in Chapter 1.

One major source of difficulty concerns the level of maturity that managers ascribe to a model. In this book we have emphasized that models are frequently "rough and ready" or "quick and dirty" in the sense that they are small, focused upon a particular decision, and quickly developed to be responsive to the situation at hand. However, to many managers, a model is something that is mature in the sense that it is exquisitely crafted, professionally polished in appearance, highly intuitive, self-documenting, easy to use, completely validated, and generalizable enough to be applied in a variety of settings by many different people. This perception is at the core of many problems associated with modeling projects. To elaborate further on this, we present the framework described in Figure 11.1. It is based upon related frameworks for understanding sources of difficulty that surfaced in other disciplines by Brooks in software development and Gorry and Scott-Morton in information systems.

The upper left-hand corner of the figure describes the characteristics of that "rough-and-ready" model, which we call a **prototype model**. It is complete in the sense that it is responsive to the business situation it abstracts; it contains no obvious logic errors, and thus provisionally, is debugged; and is run-able in Excel by its author. Validation, such as it is, is based upon parameter estimates and test data, often supplied only as judgmental inputs. Finally the model is believed to have business value, but that has yet to be conclusively demonstrated.

Often there is a sense of closure, to say nothing of satisfaction, in completing a prototype model for it takes plausible inputs and produces acceptable outputs. Thus, one might reasonably conclude that the modeling effort is finished at this point. Just as for high tech-

FIGURE 11.1

The Evolution of a Model

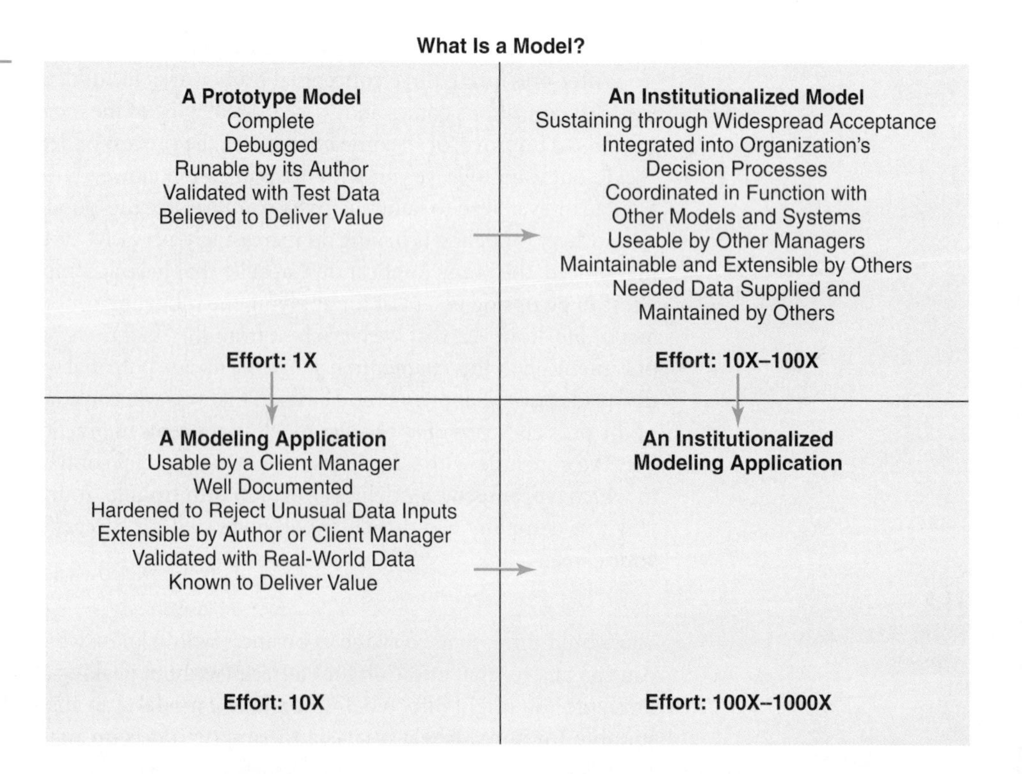

nology in which an invention is created in the proverbial garage over a weekend, the first model is often developed, say, on a laptop computer during a long flight or an airport layover. However, rarely reported is the extensive amount of effort to take that garage invention and convert it into a useful product that can be made and sold to others. Similarly, that *ad hoc* model is in reality only a prototype and is also in need of additional work. In fact, as we will see, the easy part has been finished during that airport layover, and now the real work begins of making the prototype model into something truly useful.

Making a prototype model useful means first converting it to a **modeling application**. This means converting it into something that is understandable by a client manager who may be different from its author (or understandable by the manager-modeler herself after six months in which the model's original very terse representation has been forgotten). This requires that the model must be documented, often extensively if it represents unusual abstractions, must be hardened against unexpected and unusual inputs and parameters, and most importantly, must be validated with real, as opposed to test, data. It also means that the original model has been made extensible in the sense that with little effort it may be scaled up to handle more products, more time periods, more decision alternatives, and so on, without starting the model development from scratch each time. One litmus test of the successful conversion of a prototype model into a modeling application is that its business value is unquestioned, and others can use it without "hand-holding" or tutoring by its author. As indicated in Figure 11.1, converting a prototype model to a modeling application is a much more difficult step, often requiring at least an order of magnitude more effort than creating a model itself, where effort can be defined either in terms of cost or time, as both are highly correlated.

While a modeling application is in a product sense a completed modeling endeavor, many managers define a model still more broadly as an **institutionalized model**. That is, a modeling application can be thought of as a stand-alone product that is complete, but only unto itself. An institutionalized model is one that has been integrated into the ongoing processes of the organization. By integration it is meant that it is coordinated in function with other models, decision-making processes, and systems and procedures already in use by the organization. It also means that the model is usable by other managers in different settings and whose functional responsibilities may not be exactly identical to those of the original client manager. It is also sustainable so that if the original author or client manager moves on to other responsibilities, the model's use does not die. This means the organization has accepted the responsibility for training others to use the model. In addition, this requires that it will be maintained and be made even more extensible by others in the organization who may not have been connected with the original modeling development. Finally, it means that the ongoing supply of needed data and the maintenance of a model itself against small environmental changes are the accepted responsibilities of others in the organization. Converting a prototype model to an institutionalized model means, in effect, converting a stand-alone product to an ongoing process, and correspondingly, the implementation effort is greatly amplified. This is because many others in the organization become involved, and serious resource commitments must be made that are ongoing. It is not unusual for such implementations to be one or even two orders of magnitude more effort than the creation of the original prototype model.

Of course, many managers, particularly senior managers, are not content until both additional developments are completed, creating an **institutionalized modeling application**. An institutionalized modeling application embodies all of the attributes of the other three cells in Figure 11.1, and is thus far more ambitious and risky. Unfortunately, creating an institutionalized modeling application is not additive in effort, but multiplicative. That is, the total effort to create an institutionalized modeling application can be hundred-fold to thousand-fold times more effort than that needed to create the original prototype model, a seriously daunting prospect.

It is not unusual at the initial planning stage for the author of the proposed model development to be thinking in terms of developing a prototype model while the manager funding the model development is thinking in terms of a modeling application or even an institutionalized modeling application. Thus, difficulty can follow down the road when the prototype model is delivered to someone expecting a great deal more. The stage is then set for one of the major causes of failure in modeling, especially when multiple participants are involved, where there is a *failure to manage expectations.*

11.3 THE SEPARATION OF PLAYERS CURSE

Figure 11.2 presents a second framework that is a variation of one originally proposed by one of the earliest proponents of modeling for management decision making, C. West Churchman and his colleagues. It highlights another source of difficulty created when one moves from a single person, who embodies all the functions of a decision-maker, client, modeler, and project manager, along the spectrum to the situation in which each of these functions is shouldered by a different player who may be separated from the others both physically and organizationally. These people are called **players** to signal their intended functioning as *active* participants. As you can imagine, life is much easier when all of four functions are embodied in a single person. In fact, it is for this reason that we have emphasized the importance of a manager doing his own modeling in Excel. Unfortunately, this is not always possible.

In this taxonomy the **modeler** is the person primarily responsible for the activities we have covered in this book: the development, testing, debugging, and initial evaluation of the model. The **project manager** is the person responsible for providing the resources necessary to take the modeling effort to its conclusion, either as a modeling application, or institutionalized model, or as both in an institutionalized modeling application. As such, the project manager is responsible for coordination, resource management and budgeting, and other essential project organization responsibilities. The **decision-maker** is the person who actually will use the model to support decisioning, and obviously, is a key player. The **client** is defined as the person ultimately served by the modeling project and thus provides the criteria for evaluating the success of any improved decisions. The difference between the decision-maker and the client is that the decision-maker possesses the decision rights to use the model whereas the client is only the beneficiary of the improved decision making and may be remote from actual model use.

Even in cases where all four functions are performed by a single person during development, the final implementation of the model may be spread over several people. This **separation of players** can be a source of difficulty in implementing the model. The difficulty arises because when different people take on specialized responsibilities, each will have different beliefs, preferences, agendas, skills, and motives that may not align properly

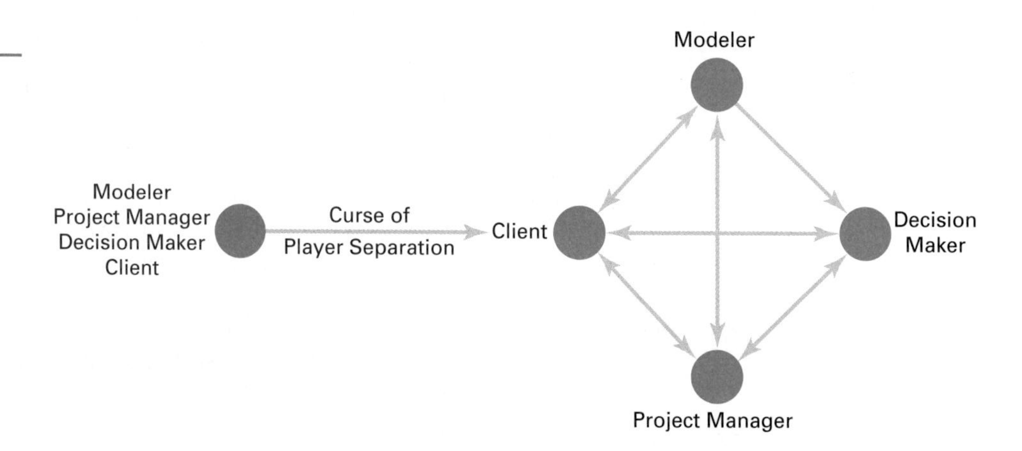

FIGURE 11.2

The Curse of Player Separation

with those most needed for a successful modeling project. Even in those rare circumstances where such alignment does occur among the players, producing what is called a **team**, there are still nontrivial activities that must be devoted to coordination and communication to maintain the effectiveness of that team. The more realistic situation, however, must anticipate some misalignment of goals, objectives, beliefs, preferences, and agendas. For example, often the decision-maker and client are separated. In this case, the decision-maker should be acting as an **agent** for the client. However, since the decision-maker may possess different preferences and rewards than that of the client, **incentive incompatibility** may result from the use of the model for the decision-maker's own purposes instead of those serving the client.

Separation of players raises a host of potential difficulties for model development. Unfortunately, the modeler in such settings may elect to specialize and thus become excessively focused upon the intellectual and technical challenges of the model building itself without paying sufficient attention to the implementation difficulties that the separation of players into functions may cause. Even in a team, such specialization can lead to gross inattention to communication and coordination.

We have used the singular in defining project manager, decision-maker, client, and modeler. Of course, any or all of these roles may be played by multiple persons, which in turn can introduce further coordination and communication problems that are manifold.

We refer to the specialization of functions in the modeling effort as the curse of player separation because so many potential problems are introduced by the behavioral, political, communication, and coordination functions caused by the separation. While our treatment here cannot do justice to the many ramifications of this curse, it should be obvious that the attention devoted to the behavioral issues of management within small groups can be of much greater importance than resolving any technicalities of the model itself, and is thus deserving of considerable additional effort over that of just building the model. Failure to deal with these potential political and coordination functions has often led to ultimate failure in modeling efforts. Importantly, the risk of failure grows geometrically as those four roles are spread over a larger and larger group of increasingly separated and specialized players. Unfortunately, it is often the case that the modeler does not have the authority nor the temperament to take responsibility for managing the many interactions that player separation introduces. In such cases, not the least of skills required is one of facilitation in small groups, and if necessary, the willingness to sacrifice some aspects of the model's sophistication and other modeling objectives if appropriate to that facilitation.

Another problem caused by separation of player function in the modeling project is diffusion of many of the ideas that originally motivated the project in the first place. For example, often the client is remote and insufficient attention is paid to defining the client and his or her needs clearly. Since the client provides the ultimate measure of effectiveness, this oversight can be deadly to the project. Also risky for the project is not to define the ultimate decision-makers clearly. Instead, the actual decision-makers are seen to be a vaguely defined group of "users." These two failures lead to a third inadequacy of the failure to define the performance measures of the project itself clearly. These performance measures need not be monetary and often are represented by milestones and a set of tangible accomplishments *as perceived by the client*, which frequently are not defined, or are ignored during the day-to-day course of model development and implementation.

The most critical component of any modeling project is the presence of a potent **crusader** to champion the modeling project among the group of clients and decision-makers. The crusader is an individual who becomes obsessively involved in seeing to it that the project is a success and will be adopted by each decision-maker and client. It is most important that the crusader be potent. Potency refers to the all-important requirement that the crusader have standing within the organization. By standing, it is meant that the crusader is accepted as being a legitimate, politically powerful, competent, and dedicated individual who is prepared to stake his or her professional reputation on the successful outcome of the modeling effort. Thus, a crusader is more than just an evangelist or spokesperson for the project, and certainly more than just a modeler or the head of the project team. Although there are exceptions, it is usually difficult for line-oriented clients and decision-makers to accept a staff-oriented player as a crusader.

Another component of the successful modeling project is someone to be a knowledgeable and credible **interpreter** of the underlying model to those whose spreadsheet or mathematical skills are insufficient to appreciate the concepts employed, or who fail to see the bigger picture or longer-run benefits of employing the model. If the project is separated over multiple players, the modeler often has a dual responsibility to be a technically proficient developer of the spreadsheet model, and also the translator of its meaning to practitioners unskilled in modeling and modeling process. Sometimes the person best at the modeling task is less well equipped to explain the model's benefits from a managerial perspective, and this interpretation responsibility must devolve onto the crusader.

A failure of the modeling process in a multiple person context often occurs because implementation is considered as an afterthought: something to be pursued after a modeling is completed. Like documentation, implementation considerations are then addressed too late in the project which in turn can threaten the ultimate success of the endeavor. Successful modeling teams facing player separation always worry about implementation issues from the *beginning* of the model development project and often condition their behavior with regard to modeling itself on those exigencies.

Finally it should be said that achieving improvements, especially among multiple players, requires behavioral changes. In case of an institutionalized model this requires organizational change. Both of these are major challenges as any practitioner will confirm. It is naive to believe that the model will sell itself or that others will accept the model and its recommendations merely because it is computer-based, is interactive, and produces pretty charts. Despite any rational improvement it offers, often the model is a threat to the stability of the existing group norms or organizational culture. Adapting models to better conform to the existing norms or culture is one option, even at the risk of reduced payoff to the modeling effort initially. In addition, education and training of all parties involved in the underlying concepts of the model, value of sensitivity analysis, necessary inadequacies in the model, and potential risks that the initial use of the model may not be immediately successful are all important considerations to be addressed during the model development and its early implementation.

Important suggestions for avoiding player separation difficulties include the obvious ones of involving the clients and decision-makers through all phases of the modeling effort, to define the project in terms of phases, each with a milestone visible to them, and the need to develop a sense of organizational ownership of the model itself that transcends the modeler. Failure to pay attention to these common aspects of business management often lead to failure of the modeling project.

11.4 THE CURSE OF SCOPE CREEP

Figure 11.3 presents the second curse, scope creep, frequently identified with modeling projects, especially those that involve development of an institutionalized model. Scope creep occurs for a variety of reasons caused by bandwagon effects. The initial modeling activity is narrow, focused, involving few players, and of manageable proportions. Unfortunately, such a narrow modeling project has the disadvantages of diseconomies of scale in the information systems and data provisioning that the model might require, low visibility within the organization because of its small-group focus, and potentially low organization-wide impact. For a variety of reasons the organization becomes excited about the possibilities of applying the efforts more broadly, not only because it picks up scale economies in data provisioning and modeling maintenance, but because more people are

Narrow Modeling Project		Wide Modeling Project
Single Model		Multiple (Replicated) Models
Single Objective		Multiple Objectives
Focused Activity		Diffused Activity
Few Players		Many Players
Few Stakeholders		Many Stakeholders
Low Effort	Curse of	High Effort
Low Cost	→	High Cost
Low Development Risk	Scope Creep	High Development Risk
Informal Coordination & Project Management		Formal Coordination & Project Management
Low Project Visibility		High Project Visibility
Scale Diseconomies in Information Systems for Model		Scale Economies in Information Systems for Model
Scale Diseconomies in Model & Database Maintenance		Scale Economies in Model & Database Maintenance
Deterioration in Model Use as Early Adopters Move on		Support for Model Use Independent of Early Adopters
Low Potential Organization-wide Impact		High Potential Organizational-wide Impact

FIGURE 11.3

The Curse of Model Scope Creep

involved who can be favorably affected by a successful modeling effort. In turn, this can lead to a much higher potential organization-wide impact and ultimately bigger payoff for the model. But this also leads to **scope creep** of the project as others suggest enhancements, features, new modules for their area, and so forth. It should be mentioned that scope of a modeling project need not always be small, but instead of a carefully planned scope, allowing unplanned scope creep can sabotage a small project and can lead ultimately to a failed project. Unfortunately, the process of getting organizational buy-in to the project and getting others involved can lead to scope creep with all of the attendant costs and delays associated with the curse of player separation.

The one obvious suggestion in controlling scope creep is to recognize that in most instances successful large modeling projects evolve from successful small ones, and that one way to prevent scope creep is to diligently circumscribe the project effort into phases, keeping the early phases small to avoid the downside risks of scope creep. The organizationally acceptable way to manage this is to never say "no" to a wider modeling project, but instead, to say that newly requested features will be postponed until a later phase after the more narrow modeling project has proven out. This requires considerable skill in arguing for more moderately paced commitments in an institutionalized modeling project in the face of compelling arguments to capture the benefits of more widespread payoff earlier rather than later. Once again, this raises issues of organizational design that transcend modeling and model development but cannot be divorced from it. An important role played by the crusader is to champion a well-defined and doable project to stave off the temptations for premature project expansion, the success of which will build credibility for a future expansion.

11.5 OTHER FREQUENT SOURCES OF IMPLEMENTATION FAILURE

In developing a model, particularly an institutionalized model, you must worry about the politics of organizational change. Information provided by a model is never politically neutral. Almost always, especially in the case of institutionalized models, use of the model causes a migration of decision rights from one set of decision-makers to another. This affects incentives and rewards within organizations, and in turn, leads to winners and losers of political power affecting the mix of players that must function together. Inadequate attention to these political issues is far more prevalent as a source of failure in modeling than the more easily addressed issues of model logic, model inadequacy, and the like.

Unfortunately, it is often the case that, following a failed project, the model itself becomes the scapegoat, and is perceived as the villain that caused the failure of the project.

That is, it is all too common to blame the model for the failure because it is an inanimate object, and thus, defenseless. Unfortunately, this can lead to undeserved and unfortunate attributions of the failure of the project as being caused by the model itself when in fact it was due to inadequacies of the whole process of developing and implementing the model. In addition, there may be legacy effects, lasting for years, which impede future modeling efforts because of the mythology surrounding a previously failed modeling project. It is most important for those involved in a new modeling project to learn about the history of the organization with any prior failures and to deal with that legacy and mythology directly.

Another problem with even a narrowly defined modeling project is the potential loss of continuity either during the development of a model itself or later during implementation caused by departure of key players, or the loss of organizational memory of a successful model as the original participants move on to other activities or even leave the organization. Over time, especially if the model has not been institutionalized, this can lead to deterioration in the use of the model as its early proponents, including the crusader, move on to other responsibilities.

A source of difficulty in modeling is the attempt to develop a modeling application before assessing issues of the data availability necessary to support that application. Despite the major gains in the creation of company databases that have occurred over past decades, much of that data consists only of the facts that are easily collected and transcribed into databases as a by-product of ongoing activities of the firm. Unfortunately, these data are often of a nature that is not applicable for modeling. A prime example is cost data. Most monetary data captured by organizations relate to transactions and their relationship to financial accounting. Modeling, on the other hand, requires access to managerial costing data involved in day-to-day use of resources. In other words, it is the day-to-day usage cost and opportunity cost data, not financial data on past transactions, that are often required for a modeling project. As a result, it is not uncommon for a perfectly reasonable model formulation to make excessive demands on the organization's ability to supply the data to make the model useful or to assure its continued use. An important consideration early in the model development phase is the matching of available data to a possibly less-adequate model as a way of avoiding implementation problems later when it becomes clear that the data are too costly or too time-consuming to collect and maintain. This is true especially in the case of an institutionalized model in which one must address the issues of the systems development and database management aspects necessary to assure that the data support function is maintained. That is, an infrastructure must be created that guarantees the data and systems will be maintained in a way that serves the users of the model. You can easily imagine how quickly a useful model could be sabotaged by an unfortunate choice regarding the provisioning of data and the systems support it requires. On the other hand, it is not uncommon for the modelers to grossly underestimate the cost and commitments necessary to provide such resources, and those costs must be weighed into the early decisions for prosecuting the modeling effort.

A more subtle and insidious shortcoming of modeling, originally suggested by Rittel and Webber, concerns the identification of shortcomings at one level of an organization as being caused by failures or inadequacies at a higher, often more abstract, level of the organization. For example, returning to the problem of getting good cost data, the root cause of inadequate cost data may be an inadequate managerial accounting system. But this, in turn, may be the result of inadequate accounting systems in general within the organization. This ultimately is a failure of organizational design. Unfortunately, one can easily be tempted to pursue the chain of abstraction trying to address ever larger and amorphous problems related to overall organizational strategy and design in order to prosecute successful completion of an otherwise straightforward modeling project. Of course, this can become a deadly spiral leading to the failure to act in light of the inadequacies that one often must accept within organizations. In the short run, the trick is to tune the model to work well given other organizational inadequacies that might be addressed more effectively at a later time.

11.6 SUMMARY

This chapter has been devoted to presenting a few frameworks and highlighting several of the potential risks that challenge anyone brave enough to apply modeling for other than their own personal benefit. Certainly a major challenge presented to a modeler and to users of spreadsheet models is with extending these ideas more broadly within the organization. Although more broad-based acceptance of modeling with spreadsheets will certainly ease this burden in future years, one cannot hold out for new developments in Excel or modeling add-ins to suffice in dealing with these challenges. Indeed, one can surmise that a major challenge to managers in the twenty-first century will relate to how organizations accommodate to the organizational changes necessary to make better use of the increasing volume of data and the application of the models we already have on hand to that data. This is much more a challenge of modeling implementation than model sophistication. Managers who understand and can appreciate the potential for modeling but who can navigate through the minefields of the organizational changes necessary to exploit those models will be the ultimate winners.

Key Terms

Prototype Model. A complete model, run-able by its author, validated with test data and believed to be valuable for supporting decision making.

Modeling Application. A prototype model that has been well documented, extensively tested and validated with real data, hardened to reject unacceptable inputs, useable by others than its author, and known to be valuable in supporting decision making.

Institutionalized Model. A prototype model that has been integrated into the organization's processes; is coordinated in function with other models, procedures, and systems; is maintained and supplied with data by others; and is sustainable after its creators depart.

Institutionalized Modeling Application. A model possessing all the features of a modeling application and an institutionalized model.

Modeler. The person who builds, tests, and validates the model.

Decision-Maker. The person who uses the model to support decision making.

Project Manager. The person responsible for converting a prototype model into one or more of the other model types.

Client. The person who benefits from the improved decision making that the model brings about.

Team. A group of players who share the same set of beliefs, preferences, rewards, and agendas regarding a decision-making situation.

Agent. A decision-maker who is charged with using the model to enhance the benefits to the client.

Incentive Incompatibility. The occurrence of a difference in the beliefs, preferences, rewards, and agendas between the agent and the client regarding decision making.

Crusader. An organizationally potent champion for a modeling project.

Interpreter. A person who educates others about the model, its use, and potential benefits.

Player. An active participant in the modeling process.

Separation of Players. The occurrence of a modeling situation in which the modeler, decision-maker, project manager, and client consist of more than one player.

Scope Creep. Continuous expansion of a modeling project by adding more models, decision alternatives, features, modules, objectives, payoff measures, and players.

Problems

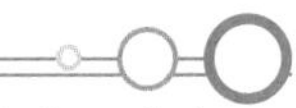

11-1. Of the four participants identified as key players in a modeling effort, who might be the best choice to be the crusader and why?

11-2. Why does scope creep occur?

11-3. Is scope creep more or less prevalent in large organizations? Why or why not?

11-4. What is your interpretation of the phrase "successful application of a model"?

11-5. Why might a staff person have a difficult time crusading for line managers to adopt and use a model?

11-6. Who make the best modelers, staff persons or line managers? Why?

11-7. The Separation of Players framework defines four players, each of which may become relatively isolated from the others. Pick one subset of three players who could be in such close contact that they become a team, leaving one in relative isolation. Elaborate on the possible implementation problems that might result from having one player less well involved in the project, and how these problems might be overcome.

11-8. The Separation of Players framework defines four players, some of whom may become relatively isolated from the others. Four players may pair up in six unique ways in which two players could be in such close contact that they become a team, leaving the other two as separate players. Pick one possible pairing in which two players are close and the other two in relative isolation from each other and the pair. Elaborate on the possible implementation problems that might result and how these problems might be overcome.

Case Study Australian Motors, Ltd.[1]

Introduction

In January of 1996, Michael Yates, acting vice president of planning at Australian Motors (AM), faced a difficult decision regarding the deployment of a new optimization model for fleet management of AM's trucks. His team had been working almost nonstop since the project started 18 months ago to develop a comprehensive linear programming model for administrating the complex process of acquiring and disposing of AM's large fleet of commercial trucks. Yates was convinced that automating the decisions to lease, and buy and sell AM's trucks had enormous potential for improving both the productivity and the effectiveness of AM's rental truck procurement in Australia, Taiwan, Singapore, Korea, and Japan. In fact, Yates had been transferred from British Financial to its AM subsidiary specifically to improve AM's asset management and had himself created the four-person team that had produced the optimization model he was now proposing AM adopt.

Yet Yates was uncomfortable with the direction the project had taken and was deeply concerned that AM's general manager of truck operations, Peter Russell, might not be willing to go along with his proposal to apply the model for fleet management company-wide. Moreover, a decision had to be reached soon or the system would not be in place in time to determine truck acquisitions for the upcoming 1997 model year. As Yates thought about the proposal, he commented:

> *You know, we have to get going with a system to assist us in managing acquisitions and disposals of our truck fleet. This new model looks like it will eliminate the uncoordinated way we do it now and could save AM an average of more than $200,000 annually for each of AM's 10 large districts. Yet, AM has never gotten involved with the development of a large-scale modeling effort, and there's little depth in the technical aspects of mathematical programming at AM, as evidenced by the questionable results from our first attempt to use it last year. If the remaining data collection and analysis for this new optimization system isn't done just right, we won't place the purchasing and leasing contracts in time for the 1997 cycle. Moreover, I don't think the district managers are going to give us another chance if we miss that time window. This whole proposal looks like an unavoidable risk for AM.*

Background

Founded in Sydney in 1960, Australian Motors targeted its business on short-term rentals of commercial delivery trucks to merchandise businesses, contractors, construction companies, and other small to medium-sized companies wishing to avoid management headaches and ownership costs of maintaining their own truck fleet. As the business grew, AM expanded into other Australian cities and more recently into Asia. AM's Asia operations consisted of four districts in Singapore, Taiwan, and Korea. AM's Japanese operations are part of a joint venture with a Japanese truck rental company, and it is organized as a separate company. During an extended recession in the late 1980s, AM's need for capital brought about a friendly acquisition of the company by British Financial, an established London-based holding company. Until recently, British Financial had provided financial backing for AM, but encouraged decentralized control of its acquisitions. However, increasing competitiveness in the truck leasing industry and continued weakness in the Australian dollar had caused AM to become one of British Financial's least profitable ventures. As a result, British Financial had begun to take a more active role in AM's operations in order to achieve better returns on its investment, most of which was used as working capital to finance AM's truck assets.

Trucks in AM's rental fleet typically comprise personnel transport vans, pick-up trucks, large and compact-sized merchandise delivery trucks, mini-vans, and other general-

[1] Inspired by a case originally authored by Professor Stephen P. Bradley whose cooperation in the production of this case is gratefully acknowledged. All names (people and companies) and data in the case have been disguised. Money is quoted in Australian dollars.

purpose trucks. In addition, many of AM's customers in Australia, Taiwan, and Japan rent larger, long-hall trucks used for pulling general freight trailers.

AM is organized into four country managers responsible for geographic districts in their country—the Japanese joint venture was an exception. Each district is a profit center, directly managed by a district manager. Each district manager has responsibility for determining the district's truck fleet management, including leasing or buy-and-sell arrangements with truck manufacturers. Country managers are responsible for review of each of their district manager's recommended truck acquisition and disposal decisions. (An exception is Singapore, where the district and country are the same.) Ownership of the trucks, if applicable, was at the district level. AM's Sydney headquarter's control of the country managers consists of a review of each district's fleet, focusing upon three performance measures: total revenues, revenue per truck, and overall district profits. As long as these figures remain acceptable and the country manager stays within AM defined policies of overall fleet composition, latitude is given in ordering district trucks.

AM requires revenue and acquisition forecasts on an annual basis. Because truck leases or ownership may occur late in the year and extend beyond the fiscal year, budgetary analysis is for a two-year planning horizon. On average AM replaces its fleet once every 18 months.

Annual fleet planning is done manually by the district managers. Relying on past sales records, local knowledge of any upcoming special events (e.g., the Sydney Olympics), each district manager forecasts monthly revenue for the coming 24-month plan. Judgment and experience play a significant role in deriving these forecasts. Target revenue per truck per month is also estimated, and from this, average fleet size by month is calculated for the coming two-year plan. The truck ordering plan proposed by a district manager presents a monthly schedule of acquisitions and disposals of trucks consistent with the forecasted fleet size each month.

Because of the many alternatives for acquiring and disposing of trucks, determination of the ordering plan by each district manager was a time-consuming trial-and-error process. There are two basic acquisition alternatives offered by each truck manufacturer, leasing and outright purchase. Within each of these alternatives a number of variations are available from different truck manufacturers. Many of these variations contain detailed restrictions and provisions, for example, limiting trucks available later in a year to a given percentage of those leased during the first half of the year.

For those trucks purchased outright, the district manager must also consider expected used truck prices up to 24 months after delivery to determine when to schedule resale of them. The scheduled disposal month depends both on the market for used trucks and on the number of similar leased trucks in the district's fleet. For example, the dates on which leased trucks are returned and the plan to replace returned trucks affects the schedule of resale dates for purchased trucks. Therefore, annual fleet management budgeting requires complex trade-offs among truck acquisition dates and disposal dates, while honoring manufacturer restrictions for each of 24 months into the future.

Generally, district managers calculate the expected cost per truck per month under each alternative schedule and recommend a plan having the lowest truck month cost. In addition, most district managers enjoy the risk of selling used trucks profitably, and tend to favor purchases of trucks instead of long-term leases, at least for types of trucks popular in their markets. Finally, country managers often modify the district proposals to incorporate requirements for a maximum number of purchased trucks or a minimum manufacturer mix.

In early 1994 several truck manufacturers announced cancellation of many of the discounts offered to fleet purchasers. This had the effect of raising the average ownership costs of AM's rental fleet by over 15%, a disastrous outcome from British Financial's perspective: AM operates on low contribution margins depending on highly leveraged financial structures to earn its return on investment.

In development since mid-1994, the linear programming model for fleet management had been used during winter 1995[2] to attempt to blunt the effects of the higher fleet costs. Unfortunately, the model met with limited success and the magnitude of its contribution to AM's performance during that year was problematic. AM's earnings in 1995, while down, showed a much lesser drop than expected. Some senior managers believed this was partially because fleet utilization had been improved somewhat, following from the introduction of the model. Other members of AM's management believed, however, that emphasis upon fleet utilization by staff management and the discipline fostered by the modeling project were responsible for the improvement, rather than the model itself. In light of these developments, AM management elected to continue to use the model, since considerable cost savings were anticipated.

In January 1996 Yates was concerned about how best to employ the linear programming model to help plan the fleet of trucks to be acquired for the 1997 model year, acquisitions for which must be finalized in the spring. In addition, many field managers had resisted use of the model. Thus, Yates was faced with the decision of what, if anything, to do with the model in planning the fleet for the upcoming 1997 model year.

History of the LP Model

The fleet planning model had its inception when John Harrington, general manager of AM, attended an executive education course in early 1994, where he saw demonstrations of spreadsheet modeling techniques, including linear pro-

[2] Northern hemisphere readers are reminded that seasons are reversed in Australia.

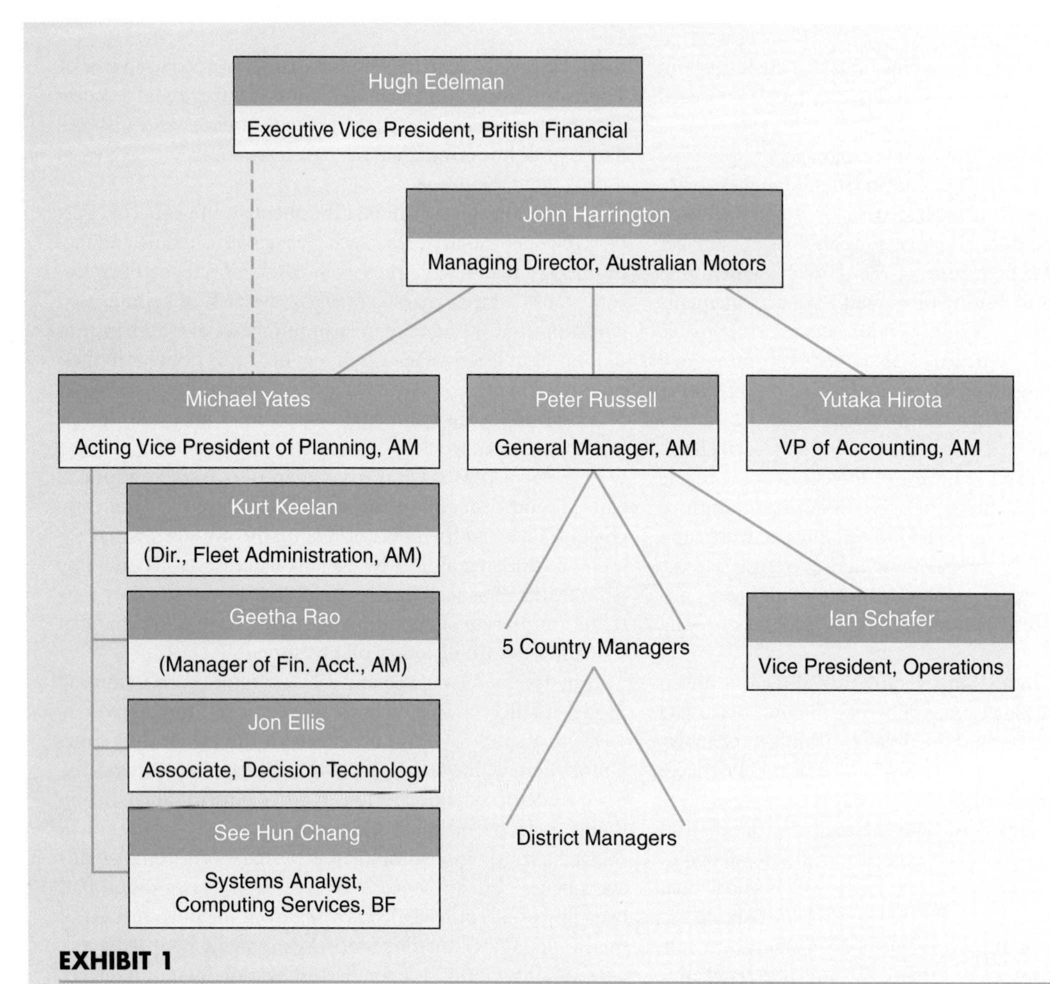

EXHIBIT 1

Partial Organization Chart

gramming (LP). Later, the prospect of using an LP model for fleet planning took hold when Michael Yates, a British financial staff analyst experienced in applying computer modeling to the petroleum industry, was sent in April 1994 to become AM's new acting vice president of planning. (See Exhibit 1.) After discussing the options with Peter Russell, general manager of AM's truck operations, Yates asked Russell to provide two people, one experienced in the field and one in accounting. Kurt Keelan and Geetha Rao, both of AM's Sydney headquarters, were assigned to the project in July 1994. An AM employee since 1975, Keelan had worked as an agent in one of AM districts, ultimately becoming a country manager. A later promotion brought him to the Sydney headquarters as AM's current director of fleet administration. Familiar with the practical problems of fleet planning and control, he was well known and respected by AM's district managers. Rao had joined AM's accounting staff group in 1990, and spent four years in general accounting while taking evening courses at the University of New South Wales. At the time of her assignment to the project, she had received her MBA in controllership and was AM's manager of financial accounting.

Data Collection and Model Formulation

Working under the direction of Yates, the team began a study of fleet operations in the Sydney District in September 1994. This location was chosen because it included AM's headquarters, and because the district was large enough—between 800 and 1,000 trucks—to identify a significant cost savings from better fleet management. Keelan and Rao concentrated upon studying the utilization of Sydney District's fleet. Decision Technology, a local consulting firm, was given the contract to develop the optimization model. Jon Ellis was the Decision Technology associate assigned to the modeling project.

From spring 1994 to fall 1995, the Keelan-Rao field study and the Ellis LP modeling work proceeded in parallel. On numerous occasions Ellis conducted discussions with Keelan and Rao to gain ideas affecting his approach to the model development. For example, Ellis utilized the results of the

Keelan-Rao study for preliminary data and for defining the variables relevant to fleet planning.

From the beginning, data collection and verification proved to be a challenge and soon became the major concern of the Keelan-Rao team. Existing data in AM's computer files consisted primarily of financial accounting items instead of the cost accounting numbers needed by the model. In addition, AM's fixed assets accounting system was developed for tax purposes and did not record detailed configuration of truck types. Instead, a labor-intensive process of searching through paper archives of truck purchase orders and lease contracts was required to correlate that information with existing accounting records in Sydney and other paper records in the districts.

As the project evolved, Yates began spending most of his time working with Ellis on building the linear programming model. By the end of 1994, the following had been accomplished (see Exhibit 8):

1. The model's decision variables and constraints had been defined;
2. A consistent set of notation, primarily used for naming rows and columns, of the model, had been completed;
3. Data definitions were determined;
4. A Java program to check input data for inconsistencies and duplicates, prepare the data for import to Microsoft Excel and to correct minor errors that had been written; and
5. A separate Visual Basic for Excel matrix generator program to arrange data into a form suitable for Solver had been developed.

As computerization of the model began to require more effort, See Hun Chang, systems analyst from British Financial's Sydney Computing Services, joined Ellis in January 1995. Chang's role was to perform the data conversions to produce the model's parameters, to help with software debugging, and to document the model and related software.

In early February 1995 the first usable results of the model were produced. Immediately, significant differences were found between fleet plans being recommended by the model and plans actually used by the Sydney District. To substantiate these findings and because the modeling effort was falling behind the schedule for recommending truck acquisitions in the spring, Yates expanded the project to all five districts in Australia.

Using existing district personnel, fleet distribution and utilization studies were started in the five districts under the direction of Keelan and Rao. Because of the learning afforded by the early experiences in the Sydney District, some of the necessary data became available within a month. To save time in determining the other parameter values necessary to run the model, the team asked the district managers to assess the data values as best they could. By March this approach was abandoned, because, except for the Sydney District, the district managers failed to respond to the team's urgent requests. Upon follow-up, the district managers claimed they did not understand what was wanted. Even the more cooperative Sydney District often provided inconsistent data. For example, Sydney District's policy specified that a minimum of 30% of its fleet was to be Toyota trucks, yet the data indicated that Sydney had allowed the fleet to drop as low as 15% Toyota. Similar misunderstandings, errors, and communication problems made it necessary for almost daily contact with the districts by the team to attempt to get trustworthy data in a reasonable time frame. By this time, Keelan and Rao had become dedicated to data gathering and refinement, a process that was now pacing the modeling project.

Data required from the field was extensive. Data for the fleet planning model involved looking ahead for 24 months to forecast expected revenues, average revenue per truck, monthly fleet size, used truck prices and number of trucks salable at those prices, variable costs and variable overhead, and any district monthly limits on the number of trucks that could be processed in and out of the fleet. Other data required were:

- Existing inventory of trucks in the fleet, broken down by truck type, month, manufacturer, and acquisition plan;
- Future monthly acquisitions by truck type, manufacturer, and plan;
- Procurement and ownership costs, such as import duties and license fees;
- Limitations on fleet composition by truck manufacturer by month;
- Acquisition costs of trucks under each of the manufacturer's plans; and
- Any exceptional needs of the districts.

Because of the lack of data and time pressure to perform, Ellis made several changes in the model during summer 1995. First the planning cycle was changed from weekly to monthly to reduce the size of the model as it was expanded to include other districts. Even with this change, the size of the model had increased to more than 200 constraints and 1,500 decision variables, requiring the purchase of an expanded "Premium Edition" version of Solver and use of the fastest Pentium-class computer available. Next, with help from Yates, Ellis began "guess-imating" the missing values for parameters and coefficients whose data were unavailable from the districts. Development costs were running somewhat higher than anticipated, and the data collection effort was now way over budget, requiring Yates to authorize more funds for the team.

By March 1995, model results for the five Australian districts were becoming available, and the managers of each district were invited to a review meeting at AM's Sydney headquarters. Also attending the meeting were Mr. Ian Schafer, AM's vice president of operations, and other headquarters personnel who would be concerned with truck operations. The meeting was led by Yates and the AM project team members Keelan, Rao, and Chang. Jon Ellis' managing partner at Decision Technology,

Sandra Bentley, also attended. The purpose of the meeting was to present the truck procurement and disposal model to the field managers, review the model's results by district, and solicit ideas. Prior to the meeting, the district managers knew nothing about the model. Their only involvement had been responding to the Keelan-Rao demands for data.

After comparisons between model-produced fleets and fleets actually budgeted for the previous year and the remaining months of 1995 were made, heated differences of opinion between the district managers on the one hand and the project team on the other were exchanged. Later, after the meeting ended, a summary was given by Schafer:

> *This industry requires rapid decision making, often based on judgment, and there was some question about the usefulness of a rigid model. Also, each district manager is somewhat of a local entrepreneur, and there is a real concern that a computer in Sydney would be running the district. The project team is viewed as a group of strangers questioning the abilities of the district managers.*

Schafer also commented that the project team had to address inadequacies in the model's structure and their working relationship with the districts. After much spirited discussion among the district managers, a number of specific objections to the model resulted:

1. The original model was based upon a monthly ordering cycle for tracking truck fleet changes, instead of a more accurate weekly cycle.
2. The monthly model assumed trucks always arrive on the first day, and are always disposed on the last day of a month. In fact, trucks enter and leave the fleet continually.
3. The model was limited to one type of truck from each truck manufacturer. Instead, a mixture of standard-sized trucks and vans, both full-sized and compacts, were being acquired. Also, the model completely ignored the long-haul trucks that carried much higher contribution margins.

During a subsequent meeting alone with Schafer, Yates promised to investigate building a weekly model including at least a dozen truck types. The effect of this proposed change upon the model would be substantial, resulting in a major escalation of the resources needed to incorporate the changes this expansion required. (See Exhibit 2.)

March 1995 was consumed with internal debates among the project team on the expansion of the model to include more truck types and a finer time grid. For the first time conflict arose from within the team. Both Keelan and Rao were opposed, claiming that the data are not available for the original model, much less a larger model. Ellis and Chang felt the current model was too simplistic and that the project team had an obligation to respond to the suggestions of the district managers for more accuracy. Yates ordered the team to undertake an investigation of the development costs and prospects for the expanded model. (See Exhibit 3.)

EXHIBIT 2 Expanded Model Size

Date:	Wed, 8 March 1995 12:30:49-0800
From:	Jon Ellis <jellis@dectech.com.au>
To:	Michael Yates <yates@britfin.com.uk>
Subject:	Model Revisions
MIME-Version:	1.0
X-Mailer:	Internet Mail Service (5.5.2650.21)
Content-Type:	text/plain

Mr. Yates:

This is a follow-up to our conversation last week in which you asked me to review the implications of expanding the model to a dozen or so truck types and converting it to a weekly cycle instead of monthly. As I mentioned, this will increase the number of variables and the number of constraints substantially.

Currently, the model has the following variable counts:

VARIABLE TYPE	NUMBER OF VARIABLES
Demand Segments	3
Total Number Revenue Variables	3
Truck Acquisition Buy/Sell Options	6
Truck Acquisition Lease Options	6
Number Truck Manufacturers	5
Total Number Truck Acquisition Variables	60
Fleet Size Costs	1
Total Number Cost Variables	61
Countries	1
Truck Types	1
Time Periods/Month	1
Number of Months	24
Total Number Variables (Multiplicative)	1,536

And it contains the following constraint counts:

CONSTRAINT TYPE	NUMBER OF CONSTRAINTS
Inventory Balance	24
Fleet Size	24
Segment Linkage	24
Demand Segment Bounds	72
Manufacturer Blend Composition	24
Blending Lease versus Buy	24
Disposal Limits	24
Second Buy Restrictions	10
Total	226
Countries	1
Truck Types	1
Time Periods/Month	1
Total Number Constraints (Multiplicative)	226

Expanding this by 12 truck types for each of four weeks per month multiplies these totals by about 50 times. My current estimate is that the expanded model would grow as shown below.

The expanded model would have the following variable counts:

VARIABLE TYPE	NUMBER OF VARIABLES
Demand Segments	3
Total Number of Revenue Variables	3
Truck Acquisition Buy/Sell Options	6
Truck Acquisition Lease Options	6
Number Truck Manufacturers	5
Total Number Truck Acq. Variables	60
Fleet Size Costs	1
Total Number of Cost Variables	61
Countries	1
Truck Types	12
Time Periods/Month	4
Number of Months	24
Total Number of Variables (Multiplicative)	73,728

The expanded model would have the following constraint counts:

CONSTRAINT TYPE	NUMBER OF CONSTRAINTS
Inventory Balance	24
Fleet Size	24
Segment Linkage	24
Demand Segment Bounds	72
Manufacturer Blend Composition	24
Blending Lease versus Buy	24
Disposal Limits	24
Second Buy Restrictions	10
Total	226
Countries	1
Truck Types	12
Time Periods/Month	4
Total Number Constraints (Multiplicative)	10,848

As you can see, this is a major expansion of the project. One alternative is to move the model to the Hitachi mainframe in computing services at British Financial's Sydney building. We will have to convert the Solver model to the format of that computer's IBM MPSX LP optimizer. I expect the conversion of the current model would take approximately two weeks.

After the software conversion, building the expanded model would take additional work. Organizing the data will require a separate proposal from Kurt. In addition, we would need to develop some tools to facilitate loading up the coefficient matrix (now bigger by about 2500-fold) and checking it for validity.

Also, checking and debugging the expanded model will take longer than previously, as we estimate each optimization run will require about 30 to 40 minutes of Hitachi CPU time, about 15 times longer than the smaller model on the Pentium took.

I hope this provides you with the information you need.

Jon

EXHIBIT 3 Expanded Model Cost Estimates

Date:	Sat, 11 March 1995 12:30:22-0100
From:	Kurt Keelan <kkeelan@am.com.au>
To:	Michael Yates <yates@britfin.com.uk>
Subject:	Model Revisions
MIME-Version:	1.0
X-Mailer:	Internet Mail Service (5.5.2650.21)
Content-Type:	text/plain

Michael:

I have confirmed that BF would recharge the cost of our using the Hitachi mainframe time to AM after all. The hourly rate is $400 per CPU hour. We estimate making over 100 runs per month during debugging and testing. Connect time is harder to forecast, but I estimate it will run about $500 per analyst per month. Disk storage and printing costs would add about $900 per month.

See Hun estimates we will need at least two additional programmers from Computing Services to help with the conversion and testing. AM would be charged $10,000 per month for each for the balance of the year. That does not include the additional modeling consultants Jon says are needed.

We are already getting lots of complaints from the district people about their providing the data for the model. I can't imagine they will be able to gear up to provide the amount of data we will require for the expanded model. We would have to help them with this. To meet your spring targets, I estimate we would need at least two staff accountants in the field for each of the five districts for the next five months. Geetha says we don't have any available staff in accounting. We could hire clerical temps at $35 per hour to do the work, but we need to resolve who is going to train and supervise them. I don't recommend we rely on the district managers to assume that responsibility.

Kurt

March 9, 1995

Mr. Michael Yates
Australian Motors, Ltd.
Sydney NSW
Australia

Dear Mr. Yates,

Decision Technology is pleased to submit this proposal to assist Australian Motors in expanding its optimization model development and converting it to run on British Financial's Hitachi mainframe.

We estimate the expansion and conversion process will require half time services of two additional Decision Technology Associates and will take approximately four months, provided data on your truck fleet costs and proposed truck acquisition are available. Jon Ellis would continue his half time role for another six months and would directly supervise the Associates.

Estimated Costs:

2 Associates @ $160 per hour for 20 hours/week × 16 weeks =	$102,400
Jon Ellis @ $250 per hour for 20 hours/week × 24 weeks =	120,000
Total	$222,400

I would continue my role as managing partner. As a tangible sign of Decision Technology's commitment to continuing this strategic partnership, any additional billings for my management of this expanded project would be absorbed by the company.

We at Decision Technology are excited at the prospects for fleet management at Australian Motors, and I look forward to working with you on this expanded project.

Sincerely,

Sandra Bentley,
Managing Partner

Date: Thur, 9 March 1995 02:30:22-0700
From: See Hun Chang <chang@britfin.com.au>
To: Michael Yates <yates@britfin.com.uk>
Subject: Computer Support
MIME-Version: 1.0
X-Mailer: Internet Mail Service (5.5.2650.21)
Content-Type: text/plain

Michael:

Connectivity from the project group at AM to the Hitachi at BF would become a problem. BF Network Services recommends that with this project AM should now upgrade its current frame relay connection to a dedicated leased T1 line ($3,500 one time + $1,600 per month) and upgrade its router to a Cisco 7510 ($25,000 one time). It would take about four weeks to install this upgrade.

They also recommend that the project database would become so large that we should consider converting it to Oracle SQL database system to facilitate updating and data maintenance. Oracle SQL is fully supported by BF on the mainframe. So, the only incremental costs will be conversion, which the new programmers can handle. We will need to spend about two weeks or so designing the database, but if we do this, I recommend the project hire a full-time database administrator.

Finally, both Kurt Keelan and Geetha Rao would have to be trained in SQL and Jon would have to adapt the model to do remote procedure calls directly to the Oracle SQL query engine. This may require additional software from IBM.

An alternative to using the Hitachi mainframe would be to purchase a SUN Ultra 4000 SPARC UNIX system and network it to a separate NT-SQL server in the same domain. The existing Pentium could be converted to become the SQL server with Microsoft software. The SPARC system is upgradeable to a multiprocessor configuration, if the expanded model requires it. Also, the SPARC could reside in the project team's current office. This would save the communications upgrade to reach the Hitachi and the mainframe use charges. An LP optimizer package called AMPL Plus can be acquired that runs on the SPARC. An advantage of using AMPL is that software exists to convert the Solver model.

Here is a rough estimate of the costs of this alternative:

SUN Ultra 4000 SPARC, dual-processor, 256MB RAM, 18.4GB Disk	$66,000
SQL Server software, NT upgrade, 9GB hard disk	18,000
AMPL optimizer plus conversion utilities	10,000
Total	$94,000

See Hun

Related matters pertaining to AM's accounting system surfaced following a memo from Geetha Rao to her former boss, Yutaka Hirota, AM's comptroller and vice president of accounting. AM's current accounting system had been developed in house over two decades and was oriented more to financial reporting. Rao argued that the considerable amount of cost data being collected for the model would be ongoing and could be a valuable source of information for cost management beyond fleet planning. But, unless AM replaced its outdated accounting system with a more modern one capable of managerial accounting, AM would evolve into supporting two separate accounting systems running on two different and incompatible computers. (See Exhibit 4.)

By the end of March Yates made the decision to reject both the proposed conversion of the model to the Hitachi mainframe and acquisition of a SPARC workstation and SQL database server. His reasoning was that, even if the substantial additional costs of the proposals were ignored, each would introduce delays and technical risks into an already late project. Ellis was instructed to expand the model to incorporate as much as possible while continuing to use the project's existing hardware and software. Based upon Ellis' further analysis, Yates informed Schafer of the revisions that could be accommodated. (See Exhibit 5.)

In June 1995, a presentation was made to AM's top management, including Harrington (AM's managing director), Schafer, and his boss, Peter Russell (general manager of the truck division). Also in attendance were Hugh Edelman (executive vice president at British Financial, in whose jurisdiction AM fell) and Sandra Bentley of Decision Technology, as well as Michael Yates. Other members of the project team were not present. Other than reflecting the recent model changes, the content of the presentation by Yates was similar to that given by the project team in the March District Manager meeting.

EXHIBIT 4 Accounting Communications

March 20, 1995

To: Yutaka Hirota

Cc: Michael Yates, Kurt Keelan

From: Geetha Rao

Subject: AM's Accounting System

As you know, we have discussed on many occasions the inadequacies of our homegrown accounting system on the HP 3000. For example, you already know how difficult and time-consuming it has become to consolidate AM's quarterly reports into the formats now required by BF's accounting group. Add to that the time I used to spend manually preparing the limited operating reports the districts want to see each month. They continue to complain that even these simple reports reach them too late in the next month to do any good.

For the last several months the project team I am now working on has been collecting district data for an LP model of fleet acquisitions and disposals. The vast majority of this data is cost accounting, never previously captured by the HP 3000 system. Yet, the data are being captured for use only for LP optimization. This data has considerable additional value for other management control uses that you need to be aware of. Moreover, the team is now considering the movement of that data to BF's mainframe to be organized under an Oracle SQL database. (An alternative proposal is to convert it to a server-based version of SQL.)

It would seem that now is the time to seriously address replacement of our accounting software. It currently runs on the HP's Image database, which is not compatible with any of the alternatives being studied by the LP project team. One suggestion would be for AM to convert its accounting system to Oracle Financials. That would be compatible with the BF accounting system. Alternatively, AM could pick an accounting system for the HP 3000 that is SQL compatible to allow ready access to the cost data being collected by the project team. Either way accounting could pick up responsibility for collecting and maintaining this new cost data, could finally migrate to a more responsive system for supplying management reports, and acquire a commercially supported accounting system rather than maintaining our own one.

I realize that the existing accounting system will be difficult to replace because it has become so tailored to AM's accounting practices over the years. But it would seem that now is the time for AM accounting to seriously undertake its replacement. Otherwise AM will end up maintaining two incompatible accounting systems, one for cost control and one for financial reporting.

I have already spoken to Michael Yates about this opportunity. He would be happy to meet with you to further explore these ideas.

May 29, 1995

To: Geetha Rao

From: Yutaka Hirota

Subject: AM's Accounting System

Thank you for the information about the LP project and the recommendation that we replace our accounting system. It is a good suggestion and we will consider it very seriously.

EXHIBIT 5 Communications to Ian Schafer

March 30, 1995

To: Ian Schafer

From: Michael Yates

Subject: Model Revisions

This is to follow up on our discussions last month about expanding the LP model to include more relevant information from the districts. It turns out that adding a dozen truck types and going to a weekly cycle will increase the size of the model by about 50 times. This would require us to re-build the model and use a much larger computer. The cost and time delays of this option are prohibitive for getting any results in time for the spring truck acquisitions.

Here is what we can do, however. We can double the model to a biweekly cycle giving two opportunities per month for truck replacements instead of once per month, as now modeled. Also, the model can be adapted to remove the beginning-of-month truck delivery and end-of-month truck disposal requirement, if you are willing to assume that trucks are delivered and disposed of uniformly throughout any one month.

Unfortunately, the model cannot accommodate more than one truck type per manufacturer. We will have to define a generic "composite" truck for each manufacturer, whose costs and revenue forecasts are an average of the desired mix of that manufacturer's trucks. This has a side benefit of reducing the amount of data that otherwise would be required while still allowing us to develop some results this winter. I realize this means that we will have to drop consideration of the long-haul cab trucks from the model. Maybe we can model those separately at some point.

We can certainly accommodate a more comprehensive LP model next year after migrating it to a larger computer system. In the meantime, please communicate these changes to the Australian district managers and tell them that Kurt will be in contact with them over the next several months as the modeling proceeds.

Date: Tues., 18 April 1995 11:07:22-0300

From: Joel Baty <jbaty@am.com.au>

To: Ian Schafer <ischafer@am.com.au>

Cc: Peter Russell <prussell@am.com.au>

Subject: The Yates Project

MIME-Version: 1.0

X-Mailer: Internet Mail Service (5.5.2650.21)

Content-Type: text/plain

Ian:

I just got off the phone with the other district managers. They confirm that the Yates team told them the same story I got yesterday. Can you believe that we're supposed to combine a half-ton pickup truck with a compact mini-delivery van? Who the hell are we going to rent a truck like that to?

We've already spent too much time responding to these Yates people and now they are asking for twice as much data. I've told Kurt Keelan that we just can't take any more time for this project of theirs.

I know you lads in Sydney have lots of idle time on your hands. But we here in Melbourne have a job to do and that comes first, doesn't it?

Edelman expressed grave concern at the costs accrued by the project to date (see Exhibit 6) and the lack of tangible savings thus far. He also expressed considerable surprise that the model was limited to Australia, ignoring the other countries where AM had truck operations. Although not enthusiastic about the model, Russell did not oppose it. After lengthy debate Harrington decided to go ahead with the rollout phase. He asked Yates how many districts could be brought into the model. Yates committed himself and his team to fleet management of AM's 10 largest truck fleets, comprising about 75% of all trucks managed by AM in Australia and Asia, for the 1996 model year.

Yates' commitment presented an enormous problem to the LP team, as fleet plans would have to be prepared within about a month to affect September orders for 1996 truck deliveries. Experience during the first half of 1995 indicated that the Keelan-Rao team would have to actively supervise data gathering. Also, no software had been developed to incorporate currency exchange rates for the other Asian districts, nor each local country's import/export restrictions for new or used trucks.

On June 20, Geetha Rao resigned from AM to accept a promotion into British Financial's Accounting group in London. She had joined the team as a one-year assignment, which was now completed, and she felt the offer from British Financial would make better use of her recent MBA in accounting. Also, the new phase of the project involving the other countries created a perfect opportunity for someone else to take over her role.

On July 1 the Decision Technology contract expired and Jon Ellis left the project team. Bentley explained that Ellis had another assignment to pursue and that his consulting assignment, the building of the model, was essentially completed. Extending it to the other countries would be more of

EXHIBIT 6 Estimated Costs of the Model[1]

Development Costs

Payments to Decision Technology	$220,000
For Software Development of Utilities	10,000
Other	30,000
	$260,000

This does not include the costs of approximately 4⅔ person-years put in by Keelan, Rao, Yates, Chang, and Keelan's 5-person team. If average burdened costs of $125,000 per person-year were used and 3 of the 4⅔ man-years allocated to development, costs breakdown is:

Development Costs	
For outside services	$260,000
Labor (3 years @ $125,000/year)	375,000
Total	$635,000
Production Costs	
Labor (1⅔ years @ $125,000/year)	208,000
Total Costs	$843,000

Kurt Keelan estimated that recurring annual costs for running each country's fleet on the model would be about $12,000. This would not include any labor costs for Keelan's team or other field personnel for data collection.

[1] Through August 1995.

a data collection effort than a modeling effort according to Bentley.

That left Chang and Keelan as the only people, beside Yates, who were acquainted with the model. The team now consisted of Sandra Bentley of Decision Technology, Kurt Keelan, and See Hun Chang. Since Chang had been working with computerization of the model, Yates assigned him to take over Ellis' role. Bentley would fill a managerial role to provide continuity. Kurt Keelan was put in sole charge of the field phase of the project. Fortunately, Yates had authorized Keelan in April to build a five-person team of some younger, more promising district personnel. They became essential for extending the data collection effort to the other countries. As had become practice earlier in the year, Chang continued the custom of supplying parameter estimates whenever field-generated data proved inadequate or missing. In addition, the team elected to simplify the model by running each country as a separate LP formulation and to ignore any country-specific import/export considerations. Chang's model documentation activities also were put on temporary hold.

By early August the first optimization runs were becoming available. Upon validation of the runs with actual 1995 plans, a new problem was identified: District managers had imposed constraints that they themselves did not follow and at other times practiced "peak cutting" of demand when trucks were not available. Of course, much of the available data continued to be missing, inconsistent, or unreliable. Kurt Keelan had Chang revise the model to put limits, more or less arbitrarily, on the degree of peak cutting done by the model and this improved model validation. It quickly became standard procedure for the team to analyze only the "cut peak" run for a district.

Unfortunately, these unforeseen developments further delayed the project. By September 1995 it was obvious that the model results would be too late to affect the 1996 model year ordering process directly, as Yates had promised. The results were distributed to the field anyway so that they could be used for subsequent ordering periods. The level of acceptance of the LP results by the district managers remained low. Feedback from Keelan's team suggested that only the Australian district managers ever looked at the results. Even they relied upon their own manual plans as a double check on model results.

An interesting development occurred in October 1995, when the Sydney District proposed a number of truck purchases in direct opposition to the model's results. Yates objected to the purchase, and Russell stopped the order until it could be resolved. Chang and Keelan worked directly with the Sydney District to rerun the model, imposing the proposed Sydney District truck order as a constraint in the model. The best plan the model could come up with, given Sydney's purchase constraint, was $110,000 more expensive than without it. This experiment convinced the Sydney district manager that the model was useful. (See Exhibit 7.)

The balance of 1995 was spent by the team developing a program to translate results of the LP model into terms more readily understood by district, country, and headquarter's management, including for the first time, some shadow price information. As of January 1996, neither documentation of the project data files nor the model had resumed. Also, Yates had received no further contact from Hirota concerning possible replacement of AM's accounting system. Finally, See Hun was pushing him for a decision to convert the model over to the SUN UNIX system.

EXHIBIT 7 Memo from Sydney District Manager

November 14, 1995

To: Peter Russell

From: Edmund Campbell

Cc: Michael Yates, Kurt Keelan, See Hun Chang

Subject: Sydney Truck Order

Peter:

I want to commend the Yates team for their extraordinary effort in quickly resolving the hold you placed upon Sydney truck purchase orders in October. I am forced to admit that our earlier proposal to buy those 55 trucks outright, instead of leasing some from one manufacturer and buying the rest from another manufacturer, was considerably more expensive.

Not only did the analysis save the district more than an estimated $100,000 over the year for that single order, but that one change reduced average truck inventories and rippled into our other truck ordering patterns for over 18 months into the future, something I never expected.

I also spent some time with Kurt Keelan going over the data file they collected for the Sydney District LP model. It is a gold mine! I have been telling you that I suspected some of the local repair shops are overcharging us, and that those new-model mini-vans have excessive warranty claims. We ran a few ratios and I think I have some hard evidence on both counts.

Also, we can use this comparative data to beat up on the manufacturer's reps when they come round to announce next year's truck lease and purchase plans. Those reps have been jerking us around with their new plans for two years now. I think we can leverage this information into negotiating some much better deals next year.

EXHIBIT 8 General Structure of the AM Model[1]

The general structure of the model can be illustrated by means of a very simplified example, which considers only a 6-month period. In the full-blown AM model, the decision variables are the number of trucks from a given manufacturer that are bought or leased in a given month. If the trucks are leased, they may be leased under different plans (for turnback) and for different periods (e.g., 6 months or 8 months). In this simplified example, consider only one manufacturer and one lease plan. The only factor left is the length of lease and consider for simplicity very short leases of 2, 3, 4, or 5 months as follows:

A_t number of trucks leased in month t for 2 months (i.e., trucks will be returned at end of period $t + 2$)

B_t number of trucks leased in month t for 3 months

C_t number of trucks leased in month t for 4 months

D_t number of trucks leased in month t for 5 months

In addition, there are the following variables:

FS_t fleet size (average number of trucks) during month t

I_t inventory (number of trucks) at the *end* of month t

The object of the model is to come up with a leasing strategy that will provide the trucks AM needs at minimum cost. However, defining this "need" is a little tricky. The exact number of trucks needed in any month is uncertain, and it would seem unwise to plan to have so many trucks on hand that no customer was ever turned away. The AM model deals with this by defining demand segments. For example, if a given city had only 100 trucks in its fleet, these 100 might be fully leased and generate a contribution margin of $1,000 per month each. If 100 additional trucks were available (a total of 200), only half the additional 100 trucks might be leased, hence generating an average of only $500 per month contribution margin each. If an additional 100 trucks were available (a total of 300), only one-tenth this last 100 trucks might be leased, generating an average of only $100 per month each. Additional trucks (above 300) could not be leased. In this case, there are three demand segments for the given month:

[1] Developed by Professor Charles Bonini.

DEMAND SEGMENT	MAXIMUM SIZE OF SEGMENT	SIZE OF FLEET	CONTRIBUTION MARGIN PER TRUCK IN SEGMENT
First	100	100	$1000
Second	100	200	500
Third	100	300	100

The model would attempt to satisfy demand only up to the point at which the expected contribution margin (revenue less variable operating costs) from a truck equaled or exceeded the cost of leasing the truck. In this simplified model, consider only two demand segments, $DS1_t$ and $DS2_t$ for each month t. Suppose over the next 6 months demand is given as:

	JANUARY	FEBRUARY	MARCH	APRIL	MAY	JUNE
Demand Segment 1 ($DS1_t$)	240	110	110	100	150	100
Demand Segment 2 ($DS2_t$)	60	80	70	80	100	50

Suppose contribution margin per truck in demand segment 1 is $1,000 per month and $800 per month in demand segment 2.

CONSTRAINTS

Month End Inventory The first set of constraints relate to the inventory of trucks on hand at the end of each month. In general this is:

Month End Inventory = Inventory at Beginning of Month + Leases during Month − Turnback or Sales During Month

Suppose, in this example, that the inventory at the beginning of January is 300 trucks, and that, as a result of previous leases, returns for January are 100, February are 120, and March are 80. Then, for

January: $I_1 = 300 + (A_1 + B_1 + C_1 + D_1) - 100$

- I_1 ↑ End of Month Inventory
- 300 ↑ Beginning Inventory
- $(A_1 + B_1 + C_1 + D_1)$ ↑ Trucks Leased for Different Periods Beginning in January
- −100 ↑ January Returns

February: $I_2 = I_1 + (A_2 + B_2 + C_2 + D_2) - 120$

March: $I_3 = I_2 + (A_3 + B_3 + C_3 + D_3) - 80 - A_1$

- A_1 ↑ Trucks Leased in January for Two Months, and Returned in March

April: $I_4 = I_3 + (A_4 + B_4 + C_4 + D_4) - (A_2 + B_1)$

- A_2 ↑ Trucks Leased in February in Two-Month Lease
- B_1 ↑ Trucks Leased in January in Three-Month Lease

May: $I_5 = I_4 + (A_5 + B_5 + C_5 + D_5) - (A_3 + B_2 + C_1)$

June: $I_6 = I_5 + (A_6 + B_6 + C_6 + D_6) - (A_4 + B_3 + C_2 + D_1)$

Fleet Size On the assumption that trucks enter and leave the fleet at a uniform rate during the month, the average fleet size during the month is the average of beginning and ending inventory. For any month t

$$FS_t = (I_{t-1} + I_t)/2$$

Segment Linkage This set of constraints relates the fleet size to the demand segments discussed earlier. For any month t, we have:

$$FS_t = DS1_t + DS2_t + \text{Surplus (one equation for each month)}$$

These equations allow the model to satisfy as many demand segments as is economically feasible (i.e., profitable). In addition, there are upper limits on the size of any demand segment:

JANUARY	FEBRUARY		JUNE
$DS1_1 \leq 240$	$DS1_2 \leq 110$	etc...	$DS1_6 \leq 100$
$DS2_2 \leq 60$	$DS2_2 \leq 80$		$DS2_6 \leq 50$

Other Constraints In the actual AM model there are several other sets of constraints that cannot be illustrated in our simplified case. These include:

1. Mix composition by manufacturer (for example, at least 51% of trucks must be Toyota)
2. Mix composition of leased versus purchased trucks
3. Limits on the number of trucks that can be disposed of in any month. For example, if no more than 100 trucks could be returned (sold) in June, the constraint would be:

$$A_4 + B_3 + C_2 + D_1 \leq 100$$

4. Second buy restrictions. The manufacturers put limits on how many trucks could be leased or bought in the second half of the year, depending on the leases or purchases in the first half.

OBJECTIVE FUNCTION

The objective function is defined to maximize the contribution from operating the fleet. For each set of variables, there is revenue or cost as follows:

VARIABLES	REVENUE OR COST
Demand Segments ($DS1_t$,$DS2_t$)	Contribution margin: Incremental profit associated with renting the trucks to customers; depends on demand segments.
Acquisitions (A_t,B_t,C_t,D_t)	Cost: Cost of the purchase or lease of a truck from the manufacturer, less the returns from sales or turnbacks.
Fleet Size (FS_t) and Inventory (I_t)	Cost: Costs associated with size of fleet (insurance,taxes, etc.)

References

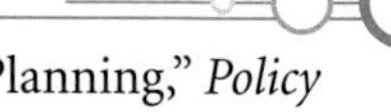

Horst, W.J. Rittel, and Melvin M. Webber, "Dilemmas in a General Theory of Planning," *Policy Sciences*, 4 (1973): 155–169.

Levasseur, R.E., "People Skills: How to Improve the Odds of a Successful Project Implementation," *Interfaces*, 23 (4 July–August 1993): 85–87.

Churchman, C.W., "Managerial Acceptance of Scientific Recommendations," *California Management Review*, 7 (Fall 1964): 31–38.

Walsham, Geoff, "Implementation of Operational Research: Some Lessons from Organizational Theory," *Operational Research*, 42, no. 5 (1990): 37–47.

Swanson, E.B., "Churchman's Theory of Design Integrity," *Interfaces*, 24 (4 July–August 1994): 54–59.

Schultz, R.L., D.P. Slevin, and J.K. Pinto, "Strategy and Tactics in a Process Model of Project Implementation," *Interfaces*, 17 (3 May–June 1987): 34–46.

Appendix A

BASIC CONCEPTS IN PROBABILITY

A.1 INTRODUCTION

Probability is the branch of mathematics that is used to model the uncertainty that occurs in nature, in science, and in business. Biologists use probability to model genetic evolution, physicists use probability to model the behavior of electrons in atoms, and economists use probability to model the behavior of stock prices. Texts such as this often use simple gambling games to motivate instruction in probability. For example, we can use probability to model the outcome of a roll of a pair of dice. The fundamental purpose of probability theory is to enable us to use what we know about simple uncertain events to calculate the probability of more complicated uncertain events. Thus, we can use our model of the probability of specific outcomes of rolling a pair of dice to calculate the probability of winning at the game of craps.

RANDOM VARIABLES

It is impossible to talk about probability without talking about random variables. Unfortunately, it is difficult to talk about random variables in a precise manner without getting into more abstract detail than this brief appendix allows or that is really required for this text. For our purposes, think of a random variable as an uncertain event that takes on a numerical value—for example, the face showing after the role of a die, the number of swimsuits sold by Newport News during July, the price of Yahoo! stock at the end of next week, the number of snowy days in Nome, Alaska, in 2005, and so on.

TYPES OF PROBABILITIES

There are two basic types of probability models: discrete and continuous. The difference between them is not important in terms of the concepts used in management science. However, each type requires the use of a different branch of mathematics. Arithmetic is really all we need to handle discrete probabilities, but integral and differential calculus must be used for continuous random variables.

A.2 DISCRETE PROBABILITIES

A. THE PROBABILITY MASS FUNCTION (PMF)

Discrete probabilities are defined with the probability mass function, $f(x)$. Specifically, $f(x)$ is the probability that the random variable of interest takes on the value x. Consider the following examples.

Example 1: A Discrete Uniform Distribution. Suppose that we continue with the example of the roll of a die, and assume that each face of the die is equally likely to appear. Then

$$\begin{aligned} f(x) &= 1/6 \qquad (x = 1, 2, 3, 4, 5, 6) \\ &= 0 \qquad (\text{otherwise}) \end{aligned}$$

The pmf for this distribution is shown in Figure A.1(a).

(a) Probability Mass Function

FIGURE A.1(a)

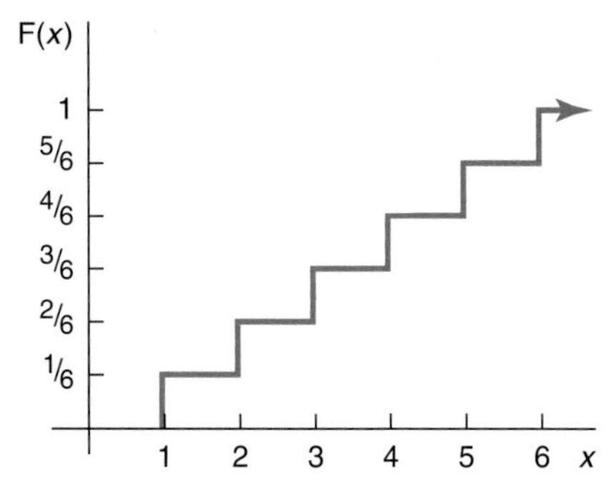

(b) Cumulative Distribution Function

FIGURE A.1(b)

Example 2: An Arbitrary Discrete Distribution. Assume that an urn contains five balls that are identical except for the numbers written on them. Two balls have a 23 on them and the other three have 37 written on them. Assume that a ball is chosen at random, that is, each ball is equally likely to be chosen. Then

$$\begin{aligned} f(x) &= 2/5 \qquad (x = 23) \\ &= 3/5 \qquad (x = 37) \\ &= 0 \qquad (\text{otherwise}) \end{aligned}$$

We note that $f(x) \geq 0$ and that $\Sigma f(x) = 1$. These two conditions must hold for any pmf.

Example 3: The Binomial Distribution. This distribution is used to model the results of a series of independent trials when, at each trial, a specific event either occurs or does not occur. (See Section A.5 B., page 610 for a definition of independence.) We encounter the binomial distribution in Chapter 9 where it is used to determine the probability of a customer with a reservation showing up for a flight departure in an airline's revenue management system. This distribution has two parameters: n, the number of trials, and p, the probability that the event occurs at each trial. It follows that $(1 - p)$ is the probability that the event does not occur. (The standard example is flipping a coin; the event is the occurrence of a head, and it is assumed that $p = 0.5$). The binomial distribution then is used to calculate the probability that the event occurs x times in n trials—for example, that there are seven heads in ten tosses of a coin. The pmf for the binomial distribution is

$$\begin{aligned} f(x) &= \binom{n}{x} p^x (1-p)^{n-x} \qquad (x = 0, 1, \cdots, n) \\ &= 0 \qquad (\text{otherwise}) \end{aligned}$$

Here the symbol $\binom{n}{x}$ is the number of ways that one can select x items out of n. It is calculated as follows:

$$\binom{n}{x} = \frac{n!}{x!(n-x)!} = \frac{(n)(n-1)\cdots(1)}{[(x)(x-1)\cdots(1)][(n-x)(n-x-1)\cdots(1)]}$$

For example, we see that the probability of seven heads in ten tosses of a coin, where the probability of a head at a single toss is 0.5 (i.e., $p = 0.5$), is

$$f(7) = \frac{(10)(9)(8)}{(3)(2)(1)} (0.5^7)(0.5^3) = 0.117$$

Example 4: The Poisson Distribution. This distribution is often used to model the number of arrivals in a specific time interval in a queuing system (Chapters 10 and 15). The pmf is

$$\begin{aligned} f(x) &= \frac{e^{-M}M^x}{x!} \qquad (x = 0, 1, 2, \cdots) \\ &= 0 \qquad (\text{otherwise}) \end{aligned}$$

where M is a parameter supplied by the manager.

B. THE CUMULATIVE DISTRIBUTION FUNCTION (CDF)

The cumulative distribution function $F(x)$ is the probability that the random variable takes on a value less than or equal to x. Since the probability mass function, $f(x)$, is the probability that the random variable takes on the value x, it follows that

$$F(x) = \sum_{j=-\infty}^{x} f(j)$$

Example 1 (continued): Discrete Uniform Distribution. If the random variable is the value showing on the throw of a fair die, then

$$\begin{aligned} F(x) &= 0 && (x < 1) \\ &= 1/6 && (1 \le x < 2) \\ &= 2/6 && (2 \le x < 3) \\ &= 3/6 && (3 \le x < 4) \\ &= 4/6 && (4 \le x < 5) \\ &= 5/6 && (5 \le x < 6) \\ &= 1 && (6 \le x) \end{aligned}$$

The CDF for this distribution is shown in Figure A.1(b).

Example 2 (continued): Arbitrary Discrete Distribution.

$$\begin{aligned} F(x) &= 0 && (x < 23) \\ &= 2/5 && (23 \le x < 37) \\ &= 1 && (37 \le x) \end{aligned}$$

A.3 CONTINUOUS PROBABILITIES

A. THE PROBABILITY DENSITY FUNCTION

Continuous probabilities are defined by the probability density function (pdf). If $f(x)$ is the pdf for a random variable, then we know that $f(x) \ge 0$ for all x, and

$$\int_{-\infty}^{\infty} f(x)\,dx = 1$$

This is the continuous analog of the fact that the pmf for a discrete random variable is always greater than or equal to 0 and must sum to 1.

B. THE CUMULATIVE DISTRIBUTION FUNCTION

The cumulative distribution function retains its definition for both continuous and discrete random variables—that is, $F(x)$ is the probability that the random variable takes on a value less than or equal to x. For continuous random variables, the relationship between the probability density function (pdf) and the cumulative distribution function (CDF) is as follows

$$F(x) = \int_{-\infty}^{x} f(r)\,dr$$

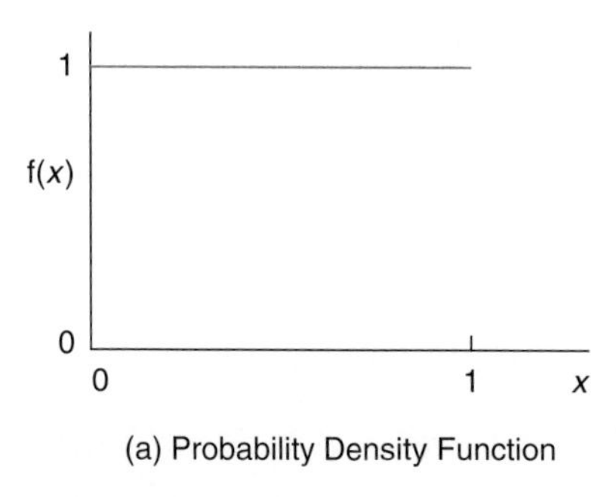

(a) Probability Density Function

FIGURE A.2(a)

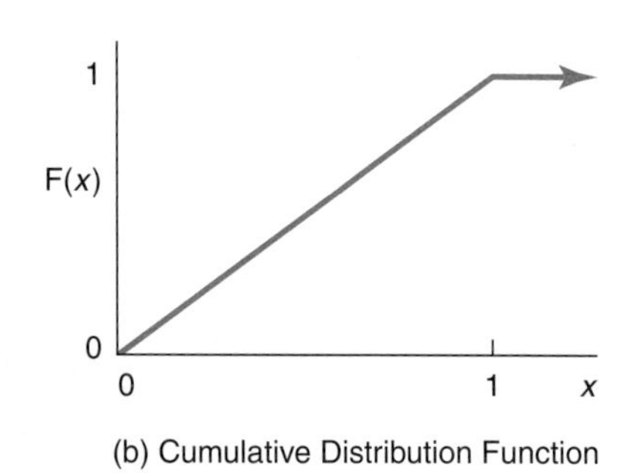

(b) Cumulative Distribution Function

FIGURE A.2(b)

Here we integrate the density function from $-\infty$ to x to determine the probability that the random variable is less than or equal to x. With discrete probabilities the concept is the same, but we sum the probability mass function rather than integrating the probability density function.

C. IMPORTANT EXAMPLES

Here we describe three distributions that play an important role in this text and in applied business problems.

Example 5: The Continuous Uniform Distribution. The uniform distribution on the interval 0 to 1 plays a crucial role in simulation, in that it is used to generate random variables (see Chapter 9).

$$\begin{aligned} \text{f}(x) &= 0 \qquad (x < 0) \\ &= 1 \qquad (0 \le x \le 1) \\ &= 0 \qquad (1 < x) \end{aligned}$$

Then by definition

$$\begin{aligned} \text{F}(x) &= \int_{-\infty}^{x} \text{f}(r)\, dr \\ &= 0 \qquad (x < 0) \\ &= x \qquad (0 \le x \le 1) \\ &= 1 \qquad (1 \le x) \end{aligned}$$

Figure A.2(a) and (b) show the pdf and the CDF for the continuous uniform distribution.

Example 6: The Exponential Distribution. The exponential distribution is used to describe the interarrival time between events in most queuing systems (Chapters 10 and 15). It is a one-parameter distribution. The parameter is typically denoted by λ. The pdf takes the form

$$\begin{aligned} \text{f}(x) &= 0 \qquad (x < 0) \\ &= \lambda e^{-\lambda x} \qquad (0 \le x) \end{aligned}$$

Using the definition for the CDF we see that

$$\begin{aligned} \text{F}(x) &= 0 \qquad (x < 0) \\ &= 1 - e^{-\lambda x} \qquad (0 \le x) \end{aligned}$$

Figure A.3 shows the pdf and the CDF for an exponential distribution with parameter $\lambda = 1$.

FIGURE A.3

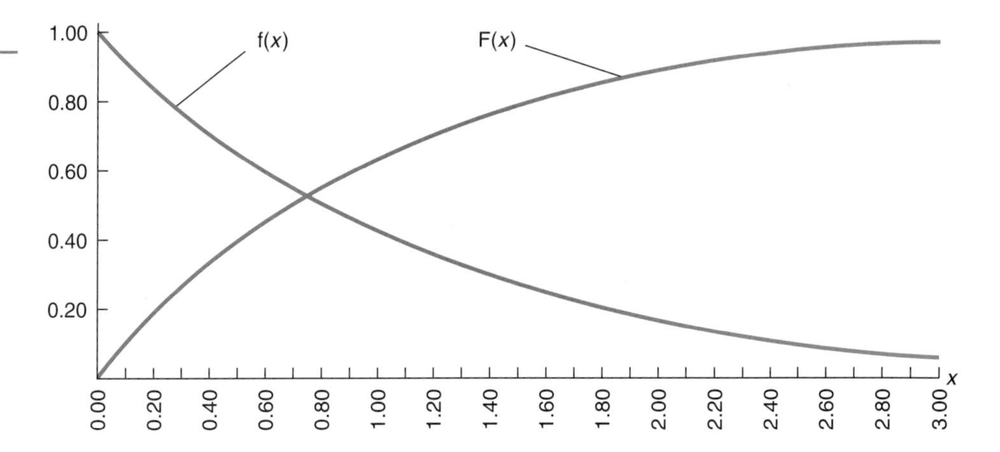

Example 7: The Normal Distribution. The normal distribution plays a fundamental role in probability and statistics. In this text, it occurs in a number of places—for example, it is used to represent uncertain demand in Chapter 9 as well as the probability that a project will be completed by a specific time in Chapter 14.

The normal is a two-parameter distribution. The parameters are μ, the mean, and σ, the standard deviation, which is required to be greater than 0. There is, of course, a mathematical expression for the density function of a normal pdf, but we will not show it here since we never make direct use of this expression. The pdf of the normal distribution is not integrable in closed form—that is,

$$\int_{-\infty}^{x} f(r)\, dr$$

cannot be written as a combination of elementary functions of x, when $f(r)$ is a normal distribution. Tables such as Table A.0 are used to evaluate $F(x)$, the CDF, for the normal distribution (represented graphically in Figure A.4). The next section is devoted to using Table A.0 to determine values for normal probabilities.

D. USING THE NORMAL TABLE

The Standard Normal Distribution Table A.0 can be used to find values for the CDF, $F(x)$, of a normal distribution with mean μ and standard deviation σ. (See Section A.4, pages 607 and 608, for a definition of μ and σ.) Actually, the table provides values for $F(x)$ for a normal distribution with $\mu = 0$ and $\sigma = 1$. (In a moment we will show how this table can be used to find values for the CDF of any normal distribution.) The values in the body of Table A.0 are the probability that a standard normal random variable (SNRV) takes on a value between the mean, 0, and the value of z shown in the row and column headings as shown in Figure A.5. Thus by looking in the row 0.4 and the column 0.05, we discover that a SNRV takes on a value between 0 and 0.45 with probability 0.1736.

Using this table and the fact that an SNRV is symmetrical about the mean allows us to find the probability that an SNRV falls into any range of numbers. Here are some examples (referring to the accompanying figure may provide some visual help in understanding the calculations).

$$\text{Prob}\{\text{SNRV} < 0.45\} = 0.5 + 0.1736 = 0.6736$$

$$\text{Prob}\{\text{SNRV} > 0.45\} = 1.0 - 0.6736 = 0.3264$$

$$\text{Prob}\{\text{SNRV} \leq -0.45\} = 0.5 - 0.1736 = 0.3264$$

You have probably observed that there are many different ways to calculate these results. For example, we knew that Prob{SNRV ≤ -0.45} = 0.3264 from the facts that Prob{SNRV > 0.45} = 0.3264 and that the normal distribution is symmetrical about the mean.

Table A.0

Areas for the Standard Normal Distribution

ENTRIES IN THE TABLE GIVE THE AREA UNDER THE CURVE BETWEEN THE MEAN AND Z STANDARD DEVIATIONS ABOVE THE MEAN. FOR EXAMPLE, FOR Z = 1.25 THE AREA UNDER THE CURVE BETWEEN THE MEAN AND Z IS 0.3944.

z	0.00	0.01	0.02	0.03	0.04	0.05	0.06	0.07	0.08	0.09
0.0	0.0000	0.0040	0.0080	0.0120	0.0160	0.0199	0.0239	0.0279	0.0319	0.0359
0.1	0.0398	0.0438	0.0478	0.0517	0.0557	0.0596	0.0636	0.0675	0.0714	0.0753
0.2	0.0793	0.0832	0.0871	0.0910	0.0948	0.0987	0.1026	0.1064	0.1103	0.1141
0.3	0.1179	0.1217	0.1255	0.1293	0.1331	0.1368	0.1406	0.1443	0.1480	0.1517
0.4	0.1554	0.1591	0.1628	0.1664	0.1700	0.1736	0.1772	0.1808	0.1844	0.1879
0.5	0.1915	0.1950	0.1985	0.2019	0.2054	0.2088	0.2123	0.2157	0.2190	0.2224
0.6	0.2257	0.2291	0.2324	0.2357	0.2389	0.2422	0.2454	0.2486	0.2518	0.2549
0.7	0.2580	0.2612	0.2642	0.2673	0.2704	0.2734	0.2764	0.2794	0.2823	0.2852
0.8	0.2881	0.2910	0.2939	0.2967	0.2995	0.3023	0.3051	0.3078	0.3106	0.3133
0.9	0.3159	0.3186	0.3212	0.3238	0.3264	0.3289	0.3315	0.3340	0.3365	0.3389
1.0	0.3413	0.3438	0.3461	0.3485	0.3508	0.3531	0.3554	0.3577	0.3599	0.3621
1.1	0.3643	0.3665	0.3686	0.3708	0.3729	0.3749	0.3770	0.3790	0.3810	0.3830
1.2	0.3849	0.3869	0.3888	0.3907	0.3925	0.3944	0.3962	0.3980	0.3997	0.4015
1.3	0.4032	0.4049	0.4066	0.4082	0.4099	0.4115	0.4131	0.4147	0.4162	0.4177
1.4	0.4192	0.4207	0.4222	0.4236	0.4251	0.4265	0.4279	0.4292	0.4306	0.4319
1.5	0.4332	0.4345	0.4357	0.4370	0.4382	0.4394	0.4406	0.4418	0.4429	0.4441
1.6	0.4452	0.4463	0.4474	0.4484	0.4495	0.4505	0.4515	0.4525	0.4535	0.4545
1.7	0.4554	0.4564	0.4573	0.4582	0.4591	0.4599	0.4608	0.4616	0.4625	0.4633
1.8	0.4641	0.4649	0.4656	0.4664	0.4671	0.4678	0.4686	0.4693	0.4699	0.4706
1.9	0.4713	0.4719	0.4726	0.4732	0.4738	0.4744	0.4750	0.4756	0.4761	0.4767
2.0	0.4772	0.4778	0.4783	0.4788	0.4793	0.4798	0.4803	0.4808	0.4812	0.4817
2.1	0.4821	0.4826	0.4830	0.4834	0.4838	0.4842	0.4846	0.4850	0.4854	0.4857
2.2	0.4861	0.4864	0.4868	0.4871	0.4875	0.4878	0.4881	0.4884	0.4887	0.4890
2.3	0.4893	0.4896	0.4898	0.4901	0.4904	0.4906	0.4909	0.4911	0.4913	0.4916
2.4	0.4918	0.4920	0.4922	0.4925	0.4927	0.4929	0.4931	0.4932	0.4934	0.4936
2.5	0.4938	0.4940	0.4941	0.4943	0.4945	0.4946	0.4948	0.4949	0.4951	0.4952
2.6	0.4953	0.4955	0.4956	0.4957	0.4959	0.4960	0.4961	0.4962	0.4963	0.4964
2.7	0.4965	0.4966	0.4967	0.4968	0.4969	0.4970	0.4971	0.4972	0.4973	0.4974
2.8	0.4974	0.4975	0.4976	0.4977	0.4977	0.4978	0.4979	0.4979	0.4980	0.4981
2.9	0.4981	0.4982	0.4982	0.4983	0.4984	0.4984	0.4985	0.4985	0.4986	0.4986
3.0	0.4986	0.4987	0.4987	0.4988	0.4988	0.4989	0.4989	0.4989	0.4990	0.4990

Reprinted with permission from Richard I. Levin and Charles A. Kirkpatrick, *Quantitative Approaches to Management, 3rd Edition*, McGraw-Hill, Inc., New York, NY, 1975.

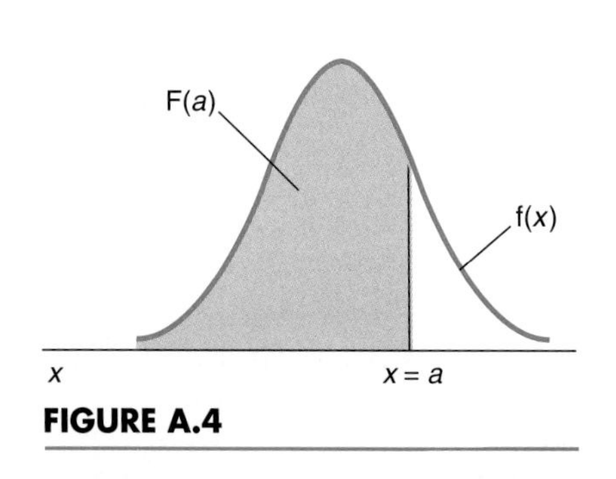

FIGURE A.4

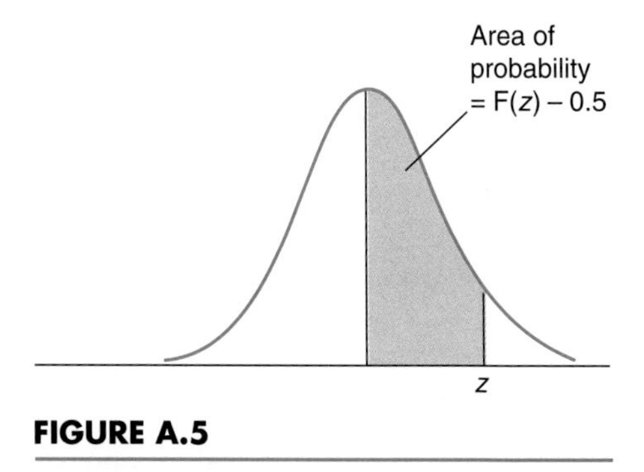

FIGURE A.5

Any Normal Random Variable Let NRV be a normal random variable with mean μ and standard deviation σ. To find the probability that this random variable falls into a range of values, we make use of this fundamental relationship.

$$\text{Prob}\{\text{NRV} \leq x\} = \text{Prob}\{\text{SNRV} \leq (x - \mu)/\sigma\}$$

Here is an example. Suppose that NRV has $\mu = 50$ and $\sigma = 100$ and we want to find the probability that NRV ≤ 95. We proceed as follows:

$$\begin{aligned}\text{Prob}\{\text{NRV} \leq 95\} &= \text{Prob}\{\text{SNRV} \leq (95 - 50)/100\} \\ &= \text{Prob}\{\text{SNRV} \leq 0.45\} = 0.6736.\end{aligned}$$

This procedure becomes second nature with a little practice.

A.4 EXPECTED VALUES

The expected cost or profit is often the objective in decisions under uncertainty—that is, in decision problems in which the payoff from a decision is a random variable. We first introduce the expected value of a random variable and then turn to the expected value of a function of a random variable.

A. EXPECTED VALUE OF A RANDOM VARIABLE

The expected value of a random variable—say, X—is typically written $E(X)$. It is called the mean of the random variable, typically denoted with the Greek letter μ. We will define $E(X)$ for both discrete and continuous random variables.

Discrete Random Variables For a discrete random variable where $f(x)$ is the probability mass function,

$$E(X) = \mu = \sum_{-\infty}^{\infty} x f(x)$$

Here are some examples.

Example 1 (continued): Discrete Uniform Distribution.

$$E(X) = 1\left(\frac{1}{6}\right) + 2\left(\frac{1}{6}\right) + 3\left(\frac{1}{6}\right) + 4\left(\frac{1}{6}\right) + 5\left(\frac{1}{6}\right) + 6\left(\frac{1}{6}\right) = 3.5$$

It is interesting to note that the expected value of a random variable does not have to be one of the values that the random variable can assume. For example, a die cannot take on the value 3.5. A physical interpretation is that the expected value is the center of gravity of the probability mass function. That is, if you think of the probabilities in a pmf as weights and place a fulcrum under the expected value, the pmf will balance. The expected value has a second intuitive interpretation. Think of a series of independent observations of a random variable. If you calculate the average of the values, you expect it to be close to the expected value.

Example 2 (continued): Arbitrary Discrete Distribution.

$$E(X) = 23\left(\frac{2}{5}\right) + 37\left(\frac{3}{5}\right) = 31.4$$

Example 3 (continued): Binomial Distribution. Here we state without providing a proof that for a binomial random variable, X, with parameters n and p,

$$E(X) = np$$

This result is intuitively appealing. If we flip a fair coin ten times, on the average we would expect to observe five heads.

Example 4 (continued): Poisson Distribution. The expected value of the Poisson distribution is M. The variance is M as well. These results are easily derived, but the derivations are not central to our purpose.

Continuous Random Variables The definition of the expected value of a continuous random variable is essentially the same as for the discrete case. Here, however, we must use the pdf and integration, that is

$$E(X) = \int_{-\infty}^{\infty} x f(x)\, dx$$

Example 5 (continued): Continuous Uniform Distribution.

$$E(X) = \int_0^1 x \cdot 1 \cdot dx = \left.\frac{x^2}{2}\right|_0^1 = \frac{1}{2}$$

It is easy to see that $\frac{1}{2}$ is the center of gravity for the density function shown in Figure A.2(a).

Example 6 (continued): Exponential Distribution.

$$E(X) = \int_0^{\infty} x\lambda e^{-\lambda x} dx = 1/\lambda$$

This integration requires a technique called integration by parts, and the details have been omitted.

B. EXPECTED VALUE OF A FUNCTION OF A RANDOM VARIABLE

The General Concept Let $G(x)$ be any function defined on x. Then for a discrete random variable X with pmf $f(x)$, the expected value of $G(x)$, $E[G(X)]$, is defined as follows:

$$E[G(X)] = \sum_{x=-\infty}^{\infty} G(x) f(x)$$

A similar definition using integrals holds for continuous random variables.

We have two main reasons for being interested in the expected value of functions of random variables. One is to define the variance of a random variable and the other is to define expected costs or profits. These topics are discussed in the following sections.

Variance and Standard Deviation of a Random Variable The variance is a measure of dispersion of the distribution of a random variable. It is typically denoted as σ^2 and is defined as follows:

$$\mathrm{Var}(X) = \sigma^2 = E[(X - E(X))^2] = \sum_{-\infty}^{\infty} (x - E(X))^2 f(x)$$

The variance plays an important role in statistics. It is the most popular measure of dispersion of the distribution of a random variable, and it is one of the two parameters of the normal distribution (see page 605). To develop a feeling for the interpretation of variance as a measure of dispersion, consider two random variables X and Y. Let $f_X(x)$ be the pmf for X and $f_Y(y)$ be the pmf for Y. Let

$$f_X(x) = \frac{1}{2} \quad (x = 4, 6)$$
$$= 0 \quad \text{(otherwise)}$$

and

$$f_Y(y) = \frac{1}{2} \quad (y = 1, 9)$$
$$= 0 \quad \text{(otherwise)}$$

Note that both random variables have an expected value of five. You should be able to verify that $\mathrm{Var}(X) = \sigma^2 = 1$ and $\mathrm{Var}(Y) = \sigma^2 = 16$. The intuitive notion is that a random variable that has a greater probability of being further from the mean will have a larger variance. That notion is consistent with this example.

The standard deviation, typically denoted by σ, is simply the square root of the variance, that is,

$$\text{Standard Deviation of } X = (\text{Variance of } X)^{1/2}$$

or

$$\sigma = (\sigma^2)^{1/2}$$

C. EXPECTED RETURN

In most business applications, management is interested in the returns (or costs) associated with the occurrence of a random event.

Discrete Random Variables To calculate the expected return, we let R(x) be the return if the random variable x occurs and use the standard definition for the expected value of a function of a random variable.

$$E[R(X)] = \sum_{x=-\infty}^{\infty} R(x)f(x)$$

Example 1 (continued): Discrete Uniform Distribution. A gambler offers to pay you $10 times the value of the face of the die that is showing if a 3, 4, 5, or 6 occur and nothing if a 1 or 2 occurs. What is the expected value of this game?

x	R(x)	f(x)	R(x)f(x)
1	0	$\frac{1}{6}$	0
2	0	$\frac{1}{6}$	0
3	30	$\frac{1}{6}$	5
4	40	$\frac{1}{6}$	$6\frac{2}{3}$
5	50	$\frac{1}{6}$	$8\frac{1}{3}$
6	60	$\frac{1}{6}$	10
		Expected Value = $\Sigma R(x)f(x) = 30$	

Continuous Random Variables The concept of finding the expected value of the function R(X) remains the same as in the discrete case. As usual, in the continuous case we must use integration and the pdf.

Example 5 (continued): Continuous Uniform Distribution. We will observe a random variable from a continuous uniform distribution on the interval 0 to 1. A gambler offers to pay 0 if the value is between 0 and 0.2 and $10 times the value of the random variable if the value is greater than 0.2 and less than or equal to 1. It follows that

$$\begin{aligned} R(x) &= 0 \qquad (x \leq 0.2) \\ &= 10x \qquad (0.2 < x \leq 1) \end{aligned}$$

Then

$$\begin{aligned} E[R(x)] &= \int_0^{.2} 0 \cdot 1 \cdot dx + \int_{.2}^{1} 10x \cdot 1 \cdot dx = 10\left(\frac{x^2}{2}\right)\Bigg|_{0.2}^{1} \\ &= 4.8 \end{aligned}$$

A.5 MULTIVARIATE DISTRIBUTIONS

This section introduces the mathematics and the concepts that are used when there is more than one random variable under consideration. Such situations are common in practice. In a PERT network (Chapter 14), the time required to complete a path in a project is equal to the sum of the times required to complete each activity on that path. Similarly, the return from a portfolio of stocks (Chapter 7) is equal to the sum of the returns of the individual stocks held in the portfolio.

Multivariate random variables are introduced in CD Section 8.13 in the discussion of Bayes' Theorem, although the term multivariate is not mentioned there. It will be useful to refer to that discussion in what follows.

A. JOINT DISTRIBUTIONS

Discrete Random Variables It is useful to introduce some new notation in the discussion of multivariate random variables. Let

$f_{X,Y}(x, y)$ = the probability that the random variable X takes on the value x *and* the random variable Y takes on the value y.

Then $f_{X,Y}(x, y)$ is the *joint* probability mass function for the random variables X and Y. The word "and" is important in this definition. It indicates that both events (x, y) must happen.

The following game is introduced in CD Section 8.13.

1. A fair die is thrown.
2. The value of the die is used to determine from which of three urns we will draw a ball. Assume that each of the balls in a given urn is equally likely to be drawn.

The details are summarized in the following table.

DIE	URN	CONTENTS OF URN
1	1	28 White and 72 Black Balls
2 or 3	2	40 White and 60 Black Balls
4 or 5 or 6	3	92 White and 8 Black Balls

This game can now be used to illustrate a joint pmf. Let X be the value of the urn chosen; $Y = 1$ if a white ball is selected and $Y = 2$ if a black ball is selected. The values for $f_{X,Y}(x, y)$ are presented below.

X	Y = 1	Y = 2
1	(1/6)(28/100) = .0467	(1/6)(72/100) = .12
2	(2/6)(40/100) = .1333	(2/6)(60/100) = .20
3	(3/6)(92/100) = .4600	(3/6)(8/100) = .04

These values were derived from the definition of conditional probability:

$$f_{X,Y}(x, y) = f_X(x) f_{Y|X}(y|x)$$

A discussion of this relationship can be found in CD Section 8.13.

Continuous Random Variables Multivariate distributions also exist for continuous random variables. Indeed, the equation that defines the relationship between joint and conditional probabilities is used to define joint probability density functions and conditional probability density functions.

B. INDEPENDENT RANDOM VARIABLES

Two random variables, X and Y, are independent if

$$f_{X,Y}(x, y) = f_X(x) f_Y(y)$$

Since in general

$$f_{X,Y}(x, y) = f_{X|Y}(x|y) f_Y(y)$$

we see that X and Y are independent if

$$f_{X|Y}(x|y) = f_x(x)$$

The last equation says that knowing that the random variable Y takes on the value y tells us nothing about the probability that X will take on the value x. In other words, X and Y are independent.

C. EXPECTATION AND VARIANCE OF SUMS

The Expected Value of $X + Y$. It is always true (whether X and Y are independent or not) that

$$E(X + Y) = E(X) + E(Y)$$

The Variance of $X + Y$ The variance of $(X + Y)$ is defined as follows:

$$\text{Var}(X + Y) = \text{Var}(X) + \text{Var}(Y) + 2\text{Cov}(X, Y)$$

or

$$\sigma^2_{(X+Y)} = \sigma^2_X + \sigma^2_Y + 2\sigma_{XY}$$

The Covariance of X and Y In the previous expression, Cov(X, Y) is the covariance of X and Y. It is denoted by σ_{XY} and is itself defined as follows:

$$\text{Cov}(X, Y) = \sigma_{XY} = E([X - E(X)][Y - E(Y)])$$

The covariance of X and Y is an indication of how X and Y relate to each other, but it is difficult to have an intuitive feeling for what a particular value of the covariance means. The correlation coefficient is better suited to convey this. Note, however, that when X and Y are independent random variables $\sigma_{XY} = 0$.

The Correlation Coefficient of X and Y The correlation coefficient of X and Y is typically denoted as ρ_{XY} and is defined as follows

$$\rho_{XY} = \frac{\text{Cov}(X, Y)}{[\text{StdDev}(X)][\text{StdDev}(Y)]} = \frac{\sigma_{XY}}{\sigma_X \sigma_Y}$$

The correlation coefficient can take on values from –1 to 1. A large positive value suggests that X and Y tend to move together—that is, when X is large then Y is apt to be large as well. Negative values suggest that X and Y move in opposite directions—that is, when X is large Y is apt to be small. If $\sigma_{XY} = 0$, X and Y are said to be uncorrelated.

The Expectation and Variance for the Sum of Several Random Variables Let

$$Z = \sum_{i=1}^{N} X_i$$

That is, Z is the sum of N random variables $X_1, X_2, \ldots, X_N$. Then

$$E(Z) = \sum_{i=1}^{N} E(X_i)$$

In words, the expected value of a sum equals the sum of the expected values.

$$\text{Var}(Z) = \sum_{i=1}^{N} \text{Var}(X_i) + 2 \sum_{i=1}^{N-1} \sum_{j>i}^{N} \text{Cov}(X_i, X_j)$$

In words, the variance of the sum is equal to the sum of the variances plus two times the sum of the covariances of all possible pairs of random variables.

Appendix B

EXCEL FEATURES USEFUL FOR MODELING

This is a summary of Excel features useful for modeling. It is set up with tasks listed in the margin along with steps for completing those tasks. If you see an unfamiliar task listed, or would like a quick review, simply follow the directions on the right. More complete summaries of a topic are given in Excel's on-line Help.

Where listed, "Win" means Windows Excel as implemented on Intel-compatible computers and "Mac" means Macintosh Excel as implemented on Apple computers. Other than for minor differences in appearance, dialogs, and operating system interactions, both versions of Excel are nearly identical. One exception is in the keyboard shortcuts. Both use two-key (and on occasion three-key) shortcut combinations, denoted here by "name_of_first_key" + "name_of_second_key." In many cases, a Win keyboard shortcut involving the "Ctrl" key, such as "Ctrl+z," is effected on Mac by substituting the Command key, for example, "Command+z." Figure B.1 shows the typical layout of an Excel window. Its major components are labeled for future reference.

B.1 EXCEL WINDOW ORGANIZATION

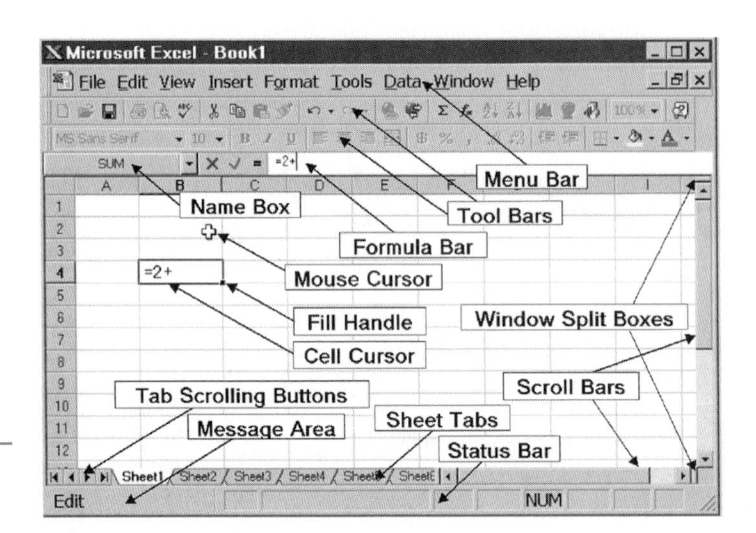

FIGURE B.1

Excel Window Organization

B.2 CONFIGURING THE WORKSHEET

Tools Options View . . .

Each of the features in Figure B.2(a) can be controlled when the "Options" item is selected from the Tools menu, and the View tab in Figure B.2(b) is chosen. If a box is checked, the item will appear on the screen display of the worksheet. (To control the *printer* output for similar features, such as grid lines, see Page Setup.) Default selections are shown in the figure. Checking the "Formulas" box will replace all worksheet cell contents by their formulas, where applicable.

Tools Options General . . .

Each of the features in Figure B.3 can be controlled when the "Options" item is selected from the Tools menu, and the General tab is chosen. It is suggested that you use defaults similar to those shown in the figure.

FIGURE B.2(a)

Options

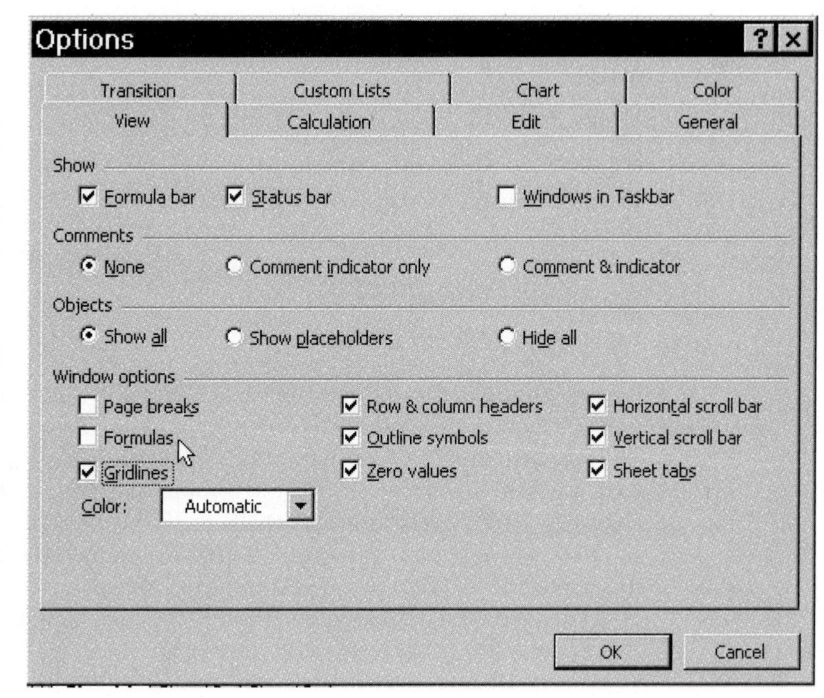

FIGURE B.2(b)

Options View

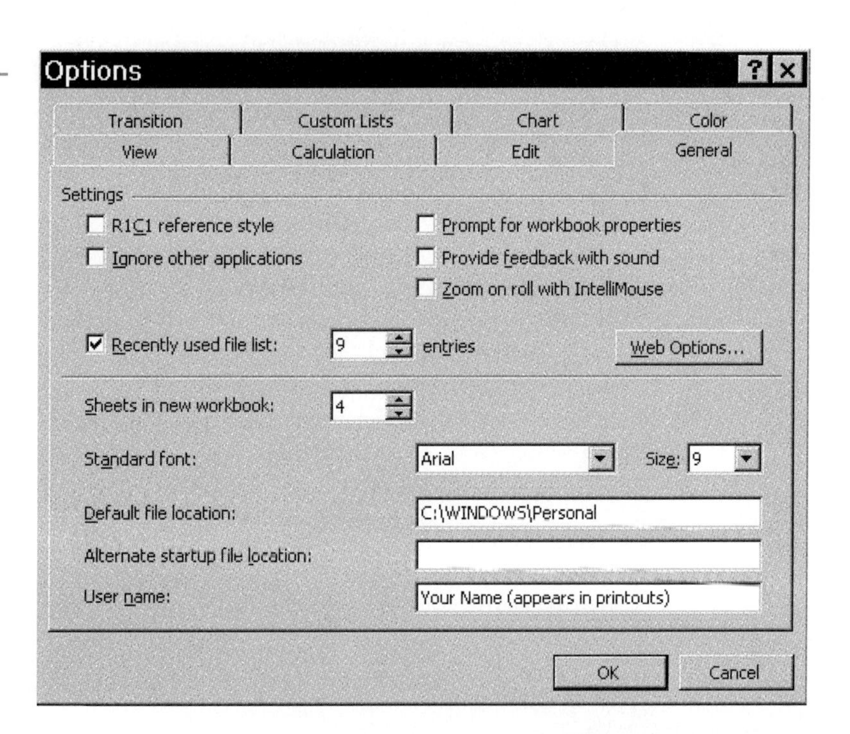

FIGURE B.3

Options General

FIGURE B.4

Command Underline "On" for Macintosh

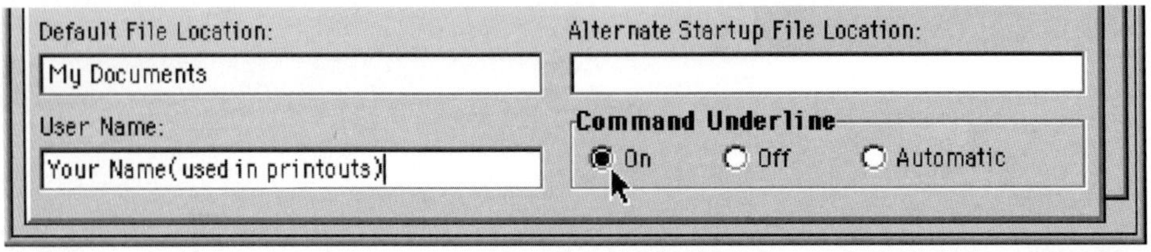

Default File Location: My Documents
Alternate Startup File Location:
User Name: Your Name(used in printouts)
Command Underline: On Off Automatic

For Mac, it is suggested that you turn "on" Command Underline, as shown in Figure B.4. It is useful for keyboard shortcuts.

Tools Options Transition . . .

Each of the features in Figure B.5 can be controlled when the Transitions tab is chosen. It is suggested that you set Alternate Menu Key to the "/" character allowing you to press "/" followed by the underlined letters in menu selection items as a fast shortcut to menuing. The suggested Save Excel file type assures backward compatibility at the cost of larger file sizes. Unchecking the Transition Navigation Keys option produces a more predictable application of Excel's keyboard shortcuts and is recommended.

Tools Options Edit . . .

Each of the features in Figure B.6 can be controlled when the Edit tab is chosen. It is suggested that you check the "Edit Directly in Cell" option to allow editing cell entries without going to the Formula Bar—just double click at the point you wish to begin editing in the cell. Unchecking "Move selection after Enter" allows multiple "What If?" projections for a single-model input cell without cursoring.

Tools Options Calculation . . .

Each of the features in Figure B.7 can be controlled when the Calculation tab is chosen. If you create large Data Tables or very large worksheet models, selecting Automatic Except for Tables or Manual, respectively, will improve response times when editing worksheets. In either case, Excel will signal whenever the worksheet needs to have its tables or formulas recomputed, that is, recalculated, by displaying "Calculate" in the Message Bar, as shown in Figure B.8. When necessary, the worksheet can be recalculated manually by pressing the F9 key (Win or Mac) or the Ctrl+= (Win or Mac) or Command+= (Mac) key combination.

FIGURE B.5

Options Transition

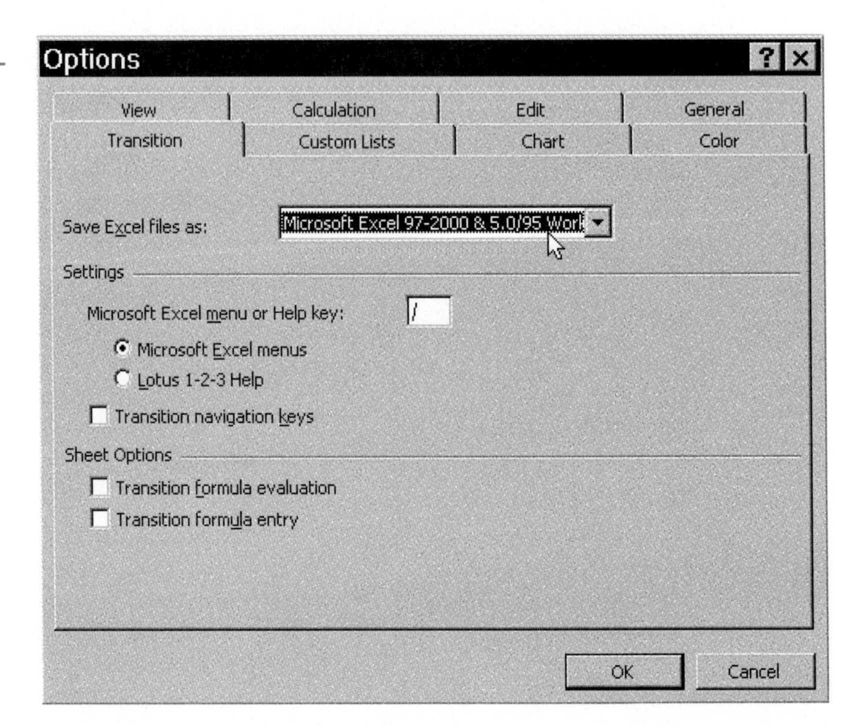

FIGURE B.6

Options Edit

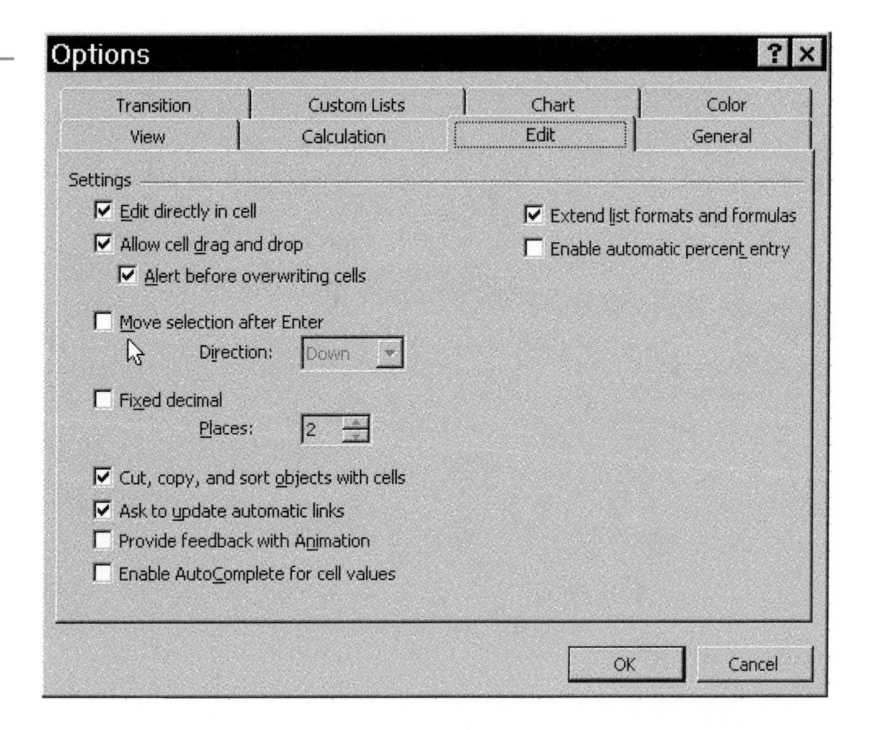

FIGURE B.7

Options Calculation

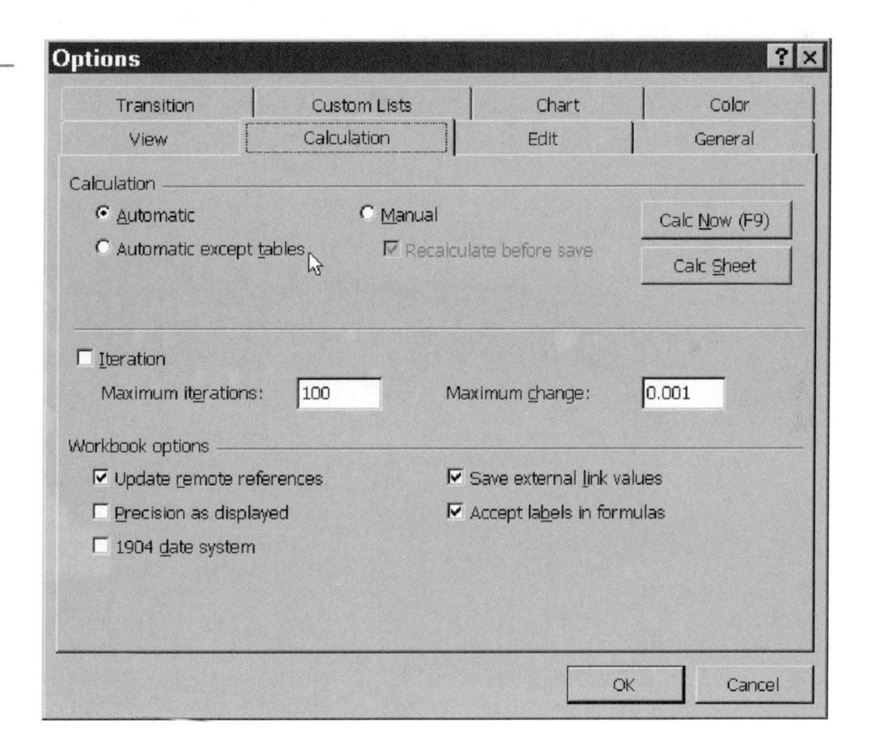

FIGURE B.8

Calculate Message

B.3 MANIPULATING WINDOWS AND WORKSHEETS

Multiple Panes

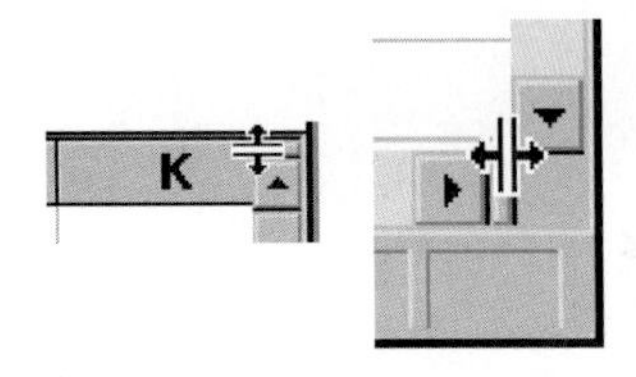

A worksheet may be split into two panes by positioning the mouse cursor over one of the Window Split boxes until it changes shape and then dragging it into the window. Repeating this for the other Window Split Box produces another two panes, as shown in Figure B.9. Additional Scroll Bars appear to allow independent scrolling of rows and columns across panes. Positioning the mouse cursor over a pane bar until it changes to and double clicking removes the pane. *Note:* The "Split" item on Window menu is equivalent to using the Window Split boxes.

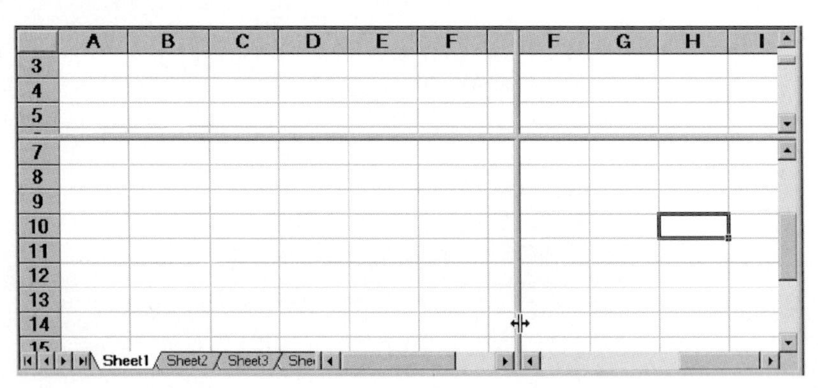

FIGURE B.9

Multiple Window Panes

Freezing Panes

The Freeze Panes item in the Window menu is similar to the use of panes in Figure B.9. In this case, however, the panes above and to the left of the cell cursor are not scrollable. This feature is often used to lock column-headings and row-stub entries into place while scrolling over large worksheet models. Place the cell cursor in the upper left cell of the area to remain unfrozen (scrollable) and select Freeze Panes from the Window menu. Rows 1 and 2 and column A will be frozen, for the example shown in Figure B.10.

FIGURE B.10

Freezing Panes

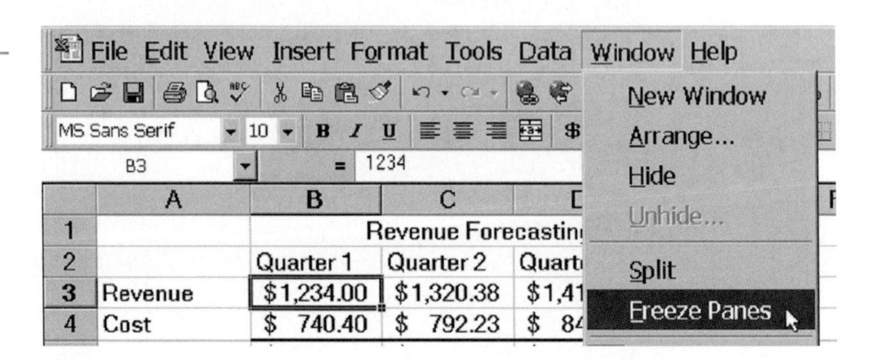

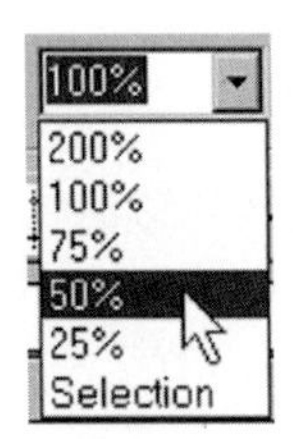

Zooming Worksheets

The Zoom tool may be used to increase or decrease the displayed size of a worksheet. Selecting small percentages displays more cells of the worksheet in the window. Selecting a range of cells and choosing the "Selection" item in the list will adjust the magnification to have the selected cells exactly fill the screen. Selecting "100%" returns the worksheet display to normal.

Multiple Windows

Selecting the New Window item from the Window menu, as shown in Figure B.11(a), opens a second window to the active workbook, which may be moved and scrolled independently of the first window. However, both are windows showing the contents of the *same* underlying workbook. Selecting the Arrange item from the Window menu, also

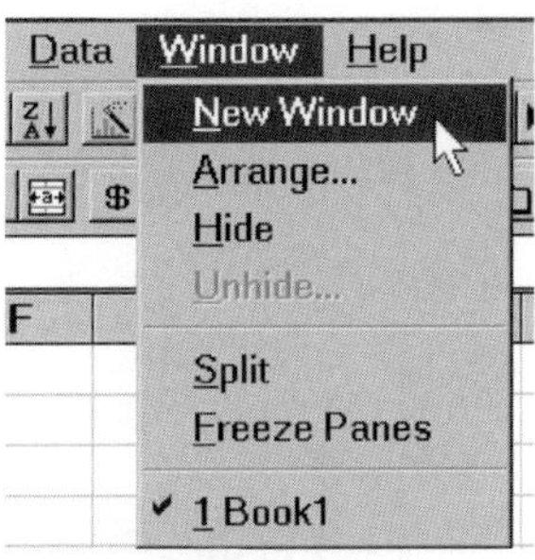

FIGURE B.11(a)

Creating a New Window

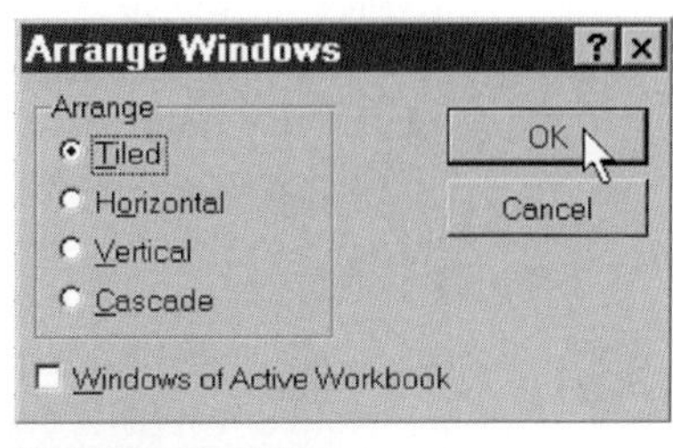

FIGURE B.11(b)

Arranging Windows

shown in Figure B.11(b), and clicking the Tiled option in the Arrange Windows dialog will divide the screen into equal-sized areas holding each window, as shown in Figure B.12. Multiple windows to a workbook offer additional flexibility, for example, displaying other worksheets in the same workbook. In addition, each window can be split into panes, yielding a wide variety of viewing options for large worksheet models. In the example in Figure B.12, both the worksheet and its formulas are displayed by setting the right-hand window to display worksheet formulas.

FIGURE B.12

Two Tiled Windows

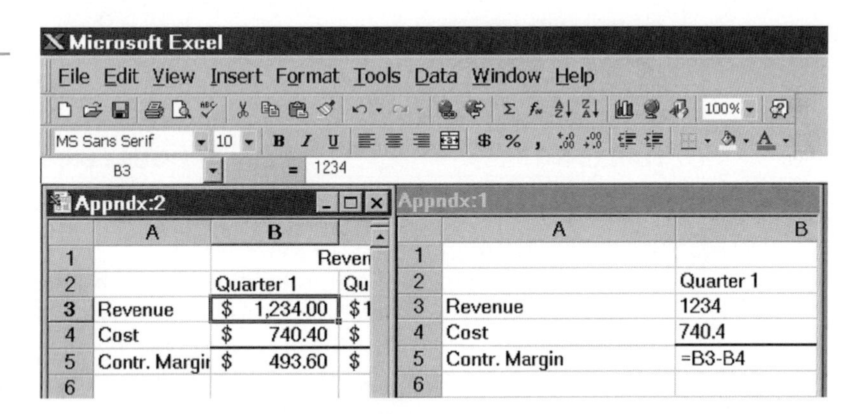

Hiding Windows

Windows may be hidden temporarily to get them out of the way by selecting the Hide item in the Window menu. The Unhide item on the same menu reverses this operation to bring the window back. See Figure B.11a.

Hiding Worksheets

Similar to hiding windows, worksheets within a workbook may be hidden for convenience. Selecting the "Sheet Hide" item on the Format menu will hide the active worksheet. The adjacent Unhide item in the same menu reverses this operation. (See Figure B.13.)

Renaming Worksheets

Selecting "Sheet Rename" on the Format menu (or double clicking the worksheet name tab) allows editing the worksheet default name. (See Figure B.14.)

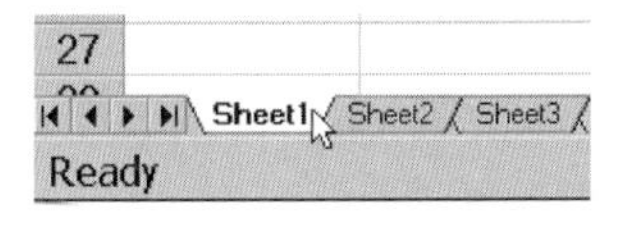

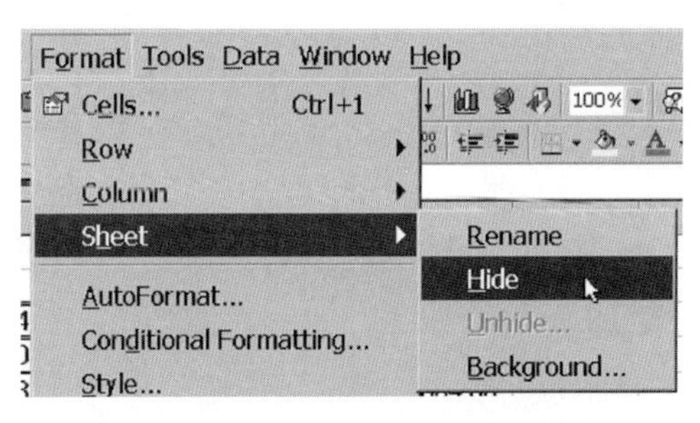

FIGURE B.13

Hiding the Active Worksheet

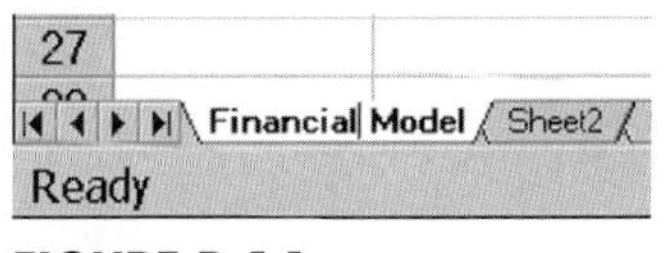

FIGURE B.14

Renaming a Worksheet

B.4

SELECTING CELLS

One row or column

To select one row or column of cells, click the row or column heading, as shown in Figure B.15.

Multiple contiguous rows or columns

To select multiple contiguous rows or columns, click-drag across row or column headings, as shown in Figure B.16.

Entire worksheet

To select an entire worksheet click the blank box in the upper-left corner of the worksheet grid, as shown in Figure B.17.

A range of cells

To select a range of cells, drag across the range of cells, as shown in Figure B.18, or

1. Select the first cell,
2. Hold down SHIFT key or depress F8 key to turn Extend mode on,
3. Press the arrow keys to extend selection, and
4. Release SHIFT key or depress F8 key to turn Extend mode off.

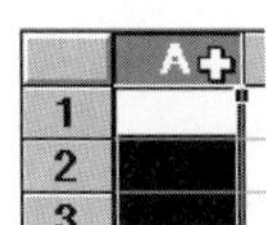

FIGURE B.15

One Row or Column

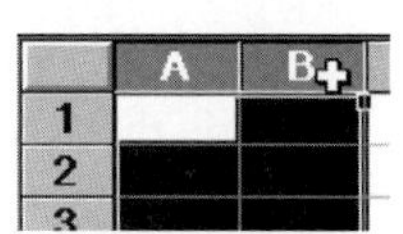

FIGURE B.16

Multiple Contiguous Rows or Columns

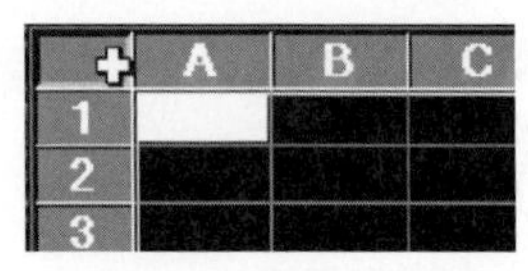

FIGURE B.17

Entire Worksheet

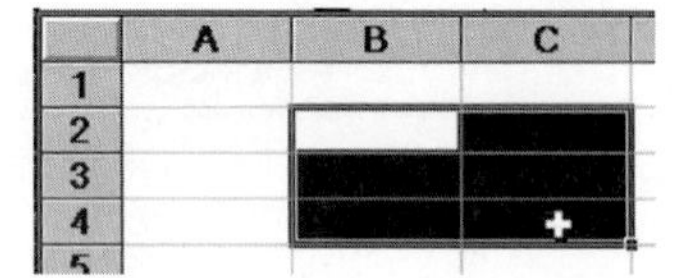

FIGURE B.18

A Range of Cells

Discontiguous cells, rows, or columns

To select discontiguous cells, rows, or columns, click-drag across the first set of cells, rows, or columns. Then, while holding down the Ctrl key (Win) or Command key (Mac), use the mouse to drag across the next set of cells, rows, or columns, and so forth. (See Figure B.19.) Alternatively,

1. Select the first cell or range of cells,
2. Press SHIFT+F8 to turn Add mode on,
3. Select first cell of next selection,
4. Depress F8 Function key to turn Extend mode on,
5. Repeat steps 2, 3, and 4 above for each new selection, and
6. Depress F8 Function key to turn Add mode off.

To select a range

To select a rectangular range, select any cell within the rectangular range of non-empty cells, as shown in Figure B.20. Press Ctrl+Shift+8. (Use the "8" key on the main keyboard, not the keypad.)

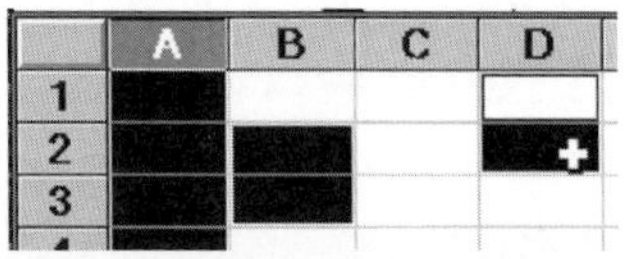

FIGURE B.19

Discontiguous Selections

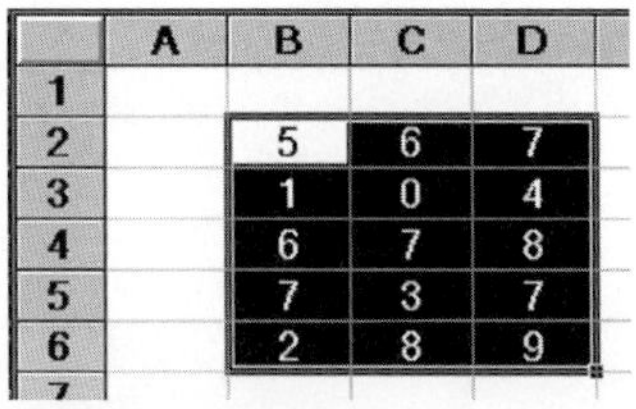

FIGURE B.20

Selecting a Rectangular Range

To move cell cursor to the edge of a range

Click the first cell within the range, press Ctrl+ARROW (Win or Mac), or press Command+ARROW (Mac), where "ARROW" is a keyboard arrow key in the desired direction (left, right, up, or down). (The Transition Navigation Keys setting under Options should be "off" for all arrow keys to work.)

To select cells from cell cursor to the edge of a range

Click the first cell within the range, press Ctrl + Shift + ARROW (Win or Mac), or press Command + Shift + ARROW (Mac), where "ARROW" is a keyboard arrow key in the desired direction (left, right, up, or down). (The Transition Navigation Keys setting under Options should be "off.") Repeating the command for the opposite arrow key direction will reverse the previous direction, depending on the ARROW key pressed. Then, pressing Shift + ARROW will augment the selection in the ARROW direction. With cell cursor starting on cell B2, Ctrl+Shift+↓ was pressed in the example in Figure B.21. If Shift+← were then pressed the selection would extend to include A2:B4.

FIGURE B.21

Extending Selections

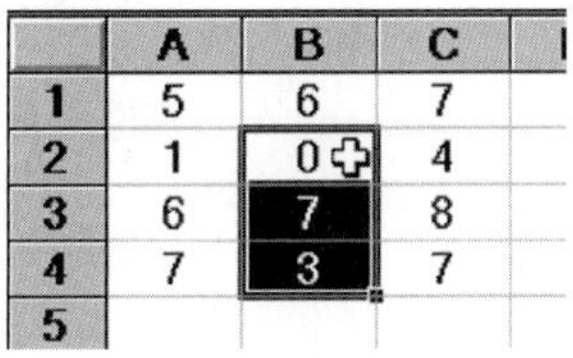

	A	B	C
1	5	6	7
2	1	0	4
3	6	7	8
4	7	3	7
5			

B.5 EDITING CELLS

Editing Cell Contents

Editing of a cell's formula or content is evoked by selecting the cell, clicking in the Formula Bar and deleting (delete or backspace key) or inserting characters (by typing). Depress the ENTER key to finish editing the cell, or depress the "Esc" key to abort editing the cell, returning it to its previous contents. Alternatively, double click on the cell to edit directly within the cell itself, as shown in Figure B.22. (Available only if enabled by an Options setting; see Figure B.6.)

Click the fx tool during formula entry to insert a predefined Excel function via the Function Wizard, described later. Clicking the Name Box will repeat application of a recently used function (in the example in Figure B.23, the IF( ) function will be inserted); clicking the Name Box drop-down arrow will present a list of recently used functions for insertion into the formula.

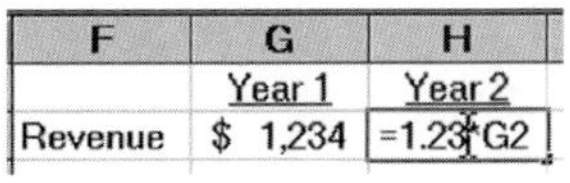

F	G	H
	Year 1	Year 2
Revenue	$ 1,234	=1.23*G2

FIGURE B.22

Editing Cells

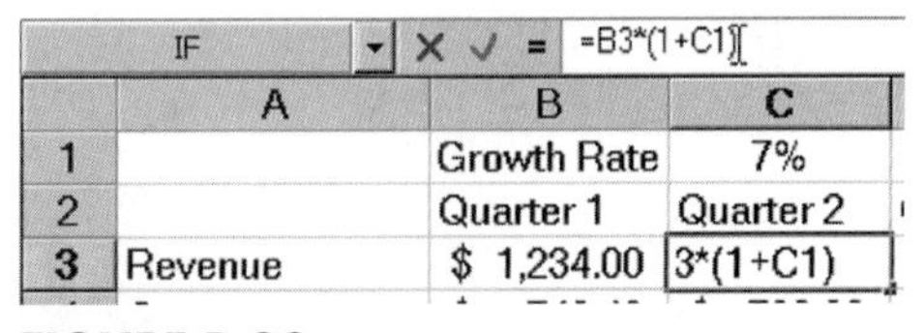

FIGURE B.23

Formula Editing

As shown in Figure B.24, clicking the = tool opens the cell for formula editing and displays the Formula Result bar. When showing, the Formula Result bar will calculate the value of the formula as you enter it, as shown in Figure B.25.

Absolute Cell References

In formulas, absolute references for cells are designated by dollar signs ($) before the row number and/or before the column letter. For example, $E$5 is an absolute reference. When included in a formula that is being copied or cut, it will always address the same E5 cell, no matter where the formula is pasted. Absolute references also can apply to just the row or just the column. For instance, E$5 will always refer to row 5, no matter where it is

FIGURE B.24

Edit Formula Tool

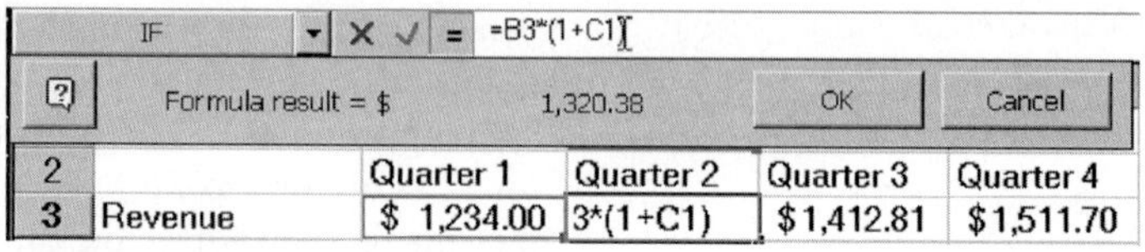

FIGURE B.25

Formula Result Bar

pasted. Likewise, $E5 will always refer to column E, no matter where it is pasted. This is useful when using the "Fill Down" and "Fill Right" commands. The $ characters may be typed directly into formulas when entering cell references, or select the cell address in the formula and press the F4 key (Win) or the Command+t key combination (Mac) to automatically insert the $ characters. Repeated pressing of the F4 key will cycle through all possible $ placements in the reference.

Relative Cell References

In formulas, relative references occur when no $ character(s) are used in cell address appearing in a formula, causing Excel to remember the cell reference relative to the cell in which the formula or reference is contained. Using a formula with relative references and copying it (via the "Fill Down" command or Copy and Paste), avoids typing in each cell's formula by hand. For example, if the formula in cell G10 is "=F10+G9". and that formula is copied to cell G11 it becomes "=F11+G10" because relative references are maintained when copying.

Cut

On the Edit menu, or via Ctrl-X (Win) or Command+X (Mac), or via the tool, this command allows you to remove the contents and formatting from a cell or range of cells or text from the Formula Bar to the Clipboard, usually in preparation for Pasting elsewhere.

Copy

On the Edit menu, or via Ctrl-C (Win) or Command+C (Mac), or via the tool, this command allows you to copy the contents and formatting of a cell or range of cells or text from the Formula Bar to the Clipboard, usually in preparation for Pasting elsewhere.

Paste

On the Edit menu, or via Ctrl-V (Win) or Command+V (Mac), or via the tool, this command places a selection from the Clipboard starting at the active cell overwriting any existing cell contents or inserts Clipboard text if the insertion point is active in the Formula Bar.

Moving/Copying a range of cells

If you position the cursor over the border of a selection and then click-drag, the selection will be moved to the new location, as if cut and pasted, as shown in Figure B.26. If you hold down SHIFT and click-drag, it will be inserted to the new location. If you hold down Ctrl (Win) or Command (Mac) and click-drag, the selection will be copied.

FIGURE B.26

Moving or Copying Selected Cells

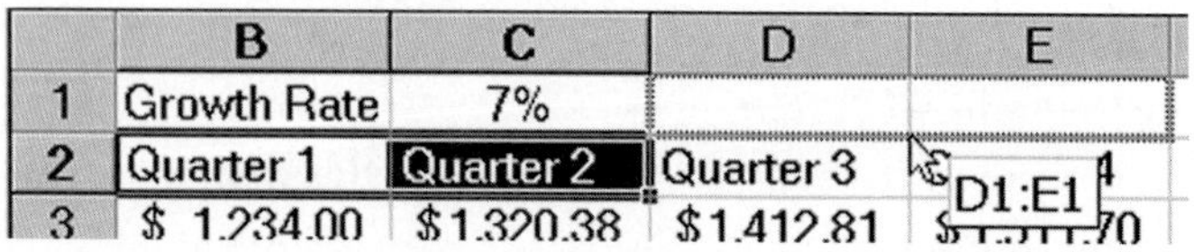

Copy Picture

Copy Picture is used to insert Excel items as a bit-mapped "picture" into other applications. Select the graphic object or range of cells you wish to copy as a picture object. Hold down the SHIFT key and select Copy Picture from the Edit menu. A dialog box will appear for selecting Copy Picture options. (See Figure B.27(a) and (b).) The "As Shown on Screen" option copies the picture just as it appears on the screen, including grid lines if present, to another worksheet or to another application via the Clipboard. The default Picture "metafile" format requires less memory but may not print fonts properly on printers lacking scalable fonts if the object is rescaled. The Bitmap format requires more memory and has lower resolution, but will print on any printer if the object is rescaled. The "As Shown when Printed" option copies the picture to another worksheet or to another application via

FIGURE B.27(a)

Copy Picture

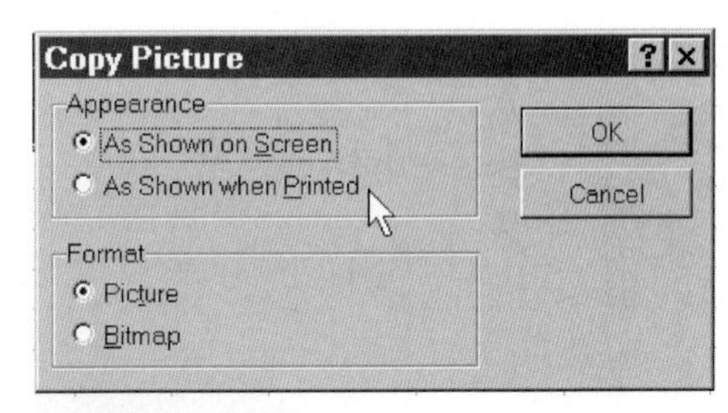

FIGURE B.27(b)

Copy Picture Options

the Clipboard as it would appear when printed. Grid lines and row and column headings will be copied if they are so designated in the worksheet's "Page Setup" options.

Undoing or Redoing a Command

Most Excel commands may be undone, or reapplied to another selection by clicking one of the two tools shown, respectively. Shortcut keys are Ctrl+z (undo) and Ctrl+y (redo) for Win and Command+z (undo) and Command+y (redo) for Mac. Excel supports multiple levels of undo or redo commands; the list of commands is presented by the drop-down button arrows on the two tools.

Shortcut Menus

A menu of popular commands is presented when the right mouse button is clicked (Win) or the Command+Option+mouse_button (Mac) is clicked. Depending upon where the mouse cursor is pointing (cell, object, chart, toolbar, row or column heading, etc.), one of several shortcut menus is displayed. Figure B.28 shows two examples, one giving cell commands and one giving column commands.

FIGURE B.28

Shortcut Menus

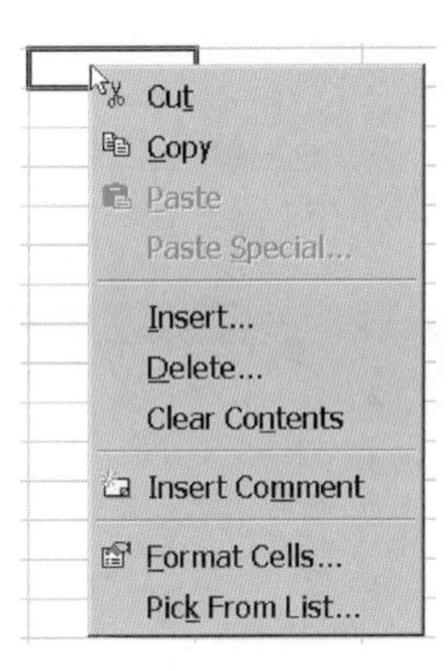

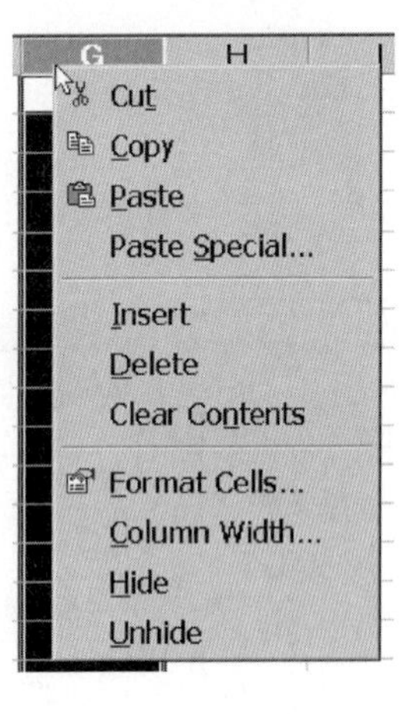

B.6 FILLING CELLS

Fill Left/Right Fill Up/Down

On the Edit menu, Fill is useful for copying formulas and other cell contents to cells adjacent and to the left/right/up/down of the source cell(s). (See Figure B.29.) Type the first entry, select the range of cells to fill, including the first entry, and choose Fill Right/Left/Up/Down from the Edit menu to fill out the rest of the selected cells.

Fill Series

Useful for copying a progression of values from the source cell, this command fills in a row or column of numbers or dates in a specified order, as shown in Figure B.30(a). Select the cell where the series will start, then choose "Fill Series" from the Edit menu.

Specify whether the series should progress in a row or in a column, the type of series: linear, growth, or date, and if a date, then the date unit. Specify the Step Value and the Stop

FIGURE B.29

Filling Cells

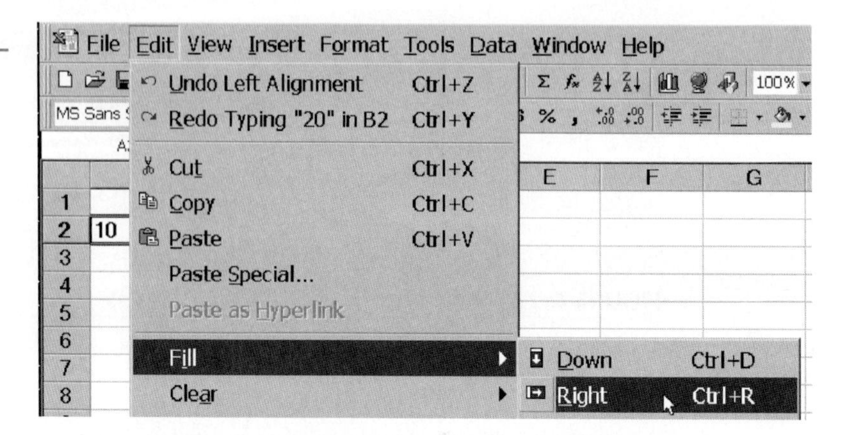

FIGURE B.30(a)

Fill Series

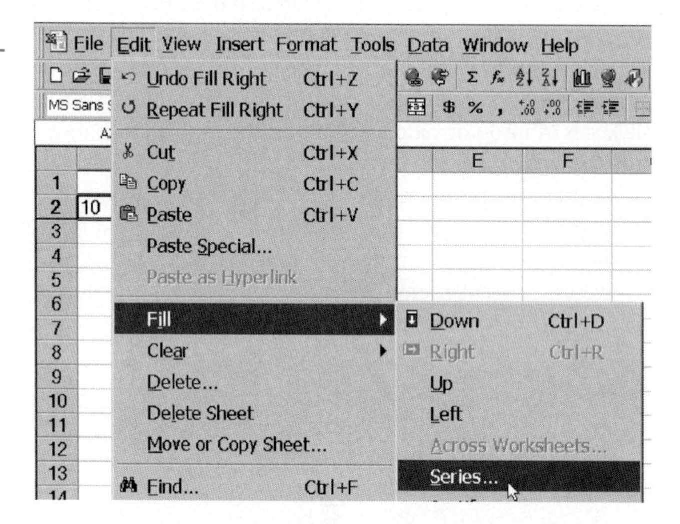

FIGURE B.30(b)

Fill Series Options

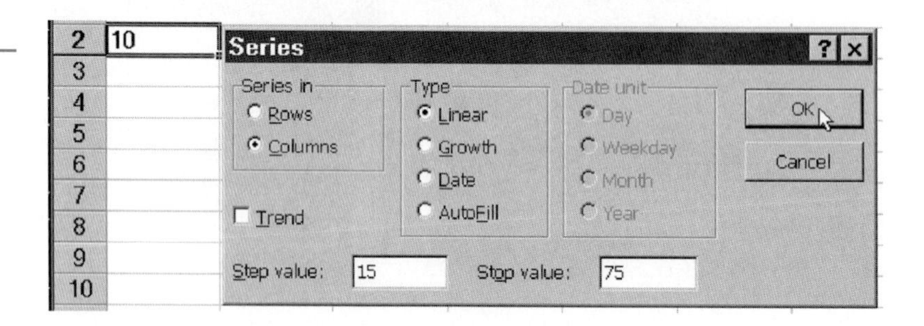

Value, and click OK. Alternatively, highlight the range of cells to be filled with the series, omit the Stop Value in the dialog box, and click OK. (Most of the common Series fills can be more easily handled by the AutoFill shortcut, described below.) The example in Figure B.30(b) creates a column of values starting at 10, incrementing each row entry by 15 and stopping at 75.

AutoFill

Select one or more cells containing a partial series of data. Move the cursor over the "Fill Handle" in the lower right of the selection until it changes to a cross hair, as shown in Figure B.31(a).

FIGURE B.31(a)

AutoFill

Then (in this example) click-drag to the right to Fill Right (overwriting the old contents of any cells dragged over). If you have selected a recognizable number series or common series of text entries, Excel will "AutoFill" the balance of the series, as shown in Figure B.31(b).

FIGURE B.31(b)

AutoFill

To defeat AutoFill and simply copy the cells, depress Ctrl while click-dragging. If you depress SHIFT while click-dragging, new empty cells will be inserted instead of overwriting existing cells. Also, as shown in Figure B.31(c), if you drag the fill handle inside the range of a selection and release, the grayed cells will be cleared.

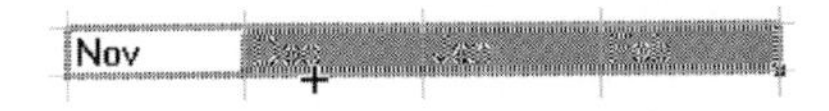

FIGURE B.31(c)

Clearing Cells

AutoFill can be applied to entire rows or columns. (If you select a row or column, the Fill Handle moves to the first cell.)

The table below shows examples of AutoFill operations on selected cells.

Data Selected	Series Created
1, 2	3, 4, 5, 6, . . .
1, 3	5, 7, 9, 11, . . .
100, 95	90, 85, . . .
Mon	Tue, Wed, Thu, . . .
Qtr2	Qtr3, Qtr4, Qtr1, Qtr2, . . .
1st Period	2nd Period, 3rd Period, . . .
text1, textA	text2, textA, text3, textA, . . .
Jan-00, Apr-00	Jul-00, Oct-00, Jan-01, . . .
1, 3, 4	5.66, 7.16, 8.66, . . . (best-fit linear trend)

B.7 FORMATTING CELLS

Row Height

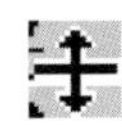

Move the cursor over the line separating the row headings until it changes to a crossbar, (Figure B.32). When it has changed, double click to AutoFit height (see AutoFit below), or click-drag the line to the desired new row height.

To define the row height of a range of several rows, select the row headings, and drag one of the row separator lines. All selected rows will take the same height. Alternatively, define the row height (of a row or a range of selected rows) by selecting "Row Height" from the Format menu (Figure B.32) and type the number of the desired height (in "points" of

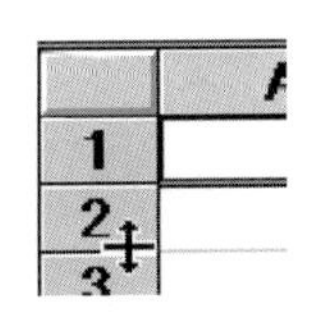

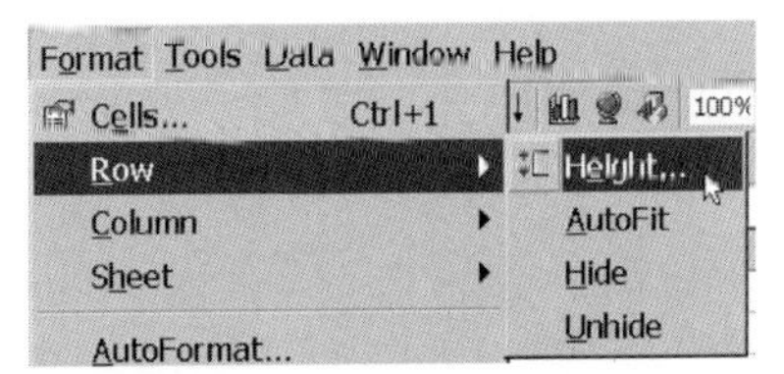

FIGURE B.32

Setting Row Height

FIGURE B.33

Setting Column Width

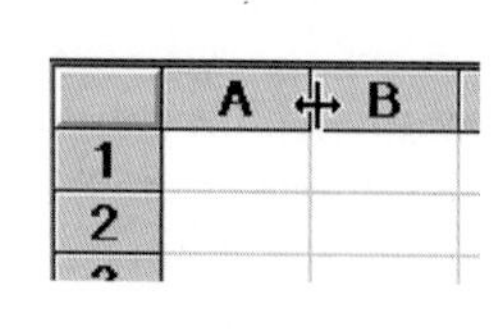

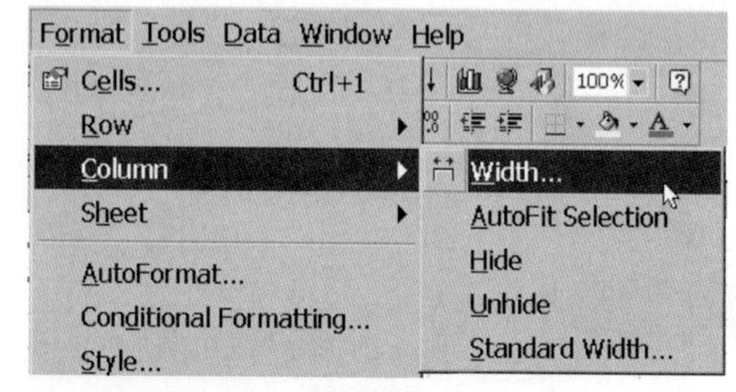

font measure). Typing a "0" for the height is the same as selecting the "Row Hide" item. Selecting "Row Unhide" reverses this latter operation.

Column Width

Move the cursor over the line separating the column headings slowly until it changes to a crossbar, (Figure B.33). When it has changed, double click to AutoFit (see AutoFit section that follows), or drag the line to the desired width.

To define the column width of a range of several columns, select the column headings, and drag one of the column separator lines. All selected columns will take the same width. Alternatively, define the column width (of a column or range of selected columns) by selecting "Column Width" in the Format menu (see Figure B.33) and typing the number of the desired width (in number of characters). Typing a "0" for the width is the same as selecting the "Column Hide" item. Selecting "Column Unhide" reverses this latter operation. Also, Copy and Paste Special can copy column width to new columns.

Column AutoFit Width (Row Autofit Height)

Move the cursor over the line separating the column headings until it changes to a crossbar (Figure B.33). When it has changed, double click to automatically size the column to the width of the widest cell contents in that column. Or select cells of interest and choose the "Column AutoFit Selection" item from the Format menu to widen the column to the width of the widest selected cell's contents. (These operations described for columns work similarly for changing the height of rows.)

Formatting Numeric Cells

Select a cell, row, or column, or select a range of cells, rows, or columns, and if applicable, click one of the tools in Figure B.34 for popular numeric format styles. Note the right two tools in Figure B.34 increase or decrease the decimal precision displayed for numbers. (Excel's internal precision of the numbers is never altered by formatting.)

FIGURE B.34

Formatting Numeric Cells

Changing Cell Fonts

Select a cell, row, or column, or select a range of cells, rows, or columns, and click one of the tools in Figure B.35 to Bold, Italicize, or Underline cell contents or select a font/size item from the appropriate list.

FIGURE B.35

Changing Cell Fonts

Cell Alignment

Select a cell, row, or column, or a range of cells, rows, or columns, and click on one of the tools in Figure B.36 that defines alignment.

FIGURE B.36

Cell Alignment Tools

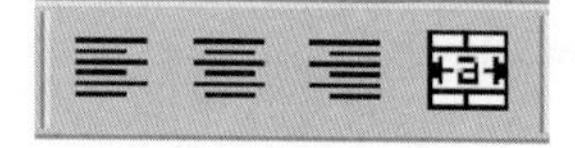

The rightmost tool, also shown in Figure B.37, merges selected cells and centers the leftmost cell contents in the merged cells, useful for report labeling. Merge and Center also works across rows. ***Note:* Because of a bug in Excel, do *not* merge any cells in a worksheet containing a model to be optimized with Solver.** The Format Cells command, described below, must be used to remove the Merge and Center operation.

FIGURE B.37

Merge and Center Across Cells

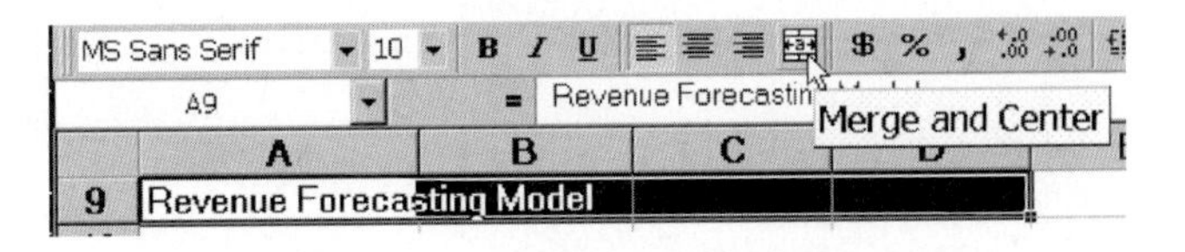

Cell Borders

Select a cell, row, or column, or a range of cells, rows, or columns, and click on one of the tools in the Border Drop-down Pallet shown in Figure B.38 that defines common border styles. The last border tool selected will become the tool's default.

FIGURE B.38

Cell Borders

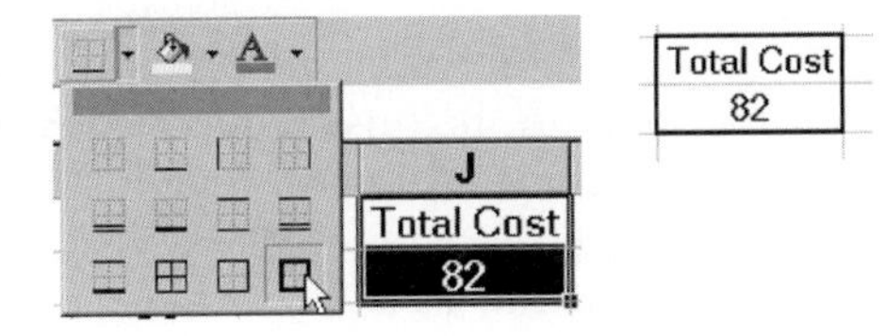

Detailed Cell Formatting

Figure B.39(a) shows more complete cell formatting options than available from the Toolbar. Select a cell, row, or column, or select a range of cells, rows, or columns, and choose "Cells" from the Format menu or press Ctrl+1 (Win) or Command+1 (Mac). Click on each of the desired format tab(s) in the dialog, and select the format option within the dialog.

FIGURE B.39(a)

Detailed Cell Formatting Options

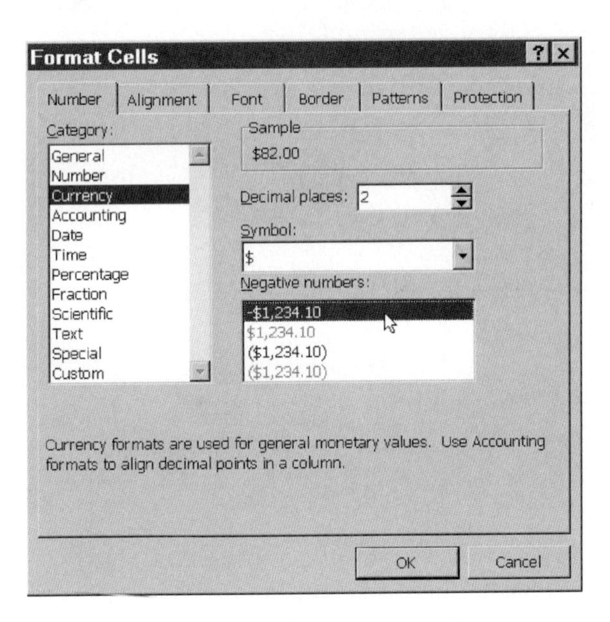

Report formatting and model management is improved if long labels are *not* split across cells. For long labels use the Alignment tab dialog to "Wrap Text" each label within its cell, and optionally, center the labels horizontally and vertically, as shown in the first example in Figure B.39(b). *Note:* You can override the Wrap Text break point and force

FIGURE B.39(b)

Wrapping Labels

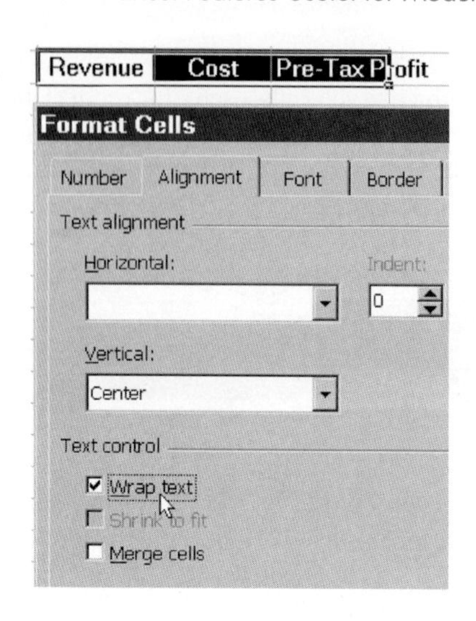

Revenue	Cost	Pre-Tax Profit
Revenue	Cost	Pre Tax Profit

manual break(s) in the text to be inserted by pressing Alt+ENTER (Win) or Option+Command+RETURN (Mac) at other place(s) in the label, as shown in the second example in Figure B.39(b).

Cells may also be wrapped and/or merged in the vertical direction, a trick that often results in more compact models, as illustrated in Figure B.40. ***Note:* Because of a bug in Excel do *not* merge any cells in a worksheet containing a model to be optimized with Solver.**

FIGURE B.40

Vertically Wrapped and Merged Cells

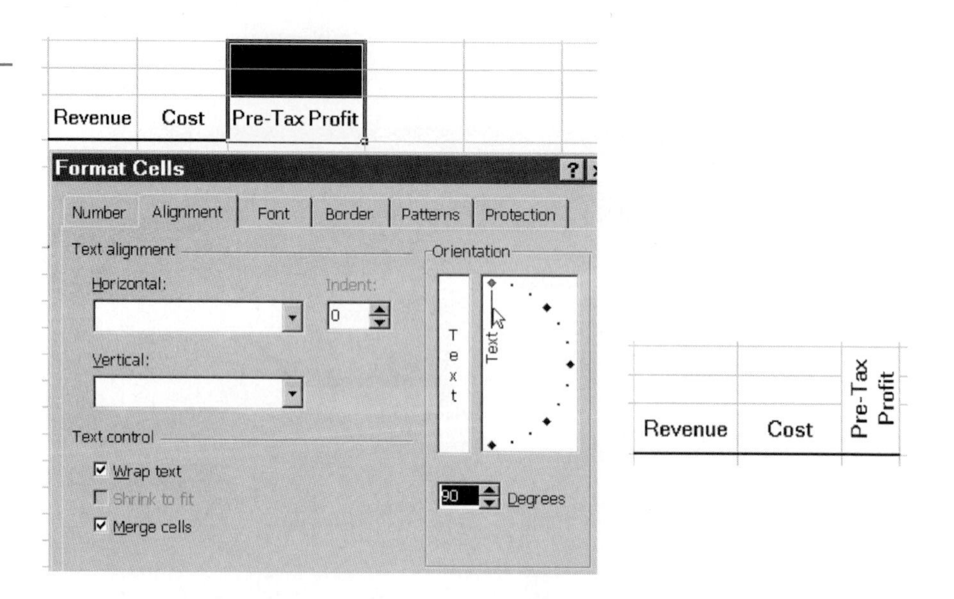

Custom Cell Formats

A variety of custom formats can be specified, as given in the example of fractional dollar formatting in Figure B.41. The Sample value in the dialog indicates how the selected cell(s) will appear. Fields separated by ";" characters apply to positive; negative; and zero values, respectively. A Custom format of ";;;" will display none of a cell's contents. Excel also supports conditional expressions enclosed in "[ ]" to select alternative formats. Also, Conditional Formatting (in the Format menu) can be selected to alter the appearance of cells depending on values in them. Refer to Excel's Help for examples of the many formatting options available.

FIGURE B.41

Custom Formatting

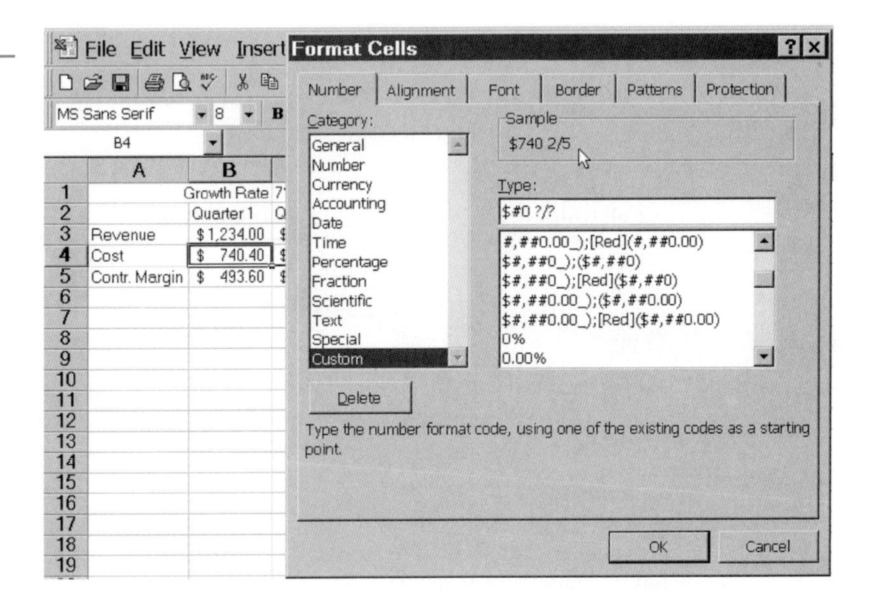

Cell Format Dressing

Character strings enclosed within quotations may be inserted before or after any field in a custom format, as shown in Figure B.42. Called a "cell dressing," these characters will be displayed along with the other formatting information for the cell. In the example shown in Figure B.42, the cell contents of "50" will be formatted to display as "<=$50.00." Since it combines documentation of the constraint direction into the cell format, this option is particularly useful in representing the right-hand sides of constraints in Excel models to be optimized with Solver.

Cell dressings and conditional formats can be used for data validation, as indicated in the examples below. The first column gives the cell contents and the second column shows how it will be displayed.

FIGURE B.42

Cell Format Dressing

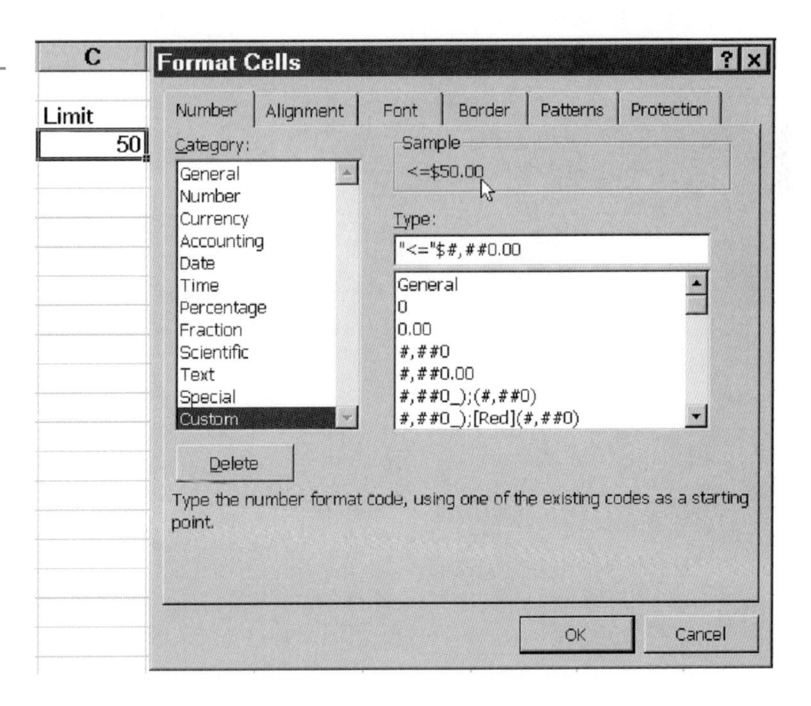

Cell Contents	Custom Format: $0.00;"Enter a Positive Number";"-"0"-" displays as
123	$123.00
–123	Enter a Positive Number
0	-0-

Cell Contents	Custom Format: [>1000]"Too Big "0.00;[<100]0.00" Too Small";0.00
1002	Too Big 1002.00
–10	–10.00 Too Small
333	333.00

Format Painter

Select a cell with the desired format, click the Format Painter tool and drag over a range of cells to apply the selected cell's format. To apply the cell's format to many different cells, double click the Format Painter tool. (When finished, cancel by clicking the tool again.)

B.8 ARRAYS OF CELLS

Definition

An array is simply a range of adjacent cells on an Excel worksheet. The notation for an array includes the top left corner cell followed by a colon (:) followed by the address of the bottom right corner cell. For example, "A1:B3" denotes an array that is two columns wide and three rows long. This array begins at cell A1, includes cells A2, A3, B1, B2, and ends with cell B3. Many Excel functions will accept arrays, that is, cell ranges, as input arguments provided that the final calculation produces a single value for the cell, such as "=SUM(A1:B3)," which adds up the contents of the six cells in the given range.

The SUMPRODUCT Function

This function multiplies corresponding cells in the given (equal-sized) arrays and returns the sum of those products, hence the name SUMPRODUCT. (See Figure B.43.) The formula is entered into the cell in the form

"=SUMPRODUCT(**array_1**,**array_2**,...)"

where **array_1**, and **array_2** are the arrays whose corresponding cells you want to multiply together and then add up the results. The array arguments must have the same dimensions, that is, the same number of rows and columns for each array (otherwise, SUMPRODUCT returns the #VALUE! error). For example, in Figure B.43, "P1, P2, P3" is the price paid for each of three items and "Q1, Q2, Q3" is the corresponding quantity of each item purchased. Total Cost is the sum of the corresponding three "price times quantity" calculations, that is, 3*2 + 4*7 + 8*6. Especially for large arrays, using the ranges of the cells in the SUMPRODUCT function is more efficient than writing a single long formula containing the intermediate calculations. *Important:* SUMPRODUCT treats array member cells that are not numeric as if they contained zeros.

FIGURE B.43

SUMPRODUCT Function

F2 | =SUMPRODUCT(B2:D2,B4:D4)

	A	B	C	D	E	F	G
1		P1	P2	P3		Total Cost	
2		3	4	8		82	
3		Q1	Q2	Q3			
4		2	7	6			

The VLOOKUP function (HLOOKUP function is similar)

The VLOOKUP function is used to map a given value into another value according to the definition given in an array of cells comprising a table. The VLOOKUP function has the following syntax:

VLOOKUP(lookup_value,table_array,col_index_num,range_lookup)

where "lookup_value" is the input value, "table_array" is the table of data, "col_index_num" is the column number to return output values from, and if present, a "range_lookup" value of FALSE means the lookup must be an exact match.

The data in Figure B.44 represent automobile insurance rates for big City drivers and small Town drivers as a function of the driver's Age. The range B3:D7 is named "Table" in the examples below.

FIGURE B.44

VLOOKUP Example

	B	C	D
2	Age	City	Town
3	16	$714	$630
4	18	$630	$588
5	21	$441	$420
6	25	$420	$420
7	60	$462	$462

Note: If not specified, "range_lookup" defaults to TRUE, that is, an exact match is not required. In this default case the values in the first column, B in Figure B.44, must be in ascending order.

VLOOKUP(16,Table,3) equals 630, that is, a 16-year-old driver living in a small town pays $630 for auto insurance.

VLOOKUP(23,TABLE,2) equals 441, that is, a 23-year-old driver living in a big city pays $441 for auto insurance. (Any lookup_value between 21 and 24.99999 will return $441 in this example.)

VLOOKUP(65,Table,3) equals 462. (Any lookup_value equal to or greater than 60 will return $462 in this example.)

VLOOKUP(15,Table,2) equals #NA, because 15 is less than the smallest value in column B.

VLOOKUP(23,Table,2,FALSE) equals #NA because "range_lookup" of FALSE requires an exact Age match.

Array Formulas: Single Cell Results

As indicated in the examples above, a formula may accept a range of cells, that is, an array, as input to calculations. Unfortunately, it is easy to defeat this simple idea of using arrays of cell references in constructing formulas. For example, suppose that instead of using "=SUM(A1:B3)" to add up the six cell values, you wish to compute their "sum of squares," that is, you wish to square the contents of each of the six cells first and then add up those squared values. The obvious formula "=SUM(A1:B3^2)" does not work—Excel returns a #VALUE! error—because the intermediate squaring operation (...^2) does not accept an array argument. Excel will accept such constructions, if you declare the cell's formula to be an "array formula." Array formulas generalize the notion of submitting arrays of cells as inputs to formula computations.

A formula is designated as an array formula by holding down the Ctrl+SHIFT keys while pressing the ENTER key to complete your formula entry. Excel signals the presence of an array formula by placing curly brackets on either side of the formula. In the example above, the sum of the squares of the array can be correctly calculated by means of an array formula "{=SUM(A1:B3^2)}".

Remember: To create an array formula, you *must* hold down the Ctrl+SHIFT keys while pressing the ENTER key when finishing formula entry *and* after each time you edit the formula. Do *not* type the curly brackets yourself.

Array Formulas: Multiple Cell Results

In addition to allowing arrays of cells as formula inputs, array formulas are also used to compute an array of formula results, that is, an array of results to be stored into a range of target cells. Although giving the same result as if a regular formula were copied to all the cells in the target range, array formulas require less memory, calculate faster, and are easier to use and maintain, especially for large models.

To use array formulas for producing arrays of results, (1) select the range of target array cells, each of which will receive one of the computed array result values, (2) create the first cell's formula by typing and/or click-dragging, as usual, (3) hold down the Ctrl+SHIFT keys while pressing the ENTER key to complete formula entry. Excel will apply the formula to all the selected target cells, using appropriate values from any input cell ranges in the formula, if given. For example, target cell range B5:E5 was selected in Figure B.45, and a single subtraction formula was typed using the indicated input cell ranges as arguments.

FIGURE B.45

Array Formula Example

IF | =B3:E3-B4:E4

	A	B	C	D	E
3	Revenue	$ 1,234.00	$1,320.38	$1,412.81	$1,511.70
4	Cost	$ 740.40	$ 792.23	$ 847.68	$ 907.02
5	Contr. Margin	=B3:E3-B4:E4			

Formula entry was completed by holding down the Ctrl+SHIFT keys while pressing the ENTER key, which causes Excel to evaluate the formula for each selected target cell in the output range B5:C5, as shown in Figure B.46. **Remember:** to use array formulas, you *must* hold down Ctrl+SHIFT while pressing the ENTER key each time you edit that array formula in the future; otherwise, it will revert to a regular formula (or yield an error message). Also, you cannot edit the formula for any subset of the cells in an array result; editing is allowed only for the whole array result.

FIGURE B.46

Completed Array Formula Example

D5 | {=B3:E3-B4:E4}

	A	B	C	D	E
3	Revenue	$ 1,234.00	$1,320.38	$1,412.81	$1,511.70
4	Cost	$ 740.40	$ 792.23	$ 847.68	$ 907.02
5	Contr. Margin	$ 493.60	$ 528.15	$ 565.12	$ 604.68

An Array Formula Example

Suppose you want to subtract each cell in the rightmost column in Figure B.47 from each cell in the bottom row, a requirement for several Network Models in Chapter 5.

FIGURE B.47

An Array Example

				10
				15
				35
				40
22	24	39	42	

The common approach uses the "Transpose" option in the Paste Special dialog from the Edit menu to copy the rightmost column as a new pasted row and then perform the subtraction for the cells in the two rows. Array formulas can do this in one operation. First, highlight the result cells, B19:E19. Then create the formula in the first cell, B19, as shown in Figure B.48.

FIGURE B.48

Another Array Formula

	B	C	D	E	F
14					10
15					15
16					35
17					40
18	22	24	39	42	
19	=B18:E18-TRANSPOSE(F14:F17)				

Complete the formula by holding down Ctrl+SHIFT while pressing the ENTER key to produce the array result for all selected cells, as shown in Figure B.49.

FIGURE B.49

Completed Array Formula Example

D19 = {=B18:E18-TRANSPOSE(F14:F17)}

	B	C	D	E	F
14					10
15					15
16					35
17					40
18	22	24	39	42	
19	12	9	4	2	

B.9 NAMING CELLS

Naming Cell Ranges

Select the cell or cell range you wish to name, and choose "Name Define" from the Insert menu, as shown in Figure B.50.

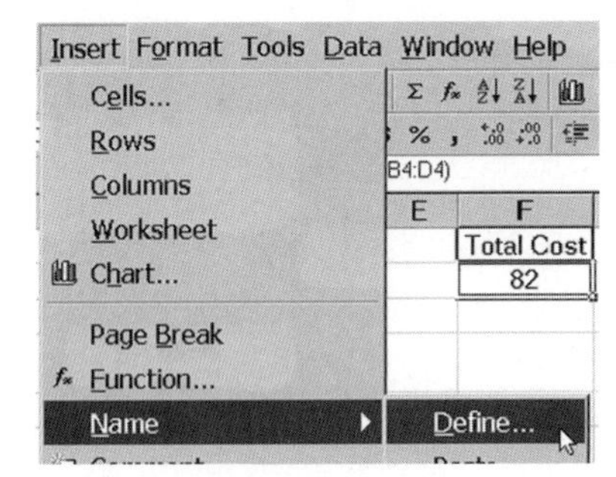

FIGURE B.50

Naming a Cell or Cell Range

Excel will guess at the desired name if there is a nearby cell containing text labels. No spaces (or special characters) are allowed in names, and so, an underline character is substituted for them such as in "Total_Cost" in Figure B.51. Click the Add button to add the name to the list of names already defined. Note that names are global to a workbook, that is, each defined name has its worksheet name pre-pended to the cell reference(s) so that a name in one worksheet can be referenced by a cell formula in another worksheet.

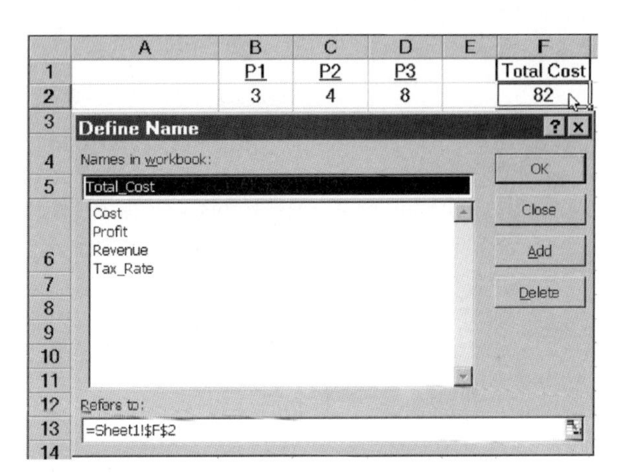

FIGURE B.51

"Total_Cost" Refers to Cell F2 on Sheet1

Alternatively, to define a name, select the cell(s), and type the name directly into the Name Box (Figure B.52).

FIGURE B.52

The Name Box

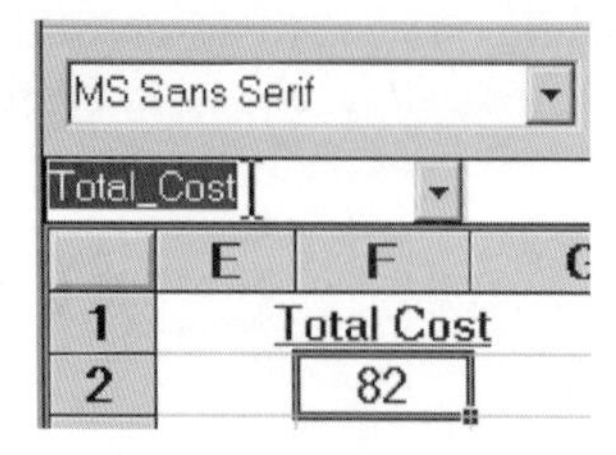

Create Names

If column (or row) label(s) are already available in adjacent cell(s), cell naming can be done directly by selecting the cells and choosing "Name Create" from the Insert menu. (See Figure B.53.)

FIGURE B.53

"Name Create" Command

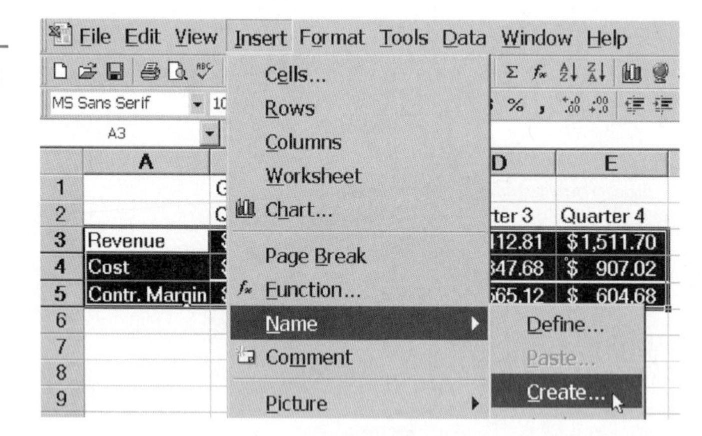

Confirm or override Excel's guess as to the location of the label(s) as shown in Figure B.54. Excel will replace spaces and special characters by underlines in creating the names. Note that all names for all sheets in a given workbook will be listed in the Define Name dialog.

FIGURE B.54

Excel's Guess for Location of Names

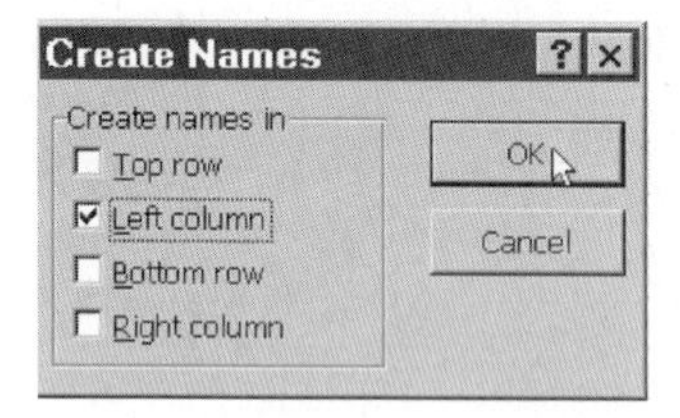

Using Names in Formulas

Using names will make your formulas easier to understand and helps document a model (Figure B.55). To use a previously defined name in a formula, you may type it directly, or select the name from the Name Box to ensure that the name is defined and spelled correctly.

FIGURE B.55

Using Names in Formulas

B6 {=Profit*(1-Tax_Rate)}

Cost
Profit
Revenue
Tax_Rate
Total_Cost

	A	B	C	D
		Year 1	Year 2	
		1,234	$ 1,518	
		567	$ 879	
4	Profit	$ 667	$ 639	
5	Tax%Rate	28%	33%	
6	Net Income	$ 480	$ 428	

Paste List

For documentation, a list of all defined names and their cell references may be pasted into the worksheet (Figure B.56).

FIGURE B.56

Paste List of Names

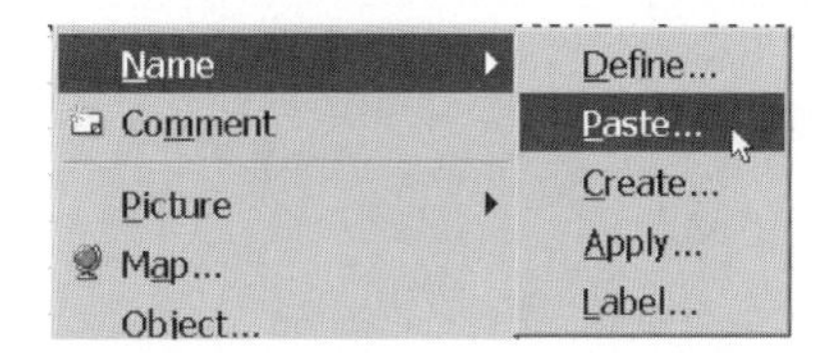

First, choose a cell in an empty region of the worksheet, select the "Name Paste" item from the Insert menu, and click the Paste List button in the Paste Name dialog (Figure B.57).

FIGURE B.57

Paste Name Dialog Box

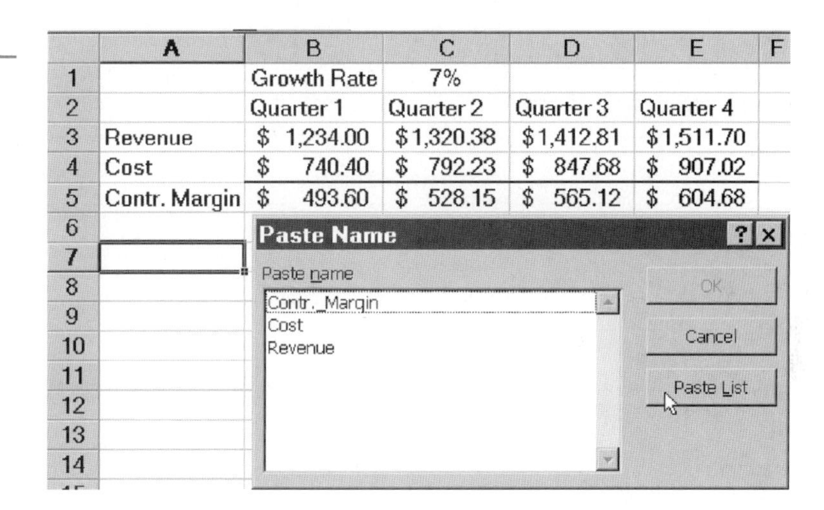

	A	B	C	D	E	F
1		Growth Rate	7%			
2		Quarter 1	Quarter 2	Quarter 3	Quarter 4	
3	Revenue	$ 1,234.00	$1,320.38	$1,412.81	$1,511.70	
4	Cost	$ 740.40	$ 792.23	$ 847.68	$ 907.02	
5	Contr. Margin	$ 493.60	$ 528.15	$ 565.12	$ 604.68	
6						
7						
8						
9						
10						
11						
12						
13						
14						

A list of all the defined names in the workbook is pasted into the active sheet. Each name has the name of the worksheet pre-pended to the defined range to avoid ambiguity (Figure B.58).

FIGURE B.58

Pasted List of Defined Names

7	Contr._Margin	='Financial Model'!$B$5:$E$5
8	Cost	='Financial Model'!$B$4:$E$4
9	Revenue	='Financial Model'!$B$3:$E$3

B.10 WIZARDS

Function Wizard

Detailed documentation of Excel's many built-in functions is given by clicking the Paste Function tool (Figure B.59). Click the Help button for additional documentation on any selected function.

Clicking OK pastes the desired function into the formula bar and opens the Formula Result bar, as shown in Figure B.60. The arguments are listed (the required arguments are boldfaced) and sample values or cell ranges may be inserted into the dialog in order to build up the formula and see the calculated result.

Chart Wizard

Excel's charting is best done by the Chart Wizard, as shown in Figure B.61: (1) select the range of data cells to chart, (2) click the Chart Wizard tool, and (3) follow the steps for the four Chart Wizard dialogs. Where present, click the Help button for additional detailed documentation for any dialog.

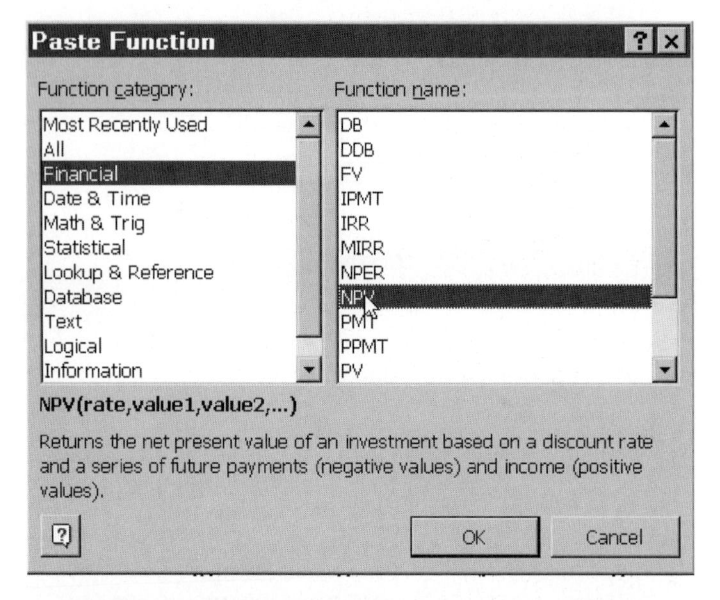

FIGURE B.59

Excel's Built-In Functions

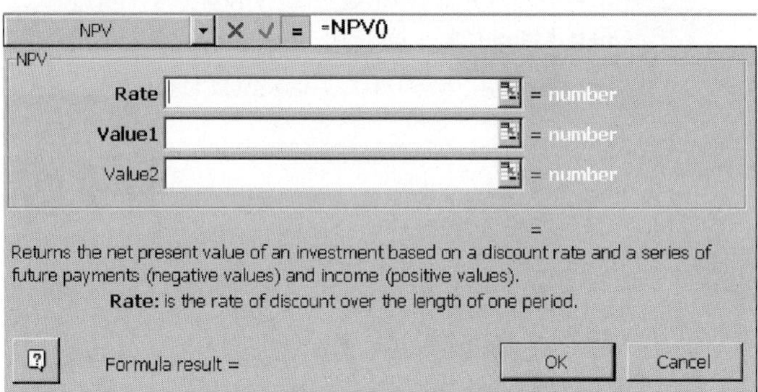

FIGURE B.60

Formula Result Bar for NPV Function

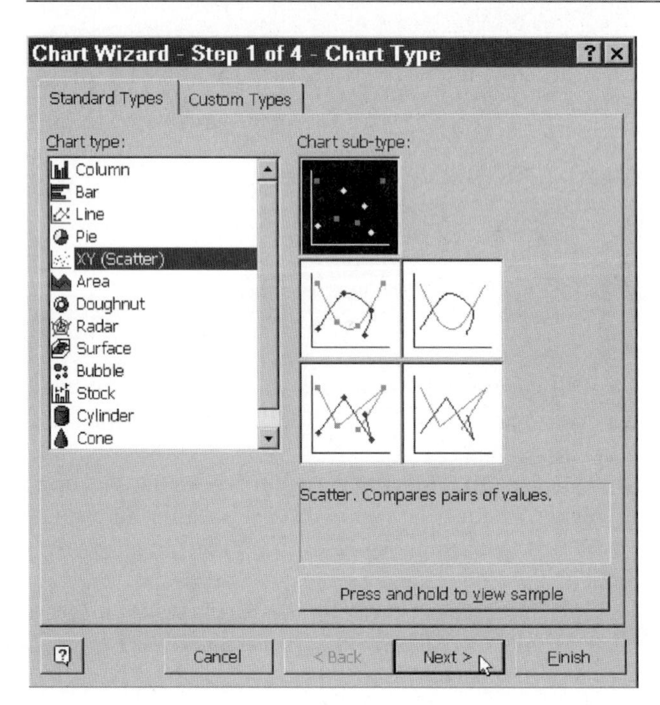

FIGURE B.61

Standard Chart Types

Charting via the Chart Wizard is greatly facilitated if the first column contains the "X-axis" data (when each data series is a column) or if the first row contains the "X-axis" data (when each data series is a row). Although work-arounds exist, it is generally much easier to rearrange the data on the worksheet to place the "X-axis" at the beginning of the data before clicking the Chart Wizard.

Important: The "XY (Scatter)" in Figure B.61 is the *only* chart type that plots the X-axis data scaled according to their values. All other chart types plot the X-axis data as if they were categorical data, that is, the X-axis data are equally spaced regardless of its values. (An exception to this occurs on Stock charts and 2D or 3D line, column, bar, and area charts in which the X-axis data are dates in days, months, or years. In this case the times/dates on the X-axis are scaled.) This is illustrated in Figure B.62 for a "Line" chart on the left and an XY (Scatter) chart of the same data on the right.

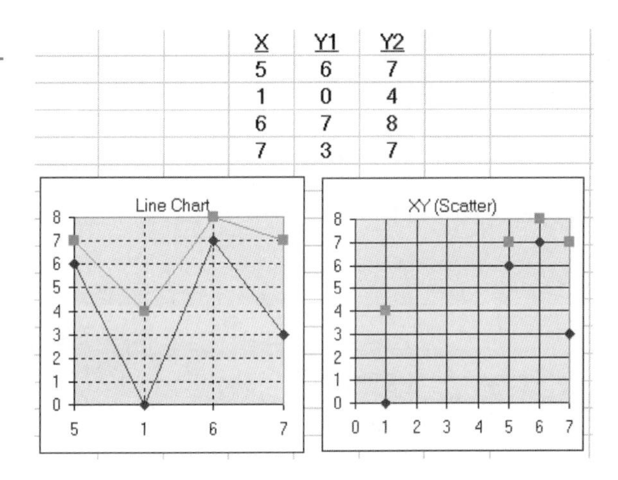

FIGURE B.62

Line Chart and Scatter Chart

Text to Columns Wizard

Pasting or importing data from another application, such as Word, into Excel often yields a single column of text, of little use if the text contains data. To parse or "break out" the data into separate Excel columns, select the text cells down the (single) column and select the "Text to Columns . . ." item from the Data menu (Figure B.63).

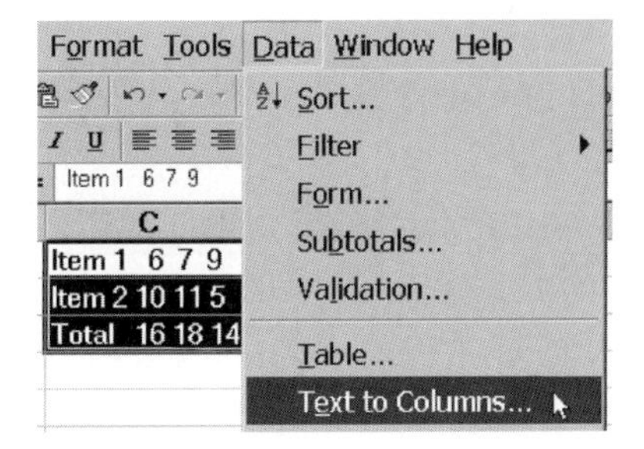

FIGURE B.63

Text to Columns Wizard

Select one of the parsing options in step 1 of the Convert Text to Columns Wizard, as shown in Figure B.64. (If available, the preferred format for the original data is "Delimited," using, for example, comma or tab separators. Otherwise, the Fixed Width option will allow most of the parsing to be done correctly.)

FIGURE B.64

Convert Text to Columns Wizard Step 1

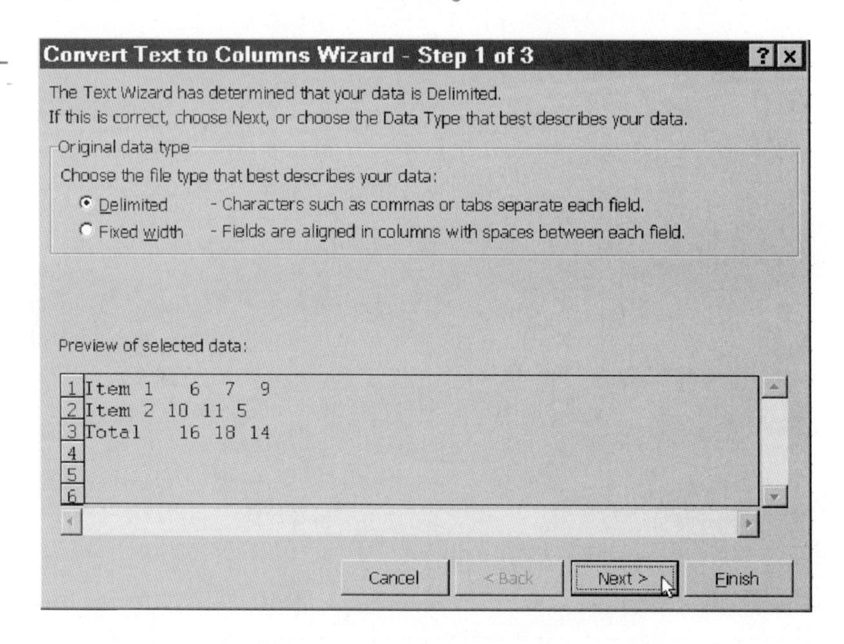

Complete step 2 in Figure B.65, as appropriate, and select data type options in step 3 (not shown).

FIGURE B.65

Convert Text to Columns Wizard Step 2

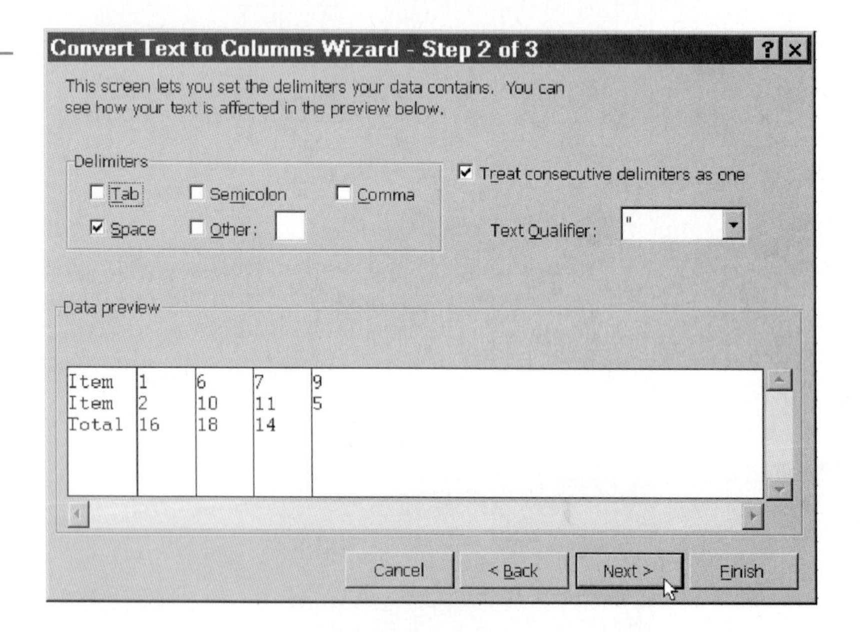

The completed breakout of text to columns is shown in Figure B.66. The results may need some manual fix-up if the source text was not of fixed width or separated by delimiters.

FIGURE B.66

Breakout of Data into Columns

C	D	E	F
Item 1	6	7	9
Item 2	10	11	5
Total	16	18	14

B.11 OTHER USEFUL COMMANDS

Sorting Rows

The two tools in Figure B.67(a) sort rows of the worksheet. If a range of cells is selected first, then the sort is done on the leftmost column in the selected range. If no range of cells is selected, then the rectangular block of contiguous non-empty cells is automatically selected, and the sort is performed for all the rows along the column containing the active cell. Since it is easy to get confused, a more step-by-step dialog is offered by selecting the "Sort" item in the Data menu (Figure B.67(b)).

FIGURE B.67(a) AND (b)

Sorting Rows

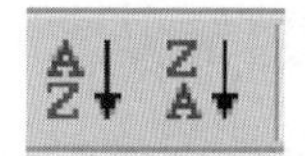

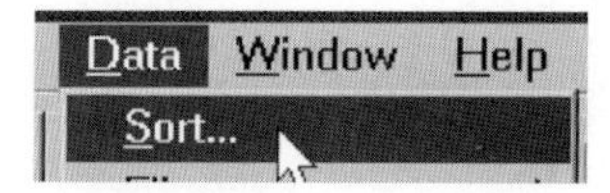

AutoSum Tool

Σ

Placing the cell cursor at the bottom of a column of non-empty cells or to the right of a row of non-empty cells and clicking the AutoSum tool will insert the formula "=SUM( )" with Excel's guess of the intended range of cells to sum highlighted (Figure B.68). If the guess is wrong, drag over the correct range before pressing the Enter key.

FIGURE B.68

AutoSum Guess

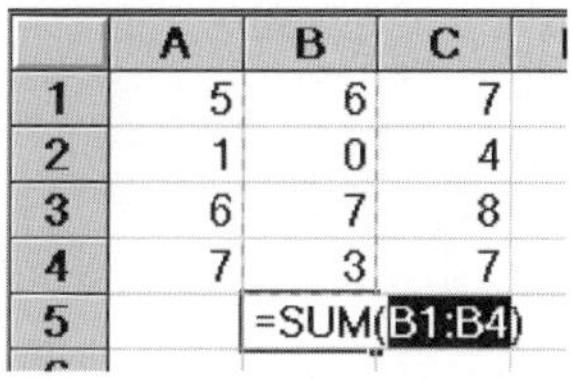

	A	B	C
1	5	6	7
2	1	0	4
3	6	7	8
4	7	3	7
5		=SUM(B1:B4)	

Spell Checking

Cell entries of a range of cells or a worksheet may be checked for spelling by clicking the Spelling tool or selecting "Spelling" from the Tools menu (Figure B.69).

FIGURE B.69

Spelling Command

Displaying Cell Formulas

To display and print formulas, it is recommended you select the "Move or Copy Sheet" item from the Edit menu, as shown in Figure B.70, to make a complete copy of your (final, debugged) worksheet model as another worksheet in your workbook (Figure B.71).

FIGURE B.70

"Move or Copy Sheet"

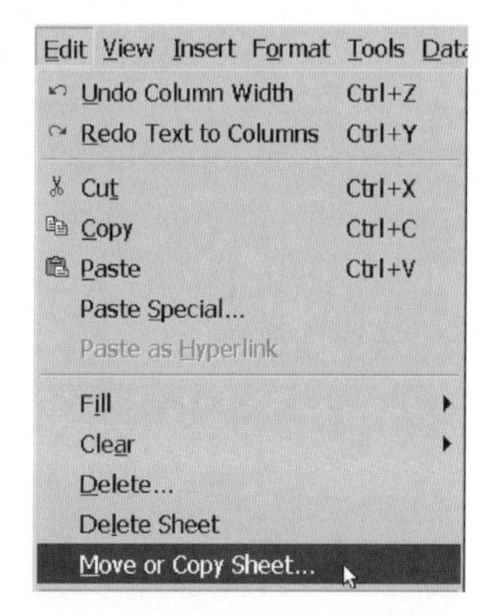

FIGURE B.71

Copying a Worksheet

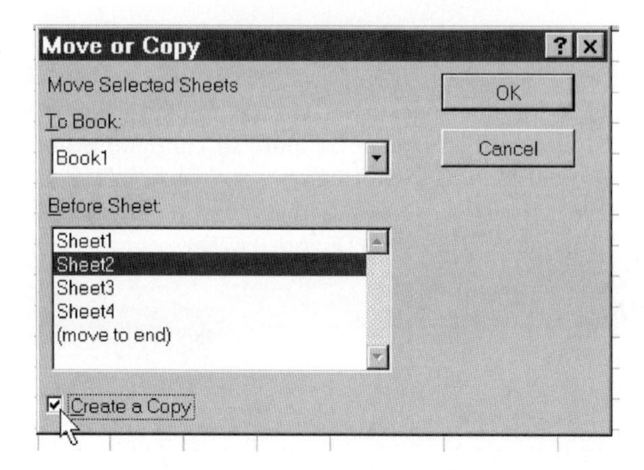

This allows independent adjustments of fonts, column widths, and so on, for the formulas that usually need to be formatted differently from that of the model's worksheet.

Switch to that copied sheet by clicking its tab. Double click its tab to change its default name to be more meaningful, such as "Sheet1 Formulas" shown in Figure B.72.

FIGURE B.72

Worksheet Formulas

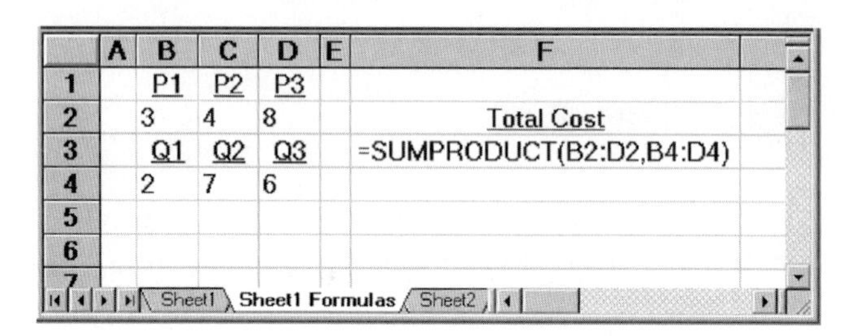

Select the "Options Display" item from the Tools menu and click the Formulas item in the View tab dialog—Pressing Ctrl+~ (Win) or Command+~ (Mac) is a useful shortcut. Next, adjust the column widths for best printing appearance, using the "Column Autofit Selection" from the Format menu, described previously. Then adjust all formats for best appearance. **Important:** If you change your original worksheet model in the future, you *must* recopy the worksheet model—this time by Copy-ing the changed cells and Paste-ing them to this sheet—to document any changed formulas or data.

Auditing Formulas

Selecting cell(s) containing formula(s) and then choosing one of the Auditing items from the Tools menu, as shown in Figure B.73, produces a visual representation that is useful for documentation and debugging.

Paste from Excel to Word

When used with a Copy command from Excel, the Paste command in Word will insert the cell contents into a spreadsheet-like Table in Word. While in a Word Table, the cell contents can be edited as separate entities. If Paste is used following a Copy as Picture command, the selection will appear as a graphic object that has limited editing options once it has been pasted, but is easy to crop or rescale.

Paste Special

This command shown in Figure B.74 is used to alter the default assumptions in a normal "Paste" command to paste just the formulas, just the values, just the formats, and so forth. You can also Add the copied formula or value(s) to the entries in the paste area, Subtract them, and so on, by clicking an Operation option. For example, to multiply the data in E4:G4 by 150, place the 150 in a cell and Copy it. Select the cells E4:G4 and choose the Paste Special item on the Edit menu.

Click the Multiply Operation in the Paste Special dialog shown in Figure B.75 and click OK. The target data items will be multiplied by the copied constant, as shown in Figure B.76.

FIGURE B.73

Auditing Formulas

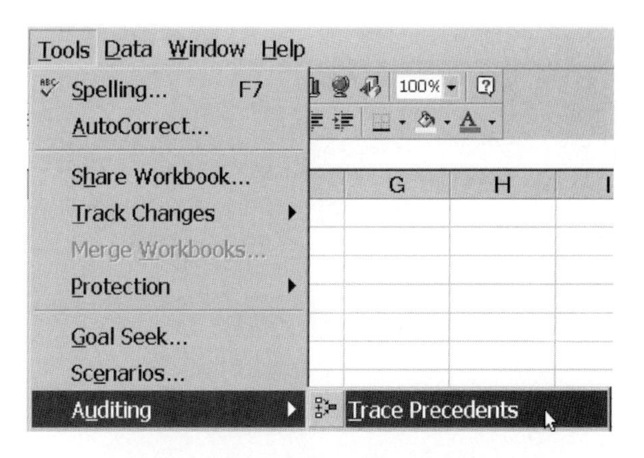

FIGURE B.74

Paste Special Example

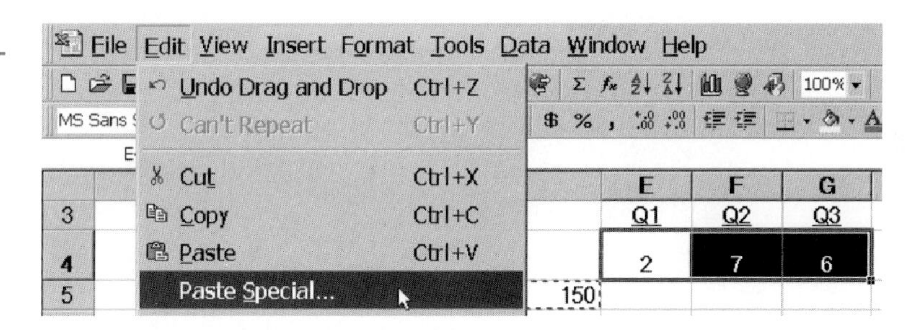

FIGURE B.75

Multiply by Copied Cell

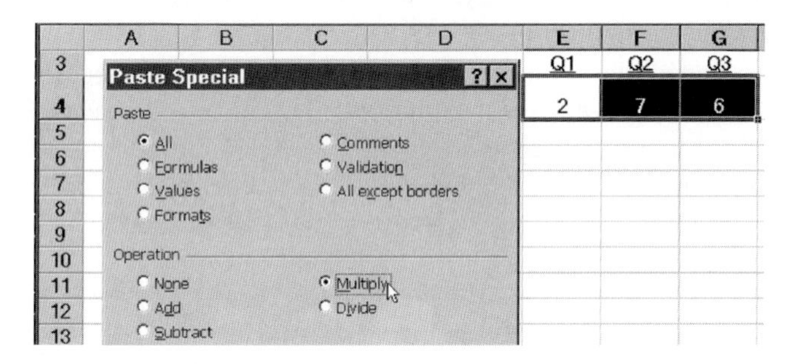

FIGURE B.76

Completed Paste Special Example

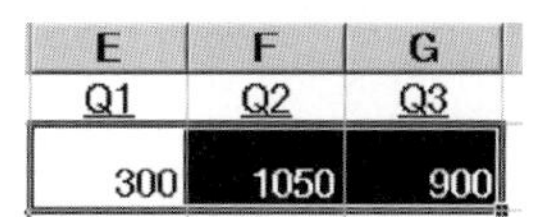

Copying a range of cells, selecting Paste Special, and checking the Transpose box pastes columns as rows and vice versa up to Excel's maximum of 256 columns. Clicking the Paste Link button pastes a pointer to the selected (source) cells into another location as a "hot" (update-able) link to the source cells (Figure B.77).

Paste from Word to Excel

If you select Paste Special after Cutting/Copying an object from Microsoft Word or similar application, the Paste Special dialog box will change to reflect the object on the

FIGURE B.77

Paste Special Dialog

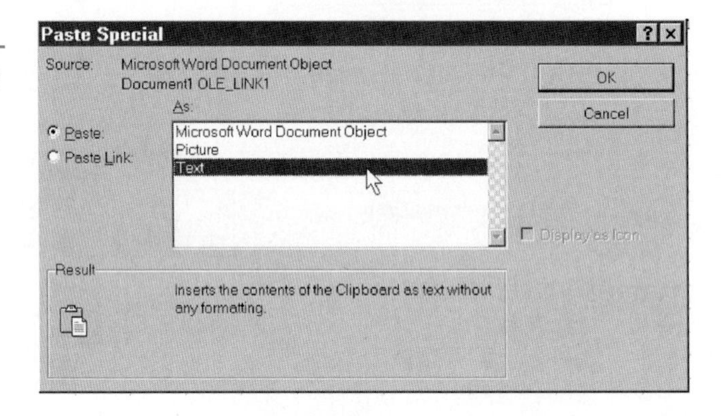

FIGURE B.78

Pasting from Word to Excel

Clipboard (Figure B.78). Paste Link maintains a "hot" link to the source document. A Document Object maintains a Microsoft OLE link to allow future editing of it in the originating application. Picture (or Bitmap) copies as a graphic object. Normally, you would select TEXT, which will paste selected characters into cell(s).

Drawing Toolbar

The drawing tools are useful for documenting a worksheet model. The drawing tools are contained in a Drawing Toolbar. To evoke it, click the Drawing tool or select the Drawing item from the View menu, as shown in Figure B.79.

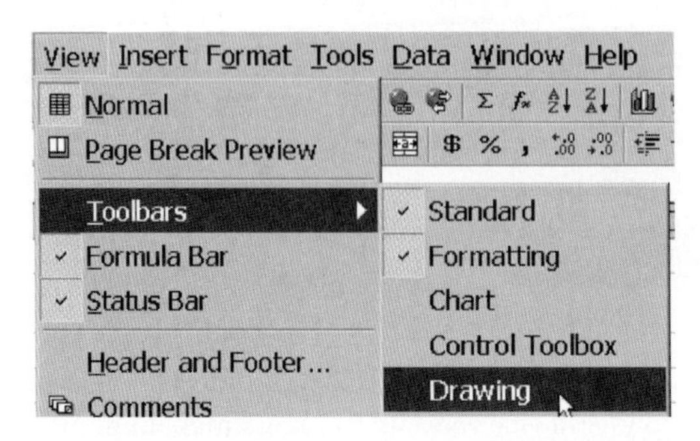

FIGURE B.79

Displaying the Drawing Toolbar

The toolbar may be moved around by clicking its leftmost end and click-dragging it.

The floating Text Box object and the arrow tools can be used to annotate a model result, or to present critical formulas (by copying the Formula Bar characters to the text

FIGURE B.80

Floating Text Box Option on Drawing Toolbar

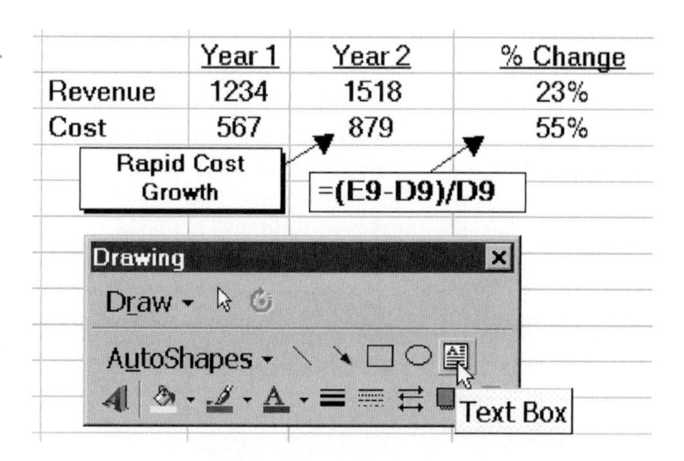

box), as shown in Figure B.80. Other drawing tools in the Drawing Toolbar may be used for more stylish effects and callouts.

Getting Help

Excel has several ways to offer help. The first is Excel Help. (*Note:* holding the cursor over any tool icon and pausing for a few seconds causes Excel to display a short description of the tool, as shown in Figure B.81.)

FIGURE B.81

Getting Help

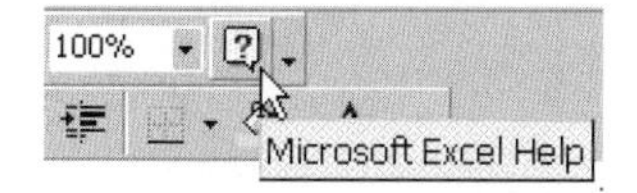

Clicking the Excel Help tool opens a dialog that allows a search of the Help system for a topic word, the display of a Tip, and the setting of Office Assistant options to indicate for which types of actions the Office Assistant should pop up to offer help (Figure B.82).

FIGURE B.82

Office Assistant

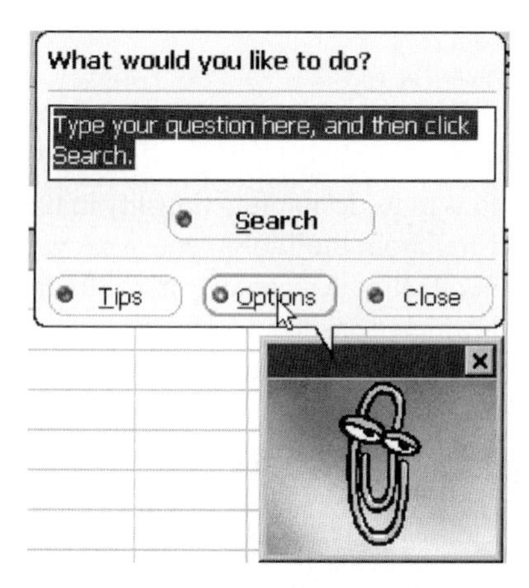

Clicking the What's This item on the Help menu (Figure B.83) changes the cursor to also show a question mark.

FIGURE B.83

What's This? Item

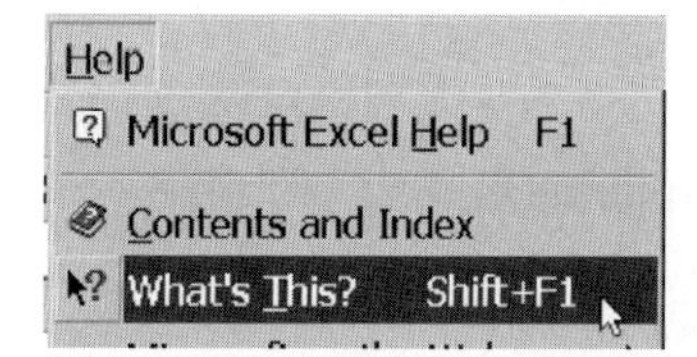

The next item you click will evoke a short description pertinent to the item you just clicked. This is a fast way to get more information on a menu item or tool.

The complete Excel Help system is available under the Help menu (Win) or under the ? menu (Mac). It is also evoked by the F1 function key (Win or Mac). In addition to an index of all help topics, selecting the Office Assistant, typing a phrase, and clicking the Search button allows a keyword search. The example in Figure B.84 shows the result of searching for the NPV function. In addition to the documentation, examples and other very useful guidelines are offered by Excel's Help system when specific Help topics are displayed.

FIGURE B.84

Result of Searching for the NPV Function

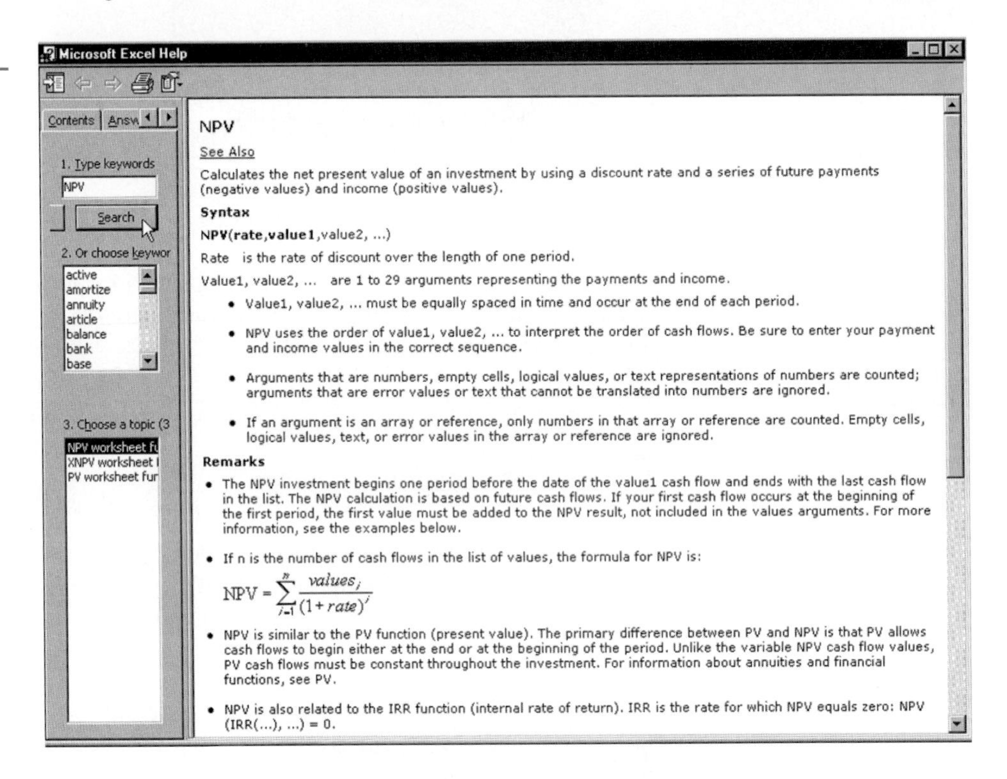

Add-Ins

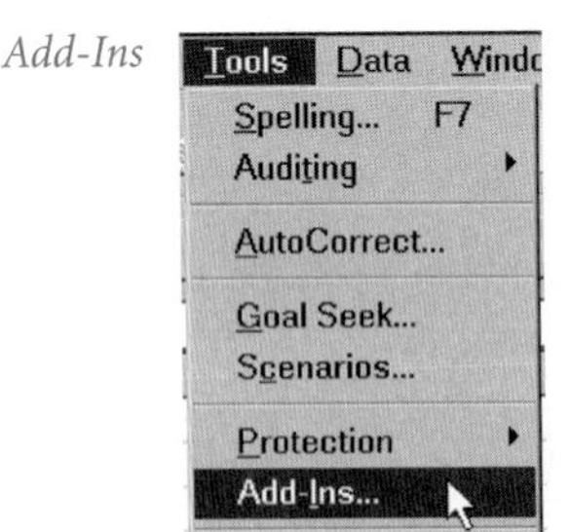

Excel supports extensions to its default functionality in the form of "Add-In" files that are managed by selecting "Add-Ins" from the Tools menu as shown in Figure B.85. Useful Add-Ins to enable are the Analysis ToolPak, which contains many financial and statistical data analysis functions; Lookup Wizard, which helps form VLOOKUP formulas; AutoSave to periodically back up your workbook; and Solver, a required add-in for optimizing worksheet models.

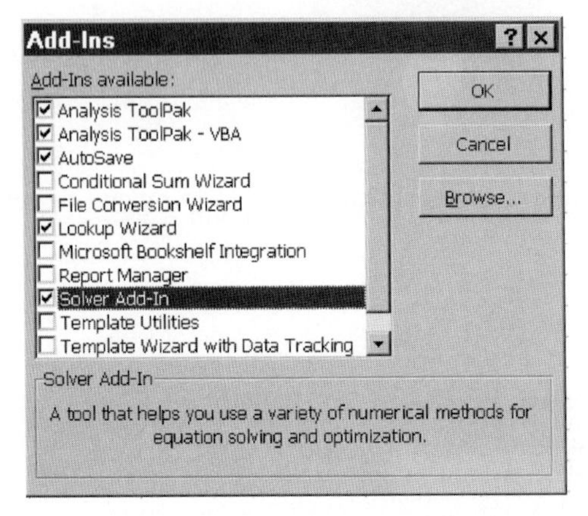

FIGURE B.85

Add-Ins Dialog

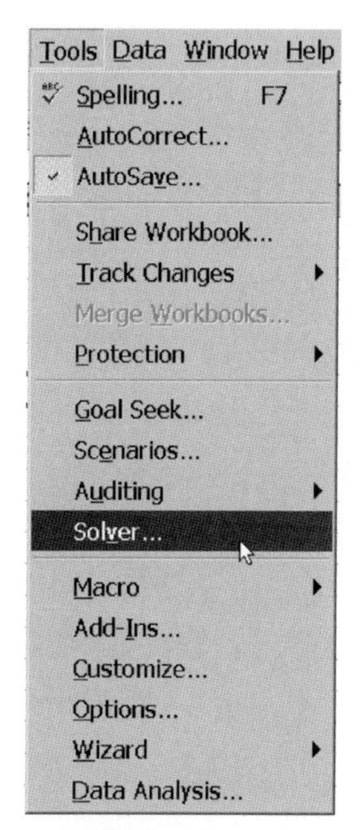

FIGURE B.86

Common Excel Add-Ins

Appndx:2

	A	B	C	D	E	F	G	H	I	J
1		Growth Rate	7%	Cost Rate	60%					
2		Quarter 1	Quarter 2	Quarter 3	Quarter 4					
3	Revenue	$ 1,234.00	$ 1,320.38	$ 1,412.81	$ 1,511.70					
4	Cost	$ 740.40	$ 792.23	$ 847.68	$ 907.02					
5	Contr. Marg	$ 493.60	$ 528.15	$ 565.12	$ 604.68					

Sheet1 / Sheet2 / Sheet3 / Sheet4

Appndx:1

	A	B	C	D	E
1		Growth Rate	0.07	Cost Rate	0.6
2		Quarter 1	Quarter 2	Quarter 3	Quarter 4
3	Revenue	1234	=B3*(1+$C$1)	=C3*(1+$C$1)	=D3*(1+$C$1)
4	Cost	=$E$1*B3	=$E$1*C3	=$E$1*D3	=$E$1*E3
5	Contr. Margin	=B3-B4	=C3-C4	=D3-D4	=E3-E4

FIGURE B.87(a)

Example Model for Data Table

	A	B	C
9		Revenue	Cont. Mar.
10	Growth Rate	$ 1,511.70	$ 604.68
11	5.0%		
12	5.5%		
13	6.0%		
14	6.5%		
15	7.0%		
16	7.5%		
17	8.0%		
18	8.5%		
19	9.0%		
20	9.5%		

FIGURE B.87(b)

Data Table Layout for One Input

Note: Availability of the Add-In files is installation dependent. For example, the Solver Add-In file is *not* installed during normal software installation of Excel via Microsoft's Setup procedure unless specifically selected as part of a Custom setup. If Solver is not present in the Tools menu nor the Add-In dialog, rerun Setup from your original Microsoft software CD-ROM to install Solver.

If the Add-In files were installed into your version of Excel, enabling, for example, the Analysis ToolPak, AutoSave, and Solver adds these extensions to basic Excel. This can be verified by the appearance of their menu items upon the Tools menu, as shown in Figure B.86.

Data Table (One-Input) (Data Table with two inputs is described in Chapter 2, Section 2.4)

A one input data table, called a Data Table 1, is a range of cells that shows the results of one or more formulas when substituting different values of a single parameter. In the example in Figure B.87(a) and (b), we want to tabulate different Quarter 4 Revenues and Contribution Margins for the model below given a collection of Growth Rate parameters. Cells B10:C10 contain the formulas "=E3" and "=E5", respectively. Data Table 1 will substitute each of the growth rates in column A into cell C1—the input cell—and tabulate the resulting model values into the corresponding cells below the formula in cells B10:C10.

To set up a one-input data table as shown in Figure B.87(b), enter the formulas that refer to the model output cells in the row above and one cell to the right of the column of parameter values (cell B10:C10 in this example). Select the range of cells containing the reference formulas and the parameter values to substitute (in this case, A10:C20), and choose "Table. . ." from the Data menu shown in Figure B.88.

FIGURE B.88

Data Table 1 Setup

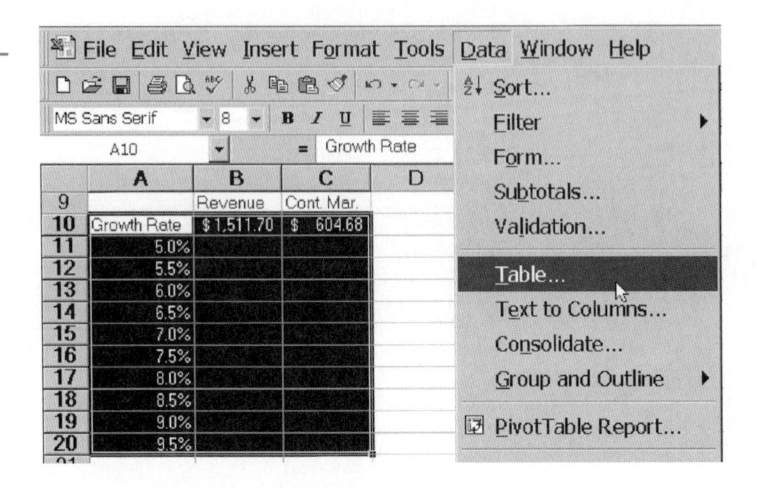

Since the values to be substituted are in a column, enter the reference to the input cell in the "Column Input Cell" dialog box, leaving the "Row Input Cell" blank as shown in Figure B.89 (it is used for the two-input Data Table 2 case). Click OK.

FIGURE B.89

Input Cell Specification for One Input Data Table

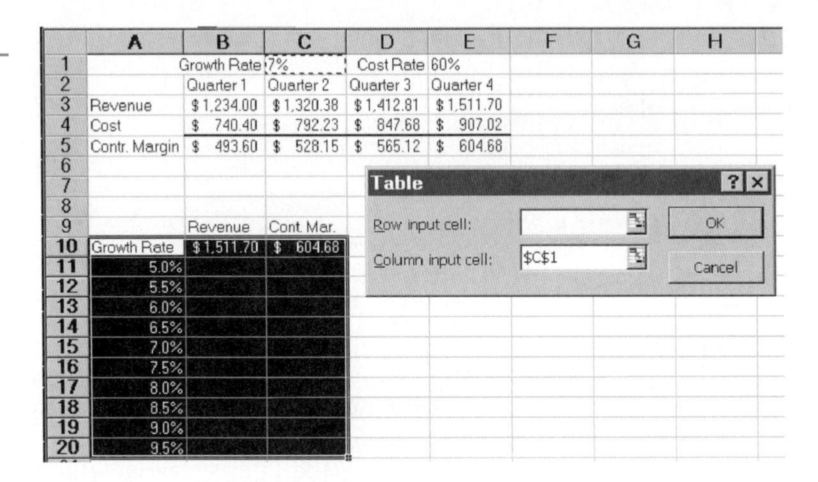

The final table should look as shown in Figure B.90. *Note:* Data Table layouts are ready-made for charting the results via the Chart Wizard.

FIGURE B.90

Final Data Table

	Revenue	Cont. Mar.
Growth Rate	$ 1,511.70	$ 604.68
5.0%	$ 1,428.51	$ 571.40
5.5%	$ 1,449.01	$ 579.61
6.0%	$ 1,469.71	$ 587.89
6.5%	$ 1,490.61	$ 596.24
7.0%	$ 1,511.70	$ 604.68
7.5%	$ 1,532.99	$ 613.20
8.0%	$ 1,554.48	$ 621.79
8.5%	$ 1,576.17	$ 630.47
9.0%	$ 1,598.07	$ 639.23
9.5%	$ 1,620.16	$ 648.06

If the Growth Rate parameter values were originally presented in a row instead of in a column, then the C1 reference would be specified in the "Row Input Cell" in Figure B.89. This and the two input Data Table 2 case are described in Chapter 2, Section 2.4.

Appendix C

Solver Tips and Messages

C.1 SOLVER INSTALLATION

Frontline Systems (http://www.frontsys.com) developed the original version of Solver for Microsoft, a version of which is bundled with Excel. In addition to developing several advanced commercial optimizer products, Frontline Systems also developed the Premium Edition Solver for Education that is contained on the book's CD-ROM. Premium Edition Solver for Education is a much more advanced version of Solver than Microsoft's and contains several bug fixes that make it preferable to Microsoft's Solver. Thus, it is recommended that you install the Premium Edition Solver for Education to replace Microsoft's Solver in your Excel installation.

You must have Microsoft's version of Solver installed before you can install the Premium Edition Solver for Education included on the book's CD-ROM. Microsoft's version of Solver is *not* installed automatically by Microsoft's Office or Excel Setup procedure. If you have Excel installed and Solver does not appear on the Tools menu, you must first rerun Setup to manually select its installation. In this case, use the Custom install option in Setup and manually check the Solver option to have Setup add Microsoft's version of the Solver add-in to your installation of Excel. In Excel 2000 open the Add-Ins item on the Tools menu and check the "Solver Add-in." You will be prompted to insert your Office CD-ROM if necessary.

Once Solver appears on the Tools menu of Excel, you may proceed to install the Premium Edition Solver for Education included on the book's CD-ROM. The file SOLVPREM.EXE contains all of the Solver files in compressed form, and running it will guide you through the installation. (Copying the Premium Edition Solver for Education files from another PC installation will not work; you must run SOLVPREM.EXE.) To uninstall the Premium Edition Solver for Education rerun SOLVPREM.EXE and select the uninstall option. It will restore Microsoft's version of Solver as it was installed originally.

As shown in Figures 3.6 and 3.7 of Chapter 3, the appearance of the Premium Edition Solver for Education Solver Parameters dialog is different from that of Microsoft's Solver, and can be configured for either of the two appearances shown in the figures by clicking the Premium button. It makes *no* difference in software which appearance version of the Solver Parameters dialog you use. The two options only affect the appearance of the dialog itself and your accessibility to the more advanced Premium options. In either version of the Parameters dialog the underlying optimizers used are the same, namely those new ones installed by the Premium Edition Solver for Education. That is, you are *not* switching between Microsoft's Solver and the Premium Edition Solver for Education by clicking the Premium and Standard buttons in the Parameters dialog. Instead, you are switching between two appearance versions of the Parameters and other dialogs, the Standard ones being closer in appearance to those of Microsoft's Solver. Since the optimizer you select from the drop-down list is more clearly documented by clicking the Premium button, producing the appearance in Figure 3.7, and the Evolutionary Solver can be accessed only from the drop-down list, it is recommended that you use the Premium appearance version of the dialog.

Table C.1

Solver Dialog Terminology

OPTIMIZATION MODELING TERMINOLOGY	SOLVER TERMINOLOGY
Objective Function	Set Cell
Decision Variables	Changing Variable Cells
Constraints	Constraints
Constraint Function (LHS, Left-Hand Side)	Constraint Cell Reference
RHS (Constraint's Right-Hand Side)	Constraint

C.2 INTRODUCTION

Solver uses slightly different terminology than elsewhere in the book. The differences are documented in Table C.1.

Listed below are the four types of model analyses that Solver can perform. Constrained optimization is the most general; the others are special cases of constrained optimization. Solver can apply each of the four types of analyses to either linear (Simplex LP) or nonlinear (GRG NLP) formulations.

1. **Find a Feasible Solution: No Cell Reference Is Given in Solver's Set Cell Box.** If the Cell Reference in the Set Cell box is empty, Solver will stop when it finds a feasible solution to the model, that is, a set of values for the Changing Variable Cells that satisfy all the constraints. If all the constraints are linear functions of the Changing Variable Cells, setting Assume Linear Model in the Solver Options or Standard Simplex LP is selected will speed up the feasible solution process.
2. **Find a Goal: No Cell Reference Is Given in Solver's Set Cell Box and Only Equality Constraints, or a Target Value for the Cell in the Set Cell Box and No Constraints.** This formulation is called a goal-seeking model. Solver handles two varieties of goal seeking: (1) traditional goal seeking (solve to find a target value given no constraints) and (2) solve to find those Changing Variable Cells values that simultaneously satisfy a system of constraints given no target value. In Solver (1) is identical in concept to Excel's Goal Seeking command except the search procedure uses a different procedure. For (2) Solver finds the solution to the system of equations represented by the constraint cells with the Changing Variable Cells as unknowns. (Solver can also solve a system of equations and inequalities, that is, constraints having lower or upper bounds. In this case, Solver finds a feasible solution, as in 1 above.) If all the constraints are linear functions of the Changing Variable Cells, setting Assume Linear Model in Solver Options or selecting Standard Simplex LP, will speed up the solution process.
3. **Find an Unconstrained Optimum: Maximization or Minimization of a Model with No Constraints.** This is often called an "unconstrained optimization" model and makes sense only if the objective function is a nonlinear function of the Changing Variable Cells—optimization of a linear objective function without constraints will always produce an unbounded solution error message. Solver will find a point along the objective function's curvature where the objective function cell reaches a maximum or minimum. If the objective function has multiple maxima or minima, Solver will find one of them (a local optimum), which may not be the global optimum. The particular local optimum found by Solver is dependent upon the initial values of the Changing Variable Cells.
4. **Find a Constrained Optimum: Maximization or Minimization of a Model with Constraints.** The most general and perhaps most common type of model involves both constraints and an objective function cell to be maximized or minimized—a "constrained optimization" model. If the objective function cell and all the con-

straints are linear functions of the Changing Variable Cells, it is a linear optimization or linear programming (LP) model, and it can be optimized faster, more reliably, and with more detailed sensitivity information by setting Assume Linear Model in Solver Options or selecting Standard Simplex LP. Otherwise, it's a nonlinear (NLP) optimization model and is optimized by Solver's Generalized Reduced Gradient (GRG) method or by Evolutionary Solver.

In the case of a nonlinear optimization model, Solver will solve for a point along the objective function's curvature where the optimum cell reaches a maximum or minimum subject to satisfying the constraints. If the objective function has multiple maxima or minima that satisfy the constraints, Solver will find one of them (a local optimum), which may not be the global optimum. The particular local optimum found by Solver that satisfies the constraints is dependent upon the initial values of the Changing Variable Cells.

Under 3 and 4 above, if there are multiple optima, repeatedly re-solving the model via some systematic search strategy with differing initial values of the Changing Variable Cells or using Evolutionary Solver are the only ways to discover the global optimum. For large models (many Changing Variable Cells) an exhaustive search or Evolutionary Solver may not be practical strategies. Thus, there is always the risk that the global optima will not be found for a nonlinear model.

Under all four conditions above, if any of the model's formulas contain nonsmooth Excel functions, such as IF( ) or VLOOKUP( ), that involve the Changing Variable Cells and influence the calculation of the model's objective function value directly or via any constraints, then you must use the Evolutionary Solver optimizer instead of the Simplex LP or the GRG Nonlinear optimizer. Evolutionary Solver is a smart search engine based upon genetic algorithm methods for finding good candidate solutions, but because random search is employed, it is not guaranteed to find an optimum solution. See Section 7.8 of Chapter 7 in the book for a general introduction to Evolutionary Solver with examples of its use.

C.3 COMMON SOLVER MODELING PROBLEMS

Solver is a very sophisticated program performing complicated calculations on the model contained in an Excel worksheet. As a result, there are numerous opportunities for mistakes or other difficulties to arise in model formulation, Solver dialog settings, Solver optimization procedures, and interpretation of Solver results. In addition, the GRG Nonlinear optimizer and Evolutionary Solver may not find a global optimum even for a correctly formulated, but not well-behaved, model. Moreover, mistakes, solution difficulties, and optimizing ill-behaved models often do *not* result in Solver error messages, a trap that frequently ensnares the unwary modeler. Even when Solver error messages do occur, their resolution is often not straightforward. Therefore, an ounce of prevention, as given in the modeling "hygiene" list below, will often avoid many frustrating hours attempting to resolve Solver difficulties once they occur.

1. Many difficulties in optimization modeling with spreadsheets are not related to Solver but to incorrect formulations. Developing the symbolic (algebraic) model on paper first will help resolve any inconsistencies. Often, writing down the symbolic model and making the Excel worksheet version mirror that model leads to a worksheet model structure that is clean, better self-documented, and easy to work with, ultimately taking less total time to develop and debug.
2. The second most common difficulty is inconsistent constraints that produce an over-constrained model, often with no feasible solution. Double check the direction of all inequality constraints ("<=" was used when you meant to use ">="). Try to avoid equality constraints unless dictated by the managerial situation being modeled or unless there is a definitional connection among the variables, for example, "Profit =

Revenue – Cost." Many times an equality constraint can be relaxed meaningfully to an inequality constraint, which will give Solver more opportunities to find an improved optimal solution.

3. A common oversight is forgetting the nonnegativity constraints on the Changing Variable Cells when the logic of the situation requires them. This is done by setting Assume Non-Negative in Solver's Options dialog or by explicity adding a nonnegativity constraint on the Changing Variable Cells (the decision variables). *Note:* Do not include both of these options. Although logically equivalent, including both creates redundant constraints that may introduce degeneracy and could cause Solver to fail to converge to an optimum for some formulations.
4. Poorly scaled models is the *most* common mistake causing Solver to stop prematurely or produce incomprehensible error messages. Poorly scaled models cause an insidious difficulty because often no messages are produced to suggest this problem, or worse yet, the Solver error messages that are produced may be entirely spurious. Linear and especially nonlinear model optimizations by Solver are very sensitive to the scaling of numbers in the model. Avoid units of measure in models that produce numbers whose differences span more than about five or six orders of magnitude. For example, a model computing Interest Expense by multiplying an Interest Rate of 12% by a Loan Balance of $60,500,000 spans nine orders of magnitude (10^9) between the Interest Rate (.12) and the Loan Balance data. This will lead to cumulating roundoff and/or truncation error as Solver optimizes the model that may result in wrong Changing Variable Cells solutions or bogus error messages. Rescaling the model's data to reduce the spread is easy and loses no generality nor accuracy in results. For the example above, rescaling the Loan Balance (and all related worksheet quantities) to be measured in millions of dollars and entering a $60.5 in the Loan Balance cell reduces the span to three orders of magnitude. For versions of Excel prior to Excel 97, the Use Automatic Scaling item in Solver Options is *inoperative* if Assume Linear Model is also checked; it works only for nonlinear models in earlier versions of Excel. For this reason alone, you are advised to upgrade older versions of Excel to more recent versions. Even for nonlinear models and recent versions of Excel, do not depend upon the automatic scaling feature. For some nonlinear models the internal rescaling generated by setting Use Automatic Scaling may not be enough to avoid this problem in unusual circumstances.
5. Finally, the use of nonsmooth functions, such as the Excel "IF( )" function, that introduce discontinuities in worksheet cell(s) will very likely invalidate responsible use of Solver if the objective function cell formula or any constraint formulas depend directly or indirectly upon the cell(s) containing those functions. Not only does the IF( ) function void linearity, but it likely introduces discontinuities into the feasible region or the set of possible objective function values. This in turn affects the partial derivative estimates computed internally by Solver that guide it toward optimality. Neither Solver nor any known optimization procedure can be guaranteed to handle such discontinuities reliably for all models. Therefore, inclusion of *any* Excel function, such as IF( ), into the worksheet model that produces a discontinuity in the graph of its output values for valid ranges of Changing Variable Cells vitiates any use of Solver's linear, integer, or nonlinear optimizers. If the model formulation requires the use of nonsmooth functions, your only option is to use Solver's Evolutionary optimizer, available in a Premium Edition Solver, such as the Premium Edition Solver for Education contained on the book's CD-ROM. However, as discussed in Section 7.8 in the book, Evolutionary Solver is not really an optimizer. Instead, it is a smart search engine for finding good model solutions based in part on randomness in its search, and it may not find the model's optimum solution or even a good solution.

C.4 USEFUL TIPS TO REMEMBER

- Several unresolved bugs in Excel 2000 outside of Solver are known to produce spurious error messages when using Solver for optimization. One documented cause of these spurious errors is triggered by use of Merged Cells in Excel worksheets. Until Microsoft fixes these problems in a future version of Excel, do *not* use Merged Cells in any worksheets/workbooks to be optimized with Solver. See the discussion in Section C.9 for a related problem with errors created by such Excel bugs.
- For nonlinear models, including those to be optimized with Evolutionary Solver, the initial values of the Changing Variable Cells (decision variables), including any values kept from a previous Solver run, become the initial Changing Variable Cells values used if Solver is rerun, that is, Solver starts its search based on the initial values contained in the Changing Variable Cells. In contrast, for linear models the initial values of Changing Variable Cells are ignored; Solver uses a separate procedure to find its own starting feasible set of values for the Changing Variable Cells.
- Although acceptable to Solver, it is poor modeling practice to put formulas as the RHS entry of the Solver Add Constraint dialog or the Solver Change Constraint dialog. Instead, put references to worksheet cells as the RHS in Solver constraint dialogs. In addition, referencing RHS cells that contain formulas may cause interpretation problems in Sensitivity Reports if the objective function or the Changing Variable Cells values are influenced by those formulas during optimization. In this latter case, it is better to include the RHS formulas as terms in the LHS formulas by algebraically moving the formulas into the calculations for the LHS, leaving a constant, such as zero, on the RHS. Then reference those RHS cells now containing constants in the Solver constraint dialog. See Section 4.12 for an extended example of this problem.
- Integer or binary constraints may only be defined directly on decision variables (Changing Variable Cells). Do not type the word "integer" nor "binary" into the RHS of such constraints in Solver dialogs. That is, Solver must fill in those fields for you when you select the constraint option "int" or "bin" from the drop-down list in the second field of the Add Constraint dialog or the Solver Change Constraint dialog. (An exception is Excel 98 on Macintosh which requires that you type in the word into the RHS of such constraints in Solver dialogs.)
- The Precision value in Solver's Options is used to assess whether a constraint is adequately satisfied. For properly scaled models (if in doubt, set Use Automatic Scaling in Solver Options) there is little reason to alter the Precision value in Solver Options. A constraint is considered satisfied if the relation it represents is within a small range of being true, called the Precision value. In any event, do not increase the Precision value in Solver Options to be a value larger than .0001, that is, 1E-4, nor smaller than .000001, that is, 1E-6.
- Do not create overlapping cell references in the LHS of different lower bound constraints or different upper bound constraints in the Constraints list box. When presented with multiple lower bound constraints (or multiple upper bound constraints) on the same cells, Solver will arbitrarily use only one of the multiple lower bound constraints (or upper bound constraints). For example, if you enter the constraints B2:B10 <= 8 and A5:C5 <= 3, then there are two upper bounds on B5, B5 <= 8 and B5 <= 3. Solver will use one of them, and you cannot influence which one Solver will use.
- Solver optimization of a model having integer constraints is computationally very intensive, and hence optimization of the model is slow. To speed up solution time Solver uses a default Tolerance value of 5% to stop when the solution's objective function value is within 5% of the true optimum. Set Tolerance to 0% to always obtain the true integer optimum at the cost of longer solution times.

- In Solver's reports the formatting for data cells is inherited from the formatting of the corresponding cells in the Excel worksheet. Often the inherited format gives insufficient precision, and for example, a datum may misleadingly show as a 0 or 1 when in fact it is a small but important fraction, such as .3 or 1.48, respectively. In particular, a too small formatting precision may lead to misinterpretation of Shadow Prices or Lagrange Multipliers in the Solver Sensitivity Report.

The following tips are for more obscure situations that can safely be ignored by most Solver users. They reflect infrequently encountered Solver difficulties and are included for completeness.

- Do not enter overlapping cell references when specifying multiple ranges separated by commas in the Changing Variable Cells field. For example, do not enter the two partially overlapping ranges F10:F20, E8:G12 into the dialog because cells F10:F12 have been specified twice.
- Using the Save Model feature in Solver Options to save multiple model formulations for a worksheet is an infrequently needed option. However, if used, do not Save Model to any other workbook or worksheet. Save Model only to the active worksheet containing the original Excel model formulation to be optimized.
- For nonlinear models, changing the Derivatives method in Solver Options away from the "Forward" default to the "Central" alternative may produce incorrect Sensitivity Report numbers in unusual circumstances.
- Do not use any Defined Names that begin with "solver" in your model's workbook.
- Do not attempt to optimize a model if the worksheet or workbook containing it is password protected.
- Do not invoke Solver while in Group Edit or Data Entry mode in Excel.
- Do not reference the Changing Variable Cells in the Solver Parameters dialog to other than the active worksheet containing your model.
- If the version of Excel for your country does not use the "." as a decimal point separator in numbers, do not record macros involving Solver optimization. Also Excel 97 may not accept multiple selections in the Changing Cells edit box in this case. An updated Solver is available at www.frontsys.com.
- Some versions of Excel will not accept more than 16 discontiguous array ranges for decision variables within Solver's Changing Variable Cells dialog box.
- Some versions of Excel will not accept dialog box entries, Solver included, if the total string length of the input exceeds 255 characters (later versions allow up to 1,024 characters). For example, this can happen with long Defined Names and many discontiguous arrays specified in Changing Variable Cells dialog.

C.5 SOLVER OPTIONS

For most small optimization models, there is rarely any reason to alter any of Solver's Options settings, except Assume Non-Negative and Use Automatic Scaling. Nevertheless, Solver Option defaults may be changed in unusual circumstances as documented below. *Note:* More general information on Solver Options settings for linear optimization is given in Section 3.4 and for nonlinear optimization is given in Section 7.6.

MAX TIME

Max Time specifies the maximum number of seconds that the Solver will run before it pauses, and has a default of 100 seconds. It includes time for model setup and to find the solution. For integer models, it is the total time taken to solve all the Branch & Bound subproblems. When Solver pauses a "Show Trial Solution" dialog is displayed offering the options of stopping or continuing without a time limitation. *Note:* You may force Solver to stop any time by pressing the Esc key.

MAX ITERATIONS

Iterations specifies the maximum number of solution iterations that Solver may perform during one optimization, and has a default of 100. For integer models, it is the maximum number of iterations for any one subproblem. When Solver pauses a "Show Trial Solution" dialog is displayed offering the options of stopping or continuing without an iterations limitation.

PRECISION

The Precision value in Solver's Options is used to assess whether a constraint is adequately satisfied—for each constraint how closely the LHS-calculated values must match the RHS in order for the constraint to be considered by Solver to be satisfied. That is, a constraint is considered satisfied if the relation it represents is within a small range of being true, called the Precision value. For an integer constraint (a Changing Variable Cell is set to be "int" or "bin"), if the difference between the cell's value and the closest integer value is less than the Precision, then the cell's value is treated as an integer.

For properly scaled models (if in doubt, set Use Automatic Scaling in Solver Options) there is little reason to alter the Precision value in Solver Options. In any event, do not increase the Precision value in Solver Options to be a value larger than .0001, that is, 1E-4, nor smaller than .000001, that is, 1E-6.

PIVOT TOLERANCE AND REDUCED TOLERANCE (STANDARD SIMPLEX LP OPTIMIZATION)

These infrequently changed options are used only for the Simplex optimization method in LP models. When Solver searches for a nonzero matrix element to pivot upon, a matrix element with an absolute value less than Pivot Tolerance is treated as zero. When Solver searches for a new nonbasic variable to enter the basis, the candidates are only those variables that have reduced costs algebraically less than the negative value of Reduced Tolerance.

SHOW ITERATION RESULTS

Checking this option pauses Solver and presents the "Show Trial Solution" dialog on every iteration during model optimization. Showing the best solution thus far, you may click on the Continue button or the Stop button. Clicking the Save Scenario button saves the current solution in a named scenario, which may be summarized later with Excel's Scenario Manager.

USE AUTOMATIC SCALING

Checking this option will scale the values of the objective and constraint functions internally to try to minimize the effects of a poorly scaled model, one with too great a range between the smallest and largest numbers. A poorly scaled model is one in which cell values differ by more than about five or six orders of magnitude. This will lead to cumulating round-off and/or truncation errors as Solver optimizes the model that may result in wrong Changing Variable Cells solutions or bogus error messages. *Note:* Do not depend upon this automatic scaling feature. For some nonlinear models the internal rescaling generated by setting Use Automatic Scaling may not be enough to avoid this problem in unusual circumstances. Also, for versions of Excel prior to Excel 97, the Use Automatic Scaling item in Solver Options is *inoperative* if Assume Linear Model is also checked.

It is recommended that this box be checked for all Solver models. However, for nonlinear models doing this *requires* that the initial values contained in the Changing Variable Cells are of the same magnitudes for those cells to contain at optimality. That is, the effectiveness of this option depends on how well these initial cell values reflect the values they will contain during the solution process.

ASSUME NON-NEGATIVE

Setting this option is equivalent to adding a nonnegativity constraint that all the Changing Variable Cells be >= 0. However, do not set this option and also add a nonnegativity constraint. Including both creates redundant constraints that may introduce degeneracy and could cause Solver to fail to converge to an optimum for some formulations.

BYPASS SOLVER REPORTS

Checking this option bypasses the extra computations by Solver to prepare for creating reports, and no reports will be selectable in the Solver Reports dialog after Solver completes its optimization. For larger models bypassing reports can noticeably speed total solution time.

CONVERGENCE (GRG NONLINEAR OPTIMIZATION)

Discussion of Convergence settings for nonlinear models is given below under Interpreting Solver Messages and in Section 7.6 of the book.

ESTIMATES, DERIVATIVES, SEARCH (GRG NONLINEAR OPTIMIZATION)

These three options control the GRG Nonlinear Solver optimizer. They are explained in Section 7.6 of the book. *Note:* Changing the Derivatives setting to Central may produce incorrect Sensitivity Report numbers for some NLP models.

MAX SUBPROBLEMS (INTEGER OPTIONS DIALOG)

This is the limit on the total number of the Branch & Bound subproblems. When exceeded Solver pauses and presents a "Show Trial Solution" dialog offering the options of stopping or continuing without a limitation. This limit should be used instead of the Iterations limit in the Solver Options dialog. The Iterations limit in the Solver Options dialog should be set high enough for the iterations needed by *each* of the individual subproblems solved during the Branch & Bound process.

MAX INTEGER SOLUTIONS (INTEGER OPTIONS DIALOG)

This is the limit on the number of candidate integer solutions found by the Branch & Bound method. When exceeded Solver pauses and presents a "Show Trial Solution" dialog offering the options of stopping or continuing without a limitation.

TOLERANCE (INTEGER OPTIONS DIALOG)

Tolerance is used by Solver only for models with integer constraints. Tolerance specifies how close the integer solution must be to the optimal integer solution before the Solver stops. To speed up solution time Solver uses a default Tolerance value of 5% to stop when the solution's objective function value is within 5% of the true optimum. Overriding this default by setting Tolerance = 0% forces Solver to continue optimizing until an optimal integer solution is found. This continuation might increase solution times by ten fold or hundred fold or much more. In a Premium Edition Solver, such as the Premium Edition Solver for Education contained on the book's CD-ROM, look for Tolerance on the Integer Options dialog, accessible from a button on the Solver Options dialog.

INTEGER CUTOFF (INTEGER OPTIONS DIALOG)

Entering an objective function value from a known solution to the model permits the Branch & Bound process to avoid having Solver optimize candidate subproblems whose objective function value can be no better than this value. *Warning:* A value that is in fact too large (maximization model) or too small (minimization model) will likely cause the Solver to skip evaluating the subproblem that produces the optimal integer solution.

SOLVE WITHOUT INTEGER CONSTRAINTS (INTEGER OPTIONS DIALOG)

Setting this option tells Solver to ignore the integer constraints in optimizing the model. When debugging an integer model, it is easier to set this option than to delete the integer constraints and add them back later.

CONVERGENCE (EVOLUTIONARY OPTIMIZATION)

Evolutionary Solver stops and displays the message "Solver has converged to the current solution" when almost all the candidate solutions in the population have similar fitness values. After the Solver has found a certain minimum number of improved solutions from the evolutionary process, the stopping condition is triggered if 99% of the population solutions have fitness values that are within Convergence tolerance of each other. If you believe that Evolutionary Solver is stopping prematurely, make the Convergence tolerance smaller. In addition, consider increasing either the Mutation Rate or the Population Size or both to increase the diversity of the population of trial solutions.

POPULATION SIZE (EVOLUTIONARY OPTIMIZATION)

This sets the number of candidate solutions kept in the population that Evolutionary Solver uses throughout the solution process. The minimum population size is 10 and the maximum is 200. A larger population size often permits a more complete exploration of the space of solutions, particularly if the mutation rate is high enough to create diversity in candidate solutions. A good starting point for this setting is 100 (the default) or 10 times the number of Changing Variable Cells.

MUTATION RATE (EVOLUTIONARY OPTIMIZATION)

The Mutation Rate is the probability that a candidate solution in the population will be mutated to create a new trial solution, which may become a new candidate solution in the population, depending on its fitness, during each iteration of the Evolutionary Solver. During Evolutionary Solver optimization, an iteration consists of a possible mutation step, a "crossover" step, a local search in the vicinity of a new candidate solution, and possibly, the elimination of an unfit solution from the population. Increasing this probability adds diversity to the population of trial solutions.

REQUIRE BOUNDS ON VARIABLES (EVOLUTIONARY OPTIMIZATION)

When selected (the default), Evolutionary Solver will produce an error message if any Changing Variable Cell does not have both a lower and an upper bound given as constraints. If the option is unchecked, the unbounded range for these cells will drastically slow down Evolutionary Solver, making it very difficult to find good candidate solutions for the population.

THE LIMIT OPTIONS DIALOG (EVOLUTIONARY OPTIMIZATION)

Clicking the Limit Options button displays the Limit Options dialog. Evolutionary Solver handles integer constraints on its own, not via Solver's Branch & Bound method for integer optimization, subject to the limits set in this dialog. However, like the Branch & Bound method, Evolutionary Solver works on a series of subproblems controlled by the options below. *Note:* Since the population often includes candidates representing infeasible solutions, the fitness value computed by Evolutionary Solver is a combination of an objective function value and a penalty amount for infeasibility. A smaller Precision value will increase this penalty.

Max Subproblems This option places a limit on the number of subproblems that may be explored by Evolutionary Solver. When exceeded Evolutionary Solver pauses and presents a "Show Trial Solution" dialog offering the options of stopping or continuing. During Evolutionary Solver optimization, an iteration consists of generating a subproblem via a possible mutation step, a "crossover" step, a local search in the vicinity of a new candidate solution, and possibly, the replacement of an unfit solution from the population by the new candidate solution. If your model is large or complex, increase the limit from its default value.

Max Feasible Solutions This option places a limit on the number of feasible solutions found by Evolutionary Solver. When exceeded Evolutionary Solver pauses and presents a "Show Trial Solution" dialog offering the options of stopping or continuing. A feasible solution is any solution that satisfies all of the constraints, including any integer constraints. If your model is large or complex, increase the limit from its default value.

Tolerance and Max Time Without Improvement Tolerance works with the Max Time Without Improvement option to limit the time the Evolutionary Solver searches for candidate solutions without making significant progress. If the percentage improvement in the best candidate solution's fitness is less than the Tolerance for the number of seconds specified in Max Time Without Improvement option, Evolutionary Solver stops and displays the Solver Results dialog. Solver Results will show the message "Solver cannot improve the current solution," or if there are no feasible solutions in the population, "Solver could not find a feasible solution." If Evolutionary Solver has stopped prematurely, either set the Tolerance value smaller (possibly to zero), or increase the number of seconds in the Max Time Without Improvement option to force Evolutionary Solver to search longer.

Solve Without Integer Constraints Setting this option tells Evolutionary Solver to ignore any integer constraints in optimizing the model. When debugging an integer model, it is easier to set this option than to delete the integer constraints and add them back later.

C.6 INTERPRETING SOLVER MESSAGES

When Solver stops, the worksheet receives the Changing Variable Cells results of the Solver solution, and Excel recalculates the worksheet to update any other cell formulas they affect. A Solver Results dialog appears with a message indicating the condition that caused the Solver optimization to terminate. The appearance of the Solver Results dialog itself does *not necessarily* mean that the optimal solution has been found by Solver; it only means that Solver has terminated its optimization procedure. Solver must terminate with one of its "successful completion" messages before it can be concluded that an optimum *may* have been found. To repeat: Completion alone of the Solver optimization process does *not* mean that the optimal solution has been found, and even if Solver terminates with one of its successful completion messages, it does not *necessarily* mean that the optimal solution has been found. For example, a linear model may have "alternative optima" only one of which will be found by Solver, or Solver may successfully terminate its optimization of a nonlinear model at a local optimum instead of the global optimum.

The Solver Results dialog that appears after Solver terminates its optimization displays a completion message. Clicking OK will keep the final Changing Variable Cells values found by Solver; clicking Cancel will restore their previous cell contents before the Solver run. Listed in the next two sections are the most common Solver messages and their meanings.

C.7 SUCCESSFUL COMPLETION MESSAGES

Solver found a solution. All constraints and optimality conditions are satisfied.

This is the most desirable Solver completion message. It means that all constraints are satisfied to within the Solver Option's Precision setting, and an optimum (maximum or minimum) value has been found for the objective function cell in the Set Cell box. For an integer model it means that an optimum value within the Tolerance setting percentage of the true optimum has been found; see below. *Note:* Because it is not really an optimizer, Evolutionary Solver will never display this message.

For a linear model (Assume Linear Model checked in Solver Options or Standard Simplex LP is selected), this message means that Solver has unambiguously found an optimal solution. It is possible that there are other solutions with the same objective function value, that is, "alternative optimal" solutions. In this case, mathematically, there are an infinite number of alternative optimal solutions (each with different values of the Changing Variable Cells), all of which produce the same optimal objective function cell value and satisfy the constraints. The infinite set of alternative optimal solutions will involve linear combinations of a finite set of extreme (corner) point alternative optimal solutions, and Solver has discovered one of the set of extreme point optimal solutions satisfying the constraints.

If the solution is nondegenerate and the model is linear, a zero Allowable Increase or Decrease entry for the Objective Coefficient range portion of the Solver Sensitivity Report signals existence of alternative optimal solutions. Other than this, no information is given in Solver reports as to the Changing Variable Cells values of any other alternative extreme (corner) point optimal solutions, and a repeated search strategy of rerunning Solver with slightly differing Objective Coefficient values is required to identify the other (extreme point) alternative optima.

For a nonlinear model (Assume Linear Model in solver Options is not checked or GRG Nonlinear is selected), this message means that Solver has found a *locally* optimal solution. There may be other sets of values for the Changing Variable Cells, which yield the same (alternative optima) or better (other local optima) values for the objective function cell. In general, there is no way to know by looking at Solver reports if the solution is a local or a global optimum nor if there are alternative optima. Repeatedly re-solving the model via some systematic search strategy that utilizes new values of initial Changing Variable Cells values is the only way to discover any other optima, and ultimately, the global optimum. However, for large models (many Changing Variable Cells) a thorough search over the space of all possible initial Changing Variable Cells values is analogous to exhaustive enumeration of the model, an impractical strategy. Thus, there is always the risk that the global optimum (or global optima in the case of alternative optimal solutions) satisfying the constraints will not be discovered. The more numerous and complex the nonlinear relationships are in the model, the more likely the global optimum (optima) will be missed.

Even if a nonlinear model's set of feasible objective function values is known mathematically to be unimodal (i.e., having only one—necessarily global—optimum), the closeness of Solver's successful-completion solution to the true solution is influenced by the Solver Options settings (for example, the Precision value), the shape of the model's nonlinear objective function and/or nonlinear constraints (having discontinuities introduced by Excel "If( )" statements, or very sharp peak(s) to name two), the initial values of the Changing Variable Cells, the model's rate of convergence toward the optimum, and the internal arithmetic accuracy of the microprocessor used.

For integer linear models (any model with at least one integer constraint) with Tolerance = X% (set in Solver Options—default is 5%), Solver has found a solution satisfying the constraints whose objective function value is *within* X% of the true optimal objective value. In particular, if Tolerance = 0% and a linear integer model was optimized, Solver has found a true integer optimal solution. If the Tolerance = X% and a nonlinear integer model was optimized, Solver has found a locally optimal integer solution within X% of a true locally optimal integer solution.

Solver found an integer solution within tolerance. All constraints are satisfied.

This message occurs when optimizing an integer model with a nonzero value for the Tolerance setting in the Solver Options dialog. Solver has found a solution satisfying the constraints with an objective value that is within the given Tolerance percent of the true optimal objective value. This may be the true integer optimal solution, but this can only be guaranteed if Tolerance is set to zero. In that case Solver will produce the message "Solver found a solution. All constraints are satisfied."

Solver has converged to the current solution. All constraints are satisfied.

This message should appear only for nonlinear models. Otherwise, review the model for unintended nonlinear relationships or poorly scaled data.

Solver has stopped because the objective function cell is changing very slowly for the last few iterations or trial solutions. That is, the value in the objective function cell named in Set Cell (or if the solution is not yet feasible, the sum of the constraint violations) is changing at a rate below a convergence rate tolerance cutoff for the last *N* trial solutions. Prior to Excel 97, the values for *N* and the convergence rate tolerance cutoff are fixed at unpublished values within Excel Solver software and were not alterable, that is, no Solver Options settings could affect them. (Indirect evidence suggests that the convergence tolerance was about .00001 and *N* was approximately 5.) Beginning with Excel 97 the Convergence box in Solver Options allows the convergence rate to be changed, but not the value of *N*. Reducing Convergence from its default of .0001 to .00001 may help to allow a model producing this message to continue to find an optimal solution.

An optimal solution *may* have been found, but it is also possible that Solver is making very slow progress toward an optimal solution, or that the precision setting (Precision in the Solver Options dialog) is too low, or that the initial values for the Changing Variable Cells were initialized too far from the optimal solution. More precisely, Solver stops if the absolute value of the relative change in the objective function is less than the convergence rate tolerance for the last *N* iterations. *Note:* A poorly scaled nonlinear model is more likely to trigger this stopping condition, even if Use Automatic Scaling in the Options dialog is checked. Although the "< 6 orders of magnitude" scaling rule for linear models is usually sufficient scaling for most nonlinear models as well, in unusual cases no more than about four orders of magnitude may be necessary to avoid this condition.

If you believe the (nonlinear) model is well formulated and scaled and that Solver has stopped prematurely, accept the final results (i.e., check the "Keep Solver solution" option in the Solver Results dialog) and then immediately rerun Solver. Keeping the Solver results will initialize the model's Changing Variable Cells to the final Solver values from the prior run, which then become the starting values for the new run. That buys you another *N* iterations to see if the convergence rate will improve or if Solver will ultimately (and slowly) converge to a solution yielding the desirable successful completion message above. Many Solver reruns may be required to get past the slow-convergence plateau, if at all. If this strategy fails, try initializing the model to a completely different set of initial Changing Variable Cells values, ones that are far removed from the region of slow convergence. The nonlinear model may converge more quickly to a (local) optimum if Solver starts toward it from a different direction. Alternatively, try decreasing the Convergence value in the Solver Options dialog or switch to using Evolutionary Solver.

For Evolutionary Solver, this message means that the fitness value for candidate solutions in the population is changing very slowly. Evolutionary Solver stops if 99% or more of the members of the population have fitness values whose percentage difference is less than the Convergence tolerance in the Solver Options dialog. Fitness values include measures of the objective function and any penalty for infeasibility, but since the Solver has found some feasible solutions, this test is weighted towards the objective function values. If Evolutionary Solver is stopping prematurely, try making the Convergence tolerance smaller (perhaps zero). Also, consider increasing either or both of the Mutation Rate and the Population Size to increase the diversity of the population of trial solutions.

C.8 UNSUCCESSFUL COMPLETION MESSAGES

Solver cannot improve the current solution. All constraints are satisfied.

This message should not appear for linear models. It appears rarely for GRG nonlinear models, and means that although an optimal solution has not been found, Solver cannot find a better set of Changing Variable Cells values than the values being displayed. One possible cause is that the model is degenerate, and Solver is cycling internally due to technical difficulties with Solver's GRG nonlinear optimization method. If this message occurs, check to see if some of the model's constraints are redundant, and therefore, can be removed from the model without affecting the optimal solution. An example of this is explicitly including nonnegativity constraints and also checking the Assume Non-Negative option. If present, removing redundant constraints may reduce or remove the degeneracy and eliminate the internal cycling. Otherwise, there are few options available other than switching to Evolutionary Solver or another optimization software package whose methods might be more immune to this rarely occurring technical difficulty.

For Evolutionary Solver, this message is common, and means that Evolutionary Solver cannot find a new candidate solution whose fitness value is a percentage improvement over the current best member's fitness of more than the Tolerance value in the time given by the Max Time Without Improvement (both set in the Limit Options dialog). Because Evolutionary Solver has no optimality test, it will usually stop with either "Solver converged to the current solution" or "Solver cannot improve the current solution" messages. If you think the message is appearing prematurely, make the Tolerance value smaller (perhaps zero), or increase the setting of the Max Time Without Improvement to more seconds.

Solver could not find a feasible solution.

Solver was unable to find a set of Changing Variable Cells values that simultaneously satisfy all the constraints to within the Solver Options Precision setting. This frequently occurring message is usually triggered when the constraints of the model are inconsistent, producing an "overconstrained" model. The most likely culprits are too many equality constraints or mistakenly choosing the wrong direction for one or more inequality constraints. Examine the worksheet for a possible mistake in the constraint formulas or the choice of constraints. An aid to help you is contained in the Solver Results dialog displaying this message. Select the Feasibility Report option to help you diagnose the source of the infeasibility.

Recent versions of Excel contain a bug outside of Solver that can also trigger the message erroneously. One known way this bug is triggered in Excel is the use of Merged Cells in the worksheet. Review your worksheet and eliminate any Merged Cells in it. Also check that the model is properly scaled. See Section C.9 for more information.

For nonlinear models, it may be that Solver could not find a feasible solution after searching in the neighborhood of the initial Changing Variable Cells values. Try initializing the Changing Variable Cells to completely different values in Excel and rerun Solver. Better yet, initialize the model's Changing Variable Cells to a feasible solution that is known to be near the optimal solution, based upon similar model results or prior knowledge, if possible. For Evolutionary Solver also consider decreasing the Precision value in its Options dialog. This will increase the infeasibility penalty and permit Evolutionary Solver to explore more solutions that are close to being feasible.

Solver encountered an error value in a target or constraint cell.

One or more of the model's formulas yielded an Excel error value, such as "#DIV/0!" or "#NUM!," on the latest Solver recalculation. Solver cannot find new trial solutions under these conditions. Find the cell containing the error and modify its formula to avoid generating such errors, thereby producing an appropriate numeric value. Also, consider adding constraints to force Solver to stay away from troublesome regions. For example, if a nonlinear model has cell A7 unconstrained, and the model has a formula containing "LOG(A7)," then Solver may investigate model behavior using values of A7<=0 for which the LOG( ) function is undefined. Adding a constraint, such as A7>=0.0001 or A7>=.02 or the like, may be required to force Solver to avoid visiting the error-generating region(s).

In earlier versions of Excel, this message appears if an invalid Defined Name is present in the Solver Parameters dialog.

Evolutionary Solver discards any candidate solution that results in such error values in the objective or the constraints, and proceeds to find another candidate solution. Thus, it never displays this message. So, if you cannot correct or avoid these error values by changing your model, one option is to abandon optimization and revert to using Evolutionary Solver to find improved solutions.

Solver stopped at user's request.

You interrupted the solution process by pressing the ESC key (Windows) or Command+. (Mac) or chose Cancel in the dialog when the Show Iterations Results was set in Solver Options.

The problem is too large for Solver to handle or too many adjustable cells or too many constraints.

There are too many Changing Variable Cells or constraints in the model. Premium Edition of Solver for Education limits the number of decision variables (Changing Variable Cells) to no more than 200.

For linear models there is no limit on the number of constraints provided there is sufficient computer memory for Solver. However, a linear model with more constraints than decision variables (Changing Variable Cells) is either overconstrained or has redundant constraints. The former reflects model logic errors and may produce the "Solver could not find a feasible solution" message. Other than increasing solution times, the latter is usually harmless but may cause difficulty in unusual circumstances (see discussion under "Solver cannot improve the current solution").

For nonlinear models the limit is 100 constraints plus up to 100 constant RHS upper bound constraints plus up to 100 constant RHS lower bound constraints directly on the Changing Variable Cells plus up to 200 integer constraints on the decision variables, if any.

Note: The limits above are relaxed for enhanced versions of Solver commercially available from its original developer, Frontline Systems (http://www.frontsys.com/).

The linearity conditions required by this Solver engine are not satisfied or The conditions for Assume Linear Model are not satisfied.

The Assume Linear Model was checked in Solver Options or Standard Simplex LP was selected, and Solver computed its trial points using linear extrapolation to arrive at the solution shown, but the final worksheet recalculation yields values for the constraints and/or the objective function cell (Set Cell) that do not agree with the linear extrapolation. Review the model logic to verify the source of the nonlinearity and correct. An aid to help you is contained in the Solver Results dialog displaying this message. Select the Linearity Report option to help you diagnose the source of the nonlinearity. Or commit to a nonlinear model formulation and abandon linear optimization.

If reviewing the model logic verifies it to be linear, then consider if poor scaling of numbers in the model caused the (spurious) message. Versions of Excel prior to Excel 97 are more susceptible to this message. Upgrading to a recent Excel version and checking Use Automatic Scaling in Solver Options will often eliminate this difficulty. For some models manual rescaling the model's data may also be necessary in recent versions of Excel.

Note: Recent versions of Excel contain a bug outside of Solver that can also trigger this message erroneously. One known way this bug is triggered in Excel is the use of Merged

Cells in the worksheet. Review your worksheet and eliminate any Merged Cells in it. (See Section C.9.)

The maximum time or iteration limit was reached.

The maximum amount of time allowed for the solution process or the maximum number of iterations (set with the Max Time and Iterations options in Solver Options) has been reached without finding a satisfactory solution. Increasing the maximum number of iterations or time may be warranted for very large models, but examine the current solution values for insights into possible modeling problems first, such as poor scaling of numbers.

The Set Cell values do not converge.

The objective function cell (Set Cell) is increasing (or decreasing) without bound, even though all the constraints are satisfied. The current worksheet values probably indicate how the solution is diverging. The most likely cause is omitted constraints in the model. Check the model for overlooked constraints or other logic errors that invalidate one or more constraints, for example, wrong direction of an inequality, and so on.

For a nonlinear model, the objective function formula may have been incorrectly specified.

Problem to solve not specified.

Needed Solver information was omitted from the Solver Parameters dialog, such as no Changing Variable Cells given, or missing Set Cell coupled with no given constraints.

There is not enough memory available to solve the problem.

This message appears when the Solver finds insufficient memory to optimize the model. Often this message appears if there are too many workbooks open in Excel or if there are too many open applications in addition to Excel. Try closing unrelated workbooks and applications. This message may also occur if the Solver model specification has become corrupted. See Section C.9.

Another Excel instance is using SOLVER.DLL. Try again later.

Solver can only be called by one instance of Excel at a time. This message appears if you click on Solve while another Excel instance is also running the Solver. Wait for the other Excel instance to finish its optimization. Otherwise there are serious operating system conflicts; reboot your computer.

Error in model. Please verify that all cells and constraints are valid.

The internal representation of the Excel model (information on the Changing Variable Cells, Set Cell, constraints, Solver Options settings, etc.) is not valid. Sources of this message might be the wrong version of the internal files SOLVER.XLA or SOLVER32.DLL is being used, or the hidden defined names used by the Solver were changed, either by you or by a user-defined Visual Basic for Applications or macro language program. This latter cause may happen if there are any Defined Names in your worksheets or workbooks beginning with "solver." If so, remove those defined names from your worksheets/workbooks.

Solver: An unexpected internal error occurred, or available memory was exhausted. Please verify that your model is correctly entered and all cells contain numeric values.

This message may occur if the Solver model specification has become corrupted. See Section C.9 for recovering from this.

In early versions of Solver, this was a "catchall" error message for difficulties not otherwise identified by Solver. A common cause of this message is that a cell range previously valid in the Solver Parameters dialog has been invalidated by subsequent deletion of some of the referenced rows or columns in the worksheet. This is more likely to occur if defined names were originally used in the Solver Parameters dialog, producing a "#Ref!" error string within the dialog box for the now-undefined references to deleted columns/rows. If so, manually edit out the "#Ref!" error string and respecify the cell range or valid Defined Name. A side effect of this "#Ref!" error is that some Solver Parameter dialog buttons may replay this message if clicked, thereby making it impossible to remove or edit out the error string that causes the error message, a frustrating dilemma. The following incantation should work in this case:

1. Dismiss the Solver Parameters dialog.
2. Select the Name Define item from Excel's Insert menu.
3. Enter the string: solver_num into the Names in Workbook field.
4. Enter a 0 into the "Refers to" field, and click OK.
5. Evoke Solver, and edit the Solver Parameters fields as usual.

C.9 LOADING AND SAVING SOLVER MODELS

Normally, a worksheet model will contain only one Solver specification, which is saved in hidden variables along with the worksheet. However, the internal specifications for a Solver optimization model can also be saved externally from Solver to a worksheet by means of the Load Model and Save Model buttons on Solver Options. This is useful if you wish to analyze the effects of several Solver optimizers on the same worksheet model and want to avoid respecifying different Solver Parameters for each one. These buttons allow you to save and restore the necessary Solver information (Changing Variable Cells, Set Cell constraints, and Solver Options settings) of a Solver model to the worksheet. The Solver information is stored as formulas in a contiguous group of cells.

To save a Solver specification to the worksheet, click any cell in an empty column on a worksheet containing a previously developed and debugged Solver model. Select Solver from the Tools menu, click Options, and click Save Model. Solver will highlight the range of cells needed to hold the cells of the Solver specifications and offer a dialog with that cell range as the default that can be overridden.

To load a new Solver specification into Solver from a worksheet, select Solver from the Tools menu, click Options, and click Load Model. Highlight the range of cells on a worksheet containing a previously saved Solver specification and click OK. Solver will read those cells containing the Solver specifications, replacing the existing specifications.

As mentioned in Section C.4, recent bugs in Excel 2000 outside of Solver can cause the internal representation of the Solver optimization specifications for a worksheet model to become corrupted. One cause of this is the use of Merged Cells in the worksheet, which should be avoided. However, other Excel bugs may also cause this problem in some cases. One recovery of this corruption involves use of the Load Model and Save Model buttons on Solver Options. Use Save Model to save the Solver specification for a suspected corrupted specification to a range of cells on the Excel worksheet. Next, immediately use Load Model to re-create the previously saved specification, except do not select the bottommost cell in the range if it is empty, and click OK to reload the specification into Solver. This may clear up a corrupted specification. Otherwise, you must use Control-C to copy your Excel model to a new workbook and re-specify the Solver Parameters from scratch.

C.10 SOLVER REPORTS

Solver produces two types of reports that are always stored as new worksheets in the active workbook, but with grid lines and row and column headings turned off. Since the reports are worksheets, the reports can be edited and copied like any other worksheet. In addition, the report cells can be referenced by other formulas or used to produce charts. The first type of report provides additional information about a just completed optimization that was successful. The second type of report provides diagnostic information when Solver encounters difficulties with the optimization.

In Solver's reports the formatting for data cells is inherited from the formatting of the corresponding cell in the Excel worksheet model. Often the inherited format gives insufficient precision, and for example, a datum may misleadingly show as a 0 or 1 when in fact it is a small but important fraction, such as .3 or 1.48, respectively. Always cursor over the data in a Solver report to avoid any misinterpretation caused by inadequate formatting precision. ***Warning:*** Inadequate formatting precision often leads to misinterpretation of Shadow Price or Lagrange Multiplier information in the Solver Sensitivity Report.

In many reports Solver constructs entries in a Name column by searching in the Excel worksheet for the first text cell to the left and the first text cell above each Changing Variable Cell and each constraint cell. If found, it then concatenates these two text strings together to form the Name entry in the report. As described in Chapter 3, laying out the Excel model in a tabular form using text labels in the leftmost column and topmost row will cause these Name entries to be most meaningful in Solver's reports.

SOLVER REPORTS DIALOG

When the Solver successfully completes its optimization of the model, or if the optimization is terminated due to an error or interrupted by you, the Solver Results dialog is displayed. To select one or more of the reports listed in the dialog's Reports list, click on the report names to select the reports you want (earlier versions of Solver required you to CTRL-click to select multiple reports). If the optimization was terminated by an error or an interruption, the Reports list will show "No reports available." If Bypass Solver Reports was checked in Solver Options, the Reports list choices will be grayed out and cannot be selected.

After selecting reports, you can choose either to "Keep Solver Solution" or "Restore Original Values," and optionally save the decision variable values in a named scenario by clicking on the Save Scenario button. Clicking on Cancel aborts generation of the reports. After you click on OK, the reports are produced as worksheets, inserted in the workbook to the left of the Solver model worksheet. An exception occurs if you checked "Return to Solver Parameters Dialog" (available only if the Premium appearance dialog was selected earlier by pressing the Premium button in the Premium Edition Solver for Education). In this case, after the reports are produced, Solver will return immediately to the Solver Parameters dialog, saving you the effort of selecting Solver from the Tools menu. This can be useful when you are trying out different options settings during debugging or model experimentation.

THE FEASIBILITY REPORT

Available whenever the Simplex LP or GRG Nonlinear optimizer cannot find a feasible solution of the model, the Feasibility Report identifies the constraints that appear to Solver to be the source of the infeasibility. There are two versions of this report, Feasibility and Feasibility-Bounds. The Feasibility report is more comprehensive and contains all the information in the Feasibility-Bounds report. Thus you need never select both reports.

To save time the Feasibility-Bounds report tries only to identify the offending constraints while keeping any upper or lower bound constraints on the variables in force, and for small models is usually adequate for diagnosing the inconsistent constraints. The Feasibility report analyzes both the constraints and any variable bounds in your model, eliminating as many of them as possible, to find the smallest subset of constraints that is infeasible. For large models this analysis may take substantial time to produce. However, it can be difficult to locate the inconsistent constraints in large models, and the Feasibility report may be necessary to obtain useful diagnostic information.

THE LINEARITY REPORT

Available only when Assume Linear Model or the Standard Simplex LP is selected and Solver's "The linearity conditions required by this Solver engine are not satisfied" error occurs, the Linearity Report helps you find and remove nonlinear relationships from the Excel model. The Linearity Report lists each Changing Variable Cell and constraint on a separate row and a column containing Yes, if the objective or constraint is a linear function or the variable occurs linearly in the model, or No, if the function is nonlinear or the variable occurs nonlinearly in the model.

THE ANSWER REPORT

The Answer Report summarizes the solution, giving the optimal values of the decision variables and constraints in the model, and shows which constraints are binding and which constraints have slack.

THE LIMITS REPORT

The Limits Report provides a limited form of sensitivity analysis by repeatedly re-optimizing the model (both maximizing and minimizing) with each Changing Variable Cell (decision variable) as the objective, and all other variables held fixed. This produces the smallest value that each decision variable can take and the largest value the variable can take while satisfying the constraints and holding all of the other variables constant.

THE SENSITIVITY REPORT

The Sensitivity Report gives sensitivity analysis information for both LP and NLP models. The shadow prices for nonbasic (defined below) Changing Variable Cells (decision variables) are called Reduced Costs for LP optimization, and Reduced Gradients for NLP optimization. The shadow prices for binding constraints are called Shadow Prices for LP optimization, and Lagrange Multipliers for NLP optimization. Sensitivity information is always interpreted as being *ceteris paribis*, that is, assessing the effect of changing only one datum while holding all other data in the model constant. Also, the occurrence of degeneracy in an optimal solution requires a more careful interpretation of the data in the Sensitivity Report than that which is summarized here.

Warning: *Inadequate formatting precision often leads to misinterpretation of the Shadow Prices or Lagrange Multipliers. In Solver's reports the formatting for data cells is inherited from the formatting of the corresponding cell in the Excel worksheet model. Often the inherited format gives insufficient precision, and for example, a Shadow Price may misleadingly show as a 0 or 1 when in fact it is a small but important fraction, such as .3 or 1.48, respectively. Always cursor over the data in the Sensitivity Report worksheet to avoid any misinterpretation caused by inadequate formatting precision.*

As described in more detail in Section 4.12, simple upper and lower bounds placed directly on the Changing Variable Cells (the decision variables) as constraints in the Constraints list box of the Solver Parameters dialog are handled differently by Solver. They are not summarized in the Constraints section of the Sensitivity report as would be expected for a constraint. Instead, when an upper or lower bound is placed directly on a decision variable and it is binding at optimality, a nonzero Reduced Cost or Reduced Gradient for that variable will appear in the Adjustable Cells section of the report. That nonzero Reduced Cost or Reduced Gradient is otherwise interpreted just as a Lagrange Multiplier or Shadow Price would be for that binding upper or lower bound constraint.

The Reduced Cost/Reduced Gradient entry in the Sensitivity Report (i.e., the Shadow Price/Lagrange Multiplier for a decision variable) is nonzero only when a decision variable's value is equal to its upper or lower bound (often zero) at optimality (and the model is nondegenerate without alternative optimal solutions). That decision variable is called nonbasic in this case because its value was set by Solver at its upper or lower bound at optimality. Forcing the variable's value away from the bound will thus always hurt the objective function value, and loosening the bound by changing its RHS will improve the objective function value. The Reduced Cost/Reduced Gradient entry in the Sensitivity Report measures the rate of change in the objective function value per unit increase in the variable's value.

The Shadow Price/Lagrange Multiplier for a constraint is nonzero only when the constraint is binding at optimality (and the solution is nondegenerate). Tightening the constraint's RHS will worsen the objective function value and loosening the RHS will improve the objective. The Shadow Price/Lagrange Multiplier measures the rate of change in the objective function value per unit increase in the constraint's RHS.

Presented only for NLP models, the Reduced Gradients/Lagrange Multipliers are partial derivatives, that is, instantaneous rates of change valid only at the single point of the optimal solution if there is any curvature involved. Presented only for LP models, the Shadow Price for each constraint remains constant over the range of Allowable Increase and Decrease in the constraint's RHS.

Presented only for LP models, the Allowable Increase and Decrease for Adjustable Cells in the Sensitivity Report gives the range of change in each objective function coefficient that produces the same optimal solution, that is, no change in the optimal values of the decision variables (Changing Variable Cells).

THE POPULATION REPORT

Available only from Evolutionary Solver, the Population Report summarizes the diversity within the population of candidate solutions created by Evolutionary Solver during its optimization search. For each variable and constraint in the model, the Population Report presents the best value found, the mean (average) and standard deviation of the values, and the maximum and minimum value of that variable or constraint in the population of candidate solutions at the end of the Evolutionary Solver run. Interpretation of these statistics is quite subjective, because Evolutionary Solver is not truly an optimizer, but a smart search engine using randomness in its exploration of the space of model solutions. For this reason, none of standard sensitivity analysis insights of optimization models can be applied. Instead, experience with performance of similar models or an extensive number of runs on a given model with Evolutionary Solver must suffice.

As a brief guide, if for example, best values vary little from run to run with widely differing initial values of the decision variables (Changing Variable Cells), and if the coefficients of variation (ratio of variables' standard deviations to their means) are small, this may suggest that your solution could be close to the global optimum. Of course, it could also suggest that a single local optimum is prominent and a wider search is needed. As another example, if the best values change substantially across multiple runs with widely differing initial values of the decision variables (Changing Variable Cells), but with small coefficients of variation, there is very likely insufficient diversity in the population. For both examples, if more exploration is warranted, this suggests (1) more runs with more widely varied initial values of the decision variables (Changing Variable Cells), and (2) increasing the Mutation Rate and/or the Population Size for additional runs on this model by Evolutionary Solver.

Appendix D

ANSWERS TO ODD-NUMBERED QUESTIONS

CHAPTER 2

2-1.

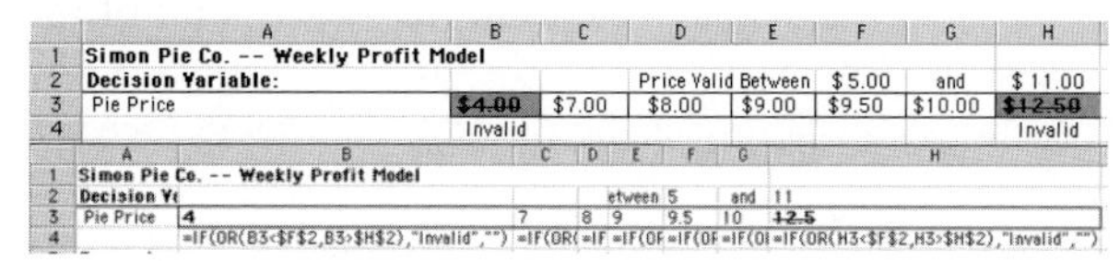

	A	B	C	D	E	F	G	H
1	Simon Pie Co. -- Weekly Profit Model							
2	Decision Variable:			Price Valid Between		$ 5.00	and	$ 11.00
3	Pie Price	~~$4.00~~	$7.00	$8.00	$9.00	$9.50	$10.00	~~$12.50~~
4		Invalid						Invalid

	A	B	C	D	E	F	G	H
1	Simon Pie Co. -- Weekly Profit Model							
2	Decision V(				etween	5	and	11
3	Pie Price	4	7	8	9	9.5	10	~~12.5~~
4		=IF(OR(B3<$F$2,B3>$H$2),"Invalid","")	=IF(OR(	=IF	=IF(OF	=IF(OF	=IF(OI	=IF(OR(H3<$F$2,H3>$H$2),"Invalid","")

2-3.

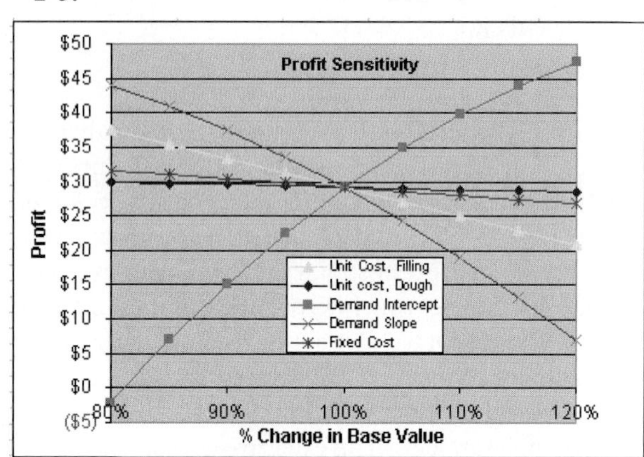

2-5. (1) About 1825 units; (2) about 1330 units. Sales Growth Rate and Price Decline % among others.

2-7. 1. $180,000

2. Recommended Price, $25.25, approximately. Profit is only mildly sensitive to up to ±5% change in price around $25.25, becoming very sensitive to larger price changes. Profit/Customer is maximum at Price of $27.50, approximately, producing a profit loss from optimum of 17%, approximately.

3. Recommended number of customers is 33,000, approximately. Profit is insensitive up to ±15% change in number of customers around 33,000.

CHAPTER 3

3-1. a-8, b-2, c-3, d-4, e-1, f-6, g-7, h-5

3-3. Maximal profit is $7200.

3-5. Maximal total return is $12,750.

3-7. Maximal profit is $82.50.

3-9. Minimal cost is $6.55 for a total of 80 pounds of fertilizer.

3-11. Minimal production time is 23,587.5 hours.

3-13. Maximal return is $880.000.

3-15. Maximal revenue is $46,630.30.

3-17. Maximal profit is $3,501.25.

3-19. Minimum number of sailors is 2,000.

3-21. Maximal return is $879,000.

3-23. Minimal cost occurs when 131.5 waiters are hired.

3-25. Maximal contribution is $201,556.

3-27. Minimal transportation cost is $3,300.

3-29. Minimal cost is $1,746,250.

3-31. Minimal generation cost is $13,600.

CHAPTER 4

4-1. A = amps; P = preamps; Assembly constraint: $12A + 4P \leq 60$; Performance constraint $4A + 8P \leq 40$.

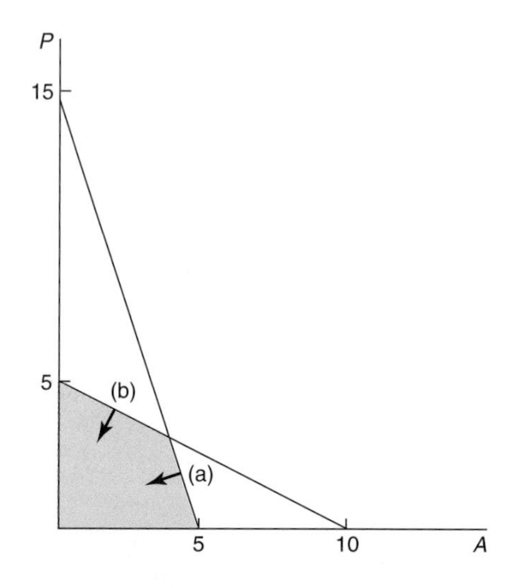

4-3.

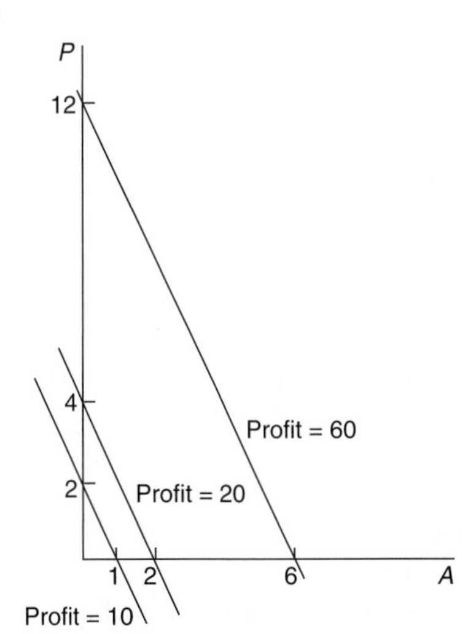

4-5. (a) $A^* = 4$, $P^* = 3$ (b) $OV = 10A^* + 5P^* = \$55$ (c) Active constraints are assembly and high-performance testing. (d) Inactive are $A \leq 6$ (with slack = 2) and $P \leq 4$ (with slack = 1).

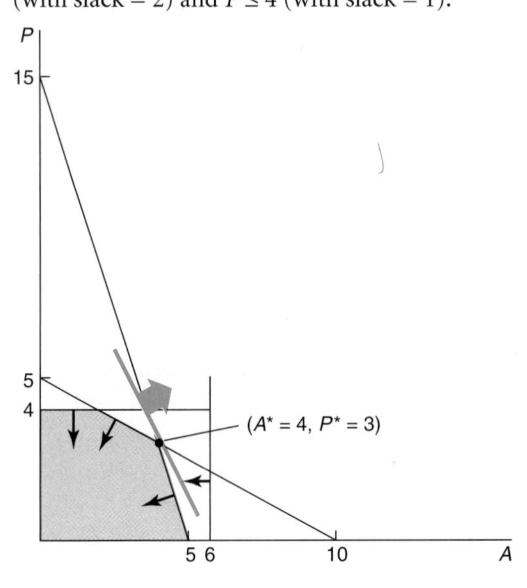

4-7. No.

4-9. Makes it infeasible.

4-11. (a) $x_1^* = 3$, $x_2^* = 1.5$, $OV = 4.5$ (b) $x_1^* = 0$, $x_2^* = 3$ (c) Four extreme (corner) points: (0, 0), (4, 0), (3, 1.5), and (0, 3)

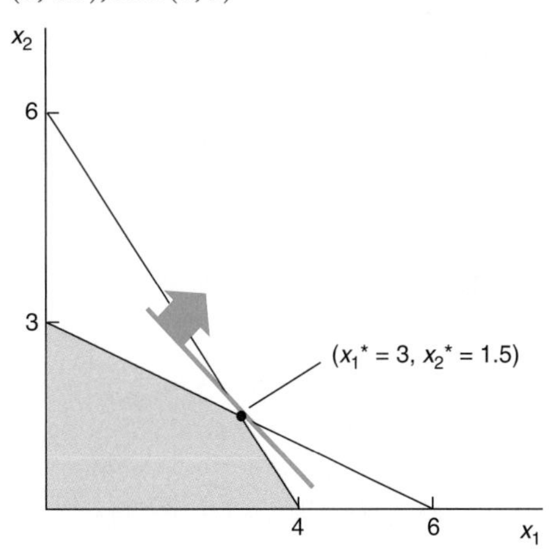

4-13. (a) $x_1^* = 6.67$, $x_2^* = 2.67$, $OV = 30.67$ (b) First constraint slack = 18.67; Second constraint slack = 0; Third constraint surplus = 0

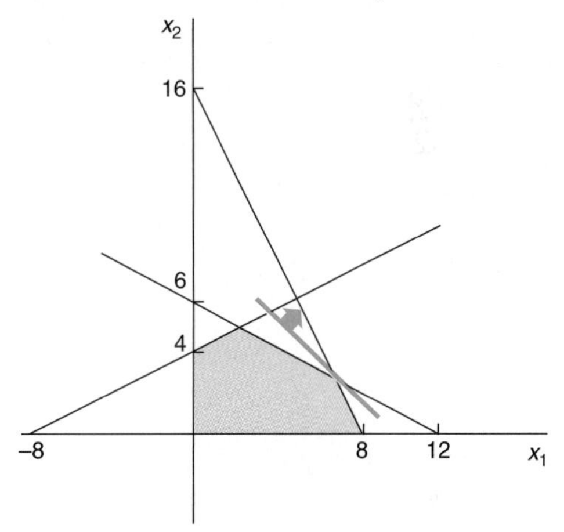

4-15. (a) $x_1{}^* = 1.091$, $x_2{}^* = 3.64$, OV = 12.73 (b) Active constraints: 2nd and 3rd; Inactive constraints: 1st and 4th (c) 1st constraint surplus = 7.091; 4th constraint slack = 12.55; other constraints have zero surplus (d) 4 (e) ($x_1{}^*= 1.091$, $x_2{}^* = 3.64$), ($x_1{}^* = 2.67$, $x_2{}^* = 1.67$)

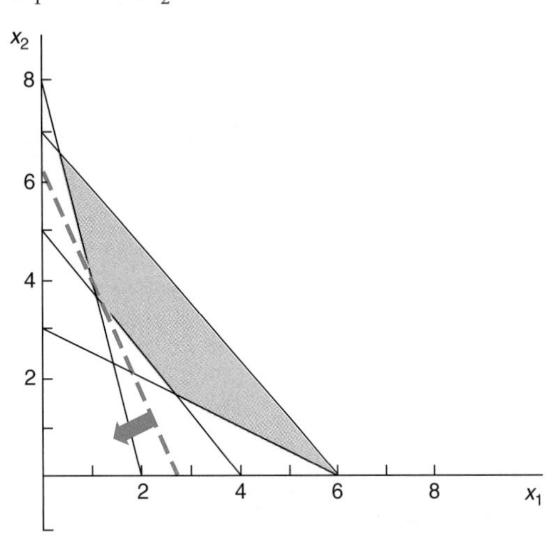

4-17. (a) $E^* = 118.4$, $F^* = 152.6$, OV = 223,684 (b) 3rd constraint (c) –18.496 (d) 0.1599 (e) 1667

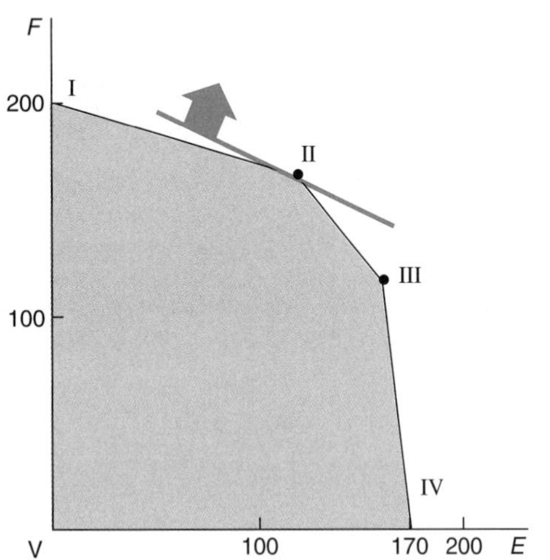

4-19. (a) New solution is $C^* = 140$, $M^* = 40$ (b) new OV = 8920

4-21. Since the relative contribution of M has increased, it is desirable to produce relatively more M. Because of the limitations on resources, this can only be done by also producing less C.

4-23. (a) $x_1{}^* = 2$, $x_2{}^* = 0$, OV = 60 (b) Increase coefficient of x_2 to 15. (c) 2; ($x_1{}^* = 2$, $x_2{}^* = 0$) and ($x_1{}^* = 1$, $x_2{}^* = 2$) (d) Can be infinitely increased. Can be decreased by 2 units. (e) A change in either direction will change the optimal solution. (f) The first constraint is binding. The second constraint is nonbinding. (g) The optimal solution changes to ($x_1{}^* = .333$, $x_2{}^* = 2.67$) and the OV changes accordingly. (h) No effect (I) Satisfies; satisfy

4-25. (a) The first is tighter (b) (2, 1) satisfies both (c) (3, 0) satisfies the second, not the first.

4-27. The second.

4-29. More; loosening

4-31. Enlarge; smaller; unchanged

4-33. No. It may not be redundant for new values of the parameters in the model.

4-35. No.

4-37. The shadow price on a nonbinding constraint is always zero. In most cases, the shadow price on a binding constraint is not zero. But if the optimal solution is degenerate, some of the binding constraints may have zero shadow prices.

4-39. The first constraint. No.

4-41. Rate of change in the OV as the RHS increases.

4-43. An increase of 72. Since 100 chairs is the minimum production and each chair requires 4 legs, the RHS can be no smaller than 400 without destroying feasibility.

4-45. The legs constraint becomes redundant for RHS ≥ 832.

4-47. Print LinksLetter = 120,000 and Ragged Edge = 0 for a total cost of $6000.

4-49.

b.

	A	B	C	D	E	F	G
1	KARMA COMPUTERS CASE						
2	Decision Variables	S	D				
3	Quantity	60	30	PROFIT			
4	Contrib. Margin	$300	$400	$30,000			
5	Subject To:			LHS		RHS	Slack
6	Schas Constr	1		60	≤	60	-0
7	Dchas Constr		1	30	≤	50	20
8	Ddrive Constr	1	2	120	≤	120	-0

c.

	A	B	C	D	E	F	G	H
1	Microsoft Excel 8.0 Sensitivity Report							
2	Adjustable Cells							
3				Final	Reduced	Objective	Allowable	Allowable
4		Cell	Name	Value	Cost	Coefficient	Increase	Decrease
5		$B$3	Quantity S	60	0	300	1E+30	100
6		$C$3	Quantity D	30	0	400	200	400
7								
8	Constraints							
9				Final	Shadow	Constraint	Allowable	Allowable
10		Cell	Name	Value	Price	R.H. Side	Increase	Decrease
11		$D$6	Schas Constr LHS	60	100	60	60	40
12		$D$7	Dchas Constr LHS	30	0	50	1E+30	20
13		$D$8	Ddrive Constr LHS	120	200	120	40	60

4-51. (a) Decrease of 6*10. (b) Increase of 90 (c) Increase of 50*6

4-53. Degenerate. The number of positive variables, including slacks, is 5, which is less than the number of constraints, 6.

4-55. (a) The solution will be on the verge of moving away from $C^* = 130$, $M^* = 60$ (alternative optimal solutions). (b) The OV = 130*80 + 60*40.

4-57. a. Since the allowable increase is 85.71, there is no change in the optimal solution. The OV increases by $50 \times .037 = 1.85$.
b. Since the solution is nondegenerate, there will be an alternative optimal solution that uses more ore from location 3.
c. New OV $= 511.11 - 118.269 \times .037 = 506.735$.

4-59. a. =SUMPRODUCT(B3:B5,B11:B13)/60 – B6
b. 7680/60 = 128 hours on 1 and 2, 4608/60 = 76.8 hours on 3; shadow prices are in dollars per minute
c. $60 \times .011 = 66$ cents
d. $1.38 per pound

4-61. a. These constraints say that the number of gallons of a vintage used cannot exceed the number of gallons available.
b. These constraints say that the balance of the number of gallons of the vintages in a Blend less the required % of the total gallons of those vintages in the Blend must be greater than zero.
c. The constraint represents the restriction that Blend A must be at least 75% Vintage 1 and 2. The percentage of Vintage 1 and 2 in Blend A is given by the following Excel expression: =(C10 + C11)/C6. Thus the constraint would be (C10 + C11)/C6 ≥ .75. But this constraint is nonlinear, so make it linear by multiplying both sides by C6. Finally, bringing all variable terms to the LHS yields the Excel formula =C10 + C11 – .75C6, which must be ≥0.
d. $54,675
e. The solution is given below. (Other alternative optimal solutions exist.)

VINTAGE

Blend	1	2	3	4	Totals
A	180	246.71		22.46	449.17
B		3.29	200	377.54	580.83
C					
Totals	180	250	200	400	1,030

f. The selling price of C would have to increase by at least the allowable increase, $22.50 (and possibly more, since the solution is degenerate), for the optimal solution to change to one in which it is optimal to produce blend C.
g. $72.50 per gallon for Vintages 1, 2, and 3 and $22.50 per gallon for Vintage 4.
h. The earthquake would destroy 100 gallons. The allowable decrease on the availability of Vintage 3 is 200 gallons. The optimal value would decline by $100 \times 72.5 = \$7,250$.

4-63. The decrease of 12 makes the optimal objective function contour coincident to the Long Dowels constraint line (see Figure 4.10). The decrease of 19,000 makes it coincident to the Heavy Seats constraint line (see Figure 4.14).

4-65. (a) It is the amount by which each of the objective function coefficients may decrease without altering the solution values of the decision variables, A, B, and C.
(b) None of the nonnegativity constraints is binding.
(c) It is the amount that each of the individual RHSs may decrease while keeping the respective shadow price the same.
(d) Four
(e) The model is degenerate.

CHAPTER 5

5-1.

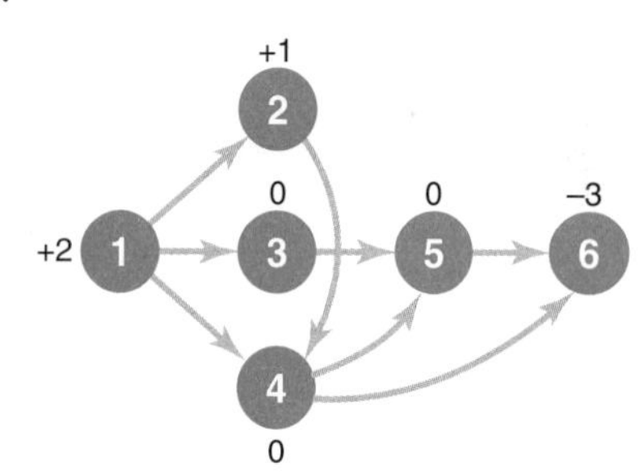

5-3.

$$
\begin{aligned}
-x_{21} + x_{14} &= 0 \\
x_{21} + x_{24} + x_{25} &= 2 \\
x_{36} &= 8 \\
-x_{14} - x_{24} + x_{47} &= -1 \\
-x_{25} - x_{65} + x_{57} &= 0 \\
-x_{36} + x_{65} &= 0 \\
-x_{47} - x_{59} &= -9
\end{aligned}
$$

5-5. Shortest path from node 1 to node 7 is 20 units.
5-7. Shortest path from node 1 to node 8 is 9 units.
5-9. (a) 5, 4, and 10, respectively
(b) 8, 6, and 11, respectively
(c) total cost = 2000
5-11. Maximal flow from node 1 to node 7 is 12 units.
5-13. Since the assignment model is a special case of the transportation model, the derivation of the transportation model below is sufficient for the assignment model.

All arcs (i, j), $i = 1, \dots, S$, $j = S + 1, \dots, S + D$ are permitted, where $i = 1, \dots, S$ denotes origins and $j = S + 1, \dots, S + D$ denotes destinations. There are SD arcs and $n = S + D$ nodes. For $j = 1, \dots, S$, there are no arc (k, j), hence $\Sigma_k x_{kj} = 0$. Also, $L_j = S_j$ = supply at j, for $j = 1, \dots, S$. For $j = S + 1, \dots, S + D$, there is no arc (j, k). Hence $\Sigma_k x_{jk} = 0$. Also, $L_j = -D_j = -$(demand at j), for $j = S + 1, \dots, S + D$. Thus, we get the supply and demand equations. Also, let $u_{ij} = \infty$, all (i, j).

5-15. Maximal flow from node 1 to node 7 is 22 units.
5-17. The shortest route from Month 1 to Month 5 costs $36 thousand.
5-19. Minimal transportation cost is $17,800.
5-21. Minimal total cost is $150,340.
5-23. Minimal total cost is $40,500.
5-25. Minimal total assignment cost is $68.
5-27. Maximal total assignment contribution is $320,000.
5-29. Minimal total assignment minutes is 99. No.
5-31. Maximal total assignment bid contribution is $96.

CHAPTER 6

6-1. (a) Max A + 3C

s.t.
$$A \le 7$$
$$4C \le 22$$
$$2A + 3C \le 19$$
$$A, C \ge 0 \text{ and integer}$$

(b) A = 1.25, C = 5.5 (c) A = 2, C = 5 (d) A = 1, C = 5; Yes (e) $1
6-3. Lower bound. LP relaxation is ILP problem without integer contraints.
6-5. Upper bound. LP relaxation is ILP problem without integer constraints.
6-7. The OV is reduced by $27.56 when solved as an ILP.
6-9. Solution time was several seconds or about 5 times longer than the LP relaxation. The OV is reduced by $0.24 when solved as an ILP.
6-11.

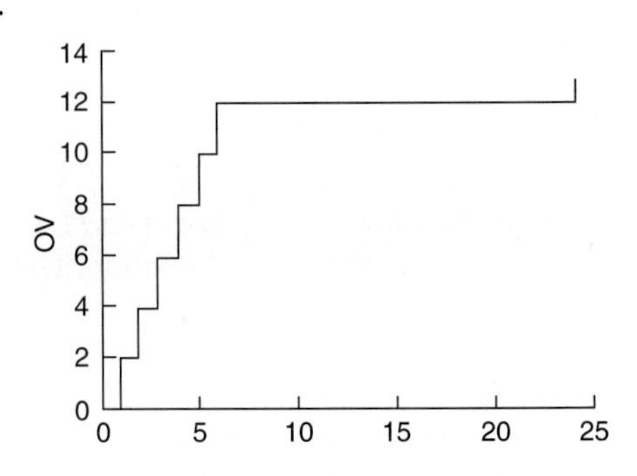

6-13. x_i = $ invested in stock i
y_i = 1 invest in stock i
0 do not invest

$$\text{Max} \sum_{i=1}^{20} r_i x_i$$

$$\text{s.t.} \quad \sum_{i=1}^{20} x_i \le 100{,}000$$
$$x_i \le 20{,}000 y_i \qquad i = 1, \dots, 20$$
$$x_i \ge 5{,}000 y_i \qquad i = 1, \dots, 20$$
$$y_i = 0, 1; \qquad x_i \ge 0, \text{ all } i$$

6-15. Cost Minimizing OV = $35,400
6-17. $y_i = 1$ make investment i
$= 0$ do not make investment i

$$\text{Max} \sum_{i=1}^{7} R_i y_i$$

s.t.
$$y_2 \le y_1$$
$$y_3 \le y_2$$
$$y_2 \le y_4$$
$$y_5 \le (1 - y_1)$$
$$y_5 \le (1 - y_2)$$
$$y_6 \le 2 - y_2 - y_3$$
$$2y_7 \le y_2 + 1 - y_3$$
$$\sum_{i=1}^{7} C_i y_i \le M$$
$$y_i = 0 \text{ or } 1 \qquad i = 1, \dots, 7$$

6-19. The minimal value of MAX(T1,T2) is 9.
6-21. Minimum OV cost = $5.4.

6-23. a. $B_1 + A_{21} + A_{41} \leq 1$
b. $B_2 \leq A_{12} + A_{52} + A_{32}$
c. $A_{21} + A_{41} \leq B_1$
d. True; e. True (See the Case Study for a fuller discussion of the formulation for models of this type.)

6-25. Minimum OV cost = $201,050.

CHAPTER 7

7-1. (a) $x^* = -7/8$ (b) $x^* = 1$
(c) Concave because the second derivative is <0 for all x.

7-3. We use the property that if the function associated with each $\leq$ constraint is convex and with each $\geq$ constraint is concave, then the constraint set will be a convex set.

$g_1(x, y) = x + y$ is a linear function, linear functions are both concave and convex.
$g_2(x, y) = -2x + y$ is concave.
$g_3(x, y) = x^2 + 2x + 1$ is convex since $\frac{\partial^2}{\partial x^2} g_3 = 2 > 0$.
$g_4(x, y) = -x^4 - 2x^2 + 60$ is concave since $\frac{\partial^2}{\partial x^2} g_4 = -12x^2 - 4 < 0$.

Thus the constraint set is convex.

7-5. The area is minimized when $r = 1$ and $h = 2$.

7-7. (a) The minimal value of the OV subject to the constraint is 26
(b) Estimated change in the OV is 27, approximately. The actual change in the OV is 37.8, approximately.

7-9. Maximal OV is $4,024.99.

7-11. From calculus, the stationary point is unique. Thus the local min must be global.

7-13. Lagrange Multiplier = .03327

7-15. Optimal Profit = $466.67

7-17. Optimal Profit = $2,864

7-19. No, there are six positive variables counting the decision, slack and surplus variables, but only five constraints.

7-21. The allowable decrease is 75% – 35.64% = 39.36%.

7-23. Max $.0891X + .2137Y + .2346Z$
Subject to:
$.0099X^2 + .0535Y^2 + .0864Z^2 + (2^*.0114)XY + (2^*.0120)XZ + (2^*.0508)YZ \leq V$
$X + Y + Z = 1$
X, Y, and Z each $>0\%$; and X, Y, and Z each $\leq 75\%$

7-25. (a) Optimal holdings of the three stocks = 19.51%, 35.37%, and 45.12%, respectively. Minimum Variance of optimal portfolio = .00922.
(b) Yes, as illustrated by this example. The negative covariance between stocks X and Z allows portfolio variance to be reduced.
(c) The Lagrange Multiplier on the minimum expected return constraint = 1.293. Thus, estimated increase in portfolio variance = .01*1.293 = .01293. Actual increase is .0325 – .00922 = .02328.

7-27. (a) 7000 (b) $420 (c) $1300 (d) $1720
(e) 183,720 (f) Larger, since annual ordering cost exceeds annual holding cost.

7-29. $Q^* = 3020.76$, $N^* = 3.02$

7-31. (a) $48,989.79 (b) 48.99 (c) 0.020 year = 5.10 days

7-33. (a) $18,974 (b) 12.65 (c) 0.079 year

7-35. (a) 90 dozen (b) 90 orders/year (c) .011 year = 4 days

7-37. (a) $Q^* = 12{,}000$; ATC = $121,800 (b) 0.5% discount: $121,432.50; 0.7% discount; $121,754.25
(c) Order 20,000 for .5% discount

7-39. (a) $Q^* = 3600$, $N^* = 3.75$, cycle time = 80 days; (b) maximum inventory = 900 gallons; (c) daily holding and setup cost = $22.50

7-41. (a) $Q^* = 1800$ gallons; annual holding and ordering cost = $13,500/yr. (b) The cost with a finite production rate is lower because inventory accumulates more slowly. (c) See plot below. (d) When $p = 45$, daily total cost = $30. When $p = 60$, daily total cost is $45. Thus, $p = 45$ is preferred.

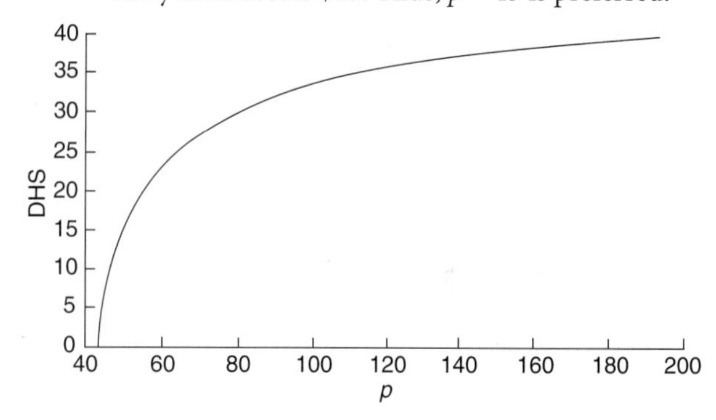

7-43. Starting at the minimum allocations of 1.1 to each division, the Maximum OV for the GRG nonlinear optimizer is 33.42. Starting Evolutionary Solver from the optimum found by the GRG optimizer produces an OV of about 860 after several minutes of computing while solving

about 40,000 subproblems. This is almost a 2500% improvement in OV. Your results will vary.

7-45. Using a VLOOKUP( ) to return divisional returns to an allocation, and starting at the minimum allocations of 1 million to each division, the Maximum OV for the GRG nonlinear optimizer is 30.4. Starting Evolutionary Solver from the optimum found by the GRG optimizer produces an OV of about 48.8 after several minutes of computing while solving about 35,000 subproblems. This is a 60% improvement in OV. Your results will vary.

CHAPTER 8

8-1. (a) 4 (b) 3 (c) 1
(d)

	STATES OF NATURE			
	1	2	3	4
1	0	3	3	21
2	8	0	8	15
3	13	0	3	5
4	15	0	0	0

(e) 3

8-3. (a) 4 (b) 4 (c) Maximizing expected net dollar return and minimizing expected regret always lead to the same optimal decision.

8-5. (a) Accept government contract (b) Accept government contract
(c)

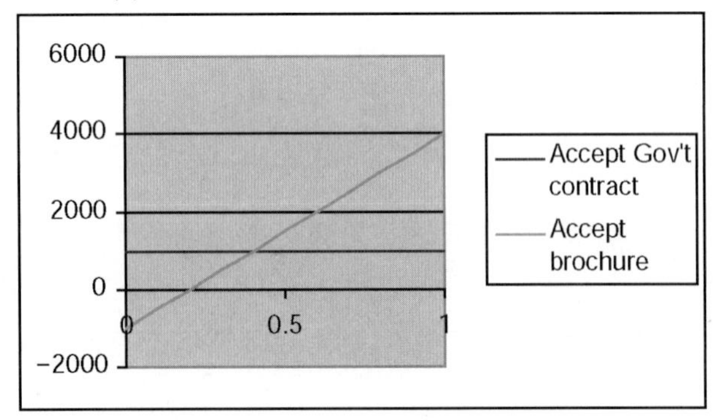

(d) 0.4 (e) Bid on brochure (f) Accept government contract (g) 1000 (h) Expected value of perfect information.

8-7. (a) Accept government contract; 1000 (b) No. The risk-averse nature of the utility function will decrease the attractiveness of bidding relative to accepting the government contract. (c) 0.73

(d) $U(666.67) = 0.66 + \frac{666.67}{1000}(0.73 - 0.66) \cong 0.71$

(e) EU(bid) = 0.66 (f) No. Not in general.

8-9. $P(\text{ordering error} \mid \text{late}) = 0.6$
$P(\text{delivery error} \mid \text{late}) = 0.4$
Therefore, look for ordering error.

8-11. (a) Optimal strategy: If "sun" forecast, go ahead. If "rain" forecast, cancel.
(b) Expected value of sample information = \$6250 – \$4750 = \$1500

8-13. $P(\text{bad risk} \mid \text{credit}) = 0.024$

8-15. Optimal strategy: 1. Compete. 2. If order is received, use current machines.

8-17. (a) Build 50 (b) Build 150 (c) Build 100 (d) Build 100 (e) EVPI = \$240,000

8-19. (a) Take 280 (b) Answers vary—trade-off between average time and worst case scenario.

8-21. (a)

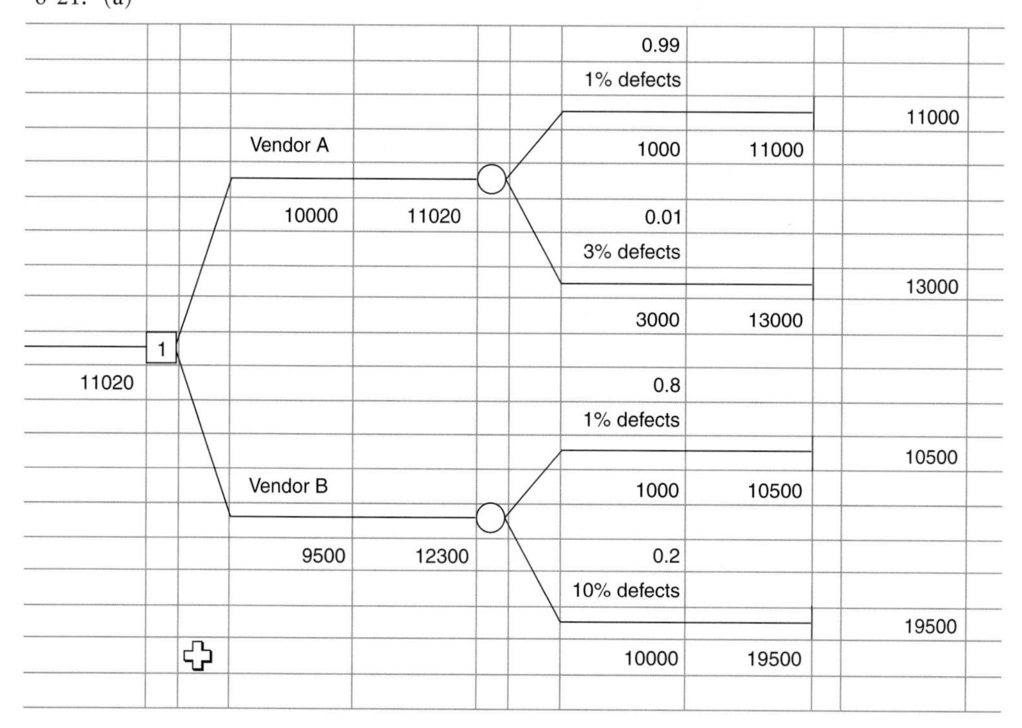

(b) Choose Vendor A

8-23. (a) Buy Q (b) Buy Q (c) Buy IBM (d) Buy Q

8-25. (a) Yes, buy insurance as long as it can be purchased at a reasonable price.

(b) Pay up to $100,000.

8-27. (a)

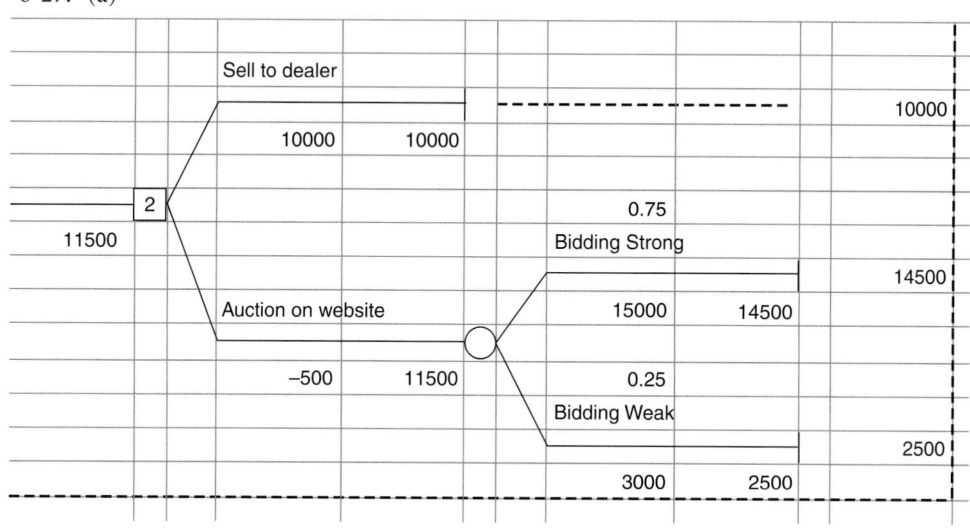

(b) The sculptor should auction his art on the web site.

8-29. (a) Flubgone, Hachoo (b) Flubgone, Hachoo

8-31. (a) Add Cargo space (b) Add Cargo space (c) Add Comfort seating

8-33. (a) $U(30) = 0.30U(70) + 0.7U(-30) = 0.3$
$U(10) = 0.1U(30) + 0.9U(-30) = 0.1$
Your utility curve is convex, and so you are risk-seeking!

(b) upper bound on $U(50) = 0.5[U(30) + U(70)] = 0.65$
lower bound on $U(50) = U(30) + 0.05[U(30) - U(10)]*20 = 0.5$

(c) upper bound on $U(25) = U(10) + .05*[U(30) - U(10)]*(25 - 10) = 0.25$
lower bound on $U(25) = \text{MAX}\{0.1 + 0.025*[U(10) - U(-30)]*(25 - 10), 0.3 + 0.025*[U(70) - U(30)]*(25 - 30)\} = \text{MAX}\{0.1375, 0.2125\} = 0.2125$

8-35. (a) $P(1/2) = 0.225$ (b) $P(A \mid 1/2) = 0.44$ (c) ER = \$188.50

8-37. (a)

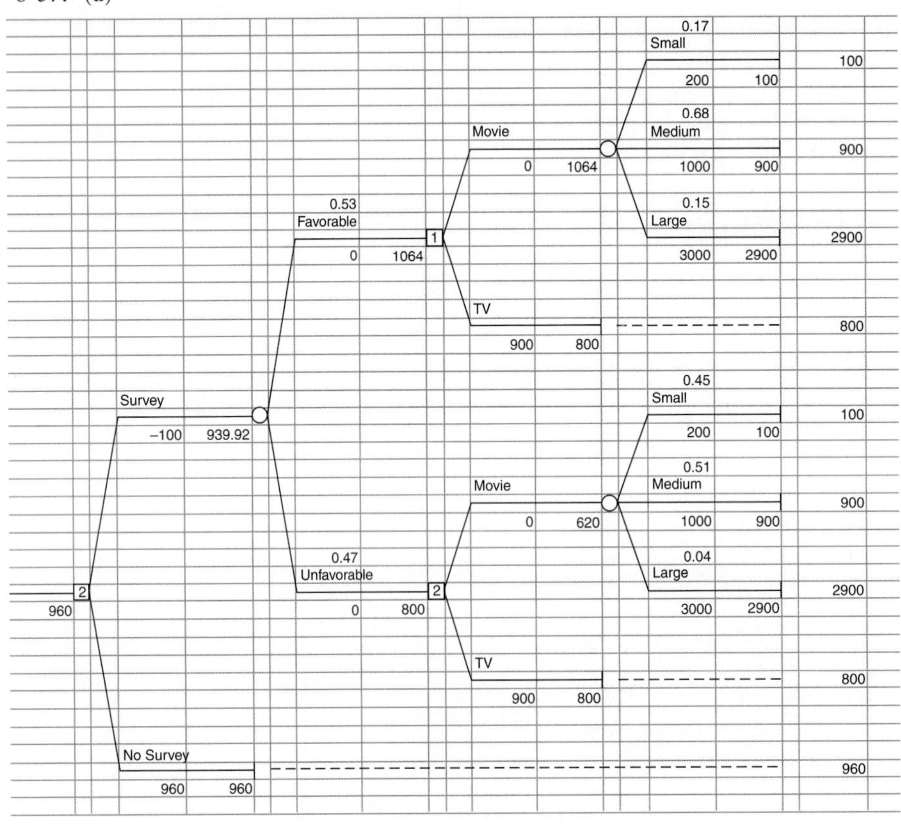

(b) No, but if she had to use the survey: If survey is favorable, sign with movie company; otherwise, sign with TV network.

(c) EVSI = (940,000 + 100,000) – 960,000 = \$80,000. Jenny should pay at most \$80,000 for the survey.

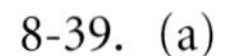

8-39. (a)

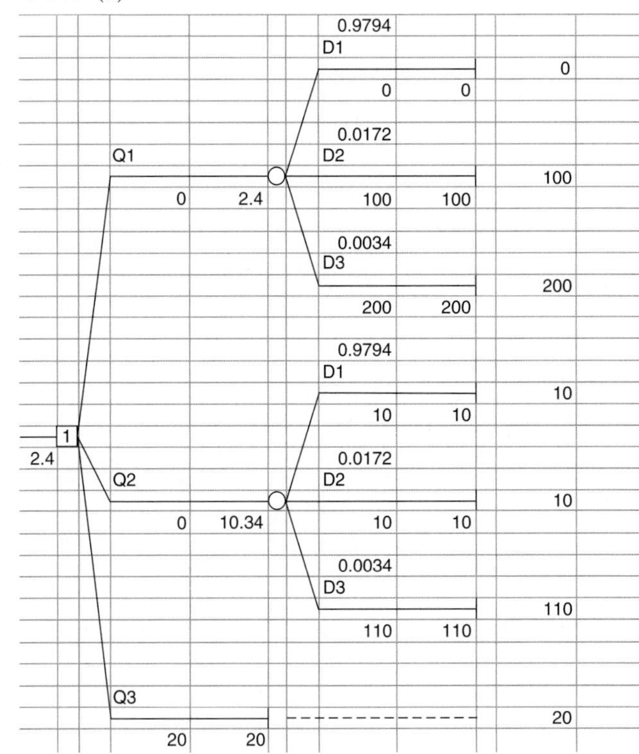

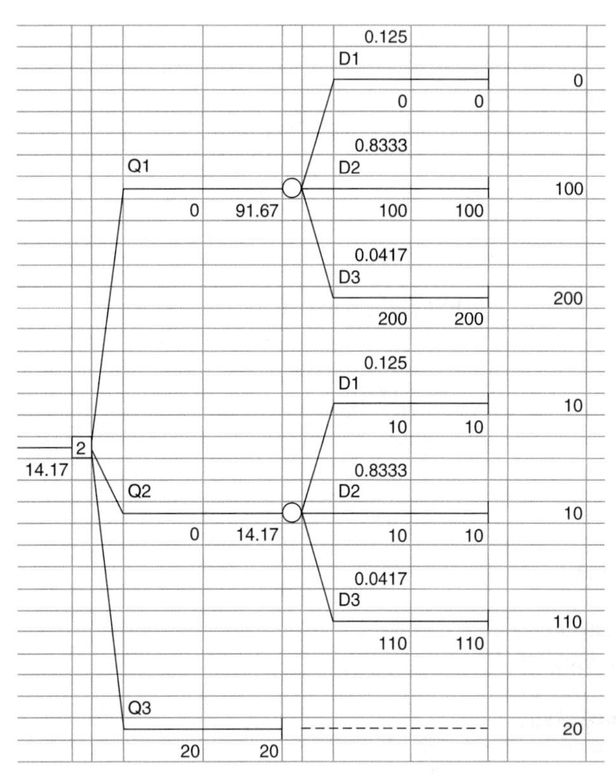

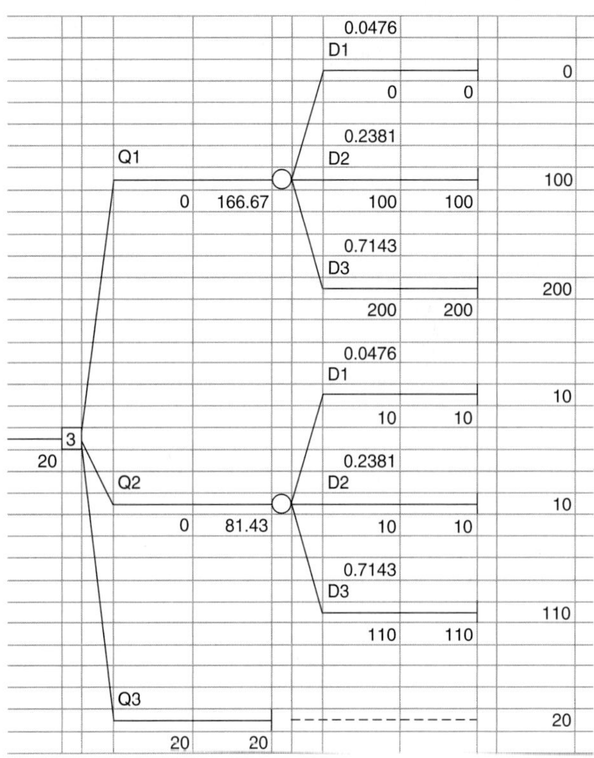

(b) EVSI = 20 – 7.38 = \$12.62

(c) \$12.62

8-41. (a)

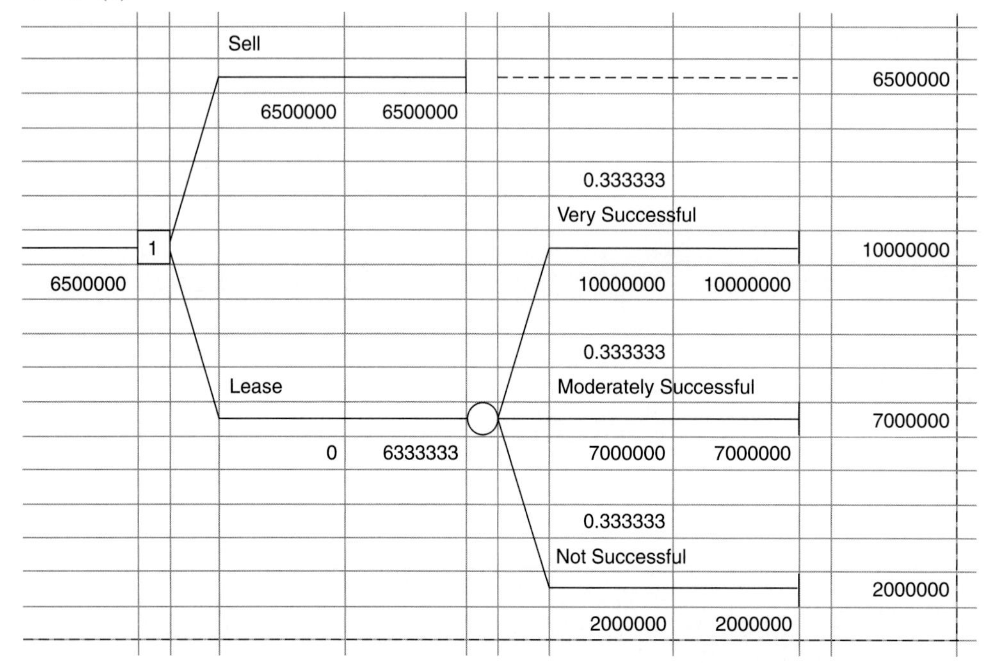

Assume equal probabilities for 3 random events.

(b) Unless Riskless can determine that the probabilities of "very successful" and/or "moderately successful" are higher than the current assumption, they should sell the property.

CHAPTER 9

9-1. Computerized war games, military exercises, training exercises.

9-3. (a)

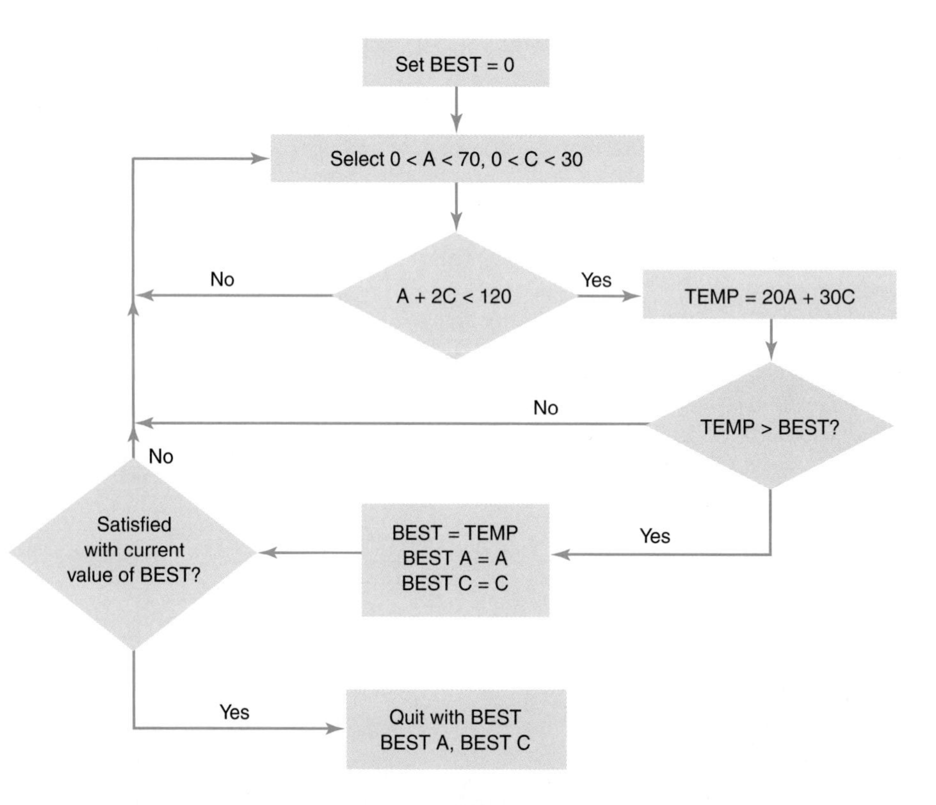

(b) A = 40, C = 30, BEST = 1700
A = 50, C = 30, BEST = 1900

9-5. False. Simplex is guaranteed to find optimum.

9-7.

EVENT	RANDOM NUMBER
Increase	0.0 – 0.299
Remain the Same	0.30 – 0.799
Decrease	0.80 – 0.999

9-9. True Expected Profit When Ordering 10 Pans

(a) ORDER QUANTITY	(b) DEMAND	(c) PROFIT	(d) PROBABILITY OF DEMAND	(e) COLUMN (c) * (d)
10	8	$ 90	.10	9.0
10	9	$110	.20	22.0
10	10	$130	.30	39.0
10	11	$133	.20	26.6
10	12	$136	.10	13.6
10	13	$139	.10	13.9
				True Expected Profit = $124.1

Simulated Average Profit from 500 trials will be different for each person (see pr9-9cb.xls), but should be relatively close to the True Expected Profit calculated here.

9-11.

x	0	1	2	3	4	5
$p(x;2)$	0.135	0.271	0.270	0.180	0.09	0.036
Cumulative	0.135	0.406	.677	.857	0.947	0.983

9-13. (a)

Sales	Relative Frequency	Random #'s
40	4/50 = 0.08	0.00 – 0.0799
41	10/50 = 0.20	0.08 – 0.2799
42	12/50 = 0.24	0.28 – 0.5199
43	9/50 = 0.18	0.52 – 0.6999
44	8/50 = 0.16	0.70 – 0.8599
45	7/50 = 0.14	0.86 – 0.9999

(b) (Using Excel alone)

WEEK	1	2	3	4	5	6	7	8	9	10
RN	.97	.02	.80	.66	.96	.55	.50	.29	.58	.51
Demand	45	40	44	43	45	43	42	42	43	42
Shortages	3		2	1	3	1			1	
Excess		2								

$$\text{Average Shortage} = \frac{3+2+1+3+1+1}{10} = 1.1$$

$$\text{Average Excess} \quad = 2/10 = 0.2$$

Using Crystal Ball with 100 iterations, we got the average shortage = 0.85 and the average excess = 0.34. Your random numbers may vary from these. Note that these estimates are closer to the true expected values (calculated in part c below) than the 10 trials in Excel alone.

(c) Expected shortage = 0.18*(43 – 42) + 0.16*(44 – 42) + 0.14*(45 – 42) = 0.92
Expected excess = 0.08*(40 – 42) + 0.20*(41 – 42) = 0.36

9-15. Best ones to maximize Mean NPV: Projects 1, 4, 5, 6; Mean NPV = $9343
Best ones to maximize 35th percentile of NPV: Projects 1, 4, 5, 6; 35th percentile of NPV = $8500. The solutions are the same in this particular example, although it is not always true. It just depends on the nature of the projects (investment required, NPV, probability of success, etc.).

9-17. (a)

NUMBER OF BRAKE JOBS	RELATIVE FREQUENCY	RANDOM NUMBERS
5	3/30 = .10	0.0 – 0.099
6	8/30 = .267	0.10 – 0.367
7	9/30 = .30	0.368 – 0.667
8	6/30 = .20	0.668 – 0.867
9	4/30 = .133	0.868 – 0.999

(b) (using Excel alone)

	RN									
	.20	.82	.74	.08	.01	.69	.36	.35	.52	.99
Demand	6	8	8	5	5	8	6	6	7	9

Simulated Average Number:

$$\frac{6+8+\cdots 7+9}{10} = 6.8 \text{ brake jobs/week}$$

Using Crystal Ball (see pr9-17cb.xls) with 100 weeks, we get an average of 6.96 jobs/week.

NOTE: Your random numbers may vary from these.

9-19. a. Probability a woman donates \$10 = (0.85)(0.8)(0.4)(0.7) = 0.1904
Probability a woman donates \$25 = (0.85)(0.8)(0.4)(0.3) = 0.0816
Probability a man donates \$10 = (0.85)(0.2)(0.7)(0.25) = 0.02975
Probability a man donates \$25 = (0.85)(0.2)(0.7)(0.75) = 0.08925
Expected return for a visit = (0.1904 + 0.02975)(10) + (0.0816 + 0.0925)(25) = 6.47275
Expected return from 3,000 households = 19,418.25

b. N = Maximum number of trials
i = Trial counter
D = Donation

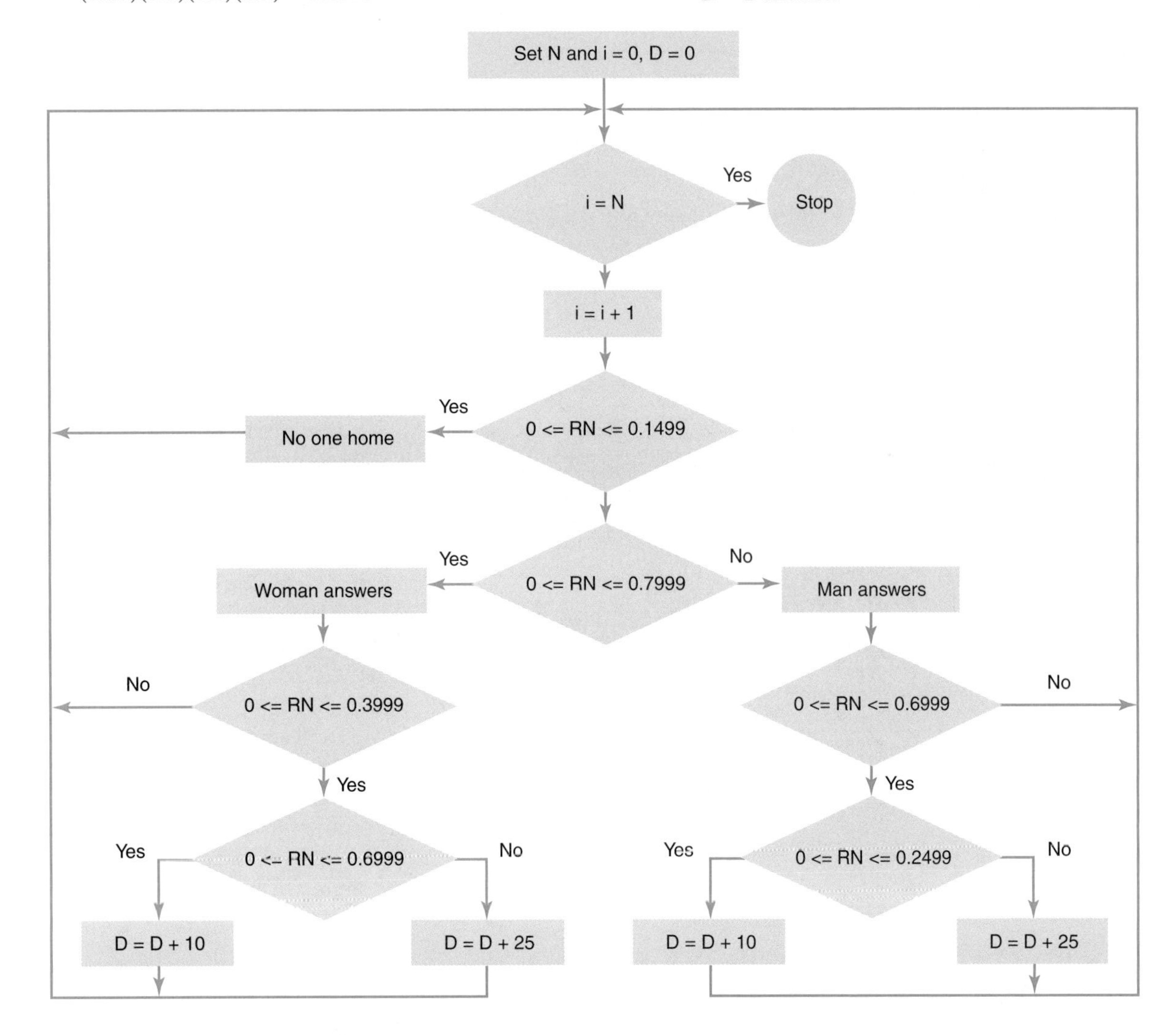

c. Using Excel alone:

i	Random Number	Event	Donation
1	0.11	No one home	0
2	0.91	Home	
	0.99	Man	
	0.57	Donation	
	0.28	$25	25
3	0.61	Home	
	0.70	Woman	
	0.33	Donation	
	0.91	$25	50
4	0.67	Home	
	0.97	Man	
	0.61	Donation	
	0.11	$10	60
5	0.50	Home	
	0.86	Man	
	0.25	Donation	
	0.6	$10	70

Total donation = $70

$$\text{Average return} = 70 \times \frac{3{,}000}{5} = \$42{,}000$$

Using Crystal Ball:
With 200 iterations, we got an average donation of $6.28. This would predict an expected return of $3000 \times 6.28 = \$18{,}840$ from 3000 households. Your numbers may vary slightly.

d. Using Excel alone:

i	Random Number	Event	Donation
1	0.49	Home	
	0.58	Woman	
	0.89	No donation	0
2	0.15	Home	
	0.12	Woman	
	0.94	No donation	0
3	0.85	Home	
	0.34	Woman	
	0.07	Donation	
	0.53	$10	10
4	0.99	Home	
	0.89	Man	
	0.10	No donation	
	0.27	$25	35
5	0.50	Home	
	0.93	Man	
	0.92	No donation	35
6	0.57	Home	
	0.50	Woman	
	0.78	No donation	35
7	.14	No one home	35
8	.70	Home	
	.90	Man	
	.24	Donation	
	.40	$25	60
9	.72	Home	
	.21	Woman	
	.01	Donation	
	.80	$25	85
10	.13	No one home	85

With 1000 iterations, we got an average donation of $7.11. This would predict an expected return of $3000 \times 7.11 = \$21{,}330$ from 3000 households. It is a little unusual that the estimate after 200 iterations is closer to the true expected value than the estimate after 1000 iterations, but this is a consequence of random sampling. Your numbers may vary slightly.
Total donation = $85

$$\text{Average return} = 85 \times \frac{3{,}000}{10} = \$25{,}500$$

9-21. Using Excel alone:
(a) The optimal number of flowers to order/day is 112 based on our 100 iterations. Your answer may vary slightly. This order quantity generates a mean payoff of $19.44.
(b) The 95% confidence interval is ($18.23; $20.65).

Using @Risk:
(a) The optimal number of flowers to order/day is 116 based on our 1000 iterations. Your answer may vary slightly. This order quantity generates a mean payoff of $19.39.
(b) The 95% confidence interval is ($18.06; $20.72).

9-23. (a) The expected daily demand = 0.2*2 + 0.3*1 + 0.5*0 = 0.7. Thus the expected demand during the 10-day sale is 0.7*10 = 7. No, you should not necessarily order the expected demand because the costs of having too few sets or too many sets are not necessarily the same.
(b) Using Excel alone, the optimal number of TV sets to order is 9 based on our 100 iterations. This order quantity generates an average profit of $1421.78. Your answer may vary slightly on both the optimal order quantity and simulated average profit.

Using @Risk:

(b) The optimal number of TV sets to order is 8 based on our 1000 iterations. This order quantity generates an average profit of $1461.70. Your answer may vary slightly on both the optimal order quantity and simulated average profit.

9-25. Using Crystal Ball:

(a) We ran 50,000 iterations.

(b) Les should bid $3.5 million below what his test shows the tract is worth. This will lead to an expected profit of $0.1211 million. Your results may vary.

Using @Risk:

(a) We ran 50,000 iterations and the convergence monitoring feature was never satisfied (using the default settings).

(b) Les should bid $3.5 million below what his test shows the tract is worth. This will lead to an expected profit of $0.1169 million. Your results may vary.

CHAPTER 10

10-1. Analog Model (Some Extend simulation models will incorporate elements of both analog and symbolic modeling.)

10-3. Increases all waiting time statistics.

10-5. Increase the simulation run length to extend over several weeks of continuous operation.

10-7. Adding the Queue Stats block to the Herrvislb.mox model of Figure 10.20 and summarizing 98 simulation runs yields Average Wait of about 6.92 ± .199 minutes and Maximum Wait of about 62.1 ± 2.56 minutes. Modifying the model to include 5% of customers returning with errors yields, after summarizing 98 simulation runs, Average Wait of about 7.85 ± .283 minutes and Maximum Wait of about 69.5 ± 3.43 minutes. (These statistics are the averages across both high and low priority customers.)Thus, average and maximum waits increase somewhat. Your results may vary.

10-9. Approximately 10% of arriving customers renege, departing after waiting 15 minutes. Summarizing 20 simulation runs, Average Wait for those not reneging falls to about 4.34 ± .01 minutes and Maximum Wait falls to exactly 15 minutes.

10-11. Modifying the Rental Office to permit Gold Card customers to bypass the Rental Station yields the following queue and resource block mean and maximum statistics, averaged over 20 simulation runs.

[24] Queue Stats

Records statistics on all queue-type blocks in the model.

Update Now | Cancel | OK

	Block	Block Name	Ave Length	Max Length	Ave Wait	Max Wait
0	Deluxe Car	Queue, Resource	0.067±0.0643	2.75±1.42	2.21±2.23	51.6±37.6
1	Econ. Car	Queue, Resource	0.0179±0.0261	1.80±0.968	0.263±0.381	10.4±12.1
2	GoldDeluxe Car	Queue, Resource	0.0111±0.0103	2.95±0.184	2.06±1.84	35.6±27.4
3	GoldEcon. Car	Queue, Resource	0.000511±0.0008	2.90±0.144	0.116±0.18	4.90±8.15
4	Waiting Line	Queue, FIFO	0.0476±0.00431	4.05±0.386	0.525±0.0434	16.2±1.63

10-13 (a) Ten simulation runs, each of 60 minutes simulated time, were made in Extend for the case of having only one worker at each window. Using a Mean and Variance block to calculate the mean total throughput time for each run, produced a 10-run mean throughput time of 8.09±3.07 minutes using a 95% confidence interval, more than double the four minute policy on average. Your results may vary.

(b) Tabulating the ratio of the number exiting within four minutes, gotten from the Histogram block data, to the total number passing through in each simulation run, gotten from the Exit block, yields percentages of between about 7% and 30% on each 60-minute run with an average across runs of about 16%. Your results may vary.

(c) The mean throughput time is minimized to approximately 3.59 minutes when two workers are assigned to each of the order and pickup windows and one worker to the pay window. Tabulating the ratio of the number exiting within four minutes, gotten from the Histogram block data, to the total number passing through in each simulation run, gotten from the Exit block, yields a percentage of about 66% averaged across 10 runs. Your results may vary.

(d) Given the limitations on maximum queue lengths, the mean throughput time is minimized to approximately 3.75 minutes when two workers are assigned to each of the order and pickup windows and one worker to the pay window, a slight increase from the results of (c). Tabulating the ratio of the number exiting within four minutes, gotten from the Histogram block data, to the total number passing through in each simulation run, gotten from the Exit block, yields a percentage of about 71% averaged across 10 runs. Your results may vary.

(e) Given the new limitations on maximum queue lengths of 3 cars at the pay window and one car at the pickup window, the mean throughput time is minimized to approximately 3.84 minutes when two workers are assigned to each of the order and pickup windows and one worker to the pay window, a slight increase from the results of (d). Given the new limitations on maximum queue lengths of 3 cars at the pickup window and one car at the pay window, the mean throughput time is minimized to approximately 3.29 minutes when two workers are assigned to each of the order and pickup windows and one worker to the pay window, a decrease from the results above. Thus, the recommended policy is to have a 3 car limit and 2 workers at the pickup window, 1 car and 1 worker at the pay window and 2 workers at the order window in order to minimize average throughput time. For this policy, tabulating the ratio of the number exiting within four minutes, gotten from the Histogram block data, to the total number passing through in each simulation run, gotten from the Exit block, yields a percentage of about 64% averaged across 10 runs. Your results may vary.

(f) Given the pooling of pay and pickup windows with maximum queue length of 4 cars, the mean throughput time is minimized to approximately 3.1 minutes when three workers are assigned to the combined pay and pickup window and two workers to the order window, a decrease from the results of (e). Thus, the new recommended policy is to pool the pay and pickup windows into one served by 3 workers with 2 workers at the order window in order to minimize average throughput time. For this policy, tabulating the ratio of the number exiting within four minutes, gotten from the Histogram block data, to the total number passing through in each simulation run, gotten from the Exit block, yields a percentage of about 90% averaged across 10 runs. Your results may vary.

10-15 (a) Assume Pat begins the year with 10 cartridges in stock, that any week's stockout incurs a penalty cost of $7000, and he follows a policy of reordering 10 cartridges whenever his inventory drops to a reorder point of 6 or less. Defining a "run" to be a single simulation of 52 weeks and using a Data Table 1 to make 100 separate 52-week runs produced a stockout percentage ranging from a low of 3.8% to a high of 25% across the 100 runs. Averaging the 100 stockout percents over the 100 52-week simulation runs yielded a mean stockout percent of 14.6%. Total costs (penalty costs plus ordering costs plus cartridge costs) ranged from a low of about $26,000 to a high of about $104,000 across the 100 runs with an average total cost over the 100 52-week simulation runs of about $66,000. From a cost standpoint this is not acceptable. For example, repeating the 100 52-week runs but reordering 10 cartridges whenever inventory drops to a reorder point of 10 or less, produced an average stockout of .8% and an average total cost of about $18,000. Your results may vary.

(b) Assuming the setup of (a) and adding uncertainty in the lead time for cartridge orders, increases stockout percentage and total costs. For example, total costs (averaged over 100 52-week simulation runs) increased to about $69,700. Holding the reorder quantity at 10 and tabulating multiple 100 52-week simulation runs for reorder point values of 7, 8, 9 10, 15, and 20 via multiple Data Table 1's, produced a minimal average total cost of about $16,800 for a reorder point of 15. Still better combinations of reorder quantity and reorder point values are possible. Your results may vary.

(c) Adding the uncertainty of copies per cartridge, makes the Excel model substantially more difficult. This is because you must not only track the number of cartridges consumed each week, given the random copies demand and given that each cartridge has a random-number-of-copies capacity, but also the inventory of a partially depleted cartridge from one week to the next. All this is in addition to calculating the beginning inventory of cartridges each week given random lead times for orders. Nevertheless, adding this additional uncertainty in cartridge life to the model of (b) and using a reorder point of 6 or less and a reorder quantity of 10, produced a slightly lower total cost averaged over 100 52-week runs as in (b) of about \$68,000. Presumably, this is due to the carryover of partially empty cartridges from one week to the next to contribute to copy supply capacity in the next week, thus allowing a marginal savings. Experimenting with several combinations of reorder quantity and reorder point values suggests a good policy would be to reorder 8 cartridges whenever the inventory drops to a reorder point of 16 or less, which yielded a total cost averaged over 100 52-week runs as in (b) of about \$15,800. Your results may vary.

CHAPTER 12

12-1. (Start III at beginning of week 1 and II at beginning of week 2) and/or (Start IX at beginning of week 5 and VII at beginning of week 7) and/or (Start IV at beginning of week 3 and III at beginning of week 4). Thus there are 7 alternative optima.

12-3. Let (i, j) mean i is assigned to j. Then the tree is

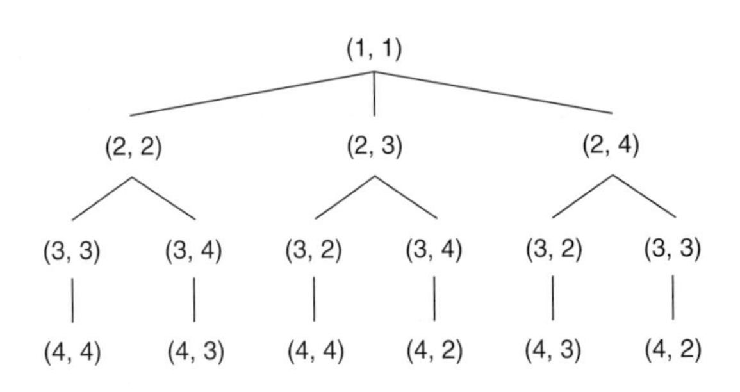

12-5. (a) Assign 4 to A. Delete row 4, column A. Assign 1 to C. Delete row 1, column C. Assign 5 to B. Delete row 5 and column B. Assign 3 to D, and assign 2 to E. Total Sales = 108.

(b) Transformed Data

	A	B	C	D	E
1	−5	−8	−2	0	−4
2	−10	−5	−7	−7	−8
3	−7	−7	−5	−1	0
4	0	0	0	0	0
5	−2	−4	−2	−2	−2

Assign 4 to A, 1 to D, 3 to E, 5 to C, 2 to B. Total Sales = 116. Sales have improved by 7.4%.

12-7.

$$\text{Min} \sum_{i=1}^{12} u_i$$

$$\begin{aligned} \text{s.t.} \quad & x_1 + u_1 - u_2 = 2 \\ & x_2 + u_3 - u_4 = 10 \\ & x_1 + u_5 - u_6 = 6 \\ & x_2 + u_7 - u_8 = 6 \\ & x_1 + u_9 - u_{10} = 1 \\ & x_2 + u_{11} - u_{12} = 3 \\ & u_i \geq 0, i = 1, \ldots, 12 \end{aligned}$$

12-9.

$$\text{Min } w_1u_1 + w_2u_2 + w_3u_3$$

$$\begin{aligned} \text{s.t.} \quad & 20x_1 + 12x_2 \leq 240 \\ & 12x_1 + 20x_2 \leq 240 \\ & x_1 + x_2 + u_1 - v_1 = 12 \\ & x_2 + u_2 - v_2 = 9 \\ & x_1 + u_3 - v_3 = 10 \\ & x_1, x_2 \geq 0, u_i, v_i \geq 0, i = 1, 2, 3 \end{aligned}$$

12-11. (a) $x_1^* = 40, x_2^* = 40$. (b) Minimize underachievement, no overachievement allowed. (c) Minimize underachievement, overachievement allowed. (d) $x_1^* = 0, x_2^* = 80$

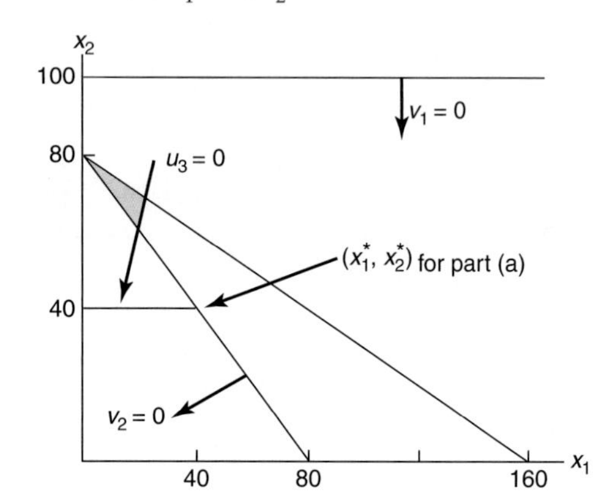

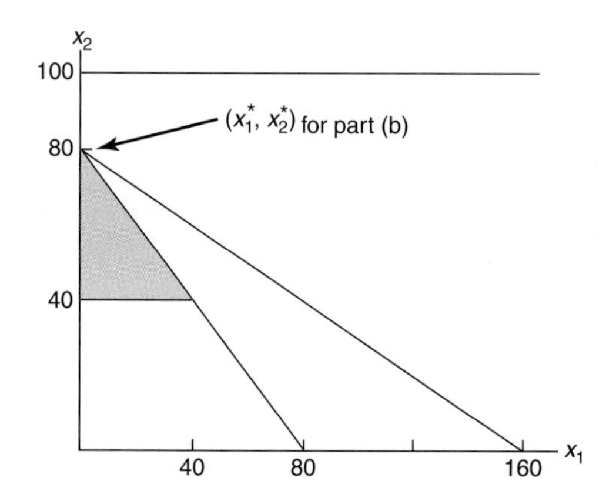

12-13. (a) $x_1^* = 100, x_2^* = 0$

(b) yes; $v_1^* = 20$ overachieved by 20

(c) The second-priority goal was exactly achieved. The third-priority goal was underachieved. $u_3^* = 45$ underachieved by 45.

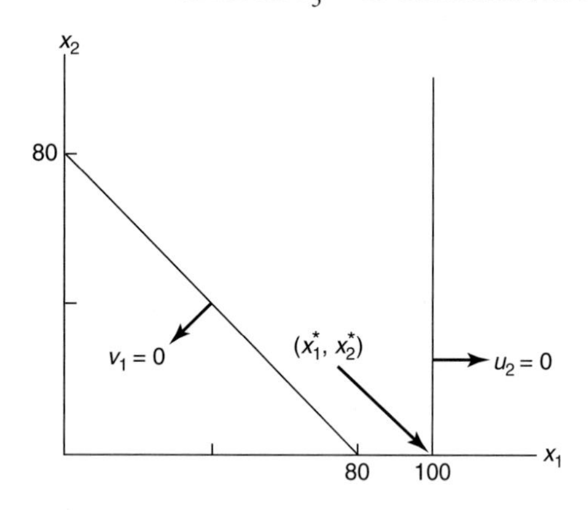

12-15. (a) $6! = 6 \times 5 \times 4 \times 3 \times 2 = 720$

(b) Sequence of jobs = D-C-A-F-E-B

Gantt Chart

Cutting: D C A F E B

0 1 2 3 4 5 6 7 8 9 10 11 12 13 14 15 16 17 18 19 20 21 22 23 24 25

Grinding: D C A F E B

0 1 2 3 4 5 6 7 8 9 10 11 12 13 14 15 16 17 18 19 20 21 22 23 24 25

Total processing time: 23 hours

12-17. (a) Mix of 70% from mine A, 15% from mine B, 15% from mine C yields lowest cost of $65.75.

(b) Assuming weights on the three deviations of 0.4 (whiteness), 0.4 (absorbency), and .2 (cost), the Solver comes up with a mix of 58.7% from mine A, 26.3% from mine B, 15% from mine C for a total cost of $72.52, and minimized weighted deviations of 1.353 (see pr12-15.xls).

12-19. (a) Greedy with maximum capacity = 4: Deliver in following order: 1 to 8; 8 to 4; 4 to 5; 5 to 6; 6 back to 1 for restocking the truck. Then 1 to 7; 7 to 3 (break tie by looking ahead one delivery); 3 to 2; 2 back to 1. Total time = 39 minutes

(b) Greedy with maximum capacity = 5: Deliver in following order: 1 to 8; 8 to 4; 4 to 5; 5 to 6; 6 to 2; 2 back to 1 for restocking the truck. Then 1 to 7; 7 to 3; 3 back to 1. Total time = 45 minutes. It's actually worse to get a larger truck!

(c) Yes, we should do better with something like dynamic programming that looks ahead or the modified greedy algorithm described in the chapter.

12-21. (a) Greedy: Job 0 to 2; 2 to 3; 3 to 1; 1 to 4. Total time = 123 minutes

12-23. (a) see pr12-23.xls (b) We can meet the goal of 35 million exposures, with a small over-achievement (7.33) of the goal of keeping the total cost below $60K.

12-25. Little Bank should be chosen as the provider of financial services (see pr12-25.xls).

12-27.

Job	**Cutting**	**Grinding**
A	3	2^3
B	4^6	5
C	2	2^2
D	1^1	1
E	5	3^5
F	3^4	4

Sequence:

Cutting

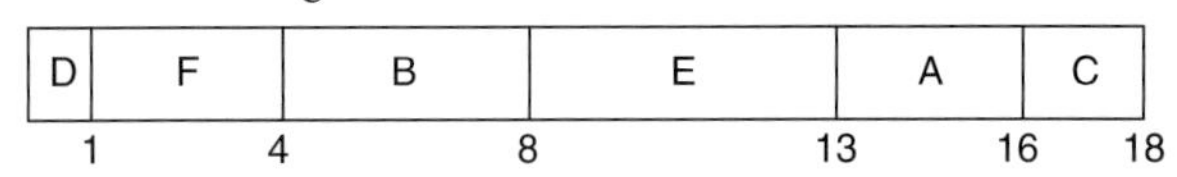

Grinding

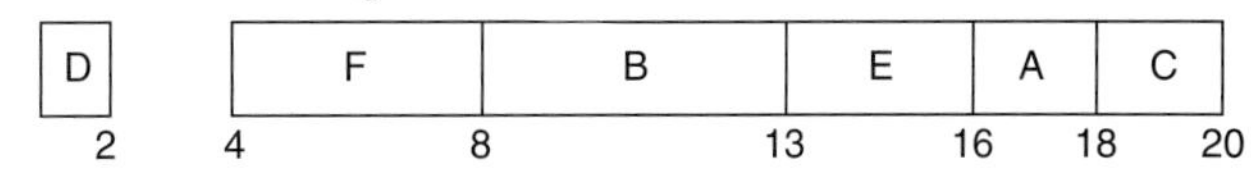

Total processing time = 20, an improvement of 3.

12-29. a. All open, cost = 224

Step 1:	Close	1	2	3	4	5
	Cost	205	189	234	205	**186**

Step 2:	Close	1&5	2&5	3&5	4&5
	Cost	167	**151**	196	177

Step 3:	Close	1&2&5	3&2&5	4&2&5
	Cost	150	161	**142**

Step 4:	Close	1&4&2&5	3&4&2&5
	Cost	177	177

Close 2, 4, 5 or open 1, 3 at a cost of 142

b. This solution is better.

12-31. (a) Regal = 0.777; Camry = 0.155; Accord = 0.069.

(b) Price = 0.179; Reliability = 0.129; Speed = 0.692.

(c) No, he's not consistent on the weights. It looks like he inadvertently switched his preference between Speed and Reliability when he entered a "0.25." He should have entered a value less than 0.1667. To fix this, he could simply enter a value like "1/10" and he is now consistent.

NOTE: The revised weights are now Price = 0.14; Reliability = 0.074; Speed = 0.786. Also, the answer to (d) is based on the revised, consistent weights.

(d) Regal.

12-33. Let A = Tree; B = Father; C = Mother; D = Rope Ladder; E = Floor; F = Boy; G = Tire Swing

First Proposal

Week	**1**	**2**	**3**	**4**	**5**	**6**	**7**	**8**	**9**
	A(6) B(3)	A(6) B(3)	A(6) C(3)	E(6) D(3)	E(6) G(3)	F(5) G(3)	F(5)	F(5)	F(5)
Total personnel	9	9	9	9	9	8	5	5	5
New Limit	8	8	8	8	8	8	8	8	8

Second Proposal

Week	**1**	**2**	**3**	**4**	**5**	**6**	**7**	**8**	**9**
	A(6)	A(6)	A(6)	E(6) D(3)	E(6) G(3)	F(5) G(3)	F(5) B(3)	F(5) B(3)	F(5) C(3)
Total personnel	6	6	6	9	9	8	8	8	8
New Limit	8	8	8	8	8	8	8	8	8

Neither D nor G can be moved in any productive way, so the heuristic terminates and we really haven't met our goal of getting the number of personnel down to 8, but we have smoothed it a little bit.

12-35. (a) See pr12-35.xls; mix of 5 Mall Outlets, 1 Internet store maximize expected return of $3.5 million (assuming integer values are required).

(b) Mix of 2 Superstores, 1 Mall Outlet, 1 Internet store maximize number of employees at 415 (assuming integer values are required).

(c) Mix of 2 Superstores, 1 Mall Outlet, 1 Internet store minimizes underachievement of both goals at 0 (assuming integer values are required).

CHAPTER 13

13-1. (a)

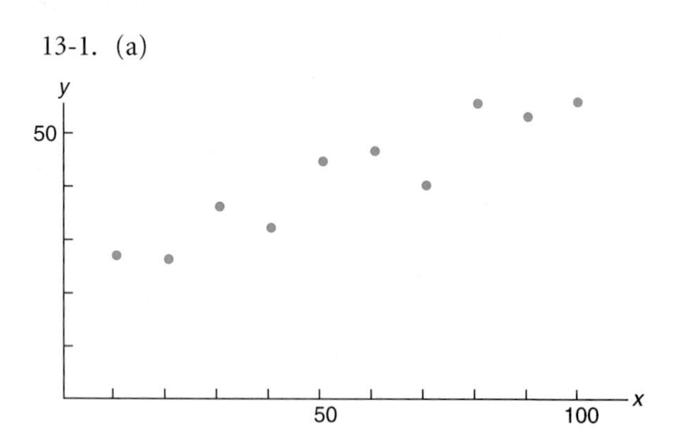

(b) Relevant data:

$$\Sigma x_i = 550, \Sigma y_i = 417$$
$$\Sigma x_i y_i = 25{,}910, \Sigma x_i^2 = 38{,}500$$
$$y = 21.87 + .361x$$

(c) $y = 21.87 + 0.361(120) = 65.19$

13-3. (a)

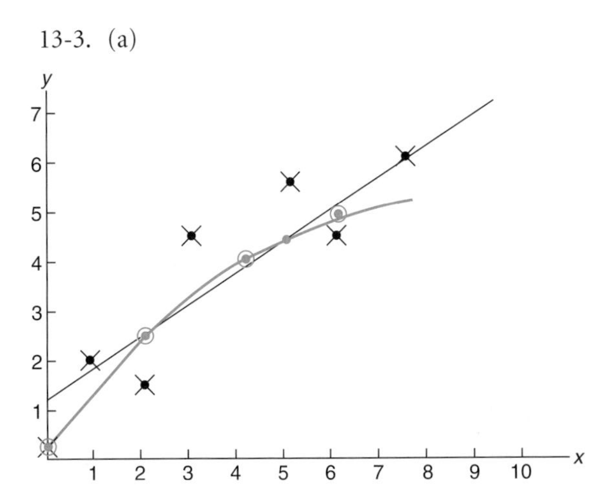

(b) Relevant data:

$$\Sigma x_i = 28, \Sigma y_i = 28, \Sigma x_i y_i = 131, \Sigma x_i^2 = 140$$
$$\Sigma x_i^3 = 784, \Sigma x_i^4 = 4676, \Sigma x_i^2 y_i = 706$$

$y = 1.29 + 0.68x$

(c) $y = 0.428 + 1.250x - 0.071x^2$

13-5. Sum of squared deviation: linear, 4.11, quadratic, 3.68

13-7. (a)

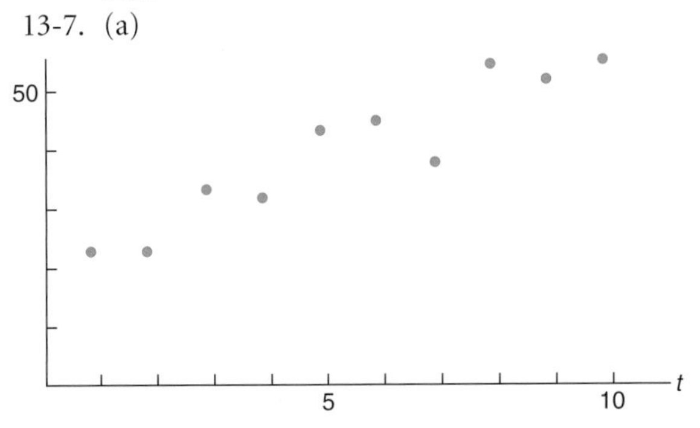

(b) $\hat{y}_{11} = 51.50$ (c) No. There seems to be a linear trend in the data and a simple moving average underestimates future demand if there is a trend.

13-9. (a) $\hat{y}_{11} = 53.9$ (b) Yes. Since there seems to be a trend, a weighted moving average with decreasing weights will underestimate demand less than a simple average. Still not as good as explicitly including the trend. (c) Optimal weights are $w_1 = 0.613$, $w_2 = 0.387$, $w_3 = w_4 = 0$. The error measure was reduced by 23.6%.

13-11. (a) $\hat{y}_{11} = 52.24$ (b) Larger. Since there seems to be a trend, we would like to put more weight on recent observations. (c) $\alpha^* = 0.799$.

13-13. The anonymity of the source of each evaluation is an advantage of the Delphi Method. This is important in this case, since some of the participants are in subordinate positions. The cost and time involved are serious disadvantages of the Delphi Method as compared to the consensus panel.

13-15. Time series. The horizon is short. It is a mature product.

13-17. Average squared error is a reasonable way of measuring how well a model forecasts. It is a standard measure and thus yields comparability over a number of models. It is, however, sensitive to large but perhaps infrequent errors. *Example:* You might prefer errors of 0, 0, 0, 11 to +5, –5, +5, –5, but the average squared error is greater in the first case.

13-19. (a) The 20-period moving average forecast has a MAD of 121.12, while the 50 period moving average forecast has a MAD of 172.44. This indicates that a more "responsive" forecast is better in a situation like this where things are always changing (see pr13-19.xls).

(b) The exponential smoothing forecast with $\alpha = 0.3$ has a MAD of 38.97, showing an even greater improvement over the moving average methods in part a.

13-21. (a)

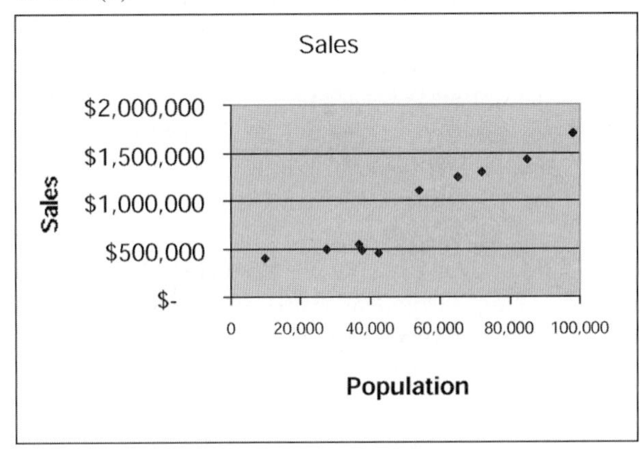

(b)

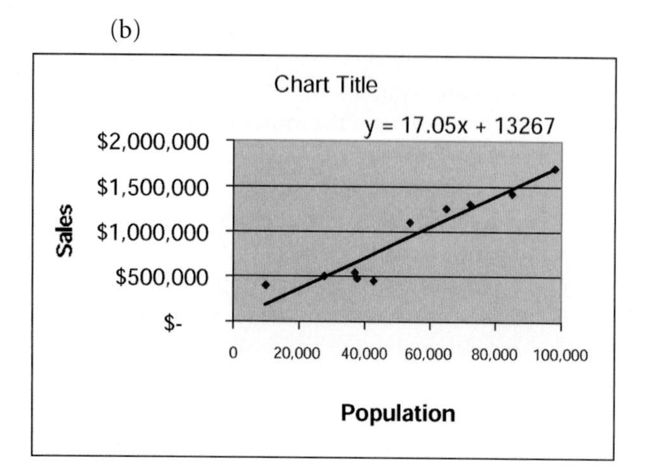

(c) The forecast would be for sales of $865, 767 for a town with 50,000 people (see pr13-21.xls).

13-23. (a) Very volatile, short term. Would need tremendous accuracy in order to do much with the forecast. Likely to use time-series model.

(b) More stable, long term. Likely to use causal model.

(c) Short to medium term. Likely to use time-series model.

(d) Short term. Definitely use a time-series model. Not likely to fluctuate very much from week to week.

13-25. Divide and conquer works basically the same for time-series forecasting models as it does for causal models. The basic idea is to choose the particular parameters (like α and β for exponential smoothing or n and the appropriate weights for moving average models) in the training set and see if they perform as well in the holdout sample. If the performance degrades in the holdout sample, you might consider simplifying the model (say from double exponential smoothing to simple exponential smoothing OR from weighted moving average to simple moving average).

13-27. (a) See pr13-27.xls. Optimal values for α = 0.836, β = 1.0.

(b) The new MSE = 19.18 and MAPE = 9.14% compared to an MSE = 29.27 and MAPE = 15.89% using single exponential smoothing.

13-29. a. See the spreadsheet pr13-29.XLS for the actual mechanics of deseasonalizing the data. The seasonal indices are:

Oct—1.118
Nov—0.933
Dec—0.714
Jan—0.804
Feb—1.02
Mar—1.201
Apr—1.099
May—1.159
Jun—1.257
Jul—0.724
Aug—0.782
Sep—1.24

b. We tried five different forecasting approaches on the deseasonalized data (Simple Exponential Smoothing, Holt's Exponential Smoothing, Linear Trend, 3 period moving average, and 6 period moving average). The Mean Absolute Deviations (MADs) for each method are summarized below:

SES (α^* = 0.18):	76,207
Holt (α^* = 0.15, β^* = 0.03):	75,048
Lin Trend (617132 – 4986.5x):	67,611
3PMA:	76,987
6PMA:	65,320

As can be seen, the 6 period moving average is the best forecasting method based on the MAD. It also is more robust than the second best performer (Linear Trend) because the Linear Trend method assumes that the number of autos sold into the future will continue to **decrease** at a rate of 4986 cars/month forever.

c. The forecast for period 44 is 459,824 × 0.933 = 429,016.

d. We can calculate the standard error as 83,643, and use it to roughly estimate our 95% confidence interval ($\pm 2s_e$) as: [429016 – 2 × 83643, 429016 + 2 × 83643] or [261,730; 596,302].

13-31. I downloaded the last 30 trading days of stock prices from 8/7/00 to 9/21/00 from the AT&T web site (www.att.com/ir/). See pr13-31.xls for the actual Holt's model. The best parameters are $\alpha = 1.0$, $\beta = 0.0$ for a MAPE of 1.59%. Using this model to forecast the next five trading days (9/22/00 to 9/28/00) gave a MAPE of 2.5%, which is quite a bit larger and reflects the fact that the stock hit a 52-week low in that week. The values for the parameters indicate that the best way to forecast the stock price is a random walk.

CHAPTER 14

14-1.

ACTIVITY	IMMEDIATE PREDECESSORS
2	—
1	2
3	1
4	3
6	4
5	1
8	1
7	8
10	8, 5
9	6, 7, 10

14-3.

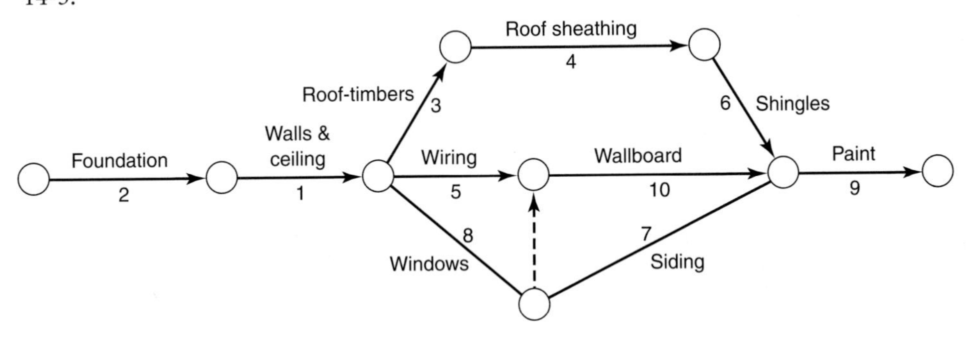

14-5.

ACTIVITY NUMBER	ACTIVITY	ES	EF	LS	LF	SLACK
2	Foundation	0	3	0	3	0
1	Walls and Ceiling	3	8	3	8	0
3	Roof Timbers	8	10	8	10	0
4	Roof Sheathing	10	13	10	13	0
6	Roof Shingles	13	21	13	21	0
5	Electrical Wiring	8	12	14	18	6
8	Windows	8	10	14	16	6
10	Inside Wall Board	12	15	18	21	6
7	Siding	10	15	16	21	6
9	Paint	21	23	21	23	0

Critical path: 2-1-3-4-6-9

14-7. (a)

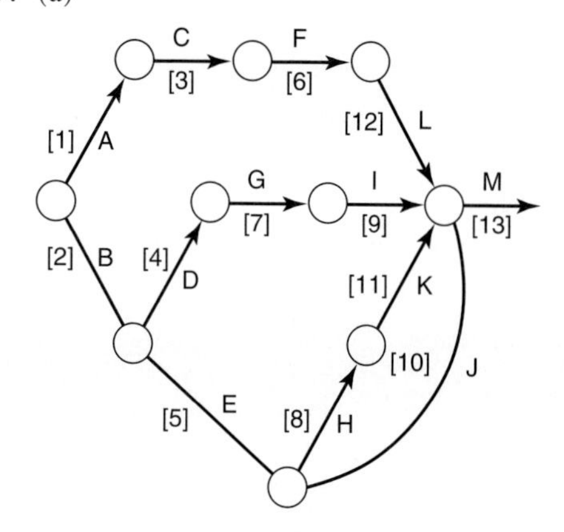

(b) and (c)

ACTIVITY	EARLIEST START	EARLIEST FINISH	LATEST START	LATEST FINISH	SLACK
A	0	1	4	5	4
B	0	2	0	2	0
C	1	4	5	8	4
D	2	6	6	10	4
E	2	7	2	7	0
F	4	10	8	14	4
G	6	13	10	17	4
H	7	15	7	15	0
I	13	22	17	26	4
J	7	17	16	26	9
K	15	26	15	26	0
L	10	22	14	26	4
M	26	39	26	39	0

Critical path: B-E-H-K-M.

(d) Savings = 9 days.

14-9. (a)

ACTIVITY	EXPECTED TIME	STANDARD DEVIATION	EARLIEST START	EARLIEST FINISH	LATEST START	LATEST FINISH	SLACK
A	3	1/3	0	3	0	3	0
B	4	2/3	3	7	3	7	0
C	2	1/3	3	5	5	7	2
D	3	2/3	7	10	13	16	6
E	3	1/3	10	13	16	19	6
F	4	1	7	11	7	11	0
G	2	0	7	9	9	11	2
H	5	1	11	16	11	16	0
I	3	2/3	11	14	13	16	2
J	3	1/3	16	19	16	19	0

b. Critical Path: A-B-F-H-J

14-11. a. $\text{Variance (A-B-F-H-J)} = \frac{1}{9} + \frac{4}{9} + \frac{9}{9} + \frac{9}{9} + \frac{1}{9} = \frac{24}{9}$

Standard Deviation = 1.63

Prob{completion time ≤20} = $\Phi[(20 - 19)/1.63] = \Phi[0.61] = 0.73$

b. Prob {completion time $\leq T$} = $\Phi[(T - 19)/1.63] = 0.95$

$$\frac{T - 19}{1.63} = 1.645$$

$T = 21.7$ weeks

14-13. Earliest Start

						DAY												DAY						
Activity Number	Activity	1	2	3	4	5	6	7	8	9	10	11	12	13	14	15	16	17	18	19	20	21	22	23
2	Foundation	6.67	6.67	6.67																				
1	Walls and Ceiling				10	10	10	10	10															
3	Roof Timbers									7.50	7.50													
4	Roof Sheathing											2.67	2.67	2.67										
6	Roof Shingles														1.63	1.63	1.63	1.63	1.63	1.63	1.63	1.63		
5	Wiring									7.50	7.50	7.50	7.50											
8	Windows									22.50	22.50													
10	Wall Board													7.33	7.33	7.33								
7	Siding											9	9	9	9	9								
9	Paint																						20	20
Daily Project Cost		6.67	6.67	6.67	10	10	10	10	10	37.50	37.50	19.17	19.17	19	17.96	17.96	1.63	1.63	1.63	1.63	1.63	1.63	20	20
Total Project Cost		6.67	13.34	20	30	40	50	60	70	107.5	145	164.17	183.34	202.34	220.30	238.26	239.89	241.52	243.15	244.78	246.41	248	268	288

Latest Start

						DAY												DAY						
Activity Number	Activity	1	2	3	4	5	6	7	8	9	10	11	12	13	14	15	16	17	18	19	20	21	22	23
2	Foundation	6.67	6.67	6.67																				
1	Walls and Ceiling				10	10	10	10	10															
3	Roof Timbers									7.50	7.50													
4	Roof Sheathing											2.67	2.67	2.67										
6	Roof Shingles														1.63	1.63	1.63	1.63	1.63	1.63	1.63	1.63		
5	Wiring															7.50	7.50	7.50	7.50					
8	Windows															22.50	22.50							
10	Wall Board																			7.33	7.33	7.33		
7	Siding																	9	9	9	9	9		
9	Paint																						20	20
Daily Project Cost		6.67	6.67	6.67	10	10	10	10	10	7.50	7.50	2.67	2.67	2.67	1.63	31.63	31.63	18.13	18.13	17.96	17.96	17.96	20	20
Total Project Cost		6.67	13.34	20	30	40	50	60	70	77.50	85	87.67	90.34	93	94.63	126.26	157.89	176.02	194.15	212.11	230.07	248	268	288

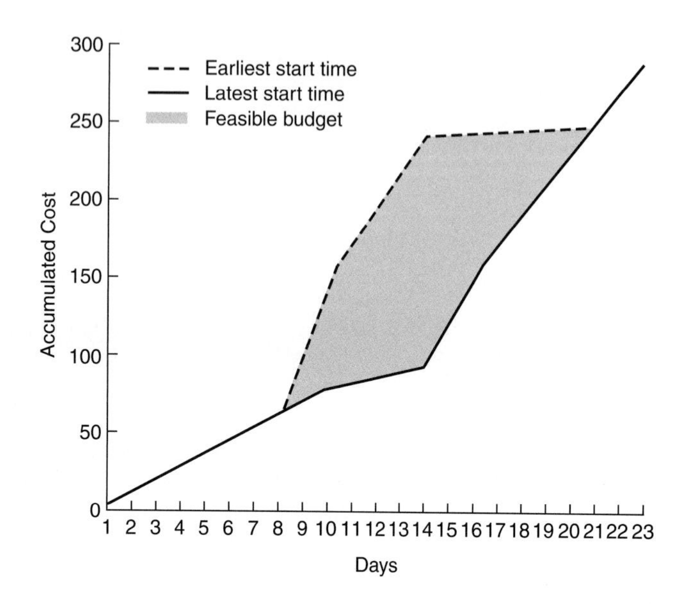

14-15.

(a)

ACTIVITY NUMBER	ACTIVITY	PERCENT COMPLETE	BUDGET	BUDGETED COST	ACTUAL COST	COST OVERRUN
2	Foundation	100	20	20	22	2
1	Walls and Ceiling	100	50	50	46	(4)
3	Roof Timbers	100	15	15	15	0
4	Roof Sheathing	100	8	8	10	2
6	Roof Shingles	25	13	3.25	4.50	1.25
5	Wiring	100	30	30	20	(10)
8	Windows	100	45	45	22.50	(22.50)
10	Inside Wall Board	100	22	22	20	(2)
7	Siding	100	45	45	40	(5)
9	Paint	0	40	0	0	0
Totals			288	238.25	200	(38.25)

(b)

ACTIVITY NUMBER	ACTIVITY	PERCENT COMPLETE	BUDGET	BUDGETED COST	ACTUAL COST	COST OVERRUN
2	Foundation	100	20	20	22	2
1	Walls and Ceiling	100	50	50	46	(4)
3	Roof Timbers	100	15	15	15	0
4	Roof Sheathing	100	8	8	10	2
6	Roof Shingles	25	13	3.25	4.50	1.25
5	Wiring	25	30	7.50	20	12.50
8	Windows	50	45	22.50	22.50	20
10	Inside Wall Board	0	22	0	20	20
7	Siding	0	45	0	40	40
9	Paint	0	40	0	0	0
Totals			288	126.25	200	73.75

14-17. a. Critical path is A-B-D-G with length 14 hours.

b. There are four possible paths. The smallest potential time per path is 5. If each can be made to have a time of 5, this will give the minimum possible time. The allocation shown below does this.

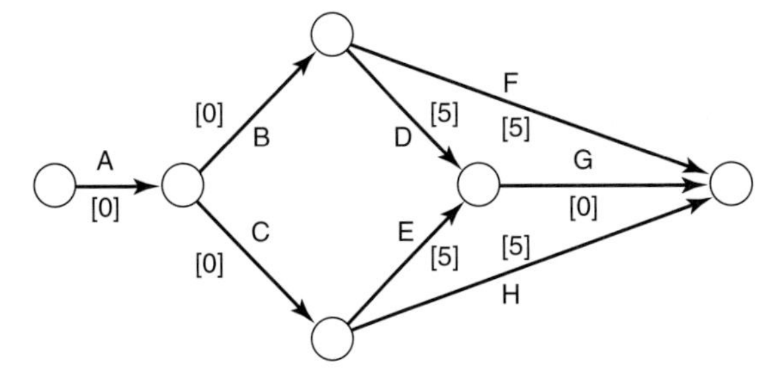

14-19.

Min 10CFOUND + 11CWALLS + 15CRTIMB + 6CRSHEA + 2CSHING + 7CWIND + 5CSIDIN + 12CWALB

s.t.

$$
\begin{aligned}
ESWALL + CFOUND &\geq 3\\
ESRTIM + CWALLS - ESWALL &\geq 5\\
ESWIR + CWALLS - ESWALL &\geq 5\\
ESWIN + CWALLS - ESWALL &\geq 5\\
ESRSHE + CRTIMB - ESRTIM &\geq 2\\
ESSHIN + CRSHEA - ESRSHE &\geq 3\\
ESPAIN + CSHING - ESSHIN &\geq 8\\
ESWALB - ESWIR &\geq 4\\
ESPAIN + CWALB - ESWALB &\geq 3\\
ESWALB + CWIND - ESWIN &\geq 2\\
ESSID + CWIND - ESWIN &\geq 2\\
ESPAIN + CSIDIN - ESSID &\geq 5\\
EFPAIN - ESPAIN &= 2
\end{aligned}
$$

$$CFOUND \leq 1, CWALLS \leq 2, CRTIMB \leq 1, CRSHEA \leq 2$$

$$CSHING \leq 4, CWIND \leq 1, CSIDIN \leq 4, CWALB \leq 1$$

$$EFPAIN + X \leq 23$$

All variables nonnegative

The last inequality represents the constraint on the total time required to complete.

23 = normal time to complete

X = desired reduction

	A	B	C	D	E	F	G	H	I	J	K	L	M	N	O	P	Q	R	S
1		CWALLS	CFOUND	CRTIMB	CRSHE/	CSHING	CSIDIN	CWIND	CWALB	ESWAL	ESRTIM	ESWIR	ESWIN	ESRSHE	ESSHIN	ESPAIN	ESWALB	ESSID	EFPAIN
2	Amount	0	0	0	0	0	0	0	0	0	0	0	0	0	0	0	0	0	0
3	Per unitCost	$ 11.00	$ 10.00	$15.00	$ 6.00	$ 2.00	$ 5.00	$ 7.00	$12.00										
4	Max Crash Days	2	1	1	2	4	4	1	1										
5																			
6	Total Cost	0																	
7																			
8	*Constraints*																		
9	Early Start Walls & Clg	0	>=	3															
10	Early Start Roof Timb	0	>=	5															
11	Early Start Wiring	0	>=	5															
12	Early Start Windows	0	>=	5															
13	Early Start Roof Sheath	0	>=	2															
14	Early Start Roof Shingl	0	>=	3															
15	Early Start Paint (Shing	0	>=	8															
16	Early Start Wall Board	0	>=	4															
17	Early StartPaint (WallB	0	>=	3															
18	Early Start Wall Board	0	>=	2															
19	Early Start Siding	0	>=	2															
20	Early Start Paint (Siding	0	>=	5															
21	Defn of EFPaint	0	=	2															
22	Early Finish PAINT Goa	0	<=	23	*(can modify by x as desired)*														

14-21. (a) 26 – 11.75 = 14.25

14-23. (a) Expected project length = 81 (critical path = B-D-E). The probability of completing it in 86 days is 99.38%. The answer is the same as for Problem 14-22 because the PERT analysis is not affected by the form of the distribution of individual activity times, but is affected by the mean and variance of those times, and these are exactly the same as in Problem 14-22.
(b) The expected project length is longer than the answer the PERT analysis gives, 86.7 versus 81.0.
(c) The probability of completion in 86 days is less, 0.6750 versus 0.9938. The reason for the differences is that sometimes A-C becomes the critical path and this increases the average length.
(d) The answers from the two simulation analyses are quite close, 86.7 versus 87.0 and 0.6750 versus 0.6550. For this example, the form of the distribution of activity times (normal versus uniform) does not seem to make much difference. What does make a difference is the (erroneous) assumption made by PERT that the path with the longest expected length will always be the critical path.

CHAPTER 15

15-1. (a) $\lambda = 0.5$ barges per hr (b) 2 hrs (c) 0.5 barges per hr

15-3. (a) $\mu = 15$ people per hr (b) 0.067 hrs per person (c) 15 people per hr

15-5. (a) $L = 2$ (b) $L_q = 4/3$ (c) $W = 1/5$ hr/person (d) $W_q = 2/15$ hr/person (e) $P_0 = 1/3$

15-7. $L = \dfrac{5}{\mu - 5}$ vs μ

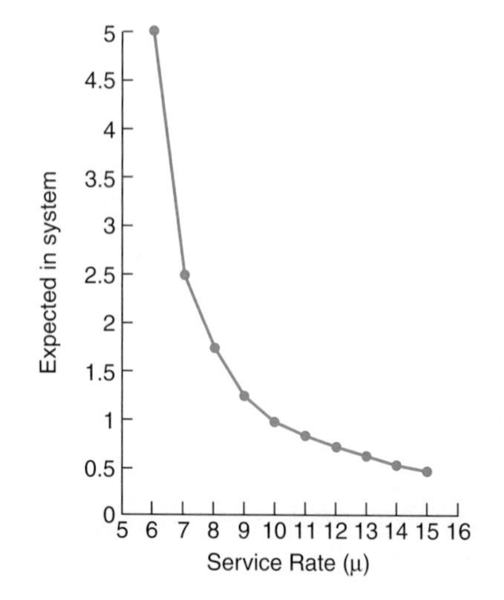

15-9. $W = L/\lambda = [\lambda/(\mu - \lambda)]/\lambda = 1/(\mu - \lambda)$

15-11. $W = W_q + \frac{1}{\mu}; \frac{1}{\mu} = 20$ minutes

$W_q = W - \frac{1}{\mu} = 30 - 20 = 10$ minutes

15-13. A three-server queue with Poisson arrivals (exponential interarrival times) and deterministic service time.

15-15. $L = \lambda W; L_q = \lambda W_q$

$1 = 1 \times 1; \frac{1}{2} = 1 \times \frac{1}{2}$

15-17. L = 1.4791

15-19. The repair person of Section 15.9 best fits the states assumptions. Here the faculty correspond to machines and the parts to repair persons. The correspondence, however, is not exact as once a machine breaks down, it enters a queue and waits for a repair person to become available. The faculty would have to redial in order to try and get service for their original request. While the equations for answering this question are given in Section 15.9, the calculations are much too painful to do by hand and we instead turn to the Q.xls template to solve the model (see pr15-19.xls).

The number of servers, 10 corresponds to the number of ports. The service rate per hour, 2, corresponds to the 30 minutes average time a faculty member spends on the computer. Distribution of service time, 1, indicates the exponential distribution. Arrival rate per hour, 0.125, corresponds to each faculty member desiring service once every 8 hours and distribution of interarrival time, 1, indicates an exponential distribution. Population size of 100, corresponds to the 100 faculty.

The queuing templates "Finite Population" indicates exponential interarrival and services time 10 servers, and 100 customers in the calling population. From this spreadsheet we can read off the answers a–e.

a. 0.0023
b. 0.0983 faculty
c. 0.0084 hrs ≅ 0.5 minutes
d. 0.5083 hours
e. 5.9745 faculty

15-21. TC(5) = $184.80 per hour.

15-23. $C_S/C_W = 1.67$

15-25. (a) $P_3 = 0.034$ (b) 0.409 (c) 5.91

15-27. (a) $L = 0.7525$ (b) $L_q = 0.2525$ (c) $W = 0.7525$ hour (d) $W_q = 0.2525$ hour (e) $P_0 = \frac{1}{2}$
(a) through (d) are less because the variability of the service time is less

15-29. (a) The spreadsheet ORDER.XLS is easily modified to answer this question (the resulting spreadsheet is pr15-29cb.xls). We basically inserted a custom distribution (90% chance of 3 hrs, 10% chance of 13 hrs). Using Crystal Ball with 5000 iterations and a Seed value of 422 gives the following results: Average completion time = 11.69 days, 99th percentile = 15.4 days. Your answers may vary slightly.

(b) Now we simply change the custom distribution to a 99% chance of 3 hrs and 1% chance of 13 hrs and rerun the simulation. Using Crystal Ball with 5000 iterations and a Seed value of 422 gives the following results: Average completion time = 8.49 days, 99th percentile = 10.8 days. Your answers may vary slightly.

If Larry continues to quote lead times so that he can be 99% sure of meeting them, he can reduce this time by 15.4 – 10.8 = 4.6 days. Thus the value of preventive maintenance is the 4.6 day reduction in lead time and the competitive advantage that brings to Sonorola.

Index

Italic *n* denotes note listing.

SITE LICENSE AGREEMENT AND LIMITED WARRANTY

READ THIS LICENSE CAREFULLY BEFORE USING THIS PACKAGE. BY USING THIS PACKAGE, YOU ARE AGREEING TO THE TERMS AND CONDITIONS OF THIS LICENSE. IF YOU DO NOT AGREE, DO NOT USE THE PACKAGE. PROMPTLY RETURN THE UNUSED PACKAGE AND ALL ACCOMPANYING ITEMS TO THE PLACE YOU OBTAINED. ***THESE TERMS APPLY TO ALL LICENSED SOFTWARE ON THE DISK EXCEPT THAT THE TERMS FOR USE OF ANY SHAREWARE OR FREEWARE ON THE DISKETTES ARE AS SET FORTH IN THE ELECTRONIC LICENSE LOCATED ON THE DISK:***

1. GRANT OF LICENSE and OWNERSHIP: The enclosed computer programs and data ("Software") are licensed, not sold, to you by Prentice-Hall, Inc. ("We" or the "Company") and in consideration of your purchase or adoption of the accompanying Company textbooks and/or other materials, and your agreement to these terms. We reserve any rights not granted to you. You own only the disk(s) but we and/or licensors own the Software itself. This license allows you to use and display the enclosed copy of the Software on up to 1 computer at a single campus or branch or geographic location of an educational institution, for academic use only, so long as you comply with the terms of this Agreement. You may make one copy for back up only.

2. RESTRICTIONS: You may not transfer or distribute the Software or documentation to anyone else. Except for backup, you may not copy the documentation or the Software. You may not reverse engineer, disassemble, decompile, modify, adapt, translate, or create derivative works based on the Software or the Documentation. You may be held legally responsible for any copying or copyright infringement which is caused by your failure to abide by the terms of these restrictions.

3. TERMINATION: This license is effective until terminated. This license will terminate automatically without notice from the Company if you fail to comply with any provisions or limitations of this license. Upon termination, you shall destroy the Documentation and all copies of the Software. All provisions of this Agreement as to limitation and disclaimer of warranties, limitation of liability, remedies or damages, and our ownership rights shall survive termination.

4. LIMITED WARRANTY AND DISCLAIMER OF WARRANTY: Company warrants that for a period of 60 days from the date you purchase this Software (or purchase or adopt the accompanying textbook), the Software, when properly installed and used in accordance with the Documentation, will operate in substantial conformity with the description of the Software set forth in the Documentation, and that for a period of 30 days the disk(s) on which the Software is delivered shall be free from defects in materials and workmanship under normal use. The Company does not warrant that the Software will meet your requirements or that the operation of the Software will be uninterrupted or error-free. Your only remedy and the Company's only obligation under these limited warranties is, at the Company's option, return of the disk for a refund of any amounts paid for it by you or replacement of the disk. THIS LIMITED WARRANTY IS THE ONLY WARRANTY PROVIDED BY THE COMPANY AND ITS LICENSORS, AND THE COMPANY AND ITS LICENSORS DISCLAIM ALL OTHER WARRANTIES, EXPRESS OR IMPLIED, INCLUDING WITHOUT LIMITATION, THE IMPLIED WARRANTIES OF MERCHANTABILITY AND FITNESS FOR A PARTICULAR PURPOSE. THE COMPANY DOES NOT WARRANT, GUARANTEE OR MAKE ANY REPRESENTATION REGARDING THE ACCURACY, RELIABILITY, CURRENTNESS, USE, OR RESULTS OF USE, OF THE SOFTWARE.

5. LIMITATION OF REMEDIES AND DAMAGES: IN NO EVENT, SHALL THE COMPANY OR ITS EMPLOYEES, AGENTS, LICENSORS, OR CONTRACTORS BE LIABLE FOR ANY INCIDENTAL, INDIRECT, SPECIAL, OR CONSEQUENTIAL DAMAGES ARISING OUT OF OR IN CONNECTION WITH THIS LICENSE OR THE SOFTWARE, INCLUDING FOR LOSS OF USE, LOSS OF DATA, LOSS OF INCOME OR PROFIT, OR OTHER LOSSES, SUSTAINED AS A RESULT OF INJURY TO ANY PERSON, OR LOSS OF OR DAMAGE TO PROPERTY, OR CLAIMS OF THIRD PARTIES, EVEN IF THE COMPANY OR AN AUTHORIZED REPRESENTATIVE OF THE COMPANY HAS BEEN ADVISED OF THE POSSIBILITY OF SUCH DAMAGES. IN NO EVENT SHALL THE LIABILITY OF THE COMPANY FOR DAMAGES WITH RESPECT TO THE SOFTWARE EXCEED THE AMOUNTS ACTUALLY PAID BY YOU, IF ANY, FOR THE SOFTWARE OR THE ACCOMPANYING TEXTBOOK. SOME JURISDICTIONS DO NOT ALLOW THE LIMITATION OF LIABILITY IN CERTAIN CIRCUMSTANCES, THE ABOVE LIMITATIONS MAY NOT ALWAYS APPLY.

6. GENERAL: THIS AGREEMENT SHALL BE CONSTRUED IN ACCORDANCE WITH THE LAWS OF THE UNITED STATES OF AMERICA AND THE STATE OF NEW YORK, APPLICABLE TO CONTRACTS MADE IN NEW YORK, AND SHALL BENEFIT THE COMPANY, ITS AFFILIATES AND ASSIGNEES. This Agreement is the complete and exclusive statement of the agreement between you and the Company and supersedes all proposals, prior agreements, oral or written, and any other communications between you and the company or any of its representatives relating to the subject matter. If you are a U.S. Government user, this Software is licensed with "restricted rights" as set forth in subparagraphs (a)-(d) of the Commercial Computer-Restricted Rights clause at FAR 52.227-19 or in subparagraphs (c)(1)(ii) of the Rights in Technical Data and Computer Software clause at DFARS 252.227-7013, and similar clauses, as applicable.

Should you have any questions concerning this agreement or if you wish to contact the Company for any reason, please contact in writing:

Director, Media Production
Pearson Education
1 Lake Street
Upper Saddle River, NJ 07458